New Perspectives on

JavaScript and AJAX

2nd Edition

Comprehensive

New Perspectives on

JavaScript and AJAX

2nd Edition

Comprehensive

Patrick Carey

Frank Canovatchel

Champlain College

COURSE TECHNOLOGY
CENGAGE Learning

Australia • Brazil • Japan • Korea • Mexico • Singapore • Spain • United Kingdom • United States

COURSE TECHNOLOGY
CENGAGE Learning™

**New Perspectives on JavaScript and AJAX,
2nd Edition—Comprehensive**

Vice President, Publisher: Nicole Jones Pinard

Executive Editor: Marie L. Lee

Associate Acquisitions Editor: Brandi Shailer

Senior Product Manager: Kathy Finnegan

Product Manager: Leigh Hefferon

Associate Product Manager: Julia Leroux-Lindsey

Editorial Assistant: Zina Kresin

Director of Marketing: Cheryl Costantini

Senior Marketing Manager: Ryan DeGrote

Marketing Coordinator: Kristen Panciocco

Developmental Editor: Robin M. Romer

Content Project Manager: Jennifer Feltri

Composition: GEX Publishing Services

Text Designer: Steve Deschene

Art Director: Marissa Falco

Cover Designer: Elizabeth Paquin

Cover Art: Bill Brown

Copyeditor: Suzanne Huizenga

Proofreader: Kathy Orrino

Indexer: Alexandra Nickerson

For product information and technology assistance, contact us at
Cengage Learning Customer & Sales Support, 1-800-354-9706
For permission to use material from this text or product, submit all requests online at **cengage.com/permissions**
Further permissions questions can be emailed to
permissionrequest@cengage.com

Some of the product names and company names used in this book have been used for identification purposes only and may be trademarks or registered trademarks of their respective manufacturers and sellers.

Microsoft and the Office logo are either registered trademarks or trademarks of Microsoft Corporation in the United States and/or other countries. Course Technology, Cengage Learning is an independent entity from the Microsoft Corporation, and not affiliated with Microsoft in any manner.

Disclaimer: Any fictional data related to persons or companies or URLs used throughout this book is intended for instructional purposes only. At the time this book was printed, any such data was fictional and not belonging to any real persons or companies.

ISBN-13: 978-1-4390-4403-2

ISBN-10: 1-4390-4403-1

Course Technology
20 Channel Center Street
Boston, Massachusetts 02210
USA

Cengage Learning is a leading provider of customized learning solutions with office locations around the globe, including Singapore, the United Kingdom, Australia, Mexico, Brazil, and Japan. Locate your local office at: **international.cengage.com/region**

Cengage Learning products are represented in Canada by Nelson Education, Ltd.

To learn more about Course Technology, visit **www.cengage.com/coursetechnology**
To learn more about Cengage Learning, visit **www.cengage.com**

Purchase any of our products at your local college store or at our preferred online store **www.ichapters.com**

Printed in the United States of America
1 2 3 4 5 6 7 8 9 13 12 11 10 09

Preface

The New Perspectives Series' critical-thinking, problem-solving approach is the ideal way to prepare students to transcend point-and-click skills and take advantage of all that the World Wide Web has to offer.

Our goal in developing the New Perspectives Series was to create books that give students the software concepts and practical skills they need to succeed beyond the classroom. With this new edition, we've updated our proven case-based pedagogy with more practical content to make learning skills more meaningful to students.

With the New Perspectives Series, students understand *why* they are learning *what* they are learning, and are fully prepared to apply their skills to real-life situations.

"I love how the tutorials in this text use applications that relate to students' interests. The step-by-step instructions allow students to create, review, and test program code in building successful applications."

—Jean Insinga
Middlesex Community
College

About This Book

This book provides comprehensive instruction in basic to advanced concepts of JavaScript programming, teaching students to apply JavaScript to create real-world applications using a practical approach.

- Step-by-step instructions help students to create customized Web calendars, count-down clocks, pull-down and pop-up menu forms, dynamic tables of contents, Lightbox-style slideshows, interactive puzzles and games, shopping cart applications, RSS news readers, and autocomplete input boxes.
- Foundational programming concepts, including variable scope, JavaScript operators, designing for loops and if statements, and working with conditional statements, are presented.
- Students learn about string objects, including number formatting and manipulating strings using regular expressions; and form validation techniques, including the ability to validate credit card data based on credit card values and patterns.
- A *new tutorial* on AJAX provides instruction on creating AJAX applications that retrieve data from text files, CGI scripts, XML documents, and JSON data structures.
- A *new tutorial* on custom objects shows students how to design their own custom objects, properties, and methods, and how to work with object prototypes and proto-typal inheritance.
- A *new tutorial* on cookies shows students how to store persistent data and how to work with single-valued and multi-valued cookies.
- Each tutorial includes additional case problems, giving students the opportunity to create more real-world applications including dynamic Web tables, drag-and-drop puzzles, Web widgets, and dynamic overlays.
- Several interactive demos are provided throughout the text to give students a hands-on experience in learning JavaScript programming concepts.
- Extended appendices on JavaScript objects, properties, and methods are provided, as well as two appendices that review the syntax of HTML and CSS.
- A robust Student Online Companion with additional material is available.

The New Perspectives Approach

"The New Perspectives Series approach, which combines definition and real-world application of content, makes it an easy choice for me when selecting textbooks. I am able to teach concepts that students can immediately apply."

—Brian Morgan
Marshall University

Context

Each tutorial begins with a problem presented in a "real-world" case that is meaningful to students. The case sets the scene to help students understand what they will do in the tutorial.

Hands-on Approach

Each tutorial is divided into manageable sessions that combine reading and hands-on, step-by-step work. Colorful screenshots help guide students through the steps. **Trouble?** tips anticipate common mistakes or problems to help students stay on track and continue with the tutorial.

InSight

InSight Boxes

New for this edition! InSight boxes offer expert advice and best practices to help students better understand how to work with JavaScript and AJAX. With the information provided in the InSight boxes, students achieve a deeper understanding of the concepts behind the features and skills presented.

Tip

Margin Tips

New for this edition! Margin Tips provide helpful hints and shortcuts for more efficient use of JavaScript and AJAX. The Tips appear in the margin at key points throughout each tutorial, giving students extra information when and where they need it.

Reality Check

Reality Checks

New for this edition! Comprehensive, open-ended Reality Check exercises give students the opportunity to practice skills by completing practical, real-world tasks, such as creating a personal Web site and creating and posting an online resume.

Review

In New Perspectives, retention is a key component to learning. At the end of each session, a series of Quick Check questions helps students test their understanding of the concepts before moving on. Each tutorial also contains an end-of-tutorial summary and a list of key terms for further reinforcement.

Apply

Assessment

Engaging and challenging Review Assignments and Case Problems have always been a hallmark feature of the New Perspectives Series. Colorful icons and brief descriptions accompany the exercises, making it easy to understand, at a glance, both the goal and level of challenge a particular assignment holds.

Reference Window

Reference

While contextual learning is excellent for retention, there are times when students will want a high-level understanding of how to accomplish a task. Within each tutorial, Reference Windows appear before a set of steps to provide a succinct summary and preview of how to perform a task. In addition, each book includes a combination Glossary/Index to promote easy reference of material.

Our Complete System of Instruction

Coverage To Meet Your Needs

Whether you're looking for just a small amount of coverage or enough to fill a semester-long class, we can provide you with a textbook that meets your needs.

- Brief books typically cover the essential skills in just 2 to 4 tutorials.
- Introductory books build and expand on those skills and contain an average of 5 to 8 tutorials.
- Comprehensive books are great for a full-semester class, and contain 9 to 12+ tutorials.

So if the book you're holding does not provide the right amount of coverage for you, there's probably another offering available. Visit our Web site or contact your Course Technology sales representative to find out what else we offer.

Online Companion

This book has an accompanying Online Companion Web site designed to enhance learning. This Web site, www.cengage.com/webdesign/np/javascript2, includes the following:

- Supplemental information tied directly to the content of each tutorial, for further student exploration and reference
- Student Data Files needed to complete the tutorials and end-of-tutorial exercises

CourseCasts – Learning on the Go. Always available...always relevant.

Want to keep up with the latest technology trends relevant to you? Visit our site to find a library of podcasts, CourseCasts, featuring a "CourseCast of the Week," and download them to your mp3 player at http://coursecasts.course.com.

Ken Baldauf, host of CourseCasts, is a faculty member of the Florida State University Computer Science Department where he is responsible for teaching technology classes to thousands of FSU students each year. Ken is an expert in the latest technology trends; he gathers and sorts through the most pertinent news and information for CourseCasts so your students can spend their time enjoying technology, rather than trying to figure it out. Open or close your lecture with a discussion based on the latest CourseCast.

Visit us at http://coursecasts.course.com to learn on the go!

Instructor Resources

We offer more than just a book. We have all the tools you need to enhance your lectures, check students' work, and generate exams in a new, easier-to-use and completely revised package. This book's Instructor's Manual, ExamView testbank, PowerPoint presentations, data files, solution files, figure files, and a sample syllabus are all available on a single CD-ROM or for downloading at http://www.cengage.com/coursetechnology.

Blackboard

Skills Assessment and Training

SAM 2007 helps bridge the gap between the classroom and the real world by allowing students to train and test on important computer skills in an active, hands-on environment. SAM 2007's easy-to-use system includes powerful interactive exams, training or projects on critical applications such as Word, Excel, Access, PowerPoint, Outlook, Windows, the Internet, and much more. SAM simulates the application environment, allowing students to demonstrate their knowledge and think through the skills by performing real-world tasks. Powerful administrative options allow instructors to schedule exams and assignments, secure tests, and run reports with almost limitless flexibility.

Online Content

Blackboard is the leading distance learning solution provider and class-management platform today. Course Technology has partnered with Blackboard to bring you premium online content. Content for use with *New Perspectives on JavaScript and AJAX, 2nd Edition, Comprehensive* is available in a Blackboard Course Cartridge and may include topic reviews, case projects, review questions, test banks, practice tests, custom syllabi, and more. Course Technology also has solutions for several other learning management systems. Please visit http://www.cengage.com/coursetechnology today to see what's available for this title.

Acknowledgments

I would like to thank the people who worked so hard to make this book possible. Special thanks to my developmental editor, Robin Romer, for her hard work and valuable insights, and to my Product Manager, Kathy Finnegan, who has worked tirelessly in overseeing this project and made my task so much easier with her enthusiasm and good humor. Other people at Course Technology who deserve credit are Marie Lee, Executive Editor; Brandi Shailer, Associate Acquisitions Editor; Leigh Hefferon, Product Manager; Julia Leroux-Lindsey, Associate Product Manager; Zina Kresin, Editorial Assistant; Jennifer Feltri, Content Project Manager; Christian Kunciw, Manuscript Quality Assurance (MQA) Supervisor; and John Freitas, Danielle Shaw, and Susan Whalen, MQA testers.

Feedback is an important part of writing any book, and thanks go to the following reviewers for their helpful ideas and comments: Sally Catlin, Indiana University—Purdue University Indianapolis; Melissa Green, College of San Mateo; Jean Insinga, Middlesex Community College; Diana Kokoska, University of Maine; Angela McFarland, B.T. Washington High School, Escambia; Brian Morgan, Marshall University; Christopher Olson, Dakota State University; James Papademas, DeVry University Chicago; and Luke Papademas, DeVry University Chicago. My thanks as well to the members of the New Perspectives HTML Advisory Board for their insights and suggestions for this new edition: Lisa Macon, Valencia Community College; Don Mangione, Baker College of Muskegon; Chuck Riden, Arizona State University; and Kenneth Wade, Champlain College.

I want to thank my wife Joan for her love and encouragement, and my six children who supported me during the course of writing this book. Thank you Catherine, Stephen, Michael, and Peter; and special thanks to my college-aged children, John and Thomas, to whom I dedicate this book.

– Patrick Carey

System Requirements

This book assumes that students have an Internet Connection, a basic text editor, and a current Web browser that supports the HTML 4.01 and XHTML 1.1 standards as well as JavaScript 1.5. The following is a list of the most recent versions of the major browsers at the time this text was published: Firefox 3.5.1, Internet Explorer 8.0, Opera 10, Safari 4.0, and Google Chrome 3.0. All Web browsers interpret HTML, CSS, and JavaScript code in slightly different ways. It is highly recommended that students have several different browsers installed on their systems for comparison purposes. Students might also want to run older versions of browsers to highlight compatibility issues. Unless otherwise noted, Web page screenshots in this book were done with Internet Explorer 7.0 and 8.0 running on Windows Vista at a screen resolution of 1024 by 768 pixels. Students using a different browser, operating system, or screen resolution might see slightly different Web pages than shown in this book.

This book does not require the use of any JavaScript library such as jQuery, the Dojo Tookit, MooTools, or the Yahoo! UI library. Use of those libraries is left to the discretion of the instructor.

Debugging software is not required but highly recommended for the programming tasks in this book. All major browsers now include developer tools to assist students in debugging code and tracing errors. Students should refer to their browser's Help files to learn how to properly install and access these developer tools.

Special Note: All tasks done in this book can be accomplished on the student's local machine with the following exceptions:

1. Because neither Safari nor Google Chrome supports the reading of cookies except over an HTTP connection to a server, students running Safari or Google Chrome will need to load their solution files to an account on a Web server or have a Web server installed for their local machines in order to complete the tasks in Tutorial 9.

2. Because AJAX applications require an HTTP connection, all students (regardless of their browsers) will need to load their solution files to a Web server or have a Web server installed for their local machines in order to complete the tasks in Tutorial 12. In addition, the Web server must include support for the Perl scripting language and students must have the ability to run CGI scripts from their server accounts.

Brief Contents

Table of Contents

Objectives

Session 1.1
- Learn the history of JavaScript
- Create a script element
- Understand basic JavaScript syntax
- Write text to a Web page with JavaScript

Session 1.2
- Learn about JavaScript data types
- Declare and work with variables
- Create and call a JavaScript function

Session 1.3
- Access an external JavaScript file
- Add comments to JavaScript code
- Learn about basic debugging techniques and tools

Programming with JavaScript

Hiding E-Mail Addresses on a Library Web Site

Case | Monroe Public Library

Kate Howard is the head of technical services at Monroe Public Library in Monroe, Ohio. One of her jobs is to maintain the library's Web site. In previous years, the library has made its staff directory, including e-mail links to library employees, available online. Kate thinks that this is an important part of making the library more accessible to everyone. However, Kate has become concerned about the security issues involved with making the staff's e-mail addresses so accessible. Kate is aware that e-mail addresses can be scanned from an HTML file and used to send junk mail to the recipients.

She would like to have some way of scrambling the e-mail addresses within the HTML code while still making them viewable when the page is rendered by a Web browser. Kate has approached you for help in writing a program to accomplish this.

Starting Data Files

Tutorial.01 →

Tutorial
mpl.jpg
mplstyles.css
mpltxt.htm
spam.js

Review
mpl2txt.htm
mplstyles.css
random.js
+ 11 graphic files

Case1
datetime.js
skymaptxt.htm
skyweb.css
+ 26 graphic files

Case2
ads.js
fronttxt.htm
random.js
styles.css
+ 7 graphic files

Case3
back.jpg
functions.js
sunday.htm - saturday.htm
todaytxt.htm
+ 2 style sheets

Case4
functions.js
logo.jpg

Session 1.1

Introducing JavaScript

You meet with Kate to discuss her goals regarding the e-mail addresses on the library's staff directory page. She shows you the content and page layout she has created.

To open the staff directory page:

▶ 1. Use your text editor to open **mpltxt.htm** from the tutorial.01\tutorial folder included with your Data Files. Enter *your name* and *the date* in the comment section at the top of the file and save the file as **mpl.htm** in the same folder.

▶ 2. Take some time to scroll through the document to become familiar with its contents and structure.

▶ 3. Open **mpl.htm** in your Web browser. Figure 1-1 shows the initial appearance of the Web page.

   Note that the staff directory table contains a column in which Kate wants to insert links to each employee's e-mail address; right now the column is empty.

Figure 1-1 ▶ **Monroe Public Library Staff page**

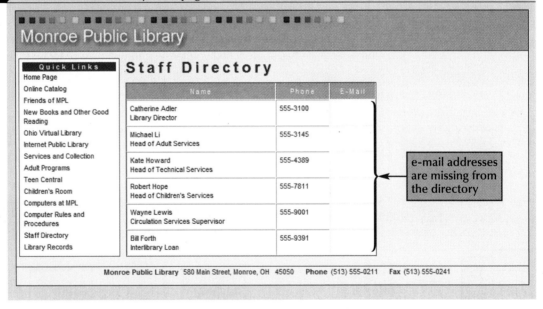

Although the staff directory page has proven invaluable in making library employees more responsive to the needs of the public, Kate is concerned about the security risks of putting e-mail addresses in that directory. Kate is most concerned about spam. **Spam** is essentially junk e-mail—messages that advertise products and services not requested by the recipient. A **spammer** is a person who sends these unsolicited e-mails, sometimes in bulk e-mailings involving tens of thousands of recipients. Aside from the annoyance of receiving unsolicited e-mail, spam costs companies thousands—and sometimes millions—of dollars each year by consuming valuable resources on mail servers and other devices forced to process the messages. Spam also reduces productivity by forcing employees to wade through numerous spam messages every day to find messages that are truly relevant.

One way that spammers collect e-mail addresses is through the use of e-mail harvesters. An **e-mail harvester** is a program that scans documents, usually Web pages, looking for e-mail addresses. Any e-mail address the harvester finds within the document code is added to a database, which can then be used for sending spam. So by putting the staff's e-mail addresses in the HTML code for the staff directory, Kate is also making them available to e-mail harvesters. See Figure 1-2.

Harvesting e-mail addresses | Figure 1-2

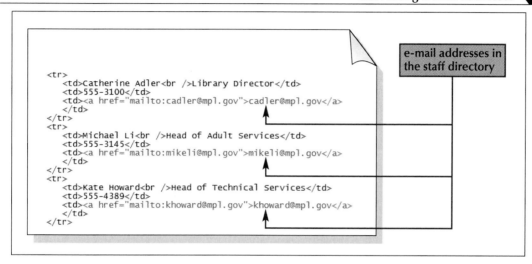

Kate would like you to scramble the e-mail addresses so that they don't appear within the Web page code; but when a browser loads and renders the page for a user, the e-mail addresses are unscrambled. See Figure 1-3. This mechanism will thwart most e-mail harvesters examining the document's HTML code while making the addresses available to users viewing the page on the Web. Note that some e-mail harvesters can still view both the underlying code and the page as they are rendered by a browser, so the proposed scrambling method is not 100% effective. However, because this technique will thwart many e-mail harvesters, Kate accepts it as a compromise solution.

Scrambling e-mail addresses | Figure 1-3

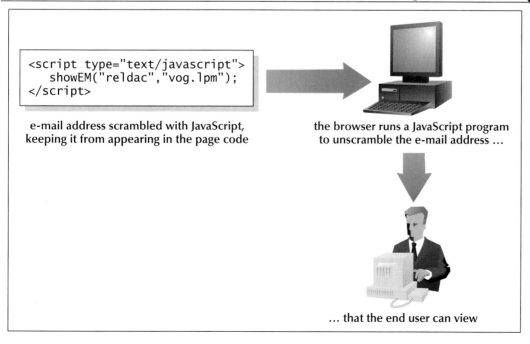

Neither HTML nor XHTML has features that allow you to scramble and unscramble the e-mail addresses from Kate's staff directory. This is not a standard function of Web browsers either. Therefore, you'll have to write a program to do this. Kate doesn't want library patrons to have to download any special applications; she wants the scrambling and unscrambling to appear behind the scenes of the library Web page. After some discussion, you decide that JavaScript is well suited to this task. You'll start on this project by first finding out just what JavaScript is and how to use it.

Server-Side and Client-Side Programming

Programming on the Web comes in two types: server-side programming and client-side programming. In **server-side programming**, a program is placed on the server that hosts a Web site. The program is then used to modify the contents and structure of Web pages. In some cases, users can interact with the program, requesting that specific information be displayed on a page, but the interaction is done remotely from the user to the server. See Figure 1-4.

| Figure 1-4 | Server-side programming |

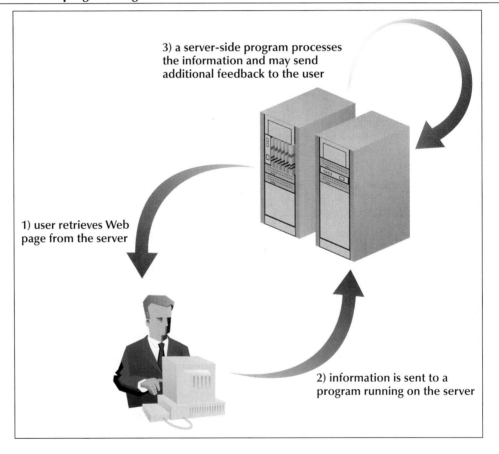

3) a server-side program processes the information and may send additional feedback to the user

1) user retrieves Web page from the server

2) information is sent to a program running on the server

There are advantages and disadvantages to this approach. A program running on a server can be connected to a database containing information not usually accessible to end users, enabling them to perform tasks not available on the client side. This enables Web pages to support such features as online banking, credit card transactions, and discussion groups. However, server-side programs use Web server resources, and in some cases a server's system administrator might place limitations on access to server-side programs to prevent users from continually accessing the server and potentially overloading the system. If the system is overloaded, an end user might have to sit through long delays as the server-side program handles multiple requests for information and action.

Client-side programming solves many of these problems by running programs on each user's computer rather than remotely off the server. See Figure 1-5.

Client-side programming ◀ Figure 1-5

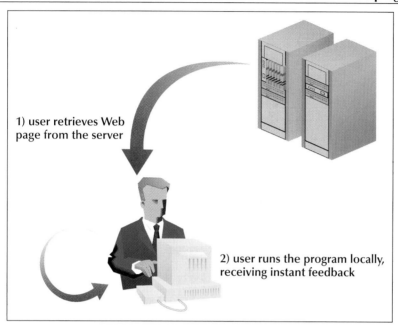

1) user retrieves Web page from the server

2) user runs the program locally, receiving instant feedback

Computing is thereby distributed so that the server is not overloaded with program-related requests. Client-side programs also tend to be more responsive because users do not have to wait for data to be sent over the Internet to a Web server. However, client-side programs can never completely replace server-side programming. For example, jobs such as running a search or processing a purchase order must be run from a central server because only the server contains the database needed to complete these types of operations.

In many cases, a combination of server-side and client-side programming is used. For example, Web forms typically use client-side programs to validate a user's entries (such as ensuring that all address information has been completely entered) and use server-side programs to submit the validated form for further processing (such as sending a purchase order to a central database). See Figure 1-6.

Figure 1-6 | **Combining client-side and server-side programming**

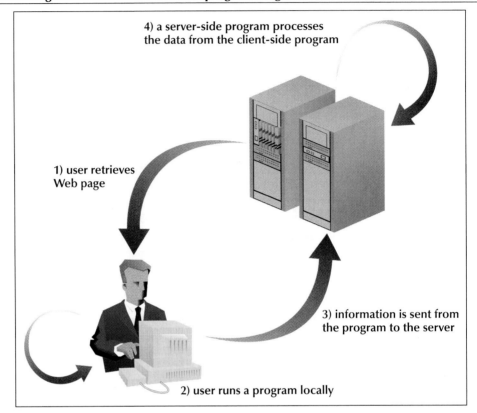

4) a server-side program processes the data from the client-side program

1) user retrieves Web page

3) information is sent from the program to the server

2) user runs a program locally

In this tutorial you'll work only with client-side programming. However, it's important to be aware that in many cases, a complete Web program includes both client-side and server-side elements.

The Development of JavaScript

Several programming languages can be run on the client side. One client-side programming language is Java. When Java was introduced, its advantages were quickly apparent and it was soon in wide use in many different browsers. However, creating a Java applet required access to the Java Development Kit (JDK), so nonprogrammers found it difficult to write their own Java applets.

To simplify this process, a team of developers from Netscape and Sun Microsystems created a subset of Java called **JavaScript**, which was different from Java in several important ways. Java is a **compiled language**, meaning that the program code must be submitted to a compiler that manipulates it, translating the code into a more basic language that machines can understand. For Java, this compiled code is the Java applet. Therefore, to create and run a program written in a compiled language, you need both the compiler and an application or operating system that can run the compiled code.

On the other hand, JavaScript is an **interpreted language**, meaning that the program code is executed directly without compiling. You need only two things to use JavaScript: 1) a text editor to write the JavaScript commands, and 2) a Web browser to run the commands and display the results. This means that JavaScript code can be inserted directly into an HTML or XHTML file, or placed in a separate text file that is linked to the Web page. JavaScript is not as powerful a computing language as Java, but it is simpler to use and meets the needs of most users who want to create programmable Web pages. Figure 1-7 highlights some of the key differences between Java and JavaScript.

Comparing Java and JavaScript ◀ Figure 1-7

Java	JavaScript
A compiled language	An interpreted language
Requires the JDK (Java Development Kit) to create the applet	Requires a text editor
Requires a Java virtual machine or interpreter to run the applet	Requires a browser that can interpret JavaScript code
Applet files are distinct from the HTML and XHTML code	JavaScript programs are integrated with HTML and XHTML code
Source code is hidden from the user	Source code is accessible to the user
Powerful, requiring programming knowledge and experience	Simpler, requiring less programming knowledge and experience
Secure; programs cannot write content to the hard disk	Secure; programs cannot write content to the hard disk; however, there are more security holes than in Java
Programs run on the client side	Programs run on the client side

Through the years, JavaScript has undergone several revisions. Internet Explorer actually supports a slightly different version of JavaScript called **JScript**. Although JScript is almost identical to JavaScript, some JavaScript commands are not supported in JScript, and vice versa. In addition, although it is tempting to use commands available in the latest JavaScript or JScript versions, these commands might prevent your programs from running on older browsers. For these reasons, you should always test your JavaScript programs on a variety of Web browsers.

Because of the proliferation of competing versions and revisions of scripting languages, the responsibility for developing a scripting standard has been transferred to an international body called the **European Computer Manufacturers Association (ECMA)**. The standard developed by the ECMA is called **ECMAScript**—though browsers still refer to it as JavaScript. Other client-side programming languages are also available to Web page designers, such as the Internet Explorer scripting language **VBScript**. However, because of the nearly universal support for JavaScript, you'll use this language for your work on the library Web site.

Working with the Script Element

JavaScript programs can be placed directly in an HTML file or they can be saved in an external text file. Placing JavaScript code in a Web page file means that users only need to retrieve one file from the server. In addition, because the code and the page it affects are both within the same file, it can be easier to locate and fix programming errors. However, if you place the code in a separate file, the programs you write can be shared by the different pages on your Web site. In this tutorial, you'll work with JavaScript code entered into an HTML file as well as code stored in an external file. You'll first examine how to insert JavaScript code directly into an HTML file.

Creating a Script Element

Scripts are entered into an HTML or XHTML file using the script element. The syntax of the script element is

```
<script type="mime-type">
   script commands
</script>
```

where *mime-type* defines the language in which the script is written and *script commands* are commands written in the scripting language. The type attribute is required for XHTML documents and should be used for HTML documents as well. The MIME type for JavaScript programs is text/javascript; meaning that for JavaScript programs, you would use the following form:

```
<script type="text/javascript">
   JavaScript commands
</script>
```

You might see other ways of entering script elements into Web page code. In earlier versions of HTML, the language attribute was used in place of the type attribute to indicate the script language. For older browsers, you indicate that the scripting language is JavaScript using the following form:

```
<script language="JavaScript">
   JavaScript commands
</script>
```

The language attribute has been deprecated and is not supported by strict applications of XHTML, so you should use the type attribute in its place if you want to conform with current standards.

Note that the script element can be used with programming languages other than JavaScript. Other client-side scripting languages are identified by using a different value for the type attribute. For example, if you use VBScript from Microsoft, the MIME type is text/vbscript. You won't use VBScript in this tutorial.

Reference Window | **Creating a Script Element**

- To place a JavaScript script element into the Web page, insert the two-sided tag
  ```
  <script type="mime-type">
     script commands
  </script>
  ```
  where *mime-type* defines the language in which the script is written and *script commands* are commands written in the scripting language.
- For JavaScript programs, set the *mime-type* to text/javascript.

Placing the Script Element

When a browser encounters a script element within a file, it treats any lines within the element as commands to be run. Script elements are processed in the order in which they appear within an HTML file; there is no limit to the number of script elements that you can use within a Web page. Scripts can be placed in either the head section or the body section of a document. When placed in the body section, a browser interprets and runs them as it loads the different elements of the Web page. Although a single page can contain many script elements, the browser still can work with them as a single unit. So JavaScript commands that are created in one script element can be referenced by commands in other script elements.

Writing a JavaScript Statement

Now that you've reviewed some of the basics involved in entering JavaScript into your HTML files, you'll examine how to enter JavaScript code. Every JavaScript program consists of a series of statements. Each **statement**—also known as a **command**—is a single line that indicates an action for the browser to take. A statement should end in a semicolon, employing the syntax

```
JavaScript statement;
```

where *JavaScript statement* is the code that the browser runs. The semicolon is the official way of notifying the browser that it has reached the end of the statement. Most browsers are very forgiving and still interpret most statements correctly even if you neglect to include the ending semicolon. However, it is good programming practice to include the semicolons and some browsers require them.

JavaScript and XML Parsers		InSight

Using JavaScript code within an XHTML file can lead to problems because XHTML parsers attempt to process the symbols in JavaScript code. Because character symbols such as angle brackets (<>) and the ampersand (&) are often used in JavaScript programs, this can lead to a page being rejected by an XHTML parser. To avoid this problem, you can place your JavaScript code within a CDATA section as follows:

```
<script type="text/javascript">
<![CDATA[
   JavaScript code
]]>
</script>
```

where *JavaScript code* is the code contained in the JavaScript program. The CDATA section marks the text of the JavaScript code as data that should not be processed by XHTML parsers. Unfortunately, the CDATA section is not well supported by current browsers.

A third alternative is not to embed your scripts within XHTML files at all, but instead to place them in external files. This practice has the added advantage of separating program code from page content. If you need to create valid XHTML documents, this is probably the best solution.

Writing Output to a Web Document

The first JavaScript program you add to Kate's document is a program that writes the text of an e-mail address into the Web page. Although you could enter the e-mail address directly, you use this opportunity to experiment with JavaScript. You also build on this simple statement as you progress through the rest of the tutorial. You insert the e-mail address for Catherine Adler as the first entry in the staff directory. Her e-mail address is cadler@mpl.gov. To write this text to the Web document, you insert the following statement:

```
<script type="text/javascript">
   document.write("cadler@mpl.gov");
</script>
```

This document.write() statement tells the browser to send the text string cadler@mpl.gov to the Web page document. To see how your browser applies this command, enter the script element and command into Kate's mpl.htm file.

To write text to the Web page using JavaScript:

▶ **1.** Return to the **mpl.htm** in your text editor.

▶ **2.** Locate the table cell after the entry for Catherine Adler and insert the following code, as shown in Figure 1-8:

```
<script type="text/javascript">
    document.write("cadler@mpl.gov");
</script>
```

Figure 1-8 ▶ **Inserting a script element**

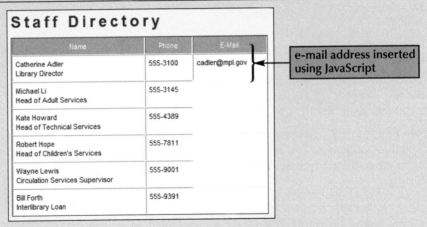

▶ **3.** Save your changes to the file and then reload **mpl.htm** in your Web browser. As shown in Figure 1-9, the text of Catherine's e-mail address should appear in the staff directory.

Figure 1-9 ▶ **Text generated by JavaScript**

Staff Directory

Name	Phone	E-Mail
Catherine Adler Library Director	555-3100	cadler@mpl.gov
Michael Li Head of Adult Services	555-3145	
Kate Howard Head of Technical Services	555-4389	
Robert Hope Head of Children's Services	555-7811	
Wayne Lewis Circulation Services Supervisor	555-9001	
Bill Forth Interlibrary Loan	555-9391	

e-mail address inserted using JavaScript

Trouble? Internet Explorer might display a yellow alert bar at the top of the browser window with a warning that it has restricted access to active content for security reasons. This is done to enable users to prevent their browsers from running unwanted scripts. To run the script, click the information bar and choose Allow Blocked Content from the pop-up menu, and then click Yes in the dialog box that follows.

Note that the placement of the script element tells the browser where to place the new text. Because the script element is placed between the opening and closing <td> tags, the text generated by the script is placed there as well. In more advanced JavaScript programs, you can direct your output to specific locations in the Web page document—but that's beyond the scope of this tutorial.

The document.write() Method

The document.write() method, which you just used to display the e-mail text, is one of the basic ways in JavaScript to send output to the Web document. Why is it called a method? In JavaScript, many commands involve working with objects in the Web page and browser. An **object** is any item—from the browser window itself to a document displayed in the browser to an element displayed within the document. Even the mouse pointer, the window scrollbars, or the browser application itself can be treated as an object. A **method** is a process by which JavaScript manipulates or acts upon the properties of an object. In this case, you've used the write() method to write new text into the document object. The document.write() method has the general syntax

```
document.write("text");
```

where *text* is a string of characters that you want written to the Web document. The text string can also include HTML tags. For example, the following statement writes the text Monroe Public Library marked as an h1 heading into a document:

```
document.write("<h1>Monroe Public Library</h1>");
```

When a browser encounters this statement, it places the text and the markup tags into the document and renders that text as if it had been entered directly into the HTML file.

Kate wants the e-mail addresses in the staff directory to appear as hypertext links. This requires placing the e-mail addresses within <a> tags and adding the href attribute value indicating the destination of each link. For example, the code to create a link for Catherine Adler's e-mail address is:

```
<a href="mailto:cadler@mpl.gov">cadler@mpl.gov</a>
```

Writing this text string requires you to include quotation marks around the href attribute value. Because text strings created with the document.write() method must be enclosed in quotes as well, you have to place one set of quotes within another. This is done by using both single and double quotation marks. If you want to write a double quotation mark as part of the code sent to the document, you enclose the quotation marks within single quotation marks. To write single quotation marks, you enclose them within a set of double quotation marks. The type of quotation mark must always be different. If you try to enclose double quotes within another set of double quotes, the browser won't know when the quoted text string begins and ends. The following JavaScript code encloses the href attribute value in single quotes and uses double quotes to mark the entire text to be written to the Web page document:

```
document.write("<a href='mailto:cadler@mpl.gov'>");
document.write("cadler@mpl.gov");
document.write("</a>");
```

Note that this example places the entire code into three separate document.write() commands. Although you could use one long text string, it might be more difficult to read and to type without making a mistake. A browser treats these consecutive commands as one long string of text to be written into the document.

Tip

Another method to write text to the Web page is the document.writeln() method, which is identical to the document.write() method except that it adds a line break to the end of the text.

Reference Window | **Writing to the Web Page**

- To write text to the Web page with JavaScript, use the method
  ```
  document.write("text")
  ```
  where *text* is the HTML code to be written to the Web page.

You're ready to add the code for the link to Catherine Adler's e-mail address.

To write the e-mail link for Catherine Adler:

▶ **1.** Return to the **mpl.htm** file in your text editor.

▶ **2.** Directly after the opening <script> element, insert the following command:

```
document.write("<a href='mailto:cadler@mpl.gov'>");
```

▶ **3.** Directly before the closing </script> tag, insert the following command:

```
document.write("</a>");
```

Figure 1-10 shows the revised code in the file.

| Figure 1-10 | Inserting several document.write() commands |

```
<tr>
    <td>Catherine Adler<br />Library Director</td>
    <td>555-3100</td>
    <td>
        <script type="text/javascript">
            document.write("<a href='mailto:cadler@mpl.gov'>");
            document.write("cadler@mpl.gov");
            document.write("</a>");
        </script>
    </td>
</tr>
```

▶ **4.** Save your changes and then reopen **mpl.htm** in your Web browser.

▶ **5.** Hover your mouse pointer over the e-mail address to verify that it is a link. As shown in Figure 1-11, the link to the e-mail address should appear in the browser's status bar.

Viewing an e-mail link

Figure 1-11

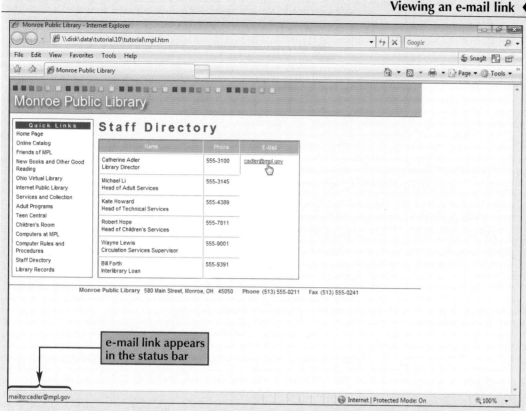

Trouble? If the link does not appear, verify that you included the opening and closing quotation marks in the JavaScript commands you just entered.

6. If you want to take a break before starting the next session, you can close any open files or programs now.

Understanding JavaScript Syntax

Besides the use of semicolons, there are some other syntax rules you should keep in mind when writing JavaScript statements. JavaScript is case sensitive so you must pay attention to whether or not letters are capitalized. For example, the following statements are not equivalent as far as JavaScript is concerned:

```
document.write("</a>");
Document.write("</a>");
```

The first command writes the HTML tag </a> to a Web page document. The second command is not recognized by a browser as a legitimate command and results in an error message. Figure 1-12 shows the error message generated by the Internet Explorer browser. The browser does not recognize the word Document (as opposed to document) and so cannot process the command. You'll examine how to handle this type of error later in this tutorial.

Figure 1-12 ▶ **An Internet Explorer error message resulting from improper case**

Like HTML, JavaScript ignores most occurrences of extra white space so you can indent your code to make it easier to read. You can see examples of this in Figure 1-10, where the newly entered statements are indented several spaces to make the commands stand out from the opening and closing <script> tags.

However, unlike HTML, you must be careful about line breaks occurring within a statement. A line break cannot be placed within the name of a JavaScript command or within a quoted text string without causing an error in the code. For example, the following line break is not allowed:

```
document.write("<a href='mailto:cadler@mpl.gov'>
cadler@mpl.gov
</a>");
```

It is good practice not to break a statement into several lines if you can avoid it. If you must break a long statement into several lines, you can indicate that the statement continues on the next line using a backslash, as follows:

```
document.write("<a href='mailto:cadler@mpl.gov'> \
cadler@mpl.gov \
</a>");
```

If the line break occurs within a quoted text string, you can also break the string into several distinct text strings placed over several lines by adding a plus symbol (+) at the end of each line, as follows:

```
document.write("<a href='mailto:cadler@mpl.gov'>" +
"cadler@mpl.gov" +
"</a>");
```

Tip

You can write a long text string to a Web page by breaking the text string into several document.write() statements.

The + symbol used in this command combines several text strings into a single text string. However, breaking a single statement into several lines is usually not recommended because of the possibility of introducing errors into the code. It should be done only with very long and complicated statements.

Supporting Non-JavaScript Browsers | InSight

For browsers that don't support scripts or that have their support for client-side scripts disabled, you can specify alternative content using the noscript element. The syntax of the noscript element is

```
<noscript>
   alternative content
</noscript>
```

where *alternative content* is the content a browser should display in place of accessing and running the script. For example, the following code displays a text message indicating that the page requires the use of JavaScript:

```
<script type="text/javascript">
   JavaScript statements
</script>
<noscript>
   <p>This page requires JavaScript. Please turn on JavaScript
      if your browser supports it and reload the page.</p>
</noscript>
```

Browsers that support client-side scripts and have that support enabled ignore the content of the noscript element.

You've completed the first phase of creating a script to scramble e-mail addresses in Kate's staff directory. At this point you've worked on learning how to create and run JavaScript code to write text to a Web document. In the next session you'll add the ability to create and work with variables and functions.

Session 1.1 Quick Check | Review

1. What is a client-side program? What is a server-side program?
2. What tag do you enter in your HTML code to create a script element for the JavaScript programming language?
3. What JavaScript command writes the text Public Library as an h2 heading to a Web document?
4. What JavaScript command would you enter to write the following tag to a Web document?
   ```
   <h2 id="sub">Public Library</h2>
   ```
5. How do you enter a single JavaScript statement on two lines?
6. Why would the following command produce an error message?
   ```
   document.Write("Monroe Public Library");
   ```
7. What code should you enter in an HTML file to display the following paragraph for browsers that don't support JavaScript?
   ```
   <p><i>JavaScript required</i></p>
   ```

Session 1.2

Working with Variables

In the previous session you learned how to write page content to a Web page using the document.write() method. Because you used this method to specify a text string explicitly, the code did little more than what you could have accomplished by entering the e-mail link directly into an HTML tag. However, the document.write() method is much more powerful and versatile when used in conjunction with variables. A **variable** is a named item in a program that stores information. Most JavaScript programs use variables to represent values and text strings. Variables are useful because they can store information created in one part of a program and use that information elsewhere. Variable values can also change as the program runs, enabling the program to display different values under varying conditions.

Declaring a Variable

It's common practice to introduce variables in your code by declaring them. **Declaring** a variable tells the JavaScript interpreter to reserve memory space for the variable. The statement to declare a variable is

```
var variable;
```

where *variable* is the name assigned to the variable. For example, the following statement creates a variable named emLink:

```
var emLink;
```

You can declare multiple variables by entering the variable names in a comma-separated list. The following statement declares three variables named emLink, userName, and emServer:

```
var emLink, userName, emServer;
```

JavaScript imposes some limits on variable names:

- The first character must be either a letter or an underscore character (_).
- The remaining characters can be letters, numbers, or underscore characters.
- Variable names cannot contain spaces.
- You cannot use words that JavaScript has reserved for other purposes. For example, you cannot name a variable document.write.

Like other aspects of the JavaScript language, variable names are case sensitive. The variable names emLink and emlink represent two different variables. One common programming mistake is to forget this important fact and to use uppercase and lowercase letters interchangeably in variable names.

Tip

To avoid programming errors, use a consistent pattern for case in variable names.

Assigning a Value to a Variable

Once a variable has been created or declared, you can assign it a value. The statement to assign a value to a variable is

```
variable = value;
```

where *variable* is the variable name and *value* is the value assigned to the variable. For example, the following statement stores the text string cadler in a variable named userName:

```
userName = "cadler";
```

You can combine the variable declaration and the assignment of a value in a single statement. The following statements declare the userName and emServer variables, and set their initial values:

```
var userName = "cadler", emServer = "mpl.gov";
```

Note that declaring a variable with the var keyword is not required in JavaScript. The first time you use a variable, JavaScript creates the variable in computer memory. The following statement both creates the director variable (if it has not already been declared in a previous statement) and assigns it an initial value:

```
director = "Catherine Adler";
```

Although it's not required, it's considered good programming style to include the var command whenever you create a variable. Doing so helps you keep track of the variables a program uses and also makes it easier for others to read and interpret your code.

> **Tip**
>
> To make your code easier to interpret, place all of your variable declarations at the beginning of your program, along with comments describing the purpose of each variable.

Declaring a JavaScript Variable | Reference Window

- To declare a JavaScript variable, run the statement
  ```
  var variable
  ```
  where *variable* is the name assigned to the variable.
- To declare a JavaScript variable and set its initial value, use
  ```
  var variable = value;
  ```
  where *value* is the initial value of the variable.

Using what you've learned about variables, you're ready to add two variables to the script element you created in the last session. The first variable, userName, will store the text string cadler, which is Catherine Adler's username on the library's mail server. The second variable, emServer, will store the text string mpl.gov, which is the domain name of the mail server. Later you'll revise this code to place different values in these variables, but you start with these two fixed values. By breaking up Catherine Adler's e-mail address into two parts, you'll make it easier to hide the e-mail address from e-mail harvesters.

To create two JavaScript variables:

1. Return to the **mpl.htm** file in your text editor.

2. Locate the script element you created in the last session. Directly below the opening <script> tag, insert the following code, as shown in Figure 1-13:
   ```
   var userName = "cadler";
   var emServer = "mpl.gov";
   ```

Figure 1-13	Declaring JavaScript variables

```
<tr>
    <td>Catherine Adler<br />Library Director</td>
    <td>555-3100</td>
    <td>
        <script type="text/javascript">
            var userName = "cadler";
            var emServer = "mpl.gov";

            document.write("<a href='mailto:cadler@mpl.gov'>");
            document.write("cadler@mpl.gov");
            document.write("</a>");
        </script>
    </td>
</tr>
```

3. Save your changes to the file.

Working with Data Types

So far, the examples you've explored have used variables that store text strings. However, JavaScript variables can store different types of information. The type of information stored in a variable is referred to as its **data type**. JavaScript supports the following data types:

- numeric value
- text string
- Boolean value
- null value

A **numeric value** is any number, such as 13, 22.5, or -3.14159. Numbers can also be expressed in scientific notation, such as 5.1E2 for the value 5.1×10^2 (or 510). Numeric values are specified without any quotation marks. So if you wished to store the value 2007 in the year variable, you would use the statement

```
year = 2007;
```

rather than

```
year = "2007";
```

A **text string** is any group of characters, such as "Hello" or "Happy Holidays!" or "421 Sunrise Lane." Text strings must be enclosed within either double or single quotation marks, but not both. The string value 'Hello' is acceptable, but the string value "Hello' is not.

A **Boolean value** indicates the truth or falsity of a statement. There are only two Boolean values: true and false. For example, the following statement sets the value of the useSafari variable to true and the value of the useIE variable to false:

```
useSafari = true;
useIE = false;
```

Tip

If a Boolean variable's value is left undefined, it is interpreted by JavaScript as having a value of false.

Boolean values are most often used in programs that must act differently based on different conditions. The useSafari variable cited above might be used in a program that tests whether a user is running the Safari browser. If the value is set to true, the program might be written to run differently for the user than if the value were set to false.

Finally, a **null value** indicates that no value has yet been assigned to the variable. This can also be done explicitly using the keyword null in assigning a value to the variable, as in the statement

```
emLink = null;
```

or implicitly by simply declaring the variable without assigning it a value, as follows:

```
var emLink;
```

In either case, the emLink variable will have a null value until it is assigned a value using one of the other data types.

In JavaScript, a variable's data type is always determined by the context in which it is used. This means that a variable can switch from one data type to another within a single program. In the following two statements, the variable Month starts out as a numeric variable with an initial value of 5, but then becomes a text string variable containing the text March:

```
Month = 5;
Month = "March";
```

When variables are not strictly tied to specific data types like this, programmers refer to the language as a **weakly typed language**; JavaScript is one such language. Other programming languages are **strongly typed languages**, forcing the programming to explicitly identify a variable's data type. In those languages, the above code would result in an error because a given variable cannot store more than one type of data.

A weakly typed language such as JavaScript relieves the programmer from the task of assigning a data type to a variable. However, this can lead to unpredictable results if you aren't careful. For example, in JavaScript the + symbol can be used with either numeric values or text strings. When used with numeric values, it returns the sum of the values—so that the code

```
var total = 5 + 4;
```

stores the value 9 in the total variable. When used with text strings, the + symbol combines the text strings—so that the code

```
var emLink = "cadler" + "@" + "mpl.gov";
```

stores the text string cadler@mpl.gov in the emLink variable. However, when used with both text strings and numeric values, the + symbol treats the numeric value as a text string so that the code

```
x = 5;
y = "4";
z = x+y;
```

stores the text string 54 in the z variable because the y variable stores "4" as a text string, not a number. This result is not readily apparent from the code without a prior understanding of how JavaScript handles text and numeric values. This is one of the limitations of a weakly typed language in which data types are inferred by the rules of the language and not by the programmer.

To see how the + symbol works with text string variables, you'll add a third variable to your script. The emLink variable will be used to store the complete e-mail address for Catherine Adler by combining the userName variable with the emServer variable.

To create the emLink variable:

1. Return to the **mpl.htm** file in your text editor.

2. Directly below the command to create the emServer variable, insert the following command, as shown in Figure 1-14:

```
var emLink = userName + "@" + emServer;
```

Figure 1-14 ► **Creating the emLink variable**

```
<script type="text/javascript">
    var userName = "cadler";
    var emServer = "mpl.gov";
    var emLink = userName + "@" + emServer;

    document.write("<a href='mailto:cadler@mpl.gov'>");
    document.write("cadler@mpl.gov");
    document.write("</a>");
</script>
```

the value stored
in the emLink
variable is
cadler@mpl.gov

► **3.** Save your changes to the file.

After you've created a variable, you can use it in JavaScript statements in place of the value it contains. The following code writes the text string Monroe Public Library to a Web page:

```
var libName = "Monroe Public Library";
document.write(libName);
```

You can also use the + symbol to combine a variable with a text string and then write the combined text string to the document. The following statements send the text string

```
<p>Welcome to the Monroe Library</p>
```

to the Web document:

```
var libName = "Monroe Library";
document.write("<p>Welcome to the "+libName+"</p>");
```

You can use the document.write() command with the variables you've already created to write the hypertext link for Catherine Adler's e-mail address. The code is as follows:

```
document.write("<a href='mailto:" + emLink + "'>");
document.write(emLink);
document.write("</a>");
```

If the text string cadler@mpl.gov is stored in the emLink variable, these commands will write the following code to the Web page:

```
<a href='mailto:cadler@mpl.gov'>
caldler@mpl.gov
</a>
```

Notice that the document.write() command nests single quotes within double quotes so that the HTML code written to the Web page includes the value of the href attribute within a set of single quotation marks. You'll add this JavaScript code to the Web page, replacing the previous document.write() commands.

To replace the document.write() commands in the script:

► **1.** Return to the **mpl.htm** file in your text editor.

► **2.** Replace the three document.write() commands in the script with the following code, as shown in Figure 1-15:

```
document.write("<a href='mailto:" + emLink + "'>");
document.write(emLink);
document.write("</a>");
```

Writing the value of the emLink variable to the Web page ◀ **Figure 1-15**

```
<script type="text/javascript">
   var userName = "cadler";
   var emServer = "mpl.gov";
   var emLink = userName + "@" + emServer;

   document.write("<a href='mailto:" + emLink + "'>");
   document.write(emLink);
   document.write("</a>");
</script>
```

▶ **3.** Save your changes to the file and then reload **mpl.htm** in your Web browser. The hypertext link for Catherine Adler's e-mail address should remain unchanged from what was shown earlier in Figure 1-11.

Creating a JavaScript Function

So far, in writing code for the staff directory page, you've focused on the e-mail address of only one person. However, five other individuals are listed in the staff directory. If you wanted to use JavaScript to write the e-mail links for the rest of the directory, you could repeat the code you used for Catherine Adler's entry five more times. However, JavaScript provides a simpler way of doing this.

When you want to reuse the same JavaScript commands throughout your Web page, you store the commands in a function. A **function** is a collection of commands that performs an action or returns a value. Every function includes a **function name**, which identifies it, and a set of commands that are run when the function is called. Some functions also require **parameters**, which are variables associated with the function. The general syntax of a JavaScript function is

```
function function_name(parameters){
   JavaScript commands
}
```

where *function_name* is the name of the function, *parameters* is a comma-separated list of variables used in the function, and *JavaScript commands* are the statements run by the function. Function names, like variable names, are case sensitive. For example, weekDay and WEEKDAY are treated as different function names. A function name must begin with a letter or underscore (_) and cannot contain any spaces. The following is an example of a function named showMsg() that writes a paragraph to a Web document:

```
function showMsg() {
   document.write("<p>Welcome to the Monroe Library</p>");
}
```

There are no parameters to this function. If you had stored the name of the library in a function parameter named libName, the showMsg() function would look as follows:

```
function showMsg(libName) {
   document.write("<p>Welcome to the" + libName +"</p>");
}
```

If the libName parameter had the value Monroe Public Library, then the HTML code

```
<p>Welcome to the Monroe Public Library</p>
```

would be sent to the Web document.

Rather than rewrite the code for generating the e-mail link for each person in the staff directory, you'll put the commands in a function named showEM(). The code for the showEM() function is as follows:

```
function showEM(userName,emServer) {
    var emLink = userName+"@" + emServer;
    document.write("<a href='mailto:" + emLink + "'>");
    document.write(emLink);
    document.write("</a>");
}
```

Compare the code for this function to the script you created in Figure 1-15. Note that userName and emServer variables from that earlier code are used here as parameters of the showEM() function.

Add the showEM() function to the document head of the mpl.htm file.

To insert the showEM() function:

▶ **1.** Return to the **mpl.htm** file in your text editor.

▶ **2.** Directly above the closing </head> tag, insert the following script element and function, as shown in Figure 1-16:

```
<script type="text/javascript">
    function showEM(userName,emServer) {
        var emLink = userName + "@"+emServer;
        document.write("<a href='mailto:" + emLink + "'>");
        document.write(emLink);
        document.write("</a>");
    }
</script>
```

Figure 1-16 ▶ **Inserting the showEM() function**

```
<title>Monroe Public Library</title>
<link href="mplstyles.css" rel="stylesheet" type="text/css" />

<script type="text/javascript">
    function showEM(userName, emServer) {
        var emLink = userName + "@" + emServer;
        document.write("<a href='mailto:" + emLink + "'>");
        document.write(emLink);
        document.write("</a>");
    }
</script>
</head>
```

Calling a Function

When a browser encounters a function, it bypasses it without executing any of the code it contains. The function is executed only when called by another JavaScript command. If the function has any parameters, the initial values of the parameters are set when the function is called. The expression to call a function and run the commands it contains has the following form:

```
function_name(parameter values)
```

where *function_name* is the name of the function and *parameter values* is a comma-separated list of values that match the parameters of the function. For example, to call the showMsg() function described earlier using the text string Monroe Public Library as the value of the libName parameter, you would run the command

```
showMsg("Monroe Public Library");
```

The HTML code

```
<p>Welcome to the Monroe Public Library</p>
```

would be written to the document.

Parameter values can also themselves be variables. The following commands store the library name in a text string variable named libText and call the showMsg() function using that variable as the parameter value:

```
var libText="Cutler Public Library";
```

```
showMsg(libText);
```

The result is that the following HTML code is written to the Web document:

```
<p>Welcome to the Cutler Public Library</p>
```

Functions can be called repeatedly with different parameter values to achieve different results. For example, the following code calls the showMsg() function twice with different parameter values to display two welcome paragraphs for the Monroe and Cutler Public Libraries:

```
var libText = "Monroe Public Library";
showMsg(libText);
var libText2 = "Cutler Public Library";
showMsg(libText2);
```

You can use a function call to run the showEM() function you just entered. To write a hypertext link for Catherine Adler's e-mail address, the function call is as follows:

```
showEM("cadler","mpl.gov");
```

As a result, the userName parameter has an initial value of cadler and the emServer parameter has the initial value of mpl.gov. You're ready to replace the commands you entered earlier to write the hypertext link for Catherine Adler's e-mail address with this function call.

To call the showEM() function:

1. Return to the **mpl.htm** file in your text editor, and scroll down the file to the script element containing the JavaScript code for Catherine Adler's e-mail address.

2. Replace all of the commands within the script element with the following command, as shown in Figure 1-17:

```
showEM("cadler","mpl.gov");
```

Figure 1-17   Calling the showEM() function

```
<tr>
    <td>Catherine Adler<br />Library Director</td>
    <td>555-3100</td>
    <td>

        <script type="text/javascript">
            showEM("cadler","mpl.gov");
        </script>

    </td>
</tr>
```

   3. Save your changes to the file and then reload **mpl.htm** in your Web browser. The link to Catherine Adler's e-mail address should once again appear in the staff table, unchanged from Figure 1-11.

Using the function call gives the same result as the code you used earlier. However, the great advantage is that you can reuse the showEM() function for other e-mail addresses in the staff directory by simply changing the parameter values. You don't have to reenter all four of the program lines. For longer programs this is a substantial improvement.

Reference Window | **Creating and Calling a JavaScript Function**

- To create a JavaScript function that performs an action, insert the structure
  ```
  function function_name(parameters){
     JavaScript commands
  }
  ```
  where *function_name* is the name of the function, *parameters* is a comma-separated list of variable names used in the function, and *JavaScript commands* are the statements run by the function.
- To create a JavaScript function that returns a value, use
  ```
  function function_name(parameters){
     JavaScript commands
     return value;
  }
  ```
  where *value* is the value returned by the function.
- To call a JavaScript function, run the command
  ```
  function_name(values)
  ```
  where *function_name* is the name of the JavaScript function and *values* is a comma-separated list of values for each of the parameters of the function.

Kate asks you to call the showEM() function for the other e-mail addresses in the staff table.

To add the remaining e-mail addresses:

   1. Return to the **mpl.htm** file in your text editor.

   2. Locate the entry for Michael Li. His e-mail address is mikeli@mpl.gov. Add the following script element to the empty table cell that directly follows the Michael Li entry:

```
<script type="text/javascript">
    showEM("mikeli","mpl.gov");
</script>
```

3. Kate Howard's e-mail address is khoward@mpl.gov. Insert the following script element in the empty table cell for her entry in the staff directory:

```
<script type="text/javascript">
   showEM("khoward","mpl.gov");
</script>
```

Trouble? You can use the copy and paste feature of your text editor because the additions you'll make to the file in these steps are so similar. If you're not sure where to place these script elements, refer to Figure 1-18.

4. Robert Hope's e-mail address is rhope@mpl.gov. Enter the following script element for his entry:

```
<script type="text/javascript">
   showEM("rhope","mpl.gov");
</script>
```

5. Wayne Lewis's e-mail address is wlewis@mpl.gov. Enter the following script element in the empty table cell for his entry:

```
<script type="text/javascript">
   showEM("wlewis","mpl.gov");
</script>
```

6. Bill Forth's e-mail address is bforth@mpl.gov. Enter the following code in the empty table cell for his entry:

```
<script type="text/javascript">
   showEM("bforth","mpl.gov");
</script>
```

Figure 1-18 shows the revised code in the mpl.htm file.

Inserting the remaining e-mail addresses   Figure 1-18

```
<tr>
   <td>Michael Li<br />Head of Adult Services</td>
   <td>555-3145</td>
   <td>
      <script type="text/javascript">
         showEM("mikeli","mpl.gov");
      </script>
   </td>
</tr>
<tr>
   <td>Kate Howard<br />Head of Technical Services</td>
   <td>555-4389</td>
   <td>
      <script type="text/javascript">
         showEM("khoward","mpl.gov");
      </script>
   </td>
</tr>
<tr>
   <td>Robert Hope<br />Head of Children's Services</td>
   <td>555-7811</td>
   <td>
      <script type="text/javascript">
         showEM("rhope","mpl.gov");
      </script>
   </td>
</tr>
<tr>
   <td>Wayne Lewis<br />Circulation Services Supervisor</td>
   <td>555-9001</td>
   <td>
      <script type="text/javascript">
         showEM("wlewis","mpl.gov");
      </script>
   </td>
</tr>
<tr>
   <td>Bill Forth<br />Interlibrary Loan</td>
   <td>555-9391</td>
   <td>
      <script type="text/javascript">
         showEM("bforth","mpl.gov");
      </script>
   </td>
</tr>
```

7. Save your changes to the file and reload **mpl.htm** in your Web browser. Figure 1-19 shows the complete list of e-mail addresses in the staff directory. Verify that each e-mail address is a hypertext link by hovering your mouse pointer over the address text and observe the destination of the link in the browser's status bar.

Figure 1-19 ▷ **The complete list of e-mail address links in the staff directory**

Name	Phone	E-Mail
Catherine Adler Library Director	555-3100	cadler@mpl.gov
Michael Li Head of Adult Services	555-3145	mikeli@mpl.gov
Kate Howard Head of Technical Services	555-4389	khoward@mpl.gov
Robert Hope Head of Children's Services	555-7811	rhope@mpl.gov
Wayne Lewis Circulation Services Supervisor	555-9001	wlewis@mpl.gov
Bill Forth Interlibrary Loan	555-9391	bforth@mpl.gov

8. If you want to take a break before starting the next session, you can close any open files and programs now.

Creating a Function to Return a Value

You created the showEM() function to perform the action of writing a text string to your Web document. The other use of functions is to return a calculated value. For a function to return a value, it must include a return statement. The syntax of a function that returns a value is

```
function function_name(parameters) {
    JavaScript commands
    return value;
}
```

where *value* is the calculated value that is returned by the function. For example, the following CalcArea() function calculates the area of a rectangular region by multiplying the region's length and width:

```
function CalcArea(length, width) {
    var area = length*width;
    return area;
}
```

In this function, the value of the area variable is returned by the function. You can then call the function to retrieve this value. The following code uses the function to calculate the area of a rectangle whose dimensions are 8 × 6 units:

```
var x = 8;
var y = 6;
var z = CalcArea(x,y);
```

The first two commands assign the values 8 and 6 to the x and y variables, respectively. The values of both of these variables are then sent to the CalcArea() function as the values of the length and width parameters. The CalcArea() function uses these values to calculate the area, which it then returns, assigning that value to the z variable. As a result of these commands, a value of 48 is assigned to the z variable.

Functions that return a value can be placed within larger expressions. For example, the following code calls the CalcArea() function within an expression that multiplies the area value by 2:

```
var z = CalcArea(x,y)*2;
```

When this command is run, the value of the CalcArea() function is returned, multiplied by 2, and then stored in the z variable. Using the above parameter values, the value of the z variable is 96.

Functions and Variable Scope | InSight

As you've seen, the commands within a function are run only when called. This has an impact on how variables within the function are treated. Every variable you create has a property known as **scope**, which indicates where you can reference a variable within the Web page. A variable's scope can be either local or global. A variable created within a JavaScript function has **local scope** and can be referenced only within that function. Variables with local scope are sometimes referred to as **local variables**. In the function you created in this session, the emLink variable has local scope and can be referenced only within the showEM() function. Parameters such as the userName and emServer parameters from the showEM() function also have local scope and are not recognized outside of the function in which they're used. When the showEM() function stops running, those variables and their values are not held in the computer memory and their values can no longer be accessed.

Variables not declared within functions have **global scope** and can be referenced from within all script elements on the Web page. Variables with global scope are often referred to as **global variables**.

You've successfully added the showEM() function to the staff directory page. In the next session you'll continue to add features to that function, including the ability to scramble and unscramble e-mail addresses to further hide them from e-mail harvesters.

Session 1.2 Quick Check | Review

1. Specify the JavaScript command to declare a variable named weekday with an initial value of Friday.
2. Describe two uses of the + symbol.
3. What are the four data types supported by JavaScript?
4. Specify the JavaScript command to write the code

   ```
   <img src='file' alt='' />
   ```

   to the Web page, where file is the value stored in the fileName variable.
5. What are the two purposes of a JavaScript function?
6. Write a JavaScript function named CalcVol() to calculate the volume of a rectangular solid. The function should have three parameters named x, y, and z, and return the value of a variable named Vol that is equal to x*y*z.
7. Write the JavaScript statement to call the CalcVol() function with values of x = 3, y = 10, and z = 4, storing the result of the function in a variable named TotalVol.
8. What is variable scope?

Session 1.3

Accessing an External JavaScript File

You show your work on the staff directory to Kate. She's happy that you were able to use JavaScript to generate the e-mail addresses, but she's still concerned that the text of each employee's username and mail server are present in the document as parameter values of the showEM() function. She would like to have those values hidden from any e-mail harvesters that might be scanning the document code. You discuss the issue with a programmer friend who sends you a file containing the following function:

```
function stringReverse(textString) {
   if (!textString) return '';
   var revString='';
   for (i = textString.length-1; i>=0; i--)
      revString+=textString.charAt(i);
   return revString;
}
```

Interpreting the code contained within this function is beyond the scope of this tutorial, but for now it is sufficient to know in general what the function does. The function has a single parameter named textString, which stores a string of characters. The function then creates a variable name revString that stores the characters from textString in reverse order, and that reversed text string is returned by the function. For example, if you called the function in the statements

```
userName = stringReverse("reldac");
emServer = stringReverse("vog.lpm");
```

the userName variable would have the value cadler, and the emServer variable would have the value mpl.gov (the text strings reldac and vog.lpm in reverse order). You show this function to Kate and she agrees that this will be sufficient to hide the actual username and server name from most e-mail address harvesters.

The stringReverse() function has already been entered for you and stored in a file named spam.js. To access JavaScript code and functions placed in external files, you employ the same script element you've been using to insert JavaScript commands directly into the staff directory document. The code to access an external script file is

```
<script src="url" type="mime-type"></script>
```

where *url* is the URL of the external document and *mime-type* is the language of the code in the external script file. For example, to access the code in the spam.js file, you would add the following script element to your Web document:

```
<script type="text/javascript" src="spam.js"></script>
```

Tip

Place all script elements that reference external files in the document head so that those programs are immediately loaded by the Web browser and can be referenced by any code within the Web page.

It's a common practice for JavaScript programmers to create libraries of functions located in external files that are easily accessible to pages on the entire Web site. Any new functions added to the external file are then instantly accessible to each Web page without having to edit the contents of those pages. External files containing JavaScript commands and functions always have the file extension .js to distinguish them from files containing script commands from other languages.

When a browser encounters a script element that points to an external file, it loads the contents of the external file into the Web document just as if the programmer had entered the code from the external file directly into the Web file. See Figure 1-20.

Using an external script file ◀ **Figure 1-20**

```
function stringReverse(textString) {          <title>Monroe Public Library</title>
    if (!textString) return '';               <link href="mplstyles.css" rel="stylesheet" type="text/css" />
    var revString='';
    for (i = textString.length-1; i>=0; i--)  <script src="spam.js" type="text/javascript"></script>
        revString+=textString.charAt(i)
    return revString;                         <script type="text/javascript">
}                                                 function showEM(userName, emServer) {
                                                      var emLink = userName + "@" + emServer;
                                                      document.write("<a href='mailto:" + emLink + "'>");
                                                      document.write(emLink);
                                                      document.write("</a>");
                                                  }
                                              </script>
                                            </head>
```

Accessing an External JavaScript File | Reference Window

- To access the code stored in an external file, add the script element
  ```
  <script src="url" type="mime-type"></script>
  ```
  to the Web page, where *url* is the URL of the external document and *mime-type* is the language of the code in the external script file.
- For JavaScript files, set the *mime-type* to text/javascript.
- JavaScript files usually have the file extension .js.

You insert a script element into the staff directory page to access the code from the spam.js file.

To access the code in the spam.js file:

▶ **1.** Return to the **mpl.htm** file in your text editor.

▶ **2.** Directly above the opening <script> tag in the head section of the file, insert the following script element, as shown in Figure 1-21:

```
<script src="spam.js" type="text/javascript"></script>
```

Inserting a link to an external script file ◀ **Figure 1-21**

```
<title>Monroe Public Library</title>
<link href="mplstyles.css" rel="stylesheet" type="text/css" />

<script src="spam.js" type="text/javascript"></script>

<script type="text/javascript">
    function showEM(userName, emServer) {
        var emLink = userName + "@" + emServer;
        document.write("<a href='mailto:" + emLink + "'>");
        document.write(emLink);
        document.write("</a>");
    }
</script>
</head>
```

Next you'll want to confirm that the stringReverse() function from the spam.js file is working correctly. To test the function, call it to reverse the text string values of the user-Name and emServer parameters in the showEM() function.

To test the stringReverse() function:

▶ **1.** Scroll down to the showEM() function.

▶ **2.** Insert the following two lines of code at the top of the function, as shown in Figure 1-22:

```
userName = stringReverse(userName);
emServer = stringReverse(emServer);
```

Figure 1-22 | Calling the stringReverse() function

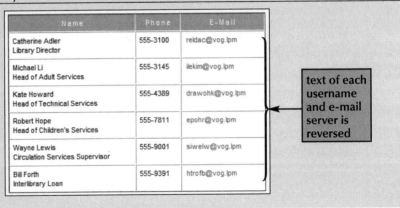

```
<script type="text/javascript">
    function showEM(userName, emServer) {

        userName = stringReverse(userName);
        emServer = stringReverse(emServer);

        var emLink = userName + "@" + emServer;
        document.write("<a href='mailto:" + emLink + "'>");
        document.write(emLink);
        document.write("</a>");
    }
</script>
```

> reverse the order of the characters in the userName and emServer parameters

▶ **3.** Save your changes to the file, and then reload **mpl.htm** in your Web browser. As shown in Figure 1-23, the text of the username and mail server portions of each employee's e-mail address appears reversed on the Web page.

Figure 1-23 | Staff directory with e-mail addresses reversed

Name	Phone	E-Mail
Catherine Adler Library Director	555-3100	reldac@vog.lpm
Michael Li Head of Adult Services	555-3145	ilekim@vog.lpm
Kate Howard Head of Technical Services	555-4389	drawohk@vog.lpm
Robert Hope Head of Children's Services	555-7811	epohr@vog.lpm
Wayne Lewis Circulation Services Supervisor	555-9001	siwelw@vog.lpm
Bill Forth Interlibrary Loan	555-9391	htrofb@vog.lpm

> text of each username and e-mail server is reversed

The stringReverse() function appears to be working correctly. Of course, you don't want the e-mail addresses to be reversed in the rendered document; you want those addresses to appear correctly. Instead, you want the code within the document reversed to thwart e-mail harvesters. This means that you need to enter the username and e-mail server names in reverse order.

To change the userName and emServer parameter values:

▶ **1.** Return to the **mpl.htm** file in your text editor.

▶ **2.** Scroll down the file to the script element for Catherine Adler's e-mail address and change the value of the userName parameter from cadler to **reldac**. Change the value of the emServer parameter from mpl.gov to **vog.lpm**.

▶ **3.** Change the parameter values for Michael Li's e-mail address to **ilekim** and **vog.lpm**.

▶ **4.** Change the parameter values for Katherine Howard's e-mail address to **drawohk** and **vog.lpm**.

▶ **5.** Change the parameter values for Robert Hope's e-mail address to **epohr** and **vog.lpm**.

▶ **6.** Change the parameter values for Wayne Lewis's e-mail address to **siwelw** and **vog.lpm**.

▶ **7.** Finally, change the parameter values for Bill Forth's e-mail address to **htrofb** and **vog.lpm**. Figure 1-24 highlights the revised code in the file.

Entering the reversed userName and emServer parameter values ◀ **Figure 1-24**

```html
<tr>
    <td>Catherine Adler<br />Library Director</td>
    <td>555-3100</td>
    <td>
        <script type="text/javascript">
            showEM("reldac","vog.lpm");
        </script>
    </td>
</tr>

<tr>
    <td>Michael Li<br />Head of Adult Services</td>
    <td>555-3145</td>
    <td>
        <script type="text/javascript">
            showEM("ilekim","vog.lpm");
        </script>
    </td>
</tr>
<tr>
    <td>Kate Howard<br />Head of Technical Services</td>
    <td>555-4389</td>
    <td>
        <script type="text/javascript">
            showEM("drawohk","vog.lpm");
        </script>
    </td>
</tr>
<tr>
    <td>Robert Hope<br />Head of Children's Services</td>
    <td>555-7811</td>
    <td>
        <script type="text/javascript">
            showEM("epohr","vog.lpm");
        </script>
    </td>
</tr>
<tr>
    <td>Wayne Lewis<br />Circulation Services Supervisor</td>
    <td>555-9001</td>
    <td>
        <script type="text/javascript">
            showEM("siwelw","vog.lpm");
        </script>
    </td>
</tr>
<tr>
    <td>Bill Forth<br />Interlibrary Loan</td>
    <td>555-9391</td>
    <td>
        <script type="text/javascript">
            showEM("htrofb","vog.lpm");
        </script>
    </td>
</tr>
```

▶ **8.** Save your changes to the file and reload **mpl.htm** in your Web browser. As shown in Figure 1-25, the text characters of the e-mail addresses for staff members now appear in the correct order.

Figure 1-25 Final staff directory page

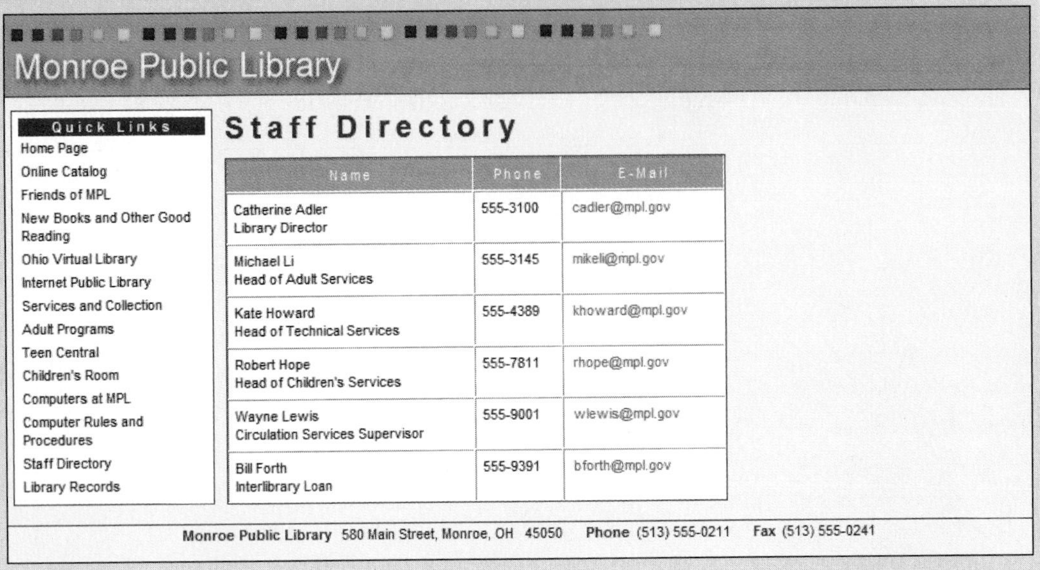

You review your progress with Kate. As she scans through the code in the HTML file, she's pleased to note that none of the e-mail addresses for the six staff members appears in any readable form. By breaking the e-mail addresses into two parts (the userName and the emServer parts) and entering the text in reverse order, you have effectively hidden the actual addresses from harvesting programs.

Commenting JavaScript Code

Kate is pleased to see how JavaScript can unscramble the e-mail addresses and present them to users in a readable form. However, she is concerned that in the future, she might forget how this program is designed to work. She would like you to add some comments to the code you created.

Inserting Single-Line and Multiline Comments

Commenting your code is an important programming practice. It helps other people who examine your code to understand what your programs are designed to do and how they work. It can even help you in the future when you return to edit the programs you've written and need to recall the programming choices you made. In JavaScript, comments can be added to script elements on either single or multiple lines. The syntax of a single-line comment is

```
// comment text
```

where *comment text* is the JavaScript comment. Single-line comments can be placed within the same line as a JavaScript command, making it easier to interpret each command in your code. The following is an example of a JavaScript statement that includes a single-line comment:

```
document.write(emLink); // write e-mail address to the Web page
```

For more extended comments, you place the comment text on several lines using the following structure:

```
/*
    comment text spanning
    several lines
*/
```

The following is an example of a multiline comment applied to a JavaScript program:

```
/*
    The showEM() function displays a link to the user's e-mail address.
    The text of the user and e-mail server names are entered in
    reverse order to thwart e-mail harvesters.
*/
```

Inserting JavaScript Comments | Reference Window

- To insert a single-line comment into a JavaScript program, use
  ```
  // comment text
  ```
  where *comment text* is the JavaScript comment. Single-line comments can be placed on the same line as a JavaScript command.
- To insert several lines of comments, use the following:
  ```
  /*
      comment text spanning
      several lines
  */
  ```

Kate would like you to add comments to the showEM() function you created.

To add comments to your JavaScript code:

▶ **1.** Return to the **mpl.htm** file in your text editor.

▶ **2.** Add the following multiline comment directly below the opening function statement for the showEM() function:

```
/*
    The showEM() function displays a link to the user's
    e-mail address.
    The text of the user and e-mail server names are entered in
    reverse order to thwart e-mail harvesters.
*/
```

▶ **3.** Add the following single-line comment to the end of the line that reverses the value of the userName parameter:

```
// reverse the text of the userName parameter
```

▶ **4.** Add the following comment to the end of the line that reverses the value of the emServer parameter:

```
// reverse the text of the emServer parameter
```

▶ **5.** Finally, add the following comment to the end of the line creating the emLink variable:

```
// combine the text of userName and emServer
```

Figure 1-26 displays these comments in the mpl.htm file.

Figure 1-26 ▶ **Adding comments to the showEM() function**

```
<script type="text/javascript">
   function showEM(userName, emServer) {
      /*
         The showEM() function displays a link to the user's e-mail address.
         The text of the user and e-mail server names are entered in
         reverse order to thwart e-mail harvesters.
      */

      userName = stringReverse(userName); // reverse the text of the userName parameter
      emServer = stringReverse(emServer); // reverse the text of the emServer parameter

      var emLink = userName + "@" + emServer; // combine the text of userName and emServer
      document.write("<a href='mailto:" + emLink + "'>");
      document.write(emLink);
      document.write("</a>");
   }
</script>
```

▶ **6.** Close the **mpl.htm** file, saving your changes.

▶ **7.** Reopen **mpl.htm** in your Web browser and verify that you have not introduced any errors by adding comments to the showEM() function.

▶ **8.** You can close any open files or programs now.

You show the commented version of the showEM() function to Kate. She agrees that it will help her better remember the purpose of the function and how the function works.

Using Comments to Hide JavaScript Code

Comments have another purpose besides documenting the code used in a JavaScript application. Older browsers that do not support JavaScript can present a problem for Web designers. If such browsers encounter JavaScript commands, they might display the program code as part of the Web page body. To avoid this problem, you can hide a script from these browsers using both HTML and JavaScript comment lines. The following is the syntax for doing this:

```
<script type="text/javascript">
   <!--Hide from nonJavaScript browsers
      JavaScript commands
   // Stop hiding from older browsers -->
</script>
```

When a Web browser that doesn't support scripts encounters this code, it ignores the <script> tag, as it does any tag it doesn't recognize. The next line it sees is the start of the HTML comment tag, which doesn't close until the arrow symbol (-->) in the second-to-last line. This means that the browser ignores the entire JavaScript program. It similarly ignores the final </script> tag.

On the other hand, a browser that does support JavaScript recognizes the <script> tag and ignores any HTML tags found between the <script> and </script> tags. Therefore, in this example, it bypasses the comment tag in the second line and processes the JavaScript program as written. The JavaScript comment, which starts with the double slash symbol (//) in the second-to-last line, is included to help other users understand and interpret your code.

Hiding JavaScript code from older browsers is not as important as it once was, so you will not add this feature to the JavaScript code for the staff directory page.

Debugging Your JavaScript Programs

As you work with JavaScript, you will inevitably encounter scripts that fail to work because of an error in the code. To fix a problem with a program, you need to debug it. **Debugging** is the process of searching code to locate a source of trouble. To debug a program, you must first determine the type of error present in your code.

There are three types of errors: load-time errors, run-time errors, and logical errors. A **load-time error** occurs when a script is first loaded by the browser. As the page loads, the browser reads through the code looking for mistakes in syntax. For example, suppose you had neglected to include the closing parenthesis, as in the following command from the showEM() function:

```
document.write("</a>";
```

In this case, you would be making a mistake in the syntax of the document.write() method. When a load-time error is uncovered, the JavaScript interpreter halts loading the script. Depending on the browser, an error message might also appear. Figure 1-27 shows the message generated by the above error in Internet Explorer. An error message can include the line number and character number of the error. This does not mean that the error occurred at this location in the document—the source of the trouble could be much earlier in the script. The message simply indicates the location at which the JavaScript interpreter was forced to cancel loading the script.

Reporting a load-time error | **Figure 1-27**

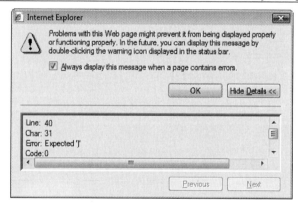

A **run-time error** occurs after a script has been successfully loaded and is being executed. In a run-time error, the mistake occurs when the browser cannot complete a line of code. One common source of a run-time error is mislabeling a variable name. For example, the line of code

```
document.write(emlink);
```

in the showEM() function would result in the run-time error shown in Figure 1-28.

Figure 1-28 ▶ **Reporting a run-time error**

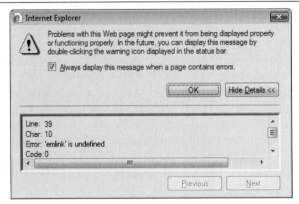

The mistake in this line of code is that there is no variable named emlink in the showEM() function—the variable name should be emLink (recall that variable names are case sensitive). When a browser attempts to write the contents of the emlink variable to the Web document, it discovers that no such variable exists and reports the run-time error. When a JavaScript interpreter catches a run-time error, it halts execution of the script and displays an error message indicating the location where it was forced to quit.

Logical errors are free from syntax and structural mistakes, but result in incorrect results. A logical error is often the hardest to fix and sometimes requires you to meticulously trace every step of your code to detect the mistake. Suppose you had incorrectly entered the line of code to create the emLink variable, placing the server name before the username, as follows:

```
var emLink = emServer + "@" + userName;
```

In this case, a browser would display the list of e-mail addresses as shown in Figure 1-29.

Figure 1-29 ▶ **Displaying a logical error**

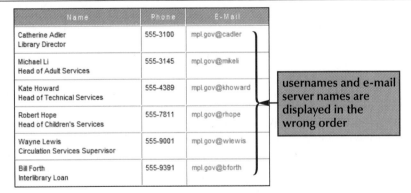

Although the browser did not report any mistakes, this is obviously not the way Kate wants e-mail addresses displayed!

Common Mistakes in JavaScript Programs | InSight

When you begin writing JavaScript programs, you will invariably encounter mistakes in your code. Some common sources of programming error include:

- Misspelling a variable name: For example, if you named a variable ListPrice, then misspellings or incorrect capitalization—such as listprice, ListPrices, or list_price—will result in the program failing to run correctly.
- Mismatched parentheses or braces: The following code results in an error because the function lacks the closing brace:
  ```
  function Area(width, height) {
      var size = width*height;
  ```
- Mismatched quotes: If you neglect the closing quotes around a text string, JavaScript treats the text string as an object or variable, resulting in an error. The following code results in an error because the closing double quote is missing from the firstName variable:
  ```
  var firstName = "Sean';
  var lastName = "Lee";
  document.write(firstName+" " + lastName);
  ```
- Missing quotes: When you combine several text strings using the + symbol, you might neglect to quote all text strings. For example, the following code generates an error because of the missing quotes around the <br /> tag:
  ```
  document.write("MidWest Student Union" + <br />);
  ```

As you become more experienced in writing JavaScript code, you'll be able to quickly spot these types of errors, making it easier for you to debug your programs.

Debugging Tools and Techniques

There are several techniques you can employ to avoid making programming mistakes and to quickly locate the mistakes you do make. One is to write **modular code**, which is code that entails breaking up a program's different tasks into smaller, more manageable chunks. A common strategy when creating modular code is to use functions that perform a few simple tasks. The different functions can then be combined and used in a variety of ways.

If you do encounter a logical error in which the incorrect results are displayed by the browser, you can monitor the changing values of your variables using an alert dialog box. An **alert dialog box** is a dialog box generated by JavaScript that displays a text message with an OK button. Clicking the OK button closes the dialog box, allowing the browser to resume running the JavaScript code. The command to create an alert dialog box is

```
alert(text);
```

where *text* is the text string that you want displayed in the dialog box. You can also use a variable name in place of a text string. For example, the command

```
alert(emLink);
```

displays the current value of the emLink variable. Figure 1-30 shows the appearance of this dialog box for the first entry in the library staff directory. Alert dialog boxes are useful in determining what is happening to your variable values while a program is running.

Figure 1-30 ▶ **Displaying a variable value in an alert dialog box**

Browsers also offer various tools for debugging JavaScript programs. Microsoft offers the **Microsoft Script Debugger**, a debugger available for use with its Internet Explorer browser running under Windows XP. The Microsoft Script Debugger is available for free from the Microsoft Web site and is also included with the Microsoft Office XP suite. When the Microsoft Script Debugger is installed on your system, it displays a prompt when it encounters a load-time or run-time error in one of your scripts. See Figure 1-31.

Figure 1-31 ▶ **Runtime Error dialog box**

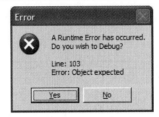

Tip

To enable script debugging on Internet Explorer, you might have to turn on script debugging from the Advanced tab on the Internet Explorer Options dialog box.

Clicking the Yes button opens the Microsoft Script Debugger window, highlighting the source of the error. As shown in Figure 1-32, the source of this particular error is that the showEM() function was referenced as showem(). Because function names are case sensitive, the browser was unable to locate the function and reported an error. You can learn more about the script debugger using the online help provided with the Microsoft Script Debugger or at the Microsoft Web site.

Microsoft Script Debugger window ◄ Figure 1-32

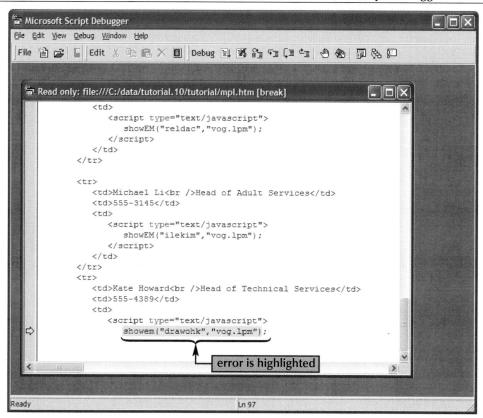

Firefox also provides the **Firefox Error Console** that displays all of the errors generated within the current document. To view the list of errors, type javascript: in the address bar as shown in Figure 1-33.

Figure 1-33 ▶ **Accessing the Firefox Error Console**

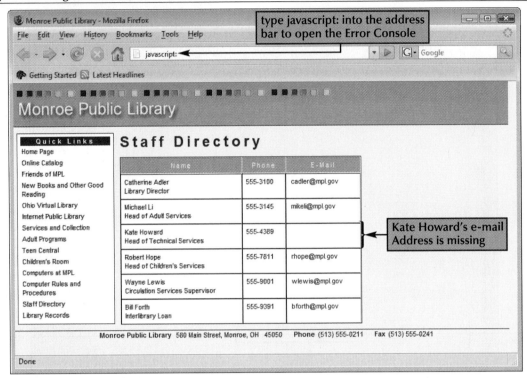

The Error Console appears as another Firefox browser window, as shown in Figure 1-34. Within the Error Console is an Evaluate box in which you can insert JavaScript commands to evaluate your code and variable values at the point at which the error occurred.

Figure 1-34 ▶ **The Firefox Error Console**

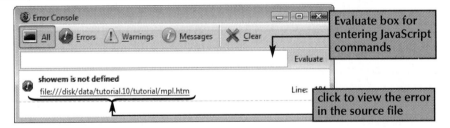

The Error Console also includes a hypertext link to another Firefox window that displays the code for the source file. The point at which the error was first detected (not necessarily the source of the error) is highlighted in this window, as shown in Figure 1-35.

Highlighting the source of the error ◀ **Figure 1-35**

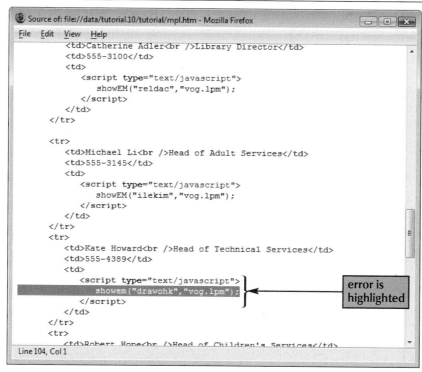

Tip

Firefox's Error Console will also display syntax errors from your CSS style sheet or other warnings generated by mistakes in the HTML code.

You can learn more about Firefox's Error Console by using the online help in the console window. Because errors inevitably creep into any programming task you undertake, it's important to be familiar with the various debugging tools available to you.

You've completed your work on the staff directory for the Monroe Public Library. Kate will call you again as other issues with the library's Web site arise.

Session 1.3 Quick Check | Review

1. Specify the code to access the JavaScript file library.js.
2. Specify the code to enter the single-line JavaScript comment Library of JavaScript functions.
3. Specify the code to enter following multiline JavaScript comment:

   ```
   The library.js file contains a collection of
   JavaScript functions for use with the file index.htm
   ```

4. What is debugging?
5. What code would you enter to display the value of the userName variable in an alert dialog box?
6. What are the three types of errors generated by mistakes in a JavaScript program?
7. Your code has a misspelled variable name. What type of error will result from the mistake?

Review | **Tutorial Summary**

In this tutorial you learned how to create and run Web page programs written in the JavaScript language. In the first session, you learned about the history of JavaScript and how it compares to Java. You then studied how to create a script element and how to use JavaScript to write text to a Web document. In the second session, you learned how to create and use variables as well as how to write and call a JavaScript function. The third session examined how to access code in external JavaScript files. The session then demonstrated how to document your code with comments. The tutorial concluded with a discussion of common scripting errors and an overview of some tools and techniques you can use to ensure that your code is error free.

Key Terms

alert dialog box	function	null value
Boolean value	function name	numeric value
client-side programming	global scope	object
command	global variable	parameter
compiled language	human input validation	run-time error
data type	interpreted language	scope
debugging	JavaScript	server-side programming
declaring	JScript	spam
ECMA	load-time error	spammer
ECMAScript	local scope	statement
e-mail harvester	local variable	strongly typed language
European Computer	logical error	text string
Manufacturers	method	variable
Association	Microsoft Script Debugger	VBScript
Firefox Error Console	modular code	weakly typed language

Practice		Review Assignments

Practice the skills you learned in the tutorial using the same case scenario.

Data Files needed for the Review Assignments: 0.jpg through 9.jpg, mpl2txt.htm, mpl.jpg, mplstyles.css, and random.js

Kate has a new assignment for you. One of the pages on the Monroe Public Library Web site is the library records page, which contains sensitive information about library patrons and the books they have checked out. Kate has created a Web form in which a staff member enters a username and password before getting access to the library records. However, Kate has heard that some hackers create programs that search for Web forms that open confidential pages. One technique of these hackers is to have automated programs that submit thousands of username/password combinations, hoping to break into the system. Kate knows that some sites use human input validation to thwart these programs.

Human input validation is a technique that requires the entry of some piece of information that humans can easily enter, but automated programs cannot. One approach is to display a series of images containing numbers or letters and request that the user enter the numbers or letters being displayed. Because most automated programs can't "see" images, they cannot answer this question; most humans, on the other hand, can enter the requested information without trouble. Kate suggests you write a program that shows five images, each displaying a random number between 0 and 9. In addition to entering a username and password, users will be required to enter the numbers they see on the screen. Figure 1-36 shows a preview of the completed Web page.

Figure 1-36

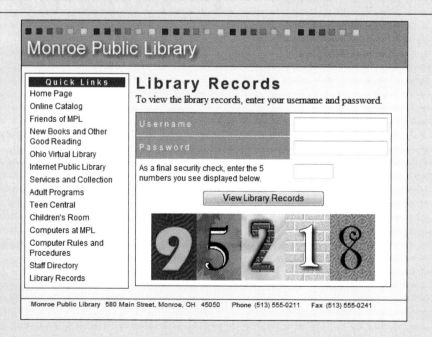

Your job is to write a script to display the random images. The images have been stored in files named 0.jpg through 9.jpg. To help you, Kate has located a file that contains a JavaScript function to return a random integer from 0 to *size*, where *size* is the largest integer to be returned. The name of the function is randomInteger, so to call the function, you use the command

```
randomInteger(size)
```

For example, to return a random integer from 0 to 5, you would run the command

```
randomInteger(5)
```

The randomInteger() function has been saved for you in the random.js file.

Complete the following:

1. Use your text editor to open **mpl2txt.htm** from the tutorial.01\review folder included with your Data Files. Enter *your name* and *the date* in the comment section of the file and save the file as **mpl2.htm** in the same folder.

2. In the head section, just above the closing </head> tag, insert a script element that accesses the code in the random.js file.

3. Add a second script element for the code that you'll add to the mpl2.htm file.

4. Within the second script element, create a function named showImg(). The purpose of this function is to write an inline image tag into the current document. The function has no parameters. Add the following statements to the function:

   a. Add the following multiline comment to the start of the function, just below the opening showImg() function statement:
   ```
   The showImg() function displays a random image from the
   0.jpg through 9.jpg files.
    The random image is designed to thwart hackers attempting to enter
   the library records database by requiring visual confirmation.
   ```

   b. Declare a variable named imgNumber equal to the value returned by the randomInteger() function. Use 9 as the value of the size parameter in the randomInteger() function.

   c. Append the statement that creates the imgNumber variable with the following single-line comment:
   ```
   Return a random number from 0 to 9.
   ```

   d. Insert a command that writes the text
   ```
   <img src='imgNumber.jpg' alt='' />
   ```
   to the document, where *imgNumber* is the value of the imgNumber variable.

5. Scroll down to the bottom of the file and locate the last table cell in the document. Within this empty table cell, insert a script element.

6. Within the script element, call the showImg() function five times. You do not need to specify a parameter value.

7. Save your changes to the file.

8. Open **mpl2.htm** in your Web browser. Verify that each time you refresh the Web page, a different sequence of five image numbers appears at the bottom of the Web form. Debug your code as necessary using any of the tools or techniques described in this tutorial.

9. Submit your completed files to your instructor.

Apply | Case Problem 1

Use the skills you learned in this tutorial to create an online star map.

Data Files needed for this Case Problem: datetime.js, mask.gif, sky0.jpg through sky23.jpg, skymaptxt.htm, skyweb.css, and skyweb.jpg

SkyWeb Astronomy Dr. Andrew Weiss of Central Ohio University maintains an astronomy page called SkyWeb for his students. On his Web site he discusses many aspects of astronomy and stargazing. One of the tools of the amateur stargazer is a planisphere, which is a handheld device composed of two flat disks: one disk shows a map of the constellations, and the other disk contains a window corresponding to the part of the sky that is visible at a given time and date. When a user rotates the second disk to the current date and time, the constellations that appear in the window correspond to the constellations currently visible in the nighttime sky.

Dr. Weiss has asked for your help in constructing an online planisphere for his Web site. He has created 24 different sky charts, named sky0.jpg through sky23.jpg, that represent 24 different rotations of the nighttime sky. He has also created an image containing a transparent window through which a user can view a selected sky chart. A preview of the completed Web page is shown in Figure 1-37.

Figure 1-37

Dr. Weiss has designed the page layout. He needs your help in creating JavaScript code to display the current date and time, and to display the correct sky chart for that date and time. To do this, you've been provided with two functions:

- The showDateTime() function, which returns the current date and time in the text string

Month Day, Year, hour:time am/pm

where *Month* is the name of the current month, *Day* is the current day, *Year* is the current year, *hour* is the current hour, *minute* is the current minute, and am/pm changes based on the current time.

- The getMap() function, which returns a number from 0 to 23. The number matches the number of the sky map image to show based on the current date and time.

Both functions have been placed in an external JavaScript file named datetime.js.

Complete the following:

1. Use your text editor to open the **skymaptxt.htm** file from the tutorial.01\case1 folder included with your Data Files. Enter *your name* and **the date** in the comment section of the file. Save the file as **skymap.htm** in the same folder.

2. Directly below the link element in the head section, insert a script element accessing the datetime.js file.

3. Below the script element, insert another script element that contains the following statements:

   a. Insert a multiline comment containing the following text:

   ```
   timeStr is a text string containing the current date and time
   mapNum is the number of the map to display in the planisphere
   ```

   b. Declare a variable named timeStr equal to the value returned from the showDateTime() function.

   c. Declare a variable named mapNum equal to the value returned from the getMap() function.

4. Scroll down the file to the div element with id value maps and replace the line

   ```
   <img id="sky" src="sky0.jpg" alt="" />
   ```

   with a script element that writes the following HTML code:

   ```
   <img id='sky' src='mapNum.jpg' alt='' />
   ```

   where *mapNum* is the value of the mapNum variable.

5. Scroll down a few lines and replace the date/time value January 1, 2011, 12:00 a.m. with a script element that writes the value of the timeStr variable to the Web page.

6. Save your changes to the file and then open **skymap.htm** in your Web browser. Verify that the planisphere displays the current date and time.

⊕ **EXPLORE** 7. If you're able to modify the date/time settings on your computer, change the date and time and then reload or refresh the page to verify that the date/time value changes and that the map also changes. Debug your code as necessary.

8. Submit your completed files to your instructor.

Apply | Case Problem 2

Use JavaScript to display random banner ads.

Data Files needed for this Case Problem: ad1.jpg through ad5.jpg, ads.js, fp.jpg, fronttxt.htm, logo.jpg, random.js, and styles.css

Ridgewood Herald Tribune Maria Ramirez manages advertising accounts for the *Ridgewood Herald Tribune* in Ridgewood, New Jersey. Recently, the paper has put more of its content online. To offset the cost of the Web site, Maria is selling ad space on the company's home page. She is looking at creating banner ads to be displayed on the paper's masthead, with each ad linked to the advertiser's Web site. Because ad space on the paper's home page is the most valuable, Maria has decided to sell space to five companies, with the selection of the banner ad determined randomly each time a user opens the page.

Maria has asked for your help in writing the JavaScript code to display banner ads randomly. She has provided a collection of functions that will be useful to you:

- The randInt() function, which returns random integers from 1 to n. To call the randInt() function, use the following expression:

  `randInt(n)`

- The adDescription() function, which returns the description of the nth ad from a list of ad descriptions. To call the function, use the following expression:

  `adDescription(n)`

- The adLink() function, which returns the URL of the nth ad of the collection. To call the function, use the following expression:

  `adLink(n)`

The random.js file contains the randInt() function. The ads.js file contains the adDescription() and adLink() functions. Figure 1-38 shows a preview of the completed Web page with one of the random banner ads displayed at the top of the page.

Figure 1-38

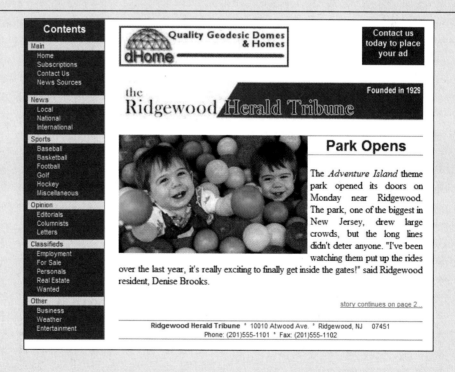

Complete the following:

1. Use your text editor to open the **fronttxt.htm** file from the tutorial.01\case2 folder included with your Data Files. Enter *your name* and *the date* in the comment section of the file. Save the file as **front.htm** in the same folder.
2. After the link element in the head section, insert a script element accessing the functions in the random.js file.
3. Insert another script element accessing the functions in the ads.js file.

4. Scroll down the file to the div element with the id ads. Replace the content of the div element with a script element containing the following statements:

   a. Declare a variable named rNumber equal to the value returned from the randInt() function using 5 as the parameter value. Append the following comment to the statement:

```
generate a random integer from 1 to 5
```

   b. Declare a variable named rAd equal to the text string returned from the adDescription() function using rNumber as the parameter value. Append the following comment to the statement:

```
description of the random ad
```

   c. Declare a variable named rLink equal to the URL returned from the adLink() function using rNumber as the parameter value. Append the following comment:

```
URL of the random ad
```

   d. Insert a command to write the text

```
<a href="url">
    <img src="adn.jpg" alt="description"/>
</a>
```

to the Web document, where *url* is the value of the rLink variable, *n* is the value of the rNumber variable, and *description* is the value of the rAd variable.

5. Save your changes to the file.

6. Open **front.htm** in your Web browser. Refresh the Web page multiple times, verifying that different banner ads appear each time the page is refreshed. Debug your code as necessary.

7. Submit your completed files to your instructor.

Challenge | Case Problem 3

Explore how to write a script to display the daily calendar of events at a student union.

Data Files needed for this Case Problem: back.jpg, friday.htm, functions.js, monday. htm, mw.css, saturday.htm, schedule.css, sunday.htm, thursday.htm, todaytxt.htm, tuesday.htm, and wednesday.htm

Midwest Student Union Sean Lee manages the Web site for the student union at MidWest University in Salina, Kansas. The student union provides daily activities for the students on campus. As Web site manager, part of Sean's job is to keep the Web site up to date on the latest activities sponsored by the union. At the beginning of each week, she revises a set of seven Web pages detailing the events for each day in the upcoming week.

Sean would like the Web site to display the current day's schedule in an inline frame within the Web page named Today at the Union. To do this, her Web page must be able to determine the day of the week and then load the appropriate file into the frame. She would also like the Today at the Union page to display the current day and date. Figure 1-39 shows a preview of the page she wants you to create.

Figure 1-39

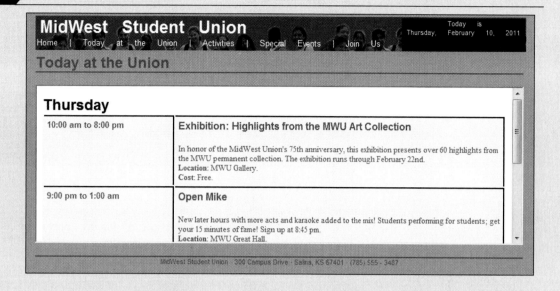

Sean has created the layout of the page, and she needs you to write the scripts to insert the current date and the calendar of events for the current day. To assist you, she has located two functions:

- The showDate() function, which returns a text string containing the current date in the format *Weekday, Month Day, Year*. The function has no parameter values.
- The weekDay() function, which returns a text string containing the name of the current weekday, from Sunday through Saturday. This function also has no parameter values.

The two functions are stored in an external JavaScript file named functions.js. The daily schedules have been stored in files named sunday.htm through saturday.htm.

Complete the following:

1. Use your text editor to open the **todaytxt.htm** file from the tutorial.01\case3 folder included with your Data Files. Enter *your name* and *the date* in the comment section of the file and save it as **today.htm**.
2. In the head section just above the closing </head> tag, insert a script element accessing the functions.js file.
3. Scroll down the file and locate the div element with the id dateBox. Within this element insert a script element. The script should run the following two commands:
   a. Write the following HTML code to the Web page:
      ```
      Today is <br />
      ```
   ⊕ EXPLORE   b. Write the text string returned by the showDate() function to the Web document.
4. Scroll down the file and locate the h2 heading Today at the Union. Within the empty paragraph that follows this heading, insert another script element. Within the script element, do the following:
   a. Insert the following multiline comment:
      ```
      Display the daily schedule in an inline frame.
      Daily schedules are stored in the files
      sunday.htm through saturday.htm.
      ```
   ⊕ EXPLORE   b. Insert a command to write the HTML code
      ```
      <iframe src='weekday.htm'></iframe>
      ```
      to the Web page, where *weekday* is the text string returned by the weekDay() function.

5. Save your changes to the document.

6. Open **today.htm** in your Web browser. Verify that it shows the current date and that the daily schedule matches the current weekday.

⊕ EXPLORE

7. If you have the ability to change your computer's date and time, change the date to different days of the week and refresh the Web page. Verify that the date and the daily schedule change to match the new date you selected. Debug your code as necessary.

8. Submit your completed files to your instructor.

| Create | **Case Problem 4** |

Test your knowledge of JavaScript by creating a splash screen displaying famous birthdays.

Data Files needed for this Case Problem: functions.js and logo.jpg

HappyBirthdayNews.com   Linda Chi is the owner of a Web site called HappyBirthdayNews.com that specializes in birthday gifts and memorabilia. To make her site more interesting for users, Linda wants to create a splash screen that displays the current date and a famous birthday occurring on that date. She has asked for your help in writing the JavaScript code to generate the welcome message. She has designed the page's style and content, and has also located the following JavaScript functions:

- The showDate() function, which returns the current date in the text string *Weekday, Month Day, Year*, where *Weekday* is the day of the week, *Month* is the name of the month, *Day* is the day of the month, and *Year* is the four-digit year value. The showDate() function has no parameters.

- The dayNumber() function, which returns the day number of the current date, ranging from 1 (the first day of the year) to 366 (the last day of the year). The dayNumber() function has no parameters.

- The showBirthDay() function, which returns a text string describing a famous birthday on the given date. The function has a single parameter—*day*—which is equal to the day number of the famous birthday you want to view.

The three functions have already been saved for you in a file named functions.js. Figure 1-40 shows one possible solution to this problem.

Figure 1-40

Complete the following:

1. Use your text editor to create the file **birthday.htm** and save it in the tutorial.01\case4 folder included with your Data Files. Create a comment section containing *your name* and *the date* as well as a brief description of the Web page.
2. Create a splash screen introducing the HappyBirthday.com Web site. The content and design of the site are up to you. You can use the **logo.jpg** graphic file as the logo for the Web site and supplement it with any other content or graphics you find.
3. Use your knowledge of JavaScript to add the following features to the Web page:
   - A page element that displays the current date
   - A page element that displays the name of a famous person born on that date
   - Any comments that document each of the variables you use in writing your JavaScript code and any functions you create
4. Save your changes to the file and then open it in your Web browser. Verify that the page displays the current date and a famous person's birthday for that date.

EXPLORE

5. If you're able to change the date on your computer's clock, change the date and refresh the Web page. Verify that the page displays the new date and a new famous birthday. Debug your code as necessary.
6. Submit your completed files to your instructor.

Review | **Quick Check Answers**

Session 1.1

1. A client-side program is a program that is run on a user's computer, usually with a Web browser. A server-side program runs off of a Web server.
2. `<script type="text/javascript"> ... </script>`
3. `document.write("<h2>Public Library</h2>");`
4. `document.write('<h2 id="sub">Public Library</h2>');`
5. Place the backslash (\) symbol at the end of the line to indicate that the statement continues on the next line.
6. JavaScript is case sensitive, so this statement should read:

   `document.write("Monroe Public Library");`
7. `<noscript>`

   `    <p><i>JavaScript required</i></p>`
   `</noscript>`

Session 1.2

1. `var weekday = "Friday";`
2. To calculate the sum of numeric values or to combine text strings into a single text string
3. numeric, text, Boolean, and null
4. `document.write("<img src='" + fileName + "' alt='' />");`
5. To perform an action or to return a value
6. `function CalcVol(x, y, z) {`

   `    Vol = x*y*z;`
   `    return Vol;`
   `}`

7. `TotalVol = CalcVol(3, 10, 4);`

8. Scope indicates where you can reference a variable within the Web page.

Session 1.3

1. `<script src="library.js" type="text/javascript"></script>`

2. `// Library of JavaScript functions.`

3. ```
/*

    The library.js file contains a collection of
    JavaScript functions for use with the file index.htm
*/
```

4. Debugging is the process of searching code to locate a source of trouble.

5. `alert(userName);`

6. load-time error, run-time error, and logical error

7. a run-time error

## Ending Data Files

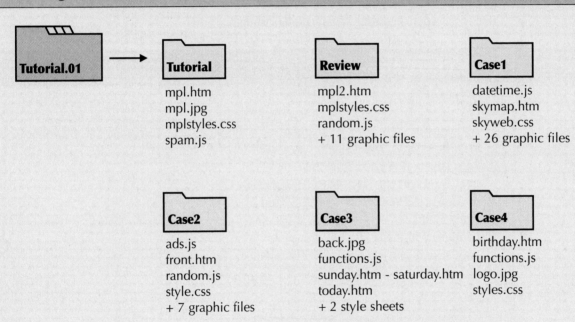

**Tutorial.01** → **Tutorial**

mpl.htm
mpl.jpg
mplstyles.css
spam.js

**Review**

mpl2.htm
mplstyles.css
random.js
+ 11 graphic files

**Case1**

datetime.js
skymap.htm
skyweb.css
+ 26 graphic files

**Case2**

ads.js
front.htm
random.js
style.css
+ 7 graphic files

**Case3**

back.jpg
functions.js
sunday.htm - saturday.htm
today.htm
+ 2 style sheets

**Case4**

birthday.htm
functions.js
logo.jpg
styles.css
```

Objectives

Session 2.1
- Work with event handlers
- Insert a value into a Web form field
- Create and work with date objects
- Extract information from date objects

Session 2.2
- Work with arithmetic, unary, conditional, and logical operators
- Understand the properties and methods of the Math object
- Understand how JavaScript works with numeric values
- Run time-delayed and timed-interval commands

Working with Operators and Expressions

Creating a New Year's Day Countdown Clock

Case | Tulsa's New Year's Bash

Every year on December 31st, Tulsa, Oklahoma, rings in the New Year with a daylong celebration. The New Year's Bash includes races, jugglers, tasting booths, live bands, and dances, and is capped by fireworks at midnight. The bash has become so big that partygoers come from miles away to join in the fun, and planning for the celebration starts early.

Hector Sadler manages promotion for the New Year's Bash. One of his responsibilities is to maintain a Web site that advertises the event and builds up anticipation for it. Hector wants to include a countdown clock on the site's home page that displays the current date and the number of days, hours, minutes, and seconds remaining before the fireworks go off. You will write the JavaScript code to create this clock for Hector.

Starting Data Files

Tutorial.02 →

Tutorial
clocktxt.htm
functxt.js
newyear.css
+ 3 graphic files

Review
datestxt.js
eventstxt.htm
tulsa.css
+ 1 graphic file

Case1
functions.js
oaetxt.htm
quiz.css
+ 6 graphic files

Case2
hometxt.htm
randtxt.js
styles.css
tips.js
+ 2 graphic files

Case3
je.css
worldtxt.htm
zonestxt.js
+ 2 graphic files

Case4
mall.txt
malltxt.htm
timetxt.js
+ 4 graphic files

Session 2.1

Introducing onevent Processing

The New Year's Bash is still six months away, but it's not too soon to sit down with Hector to discuss creating the countdown clock for the Web site. Hector envisions a clock that updates itself every second to add a dynamic effect to the site's home page. Hector already created a Web page that displays a static value for the date, time, and amount of time left until the New Year. You'll look at this file now.

To view the clock Web page:

▶ 1. Use your text editor to open **clocktxt.htm** from the tutorial.02\tutorial folder included with your Data Files, enter *your name* and *the date* in the comment section of the file, and then save the file as **clock.htm** in the same folder.

▶ 2. Scroll through the file and familiarize yourself with its contents.

▶ 3. Open **clock.htm** in your Web browser. Figure 2-1 shows the initial version of the Web page.

Figure 2-1   The initial clock page

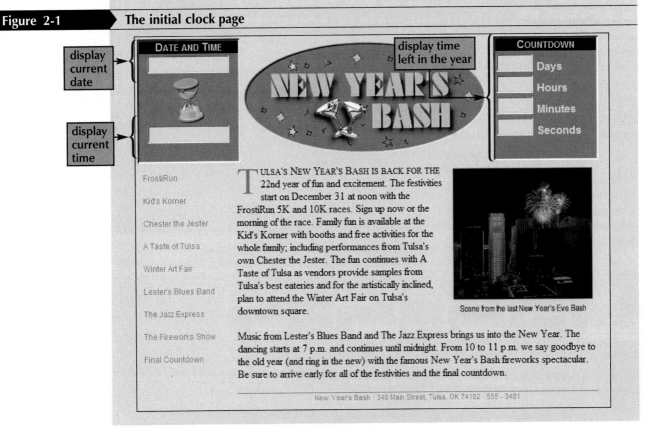

At the top of the Web page are Web form fields in which the current date, time, and countdown clock will appear. The form's name is clockform. Figure 2-2 shows the names of the fields within the form along with sample values for each field.

Form field names ◄ Figure 2-2

Hector wants these values to be constantly updated to reflect the current date and time. To do this, you'll write a JavaScript function that calculates the current date and time as well as the time remaining until New Year's Day, and then updates those values once every second. You'll start creating this function by exploring how to insert values into a Web form. The general command to insert a value into a field is

```
document.form.field.value = field_value;
```

where *form* is the name of the Web form, *field* is the name of the field, and *field_value* is the value you want to place into the field. For example, for Hector's Web page, the current date is stored in the dateNow field of the clockform Web form. To set this value to the text string 2/24/2011, you would use the following JavaScript command:

```
document.clockform.dateNow.value = "2/24/2011";
```

Similarly, to display the text 2:35:05 p.m. in the timeNow field, you would use the following JavaScript command:

```
document.clockform.timeNow.value = "2:35:05 p.m.";
```

You'll use this information as you work on Hector's Web page. You'll begin by placing sample date and time values into the clockform Web form using a JavaScript function named NYClock(). For now, you'll insert the text string "99" in the fields for days, hours, minutes, and seconds left in the year. This text string will act as a placeholder until you learn how to calculate the actual values, but including this text allows you to confirm that your code is correctly writing text to the Web form fields.

To create the NYClock() function:

► **1.** Return to the **clock.htm** file in your text editor.

► **2.** Above the closing </head> tag, insert the following embedded script, as shown in Figure 2-3:

```
<script type = "text/javascript">
   function NYClock() {
   // display the current date and time
      document.clockform.dateNow.value = "2/24/2011";
      document.clockform.timeNow.value = "2:35:05 p.m.";

   // calculate the time left until the New Year's Bash
      document.clockform.daysLeft.value = "99";
      document.clockform.hrLeft.value = "99";
      document.clockform.minLeft.value = "99";
      document.clockform.secLeft.value = "99";
   }
</script>
```

Figure 2-3 ► **Inserted NYClock function**

```
<title>Tulsa's New Year's Bash</title>
<link href="newyear.css" rel="stylesheet" type="text/css" />

<script type="text/javascript">

    function NYClock() {
    // display the current date and time
        document.clockform.dateNow.value = "2/24/2011";
        document.clockform.timeNow.value = "2:35:05 p.m.";

    // calculate the time left until the New Year's Bash
        document.clockform.daysLeft.value = "99";
        document.clockform.hrLeft.value = "99";
        document.clockform.minLeft.value = "99";
        document.clockform.secLeft.value = "99";
    }

</script>
</head>
```

writes sample dates and times to the dateNow and timeNow fields

writes placeholder values to the daysLeft, hrLeft minLeft and secLeft fields

The single-line comments make it easier to interpret the commands in the function. Be sure to enter the code exactly as shown in Figure 2-3, including matching the use of upper- and lowercase letters. Recall that JavaScript is a case-sensitive language and programs will not run correctly if the case is incorrect.

► **3.** Save your changes to the file.

Because these values will be updated constantly while the page is displayed by a user's browser, the NYClock() function needs to run when the page is initially loaded, and then repeatedly thereafter. This is in contrast to the code you wrote in the previous tutorial, which ran only once when the page was loaded by the browser. That code ran either when it was encountered within a script element or was called as part of a function. Because you'll need to control when and how often the NYClock() function is run, you must learn how to work with events.

Understanding Events and Event Handlers

An **event** is an action that occurs within a Web browser or Web document. Most objects have specific events associated with them. For example, one event associated with a Web form button is the action of being clicked by a user. Another event occurs when a user hovers the pointer over the button without clicking it. A Web document also has associated events such as the action of being loaded or unloaded by a browser. Each event can be associated with one or more JavaScript programs that run in response to the event's occurrence.

To associate a program with an event, you add an event handler to the object in which the event occurs. An **event handler** is a statement that tells browsers what code to run in response to the specified event. One way of inserting an event handler is to add it as an attribute of the element in the Web document. The syntax to insert an event handler as an attribute is:

```
<element onevent = "script" ...> ...
```

In this event handler, *element* is the name of the element, *event* is the name of an event, and *script* is a command or collection of commands to be run in response to the event. If you intend to run several commands in response to an event, it's easiest to place them within a function and run the function using a single command. One commonly used event handler, onclick, runs a program in response to a user clicking an element with the mouse button. The event handler in the following code runs the calcTotal() function when a user clicks the input button:

```
<input type = "button" value = "Total Cost" onclick = "calcTotal()" />
```

Figure 2-4 lists other event handlers you can use with the elements in a Web page. You can also view an extended list of event handlers in the appendices.

JavaScript event handlers ◄ **Figure 2-4**

Category	Event Handler	Description
Window and document event handlers	onload	The browser has completed loading the document.
	onunload	The browser has completed unloading the document.
	onerror	An error has occurred in the JavaScript program.
	onmove	The user has moved the browser window.
	onresize	The user has resized the browser window.
	onscroll	The user has moved the scroll bar within the browser window.
Form event handlers	onfocus	The user has entered an input field.
	onblur	The user has exited an input field.
	onchange	The content of an input field has changed.
	onselect	The user has selected text within an input or text area field.
	onsubmit	The user has submitted the Web form.
	onreset	The user has reset the Web form.
Mouse and keyboard event handlers	onkeydown	The user has pressed a key.
	onkeypress	The user has pressed and released a key.
	onclick	The user has clicked the mouse button.
	ondblclick	The user has double-clicked the mouse button.
	onmousedown	The user has pressed the mouse button.
	onmouseup	The user has released the mouse button.
	onmousemove	The user has moved the pointer over the element.
	onmouseout	The user has moved the pointer off of the element.

For the clock Web page, you want to run the NYClock() function when the page is loaded. Loading is one of the events associated with the Web page, and can be handled by adding the following event handler attribute to the <body> tag:

```
<body onload = "NYClock()">
```

You'll add this event handler to the clock.htm file.

To insert the onload event handler to the clock Web page:

▶ **1.** In the <body> tag of the clock.htm file, click after the word body, press the **Spacebar**, and then type the following attribute, as shown in Figure 2-5:

```
onload="NYClock()"
```

onload event handler attribute inserted in the <body> tag ◄ **Figure 2-5**

▶ **2.** Save your changes to the file.

▶ **3.** Reload **clock.htm** in your Web browser. The page opens, displaying the field values you specified in the previous set of steps. See Figure 2-6.

Figure 2-6 ▶ **Field values inserted into the clockform Web form**

Trouble? If you receive an error message when loading the page, check the code in the NYClock() function and the onload event handler. Some common programming errors that might have occurred within the NYClock() function include mismatching uppercase and lowercase letters, misspelling variable names, forgetting to close up double quotes, and forgetting to enclose command blocks and functions within curly braces.

Another way to run a JavaScript command in response to an event is to treat it as a hypertext link. This method is similar to running the command in response to a click event within an element. The syntax for running a JavaScript command as a hypertext link is

```
<a href = "javascript:script">content</a>
```

where *script* is the command (or commands) you want to run when a user clicks the link. For example, the following code runs the calcTotal() function when a user clicks the link:

```
<a href = "javascript:calcTotal()">
   Calculate total cost
</a>
```

This technique was often used for older browsers that did not support event handlers, or for elements that did not support the onclick event handler. This issue was more prevalent when event handlers were a new feature of HTML and JavaScript. Now, running JavaScript commands through hypertext links is considered a bad practice because it misuses the href attribute, which should be reserved for linked documents and not commands. However, you might see this code still being run in older Web sites.

Reference Window | **Running a Script in Response to an Event**

- To insert an event handler as an element attribute, use the syntax
  ```
  <element onevent = "script"> ...
  ```
  where *element* is the Web page element, *event* is the name of an event associated with the element, and *script* is a command to be run in response to the event.

Working with Date Objects

Now that you've created the initial form of the NYClock() function, you need some way of generating the date and time information rather than typing the values directly into the JavaScript code. To work with dates, JavaScript supports a **date object**, which contains information about a specified date and time. Date objects are created using the following command:

```
variable = new Date("month day, year hours:minutes:seconds");
```

In this command, *variable* is the name of the variable that contains the date object, and *month*, *day*, *year*, *hours*, *minutes*, and *seconds* indicate the date and time to be stored in the object. Time values are entered using 24-hour time; for example, a time of 2:35 p.m. would be entered as 14:35. The following command stores a date object in a variable named thisDate that corresponds to a date of February 24, 2011 and a time of 2:35:05 p.m.:

```
thisDate = new Date("February 24, 2011 14:35:05");
```

If you omit the hours, minutes, and seconds values, JavaScript assumes that the time is 0 hours, 0 minutes, and 0 seconds—in other words, midnight of the specified day. If you omit both the date and time information, JavaScript returns the current date and time, which it gets from the system clock on the user's computer. The following command creates a variable named thisDate that contains the current date and time:

```
thisDate = new Date();
```

You can also create a date object using the following command:

```
variable = new Date(year, month, day, hours, minutes, seconds);
```

In this command, *year*, *month*, *day*, *hours*, *minutes*, and *seconds* are the values of the date and time, and the *month* value is an integer from 0 to 11, where 0 = January, 1 = February, and so forth. Time values are again expressed in 24-hour time. The following command creates a date object for February 24, 2011, at 2:35:05 p.m.:

```
thisDate = new Date(2011, 1, 24, 14, 35, 5);
```

Creating a Date and Time Variable | Reference Window

- To store a date and time in a variable, use the JavaScript command
  ```
  variable = new Date("month day, year hours:minutes:seconds")
  ```
  where *variable* is the name of the variable that contains the date object, and *month*, *day*, *year*, *hours*, *minutes*, and *seconds* indicate the date and time to be stored in the object. Time values are entered in 24-hour time.
- To store a date and time using numeric values, use the JavaScript command
  ```
  variable = new Date(year, month, day, hours, minutes, seconds)
  ```
  where *year*, *month*, *day*, *hours*, *minutes*, and *seconds* are the values of the date and time, and the *month* value is an integer from 0 to 11, where 0 = January, 1 = February, and so forth. Time values are entered in 24-hour time.
- To create a date object containing the current date and time, use the following JavaScript command:
  ```
  variable = new Date()
  ```

Now that you've seen how to store date and time information in a variable, you'll create a variable named today that stores a date object. You'll use February 24, 2011 as the initial date and 2:35:05 p.m. as the initial time. Later in this tutorial, you'll set the value of the today variable to the current date and time. For now, using a preset date and time lets you check that any calculations based on this date are correct. You'll add the today variable to the NYClock() function you just created.

To create the today variable:

► **1.** Return to the **clock.htm** file in your text editor.

► **2.** Insert the following lines at the beginning of the NYClock() function, as shown in Figure 2-7:

```
// the today variable contains the current date and time
    var today = new Date("February 24, 2011 14:35:05");
```

| Figure 2-7 | Date object added to the NYClock() function |

variable storing the date object

```
function NYClock() {
// the today variable contains the current date and time
   var today = new Date("February 24, 2011 14:35:05");

// display the current date and time
   document.clockform.dateNow.value = "2/24/2011";
   document.clockform.timeNow.value = "2:35:05 p.m.";

// calculate the time left until the New Year's Bash
   document.clockform.daysLeft.value = "99";
   document.clockform.hrLeft.value = "99";
   document.clockform.minLeft.value = "99";
   document.clockform.secLeft.value = "99";
}
```

► **3.** Save your changes to the file.

Retrieving the Date, Month, and Hour Values

A date object stores a numeric value that is equal to the number of milliseconds (1/1000 of a second) between the specified date and time and January 1, 1970. For example, a date object with the date and time of February 24, 2011 at 2:35:05 p.m. has a hidden value equal to 1,298,579,705,000 milliseconds. Fortunately, you don't have to work with this value. Instead, JavaScript provides **date methods**, which are methods you can use to retrieve information from a date object or to change a date object's value.

To extract the day of the month from a given date object, JavaScript provides the getDate() method. The syntax to apply the getDate() method is

```
DateObject.getDate()
```

where *DateObject* is a date object (or a variable that contains a date object). For example, the following code extracts the day value from the thisDate variable and stores the result in the thisDay variable:

```
thisDate = new Date("February 24, 2011 14:35:05");
thisDay = thisDate.getDate();
```

After running these commands, the value of the thisDay variable is 24.

A similar method exists for extracting the value of the current month. This method is named getMonth(). Because JavaScript starts counting the months with 0 for January, you must add 1 to the month number returned by the getMonth() method to translate the value to the common system of numbering months from 1 to 12. The following JavaScript code extracts the current month number, increases it by 1, and stores it in a variable named thisMonth:

```
thisDate = new Date("February 24, 2011 14:35:05");
thisMonth = thisDate.getMonth()+1;
```

In this code, the value of the thisMonth variable is 2.

Finally, the getFullYear() method extracts the four-digit year value from the date object. The following code stores the value of the current year in a variable named thisYear:

```
thisDate = new Date("February 24, 2011 14:35:05");
thisYear = thisDate.getFullYear();
```

In this case, the value of the thisYear variable is 202.

Comparing the getFullYear() and getYear() Methods | InSight

The two methods to extract the year information from a date object are getFullYear() and getYear(). As you've seen, the getFullYear() method extracts the year value as a four-digit number. However, JavaScript originally used the getYear() method, which returns a two-digit year value. For example, with the getYear() method, a date object from the year 1996 returns the value 96. This approach of returning only the two-digit year value was an example of the so-called Y2K Bug in which programs that relied on two-digit year values would begin to show mistakes with the start of the new century in the year 2000.

The getYear() method is still supported by JavaScript, but it returns a four-digit year value for dates past the year 2000. For example, a date object from the year 2009 that uses the getYear() method returns 2009 and not 09. To avoid confusion between two- and four-digit year values, you should always use the getFullYear() method.

Retrieving the Hour, Minute, and Second Values

In addition to methods for extracting date, month, and hour values from a date object, JavaScript supports similar methods for extracting the hours, minutes, and seconds values from a date object. These methods are:

```
DateObject.getSeconds()
DateObject.getMinutes()
DateObject.getHours()
```

In these methods, *DateObject* is a date object or a variable containing a date object. Hours are expressed in 24-hour time. So, the code

```
thisDate = new Date("February 24, 2011 14:35:05");
thisHour = thisDate.getHours();
```

stores the value 14 in the thisHour variable. Figure 2-8 summarizes the methods for retrieving date and time values from date objects.

Figure 2-8 ▶ **Methods to extract date and time values from date objects**

Method	Retrieves	Value (when the thisDate variable stores the date object for "June 15, 2011 14:35:28")
thisDate.getSeconds()	Retrieves the seconds value	28
thisDate.getMinutes()	Retrieves the minutes value	35
thisDate.getHours()	Retrieves the hours value (in 24-hour time)	14
thisDate.getDate()	Retrieves the day of the month value	15
thisDate.getDay()	Retrieves the day of the week value (0 = Sunday, 1 = Monday, 2 = Tuesday, 3 = Wednesday, 4 = Thursday, 5 = Friday, 6 = Saturday)	3
thisDate.getMonth()	Retrieves the month value (0 = January, 1 = February, 2 = March, etc.)	5
thisDate.getFullYear()	Retrieves the four-digit year value	2011
thisDate.getTime()	Retrieves the time value, as expressed in milliseconds, since January 1, 1970	1,308,166,505,000

Reference Window | Retrieving Date and Time Values

- To retrieve the year value from a date object named DateObject, use the method
    ```
    DateObject.getFullYear()
    ```
  where *DateObject* is a variable containing a date object.
- To retrieve the month value, use the method
    ```
    DateObject.getMonth()
    ```
  where a month value of 0 equals the first month of the year (January), a month value of 1 equals the second month of the year (February), and so forth.
- To retrieve the day of the month value, use the following method:
    ```
    DateObject.getDate()
    ```
- To retrieve the day of the week value, use the method
    ```
    DateObject.getDay()
    ```
  where a value of 0 equals the first weekday (Sunday), a value of 1 equals the second weekday (Monday), and so forth.
- To retrieve the hours value, use the following method:
    ```
    DateObject.getHours()
    ```
- To retrieve the minutes value, use the following method:
    ```
    DateObject.getMinutes()
    ```
- To retrieve the seconds value, use the following method:
    ```
    DateObject.getSeconds()
    ```

Setting Date and Time Values

In addition to retrieving date and time values, you can also use JavaScript to set these values. This is most often used in programs where you have to change the value of a date object from one particular date or time to another. For example, the following code uses the setFullYear() method to change the date stored in the thisDate variable from February 24, 2011 to February 24, 2012:

```
thisDate = new Date("February 24, 2011");
thisDate.setFullYear(2012);
```

Figure 2-9 summarizes the other methods supported by JavaScript for setting date and time values.

Methods to set date and time values for date objects ◀ Figure 2-9

Method	Description
DateObject.setSeconds(*value*)	Sets the seconds value of *DateObject* to *value*
DateObject.setMinutes(*value*)	Sets the minutes value of *DateObject* to *value*
DateObject.setHours(*value*)	Sets the hours value of *DateObject* to *value*
DateObject.setDate(*value*)	Sets the day of the month value of *DateObject* to *value*
DateObject.setMonth(*value*)	Sets the month number of *DateObject* to *value* (0 = January, 1 = February, etc.)
DateObject.setFullYear(*value*)	Sets the four-digit year value of *DateObject* to *value*
DateObject.setTime(*value*)	Sets the time of *DateObject* in milliseconds since January 1, 1970

You'll create a function that uses the setFullYear() method in the next session.

Creating a Date and Time Function

You'll use the methods associated with date objects that you just learned to create functions that extract the date and time values from a date object, and then return those values in formatted text strings. The first function you'll create is named showDate() and has the following code:

```
function showDate(dateObj) {
   thisDate = dateObj.getDate();
   thisMonth = dateObj.getMonth()+1;
   thisYear = dateObj.getFullYear();
   return thisMonth + "/" + thisDate + "/" + thisYear;
}
```

The showDate() function has a single parameter named dateObj, which stores the date object to be evaluated. The function extracts the day of the month, the month number, and the four-digit year value, and returns a text string combining all of the values in the format

month/*day*/*year*

where *month* is the value of the thisMonth variable, *day* is the value of the thisDate variable, and *year* is the value of the thisYear variable. You'll call this function by placing the generated text string into the dateNow field of the Web form on the clock Web page.

The following code for the showTime() function is similar:

```
function showTime(dateObj) {
   thisSecond = dateObj.getSeconds();
   thisMinute = dateObj.getMinutes();
   thisHour = dateObj.getHours();
   return thisHour + ":" + thisMinute + ":" + thisSecond;
}
```

The showTime() function extracts the hours, minutes, and seconds values from the date object, returning the text string

hour:*minute*:*second*

Tip

JavaScript does not support daylight savings time (also known as summer time); the computer's operating system makes adjustments for daylight savings time.

where *hour* is the value of the thisHour variable, *minute* is the value of the thisMinute variable, and *second* is the value of the thisSecond variable.

You'll add both the showDate() and showTime() functions to an external JavaScript file so that you can access them from any page of Hector's Web site.

To create the showDate() and showTime() functions:

1. Use your text editor to open the **functxt.js** file from the tutorial.02\tutorial folder included with your Data Files, enter **your name** and **the date** in the comment section at the top of the file, and then save the file as **functions.js** in the same folder.

2. Below the comment section, insert the following two functions, as shown in Figure 2-10:

```
function showDate(dateObj) {
    thisDate = dateObj.getDate();
    thisMonth = dateObj.getMonth()+1;
    thisYear = dateObj.getFullYear();
    return thisMonth + "/" + thisDate + "/" + thisYear;
}

function showTime(dateObj) {
    thisSecond=dateObj.getSeconds();
    thisMinute=dateObj.getMinutes();
    thisHour=dateObj.getHours();
    return thisHour + ":" + thisMinute + ":" + thisSecond;
}
```

Figure 2-10	showDate() and showTime() functions

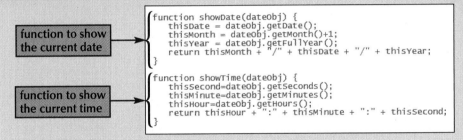

function to show the current date

function to show the current time

3. Save your changes to the file.

You can call these two functions to display the date and time text strings in the show-Date and showTime fields of the Web form. To call the functions, you first must create a link to the functions.js file.

To call the showDate() and showTime() functions:

1. Return to the **clock.htm** file in your text editor.

2. Directly above the opening <script> tag, insert the following external script element:

```
<script type="text/javascript" src="functions.js"></script>
```

3. In the embedded script element, replace the date value in the dateNow field with:

```
showDate(today)
```

4. In the embedded script element, replace the time value in the timeNow field with:

```
showTime(today)
```

Figure 2-11 shows the revised code for the clock.htm file.

Code to call the showDate() and showTime() functions | Figure 2-11

```
<script type="text/javascript" src="functions.js"></script>
<script type="text/javascript">

  function NYClock() {
  // the today variable contains the current date and time
     var today = new Date("February 24, 2011 14:35:05");

  // display the current date and time
     document.clockform.dateNow.value = showDate(today);
     document.clockform.timeNow.value = showTime(today);

  // calculate the time left until the New Year's Bash
     document.clockform.daysLeft.value = "99";
     document.clockform.hrLeft.value = "99";
     document.clockform.minLeft.value = "99";
     document.clockform.secLeft.value = "99";
  }
```

link to the external functions.js file

displays the text from the showDate() and showTime() functions in the Web form

▶ **5.** Save your changes to the file.

▶ **6.** Reopen or refresh **clock.htm** in your Web browser. Figure 2-12 shows the current values in the page's Web form. The date value has not changed but the time value is displayed in 24-hour format.

Revised countdown clock values | Figure 2-12

Hector reviews the current output and sees two things that he wants changed. The time values should be displayed in 12-hour time rather than 24-hour time. Also, a minute or second value less than 10 should have a zero placed before its value as a placeholder. In other words, instead of displaying

14:35:5

Hector wants the time to read

2:35:05 p.m.

In the next session, you'll add these features to the countdown clock and create functions to calculate the number of days, hours, minutes, and seconds remaining in the year.

Session 2.1 Quick Check | Review

1. What is an event handler?
2. What attribute would you add to a button element to run the showImage() function when the button is clicked?
3. What HTML code creates a link that runs the showImage() function when the link is clicked?

4. What JavaScript command creates a variable named examDate storing the following date and time: May 8, 2011 at 6:55:28 p.m.?
5. What command extracts the month value from the examDate variable? What value would be returned by this method?
6. What command extracts the four-digit year value from the examDate variable?
7. What command changes the day of the month value in the examDate variable from 8 to 9 (while leaving all of the other date and time values unchanged)?
8. What command creates a variable named currentTime that stores the current date and time?

Session 2.2

Working with Operators and Operands

In the previous session, you worked with date objects to display specified dates and times on a Web page. In this session, you'll learn how to perform calculations with dates and JavaScript variables. To perform a calculation, you need to insert a JavaScript statement that contains an operator. An **operator** is a symbol used to act upon an item or a variable within a JavaScript expression. The variables or expressions that operators act upon are called **operands**. An operator is a very basic concept. In fact, you've been using operators throughout this and the previous tutorial. For example, you've been using the + operator to combine text strings and add numeric values. The following statement from the showDate() function uses the + operator to increase the value of dateObj.getMonth() by 1:

```
thisMonth = dateObj.getMonth()+1;
```

You have also used the + operator to combine text strings, as in the following statement from the showDate() function, which displays dates in the format *month/date/year*:

```
thisMonth + "/" + thisDate + "/" + thisYear;
```

Using Arithmetic and Unary Operators

The + operator belongs to a group of operators called **arithmetic operators** that perform simple mathematical calculations. Figure 2-13 lists some of the arithmetic operators and gives examples of how they work.

Arithmetic operators | Figure 2-13

Operator	Description	Example
+	Combines or adds two items	Men = 20; Women = 25; Total = Men + Women;
–	Subtracts one item from another	Income = 1000; Expense = 750; Profit = Income – Expense;
*	Multiplies two items	Width = 50; Length = 20; Area = Width * Length;
/	Divides one item by another	Persons = 50; Cost = 200; CostPerPerson = Cost / Persons;
%	Calculates the remainder after dividing one value by another	TotalEggs = 64; CartonSize = 12; EggsLeft = TotalEggs % CartonSize;

The arithmetic operators shown in Figure 2-13 are also known as **binary operators** because they work with two operands in an expression. JavaScript also supports **unary operators**, which work on only one operand. Unary operators can make code more compact and efficient. One of the unary operators is the **increment operator**, which increases the value of the operand by 1. The increment operator is indicated by the ++ symbol. For example, the following two expressions increase the value of x by 1. The first uses the binary operator indicated by the + symbol, and the second uses the increment operator indicated by the ++ symbol.

```
x = x + 1;
x++;
```

A similar operator is the **decrement operator**, indicated by the -- symbol, which decreases the operand's value by 1. Thus the following two expressions have the equivalent impact of reducing the value of x by 1:

```
x = x - 1;
x--;
```

Both the increment and decrement operators can be placed either before or after the operand. The placement impacts the value ultimately assigned by JavaScript. If the operator is placed before the operand, the increment or decrement happens *before* the operand is evaluated. If the operator is placed after the operand, the operand is evaluated *after* it is incremented or decremented. For example, if the variable x has an initial value of 5, then the statement

```
y = x++;
```

assigns a value of 5 to y and 6 to x. This is because the statement combines two actions. It first assigns y the value of x using

```
y = x;
```

setting the value of y to 5. The expression then increments the value of x using

```
x = x + 1;
```

increasing the *x* value to 6. The end result is that *y* is equal to 5 and *x* is equal to 6. If you switch the order so that the increment operator appears *before* the expression as follows

```
y = ++x;
```

Tip

To avoid misinterpreting the actions of an increment or decrement operator, read the action of the operator from left to right, updating the value of the operand as you go.

then JavaScript modifies the values of *x* and *y* in the following order

```
x = x + 1;
y = x;
```

incrementing *x* by 1 and *then* assigning that value to *y*. The end result is that both *x* and *y* have a final value of 6.

Another unary operator is the **negation operator**, which changes the sign of (or negates) an item's value. Figure 2-14 summarizes the three unary operators.

Figure 2-14   **Unary operators**

Operator	Description	Example	Equivalent To
++	Increases the item's value by 1	x++	x = x + 1
--	Decreases the item's value by 1	x--	x = x - 1
-	Changes the sign of the item's value	-x	x = 0 - x

Using Assignment Operators

JavaScript statements also use operators when assigning values to items. These types of operators are called **assignment operators**. The most common assignment operator is the equal sign (=), which assigns the value of one expression to another. You can also combine the act of assigning a value and changing a value within a single operator. For example, the following two expressions both add the value of the *x* variable to the value of the *y* variable and then store the new value back in the *x* variable, creating the same result:

```
x = x + y;
x += y;
```

An assignment operator can also be used with numbers to increase a variable by a specific amount. Both of the following expressions increase the value of the *x* variable by 2:

```
x = x + 2;
x += 2;
```

Tip

Always type += for the addition assignment operator; do not insert a space between the two symbols or JavaScript will report a syntax error.

A common use of the += operator is to concatenate text strings to create a single, long text string. This is useful in situations where a text string that covers several lines might be difficult to store in a variable using a single statement. However, you can use the += operator to do this, as follows:

```
quote = "To be or not to be: ";
quote += "That is the question. ";
quote += "Whether 'tis nobler in the mind to suffer ";
quote += "the slings and arrows of outrageous fortune, ";
quote += "Or to take arms against a sea of troubles";
quote += "And by opposing end them.";
...
```

Continuing in this fashion, the quote variable eventually contains the complete text of Hamlet's soliloquy by using a series of short, simple expressions rather than one long and cumbersome expression. This technique is often used to store long text strings within a variable. Other assignment operators are described in Figure 2-15.

Assignment operators   **Figure 2-15**

Operator	Description	Example	Equivalent To
=	Assigns the value of the expression on the right to the expression on the left	x = y	
+=	Adds two expressions	x += y	x = x + y
-=	Subtracts the expression on the right from the expression on the left	x -= y	x = x - y
*=	Multiplies two expressions	x *= y	x = x * y
%=	Calculates the remainder from dividing the expression on the left by the expression on the right	x %= y	x = x % y

After you master the syntax, you can use assignment operators to create efficient and compact expressions. New JavaScript programmers might prefer to use the longer form for such expressions. However, experienced JavaScript programmers make substantial use of assignment operators to reduce program size.

Calculating the Days Left in the Year

You'll use operators and date objects to create a function that calculates the number of days remaining in the year. This function, which you'll name calcDays(), has a single parameter named currentDate that contains a date object for the current date and time. The function needs to do the following:

```
function calcDays(currentDate) {
    create a date object for January 1 of the next year
    calculate the difference between currentDate and January 1
}
```

Because you want the calcDays() function to be available to other pages of the Web site, you'll add this function structure to the functions.js file.

To create the calcDays() function:

▶ **1.** If you took a break after the previous session, make sure the clock.htm and functions.js files are open in a text editor and the clock.htm file is open in your Web browser.

▶ **2.** Return to the **functions.js** file in your text editor.

▶ **3.** At the bottom of the file, insert the following function, as shown in Figure 2-16:

```
function calcDays(currentDate) {

    // create a date object for January 1 of the next year
    // calculate the difference between currentDate and January 1
}
```

Figure 2-16 | calcDays() function

```
function calcDays(currentDate) {
    // create a date object for January 1 of the next year
    // calculate the difference between currentDate and January 1
}
```

▶ **4.** Save your changes to the file.

Next, you will enter the commands for the calcDays() function. The first line creates the January 1 date object. You need to specify a year value, so you'll use 2011 as a placeholder, as shown in the following command:

```
newYear = new Date("January 1, 2011");
```

Using 2011 as the year is only a temporary step. You really want to display the value of the current year plus 1. You can determine this value by extracting the year value from the currentDate parameter and adding 1 to it using the following command:

```
nextYear = currentDate.getFullYear()+1;
```

You'll use the setFullYear() method to set the year value of the newYear date object, as follows:

```
newYear.setFullYear(nextYear);
```

The following command calculates the time difference between New Year's Day and the current day by subtracting one date object from the other:

```
days = newYear - currentDate;
```

However, JavaScript measures time in terms of milliseconds, not days. So, this difference shows the number of milliseconds between the current date and time and the next New Year's Day. To express this value in days, you need to divide the difference by the number of milliseconds in one day. The revised expression is

```
days = (newYear - currentDate)/(1000*60*60*24);
```

because 1000 milliseconds are in one second, 60 seconds are in one minute, 60 minutes are in one hour, and 24 hours are in one day. Putting all of these commands together, the complete calcDays() function is:

```
function calcDays(currentDate) {
    // create a date object for January 1 of the next year
        newYear = new Date("January 1, 2011");
        nextYear = currentDate.getFullYear()+1;
        newYear.setFullYear(nextYear);

    // calculate the difference between currentDate and January 1
        days = (newYear - currentDate)/(1000*60*60*24);

        return days;
}
```

You'll add these commands and comments to the calcDays() function.

To revise the calcDays() function in the functions.js file:

1. Below the first comment line in the calcDays() function, add the following lines:

```
newYear = new Date("January 1, 2011");
nextYear = currentDate.getFullYear()+1;
newYear.setFullYear(nextYear);
```

2. Below the next comment line, add the following line:

```
days = (newYear - currentDate)/(1000*60*60*24);
```

3. Complete the function by adding the following command to return the value of the days variable:

```
return days;
```

Figure 2-17 shows the revised code in the calcDays() function.

Commands added to the calcDays() function ◄ **Figure 2-17**

```
function calcDays(currentDate) {
    // create a date object for January 1 of the next year
    newYear = new Date("January 1, 2011");
    nextYear = currentDate.getFullYear()+1;
    newYear.setFullYear(nextYear);

    // calculate the difference between currentDate and January 1
    days = (newYear - currentDate)/(1000*60*60*24);

    return days;
}
```

> divides by the number of milliseconds in a day

4. Save your changes to the file, and then close the file.

You can use the calcDays() function to calculate the number of days remaining in the year, displaying that value in the daysLeft field of the Web form on the New Year's Bash Web page. You'll add this function to the clock.htm file, replacing the placeholder value of 99 that you specified earlier for the number of days remaining in the year.

To add the calcDays() function to the clock.htm file:

1. Return to the **clock.htm** file in your text editor.

2. Directly above the line that sets the value of the daysLeft field, insert the following line:

```
var days = calcDays(today);
```

3. Change the line that sets the value of the daysLeft field to the following:

```
document.clockform.daysLeft.value = days;
```

Figure 2-18 highlights the revised code in the clock.htm file.

Figure 2-18 ▷ **Code to call the calcDays function**

```
function NYClock() {
  // the today variable contains the current date and time
    var today = new Date("February 24, 2011 14:35:05");

  // display the current date and time
    document.clockform.dateNow.value = showDate(today);
    document.clockform.timeNow.value = showTime(today);

  // calculate the time left until the New Year's Bash
    var days = calcDays(today);
    document.clockform.daysLeft.value = days;
    document.clockform.hrLeft.value = "99";
    document.clockform.minLeft.value = "99";
    document.clockform.secLeft.value = "99";
}
```

calls the calcDays() function to calculate the days remaining in the year

replaces the placeholder value "99" with the days variable

▷ **4.** Save your changes to the file.

▷ **5.** Reload or refresh **clock.htm** in your Web browser. The daysLeft field at the top of the page displays the calculated number of days until the New Year's Bash. See Figure 2-19.

Figure 2-19 ▷ **Days left until New Year's Day displayed**

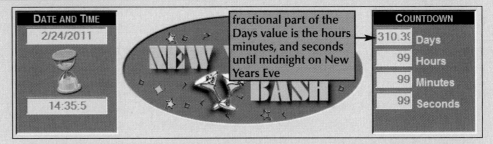

fractional part of the Days value is the hours, minutes, and seconds until midnight on New Years Eve

Trouble? If no value appears in the Days field, you might have made an error when entering the code. In your text editor, check the code in the calcDays() function against the code shown in Figure 2-17, making corrections as needed. Save the file and then repeat Step 5.

The value displayed in the daysLeft field is 310.3923, indicating that slightly more than 310 days are left until the start of the New Year's Bash. The fractional part of the value represents how much of the last day is remaining until midnight on New Year's Eve. Because Hector is interested only in the exact number of days, hours, minutes, and seconds until the party begins, you have to modify this value by extracting the days amount and then converting the fractional part to hours, minutes, and seconds. You can do this by using some of the built-in JavaScript functions for mathematical calculations.

Working with the Math Object and Math Methods

One way of performing this type of calculation is to use JavaScript's Math object. The **Math object** is an object that can be used for performing mathematical tasks and storing mathematical values.

Using Math Methods

The Math object supports several different **Math methods**, which store functions used for performing advanced calculations and mathematical operations such as generating random numbers, extracting square roots, and calculating trigonometric values. The syntax for applying a Math method is

```
Math.method(expression)
```

where *method* is the method you'll apply to an expression. For example, to calculate the square root of a number, you can use the sqrt method, which has the following syntax:

```
Math.sqrt(expression)
```

When applied to the *x* variable, the following commands result in the value 4 being stored in the *y* variable:

```
x = 16;
y = Math.sqrt(x);
```

Figure 2-20 lists the JavaScript Math methods and describes how to apply them.

Tip

Case is important in applying the Math object; you must use "Math" instead of "math" for the name of the Math object.

Math methods ◄ Figure 2-20

Math Method	Returns
Math.abs(x)	the absolute value of x
Math.acos(x)	the arc cosine of x in radians
Math.asin(x)	the arc sine of x in radians
Math.atan(x)	the arc tangent of x in radians
Math.atan2(x, y)	the angle between the x-axis and the point (x, y)
Math.ceil(x)	x rounded up to the next highest integer
Math.cos(x)	the cosine of x
Math.exp(x)	e^x
Math.floor(x)	x rounded down to the next lowest integer
Math.log(x)	the natural logarithm of x
Math.max(x, y)	the larger of x and y
Math.min(x, y)	the smaller of x and y
Math.pow(x, y)	x^y
Math.random()	a random number between 0 and 1
Math.round(x)	x rounded to the nearest integer
Math.sin(x)	the sine of x
Math.sqrt(x)	the square root of x
Math.tan(x)	the tangent of x

One of the most useful applications of JavaScript is to create dynamic pages that can change in a random fashion. A commercial Web site might need to display banner ads in a random order so that customers see a different ad each time they access the page. To create these kinds of effects, you need a script that generates a random value. JavaScript accomplishes this using the Math.random() method, which returns a random value between 0 and 1. You can enlarge the range of possible random values by multiplying the random number by the desired size of the range. To apply the range to a different interval, you add the lower boundary to the random number. So, to generate a random number from 20 to 30, you can apply the following expression:

```
20 + 10*Math.random();
```

In many cases, you will want to limit the random number to integer values. To force the random number to be an integer, you apply either the Math.ceil() method to round the value to the next highest integer or the Math.floor() method to round the value to the next lowest integer. You should not use the Math.round() method. Although the Math.round() method would round the random value to the nearest integer within the defined range, the range's lower and upper value would appear less often than the other integers. As a result, each integer would not have an equal chance of being selected. To generate a random integer from 20 to 30, you would apply the Math.floor method as follows:

```
Math.floor(20 + 11*Math.random());
```

This expression multiplies the random value by 11, not 10, because there are 11 integers in the range from 20 to 30. You can combine all of these operations in a customized function that returns a random integer for a specified range and lower boundary. The code for the function is:

```
function randInt(lower, size) {
    return Math.floor(lower + size*Math.random());
}
```

With the randInt() function, you can generate a random integer from 1 to 10 using the following expression:

```
var randInteger = randInt(1, 10);
```

To create a random integer from a different range of values, simply change the values for the lower and size parameters in the randInt() function.

Using Math Constants

Many functions require the use of mathematical constants, such as π and e. Rather than entering the numeric values of these constants directly into code, you can reference one of the built-in constants stored in the JavaScript Math object. The syntax to access one of these mathematical constants is

```
Math.CONSTANT
```

where *CONSTANT* is the name of one of the mathematical constants supported by the Math object, shown in Figure 2-21.

Math constants ◄ **Figure 2-21**

Math Constant	Description
Math.E	The natural logarithm base, e (approximately 2.7183)
Math.LN10	The natural logarithm of 10 (approximately 2.3026)
Math.LN2	The natural logarithm of 2 (approximately 0.6931)
Math.LOG10E	The base 10 logarithm of e (approximately 0.4343)
Math.LOG2E	The base 2 logarithm of e (approximately 1.4427)
Math.PI	The value π (approximately 3.1416)
Math.SQRT1_2	The value of 1 divided by the square root of 2 (approximately 0.7071)
Math.SQRT2	The value of the square root of 2 (approximately 1.4142)

For example, the formula to calculate the volume of a sphere is $4\pi r^3/3$ where r is the radius of the sphere. To reference the value of π in a calculation of the sphere's volume, you would apply the Math.PI constant. To cube the value of r, you would use the method Math.pow(r, 3). Putting these together, a function to return the volume of a sphere given the radius is:

```
function sphereVolume(radius) {
   volume = 4*Math.PI*Math.pow(radius, 3)/3;
   return volume;
}
```

To calculate the volume of a sphere that is two units in radius, you could enter the expression

```
x = sphereVolume(2);
```

and JavaScript would assign a value of 33.5103 to the x variable.

You don't need to use any Math constants for the New Year's Bash Web site. However, the countdown clock does need to display only the integer portion of the days left in the year. You can calculate this value using the Math.floor() method, which rounds a value down to the next lowest integer. For the days left value of 310.39 currently in the countdown clock, this method returns the integer value 310. You'll apply this method to the value displayed in the daysLeft field.

To apply the Math.floor() method:

► **1.** Return to the **clock.htm** file in your text editor.

► **2.** Change the statement that sets the value of the daysLeft field to the following two lines, as shown in Figure 2-22:

```
// display days rounded to the next lowest integer
document.clockform.daysLeft.value = Math.floor(days);
```

Code to apply the Math.floor() method ◄ **Figure 2-22**

```
// display days rounded to the next lowest integer
document.clockform.daysLeft.value = Math.floor(days);
document.clockform.hrLeft.value = "99";
document.clockform.minLeft.value = "99";
document.clockform.secLeft.value = "99";
}
```

> **3.** Save your changes to the file, and then reopen or refresh **clock.htm** in your Web browser. The daysLeft field displays the daysLeft value as an integer. See Figure 2-23.

| Figure 2-23 | daysLeft value displayed as an integer |

Calculating the Hours, Minutes, and Seconds Left in the Year

Next you want to calculate the hours, minutes, and seconds left in the year. The Math.floor() function determined that the number of whole days left in the year is 310. The difference between this number and 310.3923... is 0.3923..., which represents the fractional part of the current day remaining. You need to convert this value to hours. You can do this by multiplying 0.3923... by 24 (the number of hours in a single day). The JavaScript command to calculate the number of hours remaining in the current day is:

```
var hours = (days - Math.floor(days))*24;
```

Based on this calculation, the value of the hours variable is 9.4152 hours or almost 9 and a half hours. The fractional part of this value represents the minutes and seconds left within the current hour. As with the days variable in the previous set of steps, you need to round this value down to the next lowest integer using the Math.floor function, as shown in the following expression:

```
Math.floor(hours)
```

The value of the hours variable will then be equal to 9. You'll add these two expressions to the JavaScript code in the clock.htm file.

To calculate the hours left in the day:

> **1.** Return to the **clock.htm** file in your text editor.

> **2.** Below the statement that sets the value of the daysLeft field value, insert the following two lines:

```
// calculate the hours left in the current day
   var hours = (days - Math.floor(days))*24;
```

> **3.** Change the statement that sets the value of the hoursLeft field to the following, as shown in Figure 2-24:

```
// display hours rounded to the next lowest integer
document.clockform.hrLeft.value = Math.floor(hours);
```

Hours variable added to the code | Figure 2-24

```
function NYClock() {
// the today variable contains the current date and time
   var today = new Date("February 24, 2011 14:35:05");

// display the current date and time
   document.clockform.dateNow.value = showDate(today);
   document.clockform.timeNow.value = showTime(today);

// calculate the time left until the New Year's Bash
   var days = calcDays(today);

   // display days rounded to the next lowest integer
   document.clockform.daysLeft.value = Math.floor(days);

   // calculate the hours left in the current day
   var hours = (days - Math.floor(days))*24;

   // display hours rounded to the next lowest integer
   document.clockform.hrLeft.value = Math.floor(hours);
   document.clockform.minLeft.value = "99";
   document.clockform.secLeft.value = "99";
}
```

> calculates the hours left in the current day

4. Save your changes to the file, and then reopen or refresh **clock.htm** in your Web browser. The hoursLeft field displays the hours left in the current day. See Figure 2-25.

Hours left in the day | Figure 2-25

The technique to calculate the minutes left in the current hour is similar to the one you used to calculate the hours left in the current day. You multiply the difference between the hours value and whole hours value by 60 (the number of minutes in an hour) to express the fractional part in terms of minutes, as shown in the following command:

```
var minutes = (hours - Math.floor(hours))*60;
```

Finally, to calculate the seconds left in the current minute, you multiply the fractional part of the minutes variable by 60 (the number of seconds in a minute), as follows:

```
var seconds = (minutes - Math.floor(minutes))*60;
```

As with the days and hours variables, you want to display only the integer part of the minutes and seconds variables by using the Math.floor() method. You'll add these commands to the NYClock() function.

To calculate the minutes and seconds left:

1. Return to the **clock.htm** file in your text editor.

2. Below the statement that sets the value of the hrLeft field value, insert the following lines:

```
// calculate the minutes left in the current hour
var minutes = (hours - Math.floor(hours))*60;
```

3. Change the statement that sets the value of the minLeft field to:

```
// display minutes rounded to the next lowest integer
document.clockform.minLeft.value = Math.floor(minutes);
```

4. Below the statement that sets the value of the minLeft field value, insert the following lines:

```
// calculate the seconds left in the current minute
var seconds = (minutes - Math.floor(minutes))*60;
```

5. Change the statement that sets the value of the secondsLeft field to:

```
// display seconds rounded to the next lowest integer
document.clockform.secLeft.value = Math.floor(seconds);
```

Figure 2-26 highlights the changes to the code.

Figure 2-26 ▶ **Minutes and seconds variables added to the code**

```
function NYClock() {
// the today variable contains the current date and time
   var today = new Date("February 24, 2011 14:35:05");

// display the current date and time
   document.clockform.dateNow.value = showDate(today);
   document.clockform.timeNow.value = showTime(today);

// calculate the time left until the New Year's Bash
   var days = calcDays(today);

   // display days rounded to the next lowest integer
   document.clockform.daysLeft.value = Math.floor(days);

   // calculate the hours left in the current day
   var hours = (days - Math.floor(days))*24;

   // display hours rounded to the next lowest integer
   document.clockform.hrLeft.value = Math.floor(hours);

   // calculate the minutes left in the current hour
   var minutes = (hours - Math.floor(hours))*60;           ← calculates the minutes left
                                                             in the current hour
   // display minutes rounded to the next lowest integer
   document.clockform.minLeft.value = Math.floor(minutes);

   // calculate the seconds left in the current minute
   var seconds = (minutes - Math.floor(minutes))*60;       ← calculates the seconds left
                                                             in the current minute
   // display seconds rounded to the next lowest integer
   document.clockform.secLeft.value = Math.floor(seconds);
}
```

6. Save your changes to the file.

7. Reopen or refresh **clock.htm** in your Web browser. The Web form displays the time left in whole number values of days, hours, minutes, and seconds. See Figure 2-27.

Figure 2-27 ▶ **Time left in terms of days, hours, minutes, and seconds**

In some cases, the countdown value may show an extra (or missing) hour, minute, or second. Why is that? Several factors are involved. One is the presence of daylight savings time, which moves the clock forward (or backward) one hour. If your time interval crosses this event, the hour value will appear off as an hour is added to or subtracted from the time interval. Another factor is that the day is not evenly divided into seconds (that's why JavaScript measures time in milliseconds). A fraction of a second is always left over each day. As the days accumulate, these fractions of a second add up. Most time devices, such as atomic clocks, account for this accumulation by adding a "leap second" on certain days of the year. The effect of adding these leap seconds is included in any time calculations you make with JavaScript. As you can see, more is going on in calculating the time difference between one date and another than may appear at first glance.

Controlling How JavaScript Works with Numeric Values

As you perform mathematical calculations using JavaScript, you'll encounter situations in which you need to work with the properties of numeric values themselves. JavaScript provides several methods that allow you to examine the properties of numbers and specify how they're displayed on a Web page.

Handling Illegal Operations

Some mathematical operations can return results that are not numeric values. For example, you cannot divide a number by a text string. If you attempt to perform the operation

```
var x = 5/"A";
document.write(x);
```

in a script, the Web page would display the value NaN, which stands for Not a Number. This is JavaScript's way to indicate that you are attempting an operation that should involve a numeric value, but doesn't. You can check for the presence of this particular error using the function isNaN(). The syntax of the function is

```
isNaN(value)
```

where *value* is the value or variable you want to test for being numeric. The isNaN() function returns a Boolean value: true if the value is not numeric (i.e., NaN) and false if otherwise. The use of the isNaN() function is one way to locate illegal operations in code in which nonnumeric values are treated as numeric.

Another illegal operation is attempting to divide a number by 0, such as in the following code:

```
var x = 5/0;
document.write(x);
```

This code results in the value Infinity being written to the Web page. The Infinity value indicates that you've attempted a numeric calculation whose result is greater than the largest numeric value supported by JavaScript. An Infinity value also exists for operations whose result is less than the smallest numeric value. JavaScript is limited to numeric values that fall between approximately 1.8×10^{-308} and 1.8×10^{308}. Any operation that exceeds those bounds, such as dividing a number by 0, causes JavaScript to assign a value of Infinity to the result. You can check for this outcome using the function

```
isFinite(value)
```

where *value* is the value you want to test for being finite. Like the isNaN() function, the isFinite() function returns a Boolean value: true if *value* is a finite number falling within JavaScript's acceptable range and false if the numeric value falls outside that range or if *value* is not a number at all.

Specifying the Number Format

When JavaScript displays a numeric value, it displays all of the calculated digits in that value. This can result in long numeric strings of digits. For example, the code

```
var x = 1/4;
var y = 1/3;
document.write("x = " + x);
document.write("y = " + y);
```

causes the following two text strings to be written to the Web page:

```
x = 0.25
y = 0.3333333333333333
```

In most cases, you don't need to display a calculated value to 16 digits. With currency values, you usually want to display results only to two decimal places. To control the number of digits displayed by the browser, you can apply the method

```
value.toFixed(n)
```

where *value* is the value or variable and *n* is the number of decimal places that should be displayed in the output. The following examples show the toFixed() method applied to different numeric values:

```
testValue = 2.835;
testValue.toFixed(0)   // returns "3"
testValue.toFixed(1)   // returns "2.8"
testValue.toFixed(2)   // returns "2.84"
```

Note that the toFixed() method limits the number of decimals displayed by a value and converts the value into a text string. Also, the toFixed() method rounds the last digit in an expression rather than truncating it.

Converting Between Numbers and Text Strings

Sometimes you might need to convert a number to a text string and vice versa. One way to convert a number to a text string is by using the + operator to add a text string to a number. For example, the following code uses the + operator to concatenate a numeric value with an empty text string. The result is to create a text string containing the characters 123.

```
testNumber = 123;              // numeric value
testString = testNumber + "";  // text string
```

To convert a text string to a number, you can apply an arithmetic operator (other than the + operator) to the text string. The following code takes the text string "123" and multiplies it by 1. The end result is that JavaScript converts the text string "123" to the numeric value 123.

```
testString = "123";           // text string
testNumber = testString*1;    // numeric value
```

Another way of converting a text string to a numeric value is to use the parseInt() function, which extracts the leading integer value from a text string. The syntax of the parseInt() function is

```
parseInt(text)
```

where *text* is the text string or variable from which you need to extract the leading integer value. The parseInt() function determines whether the first nonblank character in the text string is a number. If it is, the function then parses the text string from left to right until the end of the number or a decimal point is encountered. Any characters in the string after that are discarded. The parseInt() function returns only the first integer in the string; it does not return decimal points or numbers to the right of a decimal. If a text string does not begin with a number, the parseInt() function returns the value NaN, indicating that there is no accessible number in the text string. The following are some sample values returned by the parseInt() function:

```
parseInt("120 lbs")                // returns 120
parseInt("206.58 lbs")             // returns 206
parseInt("weight equals 55 lbs")   // returns NaN
```

You can also use the parseFloat() function to extract numeric values other than integers from text strings. The parseFloat() function has the syntax

```
parseFloat(text)
```

where *text* is a text string or variable containing a text string. The parseFloat() function works like the parseInt() function except that it retrieves both integers and numbers with decimals. The following are sample values returned by the parseFloat() function:

```
parseFloat("120 lbs")                // returns 120
parseFloat("206.58 lbs")             // returns 206.58
parseFloat("weight equals 55 lbs")   // returns NaN
```

Because the countdown clock is not performing any calculations on values within the Web form, you don't need to use the parseInt() or parseFloat() functions in your code. However, you will use these functions in the Case Problems at the end of the tutorial. Figure 2-28 summarizes the different JavaScript methods and functions used to work with numeric values.

Numeric functions and methods ◄ **Figure 2-28**

Function or Method	Description
isFinite(*value*)	Returns a Boolean value indicating whether *value* is finite and a legal number
isNaN(*value*)	Returns a Boolean value, which has the value true if *value* is not a number
parseFloat(*string*)	Extracts the first numeric value from a text string
parseInt(*string*)	Extracts the first integer value from a text string
value.toExponential(*n*)	Returns a text string displaying *value* in exponential notation with *n* digits to the right of the decimal point
value.toFixed(*n*)	Returns a text string displaying *value* to *n* decimal places
value.toPrecision(*n*)	Returns a text string displaying *value* to *n* significant digits either to the left or to the right of the decimal point

Reference Window | Using Numeric Methods and Functions

- To display a numeric value to a set number of digits, use the function
  `value.toFixed(n)`
  where *value* is the numeric value and *n* is the number of digits to the right of the decimal place to be displayed. The toFixed() method converts the numeric value to a text string.
- To extract an integer from the beginning of a text string, use
  `parseInt(string)`
  where *string* is a text string that starts with an integer value.
- To extract a numeric value from the beginning of a text string, use
  `parseFloat(string)`
  where *string* is a text string that starts with a numeric value.
- To test whether a value represents a number, use
  `isNaN(value)`
  where *value* can be either a text string, a numeric value, or another data type. The isNaN() function returns the Boolean value true if *value* is not a number, and false if it is.

InSight | Rounding Values

Online ordering is one of the most common uses of the Web and requires calculations of monetary values. For example, suppose you needed to calculate a 2% sales tax on a customer's purchase of an item that costs $25.49. One way of doing this is to use the following code, which multiplies the price by the tax rate and stores the value in the tax variable:

```
var price = 25.49;
var taxrate = 0.02;
var tax = price*taxrate;
```

The tax value from this calculation is 0.5098, which is not an acceptable currency value. You could use the toFixed() function discussed earlier to display the result to only two decimal places. However, recall that the toFixed() function doesn't change a variable's value, only how it is displayed. Instead, you need to round the actual value of the tax variable to the hundredths digit. There are no Math methods for rounding values to specific numbers of decimal places. To round a currency value to two digits, you must first multiply the value by 100, apply the Math.round() method to round the value to the nearest integer, and then divide that result by 100. For the tax rate example, 0.5098 multiplied by 100 is 50.98; that value rounded to the nearest integer is 51; dividing that number by 100 results in a currency value of $0.51. In JavaScript, this sequence of operations can be placed in a single expression as follows:

```
Math.round(100*tax)/100;
```

In general, if *n* is the number of decimal places you want to round the value to, you multiply and divide the value by $10n$. You could use this fact to create a custom function to round values to a specified number of decimal places. The following code uses the pow() method of the Math object to create a general rounding function that rounds values to *n* decimal places:

```
function roundValue(value, n) {
    return Math.round(Math.pow(10,n)*value)/Math.pow(10,n);
}
```

The roundValue() function multiplies the value variable by a power of 10, rounds it to the nearest integer, and then divides it by the same power of 10. The end result is the value variable rounded to the number of digits specified by the n parameter. The roundValue() function also allows for a negative value for the n parameter. This has the effect of rounding a value to the nearest ten, hundred, thousand, and so forth. For example, the expression

```
roundValue(238414, -3)
```

rounds the value to the nearest thousand, returning a value of 238,000.

Working with Conditional, Comparison, and Logical Operators

Hector wants the countdown clock to display the current time using 12-hour format rather than 24-hour format. In 24-hour format, the hour values range from 0 hours (representing 12:00 a.m.) up to 23 hours (representing 11:00 p.m.). A time of 14:35 in 24-hour format is equivalent to 2:35 p.m. in 12-hour format. To convert 24-hour time to 12-hour time, the code needs to apply the following rules:

- If the hour value is less than 12, display the time as a.m.; otherwise, display the time as p.m.
- If the hour value is greater than 12, subtract 12 from the value.
- If the hour value is equal to 0, change it to 12.

Using a Conditional Operator

The code needs to run different operations based on the hours value. You can specify these options through the use of a conditional operator. A **conditional operator** is a ternary operator that tests whether a certain condition is true or not. If the condition is true, one value is returned; if the condition is not true, a different value is returned. The syntax of a conditional operator is

```
(condition) ? trueValue : falseValue
```

where *condition* is an expression that is either true or false, *trueValue* is the value returned if the condition is true, and *falseValue* is the value returned if the condition is false. You can use a conditional operator to assign a value to a variable using the statement

```
variable = (condition) ? trueValue : falseValue
```

where *variable* is the variable to which the resulting value is assigned.

Using Comparison Operators

To create expressions that have true or false values, you use comparison operators. A **comparison operator** is an operator that compares the value of one expression to another. One commonly used comparison operator is the less than operator (<), which is used to determine whether one value is less than another. The following expression demonstrates the use of the less than (<) comparison operator:

```
x < 100
```

If x is less than 100, then this expression is true; but if x is greater than or equal to 100, the expression is false. Figure 2-29 lists the comparison operators supported by JavaScript.

Figure 2-29 ▶ Comparison operators

Operator	Description	Example
==	Returns true if the values are equal	x == y
!=	Returns true if the values are not equal	x != y
>	Returns true if the value on the left is greater than the value on the right	x > y
<	Returns true if the value on the left is less than the value on the right	x < y
>=	Returns true if the value on the left is greater than or equal to the value on the right	x >= y
<=	Returns true if the value on the left is less than or equal to the value on the right	x <= y

Tip

The symbols in the == comparison operator must be entered without a space between the two = symbols.

When you want to test whether two values are equal, you use a double equal sign (==) rather than a single equal sign. The single equal sign (=) is an assignment operator and is reserved for that purpose. To test whether x is equal to 100, use the following expression:

```
x == 100
```

If x is equal to 100, then this expression returns the Boolean value true; otherwise, it returns the Boolean value false.

Using Logical Operators

JavaScript also supports **logical operators** that allow you to connect several expressions. Figure 2-30 lists the logical operators supported by JavaScript. The logical operator && returns a value of true only if both of the expressions are true. For example, the statement

```
(x < 100) && (y == 100)
```

is true only if x is less than 100 and y is equal to 100.

Figure 2-30 ▶ Logical operators

Operator	Description	Example (when x = 20 and y = 25)	Value
&&	Returns true when both expressions are true	(x == 20) && (y == 25)	TRUE
||	Returns true when at least one expression is true	(x == 20) || (y < 10)	TRUE
!	Returns true if the expression is false and false if the expression is true	!(x == 20)	FALSE

You'll use conditional, comparison, and logical operators to write code for the three rules described above to convert 24-hour time to 12-hour time. First, you need a variable named ampm that indicates whether the time is a.m. or p.m. Recall that the value of the current hour is stored in the thisHour variable. If the value of the thisHour variable is less than 12, the value of the ampm variable is a.m.; otherwise, its value is p.m. The conditional operator for this rule is:

```
ampm = (thisHour < 12) ? " a.m." : " p.m.";
```

The second rule should check whether the thisHour value is greater than 12. If so, the rule should subtract 12 from the thisHour value; otherwise, it should leave the value unchanged. You do this using the following command:

```
thisHour = (thisHour > 12) ? thisHour - 12 : thisHour;
```

The third rule should check whether thisHour is equal to 0. If so, the rule should change the value of thisHour to 12; otherwise, it should leave the value unchanged. The code for this rule is:

```
thisHour = (thisHour == 0) ? 12 : thisHour;
```

You'll add these commands to the showTime() function in the functions.js file.

To modify the showTime() function:

1. Return to the **functions.js** file in your text editor.

2. Within the showTime() function, below the statement that creates the thisHour variable, insert the following commands:

   ```
   // change thisHour from 24-hour time to 12-hour time by:
   // 1) if thisHour < 12 then set ampm to " a.m." otherwise set
   it to " p.m."
   var ampm = (thisHour < 12) ? " a.m." : " p.m.";

   // 2) subtract 12 from the thisHour variable
   thisHour = (thisHour > 12) ? thisHour - 12 : thisHour;

   // 3) if thisHour equals 0, change it to 12
   thisHour = (thisHour == 0) ? 12 : thisHour;
   ```

3. Change the return statement as follows to modify the text string returned by the function so that it displays the ampm value at the end of the text string:

   ```
   return thisHour + ":" + thisMinute + ":" + thisSecond + ampm;
   ```

   Figure 2-31 shows the revised code in the showTime() function.

Code to change the thisHour variable to 12-hour format   Figure 2-31

```
function showTime(dateObj) {
   thisSecond=dateObj.getSeconds();
   thisMinute=dateObj.getMinutes();
   thisHour=dateObj.getHours();

   // change thisHour from 24-hour time to 12-hour time by:
   // 1) if thisHour < 12 then set ampm to " a.m." otherwise set it to " p.m."
   var ampm = (thisHour < 12) ? " a.m." : " p.m.";

   // 2) subtract 12 from the thisHour variable
   thisHour = (thisHour > 12) ? thisHour - 12 : thisHour;

   // 3) if thisHour equals 0, change it to 12
   thisHour = (thisHour == 0) ? 12 : thisHour;

   return thisHour + ":" + thisMinute + ":" + thisSecond + ampm;
}
```

4. Save your changes to the file.

5. Reload or refresh **clock.htm** in your Web browser. The revised clock displays time in 12-hour format. See Figure 2-32.

Figure 2-32   ▶   **Time displayed in 12-hour format**

The time value should display minutes and seconds values with a leading zero if they are less than 10. In other words, Hector wants the clock to display 2:35:05 p.m., not 2:35:5 p.m. You can make this change by adding another conditional operator to the showTime() function. With this final modification, the statement to change the displayed value of the thisMinute variable becomes:

```
thisMinute = thisMinute < 10 ? "0"+thisMinute : thisMinute;
```

You enclose the value 0 in quotes, which causes JavaScript to treat the 0 as a text string rather than a numeric value. Also, if the value of the thisMinute variable is not less than 10, you leave it unchanged. The code to change the display of the thisSecond variable is similar:

```
thisSecond = thisSecond < 10 ? "0"+thisSecond : thisSecond;
```

You'll add these two commands to the showTime() function and then reload the Web page.

To change the minutes and seconds format:

▶ **1.** Return to the **functions.js** file in your text editor.

▶ **2.** Add the following commands, as shown in Figure 2-33:

```
// add leading zeros to minutes and seconds less than 10
thisMinute = thisMinute < 10 ? "0"+thisMinute : thisMinute;
thisSecond = thisSecond < 10 ? "0"+thisSecond : thisSecond;
```

Figure 2-33   ▶   **Code to change the format of the minutes and seconds values**

```
function showTime(dateObj) {
    thisSecond=dateObj.getSeconds();
    thisMinute=dateObj.getMinutes();
    thisHour=dateObj.getHours();

    // change thisHour from 24-hour time to 12-hour time by:
    // 1) if thisHour < 12 then set ampm to " a.m." otherwise set it to " p.m."
    var ampm = (thisHour < 12) ? " a.m." : " p.m.";

    // 2) subtract 12 from the thisHour variable
    thisHour = (thisHour > 12) ? thisHour - 12 : thisHour;

    // 3) if thisHour equals 0, change it to 12
    thisHour = (thisHour == 0) ? 12 : thisHour;

    // add leading zeros to minutes and seconds less than 10
    thisMinute = thisMinute < 10 ? "0"+thisMinute : thisMinute;
    thisSecond = thisSecond < 10 ? "0"+thisSecond : thisSecond;

    return thisHour + ":" + thisMinute + ":" + thisSecond + ampm;
}
```

▶ **3.** Save your changes, and then close the file.

4. Reload or refresh **clock.htm** in your Web browser. The revised clock displays the formatted minutes and seconds values. See Figure 2-34.

Minutes and seconds values in the revised format   **Figure 2-34**

You've completed work on the showTime() and showDate() functions. Because your purpose is to display the current date and time (and the time remaining in the year), you'll replace the test date of February 24, 2011 with the current date and time. Recall that a date object stores the current date and time when you do not specify a date/time value.

To display the current date and time:

1. Return to the **clock.htm** file in your text editor.

2. Change the command to create the today variable to the following, as shown in Figure 2-35:

```
var today = new Date();
```

Current date and time in the NYClock() function   **Figure 2-35**

```
function NYClock() {
   // the today variable contains the current date and time
   var today = new Date();          inserts the current
                                    date and time
   // display the current date and time
      document.clockform.dateNow.value = showDate(today);
      document.clockform.timeNow.value = showTime(today);
```

3. Save your changes, and then reload or reopen **clock.htm** in your Web browser. The Web page displays the current date and time as well as the time remaining in the year.

4. Refresh the Web page, and then verify that the browser updates the date/time information as well as the amount of time remaining in the year.

Running Timed Commands

You've completed the functions required for the countdown clock, but the clock is largely static, changing only when the page is loaded by the browser. Hector wants the clock to be updated constantly so that it always shows the current time and the time remaining until the New Year's Bash. To do this, you need to run the function at certain times. JavaScript provides two methods for doing this: time-delayed commands and timed-interval commands.

Working with Time-Delayed Commands

A **time-delayed command** is a JavaScript command that is run after a specified amount of time has passed. The syntax to run a time-delayed command is

```
setTimeout("command", delay);
```

where *command* is a JavaScript command and *delay* is the delay time in milliseconds before the browser runs the command. The command must be placed within either double or single quotation marks. For example, the following command sets a 5-millisecond delay before the browser runs the showClock() function:

```
setTimeout("showClock()", 5);
```

In some JavaScript programs, you may want to cancel a time-delayed command. This can occur in programs where other actions by the user remove the need to run a time-delayed command. To cancel the command, you run the command

```
clearTimeout();
```

and JavaScript will cancel the time-delayed command before it is run by the browser.

There is no limit to the number of time-delayed commands a browser can process. To distinguish one time-delayed command from another, you can assign a unique identification to each command. This ID becomes important when you want to cancel a specific command out of several time-delayed commands being processed by the browser. You store the ID value of each time-delayed command as a variable as follows

```
timeID = setTimeout("command",delay);
```

where *timeID* is a variable that stores the ID of the command. After you've assigned an ID to a time-delayed command, you can cancel it using the clearTimeout method

```
clearTimeout(timeID);
```

where once again *timeID* is the variable that stores the ID of the command.

Running Commands at Specified Intervals

The other way to time JavaScript commands is by using a **timed-interval command**, which instructs the browser to run the same command repeatedly at specified intervals. The method to run such a command is

```
setInterval("command",interval);
```

where *command* is the JavaScript command that is to be run repeatedly, and *interval* is the interval in milliseconds before the command is run again. To instruct the browser to stop running the command, you use the following method:

```
clearInterval();
```

As with time-delayed commands, you may have several timed-interval commands running simultaneously. To distinguish one timed-interval command from another, you store the time ID in a variable using the setInterval() method as follows

```
timeID = setInterval("command",interval);
```

where *timeID* is a variable that stores the ID of the timed-interval command. To halt the repeating command, you use the clearInterval() method with the *timeID* variable as follows:

```
clearInterval(timeID);
```

An important point to remember about the setTimeout() and setInterval() methods is that after a browser processes a request to run a command at a later time, the browser doesn't stop. Instead, the browser proceeds to any other commands running in the script and processes those commands without delay. For example, you might try to run three functions at 50-millisecond intervals using the following structure:

```
setTimeout("function1()",50);
setTimeout("function2()",50);
setTimeout("function3()",50);
```

However, a browser would execute this code by running all three functions almost simultaneously 50 milliseconds later. To run the functions with a separation of about 50 milliseconds between one function and the next, you would need to use three different delay times, as follows:

```
setTimeout("function1()",50);
setTimeout("function2()",100);
setTimeout("function3()",150);
```

In this case, a user's browser would run the first function after 50 milliseconds, the second function 50 milliseconds after that, and the third function after another 50 milliseconds has passed.

You have only one function to run for Hector's Web page: the NYClock() function. Because the function should run once every second, you will use the following command, which runs the NYClock() function continuously at intervals of 1000 milliseconds or one second:

```
setInterval("NYClock()", 1000)
```

You will replace the event handler in the <body> tag with this setInterval method. The revised event handler is:

```
onload = "setInterval('NYClock()', 1000)"
```

This event handler causes a browser displaying the page to run the NYClock() function one second after loading the page and then rerun that program every second thereafter. Because the event handler is enclosed in double quotation marks, you must use single quotation marks to enclose the name of the function to avoid confusion about which set of quotation marks refers to the onload attribute and which refers to the function being run.

To run the NYClock() function every second:

▶ **1.** Return to the **clock.htm** file in your text editor.

▶ **2.** Change the attribute of the onload event handler in the <body> tag to the following, as shown in Figure 2-36:

```
onload="setInterval('NYClock()',1000)"
```

Figure 2-36 **Command to run the function at timed intervals**

> runs the NYClock() function every second after the page loads

```
<body onload="setInterval('NYClock()', 1000)">
    <form name="clockform" id="clockform" action="">

    <div id="clock">
        <h4>Time</h4>
        <p>
            <input size="12" id="dateNow" name="dateNow" /><br />
            <img src="clock.jpg" alt="" /><br />
            <input size="12" id="timeNow" name="timeNow" />
        </p>
    </div>
```

3. Close the file, saving your changes.

4. Reload or reopen **clock.htm** in your Web browser. The countdown clock appears one second after the page loads, and both the countdown clock and the current time update continually as the NYClock() function is run again and again.

Reference Window | **Running Timed Commands**

- To run a command after a delay, use the method
    `timeID = setTimeout("command", delay)`
  where *command* is the command to be run, *delay* is the delay time in milliseconds, and *timeID* is a variable that stores the ID associated with the time-delayed command.
- To repeat a command at set intervals, use the method
    `timeID = setInterval("command", interval)`
  where *interval* is the time, in milliseconds, between repeating the command.
- To cancel a specific time-delayed command, use the method
    `clearTimeout(timeID)`
  where *timeID* is the ID of the time-delayed command.
- To clear all time-delayed commands, use the following method:
    `clearTimeout()`
- To cancel a repeated command, use the method
    `clearInterval(timeID)`
  where *timeID* is the ID of the repeated command.
- To clear all repeated commands, use the following method:
    `clearInterval()`

You've completed the countdown clock for the New Year's Bash. Hector will continue to work on the event's Web site and get back to you with any new projects or concerns.

Review | **Session 2.2 Quick Check**

1. How do you use a unary operator to increase the value of the thisMonth variable by 1?
2. How do you use an assignment operator to increase the value of the thisMonth variable by 1?
3. What command rounds the value of the thisMonth variable to the nearest integer?
4. What conditional operator changes the value of the thisMonth variable to 12 if it equals 11 but otherwise leaves the value unchanged?

5. What function tests whether the value of the thisMonth variable is a number?

6. What command displays the value of the thisDay variable with no decimal places?

7. What statement runs the function calcMonth() after a 0.5-second delay?

8. What statement runs the function calcMonth() every 0.5 seconds?

Tutorial Summary | Review

In this tutorial, you learned how to work with date objects, math functions, and timed commands to create a countdown clock. In the first session, you created event handlers that allow you to run functions in response to particular events occurring within a Web page and Web browser. You also set the values of fields within a Web form. The rest of the first session introduced the date object and discussed how to work with the properties and methods of dates in order to display a specified date in a Web form. In the second session, you worked with JavaScript operators to calculate the amount of time left in the year from a specified date. You used a Math object to convert this value into days, hours, minutes, and seconds. The second session then discussed how to work with numeric values in JavaScript. The session also covered how to use comparison operators to apply different possible values to a single variable. The session concluded with a discussion of timed commands, which run a function at a specified time interval.

Key Terms

arithmetic operator	decrement operator	negation operator
assignment operator	event	operand
binary operator	event handler	operator
comparison operator	increment operator	time-delayed command
conditional operator	logical operator	timed-interval command
date method	Math method	unary operator
date object	Math object	

Practice	Review Assignments

Practice the skills you learned in the tutorial using the same case scenario.

Data Files needed for the Review Assignments: datestxt.js, eventstxt.htm, logo.jpg, tulsa.css

Hector has been promoted to general manager of promotion for all of Tulsa's special events. He wants you to create something similar to the New Year's Bash countdown clock for all of the events sponsored by the city. Hector envisions a Web page displaying a list of special events that includes each event's name, the date that it will occur, and the time remaining until the event (in days, hours, minutes, and seconds). Hector wants the following events listed on the Web page:

- Heritage Day on January 14 at 10:00 a.m.
- Spring Day Rally on May 21 at 12:00 p.m.
- July 4th Fireworks on July 4 at 9:00 p.m.
- Summer Bash on September 1 at 12:00 p.m.
- Holiday Party on December 1 at 11:30 a.m.
- New Year's Bash on December 31 at 3:30 p.m.

Like the countdown clock, the contents of the Web site should be constantly updated by a user's browser. Hector has already created the Web page's design and layout, but wants you to write the JavaScript program to run the clocks. Figure 2-37 shows a preview of the completed Web page.

Figure 2-37

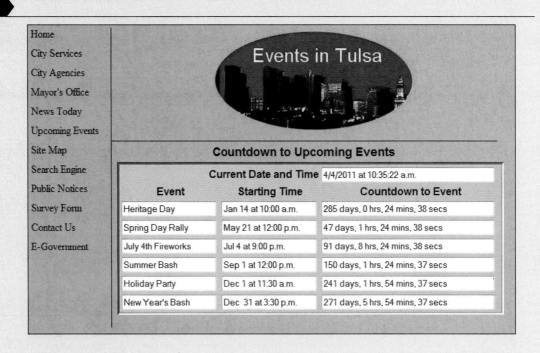

Complete the following:

1. Use your text editor to open the **eventstxt.htm** file from the tutorial.02\review folder, enter *your name* and *the date* in the head section, and then save the file as **events.htm** in the same folder. Use your text editor to open the **datestxt.js** file from the tutorial.02\ review folder, enter *your name* and *the date* in the comment section, and then save the file as **dates.js** in the same folder.

2. Go to the **dates.js** file in your text editor. The file contains a single function named showDateTime() that displays the date and time of a date object in a formatted text string. Below this function, insert a function named **changeYear()** that will change a date's year value if the date has already been passed in the current calendar year. To create the changeYear parameter, do the following:

   a. Specify two parameters for the changeYear function: today and holiday. The **today** parameter is used to store a date object representing the current date. The **holiday** parameter is used to store a date object representing one of the events in Hector's list.

   b. In the first line of the function, use the getFullYear() date method to extract the four-digit year value from the today variable and store the value in a variable named **year**.

   c. In the second line, use the setFullYear() date method to set the full year value of the holiday date object to the value of the year variable. This changes the date of the holiday event to the current year.

   d. In the third line, use a conditional operator involving the year variable. The operator's test condition is whether the value of the holiday date object is less than the today date object. If it is, the event has already passed in the current year and the value of the year variable should increase by 1. If it is not, the event has not yet occurred and the year value should remain unchanged.

   e. In the fourth line of the function, set the full year value of the holiday date object to the value of the year variable.

3. Below the changeYear() function, create a function named **countdown()** that will return a text string displaying the number of days, hours, minutes, and seconds between a starting date and a stopping date. Create the function as follows:

   a. Specify two parameters for the function: start and stop. The **start** parameter will contain a date object for the starting date. The **stop** parameter will contain a date object for the stopping date.

   b. In the first line of the function, calculate the time difference between stop and start, storing the difference in a variable named **time**.

   c. Convert the time difference into days, hours, minutes, and seconds, and return the following text string

      days **days,** *hours* **hrs,** *minutes* **mins,** *seconds* **secs**

      where *days, hours, minutes,* and *seconds* are variables that store the integer values of the days, hours, minutes, and seconds. (*Hint:* Use the commands in the NYClock() function from the tutorial as a guide for converting the time difference into days, hours, minutes, and seconds.)

4. Close the file, saving your changes.

5. Go to the **events.htm** file in your text editor. Above the closing </head> tag, insert an external script element to access the code in the dates.js file; and then, below that element, insert a second script element for code to be embedded in the events.htm file.

6. Within the embedded script element, create a function named **showCountdown()**. The showCountdown() function has no parameters. Within the function, do the following:

   a. Create a variable named **today** containing a date object. Use the current date and time shown in Figure 2-37. Create six additional date objects in variables named **Date1** through **Date6**. Assign the dates and times from the six events in Hector's list to the Date1 through Date6 variables. Use a year value of **2011** for these six dates (you'll set the current year value in a later step).

      b. Using the today variable as the parameter value, call the showDateTime() function and store the value returned by the function in the thisDay field of the eventform Web form.

      c. Using today as the first parameter value and Date1 as the second parameter value, call the changeYear() function. Calling this function sets the correct year value for the first event in Hector's list. Repeat this step for the Date2 through Date6 variables.

      d. Call the countdown() function using the today variable as the first parameter value and the Date1 variable as the second. Display the result returned by this function in the count1 field of the eventform Web form. Running this command displays the time remaining until the first event in Hector's list. Repeat this step for the other five events.

7. Add an event handler to the <body> tag that runs the showCountdown() function when the page is loaded by the browser.

8. Save your changes to the file.

9. Open **events.htm** in your Web browser. Verify that it shows the same date, time, and countdown values shown in Figure 2-37.

10. Return to the **events.htm** file in your text editor. Modify the initial value of the today variable so that it always uses the current date and time.

11. Modify the event handler in the <body> tag so that it runs the showCountdown() function every tenth of a second after the page is loaded.

12. Close the file, saving your changes.

13. Reload or refresh **events.htm** in your Web browser and verify that it shows a count-down clock with the current date and time.

14. Submit your completed files to your instructor.

Apply	**Case Problem 1**

Use JavaScript to create and run an exam timer.

Data Files needed for this Case Problem: oaetxt.htm, figa.jpg, figb.jpg, figc.jpg, figd.jpg, figures.jpg, functions.js, oae.jpg, quiz.css

Online Aptitude Exams Grunwald Testing, Inc. creates and administers a series of aptitude tests for schools, government agencies, and private firms. The company has been exploring the feasibility of putting some of its tests online. John Paulson is directing the effort and has asked you to help design a sample test page. The company's tests are graded on two measures: the number of correct answers by the respondents and the time required to complete the exam. John wants you to work on creating an online timer that starts the moment users begin work on an exam and stops once users have submitted their answers. The exam questions will be hidden from users until the clock starts. After users submit their answers, the exam questions will close and an alert box will appear showing the number of correct answers and the time, in seconds, taken to complete the exam. John has already collected some of the functions you'll need for this page in a separate file named functions.js. The file contains two functions:

- The showQuiz() function displays the quiz questions on the Web page.
- The gradeQuiz() function returns the number of correct answers in a submitted quiz, highlights the correct answers on the page, and disables the quiz, preventing users from changing their answers.

You will write the code to start and stop the quiz timer as well as to call the functions to show and grade a completed quiz. Figure 2-38 shows a preview of the exam page in action.

Figure 2-38

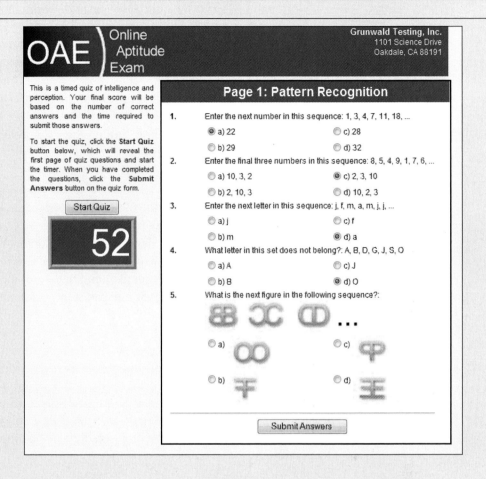

Complete the following:

1. Use your text editor to open the **oaetxt.htm** file from the tutorial.02\case1 folder, enter *your name* and *the date* in the head section, and then save the file as **oae.htm** in the same folder.

2. Above the closing </head> tag, insert an external script element that points to the functions.js file in the tutorial.02\case1 folder.

3. Below this script element, insert another script element. Within the script element, declare two variables. The first variable is named **seconds** and will store the current elapsed time that the user has worked on the exam. The second variable is named **clockId** and will reference the commands used to repeatedly update the clock value. Set the initial value of the seconds variable to 0. Do not set an initial value for the clockId variable.

4. Create a function named **runClock()** that will update the time value in the Web page's clock. There are no parameters. Add the following commands to the function:
   a. Use a unary operator to increase the value of the seconds variable by 1.
   b. Change the value of the quizclock field in the quiz form to the value of the seconds variable.

5. Create a function named **startClock()** that will start the Web page clock and then repeatedly update the elapsed time displayed in the clock. There are no parameters to this function. Add the following commands:
   a. Call the showQuiz() function to display the questions in the online exam.

     b. Call the runClock() function every second, storing the ID of this timed-interval command in the clockId variable.

6. Create a function named **stopClock()** that will stop the timer, display the user's score, and disable the exam to prevent further entry. There are no parameters to this function. Add the following commands:

     a. Halt the repeated calls to the runClock() function. (*Hint:* Use the clearInterval() method.)

     b. Call the gradeQuiz() function, storing the value returned by the function in a variable named **correctAns**.

     c. Display an alert box containing the text string

       `You have `*`correctAns`*` correct of 5 in `*`timer`*` seconds.`

       where *correctAns* is the value of the correctAns variable and *timer* is the value of the quizclock field in the quiz form.

7. Locate the input button for the Start Quiz button. Add an event handler attribute that runs the startClock() function when the button is clicked.

8. Go to the end of the file and locate the input button for the Submit Answers button. Add an event handler attribute that runs the stopClock() function when the button is clicked.

9. Save your changes to the file.

10. Open **oae.htm** in your Web browser. Verify that clicking the Start Quiz button displays the quiz questions and starts the timer. Then verify that clicking the Submit Answers button stops the timer, disables the exam, and displays an alert box with the number of correct answers and the elapsed time to complete the exam. (*Hint:* To restore the timer and the Web form to their original state, you will have to reload the page in the browser. Clicking the browser's Refresh button will not remove the Web form values or zero the timer.)

11. Submit your completed files to your instructor.

Apply | **Case Problem 2**

Use JavaScript to display a random text box.

Data Files needed for this Case Problem: hometxt.htm, logo.jpg, randtxt.js, styles.css, tips.js, work.jpg

The Home Center   Tom Vogel manages The Home Center, a Web site for do-it-yourself enthusiasts. The site contains articles, forums, and products for home repair and maintenance. Tom thinks it would be helpful for users to see a short home repair tip on the site's home page. He wants a different tip to appear each time a user loads the page, and has created a collection of 10 tips to display randomly on the page. Tom has already obtained two functions to display the tip title and text:

- The tipTitle() function returns the title of the nth tip title. The value of *n* is entered as a parameter of the function.

- The tipText() function returns the text of the nth tip of the tip collection. The value of *n* is entered as a parameter of the function.

The tipTitle() and tipText() functions have been stored in the tips.js file. You will create a function that randomly selects a tip from this collection and then writes the title and text of that tip to an appropriate spot on the Web page. A preview of the completed Web page is shown in Figure 2-39.

Figure 2-39

Search [   ]

THE HOME CENTER IS YOUR NUMBER ONE
source for do-it-yourself home improvement help
with tutorials and tips on all your home repairs,
remodeling, and redecorating. Our goal is to make
your projects easy, inexpensive, and rewarding.
Nothing matches the satisfaction of a job well done.

The Home Center

- Home

- What's New
- Home Projects
- E-Newsletter
- FAQ

- Online Store
- Product Search

- Forums
- Our Partners
- Contact Us!
- About the Home Center

You will find step-by-step instructions and money-
saving tips on all your do-it-yourself projects,
including house painting, wallpaper, carpentry,
home insulation, woodworking, electrical,
plumbing, air conditioning and heating, flooring, masonry, concrete, wood decks, interior
decorating, gardening, and the installation of energy-efficient fixtures and appliances

Be sure to visit our online store for great prices on the tools and materials you need for
your home repair projects!

**Random Tip
Using Downspouts**

To effectively get the water away from
your house, you can let your
downspout empty onto a splash block
or send the runoff to an extension
gutter. Or you can get a retractable
downspout extender that unfurls as it
fills with water, and contracts as the
water stops flowing, tucking neatly
under the downspout and remaining out
of the way of lawn mowers.

Complete the following:

1. Use your text editor to open the **hometxt.htm** file from the tutorial.02\case2 folder, enter *your name* and *the date* in the head section, and then save the file as **home.htm** in the same folder. Use your text editor to open the **randtxt.js** file, enter *your name* and *the date* in the comment section, and then save the file as **random.js** in the same folder.

 EXPLORE

2. Within the random.js file, create a function named **randInt()** that will generate a random integer within a given range. The function has two parameters: lower and upper, where lower is the lowest integer in the range and upper is the highest integer in the range. Add the following commands to the function:

   a. Declare a variable named **size** that is equal to the number of integers in the given range. (*Hint:* The size of the range is one more than the difference between the highest and lowest integer.)

   b. Use the Math.floor() and Math.random() methods as well as the lower parameter and size variable to generate a random integer. (*Hint:* See the section on generating a random integer in this tutorial for guidance.)

3. Close the file, saving your changes.

4. Go to the **home.htm** file in your text editor. Above the closing </head> tag, insert two external script elements: one that links to the tips.js file and another that links to the random.js file you just created.

5. Scroll down the document to the div element with an ID value of "tip" and replace the contents of this element with an embedded script element. Within the script element do the following:

   a. Declare a variable named **tipNum** that is equal to a random integer between 1 and 10 returned by the randInt() function you created in the random.js file.

   b. Use a series of document.write() statements to write the HTML code
   ```
   <h1>Random Tip<br />title</h1>
   <p>tip</p>
   ```
   to the Web page, where *title* is the title of the random title as generated by the tipTitle() function and *tip* is the text of the random tip as generated by the tipText() function.

6. Save your changes to the file.

7. Open **home.htm** in your Web browser and verify that a random tip appears in the floating tip box each time you reload or refresh the Web page.

8. Submit your completed files to your instructor.

Challenge | Case Problem 3

Explore how to use JavaScript to create a world clock.

Data Files needed for this Case Problem: worldtxt.htm, zonestxt.js, je.css, logo.jpg, map.jpg

Jackson Electronics Jackson Electronics is a global company that manufactures and sells quality electronic equipment and components. The company has six corporate offices at different locations around the globe, and employees must keep in constant communication with the different offices. David Lin maintains the corporate Web site and asks you for help with a problem. He wants to augment the Web page that displays the location of the corporate offices to display the local time at each location. This will give employees important information when they want to call or fax data from one office to another. To create this world clock, David needs to know how JavaScript's date object works with different time zones.

The Earth is divided into 24 time zones. Each time zone is referenced in comparison to the time kept in Greenwich, England, which is known as standard time or Greenwich mean time (GMT). You can determine how Greenwich mean time differs from your local time using the getTimezoneOffset() method. For example, if the today variable contains a date object and is run on a computer in New York, the expression

```
today.getTimezoneOffset()
```

returns the value 300 because Greenwich mean time is 300 minutes or five hours ahead of New York time. With this information, you can determine Greenwich time by adding the offset value to your computer's local time. Because JavaScript measures time in milliseconds, you must multiply the offset by the number of milliseconds in one minute. The following code calculates the number of hours using this function:

```
today.getTimezoneOffset()*60*1000
```

You can determine the time anywhere in the world if you know Greenwich time and the other location's offset from GMT. David has compiled the following list of the six corporate offices and the time difference in minutes between each of those cities and GMT:

- Office 1: Houston (–360)
- Office 2: London (0)
- Office 3: New York (–300)
- Office 4: Seattle (–480)
- Office 5: Sydney (660)
- Office 6: Tokyo (540)

The number in parentheses indicates the number of minutes the city is offset from GMT. A negative value indicates that the city is behind GMT, and a positive value indicates that it is ahead of GMT. Tokyo, for example, is 540 minutes or nine hours ahead of Greenwich.

David already designed the contents of the world map Web page, but he needs your help in programming the times for the six offices. Figure 2-40 shows a preview of the completed Web page.

Figure 2-40

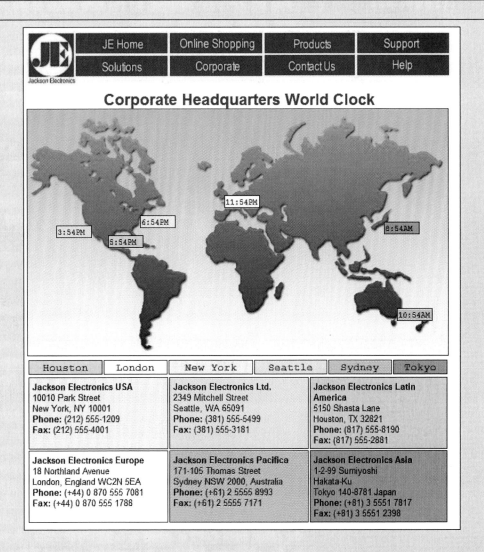

Complete the following:

1. Use your text editor to open the **worldtxt.htm** file from the tutorial.02\case3 folder, enter *your name* and *the date* in the head section, and then save the file as **world.htm** in the same folder. Use your text editor to open the **zonestxt.js** file from the tutorial.02\case3 folder, enter *your name* and *the date* in the comment section, and then save the file as **zones.js** in the same folder.

2. Within the **zones.js** file, create a function named **addTime()** that will create a new date object by adding a specified number of milliseconds to an initial time value. The function has two parameters: **oldTime** and **milliSeconds**. The oldTime parameter stores a date object representing an initial time value. The milliSeconds parameter stores the amount of time, in milliseconds, that should be added to the oldTime parameter. Add the following commands to the function:

    a. Create a date object named **newTime**, but do not specify a value for its date or time.

    b. Using the getTime() method, extract the number of milliseconds contained in the oldTime parameter and add this to the milliSeconds parameter. Store the sum in a variable named **newValue**.

⊕EXPLORE

⊕ EXPLORE

    c. Using the setTime() method, set the time value of the newTime date object to the value of the newValue variable.

    d. Return the value of the newTime date object.

3. Below the addTime() function, create a function named **showTime()** that will return a text string showing the time in 12-hour format. The function has a single parameter named **time**, which contains the date and time that you want displayed. Using the show Time() function from the tutorial as a guide, have this function return the text string

    hour:minute AM/PM

    where *hour* is the hour value in 12-hour format, *minute* is the minute value, and AM/PM is either AM or PM, depending on the time of day.

4. Save your changes to the zones.js file.

5. Go to the **world.htm** file in your text editor. Above the closing </head> tag, insert an external script element to access the functions you created in the zones.js file and then insert a second embedded script element.

6. Within the embedded script element, create a function named **worldClock()** that will calculate the time in different time zones. Within this function, do the following:

    a. Create a date object variable named **today** that is equal to the current date and time.

⊕ EXPLORE

    b. Apply the getTimezoneOffset() method to the today variable to calculate the offset of your computer's clock from GMT in minutes. Change this value to milliseconds by multiplying the value by 60 and then by 1000. Store the result in a variable named **offSet**.

    c. Call the addTime() function using today as the first parameter value and offSet as the second. Store the value returned by this function in a variable named **GMT**. The GMT variable represents the current date and time in Greenwich.

⊕ EXPLORE

    d. Calculate the current date and time at Jackson Electronics' first office (Houston). To calculate this value, call the addTime() function with GMT as the first parameter and the second parameter equal to the number of milliseconds that Houston is offset from GMT. (*Hint:* Because Houston is 360 minutes behind Greenwich, the offset from GMT is equal to (–360)*60*1000.) Store the date object returned by the addTime() function in a variable named **time1**. Repeat this step to create variables named **time2** through **time6** for the other five office locations using the offset values listed above.

    e. The current times for the six office locations are to be displayed in input fields named **place1** through **place6** in the zones Web form. To display the value of the place1 field, call the showTime() function using the time1 variable as the parameter value. Repeat this step for the five remaining input fields.

7. Add an event handler attribute to the <body> tag to run the worldClock() function when the page is loaded by the browser and every second thereafter.

8. Close the file, saving your changes.

9. Open **world.htm** in your Web browser. Verify that the page shows the current time for the six office locations and that these times are correctly offset from Greenwich.

10. Submit your completed files to your instructor.

Note: This is a simplified example of a very complex problem. Different countries apply time zones in different ways. For example, China spans several time zones but applies a uniform time throughout the country. Some countries also shift their time(s) twice a year during daylight savings time (also known as summer time) whereas others do not apply daylight savings time at all. For example, the reported times in the Case Problem will be off by one hour during daylight savings time for the Seattle, Houston, and New York clocks. To create a truly accurate world clock, you would have to take into account all the various idiosyncrasies of global timekeeping.

Create	**Case Problem 4**

Test your knowledge of JavaScript by creating a countdown clock for the opening of a shopping mall.

Data Files needed for this Case Problem: malltxt.htm, mall.txt, timetxt.js, logo.jpg, mall1.jpg, mall2.jpg, mall3.jpg

The Cutler Mall   Alice Samuels is the director of promotion for the Cutler Shopping Mall, a large new mall opening on March 23 at 9:00 a.m. in Cutler, Iowa. She asked you to design the Web page announcing the mall's opening. She's provided the text of the page as well as several graphic images; however, she also wants you to program a countdown clock that displays the days, hours, and minutes until the mall opens. The final design of the site is up to you, and you may supplement the provided material with your own.

Complete the following:

1. Use your text editor to open the **malltxt.htm** file from the tutorial.02\case4 folder, enter *your name* and *the date* in the head section, and then save the file as **mall.htm** in the same folder.
2. Insert a Web form named **mallclock** that has the following fields:
   - A **dayNow** field that displays the current date in the format month/day/year
   - A **timeNow** field that displays the time in 12-hour format
   - A **days** field that displays the number of days until the mall opens
   - An **hours** field that displays the number of hours left in the current day
   - A **minutes** field that displays the number of minutes left in the current hour; round this value to the nearest minute
3. Add the remaining content to the Web page. Refer to the **mall.txt** text file in the tutorial.02\case4 folder for the content that Alice wants you to include. Insert any styles for the Web page in an external file named **mall.css**. Link the mall.htm file to this style sheet.
4. Use your text editor to open the **timetxt.js** file from the tutorial.02\case4 folder, enter *your name* and *the date* in the comment section, and then save the file as **time.js** in the same folder.
5. In the file, add the following functions (refer to the functions and codes from the tutorial case for help in writing these functions):
   - A **daysDiff()** function that calculates the number of days, rounded down to the next lowest integer, between a starting date and a stopping date
   - An **hoursDiff()** function that calculates the number of hours left in the current day rounded down to the next lowest integer
   - A **minutesDiff()** function that calculates the number of minutes left in the current hour rounded down to the next lowest integer
   - A **showDate()** function that displays the value of a date object in the format *month/day/year*

- • A **showTime()** function that displays the value of a date object in the format *hour:minute* a.m./p.m.

6. Insert an external script element to access the functions in the time.js script file from the mall.htm file.

7. Add an embedded script to the mall.htm file to use the functions from the time.js file to create a function named **countDownClock()** that displays the current date and time in the document as well as the days, hours, and minutes remaining until the mall opening. Assume an opening date of March 23 and an opening time of 9:00 a.m. For the year, use a starting year value of the current year; but if the current date falls after March 23 of the current year, change the year value for the opening date to the next year. (*Hint:* Apply conditional operators along with the getFullYear() and setFullYear() functions to set the year value of the opening date.)

8. Have the countDownClock() function run when the page initially opens and then every 60 seconds thereafter.

9. Submit your completed files to your instructor.

Review | Quick Check Answers

Session 2.1

1. An event handler is an attribute added to an element that instructs Web browsers to run a script command or commands when an event (such as a mouse click) occurs within the element.

2. `onclick = "showImage()"`

3. `<a href = "javascript:showImage()"> ... </a>`

4. `var examDate = new Date("May 8, 2011 18:55:28");`

5. `examDate.getMonth() // The value returned would be 4.`

6. `examDate.getFullYear()`

7. `examDate.setDate(9);`

8. `currentTime = new Date();`

Session 2.2

1. `thisMonth++`

2. `thisMonth += 1;`

3. `Math.round(thisMonth)`

4. `thisMonth = (thisMonth == 11) ? 12 : thisMonth;`

5. `IsNan(thisMonth)`

6. `thisDay.toFixed(0);`

7. `setTimeout("calcMonth", 500);`

8. `setInterval("calcMonth", 500);`

Ending Data Files

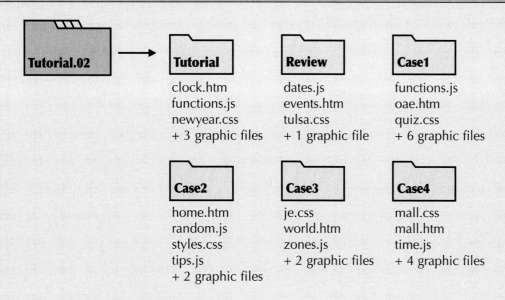

Tutorial.02 →

Tutorial

clock.htm
functions.js
newyear.css
+ 3 graphic files

Review

dates.js
events.htm
tulsa.css
+ 1 graphic file

Case1

functions.js
oae.htm
quiz.css
+ 6 graphic files

Case2

home.htm
random.js
styles.css
tips.js
+ 2 graphic files

Case3

je.css
world.htm
zones.js
+ 2 graphic files

Case4

mall.css
mall.htm
time.js
+ 4 graphic files

Objectives

Session 3.1
- Create an array
- Populate and reference values from an array
- Work with array methods

Session 3.2
- Work with For loops
- Work with While loops
- Loop through the contents of an array
- Work with If, If... Else, and multiple conditional statements

Session 3.3
- Use arrays, loops, and conditional statements to create a table
- Work with break, continue, and label commands

Working with Arrays, Loops, and Conditional Statements

Creating a Monthly Calendar

Case | The Chamberlain Civic Center

With first-class concerts, performances from Broadway touring companies, and shows from famous comics, singers, and other entertainers, the Chamberlain Civic Center (CCC) is a popular attraction in South Dakota. Maria Valdez is the new publicity director for the center. Part of her job is to oversee the development of the center's Web site. After reviewing the Web site, Maria wants you to make a few changes.

In addition to links connecting visitors to the site's main features, the CCC home page provides a brief description of the events for the current month. Maria thinks it would be helpful to place a monthly calendar at the top of the home page so that visitors could quickly see the day each event will be held. Maria does not want staff members to construct the calendar manually each month. Instead, she wants a program added to the site that displays the monthly calendar for the current date. She asks you to help write a program that automatically generates the calendar.

Starting Data Files

Tutorial.03 →

Tutorial
ccctxt.htm
caltxt.js
+ 2 CSS files
+ 3 graphic files

Review
caltxt.htm
yeartxt.js
+ 2 CSS files
+ 3 graphic files

Case1
clisttxt.htm
list.js
lhouse.css
logo.jpg

Case2
electtxt.htm
votes.js
results.css
+2 graphics files

Case3
aucttxt.htm
styles.css
logo.jpg

Case4
lunartxt.htm
lunartxt.js
moonfunc.js
atro.css
caltxt.css
+ 17 graphics files

Session 3.1

Introducing the Monthly Calendar

Maria has drawn her idea for creating the monthly calendar on a printout of the Chamberlain Civic Center's home page. The printout shows the events from the previous month, March 2011. The main text of the page contains a description of May events at the CCC. Maria wants the monthly calendar for May to appear in the upper-right corner of the page so that users can relate the events to the dates on the calendar. Figure 3-1 shows how Maria envisions the calendar on the Web page.

| Figure 3-1 | Monthly calendar to add to home page |

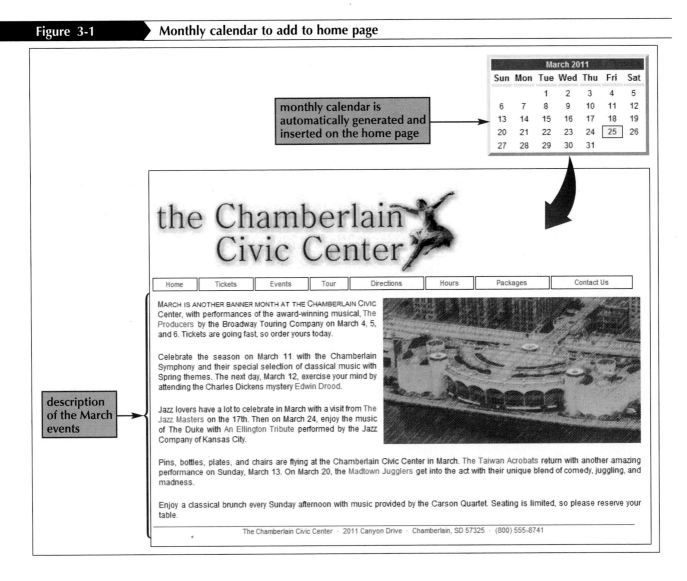

Maria wants the program you write to be easily usable on other Web pages. She envisions placing the entire JavaScript code for the calendar in an external file named calendar.js and running it from a single function. She also wants the styles for the calendar to be placed in a single external file named calendar.css. Figure 3-2 shows how these files create the monthly calendar. Accessing and displaying the monthly calendar table should then require only a minimal amount of recoding within any page at the CCC site.

Files to create and format the monthly calendar ◀ Figure 3-2

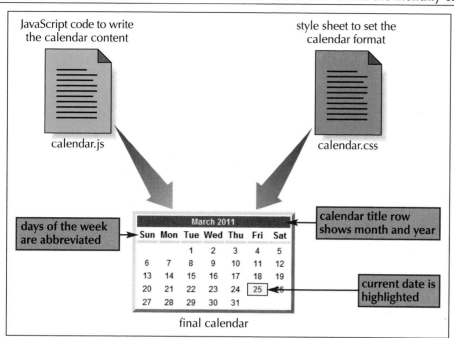

final calendar

Maria has already created the styles required for the calendar table, but has left the coding to you. You'll add links to both the calendar.js and calendar.css files on the Chamberlain Civic Center's home page.

To access the CCC files:

▶ 1. Use your text editor to open the **ccctxt.htm** and **caltxt.js** files from the tutorial.03\ tutorial folder, enter *your name* and *the date* in the comment section at the top of each file, and then save the files as **ccc.htm** and **calendar.js**, respectively.

▶ 2. Return to the **ccc.htm** file in your text editor, and then add the following code above the closing </head> tag to create links to both the calendar.css style sheet and the calendar.js JavaScript file, as shown in Figure 3-3:

```
<link href="calendar.css" rel="stylesheet" type="text/css" />
<script src="calendar.js" type="text/javascript"></script>
```

Code to link the JavaScript and style sheet files ◀ Figure 3-3

```
<title>The Chamberlain Civic Center</title>
<link href="ccc.css" rel="stylesheet" type="text/css" />

<link href="calendar.css" rel="stylesheet" type="text/css" />
<script src="calendar.js" type="text/javascript"></script>
```

▶ 3. Save your changes to the file.

Reviewing the Calendar Style Sheet

Before you start writing the code to create the monthly calendar, you will look at the styles in the calendar.css style sheet. Maria has assigned class names and IDs to different parts of the table. The five classes and IDs you'll use when creating the monthly calendar are:

- The entire calendar is set in a table with the ID **calendar_table**.
- The cell containing the calendar title has the ID **calendar_head**.
- The seven cells containing the days of the week abbreviations all belong to the class **calendar_weekdays**.
- The cells containing the dates of the month all belong to the class **calendar_dates**.
- The cell containing the current date has the ID **calendar_today**.

For each of these parts, calendar.css has a style declaration. Figure 3-4 shows the style sheet contained in the calendar.css file.

Figure 3-4   **Contents of the calendar.css style sheet**

```
#calendar_table     {float: right; background-color: white; font-size: 9pt;
                     font-family: Arial, Helvetica, sans-serif;
                     border-style: outset; border-width: 5px; margin: 0px 0px 5px 5px}

#calendar_head      {background-color: rgb(223,29,29); color: ivory; letter-spacing: 2px}

.calendar_weekdays  {width: 30px; font-size: 10pt; border-bottom-style: solid}

.calendar_dates     {text-align: center; background-color: white}

#calendar_today     {font-weight: bold; color: rgb(223,29,29); background-color: ivory;
                     border: 1px solid black}
```

As you create the code that writes this table, you need to make sure that you add the ID and class attributes to the appropriate table and cell tags. Placing this information in a separate style sheet lets you modify the table's appearance without having to rewrite the code that generates the table.

Adding the calendar() Function

Because Maria wants the calendar application to be available to any page of the CCC site, you'll place all of the commands in a single function named calendar(). The first commands you will add to the function use the document.write() method to write the HTML code for a table element with the ID calendar_table. The initial code for the calendar() function is:

```
function calendar() {
   document.write("<table id='calendar_table'>");
   document.write("</table>");
}
```

You'll call this function by adding the command in a script element within the ccc.htm file. You'll add this code to the calendar.js and ccc.htm files now.

To begin work on the calendar() function:

▶ 1. Return to the **calendar.js** file in your text editor, and then, at the bottom of the file, add the following code, as shown in Figure 3-5:

```
function calendar() {
   document.write("<table id='calendar_table'>");
   document.write("</table>");
}
```

Code for the calendar() function | Figure 3-5

```
function calendar() {
    document.write("<table id='calendar_table'>");
    document.write("</table>");
}
```

▶ **2.** Save your changes to the file.

▶ **3.** Return to the **ccc.htm** file in your text editor, and then locate the div element with the ID head. The calendar should be placed as a table element within this section of the page.

▶ **4.** Insert the following code to run the calendar() function to create the table, as shown in Figure 3-6:

```
<script type="text/javascript">
    calendar();
</script>
```

Code to call the calendar() function | Figure 3-6

```
<body>
    <div id="head">
        <script type="text/javascript">
            calendar();
        </script>
        <img src="ccc.jpg" alt="Chamberlain Civic Center" />
    </div>
```

▶ **5.** Close the file, saving your changes.

▶ **6.** Open **ccc.htm** in your Web browser, and then verify that the browser does not report any coding errors. The calendar table does not appear on the Web page because you haven't yet created any content for the table.

Trouble? If you are running Internet Explorer, you may need to allow the browser to run the script on the page.

At this point, you've completed all of the coding needed in the ccc.htm file. All of the remaining work to build the calendar() function is done in the calendar.js file. The three main tasks to complete the calendar table are:

- Creating the table header row
- Creating the table row containing the names of the days of the week
- Creating the rows containing the days of the month

In this first session, you'll learn how to create the header row for the calendar table. In the second and third sessions, you'll complete the rest of the table.

Working with Arrays

Maria wants the header row of the calendar table to display the text *Month, Year* where *Month* is the name of the month and *Year* is the four-digit year value. Recall that date objects support methods that allow you to extract the date's month number. For example, a date object storing the date March 18, 2011 has a month value of 2 (because month values start with 0 for the month of January). Maria wants the month name rather than the month number to appear in the table, but no existing date method returns the name of the month. Instead, you will have to write code to associate each month number with a month name. One way of doing this is through an array.

An **array** is a collection of data values organized under a single name. Each individual data value has a number or **index** that distinguishes it from other values in the array. The general form of an array value is

```
array[i]
```

where *array* is the name of the array and *i* is the index of a specific value in the array. The first item in any array has an index value of 0, the second item has an index value of 1, and so on. For example, the expression

```
monthName[4]
```

references the fifth (not the fourth) item in the monthName array.

Creating and Populating an Array

To create an array, you run the command

```
var array = new Array(length);
```

where *array* is the name of the array and *length* is the number of items in the array. The *length* parameter is optional. If you omit the *length* parameter, the array expands to match the number of items defined for it. When the length of an array is defined, JavaScript allots only the amount of memory needed to generate the array, so the code runs more efficiently. To create an array named monthName for the 12 month names, you can enter the command

```
var monthName = new Array(12);
```

or you can omit the array length and enter the command

Tip

Arrays without a defined length can take up more memory on your computer system.

```
var monthName = new Array();
```

After you create an array, you can populate it with values using the same commands you use for any variable. The only difference is that you must specify both the array name and the index number of the array item. The command to set the value of a specific item in an array is

```
array[i] = value;
```

where *array* is the name of the array, *i* is the index of the array item, and *value* is the value assigned to the item. For example, to insert the month names into the monthName array, you could run the following commands:

```
monthName[0]  = "January";
monthName[1]  = "February";
monthName[2]  = "March";
. . .
monthName[10]  = "November";
monthName[11]  = "December";
```

A more compact way of creating and populating an array is to specify the array values when the array is initially declared. The syntax for this statement is

```
var array = new Array(values);
```

where *values* is a comma-separated list of values. The following command creates and populates the monthName array in a single statement:

```
var monthName = new Array("January", "February", "March", "April", "May",
"June", "July", "August", "September", "October", "November", "December");
```

A final way to create an array is with an **array literal**, in which the array values are entered into a bracketed list. The expression to create an array literal is

```
var array = [values];
```

where *values* is a comma-separated list of item values. The following command creates an array literal of month names:

```
var monthName = ["January", "February", "March", "April", "May", "June",
"July", "August", "September", "October", "November", "December"];
```

Tip

Be careful when using array literals to populate an array. Some early browser versions do not support this method.

Array values do not need to all be the same data type. You can mix numeric values, text strings, and other data types within a single array, as in the following statement:

```
var x = new Array("JavaScript", 3.14, true, null);
```

Now that you've seen how to create and populate an array, you will create an array of month names to use in creating the calendar application. You will insert the array in a function named writeCalTitle() that you will use to write the header row of the calendar table. The function has a single parameter named calendarDay that will store a date object containing the date to be highlighted in the calendar. The initial code for the writeCalTitle() function is:

```
function writeCalTitle(calendarDay) {
   var monthName = new Array("January", February", "March", "April",
   "May", "June", "July", "August", "September", "October", "November",
   "December");
}
```

You'll add this function to the calendar.js file.

To create the writeCalTitle() function:

▶ **1.** Return to the **calendar.js** file in your text editor.

▶ **2.** At the bottom of the file, insert the following code, as shown in Figure 3-7, being sure that each array item value is enclosed within a set of double quotation marks and that the line does not wrap within a quoted text string:

```
function writeCalTitle(calendarDay) {
   var monthName = new Array("January", "February", "March",
   "April", "May", "June", "July", "August", "September",
   "October", "November", "December");
}
```

Code for the monthName array | **Figure 3-7**

```
function calendar() {
   document.write("<table id='calendar_table'>");
   document.write("</table>");
}

function writeCalTitle(calendarDay) {
   var monthName = new Array("January", "February", "March",
   "April", "May", "June", "July", "August", "September",
   "October", "November", "December");
}
```

array of month names

The function needs to extract the month value and year value from the calendarDay parameter using the getMonth() and getFullYear() date methods introduced in the previous tutorial. You'll store the values in variables named thisMonth and thisYear as follows:

```
var thisMonth=calendarDay.getMonth();
var thisYear=calendarDay.getFullYear();
```

Finally, the function will write the HTML code for the first table row of the monthly calendar. The monthly calendar will have seven columns, so the row containing the calendar title has to span seven columns. Recall that the heading row will also have the ID calendar_head. The HTML code for the heading row has the form

```
<tr>
   <th id='calendar_head' colspan='7'>
      Month Year
   </th>
</tr>
```

where *Month* is the month name and *Year* is the four-digit year value. The year value is simply the value of the thisYear variable. The thisMonth variable tells you the month value and ranges from 0 (for January) to 11 (for December). The month values match the index numbers from the monthName array. For example, the first item in the monthName array is January, which has an index value of 0. To retrieve the name of the month, you can use the following expression:

```
monthName[thisMonth]
```

So, the code to write the first row of the calendar table is:

```
document.write("<tr>");
document.write("<th id='calendar_head' colspan='7'>");
document.write(monthName[thisMonth]+" "+thisYear);
document.write("</th>");
document.write("</tr>");
```

You will complete the writeCalTitle() function by adding the commands to create the thisMonth and thisYear variables and to write the HTML code for the first table row.

To complete the writeCalTitle() function in the calendar.js file:

▶ **1.** Insert the following commands into the writeCalTitle() function, as shown in Figure 3-8:

```
var thisMonth=calendarDay.getMonth();
var thisYear=calendarDay.getFullYear();

document.write("<tr>");
document.write("<th id='calendar_head' colspan='7'>");
document.write(monthName[thisMonth]+" "+thisYear);
document.write("</th>");
document.write("</tr>");
```

Completed writeCalTitle() function | Figure 3-8

```
function writeCalTitle(calendarDay) {
    var monthName = new Array("January", "February", "March",
    "April", "May", "June", "July", "August", "September",
    "October", "November", "December");

    var thisMonth=calendarDay.getMonth();
    var thisYear=calendarDay.getFullYear();

    document.write("<tr>");
    document.write("<th id='calendar_head' colspan='7'>");
    document.write(monthName[thisMonth]+" "+thisYear);
    document.write("</th>");
    document.write("</tr>");
}
```

code to write the
header row of the
calendar table

2. Save your changes to the file.

Creating and Populating Arrays | Reference Window

- To create an array, run the command
  ```
  var array = new Array(length);
  ```
  where *array* is the name of the array and *length* is the number of items in the array. The optional *length* parameter limits the array to a specific size to save space.
- To set a value of an item within an array, use the command
  ```
  array[i] = value;
  ```
  where *i* is the index of the array item and *value* is the value assigned to the item.
- To create and populate an array, use the command
  ```
  var array = new Array(values);
  ```
  where *values* is a comma-separated list of values.
- To create an array literal, use the following command:
  ```
  var array = [values];
  ```

Next, you must specify a date for the calendar to display. For now, you will add a date object named calDate to the calendar() function that stores the date March 18, 2011. You will then call the writeCalTitle() function using this date as the value for the calendarDay parameter.

To revise the calendar() function:

1. Insert the following statement at the beginning of the calendar() function to create the calDate variable:

```
var calDate = new Date("March 18, 2011");
```

2. Insert the following command to call the writeCalTitle() function, as shown in Figure 3-9:

```
writeCalTitle(calDate);
```

| Figure 3-9 | Code to call the writeCalTitle() function |

```
function calendar() {
    var calDate = new Date("March 18, 2011");      ←——  test date for the
                                                         calendar table
    document.write("<table id='calendar_table'>");
    writeCalTitle(calDate);
    document.write("</table>");
}

function writeCalTitle(calendarDay) {
    var monthName = new Array("January", "February", "March",
    "April", "May", "June", "July", "August", "September",
    "October", "November", "December");

    var thisMonth=calendarDay.getMonth();
    var thisYear=calendarDay.getFullYear();

    document.write("<tr>");
    document.write("<th id='calendar_head' colspan='7'>");
    document.write(monthName[thisMonth]+" "+thisYear);
    document.write("</th>");
    document.write("</tr>");
}
```

3. Save your changes to the file.

4. Reopen or refresh **ccc.htm** in your Web browser. The calendar table appears in the upper-right corner of the page, displaying only the title March 2011. See Figure 3-10.

| Figure 3-10 | Calendar title displayed |

calendar displays only the title row → March 2011

Trouble? If the table does not appear on the Web page, your JavaScript code may contain a mistake. Check your code against the code shown in the figures. Common sources of error include forgetting to close all quoted text strings, failing to match the use of upper- and lowercase letters in function names and variable names, and misspelling function names and variable names.

Working with Array Length

To increase the size of an array, you can simply add more items to it. Unlike in other programming languages, JavaScript arrays do not need to stay at a fixed size, even if you defined a value for the *length* parameter when the array was declared. In addition, you do not have to define a value for every item in an array. The following commands create an array of 100 items even though only the first and last items actually have defined values. The other array items have null values and are not stored in memory:

```
var x = new Array();
x[0] = "start";
x[99] = "stop";
```

Arrays such as the x array with several missing or null items are called **sparse arrays**. To determine the size of an array, you can use the length property, which has the syntax

```
array.length
```

where *array* is the name of the array and *length* is one more than the highest index in the array. The value of the length property is always equal to one more than the highest index number in the array (because index numbers start with the value 0 rather than 1). For the sparse array defined above, the length is 100, even though only two items in the array have defined values.

Changing the value of the length property changes the size of an array. Increasing the array length adds more items to an array, but the items have null values until they are defined. Decreasing the array length truncates an array, removing any defined items whose indexes are not included in the new length. For example, running the command

```
monthName.length = 3;
```

on the monthName array reduces the monthName array to the following three items: January, February, and March.

Specifying Array Length | Reference Window

- To determine the size of an array, use the property
    `array.length`
  where *array* is the name of the array and *length* is one more than the highest index in the array.
- To add more items to an array, run the command
    `array[i] = value;`
  where *i* is an index value higher than the highest index currently in the array.
- To remove items from an array, run the command
    `array.length = value;`
  where *value* is an integer that is smaller than the highest index currently in the array.

Reversing an Array

Arrays are associated with a collection of methods that allow you to change their contents, order, and size. You can also use these methods to combine different arrays into a single array and to convert arrays into text strings. Though you will not need to use these methods with the calendar() function, you'll examine them for future projects. Each method is applied using the syntax

```
array.method()
```

where *array* is the name of an array and *method* is the name of the method. Some array methods have parameter values that control how they are applied to an array. You will examine a few of these array methods.

By default, array items are placed in an array either in the order in which they are defined, or explicitly by index number. JavaScript supports two methods for changing the order of these items: reverse() and sort(). The reverse() method, as the name suggests, reverses the order of items in the array, making the last items first and vice-versa. In the following set of commands, the reverse() method is used to change the order of the values in the weekDay array:

```
var weekDay = new Array("Sun", "Mon", "Tue", "Wed", "Thu", "Fri", "Sat");
weekDay.reverse();
```

After running the reverse() method, the weekDay array contains the items in the following order: Sat, Fri, Thu, Wed, Tue, Mon, and finally, Sun. So, the expression weekDay[5] returns the text string Sun.

Sorting an Array

The sort() method arranges array items in alphabetical order. This can cause problems if you apply the sort() method to data values that are not usually treated in alphabetical order. For example, applying the command

```
weekDay.sort();
```

to the weekDay array causes the array to store the weekday abbreviations in the order Fri, Mon, Sat, Sun, Thu, Tue, Wed. Also, if you apply the sort() method to numeric values, the method treats the values as text strings and sorts them in order by their first digits, rather than by their true numerical values. This sorting, which is analogous to arranging words in alphabetical order, can lead to unexpected results. For example, the following commands create and sort an array named x:

```
var x = new Array(3, 45, 1234, 24);
x.sort();
```

The sorted x array will store items in the order 1234, 24, 3, 45, because this is the order of those numbers when sorted by their first digits. To correctly sort nontextual data, you must create a **compare function** that compares the values of two adjacent items in the array at a time. The general form of the compare function is

```
function fname(a, b) {
    compare the values of a and b
    return a negative, positive, or 0 value based on the comparison
}
```

where *fname* is the name of the compare function and *a* and *b* are two parameters used by the function. The a and b parameter values are compared to determine which is greater. The function then returns a negative, positive, or 0 value based on that comparison. For example, the following compare function compares the numeric difference between the *a* and *b* parameters:

```
function numSort(a, b) {
    return a-b;
}
```

The value returned by the function is used to sort the item in the array, comparing items from the array taken two at a time. If the returned value is 0, the order of the two items remains unchanged. If the value is positive, the first of the two items is assigned a higher index than the second. If the value is negative, the second of the two items is assigned a higher index than the first. To apply a compare function to the sort() method, you use the expression

```
array.sort(function)
```

where *function* is the name of the compare function. To use the numSort() compare function in sorting the x array in numeric order, you run the following command:

```
x.sort(numSort)
```

Because of how the numSort() function works, the values of the resulting x array are now sorted in ascending numeric order rather than alphabetic, yielding the array entries: 3, 24, 45, and 1234. To sort the array in decreasing numeric order, you need a different compare function. The following function can be used to sort numeric values in decreasing numeric order:

```
function numSortDesc(a, b) {
    return b-a;
}
```

In this function, the comparison process returns the value (b–a) rather than (a–b).

Tip

You can also sort an array in descending order by sorting it and then applying the reverse() method to the sorted array.

Shuffling an Array | InSight

In some code, you may want to rearrange an array in random order. For example, you may be writing a JavaScript code to simulate a randomly shuffled deck of cards. You can shuffle an array using the same sort() method you use to place the array in a defined order. The trick is to create a compare function that randomly returns a positive, negative, or 0 value. The following compare function is a simple approach to this problem:

```
function randOrder(){
   return 0.5 - Math.random();
}
```

To randomly sort an array, you apply this function to the sort() method. For example, if you create the array

```
var poker = new Array(52);
poker[0] = "2H";
poker[1] = "3H";
...
```

containing poker cards, you can shuffle the array contents using the following command:

```
poker.sort(randOrder)
```

After running this command, the contents of the poker array will be placed in random order. This is a useful technique if you are writing an online poker program using JavaScript.

Extracting and Inserting Array Items

In some scripts, you want to extract a section of an array, known as a **subarray**. For example, you might want to extract only the names of the summer months—June, July, and August—from the monthName array. To create a subarray, you can use the slice() method, which extracts a part of an array. The original contents of the array are unaffected, but the extracted items can be stored in another array. The syntax of the slice() method is

```
array.slice(start, stop)
```

where *start* is the index of the array item at which the slicing starts and *stop* is the index before which the slicing ends. The *stop* value is optional. If no *stop* value is provided, the array is sliced to the end of the array. For example, if you want to slice the monthName array, extracting only the summer months, you use the following command:

```
summerMonths = monthName.slice(5, 8);
```

The summerMonths array will contain the values June, July, and August. Remember that arrays start with the index value 0, so the sixth month of the year (June) has an index value of 5 and the ninth month of the year (September) has an index value of 8. Related to the slice() method is the splice() method, which is a general purpose method for extracting and inserting array items. The syntax of the splice() method is

```
array.splice(start, size)
```

where *start* is the index of the array item at which to start extracting items from the array and *size* is the number of items to extract. If no *size* value is specified, items are removed up through the end of the array. For example, if you want to extract the summer months from the monthName array using the splice() method, you run the following command:

```
summerMonths = monthName.splice(5, 3);
```

One of the important differences between the slice() and splice() methods is that the splice() method extracts the selected items and also removes them from the original array. Applying the splice() method to the monthName array above creates a subarray of the summer months and removes those three months from the monthName array. This is not true of the slice() method, which leaves the contents of the monthName array unaffected.

You can also use the splice() method to insert new items into an array. To insert new array items, you use the expression

```
array.splice(start, size, values)
```

where *values* is a comma-separated list of new values to replace the old values in the array. If you want to replace the first three month names with their first letters, for example, you apply the following splice() method to the monthName array:

```
monthName(0, 3, "J", "F", "M");
```

The values in the monthName array would now be J, F, M, April, May, and so on.

In some cases, you want to work only with items at the beginning or end of an array. The most efficient methods to insert or remove those items are the push(), pop(), unshift(), and shift() methods. The push() method appends new items to the end of an array and has the syntax

```
array.push(values)
```

where *values* is a comma-separated list of values to be appended to the end of the array. To remove the last item from an array, use the pop() method, which has the following syntax:

```
array.pop()
```

The push() and pop() methods are often used with programs that employ the "last-in-first-out" principle, in which the last item added to an array is the first item that is removed. The following set of commands demonstrates how to use the push() and pop() methods to expand and contract an array of values. The most recent additions to the array are popped out first because recent additions are added to the end of an array by default.

```
var x = new Array("a", "b", "c");
x.push("d", "e"); // x now contains ["a", "b", "c", "d", "e"]
x.pop();           // x now contains ["a", "b", "c", "d"]
x.pop();           // x now contains ["a", "b", "c"]
```

The unshift() method is similar to the push() method except that it inserts new items at the start of the array. Likewise, the shift() method is akin to the pop() method except that it removes the first array item, not the last.

Using Array Methods | Reference Window

- To reverse the order of items in an array, use the method
  ```
  array.reverse()
  ```
  where *array* is the name of the array.
- To sort an array in alphabetical order, use the following method:
  ```
  array.sort();
  ```
- To sort an array in any order, use
  ```
  array.sort(function)
  ```
  where *function* is the name of a compare function that returns a positive, negative, or 0 value.
- To extract items from an array without affecting the array contents, use
  ```
  array.slice(start, stop)
  ```
  where *start* is the index of the array item at which the slicing starts and *stop* is the index before which the slicing ends. If no *stop* value is provided, the array is sliced to the end of the array.
- To add or remove items in an array, use
  ```
  array.splice(start, size)
  ```
  where *start* is the index of the array item at which the splicing starts and *size* is the number of items to splice from or into the array. If no *splice* value is specified, the array is spliced to its end.
- To add new items to the end of an array, use
  ```
  array.push(values)
  ```
  where *values* is a comma-separated list of values.
- To remove the last item from an array, use the following method:
  ```
  array.pop()
  ```

Figure 3-11 summarizes several of the other methods that can be applied to arrays. Arrays are a powerful and useful feature of the JavaScript language. The methods associated with arrays can be used to simplify and expand the capabilities of Web page scripts. Be aware, however, that older browsers might not support all of these array methods. Use these array methods with caution when you want to support a wide range of browser versions.

| Figure 3-11 | Array methods |

Array Method	Description
array.concat(*array1, array2, ...*)	Joins *array* to two or more arrays, creating a single array containing the items from all the arrays.
array.join(*separator*)	Joins all items in *array* into a single text string. The array items are separated using the text in the separator parameter. If no separator is specified, a comma is used.
array.pop()	Removes the last item from *array*.
array.push(*values*)	Appends *array* with new items, where *values* is a comma-separated list of item values.
array.reverse()	Reverses the order of items in *array*.
array.shift()	Removes the first item from *array*.
array.slice(*start, stop*)	Extracts the *array* items starting with the start index up to the *stop* index, returning a new subarray.
array.splice(*start, size, values*)	Extracts *size* items from *array* starting with the item with the index *start*. To insert new items into the array, specify the array item in a comma-separated *values* list.
array.sort(*function*)	Sorts *array* where *function* is the name of a function that returns a positive, negative, or 0. If no *function* is specified, *array* is sorted in alphabetical order.
array.toString()	Converts the contents of *array* to a text string with the array values in a comma-separated list.
array.unshift(*values*)	Inserts new items at the start of *array*, where *values* is a comma-separated list of new values.

You set up the first parts of the online calendar in this session. In the next session, you'll complete the monthly calendar by working with loops and conditional statements.

Review | Session 3.1 Quick Check

1. What is an array?
2. What command creates an array named dayNames?
3. What command both creates and populates the dayNames array with the abbreviations of the seven days of the week (starting with Sun and going through Sat)?
4. What expression returns the third value from the array dayNames?
5. What command creates the dayNames array as an array literal?
6. What command sorts the dayNames array in alphabetical order?
7. What command extracts the middle five values from the dayNames array?
8. What command converts the contents of the dayNames array to a text string with each value separated by a comma?

Session 3.2

Working with Program Loops

Now that you're familiar with the properties and methods of arrays, you'll continue working on the calendar() function. So far, you've created only the header row, which displays the calendar's month and year. The next row of the table will contain the three-letter abbreviations of the seven days of the week, starting with Sun and continuing through

Sat. Each abbreviation needs to be placed within an element with the class name calendar_weekdays. Using a document.write() command for each line of HTML, you could generate this table row with the following code:

```
document.write("<tr>");
document.write("<th class='calendar_weekdays'>Sun</th>");
document.write("<th class='calendar_weekdays'>Mon</th>");
document.write("<th class='calendar_weekdays'>Tue</th>");
document.write("<th class='calendar_weekdays'>Wed</th>");
document.write("<th class='calendar_weekdays'>Thu</th>");
document.write("<th class='calendar_weekdays'>Fri</th>");
document.write("<th class='calendar_weekdays'>Sat</th>");
document.write("</tr>");
```

This code contains a lot of repetitive text. Imagine if you had to repeat essentially the same string of code dozens, hundreds, or even thousands of times. The code would become unmanageably long. Programmers deal with this kind of situation by creating program loops. A **program loop** is a set of commands that is executed repeatedly until a stopping condition has been met. Two commonly used program loops in JavaScript are the For and While loops.

Exploring the For Loop

In a For loop, a variable known as a **counter variable** is used to track the number of times a set of commands is run. Each time through the loop, the value of the counter variable is increased or decreased by a set amount. When the counter variable reaches or exceeds a specified value, the For loop stops. The general structure of a For loop is

```
for (start; continue; update) {
    commands
}
```

where *start* is an expression that sets the initial value of a counter variable, *continue* is a Boolean expression that must be true for the loop to continue, *update* is an expression that indicates how the value of the counter variable should change each time through the loop, and *commands* is the JavaScript commands that are run each time through the loop.

Suppose you want to set a counter variable to range in value from 0 to 3 in increments of 1. You could use the following expression to set the initial value of the variable:

```
var i = 0;
```

The name of the counter variable here is i, which is a common variable name often applied in program loops. The next expression in the For loop structure defines the stopping condition for the program loop. The following expression sets the loop to continue as long as the value of the counter variable is less than 4:

```
i < 4;
```

Finally, the following update expression uses the increment operator to indicate that the value of the counter variable increases by 1 each time through the program loop:

```
i++;
```

Putting all of these expressions together, you get the following For loop:

```
for (var i = 0; i < 4; i++) {
    commands
}
```

The collection of commands that is run each time through a loop is collectively known as a **command block**, a feature you've already worked with in functions. Command blocks are easily distinguished by their opening and closing curly braces { }. If a For loop contains only a single command, you don't need the command block and can leave out the curly braces.

The following is an example of a For loop that writes the value of the counter variable to a table cell on the Web page.

```
for (var i = 0; i < 4; i++) {
    document.write("<td>" + i + "</td>");
}
```

As shown in Figure 3-12, each time through the loop, the value displayed in the table cell is changed by 1.

Figure 3-12   **For loop being run**

```
<table border="2">
    <tr>
        <script type="text/javascript">
            for (var i=0; i < 4; i++) {
                document.write("<td>" + i + "</td>");
            }
        </script>
    </tr>
</table>
```

For loop

Parts of the For Loop	Expressions	Counter Values	Code Written to the Page
start	var i=0	0	<td>0</td>
continue	i < 4	1	<td>1</td>
		2	<td>2</td>
update	i++	3	<td>3</td>

Values during the For loop

```
0 1 2 3
```

resulting table

For loops can be nested inside one another. Figure 3-13 shows the code used to create a table with three rows and four columns. This example uses two counter variables, named rowNum and colNum. The rowNum variable loops through the values 1, 2, and 3. In addition, for each value of the rowNum variable, the colNum variable loops through the values 1, 2, 3, and 4. Each time the value of the colNum variable changes, a new cell is added to the table. Each time the value of the rowNum variable changes, a new row is added to the table.

Nested For loops ◄   Figure 3-13

```
<table border="2">
    <script type="text/javascript">
        for (var rowNum=1; rowNum < 4; rowNum++) {
            document.write("<tr>");
            for (var colNum=1; colNum < 5; colNum++) {
                document.write("<td>"+rowNum+" , "+colNum+"</td>");
            }
            document.write("</tr>");
        }
    </script>
</table>
```

nested For loops

rowNum Values	colNum Values	Code Written to the Page
1		<tr>
1	1	<td>1,1</td>
1	2	<td>1,2</td>
1	3	<td>1,3</td>
1	4	<td>1,4</td>
1		</tr>
2		<tr>
2	1	<td>2,1</td>
2	2	<td>2,2</td>
2	3	<td>2,3</td>
2	4	<td>2,4</td>
2		</tr>
...		
3	4	<td>3,4</td>
3		</tr>

resulting table

1,1	1,2	1,3	1,4
2,1	2,2	2,3	2,4
3,1	3,2	3,3	3,4

The update expression is not limited to increasing the counter by 1. You can use the other operators introduced in the previous tutorial to create a wide variety of increment patterns. Figure 3-14 shows a few of the many different ways of updating the value of the For loop's counter variable.

Counter values in the For loop ◄   Figure 3-14

For Loop	Counter Values
for (var i =1 ; i <= 5; i++)	i = 1, 2, 3, 4, 5
for (var i = 5; i > 0; i--)	i = 5, 4, 3, 2, 1
for (var i = 0; i <= 360; i+=60)	i = 0, 60, 120, 180, 240, 300, 360
for (var i =1 ; i <= 64; i*=2)	i = 1, 2, 4, 8, 16, 32, 64

Using For Loops and Arrays

For loops are often used to cycle through the different values contained within an array. The general structure of accessing each value from an array is

```
for (var i = 0; i < array.length; i++) {
   commands involving array[i]
}
```

where *array* is the array containing the values to be looped through and *i* is the counter variable used in the loop. The counter variable in this case represents the index number of an item from the array. The length property is used to determine the size of the array. The last item in the array has an index value of one less than the array's length (because array indices start with zero), so you only continue the loop when the array index is less than the length value.

With this information, you can create a function that employs arrays and a For loop to create a row displaying the names of the seven days of the week. First, you need to use the following code to create an array named dayName containing the three-letter abbreviations of each day:

```
var dayName = new Array("Sun", "Mon", "Tue", "Wed", "Thu", "Fri", "Sat");
```

Then, you'll loop through the values of the dayName array, displaying each value in a header cell with the class name calendar_weekdays, as follows:

```
document.write("<tr>");
for (var i = 0;i<dayName.length;i++) {
   document.write("<th class='calendar_weekdays'>"+dayName[i]+"</th>");
}
document.write("</tr>");
```

You'll add these commands to a new function named writeDayNames(), and then apply the function to your monthly calendar.

To create the writeDayNames() function in the calendar.js file:

▶ 1. If you took a break after the previous session, make sure the calendar.js file is open in your text editor and the ccc.htm file is open in your Web browser.

▶ 2. At the bottom of the **calendar.js** file, insert the following function:

```
function writeDayNames() {
   var dayName = new Array("Sun", "Mon", "Tue", "Wed", "Thu",
                           "Fri", "Sat");
   document.write("<tr>");
   for (var i = 0;i<dayName.length;i++) {
      document.write("<th class='calendar_weekdays'> "+dayName[i]+
         "</"</th>");
   }
   document.write("</tr>");
}
```

▶ 3. Scroll up to the calendar() function, and then insert **writeDayNames()** below the command that calls the writeCalTitle() function, as shown in Figure 3-15.

Code for the writeDayNames() function | Figure 3-15

```
function calendar() {
    var calDate = new Date("March 18, 2011");

    document.write("<table id='calendar_table'>");
    writeCalTitle(calDate);
    writeDayNames();
    document.write("</table>");
}
```

```
function writeDayNames() {
    var dayName = new Array("Sun", "Mon", "Tue", "Wed", "Thu",
                            "Fri", "Sat");
    document.write("<tr>");
    for (var i=0;i < dayName.length;i++) {
        document.write("<th class='calendar_weekdays'> "+dayName[i]+"</th>");
    }
    document.write("</tr>");
}
```

function to write the days of the week

4. Save your changes to the file.

5. Reopen or refresh **ccc.htm** in your Web browser. The monthly calendar displays a second row containing the abbreviations of the seven days of the week. See Figure 3-16.

Calendar with day names | Figure 3-16

March 2011
Sun Mon Tue Wed Thu Fri Sat

day abbreviations appear in the second row

Exploring the While Loop

The For loop is only one way of creating a program loop in JavaScript. Before continuing with the calendar() function, you'll investigate a few others. Similar to the For loop is the While loop, in which a command block is run as long as a specific condition is met. Unlike the For loop, the condition in a While loop does not depend on the value of a counter variable. The general syntax of the While loop is

```
while (continue) {
    commands
}
```

where *continue* is any Boolean expression. The Boolean expression is tested before attempting to run the command block. If the expression returns a value of true, the command block is run; otherwise, the command block is skipped and the program loop ends. Every While loop includes a condition under which the loop stops. Without this stop condition, While loops would run without end, causing users' browsers to crash.

The following code shows how to create the table shown in Figure 3-12 as a While loop. In this loop, the command block is run as long as the value of the i variable remains less than 4. Each time through the command block, the loop writes the value of the i variable into a table cell and then increases the value of the i variable by 1.

```
var i = 0;
while (i < 4) {
   document.write("<td>"+i+"</td>");
   i++;
}
```

Like For loops, While loops can be nested within one another. The following code demonstrates how to create the 3 × 4 table shown in Figure 3-13 using nested While loops. Again, the initial values of the counter variables are set before the While loops are run and are updated within the command blocks.

```
var rowNum = 1;
while (rowNum < 4) {
   document.write("<tr>");
   var colNum = 1;
   while (colNum < 5) {
      document.write("<td>"+rowNum+","+colNum+"</td>");
      colNum++;
   }
   document.write("</tr>");
   rowNum++;
}
```

Tip

Use a For loop when your loop contains a counter variable. Use a While loop for a more general stopping condition.

Because For loops and While loops share many of the same characteristics, which one you choose for a given application is often a matter of personal preference. In general, For loops are used whenever you have a counter variable and While loops are used for conditions that don't easily lend themselves to using counters.

Exploring the Do/While Loop

In the For and While loops, the test to determine whether to continue the loop is made before the command block is run. JavaScript also supports a program loop called Do/While that tests the condition to continue the loop right after the latest command block is run. The structure of the Do/While loop is as follows:

```
do {
   commands
   }
while (continue);
```

For example, the following code is used to create the table shown in Figure 3-12 as a Do/While loop:

```
var i = 0;
do {
   document.write("<td>"+i+"</td>");
   i++;
   }
while (i < 4);
```

The Do/While loop is usually used when the program loop should run at least once before testing for the stopping condition.

Creating Program Loops | Reference Window

- To create a For loop, use the syntax
  ```
  for (start; continue; update) {
     commands
  }
  ```
  where *start* is an expression that sets the initial value of a counter variable, *continue* is a Boolean expression that must be true for the loop to continue, *update* is an expression that indicates how the value of the counter variable should change each time through the loop, and *commands* are the JavaScript commands that are run each time through the loop.
- To create a While loop, use the following syntax:
  ```
  while (continue) {
     commands
  }
  ```
- To create a Do/While loop, use the following syntax:
  ```
  do {
     commands
  }
  while (continue);
  ```
- To loop through the contents of an array, enter the For loop
  ```
  for (var i = 0; i < array.length; i++) {
     commands involving array[i]
  }
  ```
  where *i* is a counter variable representing the indices of the array items and *array* is the array to be looped through.

Evaluating Arrays with Customized Functions | InSight

Program loops and conditional statements are very helpful in creating customized functions to extract information from arrays. Let's look at some examples. The following function returns the maximum value from an array:

```
function maxValue(arr) {
   var maxVal = arr[0];
   for (var i = 0; i < arr.length; i++) {
      if (arr[i] > maxVal) maxVal=arr[i];
   }
   return maxVal;
}
```

The maxValue() function loops through all the entries in the arr array, testing whether each item's value is greater than the maxVal variable. The function then returns the value of max-Val, which represents the maximum value found among all of the values in the array. The statement

```
var maximumValue = maxValue(dataArray);
```

returns the maximum value from the dataArray array, storing the answer in the maximum-Value variable. To find the minimum value, revise the function with an If condition that tests whether values of arr[i] are less than the current minimum.

To return a random value from an array, the following function uses the Math.random() method along with the Math.floor() method and the length property to generate a random integer between 0 and the value of the array length:

```
function randValue(arr) {
   return arr[Math.floor(Math.random()*arr.length)];
}
```

The following statment shows how to call the function, returning a randomly chosen entry from the dataArray array:

```
var randomValue = randValue(dataArray);
```

Working with Conditional Statements

Your next task in the calendar application is to enter the table rows for the days of the month. Each table cell within those rows will contain a number for the corresponding day of the month. After reaching the last day of the month, you'll stop writing table cells and rows. This process requires some kind of program loop. The number of times this loop runs depends on the number of days in the current month. Because months have differing numbers of days, you need to create the following array containing the length of each month to use in conjunction with the loop:

```
var dayCount = new Array(31,28,31,30,31,30,31,31,30,31,30,31);
```

You'll create this array within a function named daysInMonth(). Like the writeCalTitle() function you created earlier, the daysInMonth() function has a single parameter, calendarDay, representing a date object. The function creates two variables, thisYear and thisMonth, containing the four-digit year value and month value. The thisMonth variable is used to supply the index from which the number of days in the month is returned by the function.

To start creating the daysInMonth() function:

▶ **1.** Return to the **calendar.js** file in your text editor.

▶ **2.** At the bottom of the file, insert the following code, as shown in Figure 3-17:

```
function daysInMonth(calendarDay) {
    var thisYear = calendarDay.getFullYear();
    var thisMonth = calendarDay.getMonth();
    var dayCount = new Array(31,28,31,30,31,30,31,31,30,31,30,31);
    return dayCount[thisMonth]; // return the number of days in the
    month
}
```

Figure 3-17   **Initial daysInMonth() function**

```
function writeDayNames() {
    var dayName = new Array("Sun", "Mon", "Tue", "Wed", "Thu",
                            "Fri", "Sat");
    document.write("<tr>");
    for (var i=0;i < dayName.length;i++) {
        document.write("<th class='calendar_weekdays'> "+dayName[i]+"</th>");
    }
    document.write("</tr>");
}

function daysInMonth(calendarDay) {
    var thisYear = calendarDay.getFullYear();
    var thisMonth = calendarDay.getMonth();
    var dayCount = new Array(31,28,31,30,31,30,31,31,30,31,30,31);
    return dayCount[thisMonth]; // return the number of days in the month
}
```

function to return the number of days in a given month

The dayCount array you've created has one problem: February sometimes has 29 days, not 28 days. Figure 3-18 shows the general process to determine whether a particular year is a leap year. Any year that is not divisible by 4 is not a leap year. So, a year such as 2015 is not a leap year because it is not divisible by 4. Beyond that, the situation is a little more complex. In most cases, a year that is divisible by 4 is a leap year. The only exceptions are years that occur at the turn of the century that are divisible by 100. These years are not leap years unless they are also divisible by 400. Thus, years such as 1800, 1900, and 2100 are not leap years even though they are divisible by 4. Years such as 2000 and 2400 are leap years because they are divisible by 400.

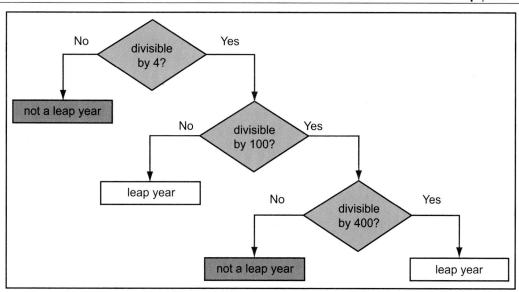

For the daysInMonth() function to determine whether February has 28 or 29 days, it must examine the year value and then set the value for the number of days in February to either 28 or 29 based on the year value. You can do this through a conditional statement. A **conditional statement** is a statement that runs a command or command block only when certain circumstances are met.

Exploring the If Statement

The most common conditional statement is the If statement. The syntax of the If statement is

```
if (condition) {
   commands
}
```

where *condition* is a Boolean expression that is either true or false, and *commands* is the command block that is run if *condition* is true. If only one command is run, you can eliminate the command block and enter the If statement as follows:

```
if (condition) command;
```

The *condition* expression uses the same comparison and logical operators you've used in the conditional operator from the previous tutorial. Unlike a comparison operator that changes the value of a variable based on a condition, a conditional statement determines whether to run a particular command or command block. For example, the following If statement sets the value of the dayCount array for February to 29 if the year value is 2012 (a leap year):

```
if (thisYear == 2012) {
   dayCount[1] = 29;
}
```

For the calendar application, you need to create a conditional expression that indicates whether the current year is a leap year. Start by looking at methods of determining whether the year is divisible by 4. One way is to use the % operator, which is also known as the modulus operator. The **modulus operator** returns the integer remainder after dividing one integer by another. For example, the expression

```
2015 % 4
```

returns the value 3 because 3 is the remainder after dividing 2015 by 4. To test whether a year value is divisible by 4, you use the conditional expression

```
thisYear % 4 == 0
```

where the thisYear variable contains the four-digit year value. The following is the complete If statement to change the value of the dayCount array for the month of February:

```
if (thisYear % 4 == 0) {
   dayCount[1] = 29;
}
```

Nesting If Statements

The above If statement works as a simple approximation, but it is not completely accurate because it doesn't take into account century years. You need to include a second test to account for the different leap year rule applicable during century years. The general structure of this nested If statement is:

```
if (thisYear % 4 == 0) {
   if statement for century years
}
```

The nested If statement needs to test for two conditions: (1) the year is not divisible by 100, and (2) the year is divisible by 400. The expressions for the two conditions are:

```
thisYear % 100 != 0
thisYear % 400 == 0
```

If either of those two conditions is true for a year evenly divisible by 4, then the year is a leap year. Note that you use the != operator to test for an inequality in the first expression. You then combine these two expressions into a single expression using the or operator (||). The combined expression is:

```
(thisYear % 100 != 0) || (thisYear % 400 == 0)
```

Finally, you place this conditional expression in a nested If statement. Following is the complete code:

```
if (thisYear % 4 == 0) {
   if ((thisYear % 100 !=0) || (thisYear % 400 == 0)) {
      dayCount[1] = 29;
   }
}
```

Under this set of nested If statements, the number of days in February is 29 only if the thisYear variable is divisible by 4 *and* only if it also is divisible by 400 or *not* divisible by 100. Take some time to compare this set of nested If statements with the chart shown in Figure 3-18 to confirm that it satisfies all possible conditions for leap years. Putting this nested If statement into the daysInMonth() function returns the number of days for any month in any given year.

By adding this nested If statement to the daysInMonth() function, you arrive at the final version of the function:

```
function daysInMonth(calendarDay) {
   var thisYear = calendarDay.getFullYear();
   var thisMonth = calendarDay.getMonth();
   var dayCount = new Array(31,28,31,30,31,30,31,31,30,31,30,31);
   if (thisYear % 4 == 0) {
      if ((thisYear % 100 !=0) || (thisYear % 400 == 0)) {
         dayCount[1] = 29; // this is a leap year
      }
   }
   return dayCount[thisMonth]; // return the number of days in the
                                 month
}
```

You'll complete the daysInMonth() function in the calendar.js file.

To create the final daysInMonth() function:

▶ **1.** In the **calendar.js** file, before the final return statement in the daysInMonth() function, insert the following nested If structure, as shown in Figure 3-19:

```
if (thisYear % 4 == 0) {
   if ((thisYear % 100 != 0) || (thisYear % 400 == 0)) {
      dayCount[1] = 29; // this is a leap year
   }
}
```

Complete daysInMonth() function ◀ Figure 3-19

```
function daysInMonth(calendarDay) {
   var thisYear = calendarDay.getFullYear();
   var thisMonth = calendarDay.getMonth();
   var dayCount = new Array(31,28,31,30,31,30,31,31,30,31,30,31);

   if (thisYear % 4 == 0) {
      if ((thisYear % 100 != 0) || (thisYear % 400 == 0)) {
         dayCount[1] = 29; // this is a leap year
      }
   }

   return dayCount[thisMonth]; // return the number of days in the month
}
```

nested If statement to test for the presence of a leap year

▶ **2.** Save your changes to the file.

Exploring the If...Else Statement

The If statement runs a command or a command block only if the conditional expression returns the value true; it does nothing if a value of false is returned. On some occasions, you may want to choose between two alternate sets of commands. In those cases, you use an If...Else structure, in which one set of commands is run if the conditional expression is true and a different set of commands is run if the expression is false. The general structure of an If...Else statement is:

```
if (condition) {
   commands if condition is true
} else {
   commands if otherwise
}
```

If only a single expression is run in response to the If statement, you can use the following abbreviated form:

```
if (condition) command if condition is true
else command if otherwise;
```

The following example shows an If...Else statement that runs one of two possible document.write() commands:

```
if (day == "Friday") document.write("Thank goodness it's Friday")
else document.write("Today is " + day);
```

In this statement, the text "Thank goodness it's Friday" is written to the document if the value of the day variable is Friday. Otherwise, the text string "Today is *day*" is written to the document, where *day* is the value of the day variable.

Like the If statement, If...Else statements can be nested. With a nested If...Else statement, you place the inner statements within command blocks. The following nested If...Else statement chooses between three possible text strings to write to a document:

```
if (day == "Friday") document.write("Thank goodness it's Friday")
else {
    if (day == "Monday") document.write("Blue Monday")
    else document.write("Today is " + day);
}
```

Some programmers advocate always using curly braces even if the command block contains only a single command. This practice visually separates one Else clause from another. Also, when reading through nested statements, it can be helpful to remember that an Else clause usually pairs with the nearest preceding If statement.

Using Multiple Else...If Statements

For more complex scripts, you may need to choose from several alternatives. In these cases, you can specify multiple Else clauses, each with its own If statement. This is not a new type of conditional structure, but rather a way of taking advantage of the syntax rules inherent in the If...Else statement. The general structure for choosing from several alternatives is

```
if (condition 1) {
    first command block
} else if (condition 2) {
    second command block
} else if (condition 3) {
    third command block
} else {
    default command block
}
```

where *condition 1, condition 2, condition 3*, and so on are the different conditions to be tested. This construction should always include a final Else clause that is run by default if none of the previous conditional expressions return the value true. When a browser runs this series of statements, it stops examining the remaining Else clauses when it encounters the first true Else clause (because there no longer is an Else condition to investigate). The following example is a structure that employs multiple Else...If conditions:

```
if (day == "Friday") {
   document.write("Thank goodness it's Friday");
}  else if (day == "Monday") {
   document.write("Blue Monday");
}  else if (day == "Saturday") {
   document.write("Sleep in today");
}  else {
   document.write("Today is "+day);
}
```

Tip

To simplify code, keep your nesting of multiple If statements to three or less (if possible). For more conditions, use the case/switch structure.

Working with Conditional Statements | Reference Window

- To test a single condition, use the construction
    ```
    if (condition) {
       commands
    }
    ```
  where *condition* is a Boolean expression and *commands* is a command block run if the conditional expression is true.
- To test between two conditions, use the following construction:
    ```
    if (condition) {
       commands if condition is true
    }  else {
       commands if otherwise
    }
    ```
- To test multiple conditions, use the construction
    ```
    if (condition 1) {
       first command block
    }  else if (condition 2) {
       second command block
    }  else if (condition 3) {
       third command block
    }  else {
       default command block
    }
    ```
  where *condition 1*, *condition 2*, *condition 3*, and so on are the different conditions to be tested. If no conditional expressions return the value true, the default command block is run.

Exploring the Switch Statement

When you need to choose from several possible conditions, a series of Else...If statements might be too cumbersome to work with. A simpler structure is the Switch statement (also known as the Case statement), in which different commands are run based upon various possible values of a variable. The syntax of a Switch statement is

```
switch (expression) {
   case label1: commands1
   break;
   case label2: commands2
   break;
   case label3: commands3
   break;
...
   default: default commands
}
```

where *expression* is an expression that returns a value other than a Boolean value; *label1*, *label2, label3*, and so on are possible values of that expression; *commands1, commands2, commands3*, and so on are the commands to run for each matching label; and *default commands* are the commands to be run if no label matches the value returned by *expression*. The previous Else...If statement could be rewritten as the following Switch statement:

```
switch (day) {
    case "Friday": document.write("Thank goodness it's Friday"); break;
    case "Monday": document.write("Blue Monday"); break;
    case "Saturday": document.write("Sleep in today"); break;
    default: document.write("Today is "+day);
}
```

Tip

Use the Switch statement for conditional statements that involve variables with several possible values.

As the browser moves through the different case values, it executes any command or command block in which the label matches the expression's value. The break statement is optional and is used to halt the execution of the Switch statement once a match has been found. For programs in which you want to allow for multiple matching cases, you can omit the break statements and JavaScript will continue moving through the Switch statements, running all matching commands.

Reference Window | **Creating a Switch Statement**

- To create a Switch statement to test for different values of an expression, use the structure
  ```
  switch (expression) {
      case label1: commands1
      break;
      case label2: commands2
      break;
      case label3: commands3
      break;

      . . .

      default: default commands
  }
  ```
  where *expression* is an expression that returns a value other than a Boolean value; *label1, label2, label3*, and so on are possible values of that expression; *commands1, commands2, commands3*, and so on are the commands to run for each matching label; and *default commands* are the commands to be run if no label matches the value returned by *expression*.

At this point, you are familiar with all of the tools you will need for completing the calendar() function. In the next session, you'll enter the code to create a monthly calendar for any date you choose.

Review **| Session 3.2 Quick Check**

1. What is a program loop? Name three types of program loops supported by JavaScript.
2. What expressions would you place in a For statement to use a counter variable named i that starts with the value 0 and continues up to 100 in increments of 10?

3. What For statement creates a table row consisting of five table cells? Assume the table cells display the text "Column *i*" where *i* is the value of the counter variable and the value of the counter variable ranges from 1 to 5 in increments of 1.

4. What is a conditional statement? What is the most commonly used conditional statement?

5. What code writes the text "Internet Explorer Browser" to the document if the Boolean variable WebBrowser equals true?

6. The WebBrowser variable has been changed to a text string variable that can equal either "IE" or "Mozilla". Write an If...Else statement to display the text "Internet Explorer Browser" if WebBrowser equals "IE" and "Mozilla Browser" otherwise.

7. The WebBrowser variable can now equal "IE", "Opera", "Safari", or "Firefox". Write a series of Else...If statements that write the name of the browser to the document. If WebBrowser equals none of the four text strings listed above, write the text "Generic Browser" to the document.

8. Answer Question 7 using a Switch statement. Use a break statement to break off from processing the Switch statement once a match has been found.

Session 3.3

Creating the calendar() Function

You are ready to complete the calendar application. You've already written the code that writes the calendar title and the row of abbreviated day names. In this session, you'll complete the calendar by adding in table rows and cells displaying the days of the month. Figure 3-20 shows a preview of the calendar you'll create for a date of March 25, 2011.

Monthly calendar | **Figure 3-20**

To complete this table, the program code must do the following:

- Calculate the day of the week in which the month starts.
- Write blank table cells for the last days of the previous month at the start of a table row.
- Loop through all of the days of the current month, writing each date in a different table cell, starting a new table row on each Sunday.

You'll place all of these commands in a function named writeCalDays(). The function will have a single parameter named calendarDay containing a date object for the current date. You'll add this function to the calendar.js file.

To insert the writeCalDays() function:

▶ 1. If you took a break after the previous session, make sure the calendar.js file is open in your text editor and the ccc.htm file is open in your Web browser.

▶ 2. At the bottom of the **calendar.js** file, insert the following function, as shown in Figure 3-21:

```
function writeCalDays(calendarDay) {
    // determine the starting day of the week
    // write blank cells preceding the starting day
    // write cells for each day of the month
}
```

Figure 3-21	Code to begin the writeCalDays() function

```
function daysInMonth(calendarDay) {
    var thisYear = calendarDay.getFullYear();
    var thisMonth = calendarDay.getMonth();
    var dayCount = new Array(31,28,31,30,31,30,31,31,30,31,30,31);

    if (thisYear % 4 == 0) {
        if ((thisYear % 100 != 0) || (thisYear % 400 == 0)) {
            dayCount[1] = 29; // this is a leap year
        }
    }

    return dayCount[thisMonth]; // return the number of days in the month
}

function writeCalDays(calendarDay) {
    // determine the starting day of the week
    // write blank cells preceding the starting day
    // write cells for each day of the month
}
```

initial
writeCalDays()
function

▶ 3. Save your changes to the file.

Setting the First Day of the Month

To loop through all of the days of the month, you'll need to keep track of the day currently being written to the calendar table. You'll store this information in a variable named dayCount. The initial value of the dayCount variable will be set to 1 and will increase up to the total number of days in the month. You can determine the total days in the month by calling the daysInMonth() function you created in the previous session. The first two lines of the writeCalDays() function are:

```
var dayCount = 1;
var totalDays = daysInMonth(calendarDay);
```

Next, you reset the value of the calendarDay variable so that it is equal to the first day of the month. This is done using the setDate() method. The command is:

```
calendarDay.setDate(1);
```

Finally, the code must determine on which day of the week this date falls. The getDay() method returns this information, with values ranging from 0 (Sunday) to 6 (Saturday). You'll store this value in a variable named weekDay. The following command declares the weekDay variable:

```
var weekDay = calendarDay.getDay();
```

You'll add these commands to the writeCalDays() function.

To declare the initial variables in the writeCalDays() function:

▶ **1.** Below the first comment line in the writeCalDays() function, insert the following commands, as shown in Figure 3-22:

```
var dayCount = 1;
var totalDays = daysInMonth(calendarDay);
calendarDay.setDate(1);              // set the date to the first
  day of the month
var weekDay = calendarDay.getDay();  // the day of week of the
  first day
```

Code to set the first day of the month ◀ Figure 3-22

```
function writeCalDays(calendarDay) {
    // determine the starting day of the week
    var dayCount = 1;
    var totalDays = daysInMonth(calendarDay);
    calendarDay.setDate(1);              // set the date to the first day of the month
    var weekDay = calendarDay.getDay();  // the day of week of the first day

    // write blank cells preceding the starting day
    // write cells for each day of the month
}
```

▶ **2.** Save your changes to the file.

Placing the First Day of the Month

Prior to the first day of the month, the calendar table should show only empty table cells. The value of the weekDay variable indicates how many empty table cells you need to create. For example, if the value of the weekDay variable is 4 (Thursday), you know that there are four blank table cells—corresponding to Sunday, Monday, Tuesday, and Wednesday—that need to be written at the start of the first table row. The following loop creates the blank table cells:

```
document.write("<tr>");
for (var i = 0; i < weekDay; i++) {
   document.write("<td></td>");
}
```

If weekDay equals 0—indicating that the month starts on a Sunday—then no blank table cells will be written because the value of the counter variable i is never less than the value of the weekDay variable. You'll insert these commands into the writeCalDays() function.

To write the initial blank cells of the first table row:

▶ **1.** Below the second comment line, insert the following For loop, as shown in Figure 3-23:

```
document.write("<tr>");
for (var i = 0; i < weekDay; i++) {
   document.write("<td></td>");
}
```

Figure 3-23 ▷ **Code to write the preceding blank table cells**

```
function writeCalDays(calendarDay) {
    // determine the starting day of the week
    var dayCount = 1;
    var totalDays = daysInMonth(calendarDay);
    calendarDay.setDate(1);              // set the date to the first day of the month
    var weekDay = calendarDay.getDay();  // the day of week of the first day

    // write blank cells preceding the starting day
    document.write("<tr>");
    for (var i=0; i < weekDay; i++) {
        document.write("<td></td>");
    }

    // write cells for each day of the month
}
```

> loop to write empty table cells to the calendar table

> **2.** Save your changes to the file.

> **3.** Reopen or refresh **ccc.htm** in your Web browser and verify that no run-time errors have been introduced by incorrectly typing any of the code. The appearance of the page remains unchanged from Figure 3-16.

Writing the Calendar Days

Now that the code determines into which table cell the initial date is placed, the rest of the function will be devoted to inserting the remaining dates. This is done using a While loop. Each time through the loop, the function should write the table cells containing the calendar dates, and, if necessary, add new rows to the table. At the end of the command block, the dayCount variable should be increased, moving to the next day in the month. The general structure of the While loop is:

```
while (dayCount <= totalDays) {
   write the table rows and cells
   move to the next day
}
```

You'll add this While loop to the writeCalDays() function.

To insert the While loop to the writeCalDays() function:

> **1.** Below the last comment line in the writeCalDays() function, insert the following While loop, as shown in Figure 3-24:

```
while (dayCount <= totalDays) {
    // write the table rows and cells
    // move to the next day
}
```

While loop for adding the calendar days | Figure 3-24

```
function writeCalDays(calendarDay) {
    // determine the starting day of the week
    var dayCount = 1;
    var totalDays = daysInMonth(calendarDay);
    calendarDay.setDate(1);          // set the date to the first day of the month
    var weekDay = calendarDay.getDay();   // the day of week of the first day

    // write blank cells preceding the starting day
    document.write("<tr>");
    for (var i=0; i < weekDay; i++) {
        document.write("<td></td>");
    }

    // write cells for each day of the month
    while (dayCount <= totalDays) {
        // write the table rows and cells
        // move to the next day
    }
}
```

loop to write the cells containing day numbers

▶ **2.** Save your changes to the file.

Each new table row in the calendar table starts with a Sunday. The first command in the While loop's command block needs to determine whether the value of the weekDay variable corresponds to a Sunday. If so, the function will write the opening <tr> tag for the table row. The If statement appears as follows:

```
if (weekDay == 0) document.write("<tr>");
```

This expression uses the same weekDay variable you used previously to determine the day on which the month started. As you proceed through the While loop, the value of this variable is constantly updated to reflect the current calendar date being written. The next step is to write a table cell containing the date. Because every date belongs to the class calendar_dates (refer to Figure 3-4), the code is:

```
document.write("<td class='calendar_dates'>"+dayCount+"</td>");
```

Finally, because every table row ends with a Saturday, you also must test whether the day being written falls on a Saturday. If this is the case, you need to write a </tr> to end the table row. The command to do this is:

```
if (weekDay == 6) document.write("</tr>");
```

In the final part of the command block for the While loop, you update the values of the dayCount, calendarDay, and weekDay variables so that the next time through the loop they point to the next day in the calendar. The commands are similar to what you used to set the initial values of these variables before the While loop, except that you increase the dayCount variable by 1 using the ++ increment operator as follows:

```
dayCount++;
calendarDay.setDate(dayCount);
weekDay = calendarDay.getDay();
```

The complete code for the While loop is:

```
while (dayCount <= totalDays) {
    // write the table rows and cells
    if (weekDay == 0) document.write("<tr>");
    document.write("<td class='calendar_dates'>"+dayCount+"</td>");
    if (weekDay == 6) document.write("</tr>");
```

```
// move to the next day
dayCount++;
calendarDay.setDate(dayCount);
weekDay = calendarDay.getDay();
}
```

After the While loop is finished running, you'll write a closing </tr> tag to ensure that the table row is closed off if the last day of the month does not fall on a Saturday. You do not need to write blank table cells at the end of the month like you did at the beginning because browsers will simply ignore any missing table cells at the end of a table row.

To add commands to the While loop:

▶ **1.** Below the first comment line within the While loop, insert the following commands:

```
if (weekDay == 0) document.write("<tr>");
document.write("<td class='calendar_dates'>"+dayCount+"</td>");
if (weekDay == 6) document.write("</tr>");
```

▶ **2.** Below the second comment line within the While loop, insert the following commands:

```
dayCount++;
calendarDay.setDate(dayCount);
weekDay = calendarDay.getDay();
```

▶ **3.** Below the While loop, insert the following command:

```
document.write("</tr>");
```

Figure 3-25 shows the revised code for the writeCalDays() function.

Figure 3-25 **Commands added to the While loop**

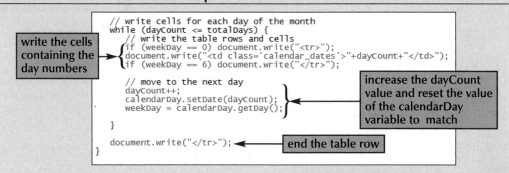

▶ **4.** Save your changes to the file.

Next, you have to run the writeCalDays() function from the calendar() function. You can then test the monthly calendar to verify that it correctly lays out the dates in the calendar.

To test the calendar() function:

▶ **1.** Scroll up to the calendar() function, and then insert the following command, as shown in Figure 3-26:

```
writeCalDays(calDate);
```

Code to call the writeCalDays() function ◀ **Figure 3-26**

```
function calendar() {
    var calDate = new Date("March 18, 2011");

    document.write("<table id='calendar_table'>");
    writeCalTitle(calDate);
    writeDayNames();
    writeCalDays(calDate);
    document.write("</table>");
}
```

▶ **2.** Save your changes to the file.

▶ **3.** Reload **ccc.htm** in your Web browser. The monthly calendar shows all of the dates laid out in different table cells and rows. See Figure 3-27.

Monthly calendar table ◀ **Figure 3-27**

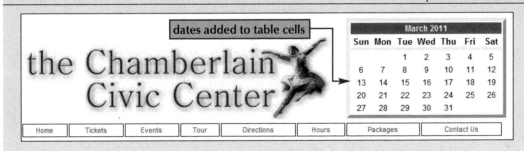

Highlighting the Current Date

Maria likes the calendar's appearance but mentions that the calendar should also highlight the current date. To indicate the current date, the corresponding table cell should have the ID calendar_today. As shown in Figure 3-4, a different style is applied to the table cell with this ID. As you loop through each day in the calendar, you need to insert an If statement that tests whether the day being written to the table represents the current date. If it does, you write the HTML code

```
<td class='calendar_dates' id='calendar_today'>day</td>
```

where *day* is the day number; otherwise, the script should write

```
<td class='calendar_dates' >day</td>
```

omitting the ID attribute. To do this test, you'll create a new variable named currentDate, setting it equal to the date value returned by applying the getDate() date object method to the calendarDay parameter. You need to create this variable before the While loop because the While loop alters the value of the calendarDay parameter as it moves through the calendar rows and cells.

To highlight the current date in the calendar:

▶ **1.** Return to the **calendar.js** file in your text editor, and then scroll down to the write-CalDays() function.

▶ **2.** Insert the following line of code as the first command in the function:

```
var currentDay = calendarDay.getDate();
```

▶ **3.** In the While loop, replace the command that writes the table cell for each day with the following If structure:

```
if (dayCount == currentDay) {
   // highlight the current day
   document.write("<td class='calendar_dates' id='calendar_
      today'>"+dayCount+"</td>");
} else {
   // display the day as usual
   document.write("<td class='calendar_dates'>"+dayCount+"</td>");
}
```

Figure 3-28 shows the final version of the writeCalDays() function.

Figure 3-28 | **Code to highlight the current day**

```
function writeCalDays(calendarDay) {
   var currentDay = calendarDay.getDate();

   // determine the starting day of the week
   var dayCount = 1;
   var totalDays = daysInMonth(calendarDay);
   calendarDay.setDate(1);                  // set the date to the first day of the month
   var weekDay = calendarDay.getDay();   // the day of week of the first day

   // write blank cells preceding the starting day
   document.write("<tr>");
   for (var i=0; i < weekDay; i++) {
      document.write("<td></td>");
   }

   // write cells for each day of the month
   while (dayCount <= totalDays) {
      // write the table rows and cells
      if (weekDay == 0) document.write("<tr>");

      if (dayCount == currentDay) {
         // highlight the current day
         document.write("<td class='calendar_dates' id='calendar_today'>"+dayCount+"</td>");
      } else {
         // display the day as usual
         document.write("<td class='calendar_dates'>"+dayCount+"</td>");
      }

      if (weekDay == 6) document.write("</tr>");

      // move to the next day
      dayCount++;
      calendarDay.setDate(dayCount);
      weekDay = calendarDay.getDay();
   }

   document.write("</tr>");
}
```

write the cell for the current day using the calendar_today ID

▶ **4.** Save your changes to the file.

▶ **5.** Reload **ccc.htm** in your Web browser. March 18 is highlighted in the calendar because this is the date specified in the calendar() function. See Figure 3-29.

Completed home page for the CCC | Figure 3-29

highlighted date specified in the calendar() function

Setting the Calendar Date

Maria is pleased with the calendar application, but wants it to display dates other than March 18, 2011. You can display specific dates by changing the value of the calDate variable in the calendar() function. Another option is to include the date value as a parameter value in the calendar() function, allowing the calendar() function to be easily used for any date. Maria asks you to make this change.

It would be ideal if the calendar() function worked like the JavaScript Date() method, creating a monthly calendar for a specified date with the command

```
calendar("March 18, 2011")
```

but producing the calendar for the current month if no date is specified, for example

```
calendar()
```

To test for the presence or absence of a parameter value, you insert an If condition that tests whether the parameter value is null. If the parameter value is null, the value of the calDate variable is set to the current date; otherwise, the calDate variable is set to the date specified in the calendarDay parameter. The revised calendar() function would appear as follows:

```
function calendar(calendarDay) {
   if (calendarDay == null) calDate = new Date()
   else calDate = new Date(calendarDay);
   ...
```

You'll edit the calendar() function to add this feature and then retest the calendar() function using both the current date and a date that you specify.

To complete and test the calendar() function:

▶ 1. Return to the **calendar.js** file in your text editor.

▶ 2. Go to the calendar() function and add the parameter **calendarDay** to the function line.

▶ 3. Replace the first line of the calendar() function with the following If statement:

```
if (calendarDay == null) calDate=new Date()
else calDate = new Date(calendarDay);
```

Figure 3-30 highlights the revised code of the calendar() function.

Figure 3-30 ▶ **Final calendar() function**

```
function calendar(calendarDay) {
    if (calendarDay == null) calDate=new Date()
    else calDate = new Date(calendarDay);

    document.write("<table id='calendar_table'>");
    writeCalTitle(calDate);
    writeDayNames();
    writeCalDays(calDate);
    document.write("</table>");
}
```

add the calendarDay parameter to the function

if no calendarDay is specified, use the current date

otherwise, use the date from the calendarDay parameter

▶ 4. Save your changes to the file.

▶ 5. Close the **calendar.js** file, and then refresh **ccc.htm** in your Web browser. Verify that the monthly calendar for the current date appears at the top of the Web page.

▶ 6. Open the **ccc.htm** file in your text editor, and then change the statement that runs the monthly calendar to the following, as shown in Figure 3-31:

```
calendar("March 25, 2011");
```

Figure 3-31 ▶ **Code to display the monthly calendar for March 25, 2011**

```
<body>
    <div id="head">
        <script type="text/javascript">
            calendar("March 25, 2011");
        </script>
        <img src="ccc.jpg" alt="Chamberlain Civic Center" />
    </div>
```

▶ 7. Close the **ccc.htm** file, saving your changes.

▶ 8. Reopen **ccc.htm** in your Web browser, and then verify that the monthly calendar for March 25, 2011 appears on the Web page.

▶ 9. Close your Web browser.

Maria is pleased with the final version of the calendar() function. Because of how the function and style sheets were designed, she can use this utility in many of the other pages on the CCC Web site with only a minimal amount of recoding in the Web documents.

Managing Program Loops and Conditional Statements

Although you are finished with the calendar() function, you should still become familiar with some features of program loops and conditional statements for future work with these JavaScript structures. You'll examine three features in more detail: the break, continue, and label commands.

Exploring the break Command

You briefly saw how to use the break command in creating a Switch statement, but the break command can be used anywhere within program code. The purpose of the break command is to terminate any program loop or conditional statement. When a browser runs a break command, it passes control to the statement immediately following it. The break statement is most often used to exit a program loop without waiting for the loop to end when the stopping condition is met. The syntax of the break command is:

```
break;
```

In some cases, you may need to create a loop that examines an array for the presence or absence of a particular value such as a customer ID number or name. The code for the loop might look as follows:

```
for (var i = 0; i< names.length; i++) {
   if (names[i] == "Valdez") {
      document.write("Valdez is in the list");
   }
}
```

Although this loop indicates whether the names array contains the text string Valdez, what would happen if the array had tens of thousands of entries? It would be time consuming to keep examining the array if Valdez was encountered within the first few array items. This is where the break command can be helpful to avoid wasting processing time. The following For loop breaks off when it encounters the Valdez text string, keeping the browser from needlessly examining the rest of the array:

```
for (var i = 0; i< names.length; i++) {
   if (names[i] == "Valdez") {
      document.write("Valdez is in the list");
      break;  // stop processing the For loop
   }
}
```

Exploring the continue Command

The continue command is similar to the break command except that instead of stopping the program loop altogether, the continue command stops processing the commands in the current iteration of the loop and jumps to the next iteration. For example, you could create a For loop to add the values from an array. The code for this For loop would be:

```
var total = 0;
for (var i = 0; i < data.length; i++) {
   total += data[i];
}
```

Each time through the loop, the value of the current entry in the data array is added to the total variable. When the For loop is finished, the total variable is equal to the sum of the values in the data array. However, what would happen if this were a sparse array containing several empty entries? In that case, when a browser encountered a missing or null value, that value would be added to the total variable; this would result in the value of the total variable also being equal to missing or null. One way to fix this problem would be to use the continue statement, jumping out of the loop if a missing or null value were encountered. The revised code would look as follows:

```
var total = 0;
for (var i = 0; i < data.length; i++) {
    if (data[i] == null) continue;  // continue with the next iteration
    total += data[i];
}
```

In this code, the value of the total variable is not updated if a null value is encountered but rather the loop jumps to the next step in the iteration.

Exploring Statement Labels

Labels are used to identify statements in JavaScript code so that you can reference those statements elsewhere in a program. The syntax of the label is

```
label: statement
```

where *label* is the text of the label and *statement* is the statement identified by the label. You've already seen labels with the Switch statement, but they can also be used with other program loops and conditional statements to provide more control over how statements are processed. Labels are often used with break and continue commands to direct a program to the statement that it should go to if it needs to break off or continue a program loop. The syntax to reference a label in such cases is simply:

```
break label;
```

or

```
continue label;
```

For example, the following nested For loop contains two labels: one for the outer loop and the other for the inner loop. The program breaks to the outer loop when the variable i is equal to the variable j:

```
//outer_loop:
for(i=1; i<4; i++) {
    document.write("<br />"+"outer "+i+": ");
    //inner_loop:
    for(j=1; j<4; j++) {
        document.write("inner "+j+" ");
        if(j==x)    //break outer_loop;
    }
}
```

As the code is run, it writes the following text to the document:

```
<br />outer 1: inner 1
<br />outer 2: inner 1
<br />outer 2: inner 2
<br />outer 3: inner 1
<br />outer 3: inner 2
<br />outer 3: inner 3
```

Some programmers discourage the use of break, continue, and label statements because they create confusing code as a script jumps in and out of loops. Most of the tasks you perform with these statements can also be performed by carefully setting up the conditions for program loops. For example, to create the same output from the above code without labels or the break command, you could define the counter variable used in the inner loop so that it is always less than or equal to the counter value of the outer loop. The following code demonstrates how this might be done:

```
for(i=1; i<4; i++) {
    document.write("<br />"+"outer "+i+": ");
    for(j=1; j<=i; j++) {
        document.write("inner "+j+" ");
    }
}
```

Tip

Avoid using break and continue statements to cut off loops unless necessary. Instead, set break conditions in the conditional expression of the loop.

Using Multidimensional Arrays | InSight

A matrix is a multidimensional array in which each item is referenced by two or more index values. The following is an example of a two-dimensional matrix consisting of three rows and four columns.

```
|  4   15    8    2  |
|  1    3   18    6  |
|  3    7   10    4  |
```

In this matrix, each value is referenced by a row index number and column index number. The value 18, for example, is located in the second row and third column and has the index numbers (2, 3).

Although matrices are commonly used in various programming languages, JavaScript does not support them. You can mimic the behavior of matrices in JavaScript by nesting one array within another. For example, the following code creates the array mArray as an array literal with another set of arrays nested within it. The values of the mArray variable match the values of the matrix shown above.

```
var mArray = [ [4, 15, 8, 2], [1, 3, 18, 6], [3, 7, 10, 4] ]
```

Values within the mArray variable can be accessed with the expression

```
mArray[x][y]
```

where x represents the index of the mArray variable and y represents an index of the nested array. For example, the expression

```
mArray[1][2]
```

returns the value 18. Proceeding in this fashion, you can treat a nested array like a matrix, allowing you to duplicate some of the features associated with matrices.

Review | **Session 3.3 Quick Check**

1. What command extracts the day of the week value from a date object variable named thisDate?
2. What day of the week value is returned for a date occurring on a Friday?
3. What command changes the thisDate variable to the fifth day of the month?
4. A function named showDate() has an optional parameter named thisDate. What expression tests whether the showDate() function was called with a value set for the thisDate parameter?
5. What command breaks out of a program loop?
6. What command forces the script to go to the next iteration of the current program loop?

Review | **Tutorial Summary**

In this tutorial, you learned how work to with arrays, program loops, and conditional statements to create an application that produces a monthly calendar for any given date. In the first session, you created and populated arrays, and you learned some JavaScript methods to sort and modify arrays. The second session dealt with program loops and conditional statements. You learned how to repeat sections of code multiple times in either For or While loops. Using the If statement, you saw how to run commands only when certain conditions are met. In the third session, you applied what you learned about program loops and conditional statements to complete the calendar application. The third session concluded with a discussion of the break, continue, and label commands.

Key Terms

array	conditional statement	program loop
array literal	counter variable	sparse array
command block	index	subarray
compare function	modulus operator	

Practice | Review Assignments

Practice | **Review Assignments**

Practice the skills you learned in the tutorial using the same case scenario.

Data Files needed for the Review Assignments: caltxt.htm, yeartxt.js, back.jpg, ccc.jpg, photo.jpg, styles.css, yearly.css

Maria finds the calendar() function you created an incredibly useful feature for the CCC Web site. However, she wants you to create a new calendar application that displays monthly calendars for the entire year on a single page. The calendar would still highlight the current date (or a date specified by the user) within the table. Figure 3-32 shows a preview of the yearly calendar that you'll create for Maria.

Figure 3-32

To combine all of the monthly calendars into one calendar, you'll use JavaScript to write a larger 3 x 4 table in which each table cell contains a monthly calendar. Maria has already created the Web page layout and a style sheet for both the Web page and the yearly calendar. You'll create the functions that generate the Web table containing the yearly calendar.

Complete the following:

1. Using your text editor, open **caltxt.htm** and **yeartxt.js** from the tutorial.03\review folder, enter *your name* and *the date* in the head section of each file, and then save the files as **calendar.htm** and **yearly.js**, respectively.

2. Go to the **yearly.js** file in your text editor. Many of the functions to create the individual monthly calendars have already been created. Insert a function named **writeMonthCell()** directly below the heading section. The purpose of this function is to place a monthly calendar within a table cell. The function has two parameters: **calendarDay** and **currentTime**. The calendarDay parameter contains a date object for the first day of the month to be displayed in the monthly calendar. The current-Time parameter contains the time value of the date that should be highlighted in the yearly table. Add the following commands to the writeMonthCell() function:

   a. Write the following HTML code to the document:
   ```
   <td class='yearly_months'>
   ```
   b. Call the writeMonth() function using calendarDay and currentTime as the parameter values. The purpose of the writeMonth() function is to write a monthly calendar into the table cell.
   c. Write a closing </td> tag to the document.

3. Above the writeMonthCell() function, insert a function named **yearly()**. The purpose of this function is to write the entire yearly calendar containing all of the separate monthly calendars as cells within the larger table. The function has a single parameter named **calDate**. Add the following commands to the function:

   a. If calDate equals null, set the calendarDay variable equal to a date object pointing to the current date and time; otherwise, calendarDay equals a date object using the text string specified in the calDate parameter.
   b. Create a variable named **currentTime** equal to the time value of the calendarDay variable. (*Hint*: Use the getTime() date object method to extract the time value from calendarDay.)
   c. Create a variable named **thisYear** equal to the four-digit year value from the calendarDay variable.
   d. Write the HTML code
   ```
   <table id='yearly_table'><tr>
     <th id='yearly_title' colspan='4'>
        this year
     </th>
   </tr>
   ```
   to the document, where *this year* is the value of the thisYear variable. This code represents the heading of the calendar table.
   e. Create a variable named **monthNum**, setting its initial value equal to –1. The purpose of the monthNum variable is to keep track of the month value of the current month being written in the calendar.
   f. Create a For loop that writes the rows of the yearly table. Create a counter variable named **i** that goes from 1 to 3 in increments of 1. The first command within the For loop should write the opening <tr> tag to the document.

g. Within the For loop you just created, add a nested For loop that writes the individual cells of the yearly table. The counter variable j of the nested For loop should go from 1 to 4 in increments of 1. In this nested For loop, add the following commands: (1) increase the value of monthNum by one; (2) use the setDate() date object method to change the day value of calendarDay to 1 (the first day of the month); (3) use the setMonth() date object method to change the month value of calendarDay to monthNum; and (4) call the writeMonthCell() function using calendarDay and currentTime as the parameter values.

h. After the nested For loop, but still within the outer loop, write a closing </tr> tag to the document.

i. After the nested loops, write a closing </table> tag to the document.

4. Locate the writeDayNames() function in the document. Within this function, change the values of the dayName array from three-letter abbreviations of the day names to the one-letter abbreviations **S, M, T, W, R, F**, and **S**.

5. Close the **yearly.js** file, saving your changes.

6. Go to the **calendar.htm** file in your text editor. In the head section of the document, add links to both the yearly.css style sheet and the yearly.js external script file.

7. Scroll down the document and locate the div element with the ID main. After the h1 heading in this element, insert an embedded script element. Within the script, run the command yearly() using the date **June 7, 2011** as the parameter value.

8. Save your changes to the file.

9. Open **calendar.htm** in your Web browser. Verify that the yearly calendar shown in Figure 3-32 is displayed on the Web page.

10. Return to the **calendar.htm** file in your text editor. Change the yearly() function so that no parameter value is specified (so that the function uses the current date). Save your changes and reload calendar.htm in your Web browser. Verify that the calendar for the current year is displayed and that the current date is the only one highlighted in the calendar.

11. Close any open files, and then submit your completed Web site to your instructor.

| Apply | **Case Problem 1** |

Use arrays, loops, and conditional statements to create a list of contributors.

Data Files needed for this Case Problem: clisttxt.htm, lhouse.css, list.js, logo.jpg

The Lighthouse   The Lighthouse is a charitable organization located in central Kentucky that matches donors with needy groups. The fundraising coordinator for The Lighthouse is Aaron Kitchen. On a Web page available only to Lighthouse staff, Aaron wants to display a list of information on recent donations, including the name and address of the donor, the amount donated, and the date of the donation. A list of donations from the last month has been downloaded from an external database and stored in a collection of arrays named firstName, lastName, street, city, state, zip, amount, and date. Aaron needs your help in displaying the data from those arrays in a Web table. He also wants a summary table that displays the total number of contributors and the total contribution amount. Figure 3-33 shows a preview of the Web page you'll create.

Figure 3-33

Complete the following:

1. Using your text editor, open **clisttxt.htm** from the tutorial.03\case1 folder, enter *your name* and *the date* in the head section, and then save the file as **clist.htm**.

2. The firstName, lastName, street, city, state, zip, amount, and date arrays have been created and populated for you in the list.js file. In the head section of the document, insert a script element that points to this file.

3. Below the script element you just created, insert another script element that contains the function **amountTotal()**. The purpose of the amountTotal() function is to return the sum of all of the values in the amount array. There are no parameters for this function. Add the following commands to the function:
   a. Declare a variable named **total**, setting its initial value to 0.
   b. Create a For loop that loops through all of the values in the amount array. At each iteration of the loop, add the current value of the array item to the value of the total variable.
   c. After the For loop is completed, return the value of the total variable.

4. Scroll down the document and locate the div element with the ID data_list. Within the div element, add a script element that contains the following commands:
   a. Write the following code to the document to create the header row for the table of contributions:
   ```
   <table border='1' rules='rows' cellspacing='0'>
      <tr>
         <th>Date</th><th>Amount</th><th>First Name</th>
         <th>Last Name</th><th>Address</th>
      </tr>
   ```
   b. Create a For loop in which the counter variable starts at 0 and, while the counter is less than the length of the amount array, increase the counter in increments of 1.
   c. Display every other row in the data list with a yellow background. To do this, within the For loop, insert an If condition that tests whether the counter variable is divisible evenly by 2 (*Hint*: Use the % modulus operator.) If the counter variable is divisible by 2, write the following HTML tag:
   ```
   <tr>
   ```
   Otherwise, write the following tag:
   ```
   <tr class='yellowrow'>
   ```

d. Next, within the For loop, write the HTML code

```
<td>date</td><td class='amt'>amount</td>
<td>firstName</td><td>lastName</td>
```

to the document, where *date*, *amount*, *firstName*, and *lastName* are the values of the date, amount, firstName, and lastName arrays for the index indicated by the current value of the For loop's counter variable.

e. Finally, within the For loop, write the HTML code

```
<td>street<br />
    city, state zip</td>
</tr>
```

to the document, where *street*, *city*, *state*, and *zip* are the values of the street, city, state, and zip arrays for the current index value.

5. Go to the div element with the ID totals. Insert a script element that writes the HTML code

```
<table border='1' cellspacing='1'>
    <tr>
        <th id='sumTitle' colspan='2'>
            Summary
        </th>
    </tr>
    <tr>
        <th>Contributors</th>
        <td>contributions</td>
    </tr>
    <tr>
        <th>Amount</th>
        <td>$total</td>
    </tr>
</table>
```

to the document, where *contributions* is the length of the amount array and *total* is the value returned by the amountTotal() function you created earlier.

6. Close the file, saving your changes.

7. Open **clist.htm** in your Web browser. Verify that a list of 35 contributions totaling $5175 is displayed in the table and that alternate rows of the contributor list have a yellow background.

8. Submit your completed Web site to your instructor.

| Apply | **Case Problem 2** |

Use arrays, loops, and conditional statements to create a horizontal bar chart.

Data Files needed for this Case Problem: electtxt.htm, votes.js, back.jpg, logo.jpg, results.css

VoterWeb   VoterWeb is an online source for election news and results from national, state, and local races. Faye Summerall is one of the managers of the Web site development team. Faye wants to add horizontal bar charts to the Web pages displaying election results. The length of each bar should correspond to the percentage of votes that the corresponding candidate receives in a given race. She has asked you to develop a JavaScript program that automatically writes the bar chart. Figure 3-34 shows a preview of the Web page for a series of Congressional races.

Figure 3-34

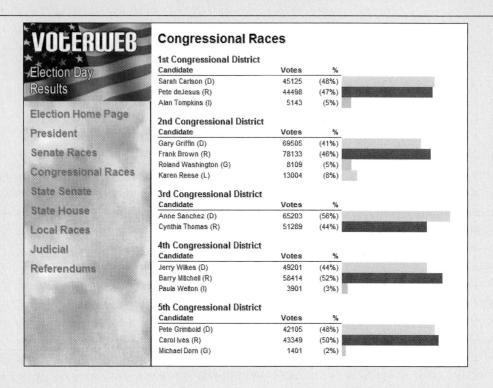

The horizontal bar charts will be created within table rows. The length of each bar will be determined by the number of blank table cells it contains. For example, to display a horizontal bar representing 45% of the vote, you'll write 45 blank table cells. The color of each bar is determined by the background color of its table cells. To apply the background color, you'll add class attributes to the blank table cells. A style in the results.css style sheet determines the background color for each class of table cells.

The data for each election has been stored in arrays in an external file named votes.js. The file includes data from five elections for different Congressional seats. The names of the races have been stored in an array named race. The name1 array contains the candidate names for the first race, the name2 array contains the candidate names for the second race, and so on through the name5 array. The party affiliations for each candidate in the first race have been stored in the party1 array, for the second race in the party2 array, and so forth. The votes1 through votes5 arrays store the votes for each candidate in each of the five races.

Complete the following:

1. Using your text editor, open **electtxt.htm** from the tutorial.03\case2 folder, enter *your name* and *the date* in the head section, and then save the file as **election.htm**.

2. Open the **votes.js** file from the tutorial.03\case2 folder in your text editor, study the contents to become familiar with the different arrays and their contents, and then close the file. Return to the **election.htm** file in your text editor, and then add a script element to the head section of the file that points to the votes.js file.

3. Insert another script element in the head section. In this script element, insert a function named **totalVotes()**. The purpose of this function is to calculate the sum of all the values within an array. The function has a single parameter, votes, representing one of the five vote arrays (vote1 through vote5). Add the following commands to the function:
   a. Declare a variable named **total**, setting its initial value to 0.
   b. Create a For loop that loops through each of the items in the votes array, adding that item's value to the total variable.
   c. After the For loop is completed, return the value of the total variable.

4. Insert another function named **calcPercent()**. The purpose of this function is to calculate a percentage, rounded to the nearest integer. The function has two parameters: **item** and **sum**. Have the function return the value of the item variable divided by sum, multiplied by 100, and then rounded to the nearest integer. (*Hint*: Use the Math.round() method to round the calculated percentage.)

5. Insert a function named **createBar()**. The purpose of this function is to write the blank table cells that make up each horizontal bar in the election results. The function has two parameters: **partyType** and **percent**. The partyType parameter stores the party affiliation of the candidate (D, R, I, G, or L). The percent parameter stores the percentage the candidate received in the election, rounded to the nearest integer. Add the following commands to the function:

   ⊕ **EXPLORE**

   a. Create a Switch statement that tests the value of the partyType parameter. If partyType equals D, store the following text string in a variable named **barText**:
   ```
   <td class='dem'> </td>
   ```
   If partyType equals R, barText should equal:
   ```
   <td class='rep'> </td>
   ```
   If partyType equals I, barText should equal:
   ```
   <td class='ind'> </td>
   ```
   If partyType equals G, barText should equal:
   ```
   <td class='green'> </td>
   ```
   Finally, if partyType equals L, barText should equal:
   ```
   <td class='lib'> </td>
   ```
   Make sure you add break commands after each case statement so that the browser does not attempt to test additional cases after it has found a match.
   b. Create a For loop in which the counter variable goes from 1 up through the value of the percent parameter in increments of 1. At each iteration, write the value of the barText variable to the Web document.

6. Insert a function named **showResults()**. The purpose of this function is to show the results of a particular race. The function has four parameters: **race**, **name**, **party**, and **votes**. The race parameter contains the name of the race. The name parameter contains the array of candidate names. The party parameter contains the array of party affiliations. Finally, the votes parameter contains the array of votes for each candidate in the race. Add the following commands to the function:
   a. Declare a variable named **totalV** equal to the value returned by the totalVotes() function using votes as the parameter value.

b. Write the HTML code

```
<h2>race</h2>
<table cellspacing='0'>
    <tr>
        <th>Candidate</th>
        <th class='num'>Votes</th>
        <th class='num'>%</th>
    </tr>
```

to the document, where *race* is the value of the race parameter.

c. Create a For loop in which the counter variable starts at 0 and, while the counter is less than the length of the name array, increase the counter in increments of 1. At each iteration of the For loop, run the commands outlined in the following five steps.

d. Write the HTML code

```
<tr>
    <td>name (party)</td>
    <td class='num'>votes</td>
```

where *name*, *party*, and *votes* are the entries in the name, party, and votes arrays for the index indicated by the counter variable.

e. Create a variable named **percent** equal to the value returned by the calcPercent() function. Use the current value from the votes array for the value of the item parameter, and totalV for the value of the sum parameter.

f. Write the HTML code

```
<td class='num'>(percent%)</td>
```

where *percent* is the value of the percent variable.

g. Call the **createBar()** function using the current value of the party array and percent as the parameter values.

h. Write a closing </tr> tag to the document.

i. After the For loop has completed, write a closing </table> tag to the document.

7. Scroll down the document. After the Congressional Races h1 heading, insert a script element containing the following commands:

a. Call the showResults() function using race[0], name1, party1, and votes1 as the parameter values.

b. Repeat the previous command for the remaining four races, using race[1] through race[4] as the parameter value for the race parameter, party2 through party5 for the party parameter, name2 through name5 for the name parameter, and votes2 through votes5 for the votes parameter.

8. Save your changes to the file, and then open **election.htm** in your Web browser. Verify that the correct percentages for each candidate appear and that a horizontal bar chart representing that percent value is displayed next to each candidate.

9. Submit your completed Web site to your instructor.

| Challenge | **Case Problem 3** |

Explore how to use JavaScript to create an auction log.

Data Files needed for this Case Problem: aucttxt.htm, logo.jpg, styles.css

Schmitt AuctionHaus David Schmitt owns Schmitt AuctionHaus, an auction center located in rural Indiana that specializes in estate and farm sales and auctions. David has been looking at ways to improve the bidding process for silent auctions in which applicants enter their name and bid for various items. David wants to create a Web page containing bidding information on various items at the auction center. The bidding could be displayed on a kiosk or terminal in the auction center, giving customers a quick look at the current status of different items for sale. David asked you to help design a Web form to track bids for a sales item. The form should include the name of the item, the current highest bid, a list of the bidding history for the item, and a form in which new bids can be entered. Because mistakes are sometimes made in entering a bid, David wants the ability to remove the last bid from the list. Figure 3-35 shows a preview of a sample page you'll create for David.

Figure 3-35

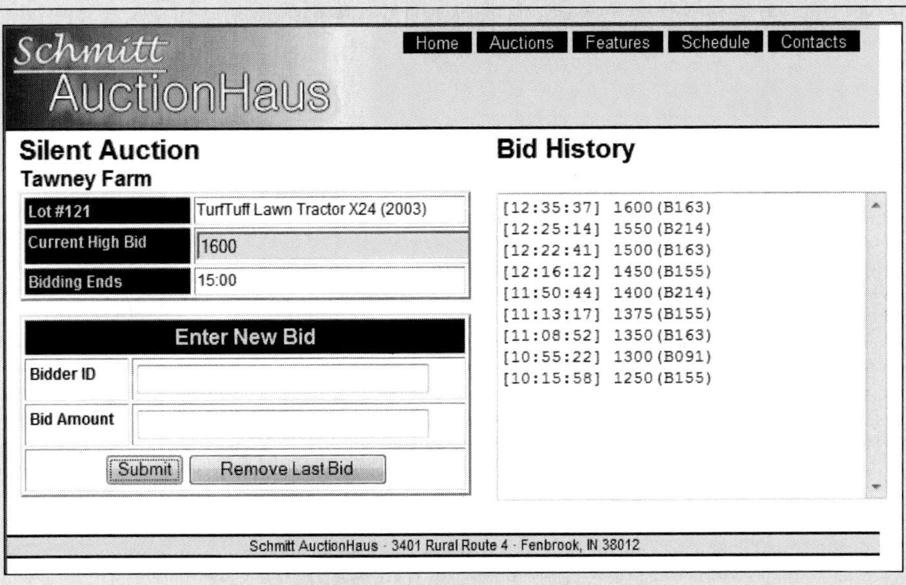

The layout and styles used on the page have already been created. You'll program the script that enters new bids and updates the box displaying the bid history and the highest current bid. You need to collect three pieces of information from each bid: the bid amount, the bidder ID, and the time when the bid was placed. You'll record this information in three arrays named bids, bidders, and bidTime, respectively.

Complete the following:

1. Using your text editor, open **aucttxt.htm** from the tutorial.03\case3 folder, enter ***your name*** and ***the date*** in the head section, and then save the file as **auction.htm**.

2. In the head section of the file, insert an embedded script element. Within the script element, create three new arrays named **bids**, **bidders**, and **bidTime**. Do not populate these arrays with any values.

3. Insert a function named **writeBid()**. The purpose of this function is to write the bidding history and the highest current bid to the Web page. There are no parameters for this function. Add the following commands to the function:

   a. Declare a variable named **historyText**, setting its initial value to an empty text string. This variable will be used to record the bidding history.

   EXPLORE

   b. Insert a For loop in which the counter variable goes from 0 through the length of the bids array in increments of 1. Each time through the loop, append the text string

   `bidTime bids (bidders) \n`

   to the historyText variable, where *bidTime*, *bids*, and *bidders* are the current items in the bidTime, bids, and bidders array based on the value of the counter variable. Note that \n is an escape character indicating a new line and causes the next entry to the historyText variable to be placed on a new line.

   EXPLORE

   c. After the For loop finishes, write the value of the historyText variable to the text area box with the name **bidList**. (*Hint*: To write text into a form field, run the command

   `document.form.field.value = text;`

   where *form* is the name of the form, *field* is the name of the form field, and *text* is the text string to be written to the field. In this example, the name of the form is bidForm and the name of the field is bidList.)

   d. Write the value of the first item in the bids array to the highBid field.

   e. Set the values of the bidId and bidAmount fields to empty text strings.

4. Create a function named **addBid()**. The purpose of this function is to add a bid to the start of the bids, bidders, and bidTime arrays. Add the following commands:

   EXPLORE

   a. Using the unshift() array method, insert the current value of the bidId field to the start of the bidders array.

   b. Use the unshift() array method to insert the current value of the bidAmount field at the start of the bids array.

   c. Declare a variable named **now** containing a date object for the current date and time.

   d. Extract the hours, minutes, and seconds values from the now variable, storing these values in variables named **hours**, **minutes**, and **seconds**.

   e. Use a conditional operator to insert leading zeroes in the minutes and seconds values if they are less than 10.

   f. Create a variable named **timeText** equal to the text

   `[hours:minutes:seconds]`

   where *hours*, *minutes*, and *seconds* are the values of the hours, minutes, and seconds variables.

   g. Using the unshift() array method, insert the value of the timeText variable at the start of the bidTime array.

   h. Call the writeBid() function. Remember that there are no parameters for this function.

5. Create a function named **removeBid()**. The purpose of this function is to remove the first entry from the bidders, bids, and bidTime arrays. Add the following commands:

   EXPLORE

   a. Using the shift() array method, remove the first entry from the bidders array.

   b. Repeat the previous step to remove the first entry from the bidders and bidTime arrays.

   c. Call the writeBid() function.

6. Scroll down the document to the Submit input button. Add an event handler attribute to run the addBid() function when the button is clicked.

7. Add an event handler attribute to the Remove Last Bid button to run the removeBid() function when the button is clicked.

8. Save your changes to the file.

9. Open **auction.htm** in your Web browser. Enter new bids in the Bidder ID and Bid Amount input fields. Click the Submit button to update the bidding history and Current High Bid field. Verify that the newest bid entries are placed at the top of the bidding history. Click the Remove Last Bid button and verify that the latest bid is removed from the list.

10. Submit your completed Web site to your instructor.

| Create | Case Problem 4 |

Use your knowledge of arrays, loops, and conditional statements to create a lunar calendar.

Data Files needed for this Case Problem: caltxt.css, lunartxt.htm, lunartxt.js, astro.css, moonfunc.js, phase0.jpg through phase15.jpg, skyweb.jpg

SkyWeb Dr. Andrew Weiss of the SkyWeb astronomy Web site is working on a Web page describing the phases and properties of the Moon. Dr. Weiss wants the page to contain a table describing the current conditions of the Moon, including the Moon phase, age (days since the last new moon), distance from the Earth, and position in the nighttime sky. He also wants the page to contain a lunar calendar for the current month. A lunar calendar is a calendar that displays the phases of the Moon on each day of the month. A preview of the page that Dr. Weiss wants you to create is shown in Figure 3-36.

Figure 3-36

Phases of the Moon

As the Moon orbits the Earth the portion we see illuminated changes from day to day. The start of each phase occurs with the **new Moon** in which the Moon does not appear illuminated from the Earth. The Moon takes 27.3 days to orbit Earth, but the lunar phase cycle (from new Moon to new Moon) is 29.5 days. This is because the Moon spends an extra 2.2 days "catching up" as the Earth travels about 45 million miles around the Sun during the time the Moon completes one orbit around Earth.

Today: August 8, 2011	
Moon's Age	9.026 days
Right Ascension	251.058°
Declination	-1.275°
In Constellation	Scorpio
Distance (Earth Radii)	57.368

Astronomers often refer to a **Lunar Calendar** to track the phases of the Moon. Generally astronomers do not want to observe the night sky during those times the Moon is highly illuminated because moonlight can obscure the light from fainter objects such as stars, planets, and nebulae. Below is a sample Lunar Calendar for the current month. Happy Moon-gazing!

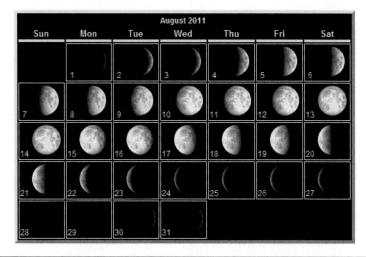

| Home Page | The Night Sky | The Moon | The Planets | The Messier Objects | Stars |

Dr. Weiss has designed the basic layout for the page. He wants you to write scripts to generate the lunar calendar as well as to insert data on the current lunar conditions in a summary table located at the top of the page. To help you in creating this page, Dr. Weiss has supplied a file named moonfunc.js containing the functions described in Figure 3-37.

Figure 3-37

Function	Description
calcMPhase(cDay)	Returns the phase number (from 0 to 15) of the Moon for the date stored in cDay
calcMAge(cDay)	Returns the age of the Moon for the date stored in cDay
calcMDist(cDay)	Returns the distance in Earth radii between the Earth and the Moon on the date stored in cDay
calcMDec(cDay)	Returns the declination (latitude on the nighttime sky) of the Moon on the date stored in cDay
calcMRA(cDay)	Returns the right ascension (longitude on the nighttime sky) of the Moon on the date stored in cDay
calcMZodiac(cDay)	Returns the name of the constellation or sign of the zodiac in which the Moon resides on the date stored in cDay

Each function has a date object parameter named cDay that you can use to return information on the Moon's status for that day. Dr. Weiss has also supplied a collection of 16 images named phase0.jpg through phase15.jpg. Each file contains an image of the Moon from a particular phase in its cycle. The file phase0.jpg contains an image of the new Moon, phase8.jpg contains an image of a full moon, and so on. Dr. Weiss points out that you can use the calcMPhase() function he's supplied to determine which of the 16 images to display for any given day.

The layout and appearance of the lunar calendar are up to you. You can also supplement the contents of this Web page with any other material you think is appropriate for the subject.

Complete the following:

1. Using your text editor, open the **caltxt.css**, **lunartxt.htm**, and **lunartxt.js** files from the tutorial.03\case4 folder. Enter *your name* and *the date* in each file. Save the files as **calendar.css**, **lunar.htm**, and **lunarcal.js**, respectively. The calendar.css file will be used to store the style sheet for the lunar calendar you'll create. The lunar.htm file contains the Web page that Dr. Weiss wants to display on the SkyWeb Web site. The lunarcal.js file will contain the functions required to create the lunar calendar.

2. Go to the **lunar.htm** file in your text editor. In the head section, add links to the **calendar.css** style sheet, the **moonfunc.js** JavaScript file, and the **lunarcal.js** JavaScript file.

3. Insert a script element in the head section containing the following:
   a. A variable named **calendarDay** containing a date object with the date set to **August 8, 2011**.
   b. A function named **writeDate()**. The purpose of this function is to display a date in the format Month Day, Year, where Month is the name of the month, Day is the day of the month, and Year is the four-digit year value. The function has a single parameter, **calendarDay**, which contains the date object to be formatted.

4. Scroll down to the summary table in the body of the document. Add the following to the table:
   a. In the table's title cell, display the text "Today: *today*", where *today* is the date from the calendarDay variable formatted using the writeDay() function.
   b. In the lunarimg cell, display the lunar image for the date in calendarDay. (*Hint*: Use the calcMPhase() function to return the phase number of the image.)

c. In the cell next to the Moon's Age label, display the text *"age days"*, where *age* is the age of the Moon on calendarDay.

d. In the cell next to the Right Ascension label, display the text *"ra°"*, where *ra* is the right ascension of the Moon on calendarDay.

e. In the cell next to the Declination label, display the text *"dec"*, where *dec* is the declination of the Moon on calendarDay.

f. In the cell next to the In Constellation label, display the text *"zodiac"*, where *zodiac* is the constellation that the Moon resides in on calendarDay.

g. In the cell next to the Distance label, display the text *"distance"*, where *distance* is the distance from the Earth to the Moon in Earth radii on calendarDay.

5. Scroll down to the lunar_cal div element. Within this element, insert a script that calls the function lunar_calendar() for the date in calendarDay.

6. Save your changes to the lunar.htm file.

7. Go to the **lunarcal.js** file in your text editor. Create a function named **lunar_calendar()** that displays a lunar calendar. The function should have a single parameter named **calendarDay** that contains the date you want to use for the calendar. You can use the calendar() function created in the tutorial as a model for your function and any supporting functions required to complete the calendar. The calendar does not have to highlight the current date.

8. Go to the **calendar.css** file in your text editor and create the styles required for your lunar calendar. You can use the calendar.css file from the tutorial as a model, or you can create a layout you choose.

9. After completing your work in the lunarcal.js and calendar.css files, open **lunar.htm** in your Web browser. Verify that the lunar calendar and the Moon data follow the information shown in Figure 3-37.

10. Submit your completed Web site to your instructor.

Review | Quick Check Answers

Session 3.1

1. An array is a collection of data values organized under a single name with each value referenced by an index number.

2. `var dayNames = new Array();`

3. `var dayNames = new Array("Sun", "Mon", "Tue", "Wed", "Thu", "Fri", "Sat");`

4. `dayNames[2]`

5. `var dayNames = ["Sun", "Mon", "Tue", "Wed", "Thu", "Fri", "Sat"];`

6. `dayNames.sort();`

7. `dayNames.slice(1,6);`

8. `dayNames.toString();`

Session 3.2

1. A program loop is a set of commands that is executed repeatedly until a stopping condition has been met. Three program loops supported by JavaScript are the For, While, and Do/While loops.

2. `for (var i = 0; i<=100; i+=10)`

3.
```
document.write("<tr>");
    for (var i=1; i<=5; i++) {
        document.write("<td>Column "+i+"</td>");
    }
document.write("</tr>");
```

4. A conditional statement is a statement that runs a command block only when certain conditions are met. The most commonly used conditional statement is the If statement.

5.
```
if (WebBrowser) document.write("Internet Explorer Browser");
```
or
```
if (WebBrowser == true) document.write("Internet Explorer Browser");
```

6.
```
if (WebBrowser == "IE") document.write("Internet Explorer Browser")
else document.write("Mozilla Browser");
```

7.
```
if (WebBrowser == "IE") document.write("Internet Explorer Browser")
else if (WebBrowser == "Opera") document.write("Opera Browser")
else if (WebBrowser == "Safari") document.write("Safari Browser")
else if (WebBrowser == "Firefox") document.write("Firefox Browser")
else document.write("Generic Browser");
```

8.
```
switch (WebBrowser) {
    case "IE": document.write("Internet Explorer Browser"); break;
    case "Opera": document.write("Opera Browser"); break;
    case "Safari": document.write("Safari Browser"); break;
    case "Firefox": document.write("Firefox Browser"); break;
    default: document.write("Generic Browser");
}
```

Session 3.3

1. `thisDate.getDay();`

2. 5

3. `thisDate.setDate(5);`

4. `if (thisDate != null) ...`

5. `break;`

6. `continue;`

Ending Data Files

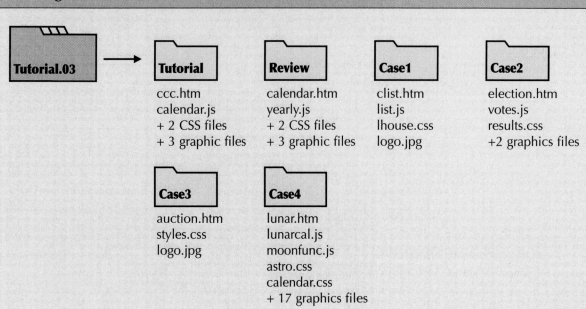

Tutorial.03 →

Tutorial
ccc.htm
calendar.js
+ 2 CSS files
+ 3 graphic files

Review
calendar.htm
yearly.js
+ 2 CSS files
+ 3 graphic files

Case1
clist.htm
list.js
lhouse.css
logo.jpg

Case2
election.htm
votes.js
results.css
+2 graphics files

Case3
auction.htm
styles.css
logo.jpg

Case4
lunar.htm
lunarcal.js
moonfunc.js
astro.css
calendar.css
+ 17 graphics files

Working with Objects and Styles

Creating a Pull-Down Menu

Case | The 221B Blog

Kyle Harris is a fan of mystery stories. His favorites are the Sherlock Holmes stories by Sir Arthur Conan Doyle. Kyle decided to create a Web site for other fans of the fictional detective called The 221B Blog, named after the street number of Holmes' Baker Street address.

On his Web site, Kyle has added a discussion forum, links to other mystery Web sites, and a place for members to post artwork, essays, and fan fiction. Kyle has also created links to the online text versions of all of the 56 short stories and four novels in the Sherlock Holmes canon. Kyle is concerned that so many links on the site's home page will be difficult for users to manage. He's seen sites in which lists of links are stored in pop-up or pull-down menus, remaining out of sight until needed by the user. Kyle wants to add a similar feature to his Web site and has asked you to help him write the code.

Starting Data Files

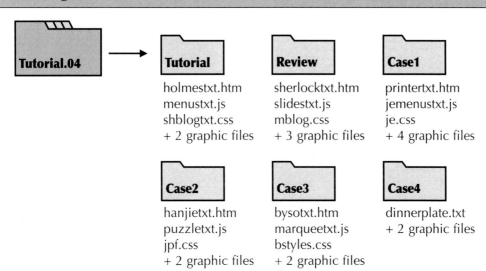

Tutorial.04 →

Tutorial
holmestxt.htm
menustxt.js
shblogtxt.css
+ 2 graphic files

Review
sherlocktxt.htm
slidestxt.js
mblog.css
+ 3 graphic files

Case1
printertxt.htm
jemenustxt.js
je.css
+ 4 graphic files

Case2
hanjietxt.htm
puzzletxt.js
jpf.css
+ 2 graphic files

Case3
bysotxt.htm
marqueetxt.js
bstyles.css
+ 2 graphic files

Case4
dinnerplate.txt
+ 2 graphic files

Session 4.1

Introducing Pull-Down Menus

Kyle asks you to help him update the home page of his 221B Blog Web site. The home page will have links to online versions of every story in the Sherlock Holmes canon. The links have been placed in separate div elements organized into five collections: *The Adventures of Sherlock Holmes*, *The Memoirs of Sherlock Holmes*, *The Return of Sherlock Holmes*, *The Case Book of Sherlock Holmes*, and *His Last Bow*. You'll open the home page to see the content of these collections and study how Kyle has organized and designed the home page.

To view the 221B Blog home page:

▶ **1.** Use your text editor to open the **holmestxt.htm** and the **shblogtxt.css** files from the tutorial.04\tutorial folder, enter *your name* and *the date* in the comment section of each file, and then save the files as **holmes.htm** and **shblog.css**, respectively.

▶ **2.** Explore the content of both files in your text editor, making note of the structure, IDs, and class names used for the different sections of the holmes.htm file.

▶ **3.** Open **holmes.htm** in your Web browser. Figure 4-1 shows the initial appearance of the Web page.

Figure 4-1 ▶ **The initial 221B Blog page**

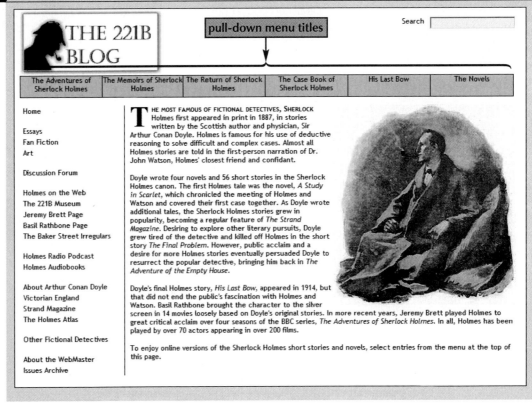

Kyle has placed the five collection titles in their own div element and given them IDs of menu1 through menu6. Each collection title has the class name menu. Kyle has also created div elements containing a list of stories and novels for each collection. The lists have been placed in separate div elements with the class name menuList and IDs ranging from menu1List to menu6List. Currently those lists are hidden, but you can reveal them by modifying the display property of the menuList class in the shblog style sheet.

To display the lists of stories and novels:

▶ **1.** Return to the **shblog.css** file in your text editor.

▶ **2.** Scroll down the style sheet and change the display property of the menuList class from none to **block**. See Figure 4-2.

Display property for the menuList class modified	Figure 4-2

displays the menuList elements as blocks

```
.menuList          {position: absolute; top: 146px; width: 140px; z-index: 2;
                    background-color: ivory; border: 1px solid black; display: block}

.menuList li       {margin: 5px}
.menuList a        {display: block; width: 132px}
.menuList a:hover  {background-color: rgb(151, 151, 151); color: white}
```

▶ **3.** Save your changes to the style sheet, and then refresh **holmes.htm** in your Web browser. The six pull-down menus are displayed in the browser window. See Figure 4-3.

Menu lists displayed on the 221B Blog home page	Figure 4-3

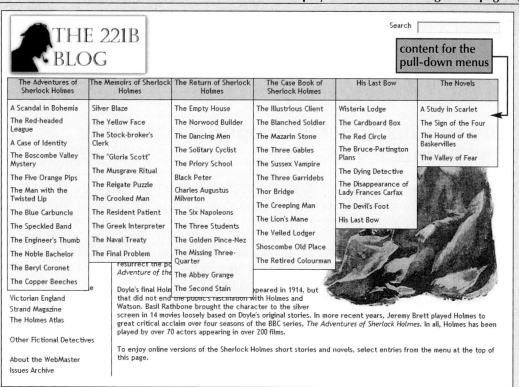

> **4.** Return to the **shblog.css** file in your text editor, change the display property of the menuList class from block back to **none**, and then save and close the file.

Each entry in the six lists will act as a hypertext link to a new page that contains the complete text of the selected story or novel. Kyle wants these titles and lists to act as pull-down menus. In a **pull-down menu**, a menu title is always visible to the user, identifying the entries in the menu. When a user clicks the title or in some cases moves the pointer over the title, the rest of the menu is displayed, often accompanied by the effect of a menu being "pulled down" from the title. See Figure 4-4. To display a different pull-down menu, users click or move the pointer over another menu title. To hide a pull-down menu, users click the menu title again or they can click or move the pointer to a spot on the main browser page.

Figure 4-4   **Pull-down menu being created**

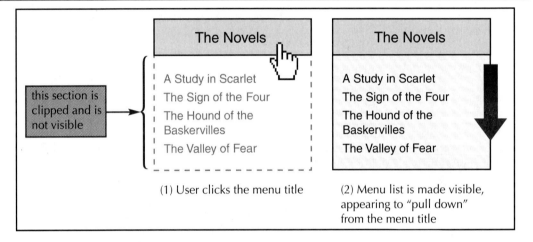

(1) User clicks the menu title

(2) Menu list is made visible, appearing to "pull down" from the menu title

To save space on the home page and to avoid obscuring the contents of the rest of the page, Kyle wants you to write a program that duplicates the pull-down menu effect for the six menu lists. You'll use JavaScript to control the action of hiding and displaying each menu list.

Introducing Objects, Properties, Methods, and Events

So far, you've used JavaScript mainly to write text strings of HTML code to the Web document. Starting with this tutorial, you'll learn how to use JavaScript to modify the contents of the document and the Web browser itself. JavaScript is an **object-based language**, which means that it is based on manipulating objects through the use of properties, methods, and events. JavaScript supports three kinds of objects. **Built-in objects** are objects intrinsic to the JavaScript language, such as the Math, array, and Date objects you've used in the previous few tutorials. **Document objects** are objects that reference elements and features of the Web document or Web browser. You'll study these kinds of objects in this tutorial. **Customized objects** are objects created by the user. You won't use customized objects with Kyle's Web page, but you'll examine how to create them later in the tutorial.

Every object has **properties** that describe its appearance, purpose, or behavior. Every object also has **methods**, which are actions that the object performs. Finally, objects can be associated with **events**, which are actions undertaken by the user or the browser that impact the object in some way.

JavaScript objects share some characteristics with common, everyday objects. An oven, for example, has certain properties, such as model name, age, size, and temperature. An oven also has associated methods, such as heating and cooking. Some of those methods change the properties of the oven, such as the oven's internal temperature or its state of cleanliness. Finally, an event that impacts an oven is when the user turns the oven on or off.

Similarly, JavaScript objects have their own set of objects, properties, methods, and events. The Web browser itself is an object, and the page you're viewing within the browser is also an object. If the page contains a form, the form is an object as are any elements within the form. A paragraph is also an object, and the text within that paragraph can be considered its own object. Each object has properties. The browser object has a property that indicates its type, such as Firefox or Internet Explorer, and another property that indicates its version number. A form object has a name or id property that distinguishes it from other forms. An object that has been placed on a page has properties for its page coordinates. Most objects also have methods. Documents can be opened or closed. The page background color can be set. The font of a paragraph can be changed in color or resized. And, of course, the user or the browser interacts with these objects by initiating events with a keyboard or mouse.

You've already been working with objects, properties, methods, and events throughout the last three tutorials. You've seen the effect of adding an onload attribute to the <body> tag to run a function in response to the event of loading the document. You've also used the onclick attribute to run code in response to the click of the mouse. The command you've used most often, the document.write() command, uses the write() method to write HTML text to the document object. In this tutorial, you'll learn about other objects and their properties, methods, and events. You'll start by examining the JavaScript objects that describe the contents of the Web browser and Web document.

Exploring the Document Object Model

All of the objects within documents and browsers need to be organized in a systematic way. This organized structure of objects is called the **document object model (DOM)**. The goal is to make every object related to the document or to the Web browser accessible to a scripting language such as JavaScript. Several document object models have been used with JavaScript. To better understand how JavaScript relates to the document object model, let's review the history of how these models developed.

Development of a Common DOM

The first document object model for the Web was introduced in Netscape Navigator 2.0. This is often referred to as the **basic model**, or in some cases, the **DOM Level 0**. The basic model did not include all objects, but it did support some common objects such as the browser window, the Web document, and the browser itself. Under the basic model, a programmer could reference these objects in the scripting language; but in most cases, the programmer could not modify their properties once the page was loaded by the browser. Only form elements could be modified after the page was loaded; the rest of the page was static and could not be changed. Internet Explorer 3.0 was the first version of Internet Explorer to support the basic model.

Netscape versions 3 and 4 further expanded the scope of the document object model by adding image rollovers and the ability to initiate programs in response to mouse and keyboard actions by the user. Internet Explorer 4.0 introduced the **IE4 DOM**, the chief feature being that all Web page elements were now part of the document object model. CSS attributes also became part of the IE4 DOM, allowing users to manipulate CSS styles with JavaScript commands. Unfortunately, the approach adopted by Internet Explorer was incompatible with the Netscape 4 approach.

The browser wars had reached a stage at which two fundamentally incompatible document object models were in use, and programmers who wanted to create dynamic Web pages had to work hard to reconcile the differences between the two models. At this point, the World Wide Web Consortium (W3C) stepped in—much like it did with HTML—to develop specifications for a common document object model.

The first specification, **DOM Level 1**, released in October 1998, provided support for all elements contained within HTML and XML documents. An update to this specification was released in September 2000 and fixed some errors from the earlier release.

The second specification, **DOM Level 2**, was released in November 2000. This specification enhanced the document object model by providing an event model that specified how events are captured as they progress through the objects in a Web browser. DOM Level 2 also extended the style sheet model to work with CSS style sheets and provided a range model to allow programmers to manipulate sections of text within a document. The DOM Level 2 specifications were placed within six different modules, allowing browser developers to support those sections of the DOM that were important to them.

The most recent specification is **DOM Level 3**, which was released in April 2004. DOM Level 3 provides a framework for working with document loading and saving, as well as for working with XML, namespaces, DTDs, and document validation. This tutorial refers to all of the DOM levels released and supported by the W3C as the **W3C DOM** unless highlighting specific aspects unique to a particular level.

Figure 4-5 summarizes the different document object models that have been introduced and supported by the browser market throughout the years.

| Figure 4-5 | Document object models |

DOM	Description
DOM Level 0 (Basic Model)	The basic DOM that supported few page and browser objects and allowed dynamic content only for form elements
DOM Level 0 + Images	The basic DOM with added support for image rollovers
Netscape 4 (layers)	The basic DOM with support for the Netscape 4 layer element and the ability to capture events within the browser
Internet Explorer 4	An expanded DOM allowing dynamic content for most page elements
Internet Explorer 5	The IE 4 DOM with additional refinements and enhancements
W3C DOM Level 1	The first DOM specification by the W3C, which supported all page and browser elements and handled all events occurring within the browser
W3C DOM Level 2	The second DOM specification, allowing for the capture of events, manipulation of CSS styles, working with element text, and document subsets
W3C DOM Level 3	The third DOM specification, providing a framework for working with document loading and saving, as well as working with DTDs and document validation

Be aware that if you're writing code that will be read by older browsers, you may be limited to supporting earlier DOM versions. At the time of this writing, current browsers support almost all of the specifications for DOM Level 1, most if not all of DOM Level 2, and partially DOM Level 3. Internet Explorer also supports the specifications for the IE4 DOM, but has some gaps in its support for DOM Levels 2 and 3. Most browsers, other than Opera, do not support the IE4 DOM at all. The scope of the tasks in these tutorials is mostly limited to the treatment of objects through DOM Level 2, unless otherwise noted. Features specific to the IE4 DOM are examined as circumstances warrant.

The Document Tree

Each document object model organizes objects into a hierarchy known as a **document tree**. Figure 4-6 shows part of this hierarchy for DOM Level 2. The topmost object in the hierarchy is the window object, which represents the browser window. Within the browser window are objects for the Web page document, each frame, the history of Web pages visited, and even the browser itself. Those objects can themselves contain yet another level of objects. For example, the document object contains objects for Web forms, images, applets, inline frames, and links. As document object models encompass more objects, the tree structure itself became more elaborate, including more of the objects within the window, browser, and document. The object hierarchy for the W3C Level 1 and Level 2 DOMs includes a structure for individual tags, tag attributes, and text strings within an HTML file.

Document tree ◀ Figure 4-6

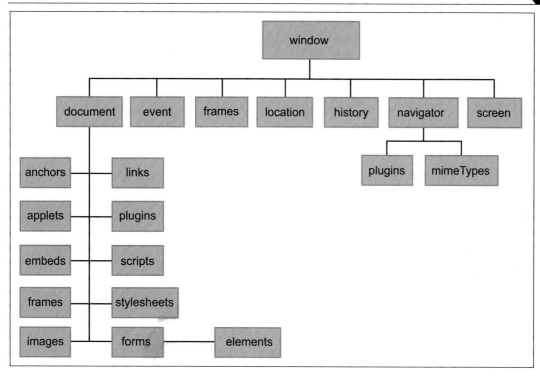

Referencing Objects

After the document object model defines how the objects within the browser and document are organized, it can be used by any scripting language, such as JavaScript. Once you understand how to work with a document object model, you can apply these lessons to several other programming languages. These tutorials explore how JavaScript interacts with the DOM, so you'll start by examining how to reference a particular element or groups of elements within a document object model using JavaScript.

Object Names

Each object is identified by an **object name**. Figure 4-7 lists the object names for some of the objects at the top of the object hierarchy. You've been using one of these objects, the document object, throughout the last three tutorials.

Figure 4-7 ▶ **Object names**

Object Name	Description
window	The browser window
document	The Web document displayed in the window
document.body	The body of the Web document displayed in the browser window
event	Events or actions occurring within the browser window
history	The list of previously visited Web sites within the browser window
location	The URL of the document currently displayed in the browser window
navigator	The browser itself
screen	The screen displaying the document

As indicated by the document tree in Figure 4-6, many objects are nested within other objects. To indicate the location of an object within the hierarchy, you separate each level using a dot. This is often referred to as **dot syntax**. The general form is

```
object1.object2.object3. ...
```

where *object1* is at the top of the hierarchy, *object2* is a child of *object1*, *object3* is a child of *object2*, and so on. To reference the document object displayed within the browser window, you could use the following nested form:

```
window.document
```

However, in most cases, you do not have to indicate an object's location within the entire hierarchy of the document tree. For example, when you simply use the document object name, JavaScript assumes that the object is located within the current browser window. If you have multiple browser windows open, you may need to explicitly indicate the window containing the document object you want to access. For now, all scripts apply to the currently active window.

Working with Object Collections

When more than one of the same type of object exists, these objects are organized into arrays called **object collections**. For example, the object reference

```
document.images
```

references all of the inline image objects in the current document (and implicitly within the current browser window). Figure 4-8 lists some other examples of object collections found with the document, navigator, and window objects.

Object collections | Figure 4-8

Object Collection	Description
document.anchors	All anchors
document.applets	All applets
document.embeds	All embed elements
document.forms	All Web forms
document.*form*.elements	All elements within a specific *form*
document.images	All inline images
document.links	All links
document.plugins	All plug-ins in the document
document.styleSheets	All style sheet elements
navigator.plugins	All plug-ins supported by the browser
navigator.mimeTypes	All mime-types supported by the browser
window.frames	All frames within the browser window

To reference a specific object within a collection, you can use either

```
collection[idref]
```

or

```
collection.idref
```

where *collection* is a reference to the object collection and *idref* is either an index number representing the position of the object in the array or the value of the name or ID assigned to the element. As with other arrays, the first object in the collection has an index number of 0. For example, if the first inline image within the document has the tag

```
<img src = "logo.jpg" id = "logoImg" />
```

you can reference the image using any of the following expressions:

```
document.images[0]
document.images["logoImg"]
document.images.logoImg
```

To avoid long object references in your code, you can store the reference in a variable. The statement

```
var firstImg = document.images[0]
```

stores the object reference to the first inline image in the variable firstImg.

Because object collections are essentially arrays, they support the length property; so you can always determine the number of items in an object collection using the following expression:

```
collection.length
```

The number of inline images within the document is returned by the following expression:

```
document.images.length
```

Finally, as with arrays, you can use a for loop to go through all of the items within the collection. The general form is

```
for (var i = 0; i< collection.length; i++) {
   commands
}
```

where *collection* is again a reference to an object collection and *commands* are commands that can be applied to each item within the collection.

Referencing Objects by Name and ID

Not all elements are associated with an object collection. For example, no object collection specifically references div elements. However, you can create object collections based on the names of element tags using the expression

```
object.getElementsByTagName(tag)
```

where *object* is an object in the document and *tag* is the name of an HTML tag nested within that object. To create an array of all div elements within the current document, you would use the following expression:

```
document.getElementsByTagName("div")
```

The getElementsByTagName() method can also be used to create an array of all elements in a document by using the * wildcard character in place of the tag name. For example, the following code creates an array of all HTML tags in the current document in the allElems variable:

```
allElems = document.getElementsByTagName("*");
```

You can also create object collections based on the ID attribute of the element. The object reference is

```
document.getElementById(id)
```

where *id* is the value of the ID attribute. So, to reference the element

```
<div id = "mainHeading">
   ...
</div>
```

from the document, you would use the following object reference:

```
document.getElementById("mainHeading")
```

Tip

Case is important with the getElementById method. A common error is to enter the code as getElementByID, incorrectly capitalizing the final letter, resulting in an error.

The getElementById () method is associated only with the document object, unlike the getElementsByTagName() method, which can be applied to any element within the document. Also, because ID values are meant to be unique, the getElementById() method returns only a single object, not an object collection.

Finally, you can create references to objects by the value of their name attribute with the expression

```
document.getElementsByName(name)
```

where *name* is the value of the name attribute. Because more than one element can share the same name (such as radio buttons within a Web form), this method returns an object collection rather than a single object. The getElementsByName() method, like the getElementById() method, is applied only to the document object.

Object References in the Internet Explorer DOM | InSight

Before the development of a common document object model, each browser put forth its own DOM—and with it, its own collection of object names and object syntax. Starting with version 4.0, Internet Explorer introduced the IE document object model. Because of the dominance of the Internet Explorer browser, programmers had to write code that would accommodate both the IE DOM as well as the DOM supported by the W3C. Versions of Internet Explorer after IE 4.0 provided more support for the W3C DOM, so you can use much of the W3C document object model; but you may occasionally need to support the IE DOM, especially if your Web site needs to work with earlier versions of the Internet Explorer browser.

One chief area of difference between the IE DOM and the W3C DOM lies in how document elements are referenced. The IE DOM supports the object reference

```
document.all
```

which references an object collection consisting of all elements within the document. To reference an element within this collection by its ID, you can use any of the following expressions:

```
document.all[id]
  document.all.id
```

Note that the document.all object collection is not supported in the W3C DOM and would cause the program to fail if it were used in a browser that did not support the IE DOM. The IE DOM also allowed object references consisting only of the object's ID value. So to reference the element with the mainHeading, ID any of the following object references would be supported under the IE DOM:

```
document.all["mainHeading"]
  document.all.mainHeading
  mainHeading
```

The IE DOM also allows references to objects by their tag name using the tags object collection

```
document.all.tags(tag)
```

where *tag* is the tag name. Thus to create an array of all paragraph elements under the IE DOM, you could enter the following expression:

```
document.all.tags("p")
```

As with the getElementsByTagName() method, you can create an array of all elements in the document by using the wildcard character * in place of the tag name. Again, the tags collection is not part of the W3C DOM and would cause the program to fail when used with non-IE browsers.

- To reference an object as part of the collection in a document, use either
    ```
    collection[idref]
    ```
  or
    ```
    collection.idref
    ```
  where *idref* is either an index number representing the position of the object in the collection or the value of the ID or name attribute assigned to that element.
- To reference a document object based on its ID, use
    ```
    document.getElementById(id)
    ```
  where *id* is the value of the element's ID attribute.
- To reference an array of elements based on the tag name, use
    ```
    object.getElementsByTagName(tag)
    ```
  where *object* is an object reference and *tag* is the name of the element tag.
- To reference an array of elements based on the value of the name attribute, use
    ```
    document.getElementsByName(name)
    ```
  where *name* is the value of the name attribute.

Working with Object Properties

Most objects are associated with one or more properties. The syntax of an object property is

```
object.property
```

where *object* is the object name and *property* is the name of a property associated with the object. To set the value of an object property, you enter the statement

```
object.property = expression
```

where *expression* is a JavaScript expression that returns a value.

Object Properties and HTML Attributes

Many of the properties associated with document objects correspond to the HTML attributes associated with document elements. For example, the img element

```
<img id = "logoImg" src = "logo.jpg" />
```

from an HTML file has the following equivalent JavaScript expression:

```
document.images["logoImg"].src = "logo.jpg";
```

The object properties that mirror HTML attributes follow certain conventions. The first is that all properties must begin with a lowercase letter. If the HTML attribute consists of multiple words, then the initial word is lowercase, but the first letter of subsequent words is an uppercase letter, also known as **camel case**. For example, the maxlength attribute from an input element in an HTML document

```
<input type = "text" id = "fName" maxlength = "15" />
```

can be expressed in camel case as follows:

```
document.getElementById("fName").maxLength = 15;
```

If the name of the HTML attribute is a reserved JavaScript name or keyword, the attribute is prefaced with the text string html. The for attribute in the label element

```
<label id = "fLabel" for = "fName">
```

is mirrored by the following JavaScript expression:

```
document.getElementById("fLabel").htmlFor = "fName";
```

One exception to this convention is the class attribute. Because the class name is reserved by JavaScript for other purposes, references to the HTML class attribute use the className property. In Kyle's document, the HTML code

```
<div id = "menu1" class = "menu">
```

which is used to mark the first menu title, has the following equivalent JavaScript expression:

```
document.getElementById("menu1").className = "menu";
```

Once you are comfortable with these conventions, you can easily transfer your knowledge of HTML elements and attributes to their equivalent JavaScript expressions involving object names and properties. Also, because the document object model mirrors the HTML code, you can modify the attribute values of most HTML elements through your JavaScript program.

The only properties you cannot change are the **read-only properties**, which have fixed values. One such property is the appVersion property of the navigator object, which identifies the Web browser version currently in use. However, keep in mind that you cannot upgrade your browser by simply running a JavaScript command to change the value of the appVersion property.

Object Properties and CSS Styles

CSS styles can also be set in the document object model through the use of the style property. The general syntax of the style property is

```
object.style.attribute
```

where *object* is a document object, and *attribute* is a CSS style attribute applicable to that object. For example, the following command mirrors the effect of applying the CSS font-size style by setting the font size of the first h1 heading in the document to 24 pixels:

```
document.getElementsByTagName("h1")[0].style.fontSize = "24px";
```

Because JavaScript does not support hyphenated letters for property names, the CSS style attribute is formatted in camel case with each hyphenated word entered with an initial capital letter.

You can use the style property to retrieve an element's style values, but only if the style is set as an inline style. For example, if the HTML file contains the tag

```
<div id = "main" style = "width: 200px">
```

you can retrieve the style value and store it in a variable using the following command:

```
widthValue = document.getElementById("main").style.width;
```

Tip

The className property and the class attribute are not limited to single values. Both the property and the attribute can store a space-separated list of class names used for assigning more than one class to the same object or element.

The widthValue variable will contain the text string 200px. If you need to extract the numeric value, you would use the parseInt() method as follows:

```
widthValue = parseInt(document.getElementById("main").style.width);
```

As with HTML attributes, one advantage of the style object is that you can apply your knowledge of CSS styles quickly and easily to your JavaScript code, allowing you to modify the appearance of your document objects through your program.

InSight | **Using Classes Versus the Style Object**

JavaScript allows styles to be changed in two ways. One approach is to modify the object's appearance by using the style object. For example, to change the font color of an element with the ID heading1 to red, you can run the following command:

```
document.getElementById("heading1").style.color = "red";
```

Another approach is to keep all style changes in a style sheet under different class names. A part of the CSS style sheet to change the font color to red might look like

```
.redText {color: red}
```

allowing the programmer to change the font color by changing the class name as follows:

```
document.getElementById("heading1").className = "redText";
```

There are several good reasons to use classes for this task rather than the style object. First, it is easier to maintain consistent styles for a Web site because all styles are confined to a style sheet rather than spread across style sheets and JavaScript programs. Second, it is usually easier to later modify a style in the style sheet rather than in what might be a long and complex JavaScript program. Finally, test speeds done by Peter-Paul Koch of quirksmode.org have shown that browsers are more responsive and apply style changes more quickly by changing the element class rather than by modifying the style properties directly.

Still, situations exist in which it would be inconvenient to create different classes for every minor change in an object's appearance. Most programmers use a combination of different classes and the style object in their JavaScript programs.

Reference Window | **Working with Object Properties**

- To set the value of an object property, use
    ```
    object.property = expression
    ```
  where *object* is the object reference, *property* is the object property, and *expression* is the value you want to assign to the property.
- To apply a CSS style to a document object, use
    ```
    object.style.attribute = expression
    ```
  where *attribute* is a CSS style attribute written in camel case and *expression* is a text string containing the value of the CSS style.

Creating an Array of Menus

You have enough information to begin writing the program that generates pull-down menus for Kyle's Web page. The first step is to create an array of all of the elements in Kyle's Web page containing menu titles. All of the menu title elements belong to the menu class. Because JavaScript does not have a built-in object collection to select objects based on their class name, you'll have to write your own. One approach is to loop through the collection of elements in the document, checking each element to determine whether it belongs to the menu class. If it does, it can be added to an array of objects sharing that class name. The code for this loop appears as follows:

```
var menus = new Array();
var allElems = document.getElementsByTagName("*");

for (var i = 0; i < allElems.length; i++) {
   if (allElems[i].className == "menu") menus.push(allElems[i]);
}
```

The code creates two variables. The menus variable starts as an empty array. The allElems variable stores the object collection containing all elements in the Web document. The for loop then loops through each object in the allElems collection and uses the push() method to push each object belonging to the menu class into the menus array. The end result is that the menus array is populated only with document objects that belong to the menu class.

You'll place this code in a new function named init() that you'll add to an external JavaScript file.

To create the init() function:

► 1. Use your text editor to open the **menustxt.js** file from the tutorial.04\tutorial folder, enter *your name* and *the date* in the comment section, and then save the file as **menus.js**.

► 2. Directly below the comment section, insert the following text, as shown in Figure 4-9:

```
function init() {
   var menus = new Array();
   var allElems = document.getElementsByTagName("*");

   for (var i = 0; i < allElems.length; i++) {
      if (allElems[i].className == "menu") menus.push(allElems[i]);
   }
}
```

Code for the init() function | Figure 4-9

```
function init() {
   var menus = new Array();
   var allElems = document.getElementsByTagName("*");

   for (var i=0; i < allElems.length; i++) {
      if (allElems[i].className == "menu") menus.push(allElems[i]);
   }
}
```

► 3. Save your changes to the file.

In this session, you have learned about the document object model, objects, and properties. In the next session, you'll continue to develop a program to create a system of pull-down menus for Kyle's Web site.

1. What is the document object model?
2. What is the object name for the user's Web browser?
3. What expression references the second hypertext link in the document?
4. An element from the Web document has the ID value footer. Provide an expression referencing this object.
5. What expression references the second paragraph element from the Web document?
6. What JavaScript command sets the action attribute of the first form in a document to the following text string: http://www.avalon.com/mailer.cgi?
7. What JavaScript command changes the second div element in the document to the blueBackground class?
8. What JavaScript command applies a 2 pixel solid black border to the document element with the ID main?
9. Specify the program code to loop through all of the hypertext links in a document, changing their text decoration style to none.

Session 4.2

Exploring Object Methods

After exploring the syntax of JavaScript objects and properties, you continue your work on the pull-down menu program for Kyle's Web site. The next step in exploring JavaScript's document object model is to learn how to work with object methods. You've been using object methods throughout the last three tutorials, but it's time to formalize that understanding. The syntax for applying a method to an object is

```
object.method(parameters)
```

where *object* is the name of the object, *method* is the method to be applied, and *parameters* is a comma-separated list of parameter values used with the method. In the previous tutorials, you applied the write method to the document object to write text into the page. In that case, there was only one parameter value, consisting of the text string to be written into the document. Figure 4-10 provides other examples of applying methods to objects. Note that not every method requires a parameter.

Examples of object methods   Figure 4-10

Expression	Action
location.reload()	Reload the current page in the browser
document.forms[0].reset()	Reset the first form in the Web page
document.forms[0].submit()	Submit the first form in the Web page
document.write("Sherlock Holmes Novels")	Write "Sherlock Holmes Novels" to the Web page
history.back()	Go back to the previous page in the browser's history list
thisDay.getFullYear()	Return the four-digit year value from the thisDay date object
Math.rand()	Return a random value using the Math object
navigator.javaEnabled()	Return a Boolean value indicating whether Java is enabled in the browser
window.close()	Close the browser window
window.print()	Print the contents of the browser window
window.scroll(x, y)	Scroll the browser window to the (x, y) coordinate

Working with Object Methods | Reference Window

- To apply a method to an object, use

  ```
  object.method(parameters)
  ```

  where *object* is the object reference, *method* is the method to be applied, and *parameters* is a comma-separated list of parameter values used by the method.

Working with Event Handlers

Finally, you'll examine how to use JavaScript to apply an event to an object. All objects can be affected by events initiated by the user or browser. In previous tutorials, you used event handlers with the HTML attribute

```
<element onevent = "script" ...>
```

where *element* is the name of an HTML element, *event* is a user- or browser-initiated event, and *script* is a JavaScript command or function to be run in response to the event. The on*event* attribute can also be treated as a property of a JavaScript object so that you can assign the same event handler using the statement

```
object.onevent = function;
```

where *object* is an object in the document or browser and *function* is a JavaScript function run in response to the event. For example, the HTML tag

```
<div id = "heading1" onclick = "showlogo()">
```

is mirrored by the following JavaScript command:

```
document.getElementById("heading1").onclick = showlogo;
```

JavaScript assigns only the name of the function to the on*event* property. It doesn't call the function itself. So the following statement would be rejected as a violation of JavaScript syntax:

```
document.getElementById("heading1").onclick = showlogo();
```

Using an event handler as an object property provides programmers with greater flexibility in designing scripts. The function assigned to an event can be changed at one or more points in a program or modified in response to other events initiated by the user or browser. Also, a Web page could contain dozens or hundreds of elements requiring event handlers. Rather than assigning event handlers as attributes to each element tag, a program could loop through this collection of elements, assigning the event handlers automatically.

The other important advantage of treating an event handler as an object property is that it removes scripting from the HTML code, placing it within the external script file. An important goal in Web site design is to separate document content (HTML) from document design (CSS) from document programming (JavaScript). The HTML file should contain little or no style attributes and little or no scripting. Placing event handlers in HTML tags violates this principle; so whenever possible, event handlers should be placed within an external JavaScript file.

One main disadvantage of treating an event handler as object property is the difficulty of passing parameter values to the function assigned to the event. In addition, you can assign only one function at a time to a particular object and event. You can work around this limitation by having the function assigned to the event call two or more other functions when it is run.

In the previous session, you began to write the init() function, which generates the collection of menuList elements found in Kyle's document. You'll run this function immediately after the page loads. If you were using event handlers as attributes, you could add the onload attribute to the <body> tag as follows:

```
<body onload = "init()">
```

In JavaScript, to run the init() function when the page is finished loading into the browser window, you run the following statement:

```
window.onload = init;
```

You'll add this command to the menus.js file, and then link the JavaScript file to Kyle's Web page.

> **Tip**
>
> Event handlers can be assigned to document objects only *after* the object has been loaded by the browser.

To add the onload event handler:

▶ **1.** If you took a break after the previous session, make sure the menus.js file is open in a text editor and the holmes.htm file is open in your Web browser.

▶ **2.** Return to the **menus.js** file in your text editor, and then directly above the init() function, insert the following command, as shown in Figure 4-11:

```
window.onload = init;
```

Code for the event handler object ◀ **Figure 4-11**

```
window.onload = init;         runs the init() function after the page
                              is loaded into the browser window
function init() {
   var menus = new Array();
   var allElems = document.getElementsByTagName("*");

   for (var i = 0; i < allElems.length; i++) {
      if (allElems[i].className == "menu") menus.push(allElems[i]);
   }
}
```

▶ 3. Save your changes to the file, and then return to the **holmes.htm** file in your text editor.

▶ 4. Link to the menus.js file by adding the following tag to the head section of the document:

```
<script type = "text/javascript" src = "menus.js"></script>
```

▶ 5. Close the file, saving your changes. With the onload event handler added to the JavaScript file, you do not need to modify the holmes.htm file anymore. All modifications and additions to your program can be done from within the menus.js file.

▶ 6. Reopen or refresh **holmes.htm** in your Web browser. The Web page loads without any errors being reported by your browser.

Trouble? If your browser reports an error, you may have made a mistake in entering the init() function in the previous session. Open the menus.js file in a text editor, compare your code to the code shown in Figure 4-11, making sure that your code matches both uppercase and lowercase letters and that all text strings are closed with quotation marks. Repeat Steps 5 and 6.

Programming a Pull-Down Menu

You can begin to write the code to create pull-down menus for Kyle. The pull-down menus are opened by clicking any of the six menu titles on Kyle's Web page. You've already created the menus array containing the menu title objects. You use JavaScript to add onclick event handlers to each of the titles to run the changeMenu() function when the title is clicked. The code to create the onclick event handlers is:

```
for (var i = 0; i < menus.length; i++) {
   menus[i].onclick = changeMenu;
}
```

This code loops through all of the items in the menus array. For each item, it adds the onclick event handler, associating the changeMenu() function (which you'll create shortly) with the action of clicking the menu title. Nothing in the code you just entered specifies how many menus are present in the document. This code works for any number of pull-down menus. Kyle could later insert additional pull-down menus to his page or apply this code to other Web pages as long as the menu titles all belong to the menu class.

You'll add the above code to the init() function now.

To add event handlers to the menus:

▶ **1.** Return to the **menus.js** file in your text editor, and then, at the end of the init() function, add the following code:

```
for (var i = 0; i < menus.length; i++) {
    menus[i].onclick = changeMenu;
}
```

▶ **2.** Below the init() function, insert the following code for the changeMenu() function:

```
function changeMenu() {
    // this function changes the pull-down menu displayed in the document

}
```

Figure 4-12 highlights the newly inserted code.

Figure 4-12 ▶ **Event handlers added to the menu titles**

```
function init() {
    var menus = new Array();
    var allElems = document.getElementsByTagName("*");

    for (var i = 0; i < allElems.length; i++) {
        if (allElems[i].className == "menu") menus.push(allElems[i]);
    }

    for (var i = 0; i < menus.length; i++) {
        menus[i].onclick = changeMenu;
    }
}

function changeMenu() {
    // this function changes the pull-down menu displayed in the document
}
```

loops through the menus array, adding an onclick event handler to each menu title

initial code for the changeMenu() function

▶ **3.** Save your changes to the file.

The purpose of the changeMenu function is to change the pull-down menu from one menu list to another. To do that, you need to keep track of what, if any, pull-down menus are currently displayed in the document. You'll store this information in a variable named activeMenu that contains the object reference of the current pull-down menu. If no pull-down menu is being displayed, the value of the activeMenu variable is set to null.

You'll add this variable to the menus.js file, setting its initial value to null.

To create the activeMenu variable:

▶ **1.** Return to the **menus.js** file in your text editor.

▶ **2.** Directly above the init() function, insert the following declaration for the active-Menu variable, as shown in Figure 4-13:

```
var activeMenu = null;
```

activeMenu variable inserted ◀ Figure 4-13

```
var activeMenu = null;◀

function init() {
   var menus = new Array();
   var allElems = document.getElementsByTagName("*");

   for (var i = 0; i < allElems.length; i++) {
      if (allElems[i].className == "menu") menus.push(allElems[i]);
   }

   for (var i = 0; i < menus.length; i++) {
      menus[i].onclick = changeMenu;
   }
}
```

the activeMenu variable stores the object reference of the pull-down menu

▶ **3.** Save your changes to the file.

The activeMenu variable is defined outside of the context of the init() function to give it global scope, allowing you to reference it in any of the functions within the menus.js file. The initial value of the activeMenu is set to null because, when the page opens, no pull-down menu is visible in the document.

Using the `this` Keyword

As users click different menu titles, the value of the activeMenu variable will be changed and updated in the changeMenu() function. Kyle assigned the menu titles ID values of menu1 through menu6, and he assigned the corresponding pull-down menu lists ID values of menu1List through menu6List. If you know the ID of the menu title the user clicked, you can derive the ID of the corresponding menu list by simply adding the text string List. Because any of the six menu titles in Kyle's document can activate the change-Menu() function, how do you know which one the user clicked? To determine that, you use JavaScript's keyword `this`. The **`this` keyword** references the currently active object in the Web browser. When the changeMenu() function is run, the currently active object is the menu title that was just clicked by the user. From the `this` keyword, you can determine the ID of that menu title using the expression

```
this.id
```

which for Kyle's Web page is equal to one of the text strings from menu1 through menu6. Therefore, the ID of the corresponding pull-down menu is:

```
this.id + "List"
```

Using this information, you'll add the following code to the changeMenu() function:

```
closeOldMenu();

menuID = this.id + "List";
activeMenu = document.getElementById(menuID);
activeMenu.style.display = "block";
```

The first line of this code calls a function named closeOldMenu() to close the currently displayed menu. The next two lines set the object reference of the activeMenu variable to point to the new pull-down menu. Finally, the last line displays the new pull-down menu by changing its CSS display style to block.

You'll add these lines of code to the changeMenu() function.

To edit the changeMenu() function:

▶ **1.** Within the changeMenu() function, insert the following lines of code, as shown in Figure 4-14:

```
closeOldMenu();

menuID = this.id + "List";
activeMenu = document.getElementById(menuID);
activeMenu.style.display = "block";
```

| Figure 4-14 | Code for the changeMenu() function |

```
function changeMenu() {
    // this function changes the pull-down menu displayed in the document

    closeOldMenu();

    menuID = this.id + "List";
    activeMenu = document.getElementById(menuID);
    activeMenu.style.display = "block";
}
```

this keyword references the object that called the changeMenu() function

▶ **2.** Save your changes to the file.

Next, you'll create the closeOldMenu() function whose purpose is to close the pull-down menu that is no longer active. The function first must test whether there is an active menu to close (to avoid generating an error message if no menu is active). It does this using the following if condition:

```
function closeOldMenu() {
    if (activeMenu) {
        commands
    }
}
```

If the activeMenu variable is null (meaning that no menu is currently open), then the if condition returns a value of false; otherwise, it will return a value of true and run the command block. The commands in the command block are as follows:

```
function closeOldMenu() {
    if (activeMenu) {
        activeMenu.style.display = "none";
        activeMenu = null;
    }
}
```

Thus, if JavaScript has determined that there is an open pull-down menu, it sets the display style of the menu to none, rehiding it from the user, and then resets the activeMenu variable to null.

You'll add this function to the menus.js file, and then test your code in your browser.

Tip

You can avoid some programming errors when working with document objects by enclosing commands within if statements that verify those objects exist and are supported by your browser.

To insert the closeOldMenu() function and test your page:

▶ **1.** At the bottom of the **menus.js** file, insert the following function, as shown in Figure 4-15:

```
function closeOldMenu() {
    if (activeMenu) {
        activeMenu.style.display = "none";
        activeMenu = null;
    }
}
```

Code for the closeOldMenu() function ◀ Figure 4-15

```
function changeMenu() {
    // this function changes the pull-down menu displayed in the document

    closeOldMenu();

    menuID = this.id + "List";
    activeMenu = document.getElementById(menuID);
    activeMenu.style.display = "block";

}

function closeOldMenu() {
    if (activeMenu) {
        activeMenu.style.display = "none";
        activeMenu = null;
    }
}
```

closes the currently-opened pull-down menu

▶ **2.** Save your changes to the file.

▶ **3.** Refresh or reopen the **holmes.htm** file in your Web browser.

▶ **4.** Click each of the six menu titles at the top of the page and verify that clicking a menu title opens the corresponding pull-down menu while closing any previously opened pull-down menu. See Figure 4-16.

Pull-down menu being tested ◀ Figure 4-16

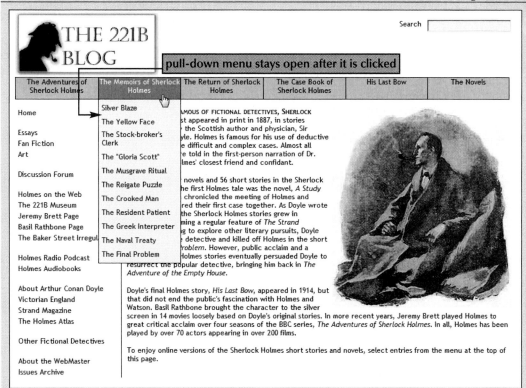

▶ **5.** Click within the page content. The pull-down menu remains open.

You need to revise the code to make the pull-down menus disappear if the user clicks elsewhere within the body of the Web page. You can do this by adding the onclick event handler to the page's logo, list of links, and main text to run the closeOldMenu() function.

To add the onclick event handlers:

▶ **1.** Return to the **menus.js** file in your text editor.

▶ **2.** At the bottom of the init() function, insert the following statements, as shown in Figure 4-17:

```
document.getElementById("logo").onclick = closeOldMenu;
document.getElementById("linkList").onclick = closeOldMenu;
document.getElementById("main").onclick = closeOldMenu;
```

Figure 4-17 ▶ **Code for the onclick event handlers**

```
function init() {
   var menus = new Array();
   var allElems = document.getElementsByTagName("*");

   for (var i = 0; i < allElems.length; i++) {
      if (allElems[i].className == "menu") menus.push(allElems[i]);
   }

   for (var i = 0; i < menus.length; i++) {
      menus[i].onclick = changeMenu;
   }

   document.getElementById("logo").onclick = closeOldMenu;
   document.getElementById("linkList").onclick = closeOldMenu;
   document.getElementById("main").onclick = closeOldMenu;

}
```

> runs the closeOldMenu() function when the user clicks within the page logo, the list of links, or the main text

▶ **3.** Save your changes to the file, and then refresh the **holmes.htm** file in your Web browser.

▶ **4.** Verify that you can close all of the pull-down menus by clicking anywhere within the page logo, main text, or list of links. If you click a blank area of the document window outside of the page content, the pull-down menu does not close.

Object Detection with JavaScript | InSight

In the closeOldMenu() function, you enclosed the commands within an if statement that veri-fied the existence of the activeMenu object. This is because you had to confirm the existence of the activeMenu object before you could apply the display style property to it. This process of confirming support for an object is known as **object detection** and has the general form

```
if (object) {
    commands
}
```

where *object* is a JavaScript reference to an object and *commands* are commands that apply if that object exists and is supported by the browser. If the condition of the if state-ment fails, then the browser skips all of the statements in *commands*, avoiding an error that could cause the program to fail.

For example, the following statement verifies that the browser supports the document. images collection before attempting to use that object in a for loop:

```
if (document.images) {
  for (var i = 0; i < document.images.length; i++) {
    document.images[i].style.border = "1px solid black";
  }
}
```

Object detection can also be used with methods. To detect support for a method, include the method name without the brackets. The code

```
if (window.focus) {
  commands
}
```

confirms that the browser supports the window.focus() method before attempting to run commands involving it.

Object detection is often used when reconciling inconsistencies between different object models. The IE4 DOM employs the document.all object to reference all objects found within the Web page document, but this object is not supported in the W3C DOM. To write com-mands specifically for the IE4 DOM, you could enclose them within the following if statement:

```
if (document.all) {
  IE4-specific commands
}
```

You can also employ object detection for the W3C DOM. The if condition

```
if (document.getElementById && document.createElement) {
  W3C DOM commands
}
```

can be used to confirm that the browser supports the features of the W3C DOM.

Object detection is an important tool for the JavaScript programmer and should be used whenever there is a question about the support for an object or method.

Adding Handlers for Mouse Events

Kyle has one more suggestion for the pull-down menu system. As the users move the pointer from one menu title to another, he wants the displayed pull-down menu to change with it, as shown in Figure 4-18.

Figure 4-18 ▶ **Pull-down menu changes by moving the pointer**

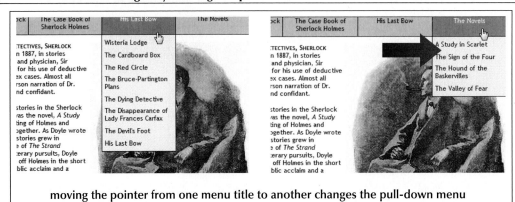

moving the pointer from one menu title to another changes the pull-down menu

To create this effect, you have to add an event handler that responds to the motions of the pointer. One such event handler is onmouseover, which is activated whenever the pointer initially moves over an object. You'll add an onmouseover event handler to the menu titles that activates the function moveMenu() in response.

Tip

To run a function in response to the pointer moving off of an object, use the onmouseout event handler.

To add the onmouseover event handler:

▶ **1.** Return to the **menus.js** file in your text editor.

▶ **2.** Within the second for loop in the init() function, add the following line of code:

```
menus[i].onmouseover = moveMenu;
```

▶ **3.** Directly below the init() function, insert the following code:

```
function moveMenu() {
    // this function moves the pull-down menu from one title to another

}
```

Figure 4-19 highlights the newly added code in the file.

Figure 4-19 ▶ **Code for the onmouseover event handler**

```
function init() {
    var menus = new Array();
    var allElems = document.getElementsByTagName("*");

    for (var i = 0; i < allElems.length; i++) {
        if (allElems[i].className == "menu") menus.push(allElems[i]);
    }

    for (var i = 0; i < menus.length; i++) {
        menus[i].onclick = changeMenu;
        menus[i].onmouseover = moveMenu;
    }

    document.getElementById("logo").onclick = closeOldMenu;
    document.getElementById("linkList").onclick = closeOldMenu;
    document.getElementById("main").onclick = closeOldMenu;

}

function moveMenu() {
    // this function moves the pull-down menu from one title to another

}
```

> runs the moveMenu() when the pointer initially moves over a menu title

▶ **4.** Save your changes to the file.

The code for the moveMenu() function is similar to the code you entered for the changeMenu() function except that it must be enclosed within an if statement to verify that a pull-down menu is already opened. Kyle wants the moveMenu() function to be run only when the user is moving the pointer from one pull-down menu to another, not just whenever the pointer moves over a menu title. The code for the moveMenu() function is therefore:

```
if (activeMenu) {
   closeOldMenu();

   menuID = this.id + "List";
   activeMenu = document.getElementById(menuID);
   activeMenu.style.display = "block";
}
```

You'll add this code to the moveMenu() function.

To edit the moveMenu() function:

▶ 1. Within the moveMenu() function insert the following code, as shown in Figure 4-20:

```
if (activeMenu) {
   closeOldMenu();

   menuID = this.id + "List";
   activeMenu = document.getElementById(menuID);
   activeMenu.style.display = "block";
}
```

Code for the moveMenu() function   **Figure 4-20**

```
function moveMenu() {
   // this function moves the pull-down menu from one title to another

   if (activeMenu) {
      closeOldMenu();

      menuID = this.id + "List";
      activeMenu = document.getElementById(menuID);
      activeMenu.style.display = "block";
   }

}
```

▶ 2. Save your changes to the file.

▶ 3. Reopen or refresh the **holmes.htm** file in your Web browser.

▶ 4. Click the menu titles for the pull-down menus and verify that as you move the pointer over the other menu titles, the browser automatically opens the corresponding menu.

▶ 5. Click outside the pull-down menus to close them.

Kyle likes the changes to the pull-down menus you created. He is pleased that you were able to create a menu system that effectively manages all of the links to the Sherlock Holmes stories and novels.

Review | Session 4.2 Quick Check

1. What is the syntax for applying an object method?
2. What object and method reload the current Web page in the browser?
3. What command runs the showMenu() function whenever the user clicks the element with the ID value pullMenu?
4. What JavaScript code runs the showLinks() function whenever a user clicks a hypertext in the Web document?
5. What is the syntax error in the following code?:

   ```
   document.getElementById("slide").onclick = loadImage();
   ```

6. What is object detection?
7. What code runs the command showMenu(), but only if the user's browser supports the IE4 DOM?
8. What JavaScript command runs the showMenu() function when the user initially moves the pointer over the element with the ID value pullMenu?

Session 4.3

Animating a Pull-Down Menu

Kyle has been reviewing the Web site and the site's home page. The pull-down menu code you wrote works well. Kyle has one more request: He wants you to add the illusion of the menu being pulled down or unrolled from the menu title so that the menu would appear in stages rather than all at once, as shown in Figure 4-21. Kyle thinks this would add some visual appeal to the site's home page.

Figure 4-21 | **Animated pull-down menu**

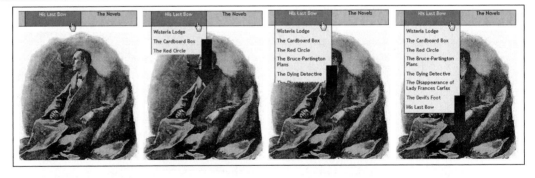

You can create this effect in several ways. One way is to use the CSS clip style. Recall that the clip style makes only part of an object visible by "clipping" a rectangular section out of the object. The syntax of the clip style is

```
clip: rect(top, right, bottom, left)
```

where *top*, *right*, *bottom*, and *left* define the coordinates of the top, right, bottom, and left corners of the clipping rectangle. For example, the following style creates a clipping rectangle that is located in the upper-left corner of the object and is 150 pixels wide and 200 pixels high:

```
clip: rect(0px, 150px, 200px, 0px)
```

For Kyle's pull-down menus, you want to start with a clipping rectangle that is located in the upper-left corner of the object with a width at least as great as the width of the menu and a height of 0 pixels. You would then gradually increase the height of the rectangle, leaving the other dimensions unchanged.

The initial size of the clipping rectangle can be set by adding the following command to the changeMenu() and moveMenu() functions:

```
activeMenu.style.clip = "rect(0px, 150px, 0px, 0px)";
```

The value of the *right* parameter is set to 150 pixels to ensure that the entire width of the menu is displayed. The rest of the parameters are set to 0 pixels to hide the menu from the user. You'll add this command to both functions.

To apply the clip style:

1. If you took a break after the previous session, make sure the menus.js file is open in a text editor and the holmes.htm file is open in a Web browser.

2. Return to the **menus.js** file in your text editor.

3. Within the changeMenu() and moveMenu() functions, insert the following command, as shown in Figure 4-22:

```
activeMenu.style.clip = "rect(0px, 150px, 0px, 0px)";
```

Clip style applied — Figure 4-22

```
function moveMenu() {
    // this function moves the pull-down menu from one title to another

    if (activeMenu) {
        closeOldMenu();

        menuID = this.id + "List";
        activeMenu = document.getElementById(menuID);
        activeMenu.style.clip = "rect(0px, 150px, 0px, 0px)";
        activeMenu.style.display = "block";
    }

}


function changeMenu() {
    // this function changes the pull-down menu displayed in the document

    closeOldMenu();

    menuID = this.id + "List";
    activeMenu = document.getElementById(menuID);
    activeMenu.style.clip = "rect(0px, 150px, 0px, 0px)";
    activeMenu.style.display = "block";

}
```

4. Save your changes to the file.

When a user opens a pull-down menu, JavaScript should repeatedly apply the clip style to the menu, increasing the value of the *bottom* parameter until it exceeds a certain value after which point the entire object is displayed. You can repeatedly modify the clip style by placing the command to do so within a function and then running that function at timed intervals using the setInterval() method. The general form of the function, which we'll call rollDown(), is:

```
function rollDown() {
    increase the clip height value
    if the height is less than the maximum value
        clip the menu
    else
```

```
        stop running the function
}
```

To run this function, you need to add two more global variables to the menus.js file. One is the clipHgt variable, which keeps track of the current value of the height of the clipping rectangle. The other is the timeID variable, which stores the ID of the timed interval function so that it can be halted once the entire menu is displayed. You'll add both of these variables to the file.

To add the clipHgt and timeID variables:

▶ **1.** Scroll to the top of the **menus.js** file.

▶ **2.** Directly above the init() function, insert the following two variable declarations, as shown in Figure 4-23:

```
var clipHgt = 0;
var timeID;
```

Figure 4-23 | **Code for the clipHgt and timeID variables**

```
var activeMenu = null;
var clipHgt = 0;
var timeID;
```

The initial value of the clipHgt is set to 0 because the pull-down menus will start out clipped to a rectangle with a height of 0 pixels.

The code for the rollDown() function is:

```
function rollDown() {
    clipHgt = clipHgt + 10;
    if (clipHgt < 400) {
        activeMenu.style.clip = "rect(0px, 150px," + clipHgt + "px, 0px)";
    } else {
        clearInterval(timeID);
        clipHgt = 0;
    }
}
```

Every time the function is run, the value of the clipHgt variable is increased by 10. As long as the clipping height is less than 400, the activeMenu object is clipped up to the height of the clipHgt value. Once the clipHgt value exceeds 400, the clearInterval() method is called, halting the timed execution of the function, and the clipHgt variable value is reset to 0. A maximum value of 400 was chosen for the clipHgt variable because all of the menu lists on Kyle's Web page are less than 400 pixels in height.

You'll add the rollDown() function to the file.

Tip

Clipping an object beyond the object's borders has no impact on how the object is displayed by the browser.

To add the rollDown() function:

▶ **1.** At the bottom of the **menus.js** file, insert the following function, as shown in Figure 4-24:

```
function rollDown() {
    clipHgt = clipHgt + 10;
    if (clipHgt < 400) {
        activeMenu.style.clip = "rect(0px, 150px," + clipHgt + "px,
            0px)";
    } else {
```

```
            clearInterval(timeID);
            clipHgt = 0;
        }
    }
```

Code for the rollDown() function   Figure 4-24

```
function closeOldMenu() {
    if (activeMenu) {
        activeMenu.style.display = "none";
        activeMenu = null;
    }
}

function rollDown() {
    clipHgt = clipHgt + 10;
    if (clipHgt < 400) {
        activeMenu.style.clip = "rect(0px, 150px," + clipHgt + "px, 0px)";
    } else {
        clearInterval(timeID);
        clipHgt = 0; .
    }
}
```

increases the clipping
height by 10 pixels

if the height is less
than 400 pixels, clips
the menu

otherwise stops running the rollDown()
function and resets the clipHgt value to 0

▶ **2.** Save your changes to the file.

To complete the illusion of a menu unrolling as the height of the clipping rectangle increases, you'll call the rollDown() function every millisecond using the setInterval() method. To keep track of the function, you'll store the ID of the timed function in the timeID variable you declared earlier.

You'll add the setInterval() method to both the moveMenu() and changeMenu() functions.

To call the rollDown() function:

▶ **1.** Within the moveMenu() and changeMenu() functions, insert the following command directly after the statement that sets the display style of the activeMenu object to display, as shown in Figure 4-25:

```
timeID = setInterval("rollDown()", 1);
```

Code to call the rollDown() function   Figure 4-25

```
function moveMenu() {
    // this function moves the pull-down menu from one title to another

    if (activeMenu) {
        closeOldMenu();

        menuID = this.id + "List";
        activeMenu = document.getElementById(menuID);
        activeMenu.style.clip = "rect(0px, 150px, 0px, 0px)";
        activeMenu.style.display = "block";
        timeID = setInterval("rollDown()", 1);
    }

}

function changeMenu() {
    // this function changes the pull-down menu displayed in the document

    closeOldMenu();

    menuID = this.id + "List";
    activeMenu = document.getElementById(menuID);
    activeMenu.style.clip = "rect(0px, 150px, 0px, 0px)";
    activeMenu.style.display = "block";
    timeID = setInterval("rollDown()", 1);

}
```

runs the rollDown()
function once every
millisecond until it
is cleared

Finally, you need to turn off the rollDown() function whenever your program closes a pull-down menu. This prevents a situation where the rollDown() function is running for a menu that has already been closed. To turn off the function, you'll add a clearInterval() method to the closeOldMenu() function.

▶ **2.** Scroll down to the closeOldMenu() function, and then insert the following command, as shown in Figure 4-26:

```
clearInterval(timeID);
```

Figure 4-26 ▶ **Code to clear the rollDown() function timer**

```
function closeOldMenu() {
    if (activeMenu) {
        clearInterval(timeID);
        activeMenu.style.display = "none";
        activeMenu = null;
    }
}
```
clears the timer, halting the operation of the rollDown() function

---

▶ **3.** Close the **menus.js** file, saving your changes.

▶ **4.** Reopen or refresh **holmes.htm** in your Web browser.

▶ **5.** Click the menu titles on the Web page and verify that each pull-down menu is opened with the illusion of being rolled out or pulled down on the Web page.

Kyle is pleased with the pull-down menu effect you created. The rolling down effect is exactly what he wanted.

Creating Other Types of Menus

Pull-down menus are only one type of menu you can create with JavaScript. Menu styles fall into four general classes: pull-downs, pop-ups, sliding, and tabbed.

Creating Pop-Up Menus

Pop-up menus are closely associated with pull-down menus. In a **pop-up menu**, a user clicks an object on the page and the menu appears, sometimes elsewhere on the page. Unlike pull-down menus, pop-up menus are not usually associated with a menu bar or a list of menu titles. To close a pop-up menu, a user clicks either the menu itself or another item on the page.

One common way to create a pop-up menu for the Web is to place the menu contents within a set of <div> container tags, hidden on the page using the visibility style attribute. When a user clicks an object on the page, a JavaScript program is run that unhides the menu. To rehide the menu, a second JavaScript program is run that changes the menu's visibility property back to hidden.

Creating Sliding Menus

In a **sliding menu**, a menu is partially hidden either off the Web page or behind another object. When the user clicks the visible part of the menu, the menu "slides" into a fully visible position, as shown in Figure 4-27.

Sliding menu   Figure 4-27

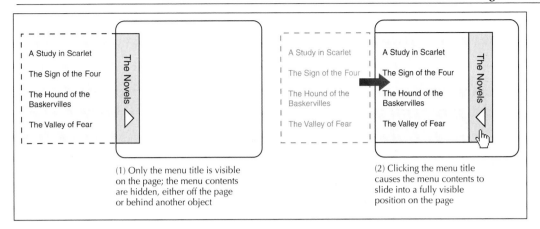

(1) Only the menu title is visible
on the page; the menu contents
are hidden, either off the page
or behind another object

(2) Clicking the menu title
causes the menu contents to
slide into a fully visible
position on the page

To create a sliding menu, use the positioning styles of the object to place it in a location where it is partially obscured. To place the object off the page, use absolute positioning and set the top and left styles to negative values. For example, the style declaration

```
position: absolute; top: -50px; left: -10px;
```

sets the object 50 pixels above and 10 pixels to the left of the visible browser window. To place a sliding menu behind another object, use the z-index style to set it below the other image on the page.

Once the sliding menu has been partially obscured, you can move the image across the page by modifying the values of the top or left style. For example, to set the top position to 20 pixels, you can apply the command

```
object.style.top = "20px";
```

where *object* is the document reference to an object. To create the illusion of moving an object across the page, you can employ the same technique of calling a function at timed intervals that you used with the rolling down effect on Kyle's Web page. The following code demonstrates how you can move an object horizontally across the page at the rate of 5 pixels every millisecond.

```
timeID = setInterval("moveItemRight()", 1);

function moveItemRight() {
    currentPos = parseInt(object.style.left);
    if ((currentPos + 5) <= 250) {
        object.style.left = leftPos + 5 + "px";
    } else {
        clearInterval(timeID);
    }
}
```

In this code, the object continues to move right until its left coordinate exceeds 250 pixels, at which time the moveItemRight() function will no longer be called by the browser. To keep track of the current position of the object, you use the parseInt() method to extract the numeric value from the object's left property. For example, if the value of the left property is 150px, the value of the currentPos variable will be 150.

Creating Tabbed Menus

In a **tabbed menu**, several menus are stacked on the page with one part of each menu visible to the user. When you click the visible part of a menu, the selected menu moves to the top of the stack, making its contents visible to the user, as shown in Figure 4-28.

Figure 4-28 ▶ **Tabbed menu**

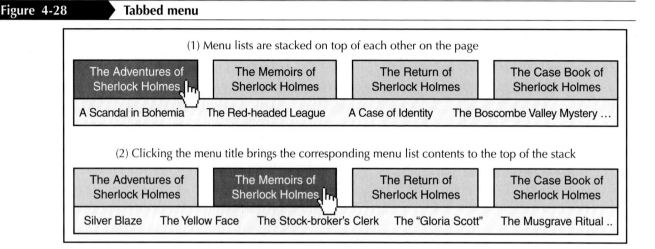

To create a tabbed menu system, you need to ensure that part of each menu is always visible, no matter where it is located in the stack. To move items to the top of the stack, you can simply change the value of the z-index style for the selected menu, setting the value to one higher than the z-index value of the menu currently on top of the stack. For example, if menu3List is on top of the stack and you want to move menu5List to the top, you could run this set of commands

```
menu3List = document.getElementById("menu3List");
menu5List = document.getElementById("menu5List");
maxZ = menu3List.style.zIndex;
menu5List.style.zIndex = maxZ+1;
```

and the menu5List object would be displayed on top of the menu3List object. An important point to remember is that when referencing a style such as the z-index style, the initial style value must be set either within the JavaScript program or as an inline style.

Retrieving Style Sheet Values | InSight

The style property can be used to set styles and to retrieve inline style values, but it cannot retrieve style values set in an external style sheet. This is because the style that the browser ultimately applies to an object is a computed value determined by resolving competing style declarations within the style sheet, the HTML code, and the browser itself. To access a computed style, the W3C DOM supports the getComputedStyle method

```
document.defaultView.getComputedStyle(object, pseudo)
```

where *object* is the reference to an object in the document and *pseudo* is a CSS pseudo-element within the object. If no pseudo-element exists, you can set the value of the *pseudo* parameter to null. For example, the following code retrieves the computed styles for the menu object:

```
menu = document.getElementById("menu");
mStyles = document.defaultView.getComputedStyle(menu, null);
```

To retrieve a specific style value for an object, you apply the getPropertyValue method

```
getPropertyValue(style)
```

where *style* is the name of a CSS style property. Therefore, to retrieve the value of the width property for the menu object, you apply the following command:

```
menuWidth = mStyles.getPropertyValue("width")
```

The IE DOM doesn't support these methods. Instead, to retrieve the computed style, you apply the following currentStyle method:

```
object.currentStyle[style]
```

Thus, to retrieve the width property for the menu object under the IE DOM, you use:

```
menuWidth = menu.currentStyle["width"]
```

If you're creating a Web site under both document object models, you can resolve the syntax differences between the two DOMs by applying object detection. The general code has the form

```
if (window.getComputedStyle) {
   W3C DOM
} else if (object.currentStyle) {
   IE DOM
}
```

where *object* is the object containing the CSS styles you want to retrieve and *W3C DOM* and *IE DOM* are the commands applicable under the W3C and IE document object models.

At this point, you've completed your work on Kyle's Web page. Through the use of JavaScript objects, properties, and methods, you've placed a large list of links on the page. Kyle is pleased with the final project.

Session 4.3 Quick Check | Review

1. What command applies a clipping rectangle to the mainDIV element located in the top-left corner of the object, having a width of 100 pixels and a height of 50 pixels?
2. What command repeats the function slideMenu() every second?
3. What command increases the value of the top coordinate of the Menu1 object by 5 pixels?
4. What command increases the z-index of the Menu1 object by 1?

5. The width value of the menu1 object has been set to 100 pixels in an external style sheet. What value is returned by the following expression?:

```
document.getElementById("menu1").style.width
```

6. You want to retrieve the value of the font-size attribute for the Menu1 object based on the value set in the Web page's external style sheet. Specify the commands to do this under the W3C DOM and the IE DOM.

Review | Tutorial Summary

This tutorial introduced the concept of the JavaScript object. The first session covered the fundamentals of objects, including the relation of Web elements and features to the document object model. You examined how to access object collections from the DOM and how to reference Web page elements based on tag name, ID value, and name value. You then learned how to create an array of Web page elements all sharing the same class value. The second session focused on how to use knowledge of objects, properties, and events to create an interactive pull-down menu system for a Web page. You explored the use of event handlers as object properties and saw how to employ the onclick and onmouseover event handlers in a JavaScript program. The third session refined the pull-down menu system created in the second session by adding animation using the setInterval() method and the CSS clip style. In this session, you explored how to write code for sliding menus and tabbed menus.

Key Terms

basic model	DOM Level 2	object-based language
built-in object	DOM Level 3	pop-up menu
camel case	dot syntax	property
document object	event	pull-down menu
document object model	IE4 DOM	read-only property
(DOM)	method	sliding menu
document tree	object collection	tabbed menu
DOM Level 0	object detection	this keyword
DOM Level 1	object name	W3C DOM

Practice | Review Assignments

Practice the skills you learned in the tutorial using the same case scenario.

Data Files needed for the Review Assignments: sherlocktxt.htm, slidestxt.js, arrow.gif, logo.jpg, mblog.css, sh.jpg

Kyle has made some modifications to the page layout of his Web site. Rather than having two sets of links—one at the top and one at the bottom—he has placed all of the links in the left page margin. There are still a lot of links on the page. Kyle wants you to design a sliding menu system in which hidden menus slide horizontally across the page to be revealed to the user. A preview of the completed page is shown in Figure 4-29.

Figure 4-29

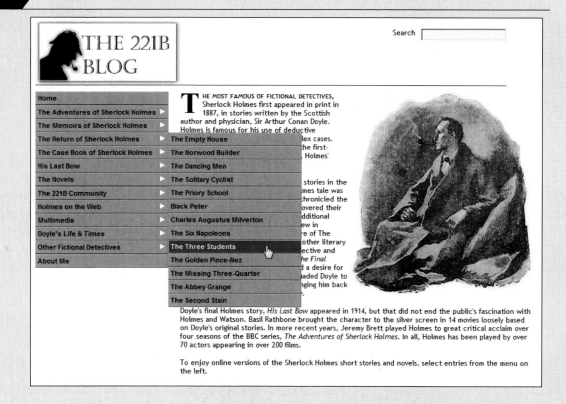

The structure of the links on this revised page has also changed. Rather than having menu titles and menu lists placed in separate div containers, Kyle opted to create a series of nested ordered lists containing the links. You'll have to take this new structure into account when you write your program.

Kyle also wants to change how the menus are activated. Menus should be displayed when the user clicks the menu title from the list of links. Menus should close whenever: (a) the user clicks another menu title, (b) the user clicks the main part of the page or the page head, and (c) the user clicks the same menu title twice. He does not want menu titles to be activated by the motions of the pointer.

Complete the following:

1. Using your text editor, open **sherlocktxt.htm** and **slidestxt.js** from the tutorial.04\ review folder, enter *your name* and *the date* in the head section of each file, and then save the files as **sherlock.htm** and **slides.js**, respectively.

2. Study the code of the **sherlock.htm** file in your text editor to understand the structure of the list of links on the page. Then, link the file to the **slides.js** JavaScript file and close it.

3. Return to the **slides.js** file in your text editor. Below the comments, insert a command to run the function makeMenus() when the browser has completed loading the page.

4. Add the following three global variables to the file:
   - **currentSlide** used to reference the sliding menu currently displayed in the document. Set its initial value to null.
   - **timeID** used to reference timed interval commands. Set its initial value to null.
   - **leftPos** used to store the left coordinate of the active sliding menu. Set its initial value to 0.

5. Add the **makeMenus()** function. The purpose of this function is to create a reference to all sliding menus in the document and to apply event handlers to objects in the document. Add the following commands to the function:
   a. Create an instance of the array object named **slideMenus**.
   b. Use the getElementsByTagName() method to store all of the elements in the document in an array named **allElems**.
   c. Loop through the elements in the allElems array, pushing all of the elements belonging to the slideMenu class into the slideMenus array.
   d. Loop through all of the items in the slideMenus array and apply the onclick event handler to those objects to run the showSlide() function. Also, for each object in the slideMenus array, reference the first ul element within that object and set the value of the ul elements left style property to 0px. This command moves all sliding menus (enclosed in unordered lists) to the far left of the page.
   e. Add onclick event handlers to the elements with ID values of head and main, running the closeSlide() function.

6. Add the **showSlide()** function to the file. The purpose of this function is to display a sliding menu on the Web page. In the first line of the function, create a variable named **slideList** that stores an object reference to the first ul element nested within the current object (as referenced by the `this` keyword).

7. Add an if statement to the showSlide() function. The purpose of the if statement is to test whether a sliding menu is currently displayed on the page. If the currentSlide object is not equal to null and the ID of the currentSlide is equal to the ID of the slideList variable, then run the closeSlide() function; otherwise, do the following:
   a. Run the closeSlide() function.
   b. Set the currentSlide variable equal to the slideList variable.
   c. Set the display style of the currentSlide variable to block.
   d. Run the moveSlide() function repeated at intervals of 1 millisecond. Store the ID of the timed function in timeID.

8. Add the **closeSlide()** function. The purpose of this function is to close any active sliding menu. Use object detection to confirm that the currentSlide variable is not equal to null and then run the following commands:
   a. Clear the timed function referenced by the timeID variable.
   b. Set the left style of the currentSlide object to 0px and set the display style to none.
   c. Set the value of currentSlide to null.

9. Add the **moveSlide()** function. The purpose of this function is to move a sliding menu horizontally across the page until the left coordinate of the menu exceeds 220 pixels. Add the following commands to the function:

   a. Increase the value of the leftPos variable by 5.

   b. If the value of the left position of the currentSlide object is less than or equal to 220, then set the left style of that object to the coordinates *leftPos*px where *leftPos* is the value of the leftPos variable.

   c. Otherwise, clear the timed function referenced by the timeID variable and reset the value of the leftPos variable to 0.

10. Close the file, saving your changes.

11. Open **sherlock.htm** in your Web browser. Click the links from the list containing a white triangle and verify that clicking those titles results in a submenu containing additional links sliding across the page. Also, verify that you can close a menu by clicking another title, clicking the same title twice, or clicking elsewhere in the main body of the Web page.

12. Submit the completed project to your instructor.

Apply	**Case Problem 1**

Use JavaScript to create a tabbed menu system.

Data Files needed for this Case Problem: printertxt.htm, jemenustxt.js, back.jpg, back2.jpg, je.css, logo.jpg, printer.jpg

Jackson Electronics Tara Dawson is in charge of Web site development for the product portion of the Jackson Electronics (JE) Web site. Recently the company began an overhaul of the site's design. One goal of the overhaul is to improve navigation of the site by placing links to different pages within a system of online menus. Tara asked you to work on the design of the home page describing JE's printer products.

Tara wants you to program a tabbed menu at the top of the page that will direct customers to the main sections of the JE Web site. This menu appears on every page in the site. Another list of links will direct users to pages directly related to the different JE printer products. Figure 4-30 shows a preview of the page's Electronics menu after the user clicked the Electronics tab on the menu.

Figure 4-30

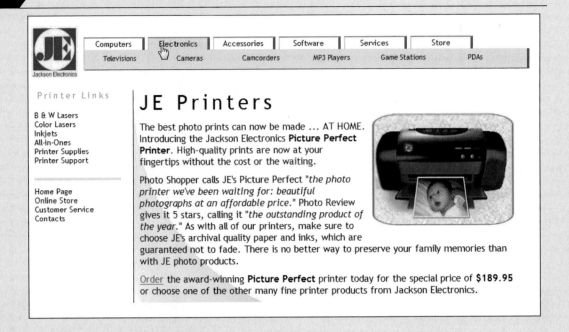

Complete the following:

1. Using your text editor, open the **printertxt.htm** and **jemenustxt.js** files from the tutorial.04\case1 folder, enter *your name* and *the date* in the comment section of each file, and then save the files as **printer.htm** and **jemenus.js**, respectively.

2. Examine the HTML code in the printer.htm file so that you are familiar with the structure of the list of links that make up the tabbed menu. When you're finished, link the file to the **jemenus.js** JavaScript file, and then close the printer.htm file.

3. Return to the **jemenus.js** file in your text editor. At the top of the file, create two global variables. The first, **currentTab**, will reference the current menu tab being displayed on the page. Set its initial value to null. The second variable, **maxZ**, will store the z-index of the currently displayed tab. Set its initial value to 1.

4. Add an event handler to run the setTabs() function after the page loads.

5. Create the **setTabs()** function. The purpose of this function is to create an array of all menu tabs in the document and to initialize the value of the currentTab object. Within the function, do the following:

   a. Declare an empty array named **menuTabs**.

   b. Use the getElementsByTagName() method to store all of the elements in the document in an array named **allElems**.

   c. Loop through the elements in the allElems array, pushing all of the elements belonging to the tab class into the menuTabs array.

   d. Set the currentTab object equal to the first item in the menuTabs array.

   e. For every item in the menuTabs array, add an onclick event handler that runs the showTab function.

6. Create the **showTab()** function. The purpose of this function is to show the currently selected tab and hide the old tab menu. Add the following commands to the function:

   a. Set the background color of the currentTab object to white.

   b. Increase the value of the maxZ variable by 1.

c. Declare a variable named tabList that references the first ul element nested within the this object.

d. Set the z-index value of the tabList object to the value of the maxZ variable.

e. Point the currentTab object to the tabList object.

f. Set the background color of the currentTab object to the color value (221, 221, 255).

7. Save your changes to the file.

8. Open the **printer.htm** file in your browser and verify that as you click different menu tabs at the top of the page, the browser displays a different submenu within the tab.

9. Submit the completed project to your instructor.

| Apply | **Case Problem 2** |

Use JavaScript to make an online puzzle interactive.

Data Files needed for this Case Problem: hanjietxt.htm, puzzletxt.js, blackbar.gif, jpf.css, jpf.jpg.

The Japanese Puzzle Factory Rebecca Peretz has been working on The Japanese Puzzle Factory Web site for several months. Created for people like her who share a love for Japanese logic puzzles, Rebecca is interested in using JavaScript to create online interactive puzzles.

Rebecca has asked you to help her create an online version of a hanjie puzzle. In a hanjie puzzle, users are presented with a blank grid in which they must click certain cells to reveal a hidden image. Each cell in the grid can be either dark or left blank. The clues to which cells darken are given by the headings of each table row or column, which lists the blocks of cells within the row or column that are to be darkened. For example, a column heading of 3 8 1 indicates that within the column there is a block of three dark cells, followed by a block of eight dark cells, and then a single dark cell. The space between the darkened blocks of cells can vary and is determined by the user, who studies the clues found in other row and column headings.

Rebecca has created a Web page containing a hanjie puzzle. The grid has been placed in a 20 × 25 table with row and column headings indicating the blocks of cells within each row or column to be darkened. The initial grid is blank. Rebecca wants users to be able to darken a table cell by clicking it. She also wants users to be able to check their progress by clicking a form button on the Web page. Users should also be able to reveal the puzzle's solution by clicking a form button. A preview of the Web page is shown in Figure 4-31.

Figure 4-31

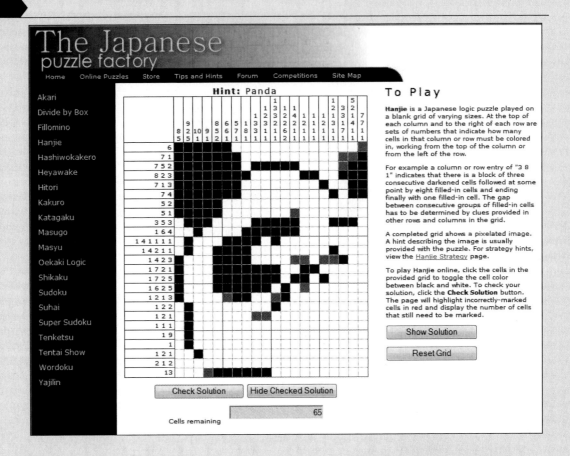

Rebecca has already written the HTML code for the puzzle page and has completed the CSS style sheet formatting the page's appearance and layout. She needs you to write the JavaScript code to make the puzzle interactive.

Complete the following:

1. Using your text editor, open the **hanjietxt.htm** and **puzzletxt.js** files in the tutorial.04\ case2 folder, enter *your name* and *the date* in the comment section of each file, and then save the files as **hanjie.htm** and **puzzle.js**, respectively.

2. Go to the **hanjie.htm** file in your text editor, study the contents and structure of the file, add a link to the **puzzle.js** external script file, and then close the file, saving your changes.

3. Return to the **puzzle.js** file in your text editor, and then add an event handler to the file, running the function setPuzzle() when the page is loaded.

4. Declare a global variable named **allCells**. The purpose of this variable will be to store the object collection of all of the cells in the hanjie puzzle grid.

5. Create the **setPuzzle()** function. The purpose of this function is to set the value of the allCells variable and to add event handlers to all of the cells within the puzzle. Add the following commands to this function:

   a. The cells in the hanjie puzzle have been stored in a table element with the ID name puzzleCells. Create a variable named **puzzleTable** that points to this object.

   b. Set the value of the allCells variable to point to all of the td elements within puzzleTable.

    c. Loop through the allCells object collection and for each item in the collection, set the background color to white and add an event handler that runs the change-Color() function when the cell is clicked.

    d. Within the Web page there are four input buttons with ID names of solution, hide, check, and uncheck. For the solution button, add an onclick event handler that runs the showSolution() function. For the hide button, add an onclick event handler to run the hideSolution() function. For the check button, add an onclick event handler to run the checkSolution() function. Finally, for the uncheck button, add an onclick event handler to run the uncheckSolution() function.

6. Create the **changeColor()** function. The purpose of this function is to toggle the background color of the active cell between black and white. Add a command to the function containing a conditional operator that tests whether the background style of the active object is equal to black. If it is, change the background color to white; otherwise, change the background color to black.

7. Create the **showSolution()** function. The purpose of this function is to reveal the hidden solution to the hanjie puzzle. The cells from the puzzle that should be filled in all belong to the dark class. To create the showSolution() function, add the following commands:

    a. Create a loop that loops through all of the objects within the allCells object collection.

    b. For each item within the allCells object collection, test whether the class name of the object is equal to dark. If so, change the background color to black; otherwise, change the background color to white.

    c. After the loop has completed, set the value of the checkCount field to 0.

8. Create the **hideSolution()** function. The purpose of this function is to reset the hanjie puzzle, hiding the solution and any guesses made by the user. Add the following commands to the function:

    a. Loop through all of the objects within the allCells object collection. For each item in the collection, set the background color to white.

    b. After the loop has completed, set the value of the checkCount field to an empty text string.

9. Create the **checkSolution()** function. The purpose of this function is to check whether the user's solution matches the actual solution of the hanjie puzzle. The function should display all incorrectly clicked cells in red. It should also count and display the number of cells that should be clicked but aren't. Add the following commands to the function:

    a. Declare a variable named **checkCount** and set its initial value to 0. The check-Count variable will keep track of the number of unclicked cells in the hanjie puzzle solution.

    b. Create a loop that loops through all of the objects in the allCells object collection.

    c. Within the loop, insert an if statement that tests whether the background color of the current item is black and the class name is not equal to dark; if so, change the background color to red. Otherwise, test whether the class name is equal to dark and the background color is white; if so, increase the value of the checkCount variable by 1.

    d. After the loop is finished, display the value of the checkCount variable in the checkCount field.

10. Create the **uncheckSolution()** function. The purpose of this function is to hide the results of checking the user's solution. Add the following commands to the function:
    a. Loop through all of the objects in the allCells object collection.
    b. For every object in the collection, test whether the background color is equal to red; if so, change the background color to black.
    c. After the loop is completed, display an empty text string in the checkCount field.
11. Close the **puzzle.js** file, saving your changes.
12. Open the **hanjie.htm** file in your Web browser. Click different cells within the puzzle, verifying that you can toggle the background color of each cell between white and black. Click the Show Solution button and verify that it reveals the hidden solution to the hanjie puzzle. Click the Reset Grid button and verify that it hides the puzzle's solution. Click some cells on the puzzle, attempting to solve or partially solve the puzzle, and then click the Check Solution button. Verify that cells that should not be selected are highlighted with a red background color, and that the number of unclicked cells appears in the Cells remaining input box. Click the Hide Checked Solution button and verify that the puzzle returns to your original solution.
13. Submit the completed Web site to your instructor.

| Challenge | **Case Problem 3** |

Explore how to use JavaScript to create a scrolling marquee.

Data Files needed for this Case Problem: bysotxt.htm, marqueetxt.js, bstyles.css, byso.jpg, bysologo.jpg

Boise Youth Symphony Orchestra Denise Young is the artistic director of the Boise Youth Symphony Orchestra from Boise, Idaho. She's asked for your help in writing JavaScript programs to augment the content of the group's Web site. One element that Denise wants to add to the site's home page is a list of upcoming concerts and events. Such lists can be long and cumbersome, and Denise has heard that she should keep the site's home page content to not much more than one full screen in height. She wants to place the list of upcoming events in a vertically scrolling marquee. A preview of the page with the scrolling marquee created using JavaScript is shown in Figure 4-32.

Figure 4-32

The marquee has been placed in a div container element. Descriptions of each event within the marquee have also been placed within their own separate div containers and positioned within the marquee using absolute positioning. To create the scrolling marquee, you'll use JavaScript to alter the top position of each event, rerunning the function at timed intervals to create the illusion of text moving vertically within the marquee box. All of the CSS styles and HTML tags have already been written for you. You need to write the JavaScript program to create the marquee effect.

Complete the following:

1. Using your text editor, open the **bysotxt.htm** and **marqueetxt.js** files from the tutorial.04\case3 folder, enter *your name* and *the date* in the comment section of each file, and then save the files as **byso.htm** and **marquee.js**, respectively.

2. Examine the HTML code in the byso.htm file. Pay close attention to how the different events within the marquee box are structured. Also compare the structure of the document with the styles contained in the bstyles.css style sheet file. When you understand how the marquee content is structured and laid out, link the file to the marquee.js JavaScript file.

3. Return to the **marquee.js** file in your text editor. Within the file, create three global variables named **timeID**, **marqueeTxt**, and **marqueeOff**. The timeID variable will store the ID of the time interval function used to scroll the marquee text. The marqueeTxt variable will store the array of text items in the marquee. The marqueeOff variable will store a Boolean value indicating if the marquee is not running. Set its initial value to true.

4. Have the browser run the defineMarquee() function when the page loads.

5. Create the **defineMarquee()** function. The purpose of this function is to set up the marquee object and define the event handlers that run the marquee. Add the following to the function:

   a. Populate the contents of the marqueeTxt array with all of the elements from the document that belong to the marqueeTxt class.

EXPLORE

   b. For every item in the marqueeTxt array, store the value of the top style from the CSS style sheet in a variable named **topValue**. (*Hint:* To extract the values from the style sheet, use object detection to determine the calculated CSS style value. Refer to the InSight in Session 4.3 for more information.) After you have calculated a value for the topValue variable, store that value in the top style property for the current item in the marqueeTxt array.

EXPLORE

   c. The Web page has two form buttons with ID values of startMarquee and stopMarquee. Add event handlers to these buttons to run the startMarquee() and stopMarquee() functions, respectively.

6. Create the **startMarquee()** function. The purpose of this function is to start the marquee scrolling. Add the following commands to the function:

   a. Insert an if condition that tests whether the value of the marqueeOff variable is true.

   b. If marqueeOff is true, then run the moveText() function at intervals of 50 milliseconds. Store the ID of the time interval in the timeID variable. Set the value of the marqueeOff variable to false.

7. Create the **stopMarquee()** function. The purpose of this function is to pause the marquee. Add the following commands to the function:

   a. Clear the time interval function indicated by the timeID variable.

   b. Reset the marqueeOff variable to true.

EXPLORE

8. Create the **moveText()** function. The purpose of this function is to move the text within the marquee in a vertical direction. Add the following commands to the function:

   a. Create a for loop that loops through each item in the marqueeTxt array.

   b. For each item, store the value of the top style in the variable topPos. Be sure to use the parseInt() method to extract the numeric value from the text string.

   c. If the value of topPos is less than –110, set the value of the top style for the marquee item to 700px; otherwise, decrease the value of the top style by 1. The value of –110 was chosen to allow the text to scroll up and off of the marquee box and out of sight from the user. The 700-pixel value was chosen to move the marquee text back down and below the marquee box, allowing it to scroll back into view from the bottom of the box.

9. Save your changes to the file.

EXPLORE

10. Open the **byso.htm** file in your Web browser. Click the Start Marquee button and verify that the text scrolls vertically up through the marquee box, reappearing again at the bottom of the box. Click the Pause Marquee button and verify that the scrolling action is paused until the Start Marquee button is pressed again.

11. Submit the completed project to your instructor.

Create	**Case Problem 4**

Test your knowledge of objects, properties, and methods by designing a menu system for a cooking Web site.

Data Files needed for this Case Problem: dinnerplate.txt, dplogo.jpg, torte.jpg

DinnerPlate Tara Anderson runs a Web site called *dinnerplate.com* in which people who share her love for cooking can post their favorite recipes, share tips, and learn about the art and science of cooking. Tara wants to put several links on the site's home page, linking her users to specific recipes for breakfast, lunch, and dinner, as well as recipes organized by food groups and dietary concerns. Worried that so many links will overwhelm the page layout, Tara would like to place these links in a simple-to-use menu system, written in JavaScript. Knowing that you have worked with JavaScript in the past, Tara has asked for your help in redesigning her home page with a JavaScript menu application.

Complete the following:

1. Use your text editor to create three files named **dinner.css**, **dinnerplate.htm**, and **menus.js**. Enter *your name*, *the date*, and a brief description of the files in the comment section of each document. Save the files in the tutorial.04\case4 folder.
2. The content for the dinnerplate.htm file is located in the **dinnerplate.txt** file. Use this content to design the site's home page. The design and layout of the page are up to you. You can also supplement the Web page with any additional content or features you decide are appropriate. The links on the page can all point to # to avoid having to create an extended folder of Web pages.
3. Place any formatting styles in the **dinner.css** file. Link the home page to both the dinner.css file and the menus.js file.
4. Add JavaScript commands to the **menu.js** file to create a menu system for the list of links in the dinnerplate.htm file. You can choose any type of menu system that you believe will work with the content of the page. Document your code to make it easy for other users to understand and interpret your program.
5. Test your code against the list of links in the **dinnerplate.htm** file, verifying that you can open and close the menus in a simple and intuitive way.
6. Submit the completed Web site to your instructor.

Review	**Quick Check Answers**

Session 4.1

1. The document object model is the organized structure of objects found within a Web document and within the Web browser.
2. `navigator`
3. `document.links[1]`
4. `document.getElementById("footer")`
5. `document.getElementsByTagName("p")[1]`
6. `document.forms[0].action = "http://www.avalon.mailer.cgi";`
7. `document.getElementsByTagName("div")[1].className = "blueBackground";`
8. `document.getElementById("main").style.border = "2px solid black";`
9. ```
for (var i = 0; i < document.links.length; i++) {
    document.links[i].style.textDecoration = "none";
}
```
```

Session 4.2

1. `object.method()`

   where *object* is the name of the object and *method* is a method that applies to the object.

2. `location.reload()`

3. `document.getElementById("pullMenu").onclick = showMenu;`

4.
```
for (var i = 0; i < document.links.length; i++) {
    document.links[i].onclick = showLinks;
}
```

5. You do not include the parentheses when assigning a function to an event handler. The correct form of the expression is:

   `document.getElementById("slide").onclick = loadImage;`

6. Object detection is the confirmation that an object exists or is supported by the browser before attempting to use it in an expression.

7. `if (document.all) showMenu();`

8. `document.getElementById("pullMenu").onmouseover = showMenu;`

Session 4.3

1. `document.getElementById("mainDIV").style.clip = "rect(0px, 100px, 50px, 0px)";`

2. `setInterval("slideMenu()", 1000);`

3. `document.getElementById("Menu1").style.top =`
   `parseInt(document.getElementById("Menu1").style.top) + 5 + "px";`

4. `document.getElementById("Menu1").style.zIndex += 1;`

5. No value is returned. The problem is that you cannot use the style property to read CSS style values from a style sheet. You can only read style values set in other JavaScript commands or with the style attribute in an inline style.

6. For the IE DOM, use:

   `document.getElementById("Menu1").currentStyle("font-size")`

   For the W3C DOM, use:

   `document.defaultView.getComputedStyle(document.`
   `getElementById("Menu1"), null).getPropertyValue("font-size")`

Ending Data Files

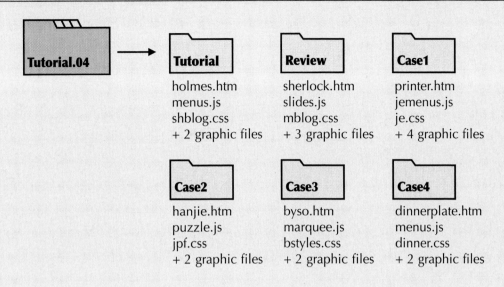

Tutorial.04 →

Tutorial
holmes.htm
menus.js
shblog.css
+ 2 graphic files

Review
sherlock.htm
slides.js
mblog.css
+ 3 graphic files

Case1
printer.htm
jemenus.js
je.css
+ 4 graphic files

Case2
hanjie.htm
puzzle.js
jpf.css
+ 2 graphic files

Case3
byso.htm
marquee.js
bstyles.css
+ 2 graphic files

Case4
dinnerplate.htm
menus.js
dinner.css
+ 2 graphic files

Objectives

Session 5.1
- Understand how to reference form element objects
- Extract data from Web form fields
- Create a calculated field

Session 5.2
- Understand the principles of form validation
- Perform a client-side validation
- Work with string objects

Session 5.3
- Work with regular expressions
- Apply regular expressions to zip code fields
- Validate credit card numbers

Working with Forms and Regular Expressions

Validating a Web Form with JavaScript

Case | GPS-ware

GPS-ware is a company that specializes in mapping and global positioning software and hardware. The company is in the planning stages of making its products available online. Carol Campbell is heading the development effort and asks you to help develop a Web form for domestic sales.

A GPS-ware employee has already created three Web forms for the Web site. The forms include fields in which users enter the details of their purchases, delivery information, and credit card data. Carol wants the forms to automatically calculate the cost of a user's order and validate any data the user has entered. All of this should be done before the form is submitted to the Web server for processing.

Starting Data Files

Tutorial.05 →

Tutorial
done.htm
form1txt.htm
form2txt.htm
form3txt.htm
contacttxt.js
ordertxt.js
paytxt.js
gpsware.css
+ 2 graphic files

Review
done.htm
ordertxt.htm
formtxt.js
gps.css
+ 2 graphic files

Case1
mpltxt.htm
linkstxt.js
mplstyles.css
mpl.jpg

Case2
done.htm
exptxt.htm
reporttxt.js
exp.css
+ 3 graphic files

Case3
conftxt.htm
sumtxt.htm
formstxt.js
conf.css
summary.css
+ 4 graphic files

Case4
info.txt
functions.js
+ 2 graphic files

Demo
demo_form1.htm
demo_form2.htm
demo_regcodes.htm
demo_regexp.htm
+ 3 graphic files

JVS 216 JavaScript Tutorial 5 Working with Forms and Regular Expressions

Session 5.1

Working with Forms and Fields

GPS-ware has three forms related to online ordering that you'll be working with. Figure 5-1 shows the structure of these forms. Customers enter order information in the first form, delivery information in the second form, and method of payment in the third form.

Figure 5-1   GPS-ware online ordering forms

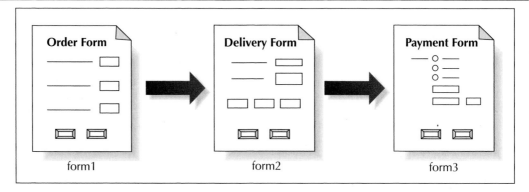

You'll open the files used on the GPS-ware Web site.

To open the order forms:

▶ 1. Use your text editor to open the **form1txt.htm**, **form2txt.htm**, **form3txt.htm**, **ordertxt.js**, **contacttxt.js**, and **paytxt.js** files from the tutorial.05\tutorial folder, enter *your name* and *the date* in the comment section of each file, and then save the files as **form1.htm**, **form2.htm**, **form3.htm**, **order.js**, **contact.js**, and **payment.js**, respectively.

▶ 2. Close all the files except form1.htm and order.js, return to the **form1.htm** file in your text editor, and then review the HTML code used in the file.

▶ 3. In the head section of the document, insert the following code to create a link to the order.js JavaScript file:

```
<script type = "text/javascript" src = "order.js"></script>
```

▶ 4. Close the file, saving your changes.

▶ 5. Open **form1.htm** in your Web browser. Figure 5-2 shows the current content and layout of the page, including the names assigned to the different form elements.

GPS-ware order form and element names | Figure 5-2

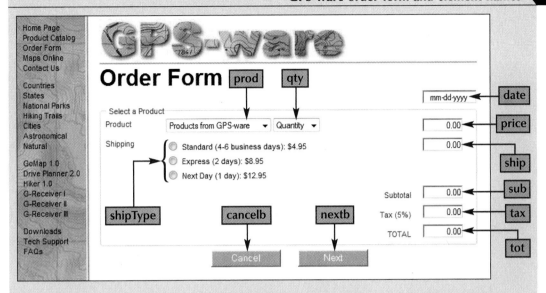

The date field and any fields that display the cost of the product, tax, or shipping are set to read-only. You cannot enter data in the fields; the values can only be set using JavaScript.

Customers use the order form to select a GPS-ware product to purchase, indicating the product name, quantity, and shipping method. Customers can choose from three shipping options: standard, which costs $4.95 and arrives in four to six business days; express, which costs $8.95 and arrives in two days; and overnight, which costs $12.95. The company also charges a 5% tax on online orders. Carol wants this form to calculate the cost of the purchased items, add the shipping cost, determine the tax, and then calculate the total order cost. All of these calculations should be done automatically by the browser. At the top of the form is a date field, which will display the current date. Carol wants the Web browser to enter this information automatically as well.

To set up the form, you'll create a function named startForm() that runs automatically after the page is loaded. You'll place this function and other JavaScript functions used with the form1.htm file in the order.js file.

To insert the startForm() function:

1. Return to the **order.js** file in your text editor.

2. Directly below the comment section, add the following statement to run the startForm() function when the page is loaded:

   ```
   window.onload = startForm;
   ```

3. Below the todayTxt() function, insert the following code for the startForm() function, as shown in Figure 5-3:

   ```
   function startForm() {
   }
   ```

Figure 5-3 ▶ **Code for the startForm() function**

```
window.onload = startForm;

function todayTxt() {
    var Today = new Date();
    return Today.getMonth() + 1 + "-" + Today.getDate() + "-" + Today.getFullYear();
}

function startForm() {
}
```

▶ **4.** Save your changes to the file.

Referencing a Web Form

To program the behavior and contents of a Web form, you must work with the properties and methods of the form object and the elements it contains. As shown in Figure 5-4, Web forms and their elements are part of the hierarchy of objects within a Web document.

Figure 5-4 ▶ **Forms hierarchy**

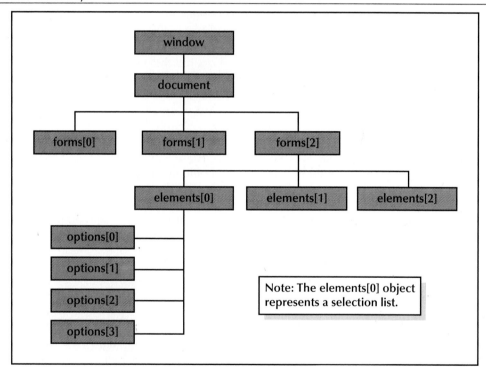

Because a Web page can contain multiple Web forms, JavaScript supports an object collection for forms. You can access a form within the current document using the object reference

```
document.forms[idref]
```

where *idref* is the ID or index number of the form. JavaScript also allows you to reference a form by its name attribute, using the object reference

```
document.webform
```

where *webform* is the value of the name attribute assigned to the form. In addition, you can always use the document.getElementById() method to reference a form based on the value of its ID attribute.

Carol assigned the ID form1 to the form, and this form is the first (and only) form on the Web page. Based on this information, you can access the form using either of the following object references:

```
document.forms[0]
```

or

```
document.forms["form1"]
```

Referencing a Form Element

The elements within a form, including all input fields, buttons, and labels, are organized into an elements collection. You can reference a form element by its position in the elements collection as follows

```
formObject.elements[idref]
```

where *formObject* is the reference to the form, and *idref* is the index number of the element within the form or the value of the name or ID attribute for the element. You can also reference the element using the syntax

```
formObject.idref
```

where *idref* is either the name or the ID of the element. For example, the first element in Carol's order form is the date input box. To reference this object, you use any of the following expressions:

```
document.forms[0].elements[0]
document.forms[0].elements["date"]
document.forms[0].date
```

If the element is a selection list, it contains its own object collection consisting of the options within the list. Likewise, option buttons belonging to the same group have a unique syntax. You'll examine how to work with both selection lists and option buttons later in this session.

Figure 5-5 lists the object references for the fields and buttons in Carol's order form. The object references are drawn from the element names, which were displayed earlier in Figure 5-2.

Tip

Because XHTML under the strict DTD does not support the name attribute of the form element, you must use the ID attribute to identify form elements.

Figure 5-5 ▷ **Objects in the order form**

Object	Reference
order form	document.forms[0]
date field	document.forms[0].date
product selection list	document.forms[0].prod
quantity selection list	document.forms[0].qty
price of the product field	document.forms[0].price
group of shipping options	document.forms[0].shipType
shipping cost field	document.forms[0].ship
subtotal field	document.forms[0].sub
tax field	document.forms[0].tax
total field	document.forms[0].tot
cancel button	document.forms[0].cancelb
next button	document.forms[0].nextb

Reference Window | **Referencing Form Objects**

- To access a Web form, use the object reference
    ```
    document.forms[idref]
    ```
    where *idref* is the ID or index number of the form. You can also use
    ```
    document.fname
    ```
    where *fname* is the name of the form.
- To reference an element within a form, use the object reference
    ```
    formObject.elements[idref]
    ```
    where formObject is the object reference to the form and *idref* is the ID or index number
    of the form element. You can also use
    ```
    formObject.ename
    ```
    where *ename* is the name of the form element.

Working with Input Fields

The first task on Carol's list is to display the current date in the Web form. To change the value of the date field, you need to work with the properties and methods of input fields.

Setting the Field Value

You use the value property to set the value contained in a field such as an input box. The general syntax of the value property is

```
formObject.element.value = fieldvalue;
```

where *formObject* is a reference to the Web form, *element* is the object reference to an element within the form, and *fieldvalue* is the value you want placed in the field. For example, to have the date field display the text string 6-23-2011, you would run the following command:

```
document.forms[0].date.value = "6-23-2011";
```

The value property is one of many properties and methods associated with input fields. Figure 5-6 shows some of the others.

Properties and methods of the input field ◀ Figure 5-6

Property	Description
defaultvalue	The default value that is initially displayed in the field
form	References the form containing the field
maxlength	The maximum number of characters allowed in the field
name	The name of the field
size	The width of the input field in characters
type	The type of input field (button, check box, file, hidden, image, password, radio, reset, submit, text)
value	The current value of the field

Method	Description
blur()	Remove the focus from the field
focus()	Give focus to the field
select()	Select the field

Working with Fields
| Reference Window

- To set the value of a form field, use the object property
    ```
    field.value = fieldValue
    ```
  where *field* is the reference to the form field and *fieldValue* is the value you want to assign to the field.
- To move the focus to a form field, use the following method:
    ```
    field.focus()
    ```

Carol created a function named todayTxt() that returns a text string with the current date in the format *mm-dd-yyyy*. She's already stored this function in the order.js file. Using this function, you can display the current date in the date field with the following command:

```
document.forms[0].date.value = todayTxt();
```

You'll add this command to the startForm() function.

To display the current date in the form:

▶ **1.** Within the startForm() function in the order.js file, insert the following command:

```
document.forms[0].date.value = todayTxt();
```

▶ **2.** Save your changes to the file.

Navigating Between Fields

Carol wants the product selection list to be selected automatically when the form opens, so it is ready for data entry. When a form element is selected either by clicking it or moving into it using keyboard buttons or arrows, it receives the **focus** of the browser. To program this action, you use the focus() method, which has the following general syntax:

```
formObject.element.focus();
```

Running this command makes the *element* the selected object in the Web form. Java-Script can also deselect a form object by using the blur() method, which has the following general syntax:

```
formObject.element.blur();
```

Using the focus() and blur() methods, you can alternately select and deselect elements in the Web form, controlling the user's navigation through the form. The product selection list has the field name prod. So to force this field to be selected automatically when the page opens, you run the following command:

```
document.forms[0].prod.focus();
```

You'll add this command to the startForm() function.

Tip

Applying the blur() method to an object deselects that object on the Web page without selecting anything else. You can also blur a field by applying the focus to another object on the page.

To select the product selection list:

1. In the **order.js** file, add the following command to the end of the startForm() function, as shown in Figure 5-7:

   document.forms[0].prod.focus();

Figure 5-7 Focus set to the prod field

```
function startForm() {
    document.forms[0].date.value = todayTxt();
    document.forms[0].prod.focus();
}
```

2. Save your changes to the file, and then reload **form1.htm** in your Web browser. The current date appears in the date field and the product selection list is selected. See Figure 5-8.

Figure 5-8 Current date and focus added to the form

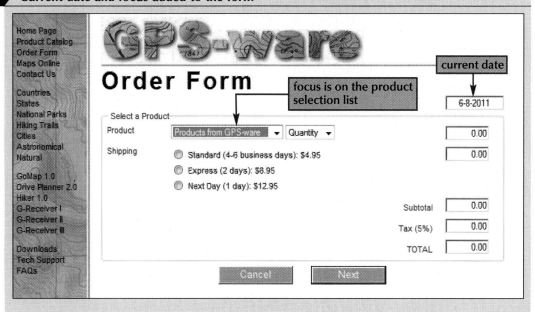

Working with Selection Lists

In the rest of the form, you need to create functions to calculate the cost of a customer's order. This involves: (1) determining the price of the order (equal to the price of the product multiplied by the quantity ordered), (2) determining the shipping cost, (3) calculating the sales tax, and (4) adding all of these costs to determine the grand total. You'll start by creating a function to calculate the price of the order.

The product prices and quantities are both placed within selection lists. However, unlike an input box, no value property exists for an entire selection list, only for each option within the list. For example, the product selection list contains the following options and values:

```
<select name = "prod" id = "prod">
   <option value = "0">Products from GPS-ware</option>
   <option value = "19.95">GoMap 1.0 ($19.95)</option>
   <option value = "29.95">Drive Planner 2.0 ($29.95)</option>
   <option value = "29.95">Hiker 1.0 ($29.95)</option>
   <option value = "149.50">G-Receiver I ($149.50)</option>
   <option value = "199.50">G-Receiver II ($199.50)</option>
   <option value = "249.50">G-Receiver III ($249.50)</option>
</select>
```

JavaScript organizes all of the options into an options collection contained within the selection list object. The syntax to reference a particular option in the collection is

```
selection.options[idref]
```

where *selection* is the reference to the selection list object and *idref* is the index number or ID of the option. Each option in the selection list supports text and value properties specifying the text and value associated with the option. Figure 5-9 shows the text and value properties for the different options in the product selection list.

Properties in the product selection list | Figure 5-9

object	object.text	object.value
document.forms[0].prod.options[0]	Products from GPS-ware	0
document.forms[0].prod.options[1]	GoMap 1.0 ($19.95)	19.95
document.forms[0].prod.options[2]	Drive Planner 2.0 ($29.95)	29.95
document.forms[0].prod.options[3]	Hiker 1.0 ($29.95)	29.95
document.forms[0].prod.options[4]	G-Receiver I ($149.50)	149.50
document.forms[0].prod.options[5]	G-Receiver II ($199.50)	199.50
document.forms[0].prod.options[6]	G-Receiver III ($249.50)	249.50

Figure 5-10 summarizes the properties of both selection list objects and selection list option objects.

Figure 5-10 ▶ **Properties of selection list and selection list options**

selection list	Property	Description
	length	The number of options in the list
	name	The name of the selection list
	options	The collection of options in the list
	selectedIndex	The index number of the currently selected option in the list

selection list option	Property	Description
	defaultSelected	A Boolean value indicating whether the option is selected by default
	index	The index value of the option
	selected	A Boolean value indicating whether the option is currently selected
	text	The text associated with the option
	value	The value associated with the option

Because there is no value property for the entire selection list, you use the value or text of the selected option in any calculations you need to perform. To determine the currently selected option in a list, you use the selectedIndex property of the selection list object. The following code demonstrates how you would determine the price associated with a product selected by a customer:

```
product = document.forms[0].prod;
pIndex = product.selectedIndex;
productPrice = product.options[pIndex].value;
```

In this code, the product variable stores the object reference to the product selected in the form1 Web form. The pIndex variable stores the index of the currently selected option (whatever that may be). Finally, the productPrice variable stores the value of that selected option, which is the product's price. The code to determine the quantity ordered is similar:

```
quantity = document.form1.qty;
qIndex = quantity.selectedIndex;
quantityOrdered = quantity.options[qIndex].value;
```

To calculate the total price for a given product, you multiply the price of the product by the quantity ordered. The following calcPrice() function performs the necessary calculation to determine the price, and then displays the value in the price field of the Web form:

```
function calcPrice() {
   product = document.forms[0].prod;
   pIndex = product.selectedIndex;
   productPrice = product.options[pIndex].value;

   quantity = document.forms[0].qty;
   qIndex = quantity.selectedIndex;
   quantityOrdered = quantity.options[qIndex].value;

   document.forms[0].price.value = productPrice*quantityOrdered;
}
```

You'll add this function to the order.js file.

To add the calcPrice() function:

▶ **1.** Return to the **order.js** file in your text editor.

▶ **2.** At the bottom of the file, insert the following calcPrice() function, as shown in Figure 5-11:

```
function calcPrice() {
    product = document.forms[0].prod;
    pIndex = product.selectedIndex;
    productPrice = product.options[pIndex].value;

    quantity = document.forms[0].qty;
    qIndex = quantity.selectedIndex;
    quantityOrdered = quantity.options[qIndex].value;

    document.forms[0].price.value = productPrice*quantityOrdered;
}
```

Code for the calcPrice() function ◀ **Figure 5-11**

```
function calcPrice() {
    product = document.forms[0].prod;
    pIndex = product.selectedIndex;
    productPrice = product.options[pIndex].value;

    quantity = document.forms[0].qty;
    qIndex = quantity.selectedIndex;
    quantityOrdered = quantity.options[qIndex].value;

    document.forms[0].price.value = productPrice*quantityOrdered;
}
```

code to return the price of the selected product

code to return the index of the selected quantity

cost is equal to the product price multiplied by the quantity ordered

▶ **3.** Save your changes to the file.

You want to run the calcPrice() function whenever a user selects a new option from either the product or the quantity selection lists. One way of doing this is to use the onchange event handler, which runs a command whenever the selected option in the list changes. You can add the onchange event handler to the product and quantity selection lists to associate the calcPrice() function with the action of changing the prod or qty selection, as follows:

```
document.forms[0].prod.onchange = calcPrice;
document.forms[0].qty.onchange = calcPrice;
```

You'll add these two commands to the startForm() function, and then test them by reloading the form1 Web page.

To apply the onchange event handler:

▶ **1.** Scroll the order.js file up to the startForm() function.

▶ **2.** Within the startForm() function, add the following commands, as shown in Figure 5-12:

```
document.forms[0].prod.onchange = calcPrice;
document.forms[0].qty.onchange = calcPrice;
```

Figure 5-12 **Code to insert the onchange event handler**

```
function startForm() {
    document.forms[0].date.value = todayTxt();
    document.forms[0].prod.focus();

    document.forms[0].prod.onchange = calcPrice;
    document.forms[0].qty.onchange = calcPrice;
}
```

> runs the calcPrice() function when the selected product or the selected quantity changes

▶ **3.** Save your changes to the file, and then reload **form1.htm** in your Web browser.

▶ **4.** Select **Hiker 1.0 ($29.95)** from the selection list in the product list box, and then select **2** from the quantity list box. As you select these options (changing the selected options in the list), the value in the price field is updated. See Figure 5-13.

Figure 5-13 **Order price calculated based on the selected product and quantity**

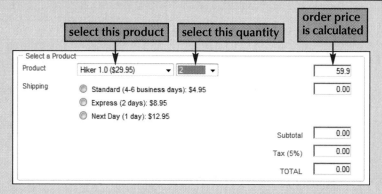

select this product   select this quantity   order price is calculated

Select a Product
Product   Hiker 1.0 ($29.95)   ▼ 2 ▼   59.9
Shipping   ◉ Standard (4-6 business days): $4.95   0.00
           ◉ Express (2 days): $8.95
           ◉ Next Day (1 day): $12.95

                                    Subtotal   0.00
                                    Tax (5%)   0.00
                                    TOTAL   0.00

▶ **5.** Select other product and quantity options, verifying that the price field automatically changes in response. For some product/quantity combinations, the value in the price field is not displayed with a two-digit cents value. You'll learn to format the calculated output to always show the price in dollars and cents later in this session.

Reference Window | **Working with Selection Lists**

- To determine which option in a selection list has been selected, use the object property
    `selection.selectedIndex`
  where *selection* is the selection list object.
- To extract the text of an option in a selection list, use the object reference
    `selection.options[idref].text`
  where *idref* is the index number or ID of the option.
- To extract the value of an option in a selection list, use the following object reference:
    `selection.options[idref].value`

Some selection lists are set up to collect multiple selections. In those cases, the selectedIndex property returns only the index number of the first selected item. If you want to determine the indices of all the selected items, you must create a for loop that runs through all of the options in the list, checking each to determine whether the selected property is true (indicating that the option was selected by the user). If the option is selected, it can then be added to an array of the selected options using the push() method. The general structure of the for loop is

```
var selectedOpt = new Array();
for (var i = 0; i < selection.options.length; i++) {
    if (selection.options[i].selected) {
        selectedOpt.push(selection.options[i]);
    }
}
```

where *selection* is a selection list object within a Web form. After this code is run, the selectedOpt array will contain all of the options within the selection list that have been chosen by the user. To work with the selected options, you can create a for loop that loops through all of the items in the selectedOpt array to extract the text and value properties from each.

Working with Option Buttons and Check Boxes

Your next task is to display the cost of the shipping option that a user selects. Carol has placed the shipping options within a group of option buttons using the following HTML tags:

```
<input type = "radio" name = "shipType" id = "ship1" value = "4.95" />
<input type = "radio" name = "shipType" id = "ship2" value = "8.95" />
<input type = "radio" name = "shipType" id = "ship3" value = "12.95" />
```

Carol wants you to write a program that will enter the shipping value into the Web form whenever the user clicks one of these three option buttons.

Using Option Buttons

Because each option button in a group shares a common name value, JavaScript places the individual buttons within that group into an array. Individual option buttons have the reference

options[idref]

where *options* is the name assigned to the group of option buttons and *idref* is either the index number or the ID of the individual option button within that group. In Carol's form, either of the following object references could be used for the first shipType option button:

```
document.forms[0].shipType[0]
document.forms[0].shipType["ship1"]
```

Figure 5-14 describes some of the properties associated with option buttons.

Figure 5-14 ▸ **Properties of option buttons**

Property	Description
checked	A Boolean value indicating whether the option button is currently selected
defaultChecked	A Boolean value indicating whether the option button is selected by default
name	The name of the option button
value	The value associated with the option button

You can use a for loop to move through all of the option buttons within the group. You'll use this for loop to assign an onclick event handler to each button, running the calcShipping() function (which you'll create shortly) when the button is clicked. The JavaScript code for the for loop is:

```
for (var i = 0; i < document.forms[0].shipType.length; i++) {
   document.forms[0].shipType[i].onclick = calcShipping;
}
```

You'll add this code to the startForm() function.

To add onclick event handlers to the shipType option buttons:

1. Return to the **order.js** file in your text editor.

2. Within the startForm() function, insert the following code, as shown in Figure 5-15:

```
for (var i = 0; i < document.forms[0].shipType.length; i++) {
   document.forms[0].shipType[i].onclick = calcShipping;
}
```

Figure 5-15 ▸ **onclick event handlers added to the shipType field**

```
function startForm() {
   document.forms[0].date.value = todayTxt();
   document.forms[0].prod.focus();

   document.forms[0].prod.onchange = calcPrice;
   document.forms[0].qty.onchange = calcPrice;

   for (var i = 0; i < document.forms[0].shipType.length; i++) {
      document.forms[0].shipType[i].onclick = calcShipping;
   }
}
```

every time a shipping type option button is clicked, the browser runs the calcShipping() function

3. Save your changes to the file.

The calcShipping() function takes the value of the clicked option button and places it in the ship field of the Web form. The code for the function is:

```
function calcShipping() {
   document.forms[0].ship.value = this.value;
}
```

The function uses the this keyword to reference the option button that was clicked, running the calcShipping() function. You'll add this function to the order.js file and test it in your Web browser.

To add and test the calcShipping() function:

▶ **1.** Scroll to the bottom of the file, and then insert the following function, as shown in Figure 5-16:

```
function calcShipping() {
    document.forms[0].ship.value = this.value;
}
```

Code for the calcShipping() function ◀ **Figure 5-16**

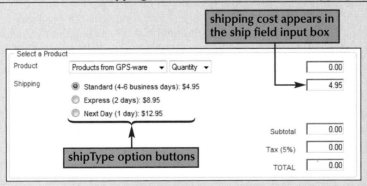

```
        document.forms[0].price.value = productPrice*quantityOrdered;
    }
    function calcShipping() {
        document.forms[0].ship.value = this.value;
    }
```

the this keyword references the currently selected object

▶ **2.** Save your changes to the file, and then reload **form1.htm** in your Web browser.

▶ **3.** Click the **Standard** option button, and then verify that 4.95 appears in the ship field input box. See Figure 5-17.

Shipping cost based on the selected shipping option button ◀ **Figure 5-17**

shipping cost appears in the ship field input box

Select a Product

| Product | Products from GPS-ware ▾ | Quantity ▾ | | 0.00 |

Shipping
  ◉ Standard (4-6 business days): $4.95 — 4.95
  ◯ Express (2 days): $8.95
  ◯ Next Day (1 day): $12.95

shipType option buttons

Subtotal	0.00
Tax (5%)	0.00
TOTAL	0.00

▶ **4.** Click the other shipping option buttons and verify that the corresponding shipping cost appears in the ship field's input box.

Reference Window | Working with Option Button Groups

- To reference a specific option button within a group, use the object reference
    `options[idref]`
  where *options* is the reference to the option button group and *idref* is the ID or index number of the option button.
- To determine whether an option button is currently checked, use the object property
    `options[idref].checked`
  which returns the Boolean value true if the button is checked.
- To determine which button in the option button group is checked, create a for loop that examines each option button's checked property, returning the index of the checked button.

Working with Check Boxes

Carol's order form contains no check boxes, which work the same way as option buttons. Like an option button, a check box supports the checked property, indicating whether the box is checked. In addition, the value associated with a check box is stored in the value property of the check box object. However, this value is applied only when the check box is checked; if a check box is not checked, its field has no value assigned to it. As with option buttons, you can run a function in response to the click event by applying the onclick event handler to the check box. However, unlike option buttons, each entry field has only one check box.

Creating Calculated Fields

To complete Carol's Web form, you need to calculate the form's remaining values: the subtotal (the product price plus the shipping cost), the sales tax, and the total cost of the order (the subtotal plus the sales tax). JavaScript treats the contents of input fields as text strings. This means you cannot simply add the input field values together because JavaScript would append the text strings rather than add the values they represent. For example, if the value in the price field is 39.9 and the value in the ship field is 9.95, adding the two field values returns the text string 39.99.95. If you want to treat the contents of input fields as numeric values, you must first convert them from text strings to numbers.

One way of converting a text string to a numeric value is to use the parseFloat() method. Recall that the parseFloat() method extracts the leading numeric value from a text string, returning a number instead of a text string in the process. The following set of commands uses the parseFloat() method to add the numeric values stored in the price and ship fields, storing the result in the sub field:

```
priceVal = parseFloat(document.forms[0].price.value);
shipVal = parseFloat(document.forms[0].ship.value);
document.forms[0].sub.value = priceVal + shipVal;
```

You'll use these commands in a function named calcTotal(), which calculates the values of the subtotal, tax, and total fields.

To create the calcTotal() function:

▶ **1.** Return to the **order.js** file in your text editor.

▶ **2.** Scroll to the bottom of the file, and then insert the following function, as shown in Figure 5-18:

```
function calcTotal() {
    priceVal = parseFloat(document.forms[0].price.value);
    shipVal = parseFloat(document.forms[0].ship.value);
    document.forms[0].sub.value = priceVal + shipVal;
}
```

Code for the calcTotal() function ◀ **Figure 5-18**

```
function calcShipping() {
    document.forms[0].ship.value = this.value;
}

function calcTotal() {
    priceVal = parseFloat(document.forms[0].price.value);
    shipVal = parseFloat(document.forms[0].ship.value);
    document.forms[0].sub.value = priceVal + shipVal;
}
```

subtotal is equal to the cost of the item ordered plus the shipping cost

You need to calculate the sales tax on the purchase, which is 5% of the subtotal, and the total cost of the sale, which is the cost of the sales tax plus the purchase cost. These two values are stored in the tax and tot fields, respectively. The code to calculate and store these values is:

```
taxVal = 0.05*(priceVal + shipVal);
document.forms[0].tax.value = taxVal;
document.forms[0].tot.value = priceVal + shipVal + taxVal;
```

You'll add these statements to the calcTotal() function.

To complete the calcTotal() function:

▶ **1.** Insert the following commands in the calcTotal() function, as shown in Figure 5-19:

```
taxVal = 0.05*(priceVal + shipVal);
document.forms[0].tax.value = taxVal;

document.forms[0].tot.value = priceVal + shipVal + taxVal;
```

Code to calculate 5% sales tax and the total price ◀ **Figure 5-19**

```
function calcTotal() {
    priceVal = parseFloat(document.forms[0].price.value);
    shipVal = parseFloat(document.forms[0].ship.value);
    document.forms[0].sub.value = priceVal + shipVal;

    taxVal = 0.05*(priceVal + shipVal);
    document.forms[0].tax.value = taxVal;

    document.forms[0].tot.value = priceVal + shipVal + taxVal;
}
```

total cost is equal to the sum of the cost of the item(s) ordered plus the shipping cost plus sales tax

▶ **2.** Save your changes to the file.

You want to run the calcTotal() function whenever a customer makes a selection on the form. This occurs when a product or quantity is picked from a selection list or when a shipping option is selected. Because you have already created event handlers for each of those actions to run the calcPrice() and calcShipping() functions, you can simply add a command to the end of those functions to run calcTotal().

To run the calcTotal() function:

▶ **1.** Scroll up the file and insert the following command into both the calcPrice() and calcShipping() functions, as shown in Figure 5-20:

```
calcTotal();
```

Figure 5-20 | Code to call the calcTotal() function

```
function calcPrice() {
    product = document.forms[0].prod;
    pIndex = product.selectedIndex;
    productPrice = product.options[pIndex].value;

    quantity = document.forms[0].qty;
    qIndex = quantity.selectedIndex;
    quantityOrdered = quantity.options[qIndex].value;

    document.forms[0].price.value = productPrice*quantityOrdered;

    calcTotal();
}

function calcShipping() {
    document.forms[0].ship.value = this.value;

    calcTotal();
}
```

> calls the calcTotal() function to update the total value displayed on the Web form

▶ **2.** Save your changes to the file, and then reload **form1.htm** in your Web browser.

▶ **3.** Select **Drive Planner 2.0 ($29.95)** from the product selection list, select **2** from the quantity selection list, and then click the **Standard (4–6 business days): $4.95** option button. As you select each option, the subtotal, tax, and total values automatically update in the Web form. See Figure 5-21.

Figure 5-21 | Subtotal, tax, and total values updated based on the selected options

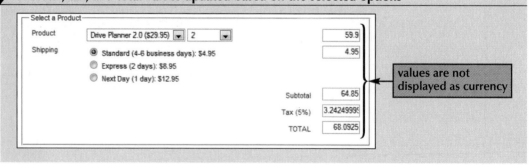

Select a Product
Product	Drive Planner 2.0 ($29.95)	2		59.9
Shipping	⦿ Standard (4-6 business days): $4.95			4.95
	◯ Express (2 days): $8.95			
	◯ Next Day (1 day): $12.95			

> values are not displayed as currency

Subtotal 64.85
Tax (5%) 3.24249999
TOTAL 68.0925

Using the options you selected, the form automatically calculates the subtotal value to be $64.85, the tax value to be approximately $3.24, and the total cost of the order to be about $68.09. Because of how numeric values are stored and calculated, the sales tax and the total price are displayed beyond two-decimal-point accuracy. All the monetary values need to be displayed only to two decimal places because they represent dollars and cents. To do this, you can apply the toFixed() method to the numeric values, which converts a number to a text string, displaying the value to a specified number of digits. Recall that the syntax of the toFixed() method is

```
value.toFixed(n)
```

where *value* is the numeric value and *n* is the number of digits displayed by the browser. You'll apply this method to the values calculated by JavaScript.

To apply the toFixed() method:

▶ **1.** Return to the **order.js** file in your text editor.

▶ **2.** In the calcPrice() function, change the statement that sets the value of the price field to:

```
document.forms[0].price.value = (productPrice*quantityOrdered).
  toFixed(2);
```

▶ **3.** In the calcTotal() function, change the statements that set the values of the sub, tax, and tot field to the following:

```
document.forms[0].sub.value = (priceVal + shipVal).toFixed(2);
document.forms[0].tax.value = taxVal.toFixed(2);
document.forms[0].tot.value = (priceVal + shipVal + taxVal).
toFixed(2);
```

You do not have to make any changes to the calcShipping() function because the three shipping values stored in the selection list are already in currency format. Figure 5-22 shows the revised code.

toFixed() method applied to currency values ◀ **Figure 5-22**

```
function calcPrice() {
    product = document.forms[0].prod;
    pIndex = product.selectedIndex;
    productPrice = product.options[pIndex].value;          displays the value to
                                                           two decimal places
    quantity = document.forms[0].qty;
    qIndex = quantity.selectedIndex;
    quantityOrdered = quantity.options[qIndex].value;

    document.forms[0].price.value = (productPrice*quantityOrdered).toFixed(2);

    calcTotal();
}

function calcShipping() {
    document.forms[0].ship.value = this.value;

    calcTotal();
}

function calcTotal() {
    priceVal = parseFloat(document.forms[0].price.value);
    shipVal = parseFloat(document.forms[0].ship.value);
    document.forms[0].sub.value = (priceVal + shipVal).toFixed(2);

    taxVal = 0.05*(priceVal + shipVal);
    document.forms[0].tax.value = taxVal.toFixed(2);

    document.forms[0].tot.value = (priceVal + shipVal + taxVal).toFixed(2);
}
```

▶ **4.** Save your changes to the file, and then reload **form1.htm** in your Web browser.

▶ **5.** Select **G-Receiver I ($149.50)** from the product selection list, select **3** from the quantity selection list, and then click the **Next Day (1 day): $12.95** shipping option button. Figure 5-23 shows the resulting values in the order form.

Figure 5-23 **Currency values formatted to two decimal places**

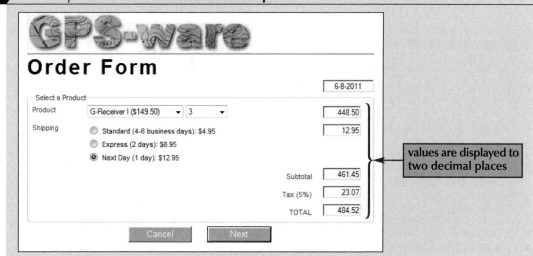

values are displayed to two decimal places

6. Continue to experiment with different order options to verify that the form correctly calculates the total price of each order.

You've created all the calculated fields needed for the order form of Carol's Web site. In the next session, you'll explore ways to ensure that Web forms are correctly filled out and to notify users of errors when they're not.

Review | **Session 5.1 Quick Check**

1. Specify the object reference to the second Web form in a document.

2. Specify the object reference to the lastname input field found in the register Web form.

3. What command changes the value of the lastname field to Carol Campbell? What command moves the cursor to the lastname field?

4. Specify the object reference to the fourth option in the statename selection list. Assume that the name of the Web form is register.

5. What expression returns the index number of the selected option from the statename selection list?

6. What expression indicates whether the contactme check box field in the register Web form is selected?

7. What expression converts the value 3.14159 to a text string displaying the value rounded to two decimal places?

Session 5.2

Working with Form Validation

Carol appreciates the order form's ability to automatically calculate the different costs associated with an order, but she is concerned that the form contains nothing to prevent customers from filling it out incorrectly. For example, users could submit an order without specifying a shipping option. Carol wants the form to contain some checks on whether a customer has correctly filled it out.

Carol is requesting one type of **form validation**, a process by which the server or a user's browser checks a form for data entry errors. On the Web, validation can occur on the client side or the server side. As shown in Figure 5-24, **server-side validation** sends a form to the Web server for checking. If an error is found, the user is notified and asked to resubmit the form. In **client-side validation**, the Web browser checks the form, which is not submitted to the server until it passes inspection.

Server-side and client-side validation — Figure 5-24

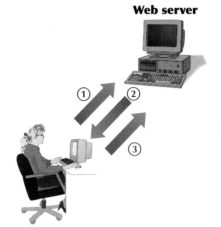

Server-side validation

1) The user submits the form to the Web server.

2) The Web server validates the user's responses and, if necessary, returns the form to the user for correction.

3) After correcting any errors, the user resubmits the form to the Web server for another validation.

Client-side validation

1) The user submits the form, and validation is performed on the user's computer.

2) After correcting any errors, the user submits the form to the Web server.

In practice, server-side and client-side validation are used together. Client-side validation provides immediate feedback to users and lessens the load on servers by distributing some of the validation tasks to users' computers. The server then has the task of performing a final check on submitted data before processing it. Carol is aware that GPS-ware's Web server might handle hundreds of orders per hour on a good business day, and anything that can be done to reduce the load on the server helps. Carol wants you to ensure that, before the form can be submitted to the server, a customer has:

1. selected a GPS-ware product
2. selected a quantity of the product to order
3. selected a shipping option

If these conditions are not met, Carol wants the user's browser to alert the customer of the problem and refuse to submit the form to the server.

Submitting a Form

When a user completes a form and then clicks the submit button, the form initiates a submit event. By default, the browser initiates the action indicated in the form's action and method attributes. The code for the <form> tag in the form1.htm file is

```
<form id = "form1" method = "post" action = "form2.htm">
```

so that when the form is successfully completed by the user, the browser will use the post method to submit the form and retrieve the form2.htm file. Clicking the Next button submits the form for processing.

To control this submission process, JavaScript provides the onsubmit event handler that can be added to the form element. The syntax of the onsubmit event handler is

```
formObj.onsubmit = function;
```

where *function* is a function that returns the Boolean value true or false. If the function returns a value of false, the submit event is cancelled, whereas a value of true allows the submit event to continue unabated. For the order form, you'll create a function named checkForm1() that will verify that all of the form data has been correctly entered. You'll create an onsubmit event handler to run this function now.

To apply an onsubmit event handler:

1. Return to the **order.js** file in your text editor.

2. Go to the startForm() function, and then at the end of the function insert the following statement, as shown in Figure 5-25:

   ```
   document.forms[0].onsubmit = checkForm1;
   ```

Figure 5-25 | Code for the onsubmit event handler

```
function startForm() {
    document.forms[0].date.value = todayTxt();
    document.forms[0].prod.focus();

    document.forms[0].prod.onchange = calcPrice;
    document.forms[0].qty.onchange = calcPrice;

    for (var i = 0; i < document.forms[0].shipType.length; i++) {
        document.forms[0].shipType[i].onclick = calcShipping;
    }

    document.forms[0].onsubmit = checkForm1;
}
```

browser runs the checkForm1() function when the form is submitted

Next, you will create the checkForm1() function. The initial form of the function is:

```
function checkForm1() {
    if (document.forms[0].prod.selectedIndex == 0) {
        return false;}
    else if (document.forms[0].qty.selectedIndex == 0) {
        return false;}
    else if (document.forms[0].ship.value == "0.00") {
        return false;}
    else return true;
}
```

The checkForm1() function tests three if conditions. It first tests whether a product has been selected by examining the selectedIndex property. A value of 0 indicates the user has not selected a product. It then tests whether a quantity has been selected by once again examining the value of the selectedIndex property. Finally, it tests whether the value of the ship field is equal to 0.00, which indicates that the user has not selected a shipping option. If any of those three conditions is satisfied, the function returns the value of false, which cancels the form submission. On the other hand, if none of the conditions is satisfied, indicating that the user has selected a product, a quantity, and a shipping option, the function returns a value of true and the form is submitted by the browser.

You'll add the checkForm1() function to the order.js file.

To insert the checkForm1() function:

▶ **1.** At the bottom of the file, insert the following code, as shown in Figure 5-26:

```
function checkForm1() {
   if (document.forms[0].prod.selectedIndex == 0) {
      return false;}
   else if (document.forms[0].qty.selectedIndex == 0) {
      return false;}
   else if (document.forms[0].ship.value == "0.00") {
      return false;}
   else return true;
}
```

Code for the checkForm1() function ◀ **Figure 5-26**

```
   document.forms[0].tot.value = (priceval + shipVal + taxval).toFixed(2);
}

function checkForm1() {
   if (document.forms[0].prod.selectedIndex == 0) {
      return false;}
   else if (document.forms[0].qty.selectedIndex == 0) {
      return false;}
   else if (document.forms[0].ship.value == "0.00") {
      return false;}
   else return true;
}
```

verifies that the user has selected a product, a quantity, and a shipping option

▶ **2.** Save your changes to the file.

Alerting the User

It is not enough to simply reject forms that have been improperly filled out. You also need to notify users of their error so they can correct the mistake. One way of notifying the user is through an alert box. An **alert box** is a dialog box that displays an informative message to the user along with an OK button that closes the box when clicked. Alert boxes are created using the method

```
alert(message);
```

where *message* is the text that appears in the dialog box. For example, to create an alert box that displays the message "You must select a GPS-ware product", you would run the following command:

```
alert("You must select a GPS-ware product");
```

You'll add similar alert messages to each of the three conditions under which the form would be rejected by the browser.

To insert the alert boxes:

▶ **1.** Directly before the first return false; line in the checkForm1() function, insert the following command:

```
alert("You must select a GPS-ware product");
```

▶ **2.** Directly before the second return false; line, insert the following command:

```
alert("You must select a quantity to order");
```

▶ **3.** Directly before the last return false; line, insert the following command:

```
alert("You must select a shipping option");
```

Figure 5-27 highlights the inserted code for the three alert boxes.

Figure 5-27 | **Code to add alert boxes**

```
function checkForm1() {
    if (document.forms[0].prod.selectedIndex == 0) {
        alert("You must select a GPS-ware product");
        return false;}
    else if (document.forms[0].qty.selectedIndex == 0) {
        alert("You must select a quantity to order");
        return false;}
    else if (document.forms[0].ship.value == "0.00") {
        alert("You must select a shipping option");
        return false;}
    else return true;
}
```

displays an alert box

▶ **4.** Save your changes to the file, and then reload **form1.htm** in your Web browser.

▶ **5.** Click the **Next** button without selecting any products, quantities, or shipping options on the form. The browser displays an alert box indicating that you have not selected a product to order, which is the first mistake found in the form. See Figure 5-28.

Figure 5-28 | **Web form being validated**

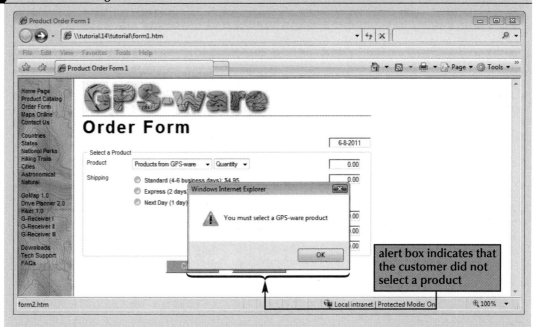

alert box indicates that the customer did not select a product

> **6.** Click the **OK** button to close the alert box.
>
> **7.** Continue to test the form by omitting one of three required pieces of information, submit the form, and then verifying that the browser fails to accept the form.
>
> **8.** Correctly complete the order form, and then click the **Next** button. Verify that the browser accepted the completed form and displayed the second of Carol's three Web forms.

Due to the way that the code for the checkForm1() function is written, only the first error that JavaScript discovers will be reported to the user. Even if you omit all three items in the order, only the lack of a chosen product will be reported.

Resetting a Form

The other event associated with Web forms is the reset event, which occurs when a user clicks a form reset button. Clicking the reset button has the effect of resetting all form fields to their default values. You can control how the reset event is handled by adding an onreset event handler to the form element in the same way that you use the onsubmit event handler to manage form submission.

In Carol's order form, the Cancel button plays the role of the reset button. However, Carol wants to modify what happens when the form is reset. Recall that the first action this form takes is to insert the current date into the date field. Carol wants the reset button to both reset the fields to their default values and rerun the startForm() function, which inserts the current date into the date field. You can perform both of these actions by having the browser reload the document when the reset event is initiated. When the page is reloaded, the startForm() function runs automatically and the fields return to their default values. To reload the current page, you run the following command:

```
location.reload();
```

You'll add this command to a function named resetForm1(), and then attach that function to the onreset event handler for the Web form.

> ### Tip
> You can use JavaScript to highlight missing or erroneous data values by modifying the display style of the input fields in the Web form. For example, modify the border style to highlight incorrect or missing data values with a red border.

To apply the onreset event handler:

> **1.** Return to the **order.js** file in your text editor.
>
> **2.** Add the following command to the bottom of the startForm() function:
>
> ```
> document.forms[0].onreset = resetForm1;
> ```
>
> **3.** Directly below the startForm() function, insert the following function, as shown in Figure 5-29:
>
> ```
> function resetForm1() {
>     location.reload();
> }
> ```

Figure 5-29 ▶ **Code to insert the onreset event handler**

```
function startForm() {
    document.forms[0].date.value = todayTxt();
    document.forms[0].prod.focus();

    document.forms[0].prod.onchange = calcPrice;
    document.forms[0].qty.onchange = calcPrice;

    for (var i = 0; i < document.forms[0].shipType.length; i++) {
        document.forms[0].shipType[i].onclick = calcShipping;
    }

    document.forms[0].onsubmit = checkForm1;
    document.forms[0].onreset = resetForm1;
}

function resetForm1() {
    location.reload();
}
```

> runs the resetForm1() function when the form is reset

▶ **4.** Close the file, saving your changes.

▶ **5.** Reload **form1.htm** in your Web browser.

▶ **6.** Select a product to order, a quantity, and a shipping option, and then click the **Cancel** button at the bottom of the form. Verify that the page reloads, setting the fields to their default values and displaying the current date in the date field. The product selection list is the selected field in the form.

Reference Window | **Validating a Web Form**

- To validate a Web form when it is submitted, add the event handler
    formObj.onsubmit = *function*;
  to the form element, where *function* is a function that returns a Boolean value. A value of false cancels the submission of the form, whereas a value of true allows the form to be submitted.
- To control the resetting of a form, add the event handler
    formObj.onreset = *function*;
  where *function* is a function that is run when the reset event is initiated.

Working with Text Strings

You've completed your work on the first Web form. The second form collects contact information from the user for delivering the purchased item. As with the form1.htm file, all JavaScript code for this file will be stored in the external JavaScript file contact.js. You'll create a link to this file now.

To view the form2.htm file:

▶ **1.** Open the **form2.htm** file in your text editor.

▶ **2.** In the head section of the document, create a link to the contact.js script file.

▶ **3.** Review the contents and code of the file, and then close the file, saving your changes.

▶ **4.** Open **form2.htm** in your Web browser. Figure 5-30 shows the initial layout of the file.

Delivery form and element names | **Figure 5-30**

Figure 5-31 lists the object references for each element in the form.

Objects in the delivery form | **Figure 5-31**

Object	Reference
first name field	document.forms[0].fname
last name field	document.forms[0].lname
street text area box	document.forms[0].street
city field	document.forms[0].city
state selection list	document.forms[0].state
ZIP code field	document.forms[0].zip
previous button	document.forms[0].prevb
next button	document.forms[0].nextb

Although this form requires no calculations, Carol wants you to implement the following validation checks before the form is accepted by the browser:

1. A customer must specify a first name, last name, street address, and city.
2. If a zip code is entered, it should consist of five digits with no nonnumeric characters.

Because you need to apply these validation checks to text strings, you'll take a deeper look at the properties and methods of text strings.

Using the String Object

JavaScript can store a text value in an object called a **String object**. The most common way to create a String object is to use the object constructor

```
stringVariable = new String(text);
```

where *stringVariable* is a variable that stores the text string, and *text* is the text of the string. This approach has the advantage of explicitly identifying a variable as containing a text string, rather than having JavaScript implicitly create a String object based on the content of a variable.

Calculating the Length of a Text String

One of the properties associated with String objects is the length property, which returns the number of characters in the text string, including all white spaces and nonprintable characters. For example, the following code uses the length property to calculate the number of characters in the stringVar variable:

```
stringVar = "GPS-ware Products";
lengthValue = stringVar.length;
```

After running this code, the lengthValue variable will have the value 17.

The length property is commonly used for functions that process text strings one character at a time and need a way of knowing when to stop. You can also use the length property to validate the entries in Web forms. Carol wants to require customers to enter a first and last name, a street address, and a city. Because these are required values, the length of the text entered in each of these fields must be greater than 0. You'll use the length property to verify this condition for each of these fields in your first set of validation checks for the delivery form, storing those tests in a function named checkForm2(). As with the earlier checkForm1() function, you'll have the browser display an appropriate alert dialog box the first time it encounters an invalid field. The following is the initial code for the checkForm2() function:

```
function checkForm2() {
   if (document.forms[0].fname.value.length == 0)
      {alert("You must enter a first name");
       return false;}
   else if (document.forms[0].lname.value.length == 0)
      {alert("You must enter a last name");
       return false;}
   else if (document.forms[0].street.value.length == 0)
      {alert("You must enter a street address");
       return false;}
   else if (document.forms[0].city.value.length == 0)
      {alert("You must enter a city name");
       return false;}
   else return true;
}
```

The checkForm2() function only verifies that an entry has been made in these fields; it does not test whether those entries make any sense. You'll add the checkForm2() function to the contact.js file.

To insert the checkForm2() function:

▶ 1. Open the **contact.js** file in your text editor.

▶ 2. Below the comment section, insert the following code, as shown in Figure 5-32:

```
function checkForm2() {
   if (document.forms[0].fname.value.length == 0)
      {alert("You must enter a first name");
       return false;}
   else if (document.forms[0].lname.value.length == 0)
      {alert("You must enter a last name");
       return false;}
```

```
        else if (document.forms[0].street.value.length == 0)
          {alert("You must enter a street address");
           return false;}
        else if (document.forms[0].city.value.length == 0)
          {alert("You must enter a city name");
           return false;}
        else return true;
    }
```

Code for the checkForm2() function ◄ Figure 5-32

```
function checkForm2() {
    if (document.forms[0].fname.value.length == 0)
      {alert("You must enter a first name");
       return false;}
    else if (document.forms[0].lname.value.length == 0)
      {alert("You must enter a last name");
       return false;}
    else if (document.forms[0].street.value.length == 0)
      {alert("You must enter a street address");
       return false;}
    else if (document.forms[0].city.value.length == 0)
      {alert("You must enter a city name");
       return false;}
    else return true;
}
```

> verifies that the user entered something in the fname, lname, street, and city fields

▶ **3.** Because this is a long piece of code, take some time to ensure that you have entered the code correctly. Make sure that you enclosed all command blocks within curly braces {} and that you used the == symbol rather than a single = symbol in the conditional statements.

You want the checkForm2() function to run when the user submits the delivery form. To do that, you once again add an onsubmit event handler to the form element when the page is initially loaded by the browser.

To insert the onsubmit event handler:

▶ **1.** Directly above the checkForm2() function, insert the following code, as shown in Figure 5-33:

```
window.onload = startForm;

function startForm() {
    document.forms[0].onsubmit = checkForm2;
}
```

Code to call the checkForm2() function ◄ Figure 5-33

```
window.onload = startForm;

function startForm() {
    document.forms[0].onsubmit = checkForm2;
}

function checkForm2() {
    if (document.forms[0].fname.value.length == 0)
      {alert("You must enter a first name");
       return false;}
```

> runs the checkForm2() function when the user submits the form

▶ **2.** Save your changes to the file, and then reload **form2.htm** in your Web browser.

As with the previous form, the Next button submits the form for processing. In this case, submitting the form causes the browser to load the form3.htm file.

3. Click the **Next** button without entering any contact information in the first name, last name, street, or city fields. Verify that the browser displays an alert box, indicating that you have not specified a first name.

4. Click the **OK** button to close the alert box, and then continue to test the form by omitting different required fields and clicking the **Next** button. Verify that you must enter all the required information before the browser will accept the completed form.

Tip

A common form design is to place asterisks next to each required field as a visual clue to the user indicating which fields are required.

Working with String Object Methods

Carol's second validation check involves examining the digits in the zip field. At the moment Carol is only considering five-digit postal codes, so this field should be five characters long and consist only of numeric characters. (You will look at how to validate extended postal codes that include a dash and additional digits in the next session.)

To validate the zip code, you'll create a function named checkZip(). The checkZip() function will return a Boolean value of true if the text string matches the pattern for zip codes and false if otherwise. The initial version of this function will check only the length of the text string. Because the zip field is not a required field in Carol's form, you'll allow valid text strings to contain either zero or five digits; any other length will be invalid. The initial code for the checkZip() function is:

```
function checkZip(zip) {
    if (zip.length != 0 && zip.length != 5) return false
    else return true;
}
```

You'll add this function to the contact.js file.

To insert the checkZip() function:

1. Return to the **contact.js** file in your text editor.

2. At the bottom of the file, insert the following function, as shown in Figure 5-34:

```
function checkZip(zip) {
    if (zip.length != 0 && zip.length != 5) return false
    else return true;
}
```

| Figure 5-34 | Initial checkZip() function |

```
        else if (document.forms[0].city.value.length == 0)
            {alert("You must enter a city name");
             return false;}
        else return true;
    }

    function checkZip(zip) {
        if (zip.length != 0 && zip.length != 5) return false
        else return true;
    }
```

verifies that the length of the zip code is either 0 or 5

3. Save your changes to the file.

The checkZip() function can confirm that the zip code contains five characters, but it does not check whether each of those characters are digits. To do that, you'll use some of the JavaScript methods associated with string objects.

JavaScript supports methods that allow you to examine the individual characters within a text string. A character is identified by its placement in the text string. Like arrays and object collections, the first character has an index value of 0, the second has an index value of 1, and so on. If you want to reference a character with a particular index, use the charAt() method

```
string.charAt(i)
```

where *string* is the string object and *i* is the index of the character. For example, the expression

```
"GPS-ware".charAt(2)
```

returns the third character from the text string, which in this case is an uppercase S. The charAt() method extracts only a single character. To extract longer text strings, known as **substrings**, use the slice() method

```
string.slice(start, end)
```

where *start* is the starting index and *end* is the index at which the slicing stops. If you do not specify an *end* value, the substring is extracted to the end of the text string. For example, the statement

```
"GPS-ware Products For Sale".slice(9,17)
```

returns the substring Products, because it starts at index number 9 and ends right before index number 17. You can also extract substrings based on their length using the method

```
string.substr(start, length)
```

where *length* is the number of characters in the substring. If you do not specify a *length* value, JavaScript extracts the substring to the end of the string. To extract the word Products from the previous text string, you can also use:

```
"GPS-ware Products For Sale".substr(9,8)
```

Both the slice() and substr() methods are limited in that they create only a single substring. In some cases, you may need to break a text string into several substrings. For example, you may need to break a long sentence into individual words. Another common use would be to break a field in which customers enter both their first and last names into two strings. Rather than run the substr() or slice() methods several times on the same text string, you can create an array of substrings in a single expression using the method

```
strArray = string.split(str)
```

where *strArray* is the array that will store the substrings and *str* is a text string that marks the break between one substring and another, which is known as a **delimiter**. The command

```
words = "GPS-ware Products For Sale".split(" ")
```

splits the text string at each occurrence of a blank space, storing the substrings in the words array. The substrings stored in the words array are:

```
words[0] = "GPS-ware"
words[1] = "Products"
words[2] = "For"
words[3] = "Sale"
```

The characters specified in the delimiter are not placed in the substrings. This is one technique you can use to remove character strings from a large text string.

Other string object methods are used to search for the occurrence of particular substrings within larger text strings. The most often used method is the indexOf() method, which has the following syntax:

```
string.indexOf(str, start)
```

The indexOf() method returns the index value of the first occurrence of the substring *str* within *string*. The *start* parameter is optional and indicates from which character to start the search. The default value of the *start* parameter is 0, indicating that the search should start with the first character. For example, the expression

```
"GPS-ware Products For Sale".indexOf("P")
```

Tip

You can use the indexOf() method to test for the presence or absence of a character. If the method returns the value −1, the character does not appear in the text string.

returns the value 1 because the first occurrence of an uppercase P in the text occurs as the second character in the text string. To locate the next occurrence of P, you can set the *start* value to 2 so that the search starts with the third character in the string. The expression

```
"GPS-ware Products For Sale".indexOf("P",3)
```

returns the value 9. If no occurrence of the substring exists, the indexOf() method returns the value −1. For this reason, the indexOf() method is often used to test whether a text string contains a particular substring.

Reference Window | **Working with String Objects**

- To determine the number of characters in a text string, use the object property
  ```
  string.length
  ```
  where *string* is a text string object.
- To extract a character from a text string, use the method
  ```
  string.charAt(i)
  ```
  where *i* is the index of the character. The first character in the text string has an index number of 0.
- To extract a substring from a text string, use the method
  ```
  string.slice(start, end)
  ```
  where *start* is the starting index and *end* is the index at which the substring stops. If you do not specify an *end* value, the substring is extracted to the end of the string.
- To split a string into several substrings, use the command
  ```
  strArray = string.split(str)
  ```
  where *strArray* is the array that will store the substrings and *str* is a text string that marks the break between one substring and another.
- To search a string, use the method
  ```
  string.indexOf(str, start)
  ```
  where *str* is the substring to search for within the larger string and *start* is the index of the character from which to start the search. If you do not specify a *start* value, the search starts with the first character in the string.

Figure 5-35 summarizes the different string object methods used to extract information from text strings.

Methods to extract strings | Figure 5-35

Method	Description	Example (text= "GPS-ware Products")
`string.charAt(i)`	Returns the *i*th character from *string*	`text.charAt(4);` // returns "w"
`string.charCodeAt(i)`	Returns the *i*th character's Unicode value from the *string*	`text.charCodeAt(4);` // returns 119
`string.concat` `(str2, str3, ...)`	Appends *string* with the text strings *str2*, *str3*, etc.	`text.concat(" Sale");` // returns "GPS-ware Products Sale"

`String.fromCharCode`
`(n1, n2, ...)`
	Returns a text string consisting of characters whose Unicode values are *n1*, *n2*, etc.	`String.fromCharCode`
		`(71,80,83);`
		// returns "GPS"

`string.indexOf` `(str, start)`	Searches *string*, beginning at the *start* index number, returning the index number of the first occurrence of *str*; if no *start* value is specified, the search begins with the first character	`text.indexOf("P",5);` // returns 9
`string.lastIndexOf` `(str,start)`	Searches *string*, beginning at the *start* index number, returning the index number of the last occurrence of *str*; if no *start* value is specified, the search begins with the first character	`text.lastIndexOf("P");` // returns 9
`string.slice` `(start, end)`	Extracts a substring from *string*, between the *start* and *end* index values; if no *end* value is specified, the substring extends to the end of the string	`text.slice(4,8);` // returns "ware"

`string.split(str)`	Splits *string* into an array of string characters at each occurrence of *str*	`word=text.split(" ");`
		// word[0] = "GPS-ware"
		// word[1] = "Products"

`string.substr` `(start, length)`	Returns a substring from *string* starting at the *start* index value and continuing for *length* characters; if no *length* value is specified, the substring continues to the end of *string*	`text.substr(9,4);` // returns "Prod"
`string.substring` `(start, end)`	Extracts a substring from *string*, between the *start* and *end* index values; if no *end* value is specified, the substring extends to the end of the string (identical to the slice() method)	`text.substring(4,8);` // returns "ware"

To further explore the string extraction methods, you'll use the charAt() and indexOf() methods to create a function that determines whether a text string is composed of only numeric characters. The code for the isNonNumeric() function is:

```
function isNonNumeric(tString) {
   validchars = "0123456789";
   for (var i = 0; i < tString.length; i++) {
      char = tString.charAt(i);
      if (validchars.indexOf(char) == -1) return true;
   }
   return false;
}
```

This function first stores the digits from 0 to 9 in a text string stored in the validchars variable. The code then loops through each of the characters in the tString variable, extracting the character at each index using the charAt() method. Each character is then tested using the indexOf() method to determine whether it matches one of the characters in the validchars text string. If it cannot be found in that text string, the indexOf() method returns the value –1, and you know that the text string contains at least one nonnumeric character. The function will then halt, returning the value true. If the loop concludes without locating at least one nonnumeric character, the function returns the value false.

You'll add this command to the contact.js file.

To insert the isNonNumeric() function:

▶ **1.** Below the checkZip() function, insert the following code, as shown in Figure 5-36:

```
function isNonNumeric(tString) {
   validchars = "0123456789";

   for (var i = 0; i < tString.length; i++) {
      char = tString.charAt(i);
      if (validchars.indexOf(char) == -1) return true;
   }

   return false;
}
```

Figure 5-36 ▶ **Code for the isNonNumeric() function**

```
function checkZip(zip) {
   if (zip.length != 0 && zip.length != 5) return false
   else return true;
}

function isNonNumeric(tString) {
   validchars = "0123456789";

   for (var i = 0; i < tString.length; i++) {
      char = tString.charAt(i);
      if (validchars.indexOf(char) == -1) return true;
   }

   return false;
}
```

function returns the value true if tString contains a non-numeric character

▶ **2.** Save your changes to the file.

Next, you'll call this function from the checkZip() function to determine whether the zip code value entered by the customer consists of only numeric characters. If the isNonNumeric() function returns the value of true, it indicates that nonnumeric characters appear in the zip code entered by the user, and the zip code should be rejected as false.

To modify the checkZip() function:

▶ **1.** Add and revise the following code from the checkZip() function, as shown in Figure 5-37:

```
else if (isNonNumeric(zip)) return false
else return true;
```

Code to check the zip code validity   ◀   **Figure 5-37**

```
function checkZip(zip) {
    if (zip.length != 0 && zip.length != 5) return false
    else if (isNonNumeric(zip)) return false
    else return true;
}
```

> verifies that the zip field contains only numeric characters

▶ **2.** Add the following code to the function to call the checkZip() function from within the checkForm2() function to confirm that the user has entered a valid zip code before the form is submitted, as shown in Figure 5-38:

```
else if (checkZip(document.forms[0].zip.value) == false)
   {alert("Invalid zip code");
    return false;}
```

Code to call the checkZip() function   ◀   **Figure 5-38**

```
function checkForm2() {
    if (document.forms[0].fname.value.length == 0)
       {alert("You must enter a first name");
        return false;}
    else if (document.forms[0].lname.value.length == 0)
       {alert("You must enter a last name");
        return false;}
    else if (document.forms[0].street.value.length == 0)
       {alert("You must enter a street address");
        return false;}
    else if (document.forms[0].city.value.length == 0)
       {alert("You must enter a city name");
        return false;}
    else if (checkZip(document.forms[0].zip.value) == false)
       {alert("Invalid zip code");
        return false;}
    else return true;
}
```

> verifies that a valid zip code has been entered

▶ **3.** Save your changes to the file, and then reload **form2.htm** in your browser.

▶ **4.** Enter text into the first name, last name, street, and city fields, and then click the **Next** button to submit the delivery form. Your browser displays the contents of Carol's third Web form.

▶ **5.** Return to the **form2.htm** page, enter the value **abcde** into the zip field, and then click the **Next** button. Your browser displays an alert box and fails to accept the form.

▶ **6.** Repeat Step 5, entering the values **123**, **1234a**, and **12345** into the zip field. Your browser displays an alert box and fails to accept the form for the zip code values 123 and 1234a, but accepts the form for the zip code value 12345.

Arrays often contain text values. One of the string methods supported by JavaScript allows you to extract these text strings, placing them within a single String object. The syntax of the toString() method is

```
array.toString()
```

where *array* is the array containing a collection of text values. The values from the array are returned in a comma-separated text string list. For example, if the array contains the abbreviated days of the week

```
wDay = new Array('Sun','Mon','Tue','Wed','Thu','Fri','Sat');
```

then running the command

```
wDayStr = wDay.toString();
```

stores the following text string in the wDayStr variable:

```
"Sun,Mon,Tue,Wed,Thu,Fri,Sat"
```

The toString() method can also be used with objects other than arrays. When used with other objects, the toString() method returns a text string representing the object. For example, when applied to a Date object, the toString() method returns the date value as a text string. When used with a numeric value, the toString() method returns the value as a text string.

Formatting Text Strings

Another set of JavaScript methods allows you to format a text string's appearance. For example, to display a text string in all uppercase letters, you would use the method

```
string.toUpperCase()
```

where *string* is the string object. To change the text GPS-ware to all uppercase letters, you would use the following JavaScript expression:

```
"GPS-ware".toUpperCase()
```

Figure 5-39 lists other formatting methods for string objects along with their equivalent HTML tags. Running these methods does not add the HTML tags to the object, but rather achieves the same effects that you would get if you applied those formatting tags to the text string.

You may notice that many of the HTML tags shown in Figure 5-39 have been deprecated in favor of style sheets. In the same way, the string formatting methods are not often used in preference to formatting text strings using the style object. The most common formatting methods are the toUpperCase() and toLowerCase() methods. At this point, you don't need to do any text formatting for Carol's Web forms.

Methods to format strings ◀ Figure 5-39

Method	Description	HTML Equivalent
string.anchor(*text*)	Creates an anchor with the anchor name *text*	`<a name="text">string</a>`
string.big()	Changes the size of the *string* font to big	`<big>string</big>`
string.blink()	Changes *string* to blinking text	`<blink>string</blink>`
string.bold()	Changes the font weight of *string* to bold	`<bold>string</bold>`
string.fixed()	Changes the font of *string* to a fixed width font	`<tt>string</tt>`
string.fontcolor(*color*)	Changes the color of *string* to the hexadecimal *color* value	`<font color="color">string</font>`
string.fontsize(*value*)	Changes the font size of *string* to *value*	`<font size="value">string</font>`
string.italics()	Changes *string* to italics	`<i>string</i>`
string.link(*url*)	Changes *string* to a link pointing to *url*	`<a href="url">string</a>`
string.small()	Changes the size of the *string* font to small	`<small>string</small>`
string.strike()	Adds strikethrough characters to *string*	`<strike>string</strike>`
string.sub()	Changes *string* to a subscript	`<sub>string</sub>`
string.sup()	Changes *string* to a superscript	`<sup>string</sup>`
string.toLowerCase()	Changes *string* to lowercase letters	
string.toUpperCase()	Changes *string* to uppercase letters	

In the next session, you'll continue to explore how to validate text entries through the use of regular expressions and how to validate financial data.

Session 5.2 Quick Check | Review

1. What is server-side validation? What is client-side validation?
2. A function named testForm() validates a Web form. What event handler should you add to the form element to run the validation before the form is submitted?
3. What expression returns the number of characters in the username string object?
4. What expression returns the first character from the username string? What expression returns the last character from the string?

5. What expression returns the first five characters from the username string?

6. E-mail addresses are usually written in the format *username@domain*. Write code that breaks an e-mail variable into two text strings: one containing *username* and the other containing *domain*.

7. Government e-mail addresses will often end with .gov. What expression tests whether the e-mail string object contains the .gov substring?

8. What expression changes the username string object to uppercase letters?

Session 5.3

Introducing Regular Expressions

Carol likes the form validation functions you created for the delivery form, but she is concerned about the function that validates the zip code. Domestic zip codes come in two forms: five digits (*nnnnn*) and five digits followed by a hyphen and four more digits (*nnnnn-nnnn*). In recent years, the second version has become more common and Carol wants the validation functions to support either format. Although you could revise the checkZip() function to accommodate the extended zip code format, a more flexible approach is to use a regular expression.

A **regular expression** is a text string that defines a character pattern. One use of regular expressions is **pattern matching**, in which a text string is tested to see whether it matches the pattern defined by a regular expression. In the zip code example, you might create a regular expression for the pattern of five digits followed by a hyphen and another four digits, and then verify that a customer's zip code matches that pattern. Pattern matching is just one use of regular expressions. They can also be used to extract substrings, insert new text, or replace old text. The greatest advantage of regular expressions is that the code is compact and powerful, so that what might take several lines of code using other methods can be done in a single line with a regular expression. However, with this power comes complexity: The syntax of regular expressions can be intimidating to new programmers, taking time and practice to master.

Creating a Regular Expression

You create a regular expression in JavaScript using the command

```
re = /pattern/;
```

where *pattern* is the text string of the regular expression and *re* is the object that stores the regular expression. This syntax for creating regular expressions is sometimes referred to as a **regular expression literal**. A regular expression is treated by a JavaScript interpreter as an object with a collection of properties and methods that can be applied to it. You'll explore some of those properties and methods later in this session. For now, you'll work on understanding the language of regular expressions. To help you understand regular expressions, you'll use a demo page in which you can enter a regular expression and apply pattern matching against a sample text string. Before continuing with Carol's order forms, you'll explore how to write and interpret regular expression patterns.

To view the regular expressions demo:

▶ **1.** In your Web browser, open the **demo_regexp.htm** file from the tutorial.05\demo folder. The demo page contains a text box in the upper-left corner into which you enter sample text. Below the text box, you can enter a predefined regular expression or type your own. To match the regular expression against the sample text, you click the Pattern Test button.

▶ **2.** Type the following text into the text box in the upper-left corner of the page, as shown in Figure 5-40:

```
GPS-ware Products Are Prepared With Care
```

Regular expression sdemo page ◀ **Figure 5-40**

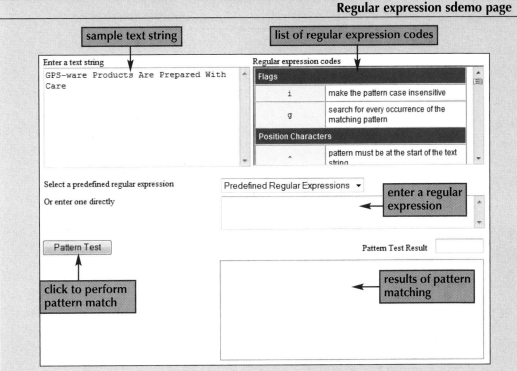

Matching a Substring

The most basic regular expression consists of a substring that you want to locate in the text string. The regular expression to match the first occurrence of a substring is

/chars/

where *chars* is the text of the substring. Regular expressions are case sensitive, so *chars* must match the uppercase and lowercase letters of the substring you are searching for. To see how this applies to the text string you have already entered on the demo page, you'll create regular expressions to locate the occurrences of the substrings "are" and "Are".

To match a simple substring:

▶ **1.** Click the **Or enter one directly** text box for the regular expression (located directly below the drop-down list box), and then type **/are/**.

2. Click the **Pattern Test** button. The first occurrence of the "are" substring is highlighted and the Pattern Test Result field displays the word "match," indicating that a matching pattern has been found in the text string. See Figure 5-41.

Figure 5-41

Matched substring

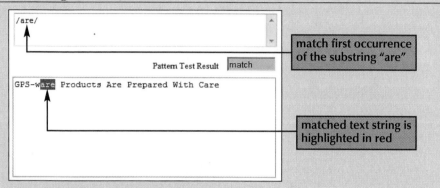

match first occurrence of the substring "are"

matched text string is highlighted in red

3. In the Or enter one directly text box, change the regular expression to **/Are/**.

4. Click the **Pattern Test** button. The pattern now matches the word "Are" occurring later in the text string.

Be aware that spaces are considered characters in a regular expression pattern. Although JavaScript allows some flexibility in the use of white space, regular expressions do not. The patterns / GPS / and /GPS/ are considered two completely different regular expressions because the substring "GPS" is surrounded by blank spaces in one pattern but not the other.

Tip

Do not insert spaces to make a regular expression more readable; adding spaces to a regular expression changes its results.

Setting Regular Expression Flags

By default, pattern matching stops after the first match is discovered; also, the matching is case sensitive. You can override both of these default behaviors by adding single character flags to the end of the regular expression. For example, to make a regular expression insensitive to case (that is, capitalization doesn't affect the results), append the regular expression pattern with the character i as follows:

```
/pattern/i
```

To allow a global search for all matches in a text string, append the regular expression with the character g as follows:

```
/pattern/g
```

Finally, to apply both at the same time, simply append both the i and g flags to the regular expression, as follows:

```
/pattern/ig
```

You'll apply these flags in the regular expression demo.

To apply global and case-insensitive flags:

▶ **1.** In the Or enter one directly text box, change the regular expression to **/are/ig**.

▶ **2.** Click the **Pattern Test** button. All examples of the text string "are" are highlighted regardless of case. See Figure 5-42.

Substring being matched using the g and i flags ◀ **Figure 5-42**

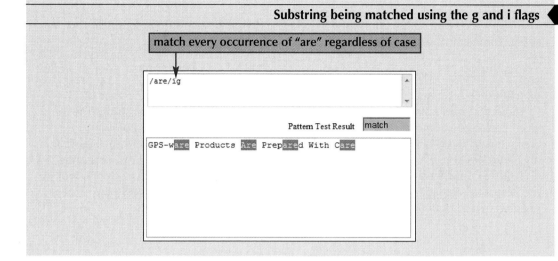

match every occurrence of "are" regardless of case

/are/ig

Pattern Test Result | match

GPS-ware Products Are Prepared With Care

Defining Character Positions

So far, you have used regular expressions to match simple text strings, which is not much more than you could have accomplished using the string object methods from the previous session. The true power (and complexity) of regular expressions comes with the introduction of special characters that allow you to match text based on the type, content, and placement of the characters in a text string. The first such characters you will consider are positioning characters. The four positioning characters are described in Figure 5-43.

Positioning characters ◀ **Figure 5-43**

Character	Description	Example
^	Indicates the beginning of the text string	/^GPS/ matches "GPS-ware" but not "Products from GPS-ware"
$	Indicates the end of the text string	/ware$/ matches "GPS-ware" but not "GPS-ware Products"
\b	Indicates the presence of a word boundary	/\bart/ matches "art" and "artists" but not "dart"
\B	Indicates the absence of a word boundary	/art\B/ matches "dart" but not "artist"

Regular expressions recognize the beginning and end of a text string, indicated by the ^ and $ characters, respectively. The following pattern uses the ^ character to mark the start of the text string:

```
/^GPS/
```

In this pattern, any text string starting with the characters "GPS" would be matched. The expression would not match the GPS substring occurring elsewhere in the text string. In the same way, the end of the text string is indicated by the $ character. The following expression matches any text string that ends with the characters "-ware":

`/-ware$/`

The ^ and $ characters are often used together to define a pattern for a complete text string. For example, the pattern

`/^GPS-ware$/`

matches only a string containing the text "GPS-ware" and nothing else.

The other positioning characters are used to locate words within a text string. The term *word* has a special meaning in regular expressions. **Words** are composed of word characters. A **word character** is any letter, number, or underscore. Symbols such as *, &, and – are not considered word characters, nor are spaces, periods, and tabs. The string "R2D2" is considered a single word, but "R2D2&C3PO" is considered two words, with the & symbol acting as a boundary between the words. In a regular expression, the presence of a word boundary is indicated with the \b symbol. The pattern

`/\bart/`

matches any word that starts with the characters "art", but does not match "art" found in other locations within a text string. For example, this pattern would match the word "artist", but not the word "dart". The \b symbol can also indicate a word boundary at the end of a word. The regular expression

`/art\b/`

matches any word that ends in "art"—such as "dart" or "heart"—but not "artist". By using the \b symbol at both the beginning and the end of a pattern, you can define a complete word. The pattern

`/\bart\b/`

matches only the word "art" and nothing else. In some cases, you want to match substrings only within words. In these situations, you use the \B symbol, which indicates the absence of a word boundary. The regular expression

`/\Bart\B/`

matches the substring "art" only when it occurs inside of a word such as in "hearts" or "darts".

Tip

Regular expression symbols have opposite meanings when expressed in upper-case letters: \B means the opposite of \b and \w means the opposite of \W.

To view the effect of word boundaries on regular expressions:

▶ **1.** In the Or enter one directly text box on the demo page, change the regular expression to **/\bare\b/gi**.

▶ **2.** Click the **Pattern Test** button. Only the word "Are" is highlighted because it is the only occurrence in the text string where "are" appears as a complete word. See Figure 5-44.

Whole word being matched ◄ **Figure 5-44**

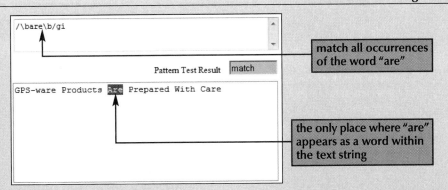

match all occurrences of the word "are"

the only place where "are" appears as a word within the text string

3. In the Or enter one directly text box, change the regular expression to **/\Bare\b/gi** and then click the **Pattern Test** button. The pattern now matches words that end in "are" and ignores words that start with "are". See Figure 5-45.

Mixed word boundaries being matched ◄ **Figure 5-45**

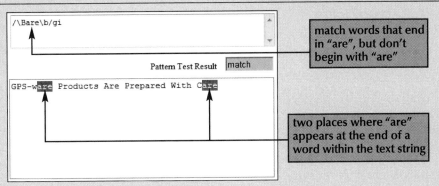

match words that end in "are", but don't begin with "are"

two places where "are" appears at the end of a word within the text string

4. In the Or enter one directly text box, change the regular expression to **/\Bare\B/gi** and then click the **Pattern Test** button to locate all instances of the substring "are" that occur within a word. The pattern now matches only the substring "are" found within the word "Prepared".

Defining Character Types and Character Classes

Another class of regular expression characters indicates character type. The three general types of characters are: word characters, digits (numbers 0 to 9), and white space characters (blank spaces, tabs, and new lines). Figure 5-46 describes the regular expression symbols for these character types.

Figure 5-46 **Character classes**

Character	Description	Example
\d	A digit (from 0 to 9)	/\dth/ matches "5th" but not "ath"
\D	A non-digit	/\Ds/ matches "as" but not "5s"
\w	A word character (an upper- or lowercase letter, a digit, or an underscore)	/\w\w/ matches "to" or "A1" but not "$x" or " *"
\W	A non-word character	/\W/ matches "$" or "&" but not "a", "B", or "3"
\s	A white space character (a blank space, tab, new line, carriage return, or form feed)	/\s\d\s/ matches " 5 " but not "5"
\S	A non-white space character	/\S\d\S/ matches "345" or "a5b" but not "5"
.	Any character	/./ matches anything

For example, digits are represented by the \d character. To match any occurrence of a single digit, you use the regular expression

/\d/

which would find matches in such text strings as 105, 6, or U2, because these all contain an instance of a single digit. If you want to match several consecutive digits, you can simply repeat the \d symbol. The regular expression

/\d\d\d/

matches the occurrence of any three consecutive digits. It would find matches in strings such as 105, 1250, or EX500. If you want to limit matches only to words consisting of three-digit numbers, you can use the \b character to mark the boundaries around the digits. The pattern

/\b\d\d\d\b/

would match strings such as 105 or 229, but not 1250 or EX500.

This barely scratches the surface of regular expressions, but you have enough information to create a regular expression for a five-digit zip code. Its pattern is:

/^\d\d\d\d\d$/

This regular expression matches only a text string that contains five digits and no other characters (recall that the ^ and $ symbols mark the beginning and end of the entire text string). You'll test this pattern now on the demo page.

To test the zip code pattern:

1. In the Enter a text string box, change the text to **12345**.

2. In the Or enter one directly text box, change the regular expression to **/^\d\d\d\d\d$/** and then click the **Pattern Test** button. The demo page highlights all of the digits in the test string indicating a complete match.

3. Continue experimenting with the pattern, trying sample text strings of **1**, **123**, and **1234a**. Verify that the demo reports a valid match only if you enter a five-digit value with no other characters or numbers.

With just one regular expression, you have achieved what took several lines of code to do in the previous session. This gives you some idea of the power of regular expressions in detecting character patterns.

No character type matches only letters. However, you can specify a collection of characters known as a **character class** to limit the regular expression to a select group of characters. The syntax to define a character class is

`[chars]`

where *chars* are characters in the class. To create a negative character class that matches any character not in the class, preface the list of characters with the caret symbol (^) as follows:

`[^chars]`

The negative character set uses the same ^ symbol that you used to mark the beginning of a text string. Although the symbol is the same, the meaning is very different in this context.

To explore working with a character class, you'll use the demo page to create character classes that match vowels and consonants.

Tip

For more general character matching, use the \w symbol, which matches any word character, or the \s symbol, which matches any white space character.

To create a character class:

1. In the Enter a text string box, change the sample text to **GPS Products For Sale**.

2. In the Or enter one directly text box, change the regular expression to **/[aeiou]/gi** and then click the **Pattern Test** button. Every vowel in the sample text string is highlighted.

3. In the Or enter one directly text box, change the regular expression to **/[^aeiou]/gi** to create a pattern that doesn't match vowels, and then click the **Pattern Test** button. The demo selects all characters in the text string other than a, e, i, o, and u.

   The regular expression still selects white space characters such as blank spaces. To remove the blank spaces from the text string, you change the regular expression by adding the \s symbol to the list of characters that are not selected.

4. In the Or enter one directly text box, change the regular expression to **\[^aeiou\s]/gi** and then click the **Pattern Test** button. Including the \s symbol in the regular expression selects only the consonants in the text string. See Figure 5-47.

All consonant characters being matched   Figure 5-47

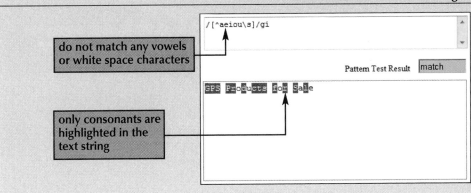

For a larger character class, you can define a range of characters by separating the starting and ending characters in the range with a hypen because characters are arranged in sequential and alphabetical order, to create a character class for all lowercase letters, you would use:

```
[a-z]
```

For uppercase letters, you would use:

```
[A-Z]
```

For both uppercase and lowercase letters, you would use:

```
[a-zA-Z]
```

You can continue to add ranges of characters to a character class. The following character class matches only uppercase and lowercase letters and digits:

```
[0-9a-zA-Z]
```

Figure 5-48 summarizes the syntax for creating regular expression character classes.

Figure 5-48 ▶ **Character classes**

Character	Description	Example
[*chars*]	Match any character in the list of characters, *chars*	/[tap]/ matches "tap" and "pat
[^*chars*]	Do not match any character in *chars*	/[^tap]/ matches neither "tap" nor "pat"
[*char1-charN*]	Match characters in the range *char1* through *charN*	/[a-c]/ matches the lowercase letters a through c
[^*char1-charN*]	Do not match characters in the range *char1* through *charN*	/[^a-c]/ does not match the lowercase letters a through c
[*a-z*]	Match lowercase letters	/[a-z][a-z]/ matches any two consecutive lowercase letters
[*A-Z*]	Match uppercase letters	/[A-Z][A-Z]/ matches any two consecutive uppercase letters
[*a-zA-Z*]	Match letters	/[a-zA-Z][a-zA-Z]/ matches any two consecutive letters
[*0-9*]	Match digits	/[1][0-9]/ matches the numbers "10" through "19"
[*0-9a-zA-Z*]	Match digits and letters	/[0-9a-zA-Z][0-9a-zA-Z]/ matches any two consecutive letters or numbers

Specifying Repeating Characters

So far, the regular expression symbols have applied to single characters. Regular expressions also include symbols that indicate the number of times to repeat a particular character. To specify the exact number of times to repeat a character, you append the character with the symbols

```
{n}
```

where *n* is the number of times to repeat the character. For example, to specify that a text string should contain only five digits, such as a zip code, you could use either

```
/^\d\d\d\d\d$/
```

or the more compact form

`/^\d{5}$/`

If you don't know how many times to repeat a character, you can use the symbol * for 0 or more repetitions, + for 1 or more repetitions, or ? for 0 repetitions or 1 repetition. Figure 5-49 describes these and other repetition characters supported by regular expressions.

Repetition characters   Figure 5-49

Repetition Character(s)	Description	Example
*	Repeat 0 or more times	/\s*/ matches 0 or more consecutive white space characters
?	Repeat 0 or 1 time	/colou?r/ matches "color" or "colour"
+	Repeat 1 or more times	/\s+/ matches 1 or more consecutive white space characters
{n}	Repeat exactly n times	/\d{9}/ matches a nine-digit number
{n, }	Repeat at least n times	/\d{9,}/ matches a number with at least nine digits
{n,m}	Repeat at least n times but no more than m times	/\d{5,9}/ matches a number with 5 to 9 digits

You'll practice using some of the repetitive symbols to create regular expressions on the demo page.

To apply a repetition pattern:

▶ 1. In the Enter a text string box, change the sample text to **To be or not to be. That is the question.**

▶ 2. In the Or enter one directly text box, change the regular expression to **/\bt[a-zA-Z]*\b/gi** to create a regular expression to match all words that begin with the letter t followed by any number of uppercase or lowercase letters, and then click the **Pattern Test** button. Words of varying length beginning with the letter t are selected. See Figure 5-50.

Repetitive characters being used   Figure 5-50

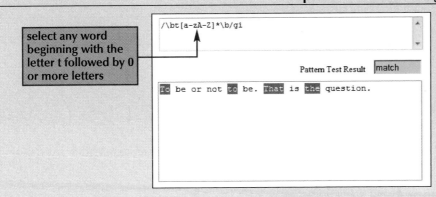

select any word beginning with the letter t followed by 0 or more letters

`/\bt[a-zA-Z]*\b/gi`

Pattern Test Result match

To be or not to be. That is the question.

▶ **3.** In the Or enter one directly text box, change the regular expression to **/\bt[a-zA-Z]{2}\b/gi** to revise the regular expression pattern to limit the number of letters after the initial letter t to two, and then click the **Pattern Test** button. The word "the" is highlighted, which is the only three-letter word beginning with the letter t.

Using Escape Sequences

Many commonly used characters are reserved by the regular expression language. The forward slash character / is reserved to mark the beginning and end of a regular expression literal. The ?, +, and * characters are used to specify the number of times a character can be repeated. What if you need to use one of these characters in a regular expression? For example, how would you create a regular expression matching the date pattern *mm/dd/yyyy* when the / character is already used to mark the boundaries of the regular expression?

In these cases, you use an escape sequence. An **escape sequence** is a special command inside the regular expression that tells the JavaScript interpreter not to interpret what follows as a character. In the regular expression language, escape sequences are marked by the backslash character \. You have been using escape sequences for several pages now—for example, you used the characters \d to represent a numeric digit, while d simply represents the letter d. The \ character can also be applied to reserved characters to indicate their use in a regular expression. For example, the escape sequence \$ represents the $ character while the escape sequence \\ represents a single \ character. Figure 5-51 provides a list of escape sequences for other special characters.

| Figure 5-51 | Escape sequences |

Escape Sequence	Represents	Example
\/	The / character	/\d\/\d/ matches "5/9" "3/1" but not "59" or "31"
\\	The \ character	/\d\\\d/ matches "5\9" or "3\1" but not "59" or "31"
\.	The . character	/\d\.\d\d/ matches "3.20" or "5.95" but not "320" or "595"
*	The * character	/[a-z]{4}*/ matches "help*" or "pass*"
\+	The + character	/\d\+\d/ matches "5+9" or "3+1" but not "59" or "39"
\?	The ? character	/[a-z]{4}\?/ matches "help?" or "info?"
|	The	character	/a|b/ matches "a|b"
\(\)	The (and) characters	/\(\d{3}\)/ matches "(800)" or "(555)"
\{ \}	The { and } characters	/\{[a-z]{4}\}/ matches "{pass}" or "{info}"
\^	The ^ character	/\d+\^\d/ matches "321^2" or "4^3"
\$	The $ character	/\$\d{2}\.\d{2}/ matches "$59.95" or "$19.50"
\n	A new line	/\n/ matches the occurrence of a new line in the text string
\r	A carriage return	/\r/ matches the occurrence of a carriage return in the text string
\t	A tab	/\t/ matches the occurrence of a tab in the text string

You'll enter an escape sequence on the demo page to create a regular expression for the date pattern.

To use an escape sequence:

▶ **1.** In the Enter a text string box, change the sample text to the date **5/21/2012**.

▶ **2.** In the Or enter one directly text box, change the regular expression to **/^\d{1,2}\/ \d{1,2}\/\d{4}$/** to match date values.

▶ **3.** Click the **Pattern Test** button. As shown in Figure 5-52, the test date you entered matches the regular expression pattern, which consists of one or two digits followed by a forward slash and then another one or two digits followed by a forward slash and then ending with four digits.

Escape sequence being used ◀ **Figure 5-52**

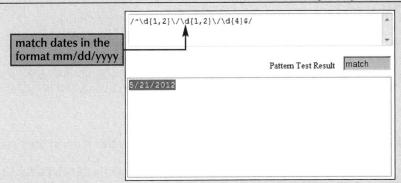

4. Test the regular expression against other text strings and verify that it matches any date in the format *mm/dd/yyyy*. The regular expression you used for the date format also matches some invalid date patterns such as 23/99/0007 or 0/0/0000 because the regular expression does not check that the month values range from 1 to 12 or that the day values range from 1 to 31.

Tip

Explore the date expressions available from the selection list on the demo page to learn more about writing expressions involving dates.

Specifying Alternate Patterns and Grouping

In some regular expressions, you may want to define two possible patterns for the same text string. You can do this by joining different patterns using the | character. The general form is

`pattern1|pattern2`

where *pattern1* and *pattern2* are two distinct patterns. For example, the expression

`/^\d{5}$|^$/`

matches a text string that either contains only five digits or is empty. You'll explore how to use the alternate character on the demo page by creating a regular expression that matches the titles Mr., Mrs., or Miss.

To specify alternate regular expression patterns:

▶ **1.** In the Enter a text string box, change the sample text to **Mr.**

▶ **2.** In the Or enter one of your own text box, change the regular expression pattern to **/Mr\.|Mrs\.|Miss/** and then click the **Pattern Test** button. The pattern test result shows a match.

▶ **3.** Repeat Steps 1 and 2 to change the sample text to **Mrs.** and then to **Miss** and verify that both regular expressions match the sample text.

Another useful technique in regular expressions is to group character symbols. Once you create a group, the symbols within that group can be treated as a single unit. The syntax to create a group is

`(pattern)`

where *pattern* is a regular expression pattern. Groups are often used with the alternation character to create regular expressions that match different variations of the same text. For example, a phone number might be entered with or without an area code. The pattern for the phone number without an area code, matching such numbers as 555-1234, is:

`/^\d{3}-\d{4}$/`

If an area code is included in the format 800-555-1234, the pattern is:

`/^\d{3}-\d{3}-\d{4}$/`

To allow the area code to be added, you place it within a group and use the ? repetition character applied to the entire area code group. The regular expression is

`/^(\d{3}-)?\d{3}-\d{4}$/`

which matches either 555-1234 or 800-555-1234. You'll try this now on the demo page.

To group a pattern:

▶ **1.** In the Enter a text string box, change the sample text to **555-1234**.

▶ **2.** In the Or enter one directly text box, change the regular expression pattern to **/^(\d{3}-)?\d{3}-\d{4}$/** and then click the **Pattern Test** button. The pattern test result shows a match. See Figure 5-53.

Figure 5-53 ▶ **Group of optional characters being created**

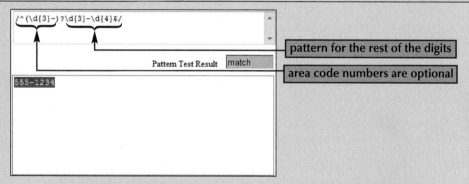

▶ **3.** In the Enter a text string box, change the phone number to **800-555-1234** and then click the **Pattern Test** button to verify that this form of the phone number also matches the regular expression.

▶ **4.** Continue to explore other test strings and regular expression patterns, and then close the demo page when you are finished.

Using the Regular Expression Object Constructor | InSight

The regular expression literal that you explored with the demo is only one way of creating a regular expression. Another approach is to create a regular expression object using the object constructor, which has the format

```
re = new RegExp(pattern, flags)
```

where *re* is a regular expression object, *pattern* is a text string of the regular expression pattern, and *flags* is a text string of the regular expression flags. The following two commands are equivalent as far as JavaScript is concerned:

```
var re = /GPS-ware/ig;
var re = new RegExp("GPS-ware","ig");
```

JavaScript treats the regular expression pattern used with the object constructor as a text string. Even though they are not regular expressions, such text strings can also contain escape sequences, which can be used to insert non-textual characters such as tabs or returns. To avoid conflict between escape sequences designed for text strings and escape sequences designed for regular expressions, you must insert an additional escape character \ for each regular expression escape sequence. The regular expression literal

```
/\b\w*\b\s\d{3}/
```

appears in the object constructor as

```
new RegExp("\\b\\w*\\b\\s\\d{3}")
```

In most cases, you will use the regular expression literal form in code. The new RegExp() operator is most often used when a script needs to retrieve the regular expression text string from another source, such as a data entry field.

Creating a Regular Expression | Reference Window

- The syntax to create a regular expression literal is
  ```
  re = /pattern/flags
  ```
  where *re* is the regular expression object, *pattern* is the regular expression pattern, and *flags* are the flags assigned to the regular expression.
- The syntax to create a regular expression with the object constructor is
  ```
  re = new RegExp(pattern, flags)
  ```
  where *pattern* is the text string of the regular expression and *flags* is the text string of the regular expression flags.

Working with the Regular Expression Object

Now that you have reviewed the syntax involved in writing a regular expression, you can use regular expressions in JavaScript programs. As noted earlier, a regular expression is treated as an object with its own collection of properties and methods. Before applying regular expressions to Carol's Web forms, you'll look at some of the methods associated with regular expressions.

Exploring Regular Expression Methods

One method associated with regular expressions is the test() method, which is used to determine whether a text string contains a substring that matches the pattern defined by a regular expression. The syntax of the test() method is

```
re.test(string)
```

where *re* is a regular expression object and *string* is the text string you want to test. The test() method returns the Boolean value true if a match is located within the text string and false otherwise. For example, the following code uses the test() method to compare the text string stored in the zipstring variable with the regular expression object stored in the regx variable:

```
zipstring = document.forms[0].zip.value;
regx = /^\d{5}$/;
testvalue = regx.test(zipstring);
```

If zipstring matches the pattern, the testvalue variable will have a value of true; otherwise, it will have a value of false. If you need to know where within the text string the match occurs, use the following search() method:

```
re.search(string)
```

The search() method returns the index of the first matching substring from *string*. If no match is found, it returns the value –1, just like the indexOf() method discussed in the previous session. All searches occur from the start of the text string. Unlike the indexOf() method, you cannot begin the search() method at a location other than the start of the text string.

You can also use regular expression methods that extract substrings from a text string. The match() method creates an array of substrings from a text string that match the pattern defined in a regular expression. The syntax of the match() method is

```
results = re.match(string)
```

where *results* is an array containing each matched substring. For example, the following set of commands extracts the individual words from the text string, placing each word in the words array:

```
regx = /\b\w+\b/g;
words = "GPS-ware Products For Sale".match(regx);
```

The global flag must be set to locate all matches in the text string. Without the g flag, only the first match is returned.

Similar to the match() method is the split() method, which breaks a text string into substrings at each location where a pattern match is found, placing the substrings into an array. You saw how to use the split() method in the previous session when it was applied to string objects. It can likewise be used with regular expressions. The following code shows how to split a text string at each word boundary followed by one or more white space characters:

```
regx = /\b\s*/g;
words = "GPS-ware Products For Sale".split(regx);
```

In this example, each element in the words array contains a word from the sample text string.

Besides pattern matching and extracting substrings, regular expressions can also be used to replace text. The syntax of the replace method is

```
string.replace(re,newsubstr)
```

where *string* is a text string containing text to be replaced, *re* is a regular expression defining the pattern of a substring, and *newsubstr* is the replacement substring. The following code shows how to apply the replace() method to change a text string:

```
oldtext = "<h1>GPS-ware Products</h1>";
regx = /h1/g;
newtext = oldtext.replace(regx,"h2");
```

In this code, the regular expression matches all of the occurrences of the h1 substring in the sample text string. When the replace() method is applied to the oldtext variable, it replaces all occurrences of h1 with h2. The result is the newtext variable that contains the text string <h2>GPS-ware Products</h2>. If you neglect to include the g flag, only the first occurrence of the substring is replaced.

Figure 5-54 summarizes the methods associated with the regular expression object.

Methods of the regular expression object ◀ Figure 5-54

Method	Description
re.compile(pattern,flags)	Compiles or recompiles a regular expression re, where pattern is the text string of the new regular expression pattern and flags are flags applied to the pattern
re.exec(string)	Executes a search on string using the regular expression re; pattern results are returned in an array and reflected in the properties of the global RegExp object
re.match(string)	Performs a pattern match in string using the re regular expression; matched substrings are stored in an array
string.replace(re, newsubstr)	Replaces the substring defined by the regular expression re in the text string string with newsubstr
string.search(re)	Searches string for a substring matching the regular expression re; returns the index of the match, or −1 if no match is found
string.split(re)	Splits string at each point indicated by the regular expression re; the substrings are stored in an array
re.test(string)	Performs a pattern match on the text string string using the regular expression re, returning the Boolean value true if a match is found and false otherwise

Tip

The replace() method is helpful in programs that revise and edit the code of HTML and XHTML documents.

Working with Regular Expressions | Reference Window

- To test whether a text string matches a regular expression, use the method
    ```
    re.test(string)
    ```
    where re is the regular expression object and string is the text string to be tested. The test() method returns the Boolean value true when a match is found and false when no match is found.
- To search a text string, use:
    ```
    re.search(string)
    ```
    The search() method returns the index of the first matching substring from the text string. If no match is found, it returns the value −1.
- To create an array of the matching substrings from a text string, use
    ```
    results = re.match(string)
    ```
    where results is an array containing each matched substring.
- To split a string into substrings, use
    ```
    results = string.split(re)
    ```
    where results is an array containing the substrings, string is the original text string, and re is a regular expression that indicates the splitting points in the text string.
- To replace a substring with a new substring, use
    ```
    string.replace(re, newsubstr)
    ```
    where string is the text string containing the text to be replaced, re is a regular expression defining the substring to be replaced, and newsubstr is the replacement substring.

Validating a Zip Code Using Regular Expressions

You'll use your knowledge of regular expressions to create a new function to validate customers' entries in the zip field. In the first line of the function, you'll create a regular expression that matches either a five-digit or a nine-digit zip code or an empty text string (when the zip code is not required for delivery). The regular expression is:

```
/^\d{5}(-\d{4})?$|^$/
```

This regular expression matches zip codes in the form *nnnnn* or *nnnnn-nnnn*; it also uses the alternation character | to allow for empty text strings. Study this regular expression until you understand how it works. You'll use this regular expression in the following function:

```
function checkZipRE(zip) {
   regx = /^\d{5}(-\d{4})?$|^$/;
   return regx.test(zip);
}
```

The second line of the function uses the test() method to determine whether a customer's zip code matches that pattern, returning the test result. Compared to the checkZip() function you created in the previous session, this more compact function tests for greater variations in zip code patterns than the original function. This demonstrates the power of regular expressions.

You'll add this function to the validation tests for Carol's delivery form.

To create the checkZipRE() function:

1. Return to the **contact.js** file in your text editor.
2. Directly below the checkForm2() function, insert the following code:

```
function checkZipRE(zip) {
   regx = /^\d{5}(-\d{4})?$|^$/;
   return regx.test(zip);
}
```

3. Change the checkForm2() function so that it calls the **checkZipRE()** function to validate the zip code field. Figure 5-55 highlights the revised code.

Figure 5-55 Code for the checkZipRE() function

code to call the checkZipRE() function

```
   else if (document.forms[0].city.value.length == 0)
      {alert("You must enter a city name");
       return false;}
   else if (checkZipRE(document.forms[0].zip.value) == false)
      {alert("Invalid zip code");
       return false;}
   else return true;
}

function checkZipRE(zip) {
   regx = /^\d{5}(-\d{4})?$|^$/;
   return regx.test(zip);
}
```

regular expression for a U.S. zip code

4. Close the file, saving your changes, and then reload **form2.htm** in your Web browser.
5. Enter sample text into the first name, last name, street, and city fields.

▶ **6.** In the zip field, enter sample zip code values in both the *nnnnn* and *nnnnn-nnnn* formats. Verify that the Web form is successfully submitted and the next form, form3. htm, is loaded when the zip code field is entered in the proper format or left blank.

You've completed the validation checks for the delivery form.

Validating Financial Data

The final of Carol's three forms is the form3.htm file, a payment form into which customers enter the credit card information that indicates how they will pay for their order. Figure 5-56 shows the contents of the payment form along with the field names.

Payment form and field names ◀ Figure 5-56

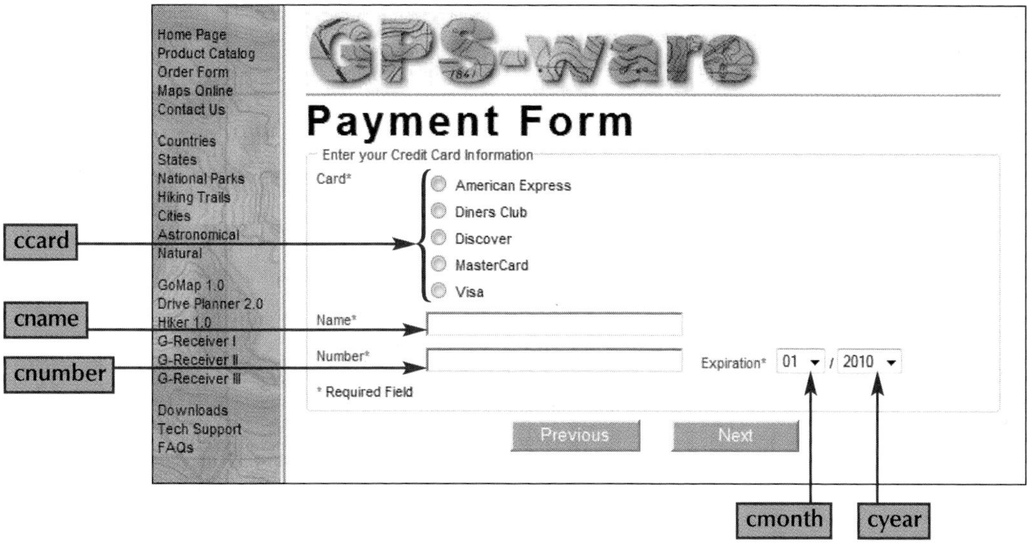

The customer's credit card data will eventually be validated on the Web server against a financial database. However, you can do some validation checks on the client side to weed out problems before they get to the server. Carol already inserted some validation checks in the payment.js file, which has already been attached to the form3.htm file. The validation checks are stored in the following two functions:

```
function checkForm3() {
   if (selectedCard() == -1)
      {alert("You must select a credit card");
       return false;}
   else if (document.forms[0].cname.value.length == 0)
      {alert("You must enter the name on your credit card");
       return false;}
   else if (document.forms[0].cnumber.value.length == 0)
      {alert("You must enter the number on your credit card");
       return false;}
   else return true;
}
```

and

```
function selectedCard() {
   card = -1;
   for (var i = 0; i < document.forms[0].ccard.length; i++) {
      if (document.forms[0].ccard[i].checked) card = i;
   }
   return card;
}
```

The checkForm3() function verifies that: (1) the customer has selected a credit card, (2) the customer has entered the name on the card, and (3) the customer has entered the number on the card. Although you have no way of knowing whether the name and number are real or accurate credit card accounts, the checkForm3() function verifies that the customer has entered something into those fields. The checkForm3() function tests whether one of the five credit cards on the payment form has been selected by calling the selectedCard() function. The selectedCard() function goes through all of the option buttons from the ccard field and returns the index number (0 to 4) of the checked option button. If no option button is checked (meaning that the customer has not selected a credit card from the list), then it returns a value of –1 and the form is not validated.

Removing Blank Spaces from Credit Card Numbers

Beyond verifying that a customer has entered something for each field, Carol wants the form to test whether the customer has entered a legitimate credit card number. Credit card numbers often appear on credit cards broken up by spaces to make it easier for cardholders to read them. Before you examine the actual card numbers, you want to remove any blank spaces that a customer entered into the credit card number field. You can do this by creating a regular expression that searches for any occurrence of white space in the credit card number field, and then by applying the replace() method to replace each occurrence of white space with an empty text string. The regular expression to match all occurrences of white space in a text string is:

```
wsregx = /\s/g
```

When applied to a text string containing spaces such as

```
123 45 6789
```

the spaces are removed, resulting in the text string

```
123456789
```

You add the g flag so that the regular expression searches the entire text string, instead of stopping at the first occurrence of white space. To replace those white spaces with empty text strings, you apply the following replace() method, storing the revised text string in the cnum variable:

```
var cnum = document.forms[0].cnumber.value.replace(wsregx,"");
```

You'll add both of these commands to a function named checkNumber() that you'll build upon to validate customers' credit card numbers.

To insert the checkNumber() function:

▶ **1.** Open the **payment.js** file in your text editor.

▶ **2.** Directly below the selectedCard() function, insert the following function, as shown in Figure 5-57:

```
function checkNumber() {
    wsregx = /\s/g;
    var cnum = document.forms[0].cnumber.value.replace(wsregx,"");
}
```

Code to remove white space from credit card numbers ◀ **Figure 5-57**

```
function selectedCard() {
    var card = -1;
    for (var i = 0; i < document.forms[0].ccard.length; i++) {
        if (document.forms[0].ccard[i].checked) card = i;
    }
    return card;
}

function checkNumber() {
    wsregx = /\s/g;
    var cnum = document.forms[0].cnumber.value.replace(wsregx,"");
}
```

regular expression that matches all white space in the text string

replaces each white space character with an empty text string

Validating Credit Card Number Patterns

Each type of credit card has a certain pattern to its numbers that uniquely identifies it. GPS-ware accepts five different credit cards: American Express, Diners Club, Discover, MasterCard, and Visa. Figure 5-58 lists the number pattern for each type of card, along with a regular expression that matches the described pattern.

Credit card number patterns ◀ **Figure 5-58**

Credit Card	Number Pattern	Regular Expression
American Express	Starts with 34 or 37 followed by 13 other digits	/^3[47]\d{13}$/
Diners Club	Starts with 300, 301, 302, 303, 304, or 305 followed by 11 digits, or starts with 36 or 38 followed by 12 digits	/^30[0-5]\d{11}$\|^3[68]\d{12}$/
Discover	Starts with 6011 followed by 12 other digits	/^6011\d{12}$/
MasterCard	Starts with 51, 52, 53, 54, or 55 followed by 14 other digits	/^5[1-5]\d{14}$/
Visa	Starts with a 4 followed by 12 or 15 other digits	/^4(\d{12}|\d{15})$/

To validate the credit card number entered by a customer, you can use the test() method with the regular expressions shown in Figure 5-58. Recall that the selectedCard() function returns the index number of the selected option button in Carol's Web form. In this case, the index numbers for the different credit card options are: 0 = American Express, 1 = Diners Club, 2 = Discover, 3 = MasterCard, and 4 = Visa. The following code uses a switch statement to define the regular expression pattern for each credit card, storing the regular expression in the cregx variable:

```
switch (selectedCard()) {
   case 0: cregx = /^3[47]\d{13}$/; break;
   case 1: cregx = /^30[0-5]\d{11}$|^3[68]\d{12}$/; break;
   case 2: cregx = /^6011\d{12}$/; break;
   case 3: cregx = /^5[1-5]\d{14}$/; break;
   case 4: cregx = /^4(\d{12}|\d{15})$/; break;
}
return cregx.test(cnum);
```

The function ends by testing the selected regular expression pattern against the credit card number stored in the cnum variable. A value of true indicates that the credit card number matches the corresponding pattern, whereas a value of false indicates that the number does not match the pattern and is invalid.

You'll add these commands to the checkNumber() function.

To create tests based on credit card number patterns:

1. Insert the following commands in the checkNumber() function, as shown in Figure 5-59:

```
switch (selectedCard()) {
   case 0: cregx = /^3[47]\d{13}$/; break;
   case 1: cregx = /^30[0-5]\d{11}$|^3[68]\d{12}$/; break;
   case 2: cregx = /^6011\d{12}$/; break;
   case 3: cregx = /^5[1-5]\d{14}$/; break;
   case 4: cregx = /^4(\d{12}|\d{15})$/; break;
}
return cregx.test(cnum);
```

Figure 5-59 Code to check credit card number patterns

```
function checkNumber() {
   wsregx = /\s/g;
   var cnum = document.forms[0].cnumber.value.replace(wsregx,"");

   switch (selectedCard()) {
      case 0: cregx = /^3[47]\d{13}$/; break;
      case 1: cregx = /^30[0-5]\d{11}$|^3[68]\d{12}$/; break;
      case 2: cregx = /^6011\d{12}$/; break;
      case 3: cregx = /^5[1-5]\d{14}$/; break;
      case 4: cregx = /^4(\d{12}|\d{15})$/; break;
   }

   return cregx.test(cnum);
}
```

credit card patterns for five credit companies

2. Save your changes to the file.

Next, you'll call this function from the checkForm3() function to add it to the list of validation checks already present in the payment form.

To check for valid credit card number patterns:

1. Add the following commands to the checkForm3() function, as shown in Figure 5-60:

```
else if (checkNumber() == false)
   {alert("Your card number is not valid");
   return false;}
```

Final checkForm3() function   **Figure 5-60**

```
function checkForm3() {
    if (selectedCard() == -1)
        {alert("You must select a credit card");
        return false;}
    else if (document.forms[0].cname.value.length == 0)
        {alert("You must enter the name on your credit card");
        return false;}
    else if (document.forms[0].cnumber.value.length == 0)
        {alert("You must enter the number on your credit card");
        return false;}
    else if (checkNumber() == false)
        {alert("Your card number is not valid");
        return false;}
    else return true;
}
```

checks that the card number is valid

▶ **2.** Save your changes to the file, and then reload **form3.htm** in your Web browser.

You'll test the form for valid credit card numbers.

▶ **3.** Enter sample text in the name field so that the form is not invalidated for lack of a cardholder name.

▶ **4.** Click each of the credit card option buttons and enter the corresponding sample credit card numbers shown in Figure 5-61. Verify that the form accepts the valid numbers and rejects the invalid ones.

Valid and invalid credit card number patterns   **Figure 5-61**

Credit Card	Valid	Invalid
American Express	34 12345 67890 127	35 12345 67890 127
Diners Club	303 12345 67890 1	310 12345 67890 1
Discover	6011 12345 67890 19	6012 12345 67890 19
MasterCard	51 12345 67890 1235	59 12345 67890 1235
Visa	4 12345 67890 12349	8 12345 67890 12349

▶ **5.** Continue testing other combinations of credit card numbers to verify that only numbers that match the card patterns described in Figure 5-58 are accepted by the browser.

Testing with the Luhn Formula

One last test that you can do on the client side weeds out mistakes a customer might make when entering the credit card number. All credit card numbers must satisfy the **Luhn Formula**, or **Mod10 algorithm**, which is a formula developed by a group of mathematicians in the 1960s to provide a quick validation check on an account number by adding up the digits in the number. Almost all institutions that employ unique account or identification numbers, including credit card companies, use numbers that satisfy the Luhn Formula. The following steps, also shown in Figure 5-62, determine whether a particular number satisfies the Luhn Formula:

1. Starting from the second to the last digit in the account number, separate every other digit into two groups, moving to the left.
2. Double the value of each digit in the first group (the group containing the first digit you selected).
3. Calculate the sum of the digits in each group.

4. Add the values of the two sums together.

5. If the total sum is evenly divisible by 10, then the number satisfies the Luhn Formula.

Figure 5-62   **Luhn Formula**

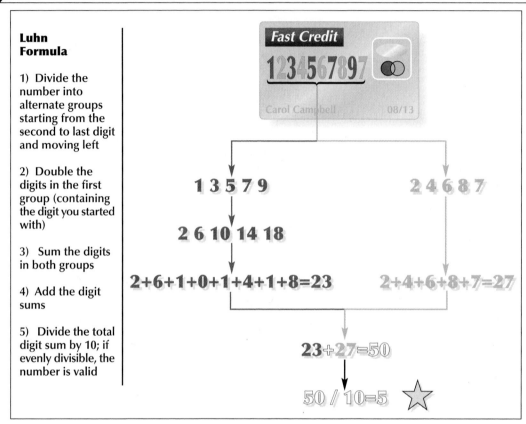

A function to calculate the Luhn Formula has already been created and is stored in the payment.js file. The code for the luhn() function is:

```
function luhn(num) {
   var luhnTotal = 0;
   for (var i = num.length-1; i >= 0; i--) {
      luhnTotal += parseInt(num.charAt(i));
      i--;
      num2 = new String(num.charAt(i)*2);
      for (j = 0; j < num2.length; j++) {
         luhnTotal += parseInt(num2.charAt(j));
      }
   }
   return (luhnTotal % 10 == 0);
}
```

The luhn() function has a single parameter, num, which contains the text string of the account number to be validated. It assumes that all white space characters have already been removed from the text string. The function loops through each digit in the text string, adding up the digit sums. Each time it encounters a digit that should be doubled, it stores the doubled digit in a string object named num2, which is then summed before continuing through the larger number string. A running total of the digit sum is stored in the luhnTotal variable. After the last digit has been added, the function uses the % operator to test whether dividing luhnTotal by 10 results in a remainder of 0. If it does, a Boolean value of true is returned by the function; otherwise, it returns a Boolean value of false. Study the code in this function. Although this function may seem daunting at first, it is composed entirely of string object methods and properties that you learned earlier in this tutorial.

You can call the luhn() function from the checkNumber() function you just created. The checkNumber() function will then have two tests: first it will check whether the selected card number matches the number pattern of the credit card company, and then it will check whether the card number fulfills the criterion of the Luhn Formula. You'll add the test for the Luhn Formula to your code.

To add a test for the Luhn Formula:

1. Return to the **payment.js** file in your text editor.

2. In the checkNumber() function, change the return statement to the following, as shown in Figure 5-63:

```
return (cregx.test(cnum) && luhn(cnum));
```

Final checkNumber() function | **Figure 5-63**

```
function checkNumber() {
    wsregx = /\s/g;
    var cnum = document.forms[0].cnumber.value.replace(wsregx,"");

    switch (selectedCard()) {
        case 0: cregx = /^3[47]\d{13}$/; break;
        case 1: cregx = /^30[0-5]\d{11}$|^3[68]\d{12}$/; break;
        case 2: cregx = /^6011\d{12}$/; break;
        case 3: cregx = /^5[1-5]\d{14}$/; break;
        case 4: cregx = /^4(\d{12}|\d{15})$/; break;
    }

    return (cregx.test(cnum) && luhn(cnum));
}
```

return value is true only if the card number matches the regular expression pattern and passes the Luhn Formula

The checkNumber() function uses the && logical operator so that a value of true is returned only if the credit card number matches the correct pattern and satisfies the Luhn Formula.

3. Close the file, saving your changes.

4. Reload **form3.htm** in your Web browser.

5. Click **American Express** from the list of credit cards, and then enter a sample cardholder name in the name field.

6. In the Number field, enter **34 12345 67890 123** and then click the **Next** button. Your browser alerts you that the number is not valid.

7. In the Number field, change the credit card number to **34 12345 67890 127** and then click the **Next** button. The number is accepted and a Web page opens, indicating that the order has been submitted successfully.

At this point, the customer's order could be sent to the Web server for further processing and validation checks. Obviously, the server would have to consult financial databases to verify that the credit card information represented a real account; but adding these validation checks on the client side allows the customer's program to filter out errors that the company's server would otherwise have to deal with.

Passing Data Between Forms

To simplify form validation for the GPS-ware Web site, Carol divided the data that she wanted collected into three separate forms. When customer input is spread out over several forms, you usually need some way of passing collected data along as customers move from one form to another. One way of doing this is with cookies, which are beyond the scope of this tutorial. Another approach is to append form data to a URL.

Appending Form Data

To append form data to a URL, you set the form's action to a URL and set the method of the form to "get". For example, the <form> tag

```
<form action = "report.htm" method = "get">
```

tells the browser to open the report.htm file using the get method when the current Web form is submitted for processing. When the report.htm file is opened by the browser, data from the calling form will be appended to its URL as follows

```
http://server/path/report.htm?field1=value1&field2=value2& ...
```

where *server* and *path* are the server and path names for the Web page; *field1*, *field2*, and so on are the names of the fields in the calling Web form; and *value1*, *value2*, and so on are the values stored in each of those fields. For example, if your Web form contains fields named firstname and lastname with values of Carol and Campbell, respectively, then the following form data is appended to report.htm's URL when it's opened in the browser:

```
http://server/path/report.htm?firstname=Carol&lastname=Campbell
```

The field/value pairs are appended to the form element after the ? character. To retrieve the form data, you must extract the substring that appears after the ? symbol, ignoring any text that appears before the ? symbol.

Extracting a Substring from a URL

You can reference the URL of the current Web page using the location object, which stores the complete text of the URL. The location object supports several properties to extract only parts of that URL. To extract only the text of the URL occurring from the ? character onward, use the following object property:

```
location.search
```

For example, the value of the location.search property for the URL noted above would consist of the following substring:

```
?firstname=Carol&lastname=Campbell
```

To remove the initial ? symbol, apply the slice() method discussed in the previous session. The expression

```
location.search.slice(1)
```

results in the following text string:

```
firstname=Carol&lastname=Campbell
```

After you have the field names and values in this substring, you can extract the form information using what you learned about string methods and regular expressions. This involves formatting the substring contents and splitting the substring into separate pieces.

Extracting Form Data from a Substring

Before you can extract form data from a substring, you must format the substring. URLs cannot contain blank spaces, so any blanks in the form data are replaced with the + symbol. For example, if a Web form contains a single field named username with a field value of Carol Campbell, the form data would be stored in the following text string:

```
username=Carol+Campbell
```

To replace every occurrence of a + symbol with a blank space, you can apply the regular expression along with the replace() method

```
plusregx = /\+/g;
formdata.replace(plusregx, " ");
```

where *formdata* is a text string containing the form data appended to a URL. You must use the escape symbol \ to reference the + character in the regular expression.

The other part of formatting the substring is to remove all escape characters from the form data. Characters such as / and : will not appear in the form data because they are reserved for use in describing the URL path. Instead of those characters, the URL will display the escape character codes: %2F for the / character and %3A for the : character. Other special characters have similar escape codes. You can remove these codes, replacing them with the actual characters using the unescape() method

```
unescape(string)
```

where *string* is the text containing escape character codes. To remove any escape codes from the form data, you would apply the following command:

```
formdata = unescape(formdata)
```

Once you've reformatted the form data string, you can split the field/value pairs. Recall that the general syntax of the field/value pairs is

```
field1=value1&field2=value2& ...
```

with each field/value pair separated by an & symbol and the fields separated from their values by an = symbol. To split the fields and values into separate substrings, you can apply the split() method to the regular expression

```
splitregx = /[&=]/g;
formArray = formdata.split(splitregx);
```

where *formArray* is an array in which each item is either a field name or a field value. The regular expression uses a group to match all occurrences of either the & symbol or the = symbol. After running these commands, the contents of *formArray* will be:

```
formArray[0] = field1
formArray[1] = value1
formArray[2] = field2
formArray[3] = value2
...
```

Tip

You can reverse the effect of the unescape() method by applying the escape() method to the text string.

At this point, you can reference each field name and field value by its location in the *formArray* and incorporate those values in your JavaScript program. Putting this all together, a function that extracts form data from a URL could appear as follows:

```
function retrieveData() {
    formString = location.search.slice(1);
    formData = formString.replace(/\+/g, " ");
    formData = unescape(formData);
    formArray = formData.split(/[&=]/g);
}
```

To see how transferring data from one form to another works in practice, you'll look at a demo page.

To view the form demo:

1. Open **demo_form1.htm** from the tutorial.05\demo folder in your Web browser.

2. Enter **your name**, **your age**, and **your city** in the appropriate fields in the form. See Figure 5-64.

Figure 5-64 | **Form data being entered**

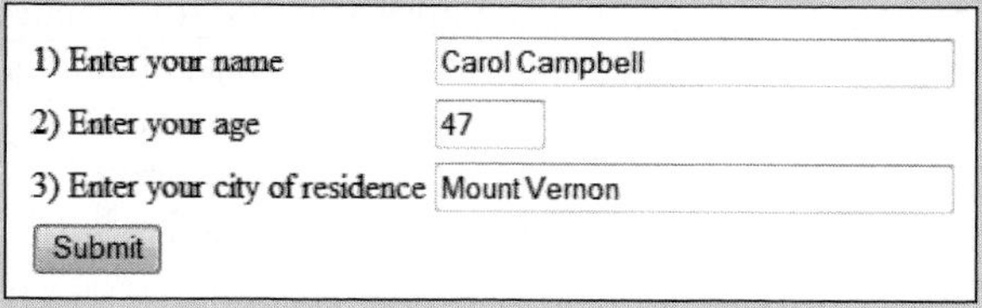

3. Click the **Submit** button. The values you entered in the first form are retrieved from the URL and displayed in the form on the second Web page. See Figure 5-65.

Figure 5-65 | **Form data retrieved from the URL**

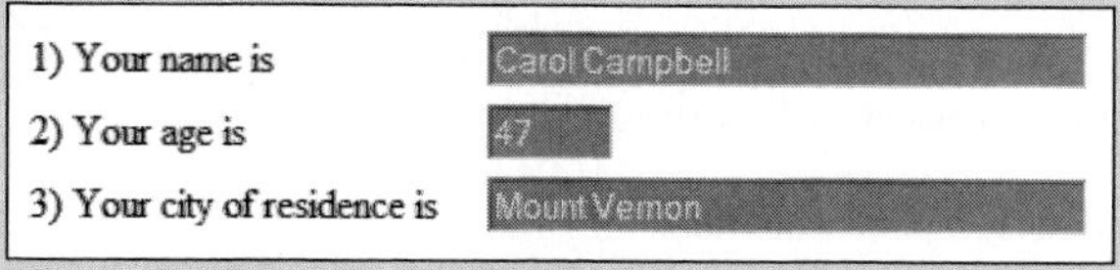

4. Close your Web browser and any open files.

At this point, you won't add the ability to pass form data to Carol's Web form, though she may want you to add this feature in the future. You've completed your work on Carol's order forms.

Review | Session 5.3 Quick Check

1. What regular expressions match every occurrence of the substring "GPS" in a text string, regardless of case?
2. What regular expression matches the first occurrence of the word "products"?
3. A Social Security number consists of nine digits. Write a regular expression to match this pattern.
4. Social Security numbers can be entered either as *ddddddddd* or *ddd-dd-dddd*. Write a regular expression to match either pattern.

5. Write a regular expression that matches any of the substrings "street", "avenue", or "lane". Make the match case insensitive and match every occurrence of the substring in the text string.

6. What JavaScript command tests whether the text string "username" matches the pattern specified in the regular expression object reuser?

7. What JavaScript command splits the text string "date" at every occurrence of the / character?

8. What is the Luhn Formula?

9. What object property extracts any form data appended to the URL of the current Web document?

Tutorial Summary | Review

This tutorial explored how JavaScript can be used to validate Web forms. In the first session, you learned how to reference different elements in a Web form, including input boxes, selection lists, and option button groups. You saw how to extract values from form fields and use them to create calculated fields. You also learned about some of the difficulties in displaying numeric values in a Web form, and techniques to create nicely formatted output. The second session introduced the concept of form validation: comparing the benefits and costs of client-side and server-side validation. You learned how to validate a form before allowing it to be processed, and you learned about the properties and methods associated with string objects. The third session introduced the language of regular expressions. You learned how to create a regular expression to match a wide variety of patterns, and you learned about the properties and methods associated with regular expression objects. In the third session, you employed regular expressions to validate both zip code and credit card data. You also learned about the Luhn Formula and how it could be used to validate credit card numbers before they are submitted to a Web server. The third session concluded with a discussion of passing data from one Web page to another, with special emphasis on passing field names and values from one Web form to another.

Key Terms

alert box	form validation	server-side validation
character class	Luhn Formula	string object
client-side validation	Mod10 algorithm	substring
delimiter	pattern matching	word
escape sequence	regular expression	word character
focus	regular expression literal	

| Practice | | Review Assignments |

Practice the skills you learned in the tutorial using the same case scenario.

Data Files needed for the Review Assignments: ordertxt.htm, formtxt.js, border.jpg, done.htm, gps.css, gpsware.jpg

Carol has a few changes she wants you to make to the first order form. Rather than displaying the GPS-ware products in a selection list, Carol wants the product names to appear as separate fields. This allows customers to purchase more than one product without having to open a second form. Also, instead of displaying the quantity to order in a selection list, Carol wants the quantity value placed in an input field, so that customers can specify any quantity in their order. Finally, Carol wants your script to confirm that a shipping option has been selected before the order is submitted to the Web server. Figure 5-66 shows a preview of the new order form.

Figure 5-66

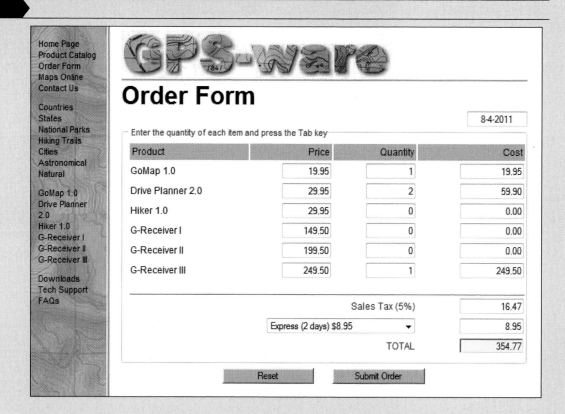

Carol wants the new form to include the following features:

- When a customer opens the form, the current date should appear in the date field.
- When a customer enters a new quantity in the Quantity column, the cost should update automatically.
- Customers should be prevented from entering anything other than digits in the Quantity column. If a value other than a digit is entered, the customer should be notified of the error and the quantity value that was entered incorrectly should be reset to 0.
- When a customer selects a shipping option, the total cost should be automatically updated to reflect the shipping price.
- The form cannot be submitted unless a shipping option has been selected.

Complete the following:

1. Use your text editor to open the **ordertxt.htm** and **formtxt.js** files from the tutorial.05\ review folder, enter *your name* and *the date* in the comment section of each file, and then save the files as **order.htm** and **form.js**, respectively.

2. Go to the **order.htm** file in your text editor, and review the contents of the file, noting the IDs and names used for the elements in the document. Insert a link to the **form.js** file in the head section of the file and close the document.

3. Go to the **form.js** file in your text editor. Below the comment section, insert an event handler to run the initForm() function when the page loads.

4. Create a function named **initForm()**. The purpose of this function is to initialize the contents of the Web page and form. Add the following commands to the function:

   a. Set the value of the date field to the value returned by the todayTxt() function.

   b. Set the focus of the Web browser on the qty1 field.

   c. Add onblur event handlers for the qty1 through qty6 fields, running the calcCost() function whenever these fields lose the focus of the Web browser.

   d. Add an onchange event handler to the shipping field, running the calcShipping() function when the value of the field changes.

5. Create a function named **productCosts()**. The purpose of this function is to return the sum of the total costs of the six GPS-ware products in the order form. The costs of items are stored in input fields named cost1 through cost6. Have the function do the following:

   a. Create a variable named **pc1** that is equal to the value of the cost1 field. Use the parseFloat() function to convert the field's value from a text string to a number.

   b. Use the same process to create variables **pc2** through **pc6**, which are equal to the numeric values of the cost2 through cost6 fields.

   c. Return the sum of the pc1 through pc6 variables.

6. Create a function named **shipExpense()**. The purpose of the shipExpense() function is to return the cost of the selected shipping option. The shipping options are stored within a selection list named shipping. Have the function do the following:

   a. Create a variable named **sindex** equal to the selected index from the shipping selection list.

   b. Return the numeric value of the option from the shipping selection list whose index is equal to the sindex variable. Be sure to use the parseFloat() function to convert the option value from a text string to a number.

7. Create a function named **calcTotal()**. The purpose of the calcTotal() function is to display the cost of the sales tax and also the total cost of the order. Add the following commands to the function:

   a. Create a variable named **ordercost** that is equal to the value returned by the productCosts() function. Create a variable named **ordertax** that is equal to 5% of the ordercost variable. Create a variable named **ordership** that is equal to the value returned by the shipExpense() function. Finally, create a variable named **ordertotal** that is equal to the sum of the ordercost, ordertax, and ordership variables.

   b. Store the value of the ordertax variable in the tax field. Display to two decimal places.

   c. Store the value of the ordertotal variable in the total field. Also display the value to two decimal places.

8. Create a function named **calcShipping()**. The purpose of the function is to display the cost of the selected shipping option and to update the total order costs. Add the following commands to the function:
   a. Store the value returned by the shipExpense() function in the shipcost field.
   b. Run the calcTotal() function.

9. Create a function named **calcCost()**. The purpose of the calcCost() function is to display the cost of the quantity of items ordered by a customer and to update the total cost of the order. This function will also test whether a customer has correctly entered an integer in one of the quantity fields. The price of each item is stored in the price*item* field, where *item* is the item number. The cost of each item is stored in the cost*item* field. And the quantity ordered by each item is stored in the qty*item* field. For the order.htm file, the value of *item* ranges from 1 to 6. To complete the calcCost() function, add the following commands:
   a. Create a variable named **iNum** that is equal to the ID of the currently selected object, using the slice() method to slice off the first three characters from the ID. (*Hint*: Use the this keyword to reference the currently selected object.)
   b. Create a variable named **price** that references the price*item* field, where *item* is the value of the iNum variable (*Hint*: Use the document.forms[0].elements collection along with the field's name to reference the price*item* field.)
   c. Create a variable named **qty** that references the qty*item* field.
   d. Create a variable named **cost** that references the cost*item* field.
   e. Create a regular expression object named **reqty** for a text string containing one or more digits and no other characters.
   f. Still within the calcCost() function, test whether the value of the qty object matches the pattern defined by the reqty regular expression. If the pattern matches, then: (1) Set the value of the cost object equal to the value of the price object multiplied by the value of the qty object. Display the value of the cost object to two decimal places; (2) Run the calcTotal() function. If the pattern does not match (meaning that the customer has not entered a quantity value in integers), then: (i) Display the alert message **Please enter a digit greater than or equal to 0**, (ii) Set the value of the qty object to 0, and (iii) Set the focus back to the qty object using the focus() method.

10. Create a function named **validateForm()**. The purpose of this function is to ensure that the form has been filled out correctly before it is submitted. Add the following commands to the function:
   a. Test whether the selected index in the shipping field is equal to 0. If it is (meaning that no shipping method has been chosen by the customer), then: (1) Display the alert message **You must select a shipping option**, and (2) Return the value false.
   b. Otherwise, return the value true.

11. Create a function named **resetForm()**. This function will run until the form is reset. Add a command to the function to reload the current document.

12. Close the **form.js** file, saving your changes. Open **order.htm** in your Web browser and verify that it correctly updates the total cost of the order as you change the values in the quantity column. Also verify that the form will not accept any quantity values other than integers. Check that the cost of shipping changes to reflect the shipping method selected by the customer, and that the form cannot be submitted unless a shipping method has been selected. Verify that clicking the Reset button reloads the Web page.

13. Submit your completed files to your instructor.

Apply | Case Problem 1

Use JavaScript to create a select and go navigation list.

Data Files needed for this Case Problem: mpltxt.htm, linkstxt.js, mpl.jpg, mplstyles.css

The Monroe Public Library At the Monroe Public Library, Denise Kruschev works on the library's Web site. One of her responsibilities is to add content to the site that will be of interest to the library's patrons. Denise's latest assignment is to create a Web page containing links to hundreds of government Web sites. She knows that a long list of links will fill the page, making the page difficult to use. Instead, Denise wants to use "select and go navigation," in which the links are placed within a selection list. When a user selects a link from the list, the linked page should open automatically. Denise already set up the selection lists, but she asks you to help write the JavaScript program. Figure 5-67 shows a preview of the Web page.

Figure 5-67

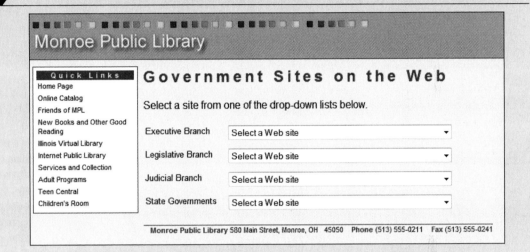

Complete the following:

1. Use your text editor to open the **mpltxt.htm** and **linkstxt.js** files from the tutorial.05\ case1 folder, enter *your name* and *the date* in the comment section of each file, and then save the files as **mpl.htm** and **links.js**, respectively.

2. Go to the **mpl.htm** file in your text editor and create a link to the **links.js** file.

3. Scroll through the mpl.htm file, studying the code. Each option in the selection list contains a value referencing the URL of a government Web site. Close the file, saving your changes.

4. Go to the **links.js** file in your text editor and insert an event handler to run the init() function when the page is loaded.

5. Create the **init()** function. Within this function do the following:

   a. Create a variable named **allSelect** that references all of the selection elements in the document.

   b. For each item within the allSelect object collection, add an onchange event handler that runs the loadLink() function when the selection list changes.

6. Create the **loadLink()** function. The purpose of this function is to cause the browser to load a URL from a selection list. Add the following commands to the function:

   a. Create a variable named **sIndex** that points to the index of the selected option in the current selection list. (*Hint*: Use the this keyword to reference the current selection list.)

⊕ EXPLORE

   b. Web pages can be loaded using the command
   ```
   location.href = url;
   ```
   where *url* is the URL of the Web page. Enter this command into the function using the value of the selected option from the selection list as the value of *url*. (*Hint*: Use the sIndex variable to point to the selected option from the current selection list.)

7. Save your changes to the file.

8. Open **mpl.htm** in your Web browser. Verify that by clicking the links from the selection lists on the page you can bring up the corresponding government Web sites.

9. Submit your completed files to your instructor.

Apply	Case Problem 2

Use JavaScript to create an online travel expense report.

Data Files needed for this Case Problem: exptxt.htm, reporttxt.js, back.jpg, done.htm, exp.css, links.jpg, logo.jpg

DeLong Enterprises   Kay Ramirez is the payroll manager for DeLong Enterprises, a manufacturer of computer components. The company has been busy putting corporate information on the company's intranet. Kay is heading a project to put all of the payroll-related forms and reports online. She asks you to help write a program for the online travel expense form. The travel expense report form requires employees to itemize their various travel expenses for corporate trips. Kay wants scripts added to the form to ensure that all of the required data is entered in the correct format. If a required data field is left blank or if data is entered in an improper format, Kay wants the program to highlight the field in yellow and refuse submission of the form to the corporate Web server. Kay wants the form to support the following features:

- The employee must enter a last name, a first name, a Social Security number, an address for the reimbursement check, and a summary of the trip.
- The employee must enter the account ID number in the format ACT*nnnnnn*, the department ID number in the format DEPT*nnn*, and the project ID number in the format PROJ*nnnnn*.
- For each day in which the employee has recorded an expense, the travel date must be entered.
- When the employee enters a travel, lodging, or meal expense, the subtotal of expenses for that day and the total cost of the trip should update automatically.
- Travel expenses must be entered as digits (either with or without the two-digit decimal place) and displayed to two digits.

A preview of the completed form is displayed in Figure 5-68.

Figure 5-68

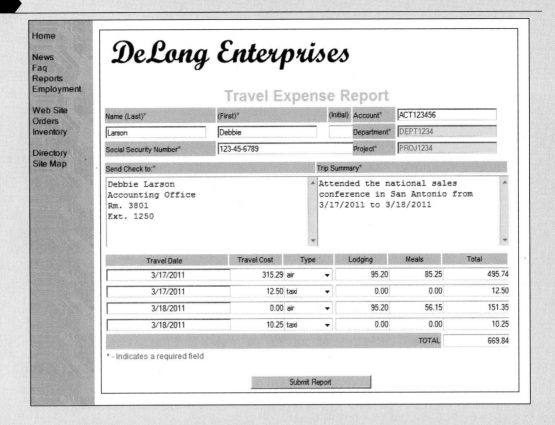

Complete the following:

1. Use your text editor to open the **exptxt.htm** and **reporttxt.js** files from the tutorial.05\case2 folder, enter *your name* and *the date* in the comment section of each file, and then save the files as **exp.htm** and **report.js**, respectively.

2. Go to the **exp.htm** file in your text editor, insert a link to the **report.js** script file in the head section of the document, review the content and elements used in the document, and then close the file, saving your changes.

3. Return to the **report.js** file in your text editor, and then add an event handler to the file, running the initPage() function when the page is loaded by the browser.

4. Insert the **initPage()** function. The purpose of this function is to set up the initial conditions for the exp.htm page. Add the following commands to the function:

   a. Declare an array variable named **dataFields**. This array will point to the input elements in the expense report for daily expenses of travel, lodging, and meals.

   b. The input elements for the daily travel, lodging, and meal expenses all belong to the expenseEntry class. Use a For loop to populate the content of the dataFields array with the object collection of all elements belonging to the expenseEntry class.

   c. For each item in the dataFields array, add an onblur event handler that runs the update() function whenever the focus leaves the dataFields element.

   d. Add an event handler to the Web form that runs the validateForm() function when the form is submitted to the browser.

5. Create a function named **testLength()**. The purpose of the testLength() function is to test whether the user has entered any text in a required field. If no text has been entered, the function should highlight the field and return the value false. If any text has been entered, the function should remove any highlighting and return the value true. The function has a single parameter named **field** that represents the field object to be tested. To complete the function, insert the following commands:

   a. Insert a conditional expression that tests whether the length of the field value is equal to 0.

   b. If the length is equal to 0, then: (i) Change the background color of the field object to yellow and (ii) Return the Boolean value false; otherwise: (i) Change the background color of the field object to white and (ii) Return the Boolean value true.

6. Create a function named **testPattern()**. The purpose of this function is to compare the value of a field against a regular expression pattern. If the field's value does not match the regular expression, the function should highlight the field on the form and return the Boolean value false. If the field's value does match the regular expression, the function should remove any highlighting and return the Boolean value true. The function has two parameters: the **field** parameter, representing the field object to be tested; and **regx**, a regular expression containing the pattern used for the testing. To complete the testPattern() function, insert the following commands:

   a. Insert a conditional expression that employs the test() method to test whether the value of the field object matches the regular expression contained in the regx parameter.

   b. If the test() method returns the value false, then: (i) Change the background color of the field object to yellow, (ii) Change the color of the field object to red, and (iii) Return the Boolean value false; otherwise: (i) Change the background color of the field object to white, (ii) Change the color of the field object to black, and (iii) Return the Boolean value true.

7. Create a function named **validateForm()**. The purpose of this function is to validate the form before it can be submitted to the server by calling the testPattern() and testLength() functions you just created. The function has no parameters. Add the following commands to the function:

   a. Create a variable named **isValid**. The purpose of this variable is to record whether the form is valid or not. Set the initial value of the isValid variable to true.

   b. Call the testLength() function with the lname field object as the parameter. (*Hint*: Use the object reference document.forms[0].lname.) If the value returned by the testLength() function is false, set the value of the isValid variable to false. Repeat this step for the fname, address, and summary fields.

   c. Call the testPattern() function with a reference to the account field as the field parameter value. For the regx parameter, insert a regular expression literal that matches a text string containing only the text "ACT" followed by six digits. If the value returned by the testPattern() function is false, set the value of the isValid variable to false.

   d. Call the testPattern() function with the department field for the field parameter. The regx parameter should contain a regular expression literal for a text string containing only the characters "DEPT" followed by three digits. If the value of the testPattern() function is false, set the value of the isValid variable to false.

   e. Repeat the previous step for the project field, using a regular expression that matches a text string containing only the characters "PROJ" followed by five digits.

f. Call the testPattern() function for the ssn field (containing the Social Security number of the employee). The regular expression should match either a nine-digit number or a text string in the form *nnn-nn-nnnn*. If the testPattern() function returns the value false, set the value of the isValid variable to false.

g. Insert a conditional statement that tests whether the value of the isValid variable is false. If it is false, then display the following alert message: **Please fill out all required fields in the proper format.**

h. Return the value of the isValid variable.

8. Add a function named **calcRow()**. The purpose of this function is to return the subtotal of the expenses within a single row in the travel expense table. The function has a single parameter named **row**, which represents the number of the table row (from 1 to 4) upon which the calculations will be performed. Add the following commands to the function:

a. Create a variable named **travel** that is equal to the numeric value of the travel*row* field, where *row* is the value of the row parameter. (*Hint*: Use the object reference document.forms[0].elements["travel"+*row*].value.) Be sure to use the parseFloat() function to convert the field value to a number. In the same fashion, create a variable named **lodge** that is equal to the numeric value of the lodge*row* field and a variable named **meal** that is equal to the numeric value of the meal*row* field.

b. Return the sum of the travel, lodge, and row variables.

9. Create a function named **calcTotal()**. The purpose of this function is to return the total of all expenses in the travel expense table by calling the calcRow() function for each of the four rows in the table. The function has no parameters. Add the following commands to the function:

a. Create a variable named **totalExp** and set its initial value to 0.

b. Insert a For loop with a counter that runs from 1 to 4.

c. Within the For loop, increase the value of the totalExp variable by the value returned by the calcRow() function using the value of the counter as the value of the row parameter.

d. Return the value of the totalExp variable.

10. Create a function named **update()**. The purpose of this function is to update the expense values displayed throughout the table and to verify that the employee has entered a valid expense amount. The function will be called whenever the employee exits from one of the 12 expense fields in the table (initiating the blur event). Add the following commands to the function:

a. Create a variable named **numRegExp** that contains the regular expression literal /^\d*(\.\d{0,2})?$/. This pattern matches any text string that only contains a number with or without two decimal place accuracy.

b. Insert a conditional statement that tests whether the value property of the currently selected object matches the numRegExp pattern. (*Hint*: Use the this keyword to reference the currently selected object.)

c. If the condition is met (meaning that the employee has entered a valid expense amount), then run the following commands: (i) Use the toFixed() method to display the value of the current object to two decimal places, (ii) Insert a For loop with a counter that runs from 1 to 4. Within the For loop, set the value of the sub*i* field to the value returned by the calcRow() function, where *i* is the value of the For loop counter. Format the value to appear to two decimal places. (iii) Set the value of the total field equal to the value returned by the calcTotal() function. Display the total field value to two decimal places.

    d. If the condition is not met (meaning that the user has entered an invalid number), then: (i) Display the alert message **Invalid currency value**, (ii) Change the value property of the current object to **0.00**, and (iii) Return the focus to the current object.

11. Save your changes to the file. Open **exp.htm** in your Web browser. Test the operation of the travel expense table, verifying that it automatically updates the travel expenses as you add new values to the table.

12. Test the form validation commands by attempting to submit the form under the following conditions: (i) Without all of the required fields filled out and (ii) With invalid entries for the account, department, project, and Social Security number fields. The form should highlight the errors and alert you of the mistakes.

13. Submit your completed files to your instructor.

| Challenge | Case Problem 3 |

Explore how to pass data between Web forms.

Data Files needed for this Case Problem: conftxt.htm, sumtxt.htm, back.jpg, conf.css, edge.jpg, formstxt.js, links.jpg, logo.jpg, summary.css

The CGIP Conference   Rajiv Rammohan is a Web site consultant for the annual conference of Computer Graphics and Image Processing. This year, the conference is putting all of its registration forms and documents online. Rajiv is working on the form in which participants will enter their registration information. Rajiv wants the form to have the following features.

- The participant must enter a first name, a last name, an address, an e-mail address, and a phone number.

- Phone numbers must follow the pattern *nnn-nnn-nnnn*.

- The participant can indicate whether he or she is a member of the ACGIP to receive a discount on the registration fee.

- The form should calculate the total registration fee. The fee is equal to $145 plus $30 for every person attending the conference banquet. ACGIP members receive a $25 discount on the registration fee.

When a form is submitted, Rajiv wants the browser to display a page summarizing all of the participant's registration information and selections. Figure 5-69 shows a preview of both the registration form and the summary page.

| Figure 5-69 |

Complete the following:

1. Use your text editor to open the **conftxt.htm, sumtxt.htm**, and **formstxt.js** files from the tutorial.05\case3 folder, enter *your name* and *the date* in the comment section of each file, and then save the files as **conf.htm, summary.htm**, and **forms.js**, respectively.

2. Go to the **conf.htm** file in your text editor, and examine the contents of the file and the Web form. Note that the form has a hidden field named total. In this field, you'll store the total cost of the registration.

3. Link the file to the **forms.js** script file, and then close conf.htm, saving your changes.

4. Go to the **forms.js** file in your text editor, and then add an event handler to run the init() function when the page is loaded. Below this statement, add the init() function, which consists of a single command to assign the submitForm() function to the onsubmit event handler for the first Web form in the document. You'll create the submitForm() function shortly.

5. Create a function named **calcCost()**. The purpose of this function is to calculate the total registration fee. Add the following commands to the function:

   a. Create a variable named **cost** and set its initial value to 145, the default cost of the conference.

   b. Retrieve the value of the selected index property from the guests selection list. This value indicates the number of guests invited to the banquet. Multiply the selected index value by 30 and add this to the cost variable.

   c. If the first member radio button is checked, subtract 25 from the value of the cost variable.

   d. Set the value of the hidden total field on the Web form equal to the value of the cost variable.

6. Create a function named **testLength()**. The purpose of the function is to test whether the user has entered any text in a required field. The function has a single parameter named **field** that represents the field object to be tested. To complete the function:

   a. Insert a conditional expression that tests whether the length of the field value is equal to 0.

   b. If the length is equal to 0, then: (i) Change the background color of the field object to yellow and (ii) Return the Boolean value false. Otherwise: (i) Change the background color of the field object to white and (ii) Return the Boolean value true.

7. Create a function named **testPattern()**. The purpose of this function is to compare the value of a field against a regular expression pattern. The function has two parameters: the field parameter, representing the field object to be tested; and reg, a regular expression literal containing the pattern used for the testing. To complete the testPattern() function:

   a. Insert a conditional statement that employs the test() method to test whether the value of the field object matches the regular expression contained in the reg parameter.

   b. If the test() method returns the value false, then: (i) Change the background color of the field object to yellow, (ii) Change the color of the field object to red, and (iii) Return the Boolean value false. Otherwise: (i) Change the background color of the field object to white, (ii) Change the color of the field object to black, and (iii) Return the Boolean value true.

8. Create a function named **submitForm()**. The purpose of this function is to validate the form and calculate the total registration fee. Add the following commands to the function:

   a. Create a variable named **valid**. Set the initial value of the variable to true.

   b. Call the testLength() function using the fname field as the parameter. If the function returns the value false, change the value of the valid variable to false. Repeat this step for the lname, address, and email fields.

   c. The phone number is divided into three fields named phone1, phone2, and phone3, representing the area code, exchange, and local number. The phone1 and phone2 fields should both contain only three digits. The phone3 field should contain only four digits. Call the testPattern() function for each field along with the appropriate regular expression literal to test whether the entries in these fields match the specified patterns. If the value returned by the testPattern() function is false for any of the fields, set the value of the valid variable to false.

   d. Insert a conditional statement that tests whether neither of the member radio buttons is checked. If neither has been checked, then: (i) Change the background color of each member radio button to yellow, and (ii) Set the value of the valid variable to false. (*Hint*: To test whether neither radio button has been checked, use the condition: ((*form*.member[0].checked || *form*.member[1].checked) == false) where *form* is the object reference to the registration form.)

   e. If the valid variable is false, then display the alert message **Enter all required information in the appropriate format**; otherwise, run the calcCost() function.

   f. Return the value of the valid variable.

9. Save your changes to the forms.js file, and then open the **conf.htm** file in your Web browser. Verify that the form cannot be submitted unless all of the required fields are filled out, the phone number is entered in the appropriate format, and the user has indicated whether he or she is a member of the ACGIP. A valid form should open the summary.htm file with a list of field names and values appended to the URL. Note that browsers differ in how they change the background color of option buttons. If you are running Internet Explorer, the background color of the option buttons changes to yellow. If you are running Firefox, the background color of the option buttons does not turn yellow. If you are running Opera, the internal color of the option buttons changes.

⊕ EXPLORE   10. Go to the **summary.htm** file in your text editor. Add an embedded script element to the head section of the document. Add the following commands to the script element:

   a. Create a variable named **searchString** that is equal to everything but the first character of the location.search object.

   b. Use the replace() method to replace every occurrence of the + character in the searchString variable with a blank space. Store the revised text string in a variable named **formString**.

   c. Apply the unescape() method to the formString variable to remove any escape characters from the string. Store the revised text string in a variable named **dataString**.

   d. Use the split() method to split the dataString at every occurrence of a & or = character. Store the substrings in an array named **data**.

⊕ EXPLORE   11. Scroll down the file to see that embedded script elements have already been entered for you on the Web page. You need to write the field values from the data array you created in the last step into the appropriate places on the Web page. Field values are stored in data[1], data[3], data[5], and so on, where the index is an odd number. The total cost of the conference is stored in data[1]. In the first script element, use the document.write() method to write the value of data[1] preceded by a $ character. The participant's first name and last name are stored in data[3] and data[5], respectively. In the second script element, write the values data[3] and data[5], separated by a blank space.

⊕ EXPLORE   12. The next row in the table displays the participant's address. This value is stored in data[7]. However, the value came from a textarea field that could contain multiple lines of text. Each line return must be converted into <br /> tags to preserve the appearance of the address text. To write the participant's address, do the following:

   a. Create a regular expression literal named **reg** that matches the occurrence of every new line character. (*Hint*: Use the \n escape sequence to represent the new line character.)

   b. Use the replace() method with the reg regular expression object to replace every occurrence of the new line character in the data[7] text string with the substring <br />. Store the revised text string in a variable named **address**.

   c. Write the address variable to the document.

13. Write the remaining field values to the remaining table cells. Use data[9] for the e-mail address; data[11], data[13], and data[15] for the phone number; data[17] for the number of banquet guests; and data[19] for ACGIP membership.

14. Save your changes to the file.

15. Reopen **conf.htm** in your Web browser. Fill out the form correctly, including a multi-line address in the address field. Submit the form. Verify that the field values and total cost of the conference are written to the table cells on the summary page. Also verify that the summary page retains the line breaks in the address field.

16. Submit your completed files to your instructor.

Create	**Case Problem 4**

Create an order form for a commercial Web site.

Data Files needed for this Case Problem: back.jpg, functions.js, info.txt, logo.jpg

Wizard Works   Wizard Works is a leading seller of custom and brand name fireworks in the United States. Roger Blaine supervises the company's Web site development team. He asks you to work on the order form for the company's line of custom fountains. Roger wants the following elements to appear on the form:

- Data entry fields from which the customer can select an item to order and the quantity of the item
- Data entry fields from which the customer can select a shipping option (standard for $4.95, express for $8.95, or next day for $12.95)
- Data entry fields for the customer's first name, last name, address, and phone number
- Data entry fields for the customer's credit card type (Wizard Works accepts American Express, Diners Club, Discover, MasterCard, and Visa), name of the cardholder, credit card number, and expiration date

The final design of the order form is up to you. Roger has provided several files to aid you in creating the order form. You can supplement this material with material of your own.

Complete the following:

1. Use your text editor to create the following files: **works.htm**, **done.htm**, **ww.css**, and **valid.js**. Enter a comment section in each file describing the purpose of the file and containing *your name* and *the date*.

2. Using the material found in the **info.txt** file in the tutorial.05\case4 folder, create the content for the works.htm file. Place the design styles in the ww.css file. Place the JavaScript code to work with the order in the valid.js file. Note that another JavaScript file, functions.js, is also available for your use in creating your Web page.

3. Add links to the works.htm file connecting that document to the ww.css file, the valid.js file, and the functions.js file.

4. Design the form so that it opens the done.htm file using the post method when the form is successfully submitted to the browser. Edit the done.htm file, so that it displays a message that the order form has been correctly filled out.

5. Go to the valid.js file and create functions to do the following:

   a. Automatically calculate the total cost of the order, including the shipping cost. The cost of the order should be formatted to two decimal places.

   b. Confirm that the customer has ordered an item, selected a quantity, specified a shipping option, and entered a first name, last name, address, phone number, cardholder name, and card number.

   c. Confirm that the phone number uses one of the following patterns: *(ddd) ddd-dddd, ddd-ddd-dddd, or ddd ddd dddd.*

   d. Confirm that the customer has selected a credit card type, entered a credit card name, and entered a credit card number that both matches the number pattern for the selected card and fulfills the Luhn Formula.

   e. Use regular expressions to test whether the credit card numbers match the card patterns specified by the card company. See the info.txt file for information on the appropriate number patterns for each card.

   f. If the form is valid, have the browser submit the form; otherwise, indicate to the customer that the form is invalid.

6. Test your Web form, verifying that it performs all calculations and validation tasks correctly. You can use the list of credit card numbers shown in Figure 5-61 to test your validation rules for both the pattern of the numbers and the numbers' adherence to the Luhn Formula.

7. Submit your completed files to your instructor.

Review | Quick Check Answers

Session 5.1

1. `document.forms[1]`
2. `document.forms["register"].elements["lastname"]`
   or
   `document.register.lastname`
3. `document.register.lastname.value = "Carol Campbell";`
4. `document.register.lastname.focus();`
5. `document.register.statename.option[3]`

6. `document.register.statename.selectedIndex`

7. `document.register.contactme.checked`

8. `3.14159.toFixed(2)`

Session 5.2

1. Server-side validation is validation that occurs on the Web server. Client-side validation is the validation of a data entry form that occurs on the user's Web browser.

2. `formObj.onsubmit = testForm;`

3. `username.length`

4. `username.charAt(0)`

  `username.charAt(username.length-1)`

5. `username.slice(0,5)`

6. `words = email.split("@")`

  words[0] contains the *username*; words[1] contains the *domain*

7. `email.indexOf("gov")`

8. `username.toUpperCase()`

Session 5.3

1. `/GPS/gi`

2. `/\bproducts\b/`

3. `/^\d{9}$/`

4. `/^\d{9}$|^\d{3}-\d{2}-\d{4}$/`
  or
  `/^\d{3}-?\d{2}-?\d{4}$/`
  Other solutions are also possible.

5. `/(street|avenue|lane)/ig`

6. `reuser.test(username)`

7. `date.split(/\//g)`

8. The Luhn Formula is a formula developed by a group of mathematicians in the 1960s to provide a quick validation check for a number string. It calculates the sum of digits in an account number to verify that the number is valid.

9. `location.search`

Ending Data Files

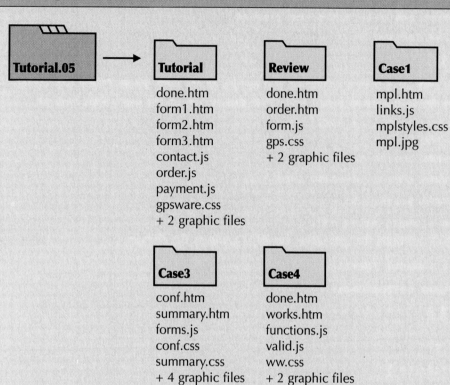

Tutorial.05 →

Tutorial
done.htm
form1.htm
form2.htm
form3.htm
contact.js
order.js
payment.js
gpsware.css
+ 2 graphic files

Review
done.htm
order.htm
form.js
gps.css
+ 2 graphic files

Case1
mpl.htm
links.js
mplstyles.css
mpl.jpg

Case2
done.htm
exp.htm
report.js
exp.css
+ 3 graphic files

Case3
conf.htm
summary.htm
forms.js
conf.css
summary.css
+ 4 graphic files

Case4
done.htm
works.htm
functions.js
valid.js
ww.css
+ 2 graphic files

Working with the Event Model

Creating a Drag-and-Drop Jigsaw Puzzle

Case | Kiddergarden

Peter Burnham is the owner of Kiddergarden, a family-friendly Web site containing games, puzzles, stories, and other activities for young children and their parents. Pete recently asked you to help develop content for the site. One of the first projects he wants you to create is an online jigsaw puzzle.

To create the jigsaw puzzle with JavaScript, you need to write code that allows the user to drag and drop objects from one location on the Web page to another. Creating this effect requires you to work with the properties and features of the JavaScript event model, as the layout of the page responds to the actions of the user's mouse.

Starting Data Files

Tutorial.06 →

Tutorial
jigsawtxt.htm
jpuzzletxt.js
kgfunctxt.js
kg.css
+ 29 graphic files

Review
blockstxt.htm
libtxt.js
slidetxt.js
sbblocks.css
+ 29 graphic files

Case1
booktxt.htm
comtxt.js
bw.css
+ 2 graphic files

Case2
badgertxt.htm
flibtxt.js
slidetxt.js
styles.css
+ 15 graphic files

Case3
crosstxt.htm
makepuzzle.js
runtxt.js
pcg.css
puzzle.css
+ 4 graphic files

Case4
library.js
pm.txt
+ 18 graphic files

Session 6.1

Setting Up the Jigsaw Puzzle

Pete has started working on the online jigsaw puzzle. He has already designed the Web page on which you will insert the puzzle. He also has already created some of the scripts to set up the puzzle. Before starting, you'll review his work.

To view Pete's files:

1. Use your text editor to open the **jigsawtxt.htm**, **jpuzzletxt.js**, and **kgfunctxt.js** files from the tutorial.06\tutorial folder, enter *your name* and *the date* in the comment section of each file, and then save the files as **jigsaw.htm**, **jpuzzle.js**, and **kgfunctions.js**, respectively.

2. Return to the **jigsaw.htm** file in your text editor.

3. Study the contents of the file, paying attention to the document's structure.

4. Open **jigsaw.htm** in your Web browser. Figure 6-1 shows the initial layout and contents of the file.

| Figure 6-1 | Initial jigsaw.htm page |

puzzle grid

puzzle pieces

The puzzle is divided into two sections. The left section contains the puzzle grid. Each square in the puzzle grid is represented by a div element positioned absolutely on the page. There are 25 grid pieces with IDs of grid0 through grid24. Each grid piece belongs to the grid class. The styles to place the grid pieces are defined in the kg.css style sheet.

The right section includes 25 div elements that will contain the individual puzzle pieces. The 25 pieces have IDs ranging from piece0 through piece24, each belonging to the pieces class. Like the grid squares, the puzzle pieces have been placed on the Web page using absolute positioning. At this point, no images are displayed on the puzzle pieces. Pete already split the puzzle image into 25 equally sized JPEG files named piece0.jpg through piece24.jpg. To display these images on the puzzle pieces, you'll set the background-image style of each piece to point to a different JPEG file.

Pete has written a function in the jpuzzle.js file to initialize the properties of the grid and puzzle pieces. The current code in the file includes the following:

```
var grids = new Array();
var pieces = new Array();

window.onload = init;

function init() {
   var allElem = document.getElementsByTagName("*");

   for (var i = 0; i < allElem.length; i++) {
      if (allElem[i].className == "grid") grids.push(allElem[i]);
      if (allElem[i].className == "pieces") pieces.push(allElem[i]);
   }

}
```

The code populates the grids and pieces array with elements that have class names of grid and pieces, respectively. To add background images to the 25 elements in the pieces array, you can add the following loop to the init() function:

```
for (var i = 0; i < pieces.length; i++) {
   pieces[i].style.backgroundImage = "url(piece" + i + ".jpg)";
}
```

You'll insert this code in the jpuzzle.js file, and then link this script file to the jigsaw.htm page.

To apply background images to the puzzle pieces:

▶ **1.** Return to the **jpuzzle.js** file in your text editor.

▶ **2.** Within the init() function, insert the following for loop, as shown in Figure 6-2:

```
for (var i = 0; i < pieces.length; i++) {
   pieces[i].style.backgroundImage = "url(piece" + i + ".jpg)";
}
```

Code to add background images to the puzzle pieces   **Figure 6-2**

```
function init() {

   var allElem = document.getElementsByTagName("*");

   for (var i = 0; i < allElem.length; i++) {
      if (allElem[i].className == "grid") grids.push(allElem[i]);
      if (allElem[i].className == "pieces") pieces.push(allElem[i]);
   }

   for (var i = 0; i < pieces.length; i++) {
      pieces[i].style.backgroundImage = "url(piece" + i + ".jpg)";
   }

}
```

sets the background image for each puzzle piece

▶ **3.** Save your changes to the file.

▶ **4.** Return to the **jigsaw.htm** file in your text editor.

▶ **5.** Within the head section of the file, insert a script element to link the Web page to the jpuzzle.js script file.

▶ **6.** Save your changes to the file, and then reload **jigsaw.htm** in your Web browser. The 25 puzzle pieces display a different background image, presenting the complete puzzle to the user. See Figure 6-3.

Figure 6-3 | Jigsaw puzzle image

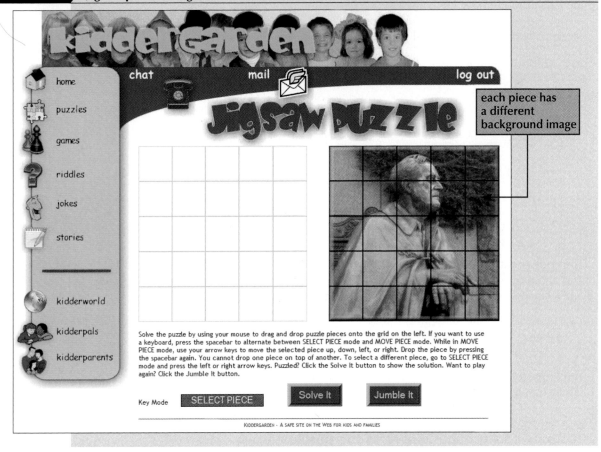

Pete wants the background images to appear in random order. To do this, you'll create an array of integers from 0 up to the number of puzzle pieces, sorted in random order. Pete has already written code to randomize the contents of an array. The code

```
function randomArray(size) {
   var ra = new Array(size);
   for (var i = 0; i < ra.length; i++) ra[i] = i;
   ra.sort(randOrder);
   return ra;
}

function randOrder() {
   return 0.5 - Math.random();
}
```

contains a function named randomArray() that returns an array of integers ranging from 0 up to the value of the size parameter in random order. Pete saved this function and other functions in the kgfunctions.js file. The kgfunctions.js file will act as a library of functions that Pete can use in a variety of programs. You'll link the jigsaw.htm file to this script file and use the randomArray() function to randomize the order of the puzzle piece images.

To randomize the order of the puzzle piece images:

▶ 1. Return to the **jpuzzle.js** file in your text editor, and then scroll down to the init() function.

▶ 2. Directly before the second for loop that sets up the background images, add the following line to create an array of random integers ranging from 0 up to the length of the pieces array:

```
var randomIntegers = randomArray(pieces.length);
```

▶ 3. In the command to set the background image, change i to the following:

```
randomIntegers[i]
```

Figure 6-4 highlights the newly inserted and revised code in the file.

Code to create random background images   Figure 6-4

creates an array of random integers from 0 up to pieces.length

random integer

```
for (var i = 0; i < allElem.length; i++) {
    if (allElem[i].className == "grid") grids.push(allElem[i]);
    if (allElem[i].className == "pieces") pieces.push(allElem[i]);
}
var randomIntegers = randomArray(pieces.length);
for (var i = 0; i < pieces.length; i++) {
    pieces[i].style.backgroundImage = "url(piece" + randomIntegers[i] + ".jpg)";
}
```

▶ 4. Save your changes to the file.

▶ 5. Return to the **jigsaw.htm** file in your text editor, and then insert a script element in the head section of the file, linking the file to the kgfunctions.js file.

▶ 6. Close the file, saving your changes, and then reload **jigsaw.htm** in your Web browser. The puzzle piece images are randomized. See Figure 6-5.

Figure 6-5 | **Puzzle pieces in jumbled order**

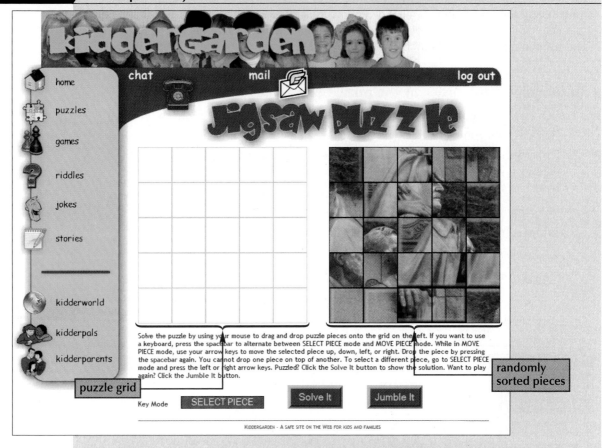

Trouble? If the pieces on your Web page do not match the placement shown in Figure 6-5, this is because the pieces are displayed in random order.

Finally, the code to manage the jigsaw puzzle requires you to work with the position and dimensions of the grid and puzzle pieces. Pete placed this information in the kg.css file. This information is not available to the JavaScript code unless you retrieve it. The kgfunctions.js file contains the following function to retrieve the value of any style applied to a specified object:

```
function getStyle(object, styleName) {
   if (window.getComputedStyle) {
      return document.defaultView.getComputedStyle(object,
null).getPropertyValue(styleName);
   } else if (object.currentStyle) {
      return object.currentStyle[styleName]
   }
}
```

Tip

Make the JavaScript code as generic as possible so it can be applied to a variety of Web pages and layouts. Confine code that explicitly defines an object's size or Web page position to the page's style sheet. The number of objects within a collection should be determined solely by the code for the HTML file.

In this function, the object parameter refers to an object in the current document and the styleName parameter is the name of a CSS style. Recall that the W3C DOM and the IE DOM use different approaches to retrieve calculated styles from the browser. The W3C DOM uses the getComputedStyle and getPropertyValue methods, whereas the IE DOM uses the currentStyle method. This function uses object detection to apply whichever method is supported by the user's browser.

To retrieve the value of the width property for the first puzzle piece in Pete's document, you could apply the following expression:

```
getStyle(pieces[0],"width");
```

You'll add code to the init() function in the jpuzzle.js that loops through each puzzle piece and grid object, and applies the getStyle() function to retrieve and set the top, left, width, and height style values for each item.

To retrieve and set the size and location of the grid and puzzle pieces:

1. Return to the **jpuzzle.js** file in your text editor.

2. Add the following code to the second for loop within the init() function to retrieve and set the top, left, width, and height style values for each puzzle piece:

```
pieces[i].style.top = getStyle(pieces[i],"top");
pieces[i].style.left = getStyle(pieces[i],"left");
pieces[i].style.width = getStyle(pieces[i],"width");
pieces[i].style.height = getStyle(pieces[i],"height");
```

3. Insert the following for loop at the bottom of the init() function to retrieve and set the top, left, width, and height style values for each grid object:

```
for (var i = 0; i < grids.length; i++) {
   grids[i].style.top = getStyle(grids[i],"top");
   grids[i].style.left = getStyle(grids[i],"left");
   grids[i].style.width = getStyle(grids[i],"width");
   grids[i].style.height = getStyle(grids[i],"height");
}
```

Figure 6-6 shows the inserted code.

Code to retrieve and set the size and location styles　　**Figure 6-6**

```
var randomIntegers = randomArray(pieces.length);
for (var i = 0; i < pieces.length; i++) {
   pieces[i].style.backgroundImage = "url(piece" + randomIntegers[i] + ".jpg)";
   pieces[i].style.top = getStyle(pieces[i],"top");
   pieces[i].style.left = getStyle(pieces[i],"left");
   pieces[i].style.width = getStyle(pieces[i],"width");
   pieces[i].style.height = getStyle(pieces[i],"height");
}

for (var i = 0; i < grids.length; i++) {
   grids[i].style.top = getStyle(grids[i],"top");
   grids[i].style.left = getStyle(grids[i],"left");
   grids[i].style.width = getStyle(grids[i],"width");
   grids[i].style.height = getStyle(grids[i],"height");
}
}
```

retrieves and sets the position and size of each puzzle piece

retrieves and sets the position and size of each grid object

the getStyle() function retrieves the style values from the style sheet

4. Save your changes to the file.

At this point, you've retrieved and set all of the properties for the puzzle pieces and grid on Pete's jigsaw puzzle page. Your next task is to start writing code so the user can interact with those objects.

Introducing the Event Model

Pete sketched his idea for the operation of the jigsaw puzzle, as shown in Figure 6-7. He wants users to be able to drag each puzzle piece from its initial location in the right section of the page onto one of the 25 grid pieces in the left section. Clicking a piece selects it, the motions of the mouse pointer move the piece, and then releasing the mouse button drops the piece in its new location on the page.

| Figure 6-7 | Puzzle piece being dragged onto the grid |

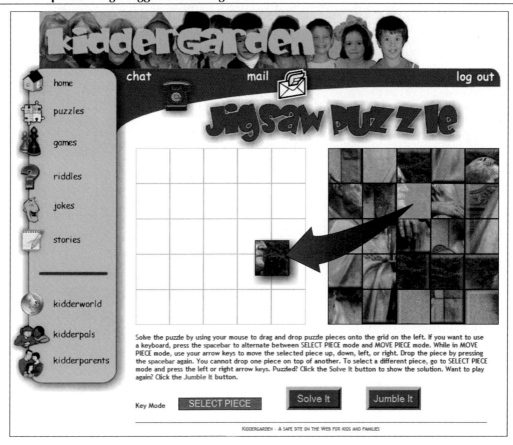

To give users this ability, the code must be able to change the position of the selected puzzle piece based on the motions of the pointer. This requires the code to work with the actions and events associated with the user's mouse.

So far, you have worked with user-initiated events in two ways. One way is by adding an on*event* attribute to the HTML code of the document. The code

```
<div id = "piece0" class = "pieces" onclick = "movePiece()">
</div>
```

binds a function named movePiece() to the action of clicking the piece0 object. One problem with this approach is that it places JavaScript code directly in the HTML file, whereas ideally page content and the code that modifies it should be separated as much as possible.

The second way is by applying an event handler as a value of the onclick property, as in the following JavaScript statement:

```
pieces[0].onclick = movePiece;
```

This way of applying an event handler is also known as **traditional binding** because it binds the movePiece() function to the click action. In most cases, traditional binding works well, but it is limited to binding only one function with a specific event. For example, the statements

```
pieces[0].onclick = movePiece;
pieces[0].onclick = dropPiece;
```

contradict each other under traditional binding. The last event handler specified in the code supersedes any earlier event handlers. In this case, the browser will run only the dropPiece() function in response to the click event on pieces[0]. If you're working on a small contained Web site, this problem may be manageable. The problem becomes unmanageable, however, if you are working on a large sprawling Web site that involves hundreds or thousands of files. When you apply an event handler using traditional binding, you might not even be aware that you're overwriting another event handler elsewhere in the site.

One way of dealing with this problem is to place the two functions within a third function that is then attached to the event. The following code shows an example of this approach:

```
pieces[0].onclick = runProgram;

function runProgram() {
   movePiece();
   dropPiece();
}
```

This approach works as long as the code does not need to use the `this` keyword. Recall that the `this` keyword returns the object that called the event handler. In most programs involving event handlers, you want to know this information. In the previous code samples, pieces[0] was the object that invoked the event handler, so you could always reference it using the `this` keyword. In this case, the movePiece() and dropPiece() functions are not directly called by the pieces[0] object, but rather by the runProgram() function. This makes a big difference in how the `this` keyword is interpreted because now it doesn't refer to pieces[0] at all, but instead refers to the object in which the runProgram() function resides, which for JavaScript is the window object. So with this code, there is no immediate way of associating the movePiece() and dropPiece() functions with the object that initiated them, which would be a problem if your program requires that information.

Another type of function supported by JavaScript is an anonymous function. As the name implies, an **anonymous function** is a function without a name. The general syntax of an anonymous function is

```
function (parameters) {
   function code
}
```

where *parameters* are the parameters of the function and *function code* are the commands executed by the function. The advantage of anonymous functions is that you can insert them anywhere you would place an expression. For example, if you want to display a couple of alert boxes when the Web page is loaded, you could put the command to display the alert boxes in the following statement:

```
window.onload = function () {
   alert("Page Loaded");
   alert("Proceed with data entry");
}
```

You will often find anonymous functions used with event handlers in situations where the function code needs to be run only once and nowhere else in the code. Rather than cluttering the code with additional functions, you can keep all of the function commands directly inline with the event handler.

The W3C and IE Event Models

Because of the limitations associated with traditional binding of events and objects, a third approach to working with user-initiated events is to use an **event model**, which is a model that describes how events interact with objects. There are two event models. One used by the World Wide Web Consortium (W3C) and the other used by the Internet Explorer browser. Because these event models are incompatible in many areas, your JavaScript code needs to reconcile the differences between the two models. The **IE event model** is supported by Internet Explorer and Opera. The **W3C event model** is supported by Firefox, Netscape, Safari, Opera, and other major browsers.

One key difference involves how events are initiated and propagated throughout the document.

Event Bubbling and Event Capturing

Consider the object hierarchy shown in Figure 6-8 that involves several nested objects. If the user clicks the innermost span object, which element receives the click event? Under the IE event model, each object receives the event though at different points in time.

Event bubbling in the IE event model | Figure 6-8

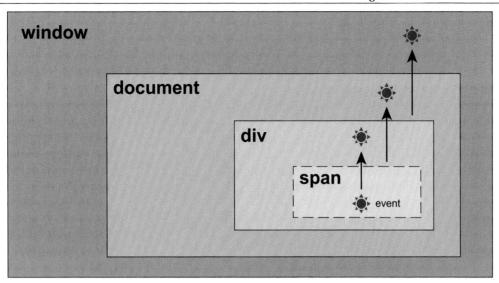

Internet Explorer does this by applying **event bubbling**, in which an event is initiated at the bottom of the object tree and rises to the top of the hierarchy. As shown in Figure 6-8, the event is first recognized by the span object, then the div object, then the Web page document, and finally the browser window itself.

Another way of propagating events through the document is by event capturing, as shown in Figure 6-9. In **event capturing**, events are initiated at the top of the object hierarchy and drop down the object tree to the lowest object. In Figure 6-9, the window object is the first object in which the event is noticed, followed by the document object, then the div element, and finally the span element. Event capturing is not supported in the IE event model but was introduced in an early version of the Netscape browser.

Event capturing | Figure 6-9

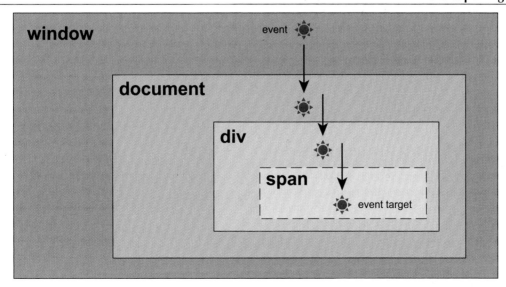

The W3C event model supports both event bubbling and event capturing, as shown in Figure 6-10. Under the W3C event model, an event starts at the top of the object hierarchy and moves down the object tree until it reaches the target of the event. At that point, the event bubbles back up the object hierarchy.

| Figure 6-10 | Event propagation in the W3C event model |

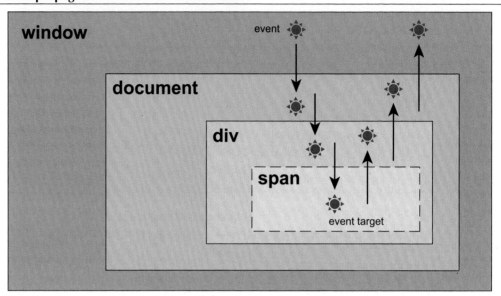

Under the W3C event model, the progress that an event makes through the DOM is split into three phases:

- A **capture phase** as the event moves down the object hierarchy
- A **target phase** in which the event reaches the object from which the event originated
- A **bubbling phase** in which the event moves back up the object hierarchy

The W3C event model is particularly powerful because it allows you to run a function that responds to an event at any phase in this process.

Attaching and Listening for Events

As an event propagates through the object hierarchy (either by bubbling or capturing or both), you can use JavaScript to assign a function to the event as it passes. The IE event model accomplishes this using the attachEvent method

```
object.attachEvent(onevent, function)
```

where *object* is the object receiving the event, on*event* is the text string describing the event, and *function* is the function that runs in response to the event. Unlike traditional event binding, you can attach multiple functions to the same event. For example, the following code attaches both the movePiece() and dropPiece() functions to the action of clicking the pieces[0] object:

```
pieces[0].attachEvent("onclick", movePiece);
pieces[0].attachEvent("onclick", dropPiece);
```

When the pieces[0] object is clicked, both functions will be run in response. So there is no problem with one event handler overwriting another.

Tip

The order in which an event ascends and descends through the objects in the DOM is based on the object hierarchy, not the placement of the objects on the Web page.

The W3C event model does not support the attachEvent method. Instead, it uses the addEventListener method

```
object.addEventListener(event, function, capture)
```

where *object* is the object receiving the event, *event* is a text string naming the event, *function* is a function that runs in response to the event, and *capture* is a Boolean value that tells the browser when to listen for the occurrence of the event. A *capture* value of true tells the browser to listen for the event during the capture phase, whereas a *capture* value of false tells the browser to listen during the bubbling phase. To run both the move-Piece() and dropPiece() functions under the W3C event model, you could apply the following code:

```
pieces[0].addEventListener("click", movePiece, false);
pieces[0].addEventListener("click", dropPiece, false);
```

In this case, both functions would run in response to a mouse click event occurring within the pieces[0] object. Note that the *capture* value is set to false for both event handlers so that the functions are triggered during the bubbling phase.

For the jigsaw puzzle page, you'll reconcile the syntax difference between the IE and W3C event models using the following addEvent() function:

```
function addEvent(object, evName, fnName, cap) {
    if (object.attachEvent)
        object.attachEvent("on" + evName, fnName);
    else if (object.addEventListener)
        object.addEventListener(evName, fnName, cap);
}
```

The function has four parameters: object representing the object receiving the event, evName containing the name of the event, fnName specifying the function associated with the event, and cap specifying whether the event is in the capture phase or the bubbling phase. Note that the function uses object detection to determine which event model is supported by the user's browser. You can apply this function to the click events for the pieces[0] object as follows

```
addEvent(pieces[0], "click", movePiece, false);
addEvent(pieces[0], "click", dropPiece, false);
```

and the browser will correctly bind the two functions to the click event under either event model.

You'll add this function to the kgfunctions.js file.

> **Tip**
>
> The attachEvent method identifies events with the name on*event*; the addEventListener method uses the event name *event* without the "on" prefix. Label events for the IE event model as onclick or onload, and use click or load for the W3C event model. Event names should be in lowercase letters.

To insert the addEvent() function:

▶ **1.** Go to the **kgfunctions.js** file in your text editor.

▶ **2.** Scroll to the bottom of the file, and then insert the following code, as shown in Figure 6-11:

```
function addEvent(object, evName, fnName, cap) {
    if (object.attachEvent)
        object.attachEvent("on" + evName, fnName);
    else if (object.addEventListener)
        object.addEventListener(evName, fnName, cap);
}
```

Figure 6-11 ▷ **Code to add event handlers with the addEvent() function**

```
function randOrder(){
    return 0.5 - Math.random();
}

function addEvent(object, evName, fnName, cap) {
    if (object.attachEvent)
        object.attachEvent("on" + evName, fnName);
    else if (object.addEventListener)
        object.addEventListener(evName, fnName, cap);
}
```

attaches a function to the event under the IE event model

adds an event to the function under the W3C event model

Removing Events

Both event models allow you to remove event handlers from objects. The IE event model uses the detachEvent method

```
object.detachEvent(onevent, function)
```

where again *object* is the object in which the event occurs, *event* is the name of the event, and *function* is the function previously attached to the object. To detach the movePiece() function from the mouse click event on pieces[0], you run the following command:

```
pieces[0].detachEvent("onclick", movePiece);
```

The W3C event model employs the removeEventListener method

```
object.removeEventListener(event, function, capture)
```

where *object*, *event*, *function*, and *capture* have the same meanings as they did for the addEventListener method. Likewise, the command

```
pieces[0].removeEventListener("click", movePiece, false);
```

removes the click event handler from the pieces[0] object, but only during the bubbling phase of the event model. An event handler that was added for the capture phase would not be affected by this command.

To create a function to remove event handlers from an object that works for both event models, you use object detection, as shown in the following code:

```
function removeEvent(object, evName, fnName, cap) {
    if (object.detachEvent)
        object.detachEvent("on" + evName, fnName);
    else if (object.removeEventListener)
        object.removeEventListener(evName, fnName, cap);
}
```

You will add this function to the kgfunctions.js file.

To insert the removeEvent() function:

▶ **1.** Scroll to the bottom of the **kgfunctions.js** file, and then insert the following code below the addEvent() function, as shown in Figure 6-12:

```
function removeEvent(object, evName, fnName, cap) {
    if (object.detachEvent)
        object.detachEvent("on" + evName, fnName);
    else if (object.removeEventListener)
        object.removeEventListener(evName, fnName, cap);
}
```

Code to remove event handlers with the removeEvent() function   **Figure 6-12**

```
function addEvent(object, evName, fnName, cap) {
    if (object.attachEvent)
        object.attachEvent("on" + evName, fnName);
    else if (object.addEventListener)
        object.addEventListener(evName, fnName, cap);
}
function removeEvent(object, evName, fnName, cap) {
    if (object.detachEvent)
        object.detachEvent("on" + evName, fnName);
    else if (object.removeEventListener)
        object.removeEventListener(evName, fnName, cap);
}
```

removes a function from the event under the IE event model

removes a function from an event under the W3C event model

▶ **2.** Save your changes to the file.

You will verify that the cross-browser functions work by creating a simple function to display an alert dialog box whenever the user presses the mouse button within one of those puzzle pieces.

To test the addEvent() function:

▶ **1.** Return to the **jpuzzle.js** file in your text editor.

▶ **2.** Add the following line to the second for loop that sets the properties of the items in the pieces array:

```
addEvent(pieces[i], "mousedown", mouseGrab, false);
```

▶ **3.** Directly below the init() function, insert the following function:

```
function mouseGrab() {
    alert("Puzzle piece clicked");
}
```

Figure 6-13 highlights the code added to the file.

Figure 6-13 ▶ **Code to respond to the mousedown event with the mouseGrab() function**

```
var randomIntegers = randomArray(pieces.length);
for (var i = 0; i < pieces.length; i++) {
    pieces[i].style.backgroundImage = "url(piece" + randomIntegers[i] + ".jpg)";
    pieces[i].style.top = getStyle(pieces[i],"top");
    pieces[i].style.left = getStyle(pieces[i],"left");
    pieces[i].style.width = getStyle(pieces[i],"width");
    pieces[i].style.height = getStyle(pieces[i],"height");

    addEvent(pieces[i], "mousedown", mouseGrab, false);
}

for (var i = 0; i < grids.length; i++) {
    grids[i].style.top = getStyle(grids[i],"top");
    grids[i].style.left = getStyle(grids[i],"left");
    grids[i].style.width = getStyle(grids[i],"width");
    grids[i].style.height = getStyle(grids[i],"height");
}

}

function mouseGrab() {
    alert("Puzzle piece clicked");
}
```

runs the mouseGrab() function in response to pressing the mouse button down within the puzzle piece

mouseGrab() function

▶ **4.** Save your changes to the file, and then reload **jigsaw.htm** in your Web browser.

▶ **5.** Click the puzzle pieces on the page and verify that each time you press the mouse button on a piece, an alert dialog box appears.

Reference Window | **Working with Document Events**

IE Event Model
- To attach a function to an object, run
  ```
  object.attachEvent(onevent, function);
  ```
  where *object* is the object receiving the event, on*event* is the text string of the event handler, and *function* is the function that runs in response to the event. Multiple functions can be attached to the same event in the same object.
- To detach a function, run the following:
  ```
  object.detachEvent(onevent, function);
  ```

W3C Event Model
- To run a function when an event reaches an object, use
  ```
  object.addEventListener(event, function, capture);
  ```
  where *object* is the object receiving the event, *event* is the text string describing the event, *function* is the function to run in response to the event, and *capture* equals true if the event is moving down the document tree and false if the event is bubbling up the tree.
- To stop listening for an event, run the following:
  ```
  object.removeEventListener(event, function, capture);
  ```

Tracking Event Handlers | InSight

Complex applications may have several event handlers associated with each object. For some applications, you may need to know whether a function has already been attached to an event. With traditional event binding, you can determine this by examining the event handler property. For example, if you create the following event handler for the pieces[0] array object

```
pieces[0].onclick = movePiece;
```

you can display the contents of the movePiece() function in an alert box using the following command:

```
alert(pieces[0].onclick)
```

If the expression returns a null or undefined value, you know that no function has been registered with the event. If a function has been registered with the event, the alert box will display the function's code.

The situation is different with the attachEvent or addEvent methods. With those methods, you cannot retrieve a list of functions registered with that event. This issue is dealt with in Level 3 of the W3C DOM, which introduces the eventListenerList attribute, which creates a list of event handlers registered to an object. There is not a great deal of browser support for the eventListenerList attribute at the time of this writing, so you should not rely upon it.

In this session, you set up the jigsaw puzzle and added cross-browser functions to handle events in the IE and W3C event models. In the next session, you'll work with mouse events to give users the ability to drag and drop puzzle pieces.

Session 6.1 Quick Check | Review

1. Specify code that uses an anonymous function to display an alert box with the message Click Detected whenever the user clicks the mouse in the Web page document.
2. How do events propagate through the document tree under the IE event model?
3. Under the IE event model, what command attaches the function calcTotal() to the Total object in response to the click event?
4. What command detaches the function in the previous question?
5. Describe how events propagate under the W3C event model.
6. Under the W3C event model, what command runs the calcTotal() function when the Total object is clicked during the bubbling phase?
7. What command removes the function in the previous question?

Session 6.2

Introducing the Event Object

In the previous session, you examined how events propagate and are handled within the IE and W3C event models. However, this is only part of what is involved with an event model. You also need to get information about an event itself. If a user has clicked a mouse button in a document, you may need to know where the pointer was located in the browser window when this happened. If the user has pressed a key on the keyboard, you may want to know which key was pressed. Information about the event is stored in an **event object**. The two event models provide different ways of working with event objects. First, let's look at the event object under the IE event model.

Working with IE Event Object

In the IE event model, the event object has the object reference

```
window.event
```

or, more simply:

```
event
```

Under the IE event model, the event object is a global object—one that is never declared by you, but is accessible in any function you write. This system works because only one event is being processed at any given time in your code. So under the IE event model, there is no need to reference multiple event objects.

The event object supports a wide variety of properties. A partial list is described in Figure 6-14.

| Figure 6-14 | Common properties of the IE event object |

Property	Description
event.button	Returns the number indicating which mouse button the user pressed (1 = left, 2 = right, 4 = middle)
event.cancelBubble	Set this property to true to cancel event bubbling; set it to false to continue event bubbling
event.fromElement	For mouseover and mouseout events, returns the object from which the pointer is moving
event.returnValue	Set this property to false to cancel the default action of the event; set it to true to retain the default action
event.srcElement	Returns the object in which the event was generated
event.toElement	For mouseover and mouseout events, returns the object to which the pointer is moving
event.type	Returns a text string indicating the type of event

Different events can call the same function. For example, your code may call the movePiece() function in response to both a mouse click and the act of pressing down a keyboard key. If you want to know which of these two events initiated the function, you can use the type property, as in the following expression:

```
event.type
```

This expression returns the value click if the function is run in response to the mouse click event, and returns the value keydown if the event that initiated the function is the user pressing a keyboard key down.

Working with the W3C Event Object

The W3C event model uses a different event object than the IE event object. In the W3C event model, the event object is inserted as the parameter of whatever function responds to the event. You can give the event object any parameter name, but the standard practice is to name the parameter e. For example, to run the movePiece() function when a user presses the mouse button anywhere within the document, you could insert the Java-Script commands

```
document.addEventListener("mousedown", movePiece, false);

function mouseGrab(e) {
    commands
}
```

and the browser will run the mouseGrab() function in response to the mousedown event. Information about the event is stored in the e parameter of the mouseGrab() function. Because functions are called by specific events, no confusion exists over which event the e parameter is referring to. Figure 6-15 lists some of the common properties associated with the W3C event object.

Common properties of the W3C event object ◀ **Figure 6-15**

Property	Description
evt.bubbles	Returns a Boolean value indicating whether *evt* can bubble
evt.button	Returns the number of the mouse button pressed by the user (0 = left, 1 = middle, 2 = right)
evt.cancelable	Returns a Boolean value indicating whether *evt* can have its default action canceled
evt.currentTarget	Returns the object that is currently handling the event
evt.eventPhase	Returns the phase in the propagation of *evt* (1 = capture, 2 = target, 3 = bubbling)
evt.relatedTarget	For mouseover events, returns the object that the mouse left when it moved over the target of the event; for mouseout events, returns the object that the mouse entered when leaving the target
evt.target	Returns the object that initiated the event
evt.timeStamp	Returns the date and time that the event was initiated
evt.type	Returns a text string indicating the event type

Like the IE event model, the W3C event model supports the type property to return the type of event that called the function. Again, the expression

```
evt.type
```

returns the type of event, where *evt* is the parameter of the event handler function.

Reconciling the Two Event Objects

You can reconcile the two event objects using the || (or) logical operator. The basic code is

```
function function(e) {
    var evt = e || window.event;
    commands
}
```

where *function* is the name of the function called by the event handler. The evt variable stores either the W3C event object as indicated by the e parameter or the window.event object. Thus under either event model, evt will point to the event object. To see this effect in action, revise the mouseGrab() function you created in the previous session to display the type of event initiated by the user.

To revise the mouseGrab() function:

1. If you took a break after the previous session, make sure the jpuzzle.js and kgfunctions.js files are open in a text editor, and the jigsaw.htm file is open in your Web browser.

2. Return to the **jpuzzle.js** file in your text editor.

3. Add the **e** parameter to the mouseGrab() function.

4. Insert the following command in the function:

   ```
   var evt = e || window.event;
   ```

5. Change the command to display the alert box to:

   ```
   alert("Event: " + evt.type);
   ```

   Figure 6-16 highlights the new code in the file.

Figure 6-16 ▶ **Code to reconcile the two event objects**

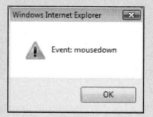

```
function mouseGrab(e) {
    var evt = e || window.event;

    alert("Event: " + evt.type);
}
```

> uses either the e parameter or the window.event object, depending on which is supported by the user's browser

6. Save your changes to the file, and then reload **jigsaw.htm** in your Web browser.

7. Click the puzzle pieces on the page and verify that each time you press the mouse button, an alert dialog box like the one shown in Figure 6-17 appears.

Figure 6-17 ▶ **Alert dialog box**

(Windows Internet Explorer dialog box: "Event: mousedown" with OK button)

Locating the Source of an Event

It is often important to know in what object a particular event was initiated. For the jigsaw puzzle, it will be particularly important to know which of the 25 puzzle pieces were clicked by the user. The IE and W3C event models use different properties to determine the source of an event. Recall that in the IE event model, events bubble up from the first object affected at the bottom of the object tree. That object is the source of the event and is returned by the IE event model's srcElement property.

The W3C event model references the source of an event using the target property, which points to the target of the event as it moves up and down the object tree. You can work with both properties using the || (or) expression, as in the following code:

```
var eventSource = e.target || event.srcElement
```

Here, the browser will use the object reference from the event model it supports. You'll use this expression in the moveGrab() function to store the reference of the puzzle piece clicked by the user in a variable named mousePiece. Because you'll be referencing this piece in other functions, you'll set up the mousePiece variable as a global variable.

To locate the source of the mousedown event:

▶ **1.** Return to the **jpuzzle.js** file in your text editor, and then directly below the statement to declare the pieces array, insert the following line:

```
var mousePiece = null;
```

▶ **2.** Scroll down the file, and then directly below the statement to declare the evt variable, add the following line to the mouseGrab() function:

```
mousePiece = evt.target || evt.srcElement;
```

You use evt as the object reference because the code already reconciled the difference between the two event models in how they reference the event object.

▶ **3.** Change the command to display the alert box to the following:

```
alert("Event: " + evt.type + " on " + mousePiece.id);
```

The value of the id property is taken from the id attribute in the jigsaw.htm file. Pieces have id attribute values ranging from piece0 to piece24. Figure 6-18 highlights the changed code.

Code to create the mousePiece variable ◀ **Figure 6-18**

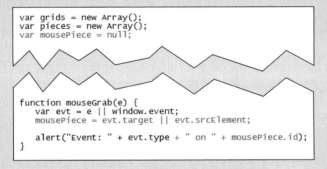

```
var grids = new Array();
var pieces = new Array();
var mousePiece = null;

function mouseGrab(e) {
    var evt = e || window.event;
    mousePiece = evt.target || evt.srcElement;

    alert("Event: " + evt.type + " on " + mousePiece.id);
}
```

▶ **4.** Save your changes to the file, and then reload **jigsaw.htm** in your Web browser.

▶ **5.** Click the puzzle pieces on the page and verify that the browser displays an alert box similar to the one shown in Figure 6-19.

Alert dialog box displaying the event and its source ◀ **Figure 6-19**

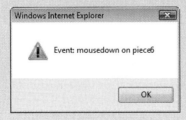

InSight | **Event Propagation and the `this` Keyword**

Events propagate through the object hierarchy under both event models. In the IE event model, the event bubbles up from the bottom of the object tree. In the W3C event model, events move down and then up the object tree. As you have seen, you can use the IE event model's srcElement property to indicate the source of the event bubbling, or the W3C event model's target property to indicate the target of the event. But how do you track the course of the event as it propagates through the object tree?

Under the W3C event model, the `this` keyword will return the object currently handling the event. You can also use the currentTarget property of the event object to return this information. If you need to know whether the object is reacting to the event during the capture phase or the bubbling phase, you can use the eventPhase property. Thus, under the W3C event model, you can always determine which object is currently handling the event and when it's being handled in the event propagation.

Unfortunately, the IE event model is not so accommodating. Because the window.event object in the IE event model is a global object, it does not contain information about individual objects that may be handling the event as it bubbles through the object hierarchy. The `this` keyword points not to the object handling the event, but rather to the window object. This is a huge limitation of the IE event model. This is not a problem if you use traditional binding in which the `this` keyword will point to the object handling the event, but you have to deal with the limitations of traditional binding, such as the inability to assign more than one function to a particular event.

JavaScript programmers have tackled this problem and have written several customized functions to overcome the limitations of the IE event model and inconsistencies between the two event models. You can find many of these functions on the Web.

Reference Window | **Working with the Event Object**

IE Event Model
- To reference the event object, use the following property:
  ```
  window.event
  ```
  or
  ```
  event
  ```
- To return the object that initiated the event bubbling, use the following property:
  ```
  event.srcElement
  ```

W3C Event Model
- To reference the event object, use
  ```
  evt
  ```
  where *evt* is the parameter of the function assigned to the event.
- To return the object that initiated an event, use the following property:
  ```
  evt.target
  ```
- To return the object that is currently handling an event, use the property
  ```
  evt.currentTarget
  ```
  or use the keyword
  ```
  this
  ```

Working with Mouse Events

You are ready to write a script to enable users to drag and drop the jigsaw puzzle pieces. You've already created the mouseGrab() function that will run whenever the user presses down the mouse button within one of the puzzle pieces. The function already identifies the piece that was selected by the user; but to create the drag-and-drop effect, you also need to know where on the page the pointer and the piece are located.

Determining the Mouse Position

The location of the puzzle piece is given by the top and left style properties that you retrieved and set in the previous session. The location of the pointer can be determined from the properties of the event object. Not surprisingly, the two event models support different properties to determine an event's location. Figure 6-20 summarizes these properties and their support in the two event models. For actual browser support, you must test these properties against your specific browser.

Location properties of the event object — Figure 6-20

Property	Returns	Event Model
evt.clientX evt.clientY	Returns the x and y coordinates of the event, evt, within the browser window	IE, W3C
evt.screenX evt.screenY	Returns the x and y coordinates of the event within the computer screen	IE, W3C
evt.offsetX evt.offsetY	Returns the x and y distances of the event from the object in which the event was initiated	IE
evt.x evt.y	Returns the x and y coordinates of the event relative to the element that initiated the event	IE
evt.pageX evt.pageY	Returns the x and y coordinates of the event within the document	W3C
evt.layerX evt.layerY	Returns the x and y coordinates of an event relative to its absolutely positioned parent element	W3C

The only properties supported by both event models are the screenX, screenY and the clientX, clientY properties. The screenX, screenY properties provide the coordinates of the event within the entire computer screen. The clientX, clientY properties provide the location of the event within the browser window.

Only the W3C event model provides the pageX, pageY properties to retrieve the location of the event within the document. Although the IE event model doesn't support the pageX, pageY properties, you can duplicate those values with the following code:

```
pageX = event.clientX +
        document.documentElement.scrollLeft +
        document.body.scrollLeft;
pageY = event.clientY +
        document.documentElement.scrollTop +
        document.body.scrollTop;
```

In this code, the location of the event within the browser window is added to however much of the remaining page is scrolled off to the left or top of the document window. The resulting pageX and pageY values are the x and y coordinates of the event within the entire document.

Tip

All location properties of the event object are measured in pixels.

For the puzzle page, you only need to know the location of the pointer relative to the browser window, not the Web page. You'll use the clientX and clientY properties to record the position of the pointer when the user presses the mouse button on the puzzle piece, storing the coordinates in the mouseX and mouseY variables.

To locate the coordinates of the mousedown event:

▶ **1.** Return to the **jpuzzle.js** file in your text editor.

▶ **2.** Directly below the statement that sets the value of the mousePiece variable in the mouseGrab() function, insert the following lines:

```
var mouseX = evt.clientX; // x-coordinate of pointer
var mouseY = evt.clientY; // y-coordinate of pointer
```

▶ **3.** Delete the line displaying the alert dialog box because you no longer need it in your program. Figure 6-21 shows the revised code of the mouseGrab() function.

Figure 6-21 ▶ **Code to retrieve the location of the pointer**

```
function mouseGrab(e) {
    var evt = e || window.event;
    mousePiece = evt.target || evt.srcElement;

    var mouseX = evt.clientX; // x-coordinate of pointer
    var mouseY = evt.clientY; // y-coordinate of pointer
}
```
→ position of the pointer at the moment the mouse button is pressed down

The next item to add to the mouseGrab() function is code to calculate the distance between the pointer and the selected puzzle piece. You'll need this information to keep the piece a constant distance from the pointer as it moves across the page. The current coordinates of the puzzle piece are stored in the top and left style properties. Because both these styles and the mouse position are measured in pixels, you can calculate the distance between them using the following statements:

```
diffX = parseInt(mousePiece.style.left) - mouseX;
diffY = parseInt(mousePiece.style.top) - mouseY;
```

Figure 6-22 shows the representation of the diffX and diffY variables based on the layout of the jigsaw puzzle page. Because the left and top style values include the px substring (as in "280px"), you need to use the parseInt method to extract the numeric value of the coordinate.

Figure 6-22 ▶ **Distance from the pointer to the puzzle piece**

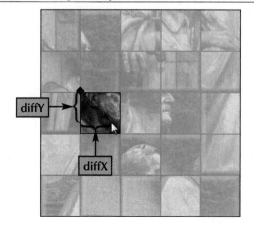

Because diffX and diffY will be used in other functions in this application, you'll declare them as global variables.

To create the diffX and diffY variables:

▶ **1.** Scroll to the top of the **jpuzzle.js** file, and directly below the declaration of the mousePiece variable, insert the following lines:

```
var diffX = null;
var diffY = null;
```

▶ **2.** Scroll down and within the mouseGrab() function, insert the following, as shown in Figure 6-23:

```
/* Calculate the distance from the pointer to the piece */
diffX = parseInt(mousePiece.style.left) - mouseX;
diffY = parseInt(mousePiece.style.top) - mouseY;
```

| Code to calculate the value of the diffX and diffY variables | Figure 6-23 |

```
var grids = new Array();
var pieces = new Array();
var mousePiece = null;
var diffX = null;
var diffY = null;

function mouseGrab(e) {
    var evt = e || window.event;
    mousePiece = evt.target || evt.srcElement;

    var mouseX = evt.clientX; // x-coordinate of pointer
    var mouseY = evt.clientY; // y-coordinate of pointer

    /* Calculate the distance from the pointer to the piece */
    diffX = parseInt(mousePiece.style.left) - mouseX;
    diffY = parseInt(mousePiece.style.top) - mouseY;
}
```

▶ **3.** Save your changes to the file.

The final task in the mouseGrab() function is to assign event handlers that will run whenever the pointer is moved or the mouse button is released. You'll assign a function named mouseMove() to the action of moving the pointer, and a function named mouseDrop() to the action of releasing the mouse button. The code to assign these two functions is:

```
addEvent(document, "mousemove", mouseMove, false);
addEvent(document, "mouseup", mouseDrop, false);
```

You'll add these two commands to the mouseGrab() function.

To create event handlers for the mousemove and mouseup events:

▶ **1.** Within the mouseGrab() function, add the following event handlers, as shown in Figure 6-24:

```
/* Add event handlers for mousemove and mouseup events */
addEvent(document, "mousemove", mouseMove, false);
addEvent(document, "mouseup", mouseDrop, false);
```

Figure 6-24 — **Code to add event handlers for the mousemove and mouseup events**

```
function mouseGrab(e) {
   var evt = e || window.event;
   mousePiece = evt.target || evt.srcElement;

   var mouseX = evt.clientX; // x-coordinate of pointer
   var mouseY = evt.clientY; // y-coordinate of pointer

   /* Calculate the distance from the pointer to the piece */
   diffX = parseInt(mousePiece.style.left) - mouseX;
   diffY = parseInt(mousePiece.style.top) - mouseY;

   /* Add event handlers for mousemove and mouseup events */
   addEvent(document, "mousemove", mouseMove, false);
   addEvent(document, "mouseup", mouseDrop, false);
}
```

▶ **2.** Save your changes to the file. The mouseGrab() function is complete.

Reference Window | **Locating an Event**

- To locate the x and y coordinates of an event within the computer screen, use the properties
  ```
  evt.screenX
  evt.screenY
  ```
  where *evt* is the event object in either the IE or W3C event model.
- To locate the x and y coordinates of an event within the browser window, use the following properties:
  ```
  evt.clientX
  evt.clientY
  ```
- To locate the x and y coordinates of an event within the Web page, use the properties
  ```
  evt.pageX
  evt.pageY
  ```
  where *evt* is the W3C event object. For the IE event model, use the following expression for the x-coordinate:
  ```
  event.clientX + document.documentElement.scrollLeft
  + document.body.scrollLeft
  ```
  For the y coordinate, use the following expression:
  ```
  event.clientY + document.documentElement.scrollTop
  + document.body.scrollTop;
  ```

Creating a Function for Mouse Movement

Your next task is to create the mouseMove() function, which will allow users to move puzzle pieces from one location to another. To move mousePiece across the Web page, the mouseMove() function needs to perform the following tasks:

- Determine the current location of the pointer.
- Maintain mousePiece at a constant distance from the pointer.

Keeping the piece a constant distance from the pointer as it moves across the page, as shown in Figure 6-25, will create the illusion that the pointer is dragging the puzzle piece.

Puzzle piece maintains a constant distance from the pointer ◄ **Figure 6-25**

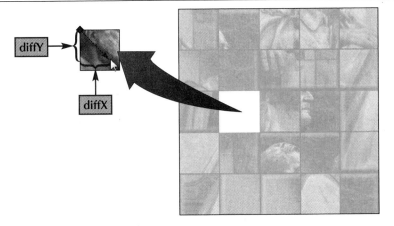

The distance between the puzzle piece and the pointer has already been stored in the diffX and diffY variables calculated in the mouseGrab() function. To set the new location of mousePiece, you add the values of diffX and diffY to the current location of the pointer, using the commands

```
mousePiece.style.left = mouseX + diffX + "px";
mousePiece.style.top = mouseY + diffY + "px";
```

where mouseX and mouseY are the current coordinates of the pointer. You have to add the px unit to the left and top styles to indicate to the browser that these coordinates are measured in pixels.

You'll add these commands to a mouseMove() function that you'll create now.

To create the mouseMove() function:

▶ **1.** Directly below the mouseGrab() function, insert the following function, as shown in Figure 6-26:

```
function mouseMove(e) {
    var evt = e || window.event;
    var mouseX = evt.clientX;
    var mouseY = evt.clientY;

    mousePiece.style.left = mouseX + diffX + "px";
    mousePiece.style.top = mouseY + diffY + "px";
}
```

Code to move the puzzle piece with the mouseMove() function ◄ **Figure 6-26**

```
    /* Add event handlers for mousemove and mouseup events */
    addEvent(document, "mousemove", mouseMove, false);
    addEvent(document, "mouseup", mouseDrop, false);
}

function mouseMove(e) {
    var evt = e || window.event;
    var mouseX = evt.clientX;
    var mouseY = evt.clientY;

    mousePiece.style.left = mouseX + diffX + "px";      new location of
    mousePiece.style.top = mouseY + diffY + "px";       the puzzle piece
}
```

▶ **2.** Save your changes to the file.

Dropping the Puzzle Piece

The next function to create for the jigsaw puzzle is the mouseDrop() function. This function runs whenever the user releases the mouse button, initiating the mouseup event. In response, the mouseDrop() function will cause the browser to stop running the mouse-Move() function. With the mouseMove() function no longer being called, the puzzle piece will stop following the pointer across the page, making it appear that the piece was dropped on the page. To halt the mouseMove() function, you'll use the removeEvent() function you created in the previous session. The code for the mouseDrop() function is:

```
function mouseDrop(e) {
    removeEvent(document, "mousemove", mouseMove, false);
    removeEvent(document, "mouseup", mouseDrop, false);
}
```

This code first removes the event handler for the mousemove event, halting the mouse-Move() function. It then removes the event handler for the mouseup event (you want the mouseDrop() function to be run only when you're in the process of moving a puzzle piece). You'll add this function to the jpuzzle.js file.

To create and test the mouseDrop() function:

1. Directly below the mouseMove() function, insert the following function, as shown in Figure 6-27:

```
function mouseDrop(e) {
    removeEvent(document, "mousemove", mouseMove, false);
    removeEvent(document, "mouseup", mouseDrop, false);
}
```

| Figure 6-27 | Code to drop the puzzle piece with the mouseDrop() function |

```
        mousePiece.style.left = mouseX + diffX + "px";
        mousePiece.style.top = mouseY + diffY + "px";
    }

    function mouseDrop(e) {
        removeEvent(document, "mousemove", mouseMove, false);
        removeEvent(document, "mouseup", mouseDrop, false);
    }
```

stops moving the puzzle piece with the mouse

removes the mouseup event handler

2. Save your changes to the file, and then reload **jigsaw.htm** in your Web browser.

3. Move the pointer over any of the 24 puzzle pieces in the right section, and then press and hold down the mouse button.

4. Move the pointer to the grid in the left section and verify that the puzzle piece moves across the page, following the pointer. See Figure 6-28.

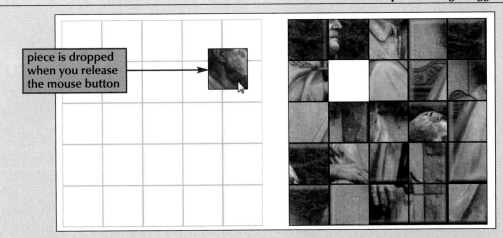

piece is dropped when you release the mouse button

5. Release the mouse button, and verify that the puzzle piece drops and remains at the new page location.

Refining the Jigsaw Puzzle

Pete reviews the jigsaw.htm page. While working with the puzzle, he notices that in some instances, the piece being moved disappears behind other objects on the page, as shown in Figure 6-29. He wants you to make sure the dragged puzzle piece always appears on top.

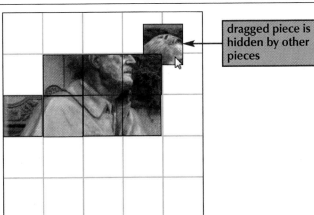

dragged piece is hidden by other pieces

Keeping Dragged Items on Top

To keep the dragged puzzle piece on top, you'll create a variable named maxZ that stores the maximum value of the z-index style for objects on the page. Each time you grab a piece, the value of maxZ is increased by 1 and then applied to the z-index style of the newly selected piece. As the piece is dragged across the page, it will have the highest z-index of any object on the page and will always appear on top of other objects.

You'll declare maxZ as a global variable, setting its initial value to 1.

To create and apply the maxZ variable:

▶ 1. Return to the **jpuzzle.js** file in your text editor, and then directly below the declaration of the diffY variable, insert the following line:

```
var maxZ = 1;
```

▶ 2. Scroll down to the mouseGrab() function, and then insert the following two lines, as shown in Figure 6-30:

```
maxZ++;
mousePiece.style.zIndex = maxZ; // place the piece above
other objects
```

Figure 6-30 ▶ **Code to declare the maxZ variable**

```
var diffx = null;
var diffY = null;
var maxZ = 1;




function mouseGrab(e) {
    var evt = e || window.event;
    mousePiece = evt.target || evt.srcElement;

    maxZ++;
    mousePiece.style.zIndex = maxZ; // place the piece above other objects

    var mouseX = evt.clientX; // x-coordinate of pointer
    var mouseY = evt.clientY; // y-coordinate of pointer
```

▶ 3. Save your changes to the file.

▶ 4. Reload **jigsaw.htm** in your Web browser, and verify that the currently selected puzzle piece always remains on top of the other objects on the page.

Preventing Hidden Pieces

A second problem Pete foresees occurs when one puzzle piece is dropped on top of another piece, hiding it from the user. Pete wants you to add a feature that prevents the user from dropping one piece upon another. To do this, you'll use the withinIt() function that Pete already created and stored in the kgfunctions.js file. The withinIt() function shown below compares the position of two objects:

```
function withinIt(object1, object2) {
   var within = false;
   var x1 = parseInt(object1.style.left);
   var y1 = parseInt(object1.style.top);

   var left = parseInt(object2.style.left);
   var top = parseInt(object2.style.top);
   var width = parseInt(object2.style.width);
   var height = parseInt(object2.style.height);

   var bottom = top + height;
   var right = left + width;

   if ((x1 > left && x1 < right) && (y1 > top && y1 < bottom)) within = true;
   return within;
}
```

If the upper-left corner of the first object falls within the boundaries of the second, the function returns the value true; otherwise, it returns the value false.

You'll use this function to confirm that the piece you're dropping will not cover another puzzle piece. The following dropValid() function does this by looping through all of the items in the pieces array, comparing the position of the specified object to the position of each piece:

```
function dropValid(object) {

   for (var i = 0; i < pieces.length; i++) {
      if (withinIt(object, pieces[i])) return false;
   }

   return true;
}
```

If the object falls within the boundary of any piece in the array, the dropValid() function returns the value false. If the for loop concludes without finding a match, the function returns the value true. Only a true value will indicate that the object will not cover any puzzle piece.

You'll add the dropValid() function to the jpuzzle.js file, and then call it from within the mouseDrop() function to check that the dragged piece can be dropped without hiding another puzzle piece.

To insert and call the dropValid() function:

▶ **1.** Return to the **jpuzzle.js** file in your text editor, and then directly below the init() function, insert the following function:

```
function dropValid(object) {

   for (var i = 0; i < pieces.length; i++) {
      if (withinIt(object, pieces[i])) return false;
   }

   return true;
}
```

▶ **2.** Scroll down to the mouseDrop() function, and after the opening function line, insert the following statement:

```
if (dropValid(mousePiece)) {
```

▶ **3.** Indent the next two lines of code, and then insert } (a closing curly brace) to complete the if statement. Figure 6-31 shows the revised code.

Figure 6-31 ▶ **Code to ensure that the piece can be dropped with the dropValid() function**

```
    for (var i = 0; i < grids.length; i++) {
        grids[i].style.top = getStyle(grids[i],"top");
        grids[i].style.left = getStyle(grids[i],"left");
        grids[i].style.width = getStyle(grids[i],"width");
        grids[i].style.height = getStyle(grids[i],"height");
    }

}

function dropValid(object) {

    for (var i = 0; i < pieces.length; i++) {
        if (withinIt(object, pieces[i])) return false;
    }

    return true;
}
```

> verifies that the upper-left corner of the object does not fall within any puzzle piece

```
function mouseDrop(e) {
    if (dropValid(mousePiece)) {
        removeEvent(document, "mousemove", mouseMove, false);
        removeEvent(document, "mouseup", mouseDrop, false);
    }
}
```

> validates the position of the piece before dropping it

▶ **4.** Save your changes to the file, and then reload **jigsaw.htm** in your Web browser.

▶ **5.** Verify that you can drop puzzle pieces everywhere on the Web page except where the upper-left corner of the piece covers another puzzle piece.

Snapping a Piece to the Puzzle Grid

Pete wants the jigsaw pieces to snap into position on the grid to make it easier for users to view the completed puzzle and to line up all individual pieces. To apply this effect, you'll use the withinIt() function again to determine whether a puzzle piece has been dropped on top of any of the 25 grid pieces in the left section of the Web page. If this has happened, you'll line up the piece with the grid square.

The following function accomplishes this task by looping through all of the items in the grids array, comparing the position of each grid square to the position of the specified object:

```
function alignPiece(object) {
    for (var i = 0; i < grids.length; i++) {
        if (withinIt(object, grids[i])) {
            object.style.left = grids[i].style.left;
            object.style.top = grids[i].style.top;
            break;
        }
    }
}
```

If the withinIt() function returns a value of true, the top and left style values of the object are set to the top and left style values of the grid square, snapping it into place.

You'll add the alignPiece() function to the jpuzzle.js file, and then apply it to any puzzle piece dropped on the Web page by calling the function from within the mouse-Drop() function.

To insert and call the alignPiece() function:

▶ **1.** Return to the **jpuzzle.js** file in your text editor, and then directly below the dropValid() function, insert the following function:

```
function alignPiece(object) {
    for (var i = 0; i < grids.length; i++) {
        if (withinIt(object, grids[i])) {
            object.style.left = grids[i].style.left;
            object.style.top = grids[i].style.top;
            break;
        }
    }
}
```

▶ **2.** Scroll down to the mouseDrop() function and directly before the first removeEvent statement, insert the following:

```
alignPiece(mousePiece);
```

Figure 6-32 shows the inserted code.

Code to snap a piece to the grid with the alignPiece() function ◀ **Figure 6-32**

```
function dropvalid(object) {

    for (var i = 0; i < pieces.length; i++) {
        if (withinIt(object, pieces[i])) return false;
    }

    return true;
}
function alignPiece(object) {
    for (var i = 0; i < grids.length; i++) {
        if (withinIt(object, grids[i])) {
            object.style.left = grids[i].style.left;
            object.style.top = grids[i].style.top;
            break;
        }
    }
}
```

checks whether the upper-left corner of the object falls within any grid square

```
function mouseDrop(e) {
    if (dropvalid(mousePiece)) {
        alignPiece(mousePiece);
        removeEvent(document, "mousemove", mouseMove, false);
        removeEvent(document, "mouseup", mouseDrop, false);
    }
}
```

snaps the dropped piece to the grid

▶ **3.** Save your changes to the file, and then reload **jigsaw.htm** in your Web browser.

▶ **4.** Verify that when you drop a puzzle piece onto the grid, the upper-left corner of the piece automatically aligns to the grid square.

InSight | **Tracking Mouse Movements**

Because many JavaScript applications involve the pointer moving into and out of objects, both the IE and the W3C event models include special event properties to help track the movements of the mouse. You will usually be concerned with two events: onmouseover occurring when the mouse initially moves over an object, and onmouseout occurring when the mouse initially moves out from an object.

You may need to know what object the mouse is coming from or going to during these events. Under the W3C event model, this information is stored in the relatedTarget property

```
evt.relatedTarget
```

where *evt* is the parameter of the event handler function. The relatedTarget property will reference the object the mouse is either going from (during the onmouseover event) or going to (during the onmouseout event). The IE event model uses two properties to convey this information. The following property determines what object the pointer is coming from during the onmouseover event:

```
event.fromElement
```

The following property determines what object the mouse is going to during the onmouse-out event:

```
event.toElement
```

One source of confusion with the onmouseover and onmouseout events is that they will run whenever the pointer moves in or out of the object, or in or out of any of the nested elements of the object. A Web page that involves several levels of nested elements may cause the event handlers to run at incorrect moments. Because of this problem, the IE event model also supports the onmouseenter and onmouseleave events. These events run only for the specified object and not for any elements nested within that element. The W3C event model has no equivalent property.

Pete is pleased with the refinements you made to the jigsaw puzzle so far. In the next session, you'll continue to work with the properties of the jigsaw puzzle and you'll explore how to work with keyboard events.

Review | **Session 6.2 Quick Check**

1. What is the reference for the event object in Internet Explorer? What is the reference in the W3C event model?
2. What property determines the type of event associated with the event object?
3. What properties determine the screen coordinates of an event?
4. What properties determine the window coordinates of an event?
5. What technique ensures that a dragged item will always be on top as it moves across a Web page?
6. What does the `this` keyword reference under the IE event model? What does it reference under the W3C event model?
7. Under both the IE and W3C event models, what event property determines what object the mouse is coming from during the mouseover event?
8. Under both the IE and W3C event models, what event property determines what object the mouse is going to during the mouseout event?

Session 6.3

Formatting a Drag-and-Drop Action

Pete wants the Web page to provide users with more visual feedback. For example, when a user hovers the pointer over one of the puzzle pieces, he wants the pointer to change to 🖑 to indicate that the object is clickable. When an object is being moved across the page, Pete wants the pointer to change to ✣ .

Setting the Cursor Style

To set the style of the pointer as it hovers over an object, you can apply the cursor style

```
object.style.cursor = cursorType;
```

where *object* is an object on the Web page and *cursorType* identifies the style of cursor applied to the pointer. Figure 6-33 lists the different *cursorType* values and the appearance of the cursor under the Windows operating system (the pointer will appear differently under different operating systems and setups).

Mouse cursor styles   Figure 6-33

Cursor	Style	Cursor	Style
+	crosshair	↕	n-resize
↖	default	↗	ne-resize
↖?	help	↔	e-resize
✣	move	↘	se-resize
🖑	pointer	↕	s-resize
I	text	↙	sw-resize
○	wait	↔	w-resize
	url(*url*) where *url* is the URL of a file containing the cursor image	↖	nw-resize

You can also set a cursor style directly in the CSS style sheet using the following style declaration:

```
cursor: cursorType
```

In addition to the types listed in Figure 6-33, the cursor style supports an auto *cursorType* value, which allows the user's browser to determine the appearance of the pointer. Many browsers also support an extended list of cursor styles not shown in Figure 6-33. Check your browser documentation for more information.

Setting Cursor Styles

- To change the appearance of a pointer, use the cursor style

  `object.style.cursor = cursorType;`

  where *object* is an object on the Web page and *cursorType* is the type of cursor to be displayed when the pointer hovers over the object.
- To change the pointer using CSS, add the following style to the style declaration for the element:

  `cursor: cursorType`

Pete wants to set the cursor style for each of the puzzle pieces as 🖑. When the user is dragging the piece, he wants the cursor to change to ✥ . After the customer drops the puzzle piece, the cursor style should return to 🖑. To make this change, you'll add commands to the init(), mouseGrab(), and mouseDrop() functions that set the cursor style when the page loads, during the mousedown event, and after the piece has been dropped during the mouseup event.

To set the cursor style:

1. If you took a break after the previous session, make sure the jpuzzle.js and kgfunctions.js files are open in a text editor, and the jigsaw.htm file is open in your Web browser.

2. Return to the **jpuzzle.js** file in your text editor, scroll down to the init() function, and then within the for loop that retrieves and sets the style properties for the puzzle pieces, add the following command:

   `pieces[i].style.cursor = "pointer";`

3. Scroll down to the mouseGrab() function and below the statement that sets the z-index style, add the following command:

   `mousePiece.style.cursor = "move";`

4. Scroll down to the mouseDrop() function and at the end of the command block for the if statement, insert the following command:

   `mousePiece.style.cursor = "pointer";`

   Figure 6-34 highlights the revised code in the file.

```
function init() {

   var allElem = document.getElementsByTagName("*");

   for (var i = 0; i < allElem.length; i++) {
      if (allElem[i].className == "grid") grids.push(allElem[i]);
      if (allElem[i].className == "pieces") pieces.push(allElem[i]);
   }

   var randomIntegers = randomArray(pieces.length);
   for (var i = 0; i < pieces.length; i++) {
      pieces[i].style.backgroundImage = "url(piece" + randomIntegers[i] + ".jpg)";
      pieces[i].style.top = getStyle(pieces[i],"top");
      pieces[i].style.left = getStyle(pieces[i],"left");
      pieces[i].style.width = getStyle(pieces[i],"width");
      pieces[i].style.height = getStyle(pieces[i],"height");
      pieces[i].style.cursor = "pointer";


function mouseGrab(e) {
   var evt = e || window.event;
   mousePiece = evt.target || evt.srcElement;

   maxZ++;
   mousePiece.style.zIndex = maxZ;  // place the piece above other objects
   mousePiece.style.cursor = "move";


function mouseDrop(e) {
   if (dropValid(mousePiece)) {
      alignPiece(mousePiece);
      removeEvent(document, "mousemove", mouseMove, false);
      removeEvent(document, "mouseup", mouseDrop, false);
      mousePiece.style.cursor = "pointer";
   }
}
```

▶ **5.** Save your changes to the file, and then reopen **jigsaw.htm** in your Web browser.

▶ **6.** Verify that as you drag and drop the puzzle pieces, the mouse cursor changes between 👆 and ✛.

Trouble? If you don't see a change in the pointer's appearance, you might be using the Safari or Opera browsers. At the time of this writing, the Safari and Opera browsers do not support the move cursor style.

Highlighting the Grid Square

Pete also wants the jigsaw puzzle page to highlight the grid square that the selected piece is being dragged over. This will help users to see which grid square the piece will be dropped into if the mouse button is released. Although it might seem that you could highlight the grid square because the pointer is hovering over it, this is not the case. The pointer is hovering over the puzzle piece, and the actions of the mouse then bubble up from the puzzle piece to the document object and then to the browser window. Even though the grid square and puzzle piece appear in close proximity on the page, they are actually separated in terms of the object hierarchy.

Instead, you can employ the same concepts you used in the previous session to determine which grid square the piece is hovering over. The following code shows how to highlight squares in the puzzle grid:

```
var hoverGrid = null;
function highlightGrid(object) {
   if (hoverGrid) hoverGrid.style.backgroundColor = "";

   for (var i = 0; i < grids.length; i++) {
      if (withinIt(object, grids[i])) {
         hoverGrid = grids[i];
         hoverGrid.style.backgroundColor = "rgb(192, 255, 192)";
         break;
      }
   }
}
```

The first line declares a global variable named hoverGrid. The hoverGrid variable will reference which of the 25 grid squares the puzzle piece is currently hovering over. The highlightGrid() function is then employed to highlight that grid square. To ensure that only one grid square is highlighted at a time, the function starts by removing the background color of the current hoverGrid square, if it exists. The function then loops through all of the grid squares, testing whether the object lies within the boundaries of any of the squares. If it finds a match, it sets hoverGrid to point to the selected square, changes the background color of that square to a light green, and discontinues the for loop. The effect is that only one grid square will be displayed with a light green background at a time, and only when the object is hovering over it.

To see this function in action, you'll add it to the jpuzzle.js file.

To add the highlightGrid() function:

▶ 1. Return to the **jpuzzle.js** file in your text editor, and then below the declaration for the maxZ variable, insert the following line:

```
var hoverGrid = null;
```

▶ 2. Below the alignPiece() function, insert the following function:

```
function highlightGrid(object) {
   if (hoverGrid) hoverGrid.style.backgroundColor = "";

   for (var i = 0; i < grids.length; i++) {
      if (withinIt(object, grids[i])) {
         hoverGrid = grids[i];
         hoverGrid.style.backgroundColor = "rgb(192, 255, 192)";
         break;
      }
   }
}
```

Figure 6-35 highlights the added code.

Code to highlight grid squares with the highlightGrid() function ◀ **Figure 6-35**

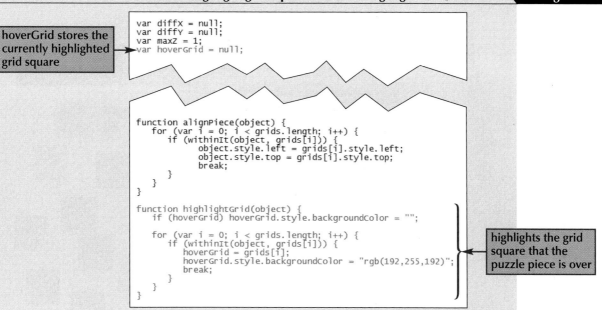

hoverGrid stores the currently highlighted grid square

```
var diffX = null;
var diffY = null;
var maxZ = 1;
var hoverGrid = null;
```

```
function alignPiece(object) {
    for (var i = 0; i < grids.length; i++) {
        if (withinIt(object, grids[i])) {
            object.style.left = grids[i].style.left;
            object.style.top = grids[i].style.top;
            break;
        }
    }
}

function highlightGrid(object) {
    if (hoverGrid) hoverGrid.style.backgroundColor = "";

    for (var i = 0; i < grids.length; i++) {
        if (withinIt(object, grids[i])) {
            hoverGrid = grids[i];
            hoverGrid.style.backgroundColor = "rgb(192,255,192)";
            break;
        }
    }
}
```

highlights the grid square that the puzzle piece is over

You want the highlightGrid() function to run as the user drags a puzzle piece across the Web page.

▶ **3.** Scroll down to the mouseMove() function and at the end of the function, insert the following statement, as shown in Figure 6-36:

```
highlightGrid(mousePiece);
```

Code to apply the highlightGrid() function while moving a puzzle piece ◀ **Figure 6-36**

```
function mouseMove(e) {
    var evt = e || window.event;
    var mouseX = evt.clientX;
    var mouseY = evt.clientY;

    mousePiece.style.left = mouseX + diffX + "px";
    mousePiece.style.top = mouseY + diffY + "px";
    highlightGrid(mousePiece);
}
```

highlights the grid square under the moving piece

▶ **4.** Save your changes to the file, and then reload **jigsaw.htm** in your Web browser.

▶ **5.** Drag a puzzle piece over the puzzle grid and verify that the background color of the grid squares changes to light green, as shown in Figure 6-37.

Figure 6-37 | **Highlighted grid square**

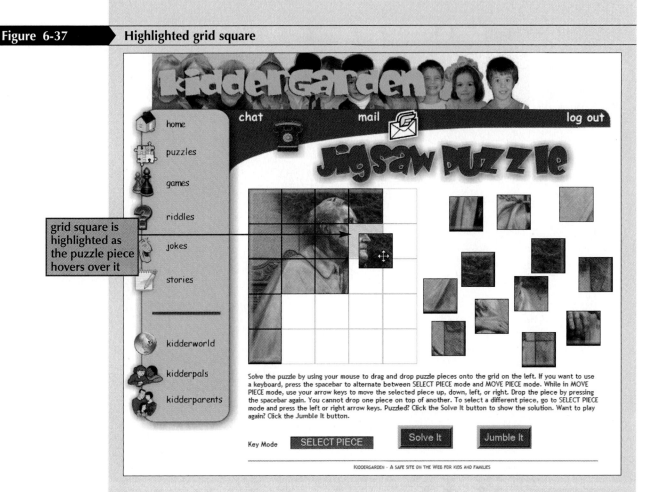

grid square is highlighted as the puzzle piece hovers over it

Pete is pleased with the addition of the mouse cursor style and the highlighted grid square. Both changes make it easier for users to interact with the jigsaw puzzle and avoid mistakes.

Specifying Mouse Buttons in Scripts

In writing code for the mouse actions in the jigsaw puzzle, you implicitly assumed that the user was pressing the left or primary mouse button. However, most mice have more than one button. Both the IE and the W3C event models provide support for three mouse buttons (left, middle, and right). You can determine which button was pressed using the button property

```
evt.button
```

where *evt* is the event object in either of the event models. The event models differ in the values returned by this property. In the W3C event model, the button values are 0 = left, 1 = middle, and 2 = right. In the IE event model, these values are 1 = left, 2 = right, and 4 = middle. Rarely will you write a script for the right and middle buttons because they often have default actions associated with them. For example, the right mouse button usually displays a shortcut menu for the highlighted object. You may not wish to interfere with these default actions.

The IE event model has an advantage over the W3C event model in that it allows for multiple buttons to be pressed. If the user clicks two or more buttons simultaneously, the sum of the button values is returned by the button property. So a user who presses both the right and middle buttons simultaneously will send the value 6 (2 + 4) to the event handler. Thus, under the IE event model, you can write scripts that involve two or more buttons being pressed simultaneously. The W3C event model does not support more than one button being pressed at time.

Working with Keyboard Events

Pete wants the site to be accessible to as many people as possible. He knows that some users have disabilities that make it difficult or even impossible for them to use a computer mouse. So, Pete wants users to also be able to play with the jigsaw puzzle using only the keyboard.

He sees keyboard activity working in two possible modes, as Figure 6-38 demonstrates. In Move Piece mode, the user moves a selected puzzle piece around the Web page by pressing any of the four keyboard arrow keys. In Select Piece mode, those same arrow keys are used to select different pieces from the puzzle. As you can see, what the arrow keys do depends on what mode is active.

Figure 6-38 ▶ Keyboard keys used in the jigsaw puzzle

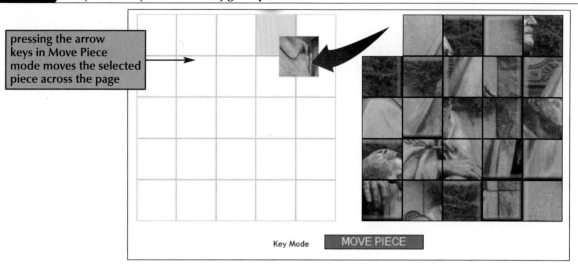

pressing the arrow keys in Move Piece mode moves the selected piece across the page

Key Mode   MOVE PIECE

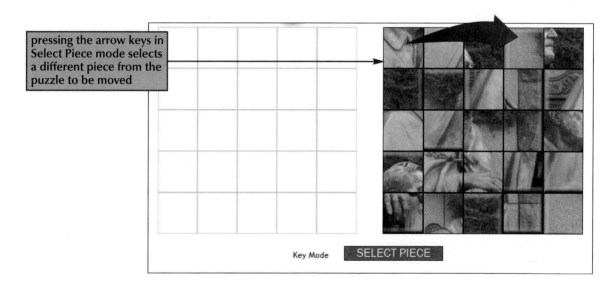

pressing the arrow keys in Select Piece mode selects a different piece from the puzzle to be moved

Key Mode   SELECT PIECE

Pete wants users to be able to switch between the two modes by pressing the Spacebar. If the user is in Move Piece mode, pressing the Spacebar has the added effect of dropping the piece in place on the Web page. To create the code for the two modes, you have to work with keyboard events.

Reviewing Keyboard Events

To make his program work, Pete wants to capture the action of a user pressing a keyboard key. Three distinct events occur in rapid succession when the user presses a key. These are:

1. **keydown** in which the user presses the key down
2. **keypress** which follows immediately after the onkeydown event
3. **keyup** which occurs after the key has been released by the user

The keydown and keypress events appear to be very similar; the difference between them lies in the difference between keyboard keys and the characters they generate. The keydown and keyup events occur as a result of a press and release of a physical keyboard key. The keypress event occurs very soon after the keydown event, at the moment when the computer generates a character in response to a keyboard action. Browsers treat the distinction between the keydown and keypress events somewhat inconsistently, which can be a source of frustration for programmers trying to create cross-browser compatible scripts. In DOM Level 3 (still to be adopted by most browsers), the keypress event has been replaced by the textinput event, which occurs whenever text is input by the user (by keyboard or not).

For the jigsaw puzzle, you want to capture the user action on the Spacebar and the four arrow keys, but not the characters that these keys generate (the four arrow keys usually do not generate characters anyway). So you'll create an event handler in response to the keydown event. Keyboard events usually occur in HTML elements that accept text entries such as input boxes or text area fields. Other than data entry fields, the keyboard events are associated with the entire document. The jigsaw puzzle contains no data entry fields, so you'll apply the following event handler to any keydown event occurring within the document:

```
document.onkeydown = keyGrab;
```

Under this event handler, whenever a user presses a key, the browser will run the keyGrab() function (which you will create shortly). You'll add this event handler to the init() function in the jpuzzle.js file.

Tip

To capture the key the user pressed, use the onkeydown event. To work with the character produced by pressing the key, use the onkeypress event.

To create an event handler for the onkeydown event:

1. Return to the **jpuzzle.js** file in your text editor.

2. Scroll down to the init() function and at the bottom of the function, insert the following command, as shown in Figure 6-39:

```
document.onkeydown = keyGrab;
```

Code to create an event handler for the keydown event   Figure 6-39

```
for (var i = 0; i < grids.length; i++) {
    grids[i].style.top = getStyle(grids[i],"top");
    grids[i].style.left = getStyle(grids[i],"left");
    grids[i].style.width = getStyle(grids[i],"width");
    grids[i].style.height = getStyle(grids[i],"height");
}

document.onkeydown = keyGrab;
}
```

runs the keyGrab() function whenever the user presses a key

Keyboard Event Properties

Both the IE and the W3C event models support several properties that provide information about the key that was pressed or the character produced by the keyboard event. Figure 6-40 summarizes these different keyboard event properties.

Figure 6-40 **Keyboard event properties**

Property	Description	Event Model
evt.altKey	Returns a Boolean value indicating whether the Alt key was pressed during the event, where evt is the event object	IE, W3C
evt.ctrlKey	Returns a Boolean value indicating whether the Ctrl key was pressed	IE, W3C
evt.shiftKey	Returns a Boolean value indicating whether the Shift key was pressed	IE, W3C
evt.metaKey	Returns a Boolean value indicating whether any meta key was pressed	W3C
evt.keyCode	Returns a key code indicating which key was pressed during the keyup and keydown events	IE, W3C
evt.charCode	Returns the ASCII character code indicating which character was produced during the keypress event	W3C
evt.which	Returns the ASCII character code indicating which key was pressed during the keydown, keypress, and keyup events	W3C

For example, to determine which key the user pressed, you can apply the keyCode property

```
evt.keyCode
```

to the event object, where evt is the event object under either event model. The keyCode property returns a code number identifying the key pressed by the user. Although there is no W3C specification for key code values, browsers have adopted a common set of code numbers partly based on ASCII codes. Figure 6-41 lists some of the key code values for the different keyboard keys.

Figure 6-41 **Key code values**

Key(s)	Key Code(s)	Key(s)	Key Code(s)
[0 – 9]	48 – 57	page up	33
[a – z]	65 – 90	page down	34
backspace	8	end	35
tab	9	home	36
enter	13	left arrow	37
shift	16	up arrow	38
ctrl	17	right arrow	39
alt	18	down arrow	40
pause/break	19	insert	45
caps lock	20	delete	46
esc	27	[f1 – f12]	112 – 123
space	32	num lock	144

To test the keyCode property, you'll add the keyGrab() function to the jpuzzle.js file and use it to report the key code for whatever key the user presses.

To report key code values:

▶ **1.** Directly below the init() function in the **jpuzzle.js** file, insert the following code, as shown in Figure 6-42:

```
function keyGrab(e) {
    var evt = e || window.event;
    alert("Key Code: " + evt.keyCode);
}
```

Code to display key code values ◀ **Figure 6-42**

```
        document.onkeydown = keyGrab;

}
function keyGrab(e) {
    var evt = e || window.event;
    alert("Key Code: " + evt.keyCode);
}
```

▶ **2.** Save your changes to the file, and then reload **jigsaw.htm** in your Web browser.

▶ **3.** Press the **Spacebar** on your keyboard and verify that an alert box similar to that shown in Figure 6-43 appears in your browser.

Alert dialog box showing the Spacebar key code value ◀ **Figure 6-43**

> Windows Internet Explorer
>
> ⚠ Key Code: 32
>
> OK

▶ **4.** Continue pressing other keyboard keys to determine the key code values associated with each key.

▶ **5.** Return to the **jpuzzle.js** file in your text editor, and then delete the line in the keyGrab() function that displays the alert box. You do not need the alert box for the program you will write.

Keyboard Events and Properties | Reference Window

- To run a command when the user presses down a key, use the onkeydown event handler.
- To run a command when the user releases a key, use the onkeyup event handler.
- To run a command when the user enters a character from the keyboard, use the onkeypress event handler.
- To retrieve the code of the key pressed by the user during the keydown or keyup event, use the property
    ```
    evt.keyCode
    ```
  where *evt* is the event object.

Toggling Between Modes in the Jigsaw Puzzle

Now that you've seen how to retrieve the code value of the key pressed by the user, you can use that information to add keyboard events to the jigsaw puzzle program. Users will require a visual clue as to which puzzle piece is the active piece—the one that will be affected by the actions of the keyboard. Pete suggests that the active piece should have a red border in Select Piece mode and a green border in Move Piece mode.

To keep track of the active piece, you'll create three global variables. The first, keyPiece, contains a reference to the currently active piece. The second variable, keyIndex, contains the index number of the current piece. The third global variable, selectMode, is a Boolean variable that indicates whether the user is in Select Piece mode or Move Piece mode. Its initial value should be set to true, indicating that the user is in Select Piece mode.

You'll add these three variables and set the initial appearance of the active puzzle piece.

To create the keyPiece, keyIndex, and selectMode variables:

1. Scroll to the top of the **jpuzzle.js** file and below the declaration of the mousePiece variable, insert the following global variables:

```
var keyPiece = null;
var keyIndex = null;
var selectMode = true;
```

2. Scroll down to the init() function and below the statement for the onkeydown event handler, insert the following global variables:

```
keyPiece = pieces[0];
keyIndex = 0;
keyPiece.style.borderColor = "red";
```

Figure 6-44 highlights the revised code.

Figure 6-44 ▶ **Code to set global variables for the keyboard pieces**

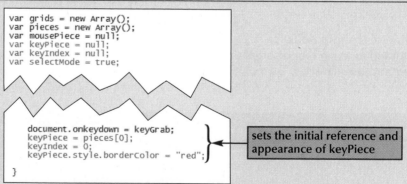

3. Save your changes to the file, and then reload **jigsaw.htm** in your Web browser.

4. Verify that the first piece in the puzzle has a red border.

Recall that Pete wants users to be able to switch between Select Piece mode and Move Piece mode by pressing the Spacebar. When they switch modes, the border color of keyPiece should change between red and green. Another visual clue is that an input box on the Web page with the id attribute keyMode should change its text between SELECT PIECE and MOVE PIECE and change its background color between red and green. To accomplish this, you'll add the following function to the file:

```
function toggleMode() {
   selectMode = !selectMode;
   var modeBox = document.getElementById("keyMode");

   if (selectMode) {
      keyPiece.style.borderColor = "red";
      modeBox.value = "SELECT PIECE";
      modeBox.style.backgroundColor = "red";
   } else {
      keyPiece.style.borderColor = "rgb(151, 255, 151)";
      modeBox.value = "MOVE PIECE";
      modeBox.style.backgroundColor = "green";
   }
}
```

The toggleMode() function first switches the value of the selectMode variable. It then creates a reference to the keyMode box on the Web page. Based on the value of select-Mode, it then changes the border color of keyPiece and the text and background color of the keyMode box.

You'll add this function to the jpuzzle.js file, and then run it in response to the user pressing the Spacebar.

To create the toggleMode() function:

▶ 1. Return to the **jpuzzle.js** file in your text editor, and then below the keyGrab() function, insert the following function:

```
function toggleMode() {
   selectMode = !selectMode;
   var modeBox = document.getElementById("keyMode");

   if (selectMode) {
      keyPiece.style.borderColor = "red";
      modeBox.value = "SELECT PIECE";
      modeBox.style.backgroundColor = "red";
   } else {
      keyPiece.style.borderColor = "rgb(151, 255, 151)";
      modeBox.value = "MOVE PIECE";
      modeBox.style.backgroundColor = "green";
   }
}
```

Next you want to run the toggleMode() function whenever the user presses the Spacebar key, which has a key code value of 32.

▶ 2. Add the following line to the keyGrab() function, as shown in Figure 6-45:

```
if (evt.keyCode == 32) toggleMode();
```

Figure 6-45   **The initial toggleMode() function**

```
function keyGrab(e) {
    var evt = e || window.event;

    if (evt.keyCode == 32) toggleMode();
}
function toggleMode() {
    selectMode = !selectMode;
    var modeBox = document.getElementById("keyMode");

    if (selectMode) {
        keyPiece.style.borderColor = "red";
        modeBox.value = "SELECT PIECE";
        modeBox.style.backgroundColor = "red";
    } else {
        keyPiece.style.borderColor = "rgb(151, 255, 151)";
        modeBox.value = "MOVE PIECE";
        modeBox.style.backgroundColor = "green";
    }
}
```

runs the toggleMode()
function whenever the user
presses the Spacebar

switches between
Select Piece and
Move Piece modes

▶ **3.** Save your changes to the file, and then reload **jigsaw.htm** in your Web browser.

▶ **4.** Press the **Spacebar** key repeatedly and verify that the border color of the active puzzle piece and the text and color of the keyMode input box switch between Select Piece mode and Move Piece mode. See Figure 6-46.

Figure 6-46   **Select Piece and Move Piece modes**

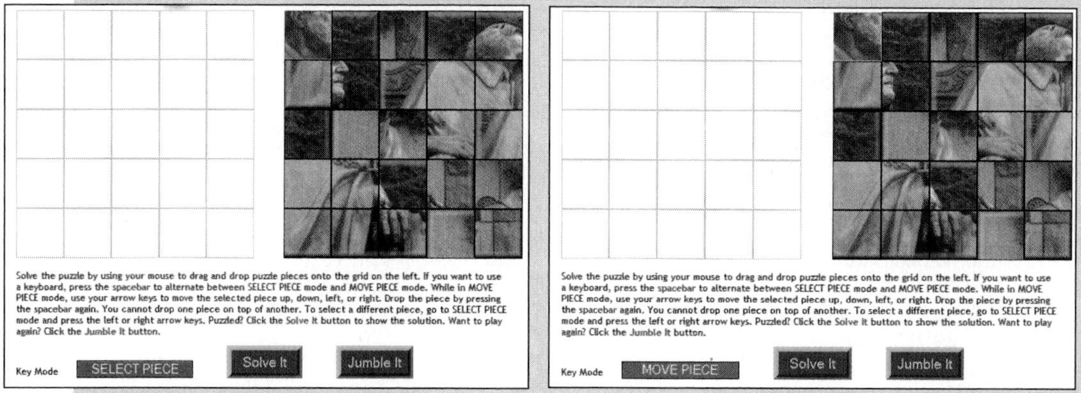

Select Piece mode   Move Piece mode

Now that you can toggle between the two modes, you can work on the actions of the keyboard within each mode. You'll start by writing a function to select a different puzzle piece by using the arrow keys.

Selecting a Piece with the Keyboard

Pete wants users to be able to select a different puzzle piece by pressing the Left and Right arrow keys. If the user presses the Left arrow key, the active piece should switch to the preceding puzzle piece. For example, if the active puzzle piece is piece23, pressing the Left arrow key should select piece22. If the user presses the Right arrow key, the next puzzle piece in the array should be selected. To keep track of the index number of the puzzle pieces, you've already created the keyIndex variable, setting its initial value to 0 (the first piece in the array). Thus, the function to select a piece is:

```
function selectPiece(diffIndex) {
    keyPiece.style.borderColor = "black";
    keyIndex = keyIndex + diffIndex;
```

Tutorial 6 Working with the Event Model | JavaScript   JVS 343

```
      keyPiece = pieces[keyIndex];
      keyPiece.style.borderColor = "red";
}
```

The selectPiece() function has a single parameter, diffIndex, which stores the amount by which the keyIndex value will change. The first line of the function changes the border color of the currently active piece back to its default of black (because it will no longer be the active piece after the function is run). You then change the value of keyIndex by diffIndex. For the jigsaw puzzle application, you'll limit the values of diffIndex to either −1 or 1 so this function will either increase or decrease keyIndex by 1. The function then changes keyPiece to the item in the pieces array with an index value of keyIndex. The function concludes by setting the border color of the new keyPiece to red.

A problem with the current selectPiece() function is that it's possible to go beyond the boundary of the pieces array. For example, if keyPiece is the last item in the array, attempting to move beyond that item will result in an error message. A similar problem occurs if trying to move before the first item in the array. You can correct this problem with the following if condition:

```
if (keyIndex == -1) keyIndex = pieces.length - 1;
else if (keyIndex == pieces.length) keyIndex = 0;
```

This if condition tests whether the value of keyIndex equals −1. If so, it sets the keyIndex value to match the last item in the array, effectively moving the user from the first puzzle piece to the last puzzle piece. Similarly, if the keyIndex value has gone beyond the end of the array, it moves it back to the beginning. As a result, users can never move off the values in the array.

The selectPiece() function will be run in response to the user pressing either the Left or Right arrow key. If the user presses the Right arrow key, the function runs with a parameter value of 1 in the command

```
selectPiece(1)
```

causing the browser to select the next item in the pieces array as the keyPiece. Similarly, pressing the Left arrow key runs the function with a parameter value of −1 in the command

```
selectPiece(-1)
```

causing the browser to select the previous piece from the pieces index.

You'll add the selectPiece() function and event handlers for the Left and Right arrow keys to the jpuzzle.js file.

To create the selectPiece() function:

▶ **1.** Return to the **jpuzzle.js** file in your text editor and directly below the keyGrab() function, insert the following function:

```
function selectPiece(diffIndex) {
   keyPiece.style.borderColor = "black";

   keyIndex = keyIndex + diffIndex;
   if (keyIndex == -1) keyIndex = pieces.length - 1;
   else if (keyIndex == pieces.length) keyIndex = 0;

   keyPiece = pieces[keyIndex];
   keyPiece.style.borderColor = "red";
}
```

▶ **2.** Add the following two lines to the keyGrab() function, as shown in Figure 6-47:

```
else if (selectMode && evt.keyCode == 37) selectPiece(-1);
else if (selectMode && evt.KeyCode == 39) selectPiece(1);
```

Figure 6-47

Code to select a puzzle piece with the selectPiece() function

```
function keyGrab(e) {
    var evt = e || window.event;

    if (evt.keyCode == 32) toggleMode();
    else if (selectMode && evt.keyCode == 37) selectPiece(-1);
    else if (selectMode && evt.keyCode == 39) selectPiece(1);
}

function selectPiece(diffIndex) {
    keyPiece.style.borderColor = "black";

    keyIndex = keyIndex + diffIndex;
    if (keyIndex == -1) keyIndex = pieces.length - 1;
    else if (keyIndex == pieces.length) keyIndex = 0;

    keyPiece = pieces[keyIndex];
    keyPiece.style.borderColor = "red";
}
```

calls the selectPiece() function when the user presses the Left arrow or Right arrow key

changes the value of keyIndex

sets the new location of keyPiece

3. Save your changes to the file, and then reload **jigsaw.htm** in your Web browser.

4. With the puzzle still in Select Piece mode, repeatedly press the **Left arrow** key and then the **Right arrow** key, verifying that the identity of the active puzzle piece changes in response.

Moving a Piece with the Keyboard

Finally, you want users to be able to move a puzzle piece using only the Left, Right, Up, and Down arrow keys. To facilitate the movement of the keyPiece, you'll add the following function:

```
function keyMove(moveX, moveY) {
    keyPiece.style.left = parseInt(keyPiece.style.left) + moveX + "px";
    keyPiece.style.top = parseInt(keyPiece.style.top) + moveY + "px";
    highlightGrid(keyPiece);
}
```

The keyMove() function has two parameters, moveX and moveY, that indicate the number of pixels to move in the x and y directions. Positive values of moveX and moveY move the piece to the right and down; negative values move the piece to the left and up. The keyPiece is moved by modifying the value of its left and top style properties. As with the code to move the puzzle piece using the mouse, the keyMove() function will also highlight any grid square that the user moves the puzzle piece over.

Pete wants the selected puzzle piece to move 8 pixels at a time in any of four directions. To move the puzzle piece 8 pixels to the left when the user presses the Left arrow key (key code 37), you run the following command:

```
if (!selectMode && evt.keyCode == 37) keyMove(-8, 0);
```

The if condition also must confirm that the user is not in Select Piece mode before moving the puzzle piece. Commands to move the piece in the up, right, and down directions are similar:

```
if (!selectMode && evt.keyCode == 38) keyMove(0, -8);
if (!selectMode && evt.keyCode == 39) keyMove(8, 0);
if (!selectMode && evt.keyCode == 40) keyMove(0, 8);
```

You'll add the keyMove() function and the commands to run it in response to the keyboard events to the jpuzzle.js file.

To create the keyMove() function:

1. Return to the **jpuzzle.js** file in your text editor and then directly below the keyGrab() function, insert the following function:

```
function keyMove(moveX, moveY) {
   keyPiece.style.left = parseInt(keyPiece.style.left) +
moveX + "px";
   keyPiece.style.top = parseInt(keyPiece.style.top) + moveY
+ "px";
   highlightGrid(keyPiece);
}
```

2. Add the following four lines to the keyGrab() function, as shown in Figure 6-48:

```
else if (!selectMode && evt.keyCode == 37) keyMove(-8, 0);
else if (!selectMode && evt.keyCode == 38) keyMove(0, -8);
else if (!selectMode && evt.keyCode == 39) keyMove(8, 0);
else if (!selectMode && evt.keyCode == 40) keyMove(0, 8);
```

Code to move a keyboard piece with the movePiece() function | Figure 6-48

```
function keyGrab(e) {
   var evt = e || window.event;

   if (evt.keyCode == 32) toggleMode();
   else if (selectMode && evt.keyCode == 37) selectPiece(-1);
   else if (selectMode && evt.keyCode == 39) selectPiece(1);
   else if (!selectMode && evt.keyCode == 37) keyMove(-8, 0);    ← Left arrow key
   else if (!selectMode && evt.keyCode == 38) keyMove(0, -8);    ← Up arrow key
   else if (!selectMode && evt.keyCode == 39) keyMove(8, 0);     ← Right arrow key
   else if (!selectMode && evt.keyCode == 40) keyMove(0, 8);     ← Down arrow key
}

function keyMove(moveX, moveY) {
   keyPiece.style.left = parseInt(keyPiece.style.left) + moveX + "px";
   keyPiece.style.top = parseInt(keyPiece.style.top) + moveY + "px";
   highlightGrid(keyPiece);
}
```

3. Save your changes to the file, and then reload **jigsaw.htm** in your Web browser.

4. Press the **Spacebar** to switch to Move Piece mode. Then press and hold down any of the four arrow keys to move the selected puzzle piece across the page, verifying that when the piece is over a grid square, the square is highlighted.

5. Press the **Spacebar** to return to Select Piece mode, and then drop the active piece onto the Web page.

6. Continue to work with the Spacebar and the arrow keys to verify that you can select different pieces from the puzzle and move them using only the keyboard keys.

The keyboard interface still needs some fine-tuning. The active piece does not always appear on top of other pieces when it is being moved using the keyboard, and it doesn't snap into place when dropped onto the grid. You can fix these problems by inserting the same functions and variables you added when programming the puzzle for use with a mouse. The maxZ variable ensures that keyPiece is always on top of other pieces. The dropValid() and alignPiece() functions ensure that one piece doesn't drop on top of another piece, and that any dropped piece aligns with the puzzle grid.

To complete the keyboard interface for the puzzle:

1. Return to the **jpuzzle.js** file in your text editor, and then scroll down to the toggleMode() function.

Tip

Always look for ways to reuse variables and code in different parts of your programming rather than duplicating the code.

▶ **2.** Insert the following expression at the beginning of the line to toggle the value of the selectMode variable to toggle the keyboard mode if the puzzle piece is located in a valid place to drop:

```
if (dropValid(keyPiece))
```

▶ **3.** Directly after the command to set the border color of keyPiece to red, insert the following command to align any dropped piece to the grid:

```
alignPiece(keyPiece);
```

▶ **4.** After the statement that sets the border color of keyPiece to the color value rgb(151, 255, 151), add the following command to keep keyPiece on top of all other objects when it is in motion by setting its zIndex value to maxZ:

```
maxZ++;
keyPiece.style.zIndex = maxZ;
```

Figure 6-49 highlights the new code inserted in the toggleMode() function.

Figure 6-49 ▶ **Completed toggleMode() function**

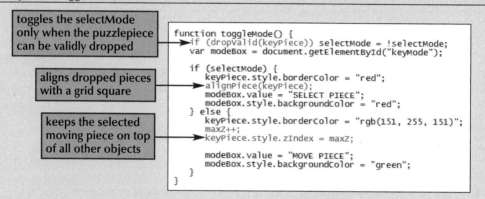

toggles the selectMode only when the puzzlepiece can be validly dropped

aligns dropped pieces with a grid square

keeps the selected moving piece on top of all other objects

```
function toggleMode() {
    if (dropValid(keyPiece)) selectMode = !selectMode;
    var modeBox = document.getElementById("keyMode");

    if (selectMode) {
        keyPiece.style.borderColor = "red";
        alignPiece(keyPiece);
        modeBox.value = "SELECT PIECE";
        modeBox.style.backgroundColor = "red";
    } else {
        keyPiece.style.borderColor = "rgb(151, 255, 151)";
        maxZ++;
        keyPiece.style.zIndex = maxZ;

        modeBox.value = "MOVE PIECE";
        modeBox.style.backgroundColor = "green";
    }
}
```

▶ **5.** Save your changes to the file, and then reload **jigsaw.htm** in your Web browser.

▶ **6.** Use your keyboard to select and move puzzle pieces, verifying that no moving piece is hidden behind another piece, that a piece cannot be dropped on top of another piece, and that pieces dropped onto the puzzle grid align with a grid square.

Understanding the keypress Event and Character Codes

The keydown event you used in the jigsaw puzzle program responds to the user pressing a key, but not necessarily typing a character. This distinction is important. A keyboard has a key for the letter A, but it makes no distinction between uppercase and lowercase letters. The keyCode property will indicate which letter key was pressed, but not whether the user typed A or a.

To determine what character the user typed, you use the keypress event along with the charCode property. The charCode property returns the character's ASCII code. The following expression returns the ASCII code of whatever character was typed by the user:

```
evt.charCode
```

where *evt* is the event object created from the keypress event. If the user typed a lower-case a, this expression will return a value 97, whereas typing an uppercase A will result in a value of 65. The charCode property should be used only with keys that actually produce characters. It should not be used with keys such as Shift or Ctrl, and the browser will usually return an undefined value for those keys. If you don't want to work with the ASCII codes, JavaScript allows you to convert these character codes into actual characters using the expression

```
String.fromCharCode(code)
```

where *code* is the ASCII code of the character.

One problem facing JavaScript programmers is that character codes are not handled equally by all browsers. Internet Explorer doesn't support the charCode property at all. Instead, the IE event model uses the keyCode property combined with the keypress event to determine the character typed by the user. This works for most browsers except Firefox, which returns a value of 0 if the keyCode property is used with the keypress event. Under Firefox, you use the which property to retrieve the character code of the pressed key.

This sounds confusing (and it is), but you can reconcile these differences in the following code which using object detection and values of the which property to determine which code value to use in determining the character typed by the user:

```
var evt = e || window.event;
if (evt.which == null)
    char = String.fromCharCode(evt.keyCode);
else if (evt.which > 0)
    char = String.fromCharCode(evt.which);
```

After these commands, the char variable will contain a text string representing the character entered by the keyboard under either event model and for any of the major browsers. The inconsistencies involved with characters and the keypress event are being dealt with in DOM Level 3 of the event model. How soon these changes are reflected in the browser market remains to be seen. However, for the jigsaw puzzle page, you're working with the only Spacebar and the four arrow keys, so you don't have to worry about interpreting the characters typed by the user.

Using Modifier Keys | InSight

In addition to keyboard characters, keyboards contain modifier keys. A **modifier key** is a keyboard key that is pressed along with a letter key to run special commands or to access program menus. For example, in many browsers, holding down the Ctrl key while pressing the P key runs the Print command. Most browsers support three modifier keys: Ctrl, Alt, and Shift. JavaScript uses these properties of the event object

```
evt.altKey;
evt.ctrlKey;
evt.shiftKey;
```

to determine the state of these keys, where *evt* is the event object for a keydown, keypress, or keyup event. Each of these properties returns a Boolean value that indicates whether the modifier key is being pressed during the event. By examining the keyCode and ctrlKey properties, you can determine whether the user is holding down the Ctrl key while pressing the P key. In addition to the three modifier keys, the W3C event model also supports the event object property

```
evt.metaKey;
```

to determine whether a Meta key is being pressed during a keyboard event. The Meta key is found on a UNIX workstation, and is usually equivalent to the Alt key on PC keyboards or the Command key on Macintosh keyboards.

Controlling and Canceling Events

Pete has been working with the keyboard interface to the jigsaw puzzle and he noticed one problem. In his browser, the arrow keys also control horizontal and vertical scrolling within the document window. Sometimes when Pete presses an arrow key to move a puzzle piece, the browser responds by both moving the piece and scrolling the window. He finds this distracting and wants you to suspend the default action of scrolling the browser window while the user is moving the piece.

Controlling Event Propagation

JavaScript supports several methods for controlling and canceling events occurring within a browser. At the most basic level, you can control how an event propagates through the object hierarchy. Because the two event models approach event propagation differently, they also use different methods to control that propagation.

You can cancel event bubbling under the IE event model by using the following cancelBubble property of IE's event object:

```
event.cancelBubble = true;
```

Once bubbling has been canceled, any objects higher up on the object tree will not receive the event. For example, in the following code, the browser calls the showLink() function whenever the user hovers the pointer over the first hypertext link in the document:

```
document.links[0].onmouseover = showLink;
function showLink() {
    commands
    event.cancelBubble = true;
}
```

The function runs some commands and then cancels event bubbling. This means that if the link has been nested within other elements on the page, none of the higher elements will "see" the mouseover event.

To turn event bubbling back on, you change the value of the cancelBubble property to false, using the following command:

```
event.cancelBubble = false;
```

Remember that because the IE event object is a global object, turning off event bubbling for one event turns it off for all events.

The corresponding property in the W3C event model is the method

```
evt.stopPropagation()
```

which stops an *evt* event object from propagating through the object tree. The stopPropagation() method is only applied during the bubbling phase. It cannot be applied during the capture phase. Unlike the cancelBubble property, the stopPropagation() method applies only to the current event being processed rather than all events in the document.

Canceling an Action

Many events have default actions associated with them. Hovering the pointer over a link changes the text of the window status bar; clicking a submit button in a Web form submits the contents of the form for processing. You've learned that you cancel form submission by having the onsubmit event handler return a value of false. This approach applies to other events as well. For example, you can disable a hypertext link by setting up an event handler that returns the value false when the link is clicked, as in the following code:

```
document.links[0].onclick = disableLink;
function disableLink() {
    return false;
}
```

You can also cancel a default action in the IE event model by setting the returnValue property of the event object to false, as in the following statement:

```
event.returnValue = false;
```

The corresponding command in the W3C event model uses the following preventDefault() method:

```
evt.preventDefault();
```

In most situations, it is easier to create a function that returns a false value, so the return-Value property and the preventDefault() method are rarely needed.

To restore the default action associated with an event, you change the return value back to true. For example, you can re-enable a blocked hypertext link by running the following commands:

```
document.links[0].onclick = enableLink;
function enableLink() {
    return true;
}
```

Canceling the default action associated with an event is most often used to substitute custom actions for the standard actions usually undertaken by the browser, which is what Pete wants to do with the default actions associated with the Spacebar and arrow keys.

To prevent the default actions associated with the Spacebar and arrow keys, you'll add the statement

```
return false;
```

to the commands of the keyGrab() function. Because you want to disable the default actions only for these keys and not others, you'll run the return false command only in response to the users pressing the Spacebar or an arrow key.

To cancel the default keyboard actions:

▶ **1.** Return to the **jpuzzle.js** file in your text editor, and then scroll down to the keyGrab() function.

▶ **2.** For each of the seven if conditions, enclose the results of the if statement within a command block within opening and closing curly braces and insert the following command:

return false;

Figure 6-50 highlights the new code added to the keyGrab() function.

Figure 6-50

Figure 6-50 ▶ **Code to cancel keyboard events within the keyGrab() function**

```
function keyGrab(e) {
  var evt = e || window.event;

  if (evt.keyCode == 32) {toggleMode(); return false}
  else if (selectMode && evt.keyCode == 37) {selectPiece(-1); return false}
  else if (selectMode && evt.keyCode == 39) {selectPiece(1); return false}
  else if (!selectMode && evt.keyCode == 37) {keyMove(-8, 0); return false}
  else if (!selectMode && evt.keyCode == 38) {keyMove(0, -8); return false}
  else if (!selectMode && evt.keyCode == 39) {keyMove(8, 0); return false}
  else if (!selectMode && evt.keyCode == 40) {keyMove(0, 8); return false}

}
```

cancels the default action associated with the spacebar

▶ **3.** Save your changes to the file, and then reload **jigsaw.htm** in your Web browser.

▶ **4.** Verify that when you press the Spacebar or any of the four arrow keys, the default action of the Web browser is canceled. (Canceling the scrolling action in this way is not supported under the Opera browser.)

The only task remaining on the jigsaw puzzle Web page is to give users the ability to re-jumble the puzzle or to have it solved for them. Pete already created functions to do these two tasks and added them earlier to the jpuzzle.js file. You will add an event handler to the init() function to run these functions when the user clicks the Jumble It and Solve It buttons on the Web page.

To complete the jigsaw puzzle program:

▶ **1.** Return to the **jpuzzle.js** file in your text editor.

▶ **2.** Within the init() function, add the following commands, as shown in Figure 6-51:

```
document.getElementById("jumble").onclick = jumbleIt;
document.getElementById("solve").onclick = solveIt;
```

Figure 6-51 ▶ **Event handlers to run the jumbleIt() and solveIt() functions**

```
document.onkeydown = keyGrab;
keyPiece = pieces[0];
keyIndex = 0;
keyPiece.style.borderColor = "red";

document.getElementById("jumble").onclick = jumbleIt;
document.getElementById("solve").onclick = solveIt;
}
```

jumbles the pieces of the puzzle again

shows the puzzle solution

▶ **3.** Save your changes to the file, and then reload **jigsaw.htm** in your Web browser.

▶ **4.** Click the **Solve It** button and verify that it shows the puzzle solution.

▶ **5.** Click the **Jumble It** button and verify that it randomizes the puzzle again.

You have completed your work on the jigsaw puzzle page. As Kiddergarden continues to grow in popularity, Pete will be looking for other online games and puzzles to add to the Web site.

Session 6.3 Quick Check | Review

1. What style declaration displays an hourglass as the pointer? What is the equivalent JavaScript command to do this?
2. What property determines which mouse button was pressed during an event? Describe how the event models differ in their interpretations of the value returned by this property.
3. What event corresponds to a user pressing a keyboard key?
4. What is the difference between the keypress event and the keydown event?
5. What event object property determines which key was pressed by a user?
6. What key code value is generated when a user presses the Spacebar?
7. What event object property determines whether the user is pressing the Alt key?
8. What property or method halts event bubbling or propagation in the IE and W3C event models?
9. How do you cancel the default action of a browser?

Tutorial Summary | Review

In this tutorial, you learned how to work with the W3C and IE event models to capture and respond to mouse and keyboard events. The first session explored the two main event models, examining how events are propagated through the document tree. It also showed how to attach functions to events and how to enable multiple functions for the same event. The second session examined the properties of the event object under both the IE and W3C event models. It showed how to extract information about the event from the event object's properties, and how to use this information to create a drag-and-drop effect for a puzzle page. The third session continued to explore how to work with mouse events and mouse buttons. It showed how to modify the mouse cursor and how to determine which mouse button the user pressed. The third session then turned toward keyboard events, showing how to capture and respond to keyboard actions initiated by the user. The session concluded by examining how to halt the propagation of events through the object hierarchy, and how to override a browser's default response to an event.

Key Terms

anonymous function	event model	keyup
bubbling phase	event object	modifier key
capture phase	IE event model	target phase
event bubbling	keydown	traditional binding
event capturing	keypress	W3C event model

Practice the skills you learned in the tutorial using the same case scenario.

Data Files needed for the Review Assignments: block0.jpg through block24.jpg, blockstxt.htm, kgmenu.jpg, kgtitle,jpg, libtxt.js, photo.jpg, sbblocks.css, sbtitle.jpg, slidetxt.js

Pete wants you to finish a Web page he has been working on that displays a sliding block puzzle. In a sliding block puzzle, the puzzle pieces are laid out in a grid with one blank space. Pieces adjacent to the blank space (either above, below, to the left, or to the right of the space) can be swapped with the space. The goal of the puzzle is to move the blocks into their correct positions on the grid. A preview of a partially finished puzzle page is shown in Figure 6-52.

Figure 6-52

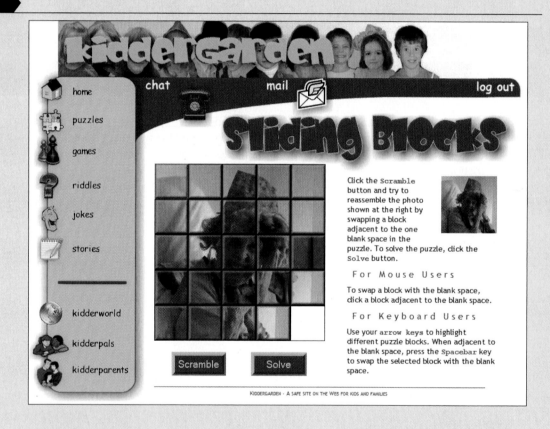

The puzzle is divided into a 5 × 5 grid, with each block in the grid contained within a div element that is 60 pixels wide by 60 pixels high. The image on each block is set as the block's background image. Starting at the upper left of the grid and moving right and then down, the div elements have the ID names block0, block1, and so on. The blank space is also a div element, with the ID name blank. The image files for the blocks are named block0.jpg through block24.jpg.

Pete wants this puzzle to work with both the mouse and the keyboard. You need to program the following actions:

- If a user clicks a block to the left of, to the right of, above, or below the blank space, that block should swap positions with the blank space.

- Any block adjacent to the blank space should display the pointer cursor when the pointer hovers over it; all other blocks should display the default cursor.
- One block in the puzzle is highlighted with a red border. A user can highlight different blocks by pressing the arrow keys on the keyboard.
- If the highlighted block is adjacent to the blank space, a user can swap the highlighted block with the blank space by pressing the Spacebar on the keyboard.

Pete also provided several JavaScript files that contain functions you can use on the Web page. Figure 6-53 summarizes the functions that you'll use in this problem.

Figure 6-53

Function	Description
scrambleIt()	Reloads the current Web page, thus rearranging the puzzle blocks
solveIt()	Places the puzzle blocks in the correct order in the puzzle
getStyle(object, styleName)	Returns the computed style value for a specified styleName applied to an object
nextTo(object1, object)	Returns a Boolean value indicating whether object1 lies next to object2
withinIt(x, y, object2)	Returns a Boolean value indicating whether the coordinate (x, y) lies within the boundaries of object
swapObjects(object1, object2)	Swaps the page positions of object1 and object2
scrambleIntegers(size)	Returns an array of integers from 0 up to one less than size, sorted in random order with even parity observed in the sorting of the integers (to ensure that the sliding blocks puzzle is solvable)
randOrder()	Returns a random value between −0.5 and 0.5

Complete the following:

1. Use your text editor to open the **blockstxt.htm**, **libtxt.js**, and **slidetxt.js** files from the tutorial.06\review folder, enter *your name* and *the date* in the comment section of each file, and then save the files as **blocks.htm**, **library.js**, and **slideblocks.js**, respectively.
2. Go to **blocks.htm** in your text editor, review the contents of the file, link the file to the library.js and slideblocks.js external script files, and then close the file, saving your changes.
3. Go to **library.js** in your text editor, and then insert a function named **addEvent()** that provides cross-browser support for assigning event handlers to events. The function should have four parameters: **object** for the object in which the event occurs, **evName** for the name of the event, **fnName** for the name of the function, and **cap**, a Boolean value indicating whether the event handler is assigned during the capture phase or the bubbling phase.
4. Insert a function named **removeEvent()** that provides cross-browser support for removing event handlers to events and objects. Use the same parameters you used for the addEvent() function. Close the library.js file, saving your changes.

5. Go to the **slideblocks.js** file in your text editor. Pete already added a global variable named blocks that contains an array of the puzzle blocks on the page and a function named init() that initializes the page and the puzzle. Add the following two global variables: **blankBlock** and **keyBlock**. You do not have to assign an initial value to either variable.

6. Add the following commands to the init() function:

    a. Declare a variable named **randomIntegers** that is equal to the array returned by the scrambleIntegers() function. Use a value equal to one less than the length of the blocks array as the parameter value for the function.

    b. Loop through the contents of the blocks array from 0 up to *one less than* the length of the blocks array. For each block item in the loop, assign the background image file block*random[i]*.jpg, where *random[i]* is the corresponding random integer from the randomIntegers array.

    c. Within the loop, assign the following event handlers to each block item: (i) the swapWithBlank() function when the block item is clicked, (ii) the highlightBlank() function when the pointer hovers over the block, and (iii) the removeHighlight-Blank() function when the user moves the pointer out from the block. Use the addEvent() function you created earlier to assign each event handler.

    d. Set the value of blankBlock to the last entry in the blocks array. Set the value of keyBlock to the first entry in the blocks array.

    e. Use the addEvent() function to run the keyEvent() function when the user presses a keyboard key.

7. Create the **swapWithBlank()** function. The purpose of this function is to swap a block clicked by the user with the adjacent blank space (if the block is adjacent to the blank space). Add the following commands to the function:

    a. Create a variable named **evt** that points to the event object for the event, under either event model.

    b. Create a variable named **mouseBlock** that references the target or the source of the event.

    c. Use the nextTo() and swapObjects() function to test whether mouseBlock is next to blankBlock. If it is, then swap the position of the two objects.

8. Create a function named **highlightBlank()**. The purpose of this function is to high-light blocks adjacent to the blank space. To complete this function:

    a. Create a variable named **evt** that points to the event object, and create a variable named **mouseBlock** that references the target or source of the event.

    b. If mouseBlock is next to blankBlock, set the style of the mouse cursor to pointer.

9. Create a function named **removeHighlightBlank()**. The purpose of this function is to remove highlighting from blocks adjacent to the blank space. To complete this function:

    a. Create a variable named **evt** that points to the event object, and create a variable named **mouseBlock** that references the target or source of the event.

    b. If mouseBlock is next to blankBlock, set the style of the mouse cursor to default.

10. Create a function named **keySwapWithBlank()**. The purpose of this function is to swap the page positions of the keyBlock and blankBlock objects. Use the nextTo() and swapObjects() functions to test whether keyBlock is next to blankBlock. If it is, swap the positions of the two objects.

11. Create a function named **selectBlock()**. The purpose of this function is to move the keyBlock from its currently selected block on the puzzle to another block (either above, below, to the left of, or to the right of the current keyBlock). The function has two parameters named **diffX** and **diffY**. Add the following commands to the function:

    a. Declare a variable named **newX** equal to the left position of the keyBlock object plus the value of diffX. Use the parseInt method to extract only the numeric value from the left style value of keyBlock.

    b. Declare a variable named **newY** equal to the top position of the keyBlock object plus the value of diffY. Again, use the parseInt method to extract only the numeric value of the top style.

    c. Declare a variable named **oldKeyBlock** equal to keyBlock.

    d. Loop through all of the items in the blocks array. For each block item, use the withinIt() function to determine whether the coordinates indicated by (newX, newY) lie within the block item. If so: (i) set keyBlock to the block item, (ii) set the border color of keyBlock to red, (iii) set the border color of oldKeyBlock to black, and (iv) break off the for loop.

12. Create a function named **keyEvent()**. The purpose of this function is to respond to the event of the user pressing down the Spacebar or one of the four arrow keys on the keyboard. To complete this function:

    a. Create a variable named **evt** that points to the event object under either event model.

    b. If the user presses the Spacebar, run the keySwapWithBlank() function and return the value false.

    c. If the user presses the Left arrow key, run the selectBlock() function with parameter values of –30 and 0. Return the value false.

    d. If the user presses the Up arrow key, run the selectBlock() function with parameter values of 0 and –30. Return the value false.

    e. If the user presses the Right arrow key, run the selectBlock() function with parameter values of 90 and 0. Return the value false.

    f. If the user presses the Down arrow key, run the selectBlock() function with parameter values of 0 and 90. Return the value false.

13. Close the file, saving your changes.

14. Open **blocks.htm** in your Web browser. Verify that you can swap a block piece adjacent to the blank space with the blank space itself. Also verify that the style of the mouse cursor is pointer for blocks adjacent to the blank space, but default elsewhere.

15. Verify that (i) pressing the arrow keys moves the highlighting from one piece to another; and (ii) pressing the Spacebar when the highlighted piece is next to the blank space swaps the position of the two.

16. Submit the completed project to your instructor.

Apply | **Case Problem 1**

Use JavaScript to create a program that limits the amount of text entered into a text area box.

Data Files needed for this Case Problem: booktxt.htm, bw.css, bwlogo.jpg, comtxt.js, leftbar.jpg

Online BookWorms Helen Ungerstatz is a manager of the Online BookWorms Web site, which is dedicated to lovers of books and reading. One of Helen's tasks is to create a comments page where users can enter short comments about books they have read. To keep the comments short and to the point, Helen wants to limit each comment to 500 characters (another place on the Web site allows extended book reviews). Helen has designed a Web page where users can enter their comments into a text area box.

One problem that Helen has encountered is that the HTML textarea element does not support a maxlength attribute to limit the length of text users can enter. Helen asks you to write a JavaScript program to do this instead. Helen also wants your program to automatically count down the number of characters left before the user reaches the 500 character maximum. A preview of the page you'll create for Helen is shown in Figure 6-54.

Figure 6-54

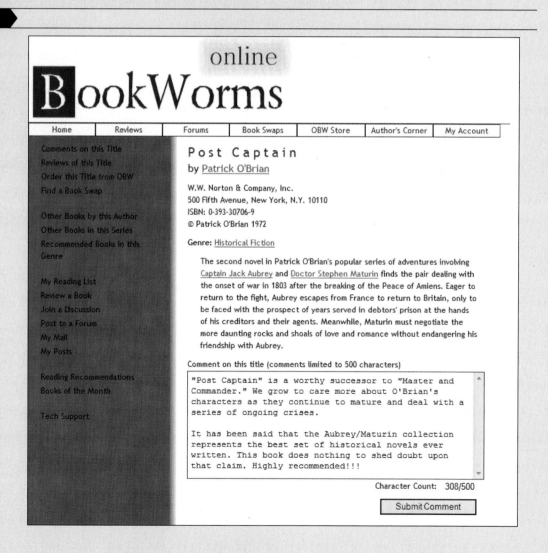

To create this application, the program needs to capture the keypress event so that you can check that space is still left in the text area box before accepting a character typed by the user, and it needs to capture the keyup event to update the count of characters in the comment box after the user has typed a character.

Complete the following:

1. Open the **booktxt.htm** and **comtxt.js** files from the tutorial.06\case1 folder in your text editor, enter *your name* and *the date* in the comment section of each file, and then save the files as **bookforum.htm** and **comments.js**, respectively.

2. Go to the **bookforum.htm** file in your text editor, study the contents and layout of the page, enter a link to the comments.js script file, and then close the file, saving your changes.

3. Go to the **comments.js** file in your text editor, declare a global variable named **maxLength** and set its value to 500, and then have the browser run the init() function when the page is loaded.

4. Create the **init()** function. The purpose of this function is to set up the event handlers for the Web page. Add the following commands to the function:

   a. Create a variable named **commentBox** that points to the textarea element with the ID comment.

   b. Create a variable named **countBox** that points to the input element with the ID wordcount.

   c. Set the value of countBox to the text string 0/*maxlength*, where *maxLength* is the value of the maxLength variable.

   d. Call the checkLength() function whenever the user presses the keyboard key within the commentBox object.

   e. Call the updateCount() function whenever the user releases a keyboard key within the commentBox object.

5. Create the **countText()** function. The purpose of this function is to return the number of non-white-space characters within the comment text area box. Add the following commands to the function:

   a. Declare a variable named **commentBox** that references the comment text area box.

   b. Store the regular expression /\s/g in the variable **commentregx**. This regular expression selects all of the white space characters within a specified text string.

   c. Use the regular expression replace() method to replace every occurrence of white space characters within the commentBox object with an empty text string, storing the resulting text string in a variable named **commentText**.

   d. Return the length of the commentText variable.

6. Create the **checkLength()** function. The purpose of this function is to confirm that users can enter a character into the comment text area box. Users can only enter a character if the number of characters currently in the box is less than the allowed maximum length, or if the keyboard key they press is either the Backspace key or the Delete key. Add the following commands to the function:

   a. Declare a variable named **evt** that points to the event object under either event model.

   b. Set an if statement with the following conditions: (i) If the value returned by the countText() function is less than maxlength, then return the value true; (ii) else if the user has typed the Backspace key or the Delete key, return the value true; (iii) otherwise, return the value false.

7. Create the **updateCount()** function. The purpose of this function is to update the character count after the user has typed characters. Add the following commands to the function:

    a. Declare the **countBox** variable that references the input element with the ID wordcount.

    b. Set the value of the **currentLength** variable returned by the countText() function.

    c. Set the value of the **countBox** object to the text string *currentLength/maxLength*, where *currentLength* is the value of the currentLength variable and *maxLength* is the value of the maxLength variable.

    d. If currentLength is less than maxLength, set the font color of the text in the countBox object to black with a background color of white; otherwise, set the font color to white on a red background.

8. Save your changes to the comments.js file.

9. Open **bookforum.htm** in your Web browser. Attempt to enter text into the comment text area box and verify that as you type non-white-space characters, the count of the characters listed for the box goes up. Also verify that if you attempt to exceed the 500-character limit, the browser prevents you from entering any characters—though it will accept input from the Backspace and Delete keys.

10. Submit your completed project to your instructor.

| Apply | | **Case Problem 2** |

Use JavaScript to create a horizontal scroll bar for an image slide show.

Data Files needed for this Case Problem: back.jpg, badgertxt.htm, bar.jpg, corner.jpg, flibtxt.js, image0.jpg – image9.jpg, links.jpg, logo.jpg, slidetxt.js, styles.css

Badger Aviation   Wayne Statz is the president and owner of Badger Aviation, an aviation company specializing in tours, charters, lessons, and shuttles in southern Wisconsin. He wants you to update the company's Web page. One of the pages you'll work with contains a slide show from one of Badger Aviation's tours of the area. Wayne wants you to create a horizontal scroll bar for the slide show that users can navigate with either the mouse or the keyboard. Figure 6-55 shows a preview of the page you'll create for Wayne.

Much of the layout is already done. Your job is to create the array of images for the slide show and program the operation of the scroll bar. The scroll button in the scroll bar has been stored in the Web page as a div element with the ID button. An external JavaScript file named functions.js contains two functions that you can use in completing this Web page: the placeIt() function places objects at specified coordinates on the page, and the getXCoord() function contains the x-coordinate of an object on the page. You'll have to create any other functions that you need.

Figure 6-55

See photos from one of our popular Dane County tours. Scroll through the slide show using your mouse or the Right and Left arrows on your keyboard.

Complete the following:

1. Use your text editor to open the **badgertxt.htm**, **flibtxt.js**, and **slidetxt.js** files from the tutorial.06\case2 folder, enter *your name* and *the date* in the comment section of each file, and then save the files as **badger.htm**, **flibrary.js**, and **slideshow.js**, respectively.

2. Go to the **badger.htm** file in your text editor, study the contents of the file, and then add links to the external script files flibrary.js and slideshow.js. Close the file, saving your changes.

3. Go to **flibrary.js** in your text editor, and then insert a function named **addEvent()** that provides cross-browser support for assigning event handlers to events. The function should have four parameters: **object** for the object in which the event occurs, **evName** for the name of the event, **fnName** for the name of the function, and **cap**, a Boolean value indicating whether the event handler is assigned during the capture phase or the bubbling phase.

4. Insert a function named **removeEvent()** that provides cross-browser support for removing event handlers to events and objects. Use the same parameters you used for the addEvent() function. Close the flibrary.js file, saving your changes.

5. Go to the **slideshow.js** file in your text editor, and then declare a global variable named **scrollButton** and a global variable named **diffX**.

6. Have the browser run the function setup() when the page is loaded.

7. Insert the **setup()** function. The purpose of this function is to set up the Web and define the event handlers. Add the following commands to the function:

   a. Point the scrollButton object to the page element with the ID button.

   b. Retrieve and set the top style value of scrollButton, using the getStyle() function from the flibrary.js file.

   c. Retrieve and set the left style value of scrollButton, also using the getStyle() function.

   d. Define the cursor style of scrollButton to use the pointer cursor.

   e. Use the addEvent() function you created for the flibrary.js file to assign the grabIt() function (which you'll create shortly) to the mousedown event occurring within the scrollButton object. Assume that the event handler is assigned during the bubbling phase.

   f. Use the addEvent() function again to assign the keyShow() function to the Web document in response to the keydown event. Again, assume that the event handler occurs during the bubbling phase.

8. Create the **grabIt()** function. The purpose of this function is to "grab" the scroll button used in the slide show. Add the following commands to the function:

   a. Declare the **evt** variable, storing within it the event object under either event model.

   b. Declare a variable named **mouseX** that stores the clientX property of the event object.

   c. Set the value of the diffX variable equal to the numerical difference between the left coordinate of the scrollButton object and the value of the mouseX variable.

   d. Use the addEvent() method to assign the mousemove event handler to the scrollButton object, running the moveIt() function in response to that event. Assume that capture is done during the bubbling phase.

   e. Use the addEvent() method to assign the dropIt() function to the scrollButton object in response to the mouseup event. Again, assume that capture is done during the bubbling phase.

9. Create the **moveIt()** function. The purpose of this function is to move the scroll button in response to the movement of the pointer. Add the following commands to the function:

   a. Declare the **evt** variable, pointing to the event object under either event model.

   b. Declare the **mouseX** variable equal to the clientX property of the event object.

   c. Declare the **buttonPosX** variable. The purpose of this variable is to define the left coordinate of the scrolling button. Set its value equal to the sum of mouseX and diffX.

   d. Run the showSlide() function (which you'll create next), using the value of the buttonPosX variable as a parameter value.

10. Create the **showSlide()** function. The purpose of this function is to move the scroll button and determine what slide show image to display on the Web page. The function has a single parameter named **x** that represents the left coordinate of the scroll button. Add the following commands to the function:

    a. If x is less than 20, set the value of x equal to 20.

    b. If x is greater than 299, set the value of x equal to 299.

    c. Set the left coordinate of the scrollButton object equal to x.

d. Declare a variable named **i** equal to (x − 20)/31 and then rounded down to the nearest integer. This converts the page coordinate to an index number. The value of the i variable is used to determine which of the nine image files to display in the slide show.

e. Set the src property of the element with the ID, photo, equal to the image file image*i*.jpg, where *i* is the value of the i variable.

11. Create the **dropIt()** function. The purpose of this function is to stop moving the scroll button in response to movements of the mouse. Use the removeEvent() function you created for the flibrary.js file to move the event handler for the mousemove event from the scrollButton object.

12. Create the **keyShow()** function. The purpose of this function is to move the scroll button in response to the user pressing either the Left or Right arrow key. Add the following commands to the function:

a. Declare the **evt** variable, pointing to the event object under either event model.

b. Declare the **key** variable, setting it equal to the keyCode property of the event object.

c. Declare the **buttonPosX** variable, setting it equal to the numeric value of the left position of the scrollButton object.

d. If the user has pressed the Left arrow key, decrease the value of the buttonPosX variable by 31. If the user has pressed the Right arrow key, increase the value of the buttonPosX variable by 31.

e. Run the showSlide() function using the value of the buttonPosX variable as the parameter value.

13. Save your changes to the file.

14. Open **badger.htm** in your Web browser. Verify that by dragging the scroll button on the Web page, you can move through the list of nine image files in the slide show. Press the Left and Right arrow keys on your keyboard and verify that you can move through the slide show using the keyboard.

15. Submit your completed project to your instructor.

Challenge	**Case Problem 3**

Explore how to use JavaScript events to create an online crossword puzzle.

Data Files needed for this Case Problem: across.gif, crosstxt.htm, down.gif, makepuzzle.js, parch.jpg, pcg.css, pcglogo.jpg, puzzle.css, runtxt.js

Park City Gazette   The *Park City Gazette*, edited by Kevin Webber, is the weekly newspaper of Estes Park, Colorado. In addition to its print offerings, the newspaper has an online version for distribution on the Web. The paper is known for its puzzles and games, so recently Kevin decided to include a puzzle in the newspaper's online edition.

Kevin wants users to be able to type their answers directly into the puzzle. They should be able to navigate the puzzle by pressing the arrow keys on their keyboard, and typing a letter should move a user to the next cell. A user should also be able to toggle whether typing is entered vertically or horizontally by pressing the Spacebar on the keyboard.

Kevin wants the current cell in the puzzle to be displayed with a yellow background. If a user enters a correct letter into a cell, the background should change to light green. If a user enters an incorrect letter, a light red background should be displayed. Blank puzzle cells should be displayed with a white background. Figure 6-56 shows a preview of a partially completed puzzle with some correct and incorrect answers.

Figure 6-56

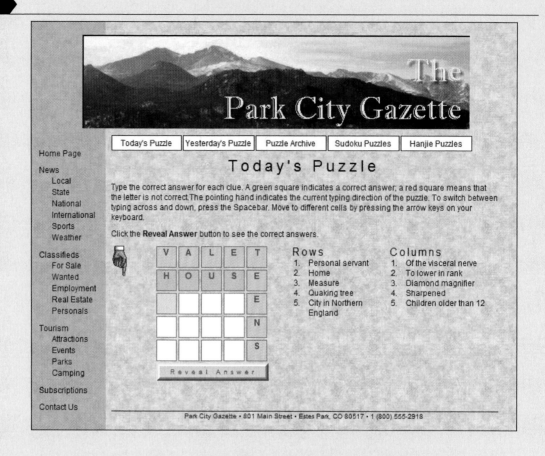

Each of the 25 cells in the puzzle is stored in a separate div element with the ID grid*xy*, where *x* represents the row number and *y* represents the column number. The row and column numbers start with 0 and go up to 4. Thus, the first cell in the puzzle has the ID grid00, the cell in the first row and second column has the ID grid01, and so on. The last cell in the puzzle has the ID grid44. You'll need to use this information to place the letters that users type in the correct cells in the puzzle.

One of Kevin's assistants already entered the HTML code for the puzzle page, and also produced some JavaScript code to generate the puzzle grid and its solution. Figure 6-57 describes the functions stored in the makepuzzle.js file.

Figure 6-57

Function	Description
writeClues()	Writes the puzzle clues onto the Web page where the puzzle clues are taken from two arrays named clues_across and clues_down
showAns()	Displays the puzzle answer; the text of the solution is contained in an array named words
writeText(object, text)	Writes the text string contained in the text parameter into the specified object

Complete the following:

1. Use your text editor to open the **crosstxt.htm** and **runtxt.js** files from the tutorial.06\case3 folder, enter *your name* and *the date* in the comment section of each file, and then save the files as **crossword.htm** and **runpuzzle.js**, respectively.

2. Go to the **crossword.htm** file in your text editor, study the contents of the file, and then add links to the external script files makepuzzle.js and runpuzzle.js. Close the file, saving your changes.

3. Go to the **runpuzzle.js** file in your text editor, and then add the following global variables to the file:

   a. **currentX** and **currentY**, representing the current column and row selected by the user from the puzzle. Set their initial values to 0.

   b. **currentCell** referencing the currently selected cell in the puzzle.

   c. **currentColor** storing the background color of the currently selected cell. Set its initial value to white.

   d. **across**, a Boolean variable indicating the direction in which data entry should occur. A value of true means that text is entered into the puzzle going across the cell. A value of false means that data entry goes down the cells. Set the initial value of the across variable to true.

   e. **keyNum**, a variable storing the keyCode value of whatever key is pressed by the user.

4. Have the browser run the init() function when the page is loaded.

5. Insert the **init()** function. The purpose of this function is to initialize the puzzle and set up the event handlers. Add the following commands to the function:

   a. Run the writeClues() function to write the puzzle clues into the Web page.

   b. Set the value of the currentCell variable to point to the grid00 cell.

   c. Set the background color of currentCell to yellow.

   d. When the user presses a keyboard key within the document, run the getKey() function.

   e. When the user clicks the Web element with the ID reveal, run the showAns() function.

   f. Change the cursor style of the reveal object to a pointer.

6. Insert the **getKey()** function. The purpose of this function is to respond to the keyboard key pressed by the user. Add the following commands to the function:

   a. Declare an event object named **evt** compatible with both event models.

   b. Store the key code of the event object in the **keyNum** variable.

   c. If the user has pressed the Spacebar key, run the toggleDirection() function and return the value false.

   d. If the user has pressed one of the arrow keys, run the moveCursor() function and return the value false.

EXPLORE
e. If the user has pressed a letter from A to Z, run the writeGuess() function and return the value false.

7. Insert the **toggleDirection()** function. The purpose of this function is to toggle the direction in which text is typed into the puzzle. Add the following commands to the function:

EXPLORE
a. If the value of the across variable is true, set the value of the across variable to false, and then change the source of the handimage inline image to the down.gif file.

b. Otherwise, change the value of the across variable to true and change the source of the handimage inline image to the across.gif file.

8. Insert the **moveCell()** function. The purpose of this function is to change the row and column number of the selected cell in the crossword puzzle to a new cell. The function has two parameters named **diffX** and **diffY**. Add the following commands to the function:

a. Increase the value of the currentX variable by diffX. Increase the value of the currentY variable by diffY.

b. If currentX is less than 0, change its value to 4. If currentY is greater than 4, set its value to 0. Repeat this for the currentY variable.

9. Insert the **moveCursor()** function. The purpose of this function is to change the selected cell in the puzzle to a new row and/or column. Add the following commands to the function:

a. Change the background color of the currentCell object to the value of the currentColor variable.

b. If the user has pressed the Left arrow key, run the moveCell() function with parameter values of –1 and 0.

c. If the user has pressed the Up arrow key, run the moveCell() function with parameter values of 0 and –1.

d. If the user has pressed the Right arrow key, run the moveCell() function with parameter values of 1 and 0.

e. If the user has pressed the Down arrow key, run the moveCell() function with parameter values of 0 and 1.

f. Change the reference of the currentCell variable to point to the element with the ID gridxy, where x is the value of the currentX variable and y is the value of the currentY variable.

g. Set the value of the currentColor variable to the background color of the current cell.

h. Set the background color of the current cell to yellow.

10. Insert the **writeGuess()** function. The purpose of this function is to write the character that the user has typed into the current cell in the puzzle grid, and then to move to the next cell in the puzzle (either across or down). Add the following commands to the function:

EXPLORE
a. Use the fromCharCode() method of the String object to store the character string represented by the keyNum variable in a variable named **outChar**.

EXPLORE
b. Use the toUpperCase() method to change the text of the outChar variable to an uppercase letter.

c. Call the writeText() function from the makepuzzle.js file to write the value of the outChar variable into the currentCell object.

    d. If the text of outChar contains the correct letter for the cell, change the background color of the current cell to light green. (*Hint*: To test whether the outChar letter is correct, compare outChar's value to the value of the words array item words[$y * 5 + x$], where y is the value of the current column and x is the value of the current row.) If the value is not correct, change the background color of the current cell to pink.

    e. If the value of the across variable is true, then move the location of the current cell to the right using the moveCell() function; otherwise, call the moveCell() function to move down.

    f. Point the currentCell object to the element with the ID grid*xy*, where *x* is the value of the currentX variable and *y* is the value of the currentY variable. Store the background color of currentCell in the currentColor variable. Change the background color of currentCell to yellow.

11. Close the runpuzzle.js file, saving your changes.

12. Load **crossword.htm** in your Web browser. Verify that (i) when you type letters using the keyboard, those letters are displayed in the puzzle grid; (ii) the current cell is displayed with a yellow background; (iii) correct letters are displayed with a light green background; (iv) incorrect letters are displayed with a pink background; (v) pressing the arrow keys moves the current cell around the puzzle grid; (vi) pressing the Spacebar toggles the typing direction and swaps the pointing hand image; and (vii) clicking the **Reveal Answer** button reveals the puzzle solution. (*Note*: The Opera browser will intercept keystrokes for the H and P letters, and attempt to display the history list and printer dialog box. You can ignore these incidents and continue to type in the puzzle solution.)

13. Submit the completed project to your instructor.

Create	Case Problem 4

Create a drag-and-drop survey form for a presidential museum.

Data Files needed for this Case Problem: library.js, pm.txt, pmlogo.jpg, pres0.jpg – pres16.jpg

Presidential Mosaic   Karen Xavier works at the Presidential Museum in Cleveland, Ohio. The museum features exhibits, talks, and displays that chronicle the history of the American presidency. One of Karen's goals is to provide interactive displays for museum patrons. She wants to establish a network of interactive kiosks scattered throughout the main floor of the museum. One of her ideas is to create interactive survey questions that patrons can answer as they tour the museum. Karen asks you to help create a Web page that contains a survey asking museum patrons who are the most popular presidents of the 20th century. Karen envisions a Web page with a list of the president names and portraits, which the museum patron can drag and drop onto a second list in the order of preference. To complete this survey page, you need to write a JavaScript program that does the following:

• Makes images of the 17 presidents from the 20th century into dragable objects

• Prevents users from dropping one presidential portrait upon another

• Includes a feature in which information about each president is displayed in a text area box when the user hovers the pointer over the presidential portrait

Karen has assembled the graphic images and the text required for the Web page. You'll use this material to create your final Web page. A preview of one possible solution to this project is shown in Figure 6-58, but you are encouraged to develop your own unique solution.

Figure 6-58

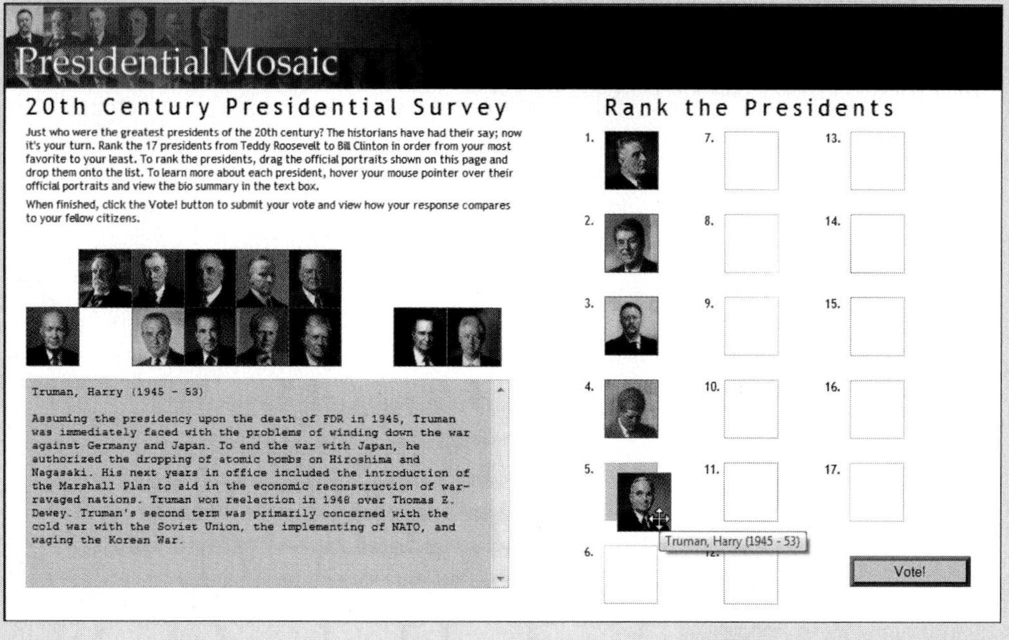

Complete the following:

1. Using the material found in the tutorial.06\case4 folder, create a Web page named **president.htm**. Include a comment section that describes the contents of your file and includes your name and the date. You may supplement the content provided for your Web page with any other content you think is appropriate for the task.

2. The design and layout of the page are up to you. Place the style definitions for your Web page in an external file named **pm.css**. Include a comment section in the file that documents its use and includes your name and the date. Link your Web page to this style sheet.

3. Create an external JavaScript file named **survey.js** that contains the code to enable users to drag and drop elements on the president.htm Web page. A few functions have been stored in the **library.js** file to help you with your program. The code should contain examples of the following features:

   a. Event handlers that involve event capturing supported under both event models

   b. Removing event handlers using a function that supports both event models

   c. Working with the properties of the event object under both event models

   d. Event handlers that respond to actions of the mouse

   e. Commands that modify the cursor style of an object

4. Link the Web page to the external JavaScript file and test the functionality of the page. Verify that you can drag and drop individual presidential portraits from their default location to their ranking on the list.

5. Submit the completed project to your instructor.

Review | **Quick Check Answers**

Session 6.1

1. `document.onclick = function () {alert("Click Detected");}`
2. From the bottom of the object hierarchy up to the top
3. `document.getElementById("Total").attachEvent("onclick", calcTotal);`
4. `document.getElementById("Total").detachEvent("onclick", calcTotal);`
5. Events are propagated from the top of the hierarchy during the capture phase, down to the event's target, and then back up the hierarchy during the bubbling phase.
6. `document.getElementById("Total").addEventListener("click", calcTotal, false)`
7. `document.getElementById("Total").removeEventListener("click", calcTotal, false)`

Session 6.2

1. IE event model: `window.event`
   W3C event model: the parameter of the event function
2. `type`
3. `screenX` and `screenY`
4. `clientX` and `clientY`
5. Increase the z-index of the object to be the maximum on the page.
6. Under the IE event model, the `this` keyword refers to the global object, which is the window itself. Under the W3C event model, the `this` keyword references whatever object is currently handling the event and calling the event function.
7. IE event model: `event.fromElement`
   W3C event model: `evt.relatedTarget`
8. IE event model: `event.toElement`
   W3C event model: `evt.relatedTarget`

Session 6.3

1. CSS: `cursor: wait`
   JavaScript: *object*`.style.cursor = "wait";`
2. Use the button property.
   The IE event model uses 1 = left, 2 = middle, 4 = right
   The W3C event model uses 0 = left, 1 = middle, 2 = right
3. `keydown`
4. The keydown event is fired when the user presses a keyboard key. The keypress event occurs immediately after the keydown event and indicates that a character has been sent to the browser from the act of pressing the key.
5. `keyCode`
6. 32
7. `altKey`
8. IE event model: `event.cancelBubble = true;`
   W3C event model: `evt.stopPropagation();`
9. Have the function handling the event return a value of false or run the following command:
   IE event model: `event.returnValue = false;`
   W3C event model: `evt.preventDefault();`

Ending Data Files

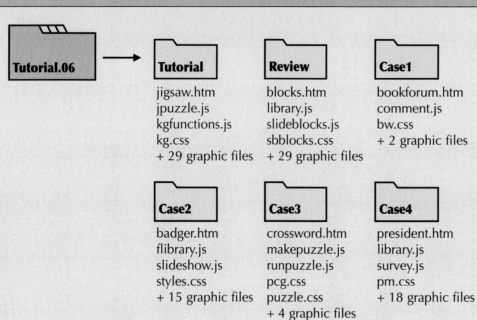

Tutorial.06 →

Tutorial
jigsaw.htm
jpuzzle.js
kgfunctions.js
kg.css
+ 29 graphic files

Review
blocks.htm
library.js
slideblocks.js
sbblocks.css
+ 29 graphic files

Case1
bookforum.htm
comment.js
bw.css
+ 2 graphic files

Case2
badger.htm
flibrary.js
slideshow.js
styles.css
+ 15 graphic files

Case3
crossword.htm
makepuzzle.js
runpuzzle.js
pcg.css
puzzle.css
+ 4 graphic files

Case4
president.htm
library.js
survey.js
pm.css
+ 18 graphic files

Working with Dynamic Content and Styles

Creating a Dynamic Table of Contents

Case | Midwest University

Norene Somerville is a professor of history at Midwest University. One of her recent projects involves putting the text of important historic documents online for her students to download and study. The Web site she's creating will support a variety of different document formats, but Norene also wants each document to be available in HTML format on a single Web page. This format makes it easier for students to print out the complete text of a document without having to navigate an entire site or install word processing or document software. However, Norene is concerned that some of the documents are very long and would be difficult to manage if placed on a single page.

She believes that a table of contents that summarizes the different sections within a document and provides links to those sections would be a great aid to students. However, Norene doesn't have the time to create such a table of contents for each document in her online library. She wants a program to automatically generate these tables of contents, and she has asked you to develop such a utility.

Starting Data Files

Tutorial.07 →

Tutorial
treattxt.htm
usconsttxt.htm
switchtxt.js
toctxt.js
+ 3 CSS files
+ 3 graphic files

Review
fed10txt.htm
keytxt.js
stylestxt.js
fedpaper.css
print.css
hlogo.jpg

Case1
french5txt.htm
engfrtxt.js
french5.js
styles.css

Case2
camtxt.htm
filtertxt.js
cstyles.css
+ 3 graphic files

Case3
statstxt.htm
tabletxt.js
tstyles.css
+ 3 graphic files

Case4
temptxt.htm
scenetxt.js
plays.css
+ 6 graphic files

Session 7.1

Introducing Dynamic Content

You and Norene discuss the table of contents utility. She has created a sample document containing the text of the United States Constitution. She feels that this would pose an ideal challenge because the document is very long and divided into different topical sections.

To view Norene's Web page:

▶ 1. Use your text editor to open the **usconsttxt.htm** and **toctxt.js** files located in the tutorial.07\tutorial folder, enter *your name* and *the date* in the comment section of each file, then save the files as **usconst.htm** and **toc.js**, respectively.

▶ 2. Return to the **usconst.htm** file in your text editor, and study the contents and structure of the file. The document contains a div element with the ID toc, in which you'll place the table of contents. It also includes a div element with the ID doc, containing the text of the document upon which the table of contents will be based.

▶ 3. Open **usconst.htm** in your Web browser. See Figure 7-1. The table of contents will be placed in the blue box in the page's left margin.

| Figure 7-1 | The initial Constitution Web page |

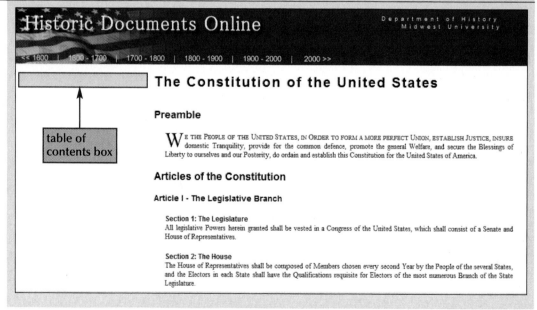

Examining the Table of Contents

Norene sketched her idea for the table of contents, as shown in Figure 7-2. Her idea is to create the table of contents as an ordered list, which is placed to the left of the source document. The table of contents utility should be automatically generated when the page is loaded by the browser, with minimal code added to the HTML document. Ideally, any table of contents application you create should be applicable to a wide selection of source documents.

Proposed table of contents layout   Figure 7-2

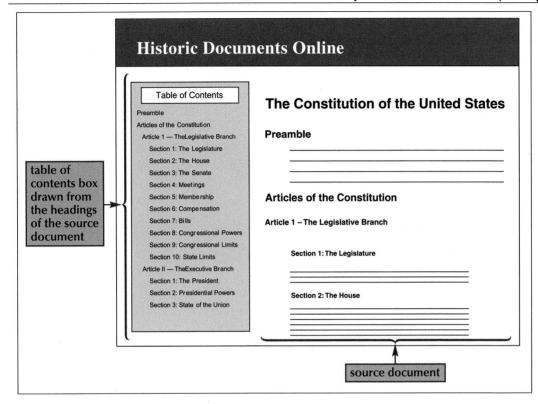

Norene suggests basing the table of contents on heading elements that are often used to break long HTML documents into topical sections. For example, the h1 heading usually marks a primary section in a document, h2 marks a secondary heading, and so on. Figure 7-3 shows the type of HTML code the table of contents application would generate. The utility would search the Web page for heading elements, copying the text of each heading into the table of contents. The table of contents would be organized as a nested ordered list with higher-level headings placed at the top of the list. For example, all h1 headings would be placed at the top level of the TOC, h2 headings would be listed within the h1 headings as the second level, and so on.

Document content converted into a table of contents   Figure 7-3

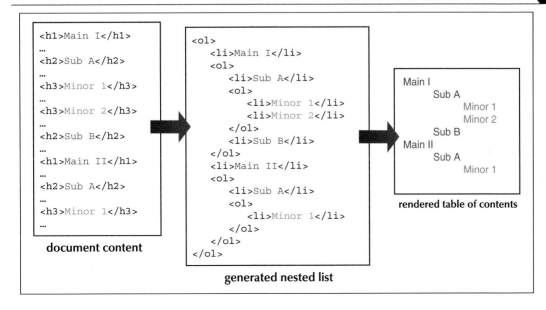

All of the JavaScript code that generates the table of contents will be located in an external file. This will allow Norene to easily apply the finished utility to other documents in her library. She created a file with some initial code, which you'll open now.

To open the toc.js JavaScript file:

▶ 1. Return to the **usconst.htm** file in your text editor, and then insert the following external script element to access the file in which you'll place the table of contents application:

```
<script src = "toc.js" type = "text/javascript"></script>
```

▶ 2. Close the file, saving your changes.

▶ 3. Return to the **toc.js** file in your text editor.

▶ 4. Add the following commands to the file, as shown in Figure 7-4, to run the makeTOC() function when the Web page is loaded:

```
addEvent(window, "load", makeTOC, false);

function makeTOC() {

}
```

Figure 7-4 ▷ **Code to run the makeTOC() function when the page loads**

```
function addEvent(object, evName, fnName, cap) {
    if (object.attachEvent)
        object.attachEvent("on" + evName, fnName);
    else if (object.addEventListener)
        object.addEventListener(evName, fnName, cap);
}

addEvent(window, "load", makeTOC, false);

function makeTOC() {

}
```

Note that this code uses the addEvent() function previously introduced to add the event under both the IE and W3C event models.

Inserting HTML Content into an Element

Generating a table of contents involves working with **dynamic content**, in which the content of the Web page is determined by the operation of a script running within the browser. Often, dynamic content is determined either by users' actions or by the content of other elements on the Web page or within the Web site. Noreen wants the table of contents to include the heading Table of Contents. One way of writing this heading into the table of contents box is to use the innerHTML property. The syntax of the innerHTML property is

```
object.innerHTML = content
```

where *object* is a Web page object and *content* is a text string containing HTML code to be written into that object. For example, to add an h1 heading to the toc element, you would run the following commands:

```
var TOC = document.getElementById("toc");
TOC.innerHTML = "<h1>Table of Contents</h1>";
```

You'll add these commands to the makeTOC() function.

To insert a heading into the TOC:

▶ **1.** Within the toc.js file, go to the makeTOC() function and insert the following commands, as shown in Figure 7-5:

```
var TOC = document.getElementById("toc");
TOC.innerHTML = "<h1>Table of Contents</h1>";
```

HTML code added to the TOC object ◀ **Figure 7-5**

```
function makeTOC() {
    var TOC = document.getElementById("toc");
    TOC.innerHTML = "<h1>Table of Contents</h1>";
}
```

▶ **2.** Save your changes to the file, and then reload **usconst.htm** in your Web browser. The table of contents displays the new heading. See Figure 7-6.

Table of contents with the h1 heading inserted ◀ **Figure 7-6**

The styles for the table of contents and the document are stored in the web.css style sheet. If you want to study the display styles that will appear as you create the table of contents throughout this tutorial, review the contents of this file.

Exploring innerText and textContent

The innerHTML property returns the HTML code found within an object, including any HTML tags, but it does not separate the text content from the text found in the markup tags. For example, if the document includes the tag

```
<div id = "doctitle">
   <h1>The Constitution of the <em>United States</em></h1>
</div>
```

the expression

```
document.getElementById("doctitle").innerHTML
```

returns

```
<h1>The Constitution of the <em>United States</em></h1>
```

In many cases, you're not interested in markup tags—only the text content of the element. Under the IE DOM, you can retrieve the text content, stripping out the HTML tags, by using the innerText property. Other browsers such as Firefox don't support this property, but instead support the textContent property, which returns the same results. You can use object detection to determine which property is supported by the user's browser, or combine the properties using the || (or) operator in the expression

```
object.innerText || object.textContent
```

where *object* is an object on the Web page. Applying this expression to content of the doctitle object described above yields the text string

```
The Constitution of the United States
```

without any markup tags from the original HTML fragment.

InSight | **Creating Dynamic Content in Internet Explorer**

The innerHTML property is not part of the official specifications for the W3C document object model, but it is part of the DOM for Internet Explorer. Because this property has proven valuable and simple to use, it is supported by all browsers. The IE DOM also supports other properties and methods to aid in the creation of dynamic content. However, these properties and methods are not as widely supported as the innerHTML property. One of these, the innerText property, has already been discussed. Another is the outerHTML property, which has the syntax

```
object.outerHTML = content;
```

where *object* is again the Web page object, but *content* is a text string of the HTML code for both the object and the content it contains. For example, if a Web page contains the element

```
<h1 id = "title">History Online</h1>
```

then the commands

```
var title = document.getElementById("title");
title.outerHTML = "<h2>Historic Documents</h2>";
```

are equivalent to replacing the h1 element with the following h2 element:

```
<h2>Historic Documents</h2>
```

Be aware that changing the element tags in addition to the element's content can result in unforeseen errors. For example, running the above code removes the title element from the document hierarchy because the ID attribute is not included in the new h2 element. Any subsequent part of the script that references the title element would result in an error. Use caution whenever you apply the outerHTML property to ensure that you don't change more of an element's content than you intended.

Working with Nodes

Although the innerHTML property writes HTML code into the document, it doesn't allow you to work with the newly inserted pieces of content as objects in their own right. A different approach is to use JavaScript to create nodes. A **node** represents an object within the Web page or Web browser. Anything in the document can be treated as a node, including every HTML tag and all of a tag's attributes. Even the tags in a document's head section, comment tags, and the <html> tag itself can be treated as nodes. The text within an HTML tag can also be treated as a node. For example, the tag

```
<h1>Table of Contents</h1>
```

consists of two nodes: one node for the h1 element and one node for the text string, Table of Contents, contained within that element.

Using a Node Tree

Nodes are arranged into a hierarchal structure called a **node tree**, which indicates the relationship between each of the nodes. Figure 7-7 shows a representation of a node tree for a simple HTML document. In the node tree, each element is treated as a separate node and the text within each element is treated as a node as well.

A document node tree — **Figure 7-7**

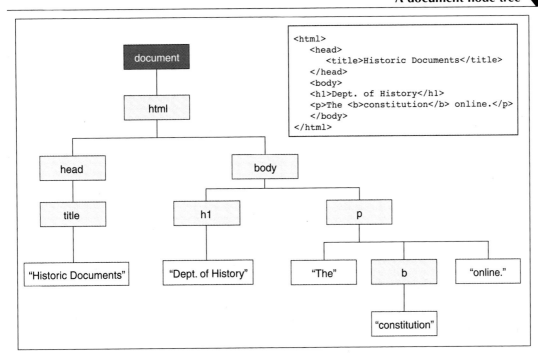

Nodes in a node tree have a familial relationship—each node can be a parent, child, and/or sibling of other nodes. To reference a node based on its relationship with the current node, use the expression

node.relationship

where *node* is the currently selected node or object and *relationship* is the relationship of another node to the current node. For example, the expression

node.parentNode

refers to the parent of *node*. In the node tree shown in Figure 7-7, the parent of the body node is the html node, and the parent of the html node is the document node. The parent of all nodes within a document is the **root node**. For HTML or XHTML documents, the root node is the html element. The root node is itself a child of the document node, which represents the entire document.

Each node can contain one or more child nodes. To reference the first child of the current node, use the following expression:

`node.firstChild`

In the node tree shown in Figure 7-7, the h1 node is the first child of the body node, and the text node "Dept. of History" is its first (and only) child. All of the child nodes are organized into the following object collection:

node.childNodes

As with other object collections, you can reference a particular object from this collection using the item's index number, as follows

```
node.childNodes[i]
```

where *i* is the index number of the child node. For example, to reference the first child of the current node, you could use either of the following expressions:

```
node.firstChild
```

or

```
node.childNodes[0]
```

To determine the total number of child nodes for a given node, you use the following length property:

```
node.childNodes.length
```

Tip

With Web documents, the order of the child nodes matches the order of the elements as they appear in the HTML or XHTML file.

The length of the childNodes collection for the paragraph element in Figure 7-7 is 3 (the two text nodes and the bold element). Figure 7-8 summarizes the rest of the familial relationships in the node tree.

Figure 7-8   **Node relationships**

Expression	Description
node.firstChild	Returns the first child of *node*
node.lastChild	Returns the last child of *node*
node.childNodes	Returns a collection containing the children of *node*
node.previousSibling	Returns the sibling prior to *node*
node.nextSibling	Returns the sibling after *node*
node.ownerDocument	Returns the root node of the document
node.parentNode	Returns the parent of *node*

Reference Window | **Determining Node Relationships**

- To access the parent of a node object, use the reference
  ```
  node.parentNode
  ```
  where *node* is a node object in the node tree.
- To reference the first and last child of a node, use the following reference:
  ```
  node.firstChild
  node.lastChild
  ```
- To reference the collection of all child nodes, use the following reference:
  ```
  node.childNodes
  ```
- To reference the previous and next sibling, use the following reference:
  ```
  node.previousSibling
  node.nextSibling
  ```

Determining Node Types, Names, and Values

The two document object models interpret white space in an HTML file differently. The W3C DOM calls for all occurrences of white space to be treated as text nodes. For example, the HTML code

```
<h1>Table of Contents</h1>
<h2>U.S. Constitution</h2>
```

contains five nodes: one node for the h1 element, one node for the h2 element, two nodes for the text contained within those two elements, and one node for the white space separating the h1 and h2 elements. The IE DOM does not treat occurrences of white space as text nodes. So under Internet Explorer, the above code contains only four nodes.

The difference between the two DOMs in how they handle white space may affect your program, so it's a good idea to determine whether a given node represents a text node, an element node, or some other type of node. The following properties provide information about a node's type, name, and value:

```
node.nodeType
node.nodeName
node.nodeValue
```

The nodeType property is an integer indicating whether the node refers to an element, a text string, a comment, an attribute, and so on. The nodeName property returns the name of the node within the document. The nodeValue property returns the node's value. Figure 7-9 displays some of the values of these three properties for the different types of nodes you'll typically encounter in a Web page document.

Tip

The nodeName property always returns element names in uppercase letters, so that an h1 element has the nodeName property value of H1.

Node types, names, and values ◄ Figure 7-9

Node	.nodeType	.nodeName	.nodeValue
Element	1	*ELEMENT NAME*	null
Attribute	2	*attribute name*	*attribute value*
Text	3	#text	*text string*
Comment	8	#comment	*comment text*
Document	9	#document	null

To see how these properties compare to a node tree, Figure 7-10 displays the nodeType, nodeName, and nodeValue property values for each of the nodes from Figure 7-7.

Nodes from the sample node tree ◄ Figure 7-10

Node	.nodeType	.nodeName	.nodeValue
Document	9	#document	null
html	1	HTML	null
head	1	HEAD	null
body	1	BODY	null
title	1	TITLE	null
"Historic Documents"	3	#text	Historic Documents
h1	1	H1	null
"Dept. of History"	3	#text	Dept. of History
p	1	P	null
"The "	3	#text	The
b	1	B	null
"constitution"	3	#text	constitution
" online"	3	#text	online

Nodes from the Sample Node Tree

Element nodes have no value. It might seem that an element node's value should be the content it contains, but that content is already its own node. If you want to change the text contained within an element, you must modify the value of that element's text node. For example, the title element contains the following text:

```
<h1 id = "title">History Online</h1>
```

To change the text of the title to "Historic Documents Online," you could run the following code under the W3C DOM:

```
var title = document.getElementById("title");
title.firstChild.nodeValue = "Historic Documents Online";
```

This code sample uses the firstChild reference because the text node is the first (and only) child of the title element.

Reference Window | **Determining Node Properties**

- To determine the type of object a node represents, use the property
    node.nodeType
  where *node* is a node object in the node tree. The nodeType property returns the value 1 for elements, 2 for attributes, and 3 for text nodes.
- To return the value of a node, use the following property:
    node.nodeValue
  For elements, the value of the nodeValue property is null. For attributes, the value represents the attribute's value. For text nodes, the value represents the text string contained in the node.
- To return the name of a node, use the following property:
    node.nodeName
  For elements, the name of the node matches the name of the element in uppercase letters. For attributes, the node name matches the attribute name. For text nodes, the node name is #text.

Creating and Attaching Nodes

To create the dynamic table of contents, you have to add new content to the Web page. The W3C DOM supports several methods to create new nodes, which are listed in Figure 7-11.

Methods to create nodes   **Figure 7-11**

Method	Description
document.createAttribute(*att*)	Creates an attribute node with the name *att*.
document.createComment(*text*)	Creates a comment node containing the comment text string *text*.
document.createElement(*elem*)	Creates an element node with the name *elem*.
document.createTextNode(*text*)	Creates a text node containing the text string *text*.
node.cloneNode(*deep*)	Creates a copy of *node*. If the Boolean parameter *deep* is true, the copy extends to all descendants of the node object; otherwise, only *node* is copied.

Using these methods, you can create a wide variety of objects that can be used in a Web page document. For example, you would use the following expression to create a text node containing the text "Historic Documents Online":

```
document.createTextNode("Historic Documents Online")
```

All of the methods described in Figure 7-11 create single nodes, with the exception of the cloneNode() method. The cloneNode() method is useful when you need to create a copy of an existing node, including any descendants of that node. The command

```
newtitle = title.cloneNode(true)
```

creates a copy of the title node, including any descendants of that node. The cloneNode() method provides a quick and easy way of creating elements and their content without having to create each node individually.

Creating Nodes | Reference Window

- To create an element node, use the method
    document.createElement(*text*)
  where *text* is the name of the element.
- To create an attribute node, use the method
    document.createAttribute(*text*)
  where *text* is the name of the attribute.
- To create a text node, use the method
    document.createTextNode(*text*)
  where *text* is the text string of the text node.
- To create a comment node, use the method
    document.createComment(*text*)
  where *text* is the text of the comment.
- To copy a preexisting node, use the method
    node.cloneNode(*deep*)
  where *node* is the preexisting node and *deep* is a Boolean value indicating whether to copy all descendants of the node (true) or only the node itself (false).

Once a node has been created, it still must be attached to another node in the document's node tree to be part of the document. Unattached nodes and node trees are known as **document fragments** and exist only in a browser's memory. They are not rendered on the Web page, although you can still access document fragments and work with them in your program. Figure 7-12 describes several methods for attaching one node to another.

Figure 7-12 ▸ **Methods to attach or remove nodes**

Method	Description
node.appendChild(*new*)	Appends a *new* child node to *node*, attaching it as the last child node
node.insertBefore(*new*, *child*)	Inserts a *new* child node into *node*, placing it before the *child* node; if no *child* is specified the *new* child node is added as the last child node
node.normalized()	Traverses all child nodes of *node*; any adjacent text nodes are merged into a single text node
node.removeChild(*old*)	Removes the child node *old* from *node*
node.replaceChild(*new*, *old*)	Replaces the child node *old* with the child node *new*

Using the properties and methods described in Figures 7-11 and 7-12, you can create elaborate node trees that contain several levels of different nodes. Figure 7-13 describes the process by which you would create the following HTML fragment using those methods:

```
<p><i>Historic</i> Documents</p>
```

Figure 7-13 ▸ **Process to create and attach nodes**

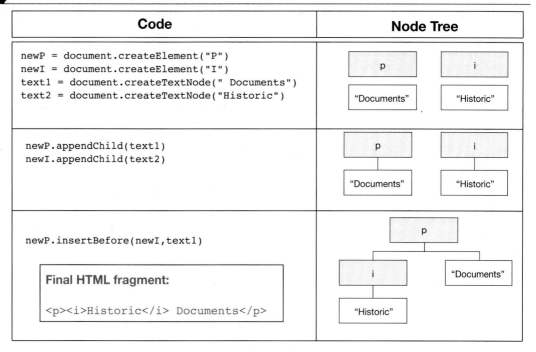

Code	Node Tree

```newP = document.createElement("P")```
```newI = document.createElement("I")```
```text1 = document.createTextNode(" Documents")```
```text2 = document.createTextNode("Historic")```	

```newP.appendChild(text1)``` ```newI.appendChild(text2)```	

```newP.insertBefore(newI,text1)```
 	
Final HTML fragment:
 	
```<p><i>Historic</i> Documents</p>```	

The approach shown in Figure 7-13 first uses the createElement() and createTextNode() methods to create four nodes: an element node for a paragraph, an element node for italicized text, a text node containing the text string "Historic", and a text node containing the text " Documents". The appendChild() method is then employed to attach the text nodes to the element nodes. The last line of code uses the insertBefore() method to insert the italicized text before the second text node. Although at first glance this approach may seem more cumbersome than simply using the innerHTML method, the advantage of nodes is that you can work with individual elements and text strings with more detail and flexibility than is possible with other methods.

Tip

When applied to a node that is already part of the document, the appendChild() and insertBefore() methods move the node from its current location in the document tree to its new location as a child node.

Attaching and Removing Nodes | Reference Window

- To append a new node as a child of a preexisting node, use the method
    ```
    node.appendChild(new)
    ```
  where *node* is the preexisting node and *new* is the new child. The new child node is appended to the end of the child nodes collection. If *new* already exists as a node in the document object tree, it is moved from its current location to the new location.
- To insert a new node at a specific location in the child nodes collection, use the method
    ```
    node.insertBefore(new, child)
    ```
  where *child* is the child node that the new node should be placed in front of. If *new* already exists as a node in the document object tree, it is moved from its current location to the new location.
- To remove a child node, use the method
    ```
    node.removeChild(old)
    ```
  where *old* is the child node to be removed.
- To replace one child node with another, use the following method:
    ```
    node.replaceChild(new, old)
    ```

Now that you've seen how to create and attach nodes, you'll create a node for an ol (ordered list) element and attach it to the table of contents on Norene's Web page. Currently, the content of the toc element consists of the elements

```
<div id = "toc">
   <h1>Table of Contents</h1>
</div>
```

which you want to change to

```
<div id = "toc">
   <h1>Table of Contents</h1>
   <ol></ol>
</div>
```

The code to create the ol list element and attach it to the table of contents is

```
var TOCList = document.createElement("ol");
TOC.appendChild(TOCList);
```

You'll add this code to the toc.js file.

To append an ordered list element to the table of contents:

1. Within the makeTOC() function in the toc.js file, insert the following code, as shown in Figure 7-14:

```
var TOCList = document.createElement("ol");
TOC.appendChild(TOCList);
```

Figure 7-14 ▶ **Code to create and attach the ol element to the table of contents**

```
function makeTOC() {
    var TOC = document.getElementById("toc");
    TOC.innerHTML = "<h1>Table of Contents</h1>";
    var TOCList = document.createElement("ol");
    TOC.appendChild(TOCList);
}
```

creates an element node for the ol element

appends the ol element to the table of contents element

2. Save your changes to the file.

Creating a List of Heading Elements

The next task is to populate the ordered list with list items, where the text of each list item matches the text of a heading element in the Constitution document. The code needs to do the following:

• Examine the child nodes of the Constitution document.
• For each child node, test whether it represents a heading element.
• If it is a heading element, extract the element's text and create a list item containing that same text.
• Append the list item as a new child of the ordered list in the table of contents.

For simplicity's sake, assume that each heading element is a child of the doc element on Norene's Web page (rather than nested within other elements) and that the heading elements contain only text and no other content.

Looping Through a Child Node Collection

There are two ways of looping through a collection of child nodes. One approach uses a counter variable that starts with a value of 0 and increases by 1 for each node, up to the length of the childNodes collection. The general form of this loop is:

```
for (var i = 0; i < node.childNodes.length; i++) {
   commands for node.childNodes[i]
}
```

In this form, the child nodes in the for loop have the object reference

```
node.childNodes[i]
```

where *node* is the parent node of the child nodes collection and *i* is the value of the counter variable in the for loop. The second approach uses familial references, starting with the first child of the parent node and then moving to each subsequent sibling until no siblings remain. The general form of this for loop is:

```
for (var n = node.firstChild; n != null; n = n.nextSibling) {
   commands for n
}
```

In this form, the current child node in the loop has the following object reference:

```
n
```

When no next sibling is available, the value of n is equal to null and the loop stops. Although both approaches yield the same results, the use of familial references is generally preferred because it does not require a browser to calculate the total length of the child nodes collection. For large documents containing thousands of nodes, this can speed up the processing time for the program. This method also provides the flexibility to insert new nodes into a document during the for loop without having to recalculate the length of the child nodes collection.

You'll use familial references in the following function to create the list of heading elements. The initial code for the function is:

```
function createList(object, list) {
    for (var n = object.firstChild; n != null; n = n.nextSibling) {
    }
}
```

This function has two parameters. The object parameter is the Web page object from which you will extract the list headings, and the list parameter contains the actual list as it is created by the createList() function. The initial code for this function simply uses a for loop to move through all of the children of the object parameter, sibling by sibling.

You'll add this function to the toc.js file.

To insert the createList() function:

▶ **1.** Below the makeTOC() function, insert the following code, as shown in Figure 7-15:

```
function createList(object, list) {
    for (var n = object.firstChild; n != null; n = n.nextSibling) {
        // loop through all of the nodes within object

    }
}
```

The createList() function   Figure 7-15

```
function makeTOC() {
    var TOC = document.getElementById("toc");
    TOC.innerHTML = "<h1>Table of Contents</h1>";
    var TOCList = document.createElement("ol");
    TOC.appendChild(TOCList);
}

function createList(object, list) {
    for (var n = object.firstChild; n != null; n = n.nextSibling) {
        // loop through all of the nodes within object

    }
}
```

creates the list items for the table of contents

▶ **2.** Save your changes to the file.

Matching the Heading Elements

Next you have to determine whether any of the child nodes of the object match one of the section headings that Norene wants to use to build her table of contents list. Recall that Norene wants to create section headings based on heading elements. To do this, you will first create an array of the element names for heading elements in the following command:

```
var sections = new Array("h1","h2","h3","h4","h5","h6");
```

The sections array is ordered from the element representing the highest level in the TOC (the h1 element) down to the lowest (the h6 element). In the Constitution document, you need to use only elements h1 through h3. However, including the full range of headings allows you to generalize the makeTOC() function for other documents in Norene's library.

Next, you want to create a function that determines whether a given node comes from one of those heading elements. The code for this function, which we'll call levelNum(), is:

```
function levelNum(node) {
    for (var i = 0; i < sections.length; i++) {
        if (node.nodeName == sections[i].toUpperCase()) return i;
    }
    return -1;
}
```

The levelNum() function uses the nodeName property to test whether a given node matches one of the elements listed in the sections array. Because element names in the nodeName property are returned in uppercase letters, you must use the toUpperCase()method to convert the element names in the section array to uppercase letters as well. The function goes through each item in the sections array and, if a match is found, returns the array index number. Thus, an h1 element returns the value 0 (indicating that it represents the highest level in the table of contents), an h2 element returns the value 1, and so on. If a node object doesn't represent a section heading, the function returns the value –1.

You'll add the sections array and the levelNum() function to the toc.js file.

> **Tip**
>
> To create a table of contents based on sections marked by elements other than headings, simply change the element names list in the sections array.

To insert the sections array and the levelNum() function:

▶ **1.** Directly above the makeTOC() function, insert the following global variable declaration:

```
var sections = new Array("h1","h2","h3","h4","h5","h6");
```

▶ **2.** Directly below the makeTOC() function, insert the following function:

```
function levelNum(node) {
    for (var i = 0; i < sections.length; i++) {
        if (node.nodeName == sections[i].toUpperCase()) return i;
    }
    return -1; // node is not a section heading
}
```

Figure 7-16 highlights the new code in the file.

The sections array and the levelNum() function | Figure 7-16

```
var sections = new Array("h1", "h2", "h3", "h4", "h5", "h6");

function makeTOC() {
    var TOC = document.getElementById("toc");
    TOC.innerHTML = "<h1>Table of Contents</h1>";
    var TOCList = document.createElement("ol");
    TOC.appendChild(TOCList);
}

function levelNum(node) {
    for (var i = 0; i < sections.length; i++) {
        if (node.nodeName == sections[i].toUpperCase()) return i;
    }
    return -1; // node is not a section heading
}
```

list of elements that can act as section headings

returns the level number of the section heading or –1 if not a section heading

The levelNum() function provides a way to determine whether a particular element within the constitution document represents a heading. The following code shows how you would extract the level number for any node:

```
var nodeLevel = levelNum(n);
if (nodeLevel != -1) {
    node represents a heading element
}
```

If the level is not equal to –1, then the node has to come from one of the six possible heading elements listed in the sections array. You'll add this if condition to the createList() function.

To create the nodeLevel variable:

1. Scroll down to the createList() function you inserted earlier and within the for loop insert the following commands, as shown in Figure 7-17:

```
var nodeLevel = levelNum(n);
if (nodeLevel != -1) {
    // node represents a section heading
}
```

if condition added to the createList() function | Figure 7-17

```
function createList(object, list) {
    for (var n = object.firstChild; n! = null; n = n.nextSibling) {
        // loop through all of the nodes within object

        var nodeLevel = levelNum(n);
        if (nodeLevel != -1) {
            // node represents a section heading

        }
    }
}
```

locates the section headings within the object

2. Save your changes to the file.

Creating the List Item Elements

Next, you'll create list item elements based on the section headings. The text of the list item should be taken from the text of the heading element. You can do that using the innerHTML property. The code is:

```
var listItem = document.createElement("li");
listItem.innerHTML = n.innerHTML;
list.appendChild(listItem);
```

You'll place these commands within the for loop of the createList() function so that for every section heading found in the source document, a corresponding list item is created for use in the table of contents.

To create the listItem variable:

▶ **1.** Directly below the comment in the for loop, insert the following code, as shown in Figure 7-18:

```
// create a list item to match
var listItem = document.createElement("li");
listItem.innerHTML = n.innerHTML;
list.appendChild(listItem);
```

Figure 7-18 **Code to create a list item for every section heading found**

```
function createList(object, list) {
    for (var n = object.firstChild; n! = null; n = n.nextSibling) {
        // loop through all of the nodes within object

        var nodeLevel = levelNum(n);
        if (nodeLevel != -1) {
            // node represents a section heading
            // create a list item to match
            var listItem = document.createElement("li");
            listItem.innerHTML = n.innerHTML;
            list.appendChild(listItem);
        }

    }
}
```

text of the list item comes from the text of the section heading

▶ **2.** Save your changes to the file.

Finally, you will call the createList() function from the makeTOC() function, specifying the constitutional document as the source document on which the TOC is based and the TOCList object as the object in which to place all of the TOC list items. Because you will reference the source document throughout this application, you will define it using a global variable named sourceDoc.

To generate the initial TOC:

▶ **1.** Directly above the makeTOC() function, insert the following global declaration to create the sourceDoc variable:

```
var sourceDoc; // document on which the TOC is based
```

▶ **2.** Within the makeTOC() function, add the following commands:

```
sourceDoc = document.getElementById("doc");

// generate list items containing section headings
createList(sourceDoc, TOCList);
```

Figure 7-19 shows the revised code.

Code to call the createList() function to generate the list items ◄ Figure 7-19

```
var sections = new Array("h1", "h2", "h3", "h4", "h5", "h6");
var sourceDoc; // document on which the TOC is based

function makeTOC() {
    var TOC = document.getElementById("toc");
    TOC.innerHTML = "<h1>Table of Contents</h1>";
    var TOCList = document.createElement("ol");
    TOC.appendChild(TOCList);

    sourceDoc = document.getElementById("doc");

    // generate list items containing section headings
    createList(sourceDoc, TOCList);
}
```

3. Save your changes to the toc.js file, and then reload **usconst.htm** in your Web browser. The table of contents contains list items whose text is taken from the section headings in the constitution document. The list items appear in uppercase letters because of a style set in the web.css file, not because of any command in the makeTOC() function. See Figure 7-20.

The initial table of contents ◄ Figure 7-20

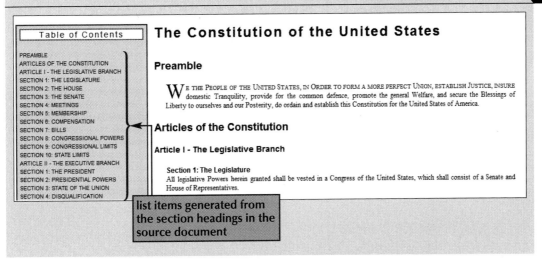

list items generated from the section headings in the source document

You've completed the initial work on the dynamic table of contents. By navigating through the node tree, you created list items matching every section heading in the constitution document. In the next session, you'll learn how to turn this table of contents list into a collection of nested lists based on the level of the different section headings.

Session 7.1 Quick Check | Review

1. What property can change the inner HTML content of an element?
2. What property extracts the text from an element, ignoring any markup tags? Provide an answer for both the IE and W3C DOMs.
3. What are nodes? What objects of an HTML file do they represent?
4. What property references the parent of a node?
5. What object references the third child node of an object?
6. For an element node representing a blockquote element, what values are returned by the nodeType, nodeName, and nodeValue properties?

7. What command creates a node containing the text string "U.S. Constitution"? Give the text string the variable name docText. What command creates an h2 element? Give the h2 element the variable name mainTitle.

8. What command places the text string you created in the previous question into the h2 element?

Session 7.2

Creating a Nested List

Norene reviewed the initial table of contents you created in the previous session. She is pleased that the table of contents extracts the text from all of the heading elements in the constitution document. However, it doesn't distinguish between main headings and subheadings. Norene wants you to revise the table of contents, making it a nested list in which lower-level headings are nested within upper-level headings. Figure 7-21 shows how the current HTML fragment generated by the createList() function needs to be modified to create a nested list of headings. All entries that match the h1 heading are placed at the top level of the table of contents, the entries for h2 headings are placed at the next lower level, and entries for h3 headings are placed at the lowest level.

Figure 7-21 **Current list being turned into a nested list**

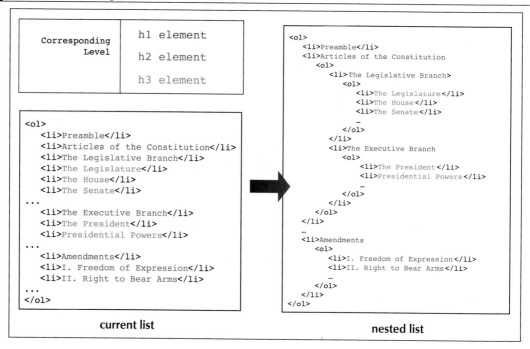

You need to modify the createList() function so that every time a list item is added to the TOC, the function determines whether to keep that item at the same level as the previous list item, to indent it as a new subheading, or to raise it up as coming from a previous main heading. To determine the level of each list item, you can use the information returned by the levelNum() function you created in the previous session. The levelNum() function returns a value of 0 for all h1 headings it encounters, 1 for all h2 headings, and

2 for all h3 headings. With that information, you can apply the following three rules to determine how a new list item should be placed in the table of contents:

1. If the level of the list item is unchanged from the level of the previous item, simply append it to the current list.
2. If the level number is higher than a previous item's level number (such as when an h3 heading follows an h2 heading), create a new nested list and append the list item to that new list.
3. If the level number is less than the previous item's level number (for example, when an h1 heading follows an h3 heading), append the list item to a list at a level higher up in the table of contents.

The key to these conditions is to record the previous item's level number. For that purpose, you'll create a new variable named prevLevel. You'll set the initial value of this variable to 0. The if condition to compare the value of prevLevel to the level of the current node has the general form:

```
if (nodeLevel == prevLevel)
    append the entry to the current list
else if (nodeLevel > prevLevel)
    append the entry to a new nested list
else if (nodeLevel < prevLevel)
    append the entry to a higher-level list
```

Recall that the nodeLevel variable contains the level of the current list item being added to the table of contents. You'll add these if conditions to the code of the createList() function.

To add the if conditions:

1. If you took a break after the previous session, make sure the toc.js file is open in a text editor and usconst.htm is loaded in your Web browser.

2. Return to the **toc.js** file in your text editor.

3. Scroll down to the createList() function, and then add the following command at the start of the function to declare and set the initial value of the prevLevel variable:

   ```
   var prevLevel = 0; // level of the previous TOC entry
   ```

4. Delete the following line:

   ```
   list.appendChild(listItem);
   ```

5. Add the following if statements in place of the line you just deleted:

   ```
   if (nodeLevel == prevLevel) {
       // append the entry to the current list
   }

   else if (nodeLevel > prevLevel) {
       // append the entry to a new nested list
   }

   else if (nodeLevel < prevLevel) {
       // append the entry to a higher-level list
   }
   ```

   Figure 7-22 shows new code in the createList() function.

Figure 7-22 **if structure for the nested list**

```
function createList(object, list) {

    var prevLevel = 0; // level of the previous TOC entry

    for (var n = object.firstChild; n!=null; n = n.nextSibling) {
        // loop through all of the nodes within object

        var nodeLevel = levelNum(n);
        if (nodeLevel != -1) {
            // node represents a section heading
            // create a list item to match
            var listItem = document.createElement("li");
            listItem.innerHTML = n.innerHTML;

            if (nodeLevel == prevLevel) {
                // append the entry to the current list
            }

            else if (nodeLevel > prevLevel) {
                // append the entry to a new nested list
            }

            else if (nodeLevel < prevLevel) {
                // append the entry to a higher-level list
            }
        }
    }
}
```

replaces the statement
to append the list item

Next, you will enter the code for each if condition. If nodeLevel equals prevLevel, then the current node is at the same level as the previous entry and you simply need to append the new entry to the current list. Figure 7-23 shows how creating and appending this node to the node tree compares to inserting the code in an HTML fragment.

Figure 7-23 **List item being added to a list**

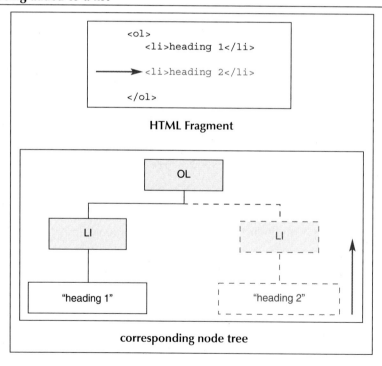

```
<ol>
    <li>heading 1</li>
    <li>heading 2</li>
</ol>
```

HTML Fragment

corresponding node tree

You'll add the command to insert the list item to the first condition in the createList() function.

To add the commands for the first condition:

▶ **1.** Add the following command to the first if condition, as shown in Figure 7-24.

```
list.appendChild(listItem);
```

List item appended under the first condition ◀ **Figure 7-24**

```
if (nodeLevel == prevLevel) {
    // append the entry to the current list
    list.appendChild(listItem);
}
```

▶ **2.** Save your changes to the file, and then reload **usconst.htm** in your Web browser. The table of contents shows only the three h1 headings because they are the headings with a level value of 0 (h1 headings). No other headings are shown because the value of the prevLevel variable was set to 0 and was not changed by the code. See Figure 7-25.

Table of contents displays only the top level headings ◀ **Figure 7-25**

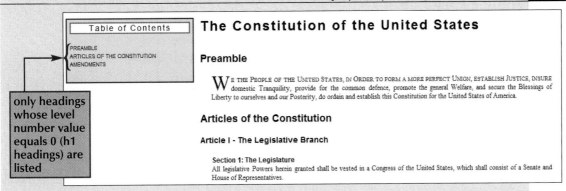

only headings whose level number value equals 0 (h1 headings) are listed

The next if condition involves the situation where the section heading is of a lower level than the one found for the previous entry (such as when an h2 heading follows an h1 heading). In that case, you want to insert the entry within a new list, nested within the previous entry. Figure 7-26 shows the HTML fragment and node tree of the new content in the table of contents.

Figure 7-26 ▶ **Nested list appended to the node tree**

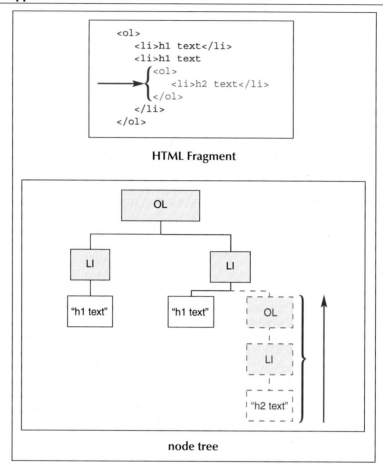

```
<ol>
    <li>h1 text</li>
    <li>h1 text
      { <ol>
          <li>h2 text</li>
      { </ol>
    </li>
</ol>
```

HTML Fragment

node tree

To do this in JavaScript, you create a new ordered list and then append the list item to it, using the following commands:

```
var nestedList = document.createElement("ol");
nestedList.appendChild(listItem);
```

The new list is then appended as a child of the previous—and last—entry in the current list, which can be done using the following command:

```
list.lastChild.appendChild(nestedList);
```

Finally, you need to make the nested list the new current list of the table of contents and set the value of the prevLevel variable to the level of the new entry. The commands to do this are:

```
list = nestedList;
prevLevel = nodeLevel;
```

You'll add these commands to the second if condition in the createList() function.

To add the commands for the second if condition:

▶ **1.** Return to the **toc.js** file in your text editor.

▶ **2.** Within the second if condition, insert the following code, as shown in Figure 7-27:

```
var nestedList = document.createElement("ol");
nestedList.appendChild(listItem);

list.lastChild.appendChild(nestedList);

list = nestedList;
prevLevel = nodeLevel;
```

Nested list appended under the second condition ◀ **Figure 7-27**

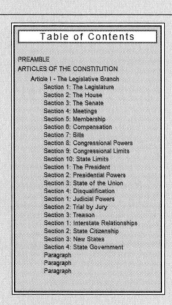

```
else if (nodeLevel > prevLevel) {
   // append the entry to a new nested list
   var nestedList = document.createElement("ol");          creates a new
   nestedList.appendChild(listItem);                       nested list

   list.lastChild.appendChild(nestedList);

   list = nestedList;                                      updates the list
   prevLevel = nodeLevel;                                  and prevLevel
}                                                          values
```

appends the nested list to the current list

▶ **3.** Save your changes to the file, and then reload **usconst.htm** in your Web browser. Figure 7-28 shows the current list of items in the table of contents with lower-level items nested within upper-level items.

Nested table of contents ◀ **Figure 7-28**

```
┌─────────────────────────────────────┐
│         Table of Contents            │
├─────────────────────────────────────┤
│ PREAMBLE                             │
│ ARTICLES OF THE CONSTITUTION         │
│    Article I - The Legislative Branch│
│        Section 1: The Legislature    │
│        Section 2: The House          │
│        Section 3: The Senate         │
│        Section 4: Meetings           │
│        Section 5: Membership         │
│        Section 6: Compensation       │
│        Section 7: Bills              │
│        Section 8: Congressional Powers│
│        Section 9: Congressional Limits│
│        Section 10: State Limits      │
│        Section 1: The President      │
│        Section 2: Presidential Powers│
│        Section 3: State of the Union │
│        Section 4: Disqualification   │
│        Section 1: Judicial Powers    │
│        Section 2: Trial by Jury      │
│        Section 3: Treason            │
│        Section 1: Interstate Relationships│
│        Section 2: State Citizenship  │
│        Section 3: New States         │
│        Section 4: State Government    │
│        Paragraph                     │
│        Paragraph                     │
│        Paragraph                     │
└─────────────────────────────────────┘
```

Don't worry that the other headings are missing from the table of contents. At this point, the createList() function only works going across the current level or down to the next level of headings. There are no commands to go up the nested list of items to higher-level headings. You'll add commands to handle that condition now.

When moving up one or more levels in the table of contents, you simply append the new list item to the correct list. Figure 7-29 shows an HTML fragment and the corresponding node tree for adding a new list item to a higher-level list.

Figure 7-29 ▶ **List item appended to a higher level list**

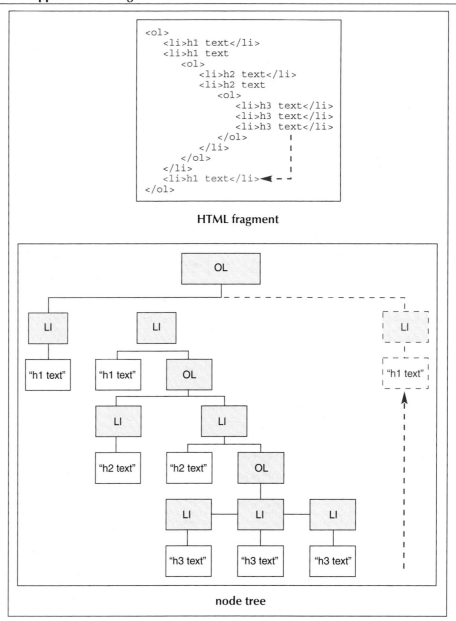

```
<ol>
    <li>h1 text</li>
    <li>h1 text
      <ol>
          <li>h2 text</li>
          <li>h2 text
            <ol>
                <li>h3 text</li>
                <li>h3 text</li>
                <li>h3 text</li>
            </ol>              |
          </li>                |
      </ol>                    |
    </li>                      |
    <li>h1 text</li>◀ - - -
</ol>
```

HTML fragment

node tree

One challenge is figuring out how many levels to go up in the node tree. Examine Figure 7-29 and notice that for each level you go up in the section headings, you go up *two* levels in the node tree. For example, to go from h3 headings back up to h1 headings, you go up four levels in the node tree. Thus, to go up the node tree, you first calculate the difference between the current level headings and the level of the new entry, which is simply the difference between the prevLevel variable and the nodeLevel variable. You can store that difference in the following levelUp variable:

```
var levelUp = prevLevel - nodeLevel;
```

To move up the node tree, you apply the parentNode property twice, for each difference in level between the two headings. That approach can be placed in the following for loop:

```
for (var i = 1; i <= levelUp; i++) {list = list.parentNode.parentNode;}
```

On each iteration, the for loop points the list object to the TOC list two levels up on the node tree. The loop stops when it has gone up the correct number of levels as indicated by the levelUp variable. Once you're at the correct level, the remaining task is to append the list item and update the value of the prevLevel variable, using the following code:

```
list.appendChild(listItem);
prevLevel = nodeLevel;
```

You'll add these commands to the third if condition in the changeList() function.

To add the commands for the third condition:

▶ **1.** Return to the **toc.js** file in your text editor.

▶ **2.** Within the third if condition, insert the following code, as shown in Figure 7-30:

```
var levelUp = prevLevel - nodeLevel;
for (var i = 1; i <= levelUp; i++) {list = list.parentNode.parentNode;}

list.appendChild(listItem);
prevLevel = nodeLevel;
```

List item appended under the third condition ◀ **Figure 7-30**

```
else if (nodeLevel < prevLevel) {
    // append the entry to a higher-level list
    var levelUp = prevLevel - nodeLevel;
    for (var i = 1; i <= levelUp; i++) {list = list.parentNode.parentNode;}

    list.appendChild(listItem);
    prevLevel = nodeLevel;
}
```
moves up two levels in the node tree

▶ **3.** Save your changes to the file, and then reload **usconst.htm** in your Web browser. The table of contents shows all three levels of headings with the h1 headings represented at the highest level of the list, followed by the h2 headings, and then followed by the h3 headings. See Figure 7-31.

Table of contents as a nested list ◀ **Figure 7-31**

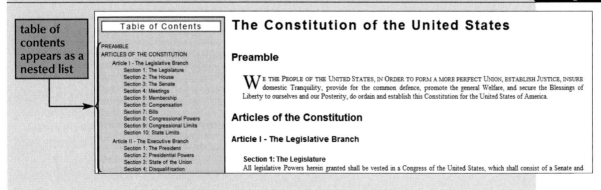

table of contents appears as a nested list

Working with Attributes

Norene is pleased with the table of contents your script generated for her document. Because this is a hypertext document, she wonders whether the entries in the table of contents could contain links to the section headings they represent.

Again, it is useful to write out the HTML code for the proposed change, even if you cannot view those markup tags in your document. Making this change involves two steps, which are illustrated in Figure 7-32:

1. Add an id attribute to each section heading (if it doesn't already have one) to mark its location on the Web page.
2. Change the content of each list item to a link pointing to the corresponding section heading.

Figure 7-32 ▶ **HTML fragment linking table of contents entries to section headings**

```
<ol>
    <li><a href = "#head1">Preamble</a></li>
    <li><a href = "#head2">Articles of the Constitution</a></li>
    <ol>
        <li><a href="#head3">Legislative Branch</a></li>
        <ol>
            <li><a href = "#head4">Section 1: The Legislature</a></li>
            <li><a href = "#head5">Section 2: The House</a></li>
            <li><a href = "#head6">Section 3: The Senate</a></li>
...
```

table of contents with links

```
<h1 id = "head1">Preamble</h1>
...
<h1 id = "head2">Articles of the Constitution</h1>
...
<h2 id = "head3">Legislative Branch</h2>
...
<h3 id = "head4">Section 1: The Legislature</h3>
...
<h3 id = "head5">Section 2: The House</h3>
...
<h3 id = "head6">Section 3: The Senate</h3>
....
```

section headings with id values

Before you can create and add the id and href attributes, you must understand how to work with attributes in the W3C DOM.

Creating Attribute Nodes

Attributes and their values are considered nodes and can be attached to element nodes. Unlike element and text nodes, attribute nodes are not part of the node tree because they are not counted as children of element nodes like text nodes are. Figure 7-33 shows how to represent the relationship between attribute nodes and the element nodes they are associated with.

Attribute nodes ◄ **Figure 7-33**

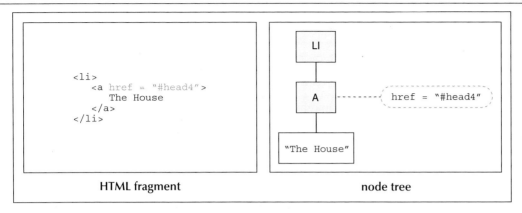

As you can see, attribute nodes have no familial relation with any node in the node tree. The W3C DOM supports several methods to create, attach, and set the values of attributes. Some of these are listed in Figure 7-34.

Methods of attribute nodes ◄ **Figure 7-34**

Method	Description
`document.createAttribute(att)`	Creates an attribute node with the name *att*
`node.getAttribute(att)`	Returns the value of an attribute *att* from a *node* to which it has been attached
`node.hasAttribute(att)`	Returns a Boolean value indicating whether *node* has the attribute *att*
`node.removeAttribute(att)`	Removes the attribute *att* from *node*
`node.removeAttributeNode(att)`	Removes an attribute node *att* from *node*
`node.setAttribute(att, value)`	Creates or changes the *value* of the attribute *att* of *node*

To create or set an attribute for an element, you use the setAttribute() method. The following code creates a list item element and then uses the setAttribute() method to set the ID value of the list item to the text string TOChead1:

```
listItem = document.createElement("li");
listItem.setAttribute("id","TOChead1");
```

The net effect of these two commands is to create the following HTML fragment:

```
<li id = "TOChead1"></li>
```

In some cases, you need to determine whether an element has a particular attribute, such as the id attribute. In these situations, you use the hasAttribute() method, which returns the Boolean value true if the element contains the attribute. For example, the expression

```
listItem.hasAttribute("id")
```

would return the value true if the list item had an id attribute, and would return false if otherwise.

For Web page elements, the simplest approach to set an attribute value is to apply the HTML attribute as a property of the object using the syntax

```
object.attr = value;
```

Tip

Attribute nodes are usually reserved for working with elements that are not part of the body of the Web page, or for use with non-HTML content such as XML data sources.

where *object* is an object reference to the HTML page element, *attr* is the name of an HTML attribute associated with the element, and *value* is the value you want to assign to the attribute.

Setting the Section Heading IDs

Now that you've learned how to work with attributes, you'll turn to the next task, which is to insert IDs into all of the section headings in the constitution document. You'll name each of the section headings

```
headi
```

where *i* is a variable that equals 1 for the first section heading, 2 for the second heading, and so on. Refer back to Figure 7-32 for an example of how the IDs of the first six section headings will be numbered. You need to be careful not to overwrite any preexisting IDs because Norene might have already placed IDs in some of the <h1> through <h3> tags. You'll first test whether an ID attribute already exists for the element and insert an ID only if it doesn't already have one. As you create section IDs, you'll store each ID in a variable named sectionId; you'll use this variable later in the code to create the hypertext references for the links. The code to insert the section heading IDs for a particular node, n, is:

```
headNum++;
if (n.id == "") {n.id = "head" + headNum;}
```

Here, headNum is a counter variable that is increased each time the code encounters a section element in the constitution document. If the element has no ID, the counter variable creates one for it.

You'll add these commands to the createList() function.

To insert the section IDs:

1. Return to the **toc.js** file in your text editor.

2. Directly below the line that declares the prevLevel variable, insert the following line to declare the headNum variable, setting its initial value to 0:

   ```
   var headNum = 0; // running count of section headings
   ```

3. At the top of the for loop within the createList() function, insert the following commands, as shown in Figure 7-35:

   ```
   // insert id for the section heading if necessary
   headNum++;
   if (n.id == "") {n.id = "head" + headNum;}
   ```

Figure 7-35 ▶ **Code to insert section IDs**

Tip

To avoid conflict with other possible ID values in the source document, you can use a JavaScript function to generate a completely random ID value.

adds IDs to section headings that don't already have one →

```
function createList(object, list) {

    var prevLevel = 0; // level of the previous TOC entry
    var headNum = 0;   // running count of section headings

    for (var n = object.firstChild; n!=null; n = n.nextSibling) {
        // loop through all of the nodes within object

        var nodeLevel = levelNum(n);
        if (nodeLevel != -1) {
            // node represents a section heading

            // insert id for the section heading if necessary
            headNum++;
            if (n.id == "") {n.id = "head" + headNum;}

            // create a list item to match
            var listItem = document.createElement("li");
            listItem.innerHTML = n.innerHTML;
```

Inserting Links

Next, you need to revise the structure of the TOC node tree to link each list item with its corresponding section in the constitution document. The href value for each link will be

```
#id
```

where *id* is the ID assigned to the section heading. You'll also set the ID of each list element to

```
TOCid
```

where *id* is again the ID of the corresponding heading element in the constitution document. This will allow you to easily match list items in the table of contents with their corresponding section headings. You'll need this information for some of the tasks you'll do in the next session. Figure 7-36 shows the node structure of the list items with and without the links.

List item being changed into a hypertext link | **Figure 7-36**

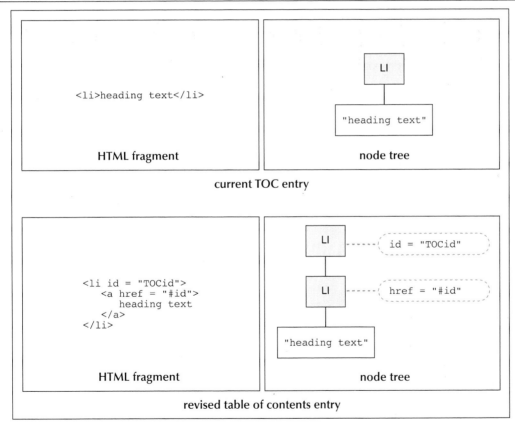

current TOC entry

revised table of contents entry

To create the new node structure, you'll replace the old commands that inserted the text of the link item with new code that inserts the item text as a hyperlink. First, you'll define an ID value for the list item, using the following command:

```
listItem.id = "TOC" + n.id;
```

Then, you'll create a hypertext link containing the text of the section head and an href attribute that points to the section head, using the following code:

```
var linkItem = document.createElement("a");
linkItem.innerHTML = n.innerHTML;
linkItem.href = "#" + n.id;
```

Finally, you'll append the hypertext link to the list item, using the following command:

```
listItem.appendChild(linkItem);
```

You'll insert these commands into the createList() function and then test the links in the table of contents.

To turn the list items into hypertext links:

▶ **1.** Within the createList() function, delete the following line:

```
listItem.innerHTML = n.innerHTML;
```

▶ **2.** Replace the deleted line with the following code, as shown in Figure 7-37:

```
listItem.id = "TOC" + n.id;

// Create a hypertext link to the section heading
var linkItem = document.createElement("a");
linkItem.innerHTML = n.innerHTML;
linkItem.href = "#" + n.id;

// Append the hypertext link to the list entry
listItem.appendChild(linkItem);
```

Figure 7-37	Code to insert hypertext links for each list item

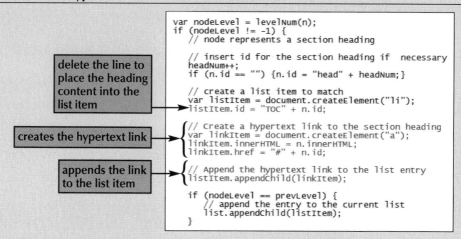

▶ **3.** Save your changes to the file.

▶ **4.** Reload **usconst.htm** in your Web browser. Each entry in the table of contents is a hypertext link. See Figure 7-38.

Table of contents as a list of links | **Figure 7-38**

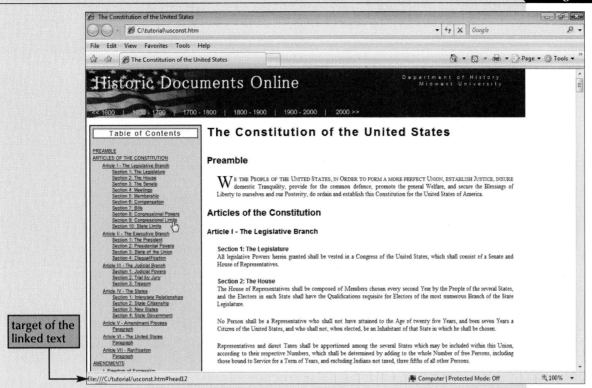

target of the
linked text

▶ **5.** Click the different links in the table of contents and verify that the browser jumps
to the corresponding section of the document.

InSight | **Inserting Element Text Under the IE DOM**

If you are supporting only the Internet Explorer browser, you can use methods in the IE DOM to insert elements at specific locations within the document tree. The syntax of these methods is

```
object.insertAdjacentHTML(position, content);
object.insertAdjacentText(position, content);
```

where *position* is a text string specifying the position in which the new HTML code or text is to be inserted relative to *object*, and *content* is the content to be inserted. The *position* parameter has four possible values:

- BeforeBegin inserts the content before the object's opening tag.
- AfterBegin inserts the content directly after the object's opening tag.
- BeforeEnd inserts the content directly before the object's closing tag.
- AfterEnd inserts the content after the object's closing tag.

For example, to insert the word Online at the end of the HTML fragment

```
<h1 id = "title">Historic Documents</h1>
```

you could run the command

```
title.insertAdjacentHTML("BeforeEnd"," Online");
```

which would change the code of the title element to

```
<h1 id = "title">Historic Documents Online</h1>
```

Keep in mind that these methods are supported only under the IE DOM. If you need to create a cross-browser Web site, use the node objects and methods to insert new text into the document.

You've completed the work for making the table of contents into a nested list of hypertext links. In the next session, you'll add more features to the table of contents, including the ability to contract and expand the table of contents and the constitution document.

Review | **Session 7.2 Quick Check**

1. What code creates two ul list elements, one nested inside of the other? Use the variable name topList for the upper list element and the variable name bottomList for the bottom list element.
2. In the previous question, what is the node reference to the topList object from a list item found in the bottom list?
3. Why are attribute nodes not part of the document node tree?
4. What node method determines whether an element contains the type attribute?
5. What command creates an input element with the variable name CBox and a type attribute value of checkbox? Use an attribute node method in your answer.
6. What commands would you add to the previous question to create the type attribute using a property rather than an attribute node method?
7. What expression would you use in the previous question to determine whether the CBox input element has a type attribute?

Session 7.3

Expanding and Collapsing a Document

Norene reviews the table of contents application. She has seen other lists in which the nested entries can be alternately hidden or displayed by clicking a plus/minus box. In a **plus/minus box**, a + symbol in the box indicates that content is hidden and a – symbol indicates that all the items are displayed. Clicking the + box reveals the hidden content and clicking the – box hides them, as shown in Figure 7-39.

Plus/minus box expands and collapses a list ◀ Figure 7-39

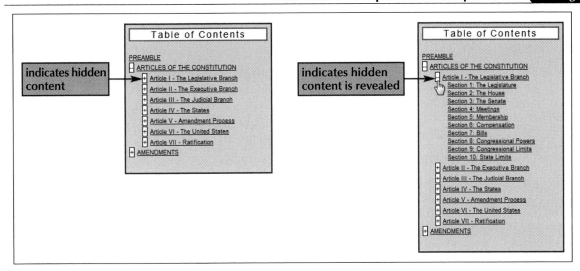

Norene wants you to add this feature to the table of contents so that users can expand or collapse the list. She also wants the contents of the document to mimic the appearance of the table of contents, so that as items are hidden in the table of contents, they are also hidden within the document. Creating this kind of dynamic content involves several of the tools and techniques you've learned in previous tutorials, including working with event objects and object styles.

Creating a Plus/Minus Box

First, you'll add the plus/minus boxes to the table of contents. Because you want to treat each plus/minus box as a distinct object, you'll place the text of the plus/minus box within a span element. Initially, the plus/minus box will display the – symbol because the TOC will open with all list items displayed to users. The following commands create the plus/minus box:

```
plusMinusBox = document.createElement("span");
plusMinusBox.innerHTML = "--";
```

Next, you must determine where to place the plus/minus boxes in Norene's table of contents. Because the boxes are designed to alternately hide and display nested lists, they should be placed before the nested list in the node tree. Figure 7-40 shows where you would place the plus/minus box if you were writing the HTML tags directly, and how it would be rendered on the Web page. Notice that the styles for the span element, including the background color and border, have already been placed in the web.css file. This means you don't have to worry about formatting the plus/minus boxes for the Web page, but you can instead focus on inserting the content.

Figure 7-40 ▶ **Plus/minus box placed before the nested list**

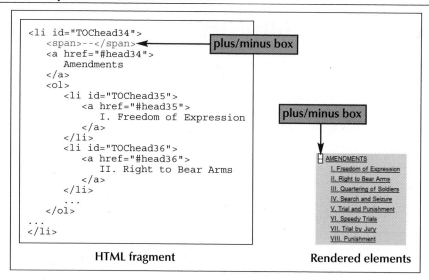

HTML fragment   Rendered elements

Figure 7-41 shows how this HTML fragment would be represented in the node tree (attribute nodes are not shown in order to simplify the diagram). As indicated in the HTML fragment and the node tree, the plus/minus box must be inserted as the first child of the last list item entry.

Figure 7-41 ▶ **Plus/minus box added to the node tree**

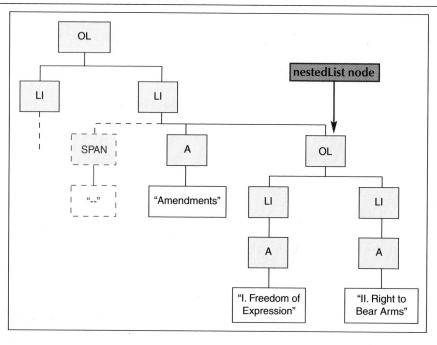

You can insert the plus/minus box using the insertBefore() method, which inserts new child nodes anywhere within a parent node. Recall that the general syntax of the insert-Before() method is

```
node.insertBefore(new, child)
```

where *node* is the parent node, *new* is a new node to be added as child of the parent, and *child* is the child node that the new node should be inserted in front of. To insert a plus/minus box, you'll use the following object reference for *node* `nestedList.parentNode`

because that reference points to the parent of the nestedList object. The *child* node in front of which you want to place the plus/minus box is the <a> tag and can be referenced by:

`nestedList.previousSibling`

Thus, to insert the plus/minus box, you would run the following command:

`nestedList.parentNode.insertBefore(plusMinusBox, nestedList.previousSibling)`

Compare this expression to the node tree diagram shown earlier in Figure 7-41 to see how the use of familiar references makes it easier to move around the contents of the node tree. You will add the commands to create the plus/minus box to the createList() function.

To create and place the plus/minus box:

▶ 1. If you took a break after the previous session, make sure the toc.js file is open in a text editor and usconst.htm is loaded in your Web browser.

▶ 2. Return to the **toc.js** file in your text editor.

▶ 3. Go to the createList() function and insert the following code within the second if condition, as shown in Figure 7-42:

```
// Add plus/minus box before the text of the nested list
var plusMinusBox = document.createElement("span");
plusMinusBox.innerHTML = "--";
nestedList.parentNode.insertBefore(plusMinusBox,
nestedList.previousSibling);
```

Code to create and place the plus/minus boxes ◀ **Figure 7-42**

```
else if (nodeLevel > prevLevel) {
    // append the entry to a new nested list
    var nestedList = document.createElement("ol");
    nestedList.appendChild(listItem);

    list.lastChild.appendChild(nestedList);

    // Add plus/minus box before the text of the nested list
    var plusMinusBox = document.createElement("span");
    plusMinusBox.innerHTML = "--";
    nestedList.parentNode.insertBefore(plusMinusBox, nestedList.previousSibling);

    list = nestedList;
    prevLevel = nodeLevel;
}
```

places a plus/minus box before each nested list

▶ 4. Save your changes to the file, and then reload **usconst.htm** in your Web browser. Plus/minus boxes appear before the nested list titles in the table of contents. See Figure 7-43.

Tip

You cannot view the HTML fragments generated by code, but you can view the node tree generated by your code under the Firefox browser by adding the DOM Inspector add-on from the Firefox Web site.

Figure 7-43 ▷ **Table of contents with plus/minus boxes**

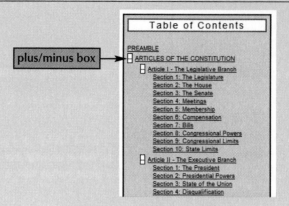

Adding an Event Handler to the Plus/Minus Boxes

You want users to be able to toggle between a plus sign and a minus sign in the plus/minus box by clicking the box. You'll use the addEvent() function already placed in the toc.js file to apply a cross-browser event handler to the plus/minus boxes. The code is:

```
addEvent(plusMinusBox, "click", expandCollapse, false);
```

The browser will run the expandCollapse() function whenever the user clicks a plus/minus box. The code of the expandCollapse() function is:

```
function expandCollapse(e) {
   var plusMinusBox = e.target || event.srcElement;

   if (plusMinusBox.innerHTML == "--") plusMinusBox.innerHTML = "+"
   else plusMinusBox.innerHTML = "--";
}
```

Each time the function is run, the text of the plus/minus box switches between a minus symbol and a plus symbol. The function uses an event object along with the target or srcElement properties to determine the box that the user clicked.

You'll add these commands to the toc.js file, and then test your code in the browser.

To insert the event handler for the plus/minus boxes:

▶ **1.** Return to the **toc.js** file in your text editor.

▶ **2.** Go to the createList() function and below the command to set the innerHTML property of the plus/minus box, insert the following function:

```
addEvent(plusMinusBox, "click", expandCollapse, false);
```

3. Below the createList() function, add the following function, as shown in Figure 7-44:

```
function expandCollapse(e) {
    var plusMinusBox = e.target || event.srcElement;

    // Toggle the plus and minus symbol
    if (plusMinusBox.innerHTML == "--") plusMinusBox.innerHTML = "+"
    else plusMinusBox.innerHTML = "--";
}
```

The expandCollapse() function ◀ Figure 7-44

```
        else if (nodeLevel > prevLevel) {
            // append the entry to a new nested list
            var nestedList = document.createElement("ol");
            nestedList.appendChild(listItem);

            list.lastChild.appendChild(nestedList);

            // Add plus/minus box before the text of the nested list
            var plusMinusBox = document.createElement("span");
            plusMinusBox.innerHTML = "--";
            addEvent(plusMinusBox, "click", expandCollapse, false);
            nestedList.parentNode.insertBefore(plusMinusBox, nestedList.previousSibling);

            list = nestedList;
            prevLevel = nodeLevel;
        }

        else if (nodeLevel < prevLevel) {
            // append the entry to a higher-level list
            var levelup = prevLevel - nodeLevel;
            for (var i = 1; i <= levelup; i++) {list = list.parentNode.parentNode;}

            list.appendChild(listItem);
            prevLevel = nodeLevel;
        }
    }
  }
}

function expandCollapse(e) {
    var plusMinusBox = e.target || event.srcElement;

    // Toggle the plus and minus symbol
    if (plusMinusBox.innerHTML == "--") plusMinusBox.innerHTML = "+"
    else plusMinusBox.innerHTML = "--";
}
```

runs the expandCollapse() function when the user clicks a plus/minus box

4. Save your changes to the file.

5. Reload **usconst.htm** in your Web browser and verify that clicking each plus/minus box toggles its symbol between a plus sign and a minus sign.

Hiding and Displaying the Nested Lists

The next action of the expandCollapse() function is to alternately hide or display the nested list associated with each plus/minus box. As shown in Figure 7-45, each nested list is placed two siblings away from the plus/minus box. You can reference the nested list using the following expression:

```
var nestedList = plusMinusBox.nextSibling.nextSibling
```

Figure 7-45 ▷ Position of the nested list relative to the plus/minus box

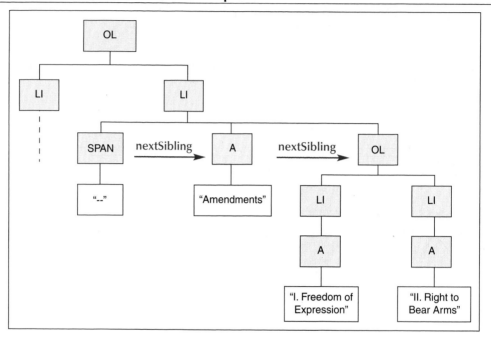

To hide the nestedList object, apply the style

```
nestedList.style.display = "none";
```

and to redisplay the object use

```
nestedList.style.display = "";
```

By not specifying a value for the display style from the object, the browser will apply whatever display style is appropriate for the object and its descendants. As with the plus and minus symbols, clicking a plus/minus box toggles the display style of the nested list between these two conditions.

You'll add commands to toggle the display style to the expandCollapse() function.

To expand and collapse the nested lists in the table of contents:

▶ 1. Return to the **toc.js** file in your text editor.

▶ 2. Scroll down to the expandCollapse() function and add the following statement after the declaration for the plusMinusBox variable:

```
var nestedList = plusMinusBox.nextSibling.nextSibling;
```

▶ 3. Add the following if statement at the end of the expandCollapse() function, as shown in Figure 7-46:

```
// Toggle the display style of the nested list
if (nestedList.style.display == "none") nestedList.style.display = ""
else nestedList.style.display = "none";
```

Code to expand and collapse the nested lists   **Figure 7-46**

```
function expandCollapse(e) {
   var plusMinusBox = e.target || event.srcElement;
   var nestedList = plusMinusBox.nextSibling.nextSibling;

   // Toggle the plus and minus symbol
   if (plusMinusBox.innerHTML == "--") plusMinusBox.innerHTML = "+"
   else plusMinusBox.innerHTML = "--";

   // Toggle the display style of the nested list
   if (nestedList.style.display == "none") nestedList.style.display = ""
   else nestedList.style.display = "none";

}
```

▶ **4.** Save your changes to the file.

▶ **5.** Reload **usconst.htm** in your Web browser and verify that as you click the plus/
minus boxes in the table of contents, the nested lists within the table of contents
are alternately hidden and redisplayed. Figure 7-47 shows the table of contents
with a mixture of hidden and displayed nested lists.

Table of contents with hidden and displayed lists   **Figure 7-47**

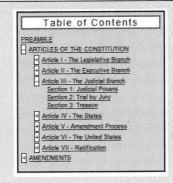

Expanding and Collapsing the Source Document

The final piece of the dynamic table of contents is to expand and collapse the document
itself so that it mimics the actions of the table of contents. One problem is that the structure of the table of contents is markedly different from the structure of the source
document. In the table of contents, different sections are nested within one another. By
contrast, in the source document all sections are siblings, with only the section headings
indicating when a section begins and ends, and the element names indicating what level
each section represents. See Figure 7-48.

Figure 7-48 ▷ **Structure of the table of contents list and the document elements**

```
<ol>
    <li>Main Head
        <ol>
            <li>Subhead
                <ol>
                    <li>Minor Subhead</li>
                    <li>Minor Subhead</li>
                </ol>
            </li>
            <li>Subhead</li>
        </ol>
    </li>
    <li>Main Head
        <ol>
            <li>Subhead
                <ol>
                    <li>Minor Subhead</li>
                </ol>
            </li>
        </ol>
    </li>
</ol>
```

```
<h1>Main Head</h1>
<p>Text</p>
<h2>Subhead</h2>
<p>Text</p>
<h3>Minor Subhead</h3>
<p>Text</p>
<h3>Minor Subhead</h3>
<p>Text</p>
<p>Text</p>
<h2>Subhead</h2>
<p>Text</p>
<p>Text</p>
<h1>Main Head</h1>
<p>Text</p>
<h2>Subhead</h2>
<p>Text</p>
<h3>Minor Subhead</h3>
<p>Text</p>
```

nested list   document elements

Your approach will be to loop through the source document, one node at a time. Each time the loop encounters a section heading, it checks whether the corresponding entry in the table of contents is displayed or hidden. If the entry is hidden, that section heading and all subsequent elements are hidden until the loop encounters another section heading. On the other hand, if the TOC entry is displayed, that section heading and all subsequent elements are displayed until the loop gets to another heading. The following code provides the general structure of this for loop:

```
var displayStatus = "";
for (var n = sourceDoc.firstChild; n != null; n = n.nextSibling) {
    var nodeLevel = levelNum(n);

    if (nodeLevel != -1) {
        // determine the display status of the TOC entry
    }
    if (n.nodeType == 1) { // node represents a page element
        // apply the current display status to the node
    }
}
```

This code starts by storing the display status in the displayStatus variable. The initial value is an empty text string indicating that the default display status of the objects will be applied by the browser. The for loop then goes through the nodes in the source document starting with the first child node and moving to the next sibling until no siblings are left. For each node, it tests whether the node is a heading element using the levelNum() function. If the value returned by the levelNum() function is not equal to –1 (indicating that the node represents one of the section headings), the code determines the display status of the TOC entry for that section heading. Also, each time through the loop, the display status is applied to the current node—but only if that node represents a Web page element.

You'll add this for loop and these if conditions to a function named expandCollapseDoc().

Tip

Before changing the display style of a node, always confirm that the node represents a Web page element by testing that the value of the nodeType property equals 1.

To insert the expandCollapseDoc() function:

▶ **1.** Return to the **toc.js** file in your text editor.

▶ **2.** At the bottom of the file, insert the following code, as shown in Figure 7-49:

```
function expandCollapseDoc() {
    var displayStatus = "";
    for (var n = sourceDoc.firstChild; n != null; n = n.nextSibling) {
        var nodeLevel = levelNum(n);

        if (nodeLevel != -1) {
            // determine the display status of the TOC entry
        }

        if (n.nodeType == 1) { // node represents a page element
            // apply the current display status to the node
        }

    }
}
```

The expandCollapseDoc() function ◀ Figure 7-49

```
function expandCollapse(e) {
    var plusMinusBox = e.target || event.srcElement;
    var nestedList = plusMinusBox.nextSibling.nextSibling;

    // Toggle the plus and minus symbol
    if (plusMinusBox.innerHTML == "--") plusMinusBox.innerHTML = "+"
    else plusMinusBox.innerHTML = "--";

    // Toggle the display style of the nested list
    if (nestedList.style.display == "none") nestedList.style.display = ""
    else nestedList.style.display = "none";

}

function expandCollapseDoc() {
    var displayStatus = "";
    for (var n = sourceDoc.firstChild; n != null; n = n.nextSibling) {
        var nodeLevel = levelNum(n);

        if (nodeLevel != -1) {
            // determine the display status of the TOC entry
        }

        if (n.nodeType == 1) { // node represents a page element
            // apply the current display status to the node
        }
    }
}
```

▶ **3.** Save your changes to the file.

You need to determine whether the corresponding entry in the table of contents is displayed. The problem is that the display status of an object cannot be determined by looking at its display style alone. This is because under CSS, display styles cascade down from objects higher up in the object hierarchy. So, for example, if an ol element is hidden on the Web page, all of the list items within that element are also hidden. The only way to determine whether an object is hidden is to move up the object hierarchy, testing each parent of the object until you arrive at the body element itself. If *any one of those parent objects* is hidden, then the object itself will be hidden. The following function provides code for moving up the object hierarchy in this way:

```
function isHidden(object) {
    for (var n = object; n.nodeName != "BODY"; n = n.parentNode) {
        if (n.style.display == "none") return true;
    }
    return false;
}
```

The isHidden() function starts with the current object and using the parentNode property moves up the object tree until it reaches the body element. At each step along the way, the function tests the display style of the current node in the loop. If the display style is set to none, the function immediately returns a value of true, indicating that the object is hidden. On the other hand, if the browser goes all the way up the object hierarchy without encountering one hidden parent, the object itself is not hidden and the function returns the value false.

You'll add the isHidden() function to the toc.js file.

To insert the isHidden() function:

▶ 1. Directly below the expandCollapseDoc() function, insert the following code, as shown in Figure 7-50:

```
function isHidden(object) {

    for (var n = object; n.nodeName != "BODY"; n = n.parentNode) {
        if (n.style.display == "none") return true;
    }

    return false;
}
```

| Figure 7-50 | The isHidden() function |

```
function expandcollapseDoc() {
    var displayStatus = "";
    for (var n = sourceDoc.firstchild; n != null; n = n.nextSibling) {
        var nodeLevel = levelNum(n);

        if (nodeLevel != -1) {
            // determine the display status of the TOC entry
        }

        if (n.nodeType == 1) { // node represents a page element
            // apply the current display status to the node
        }
    }
}

function isHidden(object) {

    for (var n = object; n.nodeName != "BODY"; n = n.parentNode) {
        if (n.style.display == "none") return true;
    }

    return false;
}
```

returns a value of true if object is not visible on the Web page

▶ 2. Save your changes to the file.

You use the isHidden() function to determine the display status of any entry in the table of contents. Recall that in the previous session, each entry was given an ID based on the ID of a section heading. If the section heading has the ID *sectionId*, then the list item has the ID TOC*sectionId*. You can use the getElementById() method to locate the list item for each section heading as follows:

```
var TOCentry = document.getElementById("TOC" + n.id);
```

To set the display status of the section heading, you then call the isHidden() function as follows:

```
if (isHidden(TOCentry)) displayStatus = "none"
else displayStatus = "";
```

Finally, you apply the value of the displayStatus variable to the current node in the source document using the following command:

```
n.style.display = displayStatus;
```

You'll add these commands to the expandCollapseDoc() function, and then call the function from within the expandCollapse() function so that the source document is expanded and collapsed simultaneously with the table of contents.

To complete the expandCollapseDoc() function:

▶ **1.** Scroll up the toc.js file to the expandCollapseDoc() function and insert the following commands below the first if condition:

```
var TOCentry = document.getElementById("TOC" + n.id);
if (isHidden(TOCentry)) displayStatus = "none"
else displayStatus = "";
```

▶ **2.** Add the following command to the second if condition:

```
n.style.display = displayStatus;
```

▶ **3.** Scroll up to the expandCollapse() function and add the following statements to the end of the function:

```
// expand and collapse the source document to match the TOC
expandCollapseDoc();
```

Figure 7-51 highlights the revised code in both functions.

Completed expandCollapse functions ◀ **Figure 7-51**

```
function expandCollapse(e) {
    var plusMinusBox = e.target || event.srcElement;
    var nestedList = plusMinusBox.nextSibling.nextSibling;

    // Toggle the plus and minus symbol
    if (plusMinusBox.innerHTML == "--") plusMinusBox.innerHTML = "+"
    else plusMinusBox.innerHTML = "--";

    // Toggle the display style of the nested list
    if (nestedList.style.display == "none") nestedList.style.display = ""
    else nestedList.style.display = "none";

    // expand and collapse the source document to match the TOC      ⎫  expands and collapses
    expandCollapseDoc();                                             ⎬  the source document
}                                                                    ⎭  to match the TOC

function expandCollapseDoc() {
    var displayStatus = "";
    for (var n = sourceDoc.firstChild; n != null; n = n.nextSibling) {
        var nodeLevel = levelNum(n);

        if (nodeLevel != -1) {
            // determine the display status of the TOC entry
            var TOCentry = document.getElementById("TOC" + n.id);    ⎫  determines whether
            if (isHidden(TOCentry)) displayStatus = "none"           ⎬  the TOC entry is visible
            else displayStatus = "";                                 ⎭
        }

        if (n.nodeType == 1) { // node represents a page element      ⎫  applies the display status
            // apply the current display status to the node          ⎬  to the current node in
            n.style.display = displayStatus;                         ⎭  the source document
        }
    }
}
```

▶ **4.** Close the file, saving your changes.

▶ **5.** Reload the **usconst.htm** file in your Web browser, and then click **plus/minus** boxes in the table of contents, verifying that the content displayed in the constitution document mimics the contents displayed in the table of contents. See Figure 7-52.

Figure 7-52 > **Documents expanded and collapsed**

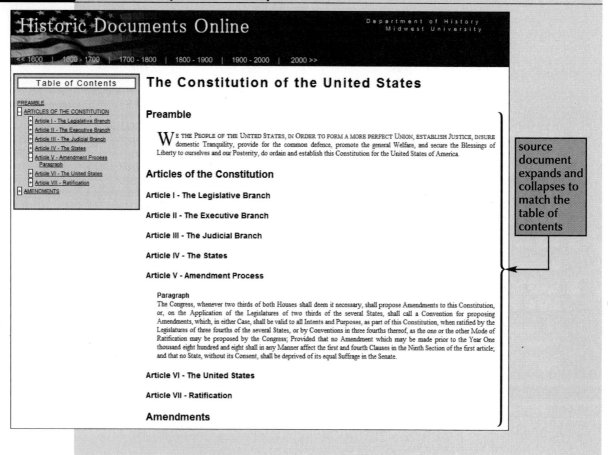

Testing the Dynamic Table of Contents

You show the dynamic table of contents application to Norene. She is pleased with the final product. She asks whether your work can be applied to other documents in her library. You test this by applying the application to a document containing the text of a 1790 peace treaty between the United States government and the Creek Indians.

To test the dynamic table of contents on a new document:

▶ **1.** Use your text editor to open the **treattxt.htm** file from the tutorial.07\tutorial folder, enter *your name* and *the date* in the comment section, and then save the file as **treaty.htm**.

▶ **2.** Above the closing </head> tag, insert the following script element to link the treaty file to the programs in the toc.js file:

```
<script src = "toc.js" type = "text/javascript"></script>
```

▶ **3.** Insert the following div element directly below the <body> tag to hold the dynamic table of contents:

```
<div id = "toc"></div>
```

4. Add the following opening tag directly before the Preamble h1 element:

```
<div id = "doc">
```

5. Directly before the </body> tag at the bottom of the file, insert the closing **</div>** tag to enclose the content of the document within a div element. Figure 7-53 highlights the code added in the file.

Revised treaty document | Figure 7-53

```
    <title>Treaty with the Creek Indians: 1790</title>
    <link href="web.css" rel="stylesheet" type="text/css" />
    <script  src = "toc.js" type = "text/javascript"></script>
</head>

<body>
    <div id = "toc"></div>

    <div id="logo"><img src="hlogo.jpg" alt="Historic Documents" /></div>
    <div id="logosub">Department of History<br />Midwest University</div>
    <div id="doctitle"><h1>Treaty with the Creek Indians: 1790</h1></div>

    <div id = "doc">
    <h1>Preamble</h1>
    <p>THE parties being desirous of establishing permanent peace and
        friendship between the United States and the said Creek Nation, and
        the citizens and members thereof, and to remove the causes of war by
        ascertaining their limits, and making other necessary, just and
        friendly arrangements: The President of the United States, by Henry
        Knox, Secretary for the Department of War, whom he hath constituted with
        full powers for these purposes, by and with the advice and consent of
        the Senate of the United States, and the Creek Nation, by the
        undersigned Kings, Chiefs and Warriors, representing the said nation,
        have agreed to the following articles. </p>


    </div>

</body>
</html>
```

6. Close the **treaty.htm** file, saving your changes, and then open the file in your Web browser. The dynamic table of contents is displayed in the left margin. See Figure 7-54.

Treaty document with the dynamic table of contents | Figure 7-54

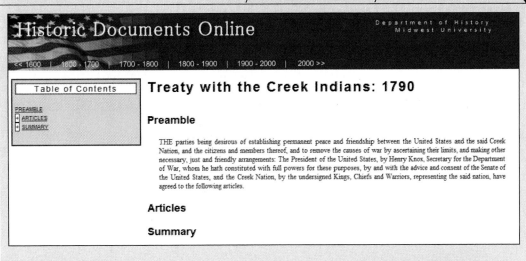

7. Click the **plus/minus** boxes to collapse and expand the document contents, and then click table of contents entries to move to the corresponding sections in the treaty.

In creating the dynamic table of contents, you made several simplifying assumptions. One was that all of the section headings in each historic document would be siblings and children of the source document. You did not allow for the possibility that a section heading would be further nested within another element. However, some applications that involve working with the node tree require a script to traverse the entire tree, touching each node. One way of doing this is through recursion. **Recursion** is a programming technique in which a function calls itself repeatedly until a stopping condition is met. The following is an example of a recursive function that counts the number of child nodes within a given node:

```
function countNodes(node, nodeCount) {
    for (var n = node.firstChild; n != null; n = n.nextSibling) {
        nodeCount++;
        countNodes(n, nodeCount);
    }
    return nodeCount;
}
```

Notice that the countNodes() function includes a for loop that loops through every child node of the given node object. For each child node the function finds, it increases the value of the nodeCount parameter by 1 and then calls *itself* to add to that total the number of children of that child node. Then, for each child node in *that set,* it calls the countNodes() function again to count the number of children in the next lower level. This process of drilling down the node tree continues until no descendant nodes remain in the node tree.

Every recursive function needs a starting point. If you wanted to count all of the nodes in Norene's source document, you would point the node parameter to the sourceDoc object and set the initial value of the nodeCount variable to 0. The expression to count all of the nodes would be:

```
countNodes(sourceDoc, 0)
```

If you apply this command to Norene's U.S. Constitution document, you would discover that the document contains 441 nodes under the W3C DOM. The IE DOM reports only 220 nodes, but that is due to the difference in how the DOMs treat white space nodes.

Switching Between Style Sheets

Norene is pleased with all of the work you have done on the dynamic table of contents. She has one last problem. Norene wants to give users the ability to easily switch their view of the documents stored on her Web site between the default Web page view you've been using, a page view more suitable for printing, and another page view that supports a larger text font. Figure 7-55 shows the document under each of these views.

Three views of the constitution document | Figure 7-55

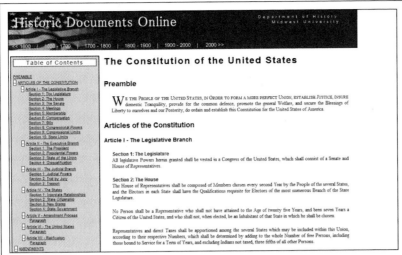

Web view

The Constitution of the United States

Preamble

W E THE PEOPLE OF THE UNITED STATES, IN ORDER TO FORM A MORE PERFECT UNION, ESTABLISH JUSTICE, INSURE DOMESTIC TRANQUILITY, PROVIDE FOR THE COMMON DEFENCE, promote the general Welfare, and secure the Blessings of Liberty to ourselves and our Posterity, do ordain and establish this Constitution for the United States of America.

Articles of the Constitution

Article I - The Legislative Branch

Section 1: The Legislature
All legislative Powers herein granted shall be vested in a Congress of the United States, which shall consist of a Senate and House of Representatives.

Section 2: The House
The House of Representatives shall be composed of Members chosen every second Year by the People of the several States, and the Electors in each State shall have the Qualifications requisite for Electors of the most numerous Branch of the State Legislature.

No Person shall be a Representative who shall not have attained to the Age of twenty five Years, and been seven Years a Citizen of the United States, and who shall not, when elected, be an Inhabitant of that State in which he shall be chosen.

Representatives and direct Taxes shall be apportioned among the several States which may be included within this Union, according to their respective Numbers, which shall be determined by adding to the whole Number of free Persons, including those bound to Service for a Term of Years, and excluding Indians not taxed, three fifths of all other Persons.

The actual Enumeration shall be made within three Years after the first Meeting of the Congress of the United States, and within every subsequent Term of ten Years, in such Manner as they shall by Law direct. The Number of Representatives shall not exceed one for every thirty Thousand, but each State shall have at Least one Representative; and until such enumeration shall be made, the State of New Hampshire shall be entitled to chuse three, Massachusetts eight, Rhode Island and Providence Plantations one, Connecticut five, New York six, New Jersey four, Pennsylvania eight, Delaware one, Maryland six, Virginia ten, North Carolina five, South Carolina five and Georgia three.

When vacancies happen in the Representation from any State, the Executive Authority thereof shall issue Writs of Election to fill such Vacancies.

The House of Representatives shall chuse their Speaker and other Officers; and shall have the sole Power of Impeachment.

Section 3: The Senate

print view

The Constitution of the United States

Preamble

W E THE PEOPLE OF THE UNITED STATES, IN ORDER TO FORM A MORE PERFECT UNION, ESTABLISH JUSTICE, insure domestic Tranquility, provide for the common defence, promote the general Welfare, and secure the Blessings of Liberty to ourselves and our Posterity, do ordain and establish this Constitution for the United States of America.

Articles of the Constitution

Article I - The Legislative Branch

Section 1: The Legislature
All legislative Powers herein granted shall be vested in a Congress of the United States, which shall consist of a Senate and House of Representatives.

Section 2: The House
The House of Representatives shall be composed of Members chosen every second Year by the People of the several States, and the Electors in each State shall have the Qualifications requisite for Electors of the most numerous Branch of the State Legislature.

No Person shall be a Representative who shall not have attained to the Age of twenty five Years, and been seven Years a Citizen of the United States, and who shall not, when elected, be an Inhabitant of that State in which he shall be chosen.

Representatives and direct Taxes shall be apportioned among the several States which may be included within this Union,

large text view

Norene already created three style sheets for the three views shown in Figure 7-55 and linked to them in the usconst.htm file. The following is the code for the three <style> tags:

```
<link type = "text/css" title = "Web" href = "web.css"
     rel = "stylesheet" />
<link type = "text/css" title = "Print" href = "print.css"
     rel = "alternate stylesheet" />
<link type = "text/css" title = "Large Text" href = "largetext.css"
     rel = "alternate stylesheet" />
```

Style sheets can be classified as persistent, preferred, and alternate. A **persistent style sheet** is a style sheet that is always active. It has a rel attribute value of stylesheet and does not have a title attribute. Persistent style sheets are loaded by the Web browser by default. A **preferred style sheet** is similar to a persistent style sheet except that it contains a title. Preferred style sheets are also turned on by default, but they also can be turned off by actions of the user. An **alternate style sheet** has a rel attribute value of alternate stylesheet and is identified by its title attribute. Alternate style sheets are not turned on by default, but the user can switch to them as alternates to the preferred style sheet.

For the usconst.htm file, Norene has created one preferred style sheet with the title Web based on the web.css file. You've been using this style sheet throughout this tutorial. The file also contains two alternate style sheets with the titles Print and Large Text, pointing to the print.css and largetext.css files, respectively. So far, those style sheets have not been activated for use in the constitution document.

Alternate style sheets can be activated in some browsers by selecting them from a menu of style sheet options. Opera has a built-in command to allow users to select their style sheet option. Firefox, on the other hand, provides an add-on to enable this functionality. Other browsers, such as Internet Explorer, do not provide a method for choosing alternate style sheets in placed or preferred sheets.

Norene wants you to provide this capability through a JavaScript program so that users running browsers other than Opera or Firefox can switch easily between style sheets. Norene envisions a program that will automatically create input buttons for each preferred or alternate style sheet listed in the HTML file. Users can then switch between the style sheets by clicking one of the input buttons on the Web page. Figure 7-56 shows a preview of this effect.

Input buttons to switch style sheets ◀ Figure 7-56

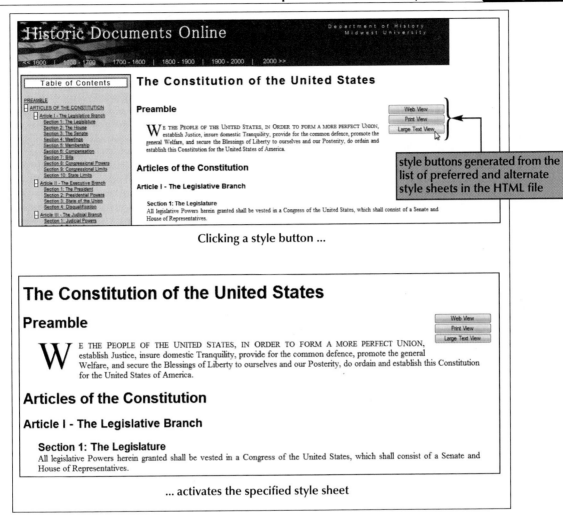

Clicking a style button ...

... activates the specified style sheet

You'll insert the code to create these input buttons in an external file named switchstyle.js and then link it to the usconst.htm file.

To create the switchstyle.js file:

1. Return to the **usconst.htm** file in your text editor, and then directly below the <script> tag to access the toc.js file, insert the following script element to access the switchstyle.js file:

```
<script src = "switchstyle.js" type = "text/javascript"></script>
```

2. Save your changes to the file.

3. Use your text editor to open the **switchtxt.js** file from the tutorial.07\tutorial folder, enter *your name* and *the date* in the comment section of the file, and then save the file as **switchstyle.js**.

   When the page is loaded by the browser, you'll run a function named makeStyle-Buttons() to generate the style buttons.

4. Add the following code to the bottom of the file:

```
addEvent(window, "load", makeStyleButtons, false);

function makeStyleButtons() {

}
```

You used the addEvent() function to provide a cross-browser solution to adding an event handler to the load event. As discussed in the previous tutorial, by adding the event handler in this way, you are not interfering with the event handler you've already created to generate the dynamic table of contents.

Working with the Link Element

So far, you've worked only with elements found in the body of a Web page. You can also access and modify elements found in the document's head. You can view the collection of all <link> tags in the current document using the following object reference:

```
document.getElementsByTagName("link")
```

From this collection of links, you want to extract only those links used for preferred or alternate style sheets. To do this, the link element needs to fulfill the following:

• Its rel attribute must equal either stylesheet or alternate stylesheet.
• It must have a style sheet title.

You'll store the link elements that fulfill these two criteria in an array named allStyles, which you'll create in the switchstyle.js file.

To create the allLinks variable:

▶ **1.** Directly above the makeStyleButtons() function in the switchstyle.js file, insert the following global variable declaration:

```
var allStyles = new Array();
```

▶ **2.** Within the makeStyleButtons() function, insert the following code to populate the allStyles array, as shown in Figure 7-57:

```
var allLinks = document.getElementsByTagName("link");

// Create an array of preferred or alternate style sheets
for (var i = 0; i < allLinks.length; i++) {
    if ((allLinks[i].rel == "stylesheet" ||
        allLinks[i].rel == "alternate stylesheet") &&
        allLinks[i].title != "") {
      allStyles.push(allLinks[i]);
    }
}
```

Code to populate the allStyles array ◀ Figure 7-57

```
addEvent(window, "load", makeStyleButtons, false);

var allStyles = new Array();

function makeStyleButtons() {
    var allLinks = document.getElementsByTagName("link");

    // Create an array of preferred or alternate style sheets
    for (var i = 0; i < allLinks.length; i++) {
        if ((allLinks[i].rel == "stylesheet" || allLinks[i].rel == "alternate stylesheet")
            && allLinks[i].title != "") {
            allStyles.push(allLinks[i]);
        }
    }
}
```

> allStyles array contains all link elements created
> for preferred or alternate style sheets

To create the buttons for each style sheet, you'll loop through all of the items in the allStyles array, creating one input button for each style sheet. The text displayed in each button will be "*style* view", where *style* is the title of the style sheet. You'll also set the title of each button to match the title of the style sheet to associate each button with its style sheet. You'll append each input button as a child of a new div element named styleBox.

You'll add this code to the makeStyleButtons() function.

To create input buttons for each titled link element in the document:

▶ **1.** Directly below the for loop you just created, insert the following code, as shown in Figure 7-58:

```
// Create buttons for each preferred or alternate style sheet
var styleBox = document.createElement("div");

for (var i = 0; i < allStyles.length; i++) {
    styleButton = document.createElement("input");
    styleButton.type = "button";
    styleButton.value = allStyles[i].title + " view";
    styleButton.title = allStyles[i].title;

    styleBox.appendChild(styleButton);
}
```

Figure 7-58 | Code to create form buttons for each style sheet

```
// Create an array of preferred or alternate style sheets
for (var i = 0; i < allLinks.length; i++) {
   if ((allLinks[i].rel == "stylesheet" || allLinks[i].rel == "alternate stylesheet")
       && allLinks[i].title != "") {
      allStyles.push(allLinks[i]);
   }
}

// Create buttons for each preferred or alternate style sheet
var styleBox = document.createElement("div");        ← box containing the style buttons

for (var i = 0; i < allStyles.length; i++) {
   styleButton = document.createElement("input");
   styleButton.type = "button";
   styleButton.value = allStyles[i].title + " view";    ← creates an input button for each style sheet
   styleButton.title = allStyles[i].title;

   styleBox.appendChild(styleButton);    ← appends each button to the style box
}
}
```

2. Save your changes to the file.

Next, you have to define the appearance of the style buttons and the style box. The style buttons will each be 120 pixels wide and the font size of the button text will be 12 pixels. The box containing the buttons will be 125 pixels wide, with top and right margins of 5 pixels and bottom and left margins of 10 pixels. The box itself will be floated on the right margin of the page. Note that the IE and W3C DOMs use different properties to apply the float style. Under the IE DOM, the property is

```
object.style.styleFloat = position;
```

where *object* is the object to be floated on the page and *position* is the margin on which the object is floated (left, right, or none). Under the W3C DOM, the float style is applied using the following property:

```
object.style.cssFloat = position;
```

To work across all browsers, you can run both commands in your script. The browser will apply the property it recognizes and ignore the one that it doesn't.

To design the appearance of the style buttons and style box:

1. Directly above the command that appends each style button to the style box, insert the following lines:

```
// Define the styles of each button
styleButton.style.width = "120px";
styleButton.style.fontSize = "12px";
```

2. At the bottom of the makeStyleButtons() function, insert the following lines:

```
// Define the styles of the box containing the buttons
styleBox.style.width = "125px";
styleBox.style.cssFloat = "right";
styleBox.style.styleFloat = "right";
styleBox.style.margin = "5px 5px 10px 10px";
```

Figure 7-59 shows the inserted code.

Design styles applied to the style buttons and box ◀ **Figure 7-59**

```
for (var i = 0; i < allStyles.length; i++) {
    styleButton = document.createElement("input");
    styleButton.type = "button";
    styleButton.value = allStyles[i].title + " view";
    styleButton.title = allStyles[i].title;

    // Define the styles of each button
    styleButton.style.width = "120px";              ◀── styles for each button
    styleButton.style.fontSize = "12px";

    styleBox.appendChild(styleButton);
}

// Define the styles of the box containing the buttons
styleBox.style.width = "125px";
styleBox.style.cssFloat = "right";                  ◀── floats the style box on
styleBox.style.styleFloat = "right";                    the right page margin
styleBox.style.margin = "5px 5px 10px 10px";
}
```

Finally, you'll attach the style box to the source document on Norene's page, placing it as the first child of that object.

To insert the style box on the Web page:

1. At the bottom of the makeStyleButtons() function, insert the following lines, as shown in Figure 7-60:

```
// Add the style box to the source document
var sourceDoc = document.getElementById("doc");
sourceDoc.insertBefore(styleBox, sourceDoc.firstChild);
```

Style box appended to the source document ◀ **Figure 7-60**

```
    // Define the styles of the box containing the buttons
    styleBox.style.width = "125px";
    styleBox.style.cssFloat = "right";
    styleBox.style.styleFloat = "right";
    styleBox.style.margin = "5px 5px 10px 10px";

    // Add the style box to the source document
    var sourceDoc = document.getElementById("doc");
    sourceDoc.insertBefore(styleBox, sourceDoc.firstChild);
}
```

2. Save your changes to the file, and then reload **usconst.htm** in your Web browser. Three input buttons have been added to the Web page, each matching one of the preferred or alternate style sheets defined in the document. See Figure 7-61.

Figure 7-61 **Style buttons for each preferred and alternate style sheet**

The Constitution of the United States

Preamble

WE THE PEOPLE OF THE UNITED STATES, IN ORDER TO FORM A MORE PERFECT UNION, establish Justice, insure domestic Tranquility, provide for the common defence, promote the general Welfare, and secure the Blessings of Liberty to ourselves and our Posterity, do ordain and establish this Constitution for the United States of America.

Initializing the Style Sheets

With the style buttons in place, you now must enable and disable the different style sheets. You can disable a style sheet using the command

```
styleSheet.disabled = true
```

and enable it with the command

```
styleSheet.disabled = false
```

where *styleSheet* is a preferred or alternate style sheet attached to the document. For Norene's application, you'll initially enable any preferred style sheet and disable any alternate style sheet. To do this, you'll add the following if statement to the for loop that creates the style buttons:

```
if (allStyles[i].rel == "stylesheet") {
   allStyles[i].disabled = false;
} else {
   allStyles[i].disabled = true;
}
```

You'll add this command to the switchstyle.js file.

To initialize the style sheets:

1. Return to the **switchstyle.js** file in your text editor.

2. Within the for loop to create the style buttons, insert the following code, as shown in Figure 7-62:

```
// Initialize the style sheets
if (allStyles[i].rel == "stylesheet") {
   allStyles[i].disabled = false;
} else {
   allStyles[i].disabled = true;
}
```

Code to initialize the style sheets   Figure 7-62

```
// Create buttons for each preferred or alternate style sheet
var styleBox = document.createElement("div");

for (var i = 0; i < allStyles.length; i++) {

   // Initialize the style sheets
   if (allStyles[i].rel == "stylesheet") {
      allStyles[i].disabled = false;
   } else {
      allStyles[i].disabled = true;
   }

   styleButton = document.createElement("input");
   styleButton.type = "button";
   styleButton.value = allStyles[i].title + " view";
   styleButton.title = allStyles[i].title;
```

Switching Between Style Sheets

The last task in your program is to enable users to enable and disable the different style sheets by clicking one of the style buttons inserted into the Web page. Because the buttons and the style sheets share the same title, you can loop through all of the style sheets contained in the allStyles array, enabling the one style sheet that matches the title and disabling the others. The code for the loop is:

```
for (var i = 0; i < allStyles.length; i++) {
   if (allStyles[i].title == this.title) {
      allStyles[i].disabled = false;
   } else {
      allStyles[i].disabled = true;
   }
}
```

This for loop uses the this keyword to reference the button clicked by the user. You'll add this for loop to a function named changeStyle(), and then add an event handler to call this function whenever one of the style buttons is clicked.

To create event handlers for the style buttons:

▶ **1.** Scroll to the bottom of the switchstyle.js file and insert the following function:

```
function changeStyle() {
   for (var i = 0; i < allStyles.length; i++) {
      if (allStyles[i].title == this.title) {
         allStyles[i].disabled = false;
      } else {
         allStyles[i].disabled = true;
      }
   }
}
```

2. Scroll up the file and insert the following code within the makeStyleButton() function, directly above the line that appends a styleButton to the styleBox:

```
// Apply an event handler to the style button
styleButton.onclick = changeStyle;
```

Figure 7-63 shows the newly inserted code.

Figure 7-63 ▶ **The changeStyle() function to switch the style sheets**

```
        // Apply an event handler to the style button
        styleButton.onclick = changeStyle;

        styleBox.appendChild(styleButton);
    }

    // Define the styles of the box containing the buttons
    styleBox.style.width = "125px";
    styleBox.style.cssFloat = "right";
    styleBox.style.styleFloat = "right";
    styleBox.style.margin = "5px 5px 10px 10px";

    // Add the style box to the source document
    var sourceDoc = document.getElementById("doc");
    sourceDoc.insertBefore(styleBox, sourceDoc.firstchild);
}

function changeStyle() {
    for (var i = 0; i < allStyles.length; i++) {
        if (allStyles[i].title == this.title) {
            allStyles[i].disabled = false;
        } else {
            allStyles[i].disabled = true;
        }
    }
}
```

runs the changeStyle() function whenever a style button is clicked

loops through all of the style sheets and enables only the one corresponding to the style button

---

3. Close the file, saving your changes.

4. Reload **usconst.htm** in your Web browser, and then verify that you can switch between the three style sheets by clicking the three style buttons on the Web page.

Working with the Style Sheets Object Collection

To complete the style sheet switcher, you had to examine the attributes of the link element. However, the link element can be used for objects other than style sheets. Instead of using the link element, you can also reference style sheets directly using the styleSheets object collection, which has the syntax

```
document.styleSheets[i]
```

where *i* is the index number of the style sheet. The first style sheet that a browser encounters has an index value of 0, the second has an index value of 1, and so on. Figure 7-64 lists the properties of the style sheet object. Some of these properties are specific to one DOM, and some properties are read-only and cannot be modified by the browser.

Properties of the style sheet object ◀ **Figure 7-64**

Property	Description
styleSheet.cssText	The text of the declarations in the style sheet (IE DOM)
styleSheet.disabled	Returns a Boolean value indicating whether the style sheet has been disabled (true) or has been enabled (false)
styleSheet.href	The url of the style sheet; for embedded style sheets, the href value is an empty text string [read-only]
styleSheet.media	A text string containing the list of media types associated with the style sheet [read-only]
styleSheet.rules	Returns the collection of rules within the style sheet (IE DOM)
styleSheet.cssRules	Returns the collection of rules within the style sheet (W3C DOM)
styleSheet.title	The title of the style sheet [read-only]
styleSheet.type	The MIME type of the style sheet [read-only]

Most browsers support the styleSheets object collection, but some do not. If you need a complete cross-browser solution, it is best to modify the attributes of the link element instead of working with the styleSheets collection.

Working with Style Sheet Rules   InSight

The style sheet object also contains an object collection that references the rules within the style sheet. In the W3C DOM, the object reference to the rules collection is

    styleSheet.cssRules

where *styleSheet* is a styleSheet object. For example, if the first style sheet on a Web page contains the declarations

```
<style type = "text/css">
    h1 {color: red}
    h2 {color: blue}
</style>
```

then the object reference

    document.styleSheets[0].cssRules[0]

refers to the style sheet declaration h1 {color: red}. In the IE DOM, style sheet rules are referenced using the following object collection:

    styleSheet.rules

You can add and remove rules from a style sheet under both DOMs. The IE DOM uses the addRule() and removeRule() methods. The equivalent methods under the W3C DOM are insertRule() and deleteRule().

Norene appreciates the work you've done adding a style switcher to her Web page. She will continue to apply the work you've done to her history site.

Review | Session 7.3 Quick Check

1. What command creates an inline image node named imgObj and then appends it as the first child of a node named listItem?
2. What command hides and removes from the page flow a page element with the ID imgObj?
3. What is recursion?
4. What are preferred and alternate style sheets? What is a persistent style sheet?
5. What are two ways of referencing style sheet objects linked to a document?
6. What command enables a *styleSheet* object? What command disables the same object?
7. What expression references the second rule from the document's third style sheet? Provide answers for both the IE and W3C DOMs.

Review | Tutorial Summary

In this tutorial, you learned how to create and manage dynamic content and styles to develop a dynamic table of contents application that could be applied to a wide variety of documents. In the first session, you learned how to apply the innerHTML property to insert new content into a page element. The first session also introduced the node tree, exploring how to navigate through a node tree, create new nodes, and attach them to a Web page document. Using this information, you created a list of section headings from a document. In the second session, you applied what you learned about node properties and methods to create a nested list of section headings. The second session also demonstrated how to work with attribute nodes and how to work with element attributes. In the third session, you created an expandable/collapsible document by applying the display style to elements within the dynamic table of contents and within the sample document. The third session also discussed how to access different style sheets created for a Web page document, showing how to create a style sheet switch to enable users to select the style sheet they want to apply to the document.

Key Terms

alternate style sheet	node tree	recursion
document fragment	persistent style sheet	root node
dynamic content	plus/minus box	
node	preferred style sheet	

Practice	**Review Assignments**

Practice the skills you learned in the tutorial using the same case scenario.

Data Files needed for the Review Assignments: fed10txt.htm, fedpaper.css, hlogo.jpg, keytxt.js, print.css, stylestxt.js

Norene has another application for you to add to her library of historic documents. Some documents are not broken into sections, so creating a table of contents would not be appropriate. For those documents, Norene wants the Web page to display a box containing a sorted list of keywords and phrases found in the document. Each keyword or phrase has been marked in the documents with a dfn (definition) element. The entries in the keyword list need to search the current historic document for the presence of these dfn elements and create links between the keyword list entries and the keywords in the document. Norene also wants the page to have a Web version and a print version, and she wants users to be able to easily switch between the two.

Figure 7-65 shows a preview of the page created for the tenth Federalist paper written by James Madison in 1787 on the danger of factions to the republic.

Figure 7-65

Norene has already provided the source document and external style sheets that format the appearance of the document and the keyword list for both the Web and the printer. You'll have to write the application that creates the content of the keyword list.

Complete the following:

1. Use your text editor to open the **fed10txt.htm**, **keytxt.js**, and **stylestxt.js** files from the tutorial.07\review folder, enter *your name* and *the date* in the comment section of each file, and then save the files as **fed10.htm**, **keywords.js**, and **styles.js**, respectively.

2. Go to the **fed10.htm** file in your text editor and study the contents of the file, paying attention to titles of the style sheets assigned to this document and the structure of the page contents. Add script elements to attach this document to the keywords.js and styles.js files, and then close the file, saving your changes.

3. Go to the **keywords.js** file in your text editor. Create a function named **makeElemList()**. The purpose of this function is to return an array containing a sorted list of the contents of elements with a common tag name. You'll use this function later to create a list of the keywords in the document. The function has a single parameter named **elem** that contains the text of the tag name. Add the following commands to the function:

   a. Store the collection of elements whose tag name equals the elem parameter in a variable named **elemList**. (*Hint:* Use the document.getElementsByTagName() method.)

   b. Declare a new array named **elemTextArr**.

   c. Create a for loop that goes through each of the objects in the elemList object collection. For each object, change the text to lowercase letters and store the content of the element in the corresponding elemTextArr array item. (*Hint:* Use the toLowerCase() String method to change the content of the object to lowercase letters.)

   d. Sort the entries in the elemTextArr array in ascending alphabetical order.

   e. Return the contents of the elemTextArr array.

4. Create a function named **setElemId()**. The purpose of this function is to create and return ID values for elements in the document that match a specific tag name and element content. You'll use this function later to insert matching ID values between the items in the keyword list and the keywords found in the document. The function has two parameters: **elem**, which contains the text of the tag name, and **elemText**, which contains the text of the element content. Add the following commands to the function:

   a. Store the collection of elements whose tag name equals the elem parameter in a variable named **elemList**.

   b. Create a for loop that goes through each of the objects in the elemList object collection.

   c. Within the for loop, test whether the content of the current elemList object, converted to lowercase letters, equals the value of the elemText parameter. If it does, test whether the ID of the object is equal to an empty text string. If the ID is missing, create a variable named **elemId** equal to the text string keyword*i*, where *i* is the value of the counter variable in the for loop, and set the ID of the object to the value of the elemId variable. If the ID is not missing, set the value of the elemId variable to the value of the ID attribute of the object.

   d. After the for loop has finished, return the value of the elemId variable. This is the ID that has been assigned to the element in the document.

5. Create a function named **makeKeyWordBox()**. The purpose of this function is to create a list of keywords drawn from the dfn elements in the historic document. There are no parameters for this function. Add the following commands:

    a. Declare a variable named **historyDoc** that references the element with the ID doc.

    b. Create an element node named **keywordBox** for a div element. Set the ID of the keywordBox to "keywords".

    c. Create an element node named **keywordBoxTitle** containing an h1 element. Set the content of the h1 element to the text string Keywords.

    d. Append keywordBoxTitle to the keywordBox node as a child.

    e. Create an element node named **ulList** containing a ul element. Append ulList as a second child of the keywordBox node. This unordered list will store the list of keywords in the document.

    f. Call the makeElemList() function using the text string dfn as the parameter value. Store the array returned by the function in a variable named keywords.

    g. Write a for loop that loops through all of the items in the keywords array that you just created. The purpose of this for loop is to create an unordered list of keywords, each one linked to a specific keyword in the document. For each item in the array, do the following: (i) Create an element node named **newListItem** that contains a list item element; (ii) Create an element node named **newLink** that contains a hypertext element; (iii) Set the content of newLink to the value of the current item in the keywords array (*Hint*: Use the reference keywords[*i*] where *i* is the value of the counter variable in the for loop.); (iv) Create a variable named **linkId** whose value is equal to the value returned by the setElemId() function using dfn and keywords[*i*] as the parameter values; (v) Change the href attribute of newLink to #*id* where *id* is the value of the linkId variable; (vi) Append newLink to newListItem and append newListItem to ulList.

    h. After the for loop has completed, append keywordBox as the first child of the historyDoc node.

6. Use the addEvent() function previously added to the file to run the makeKeyWordBox() function when the page is loaded by the browser.

7. Save your changes to the file, and then load **fed10.htm** in your Web browser. Verify that a box containing a list of keywords is displayed on the Web page with each entry in the list linked to a specific keyword within the historic document.

8. Return to the **styles.js** file in your text editor. Add a line to the bottom of the file to declare the global variable styleList as a new, empty array.

9. Use the addEvent() function to run the makeStyleListBox() function when the page is loaded by the browser.

10. Add the **makeStyleListBox()** function. The purpose of this function is to create a selection list whose entries match the list of style sheets present in the source document. Within this function, declare the variable **allLinks** matching all elements in the document with the tag name link.

11. Within the makeStyleListBox() function, add a for loop to loop through all of the entries in the allLinks object collection. If the rel attribute of the entry equals stylesheet or alternate stylesheet and the title attribute is nonempty, add the entry to the styleList array.

12. Create the selection list containing the list of style sheets by adding the following code to the makeStyleListBox() function:

    a. Create a select element node named **styleSelect**.

b. Loop through all of the entries in the styleList array. If the value of the rel attribute of the entry is not equal to stylesheet, disable the style sheet; otherwise, enable the style sheet. Also, for each entry in the array, create an option element node named **styleOption**. Set the value of the option element to the title value of the style sheet. Set the text contained within the option to "*stylesheet* view" where *stylesheet* is the title of the style sheet. Finally, append the option element to the styleSelect node.

c. After the for loop has completed, define the styles for the styleSelect element node. Set the width of the selection list to 220 pixels and float the selection list on the right margin. Set the margins around the selection list to 5 pixels above and to the right, and 10 pixels below and to the left.

13. Within the makeStyleListBox() function, add an event handler to the styleSelect object to run the changeStyle() function when the value of the selection is changed.

14. Complete the makeStyleListBox() function by declaring a variable named **sourceDoc** referencing the element with the ID doctitle. Append the styleSelect object as the first child of the sourceDoc object.

15. Create the **changeStyle()** function. The purpose of this function is to switch the style sheets employed by browser based on the choice of the user. Add the following commands to the function:

a. Create a variable named **selectedItem** that contains the index number of the selected option from the selection list of style sheets. (*Hint:* You can reference the selection list using either the this keyword if you used traditional event binding, or the event object if you used the addEvent() function to create the event handler.)

b. Create a variable named **styleOption** equal to the value of the selected option in the style sheet selection list.

c. Loop through all of the entries in the styleList array. If the title of the style sheet equals the value of styleOption, enable the style sheet; otherwise, disable the style sheet.

16. Save your changes to the file, and then reload **fed10.htm** in your Web browser. Click the selection list generated by the code in the styles.js file, and verify that you can switch styles between the Web Page and Printer views.

17. Submit the completed project to your instructor.

<table><tr><td>Apply</td><td>**Case Problem 1**</td></tr></table>

Use the skills you learned to create an English-to-French translation page.

Data Files needed for this Case Problem: engfrtxt.js, french5.js, french5txt.htm, styles.css

French 101   Professor Eve Granger teaches French 101 at a local university. She is working on a Web site containing French phrases that she wants her students to review for the weekly quiz. She's asked you to help her create the Web site. She wants a student to be able to press the mouse button down on a French phrase in the site and have the English translation appear. When the student releases the mouse button, the French phrase should reappear. Figure 7-66 shows a preview of the Web page you'll create for Professor Granger.

Figure 7-66

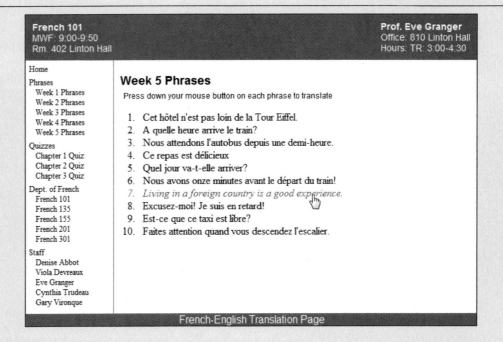

As a test case, Professor Granger has already created an external script file named french5.js that contains two arrays. The french array contains 10 French phrases. The english array contains the 10 English translations of those phrases. You'll use these arrays to insert the French phrases and their translations into the Web page. If your program works, you can then start to create similar pages that contain hundreds of translated phrases—but this is a good start.

Complete the following:

1. Use your text editor to open the **french5txt.htm** and **engfrtxt.js** files from the tutorial.07\case1 folder, enter *your name* and *the date* in the comment section of each file, and then save the files as **french5.htm** and **engfr.js**, respectively.

2. Go to the **french5.htm** file in your text editor and review the contents and structure of the file. Add two script elements that attach the french5.htm file to the french5.js and engfr.js script files. Close the french5.htm file, saving your changes.

3. Go to the **engfr.js** file in your text editor. Add a command to have the browser run the setUp() function when the page is loaded.

4. Create the **setUp()** function. The purpose of this function is to insert an ordered list of French phrases taken from the french array in the french5.js file and to add event handlers to switch these phrases to their English counterparts. Add the following commands to the setUp() function:

    a. Declare a variable named **transDoc** that references the element with the ID doc. It is within this element that you'll place the list of French phrases.

    b. Create an element node named **olElem** containing the ol element.

c. Loop through all of the items in the french array. For each item in the array, create an element node named **newLI** containing a list item element. Set the text contained within newLI to the text of the current item in the french array. Set the ID of the newLI element to *i*phrase, where *i* is the value of the index number in the array. Set the cursor style of the list item to pointer. Have the browser run the swapFE() function when the user presses the mouse button down on the list item, and run the swapEF() function when the mouse button is released. Finally, append the newLI element as a child of the olElem object.

d. After the loop has finished, append the olElem object to the transDoc object.

5. Create the **swapFE()** function. The purpose of this function is to display the English phrase in place of the French phrase selected by the user. Add the following commands to the function:

a. The swapFE() function is only run in response to the mousedown event. Store the object in which the mousedown event occurred in a variable named **phrase**.

⊕ EXPLORE

b. If the node name of the phrase object indicates that the phrase object is a text node, point the phrase object to the parent of that text node. This is done to ensure that the object being examined is the list item element containing the phrase, and not simply the text of the phrase itself.

c. Declare a variable named **phraseNum** that returns the index number of the phrase being selected. You can extract the index number by applying the parseInt() method to contents of the ID attribute of the phrase object.

d. Change the inner HTML of the phrase object to the item in the english array with an index equal to the phraseNum variable.

e. Change the font style of the phrase object to italic and the font color to the color value (155, 102, 102).

6. Create the **swapEF()** function. The purpose of this function is to display the French translation of the phrase selected by the user. The code of the function should be identical to that used in the swapFE() function, except that it should use the french array rather than the english array and the phrase text should be displayed in a normal black font.

7. Close the file, saving your changes.

8. Open **french5.htm** in your Web browser. Verify that a list of 10 French phrases appears on the Web page. Also, verify that as you press the mouse button on each phrase, the English translation appears. When you release the mouse button, the French phrase should reappear.

9. Submit the completed project to your instructor.

Challenge | Case Problem 2

Explore table objects to create a data table filter.

Data Files needed for this Case Problem: cstyles.css, dc500.jpg, linksbg.jpg, logo.jpg, camtxt.htm, filtertxt.js

MicroCity David Forrest works at MicroCity, an online store for computers and electronics. One of his jobs is to create a table listing the different digital cameras sold by MicroCity. The company carries hundreds of digital camera models, and David thinks that the data table will be too long for customers to easily view it. He wants to give customers the ability to filter the data table, showing only those models that match certain criteria. Customers should be able to select the criteria from a drop-down list box. Figure 7-67 shows a preview of a prototype for a Web page that David wants you to help him create.

Figure 7-67

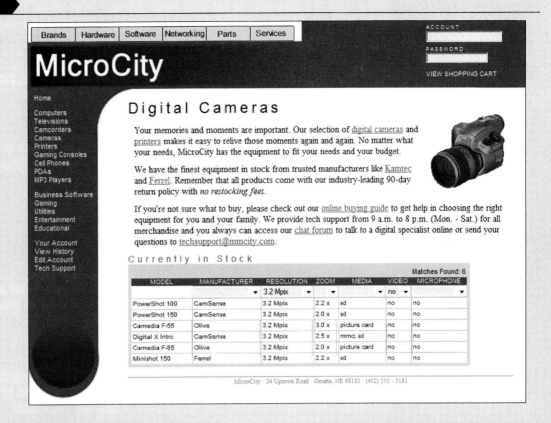

The data table shown in Figure 7-67 contains seven columns, indicating each camera's model name, manufacturer, resolution, zoom capability, storage media, and support for video, as well as whether it contains a microphone. The drop-down list boxes above the last six of those columns contain the unique values from each corresponding column. If a customer selects a zoom value of 3.0 x from the drop-down list box, only those cameras with that zoom feature should be displayed in the data table. Customers should be able to select more than one filter, and only those cameras satisfying all filter values should be shown.

The application that you'll create for Dave needs to be easily ported to other data tables on other Web pages. So any changes you make to the table need to be made using a JavaScript program, not by modifying the HTML tags in the Web page file. The application should do the following:

- Create selection list boxes for columns of values that will act as filters for the table.
- Populate each selection list with a list of unique values in the column, sorted in alphabetical order.
- Place the selection list boxes in cells in a new row of the table header.
- Filter the table in response to the user selecting a filter value from one of the selection list boxes.

This project will involve working with the structure and contents of a Web table. Web tables are organized into a hierarchy of row groups, rows, and cells within rows. The table header section of a Web table is referenced using the expression

```
table.tHead
```

where *table* is a reference to the Web table. Because Web tables can contain several tbody sections, the table bodies are referenced using the following object collection:

```
table.tBodies
```

Rows within a row group are referenced using the rows collection, and cells within a table row are referenced using the cells collection. The expression

```
table.tBodies[0].rows[2].cells[1]
```

references the second cell in the third row of the first tbody section in the Web table. You can determine the number of cells in a row or rows within a row group using the length attribute. The number of cells in the third row is

```
table.tBodies[0].rows[2].cells.length
```

and the number of rows in the row group is

```
table.tBodies[0].rows.length
```

JavaScript and HTML do not support direct object references to table columns. But if the table contains a column group, you can reference columns in that group using the expression

```
table.getElementsByTagName("col")
```

and JavaScript will return an object collection containing the col elements within the table. Once you create a column group, you can apply some of the properties of the col elements within the column group to columns within the Web table.

You'll use all of this information regarding the structure of Web table objects to complete this assignment and the next.

Complete the following:

1. Use your text editor to open the **camtxt.htm** and **filtertxt.js** files from the tutorial.07\ case2 folder, enter *your name* and *the date* in the comment section of each file, and then save the files as **cameras.htm** and **filter.js**, respectively.

2. Go to the **cameras.htm** file in your text editor and review the contents and structure of the file. Pay careful attention to the structure and contents of the Web table describing the camera products sold by MicroCity. Note that David has included a colgroup element containing seven columns: one for each column in the data table. Also notice that each col element in the colgroup contains a class attribute that is equal to filter or nofilter. The columns from the nofilter class will not have selection filters added to them, while columns belonging to the filter class will have selection lists. Create a link between this document and the external script file, filter.js, and then close the file, saving your changes.

3. Go to the **filter.js** file in your text editor. Declare the following global variables but do not set their initial values yet:
   - **filterTable** which will reference the Web table containing the camera data
   - **filterCols** which will reference the col elements within that table
   - **filterHead** which will reference the head section of filterTable
   - **filterBody** which will reference the first (and only) tbody element in filterTable

4. Use the **addEvent()** function to add an event handler that runs the init() function when the page is loaded by the browser.

5. Create the **init()** function. The purpose of the init() function is to set up the data table filters and initialize the event handler in the document. Add the following commands to the function:

   a. Set the value of filterTable to the Web table with the ID filterTable.

   b. Have the filterCols variable reference all of the col elements within filterTable.

   c. Have filterHead reference the head row group of filterTable.

   d. Have filterBody reference the first entry in the tBodies row group within filterTable.

   e. Run the addTotalsRow() function.

6. Create the **countRecords()** function. The purpose of this function is to count the number of visible rows in the table body and then enter that information into the first row of the table header. Add the following commands to the function:

   a. Declare the **rowCount** variable, setting its initial value to 0.

   b. Loop through all of the rows in the filterBody row group. If the display style of a row is equal to "", then increase the value of rowCount by 1.

   c. Return the value of the rowCount variable.

7. Create the **addTotalsRow()** function. The purpose of this function is to insert a table row that displays a count of the number of rows in the table body section of the filter table. Add the following commands to the function:

   a. Declare a variable named **newRow** that contains an element node for the tr element. Declare a variable named **newCell** that contains an element node for the td element.

   b. Set the value of the colspan attribute for newCell equal to the number of cells in the first row of the filterHead row group. (*Note:* Because of a bug in the Internet Explorer browser, you must enter the colspan attribute using the property name colSpan, not colspan.)

   c. Set the inner HTML of newCell to the text string Matches Found: *countRecords* where *countRecords* is the value returned by the countRecords() function.

   d. Append newCell to newRow.

   e. Insert newRow before the first row in the filterHead row group.

8. Save your changes to the file, and then load **cameras.htm** in your Web browser. Verify that the table now contains a new header row displaying the text "Matches Found: 24".

9. Return to **filter.js** in your text editor. Next you'll create the code that adds selection lists to table cells in a new row appended to the head section of the table. Return to the init() function, and at the bottom of the function declare a variable named **newRow** that contains a tr element node.

10. Below that command within the init() function, insert a for loop to generate cells for the new table row. The for loop loops through the entries in the filterCols object collection, creating a new table cell for each column. Each time through the loop, do the following:

    a. Create an element node named **newCell** containing a th (table heading) element.

    b. Set the style of newCell so that its contents are left-aligned and displayed in a black font on a white background.

    c. If the current item in the filterCols object collection has a class name equal to filter, then you must create a selection list for the cell. Within the command block for the if statement, do the following: (i) Declare a variable named **newSelect** and set it equal to the object returned by the createSelectionList() function. The createSelectionList() function has a single parameter value equal to *i* where *i* is the index counter used in the for loop. (ii) Append the newSelect object to newCell.

d. After the command block for the if statement, append newCell to newRow.

e. After the for loop has finished, append newRow to the filterHead row group.

11. Create the **createSelectionList()** function. The purpose of this function is to create a selection containing the unique values found within a specified column in the table. The function has a single parameter, **colIndex**, which identifies the column from which the unique values are drawn. Add the following commands to the function:

EXPLORE

a. Declare an element node for the select element. Name the node **newSelect**.

b. Create a custom property for newSelect named **cIndex**. Set the value of the cIndex property to colIndex.

c. Create an element node named **blankOption** that contains an option element. Set the inner HTML of this node to the empty string "". Append the blankOption node to the newSelect node.

d. Call the function addUniqueOptions() using parameter values newSelect and colIndex. The addUniqueOptions() function (which you'll create next) adds the remaining option elements to the newSelect selection list.

e. Set the width style value of newSelect to 100% so that it fills up its table cell.

f. Return the newSelect object.

12. Create the **addUniqueOptions()** function. The purpose of this function is to fill up the selection list with unique values found in a table column. The function has two parameters: selectionList and colIndex. The **selectionList** parameter points to an element node containing a selection list. The **colIndex** parameter indicates the index number of the column containing the data values. Add the following commands to this function:

a. Declare a new array named **uniqueList**.

b. Add a for loop that loops through the rows in the filterBody row group.

c. Within the for loop, declare a variable named **rowCell** that points to the cell in the current row from the table column. (*Hint*: Use the object reference filterBody. rows[*i*].cells[*index*] where *i* is the value of the counter variable in the for loop and *index* is the value of the colIndex parameter in the function.)

EXPLORE

d. Extract the text of the cell, using either the innerText property (for the IE DOM) or the textContent property (for the W3C DOM). Store the text string in a variable named **cellValue**.

e. Call the isUnique() function using cellValue and uniqueList as parameter values. If the function returns a value of true, then use the push() method to push the value of the cellValue variable into the uniqueList array. (*Hint:* The isUnique() function is provided for you. The function has a single purpose: It compares a given value to all of the values in a specified array. If the value is not matched in the array, the isUnique() function returns a value of true; otherwise, it returns a value of false.)

f. At this point, the uniqueList array should contain all of the unique values in the data column. Sort the array to place the values in alphabetical order.

g. Loop through all of the entries in the uniqueList array. For each item in the array, create an option element node. Set the inner HTML of the option element to the item value and then append the option element to the selectionList node.

13. Save your changes to the file, and then reload **cameras.htm** in your Web browser. The Web table should now contain a new header row with six selection lists for the six filterable columns. Click each selection list and verify that it contains a list of the unique values in the column, sorted in alphabetical order.

14. Return to the **filter.js** file in your text editor. At this point, you must program the selection lists to filter the data values in the Web table. Go to the createSelectionList() function. Directly above the statement to return the newSelect variable (the last statement in the function), insert a statement that assigns an event handler to the newSelect variable, running the doFilter() function whenever the value of the selection list changes.

15. Create the **resetTable()** function. The purpose of this function is to reset the Web table, allowing all rows in the tbody to be displayed. To complete the function, insert a for loop that loops through all of the rows in the filterBody object, setting the display style of each row to the empty text string "".

16. Create the **doFilter()** function. The purpose of this function is to loop through all of the selection lists containing the filter values, and then call a function to hide table rows that match those filter values. Add the following commands to this function:

    a. Call the resetTable()function to temporarily display all rows in the Web table.

    b. Declare a variable named **allSelects** that contains the object collection of all the select elements located in the filterHead row group. (*Hint:* Use the getElementsByTagName() method to locate the selection list elements with tag names of <select>.)

⊕ EXPLORE

    c. Loop through all of the selection list items in the allSelects object collection. For each item, store the index of the selected option in the filterIndex variable and the text of that option in the filterText variable. Store the value of the custom cIndex property you created earlier in a variable named **colIndex**.

    d. The filterText variable tells you the filter value from the selection list, and the colIndex variable tells you the column to apply the filter to. Still within the for loop, test whether filterText is equal to the empty text string "". If it is not, call the filterColumn() function using the colIndex and filterText variables as parameter values.

    e. After the for loop has run, display the text Matches Found: *countRecords* in the first cell of the first row in the filterHead row group, where *countRecords* is the value returned by the countRecords() function.

17. Create the **filterColumn()** function. The purpose of this function is to hide rows in the data table whose cells do not match a specified filter value. The function has two parameters named colIndex and fText. The **colIndex** parameter indicates the table column on which to test the filter. The **fText** parameter contains the filter text. Add the following commands to the function:

    a. Loop through all of the rows in the filterBody row group. For each entry in the loop, create a variable named **rowCell** that references a cell in the current row from the column specified by the colIndex parameter.

    b. Within the loop, create a variable named **rowCellText** that uses either the innerText property (for the IE DOM) or the textContent property (for the W3C DOM) to extract the text stored in the rowCell object.

    c. Still within the loop, test whether rowCellText equals fText. If it does not, set the display style of the current row to none.

18. Save your changes to the file, and then reload **cameras.htm** in your Web browser. Click the different selection filters in the Web table and verify that selecting different filter values limits the rows displayed in the table to only those rows that match the filters. Also, verify that the table header displays the correct number of rows in the table. Finally, verify that you can unhide a hidden row by selecting an empty string from the filter selection list.

19. Submit your completed project to your instructor.

Challenge | Case Problem 3

Explore table objects to create a sortable Web table.

Data Files needed for this Case Problem: gradient.png, gradient2.png, sasrlogo.png, statstxt.htm, tabletxt.js, tstyles.css

Sporting Abstract and Statistical Review Walter Delacreaux is the owner and operator of the Sporting Abstract and Statistical Review, a new blog and forum to report on and analyze data from the world of sports. Walter wants to fill his Web site with useful tables that other people who share his enthusiasm for statistics can review and study. He wants these tables to be as interactive as possible. One feature he wants to add to his tables is the ability to sort them in a different order by clicking a column heading. Figure 7-68 shows a preview of the Web page you'll create for Walter.

Figure 7-68

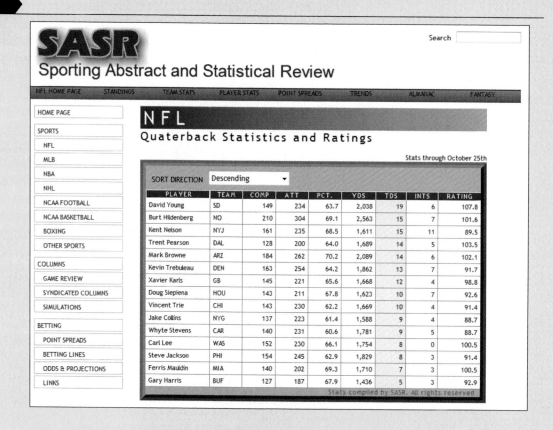

To create this application, you'll have to work with some of the objects found in Web tables. Information about these objects is provided in the introduction to Case Problem 2. You'll also have to work with some custom properties and functions. Some of these functions have been provided for you. Walter has already entered a sample table for you to work on and created the style sheet for the Web page. You will complete the project by writing the JavaScript code to enable users to sort the table with a click of the mouse button.

Complete the following:

1. Use your text editor to open the **statstxt.htm** and **tabletxt.js** files from the tutorial.07\ case3 folder, enter *your name* and *the date* in the comment section of each file, and then save the files as **stats.htm** and **tablesort.js**, respectively.

2. Go to the **stats.htm** file in your text editor and review the document's content and structure. The table of QB stats includes a column group listing the nine columns in the table. The class value associated with each col element indicates whether the column data should be treated and sorted as alphabetic characters (asort) or numeric values (numsort). Add a script element to the document, linking the file to the tablesort.js file. Close the file, saving your changes.

3. Go to the **tablesort.js** file in your text editor. Declare the following global variables but do not set their initial values yet:
   - **sortTable** which will reference the Web table containing the QB statistics
   - **sortBody** which will reference the table body within sortTable
   - **sortHead** which will reference the head section of sortTable
   - **sortCols** which will reference the col elements within the sortTable
   - **sortDirection** which indicates the direction of sorting done in the table; set its initial value to descending
   - **sortIndex** which will indicate the index number of the column on which the sorting is done; do not set an initial value for the variable

4. Use the **addEvent()** function to add an event handler that runs the setupTable() function when the page is loaded by the browser.

5. Create the **setupTable()** function. The purpose of the setupTable() function is to set up the Web table for sorting. Add the following commands to the function:
   a. Point the sortTable variable to the Web table with the ID qbstats.
   b. Have the sortCols variable reference all of the col elements within sortTable.
   c. Have sortHead reference the heading row group of sortTable.
   d. Have sortBody reference the first entry in the tBodies collection within sortTable.
   e. Create a for loop that loops through all of the cells in the first row of the sortHead row group. For each cell in the row, create an event handler that runs the sortCol() function when the cell is clicked. Also, set the cursor style of the cell to pointer. Finally, add a customer property named **colIndex** to each cell, setting the property value to the value of the counter variable used in the for loop.
   f. After the for loop is completed, run the function addSortDirection().

6. Create the **addSortDirection()** function. The purpose of this function is to insert a new table row into the head of the table with a single cell containing a drop-down selection list. The drop-down selection will be used to allow users to easily switch the direction of sorting done in the table. Add the following commands to the function:
   a. Declare variables named **newRow** and **newCell** containing element nodes for the tr and th elements, respectively.

b. Set the inner HTML of newCell to the following HTML fragment:

```
<label for = 'sortdir'>Sort Direction</label>
```

EXPLORE

c. Use the setAttribute() method to add the colSpan attribute to the newCell node. Set the value of the colSpan attribute to the length of the sortCols object collection. (*Hint:* To support Internet Explorer, you must specify the attribute as colSpan, not colspan.)

d. Set the value of the className property for newCell to sortHeader.

7. Next you must create the selection list for the new cell you just created. Continue working in the addSortDirection() function by adding the following commands:

   a. Create a select element node named **sortSelect**.

   b. Add an event handler to the sortSelect to run the toggleSort() function when the value of sortSelect is changed by the user.

   c. Create and append two option buttons to sortSelect. The first should contain the inner HTML text Descending; the second should contain inner HTML equal to the text string Ascending.

   d. Append sortSelect to the newCell node, and then append newCell to the newRow node.

   e. Insert newRow as the first child of the sortHead row group.

8. Create the **toggleSort()** function. The purpose of this function is to toggle the value of sortDirection between descending and ascending. Insert an if condition that toggles the variable between these two possible values. After the if condition, insert a command to run the runSort() function, which you'll create shortly.

9. Save your changes to the file, and then load **stats.htm** in your Web browser. Verify that the table contains a new header row containing a drop-down selection list with the entries Descending and Ascending.

10. Return to **tablesort.js** in your text editor. Go to the empty **sortCol()** function, located directly below the alphaCompare() function. The purpose of this function is to set the value of the sortIndex variable and run the sort on the table. Add the following commands to the function:

   a. Set the value of **sortIndex** to the value of the colIndex property from the table heading cell clicked by the user. (*Hint:* Use either an event object or the `this` keyword to determine the element that called the sortCol() function.)

   b. Call the runSort() function.

11. Create the **runSort()** function. The purpose of this function is to sort the table by reordering the table rows within the table body. Because you'll be sorting the entire table based on the values on one column, you'll have to create an array containing those column values and then sort it either alphabetically or numerically. In the first line of the function, declare an empty array named **sortCells**. This array will contain the data to be sorted.

12. Next you have to loop through the rows in the table body, extracting values from the column on which the sort is based. Add a for loop to the runSort() function that loops through all of the rows in the table body. Within the for loop, do the following:

   a. Declare a variable named **sortCell** that points to the cell in the current row belonging to the column to be sorted. (*Hint:* Use the object reference sortBody. rows[*i*].cells[*sortIndex*] where *i* is the value of the counter variable used in the for loop and *sortIndex* is the value of the sortIndex variable.)

EXPLORE

    b. Ignore any markup tags found within the table cells when sorting. Declare a variable named **celltxt** that is equal to the text contained within sortCell. Use either the innerText property (for the IE DOM) or the textContent property (for the W3C DOM).

    c. Some numeric values contain non-numeric characters such as commas and dollar symbols. Create a variable named **regx** that contains the regular expression

        `/(\,|\$)/g`

      and then apply this regular expression using the replace() method to celltxt in order to strip out all occurrences of commas and dollar symbols, and replace them with empty text strings.

EXPLORE

    d. Add some custom properties to sortCell. The sortCell variable contains an array of values, but you also want it to be able to reference the text value in the celltxt variable and the table row from which that value came from.

      To do so is beyond the scope of this tutorial, but a custom function has been supplied for you in the file to allow you to do this. Call the addProps() function using sortCells[*i*] for the first parameter value, celltxt for the second parameter value, and sortBody.rows[*i*] for the third parameter value, where *i* is the counter variable used in your for loop. Store the value returned by the function in sortCells[*i*].

      After calling this function, sortCells[*i*] will have two custom properties. The first, sortCells[*i*].value, will contain the value celltxt, and the second, sortCells[*i*].row, will reference the row from which celltxt came.

13. After the for loop has finished in the runSort() function, you will have an array, sort-Cells, that contains all of the values in the column to be sorted and references to the rows that those cells came from. Next, you have to add commands to the function to sort that array. Add the following commands to the function:

    a. Declare a variable named **sortType** that is equal to the className value of the *i*th entry in the sortCols object collection, where *i* is the value of the sortIndex variable.

EXPLORE

    b. If sortType equals asort, sort the sortCells array using alphaCompare() as the comparison function that determines the sorting order. If sortType equals numsort, sort the sortCells array using numCompare() as the comparison function for the sorting.

    c. If sortDirection equals ascending, then apply the reverse() method to the sortCells array to reverse the order of the array values.

    d. Loop through all of the items in the sortCells array. For each item, append the object sortCells[*i*].row to the sortBody row group, where *i* is the counter variable used in the for loop.

    e. Run the colorColumns()function.

14. Create the **colorColumns()** function. The purpose of this function is to highlight the column upon which the table has been sorted. Add the following commands to the function:

    a. Loop through all of the items in the sortCols object collection. For each item, set the backgroundColor style to white.

    b. After the loop, change the backgroundColor style of the item in the sortCols object collection whose index value equals sortIndex to the color value (232, 255, 232).

15. Close the file, saving your changes, and then reload **stats.htm** in your Web browser. Verify that you can sort the entire table by clicking the column headings for each column. Also, verify that you can sort the direction by clicking the selection list in the first header row. Finally, verify that the column upon which the sorting is based is highlighted in the table.

16. Submit the completed project to your instructor.

Challenge | **Case Problem 4**

Create a JavaScript utility to extract lines from an online play.

Data Files needed for this Case Problem: bio_out.jpg, globe_out.jpg, plays.css, plays_out.jpg, scenetxt.js, son_out.jpg, strat_out.jpg, tempest.jpg, temptxt.htm

The World of Shakespeare   Clare Daynes, a professor of English literature at Midwest University, is working on a Web site of Shakespeare's works. She would like to give students who are doing textual analysis of the plays the ability to display only those lines spoken by selected characters. She has asked you to create a utility that generates a drop-down list containing all of the characters from a particular scene, listed in alphabetical order. When a student selects a character from the list, only those lines spoken by that character should be displayed. Figure 7-69 shows a preview of a Web page that fulfills Professor Daynes's request.

Figure 7-69

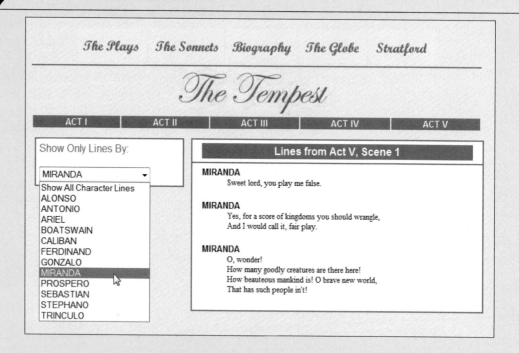

Professor Daynes has already created a Web page containing the text from the last act of *The Tempest*. The play text has been placed within a div element with the ID scene. The character names have been placed in h3 headings within that div element, with their lines following immediately after in blockquote elements. She has also created a div element with the ID characterList in which she wants the drop-down list box to be placed

She wants the content to be automatically generated by your utility. The HTML content of the list box should be

```
<p>Show Only Lines By:</p>
<select id = "cList">
   <option>Show All Character Lines</option>
   <option>Character 1</option>
   <option>Character 2</option>
...
</select>
```

where *Character 1* is the name of the first character in alphabetical order, *Character 2* is the name of the second character, and so on. To create a list of the characters from the scene, the following function has been provided for you:

```
uniqueElemText(elemName)
```

This function returns an array containing the unique text from HTML tags whose name equals *elemName*, sorted in order. For example, running the command

```
characterNames = uniqueElemText("h3")
```

creates an array named characterNames containing all of the unique character names found in h3 heading elements, sorted in alphabetical order.

Complete the following:

1. Use your text editor to open the **temptxt.htm** file from the tutorial.07\case4 folder, enter *your name* and *the date* in the comment section, and then save the file as **tempest.htm**. Create a link in the file to an external script file named **scene.js**.

2. Open the **scenetxt.js** file in your text editor, enter *your name* and *the date* in the comment section, and then save the file as **scene.js**.

3. Write a function that creates the contents of the character list box. Run the function when this page is loaded by the browser.

4. Add an event handler to the selection list you generated that runs a function to filter the contents of the scene whenever the user changes the selected character from the list.

5. Modify the function to filter the play so that it shows only the character name and succeeding lines for the selected character. All lines from other characters should be hidden. If the user selects Show All Character Lines, the entire scene should be displayed.

6. Test your Web page in your browser. Verify that only the lines from the selected character are displayed on the Web page, and that the entire scene is displayed if Show All Character Lines is selected.

7. Submit your completed Web site to your instructor.

Review | Quick Check Answers

Session 7.1

1. `innerHTML`
2. IE DOM: `innerText`
   W3C DOM: `textContent`
3. A node is part of the document object model that represents a particular type of content. Nodes can represent any element or object, including text strings, attributes, and HTML elements placed in either the head or body section of the document.
4. `parentNode`
5. `childNodes[2]`
6. The nodeType property returns the value 1. The nodeName property returns BLOCKQUOTE. The nodeValue property returns a null value.
7. `docText = document.createTextNode("U.S. Constitution");`
   `mainTitle = document.createElement("h2");`
8. `mainTitle.appendChild(docText);`

Session 7.2

1. `topList = document.createElement("ul");`
   `bottomList = document.createElement("ul");`
   `top.List.appendChild(bottomList);`
2. `listItem.parentNode.parentNode;`
3. because they are not considered child nodes of the node to which the attribute has been applied
4. `hasAttribute("type")`
5. `CBox = document.createElement("input");`
   `CBox.setAttribute("type", "checkbox");`
6. `CBox.type = "checkbox";`
7. `(CBox.type == "")`

Session 7.3

1. `listItem.insertBefore(imgObj, listItem.firstChild);`
2. `imgObj.style.display = "none";`
3. Recursion is a programming technique in which a function calls itself repeatedly until a stopping condition is met.
4. A preferred style sheet is a style sheet that has a rel attribute value of stylesheet and has been assigned a title. An alternate style sheet has a title but the rel attribute is alternate stylesheet. A persistent style sheet has the rel attribute of stylesheet but no title. Persistent styles are always loaded by the browser.

5. Use the object collection stylesheets, or reference the link element using the reference

    `document.getElementsByTagName("link")`

6. To enable the style sheet: *styleSheet*`.disabled = false;`

    To disable the style sheet: *styleSheet*`.disabled = true;`

7. W3C DOM: `document.styleSheets[2].cssRules[1]`

    IE DOM: `document.styleSheets[2].rules[1]`

Ending Data Files

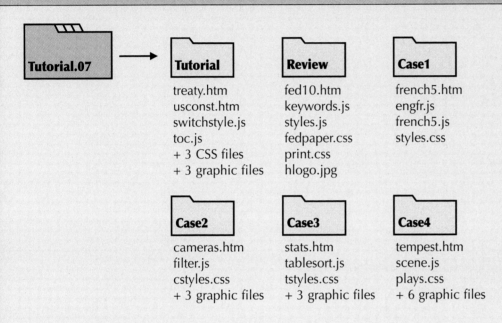

Tutorial.07 →

Tutorial

treaty.htm
usconst.htm
switchstyle.js
toc.js
+ 3 CSS files
+ 3 graphic files

Review

fed10.htm
keywords.js
styles.js
fedpaper.css
print.css
hlogo.jpg

Case1

french5.htm
engfr.js
french5.js
styles.css

Case2

cameras.htm
filter.js
cstyles.css
+ 3 graphic files

Case3

stats.htm
tablesort.js
tstyles.css
+ 3 graphic files

Case4

tempest.htm
scene.js
plays.css
+ 6 graphic files

Designing Rollovers and Slide Shows

Creating Dynamic Images

Case | Hipparchus

Alexis Richards manages a Web site named Hipparchus that contains articles and a discussion forum for people who share her interest in amateur astronomy. You have already helped Alexis set up her Web site and add new features. Now she wants you to create an interactive image gallery and slide show for users who want to view images from astronomy and space science.

Alexis doesn't want to purchase a commercial product to manage her images. Instead, you will use JavaScript to write an image gallery and slide show application. The program you write should be flexible and easily adapted to any page on her Web site. She also wants to be able to use the program without having to greatly modify the HTML code already written for her Web pages.

Starting Data Files

Tutorial.08 →

Tutorial
hipptxt.htm
slidetxt.js
galltxt.css
+ 1 CSS file
+ 49 graphic files

Review
nebulaetxt.htm
sctxt.js
controltxt.css
+ 1 CSS file
+ 52 graphic files

Case1
bookstxt.htm
adstxt.js
bannertxt.js
+ 11 HTML files
+ 2 CSS files
+ 27 graphic files

Case2
tilestxt.htm
tilestxt.js
kg.css
+ 12 graphic files

Case3
camtxt.htm
filmtxt.js
fstxt.css
+ 1 CSS file
+ 19 graphic files

Case4
summary.txt
+ 70 graphic files

Session 8.1

Setting up a Slide Show

You and Alexis discuss her interest in adding an image gallery and slide show application to the Hipparchus Web site. She has created a sample Web page describing the International Space Station (ISS) that you can use to test the JavaScript code you write. Alexis has collected 14 images of the ISS from the NASA Image Gallery for use in her slide show. She has placed thumbnails of those images in a box on the left edge of the Web page. Each thumbnail is linked to a large-resolution image file.

You will start by opening and reviewing this page.

To open and review the sample ISS Web page file:

1. Use your text editor to open the **hipptxt.htm** file from the tutorial.08\tutorial folder, enter **your name** and **the date** in the comment section of the file, and then save the file as **hipparchus.htm** in the same folder.

2. Review the HTML code in the file to become familiar with the document's structure and contents.

3. Open **hipparchus.htm** in your Web browser. Figure 8-1 shows the current appearance of the page.

Figure 8-1 | Initial hipparchus.com Web page

4. Click any of the 14 thumbnails from the slide show box and verify that your browser displays a large-resolution version of the image in a full browser window or tab.

Alexis wants you to modify this page so that users who click the thumbnail images see the large-resolution file overlaid on top of the current Web page. In addition, she wants users to be able to scroll back and forth through the images in the slide show using form buttons. A preview of the application you'll create for Alexis is shown in Figure 8-2.

Preview of the slide show application | Figure 8-2

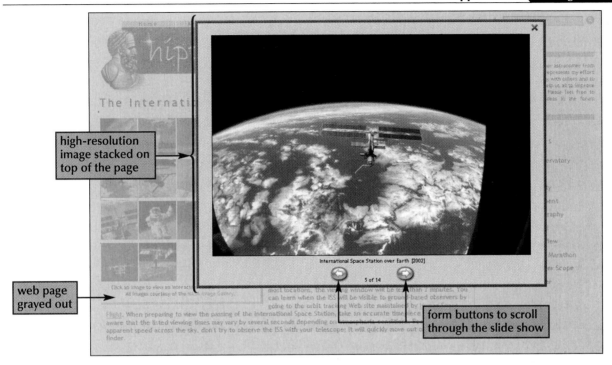

International Space Station over Earth [2002]

5 of 14

- high-resolution image stacked on top of the page
- web page grayed out
- form buttons to scroll through the slide show

Click an image to view an interactive...
All images courtesy of the NASA Image Gallery.

Marking Slide Images

The first challenge you face is marking the images in the Web page that are part of the slide show. Alexis needs a way to distinguish slide show images from other images on her Web site. She wants any inline image that is enclosed in a hypertext link *and* has a class name of slide to be considered a slide show image. You've already seen that each of the 14 thumbnails is marked as a hypertext link, so all you need to do is add a class attribute to the <img /> tags.

To mark the thumbnail images as slides:

▶ 1. Return to the **hipparchus.htm** file in your text editor.

▶ 2. Scroll down to the unordered list of 14 thumbnails and add the following attribute to each one, as shown in Figure 8-3:

```
class="slide"
```

Figure 8-3 ▶ **Slide show images marked**

slide show images
must have a class
name and be
marked as hypertext

```
<ul id="slides">
    <li><a href="slide01.jpg"><img src="slide01_thumb.jpg" class="slide"
        alt="Assembling the International Space Station [1998]" /></a></li>
    <li><a href="slide02.jpg"><img src="slide02_thumb.jpg" class="slide"
        alt="The Atlantis docks with the ISS [2001]" /></a></li>
    <li><a href="slide03.jpg"><img src="slide03_thumb.jpg" class="slide"
        alt="The Atlantis approaches the ISS [2000]" /></a></li>
    <li><a href="slide04.jpg"><img src="slide04_thumb.jpg" class="slide"
        alt="The Soyuz spacecraft undocks from the ISS [2001]" /></a></li>
    <li><a href="slide05.jpg"><img src="slide05_thumb.jpg" class="slide"
        alt="International Space Station over Earth [2002]" /></a></li>
    <li><a href="slide06.jpg"><img src="slide06_thumb.jpg" class="slide"
        alt="The International Space Station first expansion [2002]" /></a></li>
    <li><a href="slide07.jpg"><img src="slide07_thumb.jpg" class="slide"
        alt="Hurricane Ivan from the ISS [2008]" /></a></li>
    <li><a href="slide08.jpg"><img src="slide08_thumb.jpg" class="slide"
        alt="The Soyuz spacecraft approaches the ISS [2005]" /></a></li>
    <li><a href="slide09.jpg"><img src="slide09_thumb.jpg" class="slide"
        alt="The International Space Station from above [2006]" /></a></li>
    <li><a href="slide10.jpg"><img src="slide10_thumb.jpg" class="slide"
        alt="Maneuvering in space with the Canadarm2 [2006]" /></a></li>
    <li><a href="slide11.jpg"><img src="slide11_thumb.jpg" class="slide"
        alt="The International Space Station second expansion [2006]" /></a></li>
    <li><a href="slide12.jpg"><img src="slide12_thumb.jpg" class="slide"
        alt="The International Space Station third expansion [2007]" /></a></li>
    <li><a href="slide13.jpg"><img src="slide13_thumb.jpg" class="slide"
        alt="The ISS over the Ionian Sea [2007]" /></a></li>
    <li><a href="slide14.jpg"><img src="slide14_thumb.jpg" class="slide"
        alt="International Space Station fourth expansion [2009]" /></a></li>
</ul>
```

▶ **3.** Save the file.

One important consideration in writing any JavaScript application is providing a fall-back for users who run their browsers with JavaScript turned off (for security reasons). In this case, a user of a JavaScript-free browser can still view the high-resolution versions of the ISS images by clicking the thumbnail image.

Loading the Slide Images

Now that you've identified the slide show images, you are ready to begin writing the code for the slide show application. Alexis has an external JavaScript file in which you'll place all of your code.

To open the JavaScript file:

▶ **1.** Use your text editor to open the **slidetxt.js** file from the tutorial.08\tutorial folder, enter *your name* and *the date* in the comment section of the file, and then save the file as **slideshow.js** in the same folder.

▶ **2.** Return to the **hipparchus.htm** file in your text editor, and then add the following link to the head section of the document to access the code in the slideshow.js file:

```
<script src="slideshow.js" type="text/javascript"></script>
```

▶ **3.** Save the hipparchus.htm file.

The first part of your JavaScript code will be to set up the slide show. You'll place your code within a function named setupSlideshow() that runs when the page is initially loaded by the browser. Because Alexis' Web pages may have other scripts running when the page loads, you'll apply this function using the attachEvent() and addEventListener() methods of the IE and W3C event models. Alexis already placed a function named addEvent() reconciling the two event model methods into the slideshow.js file.

To run the setupSlideshow() function when the page loads:

▶ **1.** Return to the **slideshow.js** file in your text editor.

▶ **2.** Directly below the addEvent() function, insert the following code, as shown in Figure 8-4:

```
addEvent(window, "load", setupSlideshow, false);

function setupSlideshow() {

}
```

The setupSlideshow() function runs when the page loads ◀ **Figure 8-4**

```
function addEvent(object, evName, fnName, cap) {
    if (object.attachEvent)
        object.attachEvent("on" + evName, fnName);
    else if (object.addEventListener)
        object.addEventListener(evName, fnName, cap);
}

addEvent(window, "load", setupSlideshow, false);

function setupSlideshow() {

}
```

The setupSlideshow() function first needs to create an array of all slide show images in the current page. Because you already defined what constitutes a slide show image in the HTML code, you can apply this definition in your JavaScript code. The following code creates a new array named slides and then loops through the collection of inline images in the document, adding any image to the slides array that has a class name of slide and whose parent node is a hypertext link element:

```
var slides = new Array();

for (var i = 0; i < document.images.length; i++) {
    var thumb = document.images[i];
    if (thumb.className == "slide" && thumb.parentNode.tagName == "A") {
        slides.push(thumb);
    }
}
```

You will add this code to the setupSlideshow() function.

To populate the slides array:

▶ **1.** Within the setupSlideshow() function, insert the following code, as shown in Figure 8-5:

```
var slides = new Array();

// populate array of slide images
for (var i = 0; i < document.images.length; i++) {
    var thumb = document.images[i];

    if (thumb.className == "slide" && thumb.parentNode.tagName
== "A") {
        slides.push(thumb);
    }

}
```

Figure 8-5 ▶ **Array of slides created**

```
function setupSlideshow() {

    var slides = new Array();

    // populate array of slide images
    for (var i = 0; i < document.images.length; i++) {
        var thumb = document.images[i];

        if (thumb.className == "slide" && thumb.parentNode.tagName == "A") {
            slides.push(thumb);
        }

    }
}
```

> slide must have a class name of slide and be enclosed in a hypertext link

▶ **2.** Save the file.

Reference Window | **Referencing Inline Images**

- To reference the collection of inline images within a document, use the following object collection:
  ```
  document.images
  ```
- To reference a specific inline image, use
  ```
  document.images[idref]
  ```
  where *idref* is either the index number of the image object or the text of its id or name attribute.

Creating an Image Rollover

After the for loop is run, the slides array will contain all of the inline images from the current document that belong to the slide show. Alexis wants the Web page to include some visual indication of which images belong to the slide show and which are excluded. One way of doing this is with a rollover.

A **rollover** is a visual effect in which an object changes appearance in response to the pointer hovering over the object. One common way of creating a rollover is through CSS using the hover pseudo-class. For example, the following CSS styles display all hypertext links without an underline unless the user is hovering the pointer over the link:

```
a       {text-decoration: none}
a:hover {text-decoration: underline}
```

The hipparchus.com Web site contains several examples of hypertext rollovers, which you might have noticed when viewing the page in your Web browser. Alexis wants to extend this rollover effect to the slide images so that when the user hovers the pointer over the slide thumbnail, the browser displays a slightly different image. Figure 8-6 shows a grayscale thumbnail being replaced by a full-color rollover, which is what Alexis has in mind.

Image rollover ◀ Figure 8-6

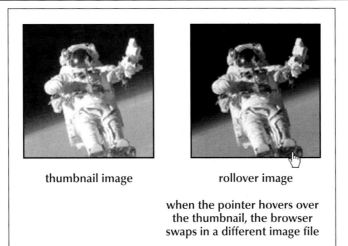

thumbnail image   rollover image

when the pointer hovers over
the thumbnail, the browser
swaps in a different image file

To create this effect, your code changes the source of the inline image from the original thumbnail to the rollover image. This can be done by changing the value of the src property

```
imgObject.src = rollover;
```

where *imgObject* is an image from the document and *rollover* is the image file for the rollover image. For example, the following code changes the source of the first inline image in the document to the rollover.jpg file:

```
document.images[0].src = "rollover.jpg";
```

Creating an Image Object

One problem with swapping in a new image is that it can slow down a user's interaction with the Web page as the browser pauses to load the new image file into memory. This can be avoided by preloading the image into an image object. An **image object** is a JavaScript object that stores an image. To create an image object, you run the command

```
var imgObject = new Image(width, height);
```

where *imgObject* is the new image, and *width* and *height* are optional parameter values that specify the size of the image. If you don't include *width* and *height* values, the browser determines the image's width and height from the image file itself.

Notice that the image object does not include a parameter for specifying the image source. That's accomplished by using the src property. For example, to create a new image object storing the rollover.jpg file, you could enter the following code:

```
var image1 = new Image();
image1.src = "rollover.jpg";
```

Besides the src property, image objects support all of the properties and attributes associated with the HTML <img> tag. Figure 8-7 summarizes some of the properties associated with image objects. In addition to the properties described in the table, you can also apply CSS styles to the image using the JavaScript style property.

Tip

If you know the image dimensions, include the width and height values to reduce the time it takes for the browser to process the image object.

Figure 8-7 | **Image object properties**

Property	Description	Example
imgObject.alt	Text alternate associated with *imgObject*	`image1.alt = "Hipparchus.com";`
imgObject.border	The size of the image border in pixels	`image1.border = 0;`
imgObject.complete	A Boolean value indicating whether the browser has completely loaded the image	`if (image1.complete) { commands}`
imgObject.height	The height of *imageObject* in pixels	`image1.height = 50;`
imgObject.hspace	The horizontal space around *imgObject* in pixels	`image1.hspace = 5;`
imgObject.id	The id associated with *imgObject*	`image1.id = "logo";`
imgObject.lowsrc	The URL of a low-resolution version of *imgObject*	`image1.lowsrc = "logo_small.jpg";`
imgObject.name	The name associated with *imgObject*	`image1.name = "logo";`
imgObject.src	The URL of the source of the image file	`image1.src = "logo.jpg";`
imgObject.vspace	The vertical space around *imgObject* in pixels	`image1.vspace = 3;`
imgObject.width	The width of *imgObject* in pixels	`image1.width = 250;`

Image objects created with the JavaScript `new Image()` command are not part of the document tree until they are attached to a particular node in the document tree, but they are loaded into the browser memory, available for quick retrieval. This means that all the rollover images are loaded into memory even as the page itself is loaded by the browser so that the user does not have to wait later on for the browser to retrieve and load the rollover image files.

Reference Window | **Creating an Image Object**

- To create an image object, run the command
  ```
  var imgObject = new Image();
  ```
  where *imgObject* is a variable that stores the image object.
- To set the dimensions of a new image object, use
  ```
  var imgObject = new Image(width, height);
  ```
  where *width* and *height* are the width and height of the image object in pixels.
- To define the source of an image object, use
  ```
  imgObject.src = url;
  ```
  where *url* is a text string containing the URL of the image file.

When a browser loads an image, it initially displays the image using the dimensions specified in the image file. You cannot determine an image's width and height before adding it to the Web page unless you access a program running on the Web server. After the image is added to the Web page, you can determine its width and height using the width and height properties of the image object.

Be aware that browsers treat the resizing process differently. If you change the width of an inline image under Firefox, Safari, or Opera, the browser automatically adjusts the height to maintain the proportions of the image. Similarly, if you change the image's height, those browsers adjust the image's width. Internet Explorer does not automatically adjust the size of an image; so if you reduce the width of an image, its height does not change in proportion and the image appears squashed. To correctly resize an image under Internet Explorer, you must determine the width-to-height ratio and then adjust the resized image accordingly.

Another effect of Internet Explorer's inability to automatically compensate for image dimension is that you cannot swap images of different sizes by simply changing the src property. Under Firefox, Safari, and Opera, the new image is displayed in the proper proportions. Under Internet Explorer, the new image takes the dimensions of the old image and can appear distorted if its dimensions are different. To solve this problem, replace the old image object with the new image object using the replaceChild() method. Internet Explorer and the other browsers will insert the new image object using that image's dimensions.

Defining Image Objects as Custom Properties

For Alexis' document, you'll define two image objects for each slide. One image object will be displayed when the pointer hovers over the thumbnail image; the other will be displayed when the pointer moves out and away from the thumbnail. One way of accomplishing this is with a custom property. A **custom property** is an object property defined by the programmer. These properties can contain text strings, numeric values, Boolean values, or other objects. For example, the following code defines a custom property named over that contains an image object and assigns that property to the image1 object:

```
image1.over = new Image();
```

The advantage of a custom property is that it becomes attached to the object and can be referenced throughout the program code. For the slide show application, you'll define two custom properties named over and out, storing image objects to be used when the pointer hovers over the thumbnail and then moves out and away from it. The code to define these properties will be stored in the createRollover() function, which has the following initial code:

```
function createRollover(thumb) {
   thumb.out = new Image();
   thumb.over = new Image();
}
```

When you run this function, the thumb object will be attached to two new image objects under the custom properties out and over. You will add this function to the slideshow.js file, and then run the function for each image in the slides array.

To insert and apply the createRollover() function:

▶ **1.** Scroll to the bottom of the slideshow.js file, and then insert the following code:

```
function createRollover(thumb) {

    thumb.out = new Image();
    thumb.over = new Image();
}
```

▶ **2.** Return to the setupSlideshow() function, and then, at the bottom of the function, insert the following code that calls the createRollover() function for each slide image:

```
for (var i = 0; i < slides.length; i++) {

    // Create a rollover for each slide
    createRollover(slides[i]);

}
```

Figure 8-8 highlights the revised code in the file.

Figure 8-8 **The createRollover() function**

```
function setupSlideshow() {

    var slides = new Array();

    // populate array of slide images
    for (var i = 0; i < document.images.length; i++) {
        var thumb = document.images[i];

        if (thumb.className == "slide" && thumb.parentNode.tagName == "A") {
            slides.push(thumb);
        }

    }

    for (var i = 0; i < slides.length; i++) {

        // Create a rollover for each slide
        createRollover(slides[i]);                   ⟩◀── creates a rollover
                                                             for each slide
    }

}

function createRollover(thumb) {

    thumb.out = new Image();                   ⟩◀── two image objects created
    thumb.over = new Image();                          for each thumbnail
}
```

▶ **3.** Save the file.

You haven't yet specified the source of the out and over images. The source of the out image is easy to determine it's the same as the thumbnail image itself and is set using the following command:

```
thumb.out.src = thumb.src;
```

Determining the source of the over image is a bit more involved. You need to have a consistent naming convention that relates the filename of the thumbnail to the filename of the rollover image. In this case, Alexis decided that the filenames of the rollover images should contain the character string _over and thumbnail images should contain the text string _thumb. For example, the first thumbnail comes from the file slide01_thumb.jpg, so the corresponding rollover image is stored in the file slide01_over.jpg. The second set of image files are named slide02_thumb.jpg and slide02_over.jpg, and so on.

Entering the source of the over image then simply involves inserting the character string _over into the thumbnail filename. This can be accomplished using the following command:

```
thumb.over.src = thumb.src.replace(/_thumb/,"_over");
```

The command uses the replace() method and the regular expression /_thumb/ to replace the _thumb character string with the character string _over. So, a text string such as slide01_thumb.jpg would be replaced with slide01_over.jpg. The new text string is then used to identify the source of the rollover image.

You will add these two commands to the createRollover() function.

Tip

The thumbnail image and the rollover image should have identical dimensions; otherwise, the browser may distort the rollover to make it match the thumbnail's dimensions.

To specify the rollover image file sources:

▶ **1.** Scroll down to the createRollover() function in the slideshow.js file, and then insert the following commands, as shown in Figure 8-9:

```
thumb.out.src = thumb.src;
thumb.over.src = thumb.src.replace(/_thumb/, "_over");
```

Source of the out and over images specified ◀ **Figure 8-9**

```
function createRollover(thumb) {

    thumb.out = new Image();
    thumb.over = new Image();

    thumb.out.src = thumb.src;
    thumb.over.src = thumb.src.replace(/_thumb/, "_over");

}
```

replaces the _thumb from the slide filename with _over

▶ **2.** Save the file.

Using Anonymous Functions

The final part of the createRollover() function is to swap the images in response to the onmouseout and onmouseover events. To do this, you will add an anonymous function to the createRollover() function. Recall from the Insight box in Tutorial 6 that anonymous functions are functions that do not have a function name, but that can be inserted within other functions. One advantage of anonymous functions is that object references carry over into the anonymous function from the containing function. This frees you from having to define variables with global scope.

The anonymous function to swap the image object in response to the pointer hovering over the thumbnail is:

```
thumb.onmouseover = function() {
    thumb.src = thumb.over.src;
}
```

Note that the thumb object reference can be used within the anonymous function because it is defined within the containing function, createRollover().

The function to display the out image when the pointer moves out and away from the thumbnail is:

```
thumb.onmouseout = function() {
    thumb.src = thumb.out.src;
}
```

Applying an Anonymous Function to an Event

- To apply an anonymous function to an object event, enter
  ```
  object.onevent = function() {
      commands
  }
  ```
  where *object* is the object, *event* is the event, and *commands* are the commands to be run in response to the event.

You will add both anonymous functions to the createRollover() function, and then test your code.

To complete the createRollover() function:

Tip

You can create a three-state rollover with two rollover images by adding a third image object to the code and displaying that image in response to the onclick event.

1. Within the createRollover() function, insert the following commands, as shown in Figure 8-10:

```
thumb.onmouseout = function() {
    thumb.src = thumb.out.src;
}

thumb.onmouseover = function() {
    thumb.src = thumb.over.src;
}
```

Figure 8-10 | Anonymous functions used to swap images

```
function createRollover(thumb) {

    thumb.out = new Image();
    thumb.over = new Image();

    thumb.out.src = thumb.src;
    thumb.over.src = thumb.src.replace(/_thumb/, "_over");

    thumb.onmouseout = function() {
        thumb.src = thumb.out.src;
    }

    thumb.onmouseover = function() {
        thumb.src = thumb.over.src;
    }

}
```

displays the out image then the pointer moves out from the slide

anonymous functions called by the mouseout and mouse over events

displays the over image when the pointer moves over the slide

2. Save the file, and then reload **hipparchus.htm** in your Web browser.

3. Move the pointer over each of the 14 images in the ISS gallery and verify that the browser swaps each thumbnail with its corresponding rollover image in response to the mouseover event. See Figure 8-11.

Image rollover **Figure 8-11**

Click an image to view an interactive slide show of the ISS.
All images courtesy of the NASA Image Gallery.

Image Rollovers without JavaScript | InSight

The technique described in this session assumes that the user will be running JavaScript. This is not always the case, as many users turn off JavaScript for security reasons. You can still create an image rollover by using only CSS. The technique involves changing the background image of the object. For example, you can apply a background image to a hypertext link with an id of slide using the following CSS style:

```
a#slide {display: block; width: 200px; height: 100px;
        background-image: url(slide.jpg);
        background-repeat: no-repeat;
        background-position: top left;
}
```

Note that the CSS style defines the hypertext link as a block-level element that is 200 pixels wide by 100 pixels high. The style also sets the background image to the slide.jpg file placed in the upper-left corner of the object with no image tiling. In general, you want the size of the hypertext link to match the size of the image.

To change the background image in response to the pointer hovering over the object, you apply the following style using the hover pseudo-class

```
a#slide:hover {background-image: url(rollover.jpg)}
```

and the browser will change the background image to the rollover.jpg file. You can use the other pseudo-classes—link, visited, and active—to create different rollovers for unvisited links, previously visited links, and active links.

CSS rollovers are quick and easy to implement, but they are not programmable. You must specify each rollover image filename in your CSS style sheet. This makes them somewhat cumbersome to use with large Web sites that incorporate dozens and perhaps hundreds of constantly changing image files.

You show the revised Web page to Alexis. She likes the rollover effect of swapping the grayscale thumbnail images for the full-color thumbnails. In the next session, you will write code to display high-resolution versions of each thumbnail overlaid on the Web page.

Review | **Session 8.1 Quick Check**

1. What object collection references all of the inline images in the current document?
2. What code would you use to change the source of the second inline image to the newlogo.png file?
3. Specify the code to store an image object in the newImage variable.
4. Specify the code to store an image object 250 pixels wide by 150 pixels high in the newImage variable.
5. Specify the code to change the source of the newImage variable to the newlogo.png file.
6. Specify the code to attach an image object to the newImage variable as a custom property named rollover.

Session 8.2

Creating an Image Gallery

In this session, you'll examine how to display a high-resolution version of the slide show thumbnails you worked with in the previous session. Currently, you can view the high-resolution images by clicking any of the thumbnail slides on the Hipparchus Web page and the browser displays the images in a new browser window or tab. Alexis doesn't want users to jump away from her Web site in this fashion, and instead prefers the images to stack on top of the current Web page. To accomplish this, you'll create a gallery containing a high-resolution image. The initial HTML code for the gallery is:

```
<div id="galleryBox">
   <img id="gallerySlide" src="slide01.jpg" />
</div>
```

Although you could enter this code directly into the hipparchus.htm file, your goal is to create an application that requires minimal rewriting of the source Web page. Instead, you'll write a function to create the gallery and then append it to the body of the current document. Initially, you'll have the gallery display the first slide image. The initial code of the createGallery() function is:

```
function createGallery() {

   var galleryBox = document.createElement("div");
   galleryBox.id = "galleryBox";

   var slide = document.createElement("img");
   slide.id = "gallerySlide";
   slide.src = "slide01.jpg";
   galleryBox.appendChild(slide);

   document.body.appendChild(galleryBox);

}
```

You will add this function to the slideshow.js file.

To insert the createGallery() function:

▶ **1.** If you took a break after the previous session, make sure the hipparchus.htm, slideshow.js, and gallery.css files are open in your text editor, and the hipparchus.htm file is open in your Web browser.

▶ **2.** Return to the **slideshow.js** file in your text editor, scroll to the bottom of the file, and then insert the following code, as shown in Figure 8-12:

```
function createGallery() {

    var galleryBox = document.createElement("div");
    galleryBox.id = "galleryBox";

    // Insert a high-resolution slide
    var slide = document.createElement("img");
    slide.id = "gallerySlide";
    slide.src = "slide01.jpg";
    galleryBox.appendChild(slide);

    document.body.appendChild(galleryBox);

}
```

Initial createGallery() function ◀ **Figure 8-12**

▶ **3.** Save the file.

Alexis has already created a style sheet for the image gallery. The style declaration for the galleryBox object is:

```
#galleryBox {position: fixed; top: 15px; left: 200px; z-index: 1000;
            background-color: rgb(250, 220, 177); padding: 2px 10px;
            border: 5px ridge rgb(244, 168, 60);
            }
```

Notice that one feature of this style declaration is that it places the gallery in the Web page using fixed positioning, which keeps the gallery box fixed at a specific location in the browser window. Also note that the z-index is set to the high value of 1000, which keeps the gallery stacked on top of other objects on the page. The result of these two styles is that the slide gallery will appear to be in a separate box on top of the Web page.

You will open the gallery style sheet and connect it to the hipparchus.htm file.

To access the style sheet for the slide gallery:

▶ **1.** Open the **galltxt.css** file from the tutorial.08\tutorial folder with your text editor, enter *your name* and *the date* in the comment section, and then save the file as **gallery.css** in the same folder.

2. Return to the **hipparchus.htm** file in your text editor, and then, in the head section of the document, insert the following link element:

```
<link type="text/css" href="gallery.css" rel="stylesheet" />
```

3. Save and close the hipparchus.htm file.

Finally, Alexis wants the application to create the gallery only when the Web page actually contains a collection of slides. You can confirm this by verifying that the length of the slides array is greater than 0. You will check for this condition in the setupSlideshow() function, and then create and test the slide gallery.

To display the slide gallery:

1. Return to the **slideshow.js** file in your text editor.

2. Add the following code to the setupSlideshow() function, as shown in Figure 8-13:

```
if (slides.length > 0) {
    createGallery();
}
```

Figure 8-13 **Code to call the createGallery() function**

```
function setupSlideshow() {

    var slides = new Array();

    // populate array of slide images
    for (var i = 0; i < document.images.length; i++) {
        var thumb = document.images[i];

        if (thumb.className == "slide" && thumb.parentNode.tagName == "A") {
            slides.push(thumb);
        }

    }

    for (var i = 0; i < slides.length; i++) {

        // Create a rollover for each slide
        createRollover(slides[i]);

    }

    if (slides.length > 0) {
        createGallery();
    }

}
```

creates the gallery only if there are slides in the document

3. Save the file, and then reopen **hipparchus.htm** in your Web browser. The first slide in the ISS slide show appears on top of the other Web page contents. See Figure 8-14.

Initial appearance of the slide gallery | **Figure 8-14**

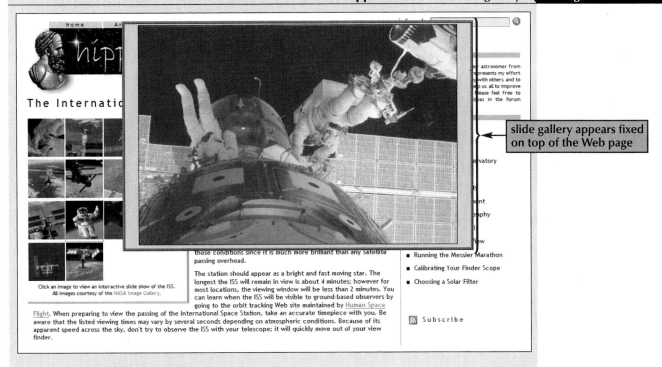

slide gallery appears fixed on top of the Web page

4. Resize the browser window, and then verify that as you scroll through the contents of the Web page, the slide gallery appears fixed in the same location within the window.

Creating Image Objects for the High-Resolution Images

The next step in designing the slide gallery is to place images from the slides array into it. Every thumbnail image on the Web page is associated with a high-resolution image. Alexis has set up the filenames so that it's easy to match each thumbnail with its high-resolution image. High-resolution images are identified by the exclusion of the text string _thumb, so that the slide01_thumb.jpg file is a thumbnail image for the slide01.jpg file, and so on. As with the rollover image object you created in the previous session, you'll create a custom property—this time to associate each thumbnail with a high-resolution version of the image. Once again, you want to preload the image objects so that the slide show runs smoothly as it switches from one image to another. The function to create and attach each thumbnail to a high-resolution image object is:

```
function createHighRes(thumb) {

    thumb.big = new Image();
    thumb.big.src = thumb.src.replace(/_thumb/, "");

}
```

In this case, the high-resolution version will be attached using a custom property named big and the source is set using the src property. The filename of the high-resolution file is determined by replacing the text string _thumb with an empty text string.

You will add this function to the slideshow.js file.

To create the setHighRes() function:

▶ **1.** Return to the **slideshow.js** file in your text editor.

▶ **2.** Insert the following function directly above the createRollover() function:

```
function createHighRes(thumb) {

    thumb.big = new Image();
    thumb.big.src = thumb.src.replace(/_thumb/, "");

}
```

▶ **3.** Call the createHighRes() function for each item in the slides array by scrolling up to the setupSlideshow() function and inserting the following code, as shown in Figure 8-15:

```
// Attach a high-resolution image object to each slide
createHighRes(slides[i]);
```

Figure 8-15	Code to set the high-resolution image objects

```
for (var i = 0; i < slides.length; i++) {

    // Create a rollover for each slide
    createRollover(slides[i]);

    // Attach a high-resolution image object to each slide
    createHighRes(slides[i]);
}

if (slides.length > 0) {
    createGallery();
}

}
function createHighRes(thumb) {

    thumb.big = new Image();
    thumb.big.src = thumb.src.replace(/_thumb/, "");
}
```

creates an image object containing the high-resolution version of the thumbnail

▶ **4.** Save the file.

Next, you want to use the big image object in the createGallery() function (rather than explicitly referencing the image file in the code). To do that, you must revise the create-Gallery() function so that it references the objects in the slides array.

To revise the createGallery() function:

▶ **1.** Go to the setupSlideshow() function, and then change the statement that calls the createGallery() function to:

```
createGallery(slides);
```

▶ **2.** Scroll down to the createGallery() function, and then change the opening function line to:

```
function createGallery(slides) {
```

▶ **3.** Change the lines that store the image source to:

```
slide.src = slides[0].big.src;
```

Figure 8-16 highlights the revised code in the file.

Revised createGallery() function ◄ Figure 8-16

```
        if (slides.length > 0) {
            createGallery(slides);
        }
    }

    function createHighRes(thumb) {

        thumb.big = new Image();
        thumb.big.src = thumb.src.replace(/_thumb/, "");

    }

    function createGallery(slides) {

        var galleryBox = document.createElement("div");
        galleryBox.id = "galleryBox";

        // Insert a high-resolution slide
        var slide = document.createElement("img");
        slide.id = "gallerySlide";
        slide.src = slides[0].big.src;
        galleryBox.appendChild(slide);

        document.body.appendChild(galleryBox);

    }
```

▶ **4.** Save the file, reload **hipparchus.htm** in your Web browser, and then verify that the Web page still shows the high-resolution version of the first slide in the image gallery.

Adding a Slide Caption

Alexis wants each slide in the gallery to be displayed with a caption. The caption text should be drawn from the value of the image's alt attribute. For example, the first slide's alt attribute value of Assembling the International Space Station [1998] should be entered as the slide's caption.

The captions will be entered into the gallery as the HTML code

```
<p id="slideCaption">caption</p>
```

where *caption* is the value of the slide's alt attribute. The following JavaScript code creates this HTML fragment:

```
var slideCaption = document.createElement("p");
slideCaption.id = "slideCaption";
slideCaption.innerHTML = slides[0].alt;
galleryBox.appendChild(slideCaption);
```

Alexis already created a style for the slide caption and added it to the gallery.css style sheet. You will add the code to generate the caption text to the createGallery() function.

Tip

Use descriptive and unique ID names in your JavaScript when creating new objects to avoid conflicts with pre-existing IDs in the user's Web page.

To create the slide caption:

▶ **1.** Return to the **slideshow.js** file in your text editor, and then, within the createGallery() function, insert the following code, as shown in Figure 8-17:

```
// Insert the slide caption
var slideCaption = document.createElement("p");
slideCaption.id = "slideCaption";
slideCaption.innerHTML = slides[0].alt;
galleryBox.appendChild(slideCaption);
```

Figure 8-17 ▸ **Code to add the slide caption**

```
function createGallery(slides) {

    var galleryBox = document.createElement("div");
    galleryBox.id = "galleryBox";

    // Insert a high-resolution slide
    var slide = document.createElement("img");
    slide.id = "gallerySlide";
    slide.src = slides[0].big.src;
    slide.index = 0;
    galleryBox.appendChild(slide);

    // Insert the slide caption
    var slideCaption = document.createElement("p");
    slideCaption.id = "slideCaption";
    slideCaption.innerHTML = slides[0].alt;
    galleryBox.appendChild(slideCaption);

    document.body.appendChild(galleryBox);

}
```

retrieves the caption text from the image's alt attribute

▸ **2.** Save the file, and then reload **hipparchus.htm** in your Web browser. The caption text is displayed below the slide image. See Figure 8-18.

Figure 8-18 ▸ **First slide with caption**

Assembling the International Space Station [1998]

This example assumed that the user created separate files for the thumbnail and the high-resolution images. One advantage to using separate files is that the thumbnail image can be cropped and reduced in size in a graphics program, making it faster to load. However, you can also create thumbnails using HTML and CSS.

One approach is to use the width and height attributes of the <img> tag to reduce the high-resolution image to thumbnail size. Note that the thumbnail image has the same file size as the high-resolution image because it comes from the same image file. Another approach is to use CSS to crop out portions of the high-resolution image to create the thumbnail. Again, this has the advantage of not requiring the Web author to create an extra file for each slide image. To crop an image with CSS, you use the clip property, which "cuts" a clipping rectangle out of the image. The style to define this clipping rectangle is

```
clip:rect(top right bottom left)
```

where *top* is the distance between the top of the rectangle and the top border of the image, *right* is the distance from the image's left border to the right side of the rectangle, *bottom* is the distance from the image top border to the bottom border of the rectangle, and *left* is the distance from the left edge of the image to the left border of the clipping rectangle. The difference between the *top* and *bottom* parameters and the *right* and *left* parameters provides the dimensions of the rectangle. For example, the following style creates a clipping rectangle that is 300 pixels wide by 150 pixels tall, and is located 100 pixels down and 50 pixels to the right of the upper-left corner of the image:

```
clip(100px 350px 250px 50px)
```

After you clip the image in the CSS style sheet, you can use JavaScript to restore the image by modifying the values of the clip style. You can also use time-based commands to "unfold" the clipped image a few pixels every few milliseconds, giving a dynamic appearance to the transitions in the JavaScript slide show.

Hiding and Viewing the Slide Gallery

So far, your code automatically displays the first slide when the Web page opens, but it covers up much of the Web page. Alexis wants you to revise the program so that users can easily open and close the slide gallery. You will start by adding an image button to the gallery box that will hide the gallery when clicked. The HTML code for the form button is:

```
<p id="galleryTitle">
    <input type="image" src="galleryclose.png" />
</p>
```

The JavaScript to generate this HTML fragment is:

```
var galleryTitle = document.createElement("p");
galleryTitle.id = "galleryTitle";

var closeButton = document.createElement("input");
closeButton.type = "image";
closeButton.src = "galleryclose.png";

galleryTitle.appendChild(closeButton);
galleryBox.appendChild(galleryTitle);
```

Tip

You can quickly create clickable images by entering the images as input image buttons and then providing an onclick event action.

As with the slide caption, Alexis already added styles to the gallery.css style sheet to format this content. You will add the code to generate the close button to the createGallery() function.

To insert the button image to close the gallery:

▶ **1.** Return to the **slideshow.js** file in your text editor, and then, within the createGallery() function, insert the following code, as shown in Figure 8-19:

```
// Insert a button to close the gallery
var galleryTitle = document.createElement("p");
galleryTitle.id = "galleryTitle";

var closeButton = document.createElement("input");
closeButton.type = "image";
closeButton.src = "galleryclose.png";

galleryTitle.appendChild(closeButton);
galleryBox.appendChild(galleryTitle);
```

Figure 8-19	Gallery close button

```
function createGallery(slides) {

    var galleryBox = document.createElement("div");
    galleryBox.id = "galleryBox";

    // Insert a button to close the gallery
    var galleryTitle = document.createElement("p");
    galleryTitle.id = "galleryTitle";

    var closeButton = document.createElement("input");
    closeButton.type = "image";
    closeButton.src = "galleryclose.png";

    galleryTitle.appendChild(closeButton);
    galleryBox.appendChild(galleryTitle);

    // Insert a high-resolution slide
    var slide = document.createElement("img");
    slide.id = "gallerySlide";
    slide.src = slides[0].big.src;
    galleryBox.appendChild(slide);
```

paragraph containing the close button

image form button

appends the button to the paragraph and the paragraph to gallery

▶ **2.** Save the file, and then reload **hipparchus.htm** in your Web browser. The slide shows a small red x in the upper-right corner of the gallery box. See Figure 8-20.

Figure 8-20	Gallery close button

close button

Assembling the International Space Station [1998]

To hide the gallery, set the display style of the gallery box to "none". By setting the display style to "none," the browser no longer displays the slide gallery but it remains part of the document structure. As with the rollover code from the first session, you'll insert the following code to hide the gallery with an anonymous function attached to the click event:

```
closeButton.onclick = function() {
   galleryBox.style.display = "none";
}
```

You will add this code to the createGallery() function, and then test it.

To test the gallery close button:

▶ **1.** Add the following code to the createGallery() function, as shown in Figure 8-21:

```
closeButton.onclick = function() {
   galleryBox.style.display = "none";
}
```

Event handler added to hide the gallery ◀ **Figure 8-21**

```
var closeButton = document.createElement("input");
closeButton.type = "image";
closeButton.src = "galleryclose.png";
closeButton.onclick = function() {
   galleryBox.style.display = "none";
}
```
sets the display style of the gallery to none when the close button is clicked

▶ **2.** Save the file, and then reload **hipparchus.htm** in your Web browser.

▶ **3.** Click the red close button located in the upper-right corner of the gallery. The gallery is hidden from the user.

Alexis wants users to be able to display the slide gallery by clicking any of the thumbnail images. To accomplish this, you'll create the showGallery() function, which will be run with the onclick event handler. You will add

```
thumb.onclick = showGallery;
```

to the createHighRes() function to associate the showGallery() function with the action of clicking one of the thumbnail images.

To call the showGallery() function:

▶ **1.** Return to the **slideshow.js** file in your text editor.

▶ **2.** Within the createHighRes() function, insert the following code, as shown in Figure 8-22:

```
// Display high-resolution image in slide gallery
thumb.onclick = showGallery;
```

Figure 8-22 ▶ Code to call the showGallery() function

Figure 8-22 ▶ Code to call the showGallery() function

```
function createHighRes(thumb) {

    thumb.big = new Image();
    thumb.big.src = thumb.src.replace(/_thumb/, "");

    // Display high-resolution image in slide gallery
    thumb.onclick = showGallery;◀──

}
```

displays the gallery when a thumbnail is clicked

▶ **3.** Save the file.

Next, you'll create the showGallery() function. The initial code of the showGallery() function is as follows:

```
function showGallery() {

    // Reveal the slide show
    document.getElementById("galleryBox").style.display = "block";

    // Halt propagation of the click event
    return false;

}
```

The first line of the function references the gallery box using the value of its ID attribute, and displays it by setting the display property to block. The function then needs to stop propagation of the click event to prevent the browser from acting on the hypertext link that encloses the thumbnail image and opening the high-resolution image in a new browser window. To halt the propagation of the click event, a value of false is returned by the function.

You will add the showGallery() function to the slideshow.js file.

To insert and test the showGallery() function:

▶ **1.** Scroll to the bottom of the slideshow.js file, and then insert the following code, as shown in Figure 8-23:

```
function showGallery() {

    // Reveal the slide show
    document.getElementById("galleryBox").style.display = "block";

    // Halt propagation of the click event
    return false;

}
```

Figure 8-23 ▶ Initial showGallery() function

```
function showGallery() {

    // Reveal the slide show
    document.getElementById("galleryBox").style.display = "block";

    // Halt propagation of the click event
    return false;

}
```

▶ **2.** Save the file.

The showGallery() function only reveals the gallery box; it does not change the slide image. To do that, you will create another function named changeSlide() that will replace the current slide image with a new slide. The changeSlide() function will also change the caption. The changeSlide() function has the following code:

```
function changeSlide(slide) {

    // Set object references
    var galleryBox = document.getElementById("galleryBox");
    var oldSlide = document.getElementById("gallerySlide");
    var slideCaption = document.getElementById("slideCaption");

    // Replace current slide with new slide
    var newSlide = oldSlide.cloneNode(true);
    newSlide.src = slide.big.src;
    galleryBox.replaceChild(newSlide, oldSlide);

    // Replace current caption with new caption
    slideCaption.innerHTML = slide.alt;

}
```

The changeSlide() function has a single parameter, which is slide, that references the slide you want to display in the gallery. The first three lines in the function set the object references to the gallery box, the slide image currently displayed in the gallery, and the paragraph containing the current slide caption. The function then replaces the current slide image with the new slide image associated with the slide parameter. Similarly, the function then replaces the current slide caption with the new caption.

You will add the changeSlide() function to the slideshow.js file.

To insert the changeSlide() function:

▶ **1.** Scroll to the bottom of the slideshow.js file, and then insert the following code, as shown in Figure 8-24:

```
function changeSlide(slide) {

    // Set object references
    var galleryBox = document.getElementById("galleryBox");
    var oldSlide = document.getElementById("gallerySlide");
    var slideCaption = document.getElementById("slideCaption");

    // Replace current slide with new slide
    var newSlide = oldSlide.cloneNode(true);
    newSlide.src = slide.big.src;
    galleryBox.replaceChild(newSlide, oldSlide);

    // Replace current caption with new caption
    slideCaption.innerHTML = slide.alt;

}
```

Figure 8-24 ▶ **Initial changeSlide() function**

```
function changeSlide(slide) {

    // Set object references
    var galleryBox = document.getElementById("galleryBox");
    var oldslide = document.getElementById("gallerySlide");
    var slideCaption = document.getElementById("slideCaption");

    // Replace current slide with new slide
    var newSlide = oldslide.cloneNode(true);
    newSlide.src = slide.big.src;
    galleryBox.replaceChild(newSlide, oldslide);

    // Replace current caption with new caption
    slideCaption.innerHTML = slide.alt;

}
```

defines the object references

replaces the current slide with the new slide image

replaces the current caption with the new slide caption

▶ **2.** Save the file.

Finally, you'll test your code by calling the changeSlide() function from the showGallery() function and running the revised code in your browser to verify that you can switch slides in the gallery by clicking thumbnail images from the Web page. The following command displays the slide associated with the clicked thumbnail:

```
changeSlide(this);
```

Note that the `this` keyword references the thumbnail that initiated the showGallery() function through the onclick event.

To call and test the changeSlide() function:

▶ **1.** Scroll up the showGallery() function, and then insert the following lines of code, as shown in Figure 8-25:

```
// Change the image based on the clicked thumbnail
changeSlide(this);
```

Figure 8-25 ▶ **Code to call the changeSlide() function**

```
function showGallery() {

    // Change the image based on the clicked thumbnail
    changeSlide(this);

    // Reveal the slide show
    document.getElementById("galleryBox").style.display = "block";

    // Halt propagation of the click event
    return false;
}
```

the this keyword references the thumbnail clicked by the user

▶ **2.** Save the file, and then reload **hipparchus.htm** in your Web browser.

▶ **3.** Click the different thumbnail images on the Web page and verify that the gallery image and caption change to reflect the selected thumbnail. You might need to close the gallery box to click some of the thumbnail images. See Figure 8-26.

Different slides selected to view | **Figure 8-26**

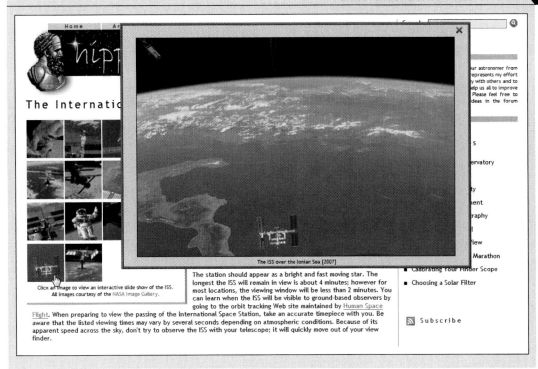

Currently, the slide gallery is displayed automatically when the page opens. You will change this by setting the display property of the gallery box to none in the gallery.css style sheet.

To hide the slide gallery when the page opens:

▶ **1.** Open the **gallery.css** file in your text editor.

▶ **2.** Add the following style to the galleryBox object, as shown in Figure 8-27:

```
display: none
```

Style changed to hide the slide gallery | **Figure 8-27**

```
#galleryBox   {position: fixed; top: 15px; left: 200px; z-index: 1000;
               background-color: rgb(250, 220, 177); padding: 2px 10px;
               border: 5px ridge rgb(244, 168, 60);
               display: none}
```

▶ **3.** Save the file, reload **hipparchus.htm** in your Web browser, and then verify that the slide gallery appears only when you click one of the thumbnails.

Alexis likes the pop-up style gallery that you created to view high-resolution versions of her slides. Next, she wants you to insert additional buttons in the gallery box to allow users to scroll forward and backward through the images in the slide show.

Review | Session 8.2 Quick Check

1. What CSS style do you use to place an object in a fixed location in the browser window?
2. Provide a regular expression and JavaScript method to replace the filename text string image01_slide.jpg with image01.jpg. Your code should be easily applicable to other similarly named image files.
3. Specify JavaScript code to insert the following HTML fragment in the current Web page document as the first child of the body element:

```
<div id="slideshow">
   <img src="slide01.jpg" alt="First Slide" />
   <p>First Slide</p>
</p>
```

   In your code, give the div element the object name slideShow; give the img element the object name slideImg; and give the paragraph the object name slideCaption.

4. Specify the code to hide the slideShow object on the Web page, but still keep it part of the Web page structure.
5. Specify the CSS style to clip an image element with the id slideImage, with a clipping rectangle that is 100 pixels wide by 150 pixels high, and that is located 50 pixels down and 75 pixels to the right of the upper-left corner of the image.
6. Specify the JavaScript code to reference the value of the alt attribute for the second inline image in the document.

Session 8.3

Navigating Through the Slide Gallery

In the previous session, you wrote code to display a high-resolution version of the thumbnail in the slide gallery. Now Alexis wants users to be able to move forward and backward through the images in the slide show. To provide this feature, you'll first add navigation buttons to the slide gallery. To create these buttons, you'll write code to add the following HTML fragment to the bottom of the slide gallery box:

```
<p id="galleryFooter">
   <input type="image" src="back.png" />
   <input type="image" src="forward.png" />
</p>
```

The styles to display the navigation buttons and the button images have already been provided by Alexis. The following code creates this HTML fragment:

```
var galleryFooter = document.createElement("p");
galleryFooter.id = "galleryFooter";

var slideBack = document.createElement("input");
slideBack.type = "image";
slideBack.src = "back.png";
galleryFooter.appendChild(slideBack);

var slideForward = document.createElement("input");
slideForward.type = "image";
slideForward.src = "forward.png";
galleryFooter.appendChild(slideForward);
```

You will add this code to the createGallery() function, and then append the gallery footer to the gallery box.

To add navigation buttons to the slide gallery:

▶ **1.** If you took a break after the previous session, make sure the hipparchus.htm, slideshow.js, and gallery.css files are open in your text editor, and the hipparchus.htm file is open in your Web browser.

▶ **2.** Return to the **slideshow.js** file in your text editor, and then scroll down to the createGallery() function.

▶ **3.** Directly above the line to append galleryBox to the document body, insert the following code to create the galleryFooter object:

```
// Create the gallery footer
var galleryFooter = document.createElement("p");
galleryFooter.id = "galleryFooter";
```

▶ **4.** Insert the following commands to create a navigation button to go to the previous slide in the slide show:

```
// Create a button to go to the previous slide
var slideBack = document.createElement("input");
slideBack.type = "image";
slideBack.src = "back.png";
galleryFooter.appendChild(slideBack);
```

▶ **5.** Insert the following commands to create a navigation button to go to the next slide in the slide show:

```
// Create a button to go to the next slide
var slideForward = document.createElement("input");
slideForward.type = "image";
slideForward.src = "forward.png";
galleryFooter.appendChild(slideForward);
```

▶ **6.** Add the following command to append the gallery footer to the gallery box:

```
galleryBox.appendChild(galleryFooter);
```

Figure 8-28 highlights the new code in the createGallery() function.

Navigation button code ◀ Figure 8-28

```
        // Insert the slide caption
        var slideCaption = document.createElement("p");
        slideCaption.id = "slideCaption";
        slideCaption.innerHTML = slides[0].alt;
        galleryBox.appendChild(slideCaption);

        // Create the gallery footer
        var galleryFooter = document.createElement("p");
        galleryFooter.id = "galleryFooter";

        // Create a button to go to the previous slide
        var slideBack = document.createElement("input");
        slideBack.type = "image";
        slideBack.src = "back.png";
        galleryFooter.appendChild(slideBack);

        // Create a button to go to the next slide
        var slideForward = document.createElement("input");
        slideForward.type = "image";
        slideForward.src = "forward.png";
        galleryFooter.appendChild(slideForward);

        galleryBox.appendChild(galleryFooter);

        document.body.appendChild(galleryBox);

}
```

gallery footer

button to go to the previous slide

button to go to the next slide

appends the footer to the slide gallery box

> **7.** Save the file, and then reload **hipparchus.htm** in your Web browser. The slide gallery box now displays a footer containing two navigation buttons. See Figure 8-29.

Figure 8-29 ▶ **Navigation buttons added to the slide gallery**

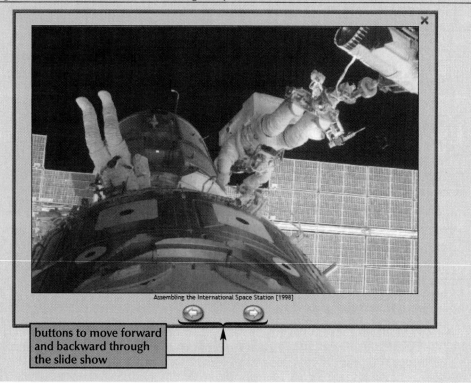

buttons to move forward and backward through the slide show

Keeping Track of the Slide Number

The next task is to program the actions of the navigation buttons. To go through the images in the slide gallery, you need to keep track of which slide is currently being displayed, and which images immediately precede and follow the current slide in the slides array. You can do this by attaching an index number to each slide as a custom property. The index number will derive its value from the position of the image in the slides array. You will revise the createHighRes() function created in the previous session, adding the custom index property to store these index numbers.

To modify the createHighRes() function:

> **1.** Return to the **slideshow.js** file in your text editor, and then scroll down to the createHighRes() function.

> **2.** Change the parameters of the function from `createHighRes(thumb)` to
>
> `createHighRes(thumb, index)`

> **3.** At the end of the function, insert the following code:
>
> ```
> // Set the index of the slide
> thumb.big.index = index;
> ```

▶ **4.** Scroll up to the setupSlideshow() function, and then change the line that calls the createHighRes() function to:

```
createHighRes(slides[i], i);
```

Figure 8-30 highlights the revised code.

Code to set the index property ◀ **Figure 8-30**

```
        for (var i = 0; i < slides.length; i++) {

            // Create a rollover for each slide
            createRollover(slides[i]);

            // Attach a high-resolution image object to each slide
            createHighRes(slides[i], i);

        }

        if (slides.length > 0) {
            createGallery(slides);
        }

    }

    function createHighRes(thumb, index) {

        thumb.big = new Image();
        thumb.big.src = thumb.src.replace(/_thumb/, "");

        // Display high-resolution image in slide gallery
        thumb.onclick = showGallery;

        // Set the index of the slide
        thumb.big.index = index;

    }
```

index values are based on the position of the slide in the slides array

adds the index value of each slide as a custom property

Examine the revised code you just entered. Notice that when the code loops through the slides array, it attaches the custom index property to each slide with the value taken from the position of the slide in the slides array. Because indexing starts with the value 0, the value of the index variable will range from 0 for the first slide up to one less than the length of the slides array. For example, the current Web page has 14 slides, so the value of the index variable is 0 for the first slide and 13 for the last slide.

The index value you derived also needs to be added as a custom property of the image that appears in the gallery box so the user always knows what image is currently being displayed. Because the gallery is created containing the first slide image, you'll set the initial value of the index to 0 and then change the index value each time the slide is changed.

To add an index property to the slide displayed in the gallery:

▶ **1.** Go to the createGallery() function in the slideshow.js file, and then insert the following command, as shown in Figure 8-31:

```
slide.index = 0;
```

Index value applied to the image displayed in the gallery ◀ **Figure 8-31**

```
        // Insert a high-resolution slide
        var slide = document.createElement("img");
        slide.id = "galleryslide";
        slide.src = slides[0].big.src;
        slide.index = 0;
        galleryBox.appendChild(slide);
```

gallery starts with the first image from the slides array so the index value is set to 0

▶ **2.** Scroll down to the changeSlide() function, and then insert the following command, as shown in Figure 8-32, to change the index values whenever the slide is changed:

```
newSlide.index = slide.big.index;
```

Figure 8-32 ▶ **Code to update the index value**

```
function changeSlide(slide) {

    // Set object references
    var galleryBox = document.getElementById("galleryBox");
    var oldSlide = document.getElementById("gallerySlide");
    var slideCaption = document.getElementById("slideCaption");

    // Replace current slide with new slide
    var newSlide = oldSlide.cloneNode(true);
    newSlide.src = slide.big.src;
    newSlide.index = slide.big.index;
    galleryBox.replaceChild(newSlide, oldSlide);

    // Replace current caption with new caption
    slideCaption.innerHTML = slide.alt;

}
```

> changes the index value to reflect the new slide in the gallery

3. Save the file.

With an index value set for the slide displayed in the gallery, you can navigate through the slide show by increasing or decreasing the index number and then loading the corresponding image from the slides array. This occurs every time the user clicks either the backward or the forward button in the gallery box. To apply this action to the backward button, you will attach the following anonymous function to the action of clicking the button:

```
slideBack.onclick = function() {
   var currentSlide = document.getElementById("gallerySlide");
   var currentIndex = currentSlide.index;

   currentIndex--;
   if (currentIndex == -1) currentIndex = slides.length -1;

   changeSlide(slides[currentIndex]);

}
```

This function first establishes a reference to the slide currently displayed in the gallery box and extracts the index number of that slide, storing it in the currentIndex variable. The function then decreases currentIndex by 1, because you're moving to the previous slide. You must then decide what to do after the display is moved all the way back to the first slide. In that case, Alexis wants the navigation buttons to work as a loop so that clicking the back button at the first slide jumps the user to the end of the slide show. To apply this, you use an if statement that tests whether the currentIndex variable is less than 0; if it is, you change its value to the length of the slides array minus 1—the index number of the last image in the slides array. Finally, you call the changeSlide() function created in the previous session to change the slide displayed in the gallery to the image in the slides array corresponding to currentIndex.

The anonymous function to move forward through the slide show is similar except that it increases the currentIndex variable by 1 and loops the slide show back to the first slide after the last slide is displayed. The following is the code for the forward button:

```
slideForward.onclick = function() {
   var currentSlide = document.getElementById("gallerySlide");
   var currentIndex = currentSlide.index;

   currentIndex++;
   if (currentIndex == slides.length) currentIndex = 0;

   changeSlide(slides[currentIndex]);

}
```

You will add both of these functions to the createGallery() function, and then test the code.

To apply code to the navigation buttons:

▶ **1.** Go to the createGallery() function, and then insert the following code, as shown in Figure 8-33, to set the operation of the back button in the slide gallery:

```
slideBack.onclick = function() {

    // Get the index of current slide
    var currentSlide = document.getElementById("gallerySlide");
    var currentIndex = currentSlide.index;

    // Decrease the index by 1
    currentIndex--;

    // If currentSlide is the first slide, go to the end
    if (currentIndex == -1) currentIndex = slides.length -1;

    // Change the image in the gallery
    changeSlide(slides[currentIndex]);

}
```

Code to set the operation of the back button ◀ Figure 8-33

```
// Create a button to go to the previous slide
var slideBack = document.createElement("input");
slideBack.type = "image";
slideBack.src = "back.png";
slideBack.onclick = function() {
    // Get the index of current slide
    var currentSlide = document.getElementById("gallerySlide");
    var currentIndex = currentSlide.index;

    // Decrease the index by 1
    currentIndex--;

    // If currentSlide is the first slide, go to the end
    if (currentIndex == -1) currentIndex = slides.length - 1;

    // Change the image in the gallery
    changeSlide(slides[currentIndex]);
}
galleryFooter.appendChild(slideBack);
```

gets the index of the current slide

decreases the value of the index

loads the new image in the gallery

▶ **2.** Directly above the command to append the slideForward object to the gallery-Footer object, insert the following code to set the operation of the forward button, as shown in Figure 8-34:

```
slideForward.onclick = function() {

    // Get the index of current slide
    var currentSlide = document.getElementById("gallerySlide");
    var currentIndex = currentSlide.index;

    // Increase the index by 1
    currentIndex++;

    // If currentSlide is the last slide, go to the start
    if (currentIndex == slides.length) currentIndex = 0;

    // Change the image in the gallery
    changeSlide(slides[currentIndex]);

}
```

Figure 8-34   Code to set the operation of the forward button

```
// Create a button to go to the next slide
var slideForward = document.createElement("input");
slideForward.type = "image";
slideForward.src = "forward.png";
slideForward.onclick = function() {

   // Get the index of current slide
   var currentSlide = document.getElementById("gallerySlide");
   var currentIndex = currentSlide.index;

   // Increase the index by 1
   currentIndex++;

   // If currentslide is the last slide, go to the start
   if (currentIndex == slides.length) currentIndex = 0;

   // Change the image in the gallery
   changeSlide(slides[currentIndex]);
}
galleryFooter.appendChild(slideForward);
```

gets the index of the current slide

loads the new image in the gallery

increases the value of the index

> **3.** Save the file, and then reload **hipparchus.htm** in your Web browser.

> **4.** Open the slide gallery, and then click the **back** and **forward** buttons in the slide gallery to verify that you can move from one slide to another.

> **5.** Click the **forward** button until you reach the last slide in the gallery, and then click the **forward** button again. The first slide at the beginning of the slide show is redisplayed as you attempt to go past the last slide in the gallery.

> **6.** Click the **back** button. The last slide at the end of the slide show is displayed as you attempt to go before the first slide in the gallery.

Displaying the Slide Number

Alexis is happy with the operation of the navigation buttons but wants the gallery to display the number of the current slide and the total number of slides in the gallery. To add this information to the gallery, you'll insert the HTML fragment

```
<span id="slideNumber">number</span> of total
```

between the back and forward buttons, where *number* is the number of the current slide being displayed and *total* is the total number of slides. This information is already stored in the index property and in the length of the slides array. Note that you have to add 1 to the value of the index value because indexing starts with the value 0, not 1.

Because the slide gallery initially contains the first image from the slides array, you can write this HTML fragment with the following code:

```
var slideNum = document.createElement("span");
slideNum.id = "slideNumber";
slideNum.innerHTML = "1";

var slideTotal = document.createTextNode(" of " + slides.length);
```

Then, you append both the span element and the text node to the gallery footer using the commands:

```
galleryFooter.appendChild(slideNum);
galleryFooter.appendChild(slideTotal);
```

You will add these commands to the createGallery() function.

To display the slide number and total slides:

▶ **1.** Return to the **slideshow.js** file in your text editor, and then go to the createGallery() function.

▶ **2.** Directly after the command to append the back button to the galleryFooter object, insert the following commands, as shown in Figure 8-35:

```
// Show the initial slide number
var slideNum = document.createElement("span");
slideNum.id = "slideNumber";
slideNum.innerHTML = "1";

// Show the total number of slides
var slideTotal = document.createTextNode(" of " + slides.length);

galleryFooter.appendChild(slideNum);
galleryFooter.appendChild(slideTotal);
```

Code to display the slide number and total slides ◀ **Figure 8-35**

```
          // Change the image in the gallery
          changeSlide(slides[currentIndex]);
     }
     galleryFooter.appendChild(slideBack);

     // Show the initial slide number
     var slideNum = document.createElement("span");
     slideNum.id = "slideNumber";
     slideNum.innerHTML = "1";

     // Show the total number of slides
     var slideTotal = document.createTextNode(" of " + slides.length);

     galleryFooter.appendChild(slideNum);
     galleryFooter.appendChild(slideTotal);
```

sets the initial slide number to 1

appends the slide number and count of total slides to the gallery footer

displays the number of images in the slides array

Every time the image displayed in the gallery changes, the slide number should change to match the current slide. Because you placed the slide number within a <span> tag with the id slideNumber, you can update this value by referencing that object and changing its text.

To change the slide number:

▶ **1.** Scroll down to the changeSlide() function.

▶ **2.** Directly after the command that declares the slideCaption variable, insert the following command to set the object reference of the slideNum variable:

```
var slideNum = document.getElementById("slideNumber");
```

▶ **3.** At the bottom of the function, insert the following command to update the text in the <span> tag so that the slide number is one more than the index value of the current slide:

```
// Update the slide number
slideNum.innerHTML = newSlide.index + 1;
```

Figure 8-36 highlights the new code in the changeSlide() function.

Figure 8-36 ▶ **Code to change the slide number**

```
function changeSlide(slide) {

    // Set object references
    var galleryBox = document.getElementById("galleryBox");
    var oldSlide = document.getElementById("gallerySlide");
    var slideCaption = document.getElementById("slideCaption");
    var slideNum = document.getElementById("slideNumber");

    // Replace current slide with new slide
    var newSlide = oldSlide.cloneNode(true);
    newSlide.src = slide.big.src;
    newSlide.index = slide.big.index;
    galleryBox.replaceChild(newSlide, oldSlide);

    // Replace current caption with new caption
    slideCaption.innerHTML = slide.alt;

    // Update the slide number
    slideNum.innerHTML = newSlide.index + 1;
}
```

> creates an object reference to the <span> tag containing the number of the current slide

> changes the slide number to match the currently displayed slide

▶ **4.** Save the file, and then reload **hipparchus.htm** in your Web browser.

▶ **5.** Navigate through the slide show and verify that the gallery contains text displaying the number of the current slide and the total count of slides. See Figure 8-37.

Figure 8-37 ▶ **Gallery with the current slide number and the total count of slides**

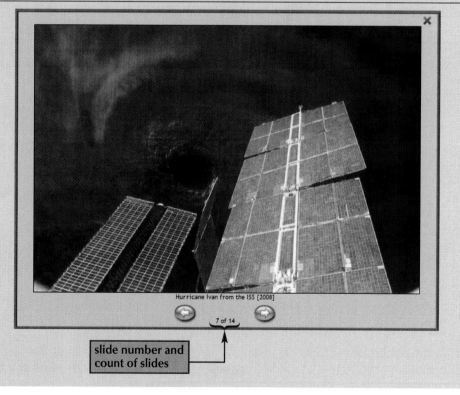

Hurricane Ivan from the ISS [2008]

7 of 14

> slide number and count of slides

Creating a Page Overlay

Alexis has spent some time working with the slide gallery. Although it is easy to use, she's concerned that the slide gallery blends in with the Web page background, making it difficult to view. She wants you to de-emphasize the Web page background while the slide gallery is active. She suggests that you display a semitransparent overlay on top of the Web page when the slide gallery is active so that users can still view the Web page while the slide gallery box is highlighted. Figure 8-38 shows the concept that Alexis has in mind for the slide show application.

Page overlay applied to a Web page — Figure 8-38

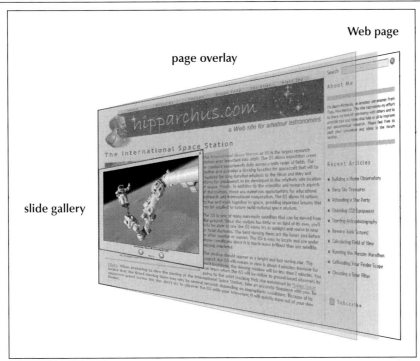

To design the page overlay effect, you'll first write the following HTML fragment to the Web page:

```
<div id = "pageOverlay"></div>
```

Note that although the overlay doesn't contain any text, it must be sized correctly to cover the Web page when the slide gallery is in use. You will create this object and append it to the document body.

To create the page overlay:

1. Return to the **slideshow.js** file in your text editor.

2. At the bottom of the file, insert the following function, as shown in Figure 8-39:

```
function createOverlay() {
    // Create an overlay to obscure the view of the Web page
    var pageOverlay = document.createElement("div");
    pageOverlay.id = "pageOverlay";

    document.body.appendChild(pageOverlay);
}
```

The createOverlay() function — Figure 8-39

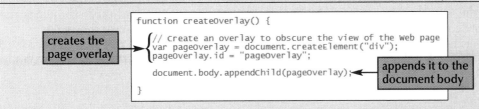

```
function createOverlay() {

    // Create an overlay to obscure the view of the Web page
    var pageOverlay = document.createElement("div");
    pageOverlay.id = "pageOverlay";

    document.body.appendChild(pageOverlay);

}
```

creates the page overlay

appends it to the document body

▶ **3.** Scroll up to the setupSlideshow() function, and then insert the following function to generate the page overlay whenever slides are present on the Web page, as shown in Figure 8-40:

```
createOverlay();
```

Figure 8-40 ▶ **Code to call the createOverlay() function**

```
if (slides.length > 0) {
    createGallery(slides);
    createOverlay();  ◀—— creates the overlay when
}                          slides are present
}
```

▶ **4.** Save the file.

You'll define the appearance of the overlay by adding new styles to the gallery.css style sheet. You want the page overlay to be fixed at the upper-left corner of the browser window so that, like the slide gallery, it does not scroll with the Web page. The window width and height will be set to 100% so that it covers the complete browser window at any size. You'll set the z-index value to 999 to display the page overlay above the Web page contents but underneath the slide gallery (which has a z-index value of 1000). For now, you'll set the background color of the page overlay to light gray with the color value (211, 211, 211). The initial display property of the pageOverlay will be set to none to hide it from the user until the gallery is displayed.

You'll add these styles to the gallery.css file.

To set the appearance of the page overlay:

▶ **1.** Go to the **gallery.css** file in your text editor.

▶ **2.** At the bottom of the file, insert the following style declaration, as shown in Figure 8-41:

```
div#pageOverlay {display: none;
                 position: fixed; top: 0px; left: 0px;
                 width: 100%; height: 100%;
                 z-index: 999;
                 background-color: rgb(211, 211, 211)
                 }
```

Figure 8-41 ▶ **Styles for the page overlay**

```
/* Styles for the semi-transparent overlay */

div#pageOverlay {display: none;
                 position: fixed; top: 0px; left: 0px;      styles to fix the
                 width: 100%; height: 100%;             ◀—— page overlay in
                 z-index: 999;                               the browser
                 background-color: rgb(211, 211, 211)        window
                 }
```

▶ **3.** Save the file.

The overlay should appear whenever the slide gallery is displayed and should be hidden whenever the slide gallery is hidden. To display the page overlay, you'll set the display style property of the pageOverlay object to block whenever the user shows the contents of the gallery in the browser window. When the user closes the slide gallery by clicking the close button, the display style of the page overlay should be reset to none to hide it from the user.

To display and hide the page overlay:

▶ **1.** Return to the **slideshow.js** file in your text editor.

▶ **2.** Scroll down to the showGallery() function, and then insert the following command to display the page overlay, as shown in Figure 8-42:

```
document.getElementById("pageOverlay").style.display = "block";
```

Code to display the page overlay ◀ **Figure 8-42**

```
function showGallery() {

    // Change the image based on the clicked thumbnail
    changeSlide(this);

    // Reveal the slide show
    document.getElementById("galleryBox").style.display = "block";
    document.getElementById("pageOverlay").style.display = "block";

    // Halt propagation of the click event
    return false;

}
```

▶ **3.** Scroll up to the createGallery() function, and then insert the following command to hide the page overlay, as shown in Figure 8-43:

```
document.getElementById("pageOverlay").style.display = "none";
```

Code to hide the page overlay ◀ **Figure 8-43**

```
function createGallery(slides) {

    var galleryBox = document.createElement("div");
    galleryBox.id = "galleryBox";

    // Insert a button to close the gallery
    var galleryTitle = document.createElement("p");
    galleryTitle.id = "galleryTitle";

    var closeButton = document.createElement("input");
    closeButton.type = "image";
    closeButton.src = "galleryclose.png";
    closeButton.onclick = function() {
        galleryBox.style.display = "none";
        document.getElementById("pageOverlay").style.display = "none";
    }
```

▶ **4.** Save the file, and then reload **hipparchus.htm** in your Web browser.

▶ **5.** Open and close the slide gallery to verify that the page overlay is displayed (hiding the contents of the Web page) when the gallery is open and that the page overlay is hidden when the gallery is closed. See Figure 8-44.

Figure 8-44   **Page overlay displayed and hidden**

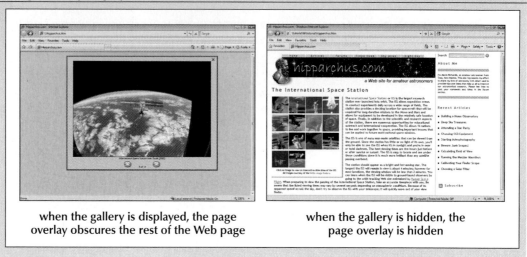

when the gallery is displayed, the page overlay obscures the rest of the Web page

when the gallery is hidden, the page overlay is hidden

Working with Opacity Values

The next step is to make the page overlay semitransparent so that the rest of the Web page can be dimly seen through it. To create the illusion of semitransparency in a Web page object, you must change the object's opacity. **Opacity** defines the percentage to which an object is nontransparent or opaque. An opaque object obscures anything it covers, whereas a transparent object allows images of underlying objects to come through. By default, all Web page objects are 100% opaque unless a different opacity value is applied.

Figure 8-45 shows an example of five different opacity percentages applied to the same object.

Figure 8-45   **Object with different opacity percentages**

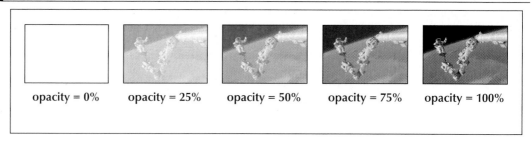

opacity = 0%   opacity = 25%   opacity = 50%   opacity = 75%   opacity = 100%

Setting Opacity with CSS

Internet Explorer and non-IE browsers allow programmers to change the opacity value through either a CSS style or a JavaScript command, but the syntax in each is different. Internet Explorer supports the use of **filters**, which are styles that affect the color, shape, or appearance of an object. One of the many filters IE supports is the alpha filter, which is used to apply transparency effects to selected objects. The alpha filter style has the following syntax:

```
filter: alpha(opacity = value)
```

The IE opacity style is only one of a library of filters supported by Internet Explorer. The general syntax of IE's filter styles is

```
filter: filter_name(params)
```

where *filter_name* is the name of the filter and *params* are parameters that control the application of the filter. You can learn more about all of the IE filters and how to apply them in Appendix G.

Non-IE browsers such as Firefox, Opera, and Safari do not support filters. Instead, those browsers set the opacity of an object by using the CSS style

```
opacity: value
```

where *value* ranges from 0 for a completely transparent object to 1 for a completely opaque object. For example, an opacity value of 75 under the IE filter style matches an opacity value of 0.75 under the CSS opacity style.

Alexis wants you to set the opacity of the page overlay to 80% by adding the appropriate styles to the gallery.css style sheet.

To set the opacity of the page overlay:

▶ **1.** Return to the **gallery.css** file in your text editor.

▶ **2.** Add the following styles to the #pageOverlay element, as shown in Figure 8-46:

```
filter: alpha(opacity = 80); opacity: 0.80
```

Page overlay opacity set   Figure 8-46

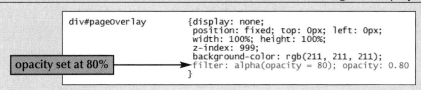

```
div#pageOverlay        {display: none;
                        position: fixed; top: 0px; left: 0px;
                        width: 100%; height: 100%;
                        z-index: 999;
                        background-color: rgb(211, 211, 211);
                        filter: alpha(opacity = 80); opacity: 0.80
                        }
```

opacity set at 80%

▶ **3.** Save and close the gallery.css file.

▶ **4.** Reload **hipparchus.htm** in your Web browser and run the gallery. The overlay is now semitransparent. See Figure 8-47.

Figure 8-47 ▶ **Slide show with semitransparent overlay**

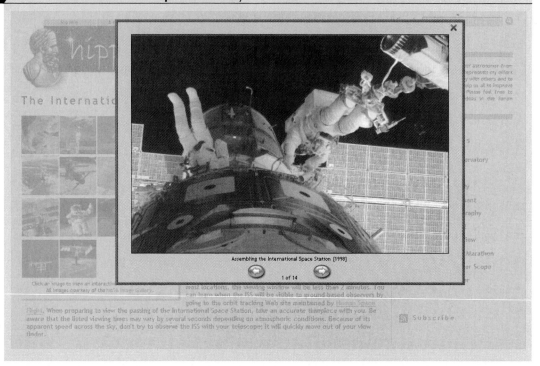

Assembling the International Space Station [1998]

1 of 14

Reference Window | **Setting Opacity with CSS**

- To set the opacity value for objects under Internet Explorer, use the style
  ```
  filter: alpha(opacity = value)
  ```
  where *value* ranges from 0 (completely transparent) to 100 (completely opaque).
- To set the opacity under non-IE browsers, use the style
  ```
  opacity: value
  ```
  where *value* ranges from 0 (completely transparent) to 1 (completely opaque).

Setting Opacity with JavaScript

The CSS opacity styles can also be set in your JavaScript program for both Internet Explorer and non-IE browsers. Internet Explorer allows users to set a filter using the command

```
object.style.filter = filter;
```

where *filter* is the CSS style of one of IE's many filters. For example, to set the opacity of the pageOverlay object to 80% using JavaScript, you could enter the following code:

```
var pageOverlay = document.getElementById("pageOverlay");
pageOverlay.style.filter = "filter: alpha(opacity = 80)";
```

Internet Explorer also supports the filters object collection, which contains all of the filters defined for a particular object. You can reference a specific filter from that collection using the expression

```
object.filters[filter].param
```

or

```
object.filters.filter.param
```

where *filter* is again the name of one of the IE filters or an index number of a filter in the collection, and *param* is a parameter value associated with that filter. Thus, you could also set the opacity of the pageOverlay object using the command

```
pageOverlay.filters["alpha"].opacity = 80;
```

or

```
pageOverlay.filters.alpha.opacity = 80;
```

Non-IE browsers set the opacity as a style property, so the JavaScript code is

```
object.style.opacity = value;
```

where *value* ranges from 0 to 1 (*not* from 0 to 100 as under Internet Explorer). To accommodate both types of browsers, you can use the following function:

```
function setOpacity(objID, value) {
   var object = document.getElementById(objID);

   object.style.filter = "alpha(opacity = " + value + ")";
   object.style.opacity = value/100;
}
```

The setOpacity() function allows users to specify the ID value of an object in the current Web page and an opacity value ranging from 0 to 100 to be applied to that object. If the browser is Internet Explorer, the function writes a text string applying the alpha filter with the specified opacity value to the object. Browsers that do not support the filter style instead apply the opacity style, dividing the opacity value by 100 so that it ranges from 0 to 1 in the command.

You will add the setOpacity() function to the slideshow.js file.

Tip

To reference the filters collection in a JavaScript command, the filter for the object must already be defined elsewhere in the program code or in the document's style sheet.

To insert the setOpacity() function:

▶ **1.** Return to the **slideshow.js** file in your text editor.

▶ **2.** Scroll to the bottom of the file, and then insert the following code, as shown in Figure 8-48:

```
function setOpacity(objID, value) {

   var object = document.getElementById(objID);

   // Apply the opacity value for IE and non-IE browsers
   object.style.filter = "alpha(opacity = " + value + ")";
   object.style.opacity = value/100;
}
```

Figure 8-48 ▷ **The setOpacity function**

```
function setOpacity(objID, value) {

    var object = document.getElementById(objID);

    // Apply the opacity value for IE and non-IE browsers
    object.style.filter = "alpha(opacity = " + value + ")";
    object.style.opacity = value/100;

}
```

Reference Window | **Setting Opacity with JavaScript**

- To set the opacity value for objects under Internet Explorer, use the object property
  ```
  object.style.filter = "alpha(opacity = value)";
  ```
  where *object* is the object and *value* is the opacity level ranging from 0 to 100.
- If filters have been defined for the object under IE, use
  ```
  object.filters["alpha"].opacity = value;
  ```
  or
  ```
  object.filters.alpha.opacity = value;
  ```
- To set the opacity under non-IE browsers, use
  ```
  object.style.opacity = value;
  ```
  where *value* ranges from 0 to 1.

Creating Fade-Ins and Fade-Outs

Alexis likes the effect of the semitransparent page overlay, but wants you to create a **fade-in effect** in which the opacity changes over time from completely transparent to completely opaque. Applying a visual effect such as changing the opacity over time is called a **transition**. To create a fade-in transition, you use JavaScript's setTimeout() method to set different opacity values at different delay times. For example, the following series of commands uses the setTimeout() method to run the setOpacity() function, changing the opacity value of the gallerySlide object from 0% up to 100% in increments of 20% over an interval of 2000 milliseconds or 2 seconds:

```
setTimeout("setOpacity('gallerySlide', 0)", 0);
setTimeout("setOpacity('gallerySlide', 20)", 400);
setTimeout("setOpacity('gallerySlide', 40)", 800);
setTimeout("setOpacity('gallerySlide', 60)", 1200);
setTimeout("setOpacity('gallerySlide', 80)", 1600);
setTimeout("setOpacity('gallerySlide', 100)", 2000);
```

Of course, it's more efficient to put these series of commands into a for loop. The following code accomplishes the same thing, but in this case it changes the opacity from 0% up to 100% in 1% increments and a time interval of 20 milliseconds between changes:

```
for (var i = 0; i <= 100; i++) {
    setTimeout("setOpacity('gallerySlide'," + i + ")", i*20);
}
```

The following fadeIn() function provides a more general application of the fade-in transition:

```
function fadeIn(objID, maxOpacity, fadeTime, delay) {

   var fadeInt = Math.round(fadeTime*1000)/maxOpacity;

   for (var i = 0; i <= maxOpacity; i++) {
      setTimeout("setOpacity('" + objID + "', " + i + ")", delay);
      delay += fadeInt;
   }

}
```

The fadeIn() function has the following four parameters:

1. The objID parameter contains the ID value of an object in the current Web page.
2. The maxOpacity value contains a value from 0 to 100 that represents the maximum opacity of the object fade-in.
3. The fadeTime parameter indicates the length of the transition in seconds.
4. The delay parameter indicates the initial time delay before starting the transition.

   The function first calculates the fadeInt variable, which stores the time interval in milliseconds between changes in the opacity level. The function then loops in 1% increments from 0% up to maxOpacity. Each time through the loop, the function runs the setOpacity() function for the object, setting the opacity value to a higher and higher level. The delay before that new opacity value is applied increases each time through the loop as well to create the visual effect of an object constantly increasing in opacity over the length of the fadeTime parameter.

   You can create a similar function to generate a **fade-out effect** in which an object changes from being opaque to completely transparent. The code for the fadeOut() function is:

```
function fadeOut(objID, maxOpacity, fadeTime, delay) {

   var fadeInt = Math.round(fadeTime*1000)/maxOpacity;

   for (var i = maxOpacity; i >= 0; i--) {
      setTimeout("setOpacity('" + objID + "', " + i + ")", delay);
      delay += fadeInt;
   }

}
```

This function assumes that the object starts at a maximum opacity, as indicated by the maxOpacity variable, and goes down to 0% opacity over the course of fadeTime seconds. Note that the for loop uses the decrement operator to decrease the value of the counter variable i, so that the opacity is always decreasing or fading out.

   You will add both the fadeIn() and fadeOut() functions to the slideshow.js file.

To insert the fadeIn() and fadeOut() functions:

▶ 1. Scroll to the bottom of the slideshow.js file, and then insert the following code for the fadeIn() function:

```
function fadeIn(objID, maxOpacity, fadeTime, delay) {

    // Calculate the interval between opacity changes
    var fadeInt = Math.round(fadeTime*1000)/maxOpacity;

    // Loop up the range of opacity values
    for (var i = 0; i <= maxOpacity; i++) {
        setTimeout("setOpacity('" + objID + "', " + i + ")", delay);
        delay += fadeInt;
    }

}
```

▶ 2. Below the fadeIn() function, insert the following code for the fadeOut() function:

```
function fadeOut(objID, maxOpacity, fadeTime, delay) {

    // Calculate the interval between opacity changes
    var fadeInt = Math.round(fadeTime*1000)/maxOpacity;

    // Loop down the range of opacity values
    for (var i = maxOpacity; i >= 0; i--) {
        setTimeout("setOpacity('" + objID + "', " + i + ")", delay);
        delay += fadeInt;
    }

}
```

Figure 8-49 shows the inserted code.

| Figure 8-49 | The fadeIn() and fadeOut() functions |

gradually fades in the object

gradually fades out the object

Applying a Fade-In

With the three functions you just entered, you can complete the slide show application by adding fade-in and fade-out effects. To create a fade-in effect for an object, you'll do the following:

1. Set the opacity of the object to 0% to make it completely transparent.
2. Add the object to the Web page in its current transparent state.
3. Fade the object into view by increasing its opacity over time to 100%.

You'll start by modifying the transition between one slide and another.

To insert a fade-in transition between slides:

▶ **1.** Go to the changeSlide() function in the slideshow.js file, and then, directly below the comment `//Replace current slide with new slide`, insert the following command:

```
setOpacity("gallerySlide", 0);
```

This command makes the slide currently displayed in the gallery completely transparent. When you clone oldSlide in the next command line, the opacity value will be copied to newSlide, making that slide transparent as well.

▶ **2.** Scroll down the function, and directly after the line to replace oldSlide with newSlide, insert the following command:

```
fadeIn("gallerySlide", 100, 0.5, 0);
```

This command reveals the new slide from its current transparent state over a half-second interval. The delay parameter is set to 0 so that the fade-in transition starts immediately. When the fade-in is completed, the slide will have an opacity value of 100%, making it completely visible in the gallery. Figure 8-50 shows the revised code in the changeSlide() function.

Code to apply a fade-in effect when changing slides ◀ **Figure 8-50**

```
function changeSlide(slide) {

    // Set object references
    var galleryBox = document.getElementById("galleryBox");
    var oldSlide = document.getElementById("gallerySlide");
    var slideCaption = document.getElementById("slideCaption");
    var slideNum = document.getElementById("slideNumber");

    // Replace current slide with new slide
    setOpacity("gallerySlide", 0);         ◀── makes the current slide
    var newSlide = oldSlide.cloneNode(true);     completely transparent
    newSlide.src = slide.big.src;
    newSlide.index = slide.big.index;
    galleryBox.replaceChild(newSlide, oldSlide);
    fadeIn("gallerySlide", 100, 0.5, 0);   ◀── after replacing the old
                                                slide with the new slide,
    // Replace current caption with new caption     fades in the new slide
    slideCaption.innerHTML = slide.alt;

    // Update the slide number
    slideNum.innerHTML = newSlide.index + 1;
}
```

▶ **3.** Save the file, and then reload **hipparchus.htm** in your Web browser.

▶ **4.** Start the slide show, and then use the navigation buttons in the gallery box to move forward and backward through the slides, verifying that each new slide is displayed by fading into the gallery box.

Next, you'll apply the fade-in transition to the entire gallery box when it's initially opened by the user. In addition to the gallery box, you'll also have to fade-in the page overlay. As with the individual slides, you first make the gallery box and the page overlay completely transparent and then you add them to the Web page before starting the fade-in effect.

To fade-in the gallery box and page overlay:

▶ **1.** Return to the **slideshow.js** file in your text editor, and then scroll down to the showGallery() function.

▶ **2.** Directly below the comment line `// Reveal the slide show`, insert the following commands to make the gallery box and page overlay transparent:

```
setOpacity("galleryBox", 0);
setOpacity("pageOverlay", 0);
```

▶ **3.** Scroll down two lines after the commands to set the display style of the gallery box and the page overlay to block, and insert the following commands to gradually reveal these objects in the browser window over a half-second time interval with no delay time before starting the transition:

```
fadeIn("galleryBox", 100, 0.5, 0);
fadeIn("pageOverlay", 80, 0.5, 0);
```

Note that the value of the maxOpacity parameter for the pageOverlay object is set to 80 to leave it semitransparent when the fade-in transition is completed. Figure 8-51 shows the final code of the showGallery() function.

Figure 8-51 ▶ **Code to reveal the gallery box and page overlay**

```
function showGallery() {

    // Change the image based on the clicked thumbnail
    changeSlide(this);

    // Reveal the slide show
    setOpacity("galleryBox", 0);
    setOpacity("pageOverlay", 0);
    document.getElementById("galleryBox").style.display = "block";
    document.getElementById("pageOverlay").style.display = "block";
    fadeIn("galleryBox", 100, 0.5, 0);
    fadeIn("pageOverlay", 80, 0.5, 0);

    // Halt propagation of the click event
    return false;

}
```

makes the gallery box and page overlay completely transparent

after setting the display style of both objects to "block" gradually reveals the object in the browser window

---

▶ **4.** Save the file, and then reload **hipparchus.htm** in your Web browser.

▶ **5.** Click any of the thumbnails to open the slide show gallery. Both the gallery box and the page overlay are gradually revealed in the browser window. See Figure 8-52.

Fade-in effect applied to the gallery box and page overlay   Figure 8-52

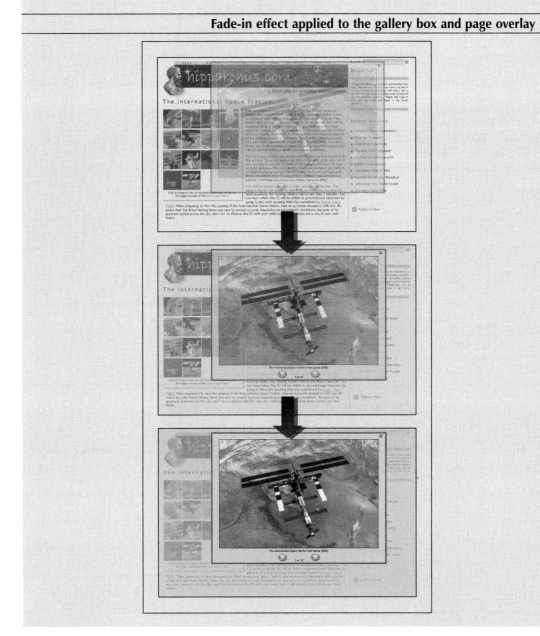

Applying a Fade-Out

Finally, Alexis wants you to fade out the gallery box and page overlay before the slide gallery is closed. The following commands immediately fade out each object over a half-second interval:

```
fadeOut("galleryBox", 100, 0.5, 0);
fadeOut("pageOverlay", 80, 0.5, 0);
```

You will add these commands to the anonymous function that closes the gallery box and page overlay.

To apply the fadeOut() function:

▶ **1.** Return to the **slideshow.js** file in your text editor, and then scroll down to the create-Gallery() function.

▶ **2.** Within the anonymous function that closes the gallery box and page overlay, insert the following commands, as shown in Figure 8-53:

```
fadeOut("galleryBox", 100, 0.5, 0);
fadeOut("pageOverlay", 80, 0.5, 0);
```

Figure 8-53 Code to apply the fadeOut() function

```
function createGallery(slides) {

    var galleryBox = document.createElement("div");
    galleryBox.id = "galleryBox";

    // Insert a button to close the gallery
    var galleryTitle = document.createElement("p");
    galleryTitle.id = "galleryTitle";

    var closeButton = document.createElement("input");
    closeButton.type = "image";
    closeButton.src = "galleryclose.png";
    closeButton.onclick = function() {
        fadeOut("galleryBox", 100, 0.5, 0);
        fadeOut("pageOverlay", 80, 0.5, 0);
        galleryBox.style.display = "none";
        document.getElementById("pageOverlay").style.display = "none";
    }
}
```

fades out the gallery box and page overlay

Before you run the revised code, note that the next two lines in the function change the display style of the gallery box and the page overlay to none, hiding them on the Web page. Because these commands will be run almost immediately, you won't see the fade-out effect as the objects already will have been hidden. To correct that, you'll run the commands to hide the gallery box and page overlay after a half-second delay. Those commands involve object references that cannot be included as parameters of the setTimeout() method, so you'll run them within an anonymous function called the setTimeout() method. The code to delay hiding the gallery box and page overlay is:

```
setTimeout(function() {
    galleryBox.style.display = "none";
    document.getElementById("pageOverlay").style.display = "none";
}, 500);
```

Note that the delay time for running these two commands is set to 500 because the set-Timeout() method expresses time in milliseconds rather than seconds. You will add these commands to the slideshow.js file and then test the fade-out transition you created.

To complete the fade-out transition:

▶ **1.** Directly below the fadeOut() commands you just entered, revise the next two lines as follows, as shown in Figure 8-54:

```
setTimeout(function() {
    galleryBox.style.display = "none";
    document.getElementById("pageOverlay").style.display = "none";
}, 500);
```

Code to delay hiding the gallery box and page overlay ◄ Figure 8-54

```
function createGallery(slides) {

    var galleryBox = document.createElement("div");
    galleryBox.id = "galleryBox";

    // Insert a button to close the gallery
    var galleryTitle = document.createElement("p");
    galleryTitle.id = "galleryTitle";

    var closeButton = document.createElement("input");
    closeButton.type = "image";
    closeButton.src = "galleryclose.png";
    closeButton.onclick = function() {
        fadeOut("galleryBox", 100, 0.5, 0);
        fadeOut("pageOverlay", 80, 0.5, 0);
        setTimeout(function() {
            galleryBox.style.display = "none";
            document.getElementById("pageOverlay").style.display = "none";
        }, 500);
    }
}
```

changes in the display style take place after a half second delay

▶ 2. Save and close the slideshow.js file.

▶ 3. Reload **hipparchus.htm** in your Web browser, click one of the thumbnails to open the slide gallery, and then click the gallery's close button to close it and verify that the fade-out transition is applied to both the gallery box and the page overlay.

Using Anonymous Functions with Timed Commands | Reference Window

- To delay the implementation of a command block, place the block in an anonymous function nested within the setTimeout() method as follows

```
setTimeout(function() {
    commands;
}, delay);
```
where *commands* are the commands to be delayed and *delay* is the delay time in milliseconds.

- To repeatedly run a command block at specified intervals, use an anonymous function and the setInterval() method as follows

```
setInterval(function() {
    commands;
}, interval);
```
where *interval* is the interval in milliseconds between implementations of the command block.

Internet Explorer Transition Filters

Internet Explorer supports a library of transition filters designed to dynamically change the appearance of an object over a specified time interval. One such transition is the blend transition, which blends one object into another. The syntax of the blend transition style is

```
filter: blendTrans(duration = value)
```

where *value* is the length of time to blend from one object to another on the Web page.

Internet Explorer also allows programmers to apply visual effects during the transition by using the revealTrans filter

```
filter: revealTrans(duration = value, transition = type)
```

where *type* is a number that represents one of IE's many transition effects. For example, the following filter style defines a transition from one object to another by wiping down the object (transition type 5) over a 2-second time interval:

```
filter: revealTrans(duration = 2, transition = 5)
```

Figure 8-55 shows a preview of how this effect appears on the Web page. You can create the same effect in non-IE browsers by changing the dimensions of the clipping rectangle around the image.

Figure 8-55 **IE wipe down transition filter**

filter: revealTrans(duration = 2, transition = 5)

First Sample Image

You can learn more about IE's transition filters and how to apply them in Appendix G.
You show Alexis the final version of the slide show application. She's pleased with the application you've constructed and likes that it can be easily adapted to any page in her Web site. Because you've placed all of the design styles and programming commands in external files, she only needs to link to those files and mark the slide images in her Web page to get her slide shows up and running.

Prepackaged Image Galleries | InSight

If you don't want to write your own application, the Web offers a wealth of prepackaged slide show programs that can be easily adapted to your Web site. Most prepackaged image galleries require minor modifications to the HTML code, but will generate the thumbnail images, rollover effects, and transition effects for you. These commercial packages also allow a single Web page to contain several distinct image galleries.

One of the more popular image galleries, and one of the first to be released, is Lightbox. To use Lightbox, you download the Lightbox files, attach three Lightbox JavaScript files to your Web page, and link to a Lightbox CSS style sheet that formats the image gallery. A slide image is generated in the Web page by adding the hypertext link

```
<a href="url" rel="lightbox" title="caption">image text</a>
```

where *url* is the URL of the slide image and *caption* is the text of the slide caption. Lightbox uses the code in this hypertext link to create the slide image object and place it in the Web page. Lightbox has evolved over the years to include support for keyboard navigation and provides a large library of transition effects.

Another popular image gallery is ThickBox, which uses the jQuery JavaScript function library to automatically generate an interactive slide show. ThickBox requires the Web page author to load several files, including two JavaScript libraries and a CSS style sheet. Thick-Box can be used for single images, inline content, inline frames, and files located on the Web server. To add a single image to a ThickBox gallery, you insert the hypertext link

```
<a href="url" title="caption" class="thickbox" rel="gallery">
    <img src="thumbnail" alt="text" />
</a>
```

in your document, where *url* is the URL of the slide image, *caption* is the slide caption, *gallery* is the name of the gallery in which the slide appears, *thumbnail* is the name of the thumbnail image file, and *text* is alternate text to be displayed in place of the thumbnail.

Take some time to explore the different image galleries available for free on the Web. You may discover that someone else has already created the tools you need to add interactive images to your Web site.

Review | Session 8.3 Quick Check

1. What opacity value makes an object completely transparent?
2. Specify the CSS style to set the opacity of an object to 40% under both Internet Explorer and non-IE browsers.
3. Specify the JavaScript code to set the opacity of an object to 40% under both Internet Explorer and non-IE browsers.
4. What is the IE filters collection?
5. Provide the code to run the following command block after a 3-second delay:
```
logo = document.getElementById("logo");
logo.style.display = "block";
```
6. Provide the general syntax of the IE transition filter to blend one object into another.
7. Provide the general syntax of the IE transition filter to reveal an object using a special visual effect.
8. Using Lightbox image gallery software, how would you add the image file photo01.jpg to the image gallery with the caption "Holiday Family Portrait"?

Review | Tutorial Summary

This tutorial explored how to work with image objects to create dynamic rollovers and interactive slide shows. The first session introduced image objects, showing how to pre-load image files to speed up the user's interaction with a Web site. The session used image objects to create rollover effects by swapping one image with another in response to the mouseover event. The first session also discussed how to create and apply custom properties, and how to use anonymous functions within event handlers. The second session built on these topics to produce the first version of an interactive slide show within a slide gallery box created whenever slides are present in the current Web document. The final session completed the slide show application and added a new style to set the opacity of Web page objects. Transition effects were also created by modifying an object's opacity over time to fade in and fade out the object.

Key Terms

custom property	filter	rollover
fade-in effect	image object	transition
fade-out effect	opacity	

Practice | Review Assignments

Practice the skills you learned in the tutorial using the same case scenario.

Data Files needed for the Review Assignments: back.png, close.png, controlltxt.css, forward.png, hipparchus.png, main.css, nebulaetxt.htm, photo01.jpg–photo15.jpg, photo01_over.jpg–photo15_over.jpg, photo01_thumb.jpg–photo15_thumb.jpg, rss.gif, sctxt.js, search.gif, stars.png

Alexis wants you to create a new interface for the slide show. She suggests a slide show application in which the navigation controls and close button appear only when the user hovers the pointer over the slide show. She also wants you to create a blend transition in which one slide fades out as another fades into the slide gallery. Figure 8-56 shows a preview of the slide show application she wants you to create and test.

Figure 8-56

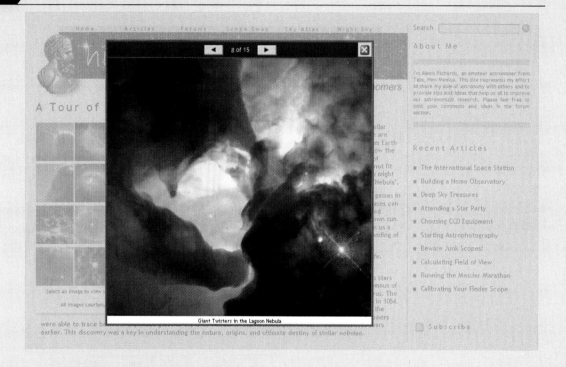

The structure of this slide show will be slightly different than the one you created in the tutorial. Alexis suggests that you design an application in which all of the high-resolution versions are added to the Web page document, stacked one on top of another. Initially, the slides will be transparent; but when the user requests a particular slide, it will fade into the Web page. If another slide is already displayed, it will fade out at the same time.

Alexis has already written several JavaScript functions for you to use in creating the slide show application, designed an appropriate style sheet, and created sample image files. You will combine all these pieces into a finished application.

Complete the following:

1. Use your text editor to open the **nebulaetxt.htm**, **sctxt.js**, and **controltxt.css** files from the tutorial.08\review folder, enter *your name* and *the date* in the comment section of each file, and then save the files as **nebulae.htm**, **slidecontrols.js**, and **controls.css**, respectively.

2. Go to the **nebulae.htm** file in your text editor, locate the list of 15 thumbnail images displayed in the Web page, and then indicate that these images are thumbnails for the slide show by adding the class name **thumb** to each <img /> tag.

3. Scroll up to the head section of the file, create links to the slidecontrols.js JavaScript file and the controls.css style sheet, and then save and close the file.

4. Go to the **slidecontrols.js** file in your text editor, and then study the functions already in the file that you'll be using to complete your slide show application.

5. Create the **makeSlides()** function. The purpose of this function is to search the current Web page for slide images and create an array of slides. The function should do the following:

   a. Create an array named **thumbs** that contains all of the inline images with the class name thumb embedded within an <a> tag.

   b. For every item within the thumbs array: (i) Add the custom property index, setting the value of the property to the thumb's position in the array. (ii) Run the createRollover() function using the current thumbnail as the parameter value. (iii) Run the createHighRes() function using the current thumbnail as the parameter value. (iv) Add an event handler that runs the showSlideshow() function whenever the thumbnail is clicked on the Web page.

   c. If the length of the thumbs array is greater than 0 (meaning that the Web page contains thumbnail images for slides), do the following: (i) Run the createSlide-Box() function using the thumbs array as the parameter value. (ii) Run the createSlideControl() function. (iii) Run the createOverlay() function.

6. Use the addEvent() function to run the makeSlides() function whenever the document is loaded into the browser window.

7. Insert the **createSlideBox()** function. The function has a single parameter named **thumbs** representing the thumbs array you created in the makeSlides() function. The purpose of the createSlideBox() function is to create div elements containing the high-resolution images. In the first part of the function, create the following div element (styles for this element already have been placed in the controls.css style sheet):

```
<div id="slideBox">
</div>
```

8. Within the createSlideBox() function, insert a for loop that creates the div element

```
<div id="slideBoxindex" class="fullSlide">
   <img src="url" />
   <br />
   caption
</div>
```

for every object in the thumbs array, where *index* is the index value of the item from the thumbs array, *url* is the src of the high-resolution image corresponding to the thumbnail image (*Hint:* Use the custom property big.src defined in the createHighRes() function), and *caption* is the value of the alt property from the item in the thumbs array. Append each div element to the slideBox element you created in the previous step, and then append the slideBox element to the document body.

9. Insert the **createSlideControl()** function. The function has a single parameter named **thumbs**. The purpose of this function is to create a control bar containing controls to close and navigate through the slide show. Add commands to create the HTML fragment

```
<div id="slideControls">
   <input id="slideBack" type="image" src="back.png" />
```

```
<span id="slideNumber">1</span> of length
<input id="slideForward" type="image" src="forward.png" />
<input id="slideBoxClose" type="image" src="close.png" />
</div>
```

where *length* is the length of the thumbs array. Styles for the slideControls box already have been created in the controls.css file. Append the slideControls box to the document body.

10. Insert the **createOverlay()** function. The purpose of this function is to create the page overlay between the slide show and the Web page contents. Have the function write the following HTML fragment and then append the object to the document body:

```
<div id="pageOverlay"></div>
```

11. Insert the **showSlideshow()** function. The purpose of this function is to display the slide show whenever one of the thumbnail images is clicked. It has no parameters. Add the following commands to the function:

    a. Use the showObject() function to display the slideBox object and the page overlay.

    b. The slide show should display the high-resolution version of whatever thumbnail is clicked. The index number of the selected thumbnail is stored in the index property. Use the showObject() function to display the element with the id slideBox*index*, where *index* is the index number of the clicked thumbnail image. (*Hint:* Use the `this` keyword and the custom index property to reference the index number.)

    c. Display the number of the current slide by setting the inner HTML of the slideNumber object to the value of the index number of the clicked thumbnail plus 1.

    d. Use the fadeIn() function to fade in the slideBox object over a 1-second interval.

    e. Use the fadeIn() function to fade in the page overlay up to 80% opacity over a 1-second interval.

    f. Return the value false to halt the propagation of the click event.

12. Add a feature to your slide show application so that the slide controls appear only when the pointer hovers over the slide box by doing the following:

    a. Go to the createSlideBox() function and add an event handler that shows the slideControls object when the pointer moves over the slide box. Add another event handler that hides the slideControls object when the pointer moves out and away from the slide box. You can use the showObject() and closeObject() function to facilitate your code.

    b. Go to the createSlideControl() function and insert an event handler that displays the slideControls object whenever the pointer moves over the slide controls.

13. Program the operation of the back button in the slide controls box. Go to the createSlideControl() function and then insert the following anonymous function to be run in response to the event of a user clicking the back button:

    a. Retrieve the index number of the current slide using the getCurrentSlideIndex() function provided in the file. Store the value in the currentIndex variable.

    b. Decrease the value of currentIndex by 1, storing the result in the nextIndex variable. If the value of nextIndex is less than 0, change its value to one less than the length of the thumbs array.

    c. Use the fadeOut() function to fade out the currently displayed slide over a 3-second interval.

d. Show the next slide using the showObject() function, and then fade in that slide using the fadeIn() function over a 3-second interval. Because the old slide and the new slide will be fading in and out at the same time, they will appear to blend in the interactive slide show.

e. To update the slide number displayed in the slide controls box, set the inner HTML property of the slideNumber object to one more than the value of the nextIndex variable.

14. Add an anonymous function to the onclick event handler for the forward button similar to what you created in Step 13 for the back button. The only differences are that the nextIndex variable should be one more than the currentIndex variable, and if nextIndex equals the length of the thumbs array, it should be changed to 0.

15. Within the createSlideControls() function, create an anonymous function that is run whenever the user clicks the close button. The function should do the following:

a. Retrieve the index number of the current slide using the getCurrentSlideIndex() function. Store the value in the currentIndex variable.

b. Use the closeObject() function to close the slideControls and slideBox objects.

c. Set the opacity of the current slide (referenced with the id slideBox*index*, where *index* is its index number) to 0, and then close it using the closeObject() function.

d. Fade out the page overlay from its maximum opacity of 80% down to 0 over a 1-second interval. After a 1-second delay, close the page overlay using the closeObject() function.

16. Save the slidecontrols.js file. Go to the **controls.css** file in your text editor, insert a style to make all objects belonging to the fullSlide class completely transparent, insert a style to make the page overlay 75% opaque, and then save the file.

17. Load **nebulae.htm** in your Web browser and test your slide show application, verifying that it does the following:

a. Whenever you hover the pointer over the thumbnail images, a full-color rollover image replaces the grayscale thumbnail.

b. When you click a thumbnail, the corresponding high-resolution image appears on the Web page with a semitransparent overlay obscuring the Web page contents.

c. Slide controls appear only when the pointer hovers over the slide.

d. The slide control shows the correct number of slides and the number of the current slide.

e. Clicking the forward and backward buttons moves you through the slide show, with the current slide fading out as the next slide is fading in.

f. Clicking the close button closes the slide box with the page overlay fading out.

18. Submit your completed project to your instructor.

| Apply | **Case Problem 1** |

Use the skills you learned to create rotating banner ads.

Data Files needed for this Case Problem: adstxt.js, banner0.jpg–banner10.jpg, bannerstyles.css, bannertxt.js, bookstxt.htm, bw.css, bwlogo.jpg, leftbar.jpg, logo0.jpg–logo10.jpg, signature.jpg, testpage0.htm–testpage10.htm

online BookWorms   Helen Ungerstatz, the manager of online BookWorms, wants your help on her Web site. To raise revenue, Helen has sold advertising space in the form of banner ads on the site's heading. The banner ads are inline images linked to the advertiser's home page. Helen wants a JavaScript program that adds the banner ads to any Web page, and then periodically rotates through the ads. Figure 8-57 shows a preview of her site's home page.

Figure 8-57

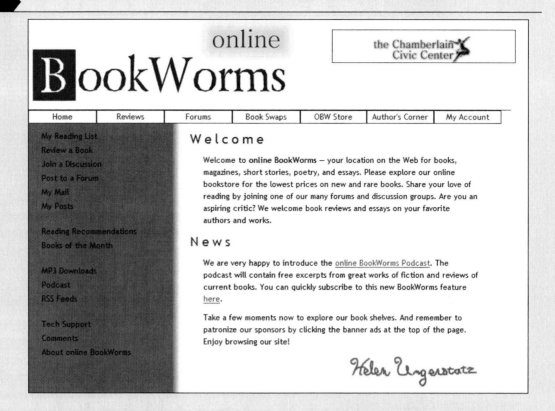

To create this application, you'll add the banner ads to a banner ad box located in the upper-right corner of the Web page. The ads will be stacked on top of each other with different z-index values. To display a different ad, your program will change the z-index numbers, bringing the bottom ad to the top of the stack. To make the application visually interesting, Helen wants the new ad to scroll down from the top, displacing the currently displayed ad.

To complete this project:

1. Use your text editor to open the **adstxt.js**, **bannertxt.js**, and **bookstxt.htm** files from the tutorial.08\case1 folder, enter *your name* and *the date* in the comment section of each file, and then save the files as **ads.js**, **banners.js**, and **books.htm**, respectively.

2. Go to the **books.htm** file in your text editor, link the document to the bannerstyles.css style sheet and the ads.js and banners.js JavaScript files, and then save the file.

3. Go to the **ads.js** file in your text editor, and then create an array named **adsURL**. The purpose of this array is to store the URLs of the home pages advertised on Helen's Web site. Add 11 items to the array containing the text strings **testpage0.htm** through **testpage10.htm**. Save and close the file.

4. Go to the **banners.js** file in your text editor, and then declare a global variable named **nextAd**. The purpose of the nextAd variable is to reference the next banner ad to be displayed in the Web page.

5. Use the addEvent() function to run the makeBannerAds() function when the page is loaded.

6. Create the **makeBannerAds()** function. The purpose of this function is to create the box containing the banner ads. Add the following commands to the function:

   a. Create the following HTML fragment:
   ```
   <div id="bannerBox">
   </div>
   ```

   b. Loop through all of the items in the adURLs array, and for each item create the HTML fragment
   ```
   <div class="bannerAd">
      <a href="url">
         <img src="bannerindex" />
      </a>
   </div>
   ```
   where *url* is the URL contained in the adURLs array and *index* is the index number of the current ad. Set the z-index number of each banner ad to the value of the counter index and append the banner ad to the bannerBox element you created in Step a.

   c. Append the bannerBox element to the document body.

   d. Run the changeBannerAd() function every 10 seconds.

7. Create the **changeBannerAd()** function. The purpose of this function is to change the ad currently displayed in the banner box. Add the following commands to the function:

   a. Loop through all of the banner ads in the banner box. Locate the banner ad with a z-index value equal to 0 and change the top position of that ad to −50 pixels (moving it above the boundaries of the banner box). Set the nextAd variable equal to this selected ad.

   b. Loop through all of the banner ads again and decrease the z-index of each ad by 1. If the new z-index value is less than 0, change it to one less than the total number of banner ads.

   c. Declare a variable named **timeDelay**, setting its initial value to 0. The purpose of the timeDelay variable is to set the time delay in moving the position of the new ad into the banner box.

   d. Create a for loop with a counter variable that starts with a value of −50 and increases by 1 up to a value of 0. The counter variable is used to store the top position of the banner ad as it moves back into the banner box. Each time through the loop, run the moveNextAd() function after timeDelay milliseconds with a parameter value equal to the value of the counter variable. Increase the value of the timeDelay variable by 15 milliseconds each time through the loop.

8. Create the **moveNextAd()** function. The function has a single parameter named **top**. The purpose of the function is to set the top position of the nextAd object. Add a command to the function to set the top position of nextAd to the value of the top parameter.

9. Save the file, and then open **books.htm** in your Web browser. Verify that the banner box appears in the upper-right corner of the Web page, the ad displayed in the banner box changes every 10 seconds, and the new ads move into the banner box by scrolling into the box from the top.

10. Submit your completed project to your instructor.

| Apply | | Case Problem 2 |

Use the skills you learned to create a matching tiles game.

Data Files needed for this Case Problem: ctitle.jpg, kg.css, kgmenu.jpg, kgtitle.jpg, tile.jpg, tileimage0.jpg–tileimage7.jpg, tilestxt.js, tilestxt.htm

Kiddergarden Pete Burnham of the children's Web site Kiddergarden wants you to help him with a new game page for the site. You will create a concentration game in which images are turned over on a board, with the object of turning over pairs of tiles containing the same image. When all of the pairs have been matched, the game is over. Pete has set up a sample Web page with a 4x4 board containing eight pairs of images. You will program the act of randomly arranging the tiles and turning the tiles over. A preview of the completed Web page is shown in Figure 8-58.

Figure 8-58

Although this sample board contains only 16 tiles with eight pairs of images, Pete wants your program to be applicable to boards of almost any size. You and Pete agree on the following parameters for setup of the game:

- Tile images will be stored in files named tileimage0.jpg up through tileimage*n*.jpg, where *n* is one less than the number of image pairs. In the current board, the eight tile images are stored in files named tileimage0.jpg through tileimage7.jpg.
- Tile images are marked in the HTML file with the class name tile and are enclosed within the <a> tag.
- A tile is turned over in the game by clicking it.
- Only two tiles can be turned over at any one time.
- If the player flips over two tiles that do not match, they will be flipped back within $\frac{8}{10}$ of a second.

- When the player flips over a matching pair of tiles, the tiles remain face up and grayed out on the board and cannot be flipped again.
- Players can view the complete solution at any time by clicking the Show Tiles button.
- Players can reload the game by clicking the Reload Tiles button.

Pete has written some JavaScript functions to aid you in writing this application.

Complete the following:

1. Use your text editor to open the **tilestxt.js**, and **tilestxt.htm** files from the tutorial.08\ case2 folder, enter *your name* and *the date* in the comment section of each file, and then save the files as **tiles.js** and **tiles.htm**, respectively.

2. Go to the **tiles.htm** file in your text editor, link the document to the tiles.js JavaScript file, study the layout of the tiles.htm file, noting the location of the 16 tile pieces on the concentration board, and then save and close the file.

3. Go to the **tiles.js** file in your text editor, and then declare the following three global variables:

   a. **flipCount**—used to track the number of tiles currently flipped over. Set its initial value to 0.

   b. **firstFlip**—used to reference the first tile flipped over.

   c. **secondFlip**—used to reference the second tile flipped over.

4. Use the addEvent() function to run the setupTiles() function when the page is loaded.

5. Create the **setupTiles()** function. The purpose of this function is to create arrays of the 16 tile pieces and the corresponding tile images. Add the following commands to the function:

   a. Declare an array named **tiles**. Populate the array with all of the images in the current document that have a class name of tile and are enclosed within the <a> tag.

   b. Create an array of tile images of the same size as the tiles array.

   c. Loop through the first half of the tileImages array. Within the first half of the array, create image objects from the image file tileimage*index*.jpg, where *index* is the value of the counter variables.

   d. Loop through the second half of the tileImages array. Create a second set of the same image objects you created in the first loop. After running the two loops, the tileImages array should be populated with pairs of matching image objects.

   e. Sort the contents of the tileImages array using the randomSort() function supplied in the file. This randomizes the order of the image objects in the tileImages array for later use in constructing the concentration board.

6. Attach each image object from the tileImages array to a board tile in the tile array by adding the following commands to the setupTiles() function:

   a. Loop through the tiles array. For each tile in the array, create a custom property named **image** that points to the corresponding tile image object from the tileImages array.

   b. Add an onclick event handler to each item in the tiles array that runs the flipTile() function.

7. Create the **flipTile()** function. The purpose of this function is to flip over the selected tile from the board, displaying the tile image attached to it. Add the following commands to the function:

    a. Insert an if condition that tests whether the flipCount variable is equal to 0. If it is, set the src of the flipped tile (referenced using the `this` keyword) to the source of the custom image property, update the value of the firstFlip variable to point to the flipped tile, and increase the value of the flipCount variable by 1.

    b. Otherwise, if flipCount equals 1, then do the following: (i) Change the source of the flipped tile to the source of the custom image property of the tile. (ii) Set the reference of the secondFlip variable to the flipped tile. (iii) Update the flipCount variable by 1. (iv) Call the checkTiles() function.

    c. After the if condition, return the value false to halt the propagation of the click event.

8. Create the **checkTiles()** function. The purpose of this function is to test whether the two flipped tiles display the same image. Add the following commands to the function:

    a. Insert an if condition that tests whether the source of the custom image property for the firstFlip variable is equal to the source of the custom image property for the secondFlip variable. If they are not equal, then run the flipBack() function after 0.8 seconds.

    b. Otherwise, if they are equal (the tiles show the same image), then: (i) Set the flipCount variable to 0. (ii) Set the opacity of firstFlip and secondFlip to 70%. (iii) Change the onclick event handlers for firstFlip and secondFlip to an anonymous function that does nothing but return the value false. You change the onclick event handler function for these two solved tiles to prevent the user from attempting to flip them again.

9. Create the **flipBack()** function. The purpose of this function is to flip back two tiles that do not match. Add the following commands to the function:

    a. Set the source of the firstFlip and secondFlip tiles to the tile.jpg image file.

    b. Change the value of flipCount back to 0.

10. Program the actions of the Reload Tiles and Show Tiles buttons. Scroll back up to the setupTiles() function, and then add the following commands:

    a. The id of the Show Tiles button is **showAll**. When this button is clicked, run an anonymous function that loops through the tiles array, changing the source of each tile to the source of the tile's custom image property, revealing the tile image attached to the tile.

    b. The id of the Reload Tiles button is **reload**. When this button is clicked, run an anonymous function that reloads the current Web page using the location.reload() property and method.

11. Save the file, and then load **tiles.htm** in your Web browser.

12. Play the concentration game and verify the following:

    a. When you click one of the 16 tiles on the board, a tile image is displayed.

    b. When you click two tiles that don't match, both tiles are flipped over after a short interval.

    c. When you click two tiles that do match, both tiles are grayed out and cannot be flipped again.

    d. When you click the Show Tiles button, the solution to the board is displayed.

    e. When you click the Reload Tiles button, a new concentration board is generated.

13. Submit the completed project to your instructor.

Challenge | Case Problem 3

Explore how to use JavaScript to create a filmstrip slide show.

Data Files needed for this Case Problem: bar.png, camshots.jpg, camtxt.htm, enlarge. png, filmtxt.js, fstxt.css, photo01.png–photo15.png, reduce.png, styles.css

CAMshots Gerry Hayward is the owner of CAMshots, a Web site for amateur photographers and digital camera enthusiasts. One of the site's most popular features is a monthly contest in which CAMshots subscribers can submit their favorite photos around a chosen theme of the month. In the past, Gerry has designed the page to contain an unordered list of links to high-resolution versions of the winning photos. He wants to revise the code so that it converts the list of links into a slide show gallery with a filmstrip of thumbnail images.

Gerry has asked you to help write the JavaScript code for this application. He wants your program to generate the thumbnail images and the large-scale images based on the image sources indicated in the hypertext links. He also wants to give users the ability to enlarge or reduce each image within the slide show by clicking buttons in the gallery box. Figure 8-59 shows a preview of the completed Web page.

Figure 8-59

Gerry has already written most of the HTML and CSS code. You will complete the application by writing the JavaScript application.

Complete the following:

1. Use your text editor to open the **camtxt.htm**, **filmtxt.js**, and **fstxt.css** files from the tutorial.08\case3 folder, enter *your name* and *the date* in the comment section of each file, and then save the files as **camshots.htm**, **filmstrip.js**, and **fs.css**, respectively.

2. Go to the **camshots.htm** file in your text editor, and then link the file to the filmstrip.js JavaScript file and the fs.css style sheet.

3. Scroll down the file and locate the list of photo links. For each entry in the list, add a rel attribute with the value **filmstrip** to the <a> tag to mark the entry as a linked image for the slide show filmstrip. Save and close the file.

4. Go to the **filmstrip.js** file in your text editor, and then enter a command to run the makeFilmStrip() function when the page is loaded.

5. Add the **makeFilmStrip()** function to the file. The purpose of this function is to create the filmstrip slide show. Within the function, declare an array named **photos** containing all of the hypertext links in the current document whose rel attribute is equal to filmstrip. If the length of the photos array is greater than 0, then the code should perform the actions described in Steps 6 through 11.

6. Create the following HTML fragment named **slideGallery**:

   ```
   <div id="slideGallery"></div>
   ```

7. Create the following HTML fragment named **thumbStrip**, and append it to slideGallery:

   ```
   <div id="thumbStrip"></div>
   ```

8. Loop through the items in the photos array and do the following:
   a. Create the following container for your thumbnail images:
      ```
      <div class="thumbBox"></div>
      ```
   b. Set the top position of the thumbnail box to 0 pixels. Set the left position to 125 x the value of the counter variable (in pixels).
   c. Within each thumbBox container, insert an image object named **thumbnail**. The source of the image should be equal to the href attribute value of the current item in the photos array. For each thumbnail image, add a custom property named **caption** that contains the text of the inner HTML of the current item in the photos array.
   d. Append each thumbnail image to a thumbBox. Append each thumbBox to the thumbStrip object.

9. Create the following HTML fragment, which provides buttons that give users the ability to reduce and expand the image displayed in the slide gallery, and then append the resizeControls object to the slideGallery object:

   ```
   <div id="resizeControls">
       <input type="image" src="reduce.png" />
       <input type="image" src="enlarge.png" />
   </div>
   ```

10. Create the HTML fragment

    ```
    <div id="photoBox">
        <img src="url" id="slidePhoto" />
        <br />
        <span>caption</span>
    </div>
    ```

    where *url* is the href attribute value of the first item in the photos array and *caption* is the value of the custom caption property for the first item in the photos array. Name this fragment **photoBox** and append it to the slideGallery object.

11. Replace the photoLinks list in the current document with the slideGallery object, and then save the file.

EXPLORE 12. Go to the **fs.css** file in your text editor. The thumbStrip object you created in Step 7 should contain a collection of div elements with the class name thumbBox, with each one containing an image element. To keep the collection of thumbnail images confined within the boundaries of thumbStrip, add a CSS style to set the overflow property of the thumbStrip object to auto. This will cause the browser to automatically insert scrollbars around thumbStrip, allowing users to scroll through the collection of thumbnails.

13. For each image element within a thumbBox, set the height to 68 pixels and the width to auto. Have the browser display a pointer cursor over the image. Set the opacity of the images to 50%. Save the file.

14. Open the **camshots.htm** file in your browser, verify that the page layout and the slide show gallery are similar to that shown in Figure 8-59, and then verify that you can use the scrollbars to scroll through the collection of thumbnail images.

15. Return to the **filmstrip.js** file in your text editor. Directly below the commands that create each thumbnail image, add the following event handlers:

    a. When the user hovers the pointer over the thumbnail image, set the opacity to 100%.

    b. When the pointer moves out from the thumbnail, change the opacity to 50%.

    c. When the user clicks the thumbnail, do the following: (i) Declare an image object named **newPhoto**. (ii) Set the source of newPhoto to the source of the clicked thumbnail. (iii) Declare a variable named **oldPhoto** that points to the first child of the photoBox object. (iv) Replace oldPhoto with newPhoto. (v) Change the text of the photoCaption object to the value of the caption property of the clicked thumbnail.

EXPLORE 16. Directly below the commands that create the reduce button from Step 9, add the following commands to create an anonymous function that is run when the user clicks the reduce button:

    a. Declare a variable named **photo** that points to the first child node of the photoBox object.

    b. Declare variables named **currentWidth** and **currentHeight** equal to the width and height of the photo object, respectively.

    c. Declare a variable named **ratio** equal to the ratio of the currentHeight to currentWidth.

    d. Declare a variable named **newWidth** equal to currentWidth minus 20.

    e. If newWidth is greater than 0, declare a variable named **newHeight** equal to currentHeight multiplied by ratio.

    f. Set the width and height of the photo object to newWidth and newHeight, respectively.

EXPLORE 17. Directly below the commands that create the expand button from Step 9, add the following commands to the onclick event handler using an anonymous function:

    a. Repeat Steps 16a through 16c.

    b. Set newWidth equal to currentWidth plus 20.

    c. The maximum width is limited by the width of the photoBox object. The maximum width is returned by the offsetWidth property of that object. Store this value in a variable named **maxWidth**.

    d. If newWidth is less than or equal to maxWidth, then set the value of newHeight to currentHeight multiplied by ratio.

e. Set the width and height of the photo object to newWidth and newHeight, respectively.

18. Save the file, and then reload **camshots.htm** in your Web browser. Verify that whenever the pointer hovers over a thumbnail, the opacity is increased to 100%. Also verify that you can switch the image displayed in the photo box by clicking a thumbnail image. Finally, confirm that when you click the reduce and expand buttons, the selected image decreases and increases in size, limited to the width of the slide gallery.

19. Submit the completed project to your instructor.

Create	**Case Problem 4**

Create a JavaScript utility to display an interactive slide show.

Data Files needed for this Case Problem: afplogo.jpg, before.jpg, close.jpg, next.jpg, sketch0.jpg–sketch21.jpg, sketch0_roll.jpg–sketch21_roll.jpg, sketch0_thumb.jpg–sketch21_thumb.jpg, summary.txt

The Amistad Freedom Project Clarence Arinze is the founder of the Amistad Freedom Project, an organization dedicated to preserving information about the 1841 United States Supreme Court case regarding the rebellion of slaves onboard the Spanish schooner Amistad in 1839. To make information about the Amistad case more accessible to the public, Clarence is attempting to put historic documents and images on a Web site. He's obtained some historical sketches of the Amistad captives made by William H. Townsend. He wants you to place these images in an interactive slide show.

Clarence has saved the sketches in JPEG format. He's included a thumbnail, rollover, and full version of each sketch. He's also written a brief caption for each sketch and provided textual material describing the origins of the sketches and of the Amistad case. You will use all of this information to design the Web page and write the JavaScript code that creates the interactive slide show.

Complete the following:

1. Using your text editor, create the following files in the tutorial.08\case4 folder: the **amistad.htm** file containing the Web page you'll create for Clarence, the **afpstyles.css** file containing the styles used for the page content, the **slides.js** file containing the code for your JavaScript application, and the **slides.css** file containing any styles required for your application. Enter *your name*, *the date*, and a *brief description* in the comment section of each file.

2. The content for your Web page can be taken from the material in the summary.txt file, although you can also supplement that information with additional material of your choosing.

3. Use the graphic files provided in the tutorial.08\case4 folder to design thumbnail, rollover, and high-resolution slide images. You may supplement these graphics with other graphics you locate on the Web or create yourself.

4. Create a slide show application displaying the Townsend sketches. The slide show application should be your own design, but include the following features:
   a. The preloading of all images used in the application
   b. Rollover effects of images displayed in the slide show
   c. Navigation tools to move forward and backward through the slide show
   d. Captions that update with each slide
   e. Transition effects as each slide is replaced with another

      f. CSS styles and JavaScript code that set or change the opacity of an object on the Web page

5. Test your code in your Web browser and verify that it provides the user with an easy-to-use interactive experience of the Townsend sketches.

6. Submit your completed project to your instructor.

Review | Quick Check Answers

Session 8.1

1. `document.images`

2. `document.images[1].src = "newlogo.png";`

3. `var newImage = new Image();`

4. `var newImage = new Image(250, 150);`

5. `newImage.src = "newlogo.png";`

6. `newImage.rollover = new Image();`

Session 8.2

1. `position: fixed`

2. `replace(/_slide/, "")`

3.
```
var slideShow = document.createElement("div");
slideShow.id = "slideshow";
var slideImg = document.createElement("img");
slideImg.src = "slide01.jpg";
slideImg.alt = "First Slide";
slideShow.appendChild(slideImg);
var slideCaption = document.createElement("p");
slideCaption.innerHTML = "First Slide";
slideShow.appendChild(slideCaption);
document.body.appendChild(slideShow);
```

4. `slideShow.style.display = "none";`

5. `clip:rect(50, 175, 200, 75)`

6. `document.images[1].alt`

Session 8.3

1. `0`

2. `opacity = 0.4; filter: alpha(opacity = 40)`

3.
```
object.style.opacity = 0.4;
object.style.filter = "alpha(opacity = 40)";
```

4. The IE filters collection is an object collection that references all filters that have been defined for an object on the Web page. The collection is only supported by Internet Explorer.

5.
```
setTimeout(function() {
    logo = document.getElementById("logo");
    logo.style.display = "block";
}, 3000);
```

6. `filter: blendTrans(duration = value)`

where *value* is the length of time to blend from one object to another on the Web page

7. `filter: revealTrans(duration = value, transition = type)`

where *value* is the length of the transition time and *type* is a number that represents one of IE's many transition effects

8.
```
<a href="photo1.jpg" rel="lightbox"
    title="Holiday Family Portrait">
    image text
</a>
```

Ending Data Files

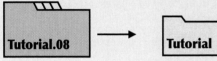

Tutorial

hipparchus.htm
slideshow.js
gallery.css
+ 1 CSS file
+ 49 graphic files

Review

nebulae.htm
slidecontrols.js
controls.css
+ 1 CSS file
+ 52 graphic files

Case1

books.htm
ads.js
banners.js
+ 11 HTML files
+ 2 CSS files
+ 27 graphic files

Case2

tiles.htm
tiles.js
kg.css
+ 12 graphic files

Case3

camshots.htm
filmstrip.js
fs.css
+ 1 CSS file
+ 19 graphic files

Case4

amistad.htm
slides.js
afpstyles.css
slides.css
+ 70 graphic files

Objectives

Session 9.1
- Learn about client-side cookies
- Set a cookie's value
- Set a cookie's expiration date
- Set a cookie's path, domain, and secure flag

Session 9.2
- Read data from a cookie
- Write cookie values to a data form
- Delete a cookie

Session 9.3
- Write a multivalued cookie
- Read a multivalued cookie
- Create a cookie to track the last visit date
- Test for browser support of cookies

Storing Data with Cookies

Creating a Registration Page

Case | CycloCrossings

Kevin Geary is the Web manager for CycloCrossings, a new and growing company that promotes long-distance bicycle touring by leading tours, publishing detailed tour maps, and selling touring equipment. Interested customers can become supporting members of CycloCrossings, which, for an annual fee, provides them with discounts on all CycloCrossings tours and merchandise. Kevin wants you to work on the new member registration page. He's created much of the code for the page, but you need to create a JavaScript program that records the member's registration information within cookies on the user's local computer.

Note: To complete this tutorial using the Safari or Google Chrome Web browsers, you must work with the files on a Web server rather than on your local machine, or install a personal Web server on your local machine that employs the HTTP communication protocol.

Starting Data Files

Tutorial.09 → Tutorial	Review	Case1	Case2	Case3	Case4
accounttxt.htm	library.js	countertxt.js	newitemstxt.js	arctictxt.htm	trivia.txt
accounttxt.js	proftxt.htm	hangerstxt.htm	sblogtxt.htm	carttxt.htm	
cooktxt.js	proftxt.js	+ 1 HTML file	+ 4 HTML files	carttxt.js	
cyclotxt.htm	ridestxt.htm	+ 1 CSS file	+ 1 CSS file	flesstxt.htm	
cyclotxt.js	ridestxt.js	+ 4 graphic files	+ 4 graphic files	glomitttxt.htm	
registertxt.htm	+ 1 HTML file			orderstxt.js	
registertxt.js	+ 3 CSS files			polyftxt.htm	
+ 1 HTML file	+ 3 graphic file			+ 3 HTML files	
+ 3 CSS files				+ 1 CSS file	
+ 5 graphic files				+ 1 JavaScript file	
				+ 10 graphic files	

Session 9.1

Introducing Cookies

Kevin already has written much of the HTML code, the CSS styles, and some of the JavaScript code you'll need to complete this project. The first page you'll develop is a membership registration page. You'll start by examining the registration file that Kevin created.

To view the registration file:

▶ 1. Use your text editor to open the **registertxt.htm**, **cooktxt.js**, and **registertxt.js** files from the tutorial.09\tutorial folder, enter *your name* and *the date* in the comment section of each file, and then save the files as **register.htm**, **cookies.js**, and **register.js**, respectively.

▶ 2. Go to the **register.htm** file in your text editor and review the HTML code.

▶ 3. Open the **register.htm** file in your Web browser. See Figure 9-1.

Figure 9-1 ▶ Initial CycloCrossings registration page

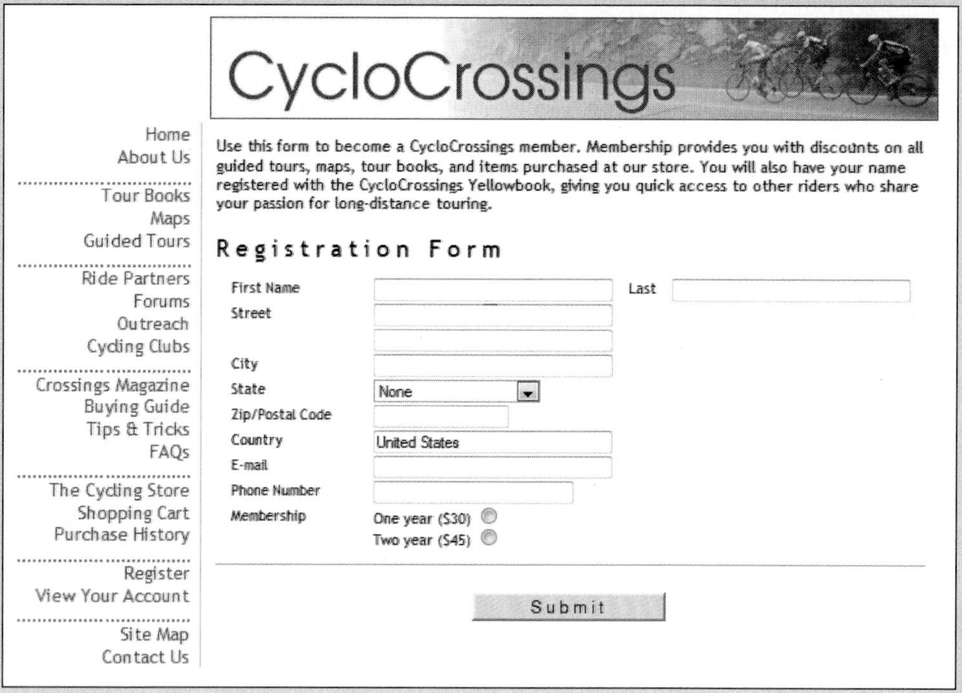

With the layout and the content of the registration page completed, Kevin wants you to write a program that will record each customer's membership information. Any membership data a customer enters should be accessible to other pages in the CycloCrossings Web site. To achieve this, you'll create cookies to store the membership information.

Understanding Cookies

One limitation of the HTTP communication protocol used on the Web is that it's a **stateless protocol**, which means that it does not record the user's interaction with the Web server. HTTP, in essence, "forgets" everything that a user may have done during previous visits or even during the current visit to the Web site. This is by design because it frees the protocol from having to maintain a complex and cumbersome record of each user's actions, speeding up the transfer of data from the server to the user.

However, sometimes you want to record the actions and data entries of the user in a permanent form. This can be achieved with cookies. A **cookie** is a text file containing data that the Web browser can retrieve and display. Cookies were first introduced in 1994 for the Netscape browser to develop shopping cart applications in which items selected by a customer are stored in memory as the customer navigates through the various pages in a commercial Web site. After the customer has finished shopping, he or she can retrieve and view all of the items placed into the shopping cart prior to purchase. Cookies quickly moved beyond that initial application to other uses, including keeping track of the number of times a user visited a Web site, the date of his or her last visit, and what parts of the Web site the user has seen and not seen.

Cookies are stored either on the Web server as **server-side cookies** or on the user's own computer as **client-side cookies**. This tutorial focuses solely on creating and retrieving client-side cookies. Client-side cookies have several important limitations. First, because a client-side cookie is basically a text file, it can only contain textual data. This means that a cookie cannot contain an executable program, it cannot access your computer's hard drive, and perhaps most important, it cannot contain a computer virus. Browsers also place limits on the size and number of client-side cookies that can be stored at any one time. In general, browsers limit developers to:

- 20 cookies per Web site domain
- 300 cookies overall
- 4 kilobytes or less for each cookie file size

In practice, browsers do exceed these limits. For example, both Firefox and Internet Explorer allow 50 cookies per domain and Opera allows 30. Keep these numbers in mind as a guideline for how to employ cookies in your Web site. If your Web site exceeds a browser's cookie limit, the browser will start removing older cookies, perhaps causing one or more Web applications to fail. The 4 kilobyte size limit per cookie is roughly equal to 4000 characters or about two pages of typewritten text, so you can store a good amount of information in a single cookie. For longer pieces of information, you must use a database located on the Web server.

Cookies and Web Browsers

Cookies are created, stored, and retrieved by the Web browser. Each browser manages cookies in a slightly different way. So a cookie that is generated while viewing a Web site under one browser is *not* available if the user then switches to a different browser. The user's browser might also be configured to block cookies for security reasons. Before testing cookies in your Web site, you should familiarize yourself with how your browser handles cookies and verify that cookies are not being blocked.

You can view information about how your browser handles cookies by opening the preference or options dialog box, usually available under the browser's File, Edit, or Tools menu. Figure 9-2 shows the options dialog boxes under Internet Explorer, Firefox, Opera, and Safari related to the use of cookies. From these dialog boxes, you can set the security options for handling cookies as well as delete already existing cookies. Firefox, Opera, and Safari allow the user to delete individual cookies related to specific Web sites. Internet Explorer only allows the user to delete all cookies at once, though third-party add-ons are available to manage individual cookies.

Figure 9-2 — **Browser dialog boxes to set cookie options**

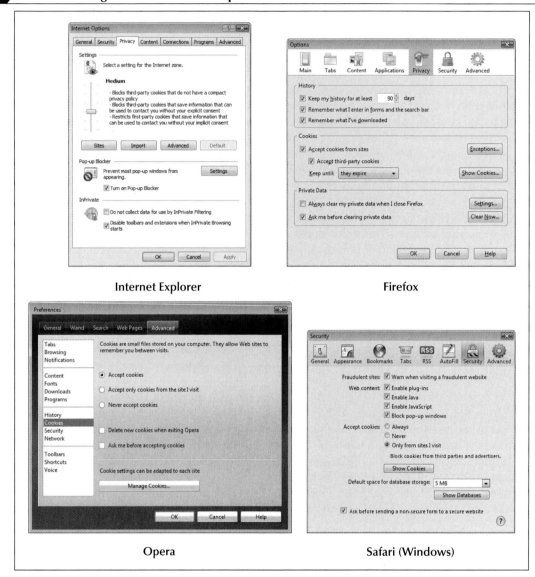

Internet Explorer

Firefox

Opera

Safari (Windows)

The major browsers also differ in how they store cookies. Internet Explorer stores each cookie in a separate file within the cookies folder. The exact location of the cookies folder depends on the version of Windows and Internet Explorer being used. Under Windows Vista, the cookies folder most likely will be stored in

```
C:\Users\username\AppData\Roaming\Microsoft\Windows\Cookies
```

where *username* is the name of the user account under Windows. Note that the cookies folder is often hidden and you need to change the Windows folder options to allow hidden files and folders to be viewable.

Firefox, Opera, and Safari save all of their cookies within a single file stored in a user profile folder associated with each application. For users of Firefox 2.0 and earlier, cookies are stored in the cookie.txt file. For users of Firefox 3.0 and later, the file is named cookies.sqlite. Opera stores cookie data in the cookies4.dat file. Safari saves cookies in the Cookies.plist file. Be aware that these filename specifications can and do change with each browser version, so it's usually best to manage the browser's cookies through the browser's options or preferences dialog box.

Tip

You can quickly locate your Internet Explorer cookies folder by doing a search for cookies using the Windows search utility.

The Structure of a Cookie

Each cookie has the general structure

`name=value;expires=date;path=directory;domain=domain-name;secure`

where *name* is the name of the cookie, *value* is the cookie's value, *date* is the date that the cookie expires or is deleted by the browser, *directory* is the directory on the Web server in which the cookie resides, *domain-name* is the domain portion of the URL in which the cookie resides, and secure indicates that the cookie should be transmitted only over a secure link. The following is a collection of cookies named firstName and lastName with the values set to Kevin and Geary, expiration date set to Thursday, April 18, 2013, belonging to the domain cyclocrossings.com with the directory path /members:

```
firstName=Kevin;expires=Thu, 18 Apr 2013 00:00:00 GMT; path=/members;
domain=cyclocrossings.com; secure

lastName=Geary;expires=Thu, 18 Apr 2013 00:00:00 GMT; path=/members;
domain=cyclocrossings.com; secure
```

A cookie only requires the *name=value* pair. The expiration date, directory, domain, and secure settings are optional and given default values by the browser if they are not set. So, the previous two cookies can also be defined as

```
firstName=Kevin;
lastName=Geary;
```

and the browser will assign the default expiration date, path, domain, and security setting. You'll explore the interpretation and use of each of those settings shortly.

Writing a Cookie Name and Value

Cookies are created in JavaScript using the document.cookie property. The document.cookie property also returns the text of all of the cookies available to the current Web document. To create a new cookie, run the command

```
document.cookie = cookie_string
```

where *cookie_string* is the text of the cookie. For example, the following commands create the firstName and lastName cookies, storing the values Kevin and Geary:

```
document.cookie = "firstName=Kevin;";
document.cookie = "lastName=Geary;";
```

Notice that the lastName cookie does not replace the firstName cookie; instead it adds the lastName cookie to the collection of cookies associated with the document.cookie property.

Using Escape Characters

The *name=value* pair must be read as a single text string with no spaces. This can be a problem if a cookie value contains a string of words, such as the full name Kevin Geary. To create a string of words, you can replace the blank spaces separating the words with an escape code that represents the blank space character. In this instance, the cookie's value becomes

```
fullName=Kevin%20Geary;
```

where %20 is an escape code that represents the blank space between the first and last names. JavaScript supports three methods to convert non-alphanumeric characters to escape codes: escape(), encodeURI(), and encodeURIComponent(). The escape() method replaces all non-alphanumeric characters with escape codes. The encodeURI() method is used primarily to encode the text of Web URLs and replaces all non-alphanumeric characters with escape codes other than those characters that might appear within a URL or URI such as /, ?, @, and +. The encodeURIComponent() method encodes many of the same characters as the encodeURI() method. Figure 9-3 lists the character codes returned by the three methods.

Figure 9-3   **Escape character codes and functions**

Character	escape()	encodeURI()	encodeURIComponent()
blank space	%20	%20	%20
!	%21	!	!
@	@	@	%40
#	%23	#	%23
$	%24	$	%24
%	%25	%25	%25
^	%5E	%5E	%5E
&	%26	&	%26
*	*	*	*
(	%28	(	(
)	%29	)	)
-	-	-	-
_	_	_	_
=	%3D	=	%3D
+	+	+	%2B
:	%3A	:	%3A
;	%3B	;	%3B
.	.	.	.
"	%22	%22	%22
'	%27	'	'
\	%5C	%5C	%5C
/	/	/	%2F
?	%3F	?	%3F
<	%3C	%3C	%3C
>	%3E	%3E	%3E
~	%7E	~	~
[	%5B	%5B	%5B
]	%5D	%5D	%5D
{	%7B	%7B	%7B
}	%7D	%7D	%7D
`	%60	%60	%60

The following code shows how to apply the escape() method to replace a blank space in the value of the nameText variable with its character code:

```
var nameText = "Kevin Geary";
document.cookie = "fullName=" + escape(nameText);
```

After running this code, the fullName cookie contains the text:

```
fullName=Kevin%20Geary
```

To remove the escape characters from a text string, you use the unescape() method

```
unescape("Kevin%20Geary")
```

which returns the text string Kevin Geary. You can also use the decodeURI() and decodeURIComponent() methods to remove escape characters created with the encodeURI() and encodeURIComponent() methods.

Inserting Escape Characters into a Text String | Reference Window

- To replace non-alphanumeric characters with escape codes, use the escape() methods.
- To replace non-alphanumeric characters with escape codes for Web URLs and URIs, use the encodeURI() and encodeURIComponent() methods.
- To replace escape codes with their corresponding non-alphanumeric characters, use the unescape(), decodeURI(), or decodeURIComponent() methods, depending on which method was used to encode the original character string.

The writeCookie() Function

For the CycloCrossings Web site, you will create a library of functions to work with cookies. The first function will be one that writes a cookie given the cookie name and value. The initial code of the writeCookie() function is:

```
function writeCookie(cName, cValue) {

    if (cName && cValue != "") {
        var cString = cName + "=" + escape(cValue);

        document.cookie = cString;
    }

}
```

The function first confirms that cName is not null and the value of the cValue parameter is not an empty text string before it writes the cookie using cName as the cookie name and cValue as the cookie value, and then uses the escape() function to replace any non-alphanumeric characters in the cookie value before writing the text of the cookie. You will add this function to the cookies.js file you created earlier.

Tip

To replace a cookie's value, write a cookie with the same name but a new value. Two cookies cannot share the same name unless they belong to different paths and/or domains.

To insert the writeCookie() function:

▶ **1.** Go to the **cookies.js** file in your text editor.

▶ **2.** At the bottom of the file, insert the following code, as shown in Figure 9-4:

```
function writeCookie(cName, cValue) {

    if (cName && cValue != "") {
        var cString = cName + "=" + escape(cValue);

        document.cookie = cString;
    }

}
```

Figure 9-4	The initial writeCookie() function

```
/* Add new code below */

function writeCookie(cName, cValue) {

    if (cName && cValue != "") {
        var cString = cName + "=" + escape(cValue);
        document.cookie = cString;
    }

}
```

replaces all non-alphanumeric characters with escape codes

▶ **3.** Save the file.

Setting the Cookie Expiration Date

Cookies are designed to expire when the current Web session is completed. When a user closes the Web browser, the browser deletes any cookies it created during the current session. This keeps the number of cookies handled by the browser to a manageable size because, as you learned earlier, browsers are limited to the number of cookies they can create. This also removes information that is no longer relevant. It is usually not of interest to record items previously placed into an online shopping cart well after the cart has been emptied and the items purchased. Cookies that expire when a Web session is completed are known as **session cookies** because they are good only for the current Web session.

However, in some cases, such as the registration data for the CycloCrossings Web site, you will want cookies to be retained from one browser session to another. Those cookies, known as **persistent cookies**, exist until a specified expiration date. Expiration dates are set by adding the following string to the cookie

```
;expires=wday, dd-mmm-yyyy hh:mm:ss GMT
```

where *wday* is the day of the week (Sun, Mon, Tue, Wed, Thu, Fri, or Sat), *dd* is the day of the month, *mmm* is the month name (Jan, Feb, Mar, Apr, May, Jun, Jul, Aug, Sep, Oct, Nov, or Dec), *yyyy* is the four-digit year value, *hh* is the hour value in 24-hour time, *mm* is the minute value, and *ss* is the second value. For example, the following text sets the cookie to expire at 2:15 p.m. on August 19th of 2013:

```
;expires=Mon, 19-Aug-2013 14:15:00 GMT
```

If the browser encounters the cookie on or after this date and time, it immediately deletes the cookie.

One way to set an expiration date is with a date object that can be converted into the appropriate date format using the toGMTString() method (see Tutorial 2 for a discussion of date objects and methods). The following code creates a date object set to the above date and time, and then converts it to the GMT string format that then can be added to a cookie:

```
var expDate = new Date("August 19, 2013 14:15:00");
expString = ";expires=" + expDate.toGMTString();
```

Expiration dates also can be set relative to the current date. For example, you can set a cookie to expire in six months by adding six months to the current date and then applying that calculated date to the cookie's expiration date, as shown in the following code:

```
var expDate = new Date();
expDate.setMonth(expDate.getMonth() + 6);
expString = ";expires=" + expDate.toGMTString();
```

Recall that using the new Date() method with a specified date returns the current date and time. The getMonth() and setMonth() methods are used here to retrieve the current month number, increase it by 6, and then apply the new month to the expDate date object. Similarly, to set an expiration date one year from the current date, you would use the setFullYear() and getFullYear() functions, as follows:

```
var expDate = new Date();
expDate.setFullYear(expDate.getFullYear() + 1);
expString = ";expires=" + expDate.toGMTString();
```

In the same fashion, you can use the other JavaScript date methods described in Tutorial 2 to set the expiration date a few days from now, a few hours from now, or whatever time interval your application requires.

You will add a parameter to the writeCookie() function to set the expiration date. Assume that the parameter is a date object that can be converted into a date string using the toGMTString() method.

To add an expiration date to the writeCookie() function:

▶ **1.** Within the cookies.js file, add the following parameter to the writeCookie() function:

```
, expDate
```

▶ **2.** Add the following line to the function that writes the expiration date only if an expiration date has been specified for the cookie:

```
if (expDate) cString += ";expires=" + expDate.toGMTString();
```

Figure 9-5 highlights the revised code in the function.

Code to write the expiration date of a cookie ◀ **Figure 9-5**

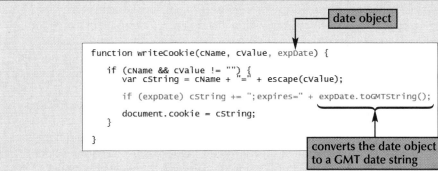

Setting the Cookie Path, Domain, and Security

The final piece to add to the writeCookie() function is to define the cookie's path, domain, and security. You will first look at the issues surrounding defining the cookie's path.

The Cookie Path

One reason that cookies are valuable is because they are not associated only with a single document, but with folders and directories. This feature allows cookies created in one Web page to be accessible to other pages in the Web site. By default, the other pages must be within the same folder as the page that created the cookie or within one of that folder's subfolders. For example, Kevin wants you to create cookies for the registration page. If he stores the register.htm file at the Web address *www.cyclocrossings.com/members/register.htm*, the file is stored in the members directory on his Web server. Any page within the members folder or subfolder can access those cookies, but a Web page located within *www.cyclocrossings.com/shoppingcart/* could not because the page resides under a different directory path.

To explicitly define where a cookie is accessible, you add the following text string to the cookie definition

```
;path=directory
```

where *directory* is the directory path in which the cookie can be read. A path such as

```
;path=/shoppingcart
```

makes the cookie available to any page within the shoppingcart folder or subfolder. Often, you want to ensure that a cookie is readable from within any folder on the Web server. This requires setting the path to the root folder of the Web server using the following expression:

```
;path=/
```

Note that if you place all Web pages within a single folder on the server, you don't have to worry about setting the cookie path. The cookie path becomes a concern only if you store your pages in different directories.

The Cookie Domain

Cookies are also restricted to work within a particular Web domain. If Kevin places the registration page within the domain *members.cyclocrossings.com*, any cookies created by the registration page will be accessible only from within that domain. One result of this restriction is that cookies cannot be accessed across domains. You cannot, for example, make cookies available at a domain such as *www.microsoft.com* or *www.whitehouse.org*; nor can JavaScript programs read cookies created by those domains. This security feature prevents other domains from "snooping" on cookies that don't belong to them.

However, many sites employ multiple domains and subdomains. The CycloCrossings Web site has several domain names, including *search.cyclocrossings.com*, *store.cyclocrossings.com*, and *news.cyclocrossings.com*. Although these domain names help customers by placing the different sections of the CycloCrossings Web site under topical domain names, cookies created under one domain are not accessible under another. To avoid this problem, you can specify the domain by adding the text string

```
;domain=domain-name
```

to the cookie definition, where *domain-name* is the name of the domain in which the cookie is active. The cookie will then be available to any page within *domain-name* and any of its subdomains. Kevin can match all of the subdomains at the CycloCrossings Web site with

```
;domain=cyclocrossings.com
```

and pages located at *search.cyclocrossings.com*, *store.cyclocrossings.com*, and *news.cyclocrossings.com* will be able to access any cookie activated by any page within the *cyclocrossings.com* domain, including cookies created by the registration page at *members.cyclocrossings.com*.

Tip

Many Web server path names are case sensitive, so you must match the use of upper- and lowercase letters in any path name you reference in cookies.

Tip

The specified domain must contain at least a second-level domain name. You can't specify a domain such as .com or .org because those are only first-level domain names.

Third-Party Cookies | InSight

Not all cookies originate from the Web server hosting the Web site. Some cookies, known as **third-party cookies**, originate from other sites on the Web, as opposed to **first-party cookies**, which are cookies associated with the domain hosting the Web site. Third-party cookies are frequently attached to banner ad images or pop-up ads that are hosted by the Web site for advertising revenue. When your browser retrieves an image from a banner ad, that third-party domain is allowed to set a cookie.

Advertising companies can use the information from these cookies to create a profile of Web users as they move from site to site across the Web. These **tracking cookies** cannot identify you personally, but they can assign you a random ID number that they can use to track your actions across the Web. In this way, an advertising company can create a profile of your interests and tailor its banner ads and pop-up ads to things that would entice you.

You can set the security features of your browser to block third-party cookies. In fact, most browsers are now configured to block such cookies by default and anti-virus programs often warn of the presence of tracking cookies. Unlike first-party cookies, which are usually critical to your interaction with a Web site, blocking a third-party cookie should have no ill effect on your Web browsing.

Setting Cookie Security

The final part of the cookie definition is defining whether or not the cookie can be sent only to a Secure Sockets Layer (SSL) using the HTTPS transfer protocol. To force the browser to employ a secure channel, you add the following text string to the cookie definition:

```
;secure
```

If you omit the secure keyword from the cookie definition, the browser will transfer the cookie using the HTTP protocol. Most cookies do not require a secure channel, so usually you will omit this flag from your cookie definition.

Now that you've seen how the other parts of the cookie definition are interpreted, you'll add those parameters to the writeCookie() function.

To complete the writeCookie() function:

1. Within the cookies.js file, add the following parameters to the writeCookie() function:

   ```
   , cPath, cDomain, cSecure
   ```

2. Add the following line to the function to test whether a path has been defined for the cookie, and if so, to add the path information to the cookie definition:

   ```
   if (cPath) cString += ";path=" + cPath;
   ```

3. Add the following line to test whether a domain has been specified for the cookie, and if so, to add the domain information to the cookie definition:

   ```
   if (cDomain) cString += ";domain=" + cDomain;
   ```

4. Add the following command to the writeCookie() function so that the final parameter, cSecure, is treated as a Boolean variable (if its value is set to true, the cookie definition should include the secure flag; otherwise, no secure flag should be added to the cookie):

   ```
   if (cSecure) cString += ";secure";
   ```

   Figure 9-6 highlights the revised code in the complete writeCookie() function.

Figure 9-6 **Code for the cookie's path, domain, and security settings**

path associated
with the cookie

Boolean value indicating
whether to transmit the
cookie over a secure
connection

domain associated
with the cookie

```
function writeCookie(cName, cValue, expDate, cPath, cDomain, cSecure) {

    if (cName && cValue != "") {
        var cString = cName + "=" + escape(cValue);

        if (expDate) cString += ";expires=" + expDate.toGMTString();
        if (cPath)   cString += ";path=" + cPath;
        if (cDomain) cString += ";domain=" + cDomain;
        if (cSecure) cString += ";secure";

        document.cookie = cString;
    }

}
```

▶ **5.** Save the cookies.js file.

▶ **6.** Return to the **register.htm** file in your text editor, and then, within the head section of the file, insert the following line to link this file to the cookies.js function library:

```
<script type="text/javascript" src="cookies.js"></script>
```

▶ **7.** Save the register.htm file.

You can use the writeCookie() function to record data values from the CycloCrossings registration page.

Reference Window | **Creating a Cookie**

- To create a cookie, enter
  ```
  document.cookie =
  name=value;expires=date;path=directory;domain=domain-name;secure
  ```
  where *name* is the name of the cookie, *value* is the cookie's value, *date* is the date that the cookie expires, *directory* is the folder in which the cookie is enabled, and *domain* is the domain in which the cookie is enabled. The expires, path, domain, and secure settings are optional.
- To create a session cookie that only exists for the current Web session, omit the expiration date.
- To create a cookie that is enabled only for files in the current folder and its subfolders, omit the path setting.
- To create a cookie that is enabled only for files in the current domain and its subdomains, omit the domain setting.
- To create a cookie that is sent over the HTTP protocol, omit the secure flag. To send the cookie over the secure HTTPS protocol, add the secure flag.

Storing Form Data in Cookies

The registration page contains several input fields that provide contact information for CycloCrossings members. Figure 9-7 lists the name of each input field. In the HTML code for the registration page, Kevin has set both the name attribute and the id attribute to the same value to make it easier to reference individual form fields in the JavaScript code.

Registration field names ◄ **Figure 9-7**

Field Name	Description
firstName	Member first name
lastName	Member last name
street1	Street address
street2	Second street address (optional)
city	City of residence
state	Two-letter state or region abbreviation
zip	Zip or postal code
country	Country of residence
email	Member e-mail address
phone	Member phone number
memberOption	CycloCrossings membership option

To save the data in the registration form, you'll loop through the elements contained in the form, saving the values entered by the user. The initial code for the saveMemberInfo() function is:

```
function saveMemberInfo() {

   var expire = new Date();
   expire.setFullYear(expire.getFullYear() + 1);

   var allFields = document.registerForm.elements;
   for (var i = 0; i < allFields.length; i++) {

   }

}
```

Note that the saveMemberInfo() function starts by creating a date object named expires that you will use to define when the cookies containing member data are set to expire. In the present code, this date will expire one year from the current date.

You will add the saveMemberInfo() function to the register.js file.

To insert the saveMemberInfo()function:

► **1.** Go to the **register.js** file in your text editor.

► **2.** At the bottom of the file, insert the following code, as shown in Figure 9-8:

```
function saveMemberInfo() {

   // Set the cookie expiration date one year hence
   var expire = new Date();
   expire.setFullYear(expire.getFullYear() + 1);

   // Loop through all of the elements in the form
   var allFields = document.registerForm.elements;
   for (var i = 0; i < allFields.length; i++) {

   }

}
```

Figure 9-8 **The saveMemberInfo() function**

```
*/

function saveMemberInfo() {

    // Set the cookie expiration date one year hence
    var expire = new Date();
    expire.setFullYear(expire.getFullYear() + 1);

    // Loop through all of the elements in the form
    var allFields = document.registerForm.elements;
    for (var i = 0; i < allFields.length; i++) {

    }
}
```

> expire stores the cookie expiration date

> the document.registerForm.elements collection contains all of the elements in the registration form

3. Save the file.

Within the for loop, you'll save each field value as a cookie, starting with the input boxes. The registration form has nine input boxes to record values for the firstName, lastName, street1, street2, city, zip, phone, and email fields. Because these input boxes all have a type attribute equal to text, the following code writes each field value into a separate cookie:

```
if (allFields[i].type == "text") {
    writeCookie(allFields[i].id, allFields[i].value, expire);
}
```

The code uses the writeCookie() function to create a new cookie with the cookie name taken from the field's id value, the cookie value taken from the field value, and the expiration date taken from the expire date object. Note that no path, domain, or security setting is required because all of the pages in this Web site are located in a single folder under a single domain name.

To store the values from the input boxes in cookies:

1. Within the for loop of the saveMemberInfo() function in the register.js file, insert the following code, as shown in Figure 9-9:

```
if (allFields[i].type == "text") {
    // Write input box value to a cookie
    writeCookie(allFields[i].id, allFields[i].value, expire);
}
```

Figure 9-9 **Code to write input box values to cookies**

```
function saveMemberInfo() {

    // Set the cookie expiration date one year hence
    var expire = new Date();
    expire.setFullYear(expire.getFullYear() + 1);

    // Loop through all of the elements in the form
    var allFields = document.registerForm.elements;
    for (var i = 0; i < allFields.length; i++) {

        if (allFields[i].type == "text") {
            // Write input box value to a cookie
            writeCookie(allFields[i].id, allFields[i].value, expire);
        }

    }
}
```

2. Save the file.

Next you'll create a cookie to store the member's state of residence. Each member selects his or her state of residence from a selection list. Because selection lists don't have a value property, you will store the index of the selected option in a cookie, using the following code:

```
if (allFields[i].nodeName == "SELECT") {
   writeCookie(allFields[i].id, allFields[i].selectedIndex, expire);
}
```

Notice that you use the nodeName property to test whether the current field in the for loop is a selection list before attempting to store the value of the selectedIndex property. You will add this code to the saveMemberInfo() function.

To save the chosen option from the selection lists:

▶ **1.** Within the for loop in the saveMemberInfo() function, insert the following code, as shown in Figure 9-10:

```
if (allFields[i].nodeName == "SELECT") {
   // Write the index number of the selected option
   writeCookie(allFields[i].id, allFields[i].selectedIndex,
expire);
}
```

Code to store the index number of selected options in a cookie ◀ **Figure 9-10**

```
function saveMemberInfo() {

    // Set the cookie expiration date one year hence
    var expire = new Date();
    expire.setFullYear(expire.getFullYear() + 1);

    // Loop through all of the elements in the form
    var allFields = document.registerForm.elements;
    for (var i = 0; i < allFields.length; i++) {

        if (allFields[i].type == "text") {
            // Write input box value to a cookie
            writeCookie(allFields[i].id, allFields[i].value, expire);
        }

        if (allFields[i].nodeName == "SELECT") {
            // Write the index number of the selected option
            writeCookie(allFields[i].id, allFields[i].selectedIndex, expire);
        }

    }
}
```

▶ **2.** Save the file.

Finally, for radio buttons and check boxes, you'll write a cookie that stores whether the button or box was checked by the user. The following code records this information:

```
if (allFields[i].type == "radio" || allFields[i].type == "checkbox") {
   writeCookie(allFields[i].id, allFields[i].checked, expire);
}
```

This code stores a Boolean value (true or false) in the cookie indicating whether the radio or checkbox was checked. You will add this code to the saveMemberInfo() function, completing the function.

To complete the saveMemberInfo() function:

▶ **1.** Add the following code to the for loop:

```
if (allFields[i].type == "radio" || allFields[i].type ==
"checkbox") {
   // Write whether the button or checkbox was checked
   writeCookie(allFields[i].id, allFields[i].checked, expire);
}
```

▶ **2.** At the end of the function, insert the following code to display an alert box, notify-ing the user that the registration data has been successfully saved:

```
alert("Registration data saved");
```

Figure 9-11 highlights the added code in the function.

Figure 9-11 ▶ **Code to store whether a radio or check box was checked**

```
function saveMemberInfo() {

   // Set the cookie expiration date one year hence
   var expire = new Date();
   expire.setFullYear(expire.getFullYear() + 1);

   // Loop through all of the elements in the form
   var allFields = document.registerForm.elements;
   for (var i = 0; i < allFields.length; i++) {

      if (allFields[i].type == "text") {
         // Write input box value to a cookie
         writeCookie(allFields[i].id, allFields[i].value, expire);
      }

      if (allFields[i].nodeName == "SELECT") {
         // Write the index number of the selected option
         writeCookie(allFields[i].id, allFields[i].selectedIndex, expire);
      }

      if (allFields[i].type == "radio" || allFields[i].type == "checkbox") {
         // Write whether the button or checkbox was checked
         writeCookie(allFields[i].id, allFields[i].checked, expire);
      }

   }

   alert("Registration data saved");

}
```

Kevin wants the saveMemberInfo() function to run whenever the user clicks the Submit button on the registration page. You will add this event handler within a function named initPage() that will run when the registration page is initially loaded by the browser. The following code sets up the page and the onclick event handler:

```
addEvent(window, "load", initPage, false);

function initPage() {

   //Add event handler to the Submit button
   document.getElementById("sbutton").onclick = saveMemberInfo;

}
```

Note that the addEvent() function is one of the functions previously included in the cookies.js file to add event handlers to the document. You will add this code to the register.js file.

To create an event handler for the registration Submit button:

▶ **1.** Add the following code directly above the saveMemberInfo() function, as shown in Figure 9-12:

```
addEvent(window, "load", initPage, false);

function initPage() {

    //Add event handler to the Submit button
    document.getElementById("sbutton").onclick = saveMemberInfo;

}
```

Event handler for the Submit button ◀ **Figure 9-12**

```
*/
addEvent(window, "load", initPage, false);

function initPage() {

    //Add event handler to the Submit button
    document.getElementById("sbutton").onclick = saveMemberInfo;
}
```

> runs the saveMemberInfo()
> function when the submit
> button is clicked

▶ **2.** Save the register.js file.

Now you can test your code by entering a set of sample data and verifying that the browser saves the form data to a set of cookies.

To run the member registration form:

▶ **1.** Go to the **register.htm** file in your text editor, and then, within the head section, link the file to the register.js script file using the following statement:

```
<script type="text/javascript" src="register.js"></script>
```

▶ **2.** Save the register.htm file.

▶ **3.** Load **register.htm** in your Web browser, and then complete the registration form, as shown in Figure 9-13.

Member registration information ◀ **Figure 9-13**

Registration Form

First Name	Kevin	Last	Geary
Street	100 North Lane		
City	Redmond		
State	Oregon		
Zip/Postal Code	97756		
Country	United States		
E-mail	kgeary@cyclocrossings.com		
Phone Number	(541) 555 - 0706		
Membership	One year ($30) ◉		
	Two year ($45) ○		

▶ **4.** Click the **Submit** button and verify that your browser does not report any errors in the JavaScript code.

If your code contains no errors, the form data should now be stored in a set of cookies maintained by the browser. But how can you be sure that the cookies were actually created? If you're using Firefox, Opera, or Safari, you can view the content of any cookie saved by the browser by going to the browser's preference or options dialog box. Internet Explorer version 7.0 and earlier does not provide this feature, but you can try to locate the cookies folder on your computer to check whether the cookies have, in fact, been created.

To simplify this process, a demo page has been created for you that will display all active cookies from the tutorial.09\tutorial folder and their contents. You will open this demo page now.

To view the demo page:

1. Use your Web browser to open the **demo_cookies.htm** file from the tutorial.09\ tutorial folder.

2. Click the **Show Cookies** button on the Web page. The demo page both displays the value of document.cookie, and lists each cookie name and its value. Notice that the cookie names match the names of the registration form fields (because the cookie names were taken from the field ids) and the cookie values are encoded as single text strings with character codes in place of any non-alphanumeric character. See Figure 9-14.

Figure 9-14 ▶ **Saved cookies from the registration form**

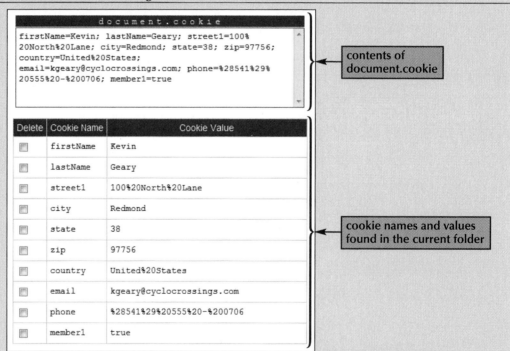

Trouble? If the Web page fails to display the cookies from the registration form, check your code in the cookies.js and register.js files against that shown in the figures. Remember that the use of upper- and lowercase letters is important.

If you are running Google Chrome or Safari on a local machine, you will not see the cookies listed in the Web page. Those browsers do not return the contents of the document.cookie property unless the cookies are sent via the HTTP protocol. Neither browser uses the HTTP protocol to retrieve local files. If you need to use one of those two browsers, you can solve this problem by loading your documents on a Web server or by installing a personal Web server on your local machine. Safari users can also view the cookies directly through the Security tab of Safari's Preference window.

You've created your first set of cookies. These cookies will remain until you manually delete them or they reach their expiration date. In the next session, you'll learn how to use JavaScript to retrieve these cookies and display their values from within any page in the CycloCrossings Web site.

Session 9.1 Quick Check | Review

1. What is the difference between client-side and server-side cookies?
2. Describe the difference between how Internet Explorer stores cookies and how Firefox, Opera, and Safari store cookies.
3. You've been asked to create a shopping cart application in which a customer can enter hundreds of items into a cart. Discuss one challenge involved in saving all of those selections in a client-side cookie.
4. What JavaScript object and property should you use to reference all of the cookies available to the current document?
5. You want to create a cookie named userName with the value Jason Stevens. Provide the text of this cookie, including the proper encoding for the blank space.
6. By default, when are cookies deleted by the browser? What would you add to a cookie string to set its expiration date to Monday, March 25, 2013 at 2:35 p.m.?
7. Provide code that creates a date object named expireDate that is equal to a date three years from now.
8. If you want all of the cookies in *www.hipparchus.com* to be available to each page in the Web site, what would you add to each cookie's text string?
9. What are third-party cookies?

Session 9.2

Retrieving a Cookie

In the previous session, you created a set of cookies to store membership data. Kevin now wants you to read those cookies and write them into a Web page that provides information to each member about his or her account with CycloCrossings. As shown earlier in Figure 9-14, the document.cookie object for the files in the tutorial.09\tutorial folder contains the following text:

```
firstName=Kevin; lastName=Geary; street=100%20North%20Lane; city=Redmond;
state=38; zip=97756; country=United%20States; email=kgeary@cyclocrossings.com;
phone=%28541%29%20555%20-%200706; member1=true
```

This text string contains all of the *name/value* pairs for each cookie separated by the = sign. Individual cookies are separated by a semicolon and a space. You may have noticed that the text string does not contain any information about the cookie's expiration date, path, domain, or security. This is because those settings are treated as commands to be run by the browser and are not directly accessible to JavaScript.

Splitting a Cookie into an Array

Because JavaScript treats the contents of the document.cookie object as one long text string, you can split the text into separate parts to retrieve information on individual cookies. One way of doing this is with the split() method introduced in Tutorial 5. The split() method breaks up a text string at each occurrence of a specified character or set of characters, saving the different substrings into an array. For document.cookie, you will split the text string at each occurrence of the text "; ". The following code splits the document.cookie object into an array named cookiesArray:

```
var cookiesArray = document.cookie.split("; ");
```

Notice that the code includes a space after the semicolon because each cookie is separated from the others by both a semicolon *and* a space. As shown in Figure 9-15, splitting document.cookie in this fashion creates an array of *name/value* pairs.

Figure 9-15 ▶ **The document.cookie object split into an array**

> **Tip**
>
> Older browsers might not support the split() method. For those browsers, you can use the indexOf() method to locate the start and end of each cookie string.

document.cookie

```
firstName=Kevin; lastName=Geary;
street1=100%20North%20Lane; city=Redmond; state=38;
zip=97756; country=United%20States;
email=kgeary@cyclocrossings.com;
phone=%28541%29%20555%20-%200706; member1=true
```

```
var cookiesArray = document.cookie.split("; ");
```

cookiesArray[0]	firstName=Kevin
cookiesArray[1]	lastName=Geary
cookiesArray[2]	street1=100%20North%20Lane
cookiesArray[3]	city=Redmond
cookiesArray[4]	state=38
cookiesArray[5]	zip=97756
cookiesArray[6]	country=United%20States
cookiesArray[7]	email=kgeary@cyclocrossings.com
cookiesArray[8]	phone=%28541%29%20555%20-%200706
cookiesArray[9]	member1=true

Each item in cookiesArray is itself a text string that can be split at the location of the = symbol to retrieve either the cookie name or the cookie value. Splitting the entry in this fashion creates an array with two items. The first item is the cookie name and the second item is the cookie value. This means that the name of the first cookie can be referenced using the expression

```
cookiesArray[0].split("=")[0]
```

returning the text firstName for the cookie you created in the previous session. The value of the firstName cookie can be retrieved using the expression

```
cookiesArray[0].split("=")[1]
```

returning the value Kevin. To remove any escape codes from the cookie's value, you apply the unescape() function to the value, as follows

```
unescape(cookiesArray[2].split("=")[1])
```

and JavaScript will return the text string 100 North Lane from the current membership data, replacing the %20 escape code with a blank space.

Retrieving a Cookie Value

Using the split() method in this fashion creates the following retrieveCookie() function to retrieve the value of a cookie given the cookie's name:

```
function retrieveCookie(cName) {
   if (document.cookie) {

      var cookiesArray = document.cookie.split("; ");
      for (var i = 0; i < cookiesArray.length; i++) {
         if (cookiesArray[i].split("=")[0] == cName) {
            return unescape(cookiesArray[i].split("=")[1]);
         }
      }

   }
}
```

The retrieveCookie() function has a single parameter, cName, that contains the name of the cookie. The function first tests whether any cookies are available. If so, the function then splits the text of document.cookie into the cookiesArray and loops through the array looking for a cookie name that matches cName. When it finds a match, it returns the value of that cookie with the escape codes removed. If no match is found, the function does not return any value.

Reading a Cookie | Reference Window

- To view the name/value pair within a cookie, retrieve the content of the document.cookie object.
- To place the cookies within document.cookie into separate items in an array, use the split() method to split the contents of document.cookie using the character string "; " as the delimiter.

You will add the retrieveCookie() function to the cookies.js file you created in the previous session.

To create the retrieveCookie() function:

▶ 1. If you took a break after the previous session, make sure the cookies.js and register.js files are open in your text editor, and the register.htm and demo_cookies.htm files are open in your Web browser.

▶ **2.** Go to the **cookies.js** file in your text editor, and insert the following code at the bottom of the file, as shown in Figure 9-16:

```
function retrieveCookie(cName) {

    if (document.cookie) {

        var cookiesArray = document.cookie.split("; ");
        for (var i = 0; i < cookiesArray.length; i++) {
            if (cookiesArray[i].split("=")[0] == cName) {
                return unescape(cookiesArray[i].split("=")[1]);
            }
        }

    }

}
```

Figure 9-16 ▶ **The retrieveCookie() function**

```
function retrieveCookie(cName) {

    if (document.cookie) {

        var cookiesArray = document.cookie.split("; ");
        for (var i = 0; i < cookiesArray.length; i++) {
            if (cookiesArray[i].split("=")[0] == cName) {
                return unescape(cookiesArray[i].split("=")[1]);
            }
        }

    }

}
```

splits document.cookie into an array and searches through to locate the cookie named cName

▶ **3.** Save the file.

With the retrieveCookie() function, you can retrieve the cookie values you created in the previous session and then write them to pages on the CycloCrossings Web site.

Writing the Cookie's Value

Kevin created an accounts page to display the membership data. He also created a file to store JavaScript code for the accounts page. You will open both of these files now.

To open the accounts files:

▶ **1.** Open the **accounttxt.htm** and **accounttxt.js** files from the tutorial.09\tutorial folder in your text editor, enter *your name* and *the date* in the comment section of each file, and then save the files as **accounts.htm** and **accounts.js**, respectively.

▶ **2.** Study the HTML code in the accounts.htm file and the layout of the page contents.

▶ **3.** Add the following elements to the head section of the accounts.htm file to link it to the cookies.js and accounts.js files:

```
<script type="text/javascript" src="cookies.js"></script>
<script type="text/javascript" src="accounts.js"></script>
```

▶ **4.** Save the accounts.htm file.

Kevin wants the membership data to be displayed within a table on the accounts page. He populated the table with several span elements that mark different pieces of member information. For example, the section in the table containing the member's first name and last name is marked with the following HTML tags:

```
<td>
   <span id="firstName"></span>
   <span id="lastName"></span>
</td>
```

To insert the member's first name and last name into these elements, you can call the retrieveCookie() function, as follows:

```
document.getElementById("firstName").innerHTML = retrieveCookie("firstName");
document.getElementById("lastName").innerHTML = retrieveCookie("lastName");
```

Note that the ids that Kevin chose for the span elements match the cookie names. This makes it easier to relate the information stored in the cookies to elements on the accounts page. Rather than specifying each cookie, you can loop through all of the span elements, inserting the appropriate cookie value, by using the following code:

```
if (retrieveCookie("lastName")) {
   var allSpans = document.getElementsByTagName("span");
   for (var i = 0; i < allSpans.length; i++) {
      var cValue = retrieveCookie(allSpans[i].id);
      if (cValue) allSpans[i].innerHTML = cValue;
   }
}
```

The code first confirms that the user has entered his or her last name in the registration page by retrieving the lastName cookie. For simplicity, you'll assume that every member has entered a last name value. In a more complex script, you might include other validation tests. You then create a collection of all span elements and loop through that collection, matching each span element with a cookie. If a cookie is associated with the span element, you then write the cookie value to the document.

You will add this code as part of a function named retrieveMemberInfo() and then run that function when the page is initially loaded.

Tip

You can make lastName a required field using the techniques described in Tutorial 5.

To retrieve the member information:

▶ **1.** Go to the **accounts.js** file in your text editor.

▶ **2.** At the bottom of the file, insert the following command to run the retrieveMemberInfo() function when the page is initially loaded by the browser:

```
addEvent(window, "load", retrieveMemberInfo, false);
```

3. Add the following code for the retrieveMemberInfo() function:

```
function retrieveMemberInfo() {

    if (retrieveCookie("lastName")) {
        // Retrieve the membership data
        var allSpans = document.getElementsByTagName("span");
        for (var i = 0; i < allSpans.length; i++) {
            var cValue = retrieveCookie(allSpans[i].id);
            if (cValue) allSpans[i].innerHTML = cValue;
        }

    }

}
```

Figure 9-17 shows the inserted code.

| Figure 9-17 | Initial retrieveMemberInfo() function |

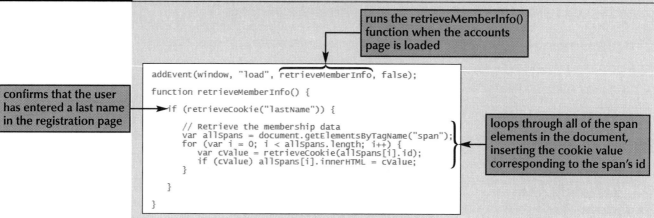

runs the retrieveMemberInfo() function when the accounts page is loaded

confirms that the user has entered a last name in the registration page

loops through all of the span elements in the document, inserting the cookie value corresponding to the span's id

4. Save the file, and then load **accounts.htm** in your Web browser. The Web page displays some of the values drawn from the cookies you created in the previous session. See Figure 9-18.

Retrieved membership information | **Figure 9-18**

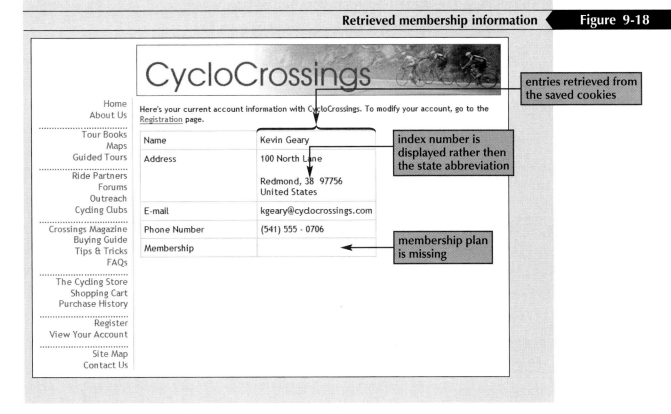

The retrieveMemberInfo() function needs more work. The index number of the state is displayed rather than the state abbreviation. Also, the page does not display the user's membership plan.

Kevin already added an array named stateAbbr to the accounts.js file containing a list of all state and province abbreviations. The array matches the list of options from the selection list on the registration page. To display the state abbreviation, you can retrieve the appropriate item using the index value stored in the state cookie, as follows:

```
var stateIndex = retrieveCookie("state");
document.getElementById("state").innerHTML = stateAbbr[stateIndex];
```

To retrieve the membership option chosen by the user, recall that the options were stored in two radio buttons named member1 and member2. If the user selects a one-year membership, a cookie named member1 is created with a value true; if the user selects a two-year membership, a cookie named member2 with a value of true is created.

You display the user's membership plan by first checking for the presence of the member1 or member2 cookie, and then writing the text describing each plan to the accounts page. The following code performs these actions:

```
if (retrieveCookie("member1") == "true")
   document.getElementById("memberOption").innerHTML = "One year ($30)";
else if (retrieveCookie("member2") == "true")
   document.getElementById("memberOption").innerHTML = "Two year ($45)";
```

Notice that we use the text string "true" rather than the Boolean value, true. This is because we are retrieving only textual content from the cookie. You will revise the retrieveMemberInfo() function to display both the state abbreviation and the user's membership plan.

To retrieve the state and membership option values:

▶ **1.** Return to the **accounts.js** file in your text editor.

▶ **2.** Scroll down to the retrieveMemberInfo() function, and then insert the following text, as shown in Figure 9-19:

```
// Retrieve the state abbreviation
var stateIndex = retrieveCookie("state");
document.getElementById("state").innerHTML = stateAbbr[stateIndex];

// Retrieve the membership option
if (retrieveCookie("member1") == "true")
   document.getElementById("memberOption").innerHTML = "One year ($30)";
else if (retrieveCookie("member2") == "true")
   document.getElementById("memberOption").innerHTML = "Two year ($45)";
```

Figure 9-19 | **Modified retrieveMemberInfo() function**

```
function retrieveMemberInfo() {

    if (retrieveCookie("lastName")) {

        // Retrieve the membership data
        var allSpans = document.getElementsByTagName("span");
        for (var i = 0; i < allSpans.length; i++) {
            var cValue = retrieveCookie(allSpans[i].id);
            if (cValue) allSpans[i].innerHTML = cValue;
        }
```

retrieves the state abbreviation →
```
        // Retrieve the state abbreviation
        var stateIndex = retrieveCookie("state");
        document.getElementById("state").innerHTML = stateAbbr[stateIndex];
```

retrieves the membership plan →
```
        // Retrieve the membership option
        if (retrieveCookie("member1") == "true")
            document.getElementById("memberOption").innerHTML = "One year ($30)";
        else if (retrieveCookie("member2") == "true")
            document.getElementById("memberOption").innerHTML = "Two year ($45)";

    }
}
```

▶ **3.** Save the file, and then reload **accounts.htm** in your Web browser. The Web page now shows both the state abbreviation and the membership plan. See Figure 9-20.

Figure 9-20 | **Full membership information**

Name	Kevin Geary
Address	100 North Lane Redmond, OR 97756 United States
E-mail	kgeary@cyclocrossings.com
Phone Number	(541) 555 - 0706
Membership	One year ($30)

Kevin wants the registration form to show the registration data you stored in the cookie so that members see their registration data on that page as well. Because the cookie names were based on the field names in the registration form, you can match each cookie with a form field. For text boxes, the value of the cookie will be inserted into the corresponding text box. The code to insert the text box values is:

```
var allInputs = document.getElementsByTagName("input");
for (var i = 0; i < allInputs.length; i++) {
   if (allInputs[i].type == "text") {
      if (retrieveCookie(allInputs[i].id)) {
         allInputs[i].value = retrieveCookie(allInputs[i].id);
      }
   }
}
```

The program first creates the allInputs collection containing all of the input tags in the registration form. It then loops through the collection and, for each input text box, it checks whether a cookie matching the input box's id value exists. If the cookie exists, it retrieves the value and places it in the input box.

For the state selection list, the state cookie stores the selected index. So, to display the selected option in the registration form, you run the following code:

```
document.getElementById("state").selectedIndex = retrieveCookie("state");
```

Finally, the two membership options are displayed as radio buttons, which have the property of being either checked or not checked. The member1 and member2 cookies store a text string value indicating the checked state. To correctly display the membership radio button as being checked or not, you use the following code:

```
if (retrieveCookie("member1") == "true")
   document.getElementById("member1").checked = true
else if (retrieveCookie("member2") == "true")
   document.getElementById("member2").checked = true;
```

You will enter this code into the initPage() function of the register.js file so that it runs whenever the registration page is loaded by the browser. As with the accounts page, you'll test whether the lastName cookie has been created by the user as a validation check before inserting the cookie values.

To display stored registration data in the registration form:

1. Return to the **register.js** file in your text editor.

2. Scroll down to the initPage() function, and then insert the following text, as shown in Figure 9-21:

```
if (retrieveCookie("lastName")) {

   var allInputs = document.getElementsByTagName("input");
   for (var i = 0; i < allInputs.length; i++) {
      if (allInputs[i].type == "text") {
         if (retrieveCookie(allInputs[i].id)) {
            allInputs[i].value = retrieveCookie(allInputs[i].id);
         }
      }
   }

   document.getElementById("state").selectedIndex =
retrieveCookie("state");

   if (retrieveCookie("member1") == "true")
      document.getElementById("member1").checked = true
   else if (retrieveCookie("member2") == "true")
      document.getElementById("member2").checked = true;
}
```

Figure 9-21 | **Code to retrieve stored registration data**

```
function initPage() {

    //Add event handler to the Submit button
    document.getElementById("sbutton").onclick = saveMemberInfo;

    if (retrieveCookie("lastName")) {

        var allInputs = document.getElementsByTagName("input");
        for (var i = 0; i < allInputs.length; i++) {
            if (allInputs[i].type == "text") {
                if (retrieveCookie(allInputs[i].id)) {
                    allInputs[i].value = retrieveCookie(allInputs[i].id);
                }
            }
        }
    }

    document.getElementById("state").selectedIndex = retrieveCookie("state");

    if (retrieveCookie("member1") == "true")
        document.getElementById("member1").checked = true
    else if (retrieveCookie("member2") == "true")
        document.getElementById("member2").checked = true;
    }

}
```

retrieves stored cookie for text input boxes

retrieves the selected state option

retrieves whether or not the radio buttons have been checked

3. Save the file, and then reload **register.htm** in your Web browser. Confirm that the registration page shows the same form data you stored earlier in the tutorial.

Deleting a Cookie

Kevin wants to know what would happen if a user without a CycloCrossings account opened the accounts page. In its current state, the page will show the introductory paragraph followed by an empty table. Kevin wants page visitors to see the following introductory paragraph:

```
You do not currently have an account with CycloCrossings. Join today
and register with us to receive discounts on all tours and merchandise.
```

He also wants the accounts table to be hidden on the page. Kevin suggests showing this content when no cookies containing membership information are found by the browser. The following code changes the introductory paragraph and hides the accounts table:

```
var nonMember = "You do not have an account with CycloCrossings. ";
nonMember += "Join today and <a href='register.htm'>register</a> ";
nonMember += "with us to receive discounts on all tours ";
nonMember += "and merchandise.";

document.getElementById("intro").innerHTML = nonMember;
document.getElementById("accountTable").style.visibility = "hidden";
```

You will add this code to the retrieveMemberInfo() function.

To revise the retrieveMemberInfo() function:

▶ **1.** Return to the **accounts.js** file in your text editor.

▶ **2.** Add the following code to the retrieveMemberInfo() function, as shown in Figure 9-22:

```
else {

    // Display text for nonmembers
    var nonMember = "You do not have an account with
CycloCrossings. ";
    nonMember += "Join today and <a
href='register.htm'>register</a> ";
    nonMember += "with us to receive discounts on all tours ";
    nonMember += "and merchandise.";

    document.getElementById("intro").innerHTML = nonMember;
    document.getElementById("accountTable").style.visibility =
"hidden";

}
```

Code to display text for nonmembers ◀ Figure 9-22

```
function retrieveMemberInfo() {

    if (retrieveCookie("lastName")) {

        // Retrieve the membership data
        var allSpans = document.getElementsByTagName("span");
        for (var i = 0; i < allSpans.length; i++) {
            var cValue = retrieveCookie(allSpans[i].id);
            if (cValue) allSpans[i].innerHTML = cValue;
        }

        // Retrieve the state abbreviation
        var stateIndex = retrieveCookie("state");
        document.getElementById("state").innerHTML = stateAbbr[stateIndex];

        // Retrieve the membership option
        if (retrieveCookie("member1") == "true")
            document.getElementById("memberOption").innerHTML = "One year ($30)";
        else if (retrieveCookie("member2") == "true")
            document.getElementById("memberOption").innerHTML = "Two year ($45)";

    } else {

        // Display text for nonmembers
        var nonMember = "You do not have an account with CycloCrossings. ";
        nonMember += "Join today and <a href='register.htm'>register</a> ";
        nonMember += "with us to receive discounts on all tours ";
        nonMember += "and merchandise.";

        document.getElementById("intro").innerHTML = nonMember;
        document.getElementById("accountTable").style.visibility = "hidden";
    }
}
```

if no cookies are available, display the text for nonmembers

▶ **3.** Save the file.

Before you can test this revised code, you must first delete the cookies you already generated for the CycloCrossings Web site.

To delete a cookie using JavaScript, you change the cookie's expiration date to a past date. Recall that when the browser encounters a cookie that has passed its expiration date, it automatically removes the cookie. The following deleteCookie() function sets the expiration date of the specified cookie to early 1970:

```
function deleteCookie(cName) {

   if (document.cookie) {

      var cookiesArray = document.cookie.split("; ");
      for (var i = 0; i < cookiesArray.length; i++) {
         if (cookiesArray[i].split("=")[0] == cName) {
            document.cookie = cName + "=;expires=Thu, 01-Jan-1970 00:00:01 GMT";
         }
      }

   }

}
```

Tip

You can use any expiration date as long as it's in the past. If you use the JavaScript setTime() method to change the expiration date to one second in the past, the browser will still delete the cookie.

When the function is run and the new expiration date is applied to the cookie, the browser will automatically delete the cookie. Note that the deleteCookie() function uses the same techniques as the retrieveCookie() function in that it creates an array of all of the cookies in document.cookie and loops through that array until it finds a match to the cName parameter. When it finds a match, the function sets the expiration date to Thursday, January 1, 1970. This date was chosen because it represents the very first second in JavaScript's system of storing dates, ensuring that the cookie will be deleted.

Reference Window | Deleting a Cookie

- To delete a cookie, set the cookie's expiration date prior to the current date and time.
- Cookies can also be deleted within the Options or Preferences dialog box of most browsers.

You will add the deleteCookie() function to your library of cookie functions in the cookies.js file.

To create the deleteCookie() function:

1. Go to the **cookies.js** file in your text editor.

2. Add the following function to the bottom of the file, as shown in Figure 9-23:

```
function deleteCookie(cName) {

   if (document.cookie) {

      var cookiesArray = document.cookie.split("; ");
      for (var i = 0; i < cookiesArray.length; i++) {
         if (cookiesArray[i].split("=")[0] == cName) {
            document.cookie = cName + "=;expires=Thu, 01-Jan-1970
00:00:01 GMT";
         }
      }

   }

}
```

The deleteCookie() function Figure 9-23

```
function deleteCookie(cName) {

    if (document.cookie) {

        var cookiesArray = document.cookie.split("; ");
        for (var i = 0; i < cookiesArray.length; i++) {
            if (cookiesArray[i].split("=")[0] == cName) {
                document.cookie = cName + "=;expires=Thu, 01-Jan-1970 00:00:01 GMT";
            }
        }

    }

}
```

sets the expiration
date to a past date to
delete the cookie

▶ **3.** Save the file.

The deleteCookie() function is also part of the demo_cookies.htm file you used in the previous session. You can explore how this function works by using the demo_cookies. htm file to delete all of the cookies currently active in the tutorial.09\tutorial folder.

To delete the CycloCrossings cookies:

▶ **1.** Open **demo_cookies.htm** in your Web browser.

▶ **2.** Click the **Show Cookies** button to list all of the cookies in the current folder.

▶ **3.** In the Delete column of the cookies table, select all of the check boxes. See Figure 9-24.

Selected cookies to delete using the demo page ◀ Figure 9-24

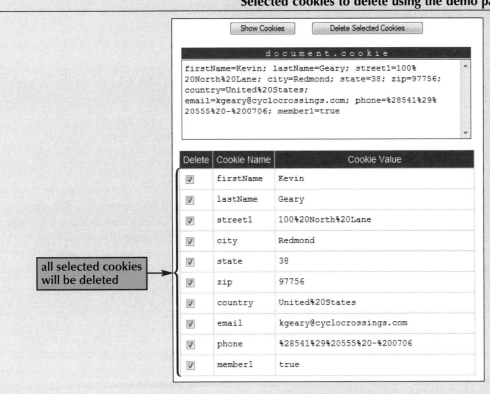

all selected cookies
will be deleted

4. Click the **Delete Selected Cookies** button. The page displays the text, No Cookies Found For This Folder.

5. Reload **accounts.htm** in your Web browser. The page now displays content for nonmembers. See Figure 9-25.

Figure 9-25 ▸ **Accounts page displayed to nonmembers**

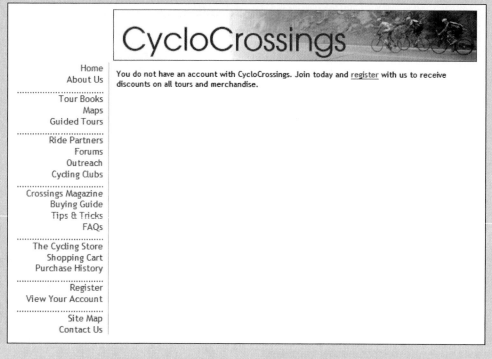

6. Go to the registration page, and then verify that the registration form contains no entered values, selected options, or clicked radio buttons.

InSight | **Bill Dortch's Cookie Library**

Cookies were introduced in 1996 for Netscape Version 2.0. Almost as soon as the browser was released, developers began to create function libraries to make it easier for programmers to interact with cookies. You have been doing that on a small and limited scale with the cookies.js file.

One of the most successful libraries was developed by Bill Dortch of Idaho Designs. His library includes functions to set cookie values, retrieve cookies, delete cookies, and change cookie expiration dates. One of the most useful aspects of Bill Dortch's Cookie Library is that it has been written and revised since the earliest browser versions and will work with all past and current browsers. The library also includes adjustments for changes in operating systems and date records.

Bill Dortch's Cookie Library is used extensively in many sites due to its rich features and overall stability. His code is in the public domain, which means that the code can be copied and reused without copyright infringement. The code is easy to locate using a Web search. If you find it difficult to program a feature involving cookies, you might locate a solution in Bill Dortch's Cookie Library or one of the many other libraries freely available on the Web.

Kevin reviews the revised accounts page as it appears to members and nonmembers. He agrees with your changes and will study your code for future revisions.

Session 9.2 Quick Check | Review

1. Explain why the expiration date, path, domain, and security do not appear when you display the contents of the document.cookie object.
2. The variable emailAddress contains a text string. What command places the contents of the variable into an array named mailArray, split at the location of the @ symbol?
3. In question 2, specify the object references to the e-mail username and mail server name if the username is located before the @ symbol and the mail server name is located after the @ symbol.
4. Name three functions used to remove the escape codes from a text string.
5. What command creates a date object named expiredDate containing a date one second prior to the current date and time?
6. Who is Bill Dortch and why is he important to the development of programming cookies with JavaScript?

Session 9.3

Storing Multiple Values in a Cookie

Kevin reviewed the CycloCrossings registration. He notes that the code requires 12 cookies to record all of the data that could be entered into the registration page. Mindful that browsers place a limit on the number of cookies that can be associated with any one Web domain, he's concerned that CycloCrossings might exceed its limit as more cookies are developed for other features in the Web site. Future assignments from Kevin will include recording payment information from CycloCrossings members, storing customer purchases from the CycloCrossings online store, and recording exchanges on the CycloCrossings forums. Kevin wants you to reduce the number of cookies allotted to the registration page. In fact, he wants you to store all the registration page data within a single cookie.

Using Subkeys

Because cookies are just text strings, you can store multiple names and values within a single cookie by including a delimiter character that separates one *name/value* pair from another. The common practice in separating these *name/value* pairs, also known as **subkeys**, is to use the structure

```
cName=field1=value1&field2=value2&field3=value3 ...
```

where *cName* is the name assigned to the cookie containing multiple values; *field1*, *field2*, *field3*, etc. are the names of the different fields within the cookie; and *value1*, *value2*, *value3*, etc. are the values of each field. For example, the data currently stored in the three cookies

```
firstName=Kevin;
lastName=Geary;
street1=100%20North%20Lane
```

Tip

When creating a client-side multivalued cookie, use the same format as the one employed for the server-side cookies created and read on your Web server.

could be stored within a single cookie named memberInfo as follows:

```
memberInfo=firstName=Kevin&lastName=Geary&street1=100%20North%20Lane
```

This format is supported by Microsoft's IIS (Internet Information Services) Active Server Pages (ASP), which uses it to read and write server-side cookies. By using this format, any client-side cookies created for the CycloCrossings Web site will also be compatible with an ASP application if Kevin decides to use that technology.

Reference Window | Storing Multiple Values in a Cookie

- To store multiple values in a cookie, format the name/value pair as
  cName=field1=value1&field2=value2&field3=value3 ...
  where *cName* is the name assigned to the cookie containing multiple values; *field1*, *field2*, *field3*, etc. are the names of the different fields within the cookie; and *value1*, *value2*, *value3*, etc. are the values of each field.

Writing a Multivalued Cookie

To create a multivalued cookie with JavaScript, you'll create a function named writeMCookie() that writes a field name and value into a multivalued cookie. The initial function line for the writeMCookie() function is:

```
function writeMCookie(cName, fName, fValue, expDate, cPath, cDomain, cSecure) {

   if (cName && fName && fValue != "") {

      var subkey = fName + "=" + escape(fValue);

   }

}
```

The function has seven parameters: cName is the name of the cookie; fName is the name of a field within the cookie; fValue is the value of that field; and expDate, cPath, cDomain, and cSecure provide the expiration date, path, domain, and security flag for the cookie, respectively. Note that the expiration date, path, domain, and security settings are applied to all fields within the cookie. If you want different settings for different fields, you must place the fields in their own cookies. The writeMCookie() function creates a subkey only if a cookie name and field name have been provided and the field value is a non-empty text string. The other parameters are optional as they were with the writeCookie() function you created earlier.

You will insert this function in the cookies.js file.

To insert the writeMCookie() function:

▶ **1.** Return to the **cookies.js** file in your text editor.

▶ **2.** Scroll to the bottom of the file, and then insert the following code, as shown in Figure 9-26:

```
function writeMCookie(cName, fName, fValue, expDate, cPath,
cDomain, cSecure) {

   if (cName && fName && fValue != "") {
```

```
            // Create the subkey
            var subkey = fName + "=" + escape(fValue);

      }

}
```

Initial writeMCookie() function ◀ **Figure 9-26**

3. Save the file.

To write this new subkey, you must first extract the cookie's value, if it exists. The following code retrieves the cookie's current value:

```
var cValue = null;
var cookiesArray = document.cookie.split("; ");
for (var i = 0; i < cookiesArray.length; i++) {
   if (cookies.Array[i].split("=")[0] == cName) {
      var valueIndex = cookiesArray[i].indexOf("=") + 1;
      cValue = cookiesArray[i].slice(valueIndex);
      break;
   }
}
```

You store the cookie's value in the cValue variable, setting its initial value to null. The code first loops through the contents of document.cookie until it locates the cookie named cName. After it finds that cookie, the code extracts the cookie's value using the slice() method and breaks off the for loop. Note that you want to slice out all of the text *after* the first = symbol because the cookie's value will contain several = symbols, one for each subkey.

You will add this code to the writeMCookie() function.

To extract the current cookie value:

1. Add the following code to the writeMCookie() function, as shown in Figure 9-27:

```
// Retrieve the current cookie value
var cValue = null;
var cookiesArray = document.cookie.split("; ");
for (var i = 0; i < cookiesArray.length; i++) {
   if (cookies.Array[i].split("=")[0] == cName) {
      var valueIndex = cookiesArray[i].indexOf("=") + 1;
      cValue = cookiesArray[i].slice(valueIndex);
      break;
   }
}
```

Figure 9-27 **Code to retrieve the current cookie value**

```
function writeMCookie(cName, fName, fValue, expDate, cPath, cDomain, cSecure) {

    if (cName && fName && fValue != "") {

        // Create the subkey
        var subkey = fName + "=" + escape(fValue);

        // Retrieve the current cookie value
        var cValue = null;
        var cookiesArray = document.cookie.split("; ");
        for (var i = 0; i < cookiesArray.length; i++) {
            if (cookiesArray[i].split("=")[0] ==  cName) {
                var valueIndex = cookiesArray[i].indexOf("=") + 1;
                cValue = cookiesArray[i].slice(valueIndex);
                break;
            }
        }

    }

}
```

loops through document.cookie and extracts the value of the cookie named cName

▶ **2.** Save the file.

The cookie may or may not have a value (after all, you could be writing this cookie for the first time) and it may or may not already have a value for the subkey you want to enter. You must account for both of these possibilities. You will start with the condition that the cookie and subkey both already exist. To set a new value for the field, you can use the following code to locate the subkey within the cookie's value and replace the current field value with the new value:

```
if (cValue) {

    var fieldExists = false;
    var cValueArray = cValue.split("&");
    for (var i = 0; i < cValueArray.length; i++) {
        if (cValueArray[i].split("=")[0] == fName) {
            fieldExists = true;
            cValueArray[i] = subkey;
            break;
        }
    }

    if (fieldExists) cValue = cValueArray.join("&")
    else cValue += "&" + subkey;

} else {

    cValue = subkey;

}
```

The code first declares the fieldExists variable, setting its initial value to false. Next, it splits the cookie value into an array at each occurrence of the & character, placing each subkey into its own array item. The code then loops through the cValueArray until it locates a subkey with a field name equal to fName. When the subkey is located, it inserts the new subkey into the array and breaks off the for loop. After the loop is finished, the cValue variable is recreated by joining the contents of the cValueArray using the & symbol as the delimiter between array items. If the fieldExists variable is still false, indicating that fName is a new field, the code appends the subkey to the current cookie value. If there is no value for the cookie, the code simply uses the subkey for the cookie's initial value.

You will add this code to the writeMCookie() function.

To insert the subkey into the cookie:

▶ **1.** Add the following code to the writeMCookie() function, as shown in Figure 9-28:

```
if (cValue) {

    var fieldExists = false;
    var cValueArray = cValue.split("&");
    for (var i = 0; i < cValueArray.length; i++) {
        if (cValueArray[i].split("=")[0] == fName) {
            fieldExists = true;
            cValueArray[i] = subkey;
            break;
        }
    }

    if (fieldExists) cValue = cValueArray.join("&")
    else cValue += "&" + subkey;

} else {

    cValue = subkey;

}
```

Code to insert a new subkey   Figure 9-28

```
function writeMCookie(cName, fName, fValue, expDate, cPath, cDomain, cSecure) {

    if (cName && fName && fValue != "") {

        // Create the subkey
        var subkey = fName + "=" + escape(fValue);

        // Retrieve the current cookie value
        var cValue = null;
        var cookiesArray = document.cookie.split("; ");
        for (var i = 0; i < cookiesArray.length; i++) {
            if (cookiesArray[i].split("=")[0] == cName) {
                var valueIndex = cookiesArray[i].indexOf("=") + 1;
                cValue = cookiesArray[i].slice(valueIndex);
                break;
            }
        }

        if (cValue) {

            var fieldExists = false;
            var cValueArray = cValue.split("&");
            for (var i = 0; i < cValueArray.length; i++) {
                if (cValueArray[i].split("=")[0] == fName) {
                    fieldExists = true;
                    cValueArray[i] = subkey;
                    break;
                }
            }

            if (fieldExists) cValue = cValueArray.join("&")
            else cValue += "&" + subkey;

        } else {

            cValue = subkey;

        }

    }
}
```

loops through cookie value looking for a matching subkey, replacing the current subkey with a revised subkey

joins the array in a single text string

or appends the new subkey to the cookie value

or sets the subkey as the cookies initial value

▶ **2.** Save the file.

The final part of the writeMCookie() function is to write the cookie text string, which includes, if specified by the user, the expiration date, path, domain, and security flag. The concluding code is:

```
var cString = cName + "=" + cValue;

if (expDate) cString += ";expires=" + expDate.toGMTString();
if (cPath)   cString += ";path=" + cPath;
if (cDomain) cString += ";domain=" + cDomain;
if (cSecure) cString += ";secure";

document.cookie = cString;
```

You will add this code to the writeMCookie() function.

To complete the writeMCookie() function:

▶ **1.** Add the following code to the writeMCookie() function, as shown in Figure 9-29:

```
var cString = cName + "=" + cValue;

if (expDate) cString += ";expires=" + expDate.toGMTString();
if (cPath)   cString += ";path=" + cPath;
if (cDomain) cString += ";domain=" + cDomain;
if (cSecure) cString += ";secure";

document.cookie = cString;
```

Figure 9-29 ▶ **Completing the writeMCookie() function**

```
            if (fieldExists) cValue = cValueArray.join("&")
            else cValue += "&" + subkey;

        } else {

            cValue = subkey;

        }

        var cString = cName + "=" + cValue;

        if (expDate) cString += ";expires=" + expDate.toGMTString();
        if (cPath)   cString += ";path=" + cPath;
        if (cDomain) cString += ";domain=" + cDomain;
        if (cSecure) cString += ";secure";

        document.cookie = cString;

    }

}
```

writes the cookie text string

▶ **2.** Save the file.

Testing the writeMCookie() Function

You can test the writeMCookie() function on sample data in the registration form. First, you have to revise the code of the register.js file so that it calls the writeMCookie() function to write the cookie containing the member information. You'll give the new cookie containing the multiple field values the name memberInfo.

To call the writeMCookie() function:

▶ **1.** Go to the **register.js** file in your text editor.

2. Scroll down to the saveMemberInfo() function, and then replace each call of the writeCookie() function with a call to the **writeMCookie()** function, inserting the following parameter value within each function call, as shown in Figure 9-30:

```
"memberInfo",
```

Code to call the writeMCookie() function ◄ **Figure 9-30**

```
function saveMemberInfo() {

    // Set the cookie expiration date one year hence
    var expire = new Date();
    expire.setFullYear(expire.getFullYear() + 1);

    // Loop through all of the elements in the form
    var allFields = document.registerForm.elements;
    for (var i = 0; i < allFields.length; i++) {

        if (allFields[i].type == "text") {
            // Write input box value to a cookie
            writeMCookie("memberInfo", allFields[i].id, allFields[i].value, expire);
        }

        if (allFields[i].nodeName == "SELECT") {
            // Write the index number of the selected option
            writeMCookie("memberInfo", allFields[i].id, allFields[i].selectedIndex, expire);
        }

        if (allFields[i].type == "radio" || allFields[i].type == "checkbox") {
            // Write whether the button or checkbox was checked
            writeMCookie("memberInfo", allFields[i].id, allFields[i].checked, expire);
        }

    }
    alert("Registration data saved");
}
```

name of the
multi-valued cookie

3. Save the file.

You will enter sample text in the CycloCrossings registration page and verify that the program writes all of the member information into a single multivalued cookie named memberInfo.

To test the writeMCookie() function:

1. Load **register.htm** in your Web browser, and then fill out the registration form as shown in Figure 9-31.

Sample member information ◄ **Figure 9-31**

Registration Form		
First Name	Diane	Last Hayward
Street	311 Fourth Street	
	Apt. #3E	
City	Woodburn	
State	Oregon	
Zip/Postal Code	97071	
Country	United States	
E-mail	dhayward@cyclocrossings.com	
Phone Number	(503) 555 - 5221	
Membership	One year ($30) ○	
	Two year ($45) ◉	

2. Click the **Submit** button to write the member information into the memberInfo cookie.

Next, you will confirm that the memberInfo cookie has been created with each entry in the registration form appearing as a separate subkey.

▶ **3.** Load the **demo_cookies.htm** file in your Web browser.

▶ **4.** Click the **Show Cookies** button. The contents of the memberInfo cookie appear in the demo Web page. See Figure 9-32.

| Figure 9-32 | Contents of the memberInfo cookie |

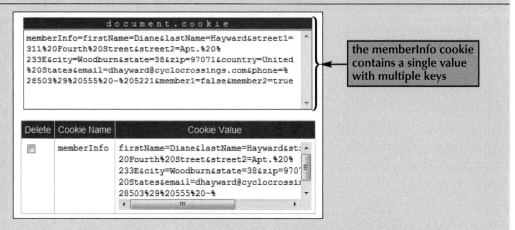

Trouble? If you are running Google Chrome or Safari, you must load the pages on a Web server or install a personal Web server on your local machine to display cookies accessible through the HTTP protocol.

Retrieving Data from a Multivalued Cookie

Next, you'll edit the accounts and registration pages so that they retrieve membership information from the subkeys in the memberInfo cookie. To do this, you'll add another function to the cookies.js library named retrieveMCookie() that retrieves the value of a specified field within a multivalued cookie. There are two stages in the retrieveMCookie() function. First, the function retrieves the entire cookie value, and then the function retrieves the value of a specific subkey within that value. The initial code for the retrieveMCookie() function is:

```
function retrieveMCookie(cName, fName) {

   if (document.cookie) {

      // Retrieve the cookie value

      // Retrieve the field value within the cookie

   }

}
```

The function has two parameters, cName and fName, which reference the cookie name and field name, respectively. You will add this function to the cookies.js file.

To insert the retrieveMCookie() function:

▶ **1.** Return to the **cookies.js** file in your text editor.

2. Scroll to the bottom of the file, and then insert the following code, as shown in Figure 9-33:

```
function retrieveMCookie(cName, fName) {

    if (document.cookie) {

        // Retrieve the cookie value

        // Retrieve the field value within the cookie

    }

}
```

The retrieveMCookie() function | Figure 9-33

```
parameter to reference          parameter to reference
the cookie name                 the field name

function retrieveMCookie(cName, fName) {
    if (document.cookie) {
        // Retrieve the cookie value
        // Retrieve the field value within the cookie
    }
}
```

3. Save the file.

To retrieve the cookie value, you again split document.cookie, placing each cookie in a separate array. You then loop through the cookies array until you match the cookie name specified in the cName parameter. Finally, you slice all of the content of that cookie after the first = symbol in separate subarrays. The code to retrieve the cookie value is as follows:

```
var cValue = null;
var cookiesArray() = document.cookie.split("; ");
for (var i = 0 ; i < cookiesArray.length; i++) {
    if (cookiesArray[i].split("=")[0] == cName) {
        var valueIndex = cookiesArray[i].indexOf("=") + 1;
        cValue = cookiesArray[i].slice(valueIndex);
        break;
    }
}
```

The value of the multivalued cookie is stored in the cValue variable. The following code then splits the text in the cValue variable into separate array items:

```
if (cValue) {
    var cValueArray = cValue.split("&");
    for (var i = 0; i < cValueArray.length; i++) {

        if (cValueArray[i].split("=")[0] == fName)
            return unescape(cValueArray[i].split("=")[1]);
    }
}
```

The code loops through the array until it locates a field name matching the fName parameter. After it locates the correct field, the code returns the value stored in the field. Note that the unescape() function removes any escape code characters in the field value. You will add the code to retrieve the field value to the retrieveMCookie() function.

To complete the retrieveMCookie() function:

▶ **1.** After the first comment within the retrieveMCookie() function, insert the following code to retrieve the cookie value:

```
var cValue = null;
var cookiesArray() = document.cookie.split("; ");
for (var i = 0 ; i < cookiesArray.length; i++) {
    if (cookiesArray[i].split("=")[0] == cName) {
        var valueIndex = cookiesArray[i].indexOf("=") + 1;
        cValue = cookiesArray[i].slice(valueIndex);
        break;
    }
}
```

▶ **2.** After the second comment in the retrieveMCookie() function, insert the following code to retrieve the field value within the cookie:

```
if (cValue) {
    var cValueArray = cValue.split("&");
    for (var i = 0; i < cValueArray.length; i++) {

        if (cValueArray[i].split("=")[0] == fName)
            return unescape(cValueArray[i].split("=")[1]);
    }
}
```

Figure 9-34 highlights the inserted code in the retrieveMCookie() function.

Figure 9-34	Code to retrieve the cookie and field values

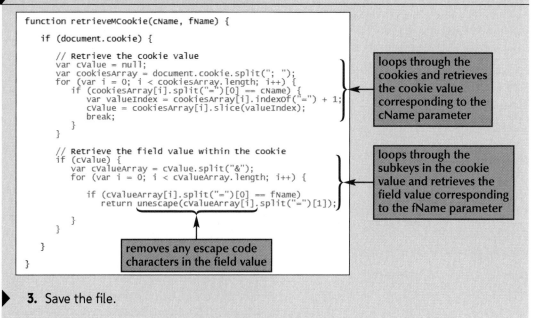

▶ **3.** Save the file.

You need to modify the retrieveMemberInfo() function in the accounts.js file so that it retrieves values from the memberInfo cookie using the field name rather than the cookie name.

To modify the retrieveMemberInfo() function:

▸ **1.** Return to the **accounts.js** file in your text editor.

▸ **2.** Within the retrieveMemberInfo() function, change every occurrence of `retrieveCookie` to **retrieveMCookie**.

▸ **3.** At the start of each call of the retrieveMCookie()function, insert the parameter value **"memberInfo"**, so that the function retrieves the field value from the memberInfo cookie. Figure 9-35 highlights the revised code in the function.

Code to call the retrieveMCookie() function ◄ **Figure 9-35**

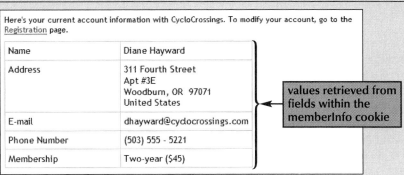

retrieves the lastName field value from the memberInfo cookie

```
function retrieveMemberInfo() {

    if (retrieveMCookie("memberInfo", "lastName")) {

        // Retrieve the membership data
        var allSpans = document.getElementsByTagName("span");
        for (var i = 0; i < allSpans.length; i++) {
            var cValue = retrieveMCookie("memberInfo", allSpans[i].id);
            if (cValue) allSpans[i].innerHTML = cValue;
        }

        // Retrieve the state abbreviation
        var stateIndex = retrieveMCookie("memberInfo", "state");
        document.getElementById("state").innerHTML = stateAbbr[stateIndex];

        // Retrieve the membership option

        if (retrieveMCookie("memberInfo", "member1") == "true")
            document.getElementById("memberOption").innerHTML = "One year ($30)";
        else if (retrieveMCookie("memberInfo", "member2") == "true")
            document.getElementById("memberOption").innerHTML = "Two year ($45)";

    } else {

        // Display text for nonmembers
        var nonMember = "You do not have an account with CycloCrossings. ";
        nonMember += "Join today and <a href='register.htm'>register</a> ";
        nonMember += "with us to receive discounts on all tours ";
        nonMember += "and merchandise.";

        document.getElementById("intro").innerHTML = nonMember;
        document.getElementById("accountTable").style.visibility = "hidden";

    }

}
```

▸ **4.** Save the file, and then reload **accounts.htm** in your Web browser, verifying that the page displays the text shown in Figure 9-36.

Sample membership information ◄ **Figure 9-36**

Here's your current account information with CycloCrossings. To modify your account, go to the Registration page.

Name	Diane Hayward
Address	311 Fourth Street Apt #3E Woodburn, OR 97071 United States
E-mail	dhayward@cyclocrossings.com
Phone Number	(503) 555 - 5221
Membership	Two-year ($45)

values retrieved from fields within the memberInfo cookie

You will make the same changes to the initPage() function in the register.js file to retrieve the registration data from the memberInfo cookie.

To modify the initPage() function:

▶ **1.** Return to the **register.js** file in your text editor.

▶ **2.** Within the initPage() function, change every occurrence of `retrieveCookie` to **`retrieveMCookie`** and add the parameter value **`"memberInfo"`**, to each call of the retrieveMCookie() function. Figure 9-37 highlights the revised code.

Figure 9-37 ▶ **Modified initPage() function**

```
function initPage() {

   //Add event handler to the Submit button
   document.getElementById("sbutton").onclick = saveMemberInfo;

   if (retrieveMCookie("memberInfo", "lastName")) {

      var allInputs = document.getElementsByTagName("input");
      for (var i = 0; i < allInputs.length; i++) {
         if (allInputs[i].type == "text") {
            if (retrieveMCookie("memberInfo", allInputs[i].id)) {
               allInputs[i].value = retrieveMCookie("memberInfo", allInputs[i].id);
            }
         }
      }

      document.getElementById("state").selectedIndex = retrieveMCookie("memberInfo", "state");

      if (retrieveMCookie("memberInfo", "member1") == "true")
         document.getElementById("member1").checked = true
      else if (retrieveMCookie("memberInfo", "member2") == "true")
         document.getElementById("member2").checked = true;
   }

}
```

▶ **3.** Save your changes to the file, and then reload **register.htm** in your Web browser, verifying that the form is automatically filled in with the correct membership values taken from the memberInfo cookie.

Kevin is pleased that your revisions place the member information within a single cookie. If the need arises, Kevin can continue adding subkeys to the memberInfo cookie, including membership dues, additional contact information, and other user preferences. The only limitation is that the size of the memberInfo cookie cannot exceed 4 kilobytes.

Creating a Welcome Back Message

Kevin wants the CycloCrossings home page to display a welcome back message to returning members. Before creating the message, you will open the CycloCrossings home page and view its contents and layout.

To view the CycloCrossings home page:

▶ **1.** Open the **cyclotxt.htm** and **cyclotxt.js** files from the tutorial.09\tutorial folder in your text editor, enter *your name* and *the date* in the comment section of each file, and then save the files as **cyclo.htm** and **cyclo.js**, respectively.

▶ **2.** Study the contents of the cyclo.htm file in your text editor.

▶ **3.** Insert the following script elements in the head section of the cyclo.htm document to link the file to the cyclo.js and cookies.js files:

```
<script type="text/javascript" src="cookies.js"></script>
<script type="text/javascript" src="cyclo.js"></script>
```

▶ **4.** Save the cyclo.htm file, and then open it in your Web browser. See Figure 9-38.

CycloCrossings home page 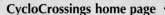 Figure 9-38

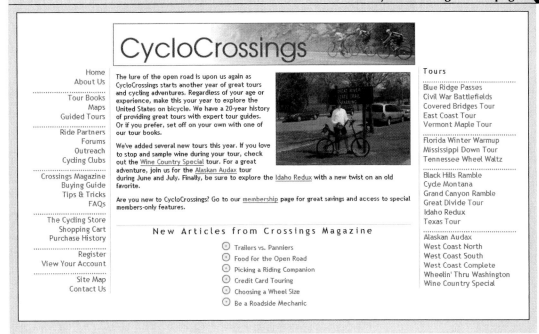

Kevin wants you to create a message that displays the member's first name, the date that the member last visited the Web site, and the date the home page was last updated. This information is provided as a courtesy to members to inform them of whether the home page was modified in their absence. Figure 9-39 shows a preview of the welcome back message.

Welcome box Figure 9-39

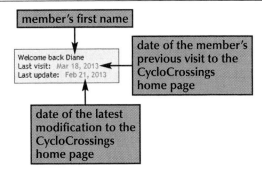

member's first name

date of the member's previous visit to the CycloCrossings home page

date of the latest modification to the CycloCrossings home page

You already have the member's first name stored in the firstName field of the member-Info cookie. You'll create a new cookie named lastVisit to store the date on which the user last visited the CycloCrossings home page. To retrieve and create the lastVisit cookie, you want the following code to run when the home page is initially opened by the browser:

```
if (retrieveCookie("lastVisit") == null) lastVisit = "First time"
    else lastVisit = retrieveCookie("lastVisit");

var today = new Date();
var currentVisit = writeDateString(today);

expire = new Date();
expire.setMonth(expire.getMonth() + 6);
writeCookie("lastVisit", currentVisit, expire);
```

The code first retrieves the last time the user visited the site from the lastVisit cookie. If there is no lastVisit cookie, the code sets the value of the lastVisit variable to First time and then retrieves the current date and time, storing it in the today variable. The writeDateString() function from the cookies.js file is used to store the date as a date string in the form *mmm dd, yyyy* where *mmm* is the three-letter month abbreviation, *dd* is the day of the month, and *yyyy* is the year. The code concludes by writing a new value to the lastVisit cookie using the current visit date as the new value and setting the cookie to expire six months from the present.

You will add this code to the cyclo.js file, placing it within a function named initPage() that will run when the home page is loaded by the browser.

To create the initPage() function:

1. Return to the **cyclo.js** file in your text editor.
2. At the bottom of the file, insert the following code for the initPage() function, as shown in Figure 9-40:

```
addEvent(window, "load", initPage, false);

function initPage() {

   // Retrieve date of last visit
   if (retrieveCookie("lastVisit") == null) lastVisit = "First time"
      else lastVisit = retrieveCookie("lastVisit");

   // Set date of current visit
   var today = new Date();
   var currentVisit = writeDateString(today);

   // Write current visit to lastVisit cookie
   expire = new Date();
   expire.setMonth(expire.getMonth() + 6);
   writeCookie("lastVisit", currentVisit, expire);

}
```

Figure 9-40 The initPage() function

```
addEvent(window, "load", initPage, false);

function initPage() {

   // Retrieve date of last visit
   if (retrieveCookie("lastVisit") == null) lastVisit = "First time"
   else lastVisit = retrieveCookie("lastVisit");

   // Set date of current visit
   var today = new Date();
   var currentVisit = writeDateString(today);

   // Write current visit to lastVisit cookie
   expire = new Date();
   expire.setMonth(expire.getMonth() + 6);
   writeCookie("lastVisit", currentVisit, expire);
}
```

tests for the presence of the lastVisit cookie

retrieves the current date

writes the current date to the lastVisit cookie

3. Save the file.

The date that the document was last modified can be accessed using the property document.lastModified, which returns a text string of the last modification date. You can convert this text string to a date object using the code

```
var lastModified = new Date(document.lastModified);
```

and then write the date in the *mmm dd, yyyy* format using the writeDateString() function. You'll write the value of this variable as well as the values of the firstName cookie and lastVisit variable into the HTML fragment

```
<div id="welcome">
   Welcome back firstName
   <br />
   Last visit: <span>lastVisit</span>
   <br />
   Last update: <span>pageUpdate</span>
</div>
```

where *firstName* is the value of the firstName cookie, *lastVisit* is the value of the lastVisit variable, and *pageUpdate* is the value of the pageUpdate variable. The styles for the welcome DIV element already have been created. The following code writes the welcome box:

```
if (retrieveMCookie("memberInfo", "lastName") != null) {

   var firstName = retrieveMCookie("memberInfo", "firstName");

   var lastModified = new Date(document.lastModified);
   var pageUpdate = writeDateString(lastModified);

   var welcome = document.createElement("div");
   welcome.id = "welcome";

   htmlString = "Welcome back " + firstName;
   htmlString += "<br />";
   htmlString += "Last visit: <span>" + lastVisit + "</span>";
   htmlString += "<br />";
   htmlString += "Last update: <span>" + pageUpdate + "</span>";

   welcome.innerHTML = htmlString;
   document.body.appendChild(welcome);

}
```

As with the retrieveMemberInfo() function, you will assume that every member has a value for the lastName field and test for its presence before writing the welcome box. You will add this code to the initPage() function in the cyclo.js file.

To create the initPage() function:

▶ **1.** Add the following code to the initPage() function in the cyclo.js file, as shown in Figure 9-41:

```
if (retrieveMCookie("memberInfo", "lastName") != null) {

    var firstName = retrieveMCookie("memberInfo", "firstName");

    var lastModified = new Date(document.lastModified);
    var pageUpdate = writeDateString(lastModified);

    var welcome = document.createElement("div");
    welcome.id = "welcome";

    htmlString = "Welcome back " + firstName;
    htmlString += "<br />";
    htmlString += "Last visit: <span>" + lastVisit + "</span>";
    htmlString += "<br />";
    htmlString += "Last update: <span>" + pageUpdate + "</span>";

    welcome.innerHTML = htmlString;
    document.body.appendChild(welcome);

}
```

Figure 9-41   **Code to write the contents of the welcome box**

```
function initPage() {

    // Retrieve date of last visit
    if (retrieveCookie("lastVisit") == null) lastVisit = "First time"
    else lastVisit = retrieveCookie("lastVisit");

    // Set date of current visit
    var today = new Date();
    var currentVisit = writeDateString(today);

    // Write current visit to lastVisit cookie
    expire = new Date();
    expire.setMonth(expire.getMonth() + 6);
    writeCookie("lastVisit", currentVisit, expire);

    if (retrieveMCookie("memberInfo", "lastName") != null) {

        var firstName = retrieveMCookie("memberInfo", "firstName");

        var lastModified = new Date(document.lastModified);
        var pageUpdate = writeDateString(lastModified);

        var welcome = document.createElement("div");
        welcome.id = "welcome";

        htmlString = "Welcome back " + firstName;
        htmlString += "<br />";
        htmlString += "Last visit: <span>" + lastVisit + "</span>";
        htmlString += "<br />";
        htmlString += "Last update: <span>" + pageUpdate + "</span>";

        welcome.innerHTML = htmlString;
        document.body.appendChild(welcome);

    }

}
```

▶ **2.** Save the file, and then reload **cyclo.htm** in your Web browser. The home page displays a welcome box in the upper-left corner with the member's name, the date of the last visit, and the date the cyclo.htm file was last modified. Because this is the first time you visited this page with the lastVisit cookie enabled, the last visit text reads "First time". See Figure 9-42.

the first time the lastVisit cookie is enabled, the welcome box will display the text string, "First Time"

Welcome back Diane
Last visit: First time
Last update: Feb 21, 2013

your date will differ

▶ **3.** Reload or refresh the **cyclo.htm** file in your Web browser, and verify that the date of the last visit updated to reflect the current date.

Trouble? If no text appears in the welcome box, you may have an error in generating the cookie. Use the demo_cookies.htm file to examine your cookie contents, and then modify your code to match that shown in Figure 9-41.

Developers often report the number of visits to their Web site. This is particularly important if the site receives advertising revenue based on its level of Web traffic. The site's home page might include a page counter that reports total visits from all users. That type of information is not available from a client-side cookie because client-side cookies can only provide information on the activities of a single user on the local computer. However, you may find it useful to report the total visits by each user to your Web site.

To create a page counter for the local user, you create a cookie named pageCount, setting its initial value to 0. Every time the page is accessed, the code retrieves the pageCount cookie, increases its value by 1, and then writes the new value to the pageCount cookie. If you want to create counters for multiple pages, you need multiple pageCount cookies—one for each page. You can also store the different page counts within different subkeys of the same multivalued cookie. By recording this information, users who visit your site infrequently can be better informed about the changes you've made to the site in their absence.

Testing for Cookie Support

All of the scripts you created for the CycloCrossings Web site assumed that the user's browser can read and write cookies. However, Kevin is aware that many users might set up their browsers to block cookies. He wants you to test and verify that the user's browser supports cookies. If not, he wants your code to display an alert message that informs the user of the need for cookies to access some features of the CycloCrossings Web site.

You can tell whether the browser has enabled cookies by using the navigator.cookieEnabled property, which returns a value of true if cookies have been enabled and false if otherwise. With older browsers that might not support the navigator.cookieEnabled property, you can verify that cookies have been enabled by creating a temporary session cookie and then retrieving it. If you can do that, then you'll know that the browser supports the creation and retrieval of other cookies as well. The following function tests for cookie support:

```
function cookiesEnabled() {

   var cookiesTest = false;

   writeCookie("tempCookie", "temp");
   if (retrieveCookie("tempCookie")) {
      cookiesTest = true;
      deleteCookie("tempCookie");
   }

   return cookiesTest;

}
```

The function starts with an initial value for the cookiesTest variable of false, and then creates a temporary cookie named tempCookie that contains a sample text string. The function then attempts to read information from the cookie it just created. If it can retrieve tempCookie, it sets the cookiesTest variable to true and deletes tempCookie (because that cookie is no longer needed). The value of the cookiesTest variable is then returned by the function. Although this function employs the writeCookie(), retrieveCookie(), and deleteCookie() functions you created for the cookies.js library, it also could be rewritten to access similar cookie functions drawn from other libraries.

Reference Window | Testing Whether Cookies Are Enabled

- To test whether cookies are enabled by a current Web browser, use the navigator.cookieEnabled object property.
- To test whether cookies are enabled for older legacy browsers, write a function that creates and retrieves a temporary session cookie and returns a Boolean value indicating whether that operation was successful or unsuccessful.

You will add the cookiesEnabled() function to the cookies.js file.

To create the cookiesEnabled() function:

▶ 1. Return to the **cookies.js** file in your text editor.

▶ 2. Scroll to the bottom of the file, and then insert the following function, as shown in Figure 9-43:

```
function cookiesEnabled() {

   var cookiesTest = false;

   writeCookie("tempCookie", "temp");
   if (retrieveCookie("tempCookie")) {
      cookiesTest = true;
      deleteCookie("tempCookie");
   }

   return cookiesTest;

}
```

Code to test for cookie support   Figure 9-43

```
function cookiesEnabled() {

    var cookiesTest = false;

    writeCookie("tempCookie", "temp");
    if (retrieveCookie("tempCookie")) {
        cookiesTest = true;
        deleteCookie("tempCookie");
    }

    return cookiesTest;

}
```

creates and retrieves a
temporary session cookie

▶ **3.** Save the file.

Next, you will add code to the cyclo.js file to test whether cookies have been enabled by the browser and display an alert message if they have not.

To test whether cookies have been enabled:

▶ **1.** Return to the **cyclo.js** file in your text editor.

▶ **2.** Scroll to the initPage() function, and then insert the following code, as shown in Figure 9-44:

```
if (cookiesEnabled() == false)
   alert("You must enable cookies to save and view member
information");
```

Code to display an alert dialog box when cookies are not enabled   Figure 9-44

```
function initPage() {

    if (cookiesEnabled() == false)
        alert("You must enable cookies to save and view member information");

    // Retrieve date of last visit
    if (retrieveCookie("lastvisit") == null) lastvisit = "First time"
    else lastvisit = retrieveCookie("lastvisit");
```

▶ **3.** Save the file, and then open **cyclo.htm** in your Web browser.

▶ **4.** Disable cookies in your Web browser, and then reload the **cyclo.htm** file, verifying that the browser displays the alert message. See Figure 9-45.

Alert dialog box   Figure 9-45

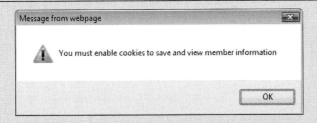

Message from webpage

⚠ You must enable cookies to save and view member information

OK

Trouble? If you're not sure how to disable cookies, view your browser's documentation. Cookie settings are usually found in the Options or Preferences command under the File or Tools menu.

▶ **5.** Re-enable cookies in your Web browser, and reload the **cyclo.htm** file, verifying that all information from the lastVisit and memberInfo cookies is displayed in the welcome box on the home page.

Although cookies have existed since 1996, they are still a source of controversy for some users and developers who are uncomfortable with Web sites storing files on the user's own machine. For that reason, some alternatives to cookies have been developed.

One approach is to attach a query string to the URL of the Web page. The query string can hold much of the same data as a session cookie. Data values can be stored in Web form fields and then passed to other pages in the Web site by opening those pages using the get method. After the browser opens another Web page, data in a query string can be retrieved and processed by processing the contents of the location.search object. For an example of using a Web form to create a query string, see Tutorial 5.

Another approach involves writing content to the window.name object. The window.name object is used to store the name of the current browser window and can contain an extended text string formatted in the same fashion as a session cookie.

Currently, there are no alternatives to client-side cookies for storing persistent data other than server-side cookies and databases. However, future versions of HTML may support other options for permanent data storage. Current specifications for HTML 5 include storage of data and variables on the user's local machine. At present, HTML 5 is not strongly supported by browsers and the specifications for the language and persistent data storage are still in development.

You've completed your work on adding cookies to the CycloCrossings Web site. Kevin still needs to create additional cookies for the Web site to track membership payment information, shopping cart purchases, and so forth, but this is a good start.

Review | **Session 9.3 Quick Check**

1. Describe how to store multiple values within a single cookie.
2. What is a subkey?
3. A cookie named siteInfo contains multiple subkeys separated by the & symbol with each name/value pair connected using the = symbol. If cookieText contains the text of the siteInfo cookie, provide code to retrieve the cookie's value storing the text in a variable named cookieValue.
4. Provide code to create an array named siteArray with each item in the array containing the text of a subkey in the cookieValue variable.
5. Explain why client-side cookies cannot be used to create a page counter of all users who visit a Web site.
6. What object property indicates whether the browser has cookies enabled?
7. What are some alternatives to client-side cookies?

Tutorial Summary | Review

In this tutorial, you learned how to create and retrieve browser cookies using JavaScript. The first session explored the different types of cookies used in Web sites and showed how to store a cookie using the document.cookie object. The session examined how to create session and persistent cookies, and how to set the path, domain, and security setting of a cookie. The second session showed how to retrieve data from a cookie using the split() method of the string object. The session also showed how to delete a cookie by setting its expiration date to a date in the past. The third session explored how to create and read from cookies containing multiple fields or subkeys. The session also looked at ways to create welcome messages for users returning to a Web site, and how to provide information on when the user last visited the site and when the site was last updated. The session concluded by exploring how to determine whether the user's browser has support for cookies enabled.

Key Terms

client-side cookie
cookie
first-party cookie
persistent cookie

server-side cookie
session cookie
stateless protocol

subkey
third-party cookie
tracking cookie

Practice the skills you learned in the tutorial using the same case scenario.

Data Files needed for the Review Assignments: ccstyles.css, cengage.jpg, cyclologo.jpg, demo.gif, demo2.gif, demo_cookies.htm, library.js, profilestyles.css, proftxt.htm, proftxt.js, ridesstyles.css, ridestxt.htm, ridestxt.js

CycloCrossings members often want to find riding partners and form touring groups. Kevin wants you to add a new page to the CycloCrossings Web site in which members can create a profile describing their cycling interests. Kevin wants the cycling preferences to be stored in a cookie that can be displayed as part of the member profile page. Figure 9-46 shows a preview of the profile page with data retrieved from cookies created from the Web site.

Figure 9-46

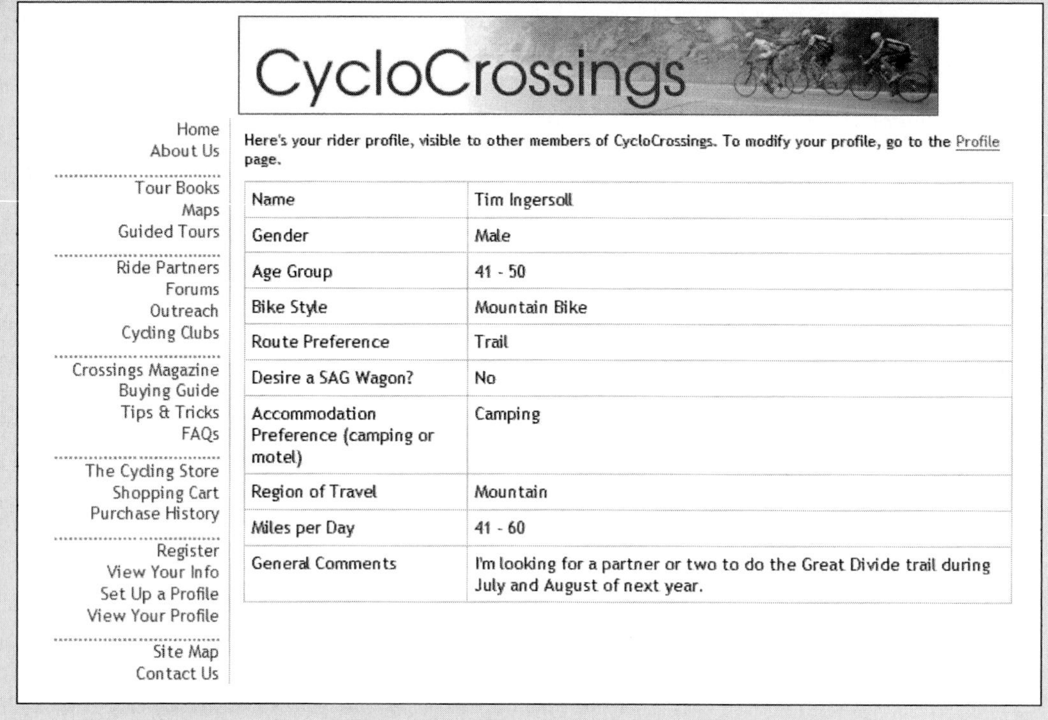

Kevin already wrote the HTML code and CSS styles for the new Web pages. He's also supplied some JavaScript functions in the library.js file to help you work with cookies. You will use these functions to write code that generates the member profile cookies and retrieves data from those cookies.

Complete the following:

1. Use your text editor to open the **proftxt.htm**, **proftxt.js**, **ridestxt.htm**, and **ridestxt.js** files in the tutorial.09\review folder, enter *your name* and *the date* in the comment section of each file, and then save the files as **profile.htm**, **profile.js**, **rides.htm**, and **rides.js**, respectively.
2. Go to the **profile.htm** file in your text editor, link the file to the library.js and profile.js script files, study the HTML code, paying attention to the use of id and name attributes in the field elements, and then save the file.
3. Go to the **library.js** file in your text editor, and then review the functions stored in the file that you'll use to complete this assignment.

4. Go to the **profile.js** file in your text editor. In this file, you'll insert code to write cookies based on the values the user enters into the profile form in the profile.htm file. Insert a command to run the initPage() function when the document is loaded in the browser window.

5. Create the **initPage()** function, adding the following commands:

   a. Apply an onclick event handler to the profile form's Submit button, running the saveProfile() function when the button is clicked.

   b. Test whether cookies have been enabled for the browser. If not, display an alert dialog box containing the following text message: **You must have cookies enabled to save your profile.** (*Hint:* Use the navigator.cookieEnabled property.)

6. Create the **saveProfile()** function. The purpose of this function is to create cookies for each of the form fields in the profile page. Create a multivalued cookie named profile using the storeCookieField() function from the library.js file, set to expire in six months and containing the following fields:

   a. The **firstName** field containing the value of the CycloCrossings member's first name

   b. The **lastName** field containing the member's last name

   c. The **gender** field containing the index number of the selected radio button from the Web form (*Hint:* Use the getOption() function to return the index number.)

   d. The **age** field containing the index number of the selected option from the selection list in the Web form (*Hint:* Use the getSelection() function to return the index number.)

   e. The **bike** field containing the index number of the selected bike type

   f. The **route** field containing the index number of the selected route type

   g. The **sag** field containing the index number of the selected sag option

   h. The **accommodation** field containing the index of the selected accommodation type

   i. The **region** field containing the index number of the selected option in the selection list in the Web form

   j. The **miles** field containing the index number of the selected option in the selection list in the Web form

   k. The **comments** field containing the value of the member's comment in the Web form

7. Add a command at the end of the saveProfile() function to display an alert box containing the text **Profile Saved** after the profile cookie has been saved.

8. Save the file and then load **profile.htm** in your Web browser. Enter the sample rider profile shown in Figure 9-46, and then click the Submit button to store the field data in the profile cookie.

9. Using the **demo_cookies.htm** file in the tutorial.09\review folder or the features of your Web browser, verify that the profile cookie has been generated correctly by your code.

10. Return to the **profile.js** file in your text editor. Edit the initPage() function so that if cookies are enabled and the profile cookie exists, it will fill out the profile form using the values from the profile cookie. Use the getCookieField() function from the library.js file to retrieve the field values, and then fill out the form by doing the following:

    a. For the firstName, lastName, and comments fields in the Web form, insert the values of the corresponding fields in the profile cookie.

b. For the gender, bikeOption, routeOption, sagOption, and accOption radio buttons, use the index number stored in the corresponding fields in the profile cookie to check the corresponding radio button in the Web form. (*Hint:* You can check a radio button in the Web form using the command

```
document.forms[0].option[index].checked = true;
```

where *option* is the name of the group of radio buttons and *index* is the index number of the selected radio button.)

c. For the age, region, and miles selection lists, display the selected option based on the index value stored in the corresponding fields in the profile cookie. (*Hint:* Use the command

```
document.forms[0].selection.selectedIndex = index;
```

where *selection* is the name of the selection list and *index* is the selected option in the list.)

11. Save the **profile.js** file, and then close and reopen **profile.htm** in your Web browser, verifying that the values from the profile cookie are automatically inserted into the form.

12. Go to the **rides.htm** file in your text editor, link the file to the library.js and rides.js script files, examine the contents of the file, and then save and close the file.

13. Go to the **rides.js** file in your text editor. Create global arrays named **genderGroup**, **ageGroup**, **bikeGroup**, **routeGroup**, **sagGroup**, **accommodationGroup**, **regionGroup**, and **milesGroup**, matching the text of the radio buttons and selection lists in the profile Web form.

14. Add a command to run the retrieveProfile() function when the page loads.

15. Create the **retrieveProfile()** function. The purpose of this function is to retrieve the fields from the profile cookie, inserting their values in the span elements in the rides.htm file. If the profile cookie exists, run the following commands:

a. Retrieve the values of the firstName, lastName, and comments fields from the profile cookie in the inner HTML of the corresponding span elements in the document.

b. Retrieve the index numbers of the gender, age, bike, route, sag, accommodation, region, and miles fields in the profile cookie, and use the index numbers and the arrays you created in Step 13 to display the text of those options in the inner HTML of the corresponding span elements in the document.

c. If the profile cookie does not exist, write the following HTML fragment into the intro paragraph on the Web page, and then set the visibility style of the profile-Table object to hidden:

```
No rider profile on record with CycloCrossings. Submit a <a
href='profile.htm'>profile</a> today to meet other riders in
your area who share your passion for touring.
```

16. Save the profile.js file, and then load **profile.htm** in your Web browser, verifying that the contents of the profile cookie are displayed in the Web page.

17. Delete the profile cookie using the features of your Web browser or the **demo_cookies.htm** Web page, and then reload the **profile.htm** file in your Web browser, verifying that the Web page displays the alternative text for users with no saved profile.

18. Submit the completed project to your instructor.

Apply	**Case Problem 1**

Use the skills you learned to create a page counter for a Web site.

Data Files needed for this Case Problem: cengage.jpg, chlogo.jpg, chphoto.jpg, chstyles.css, countertxt.js, demo.gif, demo2.gif, demo_cookies.htm, hangerstxt.htm, wall.jpg, wall2.jpg

Cliff Hangers   Debbie Chen is the owner and operator of Cliff Hangers, a climbing school located in Boulder, Colorado. She wants to supplement the contents of the school's Web site with a page counter that will inform users of the last time they visited the site and the total number of times they visited. Figure 9-47 shows a preview of the page you'll create for Debbie.

Figure 9-47

Debbie already created the content and styles for the Web site. She needs you to write the JavaScript code to generate a page-counting cookie that is updated every time a user returns to the site.

Complete the following:

1. Open the **countertxt.js** and **hangerstxt.htm** files from the tutorial.09\case1 folder in your text editor, enter *your name* and *the date* in the comment section of each file, and save the files as **counter.js** and **hangers.htm**, respectively.
2. Go to the **hangers.htm** file in your text editor, link the file to the counter.js file, and then save and close the file.
3. Go to the **counter.js** file in your text editor, and then add a command to run the set-Counter() function when the page is loaded.

4. Create the **setCounter()** function. The function will be used to update the date that the page was last visited by the user, the number of times the page was visited, and the date that the page was last modified. Steps 5 through 11 occur within the set-Counter() function.

5. Test for the existence of the lastVisit cookie. If the cookie does not exist, create a variable named **lastVisit** containing the following text string: **Welcome to Cliff Hangers**. If the cookie does exist, set the value of the lastVisit variable equal to the text string **Last Visit:** *date* where *date* is the value of the lastVisit cookie.

6. Store the current date, formatted using the writeDateString() function, in the lastVisit cookie.

7. Test for the existence of the pageCount cookie. If the cookie does not exist, create a variable named **pageCount**, setting its initial value to 1. If the cookie does exist, set the value of the pageCount variable to 1 plus the value of the pageCount cookie. Note that you must apply the parseInt() method to convert the value retrieved from the pageCount cookie from a text string into an integer before increasing it by 1.

8. Store the value of the pageCount variable in the pageCount cookie.

9. Store the date that the page was last modified in a variable named **pageUpdate**. Format the date string using the writeDateString() function.

10. Create the HTML fragment

```
<div id="pageFooter">
    <span>Visit Number: pageCount</span>
    <span>lastVisit</span>
    <span>Last Update: pageUpdate</span>
</div>
```

where *pageCount* is the value of the pageCount variable, *lastVisit* is the value of the lastVisit variable, and *pageUpdate* is the value of the pageUpdate variable.

11. Append the HTML fragment to the rightCol element in the current document.

12. Save the file, load the **hangers.htm** file in your Web browser, and then verify that the page displays the date that the page was last visited and modified in a footer at the bottom of the page; and that every time you reload or refresh the document, the page counter increases by 1.

13. Submit the completed project to your instructor.

| Apply | Case Problem 2 |

Use the skills you learned to highlight new items in a sports blog.

Data Files needed for this Case Problem: article01.htm, article02.htm, article03.htm, cengage.jpg, demo.gif, demo2.gif, demo_cookies.htm, newitem.jpg, newitemstxt.js, sblogo.jpg, sblogtxt.htm, sbstyles.css

SBlogger Steve Lavent runs a sports blog called SBlogger with news articles, columns, and stories from the world of sports. Steve wants some way to flag new content for his readers. He's asked you to write a JavaScript program that displays a "New" icon next to stories and columns that have been added to the site's home page since the last time the reader visited the site. Figure 9-48 shows a preview of the page.

Figure 9-48

SBLOGGER
Sports Blogging with a Difference

You last visited on Tue Aug 13 13:00:00 CDT 2013

News Sites
ESPN
SportsLine
Sports Illustrated
CNN
MSNBC
FOX Sports

Columnists
Thomas Bacon
Steve Carls
Debbie Eggert
Frank Franks
Bob Mitchell
Sean Smith
Tom Upham
Mary Yancy

Blogs
Captain X
Yankee Clipper
The Red Sock
Packer Heaven
FBall Blog
Couch Potato
Sports Rounder
Fat, Drunk, and ...

Check that Pen!

New Posted: August 14, 2013 14:33

ESPN is reporting that Houston running back JT Olson has come to terms with the team, signing a three-year deal for $12 million.

[more]

A Cheesy Monument

New Posted: August 13, 2013 19:48

Green Bay native Jeff Miller loves Packers QB Todd Rodgers. And he loves the Packers. And he loves cheese. So what could be more natural than carving a life-size statue of his beloved player in a huge block of gouda?

[more]

Jenkins on Ice

Posted: August 13, 2013 10:15

Retired b-baller Dennis Jenkins announced today that he has signed a contract with "Long Sleep" to have his body frozen before death ...

[more]

Headlines

Carson leads PGA

Brett Carson took a three stroke lead into the final round of the PGA Championship at Whistling Straits with a birdie on the final hole.

Gross Signs Deal

New York signed leading defenseman Steve Gross to a 2-year contract on Thursday.

Olson Out for 2 Weeks

Kansas City QB Drew Olson will miss two weeks of practice due to a sprained knee, team officials announced this morning.

Season Delayed

The start of Spain's soccer season will be delayed for two weeks because of financial problems and fallout from a league-wide drug scandal.

Steve already created a sample page with links to test articles. To create this effect, your program must retrieve the date and time the articles were posted by Steve and then compare that date and time to the date of the reader's last visit.

Complete the following:

1. Open the **newitemstxt.js** and **sblogtxt.htm** files from the tutorial.09\case2 folder in your text editor, enter *your name* and *the date* in the comment section of each file, and then save the files as **newitems.js** and **sblogger.htm**, respectively.

2. Go to the **sblogger.htm** file in your text editor, link the file to the newitems.js file, study the contents of the file, and then save and close the file.

3. Go to the **newitems.js** file in your text editor, and then add a command to run the highlightNew() function when the page is loaded.

4. Create the **highlightNew()** function. The purpose of this function is to display the date that the page was last visited and to highlight new items on the page. Steps 5 through 7 take place within the highlightNew() function.

5. Test whether the value of the lastVisit cookie is equal to null. If it is not, create a variable named **lastVisit** that contains a date object using the value of the lastVisit cookie; otherwise, set the value of the lastVisit variable to null.

6. Retrieve the current date and time and store the time value, formatted with the writeDateTime() function, in the lastVisit cookie. For the purpose of this project, use a current date of August 13, 2013 at 13:00:00.

7. If the lastVisit variable is not equal to null, do the following:

   a. Write the HTML fragment

```
<span id="lastDate">
   You last visited on lastVisit
</span>
```

where *lastVisit* is the value of the lastVisit variable. Append the HTML fragment to the document body.

b. Steve placed the posting times for all articles on the page within paragraph elements with the class name posttime. Locate all elements with this class name and place them in the **allStories** array. For items in the allStories array, retrieve the text of the item and slice the text string, starting at the ninth character, to retain only the date that the story was posted. Use the date string to create a date object variable named **storyDate**.

c. For each story, test whether the lastVisit variable is less than storyDate. If it is (indicating that the user last visited the Web site before the story was posted), create the following HTML fragment, and then append the inline image as a child of the item in the allStories array:

```
<img src="newitem.jpg" />
```

8. Save the file, load **sblogger.htm** in your Web browser, and then verify that the page displays the date that the page was last visited in the upper-right corner of the page and that the first two stories are marked as new stories.

9. Submit the completed project to your instructor.

| Challenge | **Case Problem 3** |

Explore how to use multivalued cookies to create a shopping cart application.

Data Files needed for this Case Problem: arcticb.jpg, arctictxt.htm, carttxt.htm, carttxt.js, cengage.jpg, demo.gif, demo2.gif, demo_cookies.htm, fless.jpg, flesstxt.htm, flogo.jpg, frosti.htm, fwlibrary.js, fwstyles.css, glomitt.jpg, glomitttxt.htm, gloves.htm, gloves.jpg, orderstxt.js, polyflce.jpg, polyftxt.htm, sweaters.jpg

FrostiWear   Susan Crawford is the Web site manager for FrostiWear, an online seller of winter clothing. Susan wants you to work on the shopping cart application. She's provided some sample pages describing the gloves and mittens sold by the company.

The content and design styles have already been created. You need to create the session cookies that record customer selections as they add items to the FrostiWear shopping cart. Each cookie will contain multiple values, recording the product, price, quantity, and style choices of the glove or mitten selected by the customer. Figure 9-49 shows a preview of one of four product pages that you'll be working from.

Figure 9-49

After a customer specifies the product options from the Web form and clicks the Add to Shopping Cart button, Susan wants a multivalued cookie to be created for the selected item containing all of the item's options within different subkeys. To view all the selected items, customers can go to the Shopping Cart page shown in Figure 9-50.

Figure 9-50

FrostiWear ™

| Home | Power Search | Shopping Cart | Your Account | Contact Us |

Your Shopping Cart

Product	Description	Qty	Price	Change
PolyFleece Mitts	Male Large Black	2	$39.95	Remove Item
Arctic Blast Mitts	Male XLarge Navy Blue	1	$98.95	Remove Item
Arctic Blast Mitts	Female Small White	1	$98.95	Remove Item
PolyFleece Mitts	Male Large Grey	1	$39.95	Remove Item
Glomitts	Female Medium	1	$19.95	Remove Item
Fingerless Gloves	Male Large Black	1	$29.95	Remove Item
Fingerless Gloves	Female Small Red	2	$29.95	Remove Item

Susan wants customers to have the ability to remove items from the shopping cart by using the Remove Item button on the page. Removing the item should be accomplished by removing the cookie containing the item. She's provided a library of JavaScript functions stored in the fwlibrary.js file that you can use to create, retrieve, and delete cookies. You will supplement this code with your own code to add and remove items from the shopping cart and to display the contents of the cart.

Complete the following:

1. Open the **arctictxt.htm**, **carttxt.htm**, **carttxt.js**, **flesstxt.htm**, **glomitttxt.htm**, **orderstxt.js**, and **polyftxt.htm** files from the tutorial.09\case3 folder using your text editor, enter *your name* and *the date* in the comment section of each file, and then save the files as **arctic.htm**, **cart.htm**, **cart.js**, **fless.htm**, **glomitt.htm**, **orders.js**, and **polyf.htm**, respectively.

2. Go to the **arctic.htm, fless.htm, glomitt.htm**, and **polyf.htm** files in your text editor. These four pages contain the order form for four different brands of gloves and mittens. Study the code in each file, paying attention to the field names given to each item in the order form. Link each file to the fwlibrary.js and orders.js script files, and then save and close the four files.

3. Study the contents of the **fwlibrary.js** file, which contains several functions you can use to create, retrieve, and delete cookies.

4. Go to the **orders.js** file in your text editor. In this file, you'll insert commands to add items selected from the four order forms to multivalued cookies. Add a command to run the setupOrders() function when the page is loaded. Within the setupOrders() function, insert a command to apply an onclick event handler to the submitButton element that runs the addOrder() function when the button is clicked.

5. Create the **addOrder()** function. The purpose of this function is to create a new cookie for each item selected by the customer. Steps 6 through 14 apply to commands within the addOrder() function.

6. Create a variable named **expiryDate** containing the date and time 48 hours from the present. You'll use this variable as the expiration date for the shopping cart cookies.

7. Each new item in the shopping cart will have a different cookie name. The first item will be stored in the cartItem1 cookie, the second in the cartItem2 cookie, and so on. Create a variable named **itemCount**, setting its initial value to 1. The itemCount variable will store the number of the cart item cookie.

EXPLORE

8. Write a for loop that loops through all of the cookies currently in the document.cookie object. For each cookie, extract the cookie's name, storing it in the **cookieName** variable. If cookieName contains the text string cartItem, retrieve the number of the cart item and then store it in the **cartItemNumber** variable. (*Hint:* Use the slice() method to extract text from the cookieName variable and use the parseInt() method to convert the text string to an integer.) If cartItemNumber is greater than or equal to the itemCount variable, set itemCount equal to one more than cartItemNumber. This ensures that item-Count will be higher than the highest cart item number when the for loop completes.

9. Create a variable named **newItem** that contains the text string cartItemn, where *n* is the value of the itemCount variable.

10. Using the setCookie() function, create a new cookie using the name stored in the newItem variable. Set the value of the cookie to an empty text string and set its expiration date to expiryDate.

11. Using the setField() function, store the value of the product field from the Web form in the product field of the newItem cookie. Be sure to include expiryDate as the expiration date. Do the same for the price field.

12. The remaining information in the order form is entered using selection lists. Create a variable named **allSelects** that contains all of the selection list elements in the Web page.

EXPLORE

13. For every item in allSelects, retrieve the index number of the selected option. Use the index number to retrieve the text of the selected option. (*Hint:* Use the object reference *select*.options[*index*].text, where *select* is the selection box and *index* is the selected index.) Use the setField() function to store the option text in the newItem cookie, using the id of the selection list as the field name and expiryDate as the expiration date.

14. Display to the user the alert message

    `quantity product` added to your shopping cart.
    where *quantity* is the value of the quantity field in the newItem cookie and *product* is the value of the product field in the newItem cookie.

15. Save the orders.js file, and then go to the four order forms you created in Step 2 and add items to the shopping cart using a variety of product options. Verify that the browser displays a message after each item is added to the shopping cart.

16. Using the demo_cookies.htm file or the features of your Web browser, verify that a multivalued cookie is created for each item added to the shopping cart.

17. Go to the **cart.js** file in your text editor. This page will display the contents of the shopping cart to the user. Review the code in the file, link the file to the fwlibrary.js and cart.js script files, and then save and close the file.

18. Go to the **cart.js** file in your text editor. This file contains the code to retrieve and display the cookies for the shopping cart. Add code to run the retrieveOrders() function when the page is loaded.

19. Create the **retrieveOrders()** function. The purpose of this function is to retrieve the selected items and display them in a Web table. Steps 20 through 31 all apply to commands within the retrieveOrders() function.

20. Test whether cookies are available to the document before proceeding to create the shopping cart table.

21. Create an array named **cookies** that contains all of the cookies in document.cookie.

22. Loop through the cookies array, retrieving the names of all the cookies that contain the text string cartItem. This provides a list of all the names of the cookies storing shopping cart items. Store the list of cookie names in an array named **itemsInCart**. You'll use the entries in the itemsInCart array to reference each shopping cart item.

23. If the length of the itemsInCart array is greater than 0, generate the Web table containing the shopping cart described in the following steps.

24. For the Web table, create the following HTML fragment:

```
<table id="cartTable">
    <thead>
        <tr>
            <th>Product</th>
            <th>Description</th>
            <th>Qty</th>
            <th>Price</th>
            <th>Change</th>
        </tr>
    </thead>
    <tbody>
    </tbody>
</table>
```

25. Within the <tbody> element, use a for loop to append a new row for each cookie named in the itemsInCart array.

EXPLORE 26. Within each table row in that for loop, add table cells containing the item's product name, description, quantity, and price. Steps 27 through 30 describe how to create each table cell.

27. For the product name cell, insert into the table row the HTML fragment

```
<td style="background-color: rgb(255, 255, 191)">
    product
</td>
```

where *product* is the value of the product field in the cart item cookie. (*Hint:* Use the getField() function to retrieve the field value from the appropriate cookie.)

28. For the description cell, insert into the table row the HTML fragment

```
<td>
    gender size color
</td>
```

where *gender*, *size*, and *color* are the values of the fields in the cookie. Note that not all items have values for these fields, so you must test for the existence of a field value before attempting to write it to the Web table.

29. For the quantity cell, insert the HTML fragment

```
<td style="text-align: right">
    quantity
</td>
```

where *quantity* is the value of the quantity field in the cookie.

30. For the price cell, insert the HTML fragment

```
<td style="text-align: right">
    price
</td>
```

where *price* is the value of the price field in the cookie.

EXPLORE 31. The final cell in each table row contains a form button that will remove the item from the shopping cart. The HTML fragment for the cell is

```
<td>
    <input type="button" id="cookie" class="deleteItem"
            value="Remove Item" />
</td>
```

where *cookie* is the name of the cookie that contains the shopping cart item. Use an anonymous function to add an event handler to the button that deletes the cookie named in the id attribute and reloads the Web page when the button is clicked. (*Hint:* Use the delCookie() function to delete the cookie, use the `this` keyword along with the id attribute to reference the cookie name, and use the `window.location.reload()` command to reload the Web page.)

32. Save the **cart.js** file, load **cart.htm** in your Web browser, and then verify that the page displays a shopping cart table similar to the one shown in Figure 9-48 and that clicking the Remove Item button in each table row removes the item from the shopping cart.

33. Submit the completed project to your instructor.

Create	Case Problem 4

Create a JavaScript utility that uses cookies to record an online quiz.

Data File needed for this Case Problem: trivia.txt

Trivia Masters   Todd Ferris runs Trivia Masters, an annual competition in Stevens Point, Wisconsin, in which teams of trivia buffs compete over a three-day period for fun and prizes. Todd is creating a series of online multiple choice quizzes for this year's participants to help them prepare and to advertise the competition to a wider audience. The quiz will consist of 40 questions spread over four pages. He wants your help in recording participants' answers in one or more cookies as they move through the quiz. He also wants you to create a JavaScript application that retrieves the answers from the cookie, scores the answers, and writes a summary on a Web page.

Todd provided a text file that contains the list of questions along with the correct answer to each question. You will create and design the Web site content, and write the JavaScript to generate the quiz and test the results.

Complete the following:

1. Create the following files in the tutorial.09\case4 folder: the **trivia1.htm** through **trivia4.htm** files that contain the four pages of quiz questions; the **quiz.css** style sheet that formats the appearance of the quiz pages; the **results.htm** file that contains the results of the quiz; the **score.js** file that contains the program code to score each participant's quiz; and the **results.js** file to report the results. Enter ***your name***, ***the date***, and a ***brief description*** in the comment section of each file.

2. The page content for your Web pages can be taken from the material in the **trivia.txt** file. Graphic images and logos are stored in files in the tutorial.09\case4 folder. You are free to supplement the pages with additional material of your choosing.

3. Create an application in the **score.js** file that stores the quiz results in one or more cookies. The cookie or cookies should contain the following information:
   a. The question number
   b. The correct answer to the multiple choice question
   c. The participant's answer to the multiple choice question

4. Include in the first quiz page a test that confirms that the user's browser has cookies enabled. If cookies are not enabled, display an alert message warning the user.

5. Create an application in the **results.js** file that writes the quiz results to the results.htm page. The results page should display a list of the question numbers, the correct answer, the participant's answer, and some indication of whether the answer was correct. The page should also contain a summary of the number of correct and incorrect answers.

6. Test your Web site, verifying that it records your answers and reports the results correctly.

7. Submit your completed project to your instructor.

Review | **Quick Check Answers**

Session 9.1

1. A client-side cookie is stored on the user's computer and is limited in its size and the number of cookies that can be stored for each domain and overall. Server-side cookies are stored on the Web server and are not subject to the same limitations.

2. Internet Explorer stores cookies in separate files in the cookies folder. Firefox, Opera, and Safari store all of their cookies within a single file.

3. Browsers limit the number of cookies that can be saved per domain, so you have to find a way to place information about all of those items within a smaller number of cookies.

4. `document.cookie`

5. `document.cookie = "userName=Jason%20Stevens";`

6. Cookies are deleted when the current browser session is ended. To change the expiration date, add the following text string:

   `;expire="Mon, 25-March-2013 14:35"`

7. `var expireDate = new Date();`

   `expireDate.setFullYear(expireDate.getFullYear()+3);`

8. `path=/;domain=hipparchus.com`

9. Third-party cookies are cookies from another domain, usually an advertising site, placed on a Web site in the form of a pop-up ad or an ad image that then creates a tracking cookie to track a user's movement across the Web.

Session 9.2

1. They are commands to the browser, not values to be read, and are not accessible to JavaScript.

2. `mailArray = emailAddress.split("@");`

3. `var username = mailArray[0];`

   `var servername = mailArray[1]`

4. `unescape(), decodeURI(), decodeURIComponent()`

5. `var expiredDate = new Date();`

   `expiredDate.setSeconds(expiredDate.getSeconds() - 1);`

6. Bill Dortch was a developer who created a library of functions used to work with client-side cookies. Many of the functions are still used today because they provide support for legacy browsers.

Session 9.3

1. To store multiple values in a cookie, create a set of subkeys with each subkey containing a name/value pair. A common delimiter must separate one subkey from another, and another delimiter must separate the name from the value within the subkey.

2. A subkey is a name/value pair within a multivalued cookie.

3. `var cookieValue = cookieText.slice(cookieText.indexOf("=") + 1)`

4. `var siteArray = cookieValue.split("=");`

5. Client-side cookies can only follow the actions of the user on the local machine; they cannot combine that information with information on users on other machines. To do that, you need a server-side cookie or database program.

6. `navigator.cookiesEnabled()`

7. Data can be stored in a query string as part of the URL of a Web page. Also, data can be stored in the window.name object.

Ending Data Files

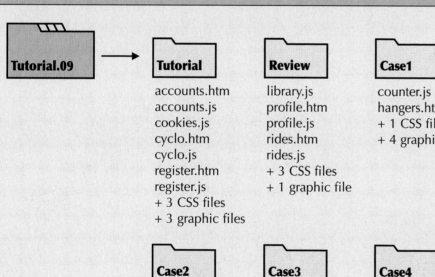

Tutorial.09 →

Tutorial
accounts.htm
accounts.js
cookies.js
cyclo.htm
cyclo.js
register.htm
register.js
+ 3 CSS files
+ 3 graphic files

Review
library.js
profile.htm
profile.js
rides.htm
rides.js
+ 3 CSS files
+ 1 graphic file

Case1
counter.js
hangers.htm
+ 1 CSS file
+ 4 graphic files

Case2
newitems.js
sblogger.htm
+ 3 HTML files
+ 1 CSS file
+ 2 graphic files

Case3
arctic.htm
cart.htm
cart.js
fless.htm
glomitt.htm
orders.js
polyf.htm
+ 2 HTML files
+ 1 CSS file
+ 1 JavaScript file
+ 7 graphics files

Case4
trivia1.htm
trivia2.htm
trivia3.htm
trivia4.htm
results.js
score.js
quiz.css

Objectives

Session 10.1
- Explore the window object
- Work with the status bar
- Work with the history and location objects

Session 10.2
- Create new browser windows
- Work with pop-up blockers
- Apply methods to the window object
- Create dialog boxes
- Exchange data between windows

Session 10.3
- Work with frames
- Control frame behavior
- Work with inline frames

Designing Pop-Up Windows and Frames

Designing a Music Web Site

Case | iMusicHistory

Teresa Jenner, a professional musician, started a music history Web site two years ago. Last month, Teresa bought a new domain name for the Web site and needs you to create scripts to redirect users automatically to the new URL from the old one. Teresa also wants to add pop-up windows for use in an online quiz and a glossary of musical terms. Finally, because part of her Web site uses frames, she wants you to write scripts to control their appearance and behavior.

Starting Data Files

Tutorial.10 →

Tutorial
concertotxt.htm
imlibrarytxt.js
imusictxt.htm
indextxt.htm
lesson3txt.htm
navtxt.htm
quiztxt.htm
sonatatxt.htm
statustxt.js
symphonytxt.htm
+ 12 HTML files
+ 4 CSS files
+ 8 graphic files

Review
atempotxt.htm
bottomtxt.htm
defaulttxt.htm
glosstxt.htm
quiz2txt.htm
+ 10 HTML files
+ 4 CSS files
+ 6 graphic files

Case1
covertxt.htm
cwjtxt.htm
formtxt.htm
+ 2 CSS files
+ 4 graphic files

Case2
braintxt.htm
iframetxt.js
+ 1 HTML file
+ 2 CSS files
+ 1 JavaScript file
+ 1 graphic file

Case3
scripttxt.js
titletxt.htm
+ 3 HTML files
+ 2 CSS files
+ 1 graphic file
+ 2 text files

Case4
allentxt.htm
birdtxt.htm
boottxt.htm
corraltxt.htm
courthousetxt.htm
indextxt.htm
schieftxt.htm
+ 1 CSS file
+ 14 graphic files

Session 10.1

Exploring the Window Object

Teresa shows you the current status of her music Web site, and conveys the changes she wants you to make. You'll start by examining the work she's done already.

To open the iMusicHistory home page:

▶ **1.** Use your text editor to open the **imusictxt.htm** file from the tutorial.10\tutorial folder, enter *your name* and *the date* in the comment section of the file, and then save the file as **imusic.htm**.

▶ **2.** Open the **imusic.htm** file in your Web browser. Some of the links on the page do not work because you do not have all of the files for the Web site. See Figure 10-1.

Figure 10-1   iMusicHistory home page

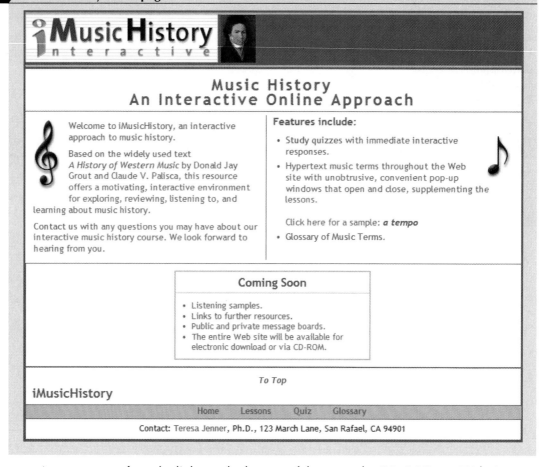

As you can see from the links on the bottom of the page, the iMusicHistory Web site has the following four main pages:

- A Home page, describing the purpose and features of the site
- A Lessons page, containing an interactive lesson on music history
- A Quiz page, containing an online quiz for students to review
- A Glossary page, containing definitions of musical terms

The first changes that Teresa wants you to make to her Web site involve the text that appears in the Web browser's status bar. Teresa wants a status bar message welcoming visitors to the site to appear as soon as the home page of the Web site loads. She also wants a description of each navigational link to appear in the status bar whenever the pointer is over a navigation link.

To create these messages in the status bar, you'll need to manipulate the appearance of the browser window. JavaScript considers the browser window an object, which it calls the **window object**. Many features of the browser window, including the text in the status bar, are properties of the window object. Figure 10-2 lists other properties of the window object. Some of these properties may already be familiar to you from programming examples in previous tutorials.

Properties of the window object ◀ Figure 10-2

Property	Description
closed	A Boolean value indicating whether the window has been closed
defaultStatus	The default message displayed in the status bar
document	The document object displayed in the window
frames	The collection of frames within the window
history	The history object, containing a list of Web sites visited within that window
innerHeight	The inner height of the window excluding all toolbars, scroll bars, and other features (not supported under Internet Explorer)
innerWidth	The inner width of the window excluding all toolbars, scroll bars, and other features (not supported under Internet Explorer)
location	The location object containing the URL of the current Web document
name	The name of the window
opener	The source browser window, which opened the current window
outerHeight	The outer height of the window including all toolbars, scroll bars, and other features (not supported under Internet Explorer)
outerWidth	The outer width of the window including all toolbars, scroll bars, and other features (not supported under Internet Explorer)
scrollbars	The scroll bar object contained in the browser window
status	The temporary or transient message displayed in the status bar
statusbar	The status bar object used for displaying messages in the browser window
toolbar	A Boolean value indicating whether the window's toolbar is visible

The command to set a property of the window object is

```
windowObject.property = value
```

where *windowObject* is a browser window, *property* is a property of the window, and *value* is the value you assign to the property. Note that you can have more than one browser window open during a session, and you can use JavaScript to work with the properties and content of those different windows. You will learn how to work with multiple windows later in this tutorial. If you're only working with the properties of the current browser window, you don't need to specify the browser window and can use the object name window or in some cases leave out the window object reference entirely. For example, to set the value of the inner height of the current browser window to 300 pixels, you would use the following command:

```
window.innerHeight = "300";
```

If the property of the window object is itself an object, you can drop the reference to the window object. The object reference

```
window.location
```

which references the location bar, is equivalent to

```
location
```

as long as you are looking at the properties and objects of the current browser window. If you want to reference the objects and properties of another window, you must include the reference to that window object in the command.

Working with the Status Bar

The borders of a browser window, including items such as the toolbars and scroll bars, are collectively referred to as the window's **chrome**. One part of the chrome that is common to all browsers is the **status bar**, which displays messages to the user about actions occurring within the window. These messages can be either permanent or transient.

Setting the Default Status Bar Message

Tip

Because the browser might not display a customized status bar, never put essential information into a status bar message.

The **permanent status bar message** is the message that appears in the status bar by default when no actions are occurring with the browser window. The command to set the text of the permanent status bar message is

```
windowObject.defaultStatus = value;
```

where *windowObject* is again the object reference to the browser window and *value* is the default message appearing in the window's status bar. This message is only permanent for the current document. After the browser loads a different page, the permanent status bar message returns to either the browser default or to the permanent message specified for the new page.

InSight	**Status Bar Messages and Counterfeit Sites**

Many current browsers disable the ability of JavaScript programs to modify permanent and transient status bar messages because of potential security issues. Modifying status bar messages can be part of an overall process of creating counterfeit Web sites that resemble legitimate sites. Counterfeit sites are sometimes created to trick unsuspecting users into revealing personal information such as contact information, passwords, and credit card numbers.

Teresa asks you to set the permanent message of the browser window's status bar under the iMusicHistory home page to "Welcome to iMusicHistory." Because this command must be run when the page is initially loaded by the browser, you'll add an event handler to the document placed in an external script file. Teresa has made a library of JavaScript functions that you'll use for the home page. The imlibrary.js file includes the addEvent() function, which you've used in several case problems from earlier tutorials.

To change the default status bar message:

1. Use your text editor to open the **imlibrarytxt.js** and **statustxt.js** files from the tutorial.10\tutorial folder, enter *your name* and *the date* in the comment section of each file, and then save the files as **imlibrary.js** and **status.js**, respectively.

2. Go to the **status.js** file, and then insert the following code, as shown in Figure 10-3, to change the default status bar message when the page is loaded by the browser:

```
addEvent(window, "load", initPage, false);

function initPage() {
   window.defaultStatus = "Welcome to iMusicHistory.com";
}
```

Code to set the status bar default text ◀ **Figure 10-3**

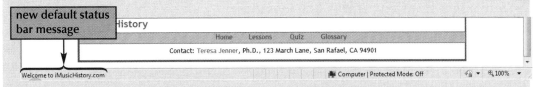

```
addEvent(window, "load", initPage, false);

function initPage() {
   window.defaultStatus = "Welcome to iMusicHistory.com";
}
```

default text displayed in the browser window's status bar

3. Save the file, and then return to the **imusic.htm** file in your text editor.

4. Add the following script elements to the head section of the file to connect the document to the two script files:

```
<script type="text/javascript" src="imlibrary.js"></script>
<script type="text/javascript" src="status.js"></script>
```

5. Save the file, and then reload **imusic.htm** in your Web browser. The browser window status bar displays the text message welcoming the user to the iMusicHistory Web site. See Figure 10-4.

Permanent status bar text ◀ **Figure 10-4**

new default status bar message

History

Home   Lessons   Quiz   Glossary

Contact: Teresa Jenner, Ph.D., 123 March Lane, San Rafael, CA 94901

Welcome to iMusicHistory.com   Computer | Protected Mode: Off   100%

Trouble? The default settings of some browsers, including Firefox and Internet Explorer 8, do not allow JavaScript to change the default status bar text. To view the revised status bar text, you must change the security settings on your browser. View your browser's documentation for more details.

Creating a Transient Status Bar Message

The iMusicHistory home page contains several links at the bottom of the page. By default, most browsers display the URL of a link in the status bar when a user hovers the pointer over the link. However, Teresa wants the message "Learn more about iMusicHistory" to appear in the status bar when users move the pointer over the Home link. This message is an example of a **transient status bar message** because it appears temporarily in response to an event occurring within the browser. After the event is over, the transient message disappears, replaced by the permanent message.

The commands to set the transient status bar message in response to a mouseover event are

```
windowObject.status = value;
return true;
```

where *value* is the text that will appear as a transient message in the status bar. Note that by default, a browser generates its own transient message for the action of hovering over a link by displaying the URL of the link. So you need to override that action. This is done by including the command

```
return true;
```

to cause the browser to set the status bar message and then halt the process of the function and the propagation of the onmouseover event. As a result, the browser does not display the default transient message, but instead displays only the message specified in the JavaScript code.

To change the transient status bar message for the Home link, you'll add the following onmouseover event handler to the link within the imusic.htm file:

```
onmouseover = "window.status='Learn more about iMusicHistory';
return true;"
```

When the user moves the pointer off the link, you want the status bar to become blank. However, by default transient status bar messages remain until another event replaces them. To remove the message, you need to also add an onmouseout event handler that changes the transient message to an empty text string. The event handler for this action is:

```
onmouseout = "window.status='';"
```

When the browser encounters a blank transient message, it understands that as a signal to display no message or to redisplay the permanent status bar message if one exists.

To create a transient status bar message:

▶ **1.** Return to the **imusic.htm** file in your text editor.

▶ **2.** Scroll down to the list of links at the bottom of the file, and then insert the following event handlers, as shown in Figure 10-5:

```
onmouseover="window.status='Learn more about
iMusicHistory';return true;"
onmouseout="window.status='';"
```

Figure 10-5 ▶ **Code to set the transient status bar message**

transient status
bar message

```
<div id="footer2">
    <p><a href="#">To Top</a></p>
    <h2>iMusicHistory</h2>
    <ul>
        <li><a href="imusic.htm"
            onmouseover="window.status='Learn more about iMusicHistory';return true;"
            onmouseout="window.status='';">Home</a>
        </li>
        <li><a href="lesson3.htm">Lessons</a></li>
        <li><a href="quiz.htm">Quiz</a></li>
        <li><a href="terms.htm">Glossary</a></li>
    </ul>
    <address>
        Contact: <a href="mailto:teresa_jenner@imusichistory.com">
        Teresa Jenner</a>, Ph.D., 123 March Lane, San Rafael, CA 94901
    </address>
</div>
</div>

</body>
</html>
```

▶ **3.** Save the file, and then reload **imusic.htm** in your Web browser.

▶ **4.** Move the pointer over the **Home** link at the bottom of the page, and then verify that the text "Learn more about iMusicHistory" appears in the status bar. See Figure 10-6.

Status bar with the transient status bar message ◀ **Figure 10-6**

▶ **5.** Move the pointer away from the link, and then verify that the default status bar text reappears.

Trouble? If you do not see any changes in the status bar, the security settings of your browser might be preventing JavaScript from changing your status bar message. In that case, your JavaScript debugger will report no error messages.

You're done working on the status bar messages for now. Later, you'll apply the techniques you learned to the other links and pages in the Web site.

Setting the Status Bar Message | Reference Window

- To change the default message displayed in the browser window's status bar, use the JavaScript command

  ```
  windowObject.defaultStatus = value
  ```
  where *windowObject* is an object reference to the browser window and *value* is the text of the status bar message.
- To change the transient or temporary message appearing in the status bar, add the following commands to the event handler function:

  ```
  windowObject.status = value;
  return true;
  ```

Working with the History and Location Objects

Previously, the iMusicHistory Web site was stored on the servers at Teresa's university and the home page was located in a file named index.htm (rather than imusic.htm). Teresa still wants to include the index.htm page in her site because some users have links or bookmarks that point to it. However, she wants the index.htm page to alert users about the change in location and provide a link to imusic.htm. Teresa also wants a link on the old home page that returns users to the previous page they visited. This way, users can easily notify the authors of pages linked to the old iMusicHistory home page that the link should be updated. Finally, if a user does nothing, Teresa wants the browser to load the new site automatically after a brief interval.

Browsers maintain information about where users have been and the pages they're currently visiting within each window. You can access this information through the location and history objects. The **location object** contains information about the page that is currently displayed in the window. The **history object** holds a list of the sites the Web browser displayed before reaching the current page in the window.

Moving Forward and Backward in the History List

In a browser window, you usually navigate the history list by clicking the Back and Forward buttons on the browser toolbar. To do the same using JavaScript, you use the following methods of the history object:

```
history.back();
history.forward();
```

The back() method causes the window to load the page before the current page in the history list; in other words, it changes the page visible in the window to the page the user was previously viewing. If a user is at the beginning of the history list, there is no page to go back to and the current page is not replaced. The forward() method loads the next page in the history list after the current page. If a user is at the end of the history list, there is no page to go to and the current page remains in the browser. Note that both of these methods access the history object within the current browser window. If you want to use history objects in other browser windows, you must specify the window object as

```
windowObject.history.back();
```

where *windowObject* is a reference to the browser window. You can also navigate to a particular page in the history object using the method

```
history.go(integer)
```

where *integer* can be a positive or negative integer value or zero, and represents how many pages the browser should move through in the history list. For example, the following command moves the user back one page in the history list:

```
history.go(-1)
```

The following command moves the user to the next page in the list:

```
history.go(1)
```

And, the following command keeps the user at the current page:

```
history.go(0)
```

A common way to implement the back() and forward() methods is as links using the HTML code

```
<a href="javascript:history.back()">Back</a>
```

and

```
<a href="javascript:history.forward()">Forward</a>
```

You'll implement this approach in Teresa's old home page. Much of the content of the revised index.htm page has been created for you and stored in the index.htm file. First, you will create a link on the index.htm page that points to the page previously visited by the user.

To create a link to previously visited pages:

► 1. Use your text editor to open the **indextxt.htm** file from the tutorial.10\tutorial folder, enter *your name* and *the date* in the comment section, and then save the file as **index.htm**.

▶ **2.** Scroll down the file and edit the hypertext link, as shown in Figure 10-7.

Link to the previously visited page ◀ **Figure 10-7**

```
<p>If a link has led you erroneously to this page, <br />
    please click <a href="javascript:history.back()">return</a>
    to go back to the previous page,<br />
    and notify the page's author of the outdated link.
</p>

</body>

</html>
```

▶ **3.** Save the file, and then load **imusic.htm** into your Web browser.

▶ **4.** Within the same tab or window, enter the address for the **index.htm** file in the address bar to replace the imusic.htm file with the index.htm file. See Figure 10-8.

Contents of the index.htm page ◀ **Figure 10-8**

> Teresa Jenner's
> Music History Course
> Has Moved
>
> You will automatically be redirected to the new
> site in 8 seconds or less.
>
> If your browser doesn't automatically redirect you,
> please click iMusicHistory.com to move to the new page.
>
> If a link has erroneously led you to this page,
> please click return to go back to the previous page,
> and notify the page's author of the outdated link.

▶ **5.** Click the **return** link on the Web page to verify that the browser reloads the imusic.htm file, which, in this case, is the previous page you opened in the browser tab or window.

Automatic Page Navigation

Your next task is to automatically redirect users' browsers to the new Web site, so that if users don't click any of the links or their Back or Forward button, the imusic.htm file will be loaded.

There are two ways to automatically redirect the user to another Web page. One way is to add a command to the <meta> tag located in the head section of an HTML file. The other is to create a JavaScript program that runs when the page is loaded and opens the new page automatically. Because users might turn off support for JavaScript in their browsers, you'll employ both methods in the index.htm file.

The HTML code to redirect a browser to a new page using the meta element is

```
<meta http-equiv="Refresh" content="sec;URL=url" />
```

where *sec* is the amount of time in seconds that will elapse before the new page opens and *url* is the new page to be loaded. For example, to load the imusic.htm page automatically after eight seconds, you add the following tag to the index.htm file:

```
<meta http-equiv="Refresh" content="8;URL=imusic.htm" />
```

Setting the time value to zero causes the redirection to occur almost instantaneously, so that often users are not even aware that a redirection has taken place. However, for Teresa's site, you will use an eight-second delay so that users have time to read the text notifying them to update their links to iMusicHistory.

Another approach to redirecting a browser to another page uses the location object

```
windowObject.location.href = url;
```

where *url* is the new page to be loaded. To automatically redirect the current browser window to the imusic.htm page, you add the following JavaScript command to the index.htm file:

```
location.href = "imusic.htm";
```

To add a delay, you can run this command with the setTimeout() method, setting a delay time of 8000 milliseconds (8 seconds), and apply the following anonymous function:

```
setTimeout( function() {
    location.href = "imusic.htm";
    }, 8000);
```

To ensure maximum compatibility with all browsers, you'll use both techniques in the outdated index.htm file.

Tip

To accommodate users that block JavaScript, include a meta element in the HTML code to redirect users to the new page.

To add automatic redirection to the index.htm page:

▶ **1.** Return to the **index.htm** file in your text editor.

▶ **2.** Directly below the title element in the head section of the document, insert the following code, as shown in Figure 10-9:

```
<meta http-equiv="Refresh" content="8;URL=imusic.htm" />

<script type="text/javascript">
    setTimeout(function() {
        location.href = "imusic.htm";
    }, 8000);
</script>
```

Figure 10-9 | Automatic redirection to the imusic.htm file

redirects after eight seconds using the meta element

redirects after eight seconds using the location.href object and the setTimeout() method

```
<title>iMusicHistory has moved</title>
<meta http-equiv="Refresh" content="8;URL=imusic.htm" />

<script type="text/javascript">
    setTimeout( function() {
        location.href = "imusic.htm";
    }, 8000);
</script>
```

▶ **3.** Save the file, and then reload the **index.htm** file in your Web browser, verifying that after about eight seconds, the browser window or tab automatically loads the imusic.htm file.

Both the <meta> tag and the JavaScript approach require the user's computer to do the redirecting. The problem with performing redirection on the client side is that it wastes browser time downloading the old HTML file and is unfriendly toward search engines. The <meta> tag and JavaScript code can also be turned off by the user for security reasons, preventing the redirection. Most Web developers recommend that automatic redirection be done on the Web server using server-side scripts. For example, the following PHP code writes an HTTP header that modifies the HTTP 301 status code to automatically redirect the user to the imusic.htm file:

```php
<?php
// Permanent redirection
header("HTTP/1.1 301 Moved Permanently");
header("Location: imusic.htm");
exit();
?>
```

Because the redirection is done solely through the server, it occurs faster and with less complication to the client-side machine. If you do not have access to scripts running on the Web server, you can always use the <meta> tag and a JavaScript program as a fallback.

Automatically Redirecting the Web Browser | Reference Window

- To redirect users automatically from one page to another, add the meta element
  ```
  <meta http-equiv="Refresh" content="sec;URL=url" />
  ```
  to the head section of the HTML file, where *sec* is the delay time in seconds and *url* is the URL of the new Web page.
- To redirect using JavaScript, run the code
  ```
  setTimeout( function() {
     location.href = url;
  }, milliseconds);
  ```
  when the page is loaded by the browser, where *url* is the URL of the new Web page and *milliseconds* is the delay time in milliseconds.
- To avoid client-side redirection, run a server-side script that modifies the HTTP 301 status code of the HTTP header.

InSight | Security Issues and the document.referrer Property

Mozilla browsers such as Firefox and Netscape also support the current, next, and previous properties of the history object. These properties return the URLs of the previous, current, and next page in a user's history list, respectively. However, use of these properties is restricted to prevent Web page authors from creating scripts to record what sites their users have been visiting. Most people would consider such tracking an invasion of privacy.

Firefox and Netscape use signed scripts to request permission to access restricted information such as the current, next, and previous properties. The process of creating a signed script involves acquiring digital certification of your identity as a legitimate developer or organization. Digital certification can come from a variety of sources on the Web, including *www.thawte.com* and *www.verisign.com*. Signed scripts are not available in Internet Explorer, however; and prior to Netscape version 4, these properties were not available at all from a script.

Another way of retrieving this information is through the document.referrer property, which records the URL of the page from which the current page was accessed. The following code uses the document.referrer property to write the name of the page from which the current page was loaded:

```
if (document.referrer) {
    document.write('You came from: ' + document.referrer);
}
```

Note that the document.referrer property works only when the current page is accessed via a link, and that some browsers disable this property for security reasons.

The document.referrer property is often used in Web commerce to provide users that come from particular Web sites with special offers or bonus points. Note that the referrer property only works for pages stored on a Web server. You cannot test it using local files loaded on your own computer.

Teresa is pleased with the messages you created for the status bar as well as your solution to redirecting visitors from her old domain to her new one. In the next session, you'll work on the online music history glossary terms, which will require creating new windows with JavaScript.

Review | Session 10.1 Quick Check

1. Explain the difference between permanent and transient status bar messages.
2. What single JavaScript command moves a user two places backward in the history list?
3. What JavaScript command(s) changes the transient status bar message to "View News page"?
4. Describe at least two methods (a JavaScript method and a non-JavaScript method) of redirecting visitors from a Web site or Web page to its new location.
5. What is the history.previous property? Describe a security concern of using this property.
6. What is the document.referrer property used for? What are two limitations of this property?

Session 10.2

Creating New Browser Windows

The iMusicHistory Web site contains a glossary of musical terms. When a user clicks a linked term, its definition on the glossary page is displayed, as shown in Figure 10-10.

Music glossary **Figure 10-10**

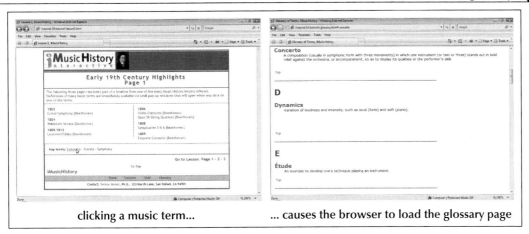

clicking a music term...   ... causes the browser to load the glossary page

Teresa is concerned that jumping from one page to another to view definitions is inconvenient and distracting. As a user goes back and forth between the two windows, it may be easy to lose track of where he or she is within the Web site. Teresa would rather see a smaller window, containing the definition, appear alongside the main window. A user could then quickly read the definition without losing contact with the main window. Figure 10-11 shows a preview of the system Teresa wants you to create.

Definition pop-up window **Figure 10-11**

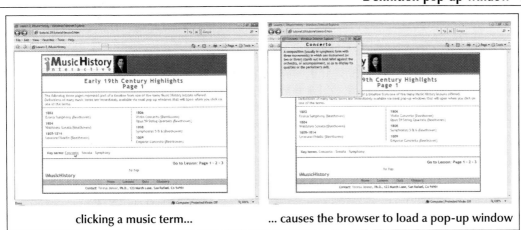

clicking a music term...   ... causes the browser to load a pop-up window

A window that opens in addition to the main browser window is called a **secondary window** or a **pop-up window**. Teresa wants you to add pop-up windows to her Web site.

Opening New Windows with HTML

By default, each new Web page that a user opens appears in the main browser window. As users move from one page to another, the contents of the browser window change accordingly. If you want a link to open the target document in a new window, you can specify the window name using the target property. The general syntax of the link element is

```
<a href="url" target="name">link text</a>
```

where *url* is the URL of the target document and *name* is the name of the secondary browser window in which the document should appear. The value of the target attribute doesn't affect the appearance or content of the new window. In fact, you need to keep track of the target attribute's value only if you intend to use the same window for other links. For example, Teresa's Web site could open a secondary window that displays biographies of the great composers. HTML tags for links to that window could appear as follows:

```
<a href="wagner.htm" target="Composer">View Wagner's biography</a>
<a href="mozart.htm" target="Composer">View Mozart's biography</a>
```

Clicking either link would open a secondary window with the target name "Composer". If the Composer window were already open, its contents would be replaced with the new page. You can assign the target any name other than one that is reserved by HTML for other purposes.

Opening New Windows with JavaScript

You can also use JavaScript to create new windows. JavaScript offers more control and many more options for creating new windows than the target property does. For example, you can control the contents of a window you create, the window size (height and width properties), its position on the screen, and whether the new window has toolbars (and which ones), a menu bar, and a status bar. In contrast, any new windows created using the target property draw their appearance (toolbars, menu bars, scroll bars, etc.) from the appearance of the main browser window.

The JavaScript command to create a new browser window is

```
window.open(url, name, features)
```

where *url* is the URL of the page to be displayed in the new window, *name* is the target name assigned to the window, and *features* is a comma-separated list of features that control the appearance and behavior of the window. If you don't need to specify a target name for the new window, you can specify an empty text string for the name value. The features list can include the size and width of the window as well as whether the window's scroll bar, toolbar, status bar, and menu bar are to be displayed.

You can store the new browser window as a JavaScript object. This is necessary if your script needs to access the window to alter its contents. To store a new window as an object, you use the command

```
var windowObject = window.open(url, name, features)
```

where *windowObject* is a variable referencing the new browser window.

Creating a Pop-up Window | Reference Window

- To create a pop-up browser window, use
  ```
  window.open(url, name, features)
  ```
  where *url* is the URL of the document to be displayed in the window, *name* is the target name assigned to the window, and *features* is a comma-separated list of window features.
- To store a pop-up window as a JavaScript object, use
  ```
  var windowObject = window.open(url, name, features)
  ```
  where *windowObject* is a variable referencing the new browser window.

Setting the Features of a Pop-up Window

Before you create a window for Teresa's glossary, you will examine the features list in more detail. The features list employs the syntax

```
feature1=value1,feature2=value2,...featureN=valueN
```

where *feature1*, *feature2*, ... are the names of the different window features, and *value1*, *value2*, ... are the values associated with those features. Figure 10-12 describes these features and their values. For example, to create a browser window that is resizable but without a menu bar, location box, and toolbar, you would use the following features list:

```
resizable=yes,menubar=no,location=no,toolbar=no
```

Tip

You can substitute the number 1 for yes and the number 0 for no in the features list.

Figure 10-12 ⟩ **Feature list values**

Feature	Description	Value
alwaysLowered	Sets the window below all other windows (not supported under Internet Explorer)	yes/no
alwaysRaised	Sets the window above all other windows (not supported under Internet Explorer)	yes/no
dependent	Defines whether the window is a dependent of the parent window that created it and closes when it closes (not supported under Internet Explorer)	yes/no
fullscreen	Displays the window in full screen mode (Internet Explorer only)	yes/no
height	Sets the window height, in pixels	integer
hotkeys	Disables keyboard hotkeys in the window (not supported under Internet Explorer)	yes/no
innerHeight	Sets the inner height of the window, in pixels (not supported under Internet Explorer)	integer
innerWidth	Sets the inner width of the window, in pixels (not supported under Internet Explorer)	integer
left	Sets the screen coordinate of the left edge of the window, in pixels (Internet Explorer only)	integer
location	Displays the location bar in the window	yes/no
menubar	Displays the menu bar in the window	yes/no
outerHeight	Sets the outer height of the window, in pixels (not supported under Internet Explorer)	integer
outerWidth	Sets the outer width of the window, in pixels (not supported under Internet Explorer)	integer
resizable	Allows users to resize the window	yes/no
screenX	Sets the screen coordinate of the left edge of the window, in pixels (not supported under Internet Explorer)	integer
screenY	Sets the screen coordinate of the top edge of the window, in pixels (not supported under Internet Explorer)	integer
scrollbars	Displays scroll bars in the window	yes/no
status	Displays the status bar in the window	yes/no
top	Sets the screen coordinate of the top edge of the window, in pixels (Internet Explorer only)	integer
titlebar	Displays the title bar (not supported under Internet Explorer)	yes/no
toolbar	Displays the window's toolbar	yes/no
width	Sets the width of the window, in pixels	integer
z-lock	Prevents the window from rising above other windows (not supported under Internet Explorer)	yes/no

A features list is not required. If you don't specify a features list, the new window adopts the characteristics of the browser window that created it. However, after you define any part of the features list, the new window follows these rules:

- If you don't specify a width or height, the width or height of the original browser window is used.
- If you don't include a particular feature of the window's chrome in the list, that feature will not appear in the window.

For example, if the features list appears as

```
width=300,height=200,resizable=yes
```

the new window will have a width of 300 pixels and a height of 200 pixels, and will be resizable, but none of the other window objects (toolbars, status bar, scroll bars, etc.) will appear.

By default, a pop-up window appears in the upper-left corner of the screen. You can specify a different location in the window.open() method. Internet Explorer uses a different feature for this compared to other browsers such as Firefox, Safari, and Opera. Internet Explorer uses features named left and top, whereas other browsers use screenX and screenY. If you wanted to place a window at the screen coordinates (200, 250)— 200 pixels from the left edge and 250 pixels down—you would specify the features as follows:

```
left=200,top=250,screenX=200,screenY=250
```

You will work with a demo page to see how JavaScript can be used to define the properties of a pop-up window.

Tip

If you don't include a features list, Firefox and Opera open the window as a new browser tab.

To view the pop-up window demo:

1. If you took a break after the previous session, make sure the imusic.htm, imlibrary.js, status.js, and index.htm files are open in your text editor, and imusic.html and index.htm are open in your Web browser.

2. Use your Web browser to open the **demo_popup.htm** file from the tutorial.10\ tutorial folder.

3. In the Web form, enter **400** in the Left edge box to set the location of the left edge of the pop-up window you'll create at 400 pixels from the left edge of the browser window. The JavaScript code to create the pop-up window changes in response.

4. Enter **35** in the Top edge box to set the location of the top edge of the pop-up window at 35 pixels from the top edge of the browser window.

5. Enter **200** in the Width box, and then enter **150** in the Height box to set the width and height of the pop-up window to 200 pixels and 150 pixels, respectively.

6. Click the **Display status bar** check box to display a status bar in the pop-up window.

7. Click the **Show pop-up window** button to display the pop-up window. See Figure 10-13.

Figure 10-13 | Pop-up Window demo page

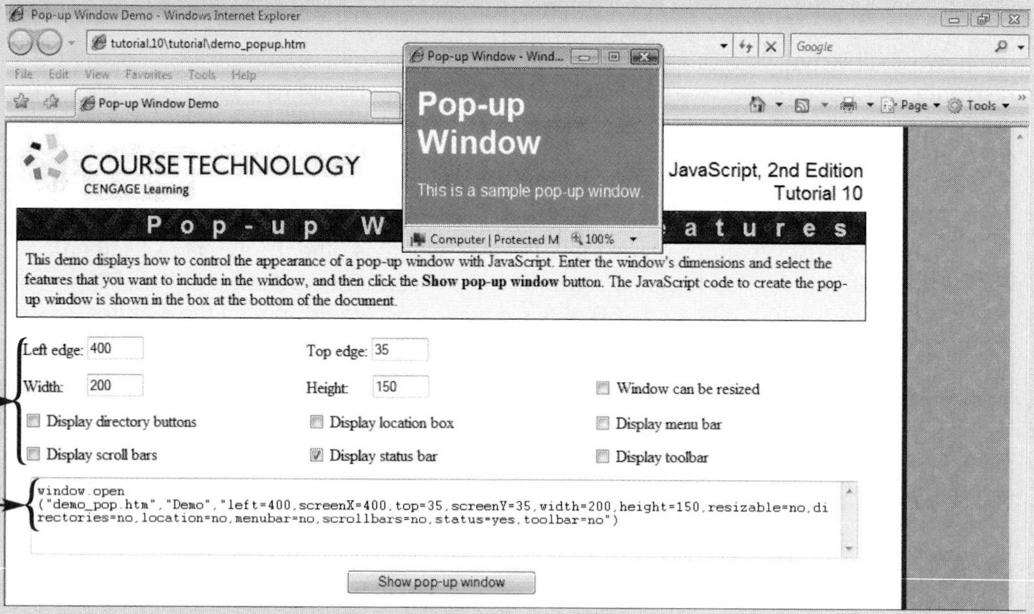

enter values and select options for the pop-up window

JavaScript code to create the pop-up window reflects the selected features

Trouble? Depending on your browser, your window will look slightly different than that shown in Figure 10-13. If you are running a pop-up blocker, you may have to turn it off to run this demo. Also, some browsers such as Firefox do not allow users to hide the location bar for security reasons. Under Internet Explorer, you might need to allow the blocked content to appear by choosing that option from the Information Bar.

8. Close the pop-up window.

9. Repeat Steps 3 through 8 to generate pop-up windows with different features, and then close the demo page.

Reference Window | Setting Pop-up Window Features

- To define the width and height of the pop-up window, add
  `width=x,height=y`
  to the features list in the window.open() method, where *x* and *y* are the width and height of the window, in pixels.
- *Internet Explorer*: To set the screen position of a pop-up, add the features
  `left=x,top=y`
  where *x* is the coordinate of the left edge, in pixels, and *y* is the coordinate of the window's top edge.
- *Other Browsers*: To set the screen position of a pop-up, add the following features:
  `screenX=x,screenY=y`
- To display the directory buttons, location box, menu bar, scroll bar, status bar, or toolbar, add the features
  `directories=value,location=value,menubar=value,scrollbars=value,`
  `status=value,toolbar=value`
  where *value* is either "yes" (to show the feature) or "no" (to hide the feature). You can also substitute the values "1" for "yes" and "0" for "no".

Working with Pop-up Blockers

Shortly after the ability to create new browser windows became a part of JavaScript, pop-up windows became a common and often annoying feature of the Web. In general, pop-ups come in two types: those that users open by clicking a link, and those that open automatically whether users want to see them or not. Many Web sites, eager to generate commercial revenue, incorporated automated pop-ups to display sponsors' advertisements. On some sites, users became inundated with so many commercial pop-up windows that it was difficult to view the contents of the Web site itself. In response to the proliferation of pop-ups, browsers and third-party software developers added **pop-up blockers** that prevent pop-up windows from opening. There are a variety of pop-up blockers used by browsers and third-party software. Some blockers make a distinction between automated pop-ups and pop-ups opened by users, and others do not. There's not a lot you can do to override pop-up blockers—and this is not something you should do if you want to create a user-friendly Web site that respects each user's preferences regarding pop-ups. However, you can use JavaScript to determine whether the pop-up window has been opened. If it hasn't, you can then have JavaScript open the linked file in the current browser window. A function that tests whether a pop-up window has failed to open has the following general form:

```
function popWin(url) {
   pop = window.open(url, name, features)
   test = (pop == null || typeof(pop) == "undefined") ? true: false;
   return test;
}
```

This function returns the value true if the pop-up fails to open and the value false if the pop-up opens without fail. The function uses a conditional operator to test whether the pop-up opens. You know that the pop-up did not open if either *pop* is null (which means that it was not created) or the type of the *pop* variable is undefined. The following code calls the popWin() function from a link on the page:

```
<a href="url" onclick="return(popWin('url'))">Link Text</a>
```

If the popWin() function returns the Boolean value true, the link code processes the onclick event, overriding the normal action of the browser to process the href attribute in response to a mouse click. However, if the popWin() function returns the value false, it cancels the click event and the browser opens the link via the href attribute in the usual way—but not as a pop-up window. In either case, a user sees the contents of the pop-up window—in one case as a pop-up, and in the other case in the current browser window. Note that the `return` keyword has the same purpose here as it did in creating a transient status bar message in the previous session: It breaks the normal behavior of the Web browser and allows you to ensure that the linked page is available to the user. If pop-up windows are an important part of your Web site, test your code against various pop-up blockers and under a variety of conditions. This helps you to ensure that the contents of your Web site are always accessible to your users, no matter what browser and pop-up blocker they may be using. Keep in mind that most pop-up blockers block only automated pop-ups and not those activated by a user clicking a link to a pop-up window.

Adding a Pop-up Window to a Web Site

Teresa has begun the process of copying the musical definitions into separate HTML files for use as pop-up windows. She already created three HTML files for the musical terms concerto, sonata, and symphony. The links for these three definitions are stored in the lesson3.htm file. Because you'll be modifying the contents of these files, you will open and save them under different names.

To open and view musical terms and definitions files:

▶ **1.** Use your text editor to open the **concertotxt.htm**, **sonatatxt.htm**, **symphonytxt.htm**, and **lesson3txt.htm** files from the tutorial.10\tutorial folder, enter *your name* and *the date* in the comment section of each file, and then save the files as **concerto.htm**, **sonata.htm**, **symphony.htm**, and **lesson3.htm**, respectively.

▶ **2.** Open the **lesson3.htm** file in your Web browser, and then open the **Concerto**, **Sonata**, and **Symphony** links at the bottom of the page to verify that the links retrieve the corresponding definitions in the glossary page, as shown earlier in Figure 10-10.

You will replace the target of these three links with pop-up windows. Teresa wants the pop-up window for the definitions to be fairly small, perhaps containing a link or button to close it, and without any features other than the scroll bar. To avoid retyping the same commands for each definition, you'll create the following function, named popWin(), to display a Web page within a pop-up window:

```
function popWin(url) {
    pop = window.open(url,"pop","width=330,height=220,scrollbars=yes");
    testpop = (pop == null || typeof(pop) == "undefined") ? true: false;
    return testpop;
}
```

In this function, the url parameter contains the URL of the document appearing in the pop-up window. Of the different features of the window, only the scroll bar will be displayed. Because the other features are not included in the list, they will not be applied to the pop-up window. As discussed earlier, this function checks whether the pop-up window has been blocked and returns a value of true if the pop-up window is blocked. You'll add this function to the imlibrary.js file so that it can be accessible to any page in Teresa's Web site.

To create the popWin() function:

▶ **1.** Go to the **imlibrary.js** file in your text editor.

▶ **2.** At the bottom of the file, insert the following code, as shown in Figure 10-14:

```
function popWin(url) {
    pop =
window.open(url,"pop","width=330,height=220, scrollbars=yes");
    testpop = (pop == null || typeof(pop) == "undefined") ? true:
false;
    return testpop;
}
```

Figure 10-14 ▶ The popWin() function

```
function popwin(url) {
    pop = window.open(url,"pop","width=330,height=220,scrollbars=yes");
    testpop = (pop == null || typeof(pop) == "undefined") ? true: false;
    return testpop;
}
```

Tip

For security reasons, pop-up windows widths and heights cannot be less than 100 pixels, which prevents Web sites from creating hidden or nearly-hidden pop-up windows.

▶ **3.** Save the file.

Next, you need to replace the hypertext links in the lesson3.htm file to call the popWin() function.

To call the popWin() function

1. Return to the **lesson3.htm** file in your text editor.

2. Insert the following script element in the head section of the file to link to the imlibrary.js script file:

   ```
   <script type="text/javascript" src="imlibrary.js"></script>
   ```

3. Scroll down the file and locate the link for the Concerto definition, and then add the following event handler to the opening <a> tag:

   ```
   onclick="return(popWin('concerto.htm'))"
   ```

4. In the link for the Sonata definition, add the following event handler to the opening <a> tag:

   ```
   onclick="return(popWin('sonata.htm'))"
   ```

5. In the link for the Symphony definition, add the following event handler to the opening <a> tag:

   ```
   onclick="return(popWin('symphony.htm'))"
   ```

   Figure 10-15 highlights the revised code in the three hypertext links.

Code to call the popWin() function   **Figure 10-15**

```
<div id="footer1">
   <p><strong>Key terms: </strong>
      <a href="glossary.htm#concerto"
         onclick="return(popWin('concerto.htm'))">Concerto</a> -
      <a href="glossary.htm#sonata"
         onclick="return(popWin('sonata.htm'))">Sonata</a> -
      <a href="glossary.htm#symphony"
         onclick="return(popWin('symphony.htm'))">Symphony</a>
   </p>
</div>
```

6. Save the file, and then reload the **lesson3.htm** file in your Web browser.

7. Click the **Concerto** link at the bottom of the page, verifying that the definition opens in its own pop-up window. See Figure 10-16.

Figure 10-16 ▶ **Pop-up window with concerto definition**

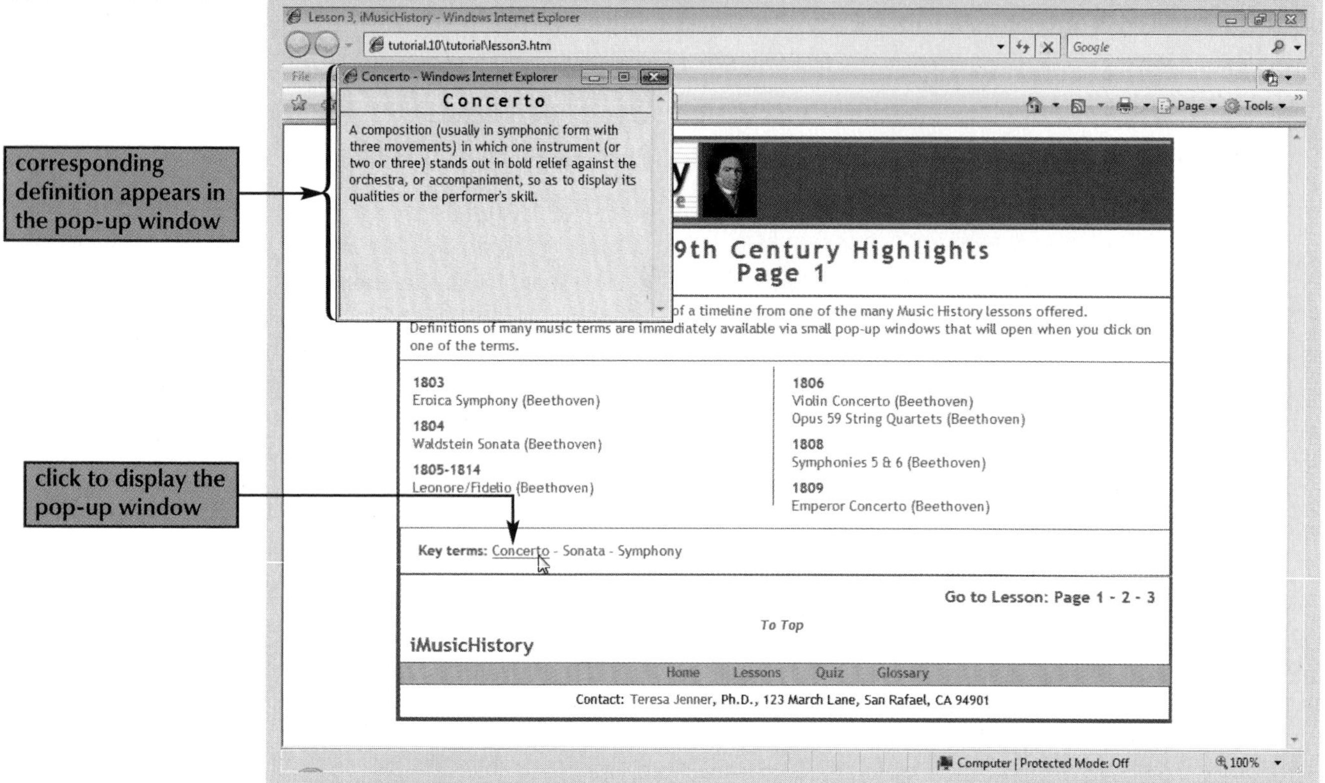

corresponding definition appears in the pop-up window

click to display the pop-up window

8. Close the pop-up window.

9. Repeat Steps 7 and 8, clicking the **Sonata** and **Symphony** links to verify that they also appear in pop-up windows.

Working with Window Methods

Teresa likes the pop-up definitions, but she is concerned that users will dislike extra windows cluttering their desktops. She thinks it would be better if the pop-up window automatically closed after the user is done looking at it—perhaps when returning to the lessons page.

You can use JavaScript to control the interaction between various browser windows, including specifying which browser window has the focus (is active) on your desktop. You can remove the focus from one window and give it to another. You can also allow users to move windows to different locations on the screen and resize them, and you can automatically close windows that are no longer needed. Most of these features are controlled by methods applied to the window object.

Window Methods

Figure 10-17 describes some of the methods you can use to manipulate windows after they are created.

Methods of the window object **Figure 10-17**

Method	Description
blur()	Removes the focus from the window
close()	Closes the window
focus()	Gives the window the focus
moveBy(dx, dy)	Moves the window dx pixels to the right and dy pixels down
moveTo(x, y)	Moves the top left corner of the window to the screen coordinates (x, y)
print()	Prints the contents of the window
resizeBy(dx, dy)	Resizes the window by dx pixels to the right and dy pixels down
resizeTo(x, y)	Resizes the window to x pixels wide and y pixels high
scrollBy(dx, dy)	Scrolls the document content in the window by dx pixels to the right and dy pixels down
scrollTo(x, y)	Scrolls the document in the window to the page coordinates (x, y)

Most often, your scripts will be used to open and close browser windows, or to add or remove the focus from a window. For example, you can use the following command to create a window object named popWin:

```
popWin = window.open("pop.htm", "Demo", "width=200,height=150")
```

If you wanted to give popWin the focus, you would use the focus() method in the following command:

```
popWin.focus();
```

The popWin window would then become the active browser window. To remove the focus from popWin, you would use the blur() method in the following command:

```
popWin.blur();
```

Finally, to close the window, you would run the following JavaScript command:

```
popWin.close();
```

You can also use the resizeBy() and resizeTo() methods to change the dimensions of the browser windows, and the moveBy() and moveTo() methods to move windows around users' screens.

Reference Window | **Applying Methods to Browser Windows**

- To give the focus to the browser window, use
  `windowObject.focus()`
  where *windowObject* is the browser window receiving the focus.
- To remove the focus from the window, use:
  `windowObject.blur()`
- To close the browser window, use:
  `windowObject.close()`
- To move the browser window, use
  `windowObject.moveBy(dx, dy)`
  where *dx* and *dy* are the distances in pixels to shift the window to the right and down, respectively. You can use negative *dx* and *dy* values to move the window left and up, respectively. Alternatively, you can use
  `windowObject.moveTo(x, y)`
  where *x* and *y* are the screen coordinates in pixels that the browser window will be moved to.
- To resize the window, use
  `windowObject.resizeBy(dx, dy)`
  where *dx* and *dy* are the amounts in pixels to increase the browser in the horizontal and vertical direction, respectively. Use negative values of *dx* and *dy* to decrease the window size. Alternatively, you can use
  `windowObject.resizeTo(x, y)`
  where *x* and *y* are the width and height, respectively, of the new browser window in pixels.

To see how you can use these methods in your Web pages, a demo page has been prepared in which you use JavaScript to open a pop-up window on your desktop, move and resize it, and then close it.

To use the pop-up window demo:

▶ 1. Open the **demo_popup2.htm** file from the tutorial.10\tutorial folder in your Web browser.

▶ 2. Click the **Show Pop-up Window** button to display the sample pop-up window. The method used to display the pop-up window appears in the text box at the bottom of the page.

▶ 3. Click the **Up**, **Down**, **Left** and **Right** buttons in the Move Window box to move the pop-up window around your screen.

▶ 4. Click the **Expand** and **Contract** buttons in the Resize Window box to expand and contract the window's width and height. Note that you cannot reduce the width or height of the pop-up window to below 100 pixels because that is not allowed by JavaScript. See Figure 10-18.

Demo page to modify a pop-up window ◀ Figure 10-18

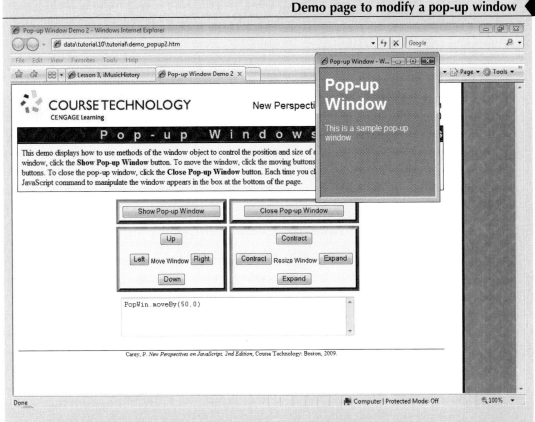

Trouble? As the focus shifts between the main browser window and the sample pop-up window, you may notice a bit of sluggishness in moving the window around your desktop. Also, depending on your browser settings, the behavior of the pop-up window might not match that shown here.

▶ **5.** Click the **Close Pop-up Window** button to close the pop-up window.

▶ **6.** Repeat Steps 2 through 5, clicking different buttons on the Web form to experiment with the window methods.

▶ **7.** Close the Web page.

The Self and Opener Keywords

When a script opens several windows, your program needs a way to distinguish one window from another. One way is through the object name you assign to each window as you create it, as in the popWin example above. Another way is through the two JavaScript keywords: self and opener.

The **self keyword** refers to the current window and is synonymous with the window keyword, but you may see it used to improve clarity when a script refers to many different windows and frames. This means that you can close the currently active window by using either of the following commands:

```
self.close();
```

or

```
window.close();
```

The **opener keyword** refers to the window or frame that used the window.open() method to open the current window. For example, when a second window is opened using JavaScript, you can close the initial or first window using the following command:

```
opener.close();
```

You will use the `self` keyword to make the pop-up window close whenever it loses the focus. You can do this by adding the following onblur event handler to the body element of each pop-up definition window:

```
onblur = "self.close()"
```

You must make this change to all three of the HTML files displayed in the definition pop-up windows.

To add the onblur event handler to the definition pop-ups:

▶ **1.** Return to the **concerto.htm** file in your text editor.

▶ **2.** Add the following event handler to the body element, as shown in Figure 10-19:

```
onblur="self.close()"
```

Figure 10-19 ▶ The onblur event handler

```
closes the window
when it loses the focus

<body onblur="self.close()">
   <h2>Concerto</h2>
   <p>A composition (usually in symphonic form with three movements) in which
      one instrument (or two or three) stands out in bold relief against the
      orchestra, or accompaniment, so as to display its qualities or the
      performer's skill.
   </p>
</body>

</html>
```

▶ **3.** Save the file, and then close it.

▶ **4.** Repeat Steps 1 through 3 for the **sonata.htm** and **symphony.htm** files.

▶ **5.** Reload the **lesson3.htm** file in your Web browser.

▶ **6.** Click each of the three definition links at the bottom of the page and verify that, after the pop-up window is displayed, clicking outside the pop-up window automatically closes it.

Trouble? If you are running Internet Explorer, you need to click the Information Bar to accept the content of the pop-up window.

Pop-up windows are only one way of displaying information on top of the current Web document. Another way is to create an overlay, which is displayed on top of the window content. **Overlays** are simply div containers that contain information to be displayed over the document content. The following HTML code contains an overlay describing the meaning of the term *concerto*:

```
<div id="overlay">
   <h2>Concerto</h2>
   <p>A composition (usually in symphonic form with three movements)
      in which one instrument (or two or three) stands out in bold
      relief against the orchestra, or accompaniment, so as to
      display its qualities or the performer's skill.
   </p>
</div>
```

This HTML fragment can be either written directly into the HTML code of the Web page or generated using JavaScript. The overlay is initially hidden from the user and then displayed by setting its display style to block and is positioned using absolute positioning styles. To display it on top of the document, its z-index style is set higher than any other document content. You can make overlays moveable by using the drag-and-drop techniques discussed in Tutorial 6. Overlays can also mimic dialog boxes through the use of Web form buttons and input controls.

Overlays have several advantages over pop-up windows. They are not affected by pop-up blockers because they're not considered new browser windows. Overlays can be designed using style sheets to have a consistent look and feel across different browsers. They require less system memory because the browser is not forced to generate a second browser window. Finally, Internet Explorer users are not distracted by the yellow security bar that usually appears when IE pop-up windows are displayed, and that must be closed before the pop-up window can be read; this is not a problem with overlays.

Because of these advantages, overlays are frequently used by Web designers in place of pop-up windows when displaying extra or temporary information within the browser window.

Creating Dialog Boxes

The next part of the iMusicHistory Web site that Teresa wants you to work on is a page containing a quiz about music history. The page consists of a series of multiple-choice questions in a Web form. You will open this file.

To open the Quiz page:

▶ **1.** Use your text editor to open the **quiztxt.htm** file from the tutorial.10\tutorial folder, enter *your name* and *the date* in the comment section, and then save the file as **quiz.htm**.

▶ **2.** Review the contents of the file.

The file contains four questions and four choices for each question. Teresa already added event handlers to each radio button in the form to run a function named answer() when a user clicks one of the choices. For example, the HTML code for the four choices in the first question is:

```
<input type="radio" name="Q1"
       onclick="answer('Robert Minute', false)" />

<input type="radio" name="Q1"
       onclick="answer('Johannes Brahms', false)" />

<input type="radio" name="Q1"
       onclick="answer('Frederic Chopin', true)" />

<input type="radio" name="Q1"
       onclick="answer('None of the above', false)" />
```

The answer function has two parameters. The first parameter contains the text of the user's guess, and the second parameter contains a Boolean value indicating whether the guess is correct. Teresa wants the answer() function to display a window containing the text of the user's choice that indicates whether the choice is correct.

A dialog box is a simple way to create a window containing customized text. JavaScript supports three types of customized dialog boxes: alert, prompt, and confirm. An **alert dialog box** displays a message along with an OK button, which a user clicks to close the dialog box. A **prompt dialog box** displays both a message and a text box in which a user can enter text. A **confirm dialog box** displays a message along with OK and Cancel buttons. The syntax to create each of these dialog boxes is

```
alert(message)
prompt(message, default)
confirm(message)
```

where *message* is the text that appears in the dialog box and *default* is the default text that appears in a prompt dialog box. Figure 10-20 shows examples of each type of dialog box. Note that different browsers display their dialog boxes with slight variations, but all browsers display dialog boxes with the following common features: a title bar, a default value (in the case of prompt dialog boxes), an OK button, and a Cancel button (in the case of prompt and confirm dialog boxes).

Sample alert, prompt, and confirm dialog boxes Figure 10-20

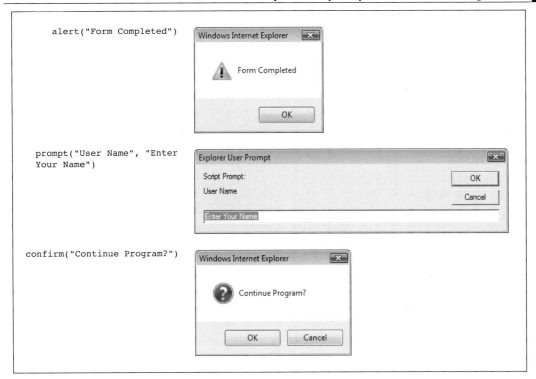

```
alert("Form Completed")
```

```
prompt("User Name", "Enter
Your Name")
```

```
confirm("Continue Program?")
```

In addition to displaying messages, the prompt and confirm dialog boxes return a value, indicating the action that the user took within the dialog box. For the prompt dialog box, the value returned is the value entered into the text box. For the confirm dialog box, the Boolean value true is returned if the user clicks the OK button, and the value false is returned if the user clicks the Cancel button.

Using Built-in Dialog Boxes | Reference Window

- To display an alert dialog box using the windows method, use
      alert(*message*)
  where *message* is the text displayed in the alert dialog box.
- To display a prompt dialog box, use
      prompt(*message*, *default*)
  where *message* is the text that appears in the dialog box and *default* is the default text appearing in the text box.
- To display a confirm dialog box, use
      confirm(*message*)
  where *message* is the text that users should confirm or cancel.

For the Quiz page, you'll use an alert dialog box that indicates whether the user has answered the question correctly. The text of the answer function is:

```
function answer(choice, guess) {
   if (guess) {
      alert(choice + " is correct!");
   } else {
      alert(choice + " is incorrect. Try again.");
   }
}
```

In this function, the guess parameter contains the Boolean value indicating whether the user responded correctly. If the guess is true, the function displays an alert dialog box containing the text of the answer followed by "is correct!" If the guess is false, the alert dialog box displays the text of the answer followed by "is incorrect. Try again." Because Teresa will be using this function on several pages in her completed Web site, you'll add it to the imlibrary.js file.

To create and run the answer() function:

1. Go to the **imlibrary.js** file in your text editor, and then insert the following code at the bottom of the file, as shown in Figure 10-21:

```
function answer(choice, guess) {
   if (guess) {
      alert(choice + " is correct!");
   } else {
      alert(choice + " is incorrect. Try again.");
   }
}
```

Figure 10-21 ▶ The answer() function

```
function answer(choice, guess) {
   if (guess) {
      alert(choice + " is correct!");
   } else {
      alert(choice + " is incorrect. Try again.");
   }
}
```

2. Save the file.

3. Return to the **quiz.htm** file in your text editor, and then insert the following script element in the head section of the file:

```
<script type="text/javascript" src="imlibrary.js"></script>
```

4. Save the file, and then load **quiz.htm** in your Web browser.

5. Click the option button for **a) Robert Minute** below the first question. Your browser displays an alert dialog box, indicating that your choice is incorrect. See Figure 10-22.

Figure 10-22 ▶ Alert dialog box for an incorrect answer

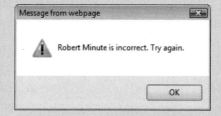

6. Click the **OK** button, and then click the option button for **c) Frederic Chopin** below the first question. Your browser displays an alert dialog box, indicating that your choice is correct. See Figure 10-23.

7. Click option buttons for the other three questions, verifying that the rest of the quiz works as planned. The correct answers are: 1-c, 2-c, 3-c, and 4-b.

Exchanging Data Between Windows

Teresa likes the alert dialog boxes you created for the Quiz page, but she wants them to be more visually interesting. Teresa asks you to add graphic images and formatted text. Although it is not possible to do this with the alert() method, you can do it by creating a customized pop-up window. To change the message for each response, you must either create a separate file for each possible response or write the HTML code directly into the pop-up window. You'll employ the latter method for Teresa's Web site.

Writing Content to a Window

One way of inserting content into a browser window is to use the document.write() method, specifying the window that will receive the new content. The syntax of the command is

```
windowObject.document.write(content);
windowObject.document.close();
```

where *windowObject* is the window object and *content* is a text string containing the HTML code that will be placed in the window. The document.close() method is used to close the input stream to the window. Some browsers require you to close this input stream before they will write the window content. When you are writing the entire HTML code in the window, you usually want to break up the *content* text string into smaller text strings. You can do this by using multiple write commands

```
windowObject.document.write(content1);
windowObject.document.write(content2);
. . .
windowObject.document.write(contentN);
windowObject.document.close();
```

where *content1* through *contentN* are separate text strings of HTML content. Alternatively, you can create a single variable containing part of the text string, and then use an assignment operator to add additional text strings to it, as follows:

```
textstring = string1;
textstring += string2;
textstring += string3;
...
textstring += stringN;
windowObject.document.write(textstring);
windowObject.document.close();
```

In this case, *textstring* is a variable that contains all of the text contained in the text strings *string1* to *stringN*. The approach you take is a matter of personal preference.

Accessing an Object Within a Window

The use of the document.write() method highlights an important point about working with the content of other browser windows. After you specify a window object, you can work with the objects contained in the window's document. For example, to access a document object based on its id value, you can use the object reference

```
windowObject.document.getElementById(id)
```

where *id* is the id of the document object. Thus, you can run a script in one window that manipulates objects and properties in another window. You can also create and attach element nodes using the command syntax

```
windowObject.document.createElement(elem)
```

where *elem* is an element node existing within the browser window. The element node will not be visible unless it is attached to another element within the document body of the window.

These objects within the browser window also include the variables and functions, which JavaScript treats as objects within that window. To access a variable defined in another browser window, you use the object reference

```
windowObject.variable
```

where *variable* is the name of the JavaScript variable. To call a function from another browser window, you use the reference

```
windowObject.function()
```

where *function* is the name of a function defined in the *windowObject* window. Note that a document must be open in a browser window for you to access the variables and functions contained in that document. For example, if your primary window opens a pop-up window, the pop-up window can access a variable named logoName from the document in the primary window using the following object reference:

```
opener.logoName
```

Recall that opener is a special JavaScript keyword that refers to the window or frame that opened the current window. In the same way, you can run a function named showLogo() contained in the original browser window using the following command:

```
opener.showLogo()
```

In this way, the variables and functions in one window can communicate with variables and functions in another browser window.

- To write text to a browser window, use

  ```
  windowObject.document.write(content);
  windowObject.document.close()
  ```

  where *windowObject* is the object reference of the browser window and *content* is the text content.
- To access an object within a browser window, use

  ```
  windowObject.document.getElementById(id)
  ```

  where *id* is the id of the object in the document within the window.
- To access a variable defined within a browser window, use

  ```
  windowObject.variable
  ```

  where *variable* is the name of a JavaScript variable defined within the window.
- To access a function defined within a browser window, use

  ```
  windowObject.function()
  ```

  where *function* is the name of a JavaScript function defined within the window.

Creating a Customized Pop-up Window

To create the customized dialog box, you'll write the HTML code

```html
<html>
<head>
   <title>iMusicHistory Quiz</title>
   <link rel="stylesheet" href="quiz.css" type="text/css" />
</head>
<body>
   <p>
      <img src="treble2.gif" alt="" />
      message
      <br />
      <input type="button" value="OK" onclick="self.close()" />
   </p>
</body>
</html>
```

for the answer window for Teresa's quiz, where *message* is the message in the pop-up window that indicates whether a student's answer is correct. Figure 10-24 shows how this pop-up window will appear for incorrect and correct answers. Note that this window mimics an alert dialog box by including a form button that uses the self.close() command to close the window.

Custom dialog boxes for incorrect and correct answers ◄ Figure 10-24

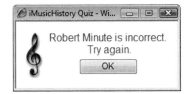 

You can also write content to a browser window by creating element and text nodes and appending them to the document contained within the browser window.

To write this content to the pop-up windows, you'll use the following function:

```
function writeContent(windowObj, choice, guess) {
   content = "<html><head><title>iMusicHistory Quiz</title>";
   content += "<link rel='stylesheet' href='quiz.css' type='text/
css' />";
   content += "</head><body><p><img src='treble2.gif' alt='' />";

   if (guess) {
      content += choice + " is correct!";
   } else {
      content += choice + " is incorrect. Try again.";
   }

   content += "<br /><input type='button' value='OK'
onclick='self.close()' />";
   content += "</p></body></html>";

   windowObj.document.write(content);
   windowObj.document.close();
}
```

The writeContent() function has three parameters. The windowObj parameter is the window object that will receive this HTML code. The choice and guess parameters have the same purpose and values as they did for the answer() function you just created. Due to the way browsers process white space in HTML code, you can insert several HTML tags on the same line, reducing the number of statements in the function. Additionally, although the HTML code is enclosed using double quotes, any attribute values within that code are enclosed in single quotes.

Because this is a complex function that could easily be mistyped, the function code has already been provided in the imlibrary.js file. You will revise the answer() function to create a customized dialog box using the writeContent() function. This involves three steps:

1. Use the window.open() method to open the pop-up window.
2. Test whether the pop-up window has been blocked or has otherwise failed to open.
3. If the pop-up window has failed to open, display alert dialog boxes as before (they are not blocked by pop-up blockers); otherwise, call the writeContent() function to display the customized dialog box.

The revised code for the answer() function is:

```
function answer(choice, guess) {

   ansWin =
window.open("","","width=250,height=100,left=250,screenX=250,top=250,
screenY=250");
   nopop = (ansWin == null || typeof(ansWin) == "undefined") ? true :
false;

   if (nopop) {
      if (guess) {
         alert(choice + " is correct!");
      } else {
         alert(choice + " is incorrect. Try again.");
      }
   } else {
      writeContent(ansWin, choice, guess);
   }
}
```

The answer() function first creates a window object named ansWin that is 250 pixels wide and 100 pixels high and placed 250 pixels to the right and below the upper-left corner of the screen. No URL or target name is specified for this window because you will be writing the HTML directly into it. The next line of the function creates the nopop variable to test whether the pop-up window opened. If the pop-up failed, you run the conditional statement you created earlier to display the appropriate alert dialog box; otherwise, the writeContent() function is run using the ansWin window as the window object, and the choice and guess variables as the second and third parameter values. In either case, a dialog box will be displayed, indicating whether the user has selected the correct answer.

To revise the answer() function:

▶ **1.** Return to the **imlibrary.js** file in your text editor and go to the answer() function.

▶ **2.** At the start of the function code, insert the following three lines:

```
ansWin =
window.open("","","width=250,height=100,left=250,screenX=250,
top=250, screenY=250");
nopop = (ansWin == null || typeof(ansWin) == "undefined") ? true
 : false;

if (nopop) {
```

▶ **3.** Indent the next five lines that display the answer result using the built-in alert() method.

▶ **4.** Insert the following three lines of code to complete the function:

```
} else {
    writeContent(ansWin, choice, guess);
}
```

Figure 10-25 highlights the revised code in the answer() function.

Revised answer() function ◀ **Figure 10-25**

```
function answer(choice, guess) {
    ansWin = window.open("","","width=250,height=100,left=250,screenX=250,top=250,screenY=250");
    nopop = (ansWin == null || typeof(answin) == "undefined") ? true : false;

    if (nopop) {
        if (guess) {
            alert(choice + " is correct!");
        } else {
            alert(choice + " is incorrect. Try again.");
        }
    } else {
        writeContent(ansWin, choice, guess);
    }
}
```

▶ **5.** Save the file.

▶ **6.** Reload **quiz.htm** in your Web browser, and then click the various answers in the Web form, verifying that the custom dialog box now appears to indicate whether the answer was correct or incorrect. Click the **OK** button to close each pop-up window before answering a different question.

InSight | **Modal and Modeless Windows**

Dialog boxes and windows can be either modal or modeless. A **modal window** is a window that prevents users from doing work in any other window or dialog box until the window is closed. A **modeless window** allows users to work in other windows and dialog boxes even as that window stays open. An alert dialog box in a browser window is an example of a modal window, because you cannot do any other work in the browser window until you close the alert dialog box. Pop-up windows, by contrast, are generally modeless. You can force a pop-up window to be modal, however, by adding the following event handler to the window's body element:

```
onblur = "self.focus()"
```

With this command, every attempt to move the focus away from the pop-up window will result in the focus returning to the window. The window becomes modal, staying active and on top until it is closed.

Starting with version 4.0, Internet Explorer introduced new methods to allow JavaScript to create modal and modeless windows. Internet Explorer 4 introduced the showModalDialog() method to create modal windows, and Internet Explorer 5 added the showModelessDialog() method for modeless windows. The syntax of the showModalDialog() method is

```
windowObject.showModalDialog(url, arguments, features)
```

where *url* is the URL of the file to display in the modal window; *arguments* is an optional parameter containing a value, variable, object, or array of values to pass to the window; and *features* is a comma-separated list of features that control the appearance of the window. The method to create a modeless dialog box is similar:

```
windowObject.showModelessDialog(url, arguments, features);
```

Both methods allow a dialog box to return values back to the browser window that called it. For example, you can create a modal or modeless dialog box containing a Web form, and then return values from that form to the original browser window. Although both the show-ModalDialog() and showModelessDialog() methods are useful ways of creating specialized pop-ups and dialog boxes, they are not supported by browsers other than Internet Explorer. So do not use them in environments where non-IE browsers may be in use. You can learn more about the showModalDialog() and showModelessDialog() methods at the Internet Explorer Web site.

You have completed your work on creating a variety of new windows, closing windows, and writing to a window via script-generated HTML. In the next session, you'll learn how to enhance the Glossary section of Teresa's iMusicHistory Web site with interactive frames.

Review | **Session 10.2 Quick Check**

1. What HTML tag creates a link that opens the file home.htm as a new window with the target name "HomePage"?
2. What JavaScript command opens the file home.htm as a pop-up window that is 300 pixels wide and 150 pixels high? You do not have to specify a value for the window's target name, but can instead use an empty text string.
3. What JavaScript command includes scroll bars and a status bar in the pop-up window described in the previous question?
4. What JavaScript command writes the following HTML tag to a window object named Home:

```
<img src="logo.jpg" alt="imhLogo" />
```

5. What JavaScript command creates an alert dialog box containing the text "Script Finished"?

6. What JavaScript command creates a confirm dialog box containing the text "Proceed"?

7. What is a modal window? What is a modeless window?

Session 10.3

Working with Frames

In this session, you'll use JavaScript to program the behavior of the frames contained in the iMusicHistory Web site. Frames enable the division of the browser window into multiple panes, with each frame displaying a separate document. Each panel is known as a frameset and is created using the HTML code

```
<frameset id="frameset">
    <frame id="fname1" name="fname1" src="url1" />
    <frame id="fname2" name="fname2" src="url2" />
    ...
    <frame id="fnameN" name="fnameN" src="urlN" />
</frameset>
```

where each frame displays a separate URL. A single window can contain multiple framesets, and framesets can be nested inside each other. Each frame element in this example contains both an id value and a name value. The name attribute is used when creating links whose targets are designed to appear in specific frames. Thus, the code for linking content to a specific frame is

```
<a href="url" target="fname"> content </a>
```

where *fname* is the name of a specific frame in the browser window. However, if you want to reference a specific frame in your JavaScript code, you need to use the id attribute rather than the name attribute. The current practice, therefore, is to use both the name and id attributes, setting them to the same value as in the following frame element:

```
<frame id="top" name="top" src="home.htm" />
```

Teresa has decided to use frames in iMusicHistory's Glossary page. One of the files displayed in the frameset is nav.htm. The nav.htm file contains the iMusicHistory logo and some navigational text that you'll use in editing Teresa's page. You will open this file, and then use your Web browser to open the Glossary page.

To view the iMusicHistory glossary:

▶ 1. If you took a break after the previous session, make sure the imusic.htm, imlibrary.js, status.js, index.htm, lesson3.htm, and quiz.htm files are open in your text editor and imusic.html, index.htm, lesson3.htm, and quiz.htm are open in your Web browser.

▶ 2. Use your text editor to open the **navtxt.htm** file from the tutorial.10\tutorial folder, enter *your name* and *the date* in the comment section, and then save the file as **nav.htm**.

▶ 3. Use your Web browser to open the **terms.htm** file located in the tutorial.10\tutorial folder, and then view the iMusicHistory glossary. See Figure 10-26.

Figure 10-26 | **The iMusicHistory glossary**

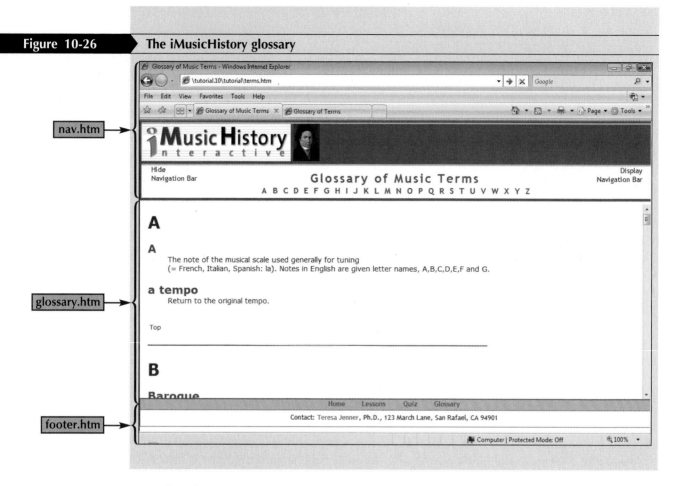

The Glossary page is composed of three frames. The header frame displays the contents of the nav.htm file, providing an alphabetic list of links to the glossary terms; the main frame displays the contents of the glossary.htm file, listing the glossary of musical terms; and the footer frame, drawn from the footer.htm file, displays a navigation bar with links to the other pages of the iMusicHistory Web site. The following is the HTML code for the Glossary frameset:

```
<frameset rows="160,*,64" id="Glossary" frameborder="0" border="0">
    <frame name="header" id="header" src="nav.htm" scrolling="no" />
    <frame name="main" id="main" src="glossary.htm" />
    <frame name="footer" id="footer" src="footer.htm" scrolling="no" />
</frameset>
```

One problem with frames is that they can take up valuable screen space. Teresa wants users to have the option of allocating more space to the list of music terms shown in the main frame. As shown in Figure 10-27, Teresa envisions users clicking links in the header frame that alternately hide and display the footer frame, providing more screen space to the definition list. To create this effect, you first must learn how JavaScript handles frames.

Footer frame being collapsed and expanded ◀ Figure 10-27

clicking the Hide Navigation Bar link ...   ... hides the footer frame

clicking the Display Navigation Bar link ...   ... reveals the footer frame

Working with the Frame and Frameset Objects

In the document object model, each frame in a frameset is part of the frames collection—an array of all the frames within the browser window. The frames collection uses the object reference

windowObject.frames[*idref*]

where *windowObject* is the browser window containing the frames and *idref* is either the id or the index number of a frame in the collection. For example, to reference the header frame in the current browser window, you could use either of the following object references:

window.frames[0]

or

window.frames["header"]

There is no frameset object in JavaScript. If you need to reference the frameset element, you must provide an id for the frameset and then use the getElementById() method to reference the frameset element. For example, to reference the Glossary frameset from within the terms.htm file, you would use the following object reference:

```
document.getElementById("Glossary")
```

Navigating Between Frames

JavaScript treats the frames in a frameset as elements in a hierarchical tree. Figure 10-28 shows a schematic diagram of the Glossary frameset. The top of the hierarchy is the browser window containing the terms.htm file and within that file is the glossary frameset. The glossary frameset contains the header, main, and footer frames, displaying the nav.htm, glossary.htm, and footer.htm files.

Figure 10-28 **The frame hierarchy**

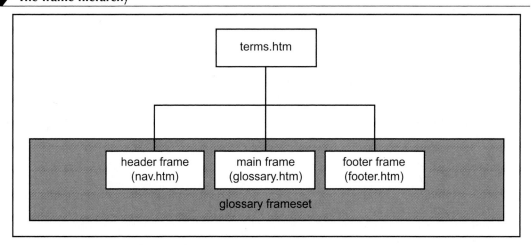

If you want to access the contents of one frame from another, you must navigate through this hierarchy of objects. JavaScript provides two keywords to do this: `parent` and `top`. The **parent keyword** refers to any object that is placed immediately above another object in the hierarchy. The browser window containing the terms.htm file is the parent object of the three frames in the Glossary frameset. To reference one of the other frames, you first go up to the parent and then down the hierarchy. Thus, to reference the main frame from within the header frame, you could use either of the following object references:

```
parent.frames[1]
```

or

```
parent.frames["main"]
```

If you have several levels of nested objects, you can stack parent references to go up through the different levels of the tree. The reference

```
parent.parent.parent.object
```

points to a child element of the parent object three levels up in the hierarchy.

If you want to go directly to the top of the hierarchy, you can use the **top** keyword. In the case of frames, the `top` keyword refers to the browser window that contains the frameset document and the frames within that frameset. When the frames are direct children of the browser window (as is the case with the Glossary frameset), the `parent` and `top` keywords are synonymous.

Note that the Glossary frameset itself is not a parent of the frames it contains. The Glossary frameset is an object within the document displayed in that window. If you need to reference the Glossary frameset directly, you must go down the document hierarchy using the document object and the getElementById() method. The complete reference to the Glossary frameset from one of the child frames is therefore:

```
parent.document.getElementById("Glossary")
```

Treating Frames as Windows

In most cases, JavaScript treats a frame as a separate browser window, meaning that most of the properties and methods you've been applying to window objects can also be applied to frame objects. For example, if you want to write content into a frame, you would use the commands

```
frameObject.document.write(content);
frameObject.document.close();
```

where *frameObject* is the object reference to the frame. To change the source of the document displayed within a frame, you use the location property

```
frameObject.location.href = url;
```

where *url* is the URL of the document to appear in the frame. The frame object also supports such window methods as setInterval() and setTimeout() for time-delayed commands, and alert() for displaying an alert box within a frame. However, you cannot close a frame the same way that you close a window. If you want to remove a frame from a frameset, you must change the frameset layout.

Changing the Content of a Frame | Reference Window

- To change a frame's source document, use the command
  ```
  frameObject.location.href = url;
  ```
  where *frameObject* is the frame object and *url* is the URL of the document to display in the frame.
- To write content into a frame, use the commands
  ```
  frameObject.document.write(content);
  frameObject.document.close();
  ```
  where *content* is a text string of HTML code to be written into the frame.
- To reference the document displayed within a frame, use the object reference
  ```
  frameObject.document.getElementById(id)
  ```
  where *id* is the id of the object in the document.

Setting the Frameset Layout

Recall that a frameset is laid out in either rows or columns using the rows and cols attribute of the <frameset> tag. To do the same thing in JavaScript, you use the rows and cols properties of the frameset object. The syntax of the commands is

```
frameset.rows = text
frameset.cols = text
```

where *frameset* is an object reference to a frameset element and *text* is a text string specifying the frame layout. Currently, the value of the row attribute for the Glossary frameset is the text string "160,*,64". To change this to "180,*,64", for example, you could use the following command:

```
document.getElementById("Glossary").rows = "180,*,64";
```

To remove or hide a frame from a frameset, you set its height (or width) value to 0 pixels. Thus, to remove the footer frame from the Glossary frameset, you could use the command

```
document.getElementById("Glossary").rows = "160,*,0";
```

and the footer frame would still be present in the frameset, but it would not be visible to users.

Collapsing and Expanding a Frame

You have the information you need to create functions to collapse and expand the glossary's footer frame. You'll add two functions as scripts embedded within the nav.htm file, named collapse() and expand(). The collapse() function reduces the height of the footer frame. The expand() function resets the footer frame's height to its original 64 pixels. Because you'll be running these functions from within the nav.htm file, you need to go up the object hierarchy to access the properties of the Glossary frameset. The code for the collapse() and expand() functions is:

```
function collapse() {
    parent.document.getElementById("Glossary").rows = "160,*,1";
}

function expand() {
    parent.document.getElementById("Glossary").rows = "160,*,64";
}
```

Note that in the collapse() function, the height of the footer frame is set to 1 pixel rather than 0 pixels. Under some browsers, setting the height to 0 pixels removes the frame entirely from the frameset. With the footer frame removed, you could not redisplay it later. To resolve this problem, you set the height to 1 pixel, which preserves the footer frame in the layout, but essentially hides it from the user. You'll call the collapse() and expand() functions from links within the nav.htm file.

To create and run the expand() and collapse() function:

▶ **1.** Return to the **nav.htm** file in your text editor.

▶ **2.** Add the following embedded script to the head section of the document, as shown in Figure 10-29:

```
<script type="text/javascript">
   function collapse() {
      parent.document.getElementById("Glossary").rows =
"160,*,1";
   }

   function expand() {
      parent.document.getElementById("Glossary").rows =
"160,*,64";
   }
</script>
```

The collapse() and expand() functions ◀ Figure 10-29

```
<title>iMusicHistory Navigation Frame</title>
<link href="imusicstyles.css" rel="stylesheet" type="text/css" />

<script type="text/javascript">
   function collapse() {
      parent.document.getElementById("Glossary").rows = "160,*,1";
   }

   function expand() {
      parent.document.getElementById("Glossary").rows = "160,*,64";
   }
</script>

</head>
```

▶ **3.** Scroll down the file to the <a> tag for the Hide Navigation Bar text link, and then insert the following attribute into the opening <a> tag:

```
href="javascript:collapse()"
```

▶ **4.** Go to the <a> tag for the Display Navigation Bar link, and then insert the following attribute into the opening <a> tag:

```
href="javascript:expand()"
```

Figure 10-30 shows the inserted code.

Code to call the collapse() and expand() functions ◀ Figure 10-30

```
<div id="navLinks">

   <div id="navLeft" class="navCol">
      <a href="javascript:collapse()">Hide <br /> Navigation Bar</a>
   </div>

   <div id="navRight" class="navCol">
      <a href="javascript:expand()">Display <br /> Navigation Bar</a>
   </div>
```

▶ **5.** Save the nav.htm file, and then reload the Glossary page in your Web browser.

▶ **6.** Click the **Hide Navigation Bar** link to verify that it hides the footer frame, and then click the **Display Navigation Bar** link to verify that it redisplays the footer frame.

Controlling Frame Behavior

Many users don't like the effect that frames can have on Web sites that they view. For example, some Web site designers either aren't aware of or don't add code to prevent external Web sites from being caught inside their frames. This can confuse viewers by making it appear that an external Web site is actually part of the frameset. Additionally, a page designed to be viewed only within a frame might be mistakenly opened outside of its frameset. Without the context that the frameset provides, such a page can be meaningless or irritating to viewers.

The iMusicHistory Web site has experienced both problems in the past. Teresa has noticed that sometimes her Web site gets stuck inside another Web site's frameset, and search engines often bring visitors to the iMusicHistory site via one of the frames in the Glossary frameset. She wants you to control the behavior of her Web site's frames to prevent these two problems from happening.

Blocking an Unwanted Frame

When a Web page gets stuck within another Web site's frame, the page appears to be a child of that browser window frameset. A demo page shows this effect in action. You will open the demo now.

To view the frame-blocking demo:

▶ **1.** Open the **demo_frameblocker.htm** file from the tutorial.10\tutorial folder in your Web browser.

▶ **2.** Click the **imusic.htm** link in the left frame. The contents of the imusic.htm file appear in the right frame of the browser window. See Figure 10-31.

Figure 10-31 **Frame Blocking demo page**

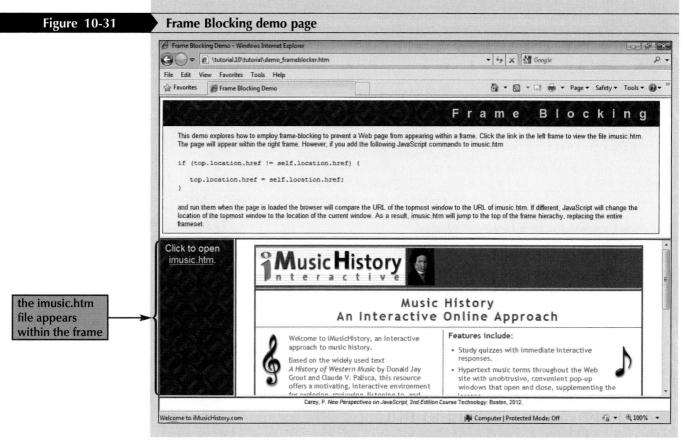

The imusic.htm file appears stuck within the frame on the demo page. If this happens to one of Teresa's pages within another framed Web site, she wants the page to move out of the frame and occupy the entire browser window. To do this, you run the following commands when the page is initially loaded by the browser:

```
if (top.location.href != self.location.href) {
    top.location.href = self.location.href;
}
```

In this code, JavaScript compares the URL of the document in the topmost window to the URL of the document in the current window or frame. If they're different, JavaScript changes the URL of the topmost window's document to the current window's document. As a result, the page cannot be forced into another site's frameset. It will always jump to the top of the hierarchy, occupying the browser window and replacing any frameset file. If the page is already at the top of the hierarchy, the code has no effect. You will try this now by running these commands when the imusic.htm file is loaded by the browser. You can test your code by rerunning the frame blocker demo.

To add frame blocking to the iMusicHistory home page:

▶ **1.** Return to the **status.js** file in your text editor.

▶ **2.** Within the initPage() function, insert the following code, as shown in Figure 10-32:

```
// Prevent the page from appearing within a frame
if (top.location.href != self.location.href) {
    top.location.href = self.location.href;
}
```

Code to block a page from appearing within a frame ◀ **Figure 10-32**

```
function initPage() {
    window.defaultStatus = "Welcome to iMusicHistory.com";

    // Prevent the page from appearing within a frame
    if (top.location.href != self.location.href) {
        top.location.href = self.location.href;
    }

}
```

▶ **3.** Save the file, and then return to the **demo_frameblocker.htm** file in your Web browser.

▶ **4.** Click the **imusic.htm** link in the left frame, and then verify that the imusic.htm file appears within the entire browser window and is no longer captured within a frame.

Forcing a Page into a Frameset

Teresa's second task involves the opposite problem: Instead of forcing a page out of a frameset, she wants to ensure that the three files that compose the Glossary frameset (nav.htm, glossary.htm, and footer.htm) are always displayed within the frameset, and never as separate Web pages. This prevents visitors from inadvertently accessing one of those pages outside the context of the iMusicHistory Glossary.

Although the problem is different, the solution is similar. It involves verifying that whenever a browser opens the nav.htm, main.htm, or footer.htm files, the topmost window is always the browser window containing the terms.htm file. The code to make this happen is:

```
if (top.location.href == self.location) {
    top.location.href="terms.htm";
}
```

Here, JavaScript checks whether the URL of the document in the topmost window is the same as that of the active window or frame. If this condition is true for a file like nav.htm, it means that the file is occupying the top browser window rather than a frame within that window. In that case, the script changes the URL of the top window so that it displays the frameset located in the terms.htm file. You will apply this code to the nav.htm file.

To force the nav.htm file to always appear within the Glossary frameset:

▶ **1.** Return to the **nav.htm** file in your text editor.

▶ **2.** Within the embedded script element at the top of the page, insert the following code, as shown in Figure 10-33:

```
// Force the page to always appear within the Glossary frameset
if (top.location.href == self.location.href) {
    top.location.href = "terms.htm";
}
```

Figure 10-33 | Code to force a page to appear within a frame

```
<script type="text/javascript">

    // Force the page to always appear within the Glossary frameset
    if (top.location.href = self.location.href) {
        top.location.href = "terms.htm";
    }

    function collapse() {
        parent.document.getElementById("Glossary").rows = "160,*,1";
    }

    function expand() {
        parent.document.getElementById("Glossary").rows = "160,*,64";
    }
</script>
```

▶ **3.** Save the file, load **nav.htm** in your Web browser, and then verify that the Web browser opens the entire frameset, not just the nav.htm file.

Reference Window | **Blocking and Forcing Frames**

- To prevent a document from appearing within a frame, run the following commands when the browser loads the page:

```
if (top.location.href != self.location.href) {
    top.location.href = self.location.href;
}
```

- To force a document to always appear within its frameset, run the commands

```
if (top.location.href == self.location.href) {
    top.location.href = url;
}
```

when the browser loads the page, where *url* is a text string containing the URL of the frameset document.

Strict applications of XHTML do not allow for the use of the target attribute. If you want to use the target attribute and still create valid XHTML documents under the strict DTD, you must employ the target attribute using JavaScript. This becomes particularly important when a Web site uses frames.

To add the target attribute to hypertext links, you can create a for loop that loops through all of the links in the document, setting the target attribute for each one. For example, the following code loops through all of the links in the document, setting each link's target attribute value to "mainframe":

```
for (var i = 0; i < document.links.length; i++) {
   document.links[i].target = "mainframe";
}
```

If you create a frame with a name and an id attribute value of mainframe, all of the links on the page appear within that frame but the document is still valid under the strict XHTML DTD. Note that for this technique to work, the user must have JavaScript enabled in the browser.

Working with Inline Frames

Another way to use frames in a Web site is by incorporating an inline frame, which appears as a separate window within the document. Recall that inline frames are created in HTML using the tag

```
<iframe src="url" id="text" name="text">
   alternate content
</iframe>
```

where *url* is the URL of the document that appears in the inline frame, the id and name attributes identify the frame, and *alternate content* is optional content that appears in the document window for browsers that don't support inline frames. As with other HTML elements, you should include both the name and id attributes to ensure maximum compatibility across browsers, setting those attributes to the same value.

Inline Frames as Document Objects and Windows

JavaScript allows you to treat an inline frame either as an object in the current document or as a frame in the frames collection. For example, if you create the inline frame

```
<iframe src="logo.htm" id="logo" name="logo"></iframe>
```

you can reference it from the current document window using the object reference

```
document.getElementById("logo")
```

or as a frame using the frames reference

```
window.frames["logo"]
```

To change the document displayed by the inline frame, you again have two choices. You can treat the frame as an object in the document and change the value of its src property, or you can treat it as a frame and change the value of the href property of its location object. Thus, to change the URL of the logo frame to point to the logo2.htm file, you could use either of the following commands:

```
document.getElementById("logo").src = "logo2.htm";
```

or

```
window.frames["logo"].location.href = "logo2.htm";
```

If you want to write content directly into an inline frame, you must treat it as part of the frames collection. To write new content into the logo inline frame, you could use the document.write() method, as follows:

```
window.frames["logo"].document.write(content)
```

Treating inline frames as frame objects is more widely supported than treating them as document objects. Some browsers, such as Opera 6.0, for example, treat inline frames only as part of the frames collection and not as objects in the document (though this is not true of more recent releases of Opera). However, if you need to manipulate the appearance or placement of an inline frame within a document, you may find it easier to work with it as an object in the document and change its style values. For example, you could float the logo inline frame on the page's left margin by simply changing the value of the float property as follows:

```
document.getElementById("logo").style.float = "left";
```

In the end, how you treat inline frames depends on the task you're trying to accomplish with your script. Fortunately, JavaScript and most browsers support either approach.

Accessing the Document Within an Inline Frame

The inline frame object references the frame itself, but not the document within the frame. If you want to access the contents of the inline frame document directly, you can use the contentWindow property

```
frameObject.contentWindow
```

to access the browser "window" containing the document, where frameObject is the reference to the frame object. From this object reference, you can then access the document within the frame using the following reference:

```
frameObject.contentWindow.document
```

With this object reference, you can access the document tree and nodes within the document. For example, the following code creates a div element node with the id intro and attaches it to the document displayed within the header inline frame:

```
var headerFrame = document.getElementById("header");
var headerDoc = headerFrame.contentWindow.document;
var newDIV = headerDoc.createElement("div");
newDIV.id = "intro";
headerDOC.body.appendChild(newDIV);
```

In addition to the document contents, you can also reference any variables or functions defined within the script elements. Because those objects belong to the "window" rather than to the document, you reference them using *frameObject*.contentWindow.*variable*

for the variable and

frameObject.contentWindow.*function*()

for the function. Thus, to run the function setup() defined for the document stored in the header frame, you could run the command

```
var headerFrame = document.getElementById("header");
var headerWin = headerFrame.contentWindow;
headerWin.setup()
```

and the browser will run the setup() function using the code found within the header frame document.

You access the document within a frame directly using the contentDocument property

frameObject.contentDocument

where *frameObject* is again the object reference to the inline frame. This property is equivalent to

frameObject.contentWindow.document

but is not supported by Internet Explorer and is not recommended for use in cross-browser environments.

Tip

To retrieve the entire HTML code of a document within a frame, use the object reference *frameObject*. contentWindow.document. body.innerHTML.

Accessing Documents Within Inline Frames | Reference Window

- To access the window object containing an inline frame document, use the object reference
     frameObject.documentWindow
  where *frameObject* is the object reference to the inline frame.
- To access the document within an inline frame, use the following object reference:
     frameObject.documentWindow.document
- To access a variable defined within a document in an inline frame, use
     frameObject.documentWindow.*variable*
  where *variable* is the name of a global variable defined within the inline frame document.
- To access a function defined within a document in an inline frame, use
     frameObject.documentWindow.*function*()
  where *function* is the name of a function defined within the inline frame document.

Because Teresa has not chosen to include inline frames in her Web site, your work on her project is finished. Teresa is pleased with the progress you've made with her Web site and wants to incorporate the work you've done on these pages into the rest of the iMusicHistory Web site.

Session 10.3 Quick Check | Review

1. What reference name accesses a frame named "Logo" located in the topmost window of the browser window hierarchy?
2. What command changes the source of the document in the Logo frame to logo.html?
3. What command writes the text string "<html></html>" to the document in the Logo frame?

4. Assume that the Logo frame is part of a frameset with the id Home. What command changes the column widths of the frames in the Home frameset to "150,150,*"?
5. The Home frameset is saved in an HTML file named home.htm. What JavaScript command(s) would you add to the logo.html file so that it always appears within the home.htm page?
6. A Web page contains an inline frame with the id report. Provide two ways of changing the source of the inline frame to the document report.htm. Assume that you are running the command from within the document containing the inline frame.
7. What object reference would you use to access a variable named username stored in the report inline frame?
8. What object reference returns the HTML code of the document contained in the report inline frame?

Review | Tutorial Summary

In this tutorial, you learned how to use JavaScript to create and format browser windows and frames. In the first session, you worked with the properties of the window's status bar, location object, and history objects. You also saw how to employ automatic page navigation using both the meta element and a JavaScript program. The second session focused on techniques to create and populate new browser windows. You learned how to use the window.open() method to create a new browser window based on a pre-existing source document. You saw how to specify the properties of that window and how to work with methods of the window object to close a pop-up window and to set the focus on it. The second session also showed how to create alert, prompt, and confirm dialog boxes. The session then showed how to write content into a pop-up window using the document.write() method and discussed how to reference variables and functions in other browser windows. The second session concluded with a discussion of specialized Internet Explorer methods to create modal and modeless dialog boxes. The third session concerned working with frames and framesets. You learned how to navigate through the object hierarchy of a frameset and how to reference the content of one frame from another. You also saw how to modify the layout of a frameset by changing the properties of the frameset object. The third session also provided a demonstration of how to use JavaScript to block frames and to force documents to remain within framesets. The tutorial concluded with a brief discussion of inline frames, showing how they can be treated either as frames in the frames collection or as objects within a document.

Key Terms

alert dialog box
chrome
confirm dialog box
history object
location object
modal window
modeless window

opener keyword
overlay
parent keyword
permanent status bar message
pop-up blocker
pop-up window

prompt dialog box
secondary window
self keyword
status bar
top keyword
transient status bar message
window object

Practice | Practice Review Assignments

Practice the skills you learned in the tutorial using the same case scenario.

Data Files needed for the Review Assignments: atempotxt.htm, bottomtxt.htm, concerto.htm, defaulttxt.htm, definitions.css, glossary.css, glosstxt.htm, header.gif, imusicstyles.css, index.htm, lesson3.htm, lesson3a.htm, lesson3b.htm, lvb.gif, nav.htm, navy8th.gif, quiz.htm, quiz2.css, quiz2.gif, quiz2txt.htm, sonata.htm, terms.htm, treble.gif, treble2.gif, symphony.htm

Teresa likes your work on the iMusicHistory Web site and wants you to apply the changes you've made to the rest of the Web site. She wants you to complete the following tasks:

- Add transient status bar messages to the other three links at the bottom of the iMusicHistory home page.
- Add a pop-up window to the iMusicHistory home page that displays the definition of the term *a tempo*, which appears on the page.
- Create a customized pop-up window and alert dialog box for the questions on the Quiz 2 Web page.
- Prevent the Quiz 2 Web page from appearing within a frame.
- Write code to ensure that the contents of the bottom.htm and glossary.htm files always appear within the context of the Glossary frameset.
- Make sure that any pop-up windows you create will behave nicely if they encounter pop-up blockers.

Figure 10-34 shows a preview of the pop-up window you'll create for the new quiz page.

Figure 10-34

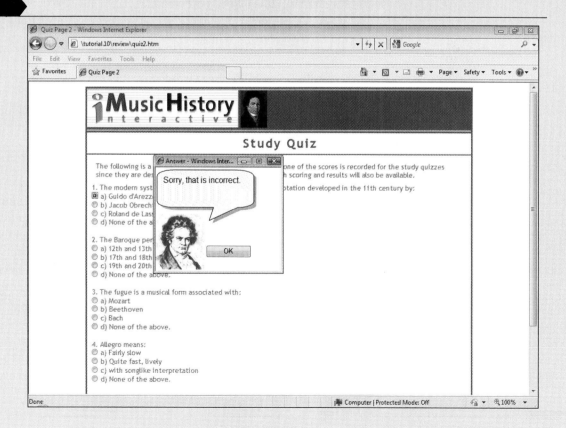

Complete the following:

1. Use your text editor to open the **defaulttxt.htm**, **atempotxt.htm**, **quiz2txt.htm**, **glosstxt.htm**, and **bottomtxt.htm** files from the tutorial.10\review folder, enter *your name* and *the date* in the comment section of each file, and then save the files as **default.htm**, **atempo.htm**, **quiz2.htm**, **glossary.htm**, and **bottom.htm**, respectively.

2. Return to the **default.htm** file in your text editor, and then add transient status bar messages to the document as follows:

   a. Go to the navigation cell text near the bottom of the document and locate the link to the lesson3.htm file. Add an onmouseover event handler to this link that displays the status bar message **Go to the Lessons page**. Add an onmouseout event handler that removes the status bar message when the pointer leaves the link.

   b. Use an onmouseover event handler to change the transient status bar message for the quiz.htm link to **Go to the First Online Quiz**. Be sure to remove this message using the onmouseout event handler.

   c. Repeat the process to change the transient status bar message for the terms.htm link to **View the Music Glossary**.

3. In the embedded script at the top of the page, insert a function named **showDef()**. The purpose of this function is to display a pop-up window. The function has a single parameter named **source** that contains the URL of the document to be displayed. Add the following commands to the showDef() function:

   a. Use the window.open() method to open a window displaying a document with a URL equal to the value of the source parameter. Leave the target name as a blank text string. The window should be 200 pixels wide by 100 pixels high, displayed at the screen coordinates (100, 100). Store the window object in a variable named **defWin**.

   b. Create a variable named **notPop** that tests whether the defWin window object was blocked. The notPop variable should have a value of true if the window was blocked and false if otherwise.

   c. Return the value of the notPop variable.

4. Scroll down to the center of the document and locate the link for the *a tempo* term. Add an onclick event handler that returns the value of the showDef() function. (*Hint*: Use the music definitions pop-ups from the tutorial as an example.)

5. Save the default.htm file, and then close it.

6. Go to the **atempo.htm** file in your text editor. Add an onblur event handler to the body element that closes the window when it loses the focus. Save and close the file.

7. Return to the **quiz2.htm** file in your text editor. Add an embedded script in the head section of the document, and within the script element, insert a function named **answer()**. The purpose of the answer() function is to write a pop-up window telling the student whether he or she answered the quiz question correctly. The answer() function should have one parameter named **correct** used to store a Boolean value indicating whether the student's answer is correct or not. Appropriate parameter values for the answer() function have already been added to onclick event handlers for the radio buttons in the form. Complete the answer() function as follows:

   a. Use the window.open() method to create a pop-up window named **popWin** that is 200 pixels wide by 200 pixels high and placed at the screen coordinates (250, 250). Specify a blank text string for the window's URL and target name.

   b. Create a variable named **notPop** that has a value of true if the popWin window failed to open and a value of false if it opened without error.

    c.   If the value of notPop is true (indicating that the pop-up window failed to open), create a conditional statement that tests whether the value of the correct parameter is true or false. If correct is true, display an alert box containing the text **Correct!** If correct is false, display an alert box with the text **Sorry, that is incorrect.**

    d.   If the value of notPop is false (indicating that a pop-up window was generated), write the HTML code

```
<html>
    <head>
        <title>Answer</title>
        <link rel='stylesheet' href='quiz2.css' type='text/css' />
    </head>
    <body>
    message
    <p>
        <input type='button' value='OK' onclick='self.close()' />
    </p>
    </body>
</html>
```

        into the popWin window, where *message* is either the HTML fragment

```
<p>Correct!</p>
```

        if the correct parameter is true or

```
<p>Sorry, that is incorrect.</p>
```

        if the correct parameter is false.

8. Add JavaScript commands to the **quiz2.htm** file so that the page cannot be placed in a frame. Save and close the file.

9. Go to the **bottom.htm** file in your text editor, add a script to the file that forces it to be displayed only within the Glossary frameset of the terms.htm file, and then save and close the file. Repeat for the **glossary.htm** file.

10. Open **default.htm** in your browser, and then verify that transient status bar messages appear for the Lessons, Quiz, and Glossary links at the bottom of the page; that clicking the *a tempo* definition link displays a pop-up window showing the term's definition; and that this pop-up window automatically closes when it loses the focus.

11. Open **quiz2.htm** in your browser, and then verify that clicking the radio buttons in the quiz form displays an appropriate pop-up window indicating whether the answer is correct, and that clicking the OK button within the pop-up window closes it.

12. Open **bottom.htm** and **glossary.htm** in your Web browser, and then verify that both files open within the context of the Glossary frameset.

13. Submit your completed Web site to your instructor.

Apply | **Case Problem 1**

Use the skills you learned to create a subscription pop-up window.

Data Files needed for this Case Problem: cover.css, cover.jpg, covertxt.htm, cwj.css, cwj.jpg, cwjtxt.htm, formtxt.htm, logo.gif, parch.jpg

The Civil War Journal   Terrence Whyte is the editor of the online version of *The Civil War Journal*, a magazine for people interested in the Civil War. Terrence wants a small pop-up window to appear when users open the home page of the online edition. The window will advertise the print version of the magazine and provide a link to a subscription form. Also, Terrence wants the status bar to display informative text for links on the page. Figure 10-35 shows a preview of the windows you'll create.

Figure 10-35

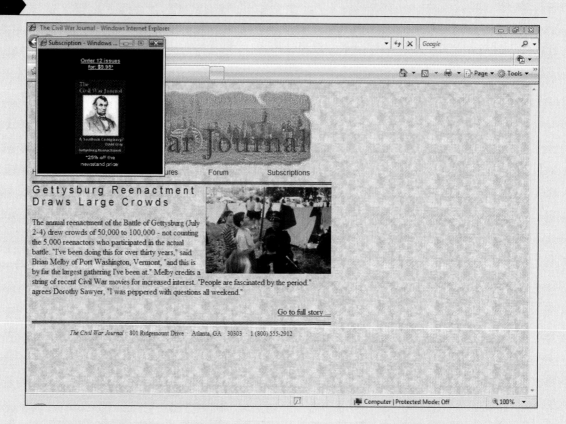

Complete the following:

1. Use your text editor to open the **cwjtxt.htm**, **covertxt.htm**, and **formtxt.htm** files from the tutorial.10\case1 folder, enter *your name* and *the date* in each file, and then save the files as **cwj.htm**, **cover.htm**, and **form.htm**, respectively.

2. Go to the **cwj.htm** file in your text editor, create the following transient status bar messages for the five links at the top of the page, configure the messages to appear in response to the onmouseover event, and then make sure the messages are removed in response to the onmouseout event:
   - Home Page: Go to the Home Page
   - News: View Current Events
   - Features: Go to Feature Articles
   - Form: Go to the Civil War Forum
   - Subscriptions: Subscribe Today!

3. In the head section of the document, insert an embedded script containing a function named **subscribe()**. The subscribe() function should open a new browser window containing the cover.htm document. Give the pop-up window a target name of **popWin**. Set the width and height of the pop-up window to 125 pixels by 240 pixels. Open the window 10 pixels down and to the right of the upper-left corner of the screen. Because this pop-up window displays only an advertisement for the magazine and not critical content, Terrence has not requested that you check for the presence of pop-up blockers.

4. Add an event handler attribute to the body element to run the subscribe() function when the page loads. Save and close the file.

5. Return to the **cover.htm** file in your text editor. Within the head section, insert an embedded script containing the showForm() function. The purpose of this function is to display the contents of the form.htm file in the main browser window. Have the function do the following:

   a. Display the form.htm file in the browser window that was used to open the cover.htm file. (*Hint*: Use the `opener` keyword to reference the main browser window and the `location.href` property to specify the document to be displayed in that window.)

   b. Close the current window.

6. Locate the linked text in the body of the document and change the value of the href attribute so that it runs the showForm() function when clicked. Save and close the file.

7. Return to the **form.htm** file in your text editor, and then create the same set of transient status bar messages that you created for the cwj.htm file. Save and close the file.

8. Open **cwj.htm** in your Web browser, verify that the status bar messages change in response to hovering the pointer over the five links at the top of the page, and verify that a subscription pop-up window appears on your screen.

9. Click the link in the subscription pop-up window. Verify that the pop-up closes and that the subscription form appears in the original browser window.

10. Submit the completed Web site to your instructor.

Challenge	**Case Problem 2**

Explore how to write content into an inline frame.

Data Files needed for this Case Problem: blank.htm, brain.css, brain.jpg, brain.js, braintxt.htm, frame.css, iframetxt.js

Anatomy 101   Jacob Terrell teaches Anatomy 101 at Thomas More College. He wants you to create a Web page on the brain. The page will display an inline image showing different parts of the human brain. As students move their pointer over a section, he wants an inline frame to display a description of that part of the brain. Figure 10-36 shows a preview of the page he wants you to create for him.

Figure 10-36

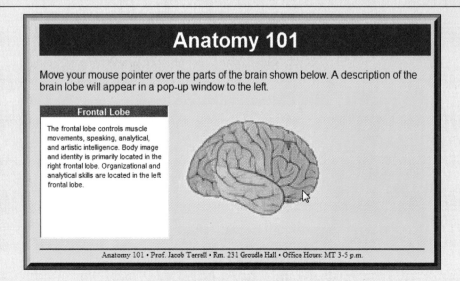

Anatomy 101

Move your mouse pointer over the parts of the brain shown below. A description of the brain lobe will appear in a pop-up window to the left.

Frontal Lobe

The frontal lobe controls muscle movements, speaking, analytical, and artistic intelligence. Body image and identity is primarily located in the right frontal lobe. Organizational and analytical skills are located in the left frontal lobe.

Anatomy 101 • Prof. Jacob Terrell • Rm. 231 Groudle Hall • Office Hours: MT 3-5 p.m.

Professor Terrell already created a document to display in the inline frame named blank. htm. As the filename implies, the document is blank save for an empty h2 element with the id docTitle and an empty paragraph element with the id docSummary. Your code will insert text strings into these two empty elements with the text content taken from two arrays named title and summary that Professor Terrell already created and stored in an external script document.

Complete the following:

1. Use your text editor to open the **braintxt.htm** and **iframetxt.js** files from the tutorial.10\ case2 folder, enter *your name* and *the date* in each file, and then save the files as **brain. htm** and **iframe.js**, respectively.

2. Review the contents of the **brain.htm** and **brain.js** files in your text editor, taking note of the contents of the title and summary arrays as well as the layout and content of the HTML file.

3. Go to the **brain.htm** file in your text editor and link the file to the **brain.js** and **iframe.js** script files. Save and close the file.

4. Go to the **iframe.js** file in your text editor, and then add a command to run the setupFrame() function when the page is initially loaded by the browser.

5. Create the **setupFrame()** function. The purpose of this function is to create event handlers and a custom property for each of the area elements in the brain.htm file. Add the following commands to the function:

   a. Create a variable named **allAreas** to reference all of the elements in the document with the area tag name.

   b. Loop through the allAreas collection and for each item in the collection: (i) Create a custom property named **index** equal to the value of the counting variable in the for loop. (ii) Add an event handler for the mouseover event that runs the writeFrame() function. (iii) Add an event handler for the mouseout event that runs the clearFrame() function.

6. Create the **writeFrame()** function. The purpose of this function is to write title and summary data to the inline frame for each part of the brain. The text of the title and summary is drawn from the title and summary arrays. Add the following commands to the function:

   a. Declare the **areaIndex** variable equal to the value of the index property for the area element that initiated on the mouseover event. (*Hint*: Use the `this` keyword to reference the area element.)

   b. Declare a variable named **frameWin** referencing the window containing the parts inline frame.

   c. Declare a variable named **frameDoc** referencing the document within the frameWin window.

   ⊕ EXPLORE d. Set the innerHTML for the element in frameDoc with the id docTitle to the value of the title array element whose index is equal to areaIndex.

   ⊕ EXPLORE e. Set the innerHTML for the element in frameDoc with the id docSummary to the value of the summary array element whose index is equal to areaIndex.

   ⊕ EXPLORE 7. Create the **clearFrame()** function. The purpose of this function is to clear the title and summary text from the document displayed in the inline frame. Apply the same commands to the clearFrame() function as you did for the writeFrame() function except set the innerHTML of the docTitle and docSummary elements to empty text strings. Save the file.

8. Load the **brain.htm** file in your Web browser. Verify that when you hover the pointer over different areas in the brain map, the title and summary text appear in the inline frame. Also, verify that when the pointer moves away from the brain map, the inline frame text disappears.

9. Submit the completed project to your instructor.

Challenge	**Case Problem 3**

Explore how to write HTML and CSS code to a frame.

Data Files needed for this Case Problem: code.css, css.htm, css.txt, demo.gif, demo.htm, html.htm, html.txt, scripttxt.js, title.css, titletxt.htm

Web Designers   Andrew Seaborn teaches a class in Web design. During the first few weeks of the course, he teaches students the basics of HTML tags and CSS style sheets. Andrew thinks it would be useful for his students to have a demo page in which they can enter HTML and CSS code directly into one set of frames and then have that code rendered as a Web page in another frame. Figure 10-37 shows a preview of the demo page you'll create.

Figure 10-37

The demo is organized into four files. The demo.htm file displays a frameset named demo containing four frames named title, htmlcode, csscode, and preview. The title frame will contain the contents of the title.htm file. You'll create the JavaScript programs for this file that you need to run the demo. The htmlcode frame contains the contents of the html.htm file. This file contains a textarea field with the id value inputhtml where you'll enter the HTML code that you want to display. The csscode frame contains the contents of the css.htm file. This file also contains a textarea field with the id value inputcss. You'll use this textarea field to enter the CSS styles that you want to apply to the elements in your HTML file. The preview pane does not contain any document at all. Instead, you'll create the document content by writing the content of the two textarea boxes into the preview frame.

Complete the following:

1. Use your text editor to open the **scripttxt.js** and **titletxt.htm** files from the tutorial.10\ case3 folder, enter *your name* and *the date* in the comment section, and then save the files as **script.js** and **title.htm**, respectively.

2. Go to the **title.htm** file in your text editor, and then link the file to the script.js external script file. Study the contents of the file, and then save and close the file.

3. Go to the **script.js** file in your text editor, and then add a command to run the setupButtons() function when the page is loaded.

4. Create the **setupButtons()** function. The purpose of this function is to add onclick event handlers to the four buttons found in the title.htm file. For the submitCode button, run the sendCode() function. For the showCode button, run the showCode() function. For the showPreview button, run the showPreview() function. For the showBoth button, run the showBoth() function.

⊕ EXPLORE

5. Create a function named **showPreview()**. The purpose of this function is to hide the htmlcode and csscode frames, providing more screen space to the preview frame. To hide those two frames, change the value of the rows attribute for the demo frameset to "100,1,*". (*Hint*: You will have to go up to the parent element of the current document to access the frameset object. Remember that the id of the frameset object is demo.)

⊕ EXPLORE

6. Insert a function named **showCode()**. The purpose of this function is to hide the preview frame and to increase the size of the textarea fields in the html.htm and css.htm documents. Add the following commands to the function:
   a. Set the value of the demo frameset's rows attribute to "100,*,1".
   b. Change the height of the textarea field in the html.htm file to 300 pixels. (*Hint*: Remember that you will have to move up to the parent object and then down to the second frame in the frames collection to reference the contents of the html.htm document. You can then use the document.getElementById() method to reference the textarea field and use the style.height property to set the textarea field's height to 300 pixels.)
   c. Change the height of the textarea field in the css.htm file to 300 pixels. Use the same techniques you employed for the textarea field in the html.htm file to reference this object. The css.htm file is stored in the third frame of the frames collection.

7. Insert a function named **showBoth()**. The purpose of this function is to show both the code and preview frames in the demo frameset. Add the following commands to the function:
   a. Set the value of the demo frameset's rows attribute to "100,210,*".
   b. Set the height of the textarea field in the html.htm document to 150 pixels.
   c. Set the height of the textarea field in the css.htm document to 150 pixels.

EXPLORE

8. Create a function named **sendCode()**. The purpose of this function is to extract whatever code has been entered into the two textarea boxes and write that code to the preview frame. To complete this function:

   a. Create a variable named **previewFrame** that references the fourth frame in the demo frameset.

   b. Create a variable named **htmlCode** that is equal to the value of the textarea field in the html.htm document. (*Hint*: The value of the textarea field can be extracted using the value property in the expression *object*.value, where *object* is the object reference to the textarea field. To reference the textarea field, you must navigate through the frames hierarchy and then down through the contents of the html.htm document.)

   c. Create a variable named **cssCode** that is equal to the value of the textarea field in the css.htm document. Write the code

   ```
   <html>
      <head>
         <title></title>
         <style type='text/css'>
            styles
         </style>
      </head>
      <body>
         html code
      </body>
   </html>
   ```

   to the document within the previewFrame object, where *styles* is the value of the cssCode variable and *html code* is the value of the htmlCode variable. Save and close the file.

9. Open the **demo.htm** file in your Web browser.

10. Copy the HTML code from the html.txt file and paste it into the textarea box in the left frame. Copy the CSS code from the css.txt file and paste it into the textarea box in the right frame.

11. Click the Submit Code button, and then verify that the preview frame displays the elements and styles from the two code frames.

12. Click the Show Only Preview button, and then verify that it hides the two code frames and increases the size of the preview pane.

13. Click the Show Only Code button, and then verify that it hides the preview frame and increases the height of the code frames and the textarea boxes they contain.

14. Click the Show Code and Preview button, and then verify that it restores the frameset layout, displaying all four frames with the textarea boxes back to their original heights.

15. Submit your completed Web site to your instructor.

| Create | **Case Problem 4** |

Create pop-up windows for a tourism Web site.

Data Files needed for this Case Problem: allen-img.jpg, allen-logo.gif, allentxt.htm, birdcage-img.jpg, birdcage-logo.gif, birdtxt.htm, boothill-img.jpg, boothill-logo.gif, boottxt.htm, corral-img.jpg, corral-logo.gif, corraltxt.htm, courthouse-img.jpg, courthouse logo.gif, courthousetxt.htm, indextxt.htm, logo.gif, map.gif, schief-img.jpg, schief-logo.gif, schieftxt.htm, styles.css

Tombstone Chamber of Commerce The Tombstone, Arizona, Chamber of Commerce has a small office in the main tourist area of Tombstone. Tony Diaz is in charge of designing a Web site that advertises the features of interest in the town. The Web site's home page will have a map of Tombstone with hot spots linked to different tourist attractions. When a user clicks a hot spot, a page describing the attraction is displayed. Tony wants you to make the following modifications to the Web site:

- Change the transient status bar message for each hot spot to a text string that describes the tourist attraction.
- Have each hot spot open a pop-up window describing the attraction.
- If a pop-up window loses the focus, have it close automatically.
- If a user is running a pop-up blocker, have links to the area attractions appear in the main browser window and not as a pop-up.

Complete the following:

1. Use your text editor to open the **allentxt.htm**, **birdtxt.htm**, **boottxt.htm**, **corraltxt.htm**, **courthousetxt.htm**, **indextxt.htm**, and **schieftxt.htm** files from the tutorial.10\case4 folder, enter *your name* and *the date* in the comment section of each file, and then save the files as **allen.htm**, **bird.htm**, **boot.htm**, **corral.htm**, **courthouse.htm**, **index.htm**, and **schief.htm**, respectively.
2. Go to the **index.htm** file and create a transient status bar message for the six hot spots in the image map. The text of each status bar message is up to you, but it should include some brief description of the tourist attraction.
3. Create a permanent status bar message for the Tombstone home page. The text of the message is up to you, but it should convey a welcome greeting to the casual tourist.
4. Create a function named **tourWin()** that generates a pop-up window. The features of the pop-up window are up to you. Include code that verifies that the pop-up window has been properly opened. If it hasn't, have the browser open the target document within the main browser window.
5. Apply the tourWin() function to the six links in the image map.
6. Add event handlers to each of the six target documents in your text editor so that if they lose their focus as pop-up windows, the browser closes them automatically.
7. Open **index.htm** in your Web browser and test the hot spot links. Verify that each link has a customized status bar message, the home page has a permanent status bar message conveying a greeting, each hot spot link opens in a customized pop-up window, and each pop-up window closes automatically when it loses the focus.
8. Submit your completed Web site to your instructor.

Session 10.1

1. A permanent status bar message appears by default in the status bar. A transient status bar message only appears in response to a particular action or event.

2. `history.go(-2)`

3. `window.status = "View News page"`

   `return true;`

4. One way is with the meta element

   `<meta http-equiv="Refresh" content="sec;URL=url" />`
   where *sec* is the amount of time in seconds that will elapse before opening the new page, and *url* is the new page to be loaded.
   Another way is to use the window.location.href property along with the setTimeout method.

5. The history.previous property provides the URL of the page previously visited by the user. However, many browsers do not allow this property because it provides information about the user's Web browsing activity and thus is a violation of privacy.

6. The document.referrer property records the URL of the page from which the current page was accessed. However, this property works only when the current page is accessed via a link, and some browsers disable it for security reasons.

Session 10.2

1. `<a href="home.htm" target="HomePage"> link text </a>`

2. `window.open("home.htm","width=300,height=150");`

3. `window.open("home.htm","width=300,height=150,scrollbars=yes,status=yes");`

   or

   `window.open("home.htm","width=300,height=150,scrollbars=1,status=1");`

4. `Home.document.write("<img src="logo.jpg" alt='imhLogo' />");`

5. `alert("Script Finished");`

6. `confirm("Proceed?");`

7. A modal window prevents users from doing anything outside the window until it is closed. A modeless window allows users to work in other windows while it's open.

Session 10.3

1. `top.frames ["Logo"]`

2. `top.frames["Logo"].location.href="logo.html";`

3. `top.frames["Logo"].document.write("<html></html>");`

4. `top.document.getElementById("Home").cols="150,150,*";`

5. `if (top.location.href == self.location) {`

   `    top.location.href = "home.htm";`

   `}`

6. `document.getElementById("report").src = "report.htm";`

   or

   `window.frames["report"].location.href = "report.htm";`

7. `document.getElementById("report").windowContent.username`

8. `document.getElementById("report").windowContent.document`

Ending Data Files

Tutorial.10 →

Tutorial
concerto.htm
imlibrary.js
imusic.htm
index.htm
lesson3.htm
nav.htm
quiz.htm
sonata.htm
status.js
symphony.htm
+ 5 HTML files
+ 4 CSS files
+ 8 graphic files

Review
atempo.htm
bottom.htm
default.htm
glossary.htm
quiz2.htm
+ 10 HTML files
+ 4 CSS files
+ 6 graphic files

Case1
cover.htm
cwj.htm
form.htm
+ 2 CSS files
+ 4 graphic files

Case2
brain.htm
iframe.js
+ 1 HTML file
+ 2 CSS files
+ 1 JavaScript file
+ 1 graphic file

Case3
script.js
title.htm
+ 3 HTML files
+ 2 CSS files
+ 1 graphic file

Case4
allen.htm
bird.htm
boot.htm
corral.htm
courthouse.htm
index.htm
schief.htm
+ 1 CSS file
+ 14 graphic files

Objectives

Exploring Object-Based Programming

Creating Custom Objects

Case | Online Games and Puzzles

Bob Voiklund supervises programming at a new Web site devoted to online games and puzzles for gaming enthusiasts. The Web site will go online in a few weeks and Bob has asked you to develop a sample Web application for an online video poker game. Bob has already written the content for the sample page and has created the style sheet; he needs you to write the JavaScript code.

Because the Web site will eventually contain several poker-style games, he wants your code to be easily adapted to applications that other people in his Web development team will create in the future. One way to create reusable objects and code is through object-based programming. Bob wants you to explore this technique as you write the code for a video poker game.

Starting Data Files

Tutorial.11 →

Tutorial
bdlibtxt.js
cardstxt.js
pokertxt.htm
pokertxt.js
+ 1 CSS file
+ 59 graphic files

Review
gamestxt.js
libtxt.js
pickemtxt.htm
pickemtxt.js
+ 1 CSS file
+ 57 graphic files

Case1
carttxt.js
shoptxt.js
spicetxt.htm
+ 1 HTML file
+ 1 CSS file
+ 2 JavaScript files
+ 4 graphic files

Case2
overlaytxt.js
schedtxt.htm
shadowstxt.js
+ 3 CSS files
+ 1 JavaScript file
+ 1 graphic file

Case3
demotxt.js
slidertxt.js
widgettxt.htm
+ 2 CSS files
+ 1 JavaScript file
+ 6 graphic files

Case4
playtxt.js
shapestxt.htm
shapestxt.js
+ 1 CSS file
+ 1 JavaScript file
+ 13 graphic files

Session 11.1

Working with Nested Functions

Bob presents his proposal for a new video poker Web game. He gives you all the files that have been developed for the application, including the HTML and CSS files. You will start by opening and reviewing these documents.

To review the poker.htm file:

▶ 1. Use your text editor to open the **bdlibtxt.js**, **cardstxt.js**, **pokertxt.js**, and **pokertxt.htm** files from the tutorial.11\tutorial folder, enter *your name* and *the date* in the comment section of each file, and then save the files as **bdlibrary.js**, **cards.js**, **poker.js**, and **poker.htm**, respectively.

▶ 2. Go to the **poker.htm** file in your text editor, and then review the HTML code to become familiar with the document's structure and contents.

▶ 3. Add the following script elements to the head section of the poker.htm file, linking Bob's Web page to the JavaScript functions stored in the three script files—bdlibrary.js, cards.js, and poker.js:

```
<script src="bdlibrary.js" type="text/javascript"></script>
<script src="cards.js" type="text/javascript"></script>
<script src="poker.js" type="text/javascript"></script>
```

▶ 4. Save the file, and then close it.

▶ 5. Open **poker.htm** in your Web browser. See Figure 11-1.

Figure 11-1 ▶ Draw poker Web page

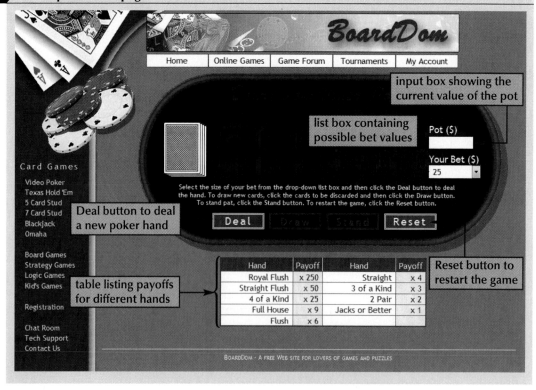

The Web page displays the poker table on which users will play video poker. Bob set up the following steps for how the game will be played:

1. The player starts the game with a predetermined amount in his or her pot. Bob suggests that players start with $500.
2. Before each hand is dealt, the player chooses an amount to bet from the drop-down list box. The pot is reduced by the amount bet. Bob has entered four betting values into a list box: $25, $50, $75, and $100.
3. The player clicks the Deal button and is dealt five cards from a poker deck.
4. The player can select any or all of the dealt cards to replace them with new cards randomly drawn from the deck. New cards are retrieved by clicking the Draw button.
5. The final poker hand is evaluated. To win, the hand needs to contain at least a pair of jacks or better. Higher-valued hands result in higher payoffs. For example, a full house (three of a kind and a pair) pays off at nine times the amount bet, so that a $50 bet would result in a $450 payoff. Bob has included a table of the payoffs for each of nine possible winning hands in the Web page.
6. After the player's winnings are added to his or her pot, a new round begins. The player can choose a new amount to bet and then click the Deal button to be dealt the next hand.
7. The game continues until the player exhausts the money in his or her pot or chooses to quit the game.

All of these operations will be stored within a single function that will automatically run whenever the user loads the Web page. Bob has already written the initial playDrawPoker() function and added it to the poker.js file.

To view the poker.js file:

▶ 1. Go to the **poker.js** file in your text editor.

▶ 2. Scroll down the file, examining the initial playDrawPoker() function. See Figure 11-2.

Initial playDrawPoker() function   Figure 11-2

runs the playDrawPoker()
function when the page is
initially loaded

references to
page objects

```
addEvent(window, "load", playDrawPoker, false);

function playDrawPoker() {

    var dealButton = document.getElementById("dealB");
    var drawButton = document.getElementById("drawB");
    var standButton = document.getElementById("standB");
    var resetButton = document.getElementById("resetB");
    var handValueText = document.getElementById("handValue");
    var betSelection = document.getElementById("bet");
    var potValue = document.getElementById("pot");

}
```

The playDrawPoker() function contains object references to all of the main features of the poker table. Bob used the addEvent() function, already defined in the bdlibrary.js file, to direct the browser to run the playDrawPoker() function when the page loads.

The first thing you'll program for the poker application is the action and appearance of the buttons on the poker table. You need to write the code that controls these buttons using nested functions.

Bob's poker table has four buttons labeled Deal, Draw, Stand, and Reset. The buttons perform the following tasks:

- The Deal button deals five cards from the poker deck into the player's hand.
- The Draw button replaces all selected cards in the player's hand with new cards from the deck.
- The Stand button signals to the dealer that the player wants to keep all of his or her cards.
- The Reset button resets the game with a fresh pot.

The Deal, Draw, and Stand buttons need to be turned on and off depending on the state of the game. For example, a player can only draw new cards or stand pat after a hand has been dealt, so both the Draw and Stand buttons are disabled before the deal. Similarly, a new hand cannot be dealt until play on the current hand is completed, so the Deal button is turned off while the current hand is in play.

Bob wants you to add code that turns the Deal, Draw, and Stand buttons off and on at different stages in the game. To disable and enable these buttons, you'll first create the following two functions:

```
function disableButton(button) {
   button.disabled = true;
   setOpacity(button, 25);
}

function enableButton(button) {
   button.disabled = false;
   setOpacity(button, 100);
}
```

Both of these functions have a single parameter named button that will reference either the Deal, Draw, or Stand buttons. The functions set the disable property of the button to true or false to disable or enable the button, respectively, and call the setOpacity() function (stored in the bdlibrary.js file) to change the opacity of the button to either gray it out or make it fully visible to the user.

These two functions could be added anywhere within the poker.js file, but you want to limit them to a local scope because Bob plans to make your code available to other programmers for use in other applications on the company's Web site. Sites that involve several programmers or multiple JavaScript applications avoid using variables and functions with global scope whenever possible. Rather than having to worry about whether a variable or function is already in use elsewhere in a large and extended application, it is better to keep the definitions local to a particular function. This ensures that code written by one programmer does not conflict with code written by another programmer.

You can limit a function to a local scope by nesting it within another function, making it invisible to any code outside of the containing function. You will nest the disableButton() and enableButton() functions within the playDrawPoker() function.

To nest functions within the playDrawPoker() function:

1. Within the poker.js file, scroll down to the playDrawPoker() function, and then insert the following code, as shown in Figure 11-3:

```
// Function to disable and gray out a form button
function disableButton(button) {
   button.disabled = true;
   setOpacity(button, 25);
}

// Function to enable and display a form button
```

```
function enableButton(button) {
   button.disabled = false;
   setOpacity(button, 100);
}
```

```
function playDrawPoker() {

    var dealButton = document.getElementById("dealB");
    var drawButton = document.getElementById("drawB");
    var standButton = document.getElementById("standB");
    var resetButton = document.getElementById("resetB");
    var handValueText = document.getElementById("handValue");
    var betSelection = document.getElementById("bet");
    var potValue = document.getElementById("pot");

    // Function to disable and gray out a form button
    function disableButton(button) {
        button.disabled = true;
        setOpacity(button, 25);
    }

    // Function to enable and display a form button
    function enableButton(button) {
        button.disabled = false;
        setOpacity(button, 100);
    }

}
```

nested functions with local scope

2. Save the file.

Players progress through the game by clicking the Deal, Draw, and Stand buttons. Each time one of these three buttons is clicked, the following occurs:

- Clicking the Deal button deals a new hand, and then: (1) turns on the Draw and Stand buttons, (2) turns off the Deal button, and (3) turns off the Bet selection list box (so that users cannot change their bets after the hand is dealt).
- Clicking the Draw button draws new cards from the deck, evaluates the player's final hand, and then: (1) turns on the Deal button (in preparation for the next hand to be dealt), (2) turns off the Draw and Stand buttons, and (3) turns on the Bet selection list box (so that users can change their bets before the next deal).
- Clicking the Stand button evaluates the players' final hand, and then: (1) turns on the Deal button, (2) turns off the Draw and Stand buttons, and (3) turns on the Bet selection list box.

You will add code to the playDrawPoker() function to turn on and off these three buttons and the Bet selection list box at appropriate points in the game.

To disable and enable the game buttons and Bet selection list:

1. Within the playDrawPoker() function, insert the following code to program the actions of the Deal button:

```
// Actions when the Deal button is clicked
dealButton.onclick = function() {

    // Enable or disable other buttons
    disableButton(dealButton);
    enableButton(drawButton);
    enableButton(standButton);
    betSelection.disabled = true;

}
```

▶ **2.** Add the following code to program the actions of the Draw and Stand buttons:

```
// Actions when the Draw button is clicked
drawButton.onclick = function() {

    // Enable or disable other buttons
    enableButton(dealButton);
    disableButton(drawButton);
    disableButton(standButton);
    betSelection.disabled = false;

}

// Actions when the Stand button is clicked
    standButton.onclick = function() {

    // Enable or disable other buttons
    enableButton(dealButton);
    disableButton(drawButton);
    disableButton(standButton);
    betSelection.disabled = false;

}
```

This code runs anonymous functions in response to the click event so that the scope of the action remains local. Figure 11-4 highlights the added code.

Figure 11-4 ▶ **Event handlers for the Deal, Draw, and Stand buttons and the Bet selection list**

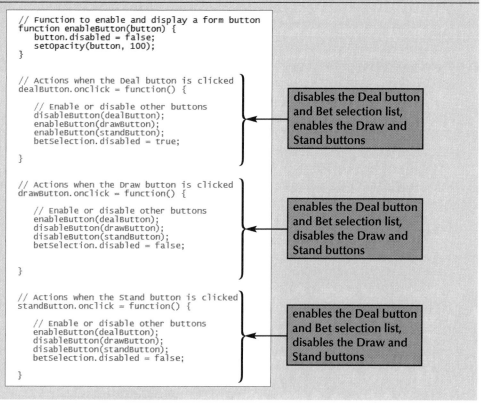

The fourth button on the Web page is the Reset button, which restarts the game. You will add an event handler that reloads the page when this button is clicked.

To program the actions of the Reset button:

▶ **1.** Add the following code to the playDrawPoker() function, as shown in Figure 11-5, to program the action of the Reset button so that it reloads the Web page when clicked:

```
// Reload the Web page when the Reset button is clicked
resetButton.onclick = function() {

    window.location.reload(true);

}
```

Event handler for the Reset button ◀ **Figure 11-5**

```
// Actions when the Stand button is clicked
standButton.onclick = function() {

    // Enable or disable other buttons
    enableButton(dealButton);
    disableButton(drawButton);
    disableButton(standButton);
    betSelection.disabled = false;

}

// Reload the Web page when the Reset button is clicked
resetButton.onclick = function() {

    window.location.reload(true);

}
}
```

▶ **2.** Save the file, and then reload **poker.htm** in your Web browser.

▶ **3.** Click the **Deal** button, and then verify that the Deal button and Bet selection list are grayed out and disabled and the Draw and Stand buttons are enabled.

   Trouble? Some browsers gray out only the drop-down arrow in the Bet selection list and not the Bet selection list value.

▶ **4.** Click either the **Draw** or **Stand** button to disable those two buttons and to re-enable the Deal button and the Bet Selection list.

▶ **5.** Click the **Reset** button to confirm that the Web page reloads with the Deal button enabled and the Draw and Stand buttons disabled.

Tip

You can avoid many user errors by enabling only those features from your application that the user is allowed to access at any particular time.

JavaScript supports three types of executable code: global code, function code, and eval code. Each type of code has a different scope and is executed in a different manner. **Global code** is any code that lies outside of a function and is automatically executed when encountered by the browser. As the name implies, global code has global scope. **Function code** is any code placed within a function and must be called to be executed. As you've seen, function code can be either local or global in scope, depending on whether the function is nested within another function. **Eval code** is any code that is passed to the browser using the eval() function. The scope of eval code is limited within the eval() function itself. The syntax of the eval() function is

```
eval(string)
```

where *string* is a text string containing executable code. The eval() function is used whenever an application needs to create executable code during run time, usually in response to an action by the user or another application. For example, the following code employs the eval() function to display the value of a variable specified by the user:

```
var varName = prompt("Enter a variable name");
var runCmd = "alert(" + varName + ")";
eval(runCmd);
```

In this code, the user is prompted for a variable name, which is stored in the varName variable. The text of the alert() command is then stored in the runCmd variable. Finally, the eval() function is called to run the stored JavaScript command.

The eval() function should be used with caution because it opens an application to untested code retrieved from outside sources. Many programmers refuse to use eval() because of this security risk and argue that any tasks done with the eval() function could be done just as well with more secure JavaScript methods. Despite these concerns, use of the eval() function is common throughout the Web, especially in recent years with applications that use the eval() function to retrieve and parse JavaScript code stored on Web servers.

Introducing Custom Objects

JavaScript is an object-based programming language that involves working with the properties and methods associated with objects. There are three kinds of JavaScript objects. **Native objects** are part of the JavaScript language, such as the Date, Array, or Image objects. **Host objects** are objects provided by the browser for use in interacting with the Web document, such as the window, document, or form objects. **Custom objects**, also known as **user-defined objects**, are objects created by the user for specific programming tasks.

Every object in JavaScript is defined using a function known as the **object constructor** or **constructor**. The definition itself is known as the **object class**. Finally, a specific case of an object class is known as the **object instance** or **instance**. Creating an object from an object class is known as **instantiating** an object. These terms have their counterparts in the real world. For example, a company that manufactures automobiles is a constructor, the make and model of a car is the object class, and a particular car that you might own and drive is an object instance.

For your application, you'll create four custom objects representing different elements in a video poker game. You need object classes representing a poker card, a poker hand, a poker deck, and the game of video poker itself. Each object class will have its own collection of properties and methods that mirror the way the game is played in the real world. There are several ways to create custom objects. You'll start by examining how to create new objects derived from native JavaScript objects.

Tip

All native object names start with an uppercase letter, all host object names start with a lowercase letter, and the format of custom object names is determined by the programmer.

The Base Object

All JavaScript objects are derived from a single fundamental **base object**. Figure 11-6 describes the properties and methods of this object.

Property or Method		Description
Property	*object*.constructor	Returns a reference to the constructor function of *object*
Method	*object*.hasOwnProperty(*prop*)	Returns a Boolean value indicating whether *object* supports the property *prop*
	object.isPrototypeOf(*object2*)	Returns a Boolean value indicating whether *object2* is an instance of *object*
	object.propertyIsEnumerable(*prop*)	Returns a Boolean value indicating whether the *prop* property of *object* is enumerable and can be used in a *for...in* loop
	object.toString()	Returns the type of *object* as the text string [object *Class*] where *Class* is the name of the object's constructor function
	object.valueOf()	Returns the value of *object* either as a text string, number, Boolean value, undefined, or null

Because native objects such as the Array and Math objects are derived from this base object, they too support these properties and methods in addition to the properties and methods unique to them. For example, to determine whether arrays support the length property, you can apply the hasOwnProperty() method

```
Array.hasOwnProperty("length")
```

which returns the Boolean value true because length is a property of the Array object. On the other hand, the expression

```
Math.hasOwnProperty("length")
```

returns the value false because the Math object supports no such method.

Custom objects can also be instantiated from the base object using the command

```
var newObj = new Object();
```

where *newObj* is a specific instance of the base object. For example, the following instance of the drawPoker object is derived from the base object:

```
var drawPoker = new Object();
```

You can think of the base object as the building block for all other JavaScript objects. After you have instantiated a custom object from the base object, you can extend it by adding your own library of custom properties and methods.

Defining an Object Property

You learned how to apply custom properties to built-in objects in Tutorial 8. In the same fashion, you can apply a property to an instance of a custom object using the command

```
object.property = value;
```

where *object* is an instance of the custom object, *property* is the name of the property, and *value* is the value assigned to the property. One property you want to add to the pokerGame object is a property that defines how much money the player currently has in his or her pot. To create such a property and set its initial value to 500, you run the following command:

```
drawPoker.currentPot = 500;
```

You can leave off the value of the property or set the value to null or undefined if you want to set the value at a later point in the application.

Defining an Object Method

To create a custom method, you associate the method with a function. The general syntax is

```
object.method = function
```

where *method* is the name of the method and *function* is the function. Note that *function* can be entered as the name of a function defined elsewhere in the code, as the following example demonstrates:

```
function alertPotValue () {
    alert (this.currentPot);
}
drawPoker.showPot = alertPotValue;
```

Or, it can be inserted directly using an anonymous function, as follows:

```
drawPoker.showPot = function() {
    alert(this.currentPot);
}
```

In both of these examples, running the command drawPoker.showPot () displays an alert dialog box with the value of the currentPot property. Note that the `this` keyword in the function text refers to the custom object to which the function has been attached.

Understanding Objects and Associative Arrays

The *object.property* and *object.method*() syntax is not the only way to access an object property or method. You can also treat any object name as an array and the name of a property or method as a value within that array. In JavaScript, the expressions

```
drawPoker.currentPot
```

and

```
drawPoker["currentPot"]
```

are equivalent because JavaScript treats objects and their properties as associative arrays. An **associative array** is an array containing a collection of keys, each associated with a value or set of values. This is in contrast to the **index arrays** you have been using in which array values are identified by their index number. For example, you can create an array of names using the indexed array

```
var names = new Array();
names[0] = "Tompkins";
names[1] = "Unger";
```

Tip

You cannot mix techniques associated with indexed and associative arrays. Expressions like names[0] to reference the first array item or names.length to return the length of the array have no meaning when applied to an associative array.

so that each value in the array is identified by its index number. However, in an associative array, each value is identified by a key value, as follows:

```
var names = new Array();
names["manager"] = "Tompkins";
names["supervisor"] = "Unger";
```

To return the text string, Tompkins, from this names array, you can use either names["manager"] or names.manager and thus you can think of manager as either an item in the names array or as a property of the names object.

As you learned in Tutorial 3, index arrays can be populated using the following more compact form:

```
var names = new Array("Tompkins", "Unger");
```

The same is true of associative arrays in which keys and values are entered using the form

```
var array = {
   "key1": value1,
   "key2": value2,
...
}
```

where *key1*, *key2*, etc. are the names of keys in the associative array and *value1*, *value2*, etc. are the corresponding values in those keys. So, the names array described above also can be entered as:

```
var names = {"manager": "Tompkins", "supervisor": "Unger"}
```

The quotation marks around the key names are optional unless the key names include spaces.

The associative array form provides a compact way to define an object using an **object literal**. For example, properties and methods of the drawPoker object can be defined in the following object literal:

Tip

Associative arrays are found in most programming languages but under different names. They're referred to as hash tables in C#, hash in Perl, maps in C++, hashmaps in Java, and dictionaries in Python.

```
var drawPoker = {
   currentPot: 500,
   currentBet: 25,
   showPot: function() {alert(this.currentPot);}
};
```

Note that the function associated with the showPot() method is nested within this object literal. This technique, known as **encapsulation**, ensures that any functions you define for a custom object will not conflict with functions defined elsewhere in the application because the scope of the function is local to the object constructor.

| InSight | Understanding for … in Loops and Associative Arrays |

Because associative arrays contain items that are not indexed, you cannot loop through the contents of an array using a counter variable. Instead, you must use the for … in structure

```
for (key in array) {
    commands
}
```

where *key* is a variable representing the keys in the associative *array*. For example, if you define the names object

```
var names = {"manager": "Tompkins", "supervisor": "Unger"}
```

using an object literal, you can generate alert boxes displaying the values of the manager and supervisor properties in the for … in loop

```
for (prop in names) {
    alert(prop + ": " + names[prop]);
}
```

and JavaScript will generate two alert boxes showing the text "manager: Tompkins" followed by "supervisor: Unger".

The for … in loop also can be applied to the properties of native and host objects. The following for … in loop is used with the event object to generate alert boxes that display all of the property values associated with the mousedown event:

```
myObject.onmousedown = function(e) {
    var evt = e || window.event;
    for (prop in evt) {
        alert(prop + ": " + evt[prop]);
    }
}
```

When applied in this fashion, a for … in loop can be a useful debugging tool, as it provides a complete picture of all the properties and methods associated with an object at any particular time.

| Reference Window | Defining a Custom Object |

- To define a custom object drawn from the base object, enter
  ```
  var newObject = new Object() {
      this.property = value;
      this.method = function;
      ...
  }
  ```
  where *newObject* is an instance of the new object, *property* is a property associated with the object, *value* is the initial value of the property, *method* is a method associated with the object, and *function* is a function run when the method is applied to the object.
- To define a custom object as an object literal, enter
  ```
  var newObject = {
      property : value,
      method : function,
      ...
  }
  ```
  where multiple properties and methods should be separated by commas.

You'll use the associative array form to create a custom object that defines the properties and methods of the draw poker game. The code to define the pokerGame object is:

```
var pokerGame = {
    currentPot: null,
    currentBet: null,

    placeBet : function() {
                this.currentPot -= this.currentBet;
            }
}
```

The pokerGame object has two properties named currentPot and currentBet that store the amount in the player's pot and the current amount of the player's bet. Both properties have initial values of null because you want to set these values within the poker game application itself. The pokerGame object also supports the placeBet() method, which uses the -= operator to subtract the current bet from the current value of the pot.

You will add this code to the cards.js file.

To create the pokerGame object:

▶ **1.** Go to the **cards.js** file in your text editor.

▶ **2.** Scroll down to the section marked "The pokerGame Object," and then insert the following code, as shown in Figure 11-7:

```
var pokerGame = {
    currentPot: null,
    currentBet: null,

    placeBet : function() {
                this.currentPot -= this.currentBet;
            }

}
```

The pokerGame object ◀ Figure 11-7

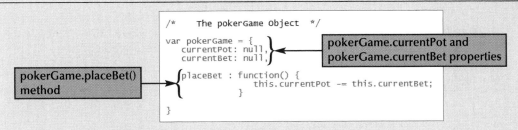

▶ **3.** Save the file, and then return to the **poker.js** file in your text editor.

▶ **4.** Near the top of the playDrawPoker() function, insert the following code, as shown in Figure 11-8, to define initial values for the currentPot and currentBet properties:

```
// Set the initial values for the pot and player's bet
pokerGame.currentPot = 500;
pokerGame.currentBet = 25;
```

Figure 11-8 — Initial values for the player's pot and bet

```
function playDrawPoker() {
    var dealButton = document.getElementById("dealB");
    var drawButton = document.getElementById("drawB");
    var standButton = document.getElementById("standB");
    var resetButton = document.getElementById("resetB");
    var handValueText = document.getElementById("handvalue");
    var betSelection = document.getElementById("bet");
    var potValue = document.getElementById("pot");

    // Set the initial values for the pot and player's bet
    pokerGame.currentPot = 500;
    pokerGame.currentBet = 25;
```

After the initial values for the pot and bet have been set, they should be changed only by the player's actions during the course of the game. The pot value is displayed in the input box on the game table and can be changed only as the player places bets and then wins or loses a hand. The bet value can be changed only by changing the selected option in the Bet selection list box. You will add code to display the current value of the pot and to change the value of the bet based on the value stored in the Bet selection list box.

To display and set the values of the currentPot and currentBet properties:

▶ **1.** Directly below the code to set the initial values of the player's pot and bet, add the following code to display the initial value of the player's pot:

```
// Display the initial pot value in the game table
potValue.value = pokerGame.currentPot;
```

▶ **2.** Directly below this code, add the following code that changes the value of the current-Bet property whenever the selected option in the Bet selection list box changes:

```
// Change the bet value from the selection list
betSelection.onchange = function() {
    pokerGame.currentBet =
    parseInt(this.options[this.selectedIndex].value);
}
```

Note that you use the parseInt() method to store a numeric value rather than a text string in the currentBet property. Figure 11-9 highlights the added code.

Figure 11-9 — Code to display the currentPot and currentBet values

```
// Set the initial values for the pot and player's bet
pokerGame.currentPot = 500;
pokerGame.currentBet = 25;

// Display the initial pot value in the game table
potValue.value = pokerGame.currentPot;                       ← displays the initial
                                                                 pot value
sets the bet value to     // Change the bet value from the selection list
match the value of        betSelection.onchange = function() {
the selected option           pokerGame.currentBet = parseInt(this.options[this.selectedIndex].value);
                          }
```

When the Deal button is clicked, the player's bet should be subtracted from the pot using the placeBet() method of the pokerGame object, but only if the player has not attempted to bet more than the value of the current pot. You will add code to event handler for the Deal button to confirm that a valid bet has been made, and then reduce the value of the pot by the amount of the bet.

To control the player's action in setting the bet:

▶ **1.** Go to the anonymous function for the Deal button's onclick event, and then, at the top of the anonymous function, insert the following if statement to verify that the current bet doesn't exceed the value of the pot:

```
if (pokerGame.currentBet <= pokerGame.currentPot) {
```

▶ **2.** Indent the next five lines that enable and disable the game buttons.

▶ **3.** Directly after the line disabling the Bet selection list, insert the following code to reduce the value of the pot by the current bet amount or to display an alert if the current bet exceeds the value of the pot:

```
// Subtract the bet from the pot
pokerGame.placeBet();
potValue.value = pokerGame.currentPot;

} else {

    alert("Reduce the size of your bet");

}
```

Figure 11-10 highlights the revised code in the file.

Code to update the value of the player's pot **Figure 11-10**

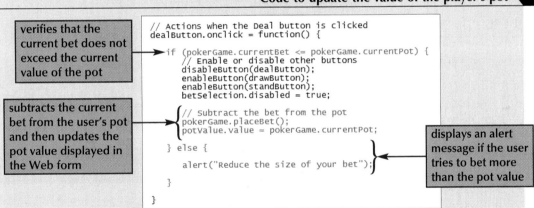

▶ **4.** Save the file, and then reload the **poker.htm** file in your Web browser.

▶ **5.** Verify that a value of **500** appears in the Pot ($) input box.

▶ **6.** Select **75** from the Your Bet ($) selection list, click the **Deal** button, and then verify that the pot value is reduced by the size of the bet and that the Bet selection list is disabled. See Figure 11-11.

Figure 11-11 ▶ Actions of the game buttons

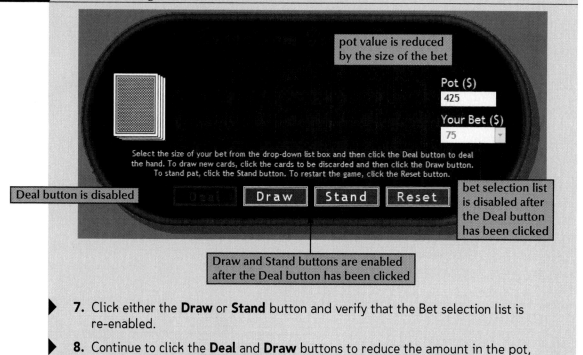

pot value is reduced
by the size of the bet

Pot ($)
425

Your Bet ($)
75

Select the size of your bet from the drop-down list box and then click the Deal button to deal
the hand. To draw new cards, click the cards to be discarded and then click the Draw button.
To stand pat, click the Stand button. To restart the game, click the Reset button.

Deal button is disabled

Deal   Draw   Stand   Reset

bet selection list
is disabled after
the Deal button
has been clicked

Draw and Stand buttons are enabled
after the Deal button has been clicked

▶ **7.** Click either the **Draw** or **Stand** button and verify that the Bet selection list is re-enabled.

▶ **8.** Continue to click the **Deal** and **Draw** buttons to reduce the amount in the pot, verifying that the browser displays an alert dialog box when you attempt to bet more than the current value of the pot.

You have completed your initial work on the poker game. In the next session, you'll add a poker deck and poker hand to the application and create custom objects for those items.

Review | **Session 11.1 Quick Check**

1. What is the result of running the following code?

```
showAlert();

function playPoker() {
   var msg = "Start Game";
   function showAlert() {
      alert(msg);
   }
}
```

2. What is the scope of a nested function?

3. What are the three types of objects supported by JavaScript?

4. Provide the code to create a custom object named pokerCard from the base JavaScript object.

5. Provide the code to create a custom object named pokerCard having a property named suit with a value of "Clubs" and a property named rank with a value of "King". Use the object literal form.

6. For the pokerCard object described in the previous question, provide the code to create a method named dropRank() that changes the rank value to "Queen".

7. What is the difference between an associative array and an indexed array?

8. How do you loop through the contents of an associative array?

Session 11.2

Creating an Object Class

In the previous session, you created a single instance of the pokerGame object. In this session, you will create objects for poker cards, poker hands, and poker decks. First, you will examine how to create the pokerCard objects. A poker deck contains 52 poker cards. To define the objects and properties of all these cards, you have to define a poker-Card object class.

Defining the Object Constructor

Object classes are defined by using the constructor function

```
function object() {
   this.prop1 = value1;
   this.prop2 = value2;
...
   this.method1 = function1;
   this.method2 = function2;
...
}
```

where *object* is the name of the object class; *prop1*, *prop2*, etc. are the properties associated with the object class; *value1*, *value2*, etc. are the default values for each property; *method1*, *method2*, etc. are the methods associated with the object class; and *function1*, *function2*, etc. are the functions applied with each method. Note that the `this` keyword is used in this context to refer to any object created with the object class.

A pokerCard object class could be defined using the constructor function

```
function pokerCard() {
   this.suit = "Club";
   this.rank = "King";
...
   this.showCard = function() {
      alert(this.rank + " of " + this.suit);
   }
}
```

with the properties of suit and rank used to store the suit and rank of the card, respectively, and the showCard() method used to display an alert box with the text of the suit and rank. Every object instantiated from this constructor function will have the default values "Club" and "King" for the suit and rank properties, respectively.

Of course, you don't want every card to be the King of Clubs, so the constructor function can also contain parameters. For example, the pokerCard object class can be created with the constructor

```
function pokerCard(suit, rank) {
   this.suit = suit;
   this.rank = rank;
...
   this.showCard = function() {
      alert(this.rank + " of " + this.suit);
   }
}
```

and the values specified for the suit and rank parameters automatically will be stored in the suit and rank properties, respectively.

> **Tip**
>
> An object class method can also reference a global function defined outside of the object class constructor.

Instantiating an Object from an Object Class

Instantiating an object from a custom class follows the same syntax that you used to create new objects from native JavaScript objects. The general form is

```
var newObject = new object();
```

where *newObject* is an instance of the object class and *object* is the name of the object class defined by the constructor function. Therefore, to create a specific instance from the pokerCard object class, you could enter the command

```
var myCard = new pokerCard("Spade", "Ace");
```

and JavaScript will create the myCard object with the value of myCard.suit equal to "Spades" and myCard.rank equal to "Ace".

Reference Window | Defining and Instantiating an Object Class

- To define a class of objects, enter the constructor function
  ```
  function object() {
      this.prop1 = value1;
      this.prop2 = value2;
  . . .
      this.method1 = function1;
      this.method2 = function2;
  . . .
  }
  ```
  where *object* is the name of the object class; *prop1*, *prop2*, etc. are the properties associated with the object class; *value1*, *value2*, etc. are the default values for each property; *method1*, *method2*, etc. are the methods associated with the object class; and *function1*, *function2*, etc. are the functions applied with each method.
- To instantiate an object from a custom class, use
  ```
  var newObject = new object();
  ```
  where *newObject* is an instance of the object class and *object* is the name of the object class defined by the constructor function.

You will add the pokerCard object class to the cards.js file.

To insert the pokerCard constructor:

▶ 1. If you took a break after the previous session, make sure the bdlibrary.js, cards.js, and poker.js files are open in your text editor, and poker.htm is open in your Web browser.

▶ 2. Return to the **cards.js** file in your text editor.

▶ 3. Scroll down to the pokerCard Object constructor section and insert the following code, as shown in Figure 11-12:

```
function pokerCard(suit, rank) {

    this.suit = suit; // Club, Diamond, Heart, or Spade
    this.rank = rank; // 2 through 10, Jack, Queen, King, or Ace

}
```

```
/*    The pokerCard Object constructor    */
function pokerCard(suit, rank) {

    this.suit = suit; // Club, Diamond, Heart, or Spade
    this.rank = rank; // 2 through 10, Jack, Queen, King, or Ace

}
```

Defining the pokerDeck Object

Next, you'll create a constructor for a poker deck object. A poker deck is essentially an array of poker cards. The constructor for the pokerDeck object is therefore:

```
function pokerDeck() {

  this.cards = new Array(52);

  var suits = new Array("Club", "Diamond", "Heart", "Spade");
  var ranks = new Array("2", "3", "4", "5", "6", "7",
                        "8", "9", "10", "Jack", "Queen",
                        "King", "Ace");

  var cardCount = 0;
  for (var i = 0; i < 4; i++) {
   for (var j = 0; j < 13; j++) {
      this.cards[cardCount] = new pokerCard(suits[i], ranks[j]);
      cardCount++;
   }
  }

}
```

Notice that the pokerDeck object has a single property named cards containing an indexed array of 52 items. The constructor then uses a for loop to populate the cards array with 52 pokerCard objects. The suit and rank of each card are determined from entries in the suits and ranks array. When the for loop is completed, the poker deck will have stored all of the cards from a standard deck sorted in suited order from Clubs through Spades and from the 2 through Ace within each suit.

Using the pokerDeck constructor, you can create an instance of a poker deck with the following command:

```
var myDeck = new pokerDeck();
```

Each card in the deck can be retrieved using the cards array property. For example, to retrieve the fifth card from the deck, you enter the expression

```
myDeck.cards[4]
```

which, in this case, retrieves the pokerCard object for the 6 of Clubs.

You will add the pokerDeck constructor to the cards.js file.

To create the pokerDeck constructor:

▶ **1.** Scroll to the pokerDeck Object constructor section and insert the following code, as shown in Figure 11-13:

```
function pokerDeck() {
```

```
        this.cards = new Array(52);
        var suits = new Array("Club", "Diamond", "Heart", "Spade");
        var ranks = new Array("2", "3", "4", "5", "6", "7",
                              "8", "9", "10", "Jack", "Queen",
                              "King", "Ace");

        // Generate the array of pokerCard objects
        var cardCount = 0;
        for (var i = 0; i < 4; i++) {
         for (var j = 0; j < 13; j++) {
            this.cards[cardCount] = new pokerCard(suits[i], ranks[j]);
            cardCount++;
         }
        }

      }
```

Figure 11-13   **The pokerDeck Object constructor**

```
/*    The pokerDeck Object constructor   */

function pokerDeck() {

   this.cards = new Array(52);
   var suits = new Array("Club", "Diamond", "Heart", "Spade");
   var ranks = new Array("2", "3", "4", "5", "6", "7",
                         "8", "9", "10", "Jack", "Queen",
                         "King", "Ace");

   // Generate the array of pokerCard objects
   var cardCount = 0;
   for (var i = 0; i < 4; i++) {
      for (var j = 0; j < 13; j++) {
         this.cards[cardCount] = new pokerCard(suits[i], ranks[j]);
         cardCount++;
      }
   }

}
```

cards property contains a collection of pokerCard objects

2. Save the cards.js file.

Almost all games require the deck to be randomly sorted. You will create a shuffle() method for the pokerDeck class that randomizes the order of the pokerCard objects in the cards array. Recall from Tutorial 3 that you can randomize an array by returning a random value to the Array's sort() method. The code for the shuffle() method is therefore:

```
this.shuffle = function() {
   this.cards.sort(function() {
      return 0.5 - Math.random();
   })
}
```

Note that this code uses a nested anonymous function to return the random value to the sort() method rather than calling an external function. You will add this method to the pokerDeck constructor.

To insert the shuffle() method:

1. Within the code for the pokerDeck constructor, insert the following code, as shown in Figure 11-14:

```
// Shuffle method to randomize the card order
this.shuffle = function() {
   this.cards.sort(function() {
      return 0.5 - Math.random();
```

```
        })
    }
```

The shuffle() method ◀ Figure 11-14

```
function pokerDeck() {
    this.cards = new Array(52);
    var suits = new Array("Club", "Diamond", "Heart", "Spade");
    var ranks = new Array("2", "3", "4", "5", "6", "7",
                          "8", "9", "10", "Jack", "Queen",
                          "King", "Ace");

    // Generate the array of pokerCard objects
    var cardCount = 0;
    for (var i = 0; i < 4; i++) {
        for (var j = 0; j < 13; j++) {
            this.cards[cardCount] = new pokerCard(suits[i], ranks[j]);
            cardCount++;
        }
    }

    // Shuffle method to randomize the card order
    this.shuffle = function() {
        this.cards.sort(function() {
            return 0.5 - Math.random();
        })
    }
}
```

> shuffle() method of the
> pokerDeck object class
> to shuffle the card order

▶ **2.** Save the cards.js file.

Now you can use the pokerDeck object class in your poker game application. You will add code to the playDrawPoker() function that creates an instance of the pokerDeck class and shuffles it at the start of play.

To create an instance of the pokerDeck object class:

▶ **1.** Return to the **poker.js** file in your text editor.

▶ **2.** Directly below the code to display the initial pot value, insert the following code to create a new shuffled deck of cards:

```
// Create a new deck of cards and shuffle it
var myDeck = new pokerDeck();
myDeck.shuffle();
```

▶ **3.** Add the following alert dialog box to confirm that your code for the pokerDeck object class is working correctly:

```
alert("The number of cards in my deck is " + myDeck.cards.length
+ ".\n" +
        "The first card is a " + myDeck.cards[0].rank + " of " +
        myDeck.cards[0].suit + "s.");
```

If your code is working correctly, the alert dialog box displays the number of cards in the deck (52), and the rank and suit of the first randomly sorted card. Figure 11-15 highlights the revised code in the file.

Code to create a new deck of shuffled cards ◀ Figure 11-15

```
// Display the initial pot value in the game table
potValue.value = pokerGame.currentPot;

// Create a new deck of cards and shuffle it
var myDeck = new pokerDeck();
myDeck.shuffle();

alert("The number of cards in my deck is " + myDeck.cards.length + ".\n" +
      "The first card is a " + myDeck.cards[0].rank + " of " +
      myDeck.cards[0].suit + "s.");
```

> creates a new
> shuffled deck

> alert dialog box to test
> the contents of myDeck

4. Save the file, and then reload **poker.htm** in your Web browser. The browser displays an alert dialog box that indicates the number of cards in the deck and the rank and suit of the first card. See Figure 11-16.

Figure 11-16 ▸ Alert dialog box displaying the deck length and contents of the first card

5. Click the **OK** button.
6. Repeat Steps 4 and 5 three times to reload the Web page, verifying that a different first card is indicated with each reload.
7. Return to the **poker.js** file in your text editor, and then delete the code you entered in Step 3 that displays the alert dialog box.
8. Save the poker.js file.

Defining the pokerHand Object

The final object class you will define is the pokerHand class. Like the pokerDeck class, the pokerHand class will contain an array of pokerCard objects. The constructor function is:

```
function pokerHand(handLength) {
   this.cards = new Array(handLength);
}
```

The constructor has a single parameter named handLength, which specifies the number of cards in the hand. You will add this constructor to the cards.js file.

To create the pokerHand constructor:

1. Return to the **cards.js** file in your text editor.
2. Within the "pokerHand Object" section, insert the following code, as shown in Figure 11-17:

```
function pokerHand(handLength) {

   this.cards = new Array(handLength);

}
```

Figure 11-17 ▸ The pokerHand object class

```
/*    The pokerHand Object constructor    */
function pokerHand(handLength) {
   this.cards = new Array(handLength);
}
```

Unlike with the pokerDeck constructor, the pokerHand constructor did not insert any card objects into the cards array. To place the cards in the array, you will add a new method to the pokerDeck constructor, one that removes cards from a poker deck and places them into a poker hand. The code for the dealTo() method is:

```
this.dealTo = function(pokerHand) {
   for (var i = 0; i < pokerHand.cards.length; i++) {
      pokerHand.cards[i] = this.cards.shift();
   }
}
```

The dealTo() method has a single parameter, pokerHand, which references the pokerHand object that will receive the cards. The code then loops through the array of cards in the poker deck and uses the shift() method to remove the first item from the array and place it in the cards array of the poker hand. As this code runs, the size of the deck is reduced by the number of cards dealt into the poker hand. This ability to have program code mimic the actions of real-world objects is one attraction of object-based programming.

To create the dealTo() method:

1. Scroll up to the constructor function for the pokerDeck object class, and then insert the following code, as shown in Figure 11-18:

```
// dealTo method to deal cards from the deck into a hand
this.dealTo = function(pokerHand) {
   for (var i = 0; i < pokerHand.cards.length; i++) {
      pokerHand.cards[i] = this.cards.shift();
   }
}
```

The dealTo() method of the pokerDeck class | **Figure 11-18**

```
function pokerDeck() {

   this.cards = new Array(52);
   var suits = new Array("Club", "Diamond", "Heart", "Spade");
   var ranks = new Array("2", "3", "4", "5", "6", "7",
                         "8", "9", "10", "Jack", "Queen",
                         "King", "Ace");

   // Generate the array of pokerCard objects
   var cardCount = 0;
   for (var i = 0; i < 4; i++) {
      for (var j = 0; j < 13; j++) {
         this.cards[cardCount] = new pokerCard(suits[i], ranks[j]);
         cardCount++;
      }
   }

   // Shuffle method to randomize the card order
   this.shuffle = function() {
      this.cards.sort(function() {
         return 0.5 - Math.random();
      })
   }

   // dealTo method to deal cards from the deck into a hand
   this.dealTo = function(pokerHand) {
      for (var i = 0; i < pokerHand.cards.length; i++) {
         pokerHand.cards[i] = this.cards.shift();
      }
   }

}
```

cards are removed from the poker deck and placed into a poker hand

2. Save the file.

Next, you will create an instance of a pokerHand object for your poker game, and then deal cards into that hand when the Deal button is clicked. Because the deck size is reduced every time you deal a hand from the poker deck, you'll verify that the deck contains at least 10 cards before dealing the new hand. If the deck contains fewer than 10 cards, you'll create a newly shuffled deck and deal the hand from that deck.

To add a poker hand to the poker game page:

▶ **1.** Return to the **poker.js** file in your text editor.

▶ **2.** Directly below the command in the playDrawPoker() function that shuffles the poker deck, insert the following code to create an instance of a pokerHand object, as shown in Figure 11-19:

```
// Define a poker hand for the game
var myHand = new pokerHand(5);
```

Figure 11-19 | Code to create a pokerHand object

```
// Display the initial pot value in the game table
potValue.value = pokerGame.currentPot;

// Create a new deck of cards and shuffle it
var myDeck = new pokerDeck();
myDeck.shuffle();

// Define a poker hand for the game
var myHand = new pokerHand(5);
```

creates an instance of the pokerHand object containing five cards

▶ **3.** Scroll down to the onclick event handler for the Deal button, and then insert the following code to get a new deck if too few cards remain in the current deck, as shown in Figure 11-20:

```
// Get a new deck if there are less than 10 cards in the current deck
if (myDeck.cards.length < 10) {
   myDeck = new pokerDeck();
   myDeck.shuffle();
}

// Deal the cards from my deck to my hand
myDeck.dealTo(myHand);
```

Figure 11-20 | Code to deal a poker hand

```
// Actions when the Deal button is clicked
dealButton.onclick = function() {

   if (pokerGame.currentBet <= pokerGame.currentPot) {
      // Enable or disable other buttons
      disableButton(dealButton);
      enableButton(drawButton);
      enableButton(standButton);
      betSelection.disabled = true;

      // Subtract the bet from the pot
      pokerGame.placeBet();
      potValue.value = pokerGame.currentPot;

      // Get a new deck if there are less than 10 cards in the current deck
      if (myDeck.cards.length < 10) {
         myDeck = new pokerDeck();
         myDeck.shuffle();
      }

      // Deal the cards from my deck to my hand
      myDeck.dealTo(myHand);

   } else {

      alert("Reduce the size of your bet");

   }
}
```

▶ **4.** Save the file. You have entered a lot of code and should verify that you have not made any typing mistakes.

▶ **5.** Reopen the **poker.htm** file in your Web browser, and then click the **Deal** button to verify that the browser does not report any program errors.

Working with Object Prototypes

The application doesn't yet show the actual cards. Bob stored image files for every card in the deck under the filename *suitrank*.png, where *suit* is the first letter of the suit in lowercase and *rank* is the first letter of the rank, also in lowercase. For example, the 2 of Clubs image is stored in the c2.png image file, the king of hearts image is stored in the hk.png file, and so forth.

You will add the imageSrc() method to the pokerCard constructor to associate each pokerCard object with an image file. The code for the method is:

```
this.imageSrc = function() {
   var fileName = this.suit.substring(0,1);

   if (this.rank == "10") fileName += "10"
   else fileName += this.rank.substring(0,1);

   fileName += ".png";
   return fileName.toLowerCase();
}
```

The function uses the substring(0,1) method to extract the first letter of the suit and rank (other than when rank = "10"), and then uses the toLowerCase() method to change the filename to lowercase letters before returning the filename text. So, for a card such as the King of Hearts, the imageSrc() function returns the text string, hk.png, the 10 of Diamonds returns the text string d10.png, and so on.

You could add this code to the constructor function for the pokerCard object class, but there are 52 instances of the pokerCard object in myDeck and each instance will store the code of the imageSrc() method. Rather than having the same code duplicated 52 times, a much more memory-efficient method is to have one copy of the code for the imageSrc() method that all instances of the pokerCard object could access. You can do that with the prototype property.

The prototype Property

When JavaScript encounters the `new` keyword in a command, it locates the corresponding constructor function and instantiates an object. However, because almost everything in JavaScript is an object, the constructor function itself is an object with its own collection of properties and methods. One property of any constructor is the **prototype** property, which stores an object that acts as a template for all new object instances created by the constructor. Prototypes are referenced using the expression

```
object.prototype
```

where *object* is the name of the constructor function. Using the prototype property, you can make new properties and methods available to all objects instantiated from the constructor function. To add a new property to a constructor, run the command

```
object.prototype.property = value;
```

where *property* is the name of the property and *value* is the default value. To add a new method, run

```
object.prototype.method = function;
```

where *method* is the name of the new method and *function* is the function object associated with the method. Any object created from the constructor function automatically supports these new properties and methods, but JavaScript needs to store the code only once in memory rather than creating duplicates for every object instance, which makes the program faster and more memory efficient.

Reference Window | **Working with Object Prototypes**

- To reference a prototype, use the expression
  ```
  object.prototype
  ```
  where *object* is the name of the constructor function.
- To apply a property to an object prototype, use
  ```
  object.prototype.property = value;
  ```
  where *property* is the name of the property and *value* is the default value.
- To apply a method to an object prototype, use
  ```
  object.prototype.method = function;
  ```
  where *method* is the name of the new method and *function* is the function object associated with the method.

To add the imageSrc() method to the pokerCard prototype, you run the commands

```
pokerCard.prototype.imageSrc = function() {
   var fileName = this.suit.substring(0,1);

   if (this.rank == "10") fileName += "10"
   else fileName += this.rank.substring(0,1);

   fileName += ".png";
   return fileName.toLowerCase();
}
```

and every object in the pokerCard class will be able to access this method. You will add this code to the cards.js file.

To add the imageSrc() method to the pokerCard prototype:

1. Return to the **cards.js** file in your text editor.

2. Directly below the pokerCard constructor function, insert the following code, as shown in Figure 11-21:

```
/* The imageSrc() method stores the image filename
   in the form "sr.png" where "s" is the
   first letter of the card suit and "r" is the
   first letter of the card rank */

pokerCard.prototype.imageSrc = function() {
   var fileName = this.suit.substring(0,1);

   if (this.rank == "10") fileName += "10"
   else fileName += this.rank.substring(0,1);

   fileName += ".png";
   return fileName.toLowerCase();
}
```

The imgSrc() method added to the pokerCard prototype ◄ Figure 11-21

```
/*    The pokerCard object constructor    */

function pokerCard(suit, rank) {

    this.suit = suit; // Club, Diamond, Heart, or Spade
    this.rank = rank; // 2 through 10, Jack, Queen, King, or Ace

}

/* The imageSrc() method stores the image filename
   in the form "sr.png" where "s" is the
   first letter of the card suit and "r" is the
   first letter of the card rank */

pokerCard.prototype.imageSrc = function() {
    var fileName = this.suit.substring(0,1);

    if (this.rank == "10") fileName += "10"
    else fileName += this.rank.substring(0,1);

    fileName += ".png";
    return fileName.toLowerCase();
}
```

applies the imgSrc() method to the pokerCard prototype

3. Save the file.

You can now use the imgSrc() method to display images on the poker Web page. Bob has set up the page so that the cards are displayed in five inline images with the class name pokerCard. First, you will create an object collection that references all of the poker card image tags in the document.

To create the collection of card images:

1. Return to the **poker.js** file in your text editor.

2. Scroll to the top of the playDrawPoker() function, and then insert the following code to populate the array of pokerCard inline image tags, as shown in Figure 11-22:

```
// Reference the collection of card images
var cardImages = new Array();
var allImages = document.getElementsByTagName("img");
for (var i = 0; i < allImages.length; i++) {
   if (allImages[i].className == "pokerCard")
      cardImages.push(allImages[i]);
}
```

Code to create the array of card images ◄ Figure 11-22

```
function playDrawPoker() {

    var dealButton = document.getElementById("dealB");
    var drawButton = document.getElementById("drawB");
    var standButton = document.getElementById("standB");
    var resetButton = document.getElementById("resetB");
    var handValueText = document.getElementById("handvalue");
    var betSelection = document.getElementById("bet");
    var potValue = document.getElementById("pot");

    // Reference the collection of card images
    var cardImages = new Array();
    var allImages = document.getElementsByTagName("img");
    for (var i = 0; i < allImages.length; i++) {
       if (allImages[i].className == "pokerCard") cardImages.push(allImages[i]);
    }
```

the cardImages array references the card images in the Web page

When the page initially loads, those inline images display a transparent GIF as a placeholder because no cards have yet been dealt. Upon dealing a new hand, the program should change the source of these images to the image files of each dealt card. You will add a command to the Deal button's onclick event handler to change the src attribute of the card images to the filename returned by the imgSrc() method.

To display the poker card images:

▶ 1. Scroll down to the Deal button's onclick event handler, and then insert the following code, as shown in Figure 11-23:

```
// Display the images for each card in the hand
    for (var i = 0; i < cardImages.length; i++) {
        cardImages[i].src = myHand.cards[i].imageSrc();
}
```

Figure 11-23 ▶ **Code to display the image of each card in the hand**

```
// Deal the cards from my deck to my hand
myDeck.dealTo(myHand, 5);

// Display the images for each card in the hand
for (var i = 0; i < cardImages.length; i++) {
    cardImages[i].src = myHand.cards[i].imageSrc();
}
```

the src property matches the file returned by the imageSrc() method for each card

▶ 2. Save the file.

▶ 3. Reload **poker.htm** in your Web browser, and then click the **Deal** button. Images of the five cards in the current hand are shown on the Web page. See Figure 11-24.

Figure 11-24 ▶ **Cards from the current hand**

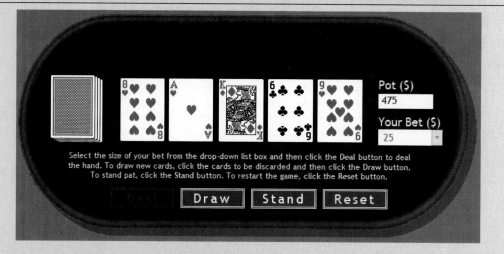

▶ 4. Click the **Draw** button, and then click the **Deal** button several times, verifying that a new hand appears on the poker table with each deal.

Prototypes and Native Objects

The prototype property also can be used with native JavaScript objects such as Array, Date, and String. This allows you to extend those JavaScript objects by creating customized properties and methods for them. For example, to make the shuffle method available to any JavaScript array, you can apply the shuffle method to the Array prototype by using the following code:

```
Array.prototype.shuffle = function() {
   this.sort(function() {
      return 0.5 - Math.random();
   })
}
```

After this code is applied to the Array prototype, any array will support the shuffle() method, as demonstrated by the following code:

```
var games = new Array("Poker", "Chess", "Go", "Checkers");
games.shuffle();
```

After the code is run, the items in the games array will be sorted in random order.

Bob wants you to start creating a library of customized methods for native JavaScript objects that can be shared with other programmers at the company. Because array sorting is a common programming task, you will create a new method for Array objects named numericSort() that sorts the contents of the Array in either ascending or descending numeric order. The code for the numericSort() method is:

```
Array.prototype.numericSort = function(ascending) {

   if (ascending) this.sort(function(a,b) {return a - b})
   else this.sort(function(a,b) {return b - a})
}
```

Tip

Use caution and restraint when adding new custom properties and methods to native objects because poorly formed code can "break" the object, making the code unusable for all native objects of that class.

The numericSort() method has a single parameter named ascending. If ascending is true, the array is sorted in ascending numeric order; if ascending is false, the array is sorted in descending numeric order. As with the shuffle() method, sorting in numeric order requires the sort() method to call a function that indicates how to swap adjacent items in the array. (See Tutorial 3 for a discussion of numeric sorting.)

You will add the code for the numericSort() method to the bdlibrary.js file in which Bob has placed other customized functions.

To create the numericSort() Array method:

▶ 1. Return to the **bdlibrary.js** file in your text editor.

▶ 2. Scroll to the bottom of the file, and then insert the following code, as shown in Figure 11-25:

```
/* Custom method to sort arrays in numeric order.
   If ascending is true, sort in ascending order,
   if ascending is false, sort in descending order */

Array.prototype.numericSort = function(ascending) {

   if (ascending) this.sort(function(a,b) {return a - b})
   else this.sort(function(a,b) {return b - a})

}
```

Figure 11-25 ▷ **The numericSort() method added to the Array object**

```
/* Add new code below */

/* Custom method to sort arrays in numeric order.
   If ascending is true, sort in ascending order,
   if ascending is false, sort in descending order */

Array.prototype.numericSort = function(ascending) {

   if (ascending) this.sort(function(a,b) {return a - b})
   else this.sort(function(a,b) {return b - a})

}
```

▶ **3.** Save the file.

InSight | **Understanding Public, Private, and Privileged Methods**

In developing methods for custom objects, you need to decide whether those methods are available to the public or available for use only within the constructor function itself. Any method that is publically available is a **public method** and includes all of the methods such as the imgSrc() method you added to the pokerCard prototype earlier in this session.

A **private method** is a method that is accessible only within the object itself and not outside of that object. The following code shows an example of a private method used within the pokerCard constructor:

```
function pokerCard() {

   function getFilename() {
     var fileName = this.suit.substring(0,1);
     if (this.rank == "10") fileName += "10"
        else fileName += this.rank.substring(0,1);
     return fileName + ".png";
   }

   this.imageSrc() = function() {
      return getFilename().toLowerCase();
   }

}
```

The getFilename() function nested within the imageSrc() method is an example of a private method because its scope is limited to the constructor function and is not accessible to any code outside of that function. Private methods are one way of ensuring that the functions and properties you create for a custom object do not conflict with code that other developers might create for your application.

A **privileged method** is a method that is able to access private variables and methods, but is itself accessible to the public. In the code sample above, the imgSrc() function is public because it is available to the public, but it is also privileged because it relies on the value returned by calling the private getFilename() function.

Private and privileged methods can be made only within the constructor function itself. Public methods can be made at any time using the object's prototype. Knowing which methods are public, private, and privileged is important to ensure that your code does not conflict with code existing elsewhere in your application.

Creating Prototypal Inheritance

In the previous session, you learned that all native JavaScript objects are derived from a single base object. In fact, any object can act as a base for new object classes through the use of prototypes. As diagrammed in Figure 11-26, an object class named Person can be used as a base for an object class named Employee, which in turn acts as a base for another object class named Staff. This hierarchy of object classes creates a **prototype chain**, ranging from the highest class in the chain, known as the **super class**, down to lower classes, or **sub classes**. Each of the properties and methods of the Person class is accessible to the Employee class and then likewise to the Staff class in a process known as **prototypal inheritance**.

Prototypal inheritance | Figure 11-26

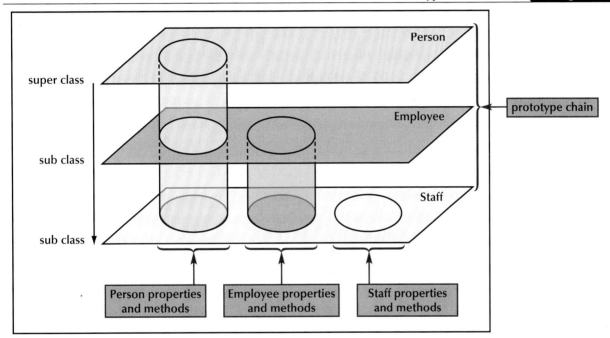

To create a prototype chain, you specify each object prototype as an instance of the object above it in the class hierarchy. To create the prototype chain shown in Figure 11-26, you first define the constructor functions for the Person, Employee, and Staff objects, as follows:

```
function Person(fName, lName) {
    this.firstName = fName;
    this.lastName = lName;
    this.fullName = function() {
        return this.lastName + ", " + this.firstName;
    }
}

function Employee(id) {
    this.empID = id;
}

function Staff(id) {
    this.staffID = id;
}
```

Next, you define the relationship between these object classes because every staff member is an employee and every employee is a person. You do this by defining the Staff and Employee prototypes as instances of a higher order object. The code that establishes the relationship between Staff, Employee, and Person is therefore:

```
Employee.prototype = new Person();
Staff.prototype = new Employee();
```

Order is important when entering the code that defines the prototype chain. You must start at the top of the hierarchy and move down to the lower sub classes. When JavaScript encounters code that references an object property or method, it attempts to resolve the code in the following order:

Tip

You can test whether an object supports a property or method by evaluating the Boolean value of the expression `"text" in object`, where *text* is the name of the property or method and *object* is the object.

1. Determine whether the property or method exists in the object instance. If not, then
2. Determine whether the property or method exists in the object prototype. If not, then
3. If the prototype is an instance of another object, determine whether the property and method exist on that object.
4. Continue moving up the prototype chain until the property or method is found or the end of the chain is reached.

Because the Staff prototype is an instance of the Employee prototype, which itself is an instance of the Person object, any instances of the Staff object will support any property method defined along that chain. For example, running the code

```
var myStaff = new Staff("WB002");
myStaff.firstName = "Bob";
myStaff.lastName = "Voiklund";

alert(myStaff.fullName());
```

displays an alert dialog box with the text "Voiklund, Bob" even though the fullName method was defined for the Person object.

Creating inheritance by instantiating a prototype from an object class is only one way of establishing relationships between objects. Other approaches exist to create more complex and powerful data structures; however, the methods to create these structures are beyond the scope of this tutorial.

You have created the custom objects for your poker game application. In the next session, you will create additional custom properties and methods for your objects that will calculate the value of the player's poker hand.

Review | **Session 11.2 Quick Check**

1. Provide the code to create an object class named Company containing a property named compID and a method named showID() that displays an alert box containing the company ID.
2. Provide code that instantiates the Company object class in the previous question and sets the compID property to the text string bdonline.
3. Revise your code in Questions 1 and 2 to allow for compID to be passed as a parameter to the Company object class.
4. Without revising the Company constructor function, supply code to add a new property named establishDate to the Company object class. Set its default value to "January 18, 2012".
5. Add a new method named showDate() to the Company object class that displays the value of the establishDate property in an alert dialog box.

6. Specify the code to create an object class named webCompany that inherits all of the properties and methods of the Company object class.

7. Provide code to add a new method named lastItem() for all JavaScript arrays to display the value of the last item in the array.

Session 11.3

Adding a Property to a Prototype

In the previous session, you completed the Deal button in Bob's poker game. Your next task is to program the actions of the Draw button. To draw new cards from the poker deck, the code has to mark the cards to be removed and then replace marked cards with new cards from the deck. You can mark the cards to be removed by adding the discard property to the pokerCard object class, setting the property's initial value to false. You will add this property now.

To add the discard property to the pokerCard class:

▶ 1. If you took a break after the previous session, make sure the bdlibrary.js, cards.js, and poker.js files are open in your text editor, and poker.htm is open in your Web browser.

▶ 2. Return to the **cards.js** file in your text editor.

▶ 3. Scroll down to the section for the pokerCard object class, and then insert the following code, as shown in Figure 11-27:

```
/* The discard property marks cards to be replaced
   by cards in the poker deck */

pokerCard.prototype.discard = false;
```

The discard property added to the pokerCard prototype **◀ Figure 11-27**

```
pokerCard.prototype.imageSrc = function() {
    var fileName = this.suit.substring(0,1);

    if (this.rank == "10") fileName += "10"
    else fileName += this.rank.substring(0,1);

    fileName += ".png";
    return fileName.toLowerCase();
}
/* The discard property marks cards to be replaced
   by cards in the poker deck */

    pokerCard.prototype.discard = false;
```

To replace a card with a new card from the deck, you'll add the following replaceFromDeck() method to the pokerDeck object class:

```
pokerCard.prototype.replaceFromDeck = function(pokerDeck) {
   this.rank = pokerDeck.cards[0].rank;
   this.suit = pokerDeck.cards[0].suit;
   pokerDeck.cards.shift(); // Delete first card from deck
}
```

The replaceFromDeck() method changes the rank and suit properties of the card to match the first card in the poker deck. It then uses the shift() method to remove the first card from the cards array in the deck. You will add this method to the poker.js file.

To add the replaceFromDeck() method to the pokerCard class:

▶ **1.** Below the code you just inserted in the cards.js file, insert the following method, as shown in Figure 11-28:

```
/* The replaceFromDeck() method replaces the card with
   the first card from the pokerDeck */

pokerCard.prototype.replaceFromDeck = function(pokerDeck) {
    this.rank = pokerDeck.cards[0].rank;
    this.suit = pokerDeck.cards[0].suit;
    pokerDeck.cards.shift(); // Delete first card from deck
}
```

Figure 11-28	The replaceFromDeck() method

```
/* The discard property marks cards to be replaced
   by cards in the poker deck */

pokerCard.prototype.discard = false;

/* The replaceFromDeck() method replaces the card with
   the first card from the pokerDeck */

pokerCard.prototype.replaceFromDeck = function(pokerDeck) {
    this.rank = pokerDeck.cards[0].rank;
    this.suit = pokerDeck.cards[0].suit;
    pokerDeck.cards.shift(); // Delete first card from deck
}
```

changes the card properties to match the first card in the deck and then removes the first card from the deck

▶ **2.** Save the cards.js file.

Players choose which cards to discard by clicking the card images on the poker table. When the card image is clicked, two things happen: (1) the card is turned facedown showing the back of the card, and (2) the discard property of the card is changed to true. If the card image is clicked again, then: (1) the card is turned faceup showing the card image, and (2) the discard property is changed to false. The code to create onclick event handlers for all of the card images is therefore:

```
for (var i = 0; i < cardImages.length; i++) {

    cardImages[i].index = i;

    cardImages[i].onclick = function() {
        if (myHand.cards[this.index].discard) {
            myHand.cards[this.index].discard = false;
            this.src = myHand.cards[this.index].imageSrc();
        } else {
            myHand.cards[this.index].discard = true;
            this.src = "cardback.png";
        }
    }

}
```

The code loops through each card image and adds a custom index property to help identify which card is being clicked. When a card is clicked, the discard property of the corresponding card in the hand is evaluated. If discard is true, the discard value is changed to false and the image of the card is displayed; if discard is false, the discard value is changed to true and an image of the back of the card is displayed. You will add this code to the poker.js file, and then test it in your Web browser.

To change the discard status and card image:

▶ 1. Return to the **poker.js** file in your text editor.

▶ 2. Below the enableButton() function, insert the following code, as shown in Figure 11-29:

```
// Actions when a card image is clicked
for (var i = 0; i < cardImages.length; i++) {

    cardImages[i].index = i;

    cardImages[i].onclick = function() {
        if (myHand.cards[this.index].discard) {
            myHand.cards[this.index].discard = false;
            this.src = myHand.cards[this.index].imageSrc();
        } else {
            myHand.cards[this.index].discard = true;
            this.src = "cardback.png";
        }
    }
}
```

An onclick event handler added to the card images ◀ Figure 11-29

records the card position with the index property

toggles the card image and discards the value when the image is clicked

```
// Function to enable and display a form button
function enableButton(button) {
    button.disabled = false;
    setOpacity(button, 100);
}

// Actions when a card image is clicked
for (var i = 0; i < cardImages.length; i++) {

    cardImages[i].index = i;

    cardImages[i].onclick = function() {
        if (myHand.cards[this.index].discard) {
            myHand.cards[this.index].discard = false;
            this.src = myHand.cards[this.index].imageSrc();
        } else {
            myHand.cards[this.index].discard = true;
            this.src = "cardback.png";
        }
    }
}
```

▶ 3. Save the poker.js file, and then reload **poker.htm** in your Web browser.

▶ 4. Click the **Deal** button to deal a hand, and then click the card images, verifying that each image toggles between the card face and the card back. See Figure 11-30.

Figure 11-30	Cards selected to be discarded

After a player has selected the cards to be discarded, he or she clicks the Draw button. When the Draw button is clicked, the browser should go through the array of cards in the current hand and replace any cards marked to be discarded with a card from the deck. After the card has been replaced, the discard property should be returned to false and the card image should be updated on the poker table. You will add code to replace the card and card image to the onclick event handler for the Draw button.

To draw new cards from the deck:

▶ **1.** Return to the **poker.js** file in your text editor.

▶ **2.** Scroll down to the onclick event handler for the Draw button, and then insert the following code, as shown in Figure 11-31:

```javascript
// Replace cards marked to be discarded with cards from myDeck
for (var i = 0; i < myHand.cards.length; i++) {

    if (myHand.cards[i].discard) {
       myHand.cards[i].replaceFromDeck(myDeck);
       myHand.cards[i].discard = false;
       cardImages[i].src = myHand.cards[i].imageSrc();
    }

}
```

Figure 11-31	Code to replace marked cards with cards from the deck

```javascript
// Actions when the Draw button is clicked
drawButton.onclick = function() {

    // Enable or disable other buttons
    enableButton(dealButton);
    disableButton(drawButton);
    disableButton(standButton);
    betSelection.disabled = false;

    // Replace cards marked to be discarded with cards from myDeck
    for (var i = 0; i < myHand.cards.length; i++) {

        if (myHand.cards[i].discard) {
           myHand.cards[i].replaceFromDeck(myDeck);
           myHand.cards[i].discard = false;
           cardImages[i].src = myHand.cards[i].imageSrc();
        }

    }

}
```

replaces marked cards with a new card from the deck and updates the card image

▶ **3.** Save the file, and then reload **poker.htm** in your Web browser.

▶ **4.** Click the **Deal** button to deal a hand, click the card images to be discarded, and then click the **Draw** button to draw new cards from the deck. See Figure 11-32.

New cards being drawn from the deck ◀ Figure 11-32

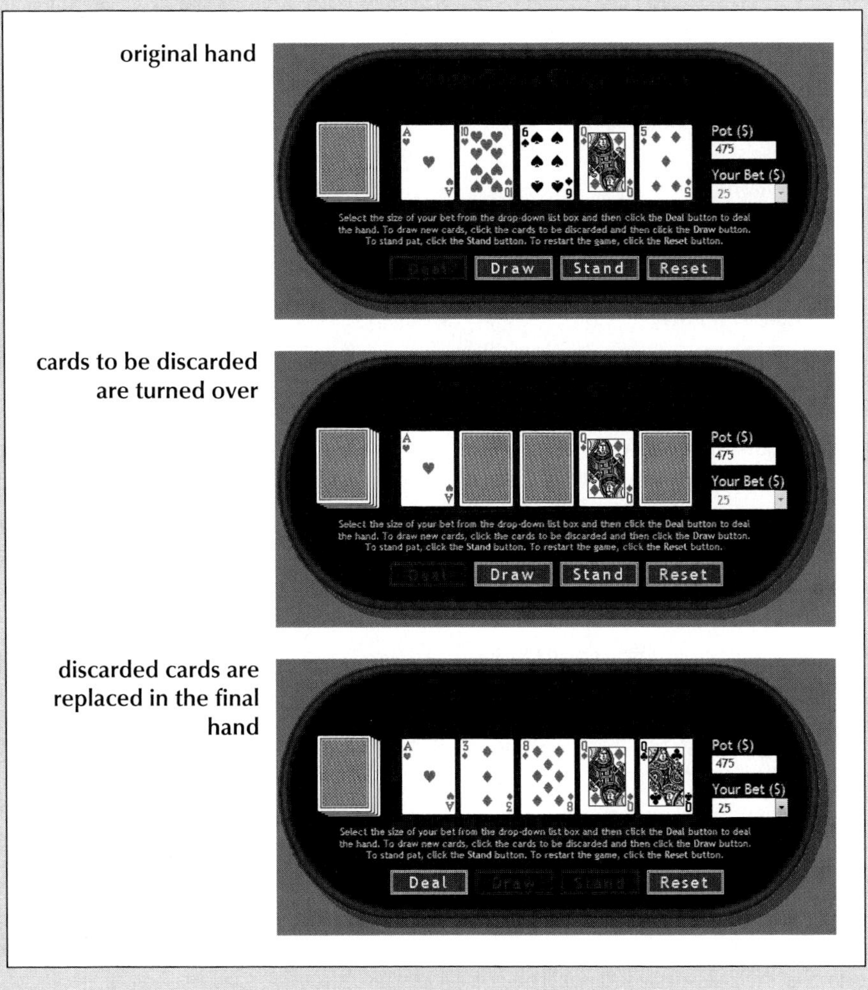

original hand

cards to be discarded are turned over

discarded cards are replaced in the final hand

Using the properties and methods of the pokerCard object, you can now discard old cards and draw new ones. The only task that remains before you have a fully functioning poker game is to evaluate the final hand and determine how much it is worth.

Tip

A custom property also can store a document element using the expression *object*.property = document. createElement- (*elem*) where *elem* is an element from the document object model.

One common source of error when working with custom methods and nested functions is failure to keep track of the changing context of the `this` keyword. Remember that the `this` keyword always refers to the current object, which is usually the object that initiated the function or method. Consider the following code:

```
var object1 = new Object();
var object2 = new Object();
object1.name = "Smith";
object2.name = "Jones";

object1.showInfo = function() {
    alert(this.name);
    function(object2) {
       alert(this.name);
    }
}
```

The command alert(this.name) is used twice in the showInfo() method. The first time, the `this` keyword refers to object1. The second time, it refers to object2 because object2 is the object that initiates the showMore() method. In more complex code involving several layers of nested functions, it is easy to lose track of the context of the `this` keyword.

One way to avoid confusion is to always store the value of the `this` keyword in a variable so that it can be easily referenced in all of the nested functions. For example, in the following code, the top-level meaning of the `this` keyword is stored in the topObject variable, which can then be referenced within the showAgain() function:

```
object1.showInfo = function() {
    var topObject = this;
    alert(topObject.name);
    object2.showAgain = function() {
       alert(this.name);
       alert(topObject.name);
    }
}
```

A good rule of thumb is to limit your use of the `this` keyword for non-nested functions or for situations where the context of the `this` keyword is completely clear to anyone studying your code.

Developing More Custom Properties and Methods

In most card games, every card has a numeric value associated with it that indicates its strength over other cards in the deck. For draw poker, Jacks have a value of 11, Queens have a value of 12, Kings have a value of 13, and number cards have a value that matches their numeric rank. Aces can have a value of either 1 or 14; but to simplify your code, you will assume that Aces can only have a value of 14. You can assign these values to each poker card using the following value() method:

```
pokerCard.prototype.value = function() {
    switch (this.rank) {
        case "Jack": return 11;
        case "Queen": return 12;
        case "King": return 13;
        case "Ace": return 14;
```

```
      default: return parseInt(this.rank);
   }
}
```

Note that for non-face cards and non-Aces, you use the parseInt() method to convert the text of the card's rank to a numeric value. You will add the value() method of the poker-Card prototype in the cards.js file.

To create the value() method of the pokerCard object:

▶ **1.** Return to the **cards.js** file in your text editor.

▶ **2.** Below the code for the replaceFromDeck() method, insert the following code, as shown in Figure 11-33:

```
/* The value() method returns the numeric rank of the
   card. Aces are assumed only to be 14 */

pokerCard.prototype.value = function() {
   switch (this.rank) {
      case "Jack": return 11;
      case "Queen": return 12;
      case "King": return 13;
      case "Ace": return 14;
      default: return parseInt(this.rank);
   }
}
```

Code to calculate the numeric rank of each card ◀ **Figure 11-33**

```
pokerCard.prototype.replaceFromDeck = function(pokerDeck) {
   this.rank = pokerDeck.cards[0].rank;
   this.suit = pokerDeck.cards[0].suit;
   pokerDeck.cards.shift(); // Delete first card from deck
}

/* The value() method returns the numeric rank of the
   card. Aces are assumed only to be 14 */

pokerCard.prototype.value = function() {
   switch (this.rank) {
      case "Jack": return 11;
      case "Queen": return 12;
      case "King": return 13;
      case "Ace": return 14;
      default: return parseInt(this.rank);
   }
}
```

Jacks have a value of 11, Queens 12, Kings 13, Aces 14; the remaining cards have their numeric rank

▶ **3.** Save the cards.js file.

Using the apply() and call() Methods

Now that you have a method that calculates the numeric value of each card, you need a method that returns the maximum value or high card found within a hand. One way of writing this method is to loop through the contents of the cards array, keeping track of the current maximum card value. At the conclusion of the for loop, the latest maximum value will be the maximum value for all cards in the hand.

JavaScript also has the Math object, which already supports a max() method that returns the maximum from a set of values. You can apply this method to the contents of an array by using the apply() and call() methods.

The apply() and call() methods are used to apply a function to an object. However, because methods are just functions associated with objects, the apply() and call() methods also allow you to apply a method defined for one object to a different object. The syntax of the apply() method is

```
function.apply(thisObj, argArray)
```

where *function* is a reference to a function, *thisObj* is the object that receives the actions of the function, and *argArray* is an array of argument values sent to the function. Both the *thisObj* and *argArray* parameters are optional. If the *thisObj* parameter is excluded, *function* will be applied to the currently selected object.

For example, in the following code, the showRank() method is defined for the pokerCard object class, but it could be applied to any object that supports the rank property:

```
function pokerCard(rank) {
    this.rank = rank;
    this.showRank = function() {
        alert(this.rank);
    }
}

function Soldier(rank) {
    this.rank = rank;
}

var newCard = new pokerCard("Ace");
var newSoldier = new Soldier("Captain");

myCard.showRank.apply(newSoldier);
```

In this case, the Soldier object class "adopts" the showRank() method to display the value of its rank property. The result of this code will be an alert dialog box showing the text "Captain". Note that no values are specified for the *thisArg* parameter.

The call() method is similar to the apply() method, having the syntax

```
function.call(thisObj, arg1, arg2, arg3, ...)
```

where *arg1*, *arg2*, *arg3*, etc. is a comma-separated list of parameter values for *function*. Therefore, you can also run the showRank() method with the following command:

```
myCard.showRank.call(newSoldier);
```

Whether you use the apply() or call() method is often a matter of personal preference. For this application, you will use the apply() method to apply the Math object's max() method to any Array object containing numeric data. You will modify the Array prototype as follows:

```
Array.prototype.max = function() {
    return Math.max.apply(this, this);
}
```

Notice that the apply() method has two parameter values, both using the `this` keyword. The first `this` keyword references the Array object itself; the second `this` keyword references the contents of the array, sending those array values as arguments to the Math object's max() method. The result is that JavaScript returns the maximum value of the values in the array. Be aware that the max() method will not work with any array. If the array contains non-numeric values or is sparse with missing or undefined values, the max() method will return a value of undefined.

Applying and Calling a Function | Reference Window

- To apply a function or method to an object, use the apply() method

    `function.apply(thisObj, argArray)`

    where *function* is a reference to a function, *thisObj* is the object that receives the actions of the function, and *argArray* is an array of argument values sent to the function.
- To call a function or method for use with an object, run

    `function.call(thisObj, arg1, arg2, arg3, ...)`

    where *arg1*, *arg2*, *arg3*, etc. is a comma-separated list of parameter values for *function*.

You will add the max() method to the Array prototype, inserting the code in the bdlibrary.js file.

To apply the max() method to any array:

▶ **1.** Return to the **bdlibrary.js** file in your text editor.

▶ **2.** At the bottom of the file, insert the following code, as shown in Figure 11-34:

```
/* Custom method to return the maximum value from
   any Array object */

Array.prototype.max = function() {
   return Math.max.apply(this, this);
}
```

The max() method added to any array ◀ **Figure 11-34**

```
Array.prototype.numericSort = function(ascending) {

   if (ascending) this.sort(function(a,b) {return a - b})
   else this.sort(function(a,b) {return b - a})

}
/* Custom method to return the maximum value from
   any Array object */
Array.prototype.max = function() {
   return Math.max.apply(this, this);
}
```

applies the max method from the Math object to any Array object

▶ **3.** Save the bdlibrary.js file.

Now that you have added the max() method to any array containing numeric values, you will use it along with the value() method to create a function that returns the maximum valued card from any poker hand. The code to apply the maxValue() method to the pokerHand object is:

```
pokerHand.prototype.maxValue = function() {
   var values = new Array();

   for (var i = 0; i < this.cards.length; i++) {
      values[i] = this.cards[i].value();
   }

   return values.max();
}
```

Tip

You should distinguish custom methods from built-in methods by adopting a naming convention, such as beginning custom method names with an underscore (_) character.

The maxValue() method first creates an array of all of the card values in the poker hand. It then uses the max() method of the Array object to return the maximum of those values. You will add this code to the cards.js file.

To create the maxValue() method:

▶ **1.** Return to the **cards.js** file in your text editor.

▶ **2.** Directly below the pokerHand constructor, insert the following code, as shown in Figure 11-35:

```
/* Return the maximum value (highest card) from
   the poker hand */

pokerHand.prototype.maxValue = function() {
   var values = new Array();

   for (var i = 0; i < this.cards.length; i++) {
      values[i] = this.cards[i].value();
   }

   return values.max();
}
```

Figure 11-35 ▶ **The maxValue() method of the pokerHand object**

```
/*     The pokerHand Object constructor     */
function pokerHand(handLength) {

   this.cards = new Array(handLength);

}

   /* Return the maximum value (highest card) from
      the poker hand */

   pokerHand.prototype.maxValue = function() {
      var values = new Array();

      for (var i = 0; i < this.cards.length; i++) {
         values[i] = this.cards[i].value();
      }

      return values.max();
   }
```

returns the maximum of the values array

loops through the cards array, storing the value of each card in the values array

Testing for Flushes and Straights

Next, you need to create methods for the pokerHand object that tests for different types of poker hands. You will start by testing whether the poker hand contains a flush or a straight. In a flush, every card in the hand must belong to the same suit. To test for a flush, you will create a method that loops through the cards in the poker hand, testing whether the suit of the current card matches the suit of the previous card. If they don't match, the loop breaks off and the method returns a value of false; if the loop concludes without finding a mismatch, the method returns a value of true. The code for the hasFlush() method is:

```
pokerHand.prototype.hasFlush = function() {

   for (var i = 1; i < this.cards.length; i++) {
      if (this.cards[i].suit != this.cards[i - 1].suit) return false;
   }
   return true;
}
```

You will add the hasFlush() method to the cards.js file.

To create the hasFlush () method:

▶ **1.** Below the code for the maxValue() method in the cards.js file, insert the following code to test for the presence of a flush, as shown in Figure 11-36:

```
/* Return true if the hand contains a flush */

pokerHand.prototype.hasFlush = function() {

    for (var i = 1; i < this.cards.length; i++) {
        if (this.cards[i].suit != this.cards[i - 1].suit) return
false;
    }

    return true;

}
```

The hasFlush() method   **Figure 11-36**

```
        return values.max();
    }

    /* Return true if the hand contains a flush */
    pokerHand.prototype.hasFlush = function() {
        for (var i = 1; i < this.cards.length; i++) {
            if (this.cards[i].suit != this.cards[i - 1].suit) return false;
        }

        return true;

    }
```

returns false if the suit of any card does not match the suit of the previous card in the array

▶ **2.** Save the cards.js file.

Next, you will create the method to test for the presence of a straight. The hasStraight() method first creates an array of each card's numeric value, with the array values sorted in ascending order. Then the method loops through the array testing whether adjacent card values differ by 1. If they don't, the loop breaks off and the method returns a value of false; if the loop concludes with each card value differing from the previous card's value by 1, the method returns a value of true, which indicates that the hand contains a straight. The code for the hasStraight() method is:

```
pokerHand.prototype.hasStraight = function() {

    var values = new Array();

    for (var i = 0; i < this.cards.length; i++) {
        values[i] = this.cards[i].value();
    }

    values.numericSort(true);

    for (var i = 1; i < values.length; i++) {
        if (values[i] != values[i - 1] + 1) return false;
    }

    return true;

}
```

This code uses the numericSort() method that you created for all Array objects in the previous session to sort the contents of the values array in ascending order. You will add the hasStraight() method to the cards.js file.

To create the hasStraight() method:

▸ 1. Below the code for the hasFlush() method in the cards.js file, insert the following method to test for the presence of a straight, as shown in Figure 11-37:

```
/* Return true if the hand contains a straight */

pokerHand.prototype.hasStraight = function() {

   var values = new Array();

   for (var i = 0; i < this.cards.length; i++) {
      values[i] = this.cards[i].value();
   }

   values.numericSort(true);

   for (var i = 1; i < values.length; i++) {
      if (values[i] != values[i - 1] + 1) return false;
   }

   return true;

}
```

Figure 11-37 — The hasStraight() method

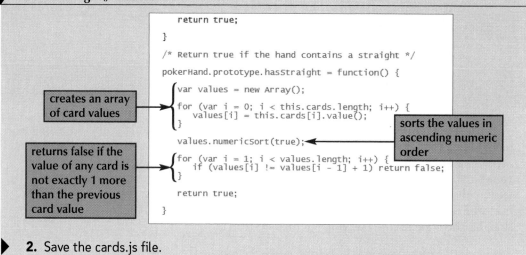

▸ 2. Save the cards.js file.

You can use the hasFlush(), hasStraight(), and maxValue() methods to test for the presence of a Royal Flush or a Straight Flush. A Straight Flush occurs whenever the hand contains a straight of cards of the same suit. A Royal Flush (the most valuable hand in poker) is a Straight Flush with an Ace as the highest card. The code for the hasRoyalFlush() and hasStraightFlush() methods are:

```
pokerHand.prototype.hasRoyalFlush = function() {
   return this.hasFlush() && this.hasStraight() && this.maxValue()
== 14;
}

pokerHand.prototype.hasStraightFlush = function() {
   return this.hasFlush() && this.hasStraight() && this.maxValue()
!= 14;
}
```

You will add these methods to the cards.js file.

To create the hasRoyalFlush() and hasStraightFlush() methods:

▶ **1.** Below the code for the hasStraight() method, insert the following code to test for the presence of a royal flush or a straight flush, as shown in Figure 11-38:

```
/* Return true if the hand contains a royal flush */

pokerHand.prototype.hasRoyalFlush = function() {
   return this.hasFlush() && this.hasStraight() &&
this.maxValue() == 14;
}

/* Return true if the hand contains a straight flush */

pokerHand.prototype.hasStraightFlush = function() {
   return this.hasFlush() && this.hasStraight() &&
this.maxValue() != 14;
}
```

The hasRoyalFlush() and hasStraightFlush() methods ◀ **Figure 11-38**

returns true if the hand has a straight flush, and the Ace is the high card

returns true if the hand has a straight flush, and the Ace is not the high card

```
      return true;
   }
   /* Return true if the hand contains a royal flush */
   pokerHand.prototype.hasRoyalFlush = function() {
      return this.hasFlush() && this.hasStraight() && this.maxValue() == 14;
   }
   /* Return true if the hand contains a straight flush */
   pokerHand.prototype.hasStraightFlush = function() {
      return this.hasFlush() && this.hasStraight() && this.maxValue() != 14;
   }
```

▶ **2.** Save the cards.js file.

With the introduction of these methods, the only remaining hands to test for are those hands that contain cards of duplicate ranks. In draw poker, duplicate ranks that pay off are (in decreasing order of value):

- Four of a Kind
- Full House (containing Three of a Kind and a pair)
- Three of a Kind
- Two Pair
- Jacks or Better (containing a pair of Jacks, Queens, Kings, or Aces)

To test for these types of hands, you will create a new method for the pokerHand object named matches(). The matches() method first creates an array of the card values sorted in numeric order. It then loops through the array testing for adjacent cards of duplicate rank. When a match is found, the matching rank is popped into a new array named duplicates containing all of the matching ranks found in the hand. The initial code for the matches() method is:

```
pokerHand.prototype.matches = function() {

   var values = new Array();
   for (var i = 0; i < this.cards.length; i++) {
      values[i] = this.cards[i].value();
   }
   values.numericSort(true);

   var duplicates = new Array();
   for (var i = 1; i < this.cards.length; i++) {
```

```
        if (values[i] == values[i - 1]) duplicates.push(values[i]);
    }

}
```

You will add this code to the cards.js file.

To insert the matches() method:

▶ **1.** Below the code for the hasStraightFlush() method in the cards.js file, insert the following method to create the duplicates array, as shown in Figure 11-39:

```
/* Return the type of duplicates in the hand (if any) */

pokerHand.prototype.matches = function() {

    var values = new Array();
    for (var i = 0; i < this.cards.length; i++) {
        values[i] = this.cards[i].value();
    }
    values.numericSort(true);

    var duplicates = new Array();
    for (var i = 1; i < this.cards.length; i++) {
        if (values[i] == values[i - 1]) duplicates.push(values[i]);
    }

}
```

| Figure 11-39 | The matches() method |

```
pokerHand.prototype.hasStraightFlush = function() {
    return this.hasFlush() && this.hasStraight() && this.maxValue() != 14;
}

/* Return the type of duplicates in the hand (if any) */

pokerHand.prototype.matches = function() {

    var values = new Array();
    for (var i = 0; i < this.cards.length; i++) {
        values[i] = this.cards[i].value();
    }
    values.numericSort(true);

    var duplicates = new Array();
    for (var i = 1; i < this.cards.length; i++) {
        if (values[i] == values[i - 1]) duplicates.push(values[i]);
    }

}
```

creates sorted array of card values

creates array of duplicate ranks found within the hand

▶ **2.** Save the cards.js file.

By examining the size and content of the duplicates array, you can determine the type of poker hand. Figure 11-40 shows the contents of the duplicates array under four poker hands. Notice that the length of the array provides information on the type of hand. If the length of the array is three, the hand is either Four of a Kind or a Full House. If the length is two, the hand is either Three of a Kind or Two Pair. Finally, if the length of the duplicates array is one (not shown in the figure), the hand is a single pair.

The contents of the duplicates array ◄ **Figure 11-40**

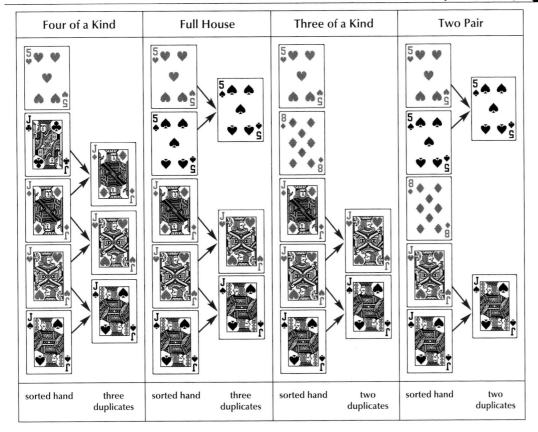

Four of a Kind	Full House	Three of a Kind	Two Pair
sorted hand three duplicates	sorted hand three duplicates	sorted hand two duplicates	sorted hand two duplicates

After you know the length of the duplicates array, the array contents tell what kind of hand it is. If the ranks are all the same, the hand is either Four of a Kind or Three of a Kind; if the ranks are different, the hand is either a Full House or Two Pair. Thus, Four of a Kind has an array length of three with the ranks all the same. Conversely, Three of a Kind has an array length of two with both ranks identical. The following code tests for all five possible winning poker hands:

```
// Check for Four of a Kind vs. Full House
if (duplicates.length == 3) {
   for (var i = 1; i < 3; i++) {
      if (duplicates[i] != duplicates[i - 1]) return "Full House";
   }
   return "Four of a Kind";
}

// Check for Three of a Kind vs. Two Pair
if (duplicates.length == 2) {
   if (duplicates[0] == duplicates[1]) return "Three of a Kind"
   else return "Two Pair";
}

// Check for Jacks or Better
if (duplicates.length == 1 && duplicates[0] >= 11) return "Jacks
or Better";

// No winning hand found
return "";
```

The code first tests for Four of a Kind versus a Full House. If duplicates of different ranks are found in the duplicates array, the code returns the text string "Full House". But if the loop concludes with all of the items in the duplicates array having the same rank, the method returns the text string "Four of a Kind". If neither hand is found, the code tests for Three of a Kind versus Two Pair, and finally for Jacks or Better. If no winning hand is found, the method returns an empty text string. Take some time to study this code, comparing the logic to the example in Figure 11-40.

You will complete the matches() method by adding this code to the cards.js file.

To complete the matches() method:

▶ **1.** Within the matches method, insert the following code, as shown in Figure 11-41:

```
// Check for Four of a Kind vs. Full House
if (duplicates.length == 3) {
    for (var i = 1; i < 3; i++) {
        if (duplicates[i] != duplicates[i - 1]) return "Full
House";
    }
    return "Four of a Kind";
}

// Check for Three of a Kind vs. Two Pair
if (duplicates.length == 2) {
    if (duplicates[0] == duplicates[1]) return "Three of a Kind"
    else return "Two Pair";
}

// Check for Jacks or Better
if (duplicates.length == 1 && duplicates[0] >= 11) return "Jacks
or Better";

// No winning hand found
return "";
```

Figure 11-41 ▶ **Code to determine the hand type**

```
/* Return the type of duplicates in the hand (if any) */

pokerHand.prototype.matches = function() {

    var values = new Array();
    for (var i = 0; i < this.cards.length; i++) {
        values[i] = this.cards[i].value();
    }
    values.numericSort(true);

    var duplicates = new Array();
    for (var i = 1; i < this.cards.length; i++) {
        if (values[i] == values[i - 1]) duplicates.push(values[i]);
    }

    // Check for Four of a Kind vs. Full House
    if (duplicates.length == 3) {
        for (var i = 1; i < 3; i++) {
            if (duplicates[i] != duplicates[i - 1]) return "Full House";
        }
        return "Four of a Kind";
    }

    // Check for Three of a Kind vs. Two Pair
    if (duplicates.length == 2) {
        if (duplicates[0] == duplicates[1]) return "Three of a Kind"
        else return "Two Pair";
    }

    // Check for Jacks or Better
    if (duplicates.length == 1 && duplicates[0] >= 11) return "Jacks or Better";

    // No winning hand found
    return "";
}
```

checks for Four of a Kind versus a Full House

checks for Three of a Kind versus Two Pair

checks for a pair of Jacks or better

otherwise returns an empty text string

▶ **2.** Save the cards.js file.

By calling all of the methods you just entered for the pokerHand object, you can create a single method named handValue() that returns a text string describing the contents of the hand. The code for the handValue() method is:

```
pokerHand.prototype.handValue = function() {

   if (this.hasRoyalFlush()) return "Royal Flush"
   else if (this.hasStraightFlush()) return "Straight Flush"
   else if (this.hasFlush()) return "Flush";
   else if (this.hasStraight()) return "Straight";
   else return this.matches();
}
```

Note that the method tests for the higher-valued hands before testing for the lower-valued hands so that the highest-valued hand is always returned by the function. You will add this method to the cards.js file.

To create the handValue() method:

1. Below the code for the matches() method, insert the following code to return the value of the poker hand, as shown in Figure 11-42:

```
/* Return the value of the poker hand */

pokerHand.prototype.handValue = function() {

   if (this.hasRoyalFlush()) return "Royal Flush"
   else if (this.hasStraightFlush()) return "Straight Flush"
   else if (this.hasFlush()) return "Flush";
   else if (this.hasStraight()) return "Straight";
   else return this.matches();

}
```

The handValue() method   Figure 11-42

```
       // No winning hand found
       return "";
    }
    /* Return the value of the poker hand */

    pokerHand.prototype.handValue = function() {

       if (this.hasRoyalFlush()) return "Royal Flush"
       else if (this.hasStraightFlush()) return "Straight Flush"
       else if (this.hasFlush()) return "Flush";
       else if (this.hasStraight()) return "Straight";
       else return this.matches();

    }
```

2. Save the cards.js file.

Next, you display the value of the poker hand on the Web page. The poker.htm file has a div container with the ID value handValueText, into which you'll place the text returned by the handValue() method. When the user clicks either the Draw or Stand button, you'll run the following evaluateHand() function:

```
function evaluateHand() {

   handValueText.innerHTML = myHand.handValue();
```

```
for (var i = 0; i < cardImages.length; i++) {
   setOpacity(cardImages[i], 25);
}


}
```

In addition to displaying the text returned by the handValue() method, the evaluate-Hand() function also grays out the card images using the setOpacity() function. Setting the opacity to 25 percent provides visual feedback to the user that the current hand is completed and it is time to deal a new hand. You will add this code as a function within the playDrawPoker() function in the poker.js file, and then call the function whenever the user clicks the Draw or Stand button.

To insert the evaluateHand() function:

▶ **1.** Return to the **poker.js** file in your text editor.

▶ **2.** After the event handler function for the Stand button, insert the following code to evaluate the player's hand and update the pot:

```
// Function to evaluate the player's hand and update the pot
function evaluateHand() {

   handValueText.innerHTML = myHand.handValue();

   for (var i = 0; i < cardImages.length; i++) {
      setOpacity(cardImages[i], 25);
   }
}
```

▶ **3.** Scroll up to the event handlers for the Draw and Stand buttons, and then add the following command within each event handler to run the evaluateHand() function:

```
evaluateHand();
```

Figure 11-43 highlights the revised code in the file.

Figure 11-43 ▶ **The evaluateHand() function**

```
// Replace cards marked to be discarded with cards from myDeck
for (var i = 0; i < myHand.cards.length; i++) {

   if (myHand.cards[i].discard) {
      myHand.cards[i].replaceFromDeck(myDeck);
      myHand.cards[i].discard = false;
      cardImages[i].src = myHand.cards[i].imageSrc();
   }

}

evaluateHand();        ◀——  evaluates the hand after the
                             Draw button is clicked
}


// Actions when the Stand button is clicked
standButton.onclick = function() {

   // Enable or disable other buttons
   enableButton(dealButton);
   disableButton(drawButton);
   disableButton(standButton);
   betSelection.disabled = false;

   evaluateHand();       ◀——  evaluates the hand after the
                               Stand button is clicked
}


// Function to evaluate the player's hand and update the pot
function evaluateHand() {

   handValueText.innerHTML = myHand.handValue();

   for (var i = 0; i < cardImages.length; i++) {   ◀——  grays out the
      setOpacity(cardImages[i], 25);                       card images
   }

}
```

When the Deal button is clicked to deal a new hand, the handValue text should be removed and the opacity of the card images reset to 100 percent. You will edit the onclick event handler for the Deal button to reset these values, and then test your changes to the poker game application.

To reset handValueText and the card image opacity:

▶ **1.** In the poker.js file, scroll up to the onclick event handler for the Deal button.

▶ **2.** After the command to subtract the current bet from the user's pot, insert the following code to remove the handValue text and reset the full opacity of the cards, as shown in Figure 11-44:

```
// Reset handValueText and set the card image opacity to 100%
handValueText.innerHTML = "";
for (var i = 0; i < cardImages.length; i++) {
   setOpacity(cardImages[i], 100);
}
```

Reset handValueText and the card image opacity ◀ **Figure 11-44**

```
// Actions when the Deal button is clicked
dealButton.onclick = function() {

    if (pokerGame.currentBet <= pokerGame.currentPot) {
       // Enable or disable other buttons
       disableButton(dealButton);
       enableButton(drawButton);
       enableButton(standButton);
       betSelection.disabled = true;

       // Subtract the bet from the pot
       pokerGame.placeBet();
       potValue.value = pokerGame.currentPot;

       // Reset handValueText and set the card image opacity to 100%
       handValueText.innerHTML = "";
       for (var i = 0; i < cardImages.length; i++) {
          setOpacity(cardImages[i], 100);
       }
```

▶ **3.** Save the file, and then reload **poker.htm** in your Web browser.

▶ **4.** Click the **Deal** button to play a new hand, and then verify that after discarding cards and clicking the Deal button and clicking the Stand button, the Web page displays the value of the hand if it is better than a pair of Jacks. See Figure 11-45.

A winning Flush hand ◀ **Figure 11-45**

▶ **5.** Continue to deal new hands, attempting to get a better result.

The only thing remaining for the game is to update the pot for winning hands. Recall that different hands provide different payouts. To start, you will add the following handOdds() method that returns the payout multiplier for hands of differing value:

```
pokerHand.prototype.handOdds = function() {

   switch (this.handValue()) {
      case "Royal Flush" : return 250;
      case "Straight Flush" : return 50;
      case "Four of a Kind" : return 25;
      case "Full House" : return 9;
      case "Flush" : return 6;
      case "Straight" : return 4;
      case "Three of a Kind" : return 3;
      case "Two Pair" : return 2;
      case "Jacks or Better" : return 1;
      default: return 0;
   }
}
```

You also must add the following payout method to the pokerGame object to update the pot value in response to a winning bet:

```
payout : function(odds) {
          this.currentPot += this.currentBet*odds;
      }
```

The odds parameter represents the odds returned by the handOdds() method, which is then multiplied by the current bet and added to the value of the current pot. You will add both of these functions to the cards.js file.

To create the handOdds() and payout() methods:

▶ **1.** Return to the **cards.js** file in your text editor.

▶ **2.** Below the handValue() method of the pokerHand object, insert the following handOdds() method, as shown in Figure 11-46:

```
/* Return the odds multiplier of the poker hand */

pokerHand.prototype.handOdds = function() {

   switch (this.handValue()) {
      case "Royal Flush" : return 250;
      case "Straight Flush" : return 50;
      case "Four of a Kind" : return 25;
      case "Full House" : return 9;
      case "Flush" : return 6;
      case "Straight" : return 4;
      case "Three of a Kind" : return 3;
      case "Two Pair" : return 2;
      case "Jacks or Better" : return 1;
      default: return 0;
   }
}
```

The handOdds() method of the pokerHand object ◀ **Figure 11-46**

```
        else if (this.hasStraight()) return "Straight";
        else return this.matches();
}


/* Return the odds multiplier of the poker hand */

pokerHand.prototype.handOdds = function() {

    switch (this.handValue()) {
        case "Royal Flush" : return 250;
        case "Straight Flush" : return 50;
        case "Four of a Kind" : return 25;
        case "Full House" : return 9;
        case "Flush" : return 6;
        case "Straight" : return 4;
        case "Three of a Kind" : return 3;
        case "Two Pair" : return 2;
        case "Jacks or Better" : return 1;
        default: return 0;
    }
}
```

3. Scroll up to the object literal defining the pokerGame object, add **,** (a comma) after the placeBet() method, and then insert the following payout() method, as shown in Figure 11-47:

```
payout :    function(odds) {
                this.currentPot += this.currentBet*odds;
            }
```

The payout() method of the pokerGame object ◀ **Figure 11-47**

```
/*      The pokerGame Object   */

var pokerGame = {
    currentPot: null,
    currentBet: null,

    placeBet : function() {
                this.currentPot -= this.currentBet;
            },

    payout :   function(odds) {
                this.currentPot += this.currentBet*odds;
            }
}
```

add a comma between the placeBet() and payout() methods

multiplies the current bet by the odds and adds that value to the pot

4. Save the cards.js file.

To complete the game, you will return to the Web page and run the handOdds() and payout() methods after the player's hand is evaluated. Bob also wants your application to automatically quit the game after the value of the pot is equal to 0.

To calculate and apply the winning odds to the current pot value:

1. Return to the **poker.js** file in your text editor, and then scroll down the evaluateHand() function.

2. Add the following commands to the end of the evaluateHand() function:

```
// Change the pot value based on the results of the hand
var payoutValue = myHand.handOdds();
pokerGame.payout(payoutValue);
potValue.value = pokerGame.currentPot;
```

> **3.** Insert the following if statement to quit the game if the pot value is 0:

```
// Quit the game if the pot is empty
if (pokerGame.currentPot == 0) {
    alert("Game Over");
    disableButton(dealButton);
}
```

Figure 11-48 highlights the added code in the function.

Figure 11-48 ▶ **Code to update the pot value and quit the poker game**

```
// Function to evaluate the player's hand and update the pot
function evaluateHand() {

    handValueText.innerHTML = myHand.handValue();

    for (var i = 0; i < cardImages.length; i++) {
        setOpacity(cardImages[i], 25);
    }

    // Change the pot value based on the results of the hand
    var payoutValue = myHand.handOdds();
    pokerGame.payout(payoutValue);
    potValue.value = pokerGame.currentPot;

    // Quit the game if the pot is empty
    if (pokerGame.currentPot == 0) {
        alert("Game Over");
        disableButton(dealButton);
    }

}
```

> **4.** Save the file, and then reload **poker.htm** in your Web browser. The poker game is fully functioning.

> **5.** Play the game, verifying that the pot is correctly increased for winning hands of a pair of Jacks or better.

Bob plays the final version of your poker game. He is pleased with the results and appreciates the work you have done creating customized objects for the game. Because your custom objects will be available to other programmers at the Web site, he wants you to add code to ensure that the correct parameter values are sent to the constructor functions that create your objects. You can do this by using properties and methods associated with the Function object.

Exploring the Function Object

Almost everything in JavaScript is an object, including functions themselves. The Function object supports its own collection of properties and methods. You have already worked with two of these methods when you used the apply() and call() methods. Figure 11-49 describes other properties and methods associated with functions.

Properties and methods of the function object ◀ **Figure 11-49**

Properties and Methods		Description
Property	*function*.name	Returns the name of the function, *function* (not currently supported by Internet Explorer or Opera)
	function.caller	Returns the function that called *function* (not currently supported by Opera)
	function.length	Returns the number of arguments expected by *function*
Method	*function*.apply(*thisObj*, *thisArray*)	Applies *function* to *thisObj* using argument values stored in the array, *thisArray*
	function.call(*thisObj*, *arg1*, *arg2*, ...)	Applies *function* to *thisObj* using arguments in the list *arg1*, *arg2*, ...
	function.toString()	Returns the code of *function* as a text string

You can use properties of the Function object to return information about constructors. For example, the command

```
var myHand = new pokerHand(5);
alert(myHand.constructor.length);
```

displays the number of arguments required by the pokerHand constructor function. In this case, the command returns a value of 1 because the pokerHand constructor has a single argument, handLength.

Note that because functions are objects, you can create new functions using the Function constructor

```
var function = new Function(arg1, arg2, ..., body);
```

where *function* is the name of the function; *arg1*, *arg2*, etc. are parameters of the function; and *body* is a text string containing the function code. For example, the following code creates a simple function that adds two values:

```
var adder = new Function("x", "y", "return x + y;");
```

Once instantiated, the adder() function then can be used like any other function created using the standard syntax shown in the earlier tutorials.

The arguments Variable

The Function object also includes an arguments variable that returns detailed information about the parameter values passed to the function. The arguments variable is similar to an array, although it is not a true array because you cannot modify its contents or add new items to it. Also, the arguments variable is only accessible within the function body, not outside of it. Figure 11-50 displays properties of the arguments variable.

Properties of the arguments variable ◀ **Figure 11-50**

Property	Description
arguments.length	Returns number of arguments passed into the function
arguments.callee	Returns a reference to the current function
arguments.caller	Returns a reference to the function that called the current function

For example, the following code uses the arguments array to loop through the array of parameter values passed to the pokerCard() function:

```
function pokerCard(suit, rank) {
   for (var i = 0; i < arguments.length) {
      alert(arguments[i]);
   }
   this.suit = suit;
   this.rank = rank;
}

var myCard = new pokerCard("Club", "Queen");
```

When the code is run, the browser displays two alert dialog boxes, showing the text string "Club" followed by "Queen" because those were the parameter values passed to the pokerCard constructor.

Testing for Errors

One use of the arguments variable is to verify that the correct number of parameter values have been passed to a function. If the number of values does not match the expected length, the user can be alerted to the problem, as the following code demonstrates:

```
function pokerCard(suit, rank) {
   if (arguments.length != 2) {
      throw new Error("This function requires 2 arguments");
   } else {
      this.suit = suit;
      this.rank = rank;
   }
}

var myCard = new pokerCard("Club");
```

Tip

If you don't have access to a debugger, you can display the error message using the alert() method in place of the throw new Error() expression.

In this code, any attempt to run the pokerCard constructor with other than two parameter values causes JavaScript to throw a run-time error using the Error object. The text stored in the Error object will appear in the browser's JavaScript debugger, providing valuable information to the other programmers about the nature and source of the error.

Another use of the arguments variable is to test the data type of each value passed to a function against a required data type. Data types can be tested in two ways. You can use the typeof() method

```
typeof(variable)
```

which returns a text string indicating the data type; or you can use the constructor property

```
variable.constructor
```

which returns the reference to the constructor function that defined the data type. Figure 11-51 shows the results returned by both approaches for different types of objects.

variable declaration	typeof(variable)	variable.constructor
var pokerDeck = new Object()	"object"	Object
var cards = new Array()	"object"	Array
var func = function() { }	undefined	Function
var suit = "Club"	"string"	String
var length = 5	"number"	Number
var discard = true	"boolean"	Boolean
var myHand = new pokerHand(5)	"object"	pokerHand

Notice that the constructor property is more robust as it distinguishes objects of different types, including variables instantiated from custom object classes. You can use the constructor property in the following code to test that the handLength parameter value is a number:

```
function pokerHand(handLength) {
   if (arguments[0].constructor != Number) {
      throw new Error("handLength value must be a number");
   this.cards = new Array(handLength);
}
```

In this code, arguments[0].constructor returns an object reference to the constructor of the first (and only) value passed to the function. If that value is not a number, JavaScript again throws a run-time error, causing the program to halt.

Returning the Data Type of a Variable | Reference Window

- To return the data type of a variable as a text string, use
    `typeof(variable)`
  where *variable* is the variable whose data type you wish to discover.
- To return the constructor of a variable, use
    `variable.constructor`
  where the constructor property returns a reference to the constructor function used to instantiate *variable*.

Now that you have seen how to test the parameter values sent to a function for both length and data type, you will add code to the pokerHand constructor to verify that calls to the pokerHand() function include a numeric value for the handLength parameter. If no numeric value is provided, the code will alert the program, throwing a run-time error.

To add error testing to the pokerHand constructor:

1. Return to the **cards.js** file in your text editor.

2. Scroll to the constructor function for the pokerHand object, and then insert the following code, as shown in Figure 11-52:

```
// Verify that only one parameter value is sent
if (arguments.length != 1) {
   throw new Error("Enter a single parameter value");
}
```

```
// Verify that the parameter value is a number
if (arguments[0].constructor != Number) {
    throw new Error("handLength value must be a number");
}
```

Figure 11-52

Code to test arguments of the pokerHand constructor

```
/*     The pokerHand object constructor     */
function pokerHand(handLength) {

    // Verify that only one parameter value is sent
    if (arguments.length != 1) {
        throw new Error("Enter a single parameter value");
    }

    // Verify that the parameter value is a number
    if (arguments[0].constructor != Number) {
        throw new Error("handLength value must be a number");
    }

    this.cards = new Array(handLength);

}
```

Trouble? If you don't have access to a JavaScript debugger, replace `throw new Error` in the above code with `alert` to display the error message in an alert dialog box.

3. Save the cards.js file.

To test whether your code will catch an error, you will add a deliberate error to the poker.js file, and then reload the page.

To add error testing to the pokerHand constructor:

1. Return to the **poker.js** file in your text editor.

2. Change the statement that creates the myHand object to the following, as shown in Figure 11-53:

```
var myHand = new pokerHand(0, 5);
```

Figure 11-53

Invalid number of parameter values

```
// Create a new deck of cards and shuffle it
var myDeck = new pokerDeck();
myDeck.shuffle();

// Define a poker hand for the game
var myHand = new pokerHand(0, 5);
```

only one parameter
value is allowed

3. Save the file, and then reload **poker.htm** in your Web browser.

4. If you have a JavaScript debugger, load the debugger and check whether it caught the run-time error. Figure 11-54 shows the error message generated by Internet Explorer 8.

Error message displayed by Internet Explorer 8 ◄ Figure 11-54

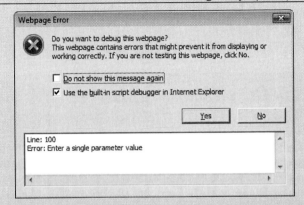

At this writing, all major browsers (Internet Explorer, Firefox, Safari, Opera, and Google Chrome) have some kind of developer tools available to the programmer, although you may have to edit your browser's preferences to view them. If you are running Internet Explorer 8, you can view a developer tools window by clicking the Yes button or by pressing F12. If you are running Firefox, you can view error messages by clicking Tools and Error Console from the Firefox menu. For additional help with debugging code in your particular browser version, see your instructor or technical resource person. If you are running Safari, you might have to enable the developer tools by selecting them from the Advanced Preferences dialog box. The developer tools for Opera and Google Chrome are available from the Tools > Advanced menu and the Pages menu, respectively.

▶ 5. Return to the **poker.js** file in your text editor, and then change the statement to create the myHand variable back to:

```
var myHand = new pokerHand(5);
```

▶ 6. Save the file, and then reload the **poker.htm** file in your Web browser, confirming that no error messages are reported by your browser.

The throw Error() command is but one part of a larger structure of testing for programming errors. The general structure for catching run-time errors is

```
try {
      JavaScript code to try;
   }
catch(err) {
      Handle run-time errors;
   }
```

The try command block is used to try and test parts of the program for errors. Any run-time errors that are generated are automatically stored in an Error object and handled within the catch command block (in this case, given the variable name err). For example, the following code catches a deliberate typing error by using Prompt() rather than prompt() to display a dialog box:

```
try {
      Prompt("Enter your username");
   }
catch(err) {
      alert("Syntax error. Prompt is not a method");
   }
```

The syntax error is caught and the program displays an alert that informs the user of the mistake in the code.

Of course, in most situations, you are not creating deliberate syntax errors and the browser will catch those anyway. The try ... catch structure becomes important when you want to catch logical errors in code, such as a missing variable value or a parameter value of an incorrect type. In those cases, you can throw an error to the catch command block, as the following code demonstrates:

```
try {
      if (username == "") throw new Error("Missing username");
   }
catch(err) {
      alert("You must supply a username");
   }
```

In this code, the catch() command block catches the error thrown when the username variable equals an empty text string and displays an alert box. If you throw an error without a corresponding catch command block, the error is sent directly to the browser, which, in this case, halts the program and displays the error message in its JavaScript debugger.

Bob wants you to create a similar test for the pokerCard constructor to confirm that users enter two parameter values, both of them text strings. The code for the error checks is:

```
// Verify that two parameter values have been sent
if (arguments.length != 2) {
   throw new Error("Enter two string values");
}

// Verify that each parameter is a text string
for (var i = 0; i < arguments.length; i++) {
   if (arguments[i].constructor != String) {
      throw new Error(arguments[i] + " must be entered as a text
string");
   }
}
```

The code first verifies that two parameter values have been sent to the function. If that test is passed, the code then checks the constructor property for each parameter value, confirming that the value is a String object. You will add this code to the cards.js file.

To create an error check for the pokerCard constructor:

▶ **1.** Return to the **cards.js** file in your text editor.

▶ **2.** Scroll down to the pokerCard constructor, and then add the following code, as shown in Figure 11-55:

```
// Verify that two parameter values have been sent
if (arguments.length != 2) {
    throw new Error("Enter two string values");
}

// Verify that each parameter is a text string
for (var i = 0; i < arguments.length; i++) {
    if (arguments[i].constructor != String) {
        throw new Error(arguments[i] + " must be entered as a text
string");
    }
}
```

| Code to test arguments of the pokerCard constructor | Figure 11-55 |

```
function pokerCard(suit, rank) {

    // verify that two parameter values have been sent
    if (arguments.length != 2) {
        throw new Error("Enter two string values");
    }

    // verify that each parameter is a text string
    for (var i = 0; i < arguments.length; i++) {
        if (arguments[i].constructor != String) {
            throw new Error(arguments[i] + " must be entered as a text string");
        }
    }

    this.suit = suit; // Club, Diamond, Heart, or Spade
    this.rank = rank; // 2 through 10, Jack, Queen, King, or Ace

}
```

▶ **3.** Save the cards.js file.

Next, you will test your code with an invalid parameter value for the pokerCard object.

To test the error checker for the pokerCard constructor:

▶ **1.** Return to the **poker.js** file in your text editor.

▶ **2.** At the top of the playDrawPoker() function, insert the following code, as shown in Figure 11-56:

```
// Test the pokerCard error code
var testCard = new pokerCard("Heart", 10);
```

| Invalid data types | Figure 11-56 |

```
function playDrawPoker() {

    // Test the pokerCard error code
    var testCard = new pokerCard("Heart", 10);
```

both parameter values
must be text strings

This code should be rejected because the second parameter value, 10, is not entered as a text string.

▶ 3. Save the file, and then reload **poker.htm** in your Web browser. As shown in Figure 11-57, the Internet Explorer 8 browser reports the parameter value error.

Figure 11-57 ▶ **Error message reported by Internet Explorer 8**

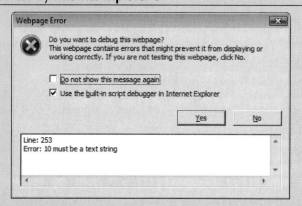

▶ 4. Return to the **poker.js** file in your text editor, delete the code you entered in Step 2, and then reload **poker.htm** in your Web browser to confirm that the poker game application is error free.

Bob is pleased with the error code you added. You can add other error checkers, including an error checker that limits the parameter values pokerCard constructor to a set of legal suit and rank values, but this is a good start.

Review | Session 11.3 Quick Check

1. Specify the code to apply the showID() method of the person object to the employee object.
2. What is the difference between the apply() method and the call() method?
3. Provide code to add the min() method of the Math object to every JavaScript array.
4. Specify the code to insert the following function using the Function constructor:
```
function circumference(radius) {
    return 2*Math.PI*radius;
}
```
5. What values will the arguments variable contain in the following code? Where can you return the values in the arguments variable:
```
function calcVol(width, length, height) {
    return width*length*height;
}

calcVol(3, 8, 2);
```
6. What do you use to create a reference to the function called the currently-active function?
7. The myJob variable is created with the following variable declaration:
```
var myJob = new job("Supervisor");
```
What value is returned by the following expression:
```
typeof(myJob)
```

8. Using the variable declaration of the previous question, what is returned by the following expression:

```
myJob.constructor
```

Tutorial Summary | Review

This tutorial showed how to use the object-based principles of JavaScript to create a new library of custom objects for an online poker game. The first session discussed the nature and scope of nested functions and how to hide function code within other functions. The session then created an instance of a custom object using the new Object() statement and demonstrated how to add properties and methods to a custom object. The second session explored techniques to create object classes using the new keyword. It also showed how to add properties and methods to those classes using a constructor function or through the use of object prototypes. The third session completed the work on the online game, and then discussed how to work with the Function object to provide error-checking capability for any custom method.

Key Terms

associative array	index array	privileged method
base object	instance	prototypal inheritance
constructor	instantiating	prototype
custom object	native object	prototype chain
encapsulation	object class	public method
eval code	object constructor	sub class
function code	object instance	super class
global code	object literal	user-defined object
host object	private method	

| Practice | **Review Assignments** |

Practice the skills you learned in the tutorial using the same case scenario.

Data Files needed for the Review Assignments: back1.png, back2.png, c2.png – cq.png, cardback.png, d2.png – dq.png, gamestxt.js, h2.png – hq.png, libtxt.js, pickem.css, pickemtxt.htm, pickemtxt.js, pokertable.png, s2.png – sq.png,

Bob wants you to use the custom objects you created for the poker game application in a new poker game called Pick 'Em Poker. The rules of the game are:

- Players are given an opening pot from which to bet.
- Before each round, players can bet a select amount from the pot.
- Three hands are dealt to the table named set1, set2, and player. Both set1 and set2 have three cards with the top card face up and the remaining two cards face down. The player hand has two cards; both are face up on the table.
- The player picks one of the two sets or the player hand, completing a five-card poker hand.
- The two hidden cards in the chosen set are revealed. The value of the completed hand and the return on the player's bet are calculated and the pot is updated.
- After the pot value is updated, the player can bet again, and then be dealt another three hands.
- The game ends when the player chooses to quit or is out of money.

Bob already designed the Web page and has a library using some of the custom objects you created for the first poker game. He wants you to write the program for Pick 'Em Poker using those custom objects and any other custom objects you'll need to complete the assignment. A preview of the completed Web page is shown in Figure 11-58.

Figure 11-58

Complete the following:

1. Use your text editor to open the **gamestxt.js**, **libtxt.js**, **pickemtxt.htm**, and **pickemtxt.js** files from the tutorial.11\review folder, enter *your name* and *the date* in the comment section of each file, and then save the files as **games.js**, **library.js**, **pickem.htm**, and **pickem.js**, respectively.

2. Go to the **pickem.htm** file in your text editor and review the code and structure of the document. Notice that the file contains three empty div containers named set1, set2, and player. This is where you'll create and insert inline images for the card images in the poker table. The set1 and set2 containers will contain three card images each. The player container will initially display two card images and then three card images moved from either set1 or set2.

3. Enter links to the library.js, games.js, and pickem.js script files in that order in the head section of the document, and then save and close the file.

4. Go to the **library.js** file in your text editor. At the bottom of the file, add a randomize() method to the prototype of the Array object to randomly sort any array. Save and close the file.

5. Go to the **games.js** file in your text editor, which contains custom objects and properties for the Pick 'Em Poker game based on your work on the draw poker game. Locate the constructor function for the pokerCard object class and add a new property named **faceDown** that indicates whether the card should be displayed facedown (true) or faceup (false) on the poker table. Set the default value of the faceDown property to true.

6. Scroll to the bottom of the file and, using the `new Object()` constructor, instantiate a new object named **pickemGame** that has the following properties and methods:
   a. A property named **account** that stores the money the user currently has in his or her account; set its value to null
   b. A property named **bet** that stores the amount of the user's current bet; set its value to null
   c. The **placeBet()** method, which reduces the value of the account property by the size of the current bet
   d. The **payout()** method, which has a single parameter named **odds** and increases the value of the account property by the value of the current bet multiplied by the odds parameter

7. Create the **addToHand()** method for the prototype of the pokerHand object. The purpose of this method is to add a new card to an existing poker hand. The method has a single parameter named **cardObj** representing a pokerCard object. The method should have a single command that uses the push() Array method to add cardObj to the end of the cards array of the pokerCard object. Save and close the file.

8. Go to the **pickem.js** file in your text editor. In this file, you will write the commands that control the action of the Pick 'Em Poker game. Study the code already in the file.

9. At the bottom of the playPickemPoker() function, set the initial values of the account and bet properties of the pickemGame object to 500 and 25, respectively.

10. Display the account property value in the potValue input box.

11. Create a new pokerDeck variable named **myDeck** and use the randomize() method to randomly sort the order of the cards array within myDeck.

12. Create new pokerHand objects named **myHand**, **mySet1**, and **mySet2** with hand sizes of 2, 3, and 3, respectively. These objects will store the cards dealt to the player's hand and the two sets of three cards players choose from later in the game.

13. Create the showCards() function nested within the playPickemPoker() function. The purpose of this function is to create inline images for cards in each of the three hands. The function has two parameters named handObject and cardHolder. The **handObject** parameter will reference one of the three hands. The **cardHolder** parameter will reference the div containers set1, set2, and player. Within this function, create a for loop that loops through each of the items in the cards array of handObject. Have the loop do the following for each card in the array:

    a. Create an inline image element named **cardImage**.

    b. Set the class name of cardImage to pokerHand.

    c. If the current card in the loop has a faceDown property equal to true, then set the src property of cardImage to the cardback.png file; otherwise, set the src property to the image file of the current card using the imageSrc() method.

    d. Create a custom property for cardImage named **card** containing a pokerCard object. Use the rank and suit properties of the current card in the loop as parameter values for this poker card object.

    e. Append cardImage as a new child of the cardHolder object.

14. Create an anonymous function to act as an event handler for the action of clicking the Deal button. Steps 15 through 22 involve commands or functions that should be nested within this function.

15. Test whether the size of the current bet is less than or equal to the value of the user's account. If the current bet is larger, display an alert box warning the user that he or she must decrease the size of the bet. If the current bet is not larger, have the code perform the actions outlined in Steps 16 through 22.

16. Initialize the table for the new round by disabling the Deal button and the bet selection list so that players cannot click the Deal button or change their initial bet before completing the current round. Set the inner HTML of the handValueText object to an empty text string. Call the deleteChildren() function for the set1, set2, and player objects to delete any card images currently displayed on the table.

17. Use the placeBet() method to subtract the current bet from the user's account and update the account value displayed in the potValue input box.

18. If fewer than eight cards remain in the deck, set the myDeck object to a new poker deck and randomize the order of the items in its cards array.

19. Use the dealTo() method to deal cards from myDeck to myHand, mySet1, and mySet2.

20. Set the faceDown property of both of the cards in myHand and the first cards in mySet1 and mySet2 to false, so that those cards will be shown face up.

21. To display the card images, call the showCards() function you created in Step 13 to display the cards from myHand in the player container, mySet1 in the set1 container, and mySet2 in the set2 container.

22. Add an event handler to the set1 object to run the moveCards() function when that container is clicked. Add the same event handler for the set2 container.

23. Create the moveCards() function placed directly below the event handler function for the Deal button. The purpose of this function is to move the cards and card images from set1 or set2 into the player's hand. Add the following to the function:

    a. Create a variable named **cardHolder** that references the object that called the moveCards() function. (*Hint*: Use the `this` keyword.) Note that the cardHolder object contains the inline images from set1 or set2.

b. Create a while loop that runs while cardHolder has child nodes (in other words, contains inline images of the cards). Within the while loop, do the following:

- Create a variable named **firstImage** that references the first child of cardHolder. This variable will reference an inline image that needs to be moved to the player container.

- Create a variable named **movedCard** that references the card property of firstImage. This variable will contain the reference to the pokerCard object that needs to be moved into the player's hand.

- Change the faceDown property of movedCard to false.

- Change the src property of firstImage to the image source file associated with movedCard. (*Hint*: Use the imageSrc() method.)

- Use the addToHand() method you created in Step 7 to add movedCard to the myHand object.

- Append firstImage as a new child node of the player container.

c. After the while loop has completed, call the evaluateHand() function to evaluate the current hand, update the amount in the player's account, and reset the poker table.

24. Save the file, and then load **pickem.htm** in your Web browser. Click the **Deal** button to deal three hands to the poker table. Click one of the two three-card sets to verify that the card images and cards are moved into the player's hand and evaluated. Continue playing the game, verifying that your account is credited with winning hands and that you cannot change your bet once the three hands have been dealt, nor that you can bet more than you have in your account or continue playing once your account is exhausted.

25. Submit the completed project to your instructor.

Apply | Case Problem 1

Apply custom objects in a shopping cart application.

Data Files needed for this Case Problem: carttxt.js, checkout.htm, checkout.js, h1checkout.png, h1salt.png, sb.css, sbback.png, sblibrary.js, sblogo.png, shoptxt.js, spicetxt.htm

The Spice Bowl   Rita Sato is a manager at the Web development team for The Spice Bowl, a new online grocery store specializing in gourmet spices. She has asked you to work on a sample Web page containing a list of specialized salts sold by the store. The Web page contains a table of select items with each table row listing a product id number (PID), a product name, a short description of a product, a product price, and a list box from which customers can select a quantity of the product to order. In addition to information about the product, each table row also contains a check box that users can select to indicate that they want to add the item to their shopping cart. Figure 11-59 shows a preview of the sample Web page that Rita has designed.

Rita wants you to create a custom store item object that contains information about the products offered on the sample Web page. The properties of the item should be retrieved from the cell values in the Web table. Items that the customer selects for purchase should be written to a multi-valued cookie using each item's product ID number as the cookie name and item properties as field values within each cookie. Cookies corresponding to any item not selected from the table should be deleted if they already exist. Note that the cookies generated in this case are per-session cookies and will be deleted when you close your browser session.

Figure 11-59

Because this project involves working with a Web table, you should review the information on creating and accessing Web table objects discussed in the introduction to Case Problem 2 of Chapter 7. Also, because part of this project involves writing data to a cookie, users of the Google Chrome or Safari Web browser should either upload these files to a Web server or install server software on their local machine.

Complete the following:

1. Use your text editor to open the **carttxt.js**, **shoptxt.js**, and **spicetxt.htm** files from the tutorial.11\case1 folder, enter *your name* and *the date* in the comment section of each file, and then save the files as **cart.js**, **shop.js**, and **spice.htm**, respectively.
2. Go to the **spice.htm** file in your text editor, and then link the file to the sblibrary.js, cart.js, and shop.js files in that order. Note that the sblibrary.js file contains a collection of functions you'll want to use in your program.
3. Study the contents of the spice.htm file, and then save and close the file.
4. Return to the **cart.js** file in your text editor. In this file, you'll enter code to create your custom objects, properties, and methods. Create a constructor function for the **storeItem** class of objects and define the **pid**, **descr**, **price**, and **qty** properties used to store each item's product ID number, description, price, and quantity ordered. Set the default value of the qty property to 1. Do not set any default values for the other properties. Save and close the cart.js file.
5. Return to the **shop.js** file in your text editor. Add code to run the startShopping() function when the page is loaded by the browser.
6. Create the **startShopping()** function below your event handler and add the commands described in the following steps.

◆ EXPLORE

7. Loop through the rows in the tbody section of the saltItems table. Within each row of the table body, do the following:

   a. Declare a variable named **newItem** as an instance of the storeItem object class.

   b. Store the text of the first cell in the row in the pid property of newItem.

   c. Store the text of the second cell in the prod property of newItem.

   d. Store the text of the third cell in the newItem's desc property.

   e. Store the text of the fourth cell in the newItem's price property.

   f. The fifth cell contains a drop-down selection list for the quantity of items ordered as the first child node of the table cell. Store the reference to this selection list in the variable **qtySelect**.

   g. Store the value of the selected option in the qtySelect object in the newItem's qty property.

   h. Associate each selection list with a particular store item (you must do this because the table contains 13 different selection lists; one for each store item) by adding a custom property to qtySelect named **currentItem**, and set it equal to the newItem variable.

   i. Add an onchange event handler to qtySelect that sets the qty property value of the currentItem property to the value of the selected option in the qtySelect selection list.

   j. The sixth cell contains a check box that customers click to move store items between the shelf and the shopping cart. Store the reference to this check box as the variable **selCheckBox**. As with the quantity selection list, every check box must be associated with a particular store item. Add the custom property **currentItem** to the selCheckBox variable and set it equal to newItem.

8. After the for loop, create an event handler for the viewCart button that does the following when the button is clicked:

   a. Create an array named **allCheckBoxes** containing all of the input elements in the current document whose type is equal to checkbox.

   b. Declare a variable named **cartCount** and set its initial value to 0.

   c. Loop through the allCheckBoxes array, and for each item in that array test whether the check box has been checked. If so, use the storeCookieField() function from the sblibrary.js file to store the values of the prod, desc, price, and qty properties of the store item corresponding to the check box. Use the currentItem property of the check box to reference the corresponding store item, and use the value of the store item's pid property as the cookie name and prod, desc, price, and qty as the field names. Increase the value of the cartCount variable by 1.

   d. If the check box has not been checked, use the removeCookie() function from the sblibrary.js file to remove any cookie whose name matches the pid property of the store item associated with the check box.

   e. After the loop has completed, alert the user of the number of items in his or her shopping cart, and then open the checkout.htm Web page.

9. Save and close the **shop.js** file. Code for the checkout.htm file has already been entered for you and you do not have to edit that file or its JavaScript code.

10. Open **spice.htm** in your Web browser. From the Web table, click check boxes to select items to add to the shopping cart. Select quantities for items from the drop-down selection lists. Click the form button to write your selections to a multi-valued cookie. Verify that the Web page indicates the number of items selected and displays the contents of the checkout page with the selected items in a table. If you make a mistake, delete the cookies by closing your Web browser to end the current session.

11. Submit the completed project to your instructor.

Apply | **Case Problem 2**

Create a custom drop shadow for any absolutely positioned object.

Data Files needed for this Case Problem: kpaf.css, kpaf.jpg, kpaflib.js, overlay.css, overlaytxt.js, schedtxt.htm, shadowstxt.js, tables.css

KPAF 620 Radio   Kyle Mitchell manages the Web site for KPAF 620, a public radio station located in Bismarck, North Dakota. Kyle has been working on a Web page listing the current nightly schedule at KPAF. He wants to create detail overlays for each entry in the schedule so that when a viewer hovers the pointer over a table cell containing a program name, a box appears over the cell displaying additional information about the program. When the user moves the pointer away from the table cell, the detail overlay disappears.

Kyle has already written the JavaScript code to display the detail overlay, but wants each overlay to contain a drop shadow to further distinguish it from the surrounding page content. A preview of the drop shadow effect is shown in Figure 11-60.

Figure 11-60

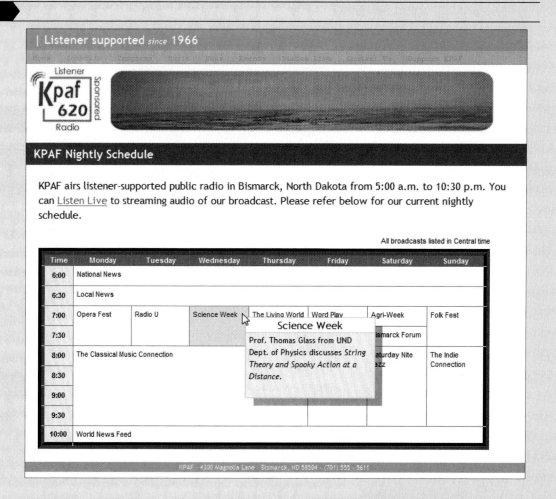

To create this effect, you'll create a drop shadow object, one in which the user can specify the color and opacity of the shadow as well as its horizontal and vertical distance from the detail overlay. The width and height of the shadow should match the width and height of the detail overlay, and the z-index values of both the overlay and its drop shadow should be set so that the drop shadow always appears beneath the overlay.

Complete the following:

1. Use your text editor to open the **overlaytxt.js**, **schedtxt.htm**, and **shadowstxt.js** files from the tutorial.11\case2 folder, enter *your name* and *the date* in the comment section of each file, and then save the files as **overlay.js**, **schedule.htm**, and **shadows.js**, respectively.

2. Return to the **schedule.htm** file in your text editor and review the code in the file. At the top of the file, insert a script element linking to the **shadows.js** file, placing it between the script elements for the kpaflib.js and overlay.js files.

3. Save the file, and then open **schedule.htm** in your Web browser. Verify that when you press your mouse button down on one of the entries in the schedule table, a detail overlay appears describing the program; and when you release the mouse button, the overlay disappears.

4. Return to the **shadows.js** file in your text editor. Create the shadow() constructor function having the following parameters: **source**, **offX**, **offY**, **r**, **g**, **b**, and **op**. The source parameter is used to reference the source of the shadow. The offX and offY parameters indicate the horizontal and vertical offset, respectively, of the shadow from its source. The r, g, and b parameters contain the red, green, and blue color values, respectively, for the shadow. Finally, the op parameter contains the opacity of the shadow on a 0 to 100 scale.

5. Add the following to the shadow constructor:

   a. Define the **srcObject** property equal to the value of the source parameter.

   b. Define the **offsetX** and **offsetY** properties equal to the values of the offX and offY parameters.

   c. Define the **color** property equal to the text string rgb(*r, g, b*) where *r*, *g*, and *b* are the values of the r, g, and b parameters.

   d. Define the **opacity** property equal to the value of the op parameter.

⊕ EXPLORE

6. Create the **addToPage()** method of the shadow prototype. The purpose of this method is to create a div element for the drop shadow with the size of the shadow based on the size of the source object. Add the following commands to the method:

   a. Create a new property for the shadow object named **divElem** and store it in a div element.

   b. Append the shadow div element to the document body.

   c. Set the id of the shadow div element equal to the id of the source object plus the text string "DropShadow".

   d. Set the background color of the shadow div element to the color property of the shadow object.

   e. Use the getStyle() method defined in the kpaflib.js file to extract the width and height values of the source object. Set the width and height values of the shadow div element to match.

   f. Use the setOpacity() method defined in the kpaflib.js file to set the opacity of the shadow div element.

   g. Set the position and display the style of the shadow div element to absolute and none, respectively.

   h. Use the getStyle() method to retrieve the z-index value of the source object. Store the z-index value in the **objectZ** variable.

   i. If objectZ is equal to auto or is undefined, let objectZ equal 1.

   j. Set the z-index style of the source object to one more than objectZ.

   k. Set the z-index style of the shadow div element to objectZ.

7. Save and close the shadows.js file.

8. Return to the **overlay.js** file in your text editor.

9. Scroll down to the mousedown event handler for the allOverlayTargets[i] object. At the end of the event handler function, add the following commands:

   a. Create an instance of the shadow object class named **myShadow** using overlay as the source object, with horizontal and vertical offsets of 13 pixels, a color value of (0, 0, 0), and an opacity of 30.

   b. Apply the addToPage() method to the myShadow object.

   c. Set the display style of the myShadow div element to block.

   d. Set the left and top styles of the myShadow div element to be offset from the left and top position of the overlay object by an amount equal to the offsetX and offsetY properties.

10. Scroll down to the mouseup event handler for the allOverlayTargets[i] object. At the end of the event handler function, add the following commands:

    a. Declare a variable named **shadowElem** whose id is equal to the id of the overlay object plus the text string "DropShadow".

    b. Remove shadowElem from the document body.

11. Save and close the overlay.js file.

12. Reopen **schedule.htm** in your Web browser. Verify that every detail overlay is displayed with a semi-transparent drop shadow located 13 pixels to the right and 13 pixels down from the overlay.

13. Submit the completed project to your instructor.

| Challenge | **Case Problem 3** |

Use the skills you learned to create a customized slider widget.

Data Files needed for this Case Problem: back.png, barimage.png, barimage2.png, barimage3.png, demotxt.js, lineimage.png, slider.css, slidertxt.js, widgettxt.htm, wm.css, wmlibrary.js, wmlogo.png

WidgetMage   Anna Lopez is the founder of WidgetMage, a Web site that specializes in designing small applications for Web pages, also known as widgets. Anna has asked you to create a slider widget. A slider is an object that allows users to enter values into an input box by dragging or sliding an indicator bar across a vertical or horizontal scale.

Anna wants you to write a JavaScript program that will allow any text input box to be converted into a slider. She's provided you with a sample Web form in which users can modify the color, opacity, or z-index of sample boxes by entering values into input boxes. She wants you to modify this page so that the values are entered using your slider widget. Figure 11-61 shows a preview of the completed page.

Figure 11-61

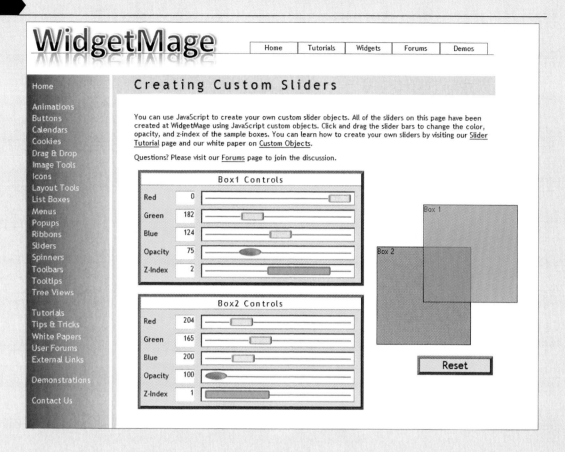

Every slider is composed of four elements: a slider box that contains the slider, a bar that the user clicks or drags across the box, a horizontal line that indicates the bar's position as it moves across the slider box, and an input box that displays the value associated with the bar's current position. See Figure 11-62.

Figure 11-62

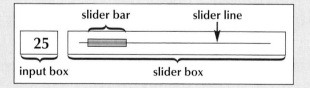

Anna already created design styles for these elements. She's also written the JavaScript code to change the appearance of the two sample boxes shown in Figure 11-61, and created a library of functions you can use in developing your slider widget. She needs you to write the code that creates the slider widget and attaches it to any input box.

To create a slider widget that can be applied to any input box, you need a way to specify the range of values that can be entered into the input box. You'll add the class attribute

```
class = "sliderInput first;last;inc;style"
```

to the <input /> tag, where *first* is the lowest value that the input box can display, *last* is the input box's highest value, *inc* is the increment from one value to the next within the input box, and *style* is the number of a style that will be used to format the appearance of the slider widget (Anna will supply you with three possible slider widget styles). Your code needs to be able to read this information from the class attribute value and apply it to the appearance and behavior of your slider widget.

Complete the following:

1. Use your text editor to open the **demotxt.js**, **slidertxt.js**, and **widgettxt.htm** files from the tutorial.11\case3 folder, enter *your name* and *the date* in the comment section of each file, and then save the files as **demo.js**, **slider.js**, and **widget.htm**, respectively.

2. The **wmlibrary.js** file is a library of functions that Anna created for you. Anna also created a style sheet in the **slider.css** file, which you'll apply to the slider widget you'll create. Study the code in both files.

3. Open the **widget.htm** file in your Web browser and observe that the appearance of the two sample boxes changes as you enter new values into the color, opacity, and z-index input boxes and press the Tab key to remove the focus from each input box.

4. Return to the **widget.htm** file in your text editor. Link the file to the **slider.css** style sheet. Between the script elements for the wmlibrary.js and demo.js files, insert a script element linked to the **slider.js** file.

⊕ EXPLORE

5. Using the class name structure described above, add class attributes to the 10 input boxes on the Web form. For the red, green, and blue input boxes, the input values range from 255 down to 0 in increments of –1 units. Use a value of 1 for *style*. For the opacity input boxes, input values range from 100 down to 0 in increments of –5 units. Use a value of 2 for *style*. For the z-index boxes, the input values range from 1 to 2 in an increment of 1 unit. Use a value of 3 for *style*. Save and close the widget.htm file.

6. Return to the **slider.js** file in your text editor. Create a constructor named **sliderBox** that defines the class of slider widgets. The constructor function has five parameters: **input**, **first**, **last**, **inc**, and **style**. The input parameter will represent the input box on the Web form that the slider widget is attached to. The first, last, inc, and style parameters will derive their values from the values entered in the input box's class attribute. Add the following to the constructor function:

   a. Create custom properties for the sliderBox object named **input**, **first**, **last**, **inc**, and **style**, and set their initial values equal to the values of the input, first, last, inc, and style parameters, respectively.

   b. Create a property named **range** that is equal to the difference between the last and first properties.

   c. Create properties named **line** and **bar**, setting their initial values to null. These properties will be used to store custom objects representing the slider line and slider bar, respectively.

⊕ EXPLORE

   d. Add a custom property to the sliderBox object named **divElem** that stores a div element with the class name sliderBox.

7. Create a constructor for an object class named **sliderLine**. This object class represents the horizontal line that appears in the slider widget. Create a property for sliderLine named **divElem** that stores a div element with the class name sliderLine.

8. Create a constructor for an object class named **sliderBar**. The constructor function has a single parameter named **style**. This object class represents the slider bar. Create a custom property for slideBar named **divElem** storing a div element with the class name sliderBar*style* where *style* is the value of the style parameter.

9. Add the **constructDOM()** method to the sliderBox prototype. The purpose of this method is to assemble the sliderBox, sliderLine, and sliderBar div objects into the HTML fragment

```
<div class = "sliderBox">
   <div class = "sliderLine">
      <div class = "sliderBarstyle"></div>
   </div>
</div>
```

where *style* is the style number that defines the appearance of your slider widget. Add the following commands to the method:

   a. Create a property for the sliderBox object named **line** containing an instance of a sliderLine object.

   b. Create a property for the sliderBox object named **bar** containing an instance of a sliderBar object using the value of the style property as the parameter value.

   c. Append the bar divElem as a child of the line divElem.

   d. Append the line divElem as a child of the slider box divElem.

10. Add the **position()** method to the sliderBar prototype. The purpose of this method is to return the current location of the slider bar. Add a command to this method to return the value of the left style property of slider bar divElem. Use the parseFloat() method to return only the numeric value, removing the distance unit. (*Hint*: To reference the slider bar position, use the expression this.divElem.style.left.)

11. Add the **setPosition()** method to the sliderBar prototype. The purpose of this method is to change the position of the slider bar. The method has a single parameter named **pos**, which specifies the left position of the slider bar in pixels. Add a command to this method to set the left style property of the slider bar divElem to the text string *pos*px, where *pos* is the value of the pos parameter.

12. Add the **getSizes()** method to the sliderBox prototype. The purpose of this method is to determine the width of the slider line and slider bar based on values entered in the slider.css style sheet, and to store those values as properties of the sliderBox object. Add the following commands to the method:

   a. Using the getStyle() method, retrieve the width of the slider line. Apply the parseFloat() method to strip out any units of measure and store the numeric value in the **lineWidth** property. (*Hint:* Use the expression this.line.divElem to reference the slider line.)

   b. Use the getStyle() and parseFloat() methods again to retrieve the width of the slider bar. Store the numeric value in the **barWidth** property. (*Hint:* Use the expression this.bar.divElem to reference the slider bar.)

   c. Create a new property for the sliderBox object named **barMaxTravel** that stores the maximum horizontal distance the bar can travel across the slider. Set its value equal to lineWidth minus barWidth.

   d. Create a new property named **ratio** that is equal to the range property of the slider box divided by the barMaxTravel property. This ratio provides a way of translating the distance that the bar can travel within the slider to the range of values found within the input box.

   e. Use the setPosition() method created in Step 11 to set the slider bar position to 0.

13. Add the **updateValue()** method to the sliderBox prototype. The purpose of this method is to change the value displayed in the input box based on the current location of the slider bar. Add the following commands to the method:

   a. Use the focus() method to give the sliderBox object the focus.

   b. Use the position() method to return the current position of the slider bar, storing the value in the variable **pos**. (*Hint*: Reference the slider bar using the expression this.bar.)

✪ **EXPLORE**   c. Convert the slider bar's position to an input box value. To do this, set the value stored in the input box to

$$(increment) \times \text{Math. round}\left(\frac{first + pos \times ratio}{increment}\right)$$

where *increment* is the value of the inc property of the slider box object, *first* is the value of the first property, *pos* is the value of the pos variable, and *ratio* is the value of the ratio property. (*Hint*: Reference the value of the input box using the expression this.input.value.)

   d. Apply the blur() method to remove the focus from the input box. (*Hint*: Reference the input box using the expression this.input.)

14. A setupEvents() method for the sliderBox prototype has already been created for you. The purpose of this method is to create the mousedown, mousemove, and mouseup event handlers for the slider bar object. Study the code for this method and then write a summary of what the code does. Save and close the slider.js file.

15. To create sliders for each input box in the Web page, return to the **demo.js** file in your text editor and use the addEvent() function to run the loadSliders() function when the page is initially loaded.

16. Add the **loadSliders()** function and create an array named **allSliderInputs** containing all of the input elements in the current document whose class name includes the substring sliderInput (*Hint:* Use the indexOf() string function to determine whether sliderInput exists as a substring of the class name.)

✪ **EXPLORE**   17. Loop through the allSliderInputs array, and for each item in the array:

   a. Split the text of the item's class name using the split() function with a single blank space, " " as the delimiter. Store the substring after the blank space into a variable named sliderParams.

   b. Use the split() function again to split sliderParams into four separate substrings at each occurrence of the semicolon character. Store the first substring in a variable named **first**, the second in a variable named **last**, the third in a variable named **inc**, and the fourth in a variable named **style**. Apply the parseFloat() method to the first, last, inc, and style variables to store the numeric value of these variables rather than their text strings.

   c. Create an instance of the sliderBox object named **mySlider** using the current item from the allSliderInputs array as the value for the input parameter, and the first, last, inc, and style variables as values for the four remaining parameters.

   d. Apply the constructDOM() method to mySlider, creating the HTML fragment that will be displayed in the page.

   e. Call the insertAfter() function in the wmlibrary.js file to insert the mySlider.divElem object directly after the current allSliderInputs item.

   f. Apply the getSizes() method to mySlider to calculate and store the size of the mySlider elements.

   g. Apply the setupEvents() method to mySlider to add all of the event handlers for the objects in the slider widget. Save the demo.js file.

18. Reopen **widget.htm** in your Web browser. Verify that all of the input boxes now have slider widgets next to them. Drag the slider bars to alter the color, opacity, and z-index values of each sample box. Verify that when you click the slider line, the slider bar jumps to the location where you clicked.

19. Submit the completed project to your instructor.

| Create | **Case Problem 4** |

Create shape objects for use with a drawing program.

Data Files needed for this Case Problem: headmenu.jpg, kblib.js, kg.css, kglogo.jpg, large.png, links.jpg, medium.png, opacity10.png, opacity30.png, opacity50.png, opacity70.png, opacity100.png, playtxt.js, shapestxt.htm, shapestxt.js, small.png, title.jpg, trash.png

Kiddergarden Pete Burnham, owner of the Kiddergarden Web site, wants you to create a page for preschoolers where they can create drawings by clicking and dragging shapes from a palette onto a Web page canvas. The kids will be able to change the size, color, and transparency of each shape. Pete already created much of the code for the Web page and style sheets. You will to finish the project by creating custom objects to represent different types of shapes and properties that describe the shape's appearance. A preview of a possible solution is shown in Figure 11-63. Pete also provided a library of JavaScript functions that you can use to complete this project.

Figure 11-63

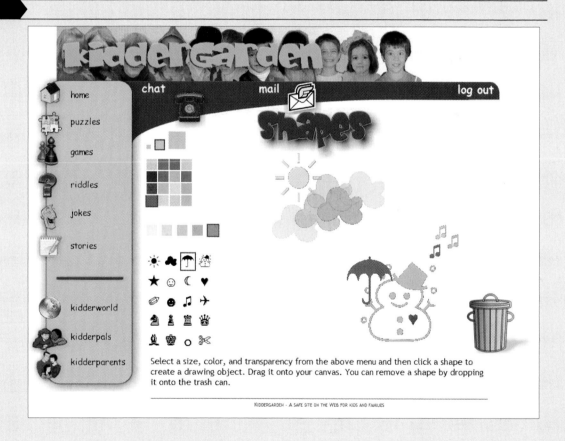

Complete the following:

1. Use your text editor to open the **playtxt.js**, **shapestxt.htm**, and **shapestxt.js** files from the tutorial.11\case4 folder, enter *your name* and *the date* in the comment sections, and then save the files as **play.js**, **shapes.htm**, and **shapes.js**, respectively.

2. The page content and design can be taken from the shapes.htm and kg.css files, but you are free to supplement this material with additional content of your own.

3. In the **shapes.js** file, write code to create a custom shape object that describes all the properties of the shapes in the drawing game, including the shape's size, color, opacity, and appearance. Add a property that associates each shape object with a div element on the Web page, methods that create that div element, and event handlers that allow you to drag and drop the shapes to different positions.

4. In the **play.js** file, insert code that runs the drawing game. Give users the ability to choose different sizes, colors, opacities, and shape designs by clicking the images that appear on the Web page. Provide visual feedback to the users so they know which option they have selected at any one time. Add code that removes created shapes from the drawing canvas when the shape is dropped onto the trash can.

5. Submit your completed project to your instructor.

Review | Quick Check Answers

Session 11.1

1. An error will result because the showAlert() function is nested within the playPoker() function and thus is "invisible" outside of that scope.

2. Nested functions are limited to the scope of the function in which they are nested.

3. native, host, and custom

4. `var pokerCard = new Object();`

5.
```
var pokerCard = {
    suit: "Clubs",
    rank: "King"
}
```

6.
```
var pokerCard = {
    suit : "Clubs",
    rank : "King"
    dropRank : function() {
        this.rank = "Queen";
    }
}
```

7. Indexed arrays are placed in sequential order through the use of an index value. Associative arrays are organized by associating each array item with a key value.

8. Use a for ... in loop.

Session 11.2

1.
```
function Company() {
    this.compID;
    this.showID = function() {
        alert(this.compID);
    }
}
```

2.
```
var myCompany = new Company();
myCompany.compID = "bdonline";
```

3.
```
function Company(id) {
    this.compID = id;
    this.showID = function() {
        alert(this.compID);
    }
}
var myCompany = new Company("bdonline");
```

4. `Company.prototype.establishDate = "January 18, 2012";`

5. ```
Company.prototype.showDate = function() {
    alert(this.establishDate);
}
```

6. `webCompany.prototype = new Company();`

7. ```
Array.prototype.lastItem = function() {
    return this[this.length - 1];
}
```

Session 11.3

1. `person.showID.apply(employee);`

2. The call method applies function arguments in a comma-separated list. The apply method applies arguments listed in an array.

3. ```
Array.prototype.min = function() {
    return Math.min.apply(this, this);
}
```

4. `var circumference = new Function("radius", "return 2*Math.PI*radius;");`

5. arguments[0] = 3, arguments[1] = 8, arguments[2] = 2. You can only reference the arguments variable from within the function.

6. Use the caller property of the Function object.

7. "object"

8. A reference to the job constructor function.

## Ending Data Files

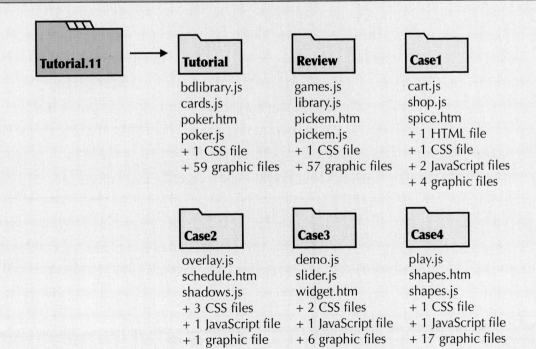

**Tutorial.11** → **Tutorial**
bdlibrary.js
cards.js
poker.htm
poker.js
+ 1 CSS file
+ 59 graphic files

**Review**
games.js
library.js
pickem.htm
pickem.js
+ 1 CSS file
+ 57 graphic files

**Case1**
cart.js
shop.js
spice.htm
+ 1 HTML file
+ 1 CSS file
+ 2 JavaScript files
+ 4 graphic files

**Case2**
overlay.js
schedule.htm
shadows.js
+ 3 CSS files
+ 1 JavaScript file
+ 1 graphic file

**Case3**
demo.js
slider.js
widget.htm
+ 2 CSS files
+ 1 JavaScript file
+ 6 graphic files

**Case4**
play.js
shapes.htm
shapes.js
+ 1 CSS file
+ 1 JavaScript file
+ 17 graphic files
```

Objectives

Session 12.1
- Explore the history of AJAX
- Create an HTTP request object
- Submit an HTTP request
- Retrieve the text of a request response

Session 12.2
- Explore the structure of XML
- Retrieve an RSS news feed
- Parse an XML document
- Study the structure of JSON objects

Session 12.3
- Upload and run a Perl CGI script
- Create an autocomplete application
- Retrieve and process JSON data

Programming with AJAX

Retrieving Online Content for a Blog

Case | Sblogger

Sports enthusiast Steve Lavent plans to create his own Web site called *Sblogger* that contains articles and commentary on the world of sports. The site will have a news feed that is continually updated with the latest scores and stories. Steve also writes his own column, sharing his sometimes-quirky insights on the world of sports. He wants browsers to automatically load his latest columns when the home page is initially opened, and he wants older columns to be accessible from an archive residing on the Web server. To create Steve's site, you will write a JavaScript application to retrieve data from Steve's Web server and then write that information directly to Steve's home page using a technology known as AJAX.

Note: To complete the tasks in this tutorial, you need access to an account on a Web server that supports Perl. You can upload the solution files to an external server, or you can work with a Web server installed on your local machine such as Windows IIS (Internet Information Services).

Starting Data Files

Tutorial.12 →

Tutorial
ajaxtxt.js
newstxt.js
sblogtxt.htm
+ 1 CSS file
+ 2 CGI scripts
+ 2 graphic files
+ 1 text file
+ 1 XML file

Review
gamestxt.htm
getscorestxt.js
libtxt.js
+ 1 CSS file
+ 1 graphic file
+ 1 text file
+ 1 XML file

Case1
getorderstxt.js
orderstxt.htm
+ 1 JavaScript file
+ 1 CSS file
+ 1 Perl file
+ 1 graphic file

Case2
bikestxt.htm
tabstxt.js
+ 1 CSS file
+ 3 HTML files
+ 1 JavaScript file
+ 8 graphic files

Case3
fwlibtxt.js
glovestxt.htm
linkstxt.js
+ 2 CSS files
+ 5 HTML files
+ 8 graphic files

Case4
authorlist.txt
intro.txt
links.txt
sflogo.png
sfpod.xml
sfreviews.pl
vinter.png

Session 12.1

Introducing AJAX

Steve already created a sample HTML file and a collection of CSS styles that he wants to use for the Sblogger Web site. You will begin by reviewing his HTML file.

To review the sblogger.htm file:

▶ 1. Use your text editor to open the **ajaxtxt.js**, **newstxt.js**, and **sblogtxt.htm** files from the tutorial.12\tutorial folder, enter *your name* and *the date* in the comment section of each file, and then save the files as **ajax.js**, **newsfeed.js**, and **sblogger.htm**, respectively.

▶ 2. Review the contents of the sblogger.htm file in your text editor, taking note of the structure and the use of the div elements.

▶ 3. Add the following script elements to the head section of the document in the order specified:

```
<script src="ajax.js" type="text/javascript"></script>
<script src="newsfeed.js" type="text/javascript"></script>
```

▶ 4. Save the file, and then close it.

▶ 5. Open **sblogger.htm** in your Web browser. Figure 12-1 shows the initial layout and contents of the page.

Figure 12-1   Initial Sblogger page

Currently, Steve's Web page has no content other than the list of links in the left sidebar and the Sblogger logo. That's okay. Steve wants the contents of this page to be updated throughout the day with articles and stories drawn from his Web server and other sources. Figure 12-2 shows a preview of the final page as envisioned by Steve.

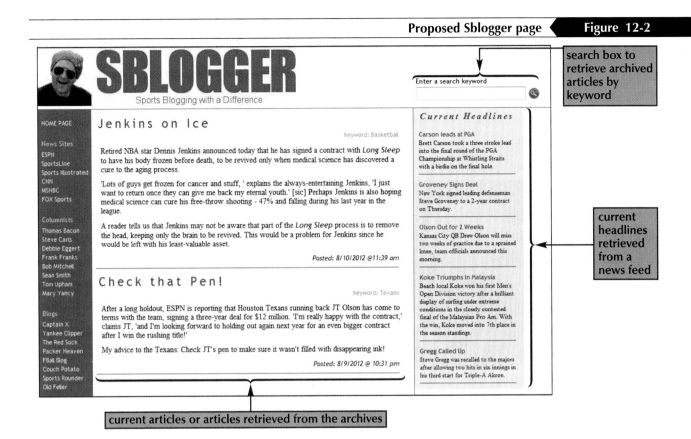

search box to retrieve archived articles by keyword

current headlines retrieved from a news feed

current articles or articles retrieved from the archives

Steve sees three areas where the Web page must be able to retrieve and display content from other sources:

- The daily commentary needs to be retrieved from a text file residing on the Sblogger Web server.
- Current headlines need to be retrieved from an online news feed.
- Archived columns need to be located after users enter a keyword in the search box, which retrieves all columns with matching keywords.

To create this type of dynamic content, you will employ AJAX programming techniques on Steve's Web site. Before writing the code, you need to understand the history and theory behind AJAX.

The History of AJAX

AJAX, which stands for **Asynchronous JavaScript and XML**, is a collection of programming techniques that allow browsers to retrieve data on demand from the Web without having to load a new Web page or reload the current page. AJAX is not a programming language. Instead, it represents the combination of several techniques to create fully interactive Web applications. The term AJAX was first coined on February 18, 2005, by Jesse James Garrett in an article entitled *AJAX: A New Approach to Web Applications*, which was posted on the Web site for the consulting firm Adaptive Path, as shown in Figure 12-3.

Figure 12-3   AJAX: A New Approach to Web Applications

It would be wrong to say that either Garrett or Adaptive Path invented AJAX. When Garrett wrote his article, AJAX-style applications such as Google Suggest and Gmail were already being developed by Google. Flickr was just coming out, providing a source for digital photo sharing. America Online's AIM Mail, another service that used AJAX principles, was about to come out.

What Garrett's article did was focus attention on this new approach to Web interactivity; AJAX combines the features of HTML, JavaScript, XML, and asynchronous communication. This is similar to how the acronym DHTML was used years earlier to focus attention on the concept of a dynamic use of HTML that combined the features of HTML, CSS, and JavaScript.

The Classic Web Application Model

To understand why AJAX represented something new in Web application development, you must first look at the traditional model used earlier in the history of the Web. In the **classic Web application model**, shown in Figure 12-4, users interact with Web servers through a Web page loaded on their browser. The Web page might have a form in which a user enters some specific pieces of information, such as a purchase order or a posted message. Submitting the form triggers an HTTP request back to the Web server. The server takes thisinformation, perhaps runs a script in response, and then generates a new HTML page, which is sent back to the user. So the level of information is exchanged in pages: one page to request information; another page to report on the results of that request.

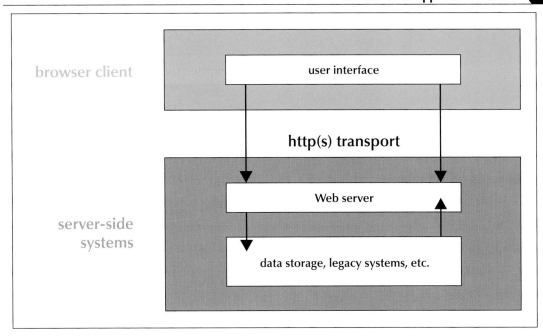

Classic Web application model ◄ Figure 12-4

This exchange of information is by its nature **synchronous** because, as illustrated in Figure 12-5, the user sends a request and must wait for a response from the server before doing anything else. While the user is waiting for a response in the form of a newly generated page, the current Web page is unavailable.

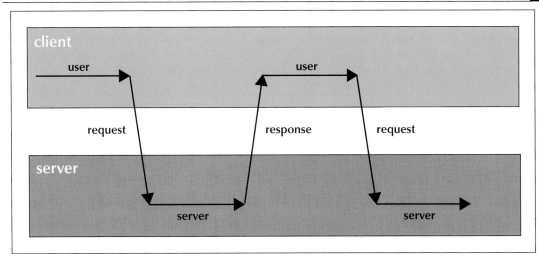

Synchronous communication ◄ Figure 12-5

The AJAX Web Application Model

The **AJAX Web application model** adds an intermediary between the user and the server-side system, called an AJAX engine. The **AJAX engine** is responsible for communicating with the server and returning any information from the server to the user interface, as shown in Figure 12-6. The user interface interacts with the AJAX engine using code written in JavaScript, but the engine communicates with the server using the same HTTP request protocol that the classic model employs to request and receive Web pages.

Figure 12-6 AJAX Web application model

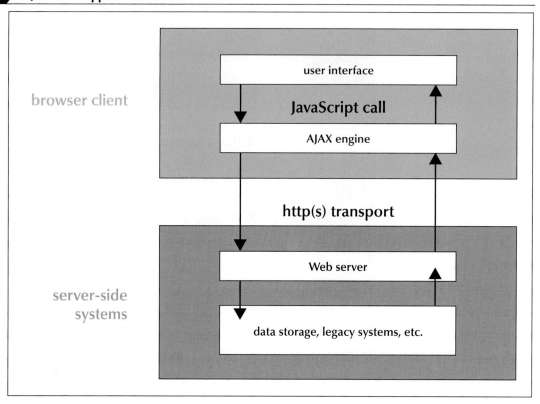

From the user's point of view, this communication is **asynchronous** because the AJAX engine is handling server requests, leaving the user free to interact with the rest of the Web page. As shown in Figure 12-7, the user does not have to wait for a response from the server to do other tasks on the Web page. In addition, several AJAX engines can be employed simultaneously to allow for exchange of data from several different sources. Also, because the server is generating only specific and smaller chunks of information and not an entire Web page, the load on the server is lessened.

Figure 12-7 Asynchronous communication

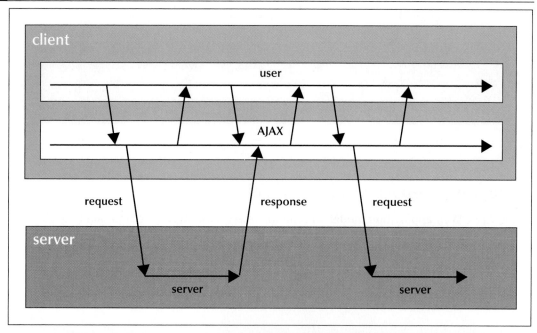

So what is AJAX? It's a way of developing Web applications that involve asynchronous communication, allowing the user to request information from the server while remaining free to do other tasks on the browser. It employs JavaScript as the scripting language for handling the interchange of information. Finally, although this aspect hasn't yet been touched on, the response from the server can be packaged in XML documents that are easily processed by JavaScript.

Limitations of AJAX

As developers learned more about the design possibilities offered by AJAX, AJAX applications quickly spread around the Internet. This created a new market for AJAX-related tools and programs. However, AJAX is not the answer to every programming need. It has some important limitations that you should be aware of before starting an AJAX project.

Perhaps the most important concern is that AJAX requires JavaScript to be running on the user's browser. Some users will disable JavaScript on the browser for security reasons, thereby disabling any AJAX application. Before writing an AJAX application, you should consider how to support users who do not run JavaScript by creating a variation of your application that relies only on the classic Web application model.

Another concern is that AJAX engines do not record the user's browser history, so you cannot use the browser's Back button to retrieve information received via an AJAX application. This also means you cannot bookmark any information returned by AJAX. As a result, you must consider whether the information that the AJAX engine is returning to the user is something the user will want to retrieve easily at a future date. If it is, you might want to use the classic Web application model in which pages can be bookmarked for future use.

AJAX applications can also pose a problem for users with special needs. Most browsers provide built-in support for keyboard users, users with poor vision or color blindness, and, in general, users who have physical problems operating a computer. You need to ensure that any AJAX application you create has not excluded an important percentage of the public.

Finally, beware of overdoing it. If you have dozens of AJAX engines running simultaneously, making calls to the Web server, communication with the server may crawl to a stop. Limit your use of AJAX to a few well chosen applications, leaving the bulk of your design to perform under the classic Web application model.

> **Tip**
>
> For AJAX applications that require longer server times to process, include a "loading" icon or other graphical feature to indicate that the application is still running and retrieving data. You can find such loading icons throughout the Web.

Exploring the XMLHttpRequest Object

For Steve's application, you'll develop an AJAX application that requests new stories, articles, and other features from the Sblogger Web server using an AJAX engine. All of these engines will be capable of retrieving and processing that information independent of one another.

The code for any AJAX application follows four basic steps:

1. Create an instance of an AJAX engine.
2. Define what server resource is opened by the engine.
3. Send any necessary data to the server.
4. Retrieve a response from the server and process it.

AJAX engines are created using the **XMLHttpRequest object**, which is a native JavaScript object that stores an HTTP request to the server. You create an instance of this object using the command

```
var req = new XMLHttpRequest();
```

where *req* is a variable containing a specific instance of the request object. This command is not supported under Internet Explorer versions 5.0 and 6.0. To support those browser versions, you must create the request as an ActiveX object using the command

```
var req = new ActiveXObject(pid);
```

where *pid* is a program ID that identifies the type of ActiveX object to be instantiated by the Internet Explorer browser. Internet Explorer 5 was the first browser to provide support for request objects through its built-in support for the XML language using an XML parser called **MSXML**. As a result, the exact program ID you need depends on which version of MSXML was installed with Internet Explorer. The following program IDs, sorted from the most recent version at the time of this writing to the earliest, can be used to create an ActiveX request object:

- Msxml2.XMLHTTP.6.0
- Msxml2.XMLHTTP.3.0
- Msxml2.XMLHTTP
- Microsoft.XMLHTTP

Tip

For versions of Internet Explorer 7.0 and higher, you can create request objects using the same XMLHttpRequest constructor employed by other browsers.

Reference Window | Creating an XMLHttpRequest Object

- To create a request object with non–IE browsers and Internet Explorer 7.0 or higher, use
  ```
  var req = new XMLHttpRequest();
  ```
  where *req* is an instance of the request object.
- For Internet Explorer 5.0 and 6.0, use
  ```
  var req = new ActiveXObject(pid);
  ```
  where *pid* is one of the following program IDs: Msxml2.XMLHTTP.6.0, Msxml2.XMLHTTP3.0, Msxml2.XMLHTTP, or Microsoft.XMLHTTP, in order from most recent to earliest.

The recommended course of action is to attempt to create an ActiveX request object with the most recent program IDs, proceeding to the earliest until an ID is found that works with the user's browser. To do this, you can insert the program IDs within an array and then loop through the array in the following structure:

```
if (typeof XMLHttpRequest == "undefined") {
   XMLHttpRequest = function() {
      var pids = ["Msxml2.XMLHTTP.6.0",
                  "Msxml2.XMLHTTP.3.0",
                  "Msxml2.XMLHTTP",
                  "Microsoft.XMLHTTP"];

      for (var i = 0; i < pids.length; i++) {
         try {
            return new ActiveXObject(pids[i]);
         } catch (e) {}
      }
      throw new Error("Unable to create request object");
   }
}
```

This code first tests whether the browser supports the XMLHttpRequest type. If it does not, the code creates its own XMLHttpRequest constructor function and attempts to create an ActiveX request object. The pids array contains each program ID supported by MSXML. The code uses a try...catch structure in an attempt to create an ActiveX request object using each pid. If the attempt is successful, the request object is returned. If the loop ends with no ActiveX request object created, the code throws an error, alerting the user of the problem and halting the execution of the program code.

When this code is added to your JavaScript library, you can create an instance of the XMLHttpRequest object using the command

```
var req = new XMLHttpRequest();
```

where the *req* variable will contain an XMLHttpRequest object for both Internet Explorer and non–IE browsers. Because you'll be creating several request objects for Steve, you will add this code to the ajax.js file so that it can be accessed throughout the Sblogger Web site.

To create the XMLHttpRequest constructor:

▶ **1.** Return to the **ajax.js** file in your text editor.

▶ **2.** At the bottom of the file, insert the following code to create a cross-browser constructor for the XMLHttpRequest object so that the file can be accessed through the Web site, as shown in Figure 12-8:

```
// XMLHttpRequest Constructor
if (typeof XMLHttpRequest == "undefined") {
   XMLHttpRequest = function() {

      // Array of MSXML PIDs
      var pids = ["Msxml2.XMLHTTP.6.0",
                  "Msxml2.XMLHTTP.3.0",
                  "Msxml2.XMLHTTP",
                  "Microsoft.XMLHTTP"];

      // Test each PID
      for (var i = 0; i < pids.length; i++) {
         try {
            return new ActiveXObject(pids[i]);
         } catch (e) {}
      }


      // Halt if unable to create request object
      throw new Error("Unable to create request object");
   }
}
```

XMLHttpRequest constructor   Figure 12-8

▶ **3.** Save the file.

The open() and send() Methods

Although browsers support different ways of creating the request object, the properties and methods associated with that object are very similar across browsers. Thus, after you instantiate a request object, almost all of your code will be compatible across different browsers and browser versions. Figure 12-9 lists some of the methods associated with the XMLHttpRequest object.

Figure 12-9	Methods of the request object

Method	Description
req.abort()	Stops any transfer of data involving the *req* request object
reg.getAllResponseHeaders()	Returns a string containing the HTTP headers received by the *req* request object
req.getResponseHeader(*header*)	Returns the text of the HTTP *header* received by the *req* request object
req.open(*method, url, async, user, pwd*)	Specifies the transaction *method* and *url* applied to the destination of the request; the *async*, *user*, and *pwd* parameters are optional and indicate whether to set up asynchronous communication, and supply a username and password for the transaction
req.overrideMimeType(*mime*)	Overrides the mime-type of the response from the server, substituting *mime* as the mime-type by which the response should be interpreted (not supported by Internet Explorer)
req.send(*content*)	Specifies any *content* to be included with the HTTP request
req.setRequestHeader(*name, value*)	Specifies a *name/value* pair to the header being sent with the HTTP request

Of the methods listed in Figure 12-9, the two that you will use in every AJAX application are the open() and send() methods. The open() method specifies what server resource you want to access with the request object and has the syntax

```
req.open(method, url, async, user, pwd)
```

where *req* is an instance of the XMLHttpRequest object, *method* specifies how data will be transferred to and from the server, *url* is the URL of the resource that will receive the request, *async* is a Boolean value that tells the browser whether to use asynchronous or synchronous communication, and *user* and *pwd* are the username and password that may be required for some secure communication channels. The *async*, *user*, and *pwd* parameters are all optional. If the *async* parameter has a default value of true, it indicates that the communication is asynchronous, allowing the AJAX application to continue without waiting for a response from the server.

The *method* parameter has two possible values: GET and POST. The **get method** sends data to the Web server by attaching a field name/value pair to the URL. For example, the URL

```
submit.cgi?topic=baseball
```

attaches a single name/value pair to a CGI script named submit.cgi running on the server with topic as the field name and baseball as the field value. You can specify this URL in the open() method

Tip

For security reasons, the *url* parameter must refer to a resource belonging to the same domain as the page containing the AJAX code. You cannot access URLs from third-party domains.

```
req.open("GET", "submit.cgi?topic=baseball")
```

and the browser will open an asynchronous connection to the CGI script using the get method. The command

```
req.open("GET", "submit.cgi?topic=baseball", false)
```

performs the same action except that the communication is synchronous, which means the code will halt until a response is received from the server.

The **post method** sends data in a separate stream from the URL. This has several advantages. Because URLs are limited in the number of characters they can contain, the post method is preferred for long data strings. The post method can also be used to transmit data in any format and is not limited to the serialized name/value format required by the get method. The command

```
req.open("POST", "submit.cgi", true, "lavent", "jr56X!")
```

opens an asynchronous connection to the submit.cgi script using the post method. Note that in this case, both a username (lavent) and a password (jr56X!) have been provided to access a secure server.

To send data to the server, you use the send() method

```
req.send(content)
```

where *content* is the data string to be sent to the server. For the post method, you also tell the server what type of data is being sent by using the setRequestHeader() method. For example, to send the same name/value pair described earlier with the post method, you would run the following two command lines:

```
req.setRequestHeader("Content-Type","application/x-www-form-
urlencoded");
req.send("topic=baseball");
```

If no content is required or if you are using the get method (which does not allow for data to be sent any way other than attaching a text string to the URL), set the *content* value to null, as in the following code:

```
req.send(null)
```

Once invoked, the send() method initiates the communication stream with the server, so it should be run after you have applied the open() and, if necessary, the setRequest-Header() methods.

Opening and Sending a Request | Reference Window

- To open a request, run
  ```
  req.open(method, url, async, user, pwd)
  ```
  where *req* is a request object, *method* is either GET or POST *url* is the URL of the server resource, *async* is an optional Boolean value that tells the browser whether to use asynchronous (true) or synchronous communication (false), and *user* and *pwd* are optional parameters that specify the username and password that may be required for secure channels. If no *async* parameter value is specified, the communication is assumed to be asynchronous.
- To send a request, run
  ```
  req.send(content)
  ```
  where *content* is data to be sent to the server. If no content is required or if the get-method is used, enter a value of null for *content*.

InSight | **HTTP Requests and Responses**

When writing an AJAX application, it is often useful to understand how HTTP transfers requests to the server and responses to the client. All HTTP requests have the general structure

```
request-line
headers

request-body
```

where *request-line* indicates the type of request, the resource to access, and the HTTP version; *headers* are lines containing additional information to be used by the server; and *request-body* is an optional section containing additional data. The HTTP request always has a blank line after the *headers* section, even if no *request-body* follows. For example, the following HTTP request specifies the get method to ask for data from the Sblogger Web server:

```
GET submit.cgi?topic=Baseball HTTP/1.1
Host: www.sblogger.com
User-Agent: Mozilla/4.0 (compatible; MSIE 8.0; Windows NT 6.0)
Connection: Keep-Alive
```

The first line supplies the URL to access and specifies HTTP/1.1 as the communication protocol. The second line provides the domain name of the host, which is followed in the third line by information about the browser initiating the request. The final line tells the server to keep the connection alive and available for future requests.

The format of the HTTP response is similar, employing the structure

```
status-line
headers

response-body
```

where *status-line* contains information on the response, *headers* contains additional information about the response, and *response-body* is an optional section that contains the text of the response. The following code shows a typical HTTP response:

```
HTTP/1.1 200 OK
Date: Sun, 5 Aug 2012 14:28:35 GMT
Content-Type: text/html;charset=ISO-8859-1
Content-Length: 91

<html>
   <head>
      <title>Sblogger</title>
   </head>
   <body>
      <h1>Welcome to Sblogger</h1>
   </body>
</html>
```

The initial lines provide information about the date of the response and the text format. The length of the response in characters is given by the Content-Length header, and the HTML code that is sent to the browser to be displayed is given in the *response-body* section.

You can view the text of an HTTP response using either the getAllResponseHeaders() or get-ResponseHeader() methods of the request object. For more control over the header included in the HTTP request, you can use the setRequestHeader() method to insert and define specific headers.

Retrieving an HTML Fragment

You are ready to start work on your first AJAX application. Steve has stored his daily commentary, encoded as an HTML fragment, in a text file named commentary.txt. The first few lines of the commentary.txt file are:

```
<h1>Jenkins on Ice</h1>
<h6>Keyword: Basketball</h6>
<p>Retired NBA star Dennis Jenkins announced today that he has signed
   a contract with <em>Long Sleep</em> to have his body frozen before
   death, to be revived only when medical science has discovered a
   cure to the aging process.</p>
...
```

Steve wants the text of this HTML fragment retrieved from the commentary.txt file and inserted into the main section of the Sblogger home page whenever the page is loaded by the browser. To do this, you'll first create a request object to retrieve the contents of this file via the get method, running this code in response to the load event of the window object.

To create a request object for the commentary.txt file:

1. Open the **commentary.txt** file in your text editor, study the code, and then close the file without saving changes.

2. Go to the **newsfeed.js** file in your text editor.

3. Insert the following command to run the getCommentary() function when the page is loaded:

   ```
   addEvent(window, "load", getCommentary, false);
   ```

4. Insert the following initial code for the getCommentary() function:

   ```
   function getCommentary() {
       var main = document.getElementById("main");

       // Request object for the commentary.txt file
       var reqCom = new XMLHttpRequest();
       reqCom.open("GET", "commentary.txt");
       reqCom.send(null);
   }
   ```

   Figure 12-10 shows the inserted code.

Code to create a request object | **Figure 12-10**

```
*/
addEvent(window, "load", getCommentary, false);

function getCommentary() {
    var main = document.getElementById("main");

    // Request object for the commentary.txt file
    var reqCom = new XMLHttpRequest();
    reqCom.open("GET", "commentary.txt");
    reqCom.send(null);
}
```

runs the getCommentary() function when the page loads

sends a request to the commentary.txt file

5. Save the file.

Processing the XMLHttpRequest Response

After a request is sent to the server, the AJAX application next needs to retrieve and interpret the server's response to that request. The interaction between the browser and the server goes through the following five stages or states:

1. **Uninitialized:** The request object is created.
2. **Loading:** The open() method is called.
3. **Loaded:** The browser successfully sends the request using the send() method, but has received no response from the server.
4. **Interactive:** The browser begins receiving a partial response from the server.
5. **Complete:** The server has completed sending a response to the browser.

You determine the current stage that the request object is in with the readyState property. Figure 12-11 describes this and other properties of the request object.

Figure 12-11 — **Properties of the request object**

Property	Description
req.onreadystatechange	Event handler that fires whenever the readyState value of the *req* request object changes
req.readyState	Integer indicating current state of the *req* request object, where: 0=uninitialized, 1=loading, 2=loaded, 3=interactive, and 4=complete
req.responseText	Text returned by the *req* request object
req.responseXML	XML document returned by the *req* request object
req.status	Numeric code returned by server indicating the communication status of the request
req.statusText	Text string returned by the server indicating the communication status of the request

Because the communication with the server is asynchronous, your AJAX application needs to "listen" for changes in the readyState property using the onreadystatechange event handler. After a completed response has been received from the server, the application can evaluate the response and use it. The general JavaScript code is:

```
req.onreadystatechange = function() {
   if (this.readyState == 4) {
      evaluate the response
   }
}
```

The server response might not be data. It might also be an error message informing the browser that the server was unable to handle the request. Before processing the response, you need to confirm that the request was successfully handled by the server by using the status property of the request object. Figure 12-12 describes values of the status property.

Figure 12-12 — **Request status code values**

Status Code	Description	Status Code	Description
100	Continue	403	Forbidden
200	OK	404	Not Found
302	Found	408	Request timeout
400	Bad request	500	Internal Server Error

For most AJAX applications, you only need to test that the status value of the request object equals 200 after the response is complete.

Only after there is a successfully completed response can you examine the content sent from the server to the AJAX application. This content is stored in two properties:

```
req.responseText
```

which returns the content as a text string, and

```
req.responseXML
```

which returns an XML document object. The next session explores the responseXML property. This session focuses solely on text content.

For simple text documents, such as the commentary.txt file, the responseText property returns the text of the file. Thus, to retrieve the text of the commentary.txt file and place that HTML fragment into the main section of Steve's Web page, you run the following code:

```
reqCom.onreadystatechange = function() {
   if (this.readyState == 4) {
      if (this.status == 200) {
         main.innerHTML = this.responseText;
      }
   }
}
```

Notice that you confirm that the response from the server is both complete and without error before inserting the response text into the main section. You will add this code to the getCommentary() function in the newsfeed.js file.

To complete the getCommentary() function:

▶ **1.** Add the following code to the getCommentary() function in the newsfeed .js file, as shown in Figure 12-13:

```
reqCom.onreadystatechange = function() {
   // Process the data when the response is
   // completed without error
   if (this.readyState == 4) {
      if (this.status == 200) {
         // Retrieve the daily commentary and
         // display it within the main section
         main.innerHTML = this.responseText;
      }
   }
}
```

Final getCommentary() function ◀ **Figure 12-13**

```
function getCommentary() {
   var main = document.getElementById("main");

   // Request object for the commentary.txt file
   var reqCom = new XMLHttpRequest();
   reqCom.open("GET", "commentary.txt");
   reqCom.send(null);

   reqCom.onreadystatechange = function() {
      // Process the data when the response is
      // completed without error
      if (this.readyState == 4) {
         if (this.status == 200) {
            // Retrieve the daily commentary and
            // display it within the main section
            main.innerHTML = this.responseText;
         }
      }
   }
}
```

confirms that the response is complete and successful

loads the html fragment in the commentary.txt file into the main div element

▶ **2.** Save the newsfeed.js file.

- To test when the server has responded to a request, run the event handler

```
req.onreadystatechange = function() {
    if (this.readyState == 4) {
        if (this.status = 200) {
            process the response
        }
    }
}
```

where *req* is a request object and *process the response* is JavaScript code to be run with the response from the server. A readyState value of 4 indicates that the response is completed, whereas a status value of 200 indicates that the response is completed with an OK status code.
- To retrieve the text of the response, use the following property:

```
req.responseText
```

- To retrieve an XML document of the response, use the following property:

```
req.responseXML
```

You can now test your AJAX application. An important point to realize about the XMLHttpRequest object is that it only works through the HTTP communication protocol. This means that you *cannot* test the code locally on your computer because that communication is done via the file: protocol. To create and test the AJAX code, you must either load your files to a Web server or install a personal Web server such as Windows **IIS (Internet Information Service)** on your computer that will run the HTTP protocol locally. This tutorial assumes that all testing is done on a Web server.

Placing an AJAX Application onto a Server

To load documents onto a Web server, you must have an account on the server. Your instructor or technical resource person can help you set up an account if you have not already done so. Web servers differ slightly in how they organize their folder structures. In general, within your account, you should find a folder named *web* or *wwwroot*. You need to install the files from the Sblogger Web site within this folder.

You can use the ftp protocol to transfer the files or, if you are using a server on your local machine, you can simply copy the files into the server's root folder. Many free ftp clients are available on the Web to upload files to a Web server account. You can also use the Internet Explorer browser to open an ftp connection to your server. You need both your username and password to access your server account. After your account is set up and accessed, you can begin transferring the files.

To load and test the Sblogger home page:

1. Using your ftp client or another file transfer program, log on to your Web server, and then, within the web folder (or another server folder if indicated by your instructor or technical resource person), insert a new folder named **tutorial.12**.

2. Within the tutorial.12 folder, create another folder named **tutorial**.

3. Within the tutorial folder, from your account on your Web server, transfer the following files from your computer's tutorial.12\tutorial folder: **ajax.js**, **commentary.txt**, **newsfeed.js**, **sblogger.htm**, **sblogo.jpg**, **sbstyles.css**, and **search.png**.

4. Use your browser to open the URL ***yourdomain*/tutorial.12/tutorial/sblogger.htm**, where *yourdomain* is your domain name and account on your Web server.

Trouble? If you don't know your domain name address, ask your instructor or technical resource person. If you are running a local server such as IIS, you might enter *http://localhost/tutorial.12/tutorial/sblogger.htm* for the URL.

As shown in Figure 12-14, your browser loads the Sblogger home page and retrieves the HTML code from the commentary.txt file, displaying the results in the main section of the page. The styles for the commentary are based on styles previously stored in the sbstyles.css file.

Daily commentary loaded into the Sblogger home page | Figure 12-14

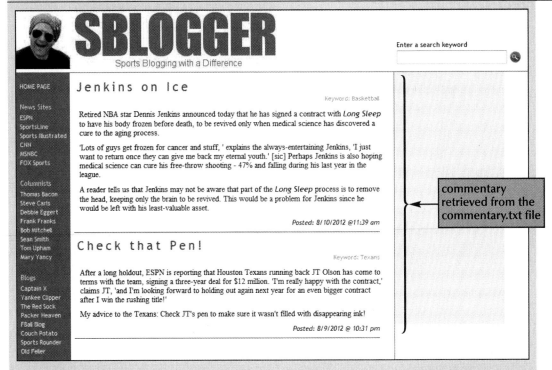

Trouble? If your browser fails to load the commentary code, check the code in both the ajax.js file and the newsfeed.js file against the code shown in Figures 12-8 and 12-13. Verify that the code matches, including the use of lowercase and uppercase letters.

Steve is pleased with your work on the daily commentary Web page. With the commentary code stored in a separate file, he can use a script to write the HTML code into that file without having to edit the home page directly. As he updates the commentary.txt file, the contents displayed on the home page will be similarly updated.

InSight | **Working with the Browser Cache**

Browsers often cache the data retrieved from external files such as the commentary.txt file in a file stored locally on the user's computer. Caching increases speed and performance because future requests can be drawn from the cache rather than the server. However, this can be a problem if the data in the external file has changed since the cache was created. Most browsers confirm that the external file data has not been changed before loading data from the cache. In some situations, however, the browser loads the cache data even though it is outdated.

If the possibility of loading old data is a concern with your AJAX application, you can force the browser to always retrieve data from the external file regardless of the contents of the browser cache by running the command

```
req.setRequestHeader("If-Modified-Since", date);
```

to add an HTTP header to your request object, where *req* is your request object and *date* is a date in the past. Because every response from the server has a time and date stamp, setting *date* to a date in the past forces the browser to always load data from the external file. For example, to keep the reqCom object you created in this session from being cached, you can run the command

```
reqCom.setRequestHeader("If-Modified-Since", "Thu, 1 Jan 1970 00:00:
01 GMT");
```

and the browser will always load the current contents of commentary.txt, whatever they may be. You can also prevent caching by using the following HTTP header:

```
req.setRequestHeader("Cache-Control", "no-cache");
```

In general, you never want to cache HTML code, but you can increase the performance of your application by caching everything else such as logo images. You can force the browser to use a cache by applying the HTTP header

```
req.setRequestHeader("Expires", date);
```

where *date* is a date far into the future. Many AJAX developers use the date string Mon, 31 Dec 2035 12:00:00 GMT Google, for example, caches its logo until 2038. By experimenting with different caching strategies, you can vastly increase the speed and performance of your AJAX applications.

In the next session, you will learn how to work with XML documents by displaying the contents of a news feed.

Review | **Session 12.1 Quick Check**

1. Describe the features of the Web application model.
2. Describe the features of the AJAX Web application model.
3. What is asynchronous communication?
4. Provide a command to open the following resource using a request object named reqAns; assuming that the communication is asynchronous and uses the get method:

   ```
   register?id=wjones&pwd=gr7#xY!
   ```

5. For the request object described in question 4, what command would you use to send the request?
6. What readyState value is returned by the server to indicate that it has received the reqAns request?
7. The server returns a status value of 404. What does this tell you about the state of the request?
8. What property do you use to view the text returned by the server?

Session 12.2

Introducing XML

Steve wants to display up-to-the-minute headlines from the world of sports on the Sblogger home page. To do this, he added a feature to his Web server to download a sports news feed. The news feed is formatted as an XML document.

XML (Extensible Markup Language) is a language used to create structured documents. You already have experience working with one markup language—HTML, the hypertext markup language. XML and HTML documents share a common structure. Elements are indicated with markup tags that contain textual content. A markup tag can contain attributes that describe a feature of the element, and a single root element contains all other elements in the document. The following is a typical XML document used to store student data:

```
<?xml version="1.0" encoding="UTF-8" ?>
<students>
    <student id="124-09" grade="junior">
        <name>Tom Aaron</name>
        <photo>taaron.jpg</photo>
    </student>
    <student id="341-08" grade="senior">
        <name>Linda Wu</name>
        <photo>lkwu.jpg</photo>
    </student>
</students>
```

The first line in this document is the **XML declaration**, which tells any application reading the document that the document is written in the XML language. A single root element named students contains information about the student body. The student, name, and photo elements and the id and grade attributes provide information about individual students. The element names are descriptive so that even without having seen an XML document before, you can easily interpret the content of this document.

Creating XML Vocabularies

Because XML is such a useful language for creating structured documents, developers have created their own markup languages, called **XML vocabularies**, built on the foundations of XML. One such XML vocabulary is **XHTML**, which is an XML version of HTML. Almost all of the Web pages that you have worked with in these tutorials are written in XHTML. A typical XHTML document has the basic structure

```
<?xml version="1.0" encoding="UTF-8" ?>
<html>
    <head>
        head elements
    </head>
    <body>
        body elements
    </body>
</html>
```

where *head elements* and *body elements* are indicated using the markup tags that you have already seen in typical HTML files. The tag names and attributes from XHTML were chosen to match those from HTML to allow for easy portability. XHTML is just one XML vocabulary. Thousands of XML vocabularies have been developed for applications ranging from chemical structures to musical scores to mathematical papers. Although the tags and attribute names may vary from one XML vocabulary to another, the basic structure of a single root element, nested elements, and element attributes remains constant across all vocabularies.

Distributing News Feeds with RSS

One of the more important XML vocabularies is the **Really Simple Syndication (RSS)** language, which is used to distribute news articles, or any content that changes on a regular basis, to a group of subscribers. Subscribers to an RSS news feed can receive periodic updates using a software program called a **feed reader** or an **aggregator**. These feed readers are often built into commonly used Internet software. One feed reader is the Apple program iTunes, which allows users to automatically retrieve audio and video feeds in the form of **podcasts** that can be played on the user's portable MP3 player or iPod. Although content delivered by the podcast is audio or video, the language that organizes and describes that content is RSS. Browsers can also act as news readers for most RSS news feeds.

Because an RSS file is written in XML, the RSS code follows the conventions of all XML documents. For example, the following RSS code is the first part of a news feed document that Steve wants to retrieve for his Web site:

```
<?xml version="1.0" encoding="UTF-8" standalone="yes" ?>

<rss version="2.0">
    <channel>
        <title>Current Headlines</title>
        <link>http://www.sblogger.com</link>
        <description>Sports News Feed</description>

        <item>
            <title>Carson leads at PGA</title>
            <link>http://www.sblogger.com/pga/pga238.html</link>
            <description>Brett Carson took a three stroke lead
                         into the final round of the PGA
                         Championship at Whistling Straits with
                         a birdie on the final hole.
            </description>
        </item>
...
    </channel>
</rss>
```

> **Tip**
>
> There are dozens more RSS elements and attributes that are not included in this scaled-down version of an RSS feed. But this example provides a taste of the basic structure and contents of an RSS document.

This news feed provides news from a golf tournament. The file begins with the XML prolog followed by the root rss element that tells the browser that this is an RSS file. The channel element is used to store information about the news "channel" or news source for all of the articles listed in the feed. The item element contains information from a specific article. A news channel might contain several such item elements. Figure 12-15 provides more information about the purpose of each element in Steve's document.

Figure 12-15 | **Elements from an RSS document**

Element	Description
channel	The root element of an RSS document, containing information about the news channel that originates the news feed
channel/title	The title of the news channel
channel/link	The URL of the news channel
channel/description	A text description of the news channel
channel/item	A news item stored on the news channel
channel/item/title	The news item title
channel/item/link	The URL of the news item
channel/item/description	A text description of the news item

Steve's sample RSS news feed is in the headlines.xml file in the tutorial.12\tutorial folder. You'll create a request object that opens this document when the Sblogger home page initially loads Steve plans to frequently update the contents of this news feed, so you'll use the setRequestHeader() method to prevent the browser from caching the feed text locally.

To create a request object for the headlines.xml document:

▶ **1.** If you took a break after the previous session, make sure the ajax.js, newsfeed.js, and sblogger.htm files are open in your text editor; the sblogger.htm file is open in your browser; and the ajax.js, commentary.txt, newsfeed.js, sblogger.htm, sblogo. jpg, sbstyles.css, and search.png files are stored in your account on your Web server in the tutorial.12/tutorial folder.

▶ **2.** Use your text editor to open the **headlines.xml** file from the tutorial.12\tutorial folder on your local computer, study the contents of the file, and then close the document without saving any changes.

▶ **3.** Return to the **newsfeed.js** file in your text editor, and then, at the bottom of the file, insert the following command to run the getHeadlines() function when the page is loaded:

```
addEvent(window, "load", getHeadlines, false);
```

▶ **4.** Enter the following initial code for the getHeadlines() function, as shown in Figure 12-16:

```
function getHeadlines() {
    var news = document.getElementById("news");

    // Request object for the headlines feed
    var reqHead = new XMLHttpRequest();
    reqHead.open("GET", "headlines.xml");
    reqHead.setRequestHeader("Cache-Control", "no-cache");
    reqHead.send(null);

    reqHead.onreadystatechange = function() {
        if (this.readyState == 4) {
            if (this.status == 200) {
                // Retrieve the headlines feed
            }
        }
    }
}
```

The getHeadlines() method   Figure 12-16

```
}
addEvent(window, "load", getHeadlines, false);

function getHeadlines() {
    var news = document.getElementById("news");

    // Request object for the headlines feed
    var reqHead = new XMLHttpRequest();
    reqHead.open("GET", "headlines.xml");
    reqHead.setRequestHeader("Cache-Control", "no-cache");
    reqHead.send(null);

    reqHead.onreadystatechange = function() {
        if (this.readyState == 4) {
            if (this.status == 200) {
                // Retrieve the headlines feed
            }
        }
    }
}
```

- runs the getHeadlines() function when the page is loaded
- stores the news feed in the news section of the Sblogger home page
- prevents the browser from caching the news feed locally
- retrieves the document once a complete and successful response has been received

▶ **5.** Save the file.

Recall that one property of the request object is the responseXML property, which returns the request response as an XML document object. You will use this property to store the contents of the headlines.xml file in a document object named newsDoc.

To create the newsDoc object:

▶ **1.** Within the getHeadlines() function, insert the following code, as shown in Figure 12-17:

```
var newsDoc = this.responseXML;
```

Figure 12-17 | **Code to retrieve the XML document object from the response**

```
reqHead.onreadystatechange = function() {
    if (this.readyState == 4) {
        if (this.status == 200) {
            // Retrieve the headlines feed
            var newsDoc = this.responseXML;
        }
    }
}
```

stores the XML document object in the newsDoc variable

▶ **2.** Save the file.

Next, you'll retrieve element values from the newsDoc document object and display them on the Sblogger home page.

InSight | **Retrieving an XHTML Document Object**

XHTML is an XML vocabulary and thus should be accessible using either the responseText or the responseXML property. However, browsers will interpret any XHTML file returned from an HTTP request as an HTML file, not as an XML file. As a result, these browsers do not store the document object via the responseXML property. This is a problem if you want your JavaScript code to be able to easily parse the contents of the XHTML document. To override the browsers' default behavior, you can force them to recognize XHTML files as XML by applying the property

```
req.overrideMimeType("text/xml")
```

to the request object before sending the request to the server. Unfortunately, this property is not supported by Internet Explorer. For Internet Explorer, you must retrieve the text of the XHTML file using the responseText property and then convert that text into an XML document using Internet Explorer's loadXML() method.

After an XHTML file has been converted into an XML document object, you can apply all of the properties and methods of the document object model to parse the contents of the document. You can explore how to retrieve XHTML files as XML documents in Case Problem 3.

Building an RSS Newsreader

One advantage of working with XML documents is that they share the same document object model as HTML documents. This means that you can create element and attribute nodes, navigate through the node tree, and apply many of the same document object methods. For example, to reference the first (and only) channel element from an RSS document, you can use the expression

```
xmlDoc.getElementsByTagName("channel")[0]
```

where *xmlDoc* is an XML document object containing RSS code. Not all of the JavaScript methods you have used for HTML documents are compatible with XML documents. You cannot, for example, use the getElementsById() method. Nor can you extract the text content of an element using the innerHTML property.

Steve wants you to create a basic news reader that will accept an RSS document and transform the contents into an HTML fragment that can then be easily inserted into the Sblogger home page. Figure 12-18 shows how he wants the content of the headlines.xml file transformed into an HTML fragment.

Tip

To retrieve an attribute value from an XML element, you must use the *elem*.getAttribute(*att*) method, where *elem* references an element in the XML document and *att* is the name of an attribute within that element.

RSS document transformed into an HTML fragment | **Figure 12-18**

RSS document
```
<channel>
    <title>Current Headlines</title>
    <link>http://www.sblogger.com</link>
    <description>Sports News Feed</description>

    <item>
        <title>Carson leads at PGA</title>
        <link>http://www.sblogger.com/pga/pga238.html</link>
        <description>Brett Carson took a three stroke lead
                into the final round of the PGA
                Championship at Whistling Straits with
                a birdie on the final hole.
        </description>
    </item>
    ...
</channel>
```

HTML fragment
```
<h1>Current Headlines</h1>
<h2>
    <a href="http://www.sblogger.com/pga/pga238.html">
        Carson leads at PGA
    </a>
</h2>
<p>Brett Carson took a three stroke lead
    into the final round of the PGA
    Championship at Whistling Straits with
    a birdie on the final hole.
</p>
...
```

Because the RSS documents could be retrieved from a variety of sources, you will create a custom news feed object that can parse RSS documents. You'll start by adding a constructor function named RSSFeed to the ajax.js file. The RSSFeed object will have three properties named title, link, and description containing the text of the news channel's title, link, and description elements, respectively. To extract the text of those elements, you'll reference the node value of the first child of each element. For example, to return the text of the channel's title, you'll use the expression

```
channel.getElementsByTagName("title")[0].firstChild.nodeValue;
```

where *channel* is a reference to the first (and only) channel element in the RSS document. The expressions to return the text of the channel's link and description are similar. You will add the RSSFeed constructor function now.

To insert the RSSFeed constructor:

▶ 1. Return to the **ajax.js** file in your text editor and scroll to the bottom of the file.

▶ 2. Insert the following code, as shown in Figure 12-19:

```
/* Constructor function for RSS news feeds */
function RSSFeed(xmlDoc) {

    // Retrieve the news feed title, link, and description
    var channel = xmlDoc.getElementsByTagName("channel")[0];
    var title = channel.getElementsByTagName("title")[0];
    var link = channel.getElementsByTagName("link")[0];

    var description =
channel.getElementsByTagName("description")[0];

    this.title = title.firstChild.nodeValue;
    this.link = title.firstChild.nodeValue;
    this.description = title.firstChild.nodeValue;

}
```

Figure 12-19 ▶ **RSSFeed constructor**

```
/* Constructor function for RSS news feeds */
function RSSFeed(xmlDoc) {

    // Retrieve the news feed title, link, and description
    var channel = xmlDoc.getElementsByTagName("channel")[0];
    var title = channel.getElementsByTagName("title")[0];
    var link = channel.getElementsByTagName("link")[0];
    var description = channel.getElementsByTagName("description")[0];

    this.title = title.firstChild.nodeValue;
    this.link = title.firstChild.nodeValue;
    this.description = title.firstChild.nodeValue;
}
```

xmlDoc contains the document object for the RSS news feed

references to the channel, title, link, and description elements

text of the title, link, and description elements

Reference Window | Reading an XML Document with AJAX

- To retrieve an XML document object, use the property
  ```
  var xmlDoc = req.responseXML
  ```
  where *req* is an instance of the request object and *xmlDoc* is the XML document object.
- To reference a collection of elements within the XML document, use the method
  ```
  var elemArr = xmlDoc.getElementsByTagName(elem)
  ```
  where *elem* is an XML element name and *elemArr* is an array of those elements in the XML document.
- To return the text of an element in an XML document, use the expression
  ```
  elemArr[i].firstChild.nodeValue
  ```
  where *i* is the index number of the element within the *elemArr* array. Note that this method assumes that the element does not contain any other child nodes.

The RSSFeed() constructor function has a single parameter named xmlDoc, which represents an XML document object. The function then creates references to the channel, title, link, and description elements in xmlDoc. Finally, it stores the text of the title, link, and description elements as custom properties of the RSSFeed object.

You will create a similar constructor function named RSSItem for each news feed item. Because a news feed item only makes sense within the context of a news feed, you'll nest the RSSItem() constructor function within the RSSFeed constructor. You will add the code for the function now.

To create the RSSItem constructor:

▶ **1.** Within the RSSFeed() function, insert the following code, as shown in Figure 12-20:

```
/* Constructor function for an RSS news item */
function RSSItem(item) {
    var title = item.getElementsByTagName("title")[0];
    var link = item.getElementsByTagName("link")[0];
    var description = item.getElementsByTagName("description")[0];

    this.title = title.firstChild.nodeValue;
    this.link = link.firstChild.nodeValue;
    this.description = description.firstChild.nodeValue;
}
```

RSSItem constructor ◀ **Figure 12-20**

```
/* Constructor function for RSS news feeds */
function RSSFeed(xmlDoc) {

    // Retrieve the news feed title, link, and description
    var channel = xmlDoc.getElementsByTagName("channel")[0];
    var title = channel.getElementsByTagName("title")[0];
    var link = channel.getElementsByTagName("link")[0];
    var description = channel.getElementsByTagName("description")[0];

    this.title = title.firstchild.nodeValue;
    this.link = title.firstChild.nodeValue;
    this.description = title.firstChild.nodeValue;

    /* Constructor function for an RSS news item */
    function RSSItem(item) {
        var title = item.getElementsByTagName("title")[0];
        var link = item.getElementsByTagName("link")[0];
        var description = item.getElementsByTagName("description")[0];

        this.title = title.firstChild.nodevalue;
        this.link = link.firstChild.nodevalue;
        this.description = description.firstChild.nodeValue;
    }
}
```

> text of each news item's title, hypertext link, and description

▶ **2.** Save the file.

The RSSItem() function has a single parameter named item to represent an item element from an RSS document. The function creates three custom properties named title, link, and description, containing the text of the item's title, hypertext link, and description, respectively.

The final property you will create for the custom RSSFeed object is the items property containing an array of RSSItem objects. You will add this property now.

To create the custom items property:

▶ **1.** Add the following code to the RSSFeed() function, as shown in Figure 12-21:

```
// Create an array of news feed items
this.items = new Array();

var feedItems = channel.getElementsByTagName("item");
for (var i = 0; i < feedItems.length; i++) {
    var feedItem = new RSSItem(feedItems[i]);
    this.items.push(feedItem);
}
```

Figure 12-21 | **Code to define the custom items property**

```
/* Constructor function for RSS news feeds */
function RSSFeed(xmlDoc) {

   // Retrieve the news feed title, link, and description
   var channel = xmlDoc.getElementsByTagName("channel")[0];
   var title = channel.getElementsByTagName("title")[0];
   var link = channel.getElementsByTagName("link")[0];
   var description = channel.getElementsByTagName("description")[0];

   this.title = title.firstChild.nodevalue;
   this.link = title.firstChild.nodevalue;
   this.description = title.firstChild.nodevalue;

   /* Constructor function for an RSS news item */
   function RSSItem(item) {
      var title = item.getElementsByTagName("title")[0];
      var link = item.getElementsByTagName("link")[0];
      var description = item.getElementsByTagName("description")[0];

      this.title = title.firstChild.nodevalue;
      this.link = link.firstChild.nodevalue;
      this.description = description.firstChild.nodevalue;
   }

   // Create an array of news feed items
   this.items = new Array();

   var feedItems = channel.getElementsByTagName("item");
   for (var i = 0; i < feedItems.length; i++) {
      var feedItem = new RSSItem(feedItems[i]);
      this.items.push(feedItem);
   }

}
```

loops through all of the item elements and creates an array of RSSItem objects

> **2.** Save the file.

The code loops through all the item elements within the news feed channel. For each element, it creates a custom RSSItem object, and then adds that object to the items array.

The final piece you need to add to your custom RSSFeed object is the parseToHTML() method, which creates the HTML fragment

```
<h1>Feed Title</h1>

<h2><a href="Item Link 1">Item Title 1</a></h1>
<p>Item Description 1</p>

<h2><a href="Item Link 2">Item Title 2</a></h1>
<p>Item Description 2</p>

. . .
```

where *Feed Title* is the title of the news feed channel, and *Item Link 1*, *Item Title 1*, *Item Description 1*, etc. are the titles, links, and descriptions of the individual news items, respectively. The parseToHTML() method is added to the RSSFeed prototype.

To create the parseToHTML() method of the RSSFeed object:

> **1.** Directly below the code for the RSSFeed() constructor function, insert the following code to write the news feed title:

```
/* Method to write the RSSFeed document to an HTML fragment */
RSSFeed.prototype.parseToHTML = function(outputNode) {

   var fTitle = document.createElement("h1")
   fTitle.innerHTML = this.title;
   outputNode.appendChild(fTitle);
```

Note that the parseToHTML() function has a single parameter named outputNode. This is the node in the Web page document in which the HTML fragment will be placed.

For each object in the items array, you need to write the HTML code for the news item and append it to outputNode.

▶ **2.** Add the following code to the parseToHTML() function:

```
for (var i = 0; i < this.items.length; i++) {
    var iTitle = document.createElement("h2");
    var iTitleLink = document.createElement("a");
    iTitleLink.innerHTML = this.items[i].title;
    iTitleLink.href = this.items[i].link;

    iTitle.appendChild(iTitleLink);
    outputNode.appendChild(iTitle);

    var iPara = document.createElement("p");
    iPara.innerHTML = this.items[i].description;
    outputNode.appendChild(iPara);
}
```

▶ **3.** Enter the closing curly brace **}** to close up the function. The code for the parseToHTML() method is complete. See Figure 12-22.

Complete parseToHTML() method ◀ **Figure 12-22**

```
/* Method to write the RSSFeed document to an HTML fragment */
RSSFeed.prototype.parseToHTML = function(outputNode) {

    var fTitle = document.createElement("h1")        ⎫
    fTitle.innerHTML = this.title;                   ⎬  writes the title of the news
    outputNode.appendChild(fTitle);                  ⎭  feed channel as an h1 heading

    for (var i = 0; i < this.items.length; i++) {
        var iTitle = document.createElement("h2");   ⎫
        var iTitleLink = document.createElement("a");⎬  writes the title of the news
        iTitleLink.innerHTML = this.items[i].title;  ⎬  item as a linked h2 heading
        iTitleLink.href = this.items[i].link;        ⎭

        iTitle.appendChild(iTitleLink);
        outputNode.appendChild(iTitle);

        var iPara = document.createElement("p");     ⎫  writes the description of the
        iPara.innerHTML = this.items[i].description; ⎬  news item into a paragraph
        outputNode.appendChild(iPara);               ⎭
    }

}
```

▶ **4.** Save the file.

Now you can apply your custom RSSFeed object to the headlines.xml document that your AJAX application has retrieved from the Web server and use it to add an HTML fragment to the Sblogger home page.

To apply the custom RSSFeed object:

▶ **1.** Return to the **newsfeed.js** file in your text editor.

▶ **2.** Scroll down to the getHeadlines() function, and then insert the following code, as shown in Figure 12-23:

```
var rssDoc = new RSSFeed(newsDoc);
rssDoc.parseToHTML(news);
```

Figure 12-23	Code to apply the custom RSSFeed object

```javascript
function getHeadlines() {
   var news = document.getElementById("news");

   // Request object for the headlines feed
   var reqHead = new XMLHttpRequest();
   reqHead.open("GET", "headlines.xml");
   reqHead.setRequestHeader("Cache-Control", "no-cache");
   reqHead.send(null);

   reqHead.onreadystatechange = function() {
      if (this.readyState == 4) {
         if (this.status == 200) {
            // Retrieve the headlines feed
            var newsDoc = this.responseXML;
            var rssDoc = new RSSFeed(newsDoc);
            rssDoc.parseToHTML(news);
         }
      }
   }
}
```

creates an RSSFeed object based on the headlines.xml file

3. Save the file.

To test and view your code, you must upload the headlines.xml file and the revised newsfeed.js and ajax.js files to your account on your Web server.

To test your RSS news reader:

1. Use your ftp client or other communication software to upload the **ajax.js**, **newsfeed.js**, and **headlines.xml** files from the tutorial.12\tutorial folder on your local computer to the tutorial.12/tutorial folder in your Web account on your Web server.

2. Use your browser to reload the URL **http://*yourdomain*/tutorial.12/tutorial/ sblogger.htm**, where *yourdomain* is your domain on your Web server. The headline text from the headlines.xml file appears in the sidebar. See Figure 12-24.

Figure 12-24	Headlines retrieved from an RSS news feed

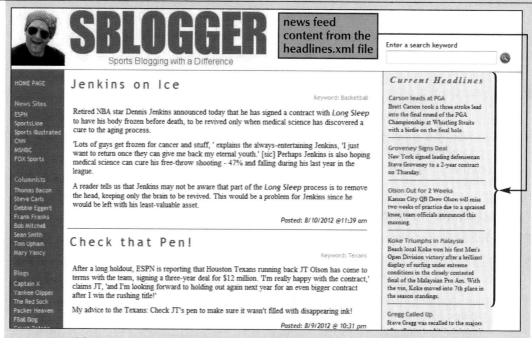

Trouble? For a local Web server such as IIS, you might have to access the file using the URL *http://localhost/tutorial.12/tutorial/sblogger.htm*.

Steve likes the news reader you created that retrieves and displays current sports headlines. In the future, he will add a script to his Web server to automatically retrieve the headlines every hour, write the news feed to the headlines.xml file, and then transfer the file to each reader's browser.

Transforming XML with XSLT | InSight

Working with the document object model is only one way to transform an XML document into HTML format. Another, more efficient approach is to use XSLT. **Extensible Stylesheet Language Transformation (XSLT)** is a style language developed for XML documents that allows developers to easily transform the contents of an XML document into another document format.

XSLT is itself an XML vocabulary and follows the same basic structure of an XML document. XSLT works by transforming a source XML document into a result document written in the chosen output format. To run the style sheet and generate the result document, you need an XSLT processor. Almost all major browsers have built-in XSLT processors, so you do not need special software to work with XSLT files.

The following is an XSLT style sheet that performs the same transformation you wrote for the parseToHTML() method:

```
<?xml version="1.0" encoding="UTF-8" ?>
<xsl:stylesheet version="1.0"
     xmlns:xsl="http://www.w3.org/1999/XSL/Transform">

   <xsl:template match="channel">
      <h1><xsl:value-of select="title" /></h1>

      <xsl:for-each select="item">
         <h2>
            <a href="{link}">
               <xsl:value-of select="title" />
            </a>
         </h2>
         <p><xsl:value-of select="description" /></p>
      </xsl:for-each>
   </xsl:template>

</xsl:stylesheet>
```

Though an exact explanation of this style sheet is beyond the scope of this tutorial, you can study the code to see how HTML elements such as h1, h2, a, and p are interspersed with markup tags from the XSLT language to create a compound document combining elements from both languages. A style sheet like this can be loaded by JavaScript using the XSLT processor built into the browser and applied to the headlines.xml file. The HTML code generated by the style sheet can then be inserted into the news section of the Sblogger home page. In general, XSLT style sheets like this one are easier to develop and maintain than scripts that rely solely on manipulating the document object model.

You can learn more about XSLT from a wide variety of tutorials freely available on the Web.

Introducing JSON

So far you have worked with two types of documents for your AJAX application: a basic text file containing HTML code and an XML document object. AJAX applications commonly involve a third document format known as JSON. **JSON (JavaScript ObjectNotation)** is a data format based on the object literal format introduced in the last tutorial. A JSON document has the general structure

```
{
    "name1": "value1",
    "name2": "value2",
    "name3": "value3"
...

}
```

where *name1*, *name2*, etc. are data field names and *value1*, *value2*, etc. are values associated with those data fields. For example, the JSON code

```
{
    "sport": "Basketball",
    "city": "Chicago",
    "name": "Bulls",
    "record": "45 - 37"
}
```

has the same general structure as the following XML code:

```
<sport>Basketball</sport>
<city>Chicago</city>
<name>Bulls</name>
<record>45 - 37</record>
```

One advantage of JSON over XML is that it is a terse language with a minimum of extraneous characters. In this simple example, the JSON code requires 71 characters, but the XML code requires 85 characters to store the same data. For larger, more complex document structures, the difference in the number of required characters is even greater.

Nested Data Structures and Array Literals

As with XML documents, JSON documents can contain several layers of nested elements. The following is an example of a JSON document with three levels of nested values:

```
{
    "teams" {
        "team1": {
            "sport": "Basketball",
            "city": "Chicago",
            "name": "Bulls",
            "record": "45 - 37"
            },
        "team2": {
            "sport": "Baseball",
            "city": "Chicago",
            "name": "Cubs",
            "record": "86 - 76"
            }
        }
}
```

The same data written in XML would appear as follows:

```
<teams>
    <team1>
        <sport>Basketball</sport>
```

```
      <city>Chicago</city>
      <name>Bulls</name>
      <record>45 - 37</record>
   </team1>
   <team2>
      <sport>Baseball</sport>
      <city>Chicago</city>
      <name>Cubs</name>
      <record>86 - 76</record>
   </team2>
</teams>
```

The JSON data requires 169 characters versus 212 characters for the XML data.

The size of a JSON data file can be further reduced through the use of array literals, expressed using the [value1, value2, ...] notation discussed in Tutorial 3. The following JSON document shows the use of both nested objects and array literals to store information about the two Chicago sports teams:

```
{
   "teams" {
      "team": {
         "city": "Chicago",
         "sport": ["Basketball", "Baseball"],
         "name": ["Bulls", "Cubs"],
         "record": ["45 - 37", "86 - 76"]
         }
      }
}
```

In this structure, the sport field contains an array of two text values: Basketball and Baseball. Similarly, the name and record fields also store their own arrays.

Finally, the following JSON file uses an array literal to store a collection of key names and values describing two cities and their sports teams:

```
{
   "teams" {
     [ {
         "city": "Chicago",
         "sport": ["Basketball", "Baseball"],
         "name": ["Bulls", "Cubs"],
         "record": ["45 - 37", "86 - 76"]
       },
       {
         "city": "Boston",
         "sport": ["Basketball", "Baseball"],
         "name": ["Celtics", "Red Sox"],
         "record": ["58 - 24", "92 - 70"]
       }
     ]
}
```

The teams field contains an array that stores two items. Each item contains a field group. Within those field groups are other fields and arrays. Following this general approach, you can add more nested fields and arrays to achieve very complicated data structures.

Referencing JSON Values

The advantage of JSON over XML is that it is easier to retrieve specific data values because JSON data structures can be treated as custom JavaScript objects with data fields referenced as object properties. For example, if you store the JSON code described above in the citySports variable

```
var citySports =
{
    "teams" :
        [ {
        "city": "Chicago",
        "sport": ["Basketball", "Baseball"],
        "name": ["Bulls", "Cubs"],
        "record": ["45 - 37", "86 - 76"]
         },
         {
        "city": "Boston",
        "sport": ["Basketball", "Baseball"],
        "name": ["Celtics", "Red Sox"],
        "record": ["58 - 24", "92 - 70"]
         }
        ]
}
```

then you can reference the name of the second sports city in this data collection using the expression

```
citySports.teams[1].city
```

returning the text string Boston. Similarly, the win/loss record of the first team listed for that city would be referenced using the expression

```
citySports.teams[1].record[0]
```

returning the text string 58 – 24. The key to writing a JSON object reference is to remember that each level of field names can be treated as a property of the field that contains it.

Although JSON has many advantages over XML, it suffers from the disadvantage of being less readable by the layperson. What XML loses due to its verbosity, it gains back by being easier to interpret. There is also a wealth of XML tools and vocabularies for the Web developer to choose from. Because both languages have their merits, many AJAX applications employ both formats.

Reading JSON Data

JSON is retrieved by an AJAX application as a simple text file. For the browser to treat a JSON data structure in terms of a custom object, it must evaluate the JSON code using the eval() function

```
var jsonData = eval( "(" + req.responseText + ")" );
```

where *jsonData* is a custom object storing the JSON data and *req* is the request object retrieving the JSON data string from the server. (For a discussion of the eval() function, see Tutorial 11.) After the JSON data has been evaluated and stored in the *jsonData* variable, you can reference individual values using either the dot notation or the array notation discussed above. For example, the reference

```
jsonData.teams[0].name[1]
```

returns the text string Cubs from the JSON data structure described above.

At this point, you will not be working with JSON data. However, in the next session, you will read data from a JSON file into Steve's Web page.

Tip

JSON values can also be referenced using array notation in place of dot notation so that the value of a data property can be referenced using either *variable.property* or *variable*["*property*"].

Reading a JSON Object with JavaScript | Reference Window

- To retrieve a document containing a JSON object, use the property
  ```
  req.responseText
  ```
  where *req* is an instance of the request object.
- To convert JSON text into a JavaScript object, use
  ```
  var jsonData = eval( "(" + req.responseText + ")" );
  ```
  where *jsonData* is a custom object storing the JSON data in terms of nested objects, properties, and methods.

In this session, you created code to retrieve and parse an RSS document. In the next session, you will learn how to build an AJAX application to retrieve older articles from the Sblogger archives.

Session 12.2 Quick Check | Review

1. What is an XML vocabulary? Provide two examples of XML vocabularies.
2. What is RSS?
3. News stories from an RSS feed are stored in what RSS element?
4. What request object property do you employ to return an XML document object?
5. Provide code to reference the link element of an RSS channel.
6. What is JSON? What are some advantages and disadvantages of JSON compared to XML?
7. In the following code, provide expressions using dot notation to reference: (a) the name of the customer, (b) the customer's city of residence, and (c) the ID of the customer's second order:

```
var contact = {"customer" : {
            "name" : "David Gillman",
            "address" : {
               "street" : "405 Main St.",
               "city" : "Columbus",
               "state" : "OH",
               "zip" : "43224"
               },
            "phone" : "(614) 555-5788",
            "orderIDs" : ["XG15", "BL20", "WID6"]
            }
      }
```

8. The reqCust request object returns a text string containing a data structure written in JSON. Provide code to store this data in a variable named contact.

Session 12.3

Working with a CGI Script

The final feature that Steve wants to provide for visitors to his home page is the ability to retrieve columns archived on the Sblogger Web server. Steve has written a CGI script that will search a collection of Sblogger articles and return the HTML code of articles that match a search keyword entered by the user. The URL to invoke this CGI script is

```
sbarchives.cgi?skey=keyword
```

where *keyword* is the search keyword. For example, making a request to the URL

```
sbarchives.cgi?skey=baseball
```

returns the HTML code for all of Steve's columns pertaining to baseball.

Introducing Perl

The sbarchives.cgi script is written in **Perl**, a common server side scripting language often used to generate and manipulate text strings. Part of the contents of the sbarchives.cgi file is shown in Figure 12-25.

Figure 12-25 The sbarchives.cgi script

Tip

If you are running a local Windows Web server such as IIS, you can install the free program ActivePerl to enable Perl support on your PC.

```perl
#!/usr/bin/perl -w

# Confirm that perl is located in the /usr/bin/perl folder on the server

#All perl scripts should use strict
use strict;

use CGI;
my $cgi_object = new CGI();

# Print out the http header
print $cgi_object->header();

# Retrieve the value of the skey parameter
my $input = $cgi_object->param('skey');

# This is the hashtable storing a sample of archived articles in HTML format
my @articles = (
    { searchkey => ."Packers",
      content => "<h1>A Cheesy Monument</h1>
                <h6>Keyword: Packers</h6>
                <p>Green Bay native Jeff Miller
                    loves Packers QB Brian Paulson. And he loves the
                    Packers. And he loves cheese. So what could be more
                    natural than carving a life-size statue of his beloved
                    player in a huge block of gouda? Speaking of natural,
                    Jeff's wife is starting to complain about the natural
                    odor of the monument. 'I suppose I'll have to give it
                    up, ' sighed Jeff.</p>
                <p>For his next creation, Jeff can do the entire porous GB
                    defense ... in swiss cheese; or he can simply do a
                    statue of beleaguered GB defense back Chris Conners in
                    toast.</p>
                <cite>Posted: 11/1/2010 @ 1:25 am</cite>"
    },

);
# Keep track of the number of hits using the count variable
my $count = 0;
foreach my $row (@articles) {
    if ( $row->{searchkey} =~ /^$input$/i) {
        $count ++;
        print "$row->{content}"
    }
}

# If no hits, print this fact
if ($count == 0) {
    print "<h1>No Articles Found</h1><p>Come back again, we're still setting
up our database!</p>";
}
```

One advantage of Perl is that it is supported by almost all Web servers. However, before you can use the sbarchives.cgi file, you need to confirm that your server supportsPerl. You must also learn the location of the Perl executable files that interpret and runany CGI script written in Perl. The code for the sbarchives.cgi file assumes that Perl is located in the /usr/bin/perl folder on the user's account on the Web server. This is perhaps the most common location. If necessary, check with your technical resource person or instructor to confirm that you have access to Perl and that it can be accessed at that address. If the Perl executable files are located elsewhere, you need to edit the sbarchives.cgi file to point to a different location.

To edit the sbarchives.cgi file (if necessary):

1. Use your text editor to open the **sbarchives.cgi** file from the tutorial.12\tutorial folder on your local computer.

2. Change the first line of the file to

   `#!location`

   where *location* is the location of the Perl executable files as indicated by your instructor or technical resource person.

3. Save the file, and then close it.

Loading a CGI Script

Next, you need to upload the sbarchives.cgi file to your Web server account. Most Web servers require all CGI scripts to be stored in the cgi-bin folder located in the user's root folder. Because Perl scripts are simple text files, you must transfer the sbarchives.cgi file using ASCII-encoding. This ensures that the server will receive the file as an ASCII text file rather than in a different format. You will upload the sbarchives.cgi file now.

To transfer the sbarchives.cgi file to your Web server account:

1. Open an ftp client or another communication utility.

2. Use the ASCII file transfer option to copy the **sbarchives.cgi** file from the tutorial.12\tutorial folder on your local computer to the cgi-bin folder located in the root folder in your Web server account.

   Trouble? If you are not sure how to specify an ASCII file transfer, refer to the documentation of your file transfer program or ask your instructor or technical resource person for help. If you are running your Web server on your local machine, such as under IIS, you can simply move the files into the cgi-bin folder under the wwwroot folder. If the cgi-bin folder does not exist under wwwroot, create that folder and move the sbarchives.cgi file into it.

Finally, CGI scripts need to be publically executable. To allow for this, you must change the file attributes for the sbarchives.cgi file. You can change file attributes using commands available in most file transfer software.

To make the sbarchives.cgi file publically executable:

1. Select the **sbarchives.cgi** file from the tutorial.12/tutorial folder in your account on your Web server.

2. Using a command from your file transfer software, change the file attributes to allow the public to execute the file. Figure 12-26 shows the Change file attributes dialog box from the free FTP client FileZilla.

Tip

If you access your Web account via a command-line interface, you change the file permissions by running the command chmod 755 sbarchives.cgi.

Figure 12-26 ▶ **Change file attributes dialog box from FileZilla**

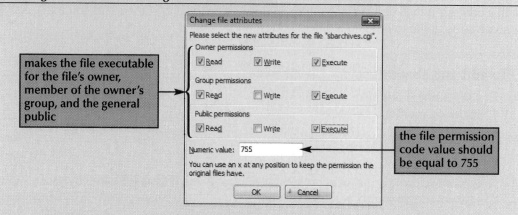

makes the file executable for the file's owner, member of the owner's group, and the general public

the file permission code value should be equal to 755

Trouble? If you are not sure how to change the file permissions, check your software's help file or contact your instructor or technical resource person.

▶ **3.** Close your file transfer software.

Before working on the Sblogger home page, you should confirm that the sbarchives. cgi script is accessible and executable. You will run the script to retrieve any articles pertaining to the Green Bay Packers.

To test the sbarchives.cgi script:

▶ **1.** Use your Web browser to open the URL **http://*yourdomain*/cgi-bin/sbarchives. cgi?skey=packers**. Your browser opens a Web page displaying an article titled, *A Cheesy Monument*. See Figure 12-27.

Figure 12-27 ▶ **Article retrieved by running the sbarchives.cgi script**

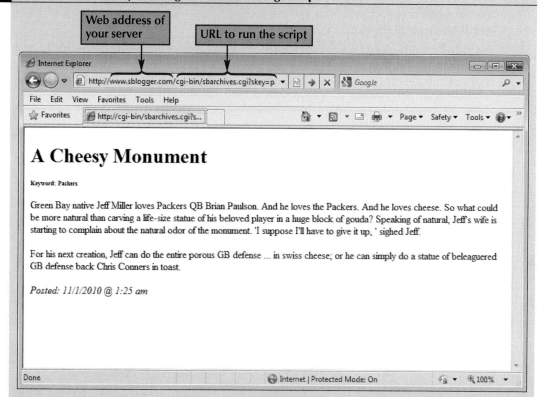

Web address of your server

URL to run the script

Trouble? If the browser displays an error message or is unable to load the file, check the following possible causes: (1) Perl is not installed on your Web server or the Perl executable files are not located in the folder specified in the first line of the sbarchives.cgi file. (2) You did not transfer the sbarchives.cgi file to your Web server as an ASCII file type. (3) You have not properly set the file permissions to allow public execution of the script. (4) You made a mistake in typing the URL.

If you are running a local Web server, you may need to set up support for Perl scripts. If you are running IIS, access the IIS Manager available under the Administrative Tools of the Windows Control Panel. Click the Handler Mappings icon to specify how IIS should handle Perl script files. View the online help for more information on supporting CGI scripts.

If you still have problems running the CGI script, ask your instructor or technical resource person for help.

▶ **2.** Test the CGI script by entering the URL **http://*yourdomain*/cgi-bin/sbarchives. cgi?skey=baseball**, and then confirm that two baseball articles are displayed.

▶ **3.** Test the CGI script by entering the URL **http://*yourdomain*/cgi-bin/sbarchives. cgi?skey=texans**, and then confirm that one football article is displayed.

With a working version of the sbarchives.cgi script installed on your Web server, you can begin writing an AJAX application to access that script and retrieve archived columns.

Loading a Perl Script to a Web Server | Reference Window

- Make sure you have an account on the Web server that includes the ability to run CGI scripts.
- Determine the location of the Perl executable files within your account.
- If necessary, change the first line of the Perl script to reflect the location of the Perl folder.
- If you are using an external Web server, use an FTP client or a file transfer program to transfer the script file to the cgi-bin folder in the root folder of your account. Use an ASCII file transfer.
- Change the protection of the script file on the server to be executable by the owner, the owner's group, and the public.

Interacting with a CGI Script

Steve has inserted a search box in the upper-right corner of the Sblogger home page. He wants users to enter a search keyword into the input box, and then retrieve articles relating to that search term by clicking the magnifying glass icon located next to the box. To program this application, you will first add an event handler to the newsfeed.js file to set up the properties of the search box.

To create the event handler in the newsfeed.js file:

▶ **1.** If you took a break after the previous session, make sure the ajax.js, newsfeed.js, and sblogger.htm files are open in your text editor; the blogger.htm file is open in your browser; and the ajax.js, commentary.txt, newsfeed.js, sblogger.htm, sblogo.jpg, sbstyles.css, and search.png files are stored in your account on your Web server in the tutorial.12/tutorial folder.

▶ **2.** Return to the **newsfeed.js** file in your text editor.

▶ **3.** Scroll to the bottom of the file, and then insert the following command to run the setupSearch() function when the page is loaded:

```
addEvent(window, "load", setupSearch, false);
```

▶ **4.** Add the following initial code for the setupSearch() function, as shown in Figure 12-28:

```
function setupSearch() {
    var main = document.getElementById("main");
    var sInput = document.getElementById("sInput");
    var sButton = document.getElementById("sButton");
}
```

Figure 12-28 ▶ **The initial setupSearch() function**

```
addEvent(window, "load", setupSearch, false);

function setupSearch() {
    var main = document.getElementById("main");
    var sInput = document.getElementById("sInput");
    var sButton = document.getElementById("sButton");
}
```

the search input box has the id sInput

stores the search results in the main section

the magnifying glass icon has the id sButton

To submit the search request, you will create a request object named reqSearch that accesses the sbarchives.cgi file using the value of the sInput box as the skeyparameter value. The request object will be created and run whenever the user clicks on the search button icon. You will add the code for this event to the setupSearch() function.

To create the event handler and request object:

▶ **1.** In the setupSearch() function, insert the following code, as shown in Figure 12-29.

```
// Retrieve articles when the search icon is clicked
sButton.onclick = function() {

    // Search key entered in the sInput box
    var key = escape(sInput.value);

    // Request object to access the archived articles
    var reqSearch = new XMLHttpRequest();
    var searchURL = "/cgi-bin/sbarchives.cgi?skey=" + key;
    reqSearch.open("GET", searchURL);
    reqSearch.send(null);
}
```

Figure 12-29 ▶ **Code to define the reqSearch object**

```
function setupSearch() {
    var main = document.getElementById("main");
    var sInput = document.getElementById("sInput");
    var sButton = document.getElementById("sButton");

    // Retrieve articles when the search icon is clicked
    sButton.onclick = function() {

        // Search key entered in the sInput box
        var key = escape(sInput.value);

        // Request object to access the archived articles
        var reqSearch = new XMLHttpRequest();
        var searchURL = "/cgi-bin/sbarchives.cgi?skey=" + key;
        reqSearch.open("GET", searchURL);
        reqSearch.send(null);
    }
}
```

encodes the search value to replace blanks and nonprintable characters

accesses the CGI script using the search key value

▶ **2.** Save the file.

Because the search key is appended to the URL, the event handler uses the escape() method to replace blanks and nonprintable characters in the text string with their character codes. Now you can process the text returned by the CGI script, placing the HTML code in the main section of the document. You will complete the event handler function and then upload the revised newsfeed.js file to your account on your Web server.

To complete the event handler function:

▶ **1.** Add the following code to the event handler function, as shown in Figure 12-30:

```
reqSearch.onreadystatechange = function() {
   if (this.readyState == 4) {
      if (this.status == 200) {
         // Retrieve the archived columns
         main.innerHTML = this.responseText;
      }
   }
}
```

Code to retrieve the HTML code from the CGI script ◀ **Figure 12-30**

```
// Retrieve articles when the search icon is clicked
sButton.onclick = function() {

   // Search key entered in the sInput box
   var key = escape(sInput.value);

   // Request object to access the archived articles
   var reqSearch = new XMLHttpRequest();
   var searchURL = "/cgi-bin/sbarchives.cgi?skey=" + key;
   reqSearch.open("GET", searchURL);
   reqSearch.send(null);

   reqSearch.onreadystatechange = function() {
      if (this.readyState == 4) {
         if (this.status == 200) {
            // Retrieve the archived columns
            main.innerHTML = this.responseText;
         }
      }
   }
}
```

places the HTML code in the main section of the Web page

▶ **2.** Save the newsfeed.js file.

▶ **3.** Copy the **newsfeed.js** file to the tutorial.12/tutorial folder in your account on your Web server, replacing the old version of the file.

▶ **4.** Use your browser to open **http://*domainname*/tutorial.12/tutorial/sblogger.htm**, where *domainname* is the domain name of your account on the Web server, and then verify that no programming errors are reported by your browser.

   Trouble? If your browser reports an error, check your code against that shown in Figures 12-29 and 12-30.

▶ **5.** Type **packers** in the search box, and then click the **magnifying glass** icon to retrieve articles related to the Green Bay Packers. The browser retrieves the response from the sbarchives.cgi script and displays it within the main section of the page. See Figure 12-31.

Figure 12-31 ▶ Article retrieved from the archives

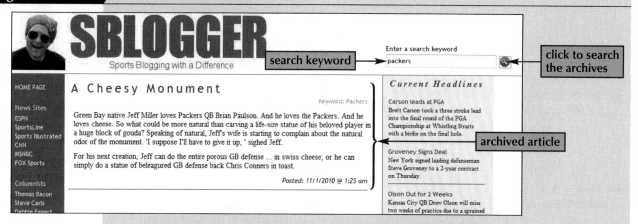

6. Continue to test the operation of the search box using the keywords **baseball**, **basketball**, and **Texans**, and confirming that your browser displays articles related to those keywords.

7. Enter the keyword **golf** (which is not related to a stored article), and then confirm that the browser displays a message indicating that it cannot locate a relevant article.

8. Click the **Home Page** link in the left sidebar to return the Web page to the original articles displayed on the home page.

Building an Autocomplete Input Box

Steve has one last feature he wants you to add to the Sblogger home page. He's concerned that users won't know what to enter in the search input box. Steve has seen Web sites that provide suggestions to the user about possible values to enter into search boxes. This can be accomplished with an autocomplete box.

An autocomplete box works by using an event handler to monitor the user's typing. In response to a partial text string typed by the user, the application sends the string to a CGI script running on the server. The script then generates a list of suggested keywords from a database that can be displayed in a suggestion box located on the Web page. Each entry in the suggestion box can be selected to insert the suggested keyword into the search box. In this way, the autocomplete feature provides useful feedback and frees the user from having to enter long search strings. Figure 12-32 shows a preview of how Steve wants the autocomplete box to work on his Web page.

Figure 12-32 ▶ Autocomplete feature for the Sblogger Web site

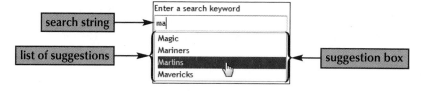

Viewing the CGI Script

Steve already created a CGI script named sbkeywords.cgi that will return an array of suggested keywords giving a text string. The URL to invoke this CGI script is

```
sbkeywords.cgi?suggest=substring
```

where *substring* is a text string containing characters from which the suggestion list is generated. Before you start writing the JavaScript code to create the autocomplete box, you will load this script into your account on your Web server and test it. As with the sbarchives.cgi file, the sbkeywords.cgi script is written in Perl and assumes that the Perl executable files are located in the /usr/bin/perl folder on your Web server.

To load and test the sbkeywords.cgi script:

▶ **1.** If your Perl files are not located in the /usr/bin/perl folder on your Web server, use your text editor to open the **sbkeywords.cgi** file from the tutorial.12\tutorial folder on your local computer, change the first line of the file to reflect the location of your Perl executable files, and then save and close the file.

▶ **2.** Transfer the **sbkeywords.cgi** file to the cgi-bin folder in your Web server account. If you are uploading the file to an external Web server using an ftp program, you should specify ASCII as the transfer type.

▶ **3.** Set the permissions of the sbkeywords.cgi file to allow it to be executed by the owner, the members of the owner's group, and the public.

Next, you will test the CGI script to display a list of all keywords that start with the letter *m*.

▶ **4.** Use your browser to open **http://*domainname*/cgi-bin/sbkeywords.cgi?suggest=m**, where *domainname* is the domain name of your account on the Web server. The CGI script returns a list of suggested keywords, all starting with the letter *m*. See Figure 12-33.

Results from running the sbkeywords.cgi script ◀ Figure 12-33

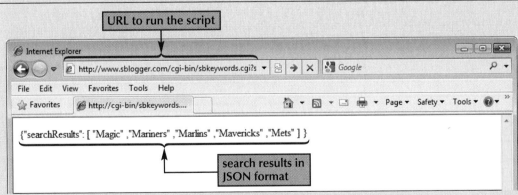

URL to run the script

{"searchResults": ["Magic" ,"Mariners" ,"Marlins" ,"Mavericks" ,"Mets"] }

search results in JSON format

▶ **5.** Try other character strings for the suggest parameter, verifying that the browser returns keywords that start with the characters in the suggest parameter.

Trouble? If only an empty list is generated, this means that no keywords start with the characters you entered in the suggest parameter. Not all character strings result in a list of suggestions. Repeat Step 5, trying a different character string.

Steve's list of suggested keywords is returned in JSON format with individual suggestions stored in an array named searchResults. For example, using the letter *m* for the suggest parameter results in the following JSON object:

```
{"searchResults": ["Magic",
                   "Mariners",
                   "Marlins",
                   "Mavericks",
                   "Mets"]
                }
```

Later on, you will use this fact to help you write code that loops through all of the items in the searchResults array to create the list of suggestions that will be displayed in the suggestion box.

Creating the Suggestion Box

Before writing the script, you will create a div element that stores the suggestion box. Also, many browsers have an autocomplete feature that automatically completes input boxes based on past entries. This would potentially interfere with the autocomplete application you plan to create. You can turn off this feature by adding the attribute

```
autocomplete="off"
```

to the search box input element. You will make both of these edits to the sblogger.htm file.

To create a div element for the Sblogger home page and turn off autocomplete:

1. Use your text editor to return to the **sblogger.htm** file from the tutorial.12\tutorial folder on your local computer.

2. Scroll down the file and locate the input element with the id attribute sInput, and then insert the following attribute:

   ```
   autocomplete="off"
   ```

3. Below the search.png input image, insert the following code for the suggestion box:

   ```
   <div id="suggestBox"></div>
   ```

   Figure 12-34 highlights the revised code.

Figure 12-34 ▶ Revised code for the Sblogger home page

```
<body>
   <div id="heading"><img src="sblogo.jpg" alt="SBLOGGER" /></div>

   <div id="search">
      <label for="sInput">Enter a search keyword</label><br />
      <input type="text" id="sInput" name="sInput" autocomplete="off"
      <input type="image" id="sButton" src="search.png" />

      <div id="suggestBox"></div>

   </div>
```

suggestion box to hold search key suggestions

prevents the browser from autocompleting the input box with previous entries

4. Save the file, and then close it.

Steve already created styles for the suggestBox element and stored them in the sbstyles. css style sheet. The suggestion box will have an initial display style equal to none so that it is hidden on the page. When displayed, the suggestion box will appear directly below the sInput input box with a width approximately equal to the width of the input box.

Writing the Event Handler

You can now begin writing the JavaScript code for the autocomplete box. Your AJAX application will send a request to the sbkeywords.cgi file every time a keyup event occurs within the search input box. The application will retrieve whatever the user has typed in and use that as the value for the suggest parameter.

A potential issue exists for fast typists. As the user types, a request is made with every keyup event, but the request and response are not instantaneous. By the time a response is received, a quick typist might have added more characters to the search box, and the suggestions list might no longer match what has been typed, confusing the user.

To resolve this issue, your application will use the setTimeout() method to add a 0.3 second delay between the keyup event and the submission of the request object. (See Tutorial 2 for a discussion of the time-delayed commands.) If the user types another character within the 0.3-second time window, the previous request is canceled before it is even sent, so that the only requests sent occur during natural pauses in the user's typing action. This technique also lessens the load on the Web server because you might not want to send a request with *every* keystroke.

To cancel a time-delayed command, you must store a time ID associated with the command. You will do that by adding a custom timeID property to the suggestBox object. When you add this property to the setupSearch() function now, you will set its initial value to null.

Tip

Another way to lessen the load on the server is not to send requests until a minimum number of characters are typed.

To define custom properties for the suggestion box:

▶ 1. Use your text editor to return to the **newsfeed.js** file from the tutorial.12\tutorial folder on your local computer.

▶ 2. Scroll down to the setupSearch() function and directly below the command to define the sButton variable, insert the following code, as shown in Figure 12-35:

```
var suggestBox = document.getElementById("suggestBox");
suggestBox.timeID = null; // time ID for delayed request
```

Code to define the suggestion box **Figure 12-35**

```
function setupSearch() {
    var main = document.getElementById("main");
    var sInput = document.getElementById("sInput");
    var sButton = document.getElementById("sButton");

    var suggestBox = document.getElementById("suggestBox");
    suggestBox.timeID = null; // time ID for delayed request
}
```

custom property to store the ID of a time-delayed command

Next, you will create an event handler for the keyup event occurring within the sInput box. When the keyup event occurs, the code will:

1. Use the clearTimeout() method to cancel the time-delay command associated with the previous keystroke.

2. Run a time-delayed command after 0.3 seconds to request a list of suggestions.

Note that before your application can run the clearTimeout() method, it must first use an if statement to confirm that a value of the timeID property exists. You will add code for this event handler to the setupSearch() function.

To create the event handler for the keyup event:

▶ **1.** Directly below the command to define the timeID custom property, insert the following code, as shown in Figure 12-36:

```
// Retrieve search suggestions after keys are typed
sInput.onkeyup = function() {

    if (suggestBox.timeID) clearTimeout(suggestBox.timeID);

    suggestBox.timeID = setTimeout(function() {

        // Submit a suggestion request after 0.3 seconds

    }, 300);
}
```

Figure 12-36 **Code to run a request after a time delay**

```
function setupSearch() {
    var main = document.getElementById("main");
    var sInput = document.getElementById("sInput");
    var sButton = document.getElementById("sButton");

    var suggestBox = document.getElementById("suggestBox");
    suggestBox.timeID = null; // time ID for delayed request

    // Retrieve search suggestions after keys are typed
    sInput.onkeyup = function() {

        if (suggestBox.timeID) clearTimeout(suggestBox.timeID);

        suggestBox.timeID = setTimeout(function() {

            // Submit a suggestion request after 0.3 seconds

        }, 300);
    }
```

if the previous time-delayed command hasn't yet been run, cancels it

event handler for the keyup event

submits a request object after a time delay

▶ **2.** Save the file.

After the 0.3-second delay, your application submits a request to the server using the same techniques you have employed for the other AJAX applications on the Sblogger home page. Before submitting the request, the application should confirm that there actually is text in the search box. If there is no text, you hide the suggestion box by setting its display style to none. If there is text, the autocomplete application sends a request to the sbkeywords.cgi script using the text value of the sInput box as the parameter value. You will add this code to the file.

To create a request object for a list of autocomplete suggestions:

▶ **1.** Within the time-delayed function you created in the last set of steps, enter the following code:

```
if (sInput.value == "") suggestBox.style.display = "none"

else {

    var reqSuggest = new XMLHttpRequest();
    var suggestURL = "/cgi-bin/sbkeywords.cgi?suggest=" +
escape(sInput.value);
    reqSuggest.open("GET", suggestURL);
    reqSuggest.send(null);
```

▶ **2.** Enter the following commands to process the request response:

```
reqSuggest.onreadystatechange = function() {
    if (this.readyState == 4) {
        if (this.status == 200) {
```

```
            // Process the request response

                }
            }
        }
    }
```

Figure 12-37 highlights the added code.

```
// Retrieve search suggestions after keys are typed
sInput.onkeyup = function() {

    if (suggestBox.timeID) clearTimeout(suggestBox.timeID);

    suggestBox.timeID = setTimeout(function() {

        // Submit a suggestion request after 0.3 seconds

        if (sInput.value == "") suggestBox.style.display = "none"

        else {

            var reqSuggest = new XMLHttpRequest();
            var suggestURL = "/cgi-bin/sbkeywords.cgi?suggest=" + escape(sInput.value);
            reqSuggest.open("GET", suggestURL);
            reqSuggest.send(null);

            reqSuggest.onreadystatechange = function() {
                if (this.readyState == 4) {
                    if (this.status == 200) {

                        // Process the request response

                    }
                }
            }
        }
    }, 300);
}
```

> if no text has been entered, hides the suggestion box

> request object for the sbkeywords.cgi script

> processes the request response

▶ 3. Save the file.

Processing the Response

As mentioned earlier, the response from the sbkeywords.cgi script is a JSON object containing an array named searchResults. You will store this object in a variable named json using the following command:

```
var json = eval("(" + this.responseText +")");
```

The array of suggested search terms can be retrieved using the following object reference:

```
json.searchResults
```

To display each entry in the searchResults array, your application will loop through the array, creating a div element for each search term. The generated HTML fragment for the suggestion box will contain the elements

```
<div id="suggestBox">
    <div class="suggestion">json.searchResults[0]</div>
    <div class="suggestion">json.searchResults[1]</div>
    <div class="suggestion">json.searchResults[2]</div>
    ...
</div>
```

where *json.searchResults[0]*, etc. are the values of the items in the searchResults array retrieved from the server. You will add this code to the newsfeed.js file.

To create the list of responses:

▶ **1.** Below the "Process the request response" comment, insert the following code to retrieve and parse the JSON data returned by the server:

```
var json = eval("(" + this.responseText +")");
```

▶ **2.** Add the following code to test whether any keywords match the text entered by the user, and then, if the length of the searchResults array is 0 (indicating no keywords match the entered text), hide the suggestion box by setting the display style to none:

```
if (json.searchResults.length == 0) {

    suggestBox.style.display = "none";

}
```

▶ **3.** Add the following code to remove any previous search results displayed by the browser, set the display style to block, and then display any new search results returned by the server on the Web page:

```
else {
    suggestBox.innerHTML = "";
    suggestBox.style.display = "block";
```

▶ **4.** Add the following code to loop through all of the items in the searchResults array and create a div element for each item, appended to the suggestion box:

```
for (var i = 0; i < json.searchResults.length; i++) {

    var suggestion = document.createElement("div");
    suggestion.className = "suggestion";
    suggestion.innerHTML = json.searchResults[i];

    suggestBox.appendChild(suggestion);

}
```

▶ **5.** Enter a closing curly brace **}** to complete the if condition. Figure 12-38 highlights the added code.

Figure 12-38 — **Code to generate the list of suggested keywords**

```
reqSuggest.onreadystatechange = function() {
    if (this.readyState == 4) {
        if (this.status == 200) {

            // Process the request response
            var json = eval("(" + this.responseText +")");          ← parses the JSON object

            if (json.searchResults.length == 0) {

                suggestBox.style.display = "none";

            } else {

                suggestBox.innerHTML = "";                          ← otherwise removes the
                suggestBox.style.display = "block";                   previous suggestions list

                for (var i = 0; i < json.searchResults.length; i++) {
                    var suggestion = document.createElement("div");
                    suggestion.className = "suggestion";
                    suggestion.innerHTML = json.searchResults[i];

                    suggestBox.appendChild(suggestion);              ← appends the list to the
                }                                                      suggestion box

            }
        }
    }
}, 300);
}
```

if no matching keywords are found, hides the suggestion box

and creates a new list of suggested keywords

▶ **6.** Save the file.

Security Issues and JSON | InSight

The eval() method is a quick and easy way to parse JSON data, but it does pose potential security risks. Because the eval() method executes whatever code might be enclosed within the JSON text string, it opens an AJAX application to malicious scripts offered from unreliable third-party Web servers. One way to protect your code is to strip out any characters that might be used for malicious code from the JSON text string. The following command uses two regular expressions and calls the test() and replace() methods to remove characters from *jsonData* that pose a security threat:

```
var my_JSON_object = !(/(/[^,:{}\[\]0-9.\-+Eaeflnr-u \n\r\t]/.test(
text.replace(/"(\\.|[^"\\])*"/g, ''))) &&
eval('(' + jsonData + ')');
```

Rather than memorizing this code, you can download the json.js library written by Web developer Douglas Crockford that contains a parseJSON() method to safely parse JSON data. The syntax of the parseJSON() method is:

```
jsonData.parseJSON()
```

where *jsonData* is a JSON text string. You can download parseJSON from *www.json.org/json.js*.

JSON has become extremely popular on the Web with third-party sources such as Flickr and Google providing JSON code that users can run remotely on their own servers. Douglas Crockford suggests that programmers obey the following principles for the safe use of JSON:

1. **Never trust the browser.** Keep all of your critical data and processes on your Web server rather than within your browser.
2. **Keep data clean.** If you are receiving JSON from a third-party source, then use parseJSON() or another method to strip out potential security risks.
3. **Beware of script tags.** The <script> tag can be used to access and run scripts from other Web servers (violating the security policy of only running code from the same server where the page originated). Do not load scripts from other sites unless you have confirmed their reliability.
4. **Don't send data to strangers.** Avoid unnecessary sharing of data from the server and browser except with a trusted resource.
5. **Use SSL.** Any time you transmit secure information, use the Secure Sockets Layer protocol to encrypt your data.

To accommodate the increasing popularity of JSON, browser manufacturers are building tools into their products to ease the process of retrieving and parsing JSON data. Eventually, these efforts will allow browsers to safely and easily request any JSON data published anywhere on the Internet.

Testing the Autocomplete Feature

The code for processing the request response is complete. You should test your AJAX application to confirm that suggested keywords appear as you enter text into the search box.

To test the autocomplete application:

▶ 1. Upload the **sblogger.htm** and **newsfeed.js** files from the tutorial.12\tutorial folder on your local computer to the tutorial.12/tutorial folder in your account on your Web server, replacing the existing files with the new versions.

▶ **2.** Use your Web browser to open the URL **http://*yourdomain*/tutorial.12/tutorial/ sblogger.htm**, where *yourdomain* is the name of your Web server domain.

▶ **3.** Click the search box on the Sblogger home page, and then type **m**. After a brief interval, a list of suggested keywords appears below the search box. See Figure 12-39.

Figure 12-39	Suggested keywords list

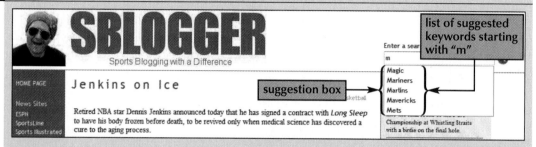

▶ **4.** Type more characters into the search box, verifying that the list of suggested keywords changes to match your entry as you type additional entries.

▶ **5.** Press the **Backspace** key, verifying that the suggestions list increases when you delete characters and the suggestion box disappears when no characters are displayed.

Selecting an Item from the Suggestion Box

Another feature of an autocomplete application is that it allows users to enter suggested keywords into the search box with a mouse click. You will add an onclick event handler for each suggestion to the setupSearch() function.

To create the onclick event handler for each suggested keyword:

▶ **1.** Return to the **newsfeed.js** file in your text editor.

▶ **2.** Scroll down to the setupSearch() function, and then, as shown in Figure 12-40, insert the following code to change the value of the search box to the suggestion text and then hide the suggestion box:

```
suggestion.onclick = function() {
   sInput.value = this.innerHTML;
   suggestBox.style.display = "none";
}
```

Figure 12-40	An onclick event handler for each suggested keyword

displays the selected keyword in the search box and then hides the suggestion box

```
for (var i = 0; i < json.searchResults.length; i++) {
   var suggestion = document.createElement("div");
   suggestion.className = "suggestion";
   suggestion.innerHTML = json.searchResults[i];

   suggestion.onclick = function() {
      sInput.value = this.innerHTML;
      suggestBox.style.display = "none";
   }

   suggestBox.appendChild(suggestion);
}
```

Steve also wants the different items in the suggestion box to be highlighted during the mouseover event. He created a class style named "activeSuggestion" in the sbstyles.css file for highlighted suggestions. You will add code to toggle the className attribute between "activeSuggestion" and "suggestion" in response to the onmouseover and onmouseout events.

To create the onmouseover and onmouseout event handlers:

▶ **1.** Directly below the onclick event handler, insert the following event handlers for the mouseover and mouseout events, as shown in Figure 12-41.

```
suggestion.onmouseover = function() {
   this.className = "activeSuggestion";
}

suggestion.onmouseout = function() {
   this.className = "suggestion";
}
```

The onmouseover and onmouseout event handlers ◀ **Figure 12-41**

```
for (var i = 0; i < json.searchResults.length; i++) {
    var suggestion = document.createElement("div");
    suggestion.className = "suggestion";
    suggestion.innerHTML = json.searchResults[i];

    suggestion.onclick = function() {
        sInput.value = this.innerHTML;
        suggestBox.style.display = "none";
    }

    suggestion.onmouseover = function() {
        this.className = "activeSuggestion";
    }

    suggestion.onmouseout = function() {
        this.className = "suggestion";
    }

    suggestBox.appendChild(suggestion);
}
```

highlights the active suggestion during a mouseover

removes the highlighting when the pointer moves out

▶ **2.** Save the newsfeed.js file.

Finally, Steve wants the suggestion box to be automatically hidden whenever the user clicks the search icon, submitting the search text to be processed by the sbarchives.cgi script. You will add this feature to the newsfeed.js file.

To complete and test the autocomplete application:

▶ **1.** Scroll down to the onclick event handler for the sButton object, and then insert the following code, as shown in Figure 12-42:

```
// Hide the suggestion box
var suggestBox = document.getElementById("suggestBox");
suggestBox.style.display = "none";
```

Code to hide the suggestion box after submitting a search ◀ **Figure 12-42**

```
// Retrieve articles when the search icon is clicked
sButton.onclick = function() {

    // Search key entered in the sInput box
    var key = escape(sInput.value);

    // Hide the suggestion box
    var suggestBox = document.getElementById("suggestBox");
    suggestBox.style.display = "none";
```

hides the suggestion box after the search icon is clicked

▶ **2.** Save the newsfeed.js file, and then close it.

▶ **3.** Upload the **newsfeed.js** file from the tutorial.12\tutorial folder on your local computer to the tutorial.12/tutorial folder in your account on your Web server, replacing the older version.

▶ **4.** Use your Web browser to open the URL **http://yourdomain/tutorial.12/tutorial/ sblogger.htm**, where *yourdomain* is the name of your Web server domain.

5. Enter **pa** into the search box to display a list of suggested keywords, and then move your pointer over the suggestion box, verifying that each selection is highlighted during the mouseover event. See Figure 12-43.

Figure 12-43 ▶ **Test of the highlighted suggestion**

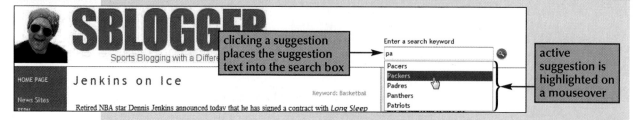

6. Click **Packers** from the list of suggestions and verify that it replaces the text in the search box.

7. Click the **magnifying glass** icon and verify that the browser retrieves an article about the Packers and that the suggestion box is automatically hidden.

| InSight | **AJAX Applications with jQuery** |

As your mastery of JavaScript progresses, you will find that others have blazed the trail by creating JavaScript libraries with customized scripts that handle many of the tasks needed for fully interactive Web sites. One of the most popular is **jQuery**, a lightweight JavaScript library containing all of the common DOM, event, and AJAX functions you have studied in these tutorials. The jQuery library is distributed as a single script file that is about 30K to 55K. You load jQuery by adding the following script element to your HTML code:

```
<script type="text/javascript" src="jQuery.js"></script>
```

One of the basic functions in jQuery is the $() used to select elements from the DOM. The $() function combines many of the features of the getElementById() and getElementsByTag-Name() methods as well as some methods associated with XML into a single function. For example, to reference all div elements belonging to the article class, you would enter the following expression:

```
$(div.article)
```

jQuery makes it easy to create AJAX applications. The simplest AJAX function offered by jQuery is the load() function, which loads an HTML file into an element within the Web page. The following command loads the contents of the commentary.txt file into the div element with the ID value main:

```
$(div#main).load("commentary.txt")
```

jQuery also supports the $.ajax() function to exchange data from a Web server. The following code creates a GET request to the sbarchives.cgi script, returning the data as HTML code stored in the responseText property of the $.ajax() function:

```
var article = $.ajax({
    url: "cgi-bin/sbarchives.cgi?skey=celtics",
    type: "GET",
    dataType: "html"
    }).responseText;
```

As you can see, writing AJAX requests in the jQuery library is quicker and more powerful than in native JavaScript code.

The jQuery library can be downloaded from the *www.jquery.com* Web site along with several online manuals and interactive tutorials to get you started on this powerful tool.

Steve is pleased with your work on the autocomplete box as well as the rest of your work on adding AJAX applications to the Sblogger home page.

Session 12.3 Quick Check | Review

1. What is Perl?
2. Where are CGI scripts often located on the user's Web server account?
3. How should you set the file permissions of a CGI script?
4. What method can you use to clean up a JSON file, making it secure and free of malicious code?
5. Provide code to create a request object named reqAccount that calls the following CGI script using the get method:

```
/cgi-bin/getaccount.php?id=smith
```

6. What is jQuery?
7. Provide code in jQuery to reference an image element whose ID attribute equals logo.

Tutorial Summary | Review

This tutorial examined how to create AJAX applications using JavaScript. The first session introduced the theory and history behind AJAX, comparing the classic Web application model to the AJAX Web application model. It discussed both the benefits and drawbacks of using AJAX. The session then showed how to create a cross-browser-compatible XMLHttpRequest object. It showed how to open a resource with the request object, and how to send a request and listen for a response from the server. The session ended by showing how to receive HTML text from a request response. The second session introduced the XML language and discussed how to retrieve and parse documents written in RSS, an XML vocabulary. It showed how to create a basic newsreader utility to work with the contents of RSS news feeds. The session concluded by examining JSON and showing how to read a JSON file. The third session began by discussing how to upload and run CGI scripts from an account on a Web server. It showed how to call a CGI script as part of an application to create an autocomplete text box. The tutorial concluded by looking at a popular JavaScript library named jQuery.

Key Terms

aggregator
AJAX (Asynchronous JavaScript and XML)
AJAX engine
AJAX Web application model
asynchronous
classic Web application model
Extensible Stylesheet Language Transformation
feed reader

get method
IIS (Internet Information Service)
JavaScript Object Notation
jQuery
JSON
MSXML
Perl
podcast
post method

Really Simple Syndication (RSS)
synchronous
XHTML
XML (Extensible Markup Language)
XML declaration
XML vocabulary
XMLHttpRequest object
XSLT

Practice	Review Assignments

Practice the skills you learned in the tutorial using the same case scenario.

Data Files needed for the Review Assignments: gamestxt.htm, gamestyles.css, getscorestxt.js, libtxt.js, results.xml, sblogo.jpg, scores.txt

Steve wants you to work on another sample page for his proposed Web site. He wants a page that loads the latest NFL news and scores. The NFL stories will come from an RSS feed, which needs to be parsed into an HTML fragment. The NFL scores will come from a JSON file, whose data needs to be retrieved and written into a series of Web tables. Figure 12-44 shows a preview of the completed Web page.

Figure 12-44

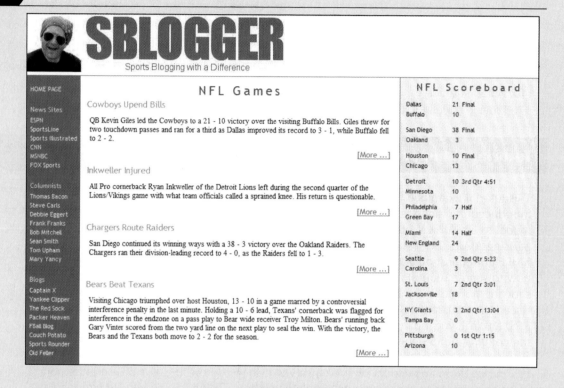

Steve has already written the HTML and CSS code for this Web site as well as some of the JavaScript code. You need to complete the project by writing the JavaScript code to retrieve the RSS feed and JSON files from your Web server and then convert them to HTML fragments.

Complete the following:

1. Use your text editor to open the **gamestxt.htm**, **getscorestxt.js**, and **libtxt.js** files from the tutorial.12\review folder, enter *your name* and *the date* in the comment section of each file, and then save the files as **games.htm**, **getscores.js**, and **library.js**, respectively.

2. Go to the **games.htm** file in your text editor and create script elements to link to the library.js and getscores.js files. Save and close the file.

3. Go to the **library.js** file in your text editor. Scroll to the bottom of the file and create a new method named **exportToHTML** for the RSSFeed prototype. The function has a single parameter named **outputNode**. The purpose of this method is to write the contents of an RSS feed into an HTML fragment. Add the following code to the method:

   a. Create an h1 heading containing the title of the RSS feed. Append this heading to the outputNode object.

   b. Loop through each of the news items in the RSS feed. For each item, write the HTML fragment

```
<h2>title</h2>
<p>description</p>
<p class="link">
   <a href = "link">[ More ]</a>
<p>
```

      where *title* is the title of the news item, *description* is the description of the news item, and *link* is a hypertext link to the complete text of the news item. Append the HTML code for each news item to the outputNode object.

4. Save and close the library.js file.

5. View the contents of the **scores.txt** file in your text editor. Take note of the structure of the object and its properties. Close the file without making or saving any changes.

6. Go to the **getscores.js** file in your text editor. Use the addEvent() function defined for you in the library.js file to add an event handler running the updateScores() function when the page is loaded.

7. Create the **updateScores()** function. The purpose of this function is to retrieve the contents of the scores.txt file and write the objects in that file into an HTML fragment. Add the following commands to the function:

   a. Create a variable named **scoresDIV** to reference the scoresDIV object on the Web page.

   b. Create a new request object named **reqScores**. Have the reqScores object open the scores.txt file using the get method.

   c. Prevent the browser from caching the contents of the scores.txt file by adding an HTTP header named **Cache-Control** to the reqScores object, setting its value to no-cache.

   d. Send the reqScores object to the Web server.

   e. When the server returns an error-free complete response, parse the response text as JSON code.

   f. Append the HTML fragment

```
<h2>title</h2>
```

      to the scoresDIV object, where *title* is the value of the sport property of the json object.

   g. Loop through all of the contents of the scores array in the json object, and then, for each item in the array, append the HTML fragment

```
<table>
   <tbody>
      <tr>
         <td>team1</td>
         <td class="num">score1</td>
         <td>time</td>
      </tr>
      <tr>
         <td>team2</td>
         <td class="num">score2</td>
         <td>time</td>
      </tr>
   </tbody>
</table>
```

      to the scoresDIV object, where *team1* and *team2* are the values of the team1 and team2 properties for the current item in the scores array, respectively; *score1* and *score2* are the values of the score1 and score2 properties, respectively; and *time* is the value of the time property.

8. Below the updateScores() function, insert an event handler to run the getStories() function when the page is loaded.

9. Create the **getStories()** function. The purpose of this function is to retrieve and display news stories from the results.xml news feed. Add the following commands to the function:

   a. Create a variable named **main** referencing the element in the document with the ID main.

   b. Create a request object named **reqStories** that opens the results.xml file using the get method.

   c. Prevent the browser from caching the contents of the results.xml file by adding an HTTP header named **Cache-Control** to the reqScores object, setting its value to no-cache.

   d. Send the reqStories object to the Web server.

   e. When a complete, error-free response is received by the server, store the XML document object returned by the server in a variable named **newsDoc**.

   f. Create an RSSFeed object named **rssDoc** using newsDoc as the parameter value.

   g. Using the exportToHTML () method you defined in the library.js file, create an HTML fragment from the newsDoc object, placing the results in the main section of the document.

10. Save and close the getscores.js file.

11. Create a folder named **review** as a subfolder of the **tutorial.12** folder in your Web server account.

12. Transfer the **games.htm**, **gamestyles.css**, **getscores.js**, **library.js**, **results.xml**, **sblogo.jpg**, and **scores.txt** files from your local computer to the tutorial.12/review folder on your Web server.

13. Use your Web browser to open **http://*domainname*/tutorial.12/review/games.htm**, where *domainname* is the domain name of your Web server account. Verify that the browser displays the articles on the game results in the main section of the page and the scores of the games in the scoresDIV section.

14. Submit your completed project to your instructor.

| Apply | **Case Problem 1** |

Use the skills you learned to retrieve online data from a customer account.

Data Files needed for this Case Problem: getorderstxt.js, orderstxt.htm, wwlibrary.js, wwlogo.jpg, wworders.pl, wwstyles.css

Wizard Works Bernard Kolbe is the online sales manager for Wizard Works, a seller of brand name fireworks and pyrotechnic effects in the Midwest. Bernard wants you to work on revamping the company's Web site. One of your first tasks is to create an AJAX application in which customers can retrieve an HTML table showing their order history with Wizard Works. Figure 12-45 shows a preview of the Web page.

Customers are required to enter their Wizard Works user ID and password and then, by clicking the View Orders button, this information will be sent to a CGI script running on the Wizard Works server. The script will return the HTML code, which you can then insert into the Web page. If the customer enters a username/password combination that does not match Wizard Works' records, the Web page should display text notifying the customer of this.

Figure 12-45

Bernard has already written the HTML code, the style sheet, and a CGI script in Perl to return a sample collection of customer orders. You need to write the JavaScript code to access this script and display its response.

Complete the following:

1. Use your text editor to open the **getorderstxt.js** and **orderstxt.htm** files from the tutorial.12\case1 folder, enter *your name* and *the date* in the comment section of each file, and then save the files as **getorders.js** and **orders.htm**, respectively.

2. Create a folder named **case1** as a subfolder of the **tutorial.12** folder in your Web server account.

3. Using your communication software, copy the **wworders.pl** file from the tutorial.12\case1 folder on your local computer into the cgi-bin folder on your Web server account. Make sure that you transfer the file as ASCII text and that you make the file executable by the owner, the owner's group, and the public.

4. Return to the **orders.htm** file in your text editor. Add script elements linking to the wwlibrary.js and getorders.js files. Examine the contents of the file, and then save and close the file.

5. Go to the **getorders.js** file in your text editor. Add an event handler to run the retrieveOrders() function when the page is loaded.

6. Add the **retrieveOrders()** function. Within this function, do the following:

   a. Create variables named **user**, **pwd**, **sButton**, and **orderHistory** to reference the elements on the Web page with ID values of userID, pwd, submitButton, and orderhistory, respectively.

    b. Add an event handler to the sButton object that runs when the button is clicked. Steps c through e should all be done within this event handler.

    c. Create variables named **userValue** and **pwdValue** equal to the values entered into the user and pwd input boxes, respectively.

    d. If userValue and pwdValue both are non-empty, create a request object named **reqOrders**. Using the get method, open the following URL with the request object

       `/cgi-bin/wworders.pl?user=userValue&pwd=pwdValue`

       where *userValue* and *pwdValue* are the values of the userValue and pwdValue variables, respectively.

    e. Send the request and then wait for a complete and error-free response from the server. When the response arrives, store the text of the response in the orderHistory object on the Web page.

7. Save the file.

8. Using your file transfer software, copy the **getorders.js**, **orders.htm**, **wwlibrary.js**, **wwlogo.jpg**, and **wwstyles.css** files from the tutorial.12\case1 folder on your local computer and paste them into the tutorial.12/case1 folder in your account on the Web server.

9. Use your Web browser to open **http://*domainname*/tutorial.12/case1/orders.htm**, where *domainname* is the domain name of your Web server account.

10. Submit each of the following user ID/password combinations into the Web form and verify that the Web page retrieves a table showing each customer's order history: **RachelWilson/kaboom** and **BernardAdams/sparkler**.

11. Submit a different username/password combination and verify that the Web browser displays a message indicating no records exist for the specified user ID and password.

12. Submit your completed project to your instructor.

Apply	**Case Problem 2**

Use the skills you learned to retrieve Web server data into a tabbed layout.

Data Files needed for this Case Problem: activetab.png, back1.png, back2.png, back3.png, bikestxt.htm, geometry.htm, inactivetab.png, pmlibrary.js, pmlogo.png, pmstyles.css, reviews.htm, specifications.htm, star.png, tabstxt.js, tour250.png

Pedal Mart Janet Schmidt is the Web development team supervisor for PedalMart, an online seller of bicycles and bike parts. Janet wants you to develop an AJAX application to retrieve product information from the Web server and insert it into a tabbed box. Rather than loading all of the content in the tabbed box when the page loads, Janet wants content to be loaded only when users click one of the tabs. She feels that will make the page load faster because the browser will not have to download all of the product information when the page loads, only product information specifically requested by the user. Figure 12-46 shows a preview of the sample page you will create.

In this sample page, Janet created three tabs containing information about bicycle specifications, geometry, and customer reviews. She stored this information in external files named specifications.htm, geometry.htm, and reviews.htm, respectively. Janet also created the styles for these documents. You need to write the JavaScript code to retrieve these documents through a request object.

Figure 12-46

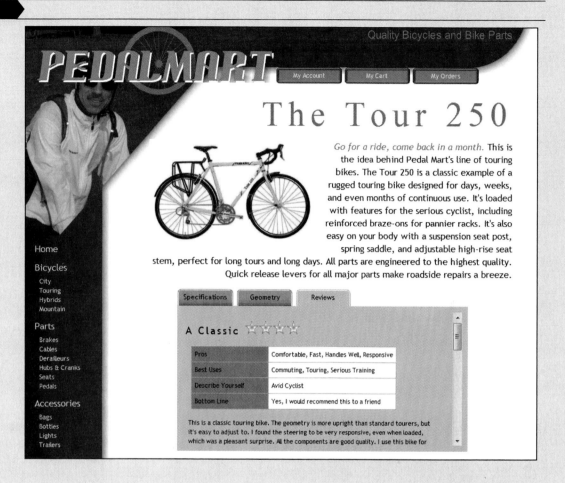

Complete the following:

1. Use your text editor to open the **bikestxt.htm** and **tabstxt.js** files from the tutorial.12\case2 folder, enter *your name* and *the date* in the comment section of each file, and then save the files as **bikes.htm** and **tabs.js**, respectively.

2. Create a folder named **case2** as a subfolder of the **tutorial.12** folder in your Web server account.

3. Return to the **bikes.htm** file in your text editor. Review the contents of the file and then create links to the pmlibrary.js and tabs.js files. Save and close the file.

4. Go to the **tabs.js** file in your text editor. Create an event handler that runs the makeTabs() function when the page is loaded.

5. Create the **makeTabs()** function. The purpose of this function is to create event handlers and request objects for the tabbed box on the Web page. Add the following commands to the function:

   a. Create a variable named **tabContent** that references the div element with the ID tabContent.

   b. Create an array named **allTabs** containing all of the div elements in the document with the class name divTab.

   c. Create a variable named **activeTab** pointing to the first tab in the allTabs array. The purpose of this variable is to indicate which tab is currently being shown in the document.

    d. For each item in the allTabs array, create an onclick event handler. When each tab is clicked, have the browser send an HTTP request using the get method to the Web server retrieving the *tabname*.htm file, where *tabname* is the name displayed on the tab in the Web page. When a response is received from the server, do the following: (i) Change the background image of activeTab to the inactivetab.png file. (ii) Change the background image of the clicked tab to the activetab.png file. (iii) Change the value of the activeTab variable to point to the tab the user clicked.

6. Save the file.

7. Using your file transfer software, copy all the files from the tutorial.12\case2 folder and paste them into the tutorial.12/case2 folder in your account on the Web server.

8. Use your Web browser to open **http://*domainname*/tutorial.12/case2/bikes.htm**, where *domainname* is the domain name of your Web server account.

9. Click the different tabs from the tabbed box and verify that the browser loads the contents for each tab.

10. Submit your completed project to your instructor.

Challenge | Case Problem 3

Explore how to use AJAX to preview hyperlinks with page overlays.

Data Files needed for this Case Problem: arctic.htm, arcticb.jpg, fless.htm, fless.jpg, flogo.jpg, frosti.htm, fwlibtxt.js, fwstyles.css, glass.png, glomitt.htm, glomitt.jpg, gloves.jpg, glovestxt.htm, linkstxt.js, overlaystyles.css, polyf.htm, polyflce.jpg, sweaters.jpg

FrostiWear Susan Crawford, the Web site manager of the FrostiWear winter clothing store, wants you to develop an AJAX application for the company Web site that can display a preview of selected hyperlinks. The application needs to access the contents of linked Web pages; retrieve the text of the main page heading, introductory paragraph, and a sample inline image; and then display them in a pop-up overlay. Figure 12-47 shows a preview of a sample page you will create.

Figure 12-47

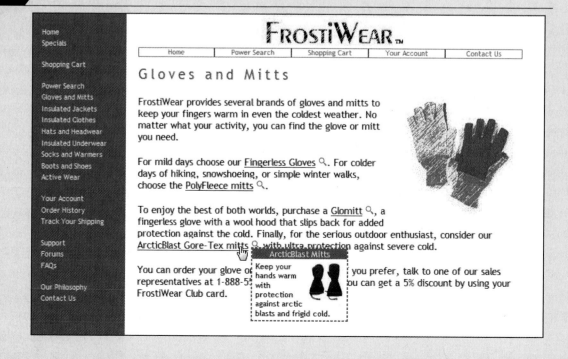

Your application needs to examine the sample Web page and locate all hypertext links marked as links capable of showing an overlay preview. Susan wants those hyperlinks displayed with a magnifying glass icon. When customers hover their pointers over the links, AJAX should send a request object to the server to retrieve information about the page contents.

Because the Web pages are written in XHTML, Susan has written a function named grabXHTMLAsXML() to ensure that all XHTML files retrieved from the request object are treated as XML documents. This will allow you to more easily parse the contents of those files to extract information needed for the pop-up overlays. Susan has already created CSS styles for the pop-up overlay you will create.

Complete the following:

1. Use your text editor to open the **glovestxt.htm**, **fwlibtxt.js**, and **linkstxt.js** files from the tutorial.12\case3 folder, enter *your name* and *the date* in the comment section of each file, and then save the files as **gloves.htm**, **fwlibrary.js**, and **links.js**, respectively.

2. Create a folder named **case3** as a subfolder of the **tutorial.12** folder in your Web server account.

3. Return to the **gloves.htm** file in your text editor. Review the contents of the file, and then do the following:

   a. Add a link to the overlaystyles.css file in the head section of the document.

   b. Add links to the fwlibrary.js and links.js script files.

   c. All links that will have pop-up overlays should be marked using the class value previewLink. Go to the main section of the Web page and add this class attribute value to the hypertext links for the fless.htm, poly.htm, glomitt.htm, and arctic.htm files.

4. Save and close the gloves.htm file.

5. Use your text editor to study the contents of the fless.htm, poly.htm, glomitt.htm, and arctic.htm files. Note that the h2 heading in each document has the id previewTitle, the inline image below the heading has the id previewImage, and the introductory paragraph has the id previewParagraph. You'll retrieve the contents of this heading, inline image, and paragraph to display in your overlay pop-ups. Close each of these four files without saving any changes.

⊕ **EXPLORE**

6. Go to the **fwlibrary.js** file in your text editor. Scroll to the bottom of the file and insert a constructor function named **linkDocument()**. The purpose of this function is to create document objects containing text drawn from an XML document. The function has a single parameter named **xmlDoc** representing an XML document object. Add the following commands to the function:

   a. Define a property named **docObj** that contains the value of the xmlDoc parameter.

   b. Loop through all of the element tags in xmlDoc. Test each element to determine whether it contains an id attribute with the value previewTitle. If so, store the text within that element in the **title** property of the linkDocument object. Test each element to determine whether it contains an id attribute with the value previewImage. If so, store the value of the src attribute in the **image** property of the linkDocument object. Finally, test each element to determine whether it contains an id attribute with the value previewParagraph. If so, store the text contained within that element in the **paragraph** property of the linkDocument. (*Hint*: To retrieve the value of the id attribute, use the getAttribute() method discussed in Tutorial 7.)

⊕ EXPLORE

7. Add a method named **makeOverlay()** to the linkDocument prototype. The purpose of this method is to use the values of the title, image, and paragraph properties to return an HTML fragment that will be used for the pop-up overlay. Add the following code to the method:

a. Create the HTML fragment

```
<div class="linkOverlay">
   <h1>title</h1>
   <img src="image" />
   <p>paragraph</p>
</div>
```

where *title*, *image*, and *paragraph* are the values of the title, image, and paragraph properties of the linkDocument object, respectively.

b. Return this HTML fragment object.

8. Save and close the fwlibrary.js file.

9. Go to the **links.js** file in your text editor and add an event handler to run the makeLinkPreviews() function when the page is loaded.

10. Create the **makeLinkPreviews()** function. The purpose of this function is to generate pop-up overlays for all hyperlinks in the document belonging to the previewLink class. The commands in Steps 12 through 14 should all be nested within this function.

11. Create the following variables in the makeLinkPreviews() function:

a. The **activeLink** variable containing the hyperlink currently previewed in the document; set its initial value to null

b. The **activeOverlay** variable referencing the pop-up overlay object displayed in the document; set its initial value to null

c. The **previewLinks** array; populate this array with all of the link elements in the Web document whose class name is previewLink

12. For each item in the previewLinks array, do the following:

a. Add the following HTML fragment after the hyperlink (*Hint*: Use the insertAfter() function defined in the fwlibrary.js file to insert this object after each hyperlink in the previewLinks array.):

```
<img src="glass.png" />
```

b. Call the showPreview() function when the mouse pointer moves over each hyperlink in the previewLinks array.

c. Call the hidePreview() function when the mouse pointer moves out from each hyperlink in the previewLinks array.

13. Create the **showPreview()** function, nested within the makeLinkPreviews() function. The purpose of this function is to display the pop-up overlay for the selected hyperlink. Add the following commands to the function:

a. Store the object representing the current event in the **evt** variable.

b. Store the object that initiated the event in the **hyperlink** variable. (*Hint*: Use either the target or the srcElement property to determine the source of the event.)

c. Store the value of the href attribute for the hyperlink variable in the **activeLink** variable.

⊕ EXPLORE

d. Create a request object to retrieve the activeLink file using a *synchronous—not an asynchronous*—connection with the get method. (*Hint*: Because this is a synchronous request, you do *not* have to add an event listener to listen for a response from the server.)

EXPLORE

e. If the browser supports the overrideMimeType() method of the request object, apply the overrideMimeType() method, changing the mime-type of the received document to text/xml.

f. Send the request to the server.

EXPLORE

g. Apply the grabXHTMLAsXML() method to the request object to convert the response from the server to an XML document. Store the XML document in the **xhtmlDoc** variable.

EXPLORE

h. Using the xhtmlDoc variable as the parameter value, create an instance of the linkDocument object named **myLink**.

i. Apply the makeOverlay() method to the myLink object, storing the result in the activeOverlay variable.

j. Store the values of the clientX and clientY properties of the event object in variables named **mouseX** and **mouseY**, respectively.

k. Set the display style of activeOverlay to block.

l. Set the top and left style values of activeOverlay to *mouseY* + 5 + "px" and *mouseX* + 5 + "px", respectively, to place the pop-up overlay on the page.

m. Append activeOverlay to the document body.

14. Nested within the makeLinkPreviews() function, insert the **hidePreview()** function. The purpose of this function is to hide and remove the pop-up overlay when the user moves the pointer off of the hyperlink. Add the following commands to the function:

a. If the activeOverlay object exists, remove it from the document body.

b. Set activeOverlay to null.

15. Save and close the file.

16. Using your file transfer software, copy all of the files from the tutorial.12\case3 folder on your local computer and paste them into the tutorial.12/case3 folder in your account on the Web server.

17. Use your Web browser to open **http://*domainname*/tutorial.12/case3/gloves.htm**, where *domainname* is the domain name of your Web server account.

18. Verify that the four hyperlinks in the main paragraph of the page appear alongside the magnifying glass icon.

19. Hover your pointer over each of the four links and verify that the browser displays a pop-up overlay with the title, main image, and introductory paragraph from the linked page. Click each link to confirm that the pop-up overlay correctly displays this content.

20. Submit your completed project to your instructor.

Create | **Case Problem 4**

Create an AJAX application to retrieve content for a Science Fiction blog.

Data Files needed for this Case Problem: authorlist.txt, intro.txt, links.txt, sflogo.png, sfpod.xml, sfreviews.pl, vinter.png

The Science Fiction Control Room Kevin Vinter is a noted science fiction author and critic. He wants to start a blog that contains selections from his published works, reviews of science fiction books and movies, and commentary on the history and culture of science fiction. You will help create interactive content for the blog using AJAX.

Kevin supplied several text files for you to use in creating a sample page. You need to write all of the JavaScript code and design the layout and style of the completed page.

Complete the following:

1. Explore the contents of the tutorial.12\case4 folder. You'll use the text and graphic files in this folder as the content for your Web page. The design and appearance of the final page are up to you and you can supplement Kevin's material with your own.

2. Using your text editor, create the following files in the tutorial.12\case4 folder: **control.htm**, **news.js**, **sflibrary.js**, and **sfstyles.css**. The control.htm file will be used for the sample page that you'll create for Kevin. JavaScript commands to retrieve data from Kevin's Web server should be entered into the sflibrary.js file. General commands for working with request objects and document objects should be entered into the sflibrary.js file. Finally, any styles used in designing your Web page should be placed in the sfstyles.css file. Enter *your name* and *the date* in a comment section of each file and include commentary that describes the purpose of the file.

3. Go to your account on your Web site and create a new subfolder named **case4** within the **tutorial.12** folder.

4. Kevin's Web site has an RSS feed stored in the sfpod.xml document. Create a request object to retrieve the contents of this file as an XML document and then parse it, showing the channel title and location in an appropriate location on the control.htm page. Link the channel title to the URL specified in the channel link element. For each news item in the sfpod.xml document, display the item's title, description, and publication date. Link the item title to the URL specified in the item link element.

⊕ **EXPLORE**

5. Kevin wants to create an archive of book reviews indexed by the author's initials. He has stored a JSON data structure in the authorlist.txt file. Create a request object that reads this JSON file, and then use it to create a drop-down list box in which each option displays the author's name and the value of the option matches the author's initials.

⊕ **EXPLORE**

6. Add an event handler to the drop-down list box that you created in the previous step that submits the request

   `/cgi-bin/sfreviews.pl?author=initials`
   to your Web server when the user selects an item from the list box, where *initials* contains the initials of the author selected from the drop-down list box. The sfreviews.pl CGI script will return HTML code for a review of a book written by the selected author. Display the book review in an appropriate spot on your Web page.

7. Copy the files for your Web site to your account on your Web server, placing them in the case4 folder. Also copy the sfreviews.pl script file to your cgi-bin folder. Make sure you transfer the file as an ASCII file and that you allow execution of the file by the owner, the owner's group, and the public.

8. Test your Web page on your server. Verify that the contents of the news feed are displayed when the page is loaded.

9. Test the author drop-down list box. Verify that when you select either Gene Wolfe or Robert Heinlein from the list box, a review of a book by that author appears on your Web page. If you select any other author, the CGI script should return a message indicating that no book reviews have been archived.

10. Submit the completed project to your instructor.

Session 12.1

1. In the Web application model, requests are sent to the server in a synchronous manner with responses returned in the form of complete Web pages.

2. In the AJAX Web application model, communication between the server and the client is performed asynchronously, allowing the user to continue to work on the client side. Also, responses are received in smaller packets via an AJAX engine rather than via an entire Web page.

3. Asynchronous communication is communication in which the user does not have to wait for a response to continue interacting with the Web page.

4. `reqAns.open("GET", "register?id=wjones&pwd=gr7#xY1")`

5. `reqAns.send(null);`

6. 4

7. The client was able to find the server resource.

8. `responseText`

Session 12.2

1. An XML vocabulary is a markup language written using XML. XML vocabularies include RSS and XHTML.

2. RSS stands for Really Simple Syndication and is an XML vocabulary used to distribute news articles or any content that changes on a regular basis to a group of subscribers.

3. The item element

4. `responseXML`

5. `var channel = `*rssDoc*`.getElementsByTagName("channel")[0];`

   `var link = channel.getElementsByTagName("link")[0]`
   where *rssDoc* is the reference to the XML document containing the RSS feed

6. JSON stands for JavaScript Object Notation and is used to send data structures via the responseText property of the request object. JSON files are more compact than XML documents and have the added advantage that they can be treated as document objects with nested fields treated as object properties.

7. a. `contact.customer.name`

   b. `contact.customer.address.city`

   c. `contact.customer.orderIDs[1]`

8. `var contact = eval( "(" + reqCust.responseText + ")" );`

Session 12.3

1. Perl is a common server side scripting language often used to generate and manipulate text strings.

2. CGI scripts are often located in the cgi-bin folder.

3. The permissions should be set to allow for execution by the script's owner, members of the owner's group, and the public.

4. The parseJSON() method

5. `reqAccount.open("GET", "/cgi-bin/getaccount.php?id=smith");`

6. jQuery is a lightweight JavaScript library containing custom methods, properties, and objects used to accomplish most common JavaScript and AJAX tasks.

7. `$(img#logo)`

Ending Data Files

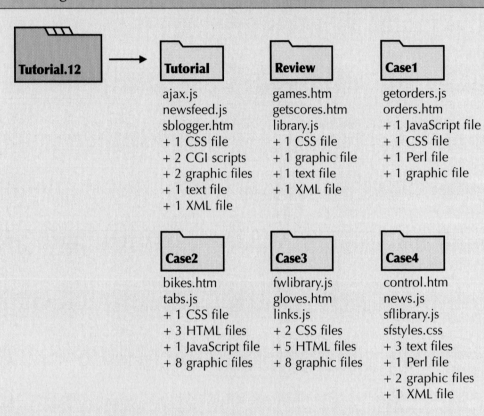

Tutorial.12 →

Tutorial
ajax.js
newsfeed.js
sblogger.htm
+ 1 CSS file
+ 2 CGI scripts
+ 2 graphic files
+ 1 text file
+ 1 XML file

Review
games.htm
getscores.htm
library.js
+ 1 CSS file
+ 1 graphic file
+ 1 text file
+ 1 XML file

Case1
getorders.js
orders.htm
+ 1 JavaScript file
+ 1 CSS file
+ 1 Perl file
+ 1 graphic file

Case2
bikes.htm
tabs.js
+ 1 CSS file
+ 3 HTML files
+ 1 JavaScript file
+ 8 graphic files

Case3
fwlibrary.js
gloves.htm
links.js
+ 2 CSS files
+ 5 HTML files
+ 8 graphic files

Case4
control.htm
news.js
sflibrary.js
sfstyles.css
+ 3 text files
+ 1 Perl file
+ 2 graphic files
+ 1 XML file

Reality Check

JavaScript is a powerful tool for creating interesting and dynamic Web pages. Because of JavaScript's popularity, hundreds of sites are available on the Web with programming tips, sample scripts, and downloadable apps to assist you in writing your own JavaScript applications.

1. Using the applications found from the various frameworks available on the Web or by writing your own code, create a Web page containing a typing test form. The design and layout of the Web page are up to you, but it should contain the following features:
   a. A Web form in which users can type the text in the typing exam
   b. Several different typing samples that users can load from text files stored on the server using an AJAX request object
   c. A start and stop button to start and stop the typing exam
   d. An input box containing a timer to time the user's typing exam
2. Use JavaScript to program the following actions on your typing exam page:
   a. The typing timer should start when the user clicks the Start button and use timed interval commands to update the value on the timer every second.
   b. Event handlers should intercept the keypress events initiated by the user and display each typed character in a div container element on the page.
   c. The Stop button should stop the typing timer when pressed.
3. Score the typing exam by writing scripts to do the following:
   a. Compare the typed characters to the characters in the typing sample. Count the number of typing errors.
   b. Highlight the mistyped characters on the Web page.
   c. Use regular expressions to loop through the number of words in the typing sample. Count up the number of words in the sample.
   d. Loop through the words typed in the typing exam. Count the number of misspelled words.
   e. Subtract the number of misspelled words from the total number of words. Divide the difference by the length of time (in minutes) needed to complete the typing exam. Report on the user's typing speed in terms of correct words per minute.
4. Write the results of the typing exam to a cookie that can then be retrieved and displayed the next time the user opens the Web page.
5. Share your typing exam with your classmates and colleagues. Evaluate each other's typing speed and level of accuracy. Report on the results of your typing tests.
6. Web sites load quicker and JavaScript programs are more responsive when the code is small and compact. Several applications are available on the Web to reduce the size of JavaScript files. Use a Web search engine to investigate these tools including the programs Squish, jscompact, JSMin, and Packers. How do these programs affect the format of a JavaScript file during the compacting process? How should you write your code to prepare it for compression?
7. Many Web sites contain prepackaged JavaScript tools also known as frameworks. Some of the more popular frameworks are Dojo, Prototype, Rico, qooxdoo, script. aculo.us, Yahoo! User Interface Library (YUI), and MooTools. Rather than creating your own programs to generate online calendars, pull-down menus, and so on, explore some of the applications available in these toolkits.

8. Write a report on one of the languages you explored in Step 7 and provide examples of three custom functions that you could use in your future JavaScript projects. Also, discuss what code in your typing exam program could be replaced by using a built-in script from one of these frameworks.

9. Document your code and describe what you've learned from creating this typing test form.

10. Submit the completed project to your instructor.

Objectives

- Understand the history of the Web and HTML
- Study the basic syntax for creating elements and attributes
- Learn to create block-level and inline elements
- Understand how to insert nontextual objects, such as inline images, into a Web page
- Study how to create and populate Web tables
- Learn how to work with Web forms and their content
- Understand how to create Web frames and inline frames

Introducing HTML and XHTML

Creating Web Pages with HTML

Appendix A

One of the most significant communications innovations in the past 50 years is the development of the Internet. In its early days in the late 1960s, the Internet was called the ARPANET and consisted of two network nodes, located at UCLA and Stanford, that were connected by a land line. Since then, the Internet has grown to include hundreds of millions of interconnected computers, cell phones, PDAs (personal digital assistants), televisions, and networks. The physical structure of the Internet uses fiber-optic cables, satellites, phone lines, and other telecommunications media to enable a worldwide community to communicate and share information.

Most early Internet tools required mastery of a bewildering array of terms, acronyms, and commands. Even navigating the network required users to be well versed in both computers and network technology. Before the Internet could be accessible to the general public, it needed to have a simple interface, which arrived in the form of the World Wide Web. The foundations for the **World Wide Web**, or **Web**, were laid in 1989 by Timothy Berners-Lee and other researchers at the CERN nuclear research facility near Geneva, Switzerland. They needed an information system that made it easy for their researchers to locate and share data and required minimal training and support. To meet this need, they developed a system of interconnected documents using hypertext. In this system, documents were stored on network computers called **servers**, which made them accessible to users running computers known as **clients**.

Hypertext is a technology that allows users to click items called **links** to open documents and other information sources. A link can open another document on your computer or, using the World Wide Web, a document on another computer located almost anywhere in the world.

The hypertext approach was just what was needed to make the Internet accessible to the general public. An end user didn't need to know exactly where in the world a linked document was located; instead, the user could simply click a mouse to open the document from the server. This approach puts any online document at a user's fingertips. It is a testament to the success of this approach that the Internet and the World Wide Web are synonymous in many users' minds.

Starting Data Files

There are no starting Data Files needed for this appendix.

Web Pages, Servers, and Browsers

Documents on the Web are known as **Web pages**. In addition to text, Web pages can contain images, video and sound clips, and even programs that users can run remotely from their computers. A Web page is stored on a **Web server**, which makes it available to the entire World Wide Web. To view a Web page, a user runs a software program called a **Web browser**, which retrieves the page from the server and displays it (see Figure A-1).

Figure A-1 ▶ **Viewing a document on the World Wide Web**

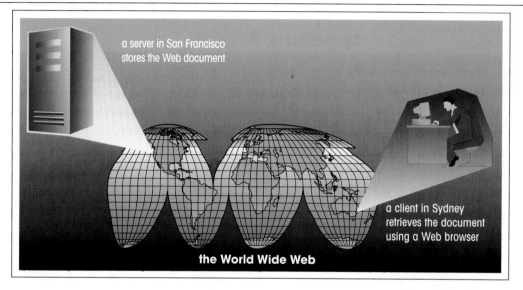

a server in San Francisco stores the Web document

a client in Sydney retrieves the document using a Web browser

the World Wide Web

The earliest browsers were text based and incapable of displaying images. Today, however, most computers support graphical browsers, which can display images, video, sound, animations, and a variety of other graphical features. Cell phones can also connect to the Web to display the latest sports scores, stock market tickers, and even rudimentary Web pages. In addition, browsers can run on teletype machines, PDAs, Braille machines, and even information devices within a car. How does a Web page work with so many combinations of browsers, clients, and devices? To understand, you have to look at how Web pages are created.

HTML: The Language of the Web

A Web page is simply a text file that is written in a language called **Hypertext Markup Language**, or **HTML**. A **markup language** describes the structure and the content of a document. Each item within such a document is set off using a **markup tag**. If the content of this appendix were stored using a markup language, markup tags would identify whether a particular block of text represented the appendix's title, a paragraph, a figure caption, and so forth.

In the early years after HTML was created, no single organization was responsible for the language. Web browser developers were free to define and modify HTML in whatever ways they thought best. Although many rules were common, competing browsers, seeking to dominate the market, introduced some differences in the language. Such changes to the language were called **extensions**. The two major browsers during the 1990s, Netscape Navigator and Microsoft Internet Explorer, added the most extensions to HTML. These extensions were providing Web page authors with more options but at the expense of complicating Web page development. The challenge for Web designers was to determine which browser or browser version supported a particular extension and to create a workaround for browsers that did not. Extensions, while often useful and necessary, diminished the promise of simplicity that made HTML so attractive in the first place.

Ultimately, a group of Web developers, programmers, and analysts formed the **World Wide Web Consortium**, or **W3C**, to create a set of standards for all browser manufacturers to follow. The W3C has no enforcement power, but because agreeing on a uniform approach to Web page creation is in the best interests of everyone, the W3C's recommendations are usually followed (though not always right away). The W3C also provides online tutorials, documentation, and quizzes that allow users to test their knowledge of HTML and other languages. For more information on the W3C and the services it offers, see its Web site at www.w3c.org.

Figure A-2 summarizes the various versions of HTML that the W3C has released. Don't worry if you don't understand all the details of these versions yet—the important thing to understand is that HTML doesn't come in only one flavor and that, as a Web page author, you might need to support a wide variety of HTML versions.

Versions of HTML and XHTML ◀ Figure A-2

Version	Date	Description
HTML 1.0	1989–1994	The first public version of HTML, which included browser support for inline images and text controls.
HTML 2.0	1995	The first version supported by all graphical browsers. It introduced interactive form elements such as option buttons and text boxes. A document written to the HTML 2.0 specification is compatible with almost all browsers on the World Wide Web.
HTML 3.0	1996	A proposed replacement for HTML 2.0 that was never widely adopted.
HTML 3.2	1997	This version included additional support for creating and formatting tables and expanded the options for interactive form elements. It also supported limited programming using scripts.
HTML 4.01	1999	This version added support for style sheets to give Web designers greater control over page layout. It added new features to tables and forms and provided support for international features. This version also expanded HTML's scripting capability and added increased support for multimedia elements.
HTML 5.0	2007	This version supports features that reflect current Web usage, including elements for Web site navigation, multimedia, and search engine indexes. HTML 5.0 removes most of the presentational elements and attributes from HTML while still maintaining backward compatibility with earlier HTML versions. HTML 5.0 is not supported by most browsers at the time of this writing.
XHTML 1.0	2001	This version is a reformulation of HTML 4.01 in XML and combines the strength of HTML 4.0 with the power of XML. XHTML brings the rigor of XML to Web pages and provides standards for more robust Web content on a wide range of browser platforms.
XHTML 1.1	2002	A minor update to XHTML 1.0 that allows for modularity and simplifies writing extensions to the language.
XHTML 2.0	2004	An updated version designed to remove most of the presentational features left in HTML.
XHTML 5.0	2007	A version of HTML 5.0 written in XML. Unlike XHTML 2.0, XHTML 5.0 is backward-compatible with XHTML 1.1. XHTML 5.0 is supported by most browsers at the time of this writing.

You also have to stay familiar with which versions of HTML are actually supported in the browser market. This could mean dealing with a collection of approaches: some that are new and meet the latest specifications and some that are older but still widely supported. Older features of HTML are often **deprecated** by the W3C, meaning that they might not be supported in current or future browsers, and you should use caution in applying them. Even though deprecated features are in the process of being phased out, this doesn't mean that you can't continue to use them; indeed, if you are supporting older browsers, you might need to. Because it's difficult to predict how quickly deprecated features will disappear from common usage on the Web, knowledge of them is crucial.

Although HTML has been instrumental in making the Web popular and accessible, the future of Web development focuses more on two other languages: XML and XHTML. **XML (Extensible Markup Language)** is another markup language used to create documents that must adhere to specific rules for content and structure. XML contrasts sharply with a language such as HTML, which allows for a wide variety of rules without a built-in mechanism for enforcing them. XML can be used to define other markup languages, and one of its applications is a stricter version of HTML called **XHTML (Extensible Hypertext Markup Language)**. XHTML is designed to confront some of the problems associated with the different and competing versions of HTML and to better integrate HTML with XML.

Even though XHTML shows great promise for the Web, HTML will not become obsolete any time soon. In addition to the considerable overlap between HTML and XHTML, the Web is full of old HTML documents and some users are still running older versions of Web browsers that might not recognize some of the features of XHTML. Where does all of this leave you as a potential Web page author? A few guidelines are helpful:

- **Become well versed in the history of HTML.** Unlike other programming and markup languages, HTML and its history play a major role in the choices you make in writing your code.
- **Know your market.** Do you have to support older browsers, or have your clients standardized on a particular browser or browser version? The answer affects how you design your pages. Become familiar with what different browsers can and cannot do.
- **Test thoroughly.** If you have to support several types of browsers and several types of devices, acquire them and use them to view your document. Don't assume that if your page works in one browser it will work in an older version of that same browser. The same browser version might even act differently on different operating systems.

Creating an HTML Document

When you consider creating an HTML document, it's useful to think of it in terms of elements. An **element** is a distinct feature of a document, such as a paragraph, a heading, or the page's title. Even a whole document itself can be considered an element. Each element is marked within the HTML file with a **tag**. Tags can be either two-sided or one-sided. A two-sided tag contains some document content. The general syntax of a two-sided tag is

```
<element>content</element>
```

where *element* is the name of the HTML element and *content* is any content it contains. For example, the following code marks the text "Welcome to Pixal Products" with the <p> tag. As you'll learn later, this directs browsers to treat the text as a paragraph element.

```
<p>Welcome to Pixal Products</p>
```

The terms "tag" and "element" are sometimes used interchangeably, but this appendix uses the term "element" to refer to an element itself, and "tag" to refer to that part of the HTML code that marks an element for a browser. So, you would mark the p element in a Web page by inserting a <p> tag in an HTML file.

The scope of a two-sided tag is identified by its **opening tag** (<p>) and its **closing tag** (</p>), with the content ("Welcome to Pixal Products") placed between them. Web browsers often allow you to omit a closing tag if the surrounding code clearly indicates the tag's content, but this practice is not recommended. XHTML requires both an opening and a closing tag.

HTML does not distinguish between uppercase and lowercase letters. So, you can type either <p> or <P> to mark a paragraph element. However, because XHTML strictly requires lowercase tag names, this appendix follows that convention, and it is strongly recommended that you do likewise to ensure that your code is consistent with current and future standards.

Unlike a two-sided tag, a **one-sided tag** contains no content. The general syntax for a one-sided tag is

```
<element />
```

where `element` is once again the element name. HTML also allows you to enter one-sided tags using the syntax `<element>` (omitting the space and the closing slash); however, because XHTML does not support this form, it is also strongly recommended that you include the space and the closing slash at all times. Elements that employ one-sided tags are called **empty elements** because they contain no content. One example of an empty element is a line break, which forces the browser to place the content that follows on a new line. To create a line break, you use the following one-sided tag:

```
<br />
```

Inserting Two-sided and One-sided Tags | Reference Window

- To create a two-sided tag, use the syntax
    ```
    <element>content</ element>
    ```
  where `element` is the name of the HTML element and `content` is any content that it contains. Element names should be in lowercase.
- To create a one-sided tag, use the syntax
    ```
    ```

A third type of tag is a comment tag. Comment tags are used to add notes to your HTML code. Comments are not required and are ignored by Web browsers, but they are useful in documenting your HTML code for yourself and others. The syntax of the comment tag is

```
<!-- comment -->
```

where `comment` is the text of your note. The following is an example of a comment tag:

```
<!-- Home page for Pixal Products -->
```

A comment can also be spread over several lines as follows:

```
<!-- Home page for
    Pixal Products
-->
```

Inserting a Comment | Reference Window

To insert a comment anywhere within your HTML file, enter
```
<!-- comment -->
```
where `comment` is the text of your comment. Comments can extend over several lines.

White Space and HTML

The fact that comments can be spread over several lines brings up an important point concerning how you enter your HTML code. As simple text files, HTML documents are composed of text characters and **white space**, which are the blank spaces, tabs, and line breaks within the file. A browser reading an HTML file treats all consecutive occurrences of white space as a single blank space. As far as a browser is concerned, there is no difference between a blank space, a tab, and a line break—or indeed between two blank spaces and a single blank space. When a browser encounters consecutive occurrences of white space, it collapses them into a single occurrence. The following three code samples are equivalent as far as a browser is concerned:

```
<p>This is an example of White Space</p>
<p>This is an example  of    White      Space</p>
<p>This is an example
   of    White
   Space</p>
```

Even though browsers ignore extra white space, careful application of white space can make your HTML code more readable—for example, by indenting lines or by separating blocks of code from one another.

Element Attributes

Elements also have attributes that provide browsers with additional information about how to treat them. Attributes are inserted into the element's opening tag using the following syntax:

```
attribute1="value1" attribute2="value2"
```

where `attribute1`, `attribute2`, and so on are the names of the attributes, and `value1`, `value2`, and so on are the values associated with those attributes. For example, you can use attributes to align the content of an element. The following code aligns the paragraph "Pixal Products" with the right page margin:

```
<p align="right">Pixal Products</p>
```

Attributes can be listed in any order, but they must be separated from one another in the opening tag by white space. As with element names, you should enter attribute names in lowercase letters and enclose attribute values within quotation marks. Although many browsers still accept attribute values without quotation marks, you can ensure maximum compatibility with all the different versions of HTML and XHTML by always including them. XHTML requires quotation marks for all attribute values.

Reference Window | **Inserting Attributes**

To add attributes to an element, insert the following into the element's opening tag
```
attribute1="value1" attribute2="value2"
```
where `attribute1`, `attribute2`, and so on are the names of the attributes, and `value1`, `value2`, and so on are the values associated with each of those attributes.

The Structure of an HTML File

Any markup document must include a **root element**, which contains all other elements in the document. For an HTML document, the root element is the html element. So, the basic structure of an HTML document is

```
<html>
    content
</html>
```

where *content* is any content included within the document. The content is divided into two sections: the head and the body. The **head element** contains information about the document, such as the document's title or keywords that a search engine on the Web might use to locate the document for others to use. The content of the head element is not displayed within the Web page, but browsers might use it in other ways—for example, the document's title is usually displayed in a browser's title bar. The **body element** contains all of the content to be displayed in the Web page. It can also contain code that tells browsers how to render that content. To mark the head and body elements, you use the <head> and <body> tags as follows:

```
<html>
    <head>
        head content
    </head>
    <body>
        body content
    </body>
</html>
```

Note that the body element is always placed after the head element.

The technique of placing one element within another is called **nesting**. When one element contains another element, you must close the inside element before closing the outside element. The following code sample is incorrect because it closes the html element before the nested body element is closed:

```
<html><head>head content</head><body>body content</html></body>
```

To correct this, you must ensure that the body element is closed before the containing element—in this case, the html element—is closed. The correct form is

```
<html><head>head content</head><body>body content</body></html>
```

Working with the Document Head

The head element also contains its own collection of nested elements. One required element is the title element, which specifies the page title that is displayed in the title bar of a user's Web browser. For example, the following code adds the page title "Pixal Products" to a document. Note that a Web document can contain only one title element.

```
<head>
    <title>Pixal Products</title>
</head>
```

The head element can also contain meta elements, which store information about the document that could be of use to programs running on Web servers. A meta element is created using the one-sided <meta /> tag as follows:

```
<meta name="text" content="text" scheme="text" http-equiv="text" />
```

where the name attribute specifies the name of a property for the page, the content attribute provides a property value, and the scheme attribute provides the format of the property value; the http-equiv attribute takes the place of the name attribute for some Web servers. For example, the following <meta /> tag stores the name of a Web page's author:

```
<meta name="author" content="Lisa Burkett" />
```

   Some Web sites use search engines to create lists of Web pages devoted to particular topics. You can give extra weight to a Web page by including a description of the page and a list of keywords in <meta /> tags such as the following:

```
<meta name="description" content="Pixal Products" />
<meta name="keywords" content="digital imaging, scanning, graphics" />
```

Note that while a Web document can contain only one title element, it can contain several meta elements. The use of meta tags to aid search engines is somewhat controversial, however. Some Web page authors have used meta tags to manipulate search engine cataloging by repeating keywords to give their pages a higher ranking. In response, many search engines have stopped reviewing meta tags entirely.

Working with Block-Level Elements

Within a document's body element, page content is marked as either a block-level element or an inline element. A **block-level element** contains content displayed in a separate section within the page, setting it off from other blocks. One common block-level element is the paragraph. **Inline elements**, on the other hand, are placed within block-level elements and are not separated from other page content as paragraphs are. In the next sections, you'll examine some of the more common block-level elements, starting with headings.

Creating Headings

Headings are titles placed within the page body, usually to mark different topics appearing on the page. HTML supports six heading elements, numbered h1 through h6. The h1 heading is reserved for the largest and most prominent headings, whereas the h6 element indicates a minor heading. The syntax to mark a heading element is

```
<hy>content</hy>
```

where y is a heading number 1 through 6 and *content* is the content of the heading. Figure A-3 illustrates the general appearance of the six heading elements. Because there is no set method for displaying headings, your browser might use slightly different fonts and sizes.

HTML headings ◀ **Figure A-3**

This is an h1 heading

This is an h2 heading

This is an h3 heading

This is an h4 heading

This is an h5 heading

This is an h6 heading

Inserting a Heading | Reference Window

To define a heading, use the syntax
```
<hy>content</hy>
```
where *y* is a heading number 1 through 6 and *content* is the content of the heading.

Creating Paragraphs

As noted earlier, paragraphs are another popular block-level element. To mark content as a paragraph, use the following tag:

```
<p>content</p>
```

where *content* is the content of the paragraph. When a browser encounters the opening <p> tag, it starts the enclosed content on a new line with blank space above it, separating the new paragraph from the preceding element. In earlier versions of HTML when standards were not firmly fixed, Web authors would often include only the opening <p> tag, omitting the closing tag entirely. Although many browsers still allow this, your Web pages will be displayed more reliably if you consistently use the closing tag. Also, if you want to write code compliant with the standards of XHTML, you must include the closing tag.

Creating a Paragraph | Reference Window

To create a paragraph, use the syntax
```
<p>content</p>
```
where *content* is the content of the paragraph.

Creating Lists

Another block-level element is the list. HTML supports three kinds of lists: ordered, unordered, and definition. You use an **ordered list** for items that have a prescribed sequential order. Ordered lists are created using the ol element in the following form:

```
<ol>
    <li>item1</li>
    <li>item2</li>
...
</ol>
```

where *item1*, *item2*, and so on are items in the list. Each <li> tag marks the content for a single list item. For example, if you wanted to enter shopping items in an ordered list, the code might look as follows:

```
<ol>
    <li>Milk</li>
    <li>Celery</li>
    <li>Bagels</li>
</ol>
```

By default, a browser displays an ordered list with numeric markers as follows:

1. Milk
2. Celery
3. Bagels

For lists in which the items do not need to be placed in any special order, you can create an **unordered list**. An unordered list has the same structure as an ordered list, except that the content of the list is contained within a <ul> tag:

```
<ul>
    <li>item1</li>
    <li>item2</li>
    ...
</ul>
```

By default, list items in an unordered list are displayed as bulleted text. So, the code

```
<ul>
    <li>Milk</li>
    <li>Celery</li>
    <li>Bagels</li>
</ul>
```

is displayed by a browser as

- Milk
- Celery
- Bagels

One list can also contain another list. The following is a combination of ordered and unordered lists:

1. Dairy
   - Milk
   - Sour cream
2. Produce
   - Celery
   - Lettuce
3. Bakery
   - Bagels
   - Bread

You create this combination of lists using the following HTML code:

```
<ol>
    <li>Dairy
        <ul>
            <li>Milk</li>
            <li>Sour cream</li>
        </ul>
    </li>
    <li>Produce
        <ul>
            <li>Celery</li>
            <li>Lettuce</li>
        </ul>
    </li>
    <li>Bakery
        <ul>
            <li>Bagels</li>
            <li>Bread</li>
        </ul>
    </li>
</ol>
```

Note that in this code some of the list items themselves contain lists.

A third list element supported by HTML is a **definition list**, which contains a list of definition terms with each term followed by a definition description. The syntax for creating a definition list is

```
<dl>
    <dt>term1</dt>
    <dd>definition1</dd>
    <dt>term2</dt>
    <dd>definition2</dd>
</dl>
```

where *term1*, *term2*, and so on are the terms in the list, and *definition1*, *definition2*, and so on are the definitions of the terms. For example, the following code creates a definition list of computer terms:

```
<dl>
    <dt>server</dt>
    <dd>A device that makes a resource available on a network</dd>
    <dt>client</dt>
    <dd>A device on a network that requests the resources stored on a
    server</dd>
</dl>
```

Web browsers typically display the definition description slightly indented from the definition term. A browser would display the above definition list as

server
    A device that makes a resource available on a network
client
    A device on a network that requests the resources stored on a server

Reference Window | Creating Lists

- To create an ordered list, use the syntax
  ```
  <ol>
      <li>item1</li>
      <li>item2</li>
      ...
  </ol>
  ```
  where *item1*, *item2*, and so on are items in the list.
- To create an unordered list, use the syntax
  ```
  <ul>
      <li>item1</li>
      <li>item2</li>
      ...
  </ul>
  ```
- To create a definition list, use the syntax
  ```
  <dl>
      <dt>term1</dt>
      <dd>definition1</dd>
      <dt>term2</dt>
      <dd>definition2</dd>
      ...
  </dl>
  ```
  where *term1*, *term2*, and so on are the terms in the list, and *definition1*, *definition2*, and so on are the definitions of the terms.

Creating a Generic Block

HTML and XHTML also support a block-level element called the **div element**, which is a generic container for any block-level content. The syntax of the div element is

```
<div>
    content
</div>
```

where `content` is any page content you want to enclose and mark as a block-level element. Browsers display the content in a block but usually do not apply any other formatting.

Using Other Block-Level Elements

HTML supports several other block-level elements that you might find useful in your Web pages. For example, the address element is used to mark contact information. Most browsers display the content of address elements in an italicized font. Long quotes can be indicated by applying the blockquote element. A browser encountering this element typically indents the quoted text. Figure A-4 shows a fuller list of block-level elements and the typical visual appearance of each.

Block-level elements ◀ **Figure A-4**

Block-Level Element	Description	Visual Appearance
<address> ... </address>	Identifies contact information	*Italicized text*
<blockquote> ... </blockquote>	Identifies a long quotation	Plain text indented from the left and the right
<center> ... </center>	Centers content horizontally within a block. **Deprecated**	Plain text, centered
<dd> ... </dd>	Identifies a definition description	Plain text
<dir> ... </dir>	Identifies a multicolumn directory list; superseded by the ul element. **Deprecated**	Plain text
<div> ... </div>	Identifies a generic block-level element	Plain text
<dl> ... </dl>	Identifies a definition list	Plain text
<dt> ... </dt>	Identifies a definition term	Plain text
<hy> ... </hy>	Identifies a heading, where y is a value from 1 to 6	**Boldfaced text of various font sizes**
<li> ... </li>	Identifies a list item in an ordered or unordered list	Bulleted or numbered text
<menu> ... </menu>	Identifies a single-column menu list; superseded by the ul element. **Deprecated**	Plain text
<ol> ... </ol>	Identifies an ordered list	Plain text
<p> ... </p>	Identifies a paragraph	Plain text
<pre> ... </pre>	Retains all white space and special characters in preformatted text	`Fixed-width text`
<ul> ... </ul>	Identifies an unordered list	Plain text

Working with Inline Elements

Now that you've examined block-level elements, let's turn to the inline elements. One type of inline element is the **character-formatting element**, which is used to define the appearance or format of text within a block. Figure A-5 describes some character-formatting elements supported by HTML.

Figure A-5   **Character-formatting elements**

Character-formatting Element	Identifies	Visual Appearance
`<abbr> ... </abbr>`	An abbreviation	Plain text
`<acronym> .. </acronym>`	An acronym	Plain text
`<b> ... </b>`	Boldface text	**Boldface text**
`<big> ... </big>`	Big text	Larger text
`<cite> ... </cite>`	A citation	*Italicized text*
`<code> ... </code>`	Program code text	`Fixed-width text`
`<del> ... </del>`	Deleted text	~~Strikethrough text~~
`<dfn> ... </dfn>`	A definition term	*Italicized text*
`<em> ... </em>`	Emphasized content	*Italicized text*
`<i> ... </i>`	Italicized text	*Italicized text*
`<ins> ... </ins>`	Inserted text	<u>Underlined text</u>
`<kbd> ... </kbd>`	Keyboard-style text	`Fixed-width text`
`<q> ... </q>`	Quoted text	"Quoted text"
`<s> ... </s>`	Strikethrough text. **Deprecated**	~~Strikethrough text~~
`<samp> ... </samp>`	Sample computer code text	`Fixed-width text`
`<small> ... </small>`	Small text	Smaller text
`<span> ... </span>`	A generic inline element	Plain text
`<strike> ... </strike>`	Strikethrough text. **Deprecated**	~~Strikethrough text~~
`<strong> ... </strong>`	Strongly emphasized content	**Boldface text**
`<sub> ... </sub>`	Subscripted text	Subscripted $_{text}$
`<sup> ... </sup>`	Superscripted text	Superscripted ^{text}
`<tt> ... </tt>`	Teletype text	`Fixed-width text`
`<u> ... </u>`	Underlined text. **Deprecated**	<u>Underlined text</u>
`<var> ... </var>`	Programming variables	*Italicized text*

For example, if you wanted to mark a section of boldface text within a paragraph, you could enter the following HTML code:

```
<p>Welcome to the <b>Home Page</b></p>
```

This code results in the following paragraph on the Web page:

Welcome to the **Home Page**

To mark those same words as italicized text, you would use

```
<p>Welcome to the <i>Home Page</i></p>
```

If you wanted the phrase "Home Page" to be marked as both boldface and italics, you could use the code

```
<p>Welcome to the <b><i>Home Page</i></b></p>
```

which would be displayed as

Welcome to the ***Home Page***

As you examine the tag list in Figure A-5, you might notice some overlap in the way the content appears in a browser. For example, if you wanted to display italicized text, you could use the <dfn>, <em>, <i>, or <var> tag (or even the <address> tag if you want to italicize a block of text). Why does HTML support so many different ways of formatting text?

The main purpose of HTML is not to format text but rather to create a structure for the content of the document. Page elements are often organized, therefore, into two types: logical elements and physical elements. A **logical element**, created with tags like <cite> and <code>, describes the nature of the enclosed content but not necessarily how that content should appear. A **physical element**, created with tags such as <b> and <i>, describes how text should appear, but it doesn't indicate the nature of the element's content.

Although it can be tempting to use logical and physical elements interchangeably, your Web pages benefit in several ways when you respect the distinction. For one, different browsers can and do display logical elements differently. For example, both Netscape's browser and Internet Explorer display text created with the <cite> tag in italics, but the text-based browser Lynx displays citation text using a fixed-width font. Some browsers, such as those that display Braille or convert HTML code into speech, don't display formatted text at all. An aural browser might increase the volume when it encounters emphasized text. Web programmers can also use logical elements to extract content information from a page—for example, a program could automatically generate a bibliography from all of the citations listed within a Web site.

In general, you should use a logical element whenever that element accurately describes the content it encloses, and use physical elements only for general content.

Working with IDs and Classes

As you add more elements to your Web page, you might need to identify distinct elements or groups of elements. You can do this using the id attribute (to identify a distinct element) and the class attribute (to mark a group of elements). The syntax of the id attribute is

```
id="text"
```

where *text* is the unique name of the id value. For example, the following code gives a paragraph the id value of "leading", which a programmer might use to indicate that this paragraph represents a leading paragraph on the page:

```
<p id="leading">Welcome to Pixal Products.</p>
```

A particular id value is associated with only one element and, therefore, can be used only once in an HTML file. To mark several elements as related, use the class attribute with the syntax

```
class="text"
```

where *text* is the name of the element class. For example, the following code uses the class attribute to indicate groupings of elements in an unordered list:

```
<ul>
    <li class="Dairy">Milk</li>
    <li class="Dairy">Sour cream</li>
    <li class="Produce">Celery</li>
    <li class="Produce">Lettuce</li>
    <li class="Bakery">Bagels</li>
    <li class="Bakery">Bread</li>
</ul>
```

The class attribute becomes useful in page design when you want to create a common format for elements that belong to the same class.

Creating Links

One of the great advantages of HTML is the ease of creating links to other documents and resources. To change content into a link, you mark the content with a two-sided <a> tag:

```
<a href="url">content</a>
```

where *url* is the address or URL of the linked resource and *content* is the page content that you want to act as a link. For example, the following code marks the text "Pixal Products" as a link pointing to the URL www.pixalproducts.com:

```
<a href="http://www.pixalproducts.com">Pixal Products</a>
```

By default, a browser opens a linked file at the top of the document; in some cases, though, you might want to link to a location farther down. To do this, you have to first mark a location within the document to which you want to be able to link. This can be done either by adding the id attribute to the element at that location in the document or by using the <a> tag to create an **anchor** at that location. The syntax for creating an anchor is

```
<a name="id"></a>
```

where *id* is the name of the anchor. Using the <a> tag to create anchors is currently being phased out in favor of using the id attribute; however, use of the <a> tag is still supported by older browsers that might not recognize the id attribute. Whichever method you use, you link to the anchor or element id using the URL

```
file#id
```

where *file* is the location and file name of the linked resource and *id* is an anchor or id within the file. For example, to link to an anchor in the home.htm file with the id or name value of "leading", you use the following URL:

```
home.htm#leading
```

Working with Images and Other Nontextual Content

Because HTML files are simple text files, nontextual objects must be stored in separate files and loaded by the browser when the page is rendered. The most common nontextual object is the graphic image, which is placed within a Web page as an **inline image**. Inline images are another example of an inline element, which must be placed within a block-level element such as a paragraph. Inline images are most widely viewable in one of two file formats: GIF (Graphics Interchange Format) or JPEG (Joint Photographic Experts Group). To mark an inline image, you use the img element

```
<img src="url" alt="text" />
```

where *url* is the location and the name of the image file, and *text* is an alternative text string that browsers can use in place of an image. It's important to include a value for the alt attribute with all inline images. Because many users run browsers that do not display images, any information conveyed by the image needs to be duplicated in text. Although HTML does not require that you use an alt attribute with your inline images, XHTML does.

Inserting an Inline Image | Reference Window

To insert an inline image, use the tag
```
<img src="url" alt="text" />
```
where *url* is the location and the name of the image file, and *text* is alternative text that browsers can use in place of the image.

If the image file is located in the same folder as the HTML file, you do not need to include any file location path information along with the file name. However, if the image file is located in another folder or on another computer, you need to include the full location path along with the file name in the src attribute.

Creating Horizontal Lines

Another graphic object that you can add to a Web page is a horizontal line. The syntax to create a horizontal line is

```
<hr />
```

There is no accepted default for the rendering of a horizontal line. Typically, the line extends across the complete width of the page with a height of 1 pixel. Some graphical browsers display the line in a solid black color; others apply a chiseled or embossed effect to the line. Text-based browsers display the line using dashes or underscores.

Working with Special Characters

Occasionally, you'll want to include special characters in your Web pages that do not appear on your keyboard. For example, a page might require mathematical symbols such as Σ or π, or you might need to include the copyright symbol © to show that the text or image is copyrighted. HTML supports the use of character symbols that are identified by a code number or name. The syntax for creating a special character is

```
&code;
```

where *code* is either a code name or a code number. Code numbers are preceded by a pound symbol (#). Figure A-6 shows some HTML symbols and the corresponding code numbers and names. Note that some older browsers support only code numbers, not code names.

Figure A-6   ▶   **Special characters and codes**

Symbol	Code	Name	Description
©	©	©	Copyright symbol
®	®	®	Registered trademark
•	·	·	Middle dot (bullet)
°	°	°	Degree symbol
			Nonbreaking space, used to insert consecutive blank spaces
<	<	<	Less-than symbol
>	>	>	Greater-than symbol
&	&	&	Ampersand

Embedding Media Clips

In recent years, as home computers have improved in speed and power and faster connections to the Web have become more readily available, it has become more practical to place video and audio clips within Web pages. Multimedia clips can be embedded within a Web document using the one-sided tag

```
<embed src="url" width="value" height="value" autostart="type" />
```

where *url* is the URL of the media clip, the width and height attributes specify the width and the height of the clip and its controls as it is rendered on the page, and the autostart attribute specifies whether to start the clip automatically when the page loads ("true") or only when the user clicks a start button on the clip's controls ("false"). Although the embed element is supported by most browsers, it is not part of the official HTML specifications, and its support might be discontinued in the future. It is also not supported by XHTML.

In place of the embed element, the current specifications for HTML and XHTML call for the use of the object element, which is a two-sided tag with the form

```
<object data="url" type="mime-type">
   page content
</object>
```

where *url* is the URL of the file containing the multimedia object, *mime-type* is a text string that defines the type of data contained in the object, and *page content* is alternate content that should be displayed in place of the object if a browser does not support the object element or the data type of the object. Figure A-7 lists the different MIME types supported by the object element.

Figure A-7   ▶   **MIME types**

Audio Object	Audio MIME Type	Text Object	Text MIME Type	Image Object	Image MIME Type	Video Object	Video MIME Type
aiff	audio/aiff	HTML file	text/html	gif	image/gif	asf	video/x-ms-asf
au	audio/basic	Plain text file	text/plain	jpg	image/jpeg	avi	video/x-msvideo
midi	audio/mid			png	image/png	mpeg	video/mpeg
mp3	audio/mpeg					quicktime	video/quicktime
wav	audio/wav						

For example, to insert a graphic image, you can use either the inline image

```
<img src="logo.jpg" alt="Pixal Products" />
```

or, equivalently, the object element

```
<object data="logo.jpg" type="image/jpeg">
   <h2>Pixal Products</h2>
</object>
```

If you wanted to embed a video clip in a Web page, you could use the following code:

```
<object data="trailer.avi" type="video/x-msvideo">
   Movie Trailer
</object>
```

Alternatively, you could use the embed element as described above. Be aware that the object element currently is not well supported by most browsers. So, you might need to use a combination of the embed element and the object element if you need to support multimedia clips in your Web pages.

Creating Web Tables

Tables are an important feature in Web page design. Tables are marked using the two-sided <table> tag. Nested within the table element is the tr element, which encloses the content of each table row. The td element, which encloses the content of each table cell, is nested within each tr element. So, the general structure of a Web table is

```
<table>
   <tr>
      <td>content</td>
      <td>content</td>
      ...
   </tr>
   <tr>
      <td>content</td>
      <td>content</td>
      ...
   </tr>
   ...
</table>
```

where *content* is the content of an individual table cell. For example, the code

```
<table>
   <tr>
      <td>First Cell</td>
      <td>Second Cell</td>
   </tr>
   <tr>
      <td>Third Cell</td>
      <td>Fourth Cell</td>
   </tr>
</table>
```

creates a table with two rows and two columns (see Figure A-8). You might have noticed that HTML includes no tag for table columns. This is because the number of columns is determined by the size of the longest row in the table. If the longest row in a table contains four td elements, the table has four columns.

Figure A-8 > **A simple Web table**

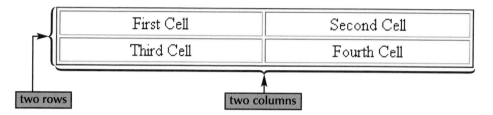

The "td" in the <td> tag stands for "table data." You can also place cell content within a th element, which marks the content as a table heading. The difference is that the content of a th element is usually centered and displayed in a boldface font by browsers.

Reference Window | **Defining the Table Structure**

- To mark a table, use the tag
    ```
    <table>content</table>
    ```
    where *content* includes the table's rows, headings, and cells.
- To create a table row, use the tag
    ```
    <tr>content</tr>
    ```
    where *content* includes the table's cells and headings.
- To create a table cell that contains a row or column heading, use the tag
    ```
    <th>content</th>
    ```
    where *content* is the content of the heading. Table headings are usually displayed in a centered, bold font.
- To create a table cell that contains table data, use the tag
    ```
    <td>content</td>
    ```
    where *content* is the cell content.

Creating Row Groups

To indicate the role that each table row plays in the table, you can organize the rows into **row groups**. HTML supports three types of row groups, identifying the table head, table body, and table footer. Because order is important in an HTML file, the table header must be listed first, followed by the table footer, and finally the table body. To mark the rows that belong to the table head, you use the syntax

```
<thead>
    table rows
</thead>
```

where `table rows` are rows of the table. Note that a table can contain only one row group for the table head. To mark the rows of a table footer, use the syntax

```
<tfoot>
    table rows
</tfoot>
```

As with the table head, a table can contain only one row group for the footer. Finally, to mark the rows of the table body, use the syntax

```
<tbody>
    table rows
</tbody>
```

A table can contain multiple table body sections. Row groups are sometimes used when tables draw their data from external sources, such as databases or XML documents. In those cases, scripts can be written in which the content of the table body rows spans several different Web pages, with the content of the table header and footer repeated on each page. Not all browsers support this capability, however.

Creating a Table Caption

Table captions provide descriptive information about a table's content. The syntax for creating a caption is

```
<caption>content</caption>
```

where *content* is the content of the caption. The <caption> tag must appear directly after the opening <table> tag. By default, a caption appears centered above a table. However, you can change the placement of a caption using the align attribute, as follows:

```
<caption align="position">content</caption>
```

where *position* equals one of the following:

- "bottom" to place the caption centered below the table
- "top" to place the caption centered above the table
- "left" to place the caption above the table, aligned with the left table margin
- "right" to place the caption above the table, aligned with the right table margin

Spanning Rows and Columns

By default, a table cell occupies the intersection of a single row and a single column; however, in some cases you might want a table cell to cover more than one row or column. Figure A-9 shows an example of table cells that need to cover several rows and/or columns.

Spanning cells   **Figure A-9**

Such cells are called **spanning cells** and are created by applying the rowspan attribute, the colspan attribute, or both attributes to a <td> or <th> tag. The syntax for these attributes is

```
<td rowspan="value" colspan="value"> ... </td>
```

or

```
<th rowspan="value" colspan="value"> ... </th>
```

where *value* is the number of rows or columns that the cell spans in the table. The direction of the spanning is downward and to the right of the cell containing the rowspan and colspan attributes. For example, to create a cell that spans two columns in a table, you enter the <td> tag as

```
<td colspan="2"> ... </td>
```

For a cell that spans two rows, the tag is

```
<td rowspan="2"> ... </td>
```

and to span two rows and two columns at the same time, the tag is

```
<td rowspan="2" colspan="2"> ... </td>
```

It's important to remember that when a table includes a cell that spans multiple rows or columns, you must adjust the number of cell tags used in the other table rows to compensate for the additional space taken up by the spanning cell. For example, if a row contains five columns but one of the cells in the row spans three columns, you need only three <td> tags within the row: two <td> tags for each of the cells that occupy a single column and a third for the cell spanning three rows.

When a cell spans several rows, you need to adjust the number of cell tags in the rows below the spanning cell. Consider the table shown in Figure A-10, which contains three rows and four columns. The first cell in the first row is a spanning cell that spans three rows. You need four <td> tags for the first row but only three <td> tags for rows two and three. This is because the spanning cell from row one occupies the cells that would normally appear in those rows.

Figure A-10	A row-spanning cell

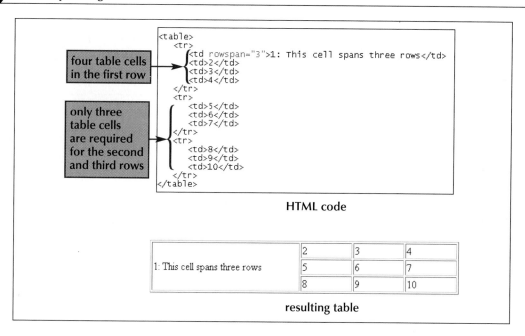

HTML code

resulting table

Creating a Spanning Cell | Reference Window

- To create a column-spanning cell, add the following attribute to the td or th element:
     colspan="value"
  where value is the number of columns to be spanned.
- To create a row-spanning cell, add the following attribute to the td or th element:
     rowspan="value"
  where value is the number of rows to be spanned.

Setting the Border, Spacing, and Padding Size

Most browsers automatically render a table to take up the least amount of space on the page. This is done by fitting the largest amount of text into each column with the least amount of line wrapping across the columns. There are several attributes you can use to override the default table size, however. These include attributes to set the size of the table border, the space between the table cells, and the space within the table cells.

By default, browsers display tables without borders. You can create a table border by adding the border attribute to the <table> tag. The syntax for creating a table border is

```
<table border="value"> ... </table>
```

where value is the width of the border in pixels. Figure A-11 shows the effect of different border sizes on a table's appearance. Note that unless you specify a border size of 0 pixels, the size of the internal borders (also called gridlines) is not affected by the border attribute.

Tables with different border sizes   Figure A-11

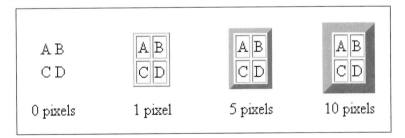

To change the amount of space between table cells, which is known as the **cell spacing**, use the cellspacing attribute:

```
<table cellspacing="value"> ... </table>
```

where value is the size of the cell spacing in pixels. If you have applied a border to your table, changing the cell-spacing value also affects the size of the interior borders. By default, the size of the cell spacing is set to 2 pixels. Figure A-12 shows how different cell-spacing values affect the appearance of these gridlines.

Figure A-12 Tables with different cell-spacing values

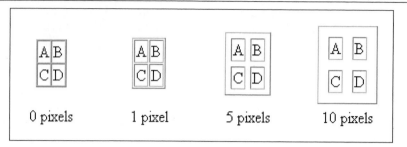

The space between the content of each table cell and the cell's border is known as **cell padding**. The default cell-padding value is 1 pixel; to set a different value for the cellpadding attribute, use

```
<table cellpadding="value"> ... </table>
```

where *value* is the size of the cell padding in pixels. Figure A-13 shows how different cell-padding values affect the appearance of the text within a table.

Figure A-13 Tables with different cell-padding values

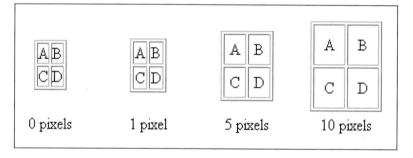

As discussed earlier, the overall size of a table is largely determined by its content. A table expands in width to match the content of its cells. If you want to set a table width to a fixed value, you use

```
<table width="value"> ... </table>
```

where *value* is the width either in pixels or as a percentage of the width of the containing element. If you specify a fixed width, the table remains constant but the table height increases to match the content. You can set a table to fill the entire width of a page by specifying a width value of 100%. Note that a browser never displays a table with a width smaller than that required to display the content. If table content requires a width of 100 pixels, for example, a browser ignores an attribute value that sets the width at 50 pixels.

The width attribute can also be applied to individual cells within a table, using the form

```
<td width="value"> ... </td>
```

or

```
<th width="value"> ... </th>
```

where *value* is the cell's width either in pixels or as a percentage of the width of the entire table. You can set the width of a column by setting the width of the first cell in the column; when you do, the remaining cells in the column adopt that width. If the content of one of the other cells exceeds that width, however, the browser expands the size of all cells in the column to match the width required to display that content. If you set different widths for two cells in the same column, the browser applies the larger value to the column.

Sizing a Table | Reference Window

- To set the size of a table, add the following attributes to the table element:
    ```
    width="value" height="value"
    ```
  where *value* is the size either in pixels or as a percentage of the containing element.
- To set cell spacing, add the following attribute to the table element:
    ```
    cellspacing="value"
    ```
  where *value* is the gap between adjacent cells in pixels. The default spacing is 2 pixels.
- To set cell padding, add the following attribute to the table element:
    ```
    cellpadding="value"
    ```
  where *value* is the size of the gap between the cell content and the cell border. The default padding is 1 pixel.

Creating Frames and Rules

By default, the table border surrounds the entire table and each of the cells within the table. You can modify this by applying the frame and rules attributes to the table element. The frame attribute defines which sides of a table have borders (the default is to apply the border to all sides). The syntax of the frame attribute is

```
<table frame="type"> ... </table>
```

where *type* is "box" (the default), "above", "border", "below", "hsides", "vsides", "lhs", "rhs", or "void". Figure A-14 shows the effect of each of these values on the appearance of the table border.

Frame values   **Figure A-14**

The rules attribute lets you define how gridlines are drawn within the table. By default, gridlines are placed around each table cell. The syntax of the rules attribute is

```
<table rules="type"> ... </table>
```

where *type* is "all" (the default), "cols", "groups", "none", or "rows". Figure A-15 shows the impact of each of these attribute values.

Figure A-15 ▶ **Rules values**

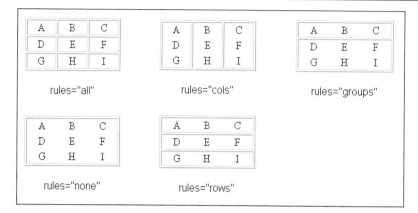

Reference Window | **Creating Frames and Rules**

- To change the frame style of a table border, add the following attribute to the table element:

      frame="*type*"

  where *type* is "box" (the default), "above", "border", "below", "hsides", "vsides", "lhs", "rhs", or "void".
- To change the rules style of the internal gridlines, add the following attribute to the table element:

      rules="*type*"

  where *type* is "all" (the default), "cols", "groups", or "none".

Working with Column Groups

Although there are no elements to create table columns, you can organize the columns that are generated by the browser into **column groups**, which allow you to format the appearance of every cell in a column. To define a column group, insert the following element after the opening <table> tag (unless there is a table caption, in which case it should follow the caption element):

```
<colgroup span="value" />
```

where *value* is the number of columns in the group. For example, you could use the following tags to organize a table with five columns into two groups—one group for the first three columns and a second group for the last two:

```
<colgroup span="3" />
<colgroup span="2" />
```

If you wanted to set the width of the first four columns to 50 pixels and the next two columns to 100 pixels, the tags for the column groups would appear as follows:

```
<colgroup span="4" width="50" />
<colgroup span="2" width="100" />
```

The colgroup element can also be expressed as a two-sided element, using the syntax

```
<colgroup>
    columns
</colgroup>
```

where *columns* are elements that define the properties for individual columns within the group. To define a single column within the group, you use the one-sided col element. The col element is useful when individual columns within a group need to have slightly different formats. For example, if you want to define a different width for each column within a column group, you could use the following:

```
<colgroup span="3">
    <col width="50" />
    <col width="100" />
    <col width="150" />
</colgroup>
```

In this case, the first column is 50 pixels wide, the second column is 100 pixels wide, and the third column in the group has a width of 150 pixels. The col element can also be used along with the span attribute to apply the same properties to several columns at the same time, as in the following example:

```
<colgroup span="5">
    <col span="2" width="50" />
    <col width="100" />
    <col span="2" width="150" />
</colgroup>
```

In this example, the column group consists of five columns: the first two columns are 50 pixels wide each, the middle column is 100 pixels wide, and the last two columns have a width of 150 pixels each.

Creating Web Forms

One of the most important uses of the Web is to collect information from users to order items, register products, or complete surveys and questionnaires. This is often done using Web forms. The data from these forms can then be sent to a program running on a Web server or client for processing. Elements of a form in which a user can enter information or otherwise interact are called **control elements**. The following are the control elements supported by Web forms:

- **input boxes** for text and numerical entries
- **selection lists** for long lists of options, usually appearing in **list boxes**
- **option buttons** (also called **radio buttons**) to select a single option from a predefined list
- **check boxes** to specify an item as either present or absent
- **group boxes** to organize form elements
- **text areas** for extended entries that can include several lines of text
- **form buttons** that can be clicked to start processing the form

A control element in which a user can enter information is also called a **field**. The information entered into a field is referred to as the **field value**. In some fields, users are free to enter anything they choose. Other fields, such as selection lists, limit the user to a predefined list of options. Figure A-16 shows a sample Web form containing different control elements and fields.

Figure A-16 Parts of a Web form

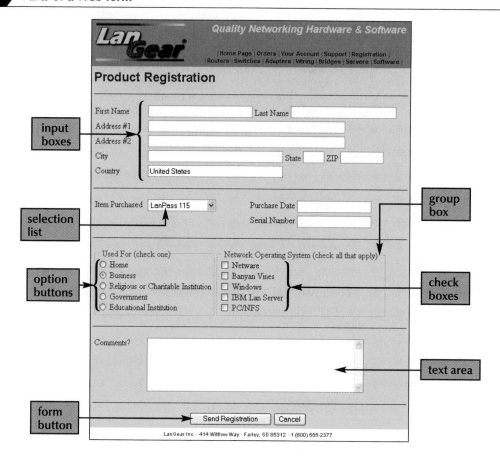

Creating a Form Element

Forms are created using the form element, which has the following structure:

```
<form attributes>
    page elements
</form>
```

where *attributes* are the attributes that control how the form is processed and *page elements* are elements placed within the form. Forms typically contain many of the control elements shown in Figure A-16 but can also contain page elements such as tables, paragraphs, inline images, and headings.

Form attributes usually tell browsers the location of the server-based program to be applied to the form's data, how that data is to be transferred to the script, and so on. In addition to not needing these attributes when first designing the form, it's also useful to omit them at first. This prevents you from accidentally running the program on an unfinished form, causing the program to process incomplete information. After you've finalized the form's appearance, you can add the final features required by the server program.

You should always specify an id or a name for a form. This is useful in situations where a page contains multiple forms and you need to differentiate one form from another. In addition, it is often required for programs that retrieve values from the form. Two attributes are available to identify a form: the id attribute and the name attribute. The syntax of these attributes is

```
<form name="name" id="id"> ... </form>
```

where *name* is the name of the form and *id* is the id of the form. Although these two attributes might appear to do much the same thing, each has its own history and role. The name attribute represents the older standard for form identification and, therefore, is often required for older browsers and Web servers. The id attribute represents the current standard for HTML and XHTML and will be the standard for all future applications. So, for maximum compatibility, the form element should include both attributes.

Creating and Formatting Input Boxes

Most of the control elements in which users are asked to insert values are marked with an input element. The general syntax of this element is

```
<input type="type" name="name" id="id" />
```

where *type* specifies the type of input field, and the name and id attributes provide the field's name and id. HTML supports 10 different input types, which are described in Figure A-17. If you omit the type attribute, the browser creates an input box.

Input types | Figure A-17

Type	Description	
type="button"	Display a button that can be clicked to perform an action from a script	button
type="checkbox"	Display a check box	✔
type="file"	Display a browse button to locate and select a file	Browse...
type="hidden"	Create a hidden field, not viewable on the form	
type="image"	Display an inline image that can be clicked to perform an action from a script	👤
type="password"	Display an input box that hides text entered by the user	*********
type="radio"	Display an option button	⦿
type="reset"	Display a button that resets the form when clicked	reset
type="submit"	Display a button that submits the form when clicked	submit
type="text"	Display an input box that displays text entered by the user	LanGear

By default, an input box displays 20 characters of text on a single line (though the actual amount of text entered into the box may be longer). To change the width of an input box, you use the size attribute:

```
<input size="value" />
```

where *value* is the size of the input box in characters. Setting the width of an input box does not limit the number of characters the box can hold. If a user tries to enter text longer than a box's width, the text scrolls to the left, hiding a portion of the field value. Although a user would not be able to see the entire text in such a case, all of it would still be sent to the server for processing.

There are times when you want to limit the number of characters a user can enter to reduce the chance of erroneous data entry. For example, if you have a Social Security number field, you know that only nine characters are required and that any attempt to enter more than nine characters is a mistake. The syntax for setting the maximum length for field input is

```
<input maxlength="value" />
```

where *value* is the maximum number of characters that can be stored in the field.

If most people enter the same value in a field, it might make sense to define a default value for that field. Default values can save time and increase accuracy for users of your Web site. To define a default value, use the syntax

```
<input value="value" />
```

where *value* is the default text or number that is displayed in the field when the Web form is opened. Even though you specify a default value, users are usually still able to enter their own values if they want.

Creating Option Buttons

Option buttons, or radio buttons, confine users to making a selection from a list of predetermined choices. A user can select only one option button at a time from a group. The syntax to create an option button is

```
<input type="radio" name="name" id="id" value="value" />
```

where *name* identifies the field containing the collection of option buttons, *id* identifies the specific option, and the value attribute indicates the value of the selected option. Note that in the case of option buttons, the name and id attributes are not redundant as they are with input boxes. In fact, the id attribute is required only if you intend to use a field label with the option button.

Although the id attribute is optional, you *must* include the name attribute because it groups distinct option buttons together. Within a group, selecting one option button automatically deselects all of the others.

There is no text attribute for an option button, so for users to understand the purpose of an option button, you must insert descriptive text next to it. If you enclose the descriptive text within a label tag, users can select the option button by clicking either the button or the label.

Figure A-18 shows an example of HTML code that creates option buttons for political party affiliations.

Figure A-18   **Creating option buttons**

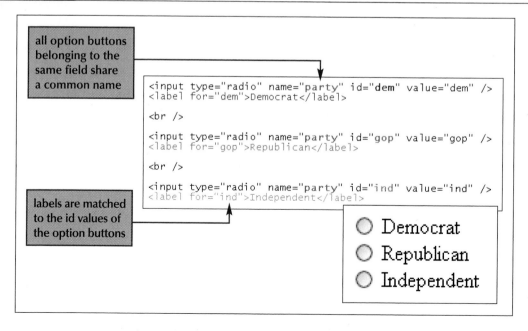

Note that in this sample code, the value sent to the server does not match the field label. For example, if a user selects the Republican option button, the value "gop" is sent to the server, paired with the field name "party". By default, no option buttons are selected. If you want an option button to be selected when the form opens, you add the checked attribute to the <input> tag:

```
<input type="radio" checked="checked" />
```

Creating an Option Button | Reference Window

- To create an option button, use the HTML tag
    ```
    <input type="radio" name="name" id="id" value="value" />
    ```
    where name identifies the field containing the option button, id identifies the specific option value, and value specifies the value sent to the server when the option button is selected. The id attribute is not required unless you intend to use a field label with the option button. The value attribute is required.
- To make a particular option button the default option, use the following attribute:
    ```
    <input type="radio" checked="checked" />
    ```
    Most browsers also accept the syntax
    ```
    <input type="radio" checked />
    ```
    although this does not follow the syntax guidelines of HTML or XHTML.

Creating Check Boxes

Check boxes are similar to option buttons except that they limit the user to only one of two possible choices. The syntax to create a check box is

```
<input type="checkbox" name="name" id="id" value="value" />
```

where the name and id attributes identify the check box and the value attribute specifies the value that is sent to the server if the check box is selected. Unlike for input boxes, the value attribute is required for every check box; unlike for option buttons, the name and id attributes should both be included even though they usually contain the same information. For example, the following code assigns the value "democrat" to the party field if the check box is selected:

```
<input type="checkbox" name="party" id="party" value="democrat" />
```

As with input boxes and option buttons, check boxes do not display any text. You add text or a label next to a check box using a separate tag. By default, a check box is not selected. To have a Web form open with a check box already selected, use the checked attribute as follows:

```
<input type="checkbox" checked="checked" />
```

Creating a Check Box | Reference Window

- To create a check box, use the HTML tag
    ```
    <input type="checkbox" name="name" id="id" value="value" />
    ```
    where the name and id attributes identify the check box field and the value attribute specifies the value sent to the server if the check box is selected.
- To specify that a check box be selected by default, use the checked attribute as follows:
    ```
    <input type="checkbox" checked="checked" />
    ```
    Most browsers also accept the syntax
    ```
    <input type="checkbox" checked />
    ```
    although this does not follow the syntax guidelines of HTML or XHTML.

Creating a Selection List

A selection list is a list box from which a user selects a particular value or set of values. Selection lists are a good idea when a field's input is a fixed set of possible responses; in such a case, a selection list helps prevent spelling mistakes and erroneous entries. You create a selection list using the <select> tag, and you specify each individual selection item with the <option> tag. The general syntax for the select and option elements is

```
<select name="name" id="id">
    <option>item1</option>
    <option>item2</option>
      .
      .
      .
</select>
```

where the name and id attributes identify the selection field, and each option element represents an individual item in the selection list. Users see the text *item1*, *item2*, and so forth as the options in the selection list. By default, a select element displays one option from the selection list along with a list arrow to view additional selection options. You can change the number of options displayed by modifying the size attribute. The syntax of the size attribute is

```
<select size="value"> ... </select>
```

where *value* is the number of items that the selection list displays in the form. By specifying a value greater than 1, you change the selection list from a list box to a list box with a scroll bar that allows a user to scroll through the selection options. If you set the size attribute to be equal to the number of options in the selection list, the scroll bar either is not displayed or is dimmed. See Figure A-19.

Figure A-19 ▶ **Size values of the selection list**

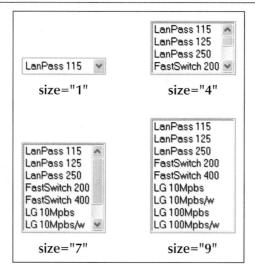

Users are not limited to a single selection from a selection list. Adding the multiple attribute to the select element enables multiple selections from the list. The syntax for this attribute is

```
<select multiple="multiple"> ... </select>
```

To make multiple selections from a selection list, a user must hold down an **access key** while making selections. The Windows operating system offers two different access keys:

- For a noncontiguous selection, press and hold the Ctrl key while you make your selections.
- For a contiguous selection, select the first item, press and hold the Shift key, and then select the last item in the range. This selects the two items as well as all the items between them.

By default, a form sends the value displayed in the list for each selected item to the server. For example, if a user selects the first option from a selection list, the text string of that option is sent to the server. Sometimes, however, you might want to send an abbreviation or a code to the server instead of the entire text string; for example, you might display descriptive text for each option in a selection list to help users make an informed choice but require only an abbreviated version for your records. You can specify the value that is sent to the server with the value attribute. The syntax is

```
<option value="value">item</option>
```

where *value* is the value associated with the selection item. You can also specify which item in the selection list is selected, or highlighted, when the form is initially displayed. The first option in the list is highlighted by default, but you can specify a different value using the following attribute:

```
<option selected="selected">item</option>
```

where the selected attribute indicates that the item is the default item in the selection list.

Creating a Selection List | Reference Window

- To create a selection list, use the code
  ```
  <select name="name" id="id">
    <option>item1</option>
    <option>item2</option>
    .
    .
    .
  </select>
  ```
  where the name and id attributes identify the selection field.
- To set the size of a selection list, use the size attribute
  ```
  <select size="value"> ... </select>
  ```
  where value is the number of items to display in the selection list at once. The default is "1".
- To allow multiple selections from the list, use the following multiple attribute:
  ```
  <select multiple="multiple"> ... </select>
  ```
- To associate a value with a selection option, use the value attribute
  ```
  <option value="value">item</option>
  ```
  where *value* is the value associated with the selection item.
- To define the default selected item, use the following selected attribute:
  ```
  <option selected="selected">item</option>
  ```

Creating a Text Area Box

An input box is limited to a single line of text. To allow users to insert several lines of text, you can instead create a text area box. The syntax to create a text area box is

```
<textarea name="name" id="id" rows="value" cols="value">
   default text
</textarea>
```

where the rows and cols attributes define the dimensions of the input box. The rows attribute indicates the number of lines in the input box—although some early browser versions show more lines than indicated by the rows attribute—and the cols attribute specifies the number of characters in each line. Although not required, you can specify default text that appears in a text area box when a form is initially displayed.

Reference Window | Creating a Text Area Box

To create a text area for extended text entry, use the tag
```
<textarea name="name" id="id" rows="value" cols="value">
   default text
</textarea>
```
where *default text* is the text that is displayed in the text area (optional) and the rows and cols attributes specify the number of lines in the text area and the number of characters in each line, respectively.

Creating a Form Button

A Web form usually contains push buttons that users can click to run a program, submit the form data for processing, or reset the form. The syntax to create a form button is

```
<input type="type" value="text" />
```

where *type* is the button type and *text* is the text that appears on the button. To create a button to submit a form to a script for processing, the type value should be set to "submit". To reset the form to its default values, the type value is "reset". For buttons that run programs or scripts when clicked, the type value is "button".

Aside from the text that a form button displays, its appearance is determined by the Web browser. For greater artistic control over the appearance of your form buttons, you can use the button element, which has the syntax

```
<button name="name" id="id" value="value" type="type">
   content
</button>
```

where the name and value attributes specify the name of the button and the value sent to a server-based program, the id attribute specifies the button's id, the type attribute specifies the button type (submit, reset, or button), and *content* is page content displayed within the button. The page content can include formatted text, inline images, and other design elements supported by HTML.

Creating Form Buttons | Reference Window

- To create a button to submit form input to a program, use the tag

      <input type="submit" name="*name*" id="*id*" value="*text*" />

  where the value attribute defines the text that appears on the button and is also sent to the program to indicate which button on the form has been clicked.
- To create a button that cancels or resets a form, set the value of the type attribute to "reset":

      <input type="reset" name="*name*" id="*id*" value="*text*" />

- To create a generic button to perform an action within a Web page, set the value of the type attribute to "button":

      <input type="button" name="*name*" id="*id*" value="*text*" />

- To create a button that can contain other Web page elements, use the code

      <button name="name" id="*id*" value="*value*">content</button>

  where the value attribute provides an initial value for the button and *content* consists of the page element(s) you want displayed in the button.

Creating a Hidden Field

In some cases, you might want to insert a field in your form to store information that you do not want displayed on the page. To do this, you can create a **hidden field**. The syntax for creating a hidden field is

```
<input type="hidden" name="name" id="id" value="value" />
```

Because the field is hidden, you can place it anywhere within the form element. A common practice is to place all hidden fields in one location, usually at the beginning of the form, to make it easier to read and interpret your HTML code. You should also include a comment describing the purpose of the field.

Working with Form Attributes

When a form is submitted, the action performed on the form values is specified by the form's action, method, and enctype attributes. The syntax of the form attributes is

```
<form action="url" method="type" enctype="type"> ... </form>
```

where `url` specifies the file name and the location of the program that processes the form, the method attribute specifies how the Web browser sends data to the server, and the enctype attribute specifies the format of the data stored in the form's fields.

There are two possible values for the method attribute: get or post. The **get method** is the default, and it appends the form data to the end of the URL specified in the action attribute. The **post method** sends form data in a separate data stream, allowing the Web server to receive the data through what is called "standard input." Because it is more flexible, most Web designers prefer the post method for sending data to the server. Because some Web servers limit the length of URLs, the post method is also safer, avoiding the possibility of data attached to a long URL being truncated by the server.

Working with Frames

Typically, as a Web site grows in size and complexity, each page is dedicated to a particular topic or group of topics: one page might contain a list of links, another page might display contact information for the company or organization, and another page might describe the business philosophy. As more pages are added to the site, the designer might want a way to display information from several pages at the same time.

One solution is to duplicate that information across the Web site, but this strategy presents problems. It requires a great deal of time and effort to repeat (or copy and paste) the same information over and over again. Also, each time a change is required, you need to repeat your edit for each page in the site—a process that could easily result in errors.

Such considerations contributed to the development of frames. A **frame** is a section of the browser window capable of displaying the content of an entire Web page. Figure A-20 shows an example of a browser window containing two frames. The frame on the left displays the content of a Web page containing a list of links; the frame on the right displays a second Web page showing a list of products. These two pages come from an old version of the NEC Web site that once utilized frames.

Figure A-20 | Frame example

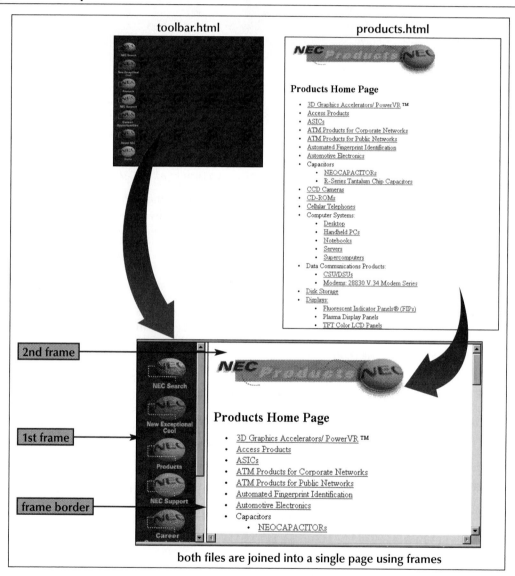

both files are joined into a single page using frames

This example illustrates a common use of frames: displaying a list of links in one frame while showing individual pages from the site in another. Figure A-21 illustrates how a list of links can remain on the screen while the user navigates through the content of the site. Using this layout, a designer can easily update the list of links because it is stored on only one page rather than having to update the link list through every page in the Web site.

Activating a link within a frame | **Figure A-21**

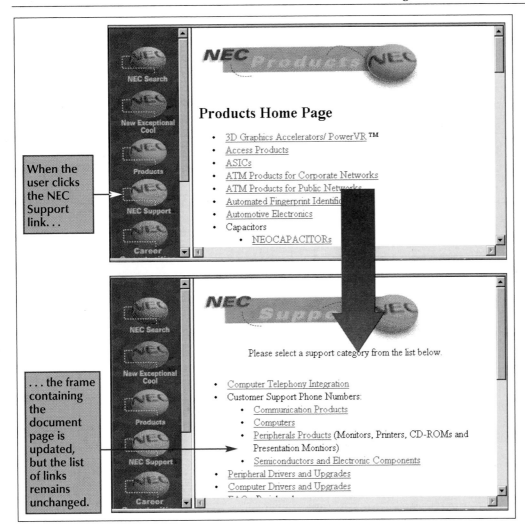

When the user clicks the NEC Support link...

...the frame containing the document page is updated, but the list of links remains unchanged.

Creating a Frameset

Within the browser window, frames are arranged in a **frameset**. The general syntax for creating a frameset is

```
<html>
<head>
<title>title</title>
</head>
<frameset>
    frames
</frameset>
</html>
```

where *frames* are the individual frames within the frameset. You'll explore how to create these frames shortly.

Note that the frameset element replaces the body element in this HTML document. Because this HTML file displays the content of other Web pages, it is not technically a Web page and, therefore, does not include a page body. A frameset is laid out in either rows or columns, but not both. Figure A-22 shows two framesets: one in which the frames are laid out in three columns and another in which they are placed in three rows.

Figure A-22 ▶ **Frame layouts in rows and columns**

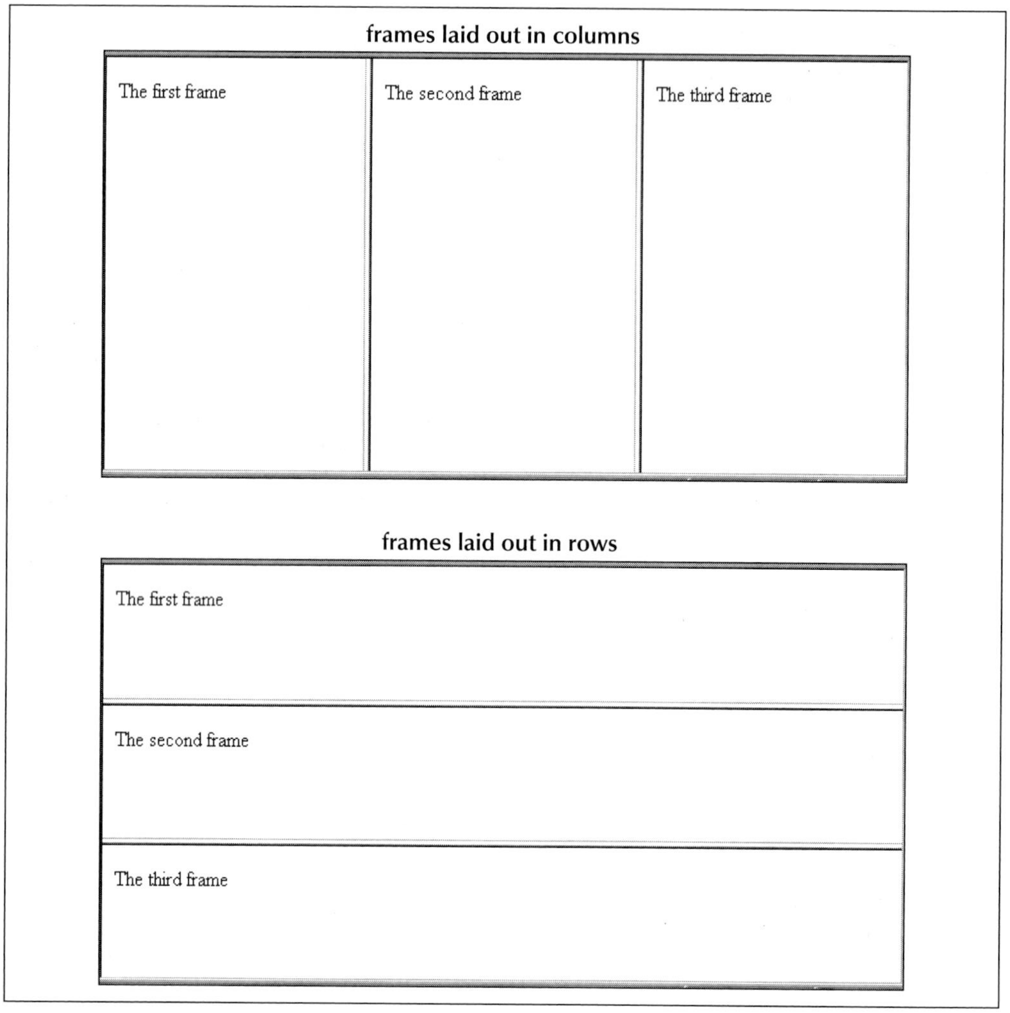

The syntax for defining the row or column frame layout is

```
<frameset rows="row1,row2,row3,...">  ...  </frameset>
```

or

```
<frameset cols="column1,column2,column3,...">  ...  </frameset>
```

where *row1*, *row2*, *row3*, and so on are the heights of the frame rows, and *column1*, *column2*, *column3*, and so on are the widths of the frame columns. There is no limit to the number of rows or columns you can specify for a frameset.

The row and column sizes can be specified in three ways: in pixels, as a percentage of the total size of the frameset, or by an asterisk (*). The asterisk instructs the browser to allocate any unclaimed space in the frameset to the given row or column. For example, the tag <frameset rows="160,*"> creates two rows of frames. The first row has a height of 160 pixels, and the height of the second row is equal to whatever space remains in the browser window. You can also combine the three methods within a single frameset. The tag <frameset cols="160,25%,*"> lays out the frames in the columns shown in Figure A-23. The first column is 160 pixels wide, the second column is 25% of the width of the display area, and the third column covers whatever space is left.

Sizing frames   Figure A-23

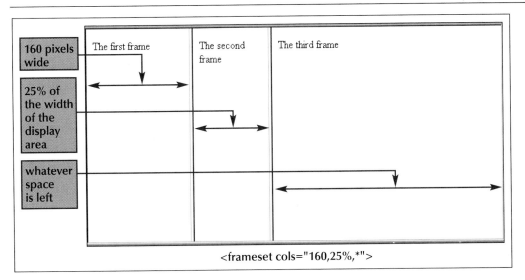

<frameset cols="160,25%,*">

It is a good idea to specify at least one of the rows or columns of your frameset with an asterisk to ensure that the frames fill up the screen regardless of the size of the browser window. You can also use multiple asterisks, which cause browsers to allocate the remaining display space equally among the frames with no defined size. For example, the tag <frameset rows="*,*,*"> creates three rows of frames of equal height.

Creating a Frameset | Reference Window

- To create frames laid out in rows, enter the tags

```
<frameset rows="row1,row2,row3,...">
   frames
</frameset>
```
where *row1*, *row2*, *row3*, and so on are the heights of the frame rows, and frames defines the frames within the frameset.

- To create frames laid out in columns, enter the tags

```
<frameset cols="column1,column2,column3,...">
   frames
</frameset>
```
where *column1*, *column2*, *column3*, and so on are the widths of the frame columns.

A frameset places frames in either rows or columns, but not both. So, if you want to create a layout containing frames in rows and columns, you must nest one frameset within a frame in another frameset. When you use this technique, the interpretation of the rows and cols attributes changes slightly. For the nested frameset, a row height of 25% does not mean 25% of the browser window but rather 25% of the height of the frame in which that frameset has been placed.

Specifying a Frame Source

Frames are marked using the one-sided <frame /> tag. Within the frame element, you use the src attribute to define which document that frame should display. The syntax is

```
<frame src="url" />
```

where url is the URL of the document. The following code creates three rows of frames displaying the documents home.htm, main.htm, and footer.htm:

```
<frameset rows="100, *, 100">
    <frame src="home.htm" />
    <frame src="main.htm" />
    <frame src="footer.htm" />
</frameset>
```

Note that frame elements can be placed only within a frameset.

Reference Window | Creating a Frame

To create a frame element, use the HTML tag
```
<frame src="url" />
```
where url is the URL of the document you want to display within the frame.

Formatting Frames

You can control several attributes of your frames: the appearance of scroll bars, the size of the margin between the source document and the frame border, and whether or not users are allowed to change the frame size. By default, a scroll bar is displayed when the content of the source page does not fit within a frame. You can override this setting using the scrolling attribute. The syntax for this attribute is

```
scrolling="type"
```

where type can be either "yes" (to always display a scroll bar) or "no" (to never display a scroll bar). If you don't specify a setting for the scrolling attribute, the browser displays a scroll bar when necessary. When working with frames, keep in mind that you should remove scroll bars from a frame only when you are convinced that the entire Web page will be visible in the frame. To do this, you should view your Web page using several different monitor settings. Few things are more irritating to Web site visitors than to discover that some content is missing from a frame and no scroll bars are available to reveal the missing content.

When a user's browser retrieves a frame's Web page, it determines the amount of space between the content of the page and the frame border. Occasionally, the browser sets the margin between the border and the content too large. Generally, you want the margin to be big enough to keep the source's text or images from running into the frame's borders. However, you do not want the margin to take up too much space because you typically want to display as much of the source as possible. The attribute for specifying margin sizes for a frame is

```
marginheight="value" marginwidth="value"
```

where marginheight specifies the amount of space, in pixels, above and below the frame source, and marginwidth specifies the amount of space to the left and right of the frame source. You do not have to specify both the margin height and the margin width. However, if you specify only one, the browser assumes that you want to use the same value for both.

Setting margin values is a process of trial and error as you determine what combination of margin sizes looks best. By default, users can resize frame borders in a browser by simply dragging a frame border. However, some Web designers prefer to freeze, or lock, frames so that users cannot resize them. The attribute for preventing frame resizing is

```
noresize="noresize"
```

Formatting a Frame | Reference Window

- To control whether a frame contains a scroll bar, add the following attribute to the frame element
  ```
  scrolling="type"
  ```
  where *type* is either "yes" (scroll bar) or "no" (no scroll bar). If you do not specify the scrolling attribute, a scroll bar appears only when the content of the frame source cannot fit within the boundaries of the frame.
- To control the amount of space between frame content and the frame boundary, add the following attribute to the frame element
  ```
  marginwidth="value" marginheight="value"
  ```
  where the width and height values are expressed in pixels. The margin width is the space to the left and right of the frame source. The margin height is the space above and below the frame source. If you do not specify a margin height or width, the browser assigns dimensions based on the content of the frame source.
- To keep users from resizing frames, add the following attribute to the frame element:
  ```
  noresize="noresize"
  ```

Working with Frames and Links

Clicking a link within a frame opens the linked file inside the same frame; however, you can specify a different location by assigning a name to each frame and then pointing the link to one of the other named frames. To assign a name to a frame, add the name attribute to the frame element. The syntax for this attribute is

```
<frame src="url" name="name" />
```

where *name* is the name assigned to the frame. Case is important in assigning names: "information" is considered a different name than "INFORMATION". Also, frame names cannot include spaces. To point the link to a specific frame, add the following attribute to the link tag:

```
target="name"
```

where *name* is the name you've assigned to a frame in your Web page. For example, you can name a frame "main" using the following code:

```
<frame src="home.htm" name="main" />
```

If you want a link's target to appear within the main frame, apply the target attribute as follows:

```
<a href="gloss.htm" target="main">Display the glossary</a>
```

In addition to frame names, you can also specify **reserved target names**, which cause a linked document to appear within a specific location in the browser. Figure A-24 lists the reserved target names supported by HTML.

Figure A-24 ▶ **Reserved target names**

Reserved Target Name	Function in a Frameset
_blank	Loads the target document into a new browser window
_self	Loads the target document into the frame containing the link
_parent	Loads the target document into the parent of the frame containing the link
_top	Loads the document into the full display area, replacing the current frame layout

For example, if you want a link target to appear in a new browser window, you could enter the following code:

```
<a href="gloss.htm" target="_blank">Display the glossary</a>
```

All reserved target names begin with the underscore character (_) to distinguish them from other target names. Note that reserved target names are case-sensitive, so you must enter them in lowercase.

Reference Window | Directing a Link to a Frame

- To assign a name to a frame, insert the attribute
    ```
    <frame name="name" />
    ```
    where name is the name of the frame.
- To point the target of a link to a named frame, use the target attribute
    ```
    target="name"
    ```
    where name is the name you assigned to the frame.
- To use the same target for all links, add the target attribute to the base element in the document head.

Using the noframes Element

To make your Web site viewable with browsers that do not support frames (known as **frame-blind browsers**) as well as by those that do, you can use the noframes element to mark a section of your HTML file for code that browsers incapable of displaying frames can use. The noframes element is nested within the frameset element as follows, and it uses the syntax shown:

```
<html>
<head>
<title>title</title>
</head>
<frameset>
    frames
    <noframes>
        <body>
            page content
        </body>
    </noframes>
</frameset>
</html>
```

where *page content* is the content that you want the browser to display in place of the frames. A document can contain only one noframes element. When a browser that supports frames processes this code, it ignores everything within the <noframes> tag and concentrates solely on the code to create the frames. When a browser that doesn't support frames processes this HTML code, however, it doesn't know what to do with the <frameset> and <noframes> tags, so it ignores them. It does know how to render whatever appears within the <body> tags, though. Using this setup, both types of browsers are supported within a single HTML file. Note that when you use the <noframes> tag, you must enclose the page content within a body element.

Supporting Frame-blind Browsers | Reference Window

To create a version of your page that does not use frames, insert the following tags within the frameset element

```
<noframes>
    <body>
        page content
    </body>
</noframes>
```

where *page content* is the content of the page you want displayed in place of the frames.

Creating Inline Frames

Another way of using frames is to create a floating frame. Introduced by Internet Explorer 3.0 and added to the HTML 4.0 specifications, a **floating frame**, or **inline frame**, is displayed as a separate box or window within a Web page in much the same way as inline images are placed within a page. The syntax for creating an inline frame is

```
<iframe src="url">
    alternate content
</iframe>
```

where *url* is the URL of the document you want displayed in the inline frame, and *alternate content* is the content you want displayed by browsers that don't support inline frames. The following code displays the content of the bio.htm file within an inline frame; for browsers that don't support inline frames, it displays a paragraph containing a link to the file:

```
<iframe src="bio.htm">
    <p>
    View the online <a href="bio.htm">bio</a> of Jeff Bester
    </p>
</iframe>
```

Figure A-25 shows an example of how such an inline frame might be rendered by a Web browser.

Figure A-25 ▶ **Example of an inline frame**

Frame-based Web sites have drawbacks that have led many Web sites to discontinue their use. A browser that opens a framed site has to load multiple HTML files before the user can view any of them, resulting in increased waiting time for potential customers. It is also very difficult to bookmark pages within a frame-based Web site or to make their content available to Internet search engines that create content-based catalogs. (In other words, if you want your content to be easily found, don't use frames.) Some browsers also have difficulty printing the pages within individual frames, although this is less of a problem than it once was. Finally, some users simply prefer layouts where the entire browser window is devoted to a single page. For these reasons, many Web designers suggest that if you still want to use frames, you should create both framed and nonframed versions for a Web site and give users the option of which one to use.

Appendix Summary | Review

In this appendix, you learned about the history and syntax of HTML. The appendix started with a discussion of the history of HTML and the Web. You then learned about the basic syntax requirements of HTML and how to insert elements and attributes. The appendix then examined block-level elements and inline elements, showing how to use those objects within a Web page. This appendix also covered the elements used to display non-textual objects such as inline images. The appendix then looked at how to create and use Web tables and Web forms. The appendix concluded with a discussion of frames and inline frames.

Key Terms

access key
anchor
block-level element
body element
cell padding
cell spacing
character-formatting element
check box
client
closing tag
column group
control element
definition list
deprecated
div element
element
empty element
Extensible Hypertext Markup
    Language
Extensible Markup Language
extension
field
field value
floating frame

form button
frame
frame-blind browser
frameset
get method
group box
head element
hidden field
HTML
Hypertext Markup Language
inline element
inline frame
inline image
input box
link
list box
logical element
markup language
markup tag
nesting
one-sided tag
opening tag
option button
ordered list

physical element
post method
radio button
reserved target name
root element
row group
selection list
server
spanning cell
tag
text area
unordered list
W3C
Web
Web browser
Web page
Web server
white space
World Wide Web
World Wide Web Consortium
XHTML
XML

Review | **Review Questions**

1. What are servers? What are clients?
2. What is hypertext?
3. What is a markup language? What is a markup tag?
4. Why was the World Wide Web Consortium created?
5. What is a deprecated feature?
6. What is XHTML? What is the relationship between HTML and XHTML?
7. What is the general syntax of a two-sided tag? Give an example of a two-sided tag.
8. What is the general syntax of a one-sided tag? Give an example of a one-sided tag.
9. What is the general syntax of a comment tag? Give an example of a comment tag.
10. What is white space? How do browsers handle occurrences of white space within an HTML file?
11. What is the root element of an HTML file? What are the two elements it contains?
12. What code would you add to an HTML file to set the Web page title to "Pixal Products Home Page"? Where should the code be placed?
13. What is a block-level element? What is an inline element?
14. What code would you use to create an h1 heading containing the text "Pixal Products"?
15. What code would you enter to create an ordered list containing the items Planes, Trains, and Automobiles?
16. What code would you enter to place the text "Pixal Products" in a generic block-level element?
17. What is a character formatting element? Provide two examples of a character formatting element.
18. What is a logical element? What is a physical element?
19. What code would you enter to create an inline image containing the image file logo.jpg with the alternate text "Pixal Products"?
20. What is general code you would enter to create a table containing two rows and three columns?
21. What is a spanning cell? What code would you enter to create a table cell that spans two rows and three columns?
22. What code would you enter to create a form with the id and name "orderForm"?
23. What code would you enter to create an input box field named "zipCode" with a size of 9 characters?
24. What code would you enter to create an option button belonging to a collection of option buttons named "gender"?
25. What code would you enter to create a check box with an id and name of "isMember" and a value of "yes"?
26. What code would you enter to create a selection list named "transport" containing the options Planes, Trains, and Automobiles?
27. What attribute would you add to a selection list to allow for multiple selections?
28. What code would you enter to create a submit button containing the text "Submit Order"?
29. Describe the difference between the get and post methods when submitting a form to be processed.
30. What is a frame? What is a frameset?
31. What code would you enter to display the file "pixal.htm" in a frame?
32. What code would you enter to create a link whose destination is the frame named "topFrame"?
33. What code would you enter to create an inline frame displaying the file "pixal.htm"?

Objectives

- Understand the history of Cascading Style Sheets
- Learn how to apply inline, embedded, and external style sheets
- Study style definitions, how they are inherited, and how they cascade through a Web site
- Learn how to work with font, text, image, and color styles
- Learn how to size and position elements on a page
- Study ids, classes, pseudo-elements, and pseudo-classes
- Understand how to create style sheets for different media types
- Learn how to create styles for printed output

Introducing Cascading Style Sheets

Formatting Web Pages with CSS

Appendix B

The primary purpose of HTML and XHTML is to create structured documents but not necessarily to describe how such documents should be rendered by Web browsers. In theory, this focus on structure ensures that HTML files are accessible by a wide variety of devices and output media. However, as HTML developed and the Web expanded worldwide, Web page authors demanded elements and attributes that would give them many of the same formatting tools found in word-processing programs. After all, for most Web pages, appearance is just as important as content. This demand resulted in the introduction of several HTML attributes and elements that describe how browsers should render a document. This development was not true to the original vision of a markup language, however; as a result, many of these elements have now been deprecated in favor of style sheets.

A **style sheet** is a collection of properties that describes how elements within a document should be rendered by the device presenting the document. The advantage of style sheets is that they separate document content from document presentation. So, by applying different style sheets, the same document can be rendered on different types of devices—from computer monitors to printers to speech-synthesized browsers—without the need to alter the content or structure of the original document.

Starting Data Files

There are no starting Data Files needed for this appendix.

Introduction to CSS

Although several style sheet languages exist, by far the most commonly used on the Web is the **Cascading Style Sheets** language, also known as **CSS**. As with HTML and XHTML, the specifications for CSS are maintained by the World Wide Web Consortium and several versions of CSS exist with varying levels of browser support. The first version of CSS, called **CSS1**, was introduced in 1996 but was not fully implemented by any browser for another three years. CSS1 introduced styles for the following document features:

- **Fonts:** Setting font size, type, and other properties
- **Text:** Controlling text alignment and applying decorative elements such as underlining, italics, and capitalization
- **Color:** Specifying background and foreground colors of different page elements
- **Backgrounds:** Setting and tiling background images for any element
- **Block-level elements:** Controlling margins and borders around blocks, setting the padding space within a block, and floating block-level elements on a page, as done with inline images

The second version of CSS, **CSS2**, was introduced in 1998. It expanded the language to support styles for the following controls:

- **Positioning:** Placing elements at specific coordinates on a page
- **Visual formatting:** Clipping and hiding element content
- **Media types:** Creating styles for different output devices, including printed media and aural devices
- **Interfaces:** Controlling the appearance and behavior of system features such as scroll-bars and mouse cursors

At present, browser support for CSS2 is mixed. Most of the styles for positioning and visual formatting are supported, but many of the other CSS2 styles are not. An update to CSS2, **CSS2.1**, was introduced by the W3C in April 2002. Although the update did not add any new features to the language, it cleaned up some minor errors that were introduced in the original specification.

Even though browsers are still trying to catch up to all of the features of CSS2, the W3C has pressed forward with the next version, **CSS3**. Still in development as of this writing, CSS3 is being designed in individual modules. This approach should make it easier for software developers to design applications that support only those features of CSS that are relevant to their products. For example, an aural browser might not need to support the CSS styles associated with printed media, so the browser's developers could concentrate only on the CSS3 modules that deal with aural properties. This setup promises to make browser development easier and the resulting browser products more compact in size and, therefore, more efficient. This is an especially important consideration in trying to fit a browser into a small handheld device such as a PDA or cell phone. CSS3 will also expand the range of styles supported by the language:

- **User interfaces:** Adding dynamic and interactive features
- **Accessibility:** Supporting users with disabilities and other special needs
- **Columnar layout:** Giving Web authors more page layout options
- **International features:** Providing support for a wide variety of languages and typefaces
- **Mobile devices:** Supporting the device requirements of PDAs and cell phones
- **Scalable vector graphics:** Making it easier for Web authors to add graphic elements to their Web pages

As with HTML and XHTML, the applicability of these features depends on the support of the browser community. Because CSS2 is still not completely supported, it is unclear how long it will take after the W3C releases the final specification for CSS3 styles before they are adopted. In addition, individual browsers have introduced their own extensions to CSS. For example, Internet Explorer has introduced styles to format inline images and to add slideshow effects to Web pages. This means that, once again, Web page designers need to be aware of compatibility issues not just between different versions of CSS but also between different versions of each browser.

Applying a Style Sheet

There are three ways of applying a style to an HTML or XHTML document:

- **Inline styles:** Each style is applied to a specific element through the use of the style attribute in the element's tag.
- **Embedded styles:** A style sheet is placed in a document's head, setting the style definitions for the document's elements.
- **External styles:** A style sheet is saved in a separate document and is applied to a group of pages in a Web site.

Each approach has its own advantages and disadvantages, and you'll probably use some combination of all three in developing your Web sites.

Using Inline Styles

An **inline style** is applied to an element by adding the style attribute to the element's markup tag. The syntax of the style attribute is

```
<element style="style1: value1; style2: value2; style3: value3; ...">
```

where `element` is the name of the element, `style1`, `style2`, `style3`, and so on are the names of the styles, and `value1`, `value2`, `value3`, etc. are the values associated with each style. For example, the inline style in the following code instructs browsers to display the h1 heading "Pixal Products" in a red font:

```
<h1 style="color: red">Pixal Products</h1>
```

Inline styles are easy to use and interpret because they are applied directly to the elements they affect. However, there are also some problems with their use. The main complication is that an inline style applies only to the specific element that it modifies. With inline styles, if you wanted all of your headings to be rendered in a sans-serif font, for example, you would have to locate all of the h1 through h6 tags in the Web site and apply the same font-family style to them. This is no small task in a large Web site with hundreds of headings spread through dozens of pages.

Using Embedded Styles

The power of style sheets becomes evident as you move the style definitions farther away from the document content. One way of doing this is to use **embedded style** definitions within the head element of a Web document using the style element. The syntax of the style element is

```
<style>
   style declarations
</style>
```

where *style declarations* are the declarations of the different styles to be applied to the document. Each style declaration is applied to a group of elements within the document called the *selector*. The style declaration has the syntax

```
selector {style1: value1; style2: value2; style3: value3; ...}
```

where *selector* identifies an element or elements within the document, and the *style*:*value* pairs follow the same syntax that you use to apply inline styles to elements. For example, to render all h1 headings in a red font, you use the selector h1 and insert the following style declaration in the document's head:

```
<head>
<title>Web Page Title</title>
<style>
    h1 {color: red}
</style>
</head>
```

Later in this appendix, you'll look at different ways of expressing the selector value to select wide-ranging groups of elements.

The style element supports several attributes that define the type of style sheet language to be used, the type of output media for which the style is designed, and a name or id that identifies the style element. The syntax of these attributes is

```
<style type="mime_type" media="media_type" title="text" id="text">
    style declarations
</style>
```

where the type attribute indicates the style sheet language, the media attribute identifies the output media, and the title and id attributes provide a label for the set of style declarations in the style element. For style declarations written in CSS, you set the *mime_type* value to "text/css".

The media attribute indicates the output media for which a style sheet is written. For example, you can create different style sheets for printed output and output directed toward a computer screen. Figure B-1 describes the different values of the media attribute.

Figure B-1 ▶ **Values of the media attribute**

Media	Used for
all	All output devices (the default)
aural	Speech and sound synthesizers
braille	Braille tactile feedback devices
embossed	Paged Braille printers
handheld	Small or handheld devices with small screens, monochrome graphics, and limited bandwidth
print	Printers
projection	Projectors
screen	Computer monitors
tty	Fixed-width devices such as teletype machines and terminals
tv	Television-type devices with low resolution, color, and limited scrollability

For example, if you wanted to create a style sheet specifically for printed output, you would use an embedded style sheet similar to the following in your HTML or XHTML file:

```
<style type="text/css" media="print">
   h1 {color: red}
</style>
```

Under this style sheet, the h1 heading is displayed in red for printed output. Note that this style sheet doesn't apply to other output media such as computer monitors. In a different medium, an h1 heading would still have the default appearance defined by that device, or it would have its appearance defined by another style sheet written for that medium. The media attribute is discussed in more detail later in this appendix.

Finally, because a single HTML file can contain several embedded style sheets, the id and title attributes provide a means of distinguishing one style sheet from another. This can be useful in a script that loads different style sheets in response to requests from users. The id and title attributes are optional; unless you need to use multiple style sheets on a particular page, you probably will not have to use them.

Creating an Embedded Style Sheet | Reference Window

To create an embedded style sheet, enter the following tags within a document's head element:

```
<style type="mime-type" media="type" title="text" id="text">
   style declarations
</style>
```

where the type attribute specifies the MIME type of the style sheet language, the media attribute specifies the output type, the title and id attributes provide labels for the style sheet, and style declarations are the individual style declarations applied to elements in the document. For CSS style sheets, use a type value of "text/css". The default media value is "all", which applies the style sheet to all output media.

Using an External Style Sheet

An **external style** sheet is a simple text file that contains only style declarations. The file can be linked to any page in a Web site, allowing the same styles to be applied to the entire site at once. So, to make all of the h1 headings in a Web site appear in a red font, you could simply add the following text to the external style sheet

```
h1 {color: red}
```

and then link that style sheet to each page. To link an external style sheet to a Web page, you add the following link element to the head element of the HTML or XHTML file:

```
<link href="url" rel="stylesheet" type="mime-type" media="media type"
    id="text" title="text" />
```

where url is the URL of the external style sheet, and the remaining attributes have the same meanings as they did for an embedded style sheet. An external style sheet written in the CSS language should have the file name extension ".css". So, to link a Web page to a style sheet named "styles.css", you would enter the following link in the head element of the Web document:

```
<link href="styles.css" rel="stylesheet" type="text/css" />
```

You can include several link elements within a single file, allowing your Web page to retrieve styles from different style sheets. This method allows you to link a Web page to separate style sheets for printed output, computer monitors, and so on (see Figure B-2).

Figure B-2 | Applying multiple style sheets to a single document

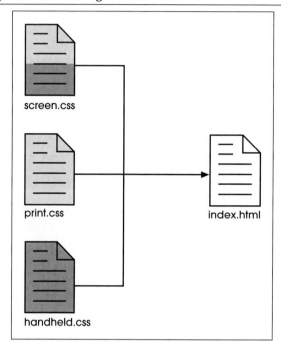

In addition, the same style sheet can be linked to several different Web pages, giving all the pages in the Web site a common look and feel. If you make a change to the style sheet, the change is automatically reflected across the Web site (see Figure B-3).

Figure B-3 | Applying a single style sheet to multiple documents

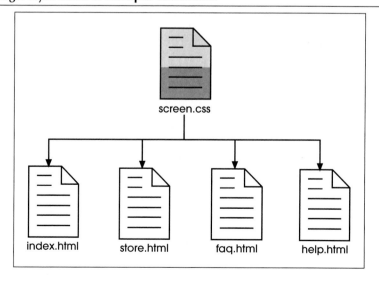

Style Comments

In addition to style declarations, an embedded or external style sheet can also contain comments that document important information about the style sheet. To add a comment, use the form

```
/* comment */
```

where *comment* is the text of the comment. For example, the following line inserts the comment "Pixal Products Style Sheet" into a style sheet:

```
/* Pixal Products Style Sheet */
```

Understanding Style Precedence

You've seen how styles can be applied inline with individual elements, how they can be embedded within a single file, and how an external style sheet can be applied to an entire Web site. With so many potential sources of styles for a single document, how does a browser determine what takes precedence when styles conflict? When styles come from several sources, they are weighted as follows (in order of increasing importance):

1. External style sheet
2. Embedded styles
3. Inline styles

So, an inline style takes precedence over an embedded style, which has precedence over an external style sheet. If two styles have the same weight, the one declared last has precedence. For example, in the embedded style

```
<style type="text/css">
   h1 {color: orange}
   h1 {color: blue}
</style>
```

the blue font color is applied to the h1 heading because it is declared last, overriding the orange color style. You can override the precedence rules by adding the !important property to the style declaration. The style sheet

```
<style type="text/css">
   h1 {color: orange !important}
   h1 {color: blue}
</style>
```

results in h1 headings being rendered in an orange font, as the orange style is given a higher weighting than the blue style. The !important property is useful in situations when you want to ensure that a particular style is always enforced no matter what its location in the order of precedence.

Note that any style can still be overridden by users who have set up their own style sheets for use with their browsers. This is often done by people with disabilities who have unique needs (such as the need for text to be displayed in large fonts with highly contrasting colors). The styles in these style sheets take precedence over a browser's default styles and the styles specified by a Web page author. So, you should make sure that your Web pages are still readable even when a user does not adopt your style sheets. The ability to view the content of your Web pages should not depend on the ability to access your style sheets.

Understanding Style Inheritance

If a style for an element is not specified, the element adopts the style of its parent element. This effect, known as **style inheritance**, causes style declarations to cascade down through the document hierarchy. For example, if you want to set the text color of every element on a page to blue, you could use the declaration

```
body {color: blue}
```

Every element within the body element (which is to say, every element that is displayed on the page) inherits this style. To override style inheritance, you specify an alternate style for one of the descendant elements of the parent. Together, the styles

```
body {color: blue}
p {color: red}
```

change the text color to blue for every element on the page except for paragraphs and any element contained within a paragraph. As with style precedence, you can override style inheritance by using the !important property.

Working with Text Styles

Now that you've learned how to apply a style to a document, you'll next examine some of the specific styles supported by CSS, starting with a look at text styles.

Choosing a Font

By default, browsers apply a single font face to Web page text—usually Times New Roman. You can specify a different font for any page element using the style

```
font-family: fonts
```

where `fonts` is a comma-separated list of specific or generic font names. A **specific font** is a font such as Times New Roman, Arial, or Garamond that is actually installed on a user's computer. A **generic font** is a name for the general description of the font's appearance. Browsers recognize five generic font names: serif, sans-serif, monospace, cursive, and fantasy. Figure B-4 shows examples of each. Note that each generic font can represent a wide range of designs.

Figure B-4   **Generic fonts**

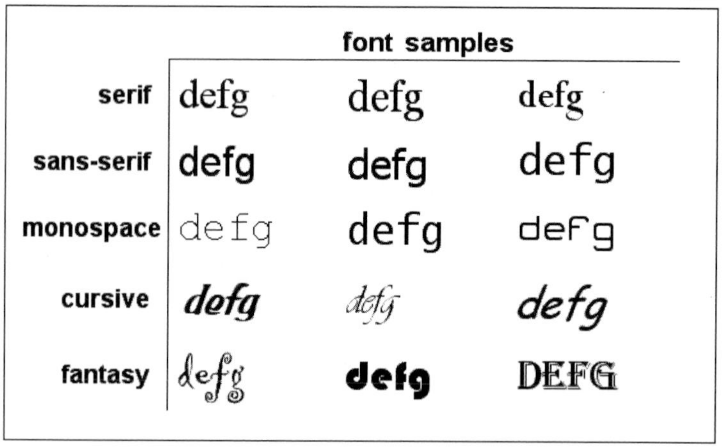

	font samples		
serif	defg	defg	defg
sans-serif	defg	defg	defg
monospace	defg	defg	defg
cursive	defg	defg	defg
fantasy	defg	defg	DEFG

When you specify a generic font, you cannot be exactly sure how the text is rendered by a given user's browser—this depends on how the browser has been configured to deal with generic fonts. This is one reason why CSS allows you to specify a list of fonts, rather than just one. You list the specific fonts you want browsers to try first, in order of preference, and then end the list with the generic font. If a browser cannot find any of the specific fonts listed, it uses the generic font as the final choice. For example, to apply a sans-serif font to the text within an element, you could use the following style:

```
font-family: Arial, Helvetica, sans-serif
```

This style tells the browser to first try to apply the Arial font. If Arial is not available, it tells the browser to look for Helvetica. If neither of those is installed, it tells the browser to use the generic sans-serif font (whatever that might be).

Choosing a Font | Reference Window

To choose a font for an element's text, use the style
```
font-family: fonts
```
where *fonts* is a comma-separated list of font names, starting with the most specific and desirable fonts and ending with a generic font name.

Setting the Font Size

As with font faces, font sizes are largely determined by a user's Web browser but can be overridden by style sheets. The style to change the font size used in an element is

```
font-size: length
```

where *length* is a length measurement. Lengths can be specified in four different ways:

- With a unit of measurement
- With a keyword description
- As a percentage of the size of the containing element
- With a keyword expressing the size relative to the size of the containing element

If you choose to specify lengths using measurement units, you can use absolute units or relative units. Because absolute and relative units are options for a lot of other styles as well, it's worthwhile to spend some time understanding them. **Absolute units** define a font size using one of the following standard units of measurement: mm (millimeter), cm (centimeter), in (inch), pt (point), or pc (pica). **Relative units** express the font size relative to the size of a standard character in the output device (whatever that might be). The two common typesetting standards are referred to as "em" and "ex." The **em unit** is equal to the width of the capital letter "M." The **ex unit** is equal to the height of a lowercase "x" (see Figure B-5).

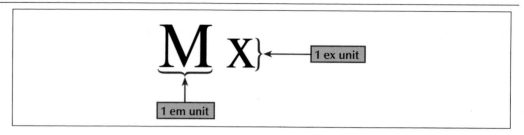

For example, to set the font size about 50% larger than the width of a capital "M" in the default font, you could set the font size as:

```
font-size: 1.5em
```

You can use relative units to make a page **scalable**, allowing the page to be rendered in the same way no matter how a particular browser has been configured. For example, one user could have a large monitor and have set the default font size for body text to 18pt. Another user could have a smaller monitor and have set the default font size to 12pt. You want your heading text to be about 50% larger than the body text for either user. You can't specify the default font size for each user's browser, but if you use a value of 1.5em for the heading, it is sized appropriately on either monitor. Note that you can achieve the same effect by expressing a font size as a percentage of an element's default font size. For example, the style

```
font-size: 150%
```

causes the heading to appear 50% larger than the default size. Because of the advantages of scalability, Web designers often opt for the em unit over an absolute unit such as point size (even though point size is the most commonly used unit in desktop publishing).

The final unit of measurement you need to examine is the **pixel**, which represents a single dot on the output device. Because a pixel is the most fundamental unit, for most length measurements browsers assume that length is expressed in pixels if no unit is specified. So, to set the font size to 20 pixels, you could use either of the following styles:

```
font-size: 20px
font-size: 20
```

In general, it's best to include the measurement unit to ensure that your style declaration is unambiguous.

Finally, you can express font sizes using seven descriptive keywords: xx-small, x-small, small, medium, large, x-large, or xx-large. Each browser is configured to display text at a particular size for each of these keywords, enabling you to achieve some uniformity across browsers.

Reference Window | **Setting the Font Size**

To set the font size, use the style
```
    font-size: value
```
where *value* is either a unit of length (specified in mm, cm, in, pt, pc, em, or ex units), a keyword (xx-small, x-small, small, medium, large, x-large, or xx-large), a percentage of the default font size, or a keyword describing the size relative to the size of the containing element (smaller or larger). The default font size unit is the pixel (px).

Controlling Spacing and Indentation

CSS supports styles that allow you to perform some basic typographic tasks, such as setting the **kerning** (the amount of space between letters) and **tracking** (the amount of space between words). The styles to control an element's kerning and tracking are

```
letter-spacing: value
word-spacing: value
```

where *value* is the size of space between individual letters or words. You specify these sizes with the same units that you use for font sizing. As with font sizes, the default unit of length for kerning and tracking is the pixel (px). The default kerning and tracking value is 0 pixels each. A positive value increases the letter and word spacing. A negative value reduces the space between letters and words.

Another typographic feature that you can set is **leading**, which is the space between lines of text. The style to set the leading for the text within an element is

```
line-height: length
```

where *length* is a specific length or a percentage of the font size of the text on the affected lines. If no unit is specified, a browser interprets the number as the ratio of the line height to the font size. The standard ratio is 1.2:1, meaning that the line height is 1.2 times the font size. To create double-spaced text, you use the style

```
line-height: 2
```

The final way to control the spacing of your text is to set the indentation used in the first line. The style is

```
text-indent: value
```

where *value* is either a length expressed in absolute or relative units or a percentage of the width of the text block. For example, an indentation value of 5% indents the first line by 5% of the width of the block. The indentation value can also be negative, extending the first line to the left of the text block to create a hanging indent.

Setting Text Spaces | Reference Window

- To set the space between letters (kerning), use the style
    ```
    letter-spacing: value
    ```
  where *value* is the space between individual letters. The default is 0 pixels.
- To set the space between words (tracking), use the style
    ```
    word-spacing: value
    ```
  where *value* is the space between individual words. The default is 0 pixels.
- To set the vertical space between lines of text (leading), use the style
    ```
    line-height: value
    ```
  where *value* is either the length between the lines, a percentage of the font size, or the ratio of the line height to the font size. The default is a ratio of 1.2:1.
- To set the indentation of the first line, use the style
    ```
    text-indent: value
    ```
  where *value* is the length of the indentation expressed either as a length or as a percentage of the width of the text block. The default is 0 pixels.

Setting Font Styles, Weights, and Other Decorative Features

Browsers often apply default font styles to particular types of elements. For example, text marked with an <address> tag usually appears in italics. You can specify font styles yourself using the style

```
font-style: type
```

where *type* is normal, italic, or oblique. The italic and oblique styles are similar in appearance but might differ subtly depending on the font in use.

You have also seen that browsers render certain elements in heavier fonts. For example, most browsers render headings in a boldface font. You can control the font weight for any page element using the style

```
font-weight: weight
```

where *weight* is the level of bold formatting applied to the text. You express weights as values ranging from 100 to 900, in increments of 100. In practice, however, most browsers cannot render nine different font weights. For practical purposes, you can assume that 400 represents normal (unbolded) text, 700 is bold text, and 900 represents extrabold text. You can also use the keywords "normal" or "bold" in place of a weight value, or you can express the font weight relative to the containing element, using the keywords "bolder" or "lighter."

Another style you can use to change the appearance of text is

```
text-decoration: type
```

where *type* is none (for no decorative changes), underline, overline, line-through, or blink. You can apply several decorative features to the same element. For example, the style

```
text-decoration: underline overline
```

places a line under and over the text in the element. Note that the text-decoration style cannot be applied to nontextual elements, such as inline images.

To control the case of the text within an element, you use the style

```
text-transform: type
```

where *type* is capitalize, uppercase, lowercase, or none (to make no changes to the text case). For example, if you wanted to capitalize the first letter of each word in an element, you could use the following style:

```
text-transform: capitalize
```

To display every letter in lowercase, you use the text-transform value "lowercase". Similarly, the setting "uppercase" displays every letter in uppercase.

Finally, you can display text in uppercase letters and a small font, using the style

```
font-variant: type
```

where *type* is normal (the default) or small-caps (small capital letters). Small-caps are often used in legal documents, such as software agreements, where the capital letters indicate the importance of a phrase or point, but the text is made small so as not to detract from other elements in the document.

Setting Font Styles

- To set a font's appearance, use the style
      font-style: *type*
  where *type* is either normal, italic, or oblique.
- To set a font's weight, use
      font-weight: *value*
  where *value* is either a value from 100 to 900 in increments of 100, or the keyword "normal" or "bold." To increase the weight of the font relative to its containing element, use the keywords "bolder" or "lighter."
- To decorate text, use the style
      text-decoration: *type*
  where *type* equals underline, overline, line-through, blink, or none.
- To change the case of the text in an element, use the style
      text-transform: *type*
  where *type* equals capitalize, lowercase, uppercase, or none.
- To display a variant of the current font, use the style
      font-variant: *type*
  where *type* equals normal or small-caps.

Aligning Element Content

CSS provides two styles for aligning the content of an element. To align text horizontally, use the style

text-align: *type*

where *type* is left, right, center, or justify (which spaces out the content to touch both the left and the right margins of the element). To vertically align an element's content, use the style

vertical-align: *type*

where *type* is one of the keywords described in Figure B-6.

Values of the vertical-alignment style **Figure B-6**

Vertical Alignment	Description
baseline	Aligns the element with the bottom of lowercase letters in surrounding text (the default)
bottom	Aligns the bottom of the element with the bottom of the lowest element in surrounding content
middle	Aligns the middle of the element with the middle of the surrounding content
sub	Subscripts the element
super	Superscripts the element
text-bottom	Aligns the bottom of the element with the bottom of the font of the surrounding content
text-top	Aligns the top of the element with the top of the font of the surrounding content
top	Aligns the top of the element with the top of the tallest object in the surrounding content

Instead of using keywords, you can specify a length or a percentage for an element to be aligned relative to the surrounding content. A positive value moves the element up, and a negative value lowers the element. For example, the style

```
vertical-align: 50%
```

raises the element by half of the line height of the surrounding content, whereas the style

```
vertical-align: -100%
```

drops the element an entire line height below the baseline of the current line.

Combining All Text Formatting in a Single Style

This appendix has covered a lot of different text and font styles. You can combine most of them into a single style declaration, using the form:

```
font: font-style font-variant font-weight font-size/line-height
    font-family
```

where *font-style* is the font's style, *font-variant* is the font variant, *font-weight* is the weight of the font, *font-size* is the size of the font, *line-height* is the height of the lines, and *font-family* is the font face. For example, the style

```
font: italic small-caps bold 16pt/24pt Arial, sans-serif
```

displays the text of the element in an italic bold Arial or sans-serif font. The font size is 16pt and the space between the lines is 24pt. The text appears in small capital letters. You do not have to include all of the properties of the font style. The only required properties are size and font-family. A browser assumes the default value for any omitted property. However, you must place any properties that you do include in the order indicated above. For example, the following is a correct style declaration to specify a 16pt bold monospace font:

```
font: bold 16pt monospace
```

However, it would *not* be correct to switch the order, placing the font-family property before the style and weight properties, as follows:

```
font: monospace bold 16pt
```

Although some browsers would be able to interpret this style correctly, others would reject it because of the flawed syntax.

Working with Color and Image Styles

CSS provides several different styles for adding color and images to your Web pages. You can define the foreground and background color for each element on a page. The foreground color is usually the color of the text in an element, although in the case of horizontal lines it defines part of the line's color. The style to define an element's foreground color is

```
color: color
```

where *color* is either a color value or a color name. Color values are entered in the form rgb (red, green, blue) where red is the red component of the color, green is the green component, and blue is the blue component. Component values range from 0 (no intensity) to 255 (highest intensity). The style to define an element's background color is:

```
background-color: color
```

If you do not define an element's color, the color is taken from the containing element. For example, if you specify red text on a gray background for a Web page's body, all elements within the page inherit that color combination unless you specify a different style. For example, if you want to display all paragraphs in white text on a black background, the style is:

```
p {color: white; background-color: black}
```

Setting Foreground and Background Colors | Reference Window

- To set an element's foreground color, use the style
    ```
    color: color
    ```
  where *color* is either a color name or a color value.
- To set an element's background color, use the style:
    ```
    background-color: color
    ```

Setting a Background Image

Almost any element can be displayed with a background image. You can set four properties on a background image:

- The source of the image file
- Where the image is placed in the background of the element
- How the image is repeated across the background of the element
- Whether the image scrolls with the display window

To apply a background image, use the style

```
background-image: url(url)
```

where *url* is the location and the name of the image file.

Controlling Image Placement

By default, background images are tiled both horizontally and vertically until they occupy the background of the entire element. You can control how browsers tile a background image using the style

```
background-repeat: type
```

where *type* equals repeat, repeat-x, repeat-y, or no-repeat. Figure B-7 shows an example of each of these repeat types. The default type value is "repeat," which causes the tiling to occur in both the vertical and horizontal directions.

Figure B-7 Values of the background-repeat style

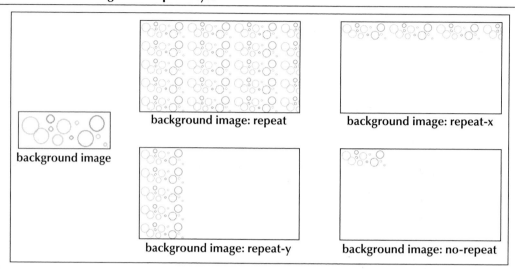

background image

background image: repeat

background image: repeat-x

background image: repeat-y

background image: no-repeat

By default, background images are placed in the upper-left corner of the space occupied by an element and then repeated from there if tiling is in effect. You can place a background image in a different location using the style

```
background-position: horizontal_position vertical_position
```

where $horizontal\_position$ and $vertical\_position$ are the horizontal and vertical coordinates of the upper-left corner of the image. For example, the style

```
background-position: 30 50
```

places the image 30 pixels to the right and 50 pixels down from the upper-left corner of the element space. If you specify only one value, a browser applies it to both the horizontal and the vertical coordinates.

To describe image position more generally, you can use a combination of six keywords: left, center, right (for the horizontal position) and top, center, bottom (for the vertical position). You can also define the position of a background image as a percentage of the width and height of the element. For example, the style

```
background-position: 50% 50%
```

places the background image at the center of the element. By default, a background image moves with the element as the page is scrolled through the browser display window. You can change this behavior using the style

```
background-attachment: attachment
```

where $attachment$ is either "scroll" (the default) to scroll the image with the page, or "fixed" to place the image at a fixed location in the display window. Fixed background images are often used to create the illusion of a **watermark**, mimicking a translucent graphic impressed into the very fabric of paper and often used in specialized stationery.

Like the font style, all of the various background image styles can be combined into a single style:

```
background: color url(url) repeat attachment position
```

where $color$ is the color name or color value of the element background, url is the URL of the background image file, $repeat$ specifies how the image is tiled in the background, $attachment$ specifies whether the image scrolls with the page, and $position$ provides the coordinates of the background image. For example, the declaration

```
body {background: yellow url(paper.gif) no-repeat fixed center center}
```

displays the image file "paper.gif" on the page body's background. The image file is centered on the page, fixed in position (so that it doesn't scroll), and is not repeated or tiled across the page body. In places where the background image is not displayed, a background color of yellow is displayed.

Inserting a Background Image | Reference Window

- To insert a background image behind an element, use the style
    ```
    background-image: url(url)
    ```
  where *url* is the file name and the location of the image file.
- To control the tiling of the background image, use the style
    ```
    background-repeat: type
    ```
  where *type* is repeat (the default), repeat-x, repeat-y, or no-repeat.
- To place the background image in a specific position behind the element, use the style
    ```
    background-position: horizontal vertical
    ```
  where *horizontal* is the horizontal position of the image and *vertical* is the vertical position. You can specify a position as the distance from the top-left corner of the element, a percentage of the element's width and height, or by using a keyword. Keyword options are top, center, or bottom for vertical position and left, center, or right for horizontal placement.
- To control whether the background image scrolls, use the style
    ```
    background-attachment: attachment
    ```
  where *attachment* is scroll (the default) or fixed.
- To place all of the background options in a single declaration, use the style
    ```
    background: color image repeat attachment position
    ```
  where *color* is the background color, *image* is the image file, *repeat* is the method of tiling the image, *attachment* defines whether the image scrolls or is fixed, and *position* defines the position of the image within the element.

Sizing Elements

By default, the size of each element is determined either by its content or by the size of its containing element. For example, the width of a paragraph expands to match the width of its containing element, and the paragraph's height is determined by its content. You can use CSS to override these default settings, specifying a different width or height for any element on a page.

Setting an Element's Width

To set the width of an element, apply the style

```
width: value
```

where *value* is expressed as a percentage of the width of the parent element or in absolute units. For example, to set the width of all paragraphs on a page to 4 inches, you use the following style declaration:

```
p {width: 4in}
```

If you do not specify a unit of measurement, browsers assume that the width is set in pixels. For example, the style

```
p {width: 250}
```

sets the width of all paragraphs to 250 pixels.

Setting an Element's Height

To set the height of an element, use the style

```
height: value
```

where *value* is the height of the element specified as a percentage of the parent element or in absolute units. If you do not specify a height, browsers expand the height of the element until all of the content is visible.

Handling Content Overflow

If you do specify a height for an element, you run the risk of not being able to fit its content into a defined space. In that case, you can control how the browser handles the extra content by applying the style

```
overflow: type
```

where *type* is visible (the default), hidden, scroll, or auto. A value of "visible" instructs browsers to increase the height of the element to fit the extra content. A value of "hidden" hides the extra content. Both the "scroll" and "auto" values instruct browsers to display scroll bars that enable users to view the extra content. The "auto" option adds scroll bars only when needed, whereas the "scroll" option adds scroll bars whether they are needed or not (see Figure B-8).

| Figure B-8 | Values of the overflow style |

overflow: visible

overflow: hidden

overflow: scroll

overflow: auto

Clipping Content

Another attribute related to overflow is the clip attribute. The clip attribute allows a Web designer to define a rectangular area through which the content of an element can be viewed. Any content that falls outside of the clip area is hidden. The syntax for the clip attribute is

```
clip: rect(top, right, bottom, left)
```

where *top*, *right*, *bottom*, and *left* define the coordinates of the rectangular region. For example, a clip value of rect(10, 175, 125, 75) defines a clip region whose top and bottom edges are 10 and 125 pixels from the top of the element and whose right and left edges are 175 and 75 pixels from the left side of the element (see Figure B-9).

Clipping an element **Figure B-9**

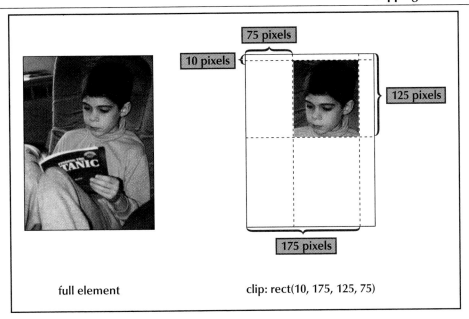

full element   clip: rect(10, 175, 125, 75)

The *top*, *right*, *bottom*, and *left* values can also be set to "auto," which shifts the clipping region to the edge of an element. For example, a clip value of rect(10, auto, 125, 75) creates a clipping rectangle whose right edge matches the right edge of the element while the rest of the edges are clipped.

Working with Borders, Margins, and Padding

For each page element, CSS defines a **box model** that identifies the different parts of the element. The box model describes four aspects of an element (see Figure B-10):

- The margin between the box and the other elements
- The border of the box
- The padding between the element's content and the border
- The element's content

Figure B-10 Parts of the box model

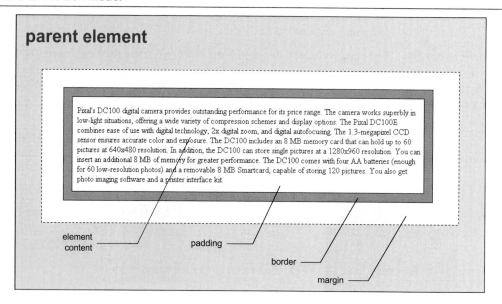

CSS provides styles to work with the margins, borders, and padding of any page element.

Working with Margins

CSS supports four styles that can be used to control the size of the margin of a page element. These attributes are

```
margin-top: value
margin-right: value
margin-bottom: value
margin-left: value
```

where *value* is the size of the margin expressed in absolute units or as a percentage of the width of the parent element. You can also use the value "auto," which instructs browsers to determine the margin size. For example, to create margins of 10 pixels on each side and 5 pixels above and below every h1 element, you use the following style:

```
h1 {margin-top: 5; margin-right: 10; margin-bottom: 5; margin-left: 10}
```

Margin sizes can also be negative, which you can use to crowd or overlap elements on a page. The four margin styles can also be combined into a single style

```
margin: top right bottom left
```

where *top*, *right*, *bottom*, and *left* are sizes of the corresponding margins. If you include only three values in the combined attribute, they are interpreted as top, right, and bottom, and browsers match the size of the left and right margins. If only two values are specified, they are applied to the top and right margins, and browsers match the bottom and left margins to those two values. If only one value is entered, browsers apply that size to all four margins.

Setting the Margin Size | Reference Window

- To set the size of the margins around an element, use the styles
    ```
    margin-top: length
    margin-right: length
    margin-bottom: length
    margin-left: length
    ```
    where *length* is a unit of length, a percentage of the width of the containing element, or the keyword "auto" (the default), which enables browsers to set the margin size.
- To combine all margin styles in a single style, use
    ```
    margin: top right bottom left
    ```
    where *top*, *right*, *bottom*, and *left* are the margins of the top, right, bottom, and left edges. If you include only three values, the margins are applied to the top, right, and bottom, and the left value matches the right one. If you specify only two values, the first value is applied to the top and bottom edges, and the second value is applied to the right and left edges. If you specify only one value, it is applied to all four edges.

Working with Borders

You can create a border around any element and define its thickness, color, and style. You can apply styles to individual border sides or to all four sides at once. Figure B-11 describes the various CSS border attributes.

Border styles | Figure B-11

Border Style	Description	Notes
border-top-width: *value*	Width of the top border	Where *value* is the width of the border in absolute or relative units or defined with the keyword "thin", "medium", or "thick"
border-right-width: *value*	Width of the right border	
border-bottom-width: *value*	Width of the bottom border	
border-left-width: *value*	Width of the left border	
border-width: *top right bottom left*	Width of any or all of the borders	
border-top-color: *color*	Color of the top border	Where *color* is a color name or color value
border-right-color: *color*	Color of the right border	
border-bottom-color: *color*	Color of the bottom border	
border-left-color: *color*	Color of the left border	
border-color: *top right bottom left*	Color of any or all of the borders	
border-top-style: *type*	Style of the top border	Where *type* is one of the nine border styles: solid, dashed, dotted, double, outset, inset, groove, ridge, or none
border-right-style: *type*	Style of the right border	
border-bottom-style: *type*	Style of the bottom border	
border-left-style: *type*	Style of the left border	
border-style: *top right bottom left*	Style of any or all of the borders	

Border widths can be expressed using units of length or with the keywords "thin," "medium," or "thick." Border color is defined using a color name or value. For border style, CSS supports the nine different types described in Figure B-12.

Figure B-12 ▶ **Border style types**

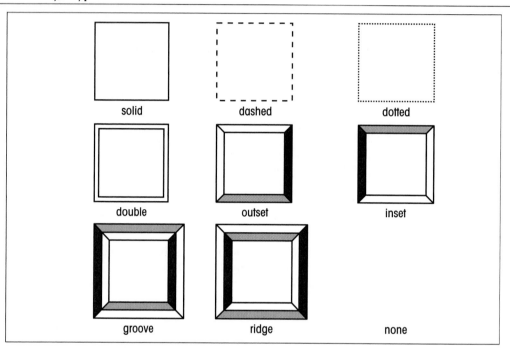

For example, to place a double border around an entire Web page, you could use the style

```
body {border-style: double}
```

All of the border attributes can be combined into a single style declaration using the style

```
border: width style color
```

To create a 5pt blue dotted border around h1 headings, you could use the style declaration

```
h1 {border-width: 5pt; border-style: dotted; border-color: blue}
```

or you could combine the attributes into the style declaration

```
h1 {border: 5pt dotted blue}
```

To work with individual borders, you can identify specific borders to format using the styles

```
border-top: width style color
border-right: width style color
border-bottom: width style color
border-left: width style color
```

There are several methods of formatting the border for a block element, but support for the different methods is inconsistent across browsers and browser versions. As always, be sure that the styles you use are supported by the browsers your audience is likely to be using.

- To set the width of an element's border, use the style
    ```
    border-width: top right bottom left
    ```
  where *top*, *right*, *bottom*, and *left* are the widths of the top, right, bottom, and left borders. To define the border width for individual sides, use the styles border-top-width, border-right-width, border-bottom-width, and border-left-width.
- To set the border color, use the style
    ```
    border-color: top right bottom left
    ```
  where *top*, *right*, *bottom*, and *left* are the colors of the top, right, bottom, and left borders. To define the border color for individual sides, use the styles border-top-color, border-right-color, border-bottom-color, and border-left-color.
- To set the border style, use
    ```
    border-style: top right bottom left
    ```
  where *top*, *right*, *bottom*, and *left* are the styles of the top, right, bottom, and left borders. Possible border style values are solid, dashed, dotted, double, outset, inset, groove, ridge, and none. To define the border style for individual sides, use the styles border-top-style, border-right-style, border-bottom-style, and border-left-style.
- To format the entire border, use the style
    ```
    border: width style color
    ```
  where *width* is the border width, *style* is the border style, and *color* is the border color. To define the border appearance for individual sides, use the styles border-top, border-right, border-left, and border-bottom.

Working with Padding

To increase the space between element content and its border, you increase the size of the padding for the block. You can do this using any of the following styles:

```
padding-top: value
padding-right: value
padding-bottom: value
padding-left: value
padding: top right bottom left
```

where the padding values can be expressed in absolute units or as a percentage of the width of the block-level element. As with the combined margin style discussed earlier, if you enter fewer than four of the values for top, right, bottom, and left, browsers match the opposite sides. For example, to set the padding of all sides to 5 millimeters, you could use the style

```
padding: 5mm
```

To set the size of the internal padding, use the style
```
padding: top right bottom left
```
where *top*, *right*, *bottom*, and *left* are the top, right, bottom, and left padding sizes. To define the padding size for only one side of an element, use the styles padding-top, padding-right, padding-bottom, and padding-left.

Positioning Elements

Each page element is placed using the default settings of a user's Web browser. You can override these settings, however, and place elements at specific coordinates on the page. The style to set the position of an element is

```
position: type; top:value; right:value; bottom:value; left:value
```

where *type* indicates the type of positioning applied to the element and the top, right, bottom, and left styles indicate the coordinates of the top, right, bottom, and left edges of the element. In practice, only the top and left coordinates are used because the bottom and right coordinates can be inferred given the element's height and width. Coordinates can be expressed in the usual CSS measurement units.

The position style has five possible values: static, absolute, relative, fixed, and inherit. The default position is static, which allows browsers to place an element based on where it flows in a document. This is essentially the same as not using any CSS positioning at all. When the position is static, any values specified for the top or left styles are ignored by the browser.

Reference Window | **Positioning an Object with CSS**

To place an object at a specific location, use the style

```
position: type; top: value; right: value; bottom: value; left:
    value
```

where *type* indicates the type of positioning applied to the element (absolute, relative, static, fixed, or inherit), and the top, right, bottom, and left styles indicate the coordinates of the top, right, bottom, and left edges of the element.

Absolute Positioning

Absolute positioning places an element at defined coordinates within its parent element. In most cases, the parent element is the document window itself, meaning that the absolute position coordinates refer to the coordinates within the window. The coordinates are specified with respect to the upper-left corner of the parent element. A positive top value places the object down from the top edge; a negative value moves the object above the top edge of the parent. Similarly, a positive left value moves the element to the right of the left edge, and a negative value moves the element to the left of the parent.

Figure B-13 shows an object that has been placed at the coordinates (100, 150)—that is, 100 pixels to the right and 150 pixels down from the upper-left corner of its containing element. Absolute positioning essentially takes the object out of the document flow. Note that the other elements in the document move up in the flow of the document, occupying the space previously taken by the absolutely positioned object.

Absolute positioning ◀ **Figure B-13**

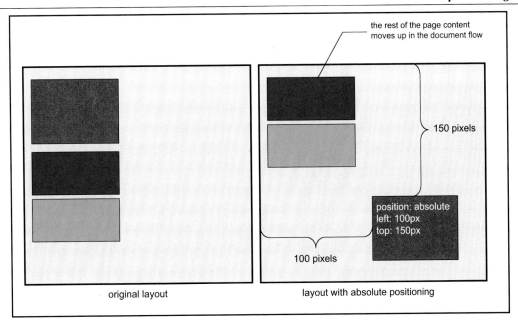

Relative Positioning

An alternative approach is to offset an element by using **relative positioning**. This approach moves an element a specific distance from where the browser would have placed it. For example, the element shown in Figure B-14 is offset 50 pixels to the left and 75 pixels down from its original location on the page. Unlike absolute positioning, relative positioning does not affect the placement of subsequent objects on the page. Other objects are placed at their original locations just as if no relative positioning had taken place. Relative positioning affects only the object being moved.

Relative positioning ◀ **Figure B-14**

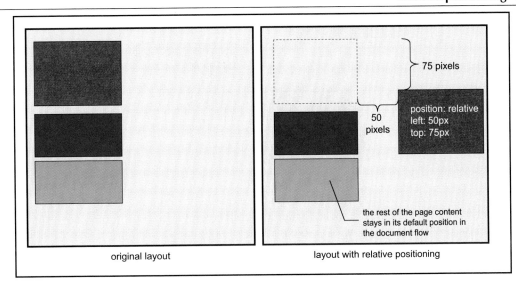

Fixed and Static Positioning

A **fixed position** places an element at a fixed location in the display window. The element remains in that location and does not scroll with other elements on the page. Similar to absolute positioning, the other elements in the document move into the space previously occupied by the element. This is different from a **static position**, which places an object in its natural position in the flow of the document as determined by the browser. Using static positioning, you allow the browser, or whatever application is rendering the document, to determine the element's location. Therefore, you do not specify a top, right, bottom, or left value when using static positioning.

Floating an Element

Another way to position an element is to float it. Floating an element places it alongside the left or right margin of the page or the containing element, allowing subsequent blocks to flow around it. The style to float an element is

```
float: margin
```

where `margin` is either left or right. Figure B-15 shows an example of an element that has been resized and is floating on the right margin of the page.

Figure B-15 ▷ **The float style**

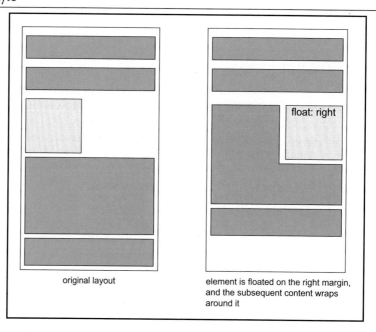

original layout

element is floated on the right margin, and the subsequent content wraps around it

You can prevent an element from wrapping around a floating element by clearing it. To clear an element, you use the style

```
clear: margin
```

where `margin` is left, right, or both. For example, if the value of the clear style for an element is set to "right," the element is not rendered on the page until the right margin is clear of all floating elements. A clear value of "both" requires both margins to be clear. Figure B-16 illustrates the flow of an element when both the float and the clear attributes are used.

The clear style ◀ **Figure B-16**

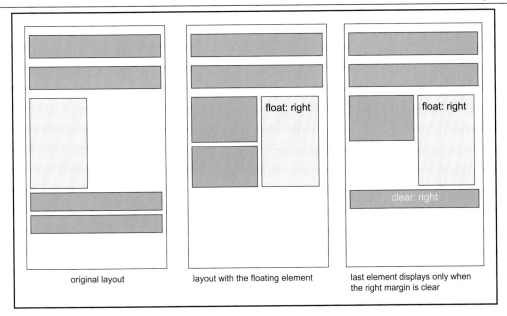

original layout

layout with the floating element

last element displays only when the right margin is clear

The clear style is most often used when you want to ensure that a page footer is always placed at the bottom of the page after all other page content has been displayed.

Floating and Clearing an Element | Reference Window

- To float an element on the left or right margin, use the style
    ```
    float: position
    ```
  where *position* is none (the default), left, or right.
- To display an element in the first available space where the specified margin is clear of floating elements, use the following style:
    ```
    clear: position
    ```

Stacking Elements

The ability to move elements to different locations on a page can lead to elements overlapping each other. By default, elements that are defined later in a document are placed on top of earlier elements. To specify a different stacking order, use the style

```
z-index: value
```

where *value* is a positive or negative integer or the value "auto." Elements are stacked based on their z-index values, with the highest z-index values placed on top. A value of "auto" uses the default stacking order. Figure B-17 shows the effect of the z-index attribute on the stacking of several different elements.

Figure B-17 | Using the z-index style

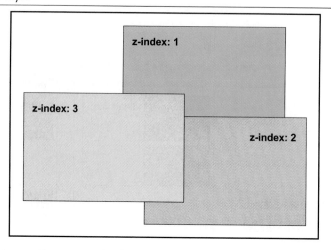

Note that the z-index attribute is applied only when elements share the same parent, and it has no effect on elements with different parent elements.

Setting the Element Display Style

Most page elements are classified as either inline elements or block-level elements. You can use CSS to change the display style applied to any element, allowing you to make inline elements appear as block-level elements and vice versa. The syntax of the display style is

```
display: type
```

where *type* is one of the CSS display types described in Figure B-18.

Setting the display style | Figure B-18

Display	Description
block	Display as a block-level element
inline	Display as an inline element
inline-block	Display as an inline element with some of the properties of a block (much like an inline image or a frame)
inherit	Inherit the display property of the element's parent
list-item	Display as a list item
none	Do not display the element
run-in	Display as either an inline or a block-level element, depending on the context
table	Display as a block-level table
inline-table	Display as an inline table
table-caption	Treat as a table caption
table-cell	Treat as a table cell
table-column	Treat as a table column
table-column-group	Treat as a group of table columns
table-footer-group	Treat as a group of table footer rows
table-header-group	Treat as a group of table header rows
table-row	Treat as a table row
table-row-group	Treat as a group of table rows

For example, to display an element as a block, you can use the following style:

```
display: block
```

Setting the Display Style | Reference Window

To define the display style of an element, use the style
```
display: type
```
where *type* is the display. Use a *type* value of "block" to format an element as a block, and use "inline" to format it is an inline element.

Hiding Elements

You can also use CSS to prevent elements from being displayed on a rendered Web page. This is useful in situations where you want one element to be displayed in a particular output medium (such as the computer screen) but not displayed in another medium (such as printed output). There are two ways of hiding an element. One is to set the value of the display style to "none," as in the style declaration

```
address {display: none}
```

which turns off the display of the address element. Alternatively, you can use the visibility style, which has the syntax

```
visibility: type
```

where *type* is visible, hidden, collapse, or inherit (the default). A value of "visible" makes an element visible; the "hidden" value hides the element; a value of "collapse" is used with the tables to prevent a row or column from being displayed; and the "inherit" value causes an element to inherit the visibility style from its parent. Unlike the display style, the visibility style hides an element, but does not remove it from the flow of elements in a page. As shown in Figure B-19, setting the display style to "none" not only hides an element, but also removes it from the page flow.

Figure B-19   Comparing the visibility and display styles

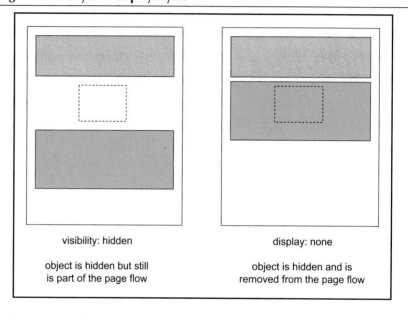

visibility: hidden

object is hidden but still
is part of the page flow

display: none

object is hidden and is
removed from the page flow

The display: none style is more appropriate for hiding elements in most cases. Use of the visibility: hidden style is usually reserved for scripts in which an element is alternatively hidden and made visible in order to create an animated effect.

Working with Selectors

Now that you've learned about some of the important styles, you'll look at how you can apply those styles to your Web sites. So far you've looked only at styles applied to individual elements. However, CSS also allows you to work with selectors that match different combinations of elements. For example, if you want to apply the same style to a collection of elements, you can group them by entering the elements in a comma-separated list. This feature allows you to replace a set of repetitive declarations, such as

```
h1 {font-family: sans-serif}
h2 {font-family: sans-serif}
h3 {font-family: sans-serif}
h4 {font-family: sans-serif}
h5 {font-family: sans-serif}
h6 {font-family: sans-serif}
```

with a single declaration, such as

```
h1, h2, h3, h4, h5, h6 {font-family: sans-serif}
```

You can also combine grouped and ungrouped selectors. In the following example, the h1 headings are displayed in a red sans-serif font, while the h2 headings are displayed in a blue sans-serif font.

```
h1, h2 {font-family: sans-serif}
h1 {color: red}
h2 {color: blue}
```

Placing common styles in a single declaration is a useful way of simplifying your style sheets.

Contextual Selectors

Sometimes you want to apply styles to elements depending on how those elements are used in a document. For example, the following style causes all boldfaced text to appear in a blue color:

```
b {color: blue}
```

However, if you wanted to apply this style only to boldfaced text within lists, you would need a way of applying a style based on the context in which an element is used. You can do this with **contextual selectors**. For example, to apply a style to an element only when it is descended from another element, you use the form

```
parent descendant {styles}
```

where *parent* is the parent element, *descendant* is a descendant of the parent, and *styles* are the styles to be applied to the descendant element. So, to apply a blue color only to boldfaced text found in lists, you use the style

```
li b {color: blue}
```

In this case li is the parent element and b is the descendant element. Any boldfaced text not contained in a list item is unaffected by this style. Note that the descendant element does not have to be direct child of the parent element. In the code

```
<li><span><b>Special</b> Orders</span> this month!</li>
```

the boldfaced text is a descendant of the list item, but it is a direct child of the span element.

Contextual selectors can also be grouped with other selectors. The following style applies a blue font to h2 headings and to boldfaced list items, but nowhere else:

```
li b, h2 {color: blue}
```

The parent/descendant form is only one example of a contextual selector. Figure B-20 shows some of the other contextual forms supported by CSS.

Simple and contextual selectors ◄ **Figure B-20**

Selector	Description
*	Matches any element in the hierarchy
e	Matches any element, *e*, in the hierarchy
e1, e2, e3, ...	Matches the group of elements *e1, e2, e3, ...*
e f	Matches any element, *f*, that is a descendant of an element, *e*
e > f	Matches any element, *f*, that is a direct child of an element, *e*
e + f	Matches any element, *f*, that is immediately preceded by a sibling element, *e*

To illustrate just how versatile these patterns can be, Figure B-21 shows six selector patterns applied to the same document tree. Selected elements are highlighted in red for each pattern. Remember that because of style inheritance, any style applied to an element is passed down the document tree.

Examples of selector patterns

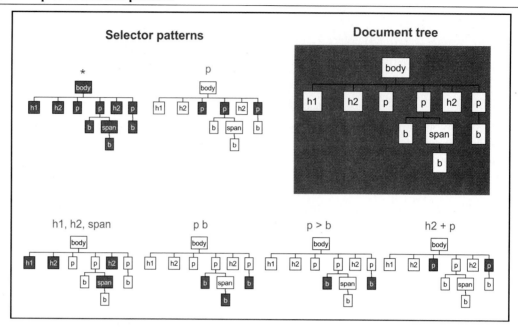

While the contextual selectors listed in Figure B-20 are part of the specifications for CSS2, they might not be well supported by many browsers. The *e > f* and *e + f* contextual selectors in particular should be used with caution.

Attribute Selectors

On occasion, you might also need to select elements based on their attribute values. For example, if you want to display link text in a blue font, you can use the following declaration:

```
a {color: blue}
```

However, this declaration makes no distinction between <a> tags used to mark links and <a> tags used to mark document anchors. HTML makes this distinction based on the presence or absence of the href attribute. To select an element based on the element's attributes you can create an **attribute selector**. For example, the selector

```
element[att] {styles}
```

selects all elements named *element* that contain an attribute named `att` and applies the `styles` in the list to them. So, to apply a blue font to link text, you use the declaration

```
a[href] {color: blue}
```

Any <a> tag used to mark anchors does not contain the href attribute and, therefore, is not affected by this style. Figure B-22 describes some of the other attribute selectors supported by CSS.

Selector	Description	Example	Interpretation
[att]	The element contains the *att* attribute	a[href]	Matches a elements containing the href attribute
[att="val"]	The element's *att* attribute equals "val"	a[href="gloss.htm"]	Matches a elements whose href attribute equals "gloss.htm"
[att~="val"]	The element's att attribute value is a space-separated list of words, one of which is exactly "val"	a[rel~="glossary"]	Matches a elements whose rel attribute contains the word "glossary"
[attl="val"]	The element's att attribute value is a hyphen-separated list of words, beginning with "val"	p[idl="first"]	Matches paragraphs whose id attribute starts with the word "first" in a hyphen-separated list of words
[att^="val"]	The element's *att* attribute begins with val (CSS3)	a[rel^="prev"]	Matches a elements whose rel attribute begins with "prev"
[att$="val"]	The element's *att* attribute ends with val (CSS3)	a[href$="org"]	Matches a elements whose href attribute ends with "org"
[att*="val"]	The element's *att* attribute contains the value val (CSS3)	a[href*="faq"]	Matches a elements whose href attribute contains the text string "faq"

As with contextual selectors, browser support for attribute selectors is mixed. For this reason, you should use attribute selectors with caution. Note that some of the attribute selectors listed in Figure B-22 are part of the proposed specifications for CSS3 and have very little browser support at the present time.

Applying Styles to IDs and Classes

CSS provides selectors to apply styles to elements based on their id and class values. To apply a style to an element based on the value of its id attribute, use the form

#id {styles}

where *id* is the id value of an element in the document. For example, if you want to center the text in the following h1 heading:

`<h1 id="company">Pixal Products</h1>`

you use the following style declaration in the embedded or external style sheet:

`#company {text-align: right}`

Recall that each id is unique and cannot be applied to more than one element. To identify a group of elements you use the class attribute. To apply a style to a group of elements based on the value of their class attribute, use the selector

.class {styles}

where *class* is the value of the class attribute for the group. Figure B-23 shows how applying a style based on class values can be used to apply the same style to a group of elements.

Figure B-23 ▶ **Applying a style to a class**

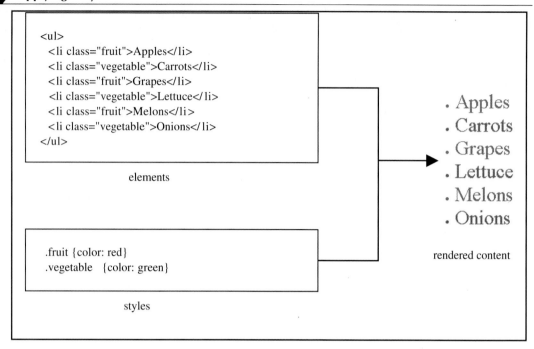

If you want to apply a style to a class of elements of a particular type, include the element name along with the class value using the form

```
element.class {styles}
```

where *element* and *class* are the element and class names, respectively. Figure B-24 demonstrates how to use the class value along with an element name to format the h1 and h2 headings described above. Note that the sans-serif font is applied to any element of the title class, but the italic font style is only applied to h2 headings in the title class.

Figure B-24 ▶ **Applying a style to a class and element**

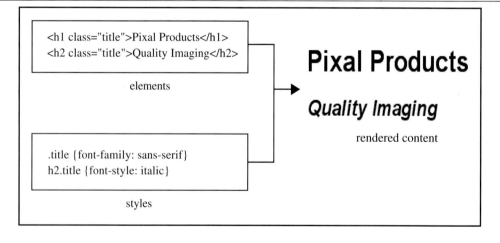

Applying Styles to ids and Classes

- To apply styles to an element with an id, use the form
    `#id {styles}`
  where `id` is the value of the id attribute for the element.
- To apply styles to a class of elements, use the form
    `class {styles}`
  where `class` is the value of the class attribute for the elements.
- To apply styles to a class of elements of a particular type, use the form
    `element.class {styles}`
  where `element` is the name of the element.

Applying Styles to Pseudo-Classes and Pseudo-Elements

Another selector form is based on pseudo-classes. A **pseudo-class** is a classification of an element based on its status, position, or current use in a document. For example, one pseudo-class indicates whether a user has previously visited a link. Another pseudo-class indicates whether the links is currently being activated or clicked. To create a style for a pseudo-class, use the style

`selector:pseudoclass {styles}`

where `selector` is an element or group of elements within the document, `pseudoclass` is the name of a pseudo-class, and `styles` are the styles you want to apply. Figure B-25 lists some of the pseudo-classes supported by CSS.

Pseudo-classes   Figure B-25

Pseudo-class	Description	Example
link	The link has not yet been visited by the user	a:link {color: red}
visited	The link has been visited by the user	a:visited {color: green}
active	The link is in the process of being activated by the user	a:active {color: yellow}
hover	The pointer is hovering over the link (CSS2)	a:hover {color: blue}
focus	The element has received the focus of the keyboard or pointer (CSS2)	input.focus {background-color: yellow}
first-child	The element is the first child of its parent (CSS2)	p:first-child {text-indent: 0}
lang	The language to be used with the element (CSS2)	q:lang(FR) {quotes: '«' '»'}

If you wanted to change the font color of all previously visited links to red, for example, you could use the style declaration

`a:visited {color: red}`

Pseudo-classes are often used to create rollover effects, in which effects are applied to elements when a user's pointer hovers over them. For example, the following styles remove the underlining from all links in a document *except* when a user hovers the pointer over a link, in which case an underline appears:

```
a {text-decoration: none}
a:hover {text-decoration: underline}
```

In some cases, two or more pseudo-classes can apply to the same element—for example, a link can be both previously visited and hovered over. In such situations, the standard cascading rules apply: the style that is more heavily weighted or declared last is applied to the element. Because of the cascading rules, order is important. The hover pseudo-class is used only if it is listed after the link and visited pseudo-classes. Similarly, the active pseudo-class should be listed last in preference to the link, visited, and hover pseudo-classes.

So far all of the selectors have been based on elements that exist somewhere in the document hierarchy. However, you can also define selectors that are not actual elements, but are instead abstracted from what you know of an element's content, use, or position. For example, a paragraph element is part of a document, but the first letter of that paragraph is not (there is no "first letter" element). You can work with this kind of abstracted element by treating it as a **pseudo-element**.

CSS supports a wide variety of pseudo-elements, including those that select the first letter or first line of an element's content. The syntax for creating a style declaration for a pseudo-element is similar to that for a pseudo-class:

```
selector:pseudoelement {styles}
```

where *selector* is an element or group of elements within a document, *pseudoelement* is an abstract element based on the selector, and *styles* are the styles that you want to apply to the pseudo-element. Figure B-26 lists some of the pseudo-elements supported by CSS.

Figure B-26 > **Pseudo-elements**

Pseudo-element	Description	Example
first-letter	The first letter of the element text	p:first-letter {font-size: 14pt}
first-line	The first line of the element text	p:first-line {text-transform: uppercase}
before	Content to be placed directly before the element (CSS2)	p:before {content: "Special!"}
after	Content to be placed directly after the element (CSS2)	p:after {content: "eof"}

For example, to display the first letter of every paragraph in a gold fantasy font, you use the declaration

```
p:first-letter {font-family: fantasy; color: gold}
```

You can use pseudo-elements to create drop-caps. To create a dropped cap, you increase the font size of an element's first letter and float it on the left margin. Dropped caps also generally look better if you decrease the line height of the first letter, enabling the surrounding content to better wrap around the letter.

Reference Window | Working with Pseudo-Classes and Pseudo-Elements

- To create a style for a pseudo-class, use the style
     `selector:pseudoclass {styles}`
  where `selector` is an element or group of elements within the document, `pseudoclass` is the name of a pseudo-class, and `styles` are the styles you want to apply to the selector. Some useful pseudo-classes are the link, visited, hover, and active pseudo-classes; these are applied to the a element to format linked, visited, hovered, and active hyperlinks.
- To create a style for a pseudo-element, use the style
  `selector:pseudoelement {styles}`
  where `selector` is an element or group of elements within the document, `pseudoelement` is the name of a pseudo-element, and `styles` are the styles you want to apply to the pseudo-element. Some useful pseudo-elements are the first-line and first-letter pseudo-elements, which represent the first line or first letter of an element's content.

Working with Different Media

By default, a style sheet is applied to all devices, and each device must determine how best to match the styles specified to its own requirements. For example, when you print a Web page, a Web browser and its built-in styles prepare the document for the printer. A user has some control over that process—for example, determining the size of the page margins or the content of the printout's header or footer.

You can use the media attribute in either the link or style element to define the output device for a specific style sheet. For example, to specify that an external style sheet named "sounds.css" should be used for aural browsers, you enter the following link element in your HTML or XHTML document:

```
<link href="sounds.css" type="text/css" media="aural" />
```

In the same way, you use the media attribute in an embedded style sheet to indicate that its styles are intended for aural devices:

```
<style type="text/css" media="aural">
...
</style>
```

The media attribute can also contain a comma-separated list of media types. The following link element links to a style sheet designed for both print and screen media:

```
<link href="output.css" type="text/css" media="print, screen" />
```

Style sheets cascade through different media types in the same way they cascade through a document tree. A style sheet in which the output device is not specified is applied to all devices, unless it is superseded by a style designed for a particular device. In the following set of embedded style sheets, h1 headings are displayed in a sans-serif font for all devices; however, text color is red for computer screens and black for printed pages:

```
<style type="text/css">
   h1 {font-family: sans-serif}
</style>
<style type="text/css" media="screen">
   h1 {color: red}
</style>
<style type="text/css" media="print">
   h1 {color: black}
</style>
```

The @media Rule

You can also specify the output media within a style sheet using the rule

```
@media type {style declarations}
```

where *type* is one of the supported media types and *style declarations* are the styles associated with that media type. For example, the following declarations set the font size of body text and h1 headings for a variety of different output media:

```
@media screen {body {font-size: 1em} h1 {font-size: 2em}}
@media print {body {font-size: 12pt} h1 {font-size: 16pt}}
@media handheld {body {font-size: 8pt} h1 {font-size: 12pt}}
@media tv {body {font-size: 16pt} h1 {font-size: 24pt}}
```

In this style sheet, the font size is smallest for a handheld device (which presumably has a limited screen area), and largest for a television (which is usually viewed from a greater distance). Similar to the media attribute, the @media rule also allows you to place media types in a comma-separated list:

```
@media screen, print, handheld, tv {h1 {font-family: sans-serif}}
```

Both the media attribute and the @media rule come with their own benefits and disadvantages. The @media rule allows you to consolidate all of your styles within a single style sheet; however, this consolidation can result in larger and more complicated files. The alternative, placing media styles in different sheets, can make those sheets easier to maintain; however, if you change the design of your site, you might have to duplicate your changes across several style sheets.

Reference Window | Creating Styles for Different Media

- To create a style sheet for a specific media, add the following attribute to either the link element or the style element
    media="*type*"
  where *type* is one or more of the following: aural, braille, embossed, handheld, print, projection, screen, tty, tv, or all. If you don't specify a value for the media attribute, the style sheet is applied to all media. Multiple types should be entered in a comma-separated list.
- To create style declarations for a specific media within a style sheet, use the following form:
    @media *type* {*style declarations*}

Supporting Older Browsers

Many older browsers do not support the media attribute, the @media rule, or many CSS2 styles. For these older browsers, the most common practice for formatting output for different media is to link each page to a **printer-friendly version** of the document, which is formatted specifically for printing. Although this approach comes with the drawback of forcing you to create and maintain duplicate copies of your pages, it provides users a choice of printed styles. They can print from the page as it appears on the computer screen or use the specially formatted print style that you design.

Media Groups

Despite the differences among various types of output media, they do share some common properties. The computer screen and the printed page are both visual media. A sound recording is not visual but aural. Output sent to a television might be both visual and aural. CSS2 organizes these different basic properties into **media groups**. There are four media groups that describe a basic facet of the output. The output media can be:

- Continuous or paged
- Visual, aural, or tactile
- Grid (for character grid devices) or bitmap
- Interactive (for devices that allow user interaction) or static (for devices that allow no interaction)

Figure B-27 shows how each output media is categorized based on the four media groups. A printout is paged (because the output comes in discrete units or pages), visual, bitmap, and static (you can't interact with it). A computer screen is continuous, visual, bitmap, and can be either static or interactive.

Media Types	Media Groups			
	continuous/ paged	**visual/aural/ tactile**	**grid/ bitmap**	**interactive/ static**
aural	continuous	aural	N/A	both
braille	continuous	tactile	grid	both
embossed	paged	tactile	grid	both
handheld	both	visual	both	both
print	paged	visual	bitmap	static
projection	paged	visual	bitmap	static
screen	continuous	visual	bitmap	both
tty	continuous	visual	grid	both
tv	both	visual, aural	bitmap	both

Media groups are important because the CSS2 specifications indicate which media group a particular style belongs to rather than the specific media device. For example, the font-size style belongs to the visual media group, meaning that you should be able to use it with handheld, print, projection, screen, tty, and tv media. The pitch style, used to define the pitch or frequency of a speaking voice, belongs to the aural media group, which means that it should be supported by aural and tv devices. Studying the media groups can help you choose the styles that apply to a given output device.

Using Print Styles

CSS2 defines printed pages by extending the box model described earlier to incorporate the entire page in a **page box**. As with other objects in the box model, you can specify the size of a page, the page margins, the internal padding, and so on. Although a page box specifies how a document should be rendered within the rectangular area of the page, it is the browser's responsibility to transfer that model to the printed sheet. The general rule to create and define a page box is

```
@page {styles}
```

where `styles` are the styles you want applied to the page. For example, the following embedded style sets the page margin for the printed output to 5 inches and displays the page's body text in a 12pt serif font:

```
<style type="text/css" media="print">
   @page {margin: 5in}
   body {font-size: 12pt; font-family: serif}
</style>
```

A page box does not support all of the measurement units you've used with the other elements. For example, pages do not support the em or ex measurement units.

Page Pseudo-Classes and Named Pages

In some cases you might need to define multiple page styles within the same document. You can do this through pseudo-classes or page names. The syntax to apply a pseudo-class to a page is

```
@page:pseudoclass {styles}
```

where *pseudoclass* is one of the three following supported types:

- **first:** for the first page of the printout
- **left:** for pages that appear on the left in double-sided printouts
- **right:** for pages that appear on the right in double-sided printouts

For example, if you are doing two-sided printing, you might want to mirror the margins of the left and right pages of the printout. The following styles result in pages in which the inner margin is set to 5 centimeters and outer margin is set to 2 centimeters:

```
@page:left {margin: 3cm 5cm 3cm 2cm}
@page:right {margin: 3cm 2cm 3cm 5cm}
```

To format specific pages other than the first, left, or right pages, you can create a named label for a page style and then apply that page to particular elements in your document. The syntax to create a page name is

```
@page name {styles}
```

where *name* is the label assigned to the page style. To access a named page, use the page style in a style declaration as follows:

```
selector {page: name}
```

For example, the following styles define a page named "large_margins" and then indicate that this page should be used for every instance of a table in a document:

```
@page large_margins {margin: 10cm}
table {page: large_margins}
```

Note that named pages can be applied only to block-level elements, meaning that you cannot apply them to inline elements. Also, if two consecutive block-level elements are assigned different page names, browsers automatically insert a page break between the elements.

Setting the Page Size

The size of the output page can be defined using the size style. With this style, Web authors can define the dimensions of the printed page, as well as whether pages should be printed in portrait or landscape orientation. The syntax of the size style is

```
size: width height orientation
```

where *width* and *height* are the width and height of the page, and *orientation* is the orientation of the page (portrait or landscape). If you don't specify the orientation, browsers assume a portrait orientation. To format a page as a standard-size page in landscape orientation with a 1-inch margin, you could use the following style:

```
@page {size: 8.5in 11in landscape; margin: 1in}
```

If you remove the orientation value, as in the style

```
@page {size: 8.5in 11in; margin: 1in}
```

browsers default to an orientation setting of portrait. You can also replace the width, height, and orientation values with the keyword "auto" (to let the browser determine the page dimensions and orientation) or "inherit" (to inherit the page size and orientation from the parent element). If a page does not fit into the dimensions specified by the style, browsers either rotate the page box 90 degrees or scale the page box to fit the sheet size.

Displaying Crop Marks

In high-quality printing, crop marks are used to define where a page should be trimmed before binding. CSS2 supports the marks property, which adds crop marks to a printed sheet. The syntax of the marks style is

```
marks: type
```

where *type* is crop, cross, inherit, or none. Figure B-28 shows examples of the crop and cross values.

Displaying crop marks **Figure B-28**

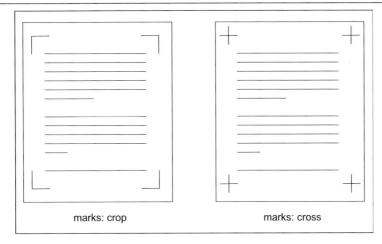

marks: crop   marks: cross

The size, style, and position of the crop marks depend on the browser.

Working with Page Breaks

CSS supports three styles that determine where page breaks should be placed in relation to the elements in a page. The page-break-before and page-break-after styles are used to place page breaks before or after a given element. The syntax of the page-break-before and page-break-after styles is

```
page-break-before: type
page-break-after: type
```

where *type* is always (to always place a page break), avoid (to never place a page break), left (to force a page break where the succeeding page is a left page), right (to force a page break where the succeeding page is a right page), auto (to allow the browser to determine whether or not to insert a page break), or inherit (to inherit the page break style of the parent element). For example, if you want tables to always appear on their own pages, you can place a page break before and after each table using the following style:

```
table {page-break-before: always; page-break-after: always}
```

You can also prevent the insertion of a page break using the page-break-inside style with the syntax

```
page-break-inside: type
```

where *type* is auto, inherit, or avoid. If you want to avoid placing a page break inside a table, you use the following style:

```
table {page-break-inside: avoid}
```

Note that the avoid type does not guarantee that there will not be a page break within the element. If the content of an element exceeds the dimensions of the sheet, the browser might be forced to insert a page break.

You can combine the various page styles to provide greater control over printed output. For example, if your document contains several wide tables, you can place the tables on separate pages in landscape orientation using the following style declarations:

```
@page table_page {8.5in 11in landscape}
table {page: table_page; page-break-before: always; page-break-inside:
    avoid; page-break-after: always}
```

Finally, you can use CSS2 to control the sizes of the widows and orphans that appear when a page break is inserted within an element. A **widow** refers to the final few lines of an element's text when they appear at the top of a page, while most of the element's text appears on the previous page. The term **orphan** describes the first few lines of an element's text when they appear at the bottom of a page, with the bulk of the element's text appearing on the next page. The styles to control widows and orphans are

```
widow: value
orphan: value
```

where *value* is the number of lines that must appear within the element before a page break is inserted. The default value is 2, which means that widows and orphans must both contain at least two lines of text. If you wanted to increase the size of widows and orphans to three lines for the paragraphs of your document, you use the following style declaration:

```
p {widow: 3; orphan: 3}
```

It's important to note that browsers might not always implement the widow and orphan values that you specify. Browsers attempt to use page breaks that obey the following guidelines:

- Insert all of the manual page breaks as indicated by the page-break-before, page-break-after, and page-break-inside styles.
- Avoid inserting page breaks where indicated in the style sheet.
- Break the pages as few times as possible.
- Make all pages that don't have a forced page break appear to have the same height.
- Avoid page breaking inside of a block-level element that has a border.
- Avoid breaking inside a table.
- Avoid breaking inside a floating element.

Only after attempting to satisfy these constraints are the recommendations of the widow and orphan styles applied.

Working with Print Styles | Reference Window

- To define a page box for a printout that indicates the page size, margins, and orientation, use the declaration

      @page {styles}

  where *styles* are the styles you want used to define the page.
- To apply a style to a particular page, use the declaration

      @page:pseudoclass {styles}

  where *pseudoclass* is first (for the first page), left (for pages that appear on the left), or right (for pages that appear on the right).
- To set the page size and orientation use the style

      size: width height orientation

  where *width* and *height* are the width and height of the page, and *orientation* is the orientation of the page (portrait or landscape).
- To display crop marks, use the style

      marks: type

  where *type* is crop, cross, inherit, or none.
- To format the page break before an element, use the style

      page-break-before: type

  where *type* is always (to always place a page break), avoid (to never place a page break), left (to force a page break where the succeeding page is a left page), right (to force a page break where the succeeding page is a right page), auto (to allow the browser to determine whether or not to insert a page break), or inherit (to inherit the page break style of the parent element).
- To format the page break after an element, use the style

      page-break-after: type

  where *type* has the same values as for the page-break-before style.
- To apply a page break inside an element, use the style

      page-break-inside: type

  where *type* is auto, inherit, or avoid.

Review | **Appendix Summary**

In this appendix, you learned about the history and syntax of Cascading Style Sheets. You saw how to apply style sheets to a Web page using inline styles, embedded styles, and external style sheets. You also saw how style definitions are inherited and cascade through the contents of a given document, as well as all of the documents in a Web site. This appendix also covered the different styles supported by CSS. You learned about the different styles that apply to fonts, text, colors, and images. You also learned how to create styles to resize elements, apply borders, and set the margin and padding size. The appendix also discussed how to use CSS to position elements on a page. In the later part of the appendix, you learned about different selector forms and how to apply styles to elements based on their uses in documents, their id values, and their class values. The appendix also covered how to work with pseudo-classes and pseudo-elements to create effects such as rollovers and dropped caps. The appendix concluded with a discussion of style sheets designed for different media output, as well as specific styles designed for printed output.

Key Terms

absolute position	ex unit	pseudo-element
absolute unit	external style	relative position
attribute selector	fixed position	relative unit
box model	generic font	scalable
Cascading Style Sheets	inline style	selector
contextual selector	kerning	specific font
CSS	leading	static position
CSS1	media group	style inheritance
CSS2	orphan	style sheet
CSS2.1	page box	tracking
CSS3	pixel	watermark
em unit	printer-friendly version	widow
embedded style	pseudo-class	

Review Questions | Review

1. What is a style sheet?
2. What is CSS?
3. What are the three ways of applying a style sheet to a document?
4. What is the syntax for applying an inline style?
5. What inline style would you add to an h1 heading to change the color of the text "Pixal Products" to blue?
6. What is the syntax for creating an embedded style sheet?
7. What is the syntax of a style declaration within an embedded or external style sheet?
8. What code would you enter to create an embedded style sheet that sets the color of all h1 headings to blue?
9. What attribute would you add to the style element to indicate that a style sheet is designed for printed media?
10. What code would you enter to create a link to the external style sheet file "styles.css"? Assume that the style sheet is designed for printed media.
11. What code would you add to a style sheet to insert the comment "printed styles"?
12. What style would you enter to apply the fonts Arial, Helvetica, or sans-serif to every h3 heading in the document?
13. What are absolute units and relative units?
14. What style would you enter to increase a font size 50% from its default size?
15. What are kerning, tracking, and leading? What are the styles to set the kerning, tracking and leading values for an element?
16. What style would you use to display text in italics?
17. What single style would you enter to display text in a bold 12pt Arial font?
18. What style declaration would you enter to change the background color of a page to the color value (212, 255, 155)?
19. What style declaration would you enter to change the background image to the image file paper.jpg?
20. What style declaration would you enter to set the width and height of the element with the id "logo" to 250 pixels wide by 100 pixels high?
21. What style declaration would you enter to add a 10 pixel blue border around the logo element, displayed in the outset border style?
22. What are absolute and relative positioning?
23. What style do you enter to float an element on a page's left margin?
24. What two styles can you enter to prevent a browser from displaying an object?
25. What selector would you enter to match all bold elements placed within address elements?
26. What selector would you use to match all elements belonging to the class "links"?
27. What is a pseudo-class? Give two examples of a pseudo-class.
28. What is a pseudo-element? Give two examples of a pseudo-element.
29. What style would you enter to define a page box with a 5-inch margin?
30. What style declaration would you enter to set the margins of the right page in a double-sided printout to 3 inches?
31. What style declaration would you enter to insert a page break before every h1 heading?

HTML and XHTML Elements and Attributes

Appendix C

This appendix provides descriptions of the major elements and attributes of HTML and XHTML. The elements and attributes represent the specifications of the W3C; therefore, they might not all be supported by the major browsers. Also, in some cases, an element or attribute is not part of the W3C specifications, but instead is an extension offered by a particular browser. Where this is the case, the element or attribute is listed with the supporting browser indicated in parentheses. Likewise, many elements and attributes have been deprecated by the W3C. Deprecated elements and attributes are supported by most browsers, but their use is discouraged.

Where appropriate, the appendix lists the version number in which each element and attribute was introduced. For example, an HTML version number of 2.0 for the <base /> tag means that it is supported by HTML 2.0 *and above*. Version numbers for XHTML refer to the support under the XHTML strict DTD. An asterisk next to the XHTML version number means that the element or attribute is supported under the XHTML transitional or frameset DTD, but not the strict DTD.

The following data types are used throughout this appendix:

- *char*   A single text character
- *char code*   A character encoding
- *color*   An HTML color name or hexadecimal color value
- *date*   A date and time in the format: *yyyy-mm-ddThh: mm:ssTIMEZONE*
- *integer*   An integer value
- *mime-type*   A MIME data type, such as "text/css", "audio/wav", or "video/x-msvideo"
- *mime-type list*   A comma-separated list of mime-types
- **option1**|option2| ... The value is limited to the specified list of *options*; a default value, if it exists, is displayed in **bold**
- *script*   A script or a reference to a script
- *styles*   A list of style declarations
- *text*   A text string
- *text list*   A comma-separated list of text strings
- *url*   The URL for a Web page or file
- *value*   A numeric value
- *value list*   A comma-separated list of numeric values

Starting Data Files

There are no starting Data Files needed for this appendix.

General Attributes

Several attributes are common to many page elements. Rather than repeating this information each time it occurs, the following tables summarize these attributes.

Core Attributes

The following four attributes, which are laid out in the specifications for HTML and XHTML, apply to all page elements and are supported by most browser versions.

Attribute	Description	HTML	XHTML
class="*text*"	Specifies the class or group to which an element belongs	4.0	1.0
id="*text*"	Specifies a unique identifier to be associated with the element	4.0	1.0
style="*styles*"	Defines an inline style for the element	4.0	1.0
title="*text*"	Provides an advisory title for the element	2.0	1.0

Language Attributes

The Web is designed to be universal and has to be adaptable to languages other than English. So, another set of attributes provides language support. This set of attributes is not as widely supported by browsers as the core attributes are. As with the core attributes, they can be applied to most page elements.

Attribute	Description	HTML	XHTML
dir="**ltr**|rtl"	Indicates the text direction as related to the lang attribute; a value of ltr displays text from left to right; a value of rtl displays text from right to left	4.0	1.0
lang="*text*"	Identifies the language used in the page content	4.0	1.0

Form Attributes

The following attributes can be applied to most form elements or to a Web form itself, but not to other page elements.

Attribute	Description	HTML	XHTML
accesskey="*char*"	Indicates the keyboard character that can be pressed along with the accelerator key to access a form element	4.0	1.0
disabled="disabled"	Disables a form field for input	4.0	1.0
tabindex="*integer*"	Specifies a form element's position in a document's tabbing order	4.0	1.0

Internet Explorer Attributes

Internet Explorer supports a collection of attributes that can be applied to almost all page elements. Other browsers do not support these attributes or support them only for a more limited collection of elements.

Attribute	Description
accesskey="*char*"	Indicates the keyboard character that can be pressed along with the accelerator key to access the page element
contenteditable="true|false|**inherit**"	Specifies whether the element's content can be modified online by the user
disabled="disabled"	Disables the page element for input
hidefocus="true|**false**"	Controls whether the element provides a visual indication of whether the element is in focus
tabindex="*integer*"	Specifies the position of the page element in the tabbing order of the document
unselectable="on|**off**"	Specifies whether the element can be selected by the user

Event Attributes

To make Web pages more dynamic, HTML and XHTML support event attributes that identify scripts to be run in response to an event occurring within an element. For example, clicking a main heading with a mouse can cause a browser to run a program that hides or expands a table of contents. Each event attribute has the form

```
event = "script"
```

where *event* is the name of the event attribute and *script* is the name of the script or command to be run by the browser in response to the occurrence of the event within the element.

Core Events

The general event attributes are part of the specifications for HTML and XHTML. They apply to almost all page elements.

Attribute	Description	HTML	XHTML
onclick	The mouse button is clicked.	4.0	1.0
ondblclick	The mouse button is double-clicked.	4.0	1.0
onkeydown	A key is pressed down.	4.0	1.0
onkeypress	A key is initially pressed.	4.0	1.0
onkeyup	A key is released.	4.0	1.0
onmousedown	The mouse button is pressed down.	4.0	1.0
onmousemove	The mouse pointer is moved within the element's boundaries.	4.0	1.0
onmouseout	The mouse pointer is moved out of the element's boundaries.	4.0	1.0
onmouseover	The mouse pointer hovers over the element.	4.0	1.0
onmouseup	The mouse button is released.	4.0	1.0

Document Events

The following list of event attributes applies not to individual elements within the page, but to the entire document as it is displayed within the browser window or frame.

Attribute	Description	HTML	XHTML
onafterprint	The document has finished printing (IE only).		
onbeforeprint	The document is about to be printed (IE only).		
onload	The page is finished being loaded.	4.0	1.0
onunload	The page is finished unloading.	4.0	1.0

Form Events

The following list of event attributes applies either to the entire Web form or fields within the form.

Attribute	Description	HTML	XHTML
onblur	The form field has lost the focus.	4.0	1.0
onchange	The value of the form field has been changed.	4.0	1.0
onfocus	The form field has received the focus.	4.0	1.0
onreset	The form has been reset.	4.0	1.0
onselect	Text content has been selected in the form field.	4.0	1.0
onsubmit	The form has been submitted for processing.	4.0	1.0

Internet Explorer Data Events

The following list of event attributes applies to elements within the Web page capable of data binding. Note that these events are supported only by the Internet Explorer browser.

Attribute	Description
oncellchange	Data has changed in the data source.
ondataavailable	Data has arrived from the data source.
ondatasetchange	The data in the data source has changed.
ondatasetcomplete	All data from the data source has been loaded.
onrowenter	The current row in the data source has changed.
onrowexit	The current row is about to be changed in the data source.
onrowsdelete	Rows have been deleted from the data source.
onrowsinserted	Rows have been inserted into the data source.

Internet Explorer Events

The Internet Explorer browser supports a wide collection of customized event attributes. Unless otherwise noted, these event attributes can be applied to any page element and are not supported by other browsers or included in the HTML or XHTML specifications.

Attribute	Description
onactive	The element is set to an active state.
onafterupdate	Data has been transferred from the element to a data source.
onbeforeactivate	The element is about to be set to an active state.
onbeforecopy	A selection from the element is about to be copied to the Clipboard.
onbeforecut	A selection from the element is about to be cut to the Clipboard.
onbeforedeactivate	The element is about to be deactivated.
onbeforeeditfocus	The element is about to become active.
onbeforepaste	Data from the Clipboard is about to be pasted into the element.
onbeforeunload	The page is about to be unloaded.
onbeforeupdate	The element's data is about to be updated.
onblur	The element has lost the focus.
oncontextmenu	The right mouse button is activated.
oncontrolselect	Selection using a modifier key (Ctrl for Windows, Command for Macintosh) has begun within the element.
oncopy	Data from the element has been copied to the Clipboard.
oncut	Data from the element has been cut to the Clipboard.
ondrag	The element is being dragged.
ondragdrop	The element has been dropped into the window or frame.
ondragend	The element is no longer being dragged.
ondragenter	The dragged element has entered a target area.
ondragleave	The dragged element has left a target area.
ondragover	The dragged element is over a target area.
ondragstart	The element has begun to be dragged.
ondrop	The dragged element has been dropped.
onerrorupdate	The data transfer to the element has been cancelled.
onfocus	The element has received the focus.
onfocusin	The element is about to receive the focus.
onfocusout	The form element has just lost the focus.
onhelp	The user has selected online help from the browser.
oninput	Text has just been entered into the form field.
onlosecapture	The element has been captured by the mouse selection.
onmouseenter	The mouse pointer enters the element's boundaries.
onmouseleave	The mouse pointer leaves the element's boundaries.
onmousewheel	The mouse wheel is moved.
onmove	The browser window or element has been moved by the user.
onmoveend	Movement of the element has ended.
onmovestart	The element has begun to move.
onpaste	Data has been pasted from the Clipboard into the element.

Attribute	Description
onpropertychange	One or more of the element's properties has changed.
onreadystatechange	The element has changed its ready state.
onresize	The browser window or element has been resized by the user.
onscroll	The scroll bar position within the element has been changed (also supported by other browsers).
onselectstart	Selection has begun within the element.
onstop	The page is finished loading.

HTML and XHTML Elements and Attributes

The following table contains an alphabetic listing of the elements and attributes supported by HTML, XHTML, and the major browsers. Some attributes are not listed in this table, but are described instead in the general attributes tables presented in the previous section of this appendix.

Element/Attribute	Description	HTML	XHTML
`<!-- text -->`	Inserts a comment into the document (comments are not displayed in therendered page)	2.0	1.0
`<!doctype>`	Specifies the Document Type Definition for a document	2.0	1.0
`<a> </a>`	Marks the beginning and end of a link	2.0	1.0
`accesskey="char"`	Indicates the keyboard character that can be pressed along with the accelerator key to activate the link	4.0	1.0
`charset="text"`	Specifies the character encoding of the linked document	4.0	1.0
`coords="value list"`	Specifies the coordinates of a hotspot in a client-side image map; the value list depends on the shape of the hotspot: shape="rect" "left, right, top, bottom"shape="circle" "x_center, y_center, radius"shape="poly" "x1, y1, x2, y2, x3, y3, ..."	4.0	1.0
`href="url"`	Specifies the URL of the link	3.2	1.0
`hreflang="text"`	Specifies the language of the linked document	4.0	1.0
`name="text"`	Specifies a name for the enclosed text, allowing it to be a link target	2.0	1.0
`rel="text"`	Specifies the relationship between the current page and the link specified by the href attribute	2.0	1.0
`rev="text"`	Specifies the reverse relationship between the current page and the linkspecified by the href attribute	2.0	1.0
`shape="rect|circle|polygon"`	Specifies the shape of the hotspot	4.0	1.0
`title="text"`	Specifies the pop-up text for the link	2.0	1.0
`target="text"`	Specifies the target window or frame for the link	4.0	1.0
`type="mime-type"`	Specifies the data type of the linked document	4.0	1.0
`<abbr> </abbr>`	Marks abbreviated text	4.0	1.0
`<acronym> </acronym>`	Marks acronym text	3.0	1.0
`<address> </address>`	Marks address text	2.0	1.0

Element/Attribute	Description	HTML	XHTML
`<applet> </applet>`	Embeds an applet into the browser (deprecated)	3.2	1.0*

`align="absmiddle|`
`absbottom|baseline|`
`bottom|center`
`|left|middle`
`|right|texttop`
`|top"`
	Specifies the alignment of the applet with the surrounding text	3.2	1.0*

`alt="text"`	Specifies alternate text for the applet (deprecated)	3.2	1.0*
`archive="url"`	Specifies the URL of an archive containing classes and other resources to be used with the applet (deprecated)	4.0	1.0*
`code="url"`	Specifies the URL of the applet's code/class (deprecated)	3.2	1.0*
`codebase="url"`	Specifies the URL of all class files for the applet (deprecated)	3.2	1.0*
`datafld="text"`	Specifies the data source that supplies bound data for use with the applet	4.0	
`datasrc="text"`	Specifies the ID or URL of the applet's data source	4.0	
`height="integer"`	Specifies the height of the applet in pixels	3.2	1.0*
`hspace="integer"`	Specifies the horizontal space around the applet in pixels (deprecated)	3.2	1.0*
`mayscript="mayscript"`	Permits access to the applet by programs embedded in the document		
`name="text"`	Specifies the name assigned to the applet (deprecated)	3.2	1.0*
`object="text"`	Specifies the name of the resource that contains a serialized representation of the applet (deprecated)	4.0	1.0*
`src="url"`	Specifies an external URL reference to the applet		
`vspace="integer"`	Specifies the vertical space around the applet in pixels (deprecated)	3.2	1.0*
`width="integer"`	Specifies the width of the applet in pixels (deprecated)	3.2	1.0*
`<area />`	Marks an image map hotspot	3.2	1.0
`alt="text"`	Specifies alternate text for the hotspot	3.2	1.0
`coords="value list"`	Specifies the coordinates of the hotspot; the value list depends on the shape of the hotspot: shape="rect" *"left, right, top, bottom"* shape="circle" *"x_center, y_center, radius"* shape="poly" *"x1, y1, x2, y2, x3, y3, ..."*	3.2	1.0
`href="url"`	Specifies the URL of the document to which the hotspot points	3.2	1.0
`nohref="nohref"`	Specifies that the hotspot does not point to a link	3.2	1.0
`shape="rect|circle|` `polygon"`	Specifies the shape of the hotspot	3.2	1.0
`target="text"`	Specifies the target window or frame for the link	3.2	1.0*
`<b> </b>`	Marks text as bold	2.0	1.0
`<base />`	Specifies global reference information for the document	2.0	1.0
`href="url"`	Specifies the URL from which all relative links in the document are based	2.0	1.0
`target="text"`	Specifies the target window or frame for links in the document	2.0	1.0*
`<basefont />`	Specifies the font setting for the document text (deprecated)	3.2	1.0*
`color="color"`	Specifies the text color (deprecated)	3.2	1.0*
`face="text list"`	Specifies a list of fonts to be applied to the text (deprecated)	3.2	1.0*
`size="integer"`	Specifies the size of the font range from 1 (smallest) to 7 (largest) (deprecated)	3.2	1.0*

Element/Attribute	Description	HTML	XHTML
`<bdo> </bdo>`	Indicates that the enclosed text should be rendered with the direction specified by the dir attribute	4.0	1.0
`<bgsound />`	Plays a background sound clip when the page is opened (IE and Opera only)		
`balance="integer"`	Specifies the balance of the volume between the left and right speakers where balance ranges from -10,000 to 10,000 (IE and Opera only)		
`loop="integer|` `infinite"`	Specifies the number of times the clip will be played (a positive integeror infinite) (IE and Opera only)		
`src="url"`	Specifies the URL of the sound clip file (IE and Opera only)		
`volume="integer"`	Specifies the volume of the sound clip, where the volume ranges from -10,000 to 0 (IE and Opera only)		
`<big> </big>`	Increases the size of the enclosed text relative to the default font size	3.0	1.0
`<blink> </blink>`	Blinks the enclosed text on and off		
`<blockquote>` `</blockquote>`	Marks content as quoted from another source	2.0	1.0
`align="left|` `center|right"`	Specifies the horizontal alignment of the content		
`cite="url"`	Provides the source URL of the quoted content	4.0	1.0
`clear="none|left|` `right|all"`	Prevents content from rendering until the specified margin is clear	3.0*	
`<body> </body>`	Marks the page content to be rendered by the browser	2.0	1.0
`alink="color"`	Specifies the color of activated links in the document (deprecated)	3.2	1.0*
`background="url"`	Specifies the background image file used for the page (deprecated)	3.0	1.0*
`bgcolor="color"`	Specifies the background color of the page (deprecated)	3.2	1.0*
`bgproperties="fixed"`	Fixes the background image in the browser window (IE only)		
`bottommargin="integer"`	Specifies the size of the bottom margin in pixels (IE only)		
`leftmargin="integer"`	Specifies the size of the left margin in pixels		
`link="color"`	Specifies the color of unvisited links (deprecated)	3.2	1.0*
`marginheight="integer"`	Specifies the size of the margin above and below the page (Netscape 4 only)		
`marginwidth="integer"`	Specifies the size of the margin to the left and right of the page (Netscape 4 only)		
`nowrap="false|true"`	Specifies whether the content wraps using normal HTML line-wrapping conventions (IE only)		
`rightmargin="integer"`	Specifies the size of the right margin in pixels (IE only)		
`scroll="yes|no"`	Specifies whether to display a scroll bar (IE only)		
`text="color"`	Specifies the color of page text (deprecated)	3.2	1.0*
`topmargin="integer"`	Specifies the size of the top page margin in pixels (IE only)		
`vlink="color"`	Specifies the color of previously visited links (deprecated)	3.2	1.0*
` `	Inserts a line break into the page	2.0	1.0
`clear="none|left|` `right|all"`	Displays the line break only when the specified margin is clear (deprecated)	3.2	1.0*
`<button> </button>`	Creates a form button	4.0	1.0
`datafld="text"`	Specifies the column from a data source that supplies bound data for the button (IE only)		
`dataformatas="html|` `plaintext|text"`	Specifies the format of the data in the data source bound with the button (IE only)		

Element/Attribute	Description	HTML	XHTML
datasrc="url"	Specifies the URL or ID of the data source bound with the button (IE only)		
name="text"	Provides the name assigned to the form button	4.0	1.0
type="submit|reset|button"	Specifies the type of form button	4.0	1.0
value="text"	Provides the value associated with the form button	4.0	1.0
<caption> </caption>	Creates a table caption	3.0	1.0
align="bottom|center|left|right|top"	Specifies the alignment of the caption (deprecated)	3.0	1.0*
valign="top|bottom"	Specifies the vertical alignment of the caption		
	Centers content horizontally on the page (deprecated)	3.2	1.0*
<cite> </cite>	Marks citation text	2.0	1.0
<code> </code>	Marks text used for code samples	2.0	1.0
<col> </col>	Defines the settings for a column or group of columns	4.0	1.0
align="left|right|center"	Specifies the alignment of the content of the column(s)	4.0	1.0
bgcolor="color"	Specifies the background color of the column(s)		
char="char"	Specifies a character in the column used to align column values	4.0	1.0
charoff="integer"	Specifies the offset in pixels from the alignment character specified in the char attribute	4.0	1.0
span="integer"	Specifies the number of columns in the group	4.0	1.0
valign="top|middle|bottom|baseline"	Specifies the vertical alignment of the content in the column(s)	4.0	1.0
width="integer"	Specifies the width of the column(s) in pixels	4.0	1.0
<colgroup> </colgroup>	Creates a container for a group of columns	4.0	1.0
align="left|right center"	Specifies the alignment of the content of the column group	4.0	1.0
bgcolor="color"	Specifies the background color of the column group		
char="char"	Specifies a character in the column used to align column group values	4.0	1.0
charoff="integer"	Specifies the offset in pixels from the alignment character specified in the char attribute	4.0	1.0
span="integer"	Specifies the number of columns in the group	4.0	1.0
valign="top|middle|bottom|baseline"	Specifies the vertical alignment of the content in the column group	4.0	1.0
width="integer"	Specifies the width of the columns in the group in pixels	4.0	1.0
<dd> </dd>	Marks text as a definition within a definition list	2.0	1.0
<del> </del>	Marks text as deleted from the document	3.0	1.0
cite="url"	Provides the URL for the document that has additional information about the deleted text	3.0	1.0
datetime="date"	Specifies the date and time of the text deletion	3.0	1.0
<dfn> </dfn>	Marks the defining instance of a term	3.0	1.0
<dir> </dir>	Contains a directory listing (deprecated)	2.0	1.0*
compact="compact"	Permits use of compact rendering, if available (deprecated)	2.0	1.0*

Element/Attribute	Description	HTML	XHTML
`<div> </div>`	Creates a generic block-level element	3.0	1.0
`align="left|center right|justify"`	Specifies the horizontal alignment of the content (deprecated)	3.0	1.0*
`datafld="text"`	Indicates the column from a data source that supplies bound data for the block (IE only)		
`dataformatas="html |plaintext|text"`	Specifies the format of the data in the data source bound with the block (IE only)		
`datasrc="url"`	Provides the URL or ID of the data source bound with the block (IE only)		
`nowrap="nowrap"`	Specifies whether the content wraps using normal HTML line-wrapping conventions	3.0*	
`<dl> </dl>`	Encloses a definition list using the dd and dt elements	2.0	1.0
`compact="compact"`	Permits use of compact rendering, if available (deprecated)	2.0	1.0*
`<dt> </dt>`	Marks a definition term in a definition list	2.0	1.0
`nowrap="nowrap"`	Specifies whether the content wraps using normal HTML line-wrapping conventions		
`<em> </em>`	Marks emphasized text	2.0	1.0
`<embed> </embed>`	Places an embedded object into the page (not part of the W3C specifications, but supported by most major browsers)		
`align="bottom|left |right|top"`	Specifies the alignment of the object with the surrounding content		
`autostart="true |false"`	Starts the embedded object automatically when the page is loaded		
`height="integer"`	Specifies the height of the object in pixels		
`hidden="true|false"`	Hides the object on the page		
`hspace="integer"`	Specifies the horizontal space around the object in pixels		
`name="text"`	Provides the name of the embedded object		
`pluginspage="url"`	Provides the URL of the page containing information on the object		
`pluginurl="url"`	Provides the URL of the page for directly installing the object		
`src="url"`	Provides the location of the file containing the object		
`type="mime-type"`	Specifies the mime-type of the embedded object		
`units="text"`	Specifies the measurement units of the object		
`vspace="integer"`	Specifies the vertical space around the object in pixels		
`width="integer"`	Specifies the width of the object in pixels		
`<fieldset> </fieldset>`	Places form fields in a common group	4.0	1.0
`align="left|center |right"`	Specifies the alignment of the contents of the field set (IE only)		
`datafld="text"`	Indicates the column from a data source that supplies bound data for the field set (IE only)		
`dataformatas="html| plaintext|text"`	Specifies the format of the data in the data source bound with the field set (IE only)		
`datasrc="url"`	Provides the URL or ID of the data source bound with the field set (IE only)		
`<font> </font>`	Formats the enclosed text (deprecated)	3.2	1.0*
`color="color"`	Specifies the color of the enclosed text (deprecated)	3.2	1.0*
`face="text list"`	Specifies the font face(s) of the enclosed text (deprecated)	3.2	1.0*
`size="integer"`	Specifies the size of the enclosed text, with values ranging from 1 (smallest) to 7 (largest); a value of +integer increases the font size relative to the font size specified in the basefont element (deprecated)	3.2	1.0*

Element/Attribute	Description	HTML	XHTML
`<form> </form>`	Encloses the contents of a Web form	2.0	1.0
`accept="mime-type list"`	Lists mime-types that the server processing the form will handle	4.0	1.0
`accept-charset="char code"`	Specifies the character encoding that the server processing the form will handle	4.0	1.0
`action="url"`	Provides the URL to which the form values are to be sent	2.0	1.0
`autocomplete="on|off"`	Enables automatic insertion of information in fields in which the user has previously entered data (IE only)		
`enctype="mime-type"`	Specifies the mime-type of the data to be sent to the server for processing; the default is "application/x-www-form-urlencoded"	2.0	1.0
`method="get|post"`	Specifies the method of accessing the URL specified in the action attribute	2.0	1.0
`name="text"`	Specifies the name of the form	2.0	1.0
`target="text"`	Specifies the frame or window in which output from the form should appear	4.0	1.0
`<frame> </frame>`	Marks a single frame within a set of frames	4.0	1.0*
`border="integer"`	Specifies the thickness of the frame border in pixels (Netscape 4 only)		
`bordercolor="color"`	Specifies the color of the frame border		
`frameborder="1|0"`	Determines whether the frame border is visible (1) or invisible (0); Netscape also supports values of yes or no	4.0	1.0*
`longdesc="url"`	Provides the URL of a document containing a long description of the frame's contents	4.0	1.0*
`marginheight="integer"`	Specifies the space above and below the frame object and the frame's borders, in pixels	4.0	1.0*
`marginwidth="integer"`	Specifies the space to the left and right of the frame object and the frame's borders, in pixels	4.0	1.0*
`name="text"`	Specifies the name of the frame	4.0	1.0*
`noresize="noresize"`	Prevents users from resizing the frame	4.0	1.0*
`scrolling="auto|yes|no"`	Specifies whether the browser will display a scroll bar with the frame	4.0	1.0*
`src="url"`	Provides the URL of the document to be displayed in the frame	4.0	1.0*
`<frameset> </frameset>`	Creates a collection of frames	4.0	1.0*
`border="integer"`	Specifies the thickness of the frame borders in the frameset in pixels (not part of the W3C specifications, but supported by most browsers)		
`bordercolor="color"`	Specifies the color of the frame borders		
`cols="value list"`	Arranges the frames in columns with the width of each column expressed either in pixels, as a percentage, or using an asterisk (to allow the browser to choose the width)	4.0	1.0*
`frameborder="1|0"`	Determines whether frame borders are visible (1) or invisible (0); (not part of the W3C specifications, but supported by most browsers; Netscape also supports values of yes or no)		
`framespacing="integer"`	Specifies the amount of space between frames in pixels (IE only)		
`rows="value list"`	Arranges the frames in rows with the height of each column expressed either in pixels, as a percentage, or using an asterisk (to allow the browser to choose the height)	4.0	1.0*

Element/Attribute	Description	HTML	XHTML
`<hi> </hi>`	Marks the enclosed text as a heading, where i is an integer from 1 (the largest heading) to 6 (the smallest heading)	2.0	1.0
`align="left| center|right| justify"`	Specifies the alignment of the heading text (deprecated)	3.0	1.0*
`<head> </head>`	Encloses the document head, containing information about the document	2.0	1.0
`profile="url"`	Provides the location of metadata about the document	4.0	1.0
`<hr />`	Draws a horizontal line (rule) in the rendered page	2.0	1.0
`align="left|center |right"`	Specifies the horizontal alignment of the line (deprecated)	3.2	1.0*
`color="color"`	Specifies the color of the line		
`noshade="noshade"`	Removes 3-D shading from the line (deprecated)	3.2	1.0*
`size="integer"`	Specifies the height of the line in pixels or as a percentage of the enclosing element's height (deprecated)	3.2	1.0*
`width="integer"`	Specifies the width of the line in pixels or as a percentage of the enclosing element's width (deprecated)	3.2	1.0*
`<html> </html>`	Encloses the entire content of the HTML document	2.0	1.0
`version="text"`	Specifies the version of HTML being used	2.0	1.1
`xmlns="text"`	Specifies the namespace prefix for the document		1.0
`<i> </i>`	Displays the enclosed text in italics	2.0	1.0
`<iframe> </iframe>`	Creates an inline frame in the document	4.0	1.0*
`align="bottom|left |middle|top |right"`	Specifies the horizontal alignment of the frame with the surrounding content (deprecated)	4.0	1.0*
`datafld="text"`	Indicates the column from a data source that supplies bound data for the inline frame (IE only)		4.0
`dataformatas="html| plaintext|text"`	Specifies the format of the data in the data source bound with the inline frame (IE only)		4.0
`datasrc="url"`	Provides the URL or ID of the data source bound with the inline frame (IE only)		4.0
`frameborder="1|0"`	Specifies whether to display a frame border (1) or not (0)	4.0	1.0*
`height="integer"`	Specifies the height of the frame in pixels	4.0	1.0*
`hspace="integer"`	Specifies the space to the left and right of the frame in pixels	4.0	1.0*
`longdesc="url"`	Indicates the document containing a long description of the frame's content	4.0	1.0*
`marginheight= "integer"`	Specifies the space above and below the frame object and the frame's borders, in pixels	4.0	1.0*
`marginwidth="integer"`	Specifies the space to the left and right of the frame object and the frame's borders, in pixels	4.0	1.0*
`name="text"`	Specifies the name of the frame	4.0	1.0*
`scrolling="auto| yes|no"`	Determines whether the browser displays a scroll bar with the frame	4.0	1.0*
`src="url"`	Indicates the document displayed within the frame	4.0	1.0*
`vspace="integer"`	Specifies the space to the top and bottom of the frame in pixels	4.0	1.0*
`width="integer"`	Specifies the width of the frame in pixels	4.0	1.0*

Element/Attribute	Description	HTML	XHTML
`<ilayer> </ilayer>`	Creates an inline layer used to display the content of an external document (Netscape 4 only)		
`above="text"`	Specifies the name of the layer displayed above the current layer (IE only)		
`background="url"`	Provides the URL of the file containing the background image (IE only)		
`below="text"`	Specifies the name of the layer displayed below the current layer (IE only)		
`bgcolor="color"`	Specifies the layer's background color (IE only)		
`clip="top, left, bottom, right"`	Specifies the coordinates of the viewable region of the layer (IE only)		
`height="integer"`	Specifies the height of the layer in pixels (IE only)		
`left="integer"`	Specifies the horizontal offset of the layer in pixels (IE only)		
`pagex="integer"`	Specifies the horizontal position of the layer in pixels (IE only)		
`pagey="integer"`	Specifies the vertical position of the layer in pixels (IE only)		
`src="url"`	Provides the URL of the document displayed in the layer (IE only)		
`top="integer"`	Specifies the vertical offset of the layer in pixels (IE only)		
`visibility="hide| inherit|show"`	Specifies the visibility of the layer (IE only)		
`width="integer"`	Specifies the width of the layer in pixels (IE only)		
`z-index="integer"`	Specifies the stacking order of the layer (IE only)		
`<img> </img>`	Inserts an inline image into the document	2.0	1.0
`align="left|right| top|texttop| middle|absmiddle| baselines|bottom| absbottom"`	Specifies the alignment of the image with the surrounding content (deprecated)	2.0	1.0*
`alt="text"`	Specifies alternate text to be displayed in place of the image	2.0	1.0
`border="integer"`	Specifies the width of the image border (deprecated)	3.2	1.0*
`controls="control"`	For video images, displays a playback control below the image (IE only)		
`datafld="text"`	Names the column from a data source that supplies bound data for the image (IE only)		
`dataformatas="html| plaintext|text"`	Specifies the format of the data in the data source bound with the image (IE only)		
`datasrc="url"`	Provides the URL or ID of the data source bound with the image (IE only)		
`dynsrc="url"`	Provides the URL of a video or VRML file (IE and Opera only)		
`height="integer"`	Specifies the height of the image in pixels	3.0	1.0
`hspace="integer"`	Specifies the horizontal space around the image in pixels (deprecated)	3.0	1.0*
`ismap="ismap"`	Indicates that the image can be used as a server-side image map	2.0	1.0
`longdesc="url"`	Provides the URL of a document containing a long description of the image	4.0	1.0
`loop="integer"`	Specifies the number of times the video will play (IE and Opera only)		
`lowsrc="url"`	Provides the URL of the low-resolution version of the image (IE and Netscape only)		
`name="text"`	Specifies the image name	4.0	1.0*

Element/Attribute	Description	HTML	XHTML
src="url"	Specifies the image source file	2.0	1.0
start="fileopen|mouseover"	Indicates when to start the video clip (either when the file is opened or when the mouse hovers over the image) (IE and Opera only)		
suppress="true|false"	Suppresses the display of the alternate text and the placeholder icon until the image file is located (Netscape 4 only)		
usemap="url"	Provides the location of a client-side image associated with the image (not well-supported when the URL points to an external file)	3.2	1.0
vspace="integer"	Specifies the vertical space around the image in pixels (deprecated)	3.2	1.0*
width="integer"	Specifies the width of the image in pixels	3.0	1.0
<input> </input>	Marks an input field in a Web form	2.0	1.0
align="left|right|top|texttop|middle|absmiddle|baseline|bottom|absbottom"	Specifies the alignment of the input field with the surrounding content (deprecated)	2.0	1.0*
alt="text"	Specifies alternate text for image buttons and image input fields	4.0	1.0
checked="checked"	Specifies that the input check box or input radio button is selected	2.0	1.0
datafld="text"	Indicates the column from a data source that supplies bound data for the input field	4.0	
dataformatas="html|plaintext|text"	Specifies the format of the data in the data source bound with the input field	4.0	
datasrc="url"	Provides the URL or ID of the data source bound with the input field	4.0	
height="integer"	Specifies the height of the image input field in pixels (not part of the W3C specifications, but supported by many browsers)		
hspace="integer"	Specifies the horizontal space around the image input field in pixels (not part of the W3C specifications, but supported by many browsers)		
ismap="ismap"	Enables the image input field to be used as a server-side image map	4.0	1.1
maxlength="integer"	Specifies the maximum number of characters that can be inserted into a text input field	2.0	1.0
name="text"	Specifies the name of the input field	2.0	1.0
readonly="readonly"	Prevents the value of the input field from being modified	2.0	1.0
size="integer"	Specifies the number of characters that can be displayed at one time in an input text field	2.0	1.0
src="url"	Indicates the source file of an input image field	2.0	1.0
type="button|checkbox|file|hidden|image|password|radio|reset|submit|text"	Specifies the type of input field	2.0	1.0
usemap="url"	Provides the location of a client-side image associated with the image input field (not well-supported when the URL points to an external file)	4.0	1.0
value="text"	Specifies the default value of the input field	2.0	1.0
vspace="integer"	Specifies the vertical space around the image input field in pixels (not part of the W3C specifications, but supported by many browsers)		
width="integer"	Specifies the width of an image input field in pixels (not part of the W3C specifications, but supported by many browsers)		

Element/Attribute	Description	HTML	XHTML
`<ins> </ins>`	Marks inserted text	3.0	1.0
`cite="url"`	Provides the URL for the document that has additional information about the inserted text	3.0	1.0
`datetime="date"`	Specifies the date and time of the text insertion	3.0	1.0
`<isindex />`	Inserts an input field into the document for search queries (deprecated)	2.0	1.0*
`action="url"`	Provides the URL of the script used to process the sindex data		1.0
`prompt="text"`	Specifies the text to be used for the input prompt (deprecated)	3.0	1.0*
`<kbd> </kbd>`	Marks keyboard-style text	2.0	1.0
`<label> </label>`	Associates the enclosed content with a form field	4.0	1.0
`datafld="text"`	Indicates the column from a data source that supplies bound data for the label (IE only)		
`dataformatas="html|` `plaintext|text"`	Specifies the format of the data in the data source bound with the label (IE only)		
`datasrc="url"`	Provides the URL or ID of the data source bound with the label (IE only)		
`for="text"`	Provides the ID of the field associated with the label	4.0	1.0
`<layer> </layer>`	Creates a layer used to display the content of external documents; unlike the ilayer element, layer elements are absolutely positioned in the page (Netscape 4 only)		
`above="text"`	Specifies the name of the layer displayed above the current layer (Netscape 4 only)		
`background="url"`	Provides the URL of the file containing the background image (Netscape 4 only)		
`below="text"`	Specifies the name of the layer displayed below the current layer (Netscape 4 only)		
`bgcolor="color"`	Specifies the layer's background color (Netscape 4 only)		
`clip="top, left,` `bottom, right"`	Specifies the coordinates of the viewable region of the layer (Netscape 4 only)		
`height="integer"`	Specifies the height of the layer in pixels (Netscape 4 only)		
`left="integer"`	Specifies the horizontal offset of the layer in pixels (Netscape 4 only)		
`pagex="integer"`	Specifies the horizontal position of the layer in pixels (Netscape 4 only)		
`pagey="integer"`	Specifies the vertical position of the layer in pixels (Netscape 4 only)		
`src="url"`	Provides the URL of the document displayed in the layer (Netscape 4 only)		
`top="integer"`	Specifies the vertical offset of the layer in pixels (Netscape 4 only)		
`visibility="hide|` `inherit|show"`	Specifies the visibility of the layer (Netscape 4 only)		
`width="integer"`	Specifies the width of the layer in pixels (Netscape 4 only)		
`z-index="integer"`	Specifies the stacking order of the layer (Netscape 4 only)		
`<legend> </legend>`	Marks the enclosed text as a caption for a field set	4.0	1.0
`align="bottom|left` `|top|right"`	Specifies the alignment of the legend with the field set; Internet Explorer also supports the center option (deprecated)	4.0	1.0*

Element/Attribute	Description	HTML	XHTML
`<li> </li>`	Marks an item in an ordered (ol), unordered (ul), menu (menu), or directory (dir) list	2.0	1.0
`type="A|a|I|i |1|disc|square |circle"`	Specifies the bullet type associated with the list item: a value of "1" is the default for ordered list; a value of "disc" is the default for unordered list (deprecated)	3.2	1.0*
`value="integer"`	Sets the value for the current list item in an ordered list; subsequent list items are numbered from that value (deprecated)	3.2	1.0*
`<link />`	Creates an element in the document head that establishes the relationship between the current document and external documents or objects	2.0	1.0
`charset="char code"`	Specifies the character encoding of the external document	4.0	1.0
`href="url"`	Provides the URL of the external document	2.0	1.0
`hreflang="text"`	Indicates the language of the external document	4.0	1.0
`media="all|aural| braille|handheld| print|projection| screen|tty|tv"`	Indicates the media in which the external document is presented	4.0	1.0
`name="text"`	Specifies the name of the link		
`rel="text"`	Specifies the relationship between the current page and the link specified by the href attribute	2.0	
`rev="text"`	Specifies the reverse relationship between the current page and the link specified by the href attribute	2.0	1.0
`target="text"`	Specifies the target window or frame for the link	4.0	1.0*
`title="text"`	Specifies the title of the external document	2.0	1.0
`type="mime-type"`	Specifies the mime-type of the external document	4.0	1.0
`<map> </map>`	Creates an element that contains client-side image map hotspots	3.2	1.0
`name="text"`	Specifies the name of the image map	3.2	1.0*
`<marquee> </marquee>`	Displays the enclosed text as a scrolling marquee (not part of the W3C specifications, but supported by most browsers)		
`behavior="alternate |scroll|slide"`	Specifies how the marquee should move		
`bgcolor="color"`	Specifies the background color of the marquee		
`datafld="text"`	Indicates the column from a data source that supplies bound data for the marquee		
`dataformatas="html| plaintext|text"`	Indicates the format of the data in the data source bound with the marquee		
`datasrc="url"`	Provides the URL or ID of the data source bound with the marquee		
`direction="down| left|right|up"`	Specifies the direction of the marquee		
`height="integer"`	Specifies the height of the marquee in pixels		
`hspace="integer"`	Specifies the horizontal space around the marquee in pixels		
`loop="integer| infinite"`	Specifies the number of times the marquee motion is repeated		
`scrollamount= "integer"`	Specifies the amount of space, in pixels, between successive draws of the marquee text		
`scrolldelay="integer"`	Specifies the amount of time, in milliseconds, between marquee actions		
`truespeed="truespeed"`	Indicates whether the scrolldelay value should be set to its exact value; otherwise any value less than 60 milliseconds is rounded up		

Element/Attribute	Description	HTML	XHTML
vspace="*integer*"	Specifies the vertical space around the marquee in pixels		
width="*integer*"	Specifies the width of the marquee in pixels		
<menu> </menu>	Contains a menu list (deprecated)	2.0	1.0*
compact="compact"	Reduces the space between menu items (deprecated)	2.0	1.0*
start="*integer*"	Specifies the starting value of the items in the menu list		
type="A|a|I|i |1|disc|square| circle|none"	Specifies the bullet type associated with the list items	3.2	1.0*
<meta> </meta>	Creates an element in the document's head section that contains information and special instructions for processing the document	2.0	1.0
content="*text*"	Provides information associated with the name or http-equiv attributes	2.0	1.0
http-equiv="*text*"	Provides instructions to the browser to request the server to perform different http operations	2.0	1.0
name="*text*"	Specifies the type of information specified in the content attribute	2.0	1.0
scheme="*text*"	Supplies additional information about the scheme used to interpret the content attribute	4.0	1.0
<nobr> </nobr>	Disables line wrapping for the enclosed content (not part of the W3C specifications, but supported by most browsers)		
<noembed> </noembed>	Encloses alternate content for browsers that do not support the embed element (not part of the W3C specifications, but supported by most browsers)		
<noframe> </noframe>	Encloses alternate content for browsers that do not support frames	4.0	1.0*
<nolayer> </nolayer>	Encloses alternate content for browsers that do not support the layer or ilayer elements (Netscape 4 only)		
<noscript> </noscript>	Encloses alternate content for browsers that do not support client-side scripts	4.0	1.0
<object> </object>	Places an embedded object (image, applet, sound clip, video clip, etc.) into the page	4.0	1.0
archive="*url*"	Specifies the URL of an archive containing classes and other resources preloaded for use with the object	4.0	1.0
align="absbottom| absmiddle|baseline |bottom|left| middle|right| texttop|top"	Aligns the object with the surrounding content (deprecated)	4.0	1.0*
border="*integer*"	Specifies the width of the border around the object (deprecated)	4.0	1.0*
classid="*url*"	Provides the URL of the object	4.0	1.0
codebase="*url*"	Specifies the base path used to resolve relative references within the embedded object	4.0	1.0
codetype="*mime-type*"	Indicates the mime-type of the embedded object's code	4.0	1.0
data="*url*"	Provides the URL of the object's data file	4.0	1.0
datafld="*text*"	Identifies the column from a data source that supplies bound data for the embedded object	4.0	
dataformatas="html| plaintext|text"	Specifies the format of the data in the data source bound with the embedded object	4.0	
datasrc="*url*"	Provides the URL or ID of the data source bound with the embedded object	4.0	

Element/Attribute	Description	HTML	XHTML
`declare="declare"`	Declares the object without embedding it on the page	4.0	1.0
`height="integer"`	Specifies the height of the object in pixels	4.0	1.0
`hspace="integer"`	Specifies the horizontal space around the image in pixels	4.0	1.0
`name="text"`	Specifies the name of the embedded object	4.0	1.0
`standby="text"`	Specifies the message displayed by the browser while loading the embedded object	4.0	1.0
`type="mime-type"`	Indicates the mime-type of the embedded object	4.0	1.0
`vspace="integer"`	Specifies the vertical space around the embedded object	4.0	1.0
`width="integer"`	Specifies the width of the object in pixels	4.0	1.0
`<ol> </ol>`	Contains an ordered list of items	2.0	1.0
`compact="compact"`	Reduces the space between ordered list items (deprecated)	2.0	1.0*
`start="integer"`	Specifies the starting value in the list (deprecated)	3.2	1.0
`type="A|a|I|i|1"`	Specifies the bullet type associated with the list items (deprecated)	3.2	1.0*
`<optgroup> </optgroup>`	Contains a group of option elements in a selection field	4.0	1.0
`label="text"`	Specifies the label for the option group	4.0	1.0
`<option> </option>`	Formats an option within a selection field	2.0	1.0
`label="text"`	Supplies the text label associated with the option	4.0	1.0
`selected="selected"`	Selects the option by default	2.0	1.0
`value="text"`	Specifies the value associated with the option	2.0	1.0
`<p> </p>`	Marks the enclosed content as a paragraph	2.0	1.0
`align="left|center |right|justify"`	Horizontally aligns the contents of the paragraph (deprecated)	3.0	1.0*
`<param> </param>`	Marks parameter values sent to an object element or an applet element	3.2	1.0
`name="text"`	Specifies the parameter name	3.2	1.0
`type="mime-type"`	Specifies the mime-type of the resource indicated by the value attribute	4.0	1.0
`value="text"`	Specifies the parameter value	3.2	1.0
`valuetype="data| ref|object"`	Specifies the data type of the value attribute	4.0	1.0
`<plaintext> </plaintext>`	Marks the enclosed text as plain text (not part of the W3C specifications, but supported by most browsers)		
`<pre> </pre>`	Marks the enclosed text as preformatted text, retaining white space from the document	2.0	1.0
`width="integer"`	Specifies the width of preformatted text, in number of characters (deprecated)	2.0	1.0*
`<q> </q>`	Marks the enclosed text as a quotation	3.0	1.0
`cite="url"`	Provides the source URL of the quoted content	4.0	1.0
`<s> </s>`	Marks the enclosed text as strikethrough text (deprecated)	3.0	1.0*
`<samp> </samp>`	Marks the enclosed text as a sequence of literal characters	2.0	1.0
`<script> </script>`	Encloses client-side scripts within the document; this element can be placed within the head or the body element or it can refer to an external script file	3.2	1.0
`charset="char code"`	Specifies the character encoding of the script	4.0	1.0
`defer="defer"`	Defers execution of the script	4.0	1.0
`event="text"`	Specifies the event that the script should be run in response to	4.0	

Element/Attribute	Description	HTML	XHTML
`for="text"`	Indicates the name or ID of the element to which the event attribute refers to	4.0	
`language="text"`	Specifies the language of the script (deprecated)	4.0	1.0*
`src="url"`	Provides the URL of an external script file	4.0	1.0
`type="mime-type"`	Specifies the mime-type of the script	4.0	1.0
`<select> </select>`	Creates a selection field (drop-down list box) in a Web form	2.0	1.0
`align="left|right| top|texttop| middle|absmiddle| baseline|bottom| absbottom"`	Specifies the alignment of the selection field with the surrounding content (deprecated)	3.0*	
`datafld="text"`	Identifies the column from a data source that supplies bound data for the selection field	4.0	
`dataformatas="html| plaintext|text"`	Specifies the format of the data in the data source bound with the selection field	4.0	
`datasrc="url"`	Provides the URL or ID of the data source bound with the selection field	4.0	
`multiple="multiple"`	Allows multiple sections from the field	2.0	1.0
`name="text"`	Specifies the selection field name	2.0	1.0
`size="integer"`	Specifies the number of visible items in the selection list	2.0	1.0
`<small> </small>`	Decreases the size of the enclosed text relative to the default font size	3.0	1.0
`<span> </span>`	Creates a generic inline element	3.0	1.0
`datafld="text"`	Identifies the column from a data source that supplies bound data for the inline element (IE only)		
`dataformatas="html| plaintext|text"`	Specifies the format of the data in the data source bound with the inline element (IE only)		
`datasrc="url"`	Provides the URL or ID of the data source bound with the inline element (IE only)		
`<strike> </strike>`	Marks the enclosed text as strikethrough text (deprecated)	3.0	1.0*
`<strong> </strong>`	Marks the enclosed text as strongly emphasized text	2.0	1.0
`<style> </style>`	Encloses global style declarations for the document	3.0	1.0
`media="all|aural| braille|handheld| print|projection| screen|tty|tv|"`	Indicates the media of the enclosed style definitions	4.0	1.0
`title="text"`	Specifies the style of the style definitions	4.0	1.0
`type="mime-type"`	Specifies the mime-type of the style definitions	4.0	1.0
`<sub> </sub>`	Marks the enclosed text as subscript text	3.0	1.0
`<sup> </sup>`	Marks the enclosed text as superscript text	3.0	1.0
`<table> </table>`	Encloses the contents of a Web table	3.0	1.0
`align="left|center |right"`	Aligns the table with the surrounding content (deprecated)	3.0	1.0*
`background="url"`	Provides the URL of the table's background image (not part of the W3C specifications, but supported by most browsers)		
`bgcolor="color"`	Specifies the background color of the table (deprecated)	4.0	1.0*
`border="integer"`	Specifies the width of the table border in pixels	3.0	1.0
`bordercolor="color"`	Specifies the table border color (IE and Netscape 4 only)		

Element/Attribute	Description	HTML	XHTML
bordercolordark= "color"	Specifies the color of the table border's shaded edge (IE only)		
bordercolorlight= "color"	Specifies the color of the table border's unshaded edge (IE only)		
cellpadding= "integer"	Specifies the space between the table data and the cell borders in pixels	3.2	1.0
cellspacing= "integer"	Specifies the space between table cells in pixels	3.2	1.0
cols="integer"	Specifies the number of columns in the table		
datafld="text"	Indicates the column from a data source that supplies bound data for the table	4.0	
dataformatas="html| plaintext|text"	Specifies the format of the data in the data source bound with the table	4.0	
datapagesize= "integer"	Sets the number of records displayed within the table	4.0	1.1
datasrc="url"	Provides the URL or ID of the data source bound with the table	4.0	
frame="above|below |**border**|box| hsides|lhs|rhs| void|vside"	Specifies the format of the borders around the table	4.0	1.0
height="integer"	Specifies the height of the table in pixels (not part of the W3C specifications, but supported by most browsers)		
hspace="integer"	Specifies the horizontal space around the table in pixels (not part of the W3C specifications, but supported by most browsers)		
rules="**all**|cols| groups|none|rows"	Specifies the format of the table's internal borders or gridlines	4.0	1.0
summary="text"	Supplies a text summary of the table's content	4.0	1.0
vspace="integer"	Specifies the vertical space around the table in pixels		
width="integer"	Specifies the width of the table in pixels	3.0	1.0
<tbody> </tbody>	Encloses the content of the Web table body	4.0	1.0
align="left|center |right|justify|char"	Specifies the alignment of the contents in the cells of the table body	4.0	1.0
bgcolor="color"	Specifies the background color of the table body		
char="char"	Specifies the character used for aligning the table body contents when the align attribute is set to "char"	4.0	1.0
charoff="integer"	Specifies the offset in pixels from the alignment character specified in the char attribute	4.0	1.0
valign="baseline| bottom|middle|top"	Specifies the vertical alignment of the contents in the cells of the table body	4.0	1.0
<td> </td>	Encloses the data of a table cell	3.0	1.0
abbr="text"	Supplies an abbreviated version of the contents of the table cell	4.0	1.0
align="**left**|center |right"	Specifies the horizontal alignment of the table cell data	3.0	1.0
background="url"	Provides the URL of the background image file		
bgcolor="color"	Specifies the background color of the table cell (deprecated)	4.0	1.0*
bordercolor="color"	Specifies the color of the table cell border (IE only)		
bordercolordark="color"	Specifies the color of the table cell border's shaded edge (IE only)		

Element/Attribute	Description	HTML	XHTML
bordercolorlight= "*color*"	Specifies the color of the table cell border's unshaded edge (IE only)		
char="*char*"	Specifies the character used for aligning the table cell contents when the align attribute is set to "char"	4.0	1.0
charoff="*integer*"	Specifies the offset in pixels from the alignment character specified in the char attribute	4.0	1.0
colspan="*integer*"	Specifies the number of columns the table cell spans	3.0	1.0
headers="*text*"	Supplies a space-separated list of table headers associated with the table cell	4.0	1.0
height="*integer*"	Specifies the height of the table cell in pixels (deprecated)	3.2	1.0*
nowrap="nowrap"	Disables line-wrapping within the table cell (deprecated)	3.0	1.0*
rowspan="*integer*"	Specifies the number of rows the table cell spans	3.0	1.0
scope="col|colgroup |row|rowgroup"	Specifies the scope of the table for which the cell provides data	4.0	1.0
valign="top|**middle** |bottom"	Specifies the vertical alignment of the contents of the table cell	3.0	1.0
width="*integer*"	Specifies the width of the cell in pixels (deprecated)	3.2	1.0*
<textarea> </textarea>	Marks the enclosed text as a text area input box in a Web form	2.0	1.0
datafld="*text*"	Specifies the column from a data source that supplies bound data for the text area box	4.0	
dataformatas="html| plaintext|text"	Specifies the format of the data in the data source bound with the text area box	4.0	
datasrc="*url*"	Provides the URL or ID of the data source bound with the text area box	4.0	
cols="*integer*"	Specifies the width of the text area box in characters	2.0	1.0
name="*text*"	Specifies the name of the text area box	2.0	1.0
readonly="readonly"	Specifies the value of the text area box, cannot be modified	4.0	1.0
rows="*integer*"	Specifies the number of visible rows in the text area box	2.0	1.0
wrap="off|**soft**|hard"	Specifies how text is wrapped within the text area box and how that text-wrapping information is sent to the server-side program; in earlier versions of Netscape Navigator, the default value is "off" (Netscape accepts the values "off," "virtual," and "physical.")		
<tfoot> </tfoot>	Encloses the content of the Web table footer	4.0	1.0
align="left|center |right|justify|char"	Specifies the alignment of the contents in the cells of the table footer	4.0	1.0
bgcolor="*color*"	Specifies the background color of the table body (not part of the W3C specifications, but supported by many browsers)		
char="*char*"	Specifies the character used for aligning the table footer contents when the align attribute is set to "char"	4.0	1.0
charoff="*integer*"	Specifies the offset in pixels from the alignment character specified in the char attribute	4.0	1.0
valign="baseline| bottom|middle|top"	Specifies the vertical alignment of the contents in the cells of the table footer	4.0	1.0
<th> </th>	Encloses the data of a table header cell	3.0	1.0
abbr="*text*"	Supplies an abbreviated version of the contents of the table cell	4.0	1.0
align="**left**|center |right"	Specifies the horizontal alignment of the table cell data	3.0	1.0
axis="*text list*"	Provides a list of table categories that can be mapped to a table hierarchy	3.0	1.0

Element/Attribute	Description	HTML	XHTML
background="url"	Provides the URL of the background image file (not part of the W3C specifications, but supported by many browsers)		
bgcolor="color"	Specifies the background color of the table cell (deprecated)	4.0	1.0*
bordercolor="color"	Specifies the color of the table cell border (IE only)		
bordercolordark="color"	Specifies the color of the table cell border's shaded edge (IE only)		
bordercolorlight= "color"	Specifies the color of the table cell border's unshaded edge (IE only)		
char="char"	Specifies the character used for aligning the table cell contents when the align attribute is set to "char"	4.0	1.0
charoff="integer"	Specifies the offset in pixels from the alignment character specified in the char attribute	4.0	1.0
colspan="integer"	Specifies the number of columns the table cell spans	3.0	1.0
headers="text"	A space-separated list of table headers associated with the table cell	4.0	1.0
height="integer"	Specifies the height of the table cell in pixels (deprecated)	3.2	1.0*
nowrap="nowrap"	Disables line-wrapping within the table cell (deprecated)	3.0	1.0*
rowspan="integer"	Specifies the number of rows the table cell spans	3.0	1.0
scope="col| colgroup|row|rowgroup"	Specifies the scope of the table for which the cell provides data	4.0	1.0
valign="top|middle |bottom"	Specifies the vertical alignment of the contents of the table cell	3.0	1.0
width="integer"	Specifies the width of the cell in pixels (deprecated)	3.2	1.0*
<thead> </thead>	Encloses the content of the Web table header	4.0	1.0
align="left|center |right|justify|char"	Specifies the alignment of the contents in the cells of the table header	4.0	1.0
bgcolor="color"	Specifies the background color of the table body		
char="char"	Specifies the character used for aligning the table header contents when the align attribute is set to "char"	4.0	1.0
charoff="integer"	Specifies the offset in pixels from the alignment character specified in the char attribute	4.0	1.0
valign="baseline| bottom|middle|top"	Specifies the vertical alignment of the contents in the cells of the table header	4.0	1.0
<title> </title>	Specifies the title of the document, placed in the head section of the document	2.0	1.0
<tr> </tr>	Encloses the content of a row within a Web table	3.0	1.0
align="left|center |right"	Specifies the horizontal alignment of the data in the row's cells	3.0	1.0
background="url"	Provides the URL of the background image file for the row		
bgcolor="color"	Specifies the background color of the row (deprecated)	4.0	1.0*
bordercolor="color"	Specifies the color of the table row border (IE only)		
bordercolordark="color"	Specifies the color of the table row border's shaded edge (IE only)		
bordercolorlight= "color"	Specifies the color of the table row border's unshaded edge (IE only)		
char="char"	Specifies the character used for aligning the table row contents when the align attribute is set to "char"	4.0	1.0
charoff="integer"	Specifies the offset in pixels from the alignment character specified in the char attribute	4.0	1.0

Element/Attribute	Description	HTML	XHTML
height="*integer*"	Specifies the height of the table row in pixels		
valign="baseline|bottom|*middle*|top"	Specifies the vertical alignment of the contents of the table row	3.0	1.0
`<tt> </tt>`	Marks the enclosed text as teletype or monospaced text	2.0	1.0
`<u> </u>`	Marks the enclosed text as underlined text (deprecated)	3.0	1.0*
`<ul> </ul>`	Contains an unordered list of items	2.0	1.0
compact="compact"	Reduces the space between unordered list items (deprecated)	2.0	1.0*
type="**disc**|square|circle"	Specifies the bullet type associated with the list items (deprecated)	3.2	1.0*
`<var> </var>`	Marks the enclosed text as containing a variable name	2.0	1.0
`<wbr />`	Forces a line-break in the rendered page (not part of the W3C specifications, but supported by many browsers)		
`<xml> </xml>`	Encloses XML content (also referred to as a "data island") or references an external XML document (IE only)		
ns="*url*"	Provides the URL of the XML data island (IE only)		
prefix="*text*"	Specifies the namespace prefix of the XML content (IE only)		
src="*url*"	Provides the URL of an external XML document (IE only)		
`<xmp> </xmp>`	Marks the enclosed text as preformatted text, preserving the white space of the source document; replaced by the pre element (deprecated)	2.0	

Cascading Style Sheets

Appendix D

This appendix describes the selectors, units, and attributes supported by Cascading Style Sheets (CSS). Version numbers indicate the lowest version that supports the given selector, unit, or attribute. This appendix focuses on CSS1 and CSS2 styles. It does not include all of the CSS3 styles due to the state of CSS3's development and current level of browser support for CSS3. You should always check your code against different browsers and browser versions to ensure that your page is being rendered correctly. Additional information about CSS can be found at the World Wide Web Consortium Web site at *www.w3.org*.

Starting Data Files

There are no starting Data Files needed for this appendix.

Selectors

The general form of a style declaration is:

selector {attribute1:value1; attribute2:value2; ...}

where *selector* is the selection of elements within the document to which the style will be applied; *attribute1, attribute2,* etc. are the different style attributes; and *value1, value2,* etc. are values associated with those styles. The following table shows some of the different forms that a selector can take.

Selector	Matches	CSS
`*`	All elements in the document	2.0
`e`	An element, *e*, in the document	1.0
`e1, e2, e3, …`	A group of elements, *e1, e2, e3,* in the document	1.0
`e1 e2`	An element *e2* nested within the parent element, *e1*	1.0
`e1 > e2`	An element *e2* that is a child of the parent element, *e1*	2.0
`e1+e2`	An element, *e2,* that is adjacent to element *e1*	2.0
`e1.class`	An element, *e1,* belonging to the *class* class	1.0
`.class`	Any element belonging to the *class* class	1.0
`#id`	An element with the id value *id*	1.0
`[att]`	The element contains the *att* attribute	2.0
`[att="val"]`	The element's *att* attribute equals *"val"*	2.0
`[att~="val"]`	The element's *att* attribute value is a space-separated list of "words," one of which is exactly *"val"*	2.0
`[att|="val"]`	The element's *att* attribute value is a hyphen-separated list of "words" beginning with "val"	3.0
`[att^="val"]`	The element's *att* attribute begins with *"val"*	3.0
`[att$="val"]`	The element's *att* attribute ends with *"val"*	3.0
`[att*="val"]`	The element's *att* attribute contains the value *"val"*	3.0
`[ns|att]`	References all *att* attributes in the *ns* namespace	3.0

Pseudo-Elements and Pseudo-Classes

Pseudo-elements are elements that do not exist in HTML code but whose attributes can be set with CSS. Many pseudo-elements were introduced in CSS2.

Pseudo-Element	Matches	CSS
`e:after {content: "text"}`	Text content, *text,* that is inserted at the end of an element, *e*	2.0
`e:before {content: "text"}`	Text content, *text,* that is inserted at the beginning of an element, *e*	2.0
`e:first-letter`	The first letter in the element, *e*	1.0
`e:first-line`	The first line in the element, *e*	1.0

Pseudo-classes are classes of HTML elements that define the condition or state of the element in the Web page. Many pseudo-classes were introduced in CSS2.

Pseudo-Class	Matches	CSS
`:canvas`	The rendering canvas of the document	
`:first`	The first printed page of the document (used only with print styles created with the @print rule)	2.0
`:last`	The last printed page of the document (used only with print styles created with the @print rule)	2.0
`:left`	The left side of a two-sided printout (used only with print styles created with the @print rule)	2.0
`:right`	The right side of a two-sided printout (used only with print styles created with the @print rule)	2.0
`:root`	The root element of the document (the html element in HTML and XHTML documents)	
`:scrolled-content`	The content that is scrolled in the rendering viewport (Netscape only)	
`:viewport`	The rendering viewport of the document (Netscape only)	
`:viewport-scroll`	The rendering viewport of the document plus the scroll bar region (Netscape only)	
`e:active`	The element, *e*, is being activated by the user (usually applies only to hyperlinks)	1.0
`e:empty`	The element, *e*, has no content (Netscape only)	
`e:first-child`	The element, *e*, which is the first child of its parent element	2.0
`e:first-node`	The first occurrence of the element, *e*, in the document tree	
`e:focus`	The element, *e*, has received the focus of the cursor (usually applies only to Web form elements)	2.0
`e:hover`	The mouse pointer is hovering over the element, *e* (usually applies only to hyperlinks)	2.0
`e:lang(text)`	Sets the language, *text*, associated with the element, *e*	2.0
`e:last-child`	The element, *e*, that is the last child of its parent element	2.0
`e:last-node`	The last occurrence of the element, *e*, in the document tree (Netscape only)	
`e:link`	The element, *e*, has not been visited yet by the user (applies only to hyperlinks)	1.0
`e:not`	Negate the selector rule for the element, *e*, applying the style to all *e* elements that do not match the selector rules (Netscape only)	
`e:visited`	The element, *e*, has been already visited by the user (to only the hyperlinks)	1.0

@ Rules

CSS supports different "@ rules" designed to run commands within a style sheet. These commands can be used to import other styles, download font definitions, or define the format of printed output.

@ Rule	Description	CSS
`@charset "encoding"`	Defines the character set encoding used in the style sheet (this must be the very first line in the style sheet document)	2.0
`@import url(url) media`	Imports an external style sheet document into the current style sheet, where *url* is the location of the external style sheet and *media* is a comma-separated list of media types (optional)	1.0
`@media media {style declaration}`	Defines the media for the styles in the *style declaration* block, where *media* is a comma-separated list of media types	2.0
`@namespace prefix url(url)`	Defines the namespace used by selectors in the style sheet, where *prefix* is the local namespace prefix (optional) and *url* is the unique namespace identifier; the @namespace rule must come before all CSS selectors (Netscape only)	
`@page label pseudo-class {styles}`	Defines the properties of a printed page, where *label* is a label given to the page (optional), *pseudo-class* is one of the CSS pseudo-classes designed for printed pages, and *styles* are the styles associated with the page	2.0

Miscellaneous Syntax

The following syntax elements do not fit into the previous categories but are useful in constructing CSS style sheets.

Item	Description	CSS
`style !important`	Places high importance on the preceding *style*, overriding the usual rules for inheritance and cascading	1.0
`/* comment */`	Attaches a *comment* to the style sheet	1.0

Units

Many style attribute values use units of measurement to indicate color, length, angles, time, and frequencies. The following table describes the measuring units used in CSS.

Units	Description	CSS
Color	**Units of color**	
name	A color name; all browsers recognize 16 base color names: aqua, black, blue, fuchsia, gray, green, lime, maroon, navy, olive, purple, red, silver, teal, white, and yellow	1.0
#*rrggbb*	The hexadecimal color value, where *rr* is the red value, *gg* is the green value, and *bb* is the blue value	1.0
#*rgb*	A compressed hexadecimal value, where the *r*, *g*, and *b* values are doubled so that, for example, #A2F = #AA22FF	1.0
rgb(*red*, *green*, *blue*)	The decimal color value, where *red* is the red value, *green* is the green value, and *blue* is the blue value	1.0
rgb(*red%*, *green%*, *blue%*)	The color value percentage, where *red%* is the percent of maximum red, *green%* is the percent of maximum green, and *blue%* is the percent of maximum blue	1.0
Length	**Units of length**	
auto	Keyword which allows the browser to automatically determine the size of the length	1.0
em	A relative unit indicating the width and the height of the capital "M" character for the browser's default font	1.0
ex	A relative unit indicating the height of the small "x" character for the browser's default font	1.0
px	A pixel, representing the smallest unit of length on the output device	1.0
in	An inch	1.0
cm	A centimeter	1.0
mm	A millimeter	1.0
pt	A point, approximately 1/72 inch	1.0
pc	A pica, approximately 1/12 inch	1.0
%	A percent of the width or height of the parent element	1.0
xx-small	Keyword representing an extremely small font size	1.0
x-small	Keyword representing a very small font size	1.0
small	Keyword representing a small font size	1.0
medium	Keyword representing a medium-sized font	1.0
large	Keyword representing a large font	1.0
x-large	Keyword representing a very large font	1.0
xx-large	Keyword representing an extremely large font	1.0
Angle	**Units of angles**	
deg	The angle in degrees	2.0
grad	The angle in gradients	2.0
rad	The angle in radians	2.0

Units	Description	CSS
Time	**Units of time**	
ms	Time in milliseconds	2.0
s	Time in seconds	2.0
Frequency	**Units of frequency**	
hz	The frequency in hertz	2.0
khz	The frequency in kilohertz	2.0

Attributes and Values

The following table describes the attributes and values for different types of elements. The attributes are grouped into categories to help you locate the features relevant to your particular design task.

Attribute	Description	CSS
Aural	**Styles for Aural Browsers**	
azimuth: *location*	Defines the location of the sound, where *location* is left-side, far-left, left, center-left, center, center-right, right, far-right, right-side, leftward, rightward, or an angle value	2.0
cue: url(*url1*) url(*url2*)	Adds a sound to an element: if a single value is present, the sound is played before and after the element; if two values are present, the first is played before and the second is played after	2.0
cue-after: url(*url*)	Specifies a sound to be played immediately after an element	2.0
cue-before: url(*url*)	Specifies a sound to be played immediately before an element	2.0
elevation: *location*	Defines the vertical location of the sound, where *location* is below, level, above, lower, higher, or an angle value	2.0
pause: *time1 time2*	Adds a pause to an element: if a single value is present, the pause occurs before and after the element; if two values are present, the first pause occurs before and the second occurs after	2.0
pause-after: *time*	Adds a pause after an element	2.0
pause-before: *time*	Adds a pause before an element	2.0
pitch: *value*	Defines the pitch of a speaking voice, where *value* is x-low, low, medium, high, x-high, or a frequency value	2.0
pitch-range: *value*	Defines the pitch range for a speaking voice, where *value* ranges from 0 to 100; a low pitch range results in a monotone voice, whereas a high pitch range sounds very animated	2.0
play-during: url(*url*) mix repeat *type*	Defines a sound to be played behind an element, where *url* is the URL of the sound file; mix overlays the sound file with the sound of the parent element; repeat causes the sound to be repeated, filling up the available time; and *type* is auto to play the sound only once, none to play nothing but the sound file, or inherit	2.0
richness: *value*	Specifies the richness of the speaking voice, where *value* ranges from 0 to 100; a low value indicates a softer voice, whereas a high value indicates a brighter voice	2.0
speak: *type*	Defines how element content is to be spoken, where *type* is normal (for normal punctuation rules), spell-out (to pronounce one character at a time), none (to suppress the aural rendering), or inherit	2.0

Attribute	Description	CSS
speak-numeral: *type*	Defines how numeric content should be spoken, where *type* is digits (to pronounce one digit at a time), continuous (to pronounce the full number), or inherit	2.0
speak-punctuation: *type*	Defines how punctuation characters are spoken, where *type* is code (to speak the punctuation literally), none (to not speak the punctuation), or inherit	2.0
speech-rate: *value*	Defines the rate of speech, where *value* is x-slow, slow, medium, fast, x-fast, slower, faster, or a value in words per minute	2.0
stress: *value*	Defines the maximum pitch, where *value* ranges from 0 to 100; a value of 50 is normal stress for a speaking voice	2.0
voice-family: *text*	Defines the name of the speaking voice, where *text* is male, female, child, or a text string indicating a specific speaking voice	2.0
volume: *value*	Defines the volume of a voice, where *value* is silent, x-soft, soft, medium, loud, x-loud, or a number from 0 (lowest) to 100 (highest)	2.0
Backgrounds	**Styles applied to an element's background**	
background: *color* url(*url*) *repeat attachment position*	Defines the background of the element, where *color* is a CSS color name or value, *url* is the location of an image file, *repeat* defines how the background image should be repeated, *attachment* defines how the background image should be attached, and *position* defines the position of the background image	1.0
background-attachment: *type*	Specifies how the background image is attached, where *type* is inherit, scroll (move the image with the page content), or fixed (fix the image and not scroll)	1.0
background-color: *color*	Defines the color of the background, where *color* is a CSS color name or value; the keyword "inherit" can be used to inherit the background color of the parent element, or "transparent" can be used to allow the parent element background image to show through	1.0
background-image: url(*url*)	Specifies the image file used for the element's background, where *url* is the URL of the image file	1.0
background-position: *x y*	Sets the position of a background image, where *x* is the horizontal location in pixels, as a percentage of the width of the parent element, or the keyword "left", "center", or "right", *y* is the vertical location in pixels, as a percentage of the height and of the parent element, or the keyword, "top", "center", or "bottom"	1.0
background-repeat: *type*	Defines the method for repeating the background image, where *type* is no-repeat, repeat (to tile the image in both directions), repeat-x (to tile the image in the horizontal direction only), or repeat-y (to tile the image in the vertical direction only)	1.0
Block-Level Styles	**Styles applied to block-level elements**	
border: *length style color*	Defines the border style of the element, where *length* is the border width, *style* is the border design, and *color* is the border color	1.0
border-bottom: *length style color*	Defines the border style of the bottom edge of the element	1.0
border-left: *length style color*	Defines the border style of the left edge of the element	1.0
border-right: *length style color*	Defines the border style of the right edge of the element	1.0
border-top: *length style color*	Defines the border style of the top edge of the element	1.0

Attribute	Description	CSS
`border-color: color`	Defines the color applied to the element's border using a CSS color unit	1.0
`border-bottom-color: color`	Defines the color applied to the bottom edge of the element	1.0
`border-left-color: color`	Defines the color applied to the left edge of the element	1.0
`border-right-color: color`	Defines the color applied to the right edge of the element	1.0
`border-top-color: color`	Defines the color applied to the top edge of the element	1.0
`border-style: style`	Specifies the design of the element's border (dashed, dotted, double, groove, inset, none, outset, ridge, or solid)	1.0
`border-style-bottom: style`	Specifies the design of the element's bottom edge	1.0
`border-style-left: style`	Specifies the design of the element's left edge	1.0
`border-style-right: style`	Specifies the design of the element's right edge	1.0
`border-style-top: style`	Specifies the design of the element's top edge	1.0
`border-width: length`	Defines the width of the element's border, in a unit of measure or using the keyword "thick", "medium", or "thin"	1.0
`border-width-bottom: length`	Defines the width of the element's bottom edge	1.0
`border-width-left: length`	Defines the width of the element's left edge	1.0
`border-width-right: length`	Defines the width of the element's right edge	1.0
`border-width-top: length`	Defines the width of the element's top edge	1.0
`margin: top right bottom left`	Defines the size of the margins around the top, right, bottom, and left edges of the element, in one of the CSS units of length	1.0
`margin-bottom: length`	Defines the size of the element's bottom margin	1.0
`margin-left: length`	Defines the size of the element's left margin	1.0
`margin-right: length`	Defines the size of the element's right margin	1.0
`margin-top: length`	Defines the size of the element's top margin	1.0
`padding: top right bottom left`	Defines the size of the padding space within the top, right, bottom, and left edges of the element, in one of the CSS units of length	1.0
`padding-bottom: length`	Defines the size of the element's bottom padding	1.0
`padding-left: length`	Defines the size of the element's left padding	1.0
`padding-right: length`	Defines the size of the element's right padding	1.0
`padding-top: length`	Defines the size of the element's top padding	1.0

Attribute	Description	CSS
Content	**Styles to attach additional content to elements**	
content: text	Generates a text string to attach to the content of the element	2.0
content: attr(attr)	Returns the value of the *attr* attribute from the element	2.0
content: close-quote	Attaches a close quote using the characters specified in the quotes style	2.0
content: counter(text)	Generates a counter using the text string *text* attached to the content (most often used with list items)	2.0
content: counters(text)	Generates a string of counters using the comma-separated text string *text* attached to the content (most often used with list items)	2.0
content: no-close-quote	Prevents the attachment of a close quote to an element	2.0
content: no-open-quote	Prevents the attachment of an open quote to an element	2.0
content: open-quote	Attaches an open quote using the characters specified in the quotes style	2.0
content: url(url)	Attaches the content of an external file indicated in the *url* to the element	2.0
counter-increment: id integer	Defines the element to be automatically incremented and the amount by which it is to be incremented, where *id* is an identifier of the element and *integer* defines by how much	2.0
counter-reset: id integer	Defines the element whose counter is to be reset and the amount by which it is to be reset, where *id* is an identifier of the element and *integer* defines by how much	2.0
quotes: text1 text2	Defines the text strings for the open quotes (*text1*) and the close quotes (*text2*)	2.0
Display Styles	**Styles that control the display of the element's content**	
clip: rect(top, right, bottom, left)	Defines what portion of the content is displayed, where *top*, *right*, *bottom*, and *left* are distances of the top, right, bottom, and left edges from the element's top-left corner; use a value of auto to allow the browser to determine the clipping region	2.0
display: type	Specifies the display type of the element, where *type* is one of the following: block, inline, inline-block, inherit, list-item, none, run-in, table, inline-table, table-caption, table-column, table-cell, table-column-group, table-header-group, table-footer-group, table-row, or table-row-group	1.0

Attribute	Description	CSS
height: *length*	Specifies the height of the element in one of the CSS units of length	1.0
min-height: *length*	Specifies the minimum height of the element	2.0
min-width: *length*	Specifies the minimum width of the element	2.0
max-height: *length*	Specifies the maximum height of the element	2.0
max-width: *length*	Specifies the maximum width of the element	2.0
overflow: *type*	Instructs the browser how to handle content that overflows the dimensions of the element, where *type* is auto, inherit, visible, hidden, or scroll	2.0
overflow-x: *type*	Instructs the browser how to handle content that overflows the element's width, where *type* is auto, inherit, visible, hidden, or scroll (IE only)	
overflow-y: *type*	Instructs the browser on how to handle content that overflows the element's height, where *type* is auto, inherit, visible, hidden, or scroll (IE only)	
text-overflow: *type*	Instructs the browser on how to handle text overflow, where *type* is clip (to hide the overflow text) or ellipsis (to display the ... text string) (IE only)	
visibility: *type*	Defines the element's visibility, where *type* is hidden, visible, or inherit	2.0
width: *length*	Specifies the width of the element in one of the CSS units of length	1.0
Fonts and Text	**Styles that format the appearance of fonts and text**	
color: *color*	Specifies the color of the element's foreground (usually the font color)	1.0
font: *style variant weight size/line-height family*	Defines the appearance of the font, where *style* is the font's style, *variant* is the font variant, *weight* is the weight of the font, *size* is the size of the font, *line-height* is the height of the lines, and *family* is the font face; the only required attributes are *size* and *family*	1.0
font-family: *family*	Specifies the font face used to display text, where *family* is sans-serif, serif, fantasy, monospace, cursive, or the name of an installed font	1.0
font-size: *value*	Specifies the size of the font in one of the CSS units of length	1.0
font-size-adjust: *value*	Specifies the aspect *value* (which is the ratio of the font size to the font's ex unit height)	2.0
font-stretch: *type*	Expands or contracts the font, where *type* is narrower, wider, ultra-condensed, extra-condensed, condensed, semi-condensed, normal, semi-expanded, extra-expanded, or ultra-expanded	2.0
font-style: *type*	Specifies a style applied to the font, where *type* is normal, italic, or oblique	1.0
font-variant: *type*	Specifies a variant of the font, where *type* is inherit, normal, or small-caps	1.0
font-weight: *value*	Defines the weight of the font, where *value* is 100, 200, 300, 400, 500, 600, 700, 800, 900, normal, lighter, bolder, or bold	1.0
letter-spacing: *value*	Specifies the space between letters, where *value* is a unit of length or the keyword "normal"	1.0
line-height: *value*	Specifies the height of the lines, where *value* is a unit of length or the keyword, "normal"	1.0

Attribute	Description	CSS
text-align: *type*	Specifies the horizontal alignment of text within the element, where *type* is inherit, left, right, center, or justify	1.0
text-decoration: *type*	Specifies the decoration applied to the text, where *type* is blink, line-through, none, overline, or underline	1.0
text-indent: *length*	Specifies the amount of indentation in the first line of the text, where *length* is a CSS unit of length	1.0
text-shadow: *color* *x y blur*	Applies a shadow effect to the text, where *color* is the color of the shadow, *x* is the horizontal offset in pixels, *y* is the vertical offset in pixels, and *blur* is the size of the blur radius (optional); multiple shadows can be added with shadow effects separated by commas	2.0
text-transform: *type*	Defines a transformation applied to the text, where *type* is capitalize, lowercase, none, or uppercase	1.0
vertical-align: *type*	Specifies how to vertically align the text with the surrounding content, where *type* is baseline, middle, top, bottom, text-top, text-bottom, super, sub, or one of the CSS units of length	1.0
white-space: *type*	Specifies the handling of white space (blank spaces, tabs, and new lines), where *type* is inherit, normal, pre (to treat the text as preformatted text), or nowrap (to prevent line-wrapping)	1.0
word-spacing: *length*	Specifies the amount of space between words in the text, where *length* is either a CSS unit of length or the keyword "normal" to use normal word spacing	1.0
Layout	**Styles that define the layout of elements**	
bottom: *y*	Defines the vertical offset of the element's bottom edge, where *y* is either a CSS unit of length or the keyword "auto" or "inherit"	2.0
clear: *type*	Places the element only after the specified margin is clear of floating elements, where *type* is inherit, none, left, right, or both	1.0
float: *type*	Floats the element on the specified margin with subsequent content wrapping around the element, where *type* is inherit, none, left, right, or both	1.0
left: *x*	Defines the horizontal offset of the element's left edge, where *x* is either a CSS unit of length or the keyword "auto" or "inherit"	2.0
position: *type*	Defines how the element is positioned on the page, where *type* is absolute, relative, fixed, static, and inherit	1.0
right: *x*	Defines the horizontal offset of the element's right edge, where *x* is either a CSS unit of length or the keyword "auto" or "inherit"	2.0
top: *y*	Defines the vertical offset of the element's top edge, where *y* is a CSS unit of length or the keyword "auto" or "inherit"	2.0
z-index: *value*	Defines how overlapping elements are stacked, where *value* is either the stacking number (elements with higher stacking numbers are placed on top) or the keyword "auto" to allow the browser to determine the stacking order	2.0
Lists	**Styles that format lists**	
list-style: *type image position*	Defines the appearance of a list item, where *type* is the marker type, *image* is the URL of the location of an image file used for the marker, and *position* is the position of the marker	1.0
list-style-image: url(*url*)	Defines image used for the list marker, where *url* is the location of the image file	1.0

Attribute	Description	CSS
list-style-type: *type*	Defines the marker type used in the list, where *type* is disc, circle, square, decimal, decimal-leading-zero, lower-roman, upper-roman, lower-alpha, upper-alpha, or none	1.0
list-style-position: *type*	Defines the location of the list marker, where *type* is inside or outside	1.0
marker-offset: *length*	Defines the distance between the marker and the enclosing list box, where *length* is either a CSS unit of length or the keyword "auto" or "inherit"	2.0
Outlines	**Styles to create and format outlines**	
outline: *color style width*	Creates an outline around the element content, where *color* is the color of the outline, *style* is the outline style, and *width* is the width of the outline	2.0
outline-color: *color*	Defines the color of the outline	2.0
outline-style: *type*	Defines the style of the outline, where *type* is dashed, dotted, double, groove, inset, none, outset, ridge, solid, or inherit	2.0
outline-width: *length*	Defines the width of the outline, where *length* is expressed in a CSS unit of length	2.0
Printing	**Styles for printed output**	
page: *label*	Specifies the page design to apply, where *label* is a page design created with the @page rule	2.0
page-break-after: *type*	Defines how to control page breaks after the element, where *type* is avoid (to avoid page breaks), left (to insert a page break until a left page is displayed), right (to insert a page break until a right page is displayed), always (to always insert a page break), auto, or inherit	2.0
page-break-before: *type*	Defines how to control page breaks before the element, where *type* is avoid left, always, auto, or inherit	2.0
page-break-inside: *type*	Defines how to control page breaks within the element, where *type* is avoid, auto, or inherit	2.0
marks: *type*	Defines how to display crop marks, where *type* is crop, cross, none, or inherit	2.0
size: *width height orientation*	Defines the size of the page, where *width* and *height* are the width and the height of the page and *orientation* is the orientation of the page (portrait or landscape)	2.0
orphans: *value*	Defines how to handle orphaned text, where *value* is the number of lines that must appear within the element before a page break is inserted	2.0
widows: *value*	Defines how to handle widowed text, where *value* is the number of lines that must appear within the element after a page break is inserted	2.0
Scrollbars and Cursors	**Styles to format the appearance of scrollbars and cursors**	
cursor: *type*	Defines the cursor image used, where *type* is n-resize, ne-resize, e-resize, se-resize, s-resize, sw-resize, w-resize, nw-resize, crosshair, pointer, move, text, wait, help, auto, default, inherit, or a URL pointing to an image file; individual browsers also support dozens of other cursor types	2.0
scrollbar-3dlight-color: *color*	Defines the *color* of the outer top and left edge of the slider (IE only)	
scrollbar-arrow-color: *color*	Defines the *color* of the scroll bar directional arrows (IE only)	

Attribute	Description	CSS
scrollbar-base-color: color	Defines the *color* of the scroll bar button face, arrow, slider, and slider tray (IE only)	
scrollbar-darkshadow-color: color	Defines the *color* of the outer bottom and right edges of the slider (IE only)	
scrollbar-face-color: color	Defines the *color* of the button face of the scroll bar arrow and slider (IE only)	
scrollbar-highlight-color: color	Defines the *color* of the inner top and left edges of the slider (IE only)	
scrollbar-shadow-color: color	Defines the *color* of the inner bottom and right edges of the slider (IE only)	
Special Effects	**Styles to create special visual effects**	
filter: *type parameters*	Applies transition and filter effects to elements, where *type* is the type of filter and *parameters* are parameter values specific to the filter (IE only)	
Tables	**Styles to format the appearance of tables**	
border-collapse: *type*	Determines whether table cell borders are separate or collapsed into a single border, where *type* is separate, collapse, or inherit	2.0
border-spacing: *length*	If separate borders are used for table cells, defines the distance between borders, where *length* is a CSS unit of length or inherit	2.0
caption-side: *type*	Defines the position of the caption element, where *type* is bottom, left, right, top, or inherit	2.0
empty-cells: *type*	If separate borders are used for table cells, defines whether to display borders for empty cells, where *type* is hide, show, or inherit	2.0
speak-header: *type*	Defines how table headers are spoken in relation to the data cells, where *type* is always, once, or inherit	2.0
table-layout: *type*	Defines the algorithm used for the table layout, where *type* is auto (to define the layout once all table cells have been read), fixed (to define the layout after the first table row has been read), or inherit	2.0

JavaScript Objects, Properties, Methods, and Event Handlers

Appendix E

This appendix defines some of the important JavaScript objects, properties, methods, and event handlers. The JavaScript object is listed first, followed by any properties, methods, and event handlers associated with it.

Where a particular object, property, method, or event handler is supported only in a specific browser, this fact is noted in the table.

As always, you should test your code against a variety of browsers to ensure support.

Starting Data Files

There are no starting Data Files needed for this appendix.

JavaScript Elements	Description
Anchor	An anchor in the document (use the anchor name)
Properties	
accessKey	The hotkey that gives the element focus
charset	The character set of the linked document
coords	The coordinates of the object, used with the shape attribute
hreflang	The language code of the linked resource
name	The name of the anchor
nameProp	The string holding the filename portion of the URL in the href
shape	The string defining the shape of the object
tabIndex	The numeric value that indicates the tab order for the object
text	The anchor text
type	Specifies the media type in the form of a MIME type for the link target
Methods	
blur( )	Removes focus from the element
handleEvent (*event*)	Causes the Event instance *event* to be processed
focus( )	Gives the element focus
Applet	A Java applet in the document
Properties	
align	Specifies alignment, for example, "left
alt	Specifies alternative text for the applet
altHTML	Specifies alternative text for the applet
archive	A list of URLs
code	The URL for the applet class file
codeBase	The base URL for the applet
height	The height of the object in pixels
hspace	The horizontal margin to the left and the right of the applet
name	The name of the applet
object	The name of the resource that contains a serialized representation of the applet
vspace	The vertical margin above and below the applet
width	The width of the object in pixels
Area	An area defined in an image map
Properties	
accessKey	The hotkey that gives the element focus
alt	Alternative text to the graphic
cords	Defines the coordinates of the object
hash	The anchor name from the URL
host	The host and domain names from the URL
hostname	The hostname from the URL
href	The entire URL
pathname	The pathname from the URL

JavaScript Elements	Description
port	The port number from the URL
protocol	The protocol from the URL
search	The query portion from the URL
shape	The shape of the object, for example, "default", "rect", "circle", or "poly"
tabIndex	Numeric value that indicates the tab order for the object
target	The target attribute of the <area> tag
Methods	
getSelection()	Returns the value of the current selection3.0
Event Handlers	
onDblClick()	Runs when the area is double-clicked
onMouseOut()	Runs when the mouse leaves the area
onMouseOver()	Runs when the mouse enters the area
`Array`	`An array object`
Properties	
index	For an array created by a regular expression match, the zero-based index of the match in the string
input	Reflects the original string against which the regular expression was matched
length	The next empty index at the end of the array
prototype	A mechanism to add properties to an array object
Methods	
concat(*array*)	Combines two arrays and stores the result in a third array named *array*
join(*string*)	Stores each element in a text string named *string*
pop( )	"Pops" the last element of the array and reduces the length of the array by 1
push(*arg1, arg2, ...*)	"Pushes" the elements in the list to the end of the array and returns the new length
reverse( )	Reverses the order of the elements in the array
shift( )	Removes the first element from an array, returns that element, and shifts all other elements down one index
slice(*array, begin,end*)	Extracts a portion of the array, starting at the index number *begin* and ending at the index number *end*; the elements are then stored in *array*
sort(*function*)	Sorts the array based on the function named *function*; if *function* is omitted, the sort applies dictionary order to the array
splice(*start,howMany,* [,item1[,item2 [,...]]])	Removes *howMany* elements from the array, beginning at index *start* and replaces the removed elements with the *itemN* arguments (if passed); returns an array of the deleted elements
toString( )	Returns a string of the comma-separated values of the array
unshift([Item1 [,item2[,...]]])	Inserts the items to the front of an array and returns the new length of the array
`Button`	`A push button in an HTML form (use the button's name)`
Properties	
accessKey	Indicates the hotkey that gives the element focus
align	Specifies the alignment of the element, for example, "right"
disabled	A Boolean indicating whether the element is disabled

JavaScript Elements	Description
enabled	Indicates whether the button has been enabled
form	The name of the form containing the button
name	The name of the button element
size	Indicates the width of the button in pixels
tabIndex	Indicates the tab order for the object
type	The value of the type attribute for the <button> tag
value	The value of the button element
Methods	
blur()	Removes focus from the button
click()	Emulates the action of clicking the button
focus()	Gives focus to the button
Event Handlers	
onBlur	Runs when the button loses the focus
onClick	Runs when the button is clicked
onFocus	Runs when the button receives the focus
onMouseDown	Runs when the mouse button is pressed
onMouseUp	Runs when the mouse button is released
Checkbox	A check box in an HTML form
Properties	
accessKey	Indicates the hotkey that gives the element focus
align	Specifies the alignment of the element, for example, "right"
checked	Indicates whether the check box is checked
defaultChecked	Indicates whether the check box is checked by default
disabled	Boolean indicating whether the element is disabled
enabled	Indicates whether the check box is enabled
form	The name of the form containing the check box
name	The name of the check box element
size	Indicates the width of the check box in pixels0
status	Boolean indicating whether the check box is currently selected
tabIndex	Indicates the tab order for the object
type	The value of the type attribute for the <input> tag
value	The value of the check box element
Methods	
blur()	Removes the focus from the check box
click()	Emulates the action of clicking on the check box
focus()	Gives focus to the check box
Event Handlers	
onBlur	Runs when the check box loses the focus
onClick	Runs when the check box is clicked
onFocus	Runs when the check box receives the focus

JavaScript Elements	Description
Date	An object containing information about a specific date or the current date; dates are expressed either in local time or in UTC (Universal Time Coordinates), otherwise known as Greenwich Mean Time

Methods

getDate()	Returns the day of the month, from 1 to 31
getDay()	Returns the day of the week, from 0 to 6 (Sunday = 0, Monday = 1, etc.)
getFullYear()	Returns the year portion of the date in four-digit format
getHours()	Returns the hour in military time, from 0 to 23
getMilliseconds()	Returns the number of milliseconds
getMinutes()	Returns the minute, from 0 to 59
getMonth()	Returns the value of the month, from 0 to 11 (January = 0, February = 1, etc.)
getSeconds()	Returns the seconds
getTime()	Returns the date as an integer representing the number of milliseconds since December 31, 1969, at 18:00:00
getTimezoneOffset()	Returns the difference between the local time and Greenwich Mean Time in minutes
getYear()	Deprecated. Returns the number of years since 1900; for example, 1996 is represented by '96'—this value method is inconsistently applied after the year 1999
getUTCDate()	Returns the UTC getDate() value
getUTCDay()	Returns the UTC getDay() value
getUTCFullYear()	Returns the UTC getFullYear() value
getUTCHours()	Returns the UTC getHours() value
getUTCMilliseconds()	Returns the UTC getMilliseconds() value
getUTCMinutes()	Returns the UTC getMinutes() value
getUTCMonth()	Returns the UTC getMonth() value
getUTCSeconds()	Returns the UTC getSeconds() value
getUTCTime()	Returns the UTC getTime() value
getUTCYear()	Returns the UTC getYear() value
setDate(*date*)	Sets the day of the month to the value specified in *date*
setFullYear(*year*)	Sets the year to the four-digit value specified in *year*
setHours(*hour*)	Sets the hour to the value specified in *hour*
setMilliseconds(*milliseconds*)	Sets the millisecond value to *milliseconds*
setMinutes(*minutes*)	Sets the minute to the value specified in *minutes*
setMonth(*month*)	Sets the month to the value specified in *month*
setSeconds(*seconds*)	Sets the second to the value specified in *seconds*
setTime(*time*)	Sets the time using the value specified in *time*, where *time* is a variable containing the number of milliseconds since December 31, 1969, at 18:00:00
setYear(*year*)	Sets the year to the value specified in *year*
toDateString()	Returns a date as a string value
toLocaleDateString()	Returns a date as a string value
toTimeString()	Returns a time as a string value

JavaScript Elements	Description
toGMTString()	Converts the current date to a text string in Greenwich Mean Time
toLocaleString()	Converts a date object's date to a text string, using the date format the Web browser is set up to use
toSource	String representing the source code of the object
toString()	String representation of a Date object
toUTCString()	Date converted to string using UTC
UTC()	Milliseconds since December 31, 18:00:00, using UTC
UTC(*date*)	Returns *date* in the form of the number of milliseconds since December 31, 1969, at 18:00:00 for Universal Coordinated Time
setUTCDate(*date*)	Applies the setDate() method in UTC time
setUTCFullYear(*year*)	Applies the setFullYear() method in UTC time
setUTCHours(*hour*)	Applies the setHours() method in UTC time
setUTCMilliseconds (*milliseconds*)	Applies the setMilliseconds() method in UTC time
setUTCMinutes(*minutes*)	Applies the setMinutes() method in UTC time
setUTCMonth(*month*)	Applies the setMonth() method in UTC time
setUTCSeconds(*seconds*)	Applies the setSeconds() method in UTC time
setUTCTime(*time*)	Applies the setTime() method in UTC time
setUTCYear(*year*)	Applies the setYear() method in UTC time
`dir`	A directory listing element in the document
Properties	
compact	A Boolean indicating whether the listing should be compacted
`div`	A `<div>` (block container) element in the document
Properties	
align	Alignment of the element
`document`	An HTML document (child of Window)
Properties	
alinkColor	The color of active hypertext links in the document
all[ ]	An array of each of the HTML tags in the document
anchors[ ]	An array of the anchors in the document
applets[ ]	An array of the applets in the document
attributes[ ]	A collection of attributes for the element
bgColor	The background color of the document
body	Reference to the `<body>` element object of the document
charset	A string containing the character set of the document
characterSet	A string containing the character set of the document
childNodes[ ]	A collection of child nodes of the object
classes.*class.tag.style*	Deprecated; the *style* associated with the element in the document with the class name *class* and the tag name *tag*
cookie	A text string containing the document's cookie values

JavaScript Elements	Description
designMode	Specifies whether design mode is on or off
dir	A string holding the text direction of text enclosed in the document
doctype	Reference to the DocumentType object for the document
documentElement	Reference to the root node of the document object hierarchy
domain	The domain of the document
embeds	An array of the embedded objects in the document
expando	A Boolean dictating whether instance properties can be added to the object (*IE only*)
fgColor	The text color used in the document
firstChild	Reference to the first child node of the element, if one exists
form	A form within the document (the form itself is also an object)
forms	An array of the forms in the document
implementation	An object with method *hasFeature(feature, level)* that returns a Boolean indicating if the browser supports the feature given in the string *feature* at the DOM level passed in the string *level*
lastChild	Reference to the last child node of the element, if one exists
lastModified	The date the document was last modified
layers	An array of layer objects
linkColor	The color of hypertext links in the document
links	An array of the links within the document
localName	A string indicating the "local" XML name for the object
location	The URL of the document
media	The media for which the document is intended
nextSibling	Reference to next sibling of the node
nodeName	A string containing the name of the node, the name of the tag to which the object corresponds
nodeValue	A string containing value within the node
ownerDocument	Reference to the document in which the element is contained
parentNode	Reference to the parent of the object
parentWindow	Reference to the window that contains the document
previousSibling	Reference to the previous sibling of the node
protocol	A string containing the protocol used to retrieve the document—its full name
referrer	The URL of the document containing the link that the user accessed to get to the current document
security	A string that contains information about the document's certificate
styleSheets[ ]	Collection of style sheets in the document
title	The title of the document
URL	The URL of the document
vlinkColor	The color of followed hypertext links
XMLDocument	Reference to the top-level node of the XML DOM exposed by the document
XSLDocument	Reference to the top-level node of the XSL DOM exposed by the document

JavaScript Elements	Description
Methods	
addEventListener (whichEvent, handler, direction)	Instructs the object to execute the function *handler* whenever an event of the type stated in *whichEvent* occurs; *direction* is a Boolean telling which phase to fire; use true for capture and false for bubbling
appendChild(newChild)	Appends *newChild* to the end of the node's childNodes[ ] list
attachEvent(whichHandler, theFunction)	Attaches the function *theFunction* as a handler specified by the string *whichHandler*
clear()	Clears the contents of the document window
cloneNode(cloneChildren)	Clones the node and returns the new clone
close()	Closes the document stream
createAttribute(name)	Returns a new attribute node of a name given by string *name*
createComment(data)	Returns a new comment node with the text given by *data*
createElement(tagName)	Returns a new element object that corresponds to *tagName*
createEventObject ([eventObj])	Creates and returns a new Event instance to pass to *fireEvent()*
createStyleSheet ([url [,index]])	Creates a new styleSheet object from the Stylesheet at the URL in the string *url* and inserts it into the document at index *index*
createTextNode(data)	Returns a new text node with value given by *data*
detachEvent(whichHandler, theFunction)	Instructs the object to stop executing *theFunction* as a handler given the string *whichHandler*
dispatchEvent(event)	Causes *event* to be processed by the appropriate handler; is used to redirect events
fireEvent(handler [, event])	Fires the event handler given by *handler*
focus()	Gives focus to the document and fires *onfocus* handler
getElementById(id)	Returns the element with *id* (or *name*) that is equal to *id*
getElementByName(name)	Gets a collection of elements with *id* (or *name*) that is equal to *name*
getElementByTagName (tagname)	Gets a collection of elements corresponding to *tagname*
getSelection()	Returns the selected text from the document
hasAttributes()	Returns a Boolean showing if any attributes are defined for the node
hasChildNodes()	Returns a Boolean showing if the node has children
insertBefore(newChild, refChild)	Inserts the node *newChild* in front of *refChild* in the *childNodes*[ ] list of *refChild*'s parent node
isSupported(feature [, version])	Returns a Boolean showing which feature and version identified in the arguments is supported
normalize()	Merges adjacent text nodes in the subtree rooted at this element
open()	Opens the document stream
recalc([forceAll])	If *forceAll* is *true*, all dynamic properties are reevaluated
removeChild(oldChild)	Removes *oldChild* from the node's children and returns a reference to the removed node
removeEventListener (whichEvent, handler, direction)	Removes the function *handler* for the event declared in *whichEvent* for the phase stated in the Boolean *direction*

JavaScript Elements	Description
replaceChild(newChild, oldChild)	Replaces the node's child node *oldChild* with the node *newChild*
setActive()	Sets the document as the current element but does not give it focus
write()	Writes to the document window
writeln()	Writes to the document window on a single line (used only with preformatted text)
Event Handlers	
onClick	Runs when the document is clicked
onDblClick	Runs when the document is double-clicked
onKeyDown	Runs when a key is pressed down
onKeyPress	Runs when a key is initially pressed
onKeyUp	Runs when a key is released
onLoad	Runs when the document is initially loaded
onMouseDown	Runs when the mouse button is pressed down
onMouseUp	Runs when the mouse button is released
onUnLoad	Runs when the document is unloaded
Error	This object gives information about the error that occurred during runtime
Properties	
description	Describes the nature of the error
lineNumber	The line number that generated the error
number	The numeric value of the Microsoft-specific error number
File, FileUpload	A file upload element in an HTML form (use the FileUpload box's name)
Properties	
accessKey	Indicates the hotkey that gives the element focus
disabled	A Boolean signifying if the element is disabled
form	The form object containing the FileUpload box
name	The name of the FileUpload box
size	The width in pixels
tabIndex	A numeric value of the width in pixels
type	The type attribute of the FileUpload box
value	The pathname of the selected file in the FileUpload box
Methods	
blur()	Removes the focus from the FileUpload box
focus()	Gives the focus to the FileUpload box
handleEvent(*event*)	Invokes the event handler for the specified *event*
select()	Selects the input area of the FileUpload box
Event Handlers	
onBlur	Runs when the focus leaves the FileUpload box
onChange	Runs when the value in the FileUpload box is changed
onFocus	Runs when the focus is given to the FileUpload box

JavaScript Elements	Description
Form	An HTML form (use the form's name)
Properties	
acceptCharset	Specifies a list of character encodings for input data to be accepted by the server processing the form
action	The location of the CGI script that receives the form values
autocomplete	Specifies whether form autocompletion is on or off
elements[ ]	An array of elements within the form
encoding	The type of encoding used in the form
enctype	Specifies the MIME type of submitted data
length	The number of elements in the form
method	The type of method used when submitting the form
name	The name of the form
target	The name of the window into which CGI output should be directed
Methods	
handleEvent(*event*)	Invokes the event handler for the specified *event*
reset()	Resets the form
submit()	Submits the form to the CGI script
urns(*urn*)	Retrieves a collection of all elements to which the behavior of string *urn* is attached
Event Handlers	
onReset	Runs when the form is reset
onSubmit	Runs when the form is submitted
Frame	A frame window (use the frame's name)
Properties	
document	The current document in the frame window
frames	An array of frames within the frame window
length	The length of the frames array
name	The name of the frame
parent	The name of the window that contains the frame
self	The name of the current frame window
top	The name of the topmost window in the hierarchy of frame windows
window	The name of the current frame window
Methods	
alert(*message*)	Displays an Alert box with the text string *message*
blur()	Removes the focus from the frame
clearInterval(*ID*)	Cancels the repeated execution
clearTimeout(*ID*)	Cancels the delayed execution *ID*
confirm(*message*)	Displays a Confirm box with the text string *message*
open(*URL, name, features*)	Opens a URL in the frame with the name *name* and a feature list indicated by *features*
print()	Displays the Print dialog box

JavaScript Elements	Description
prompt(*message, response*)	Displays a Prompt dialog box with the text string *message* and the default value *response*
setInterval(*expression, time*)	Runs an *expression* after *time* milliseconds
setTimeout(*expression, time*)	Runs an *expression* every *time* milliseconds
Event Handlers	
onBlur	Runs when the focus is removed from the frame
onFocus	Runs when the frame receives the focus
onMove	Runs when the frame is moved
onResize	Runs when the frame is resized
h1…h6	Heading level element in the document
Properties	
align	The alignment of the element, for example, "right"
head	Corresponds to the <head> element in the document
Properties	
profile	A list of the URLs for data properties and legal values
hidden	A hidden field on an HTML form (use the name of the hidden field)
Properties	
form	The name of the form containing the hidden field
name	The name of the hidden field
type	The type of the hidden field
value	The value of the hidden field
history	An object containing information about the Web browser's history list
Properties	
current	The current URL in the history list
length	The number of items in the history list
next	The next item in the history list
previous	The previous item in the history list
Methods	
back()	Navigates back to the previous item in the history list
forward()	Navigates forward to the next item in the history list
go(*location*)	Navigates to the item in the history list specified by the value of *location*; the *location* variable can be either an integer or the name of the Web page
hr	A horizontal rule element in the document
Properties	
align	Alignment of the object, for example, "right"
color	The color of the rule
noShade	A Boolean indicating that the rule is not to be shaded
size	The size (height) of the rule in pixels
width	The width of the rule in pixels

JavaScript Elements	Description
html	Corresponds to the <html> element in the document
Properties	
version	The DTD version for the document
iframe	An inline frame element in the document
Properties	
align	The alignment of the object, for example, "right"
allowTransparency	A Boolean specifying whether the background of the frame can be transparent
border	The width of the border around the frame
contentDocument	The document that corresponds to the content of this frame
contentWindow	The window that corresponds to this frame
frameBorder	String of "0" (no border) or "1" (show border)
height	The height of the frame in pixels
longdesc	The URL of a long description for the frame
marginHeight	Vertical margins in pixels
marginWidth	Horizontal margins in pixels
name	The name of the frame
width	The width of the frame in pixels
image	An inline image (use the name assigned to the image)
Properties	
align	Specifies the alignment of the object, for example, "left", "right", or "center"
alt	A string containing alternative text for the image
border	The width of the image border in pixels
complete	A Boolean value indicating whether the image has been completely loaded by the browser
height	The height of the image in pixels
hspace	The horizontal space around the image in pixels
isMap	A Boolean indicating whether the image is a server-sid image map
longDesc	The URL for a more detailed description of the image
loop	An integer indicating how many times the image is to loop when activated
lowSrc	Specifies a URL for a lower-resolution image to display
lowsrc	The value of the lowsrc property of the <img> tag
name	The name of the image
nameProp	Indicates the name of the file given in the *src* attribute of the <img> tag
src	The URL of the image
style	Reference to the inline *Style* object for the element
useMap	Contains a URL to use as a client-side image map
vspace	The vertical space around the image in pixels
width	The width of the image in pixels
Methods	
handleEvent(*event*)	Invokes the event handler for the specified *event*

JavaScript Elements	Description
Event Handlers	
onAbort	Runs when the image load is aborted
onError	Runs when an error occurs while loading the image
onKeyDown	Runs when a key is pressed down
onKeyPress	Runs when a key is pressed
onKeyUp	Runs when a key is released
onLoad	Runs when the image is loaded
implementation	Information about the DOM technologies the browser supports (child of Document)
Methods	
hasFeature(feature [, version])	A Boolean indicating if the browser supports the feature at the DOM level given in version
label	A form field label in the document
Properties	
accessKey	Indicates the hotkey that gives the element focus
form	The form that encloses the label
layer	A document layer (use the name of the layer); deprecated in favor of the standard <div> element *(NS 4.0 only)*
Properties	
above	The layer above the current layer *(NS 4.0 only)*
background	The background image of the layer *(NS 4.0 only)*
below	The layer below the current layer *(NS 4.0 only)*
bgColor	The background color of the layer *(NS 4.0 only)*
clip.bottom, clip.height, clip.left, clip.right, clip.top, clip.width	The size and position of the layer's clipping area *(NS 4.0 only)*
document	The document containing the layer *(NS 4.0 only)*
name	The value of the *name* or *id* attribute for the layer *(NS 4.0 only)*
left	The *x*-coordinate of the layer *(NS 4.0 only)*
pageX	The *x*-coordinate relative to the document *(NS 4.0 only)*
pageY	The *y*-coordinate relative to the document *(NS 4.0 only)*
parentLayer	The containing layer *(NS 4.0 only)*
siblingAbove	The layer above in the zIndex *(NS 4.0 only)*
siblingBelow	The layer below in the zIndex *(NS 4.0 only)*
src	The URL of the layer document *(NS 4.0 only)*
top	The *y*-coordinate of the layer *(NS 4.0 only)*
visibility	The state of the layer's visibility *(NS 4.0 only)*
zIndex	The zIndex value of the layer *(NS 4.0 only)*
Methods	
handleEvent(*event*)	Invokes the event handler for the specified *event* *(NS 4.0 only)*
load(*source, width*)	Loads a new URL into the layer from *source* with the specified *width* *(NS 4.0 only)*

JavaScript Elements	Description
moveAbove(*layer*)	Moves the layer above *layer* (*NS 4.0 only*)
moveBelow(*layer*)	Moves the layer below *layer* (*NS 4.0 only*)
moveBy(*x, y*)	Moves the *x* pixels in the *x*-direction, and the *y* pixels in the *y*-direction (*NS 4.0 only*)
moveTo(*x, y*)	Moves the upper-left corner of the layer to the specified0 (*x, y*) coordinate (*NS 4.0 only*)
moveToAbsolute(*x, y*)	Moves the layer to the specified coordinate (*x, y*) within the page (*NS 4.0 only*)
resizeBy(*width, height*)	Resizes the layer by the specified *width* and *height* (*NS 4.0 only*)
resizeTo(*width, height*)	Resizes the layer to the specified *height* and *width* (*NS 4.0 only*)
Event Handlers	
onBlur	Runs when the focus leaves the layer (*NS 4.0 only*)
onFocus	Runs when the layer receives the focus (*NS 4.0 only*)
onLoad	Runs when the layer is loaded (*NS 4.0 only*)
onMouseOut	Runs when the mouse leaves the layer (*NS 4.0 only*)
onMouseOver	Runs when the mouse hovers over the layer (*NS 4.0 only*)
legend	A `<legend>` (fieldset caption) element in the document
Properties	
accessKey	Indicates the hotkey
align	Specifies the alignment of the element, for example, "right"
form	The form in which the element is enclosed
link	A link within an HTML document (use the name of the link)
Properties	
accessKey	Indicates the hotkey that gives the element focus
charset	The character set of the linked document
coords	Defines the coordinates of the object
disabled	A Boolean indicating whether the element is disabled
hash	The anchor name from the link's URL
host	The host from the link's URL
hostname	The hostname from the link's URL
href	The link's URL
hreflang	Indicates the language code of the linked resource
media	The media the linked document is intended for
nameProp	Holds the filename portion of the URL in the *href*
pathname	The path portion of the link's URL
port	The port number of the link's URL
protocol	The protocol used with the link's URL
search	The search portion of the link's URL
target	The target window of the hyperlinks
text	The text used to create the link
type	Specifies the media type in the form of a MIME type for the ink target
Methods	
handleEvent(*event*)	Invokes the event handler for the specified *event*

JavaScript Elements	Description
Event Handlers	
onClick	Runs when the link is clicked
onDblClick	Runs when the link is double-clicked
onKeyDown	Runs when a key is pressed down
onKeyPress	Runs when a key is initially pressed
onKeyUp	Runs when a key is released
onMouseDown	Runs when the mouse button is pressed down on the link
onMouseOut	Runs when mouse moves away from the link
onMouseOver	Runs when the mouse hovers over the link
onMouseUp	Runs when the mouse button is released
`location`	The location of the document
Properties	
hash	The location's anchor name
host	The location's hostname and port number
href	The location's URL
pathname	The path portion of the location's URL
port	The port number of the location's URL
protocol	The protocol used with the location's URL
Methods	
Assign(*url*)	Assigns the URL in the string *url* to the object
reload()	Reloads the location
replace(*url*)	Loads a new location with the address *url*
`map`	Corresponds to a <map> (client-side image map)element in the document
Properties	
Areas[ ]	A collection of *areas* enclosed by the object
Name	String holding the name of the image map
`Math`	An object used for advanced mathematical calculations
Properties	
E	The value of the base of natural logarithms (2.7182...)
LN10	The value of the natural logarithm of 10
LN2	The value of the natural logarithm of 2
LOG10E	The base 10 logarithm of E
LOG2E	The base 2 logarithm of E
PI	The value of pi (3.1416...)
SQRT1_2	The square root of $\frac{1}{2}$
SQRT2	The square root of 2
Methods	
abs(*number*)	Returns the absolute value of *number*
acos(*number*)	Returns the arc cosine of *number* in radians
asin(*number*)	Returns the arc sine of *number* in radians

JavaScript Elements	Description
atan(*number*)	Returns the arc tangent of *number* in radians
atan2()	Returns the arc tangent of the quotient of its arguments
ceil(*number*)	Rounds *number* up to the next-highest integer
cos(*number*)	Returns the cosine of *number*, where *number* is an angle expressed in radians
exp(*number*)	Raises the value of E (2.7182...) to the value of *number*
floor(*number*)	Rounds *number* down to the next-lowest integer
log(*number*)	Returns the natural logarithm of *number*
max(*number1, number2*)	Returns the greater of *number1* and *number2*
min(*number1, number2*)	Returns the lesser of *number1* and *number2*
pow(*number1, number2*)	Returns the value of *number1* raised to the power of *number2*
random()	Returns a random number between 0 and 1
round(*number*)	Rounds *number* to the closest integer
sin(*number*)	Returns the sine of *number*, where *number* is an angle expressed in radians
sqrt(*number*)	Returns the square root of *number*
tan(*number*)	Returns the tangent of *number*, where *number* is an angle expressed in radians
toString(*number*)	Converts *number* to a text string
menu	A <menu> (menu list) element in the document
Properties	
compact	A Boolean signifying whether the list should be compacted
navigator	An object representing the browser currently in use
Properties	
appCodeName	The code name of the browser
appName	The name of the browser
appVersion	The version of the browser
cookieEnabled	A Boolean signifying whether persistent cookies are enabled
language	The language of the browser
mimeTypes	An array of the MIME types supported by the browser
oscpu	A string containing the operating system
platform	The platform on which the browser is running
plugins	An array of the plug-ins installed on the browser
preference	Allows a signed script to get and set certain Navigator preferences (*NS 4.0 only*)
userAgent	The user-agent text string sent from the client to the Web serve
Methods	
javaEnabled()	Indicates whether the browser supports Java
plugins.refresh()	Checks for newly installed plug-ins
taintEnabled()	Specifies whether data tainting is enabled
Option	An option from a selection list (use the name of the option or the index value from the options array)
Properties	
defaultSelected	A Boolean indicating whether the option is selected by default
disabled	A Boolean indicating whether the element is disabled
index	The index value of the option
label	Alternate text for the option as specified in the *label* attribute

JavaScript Elements	Description
selected	A Boolean indicating whether the option is currently selected
text	The text of the option as it appears on the Web page
value	The value of the option
param	Corresponds to an occurrence of a `<param>` element in the document
Properties	
name	The name of the parameter
type	The type of the value when *valueType* is "ref"
value	The value of the parameter
valueType	Provides more information about how to interpret value; usually "data", "ref", or "object"
Password	A password field in an HTML form (use the name of the password field)
Properties	
defaultValue	The default password
name	The name of the password field
type	The type value of the password field
value	The value of the password field
Methods	
focus()	Gives the password field the focus
blur()	Leaves the password field
select()	Selects the password field
Event Handlers	
onBlur	Runs when the focus leaves the password field
onFocus	Runs when the password field receives the focus
plugin	A plug-in object in the Web page
Properties	
description	The description of the plug-in
filename	The plug-in filename
length	The number of MIME types supported by the plug-in
name	The name of the plug-in
popup	A popup window object created by using the `createPopup()` method in IE (*IE only*)
Properties	
document	Reference to the window's document (*IE only*)
isOpen	A Boolean indicating if the window is open (*IE only*)
Radio	A radio button in an HTML form (use the radio button's name)
PropertiesZ	
accessKey	Indicates the hotkey that gives the element focus
align	A string specifying the alignment of the element, for example, "right"
alt	Alternative text for the button

JavaScript Elements	Description
checked	A Boolean indicating whether a specific radio button has been checked
defaultChecked	A Boolean indicating whether a specific radio button is checked by default
defaultValue	The initial value of the button's *value* attribute
disabled	A Boolean indicating whether the element is disabled
form	The name of the form containing the radio button
name	The name of the radio button
type	The type value of the radio button
value	The value of the radio button
Methods	
blur()	Removes the focus from the radio button
click()	Clicks the radio button
focus()	Gives focus to the radio button
handleEvent(*event*)	Invokes the event handler for the specified *event*
Event Handlers	
onBlur	Runs when the focus leaves the radio button
onClick	Runs when the radio button is clicked
onFocus	Runs when the radio button receives the focus
RegExp	An object used for searching regular expressions
Properties	
global	Specifies whether to use a global pattern match
ignoreCase	Specifies whether to ignore case in the search string
input	The search string
lastIndex	Specifies the index at which to start matching the next string
lastMatch	The last matched characters
lastParen	The last parenthesized substring match
leftContext	The substring preceding the most recent match
multiline	Specifies whether to search on multiple lines
rightContext	The substring following the most recent match
source	The string pattern
Methods	
compile()	Compiles a regular search expression
exec(*string*)	Executes the search for a match to *string*
test(*string*)	Tests for a match to *string*
Reset	A reset button in an HTML form (use the name of the reset button)
Properties	
accessKey	Indicates the hotkey that gives the element focus
align	Specifies the alignment of the element, for example, "right"
alt	Alternative text for the button

JavaScript Elements	Description
defaultValue	Contains the initial value of the button
disabled	A Boolean indicating whether the element is disabled
form	The name of the form containing the reset button
name	The name of the reset button
type	The type value of the reset button
value	The value of the reset button
Methods	
blur()	Removes the focus from the reset button
click()	Clicks the reset button
focus()	Gives the focus to the reset button
handleEvent(*event*)	Invokes the event handler for the specified *event*
Event Handlers	
onBlur	Runs when the focus leaves the reset button
onClick	Runs when the reset button is clicked
onFocus	Runs when the reset button receives the focus
screen	An object representing the user's screen
Properties	
availHeight	The height of the screen, minus toolbars or any other permanent objects
availWidth	The width of the screen, minus toolbars or any other permanent objects
colorDepth	The number of possible colors in the screen
height	The height of the screen
pixelDepth	The number of bits per pixel in the screen
width	The width of the screen
Script	Corresponds to a <script> element in the document
Properties	
charset	The character set used to encode the script
defer	A Boolean indicating whether script execution may be deferred
src	The URL of the external script
text	The contents of the script
type	The value of the type attribute
Select	A selection list in an HTML form (use the name of the selection list)
Properties	
disabled	A Boolean indicating whether the element is disabled
form	The name of the form containing the selection list
length	The number of *options* in the selection list
multiple	A Boolean indicating whether multiple *options* may be selected
name	The name of the selection list
options[ ]	An array of options within the selection list; see the options object for more information on working with individual selection list options
selectedIndex	The index value of the selected option from the selection list

JavaScript Elements	Description
size	The number of options that are visible at one time
tabIndex	Numeric value that indicates the tab order for the object
type	The type value of the selection list
value	The *value* of the currently selected option

Methods

add(element, before)	Adds the *option* referenced by the *element* to the list of options before the *option* referenced by *before*; if *before* is null, it is added at the end
blur()	Removes the focus from the selection list
focus()	Gives the focus to the selection list
handleEvent(*event*)	Invokes the event handler for the specified *event*
remove(index)	Removes the option at index *index* from the list of *options*

Event Handlers

onBlur	Runs when the focus leaves the selection list
onChange	Runs when the focus leaves the selection list and the value of the selection list is changed
onFocus	Runs when the selection list receives the focus

`String`	An object representing a text string

Properties

length	The number of characters in the string

Methods

anchor(*name*)	Converts the string into a hypertext link anchor with the name *name*
big()	Displays the string using the <big> tag
blink()	Displays the string using the <blink> tag
bold()	Displays the string using the <b> tag
charAt(*index*)	Returns the character in the string at the location specified by *index*
charCodeAt(position)	Returns an unsigned integer of the Unicode value of the haracter at index *position*
concat(*string2*)	Concatenates the string with the second text string *string2*
fixed()	Displays the string using the <tt> tag
fontColor(*color*)	Sets the color attribute of the string
fontSize(*value*)	Sets the size attribute of the string
indexOf(*string, start*)	Searches the string, beginning at the *start* character, and returns the index value of the first occurrence of the string *string*
italics()	Displays the string using the <i> tag
lastIndexOf(*string, start*)	Searches the string, beginning at the *start* character, and locates the index value of the last occurrence of the string *string*
link(*href*)	Converts the string into a hypertext link pointing to the URL *href*
match(*expression*)	Returns an array containing the matches based on the regular expression *expression*
replace(*expression, new*)	Performs a search based on the regular expression *expression* and replaces the text with *new*
search(*expression*)	Performs a search based on the regular expression *expression* and returns the index number

JavaScript Elements	Description
slice(*begin, end*)	Returns a substring between the *begin* and the *end* index values; the *end* index value is optional
small()	Displays the string using the <small> tag
split(*separator*)	Splits the string into an array of strings at every occurrence of the *separator* character
strike()	Displays the string using the <strike> tag
sub()	Displays the string using the <sub> tag
substr(*begin, length*)	Returns a substring starting at the *begin* index value and continuing for *length* characters; the *length* parameter is optional
substring(*begin, end*)	Returns a substring between the *begin* and the *end* index values; the *end* index value is optional
sup()	Displays the string using the <sup> tag
toLowerCase()	Converts the string to lowercase
toUpperCase()	Converts the string to uppercase
style	This corresponds to an instance of a <style> element in the page
Properties	
disabled	A Boolean indicating whether the element is disabled
sheet	The styleSheet object corresponding to the element
styleSheet	The styleSheet object corresponding to the element
type	The value of the *type* attribute for the style sheet
Submit	A submit button in an HTML form (use the name of the submit button)
Properties	
accessKey	String indicating the hotkey that gives the element focus
alt	Alternative text for the button
defaultValue	The initial value of the button's *value* attribute
disabled	A Boolean indicating whether the element is disabled
form	The name of the form containing the submit button
name	The name of the submit button
tabIndex	Numeric value that indicates the tab order for the object
type	The type value of the submit button
value	The value of the submit button
Methods	
blur()	Removes the focus from the submit button
click()	Clicks the submit button
focus()	Gives the focus to the submit button
handleEvent(*event*)	Invokes the event handler for the specified *event*
Event Handlers	
onBlur	Runs when the focus leaves the submit button
onClick	Runs when the submit button is clicked
onFocus	Runs when the submit button receives the focus

JavaScript Elements	Description
Text	An input box from an HTML form (use the name of the input box)
Properties	
accessKey	A string indicating the hotkey that gives the element focus
defaultValue	The default value of the input box
disabled	A Boolean indicating whether the element is disabled
form	The form containing the input box
maxLength	The maximum number of characters the field can contain
name	The name of the input box
size	The width of the field in characters
tabIndex	The numeric value that indicates t1he tab order for the object
type	The type value of the input box
value	The value of the input bo
Methods	
blur()	Removes the focus from the input box
focus()	Gives the focus to the input box
handleEvent(*event*)	Invokes the event handler for the specified *event*
select()	Selects the input box
Event Handlers	
onBlur	Runs when the focus leaves the input box
onChange	Runs when the focus leaves the input box and the input box value changes
onFocus	Runs when the input box receives the focus
onSelect	Runs when some of the text in the input box is selected
Textarea	A text area box in an HTML form (use the name of the text area box)
Properties	
accessKey	Indicates the hotkey that gives the element focus
cols	The number of columns of the input area
defaultValue	The default value of the text area box
enabled	Indicates whether a text area field is enabled using a Boolean
form	The form containing the text area box
name	The name of the text area box
rows	The number of rows of the input area
tabIndex	Numeric value that indicates the tab order for the object
type	The type value of the text area box
value	The value of the text area box
Methods	
blur()	Removes the focus from the text area box
focus()	Gives the focus to the text area box
handleEvent(*event*)	Invokes the event handler for the specified *event*
select()	Selects the text area box
Event Handlers	
onBlur	Runs when the focus leaves the text area box
onChange	Runs when the focus leaves the text area box and the text area box value changes
onFocus	Runs when the text area box receives the focus
onKeyDown	Runs when a user presses a key
onKeyPress	Runs when a user presses or holds down a key
onKeyUp	Runs when a user releases a key
onSelect	Runs when some of the text in the text area box is selected

JavaScript Elements	Description
`window`	The document window
Properties	
clipboardData	Provides access to the OS's clipboard
defaultStatus	The default message shown in the window's status bar
directories	A Boolean specifying whether the Netscape 6 "directories" button is visible.
document	The document displayed in the window
frameElement	The *Frame* in which the window is enclosed
frames	An array of frames within the window (see the frames object for properties and methods applied to individual frames)
history	A list of visited URLs
innerHeight	The height of the window's display area
innerWidth	The width of the widow's display area
length	The number of frames in the window
location	The URL loaded into the window
locationbar.visible	A Boolean indicating the visibility of the window's location bar
menubar.visible	A Boolean indicating the visibility of the window's menu bar
name	The name of the window
opener	The name of the window that opened the current window
outerHeight	The height of the outer area of the window
outerWidth	The width of the outer area of the window
pageXOffset	The *x*-coordinate of the window
pageYOffset	The *y*-coordinate of the window
parent	The name of the window containing this particular window
personalbar.visible	A Boolean indicating the visibility of the window's personal bar
screen	The browser's *screen* object
screenLeft	The *x*-coordinate in pixels of the left edge of the client area of the browser window
screenTop	The *y*-coordinate in pixels of the top edge of the client area of the browser window
scrollbars.visible	A Boolean indicating the visibility of the window's scroll bars
scrollX	How far the window is scrolled to the right
scrollY	How far the window is scrolled down
self	The current window
status	The message shown in the window's status bar
statusbar.visible	A Boolean indicating the visibility of the window's status bar
toolbar.visible	A Boolean indicating the visibility of the window's toolbar
top	The name of the topmost window in a hierarchy of windows
window	The current window
Methods	
alert(*message*)	Displays the text contained in *message* in a dialog box
back()	Loads the previous page in the window
blur()	Removes the focus from the window
captureEvents()	Sets the window to capture all events of a specified type
clearInterval(*ID*)	Clears the interval for *ID*, set with the SetInterval method
clearTimeout()	Clears the timeout, set with the setTimeout method
close()	Closes the window
confirm(*message*)	Displays a confirmation dialog box with the text *message*
createPopup(*arg*)	Creates a popup window and returns a reference to the new popup object
disableExternalCapture	Disables external event capturing
enableExternalCapture	Enables external event capturing

JavaScript Elements	Description
find(*string, case, direction*)	Displays a Find dialog box, where *string* is the text to find in the window, *case* is a Boolean indicating whether the find is case-sensitive, and *direction* is a Boolean indicating whether the find goes in the backward direction (all of the parameters are optional)
focus()	Gives focus to the window
forward()	Loads the next page in the window
handleEvent(*event*)	Invokes the event handler for the specified *event*
moveBy(*horizontal, vertical*)	Moves the window by the specified amount in the *horizontal* and *vertical* directions
moveTo(*x, y*)	Moves the window to the *x*- and *y*-coordinates
open()	Opens the window
print()	Displays the Print dialog box
prompt(*message, default_text*)	Displays a Prompt dialog box with the text *message* (the default message is *default_text*)
releaseEvents(*event*)	Releases the captured events of a specified *event*
resizeBy(*horizontal, vertical*)	Resizes the window by the amount in the *horizontal* and *vertical* directions
resizeTo(*width, height*)	Resizes the window to the specified *width* and *height*
routeEvent(*event*)	Passes the *event* to be handled natively
scroll(*x, y*)	Scrolls the window to the *x, y* coordinate
scrollBy(*x, y*)	Scrolls the window by *x* pixels in the *x*-direction and *y* pixels in the *y*-direction
scrollTo(*x, y*)	Scrolls the window to the *x, y* coordinate
setActive( )	Sets the window to be active but does not give it the focus
setCursor(*type*)	Changes the cursor to *type*
setInterval(*expression, time*)	Evaluates the *expression* every *time* milliseconds have passed
setTimeout(*expression, time*)	Evaluates the *expression* after *time* milliseconds have passed
sizeToContent( )	Resizes the window so all contents are visible
stop()	Stops the window from loading
Event Handlers	
onBlur	Runs when the window loses the focus
onDragDrop	Runs when the user drops an object on or within the window
onError	Runs when an error occurs while loading the page
onFocus	Runs when the window receives the focus
onLoad	Runs when the window finishes loading
onMove	Runs when the window is moved
onResize	Runs when the window is resized
onUnload	Runs when the window is unloaded

JavaScript Operators, Keywords, and Syntactical Elements

Appendix F

The following table lists some of the important JavaScript operators, keywords, and syntactical elements. The first operators listed in the table are the assignment operators, used to assign values to variables and to document objects. The next operators are the arithmetic operators, used for performing arithmetic calculations on variables (addition, subtraction, multiplication, and division). The comparison operators are next and are used primarily in conditional expressions and in program loops. The JavaScript keywords listed in the table are special names reserved by JavaScript. The logical operators are used for evaluating whether an expression is true or false, and are primarily used in conditional expressions and in program loops. The last part of the table contains special syntax elements for marking the end of a program or for inserting a JavaScript comment.

Starting Data Files

There are no starting Data Files needed for this appendix.

Operators	Description
Assignment	**Operators used to assign values to variables**
=	Assigns the value of the variable on the right to the variable on the left ($x = y$)
+=	Adds the two variables and assigns the result to the variable on the left ($x \mathrel{+}= y$ is equivalent to $x = x + y$)
-=	Subtracts the variable on the right from the variable on the left and assigns the result to the variable on the left ($x\mathrel{-} = y$ is equivalent to $x = x - y$)
*=	Multiplies the two variables together and assigns the result to the variable on the left ($x \mathbin{*}= y$ is equivalent to $x = x * y$)
/=	Divides the variable on the left by the variable on the right and assigns the result to the variable on the left ($x \mathbin{/}= y$ is equivalent to $x = x / y$)
&=	Combines two expressions into a single expression (x &= y is equivalent to $x = x \mathbin{\&} y$)
%=	Divides the variable on the left by the variable on the right and assigns the remainder to the variable on the left ($x \mathbin{\%}= y$ is equivalent to $x = x \mathbin{\%} y$)
Arithmetic	**Operators used for arithmetic functions**
+	Adds two variables together ($x + y$)
-	Subtracts the variable on the right from the variable on the left ($x - y$)
*	Multiplies two variables together ($x * y$)
/	Divides the variable the left by the variable on the right (x / y)
%	Calculates the remainder after dividing the variable on the left by the variable on the right ($x \mathbin{\%} y$)
++	Increases the value of a variable by 1 ($x \mathbin{++}$ is equivalent to $x = x + 1$)
&	Combines two expressions ($x \mathbin{\&} y$) Decreases the value of variable by 1 ($x \mathbin{--}$ is equivalent to $x = x - 1$)
-	Changes the sign of a variable ($- x$)
Comparison	**Operators used for comparing expressions**
==	Returns true when the two expressions are equal ($x == y$)
!=	Returns true when the two expressions are not equal ($x \mathbin{!=} y$)
!==	Returns true when the values of the two expressions are equal ($x \mathbin{!==} y$)
>	Returns true when the expression on the left is greater than the expression on the right ($x > y$)
<	Returns true when the expression on the left is less than the expression on the right ($x < y$)
>=	Returns true when the expression on the left is greater than or equal to the expression on the right ($x >= y$)
<=	Returns true when the expression on the left is less than or equal to the expression on the right ($x <= y$)

Operators	Description
Conditional	**Operators used to determine values based on conditions that are either true or false**
(condition) ? *value1 : value2*	If *condition* is true, then this expression equals *value1*; otherwise it equals *value2*
Keywords	**JavaScript keywords are reserved by JavaScript**
infinity	Represents positive infinity (often used with comparison operators)
this	Refers to the current object
var	Declares a variable
with	Allows the declaration of all the properties for an object without directly referencing the object each time
Logical	**Operators used for evaluating true and false expressions**
^	The XOR (exclusive OR) operator
!	Reverses the Boolean value of the expression
&&	Returns true only if both expressions are true (also known as an AND operator)
||	Returns true when either expression is true (also known as an OR operator)
|	Returns true if the expression is false and false if the expression is true (also known as a NEGATION operator)
Syntax	**Syntactical elements**
;	Indicates the end of a command line
/ comments */*	Used for inserting *comments* within a JavaScript command line
// comments	Used to create a line of *comments*

Exploring Filters and Transitions

Appendix G

If you are supporting only the Internet Explorer browser, you can take advantage of an IE-only style known as the filter. A **filter** is an effect that is applied to an object or page to change its appearance. Using Internet Explorer filters, you can make text or images appear partially transparent, add a drop shadow, or make an object appear to glow. Filters were introduced in Internet Explorer version 4.0 and are not supported by other browsers, so you have to use them with caution. Filters can be applied to any element with a defined height and width.

A filter is applied either by adding a filter style to the Web page's style sheet or by running a JavaScript command that applies the filter style to an object in the document. Let's first look at how to create a filter using styles.

Starting Data Files

There are no starting Data Files needed for this appendix.

Applying Filters Using CSS Styles

The syntax that Internet Explorer uses to employ the filter style differs between earlier versions of Internet Explorer and current versions of the browser. In IE version 4.0, the filter style is expressed as

```
filter: filter_name(params)
```

where *filter_name* is the name of one of the many Internet Explorer 4.0 filters, and *params* are the parameter values (if any) that apply to the filter. The syntax for filter styles employed in Internet Explorer 5.5 and above is:

```
filter: progid:DXImageTransform.Microsoft.filter_name(params)
```

In addition to the syntactical differences between the two versions, there are some differences in how different versions of Internet Explorer apply the filter style. In Internet Explorer 4.0, the filter effect is clipped when it is set too close to an object's boundary; with Internet Explorer 5.5 and above, the filter effect extends beyond an object's boundary.

Figure G-1 lists some of the filter names and parameters supported by Internet Explorer 5.5 and above.

Figure G-1   **Internet Explorer filters**

Filter Name	Parameters	Description
Alpha	style=0, 1, 2, 3 opacity=1–100 finishOpacity=1–100 startX=1–100 finishX=1–100 startY=1–100 finishY=1–100	Applies a transparency filter. A low opacity value makes the object transparent, while a high value makes the object opaque. The style parameter is used to indicate the direction of the transparency effect. The rest of the parameters control where in element the transparency is applied
BasicImage	rotation=0, 1, 2, 3 opacity=0–1 mirror=0, 1 invert=0, 1 xRay=0, 1 grayscale=0,1	Modifies the appearance of the object. The rotation parameter rotates the object (0=0 deg., 1=90 deg., 2=180 deg., 3=270 deg.). The opacity parameter sets the opacity of the object. The remaining parameters, if their values are set to "1," create a mirror image, invert the object, apply an "x-ray" effect, or display the object in grayscale
Blur	pixelRadius=*value* makeShadow =true,false shadowOpacity=0–1	Blurs the object. The pixelRadius parameter determines the amount of the blurring. The makeShadow and shadowOpacity parameters apply shadowing to the blur effect
Chroma	color=#*rrggbb*	Makes a specified color in the object transparent
DropShadow	color=#*rrggbb* offX=*value* offY=*value*	Creates a drop shadow of the specified color with a length of offX in the x-direction and offY in the y-direction
Emboss		Applies an embossing effect to the object
Engrave		Applies an engraving effect to the object
Glow	color=#*rrggbb* strength=1–255	Applies a glowing border around the object with the size of the glow determined by the strength parameter and the glow's color determined by the color parameter

Filter Name	Parameters	Description
Gradient	gradientType=0, 1 startColorStr=#rrggbb endColorStr=#rrggbb	Applies a color gradient to the object. The gradientType parameter determines the direction of the gradient, either vertical (0) or horizontal (1). The startColorStr and endColorStr parameters indicate the starting and ending colors. Intermediate colors are supplied by the filter
MotionBlur	direction=angle strength=1–255	Applies a motion blur effect. The direction parameter provides the angle of the motion, and the strength parameter indicates the length of the motion lines
Pixelate	maxSquare=value	Pixelates the object, where maxSquare is the size of the pixel
Shadow	direction=angle color=#rrggbb strength=1–255	Applies a simple drop shadow to the object with the angle of the shadow specified by the direction parameter, the color by the color parameter, and the size of the shadow determined by the strength parameter
Wave	freq=value lightStrength=value phase=value strength=value	Applies a sine-wave distortion to the object; the appearance of the wave is determined by the four parameters

For example, to apply a drop shadow filter in Internet Explorer 5.5 or above, you would add the following filter style to the element:

```
filter: progid:DXImageTransform.Microsoft.dropShadow (color=#FF0000,
offX=5, offY=10)
```

which places a red drop shadow (the hexadecimal color value of red is #FF0000) around the image with an offset of 5 pixels to the right and 10 pixels down. Figure G-2 shows some examples of other IE filter styles applied to an inline image.

Examples of IE filters | **Figure G-2**

| original image | MotionBlur
(direction = 90, strength = 100) | Pixelate
(maxSquare = 10) | Engrave() |

Internet Explorer supports both the 4.0 and 5.5 filter styles, and you may find the 4.0 styles easier to work with in some situations. Figure G-3 describes how some of the version 4.0 filters are matched with their 5.5 counterparts.

IE 4.0 Filter	IE 5.5 Filter
Alpha	progid:DXImageTransform.Microsoft.Alpha
Blur	progid:DXImageTransform.Microsoft.MotionBlur
Chroma	progid:DXImageTransform.Microsoft.Chroma
DropShadow	progid:DXImageTransform.Microsoft.dropShadow
FlipH	progid:DXImageTransform.Microsoft.BasicImage(rotation=2, mirror=1)
FlipV	progid:DXImageTransform.Microsoft.BasicImage(mirror=1)
Glow	progid:DXImageTransform.Microsoft.Glow
Gray	progid:DXImageTransform.Microsoft.BasicImage(grayscale=1)
Invert	progid:DXImageTransform.Microsoft.BasicImage(invert=1)
Light	progid:DXImageTransform.Microsoft.Light
Mask	progid:DXImageTransform.Microsoft.MaskFilter
Shadow	progid:DXImageTransform.Microsoft.Shadow
Wave	progid:DXImageTransform.Microsoft.Wave
Xray	progid:DXImageTransform.Microsoft.BasicImage(xray=1)

Filters can also be combined to create interesting visual effects. The effects are added in the order in which they are entered into the style declaration. To combine the alpha filter with a drop shadow, for example, you would enter the following set of filters:

```
filter: progid:DXImageTransform.Microsoft.Shadow(direction=135,
color=#0000FF strength=5)
progid:DXImageTransform.Microsoft.Alpha(style=0, opacity=30)
```

This code applies a drop shadow to the object, and then changes the opacity value to 30. If you switch the order of the filters, the drop shadow is added after the object is made transparent, meaning that the shadow itself is not made transparent. You can also apply the same filter several times. For example, you can add two drop shadows to the same object by applying two shadow filters.

Most browsers do not support the Internet Explorer filter styles, and they are not part of the official specifications for CSS. When other browsers encounter a style sheet that employs the filter style, they usually ignore those particular styles while processing the other styles in the sheet. You can also use IE conditional comments to apply the filter styles only to select IE browsers.

Applying a Filter Style with JavaScript

As with other style attributes, the filter style can be applied in JavaScript using the style property. The syntax for applying a filter style is

```
object.style.filter = filter_text
```

where *object* is an object in the Web page, and *filter_text* is the text of the filters applied to the object. As in a style sheet, the text string can contain multiple filters separated by spaces. For example, to apply the alpha filter to the first inline image in a document, you could use the following JavaScript command:

```
document.images[0].style.filter = "progid:DXImageTransform.Microsoft.
Alpha(style=0, opacity=30)";
```

Internet Explorer's version of JavaScript also recognizes the **filter collection**, which is the collection of all filters associated with a particular object. The reference syntax of the filter collection is

```
object.filters[idref]
```

where *object* is an object that has some filters applied to it, and *idref* is either the index number or the name of a filter within that collection. As with other arrays, the index numbering starts at 0. For example, the expression

```
document.images[0].filters[1]
```

references the second filter associated with the first inline image in the document. If you want to reference the filter by its name, you would use a reference such as

```
document.images[0].filters["DXImageTransform.Microsoft.Alpha"]
```

where Internet Explorer's Alpha filter is one of the filters applied to the first inline image in the document. One of the purposes of using JavaScript to work with filter styles is to modify the parameter values. You can reference specific parameters within each filter using the syntax

```
filter.param
```

where *filter* is a specific filter in an object's filters collection, and *param* is the name of a parameter associated with the filter. For example, to change the opacity value of the Alpha filter for the first inline image, you could run the following expression:

```
document.images[0].filters["DXImageTransform.Microsoft.Alpha"]
.opacity = 25;
```

This command works only if the Alpha filter has already been defined for the inline image.

Using a Light Filter

Another popular filter that can add visual interest to Web pages is the Light filter, which creates the illusion of a light (or multiple lights) illuminating an object. Much like a drop shadow, adding a light source can give page elements a dynamic 3D effect. The style to create a Light filter in Internet Explorer 4.0 is:

```
filter: Light()
```

In Internet Explorer 5.5 and above, the style is:

```
filter: progid:DXImageTransform.Microsoft.Light()
```

Once you've created the Light filter, the next step is to define a light source for the object. This is done not with a style declaration, but with a JavaScript command. The three methods for creating a light source are: addAmbient(), addPoint(), and addCone(). The addAmbient() method applies an overall or ambient light to the object. The syntax of the method is

```
object.filters.Light.addAmbient(red, green, blue, strength)
```

where *object* is the object being illuminated; *red*, *green*, and *blue* are the RGB color values of the light; and *strength* is the strength of the light source, expressed as a number from 0 to 100. For example, the following statement adds a red light source at highest intensity on the document's first inline image:

```
document.images[0].filters.Light.addAmbient(255,0,0,100)
```

The addAmbient() method doesn't assume a specific location for the light source. To specify a location for the light, you can use the addPoint() method, which creates a point light source hovering above the object. The syntax to add a point light source to the Light filter is

```
object.filters.Light.addPoint(x, y, z, red, green, blue, strength)
```

where *x* and *y* are the horizontal and vertical coordinates of the light source, and *z* is the height, in pixels, of the light source above the object. For example, to create a high-intensity red light source 50 pixels "above" the object at the (x,y) coordinates (50, 75), you would use the following expression:

```
document.images[0].filters.Light.addPoint(50,75,50,255,0,0,100)
```

The addPoint() method assumes that the light is shone directly down on the object. If you want the light source to shine at an angle, you need to use the addCone() method. The syntax of the addCone() method is

```
object.filters.Light.addCone(x, y, z, x2, y2, red, green, blue,
strength, spread)
```

where *x, y, z* are once again the coordinates of the light source and *x2, y2* are the coordinates of the focus of the light—where the light actually "hits" the object. The spread parameter indicates the angle (or spread) of the light between the light source and the surface of the object. The spread parameter varies from 0 to 90 degrees. The other parameters have the same meanings as those used with the addAmbient() and addPoint() methods.

You can create up to 10 light sources to illuminate a particular object. Internet Explorer assigns each light source a number. The first light source you define has a light number of 0; the second light source has a value of 1, and so on. Once a light source has been created, Internet Explorer provides several methods to manipulate it. You can move the light source to a new location, change its color, change its intensity, or remove the light altogether. To move the light source to another location, use the method

```
object.filters.Light.moveLight(light, x, y, z, absolute)
```

where *light* is the light source's light number; *x,y,* and *z* are the new coordinates of the light source; and *absolute* is a Boolean value that has the value true when the new coordinates are expressed in absolute terms, and has the value false when the coordinates are expressed relative to the present coordinates of the light source. To change the color of the light, use the method

```
object.filters.Light.changeColor(light, red, green, blue, absolute)
```

where *red, green,* and *blue* are the new RGB color values of the light source; and *absolute* is a Boolean value that is true when the color values are expressed as absolute values, and false when the color values are to be added to the light source's current color values. You can use negative color values if the absolute parameter is set to false.

To change the intensity of the light source, use the method

```
object.filters.Light.changeStrength(light, strength, absolute)
```

where *strength* is the new strength of the light source, and *absolute* is a Boolean value that is set to true if the strength parameter is expressed in absolute terms, and false if the value of the strength parameter is to be added to the light source's current strength. Once again, the strength parameter can be negative if the value of the absolute parameter is set to false.

As you create light sources, you can remove the effect of a particular light source by setting its strength parameter back to 0. You can remove all of the light sources applied to a particular object by using the following method:

```
object.filters.Light.clear()
```

Internet Explorer does not provide a method of removing a specific light source while keeping all of the others.

By combining various filter styles including the different light filters with JavaScript, you can create wonderful visual effects with very little extra programming and no need to install specialized add-ins. However, remember these effects will be visible only to users of Internet Explorer.

Introducing Transitions

A second type of special effect supported by Internet Explorer is the transition. A **transition** is a visual effect that is applied to an object over an interval of time. For example, instead of having a pop-up menu disappear instantaneously, you can apply a transition that makes the pop-up menu appear to gradually blend into the background until it disappears. Transition styles are applied using the same format you use with filter styles. The transition styles first introduced with IE 4.0, are entered as

```
filter: filter_name(params)
```

and transitions introduced with IE 5.5 are entered as

```
filter: progid:DXImageTransform.Microsoft.filter_name(params)
```

where *filter_name* is the name of a transition style and params are parameters used by that transition. Internet Explorer 4.0 supports two possible transition values for *filter_name*: blend and reveal. In IE 4.0, a **blend transition** is a transition in which one object is blended into another. The style to create a blend transition is

```
filter: blendTrans(duration = value)
```

where *value* is the amount of time, in seconds, for the blending transition to take place. Two separate objects need not be used. You can apply a blend transition on a single object by initially making the object invisible (using the visibility style) and then applying the blendTrans() filter to move it to a visible state. A **reveal transition** is a more general transition in which a visual effect is applied as one object is changed into another. The style for the reveal transition under IE 4.0 is

```
filter: revealTrans(duration = value, transition = type)
```

where *type* is a number from 0 to 23, specifying the transition effect. The various transition effects and their numeric values are listed in Figure G-4.

Figure G-4 ▶ **Internet Explorer 4.0 transition styles**

Transition	Type Number	Transition	Type Number
Box In	0	Random Dissolve	12
Box Out	1	Split Vertical In	13
Circle In	2	Split Vertical Out	14
Circle Out	3	Split Horizontal In	15
Wipe Up	4	Split Horizontal Out	16
Wipe Down	5	Strips Left Down	17
Wipe Right	6	Strips Left Up	18
Wipe Left	7	Strips Right Down	19
Vertical Blinds	8	Strips Right Up	20
Horizontal Blinds	9	Random Bars Horizontal	21
Checkerboard Across	10	Random Bars Vertical	22
Checkerboard Down	11	Random	23

Figure G-5 shows an example of the circle out transition (with transition type number equal to 3) that transitions the inline image from one image file to another.

Figure G-5 ▶ **IE 4.0 circle out transition**

initial image   revealTrans(duration = 10, transition = 3)   final image

In Internet Explorer 5.5, the blendTrans() and revealTrans() transitions were replaced by a whole library of transition effects. Figure G-6 describes some of the Internet Explorer 5.5 transitions and their parameters. In addition to the parameters listed in Figure G-6, each transition also supports the duration parameter, which indicates how many seconds the transition lasts.

Internet Explorer 5.5 transition styles ◀ **Figure G-6**

Transition Name	Parameters	Description
Barn	motion=out, in orientation=horizontal, vertical	Applies a "barn door" transition
Blinds	bands=*value* direction=up, down, left, right	Applies a "window blinds" effect
Checkboard	direction=up, down, left, right squaresX=*value* squaresY=*value*	Creates a checkboard transition. The size of the checkboard is determined by the squaresX and squaresY parameters
Fade	overlap=0–1	Fades one object into another. The overlap parameter controls the degree of overlap as the fade occurs
GradientWipe	gradientSize=0–1 wipeStyle=0, 1 motion=forward, reverse	Wipes one object into another. The gradientSize parameter controls the blurring effect. The wipeStyle parameter indicates whether to wipe left to right (0) or up to down (1)
Inset		Applies an inset transition
Iris	irisStyle=*multiple* motion=out, in	Applies an iris-opening transition effect.The style of the iris is determined by the irisStyle parameter
Pixelate	maxSquare=*value*	Applies a pixelate transition, where maxSquare is the size of the pixel
RadialWipe	wipeStyle=clock, wedge, radial	Applies a radial wipe transition
RandomBars	orientation=horizontal, vertical	Applies a random bars transition
RandomDissolve	duration=*value*	Dissolves one object into another. The duration parameter indicates the dissolve time in seconds
Slide	slideStyle=hide, push, swap bands=value	Slides one object over or into another
Spiral	gridSizeX=*value* gridSizeY=*value*	Spirals one object into another
Stretch	stretchStyle=hide, push, spin	Stretches one object into another
Strips	motion=left-up, left-down, right-up, right-down	Wipes one object over another in a diagonal direction
Wheel	spokes=*value*	Applies a wheel transition
ZigZag	gridSizeX=*value* gridSizeY=*value*	Applies a zig-zag transition

Figure G-7 shows an example of applying the IE 5.5 stretch transition to replace one inline image with another.

| Figure G-7 | ▶ | IE 5.5 stretch style transition |

    initial image   stretch (stretchStyle = push)   final image

Scripting a Transition

The code for scripting a transition follows the same syntax described earlier for filters. For example, the code to apply the RadialWipe transition with a WipeStyle value of "clock" to an object is

```
object.style.filter =
"progId:DXImageTransform.Microsoft.RadialWipe(WipeStyle=clock)"
```

where *object* is the object receiving the transition style. You can also use the filters collection to modify the parameter value of a selected transition. The following code sets the WipeStyle parameter of the RadialWipe transition to a value, of "clock":

```
object.filters["DXImageTransform.Microsoft.RadialWipe"].WipeStyle="clock";
```

Again, if you use a filters collection, you must define a filter style in the style sheet for the object.

Running a Transition

If you want to see the effect of a transition style on your object, you have to run it using a series of JavaScript commands. Running a transition involves four steps:

1. Setting the initial state of the object

2. Applying a transition to the object

3. Specifying the final state of the object

4. Playing the transition

    The initial state of the object is the status of the object before the transition. This includes such things as the visibility property of the object, the source of an inline image, or any HTML code applied to the object. Once the initial state of the object has been determined, you apply the transition by using the apply() method

```
object.filters[idref].apply();
```

where *object* is the object that you want to apply the transition and idref is either the index number or the text of the transition name. Applying the transition does not actually run the transition, because the final state of the object has not been determined yet. At this point, it simply "freezes" the object in its initial state. Once the transition has been applied, you can write code to modify the appearance of the object, but because the object is frozen, these changes will not appear in the Web page.

After you've defined the final state of the object, you use the play() method to "unfreeze" the object and run the transition effect, moving the object from its initial state to its final state. The syntax for playing a transition is

```
object.filters[idref].play(duration);
```

where *duration* is the time, in seconds, for the transition to run. Note that for IE 4.0 transitions, the duration of the transition is entered as a parameter of the transition. The following code demonstrates how to create a transition between two sources for an inline image.

```
<style type="text/css">
    #Img1 {filter: progid:DXImageTransform.Microsoft.Slide(slideStyle =
push, Bands = 1)}
</style>
<script type="text/javascript">
var img = document.getElementById("Img1");
img.onclick = transitionImage;

function transitionImage() {
    img.filters[0].apply();
    img.src = "slide2.jpg";
    img.filters[0].play(2);
}
</script>
```

This code applies the transition to an inline image file whose ID attribute is equal to "Img1". When a user clicks the inline image, the transitionImage() function is called. The apply() method applies the Slide transition to the image and freezes it. The source of the inline image is changed to the slide2.jpg file. The play() method is then invoked, running the Slide transition for two seconds. After the transition is complete, the Img1 object is left displaying a new inline image.

The IE transitions can be applied to any HTML object. The following code shows how to apply a Fade-out transition to a div element containing a quote from Hamlet:

```
<style type="text/css">
    #Hamlet {visibility: visible; position: absolute}
    #Hamlet {filter: progid:DXImageTransform.Microsoft.Fade(overlap = 1)}
</style>
<script type="text/javascript">
var Hamlet = document.getElementById("Hamlet");
Hamlet.onclick = fadeOut;
```

```
function fadeOut() {
   Hamlet.filters[0].apply();
   Hamlet.style.visibility = "hidden";
   Hamlet.filters[0].play();
}
</script>
<div id="Hamlet" onclick="fadeOut()">
   <h1>The Rest is Silence</h1>
</div>
```

In this example, the text string will fade out when the user clicks it, changing its state from visible to hidden. Because this is a div element, you must define an absolute position before the transition can be applied. The span element has a similar requirement.

Using Interpage Transitions

Internet Explorer also allows you to create transitions between one Web page and another. These transitions, known as **interpage transitions**, involve effects applied to a page when a browser either enters or exits the page. Interpage transitions are created using the meta element within the head section of the HTML file. The meta element specifies the type of transition, the duration, and whether it's applied on entering or exiting the page. The four types of transitions occur when a user initially enters the Web page, exits the page, enters the Web site, or exits the site. The syntax for the four different interpage transitions are

```
<meta http-equiv = "Page-Enter" content = "type" />

<meta http-equiv = "Page-Exit" content = "type" />

<meta http-equiv = "Site-Enter" content = "type" />

<meta http-equiv = "Site-Exit" content = "type" />
```

where *type* is one of the transitions supported by Internet Explorer and the http-equiv attribute specifies when the transition should be applied. The syntax for the transition type is the same for interpage transitions as it is for an object within a page. These transitions appear only when you go from one page to another or from one Web site to another. A user does not see a Page-Enter transition if the page is the first file the user opens when starting a Web browser.

For example, to display an inset transition with a duration of 3 seconds when a user enters the page, you would apply the following meta element:

```
<meta http-equiv="Page-Enter"
content="progid:DXImageTransform.Microsoft.Inset(duration=3)" />
```

To apply a 2-second Wheel transition upon exiting the page, you would add the following meta element to the page head:

```
<meta http-equiv="Page-Exit"
content="progid:DXImageTransform.Microsoft.Wheel(Spokes=8, duration=2)" />
```

If a browser other than Internet Explorer encounters these meta elements, it will open or exit the page as usual without attempting to apply the transition style. So, do not rely on these transitions if you plan on supporting non–IE browsers.

Review | **Appendix Summary**

This appendix examined the Internet Explorer-only styles to create filters and transitions. It showed how to use filters to add drop shadows, blurs, light illumination and other special effects to document objects. It also examined how to apply graphic transitions between one document object and another. The appendix then examined how to work with these styles under both CSS and JavaScript. The appendix concluded by examining how to use the meta element to create interpage transitions.

Key Terms

blend transition

filter

filter collection

interpage transition

reveal transition

transition

Glossary/Index

Note: Boldface entries include definitions.

Special Characters

/~(backslash), JVS 262, JVS 524

< (left angle bracket), JVS 83–84, JVS 524, JVS F2

> (right angle bracket), JVS 84, JVS 524, JVS F2

( ) (parentheses), JVS 524

 (curly brackets), JVS 524

! (exclamation point), JVS 84, JVS 524, JVS F3

" (double quotation marks), JVS 524

(hash mark), JVS 524

$ (dollar sign), JVS 255, JVS 262, JVS 524

% (percent sign), JVS 67, JVS 524, JVS F2

& (ampersand), JVS 84, JVS 524, JVS F2, JVS F3

 * (asterisk), JVS 67, JVS 69, JVS 244, JVS 261, JVS 262, JVS 524, JVS F2, JVS F3

 + (plus sign), JVS 67, JVS 68, JVS 69, JVS 261, JVS 262, JVS 524, JVS F2

 – (minus sign), JVS 67, JVS 68, JVS 69, JVS 524, JVS F2

 / (forward slash), JVS 67, JVS 262, JVS 524, JVS F2, JVS F3

 = (equal sign), JVS 68, JVS 69, JVS 84, JVS 130, JVS 524, JVS F2

 ? (question mark), JVS 261, JVS 262, JVS 524

@ (at sign), JVS 524

[ ] (square brackets), JVS 524

^ (caret), JVS 255, JVS 262, JVS 524, JVS F3

| (pipe), JVS 84, JVS 262, JVS F3

. (period), JVS 262, JVS 524

: (colon), JVS 524

; (semicolon), JVS 524, JVS F3

` and ' (single quotation mark), JVS 524

A

<a> element, JVS C6

<abbr> element, JVS C6

absolute position A style that places an element at specific coordinates within its parent element, which is usually the document window. JVS B24–B25

absolute unit A measurement unit that is fixed in size regardless of the device rendering the Web page, specified in one of five standard units of measurement: mm (millimeters), cm (centimeters), in (inches), pt (points), or pc (picas). JVS B9

access key A key on the keyboard that is held down while pressing other keys or selecting items with the pointer. JVS A33

<acronym> element, JVS C6

action, canceling, JVS 348–350

<address> element, JVS C6

aggregator. See feed reader

AJAX (Asynchronous JavaScript and XML) A collection of programming techniques that allow browsers to retrieve data on demand from the Web without having to load a new Web page or reload the current page. JVS 729–779

 AJAX Web application model, JVS 733–735

 building autocomplete input box, JVS 768–778

 CGI scripts. See CGI script

 classic Web application model, JVS 732–733

 history, JVS 731–732

 jQuery applications, JVS 778

 JSON. See JSON (JavaScript ObjectNotation)

 limitations, JVS 735

 reading XML documents with AJAX, JVS 752

 RSS newsreaders, JVS 750–757

 XML. See XML (Extensible Markup Language)

 XMLHttpRequest object. See XMLHttpRequest object

AJAX engine In the AJAX Web application model, the object responsible for communicating with the server and returning any information from the server to the user interface. JVS 733

AJAX Web application model A Web application model that adds an intermediary between the user and the server-side system, called an AJAX engine. JVS 733–735

alert box. See alert dialog box

alert dialog box A dialog box generated by JavaScript that displays a text message with an OK button, which a user clicks to close the dialog box. JVS 37–38, JVS 614

 form validation, JVS 237–239

alignment of element content, JVS B13–B14

Alpha filter, JVS G2, JVS G4

alternate style sheet A style sheet that has a rel attribute value of "alternate stylesheet" and is identified by its title attribute. JVS 418

ampersand (&)

 arithmetic operators, JVS F2

 assignment operators, JVS F2

 escape character, JVS 524

 logical operator, JVS 84, JVS F3

anchor The code to mark a location within a document to which you want to be able to link. JVS A16

Anchor element, JVS E2

anonymous function A function without a name. JVS 304

 applying to events, JVS 460

 rollovers, JVS 459–461

 with timed commands, JVS 499

appendChild() method, JVS 380, JVS 381

appending from data, JVS 276

Applet element, JVS E2

<applet> element, JVS C7

apply() method, JVS 687–690

Area element, JVS E2–E3

<area> element, JVS C7

arguments variable, JVS 703–704

arithmetic operator An operator that performs simple mathematical calculation, such as +, –, *. /, and %., JVS 66–67

ARPANET, JVS A1

array A collection of data values organized under a single name. JVS 109–120

 array methods, JVS 119–120

 creating and populating, JVS 110–114

 customized functions, JVS 127

 extracting and inserting items, JVS 117–120

 extracting text strings, JVS 250

 length, JVS 110, JVS 114–115

 For loops, JVS 124–125

 menus, JVS 178–179

 multidimensional, JVS 147

 reversing, JVS 115

 shuffling, JVS 117

 sorting, JVS 116–117

C

calculated field, forms, JVS 230–234

calendar() function, JVS 108–109, JVS 135–144

    highlighting current date, JVS 141–143

    placing first day of month, JVS 137–138

    setting calendar date, JVS 143–144

    setting first day of month, JVS 136–137

    testing, JVS 141

    writing calendar days, JVS 138–141

calling functions, JVS 689

call() method, JVS 687–690

camel case Capitalization of multiple words where the initial word is lowercase, but the first letter of subsequent words is uppercase. JVS 176–177

caption, Web table, JVS A21

<caption> element, JVS C9

capture phase Under the W3C event model, the phase in which the event moves down the object hierarchy. JVS 306

caret (^)

    escape character, JVS 524

    escape sequence, JVS 262

    logical operator, JVS F3

    text string beginning marker, JVS 255

Cascading Style Sheet (CSS) A language used to write a set of declarations describing the layout and appearance of a Web site. JVS B1–B44

    applying style sheets, JVS B3–B8

    background image, JVS B15

    borders, JVS B21–B23

    clipping content, JVS B18–B19

    color, JVS B14–15

    content overflow, JVS B18

    creating thumbnails, JVS 469

    element display style, JVS B28–B30

    element height, JVS B18

    element width, JVS B17

    embedded styles, JVS B3–B5

    external style sheets, JVS B5–B6

    hiding elements, JVS B29–B30

    image placement, JVS B15–B17

    margins, JVS B20–B21

    media, JVS B37–B39

    opacity settings, JVS 488–490

    padding, JVS B23

    positioning elements. *See* positioning elements

    print styles. *See* print style

    retrieving style sheet values, JVS 199

    selectors. *See* selector

    style comments, JVS B7

    style inheritance, JVS B8

    style precedence, JVS B7

    supporting older browsers, JVS B38

    text style. *See* text style

cell, spanning, JVS A21–A23

cell padding The space between the content of a table cell and the cell border. JVS A24

cell spacing The amount of space between table cells. JVS A23–A24

<center> element, JVS C9

CGI script, JVS 761–768

    interacting with, JVS 765–768

    loading, JVS 763–765

    Perl, JVS 762–763

    viewing, JVS 769–770

character class A collection of characters used to limit the regular expression to a select group of characters. JVS 257–260

    regular expressions, JVS 259–260

character code, JVS 346–347

character type, regular expressions, JVS 257–259

character-formatting element An inline element used to define the appearance or format of text within a block. JVS A14–A15

charAT() method, JVS 245

check box A control element for specifying an item as either present or absent. JVS 230, JVS A27

    creating, JVS A31

Checkbox element, JVS E4

Checkerboard Across transition, JVS G8

Checkerboard Down transition, JVS G8

Checkerboard transition, JVS G9

Chroma filter, JVS G2, JVS G4

chrome The borders of a browser window, including items such as the toolbars, status bar, and scroll bars. JVS 590

Circle In transition, JVS G8

Circle Out transition, JVS G8

<cite> element, JVS C9

class

    applying styles, JVS B33–B35

    HTML, JVS A15–A16

    style object versus, JVS 178

    subclasses, JVS 679

classic Web application model The classic approach in which users send data to a server and receive information from the server as whole Web pages. JVS 732–733

client A computer or other device that requests services from a server. JVS A1

client-side cookie A cookie stored on the user's own computer. JVS 521

client-side programming Programs that run on each user's computer rather than remotely off a server. JVS 5

    combining with server-side programming, JVS 5–6

client-side validation The Web browser checks the form, which is not submitted to the server until it passes inspection. JVS 235

clipping

    content, JVS B18–B19

    objects, JVS 193–194

closing tag A tag that indicates the end of a two-sided tag. JVS A4

<code> element, JVS C9

<col> element, JVS C9

<colgroup> element, JVS C9

collapsing

    documents. *See* plus/minus box

    frames, JVS 628–629

colon (:), escape character, JVS 524

color, JVS B14–B15

column, spanning, JVS A21–A23

column group An element that allows you to assign a common format to all cells within a column. JVS A26–A27

command A single line that indicates an action for the browser to take. JVS 9. *See also* statement

    running as hypertext link, JVS 58

command block The collection of commands that is run each time through a loop. JVS 122

decrement operator The unary operator that decreases the operand's value by 1, indicated by the - symbol. JVS 67

definition list A block-level element used for a list of terms with each term followed by its description or meaning. JVS A11–A12

<del> element, JVS C9

deleting. *See also* removing

    cookies, JVS 546–550

delimiter A text string that marks the break between one substring and another. JVS 245–246

deprecated When a feature of HTML or XHTML is being phased out by the W3C and might not be supported by future browsers. JVS A3–A4

<dfn> element, JVS C9

dialog box. *See also* specific dialog boxes

    built-in, JVS 615

    creating, JVS 613–617

<dir> element, JVS C9

dir element, JVS E6

display style, attribute, JVS D9–D10

displaying

    elements, setting display style, JVS B28–B30

    nested list, JVS 407–409

    page overlay, JVS 487–488

<div> element, JVS C10

div element, JVS E6

div element A block-level element that is a generic container for block-level content; can be resized and floated to create different page layouts. JVS A13

<dl> element, JVS C10

<!doctype> element, JVS C6

document element, JVS E6–E9

document event

    attributes, JVS C4

    IE and W3C event models, JVS 310

document fragment An unattached node or node tree that exists only in a browser's memory. JVS 380

document object An object that references elements and features of the Web document or Web browser. JVS 168

    inline frames as, JVS 633–634

document object model (DOM) The structure of all the objects within documents and browsers that are organized in a systematic way. JVS 169–171

    development, JVS 169–170

document tree The hierarchy into which each document object model organizes objects. JVS 171

document.writeln() method, JVS 11

document.write() method, JVS 11–13

dollar sign ($)

    escape character, JVS 524

    escape sequence, JVS 262

    text string end marker, JVS 255

DOM. *See* document object model (DOM)

DOM Level 0. *See* basic model

DOM Level 1 The first specification, released in October 1998, provided support for all elements contained within HTML and XML documents. JVS 170

DOM Level 2 The second specification, released in November 2000, enhanced the document object model by providing an event model that specified how events are captured as they progress through the objects in a Web browser. DOM Level 2 also extended the style sheet model to work with CSS style sheets and provided a range model to allow programmers to manipulate sections of text within a document. JVS 170

DOM Level 3 The most recent specification, released in April 2004, provides a framework for working with document loading and saving, as well as for working with XML, namespaces, DTDs, and document validation. JVS 170

domain, cookies, JVS 528

dot syntax The format that indicates the location of an object within the hierarchy by separating each level using a dot. JVS 172

double quotation marks (")

    escape character, JVS 524

Do/While loop, JVS 126–127

drag-and-drop action, formatting. *See* formatting drag-and-drop action

DropShadow filter, JVS G2, JVS G4

<dt> element, JVS C10

dynamic content Web page content that is determined by the operation of a script running within the browser. JVS 370–416

    attributes. *See* attribute

    creating in Internet Explorer, JVS 374

expanding/collapsing documents. *See* plus/minus box

heading element list. *See* heading element list

innerText property, JVS 373–374

inserting into elements, JVS 372–373

nested list, JVS 388–395

nodes. *See* nodes

textContent property, JVS 373–374

E

ECMA. *See* European Computer Manufacturers Association (ECMA)

ECMAScript The standard scripting language developed by the ECMA, though browsers still refer to it as JavaScript. JVS 7

element A distinct object in a Web document, such as a paragraph, a heading, or the page's title. JVS A4

    block-level. *See* block-level element

    clipping content, JVS B18–B19

    content overflow, JVS B18

    core, JVS C2

    core events, JVS B3

    display style, JVS B28–B30

    document events, JVS C4

    empty, JVS A5

    event, JVS C3

    form, JVS C2

    form events, JVS C4

    heading. *See* heading element list

    height, JVS B18

    hiding, JVS B29–B30

    HTML and XHTML, JVS C6–C23

    inline, JVS A8, JVS A14–A15

    inserting HTML content, JVS 372–373

    inserting under IE DOM, JVS 402

    Internet Explorer, JVS C3

    Internet Explorer data events, JVS C4

    Internet Explorer events, JVS C5–C6

    language, JVS C2

    list, JVS E2–E24

    logical, JVS AJVS 5

    physical, JVS AJVS 5

inserting attributes, JVS A6

opening new windows, JVS 600

retrieving HTML fragments, JVS 741

special characters, JVS A17–A18

strict, target attribute, JVS 633

structure of HTML files, JVS A7

tables. *See* Web table

versions, JVS A3

white space, JVS A6

I

<i> element, JVS C12

ID

applying styles, JVS B33–B35

HTML, JVS A15–A16

referencing objects, JVS 174–176

section heading, JVS 398

section heading IDs, JVS 398

id attribute, HTML, JVS A15–A16

IE4 DOM Introduced by Internet Explorer 4.0, the chief feature is that all Web page elements were now part of the document object model. CSS attributes also became part of the IE4 DOM, allowing users to manipulate CSS styles with JavaScript commands; incompatible with the Netscape 4 approach. JVS 169

inserting element text, JVS 402

referencing objects, JVS 175

IE event model The event model supported by Internet Explorer and Opera. JVS 304

document events, JVS 304

this keyword, JVS 316

IE event object, JVS 312

If statement, JVS 129–130

enclosing commands within, JVS 186

nesting, JVS 130–131, JVS 132

If...Else statement, JVS 131–132

<iframe> element, JVS C12

iframe element, JVS E12

IIS (Internet Information Service) A personal Web server installed on a local computer that will run the HTTP protocol locally. JVS 744

<ilayer> element, JVS C13

image

background, JVS B15–B17

inline, JVS A16–A17

placement, JVS B15–B17

image element, JVS E12–E13

image gallery, JVS 462–469

adding slide captions, JVS 467–468

creating image objects for high-resolution images, JVS 465–467

creating thumbnails with HTML and CSS, JVS 469

prepackaged, JVS 501

image object A JavaScript object that stores an image. JVS 455–459

creating, JVS 455–456

defining as custom properties, JVS 457–459

high-resolution images, JVS 465–467

<img> element, JVS C13–C14

implementation element, JVS E13

increment operator The unary operator that increases the value of the operand by 1, indicated by the ++ symbol. JVS 67–68

index A number for each individual data value that distinguishes it from other values in the array. JVS 110

index array An array whose values are identified by their index number; contrast with associative array. JVS 659

IndexOf() method, JVS 538

inheritance, prototypal, JVS 679–680

initializing a style sheet, JVS 424–425

inline element An element placed within a block-level element and not separated from other page content, flowing "in-line" with the rest of the characters in the block. JVS A8, JVS A14–A15

inline frame. *See* floating frame

inline image A graphic file placed within a Web page that is loaded as a browser renders the Web page. JVS A16–A17

inline style A style that is applied directly to an element by adding the style attribute to the element's markup tag. JVS B3

innerText property, JVS 373–374

input box A control element for text and numerical entries. JVS A27

creating and formatting, JVS A29–30

<input> element, JVS C14

input field, JVS 220–222

navigating between fields, JVS 221–222

setting field value, JVS 220–221

<ins> element, JVS C15

insertBefore() method, JVS 380, JVS 381

inserting

array items, JVS 117–120

attributes in HTML files, JVS A6

comments, JVS 32–34

HTML content, JVS 372–373

inline images, JVS A17

Inset transition, JVS G9

instance A specific object. JVS 656. *See also* object instance

instantiating The process of creating an object from an object class. JVS 656

objects from object classes, JVS 666–667

Internet Explorer

creating dynamic content, JVS 374

transition filters, JVS 499–500

Internet Explorer attribute, JVS C3

Internet Explorer data event, attributes, JVS C4

Internet Explorer event, attributes, JVS C5–C6

Internet Information Service. *See* IIS (Internet Information Service)

interpage transition A transition between one Web page and another that involves effects applied to a page when a browser either enters or exits the page. JVS G12–G13

interpreted language A language in which the program code is executed directly without compiling. JVS 6

Invert filter, JVS G4

Iris transition, JVS G9

<isindex> element, JVS C15

J

JavaScript A subscript of Java, meant to be easy for nonprogrammers to use. JVS 6

development, JVS 6–7

versions, JVS 7

JavaScript Object Notation. *See* JSON (JavaScript Object Notation)

jQuery A lightweight JavaScript library containing all of the common DOM, event, and AJAX functions. JVS 778

Jscript A slightly different version of JavaScript, supported by Internet Explorer. JVS 7

JSON (JavaScript Object Notation) A data format based on the object literal format. JVS 757–761

  nested structures and array literals, JVS 758–759

  reading JSON data, JVS 760–761

  referencing JSON variables, JVS 759–760

  security issues, JVS 775

K

<kbd> element, JVS C15

kerning A typographic feature that refers to the amount of space between characters. JVS B11

keyboard event, JVS 335–347

  character codes, JVS 346–347

  keypress event, JVS 346–347

  modifier keys, JVS 347

  moving items, JVS 344–346

  properties, JVS 337–339

  selecting items, JVS 342–344

  toggling between modes, JVS 340–342

keydown The keyboard event in which the user presses the key down. JVS 336, JVS 337

keypress The keyboard event that follows immediately after the onkeydown event. JVS 336, JVS 337, JVS 346–347

keyup The keyboard event that occurs after the key has been released by the user. JVS 336, JVS 337

L

<label> element, JVS C15

label element, JVS E13

language attribute, JVS C2

<layer> element, JVS C15

layer element, JVS E13–E14

layout

  attribute, JVS D11

  framesets, setting, JVS 628

leading A typographic feature that refers to the amount of space between lines of text. JVS B11

left angle bracket (<)

  comparison operator, JVS 84, JVS F2

  escape character, JVS 524

<legend> element, JVS C15

legend element, JVS E14

<li> element, JVS C16

Light filter, JVS G4, JVS G5–G7

line break, JavaScript, JVS 14

link An element in a hypertext document that allows a user to jump from one topic or document to another, usually by clicking it with a mouse button. JVS A1

  creating, JVS A16

  inserting, JVS 399–402

  Web forms, JVS A41–A42

link element, JVS 420–424

<link> element, JVS C16

link element, JVS E14–E15

list

  attribute, JVS D11–D12

  combined ordered and unordered, JVS A11

  creating in HTML documents, JVS A10–A12

  definition, JVS A11–A12

  heading elements. *See* heading element list

  nested, JVS 388–395

  ordered, JVS A10

  unordered, JVS A10

list box The element in which a selection list appears. JVS A27

listening for events, JVS 307–308

loading

  CGI scripts, JVS 763–765

  slide images, JVS 452–454

load-time error An error that occurs when a script is first loaded by the browser. JVS 35

local scope A variable created within a JavaScript function that can be referenced only within that function. JVS 27

local variable A variable with local scope. JVS 27

location element, JVS E15

location object Information about the page that is currently displayed in the window. JVS 593, JVS 595–597

logical element A page element that describes the nature of the content enclosed within tags such as <cite> and <code> but not necessarily how that content should appear. JVS A15

logical error An error that doesn't involve syntax and structural mistakes, but results in incorrect results. JVS 36

logical operator An operator that allows you to connect two or more Boolean expressions. JVS 84–87

looping through child node collection, JVS 382–383

Luhn Formula A formula developed by a group of mathematicians in the 1960s to provide a quick validation check on an account number by adding up the digits in the number. JVS 273–275

M

<map> element, JVS C16

map element, JVS E15

margin, styles, JVS B20–B21

marking a slide image, JVS 451–452

markup language A language that describes the structure and content of a document. JVS A2

markup tag The code used to set off each item within a document. JVS A2

<marquee> element, JVS C16–C17

Mask filter, JVS G4

math constant, JVS 74–76

Math element, JVS E15–E16

Math method A method that stores functions for performing advanced calculations and mathematical operations such as generating random numbers, extracting square roots, and calculating trigonometric values. JVS 73–74

  calculating hours, minutes, and seconds left in year, JVS 76–79

Math object An object that can be used for performing mathematical operations and storing mathematical values. JVS 72–79

media clip, HTML documents, JVS A18–A19

media group A CSS category that describes how different media devices render content.; the four media groups are continuous or paged; visual, aural, or tactile; grid or bitmap; and interactive. JVS B38–B39

@media rule, JVS B37–B39

media type, styles, JVS B37–B39

menu

    pop-up, JVS 196

    pull-down. *See* pull-down menu

    sliding, JVS 196–197

    tabbed, JVS 198

<menu> element, JVS C17

menu element, JVS E16

<meta> element, JVS C17

method A process by which JavaScript manipulates or acts upon the properties of an object; object; an action that an object performs. JVS 11, JVS 168. *See also* specific methods

    custom, JVS 686–702

    objects, JVS 180–181

    private, JVS 678

    privileged, JVS 678

    public, JVS 678

Microsoft Script Debugger A debugger available for use with its Internet Explorer browser running under Windows XP. JVS 38–39

middle alignment, JVS B13

MIME type, JVS A18

minus sign (–)

    arithmetic operator, JVS 67

    assignment operators, JVS 69, JVS F2

    escape character, JVS 524

    unary operator, JVS 68

mistake. *See* error

Mod10 algorithm. *See* Luhn Formula

modal window A window that prevents users from doing work in any other window or dialog box until the window is closed. JVS 622

modeless window A window that allows users to work in other windows and dialog boxes even as that window stays open. JVS 622

modifier key A keyboard key that is pressed along with a letter key to run special commands or to access program menus. JVS 347

modular code Code that entails breaking up a program's different tasks into smaller, more manageable chunks. JVS 37

modulus operator The % operator, which returns the integer remainder after dividing one integer by another. JVS 130

MotionBlur filter, JVS G3

mouse

    determining position, JVS 317–320

    tracking movements, JVS 328

mouse button, specifying in scripts, JVS 335

mouse event, JVS 317–323

    creating function for mouse movement, JVS 320–321

    determining mouse position, JVS 317–320

    mouseDrop() function, JVS 322–323

mouseDrop() function, JVS 322–323

moving items using keyboard, JVS 344–346

MSXML The XML parser built-in to Internet Explorer that provides support for request objects through its XML language. JVS 736

multidimensional array, JVS 147

multivalued cookie, JVS 551–562

    retrieving data, JVS 558–562

    subkeys, JVS 551–552, JVS 554–555

    testing, JVS 556–558

    writing, JVS 552–556

N

named page, print styles, JVS B40

native object A JavaScript object that is part of the JavaScript language, such as the Date, Array, or Image objects. JVS 656

    prototypes, JVS 676–678

navigating the slide gallery, JVS 476–484

    adding navigation buttons, JVS 477–478

    displaying slide numbers, JVS 482–484

    keeping track of slide number, JVS 478–482

navigation

    automatic, JVS 595–597

    between frames, JVS 626–627

    slide gallery. *See* navigating the slide gallery

navigator element, JVS E16

negation operator The unary operator that changes the sign of (or negates) an item's value. JVS 68

nested data structure, JSON, JVS 758–759

nested function, JVS 650–656

nested list, JVS 388–395

    hiding/displaying, JVS 407–409

nesting The technique of placing one element within another. JVS A7

nesting If statement, JVS 130–131, JVS 132

<nobr> element, JVS C17

node An object within the Web page or Web browser; anything in the document can be treated as a node, including every HTML tag and all of a tag's attributes. JVS 374–382

    attaching, JVS 380–382

    attribute, JVS 386–398

    creating, JVS 378–379

    looping through child node collection, JVS 382–387

    node trees, JVS 375–376

    properties, JVS 378

    relationships, JVS 376

    removing, JVS 380, JVS 381

    root, JVS 375

    types, names, and values, JVS 376–377

node tree A hierarchal structure of nodes that indicates the relationship between each of the nodes. JVS 375–376

    traversing with recursion, JVS 416

<noembed> element, JVS C17

<noframe> element, JVS C17

noframes element, JVS A42–A43

<nolayer> element, JVS C17

<noscript> element, JVS C17

null value Indicates that no value has yet been assigned to the variable. JVS 18–19

number format, specifying, JVS 80

numeric value Any number, such as 13, 22.5, or –3.14159. JVS 18, JVS 79–82

    converting between numbers and text strings, JVS 80–81

    numeric methods and functions, JVS 81JVS 82

    rounding values, JVS 82

    specifying number format, JVS 80

O

object Any item from the browser window itself to a document displayed in the browser to an element displayed within the document. JVS 11

    custom. *See* custom object

    methods, JVS 180–181

pull-down menu A menu in which a menu title is always visible to the user, identifying the entries in the menu. When a user clicks the title or in some cases moves the pointer over the title, the rest of the menu is displayed, often accompanied by the effect of a menu being "pulled down" from the title. JVS 166–168

    animating, JVS 192–196

    programming. *See* programming pull-down menu

Q

<q> element, JVS C18

question mark (?)

    escape character, JVS 524

    escape sequence, JVS 262

    repetition character, JVS 261

R

RadialWipe transition, JVS G9

radio button. *See* option button

Radio element, JVS E17–E18

random number, generating, JVS 74

RandomBars transition, JVS G9

RandomDissolve transition, JVS G9

read-only property A property you cannot change, which has a fixed value. JVS 177

Really Simple Syndication (RSS) An XML vocabulary that is used to distribute news articles, or any content that changes on regular basis, to a group of subscribers. JVS 748–757

    building RSS newsreader, JVS 750–757

    elements from RSS documents, JVS 748

recursion A programming technique in which program code calls itself repeatedly until a stopping condition is met. JVS 416

referencing

    form elements, JVS 219–220

    objects. *See* referencing objects

    Web forms, JVS 218–219

referencing objects, JVS 171–176

    IE DOM, JVS 175

    object collections, JVS 172–174

    object names, JVS 171–172

    referencing by name and ID, JVS 174–176

RegExp element, JVS E18

regular expression A text string that defines a character pattern. JVS 252–275

    creating, JVS 252–253, JVS 265

    defining character positions, JVS 255–257

    defining character types and character classes, JVS 257–260

    escape sequences, JVS 262–263

    matching substrings, JVS 253–254

    methods, JVS 265–267

    object constructor, JVS 265

    setting flags, JVS 254–255

    specifying alternate patterns and grouping, JVS 263–264

    specifying repeating characters, JVS 260–262

    validating financial data, JVS 269–275

    validating zip codes, JVS 268–269

regular expression literal The syntax for creating regular expressions. JVS 252

relative position A style that moves an element a specific distance from where the browser would have placed it. JVS B25

relative unit A measurement unit expressed relative to the size of other objects within a Web page, such as the font size relative to the size of a standard character in the output device. JVS B9

removing

    cookies, JVS 546–550

    events from event model, JVS 308–311

    nodes, JVS 380–381

repeating character, regular expressions, JVS 260–262

reserved target name A special name used in place of a frame name as a target so that the linked document appears within a specific location in the browser. JVS A41–A42

Reset element, JVS E18–E19

resetting a form, JVS 239–240

retrieving

    cookie values, JVS 539–540

    cookies. *See* retrieving cookies

    data from multivalued cookies, JVS 558–562

    HTML fragments, JVS 741

    XHTML document objects, JVS 750

retrieving cookies, JVS 537–546

    retrieving cookie values, JVS 539–540

    splitting cookies into arrays, JVS 537–538

    writing cookie values, JVS 540–546

reveal transition A more general transition in which a visual effect is applied as one object is changed into another. JVS G7

reversing arrays, JVS 115

right angle bracket (>)

    comparison operator, JVS 84, JVS F2

    escape character, JVS 524

rollover A visual effect in which an object changes appearance in response to the pointer hovering over the object. JVS 454–461

    anonymous functions, JVS 459–461

    creating image objects, JVS 455–456

    defining image objects as custom properties, JVS 457–459

    sizing and replacing images under Internet Explorer, JVS 457

    without JavaScript, JVS 461

root element The element of a markup document that contains all other elements in the document; for HTML documents, the root element is marked with the <html> tag. JVS A7

root node The parent of all nodes within a document. JVS 375

rounding values, JVS 82

row, spanning, JVS A21–A23

row group An element that allows you to assign a common format to all rows in a group; HTML supports row groups for header rows, body rows, and footer rows. JVS A20–A21

RSS. *See* Really Simple Syndication (RSS)

rule

    style sheets, JVS 427

    Web tables, JVS A25–A26

@rule, JVS D5

running a transition, JVS G10

run-time error hat occurs after a script has been successfully loaded and is being executed; occurs when the browser cannot complete a line of code. JVS 35–36

S

\<s\> element, JVS C18

\<samp\> element, JVS C18

scalable When using relative units, the ability of a page to be rendered the same way no matter what font size a browser uses. JVS B10

scope A property of a variable that indicates where you can reference the variable within the Web page. JVS 27

screen element, JVS E19

script

    CGI. *See* CGI script

    specifying mouse buttons, JVS 335

Script element, JVS E19

\<script\> element, JVS C18–C19

script element

    creating, JVS 7–8

    placing, JVS 8

    writing statements, JVS 9

scripting a transition, JVS G10–G12

scrollbar, attribute, JVS D12–D13

secondary window A window that opens in addition to the main browser window; also called a pop-up window. JVS 599. *See also* pop-up window

section heading, inserting IDs, JVS 398

security

    cookies, JVS 529–530

    document.referrer property, JVS 598

    JSON, JVS 775

Select element, JVS E19–E20

\<select\> element, JVS C19

selecting items using keyboard, JVS 342–344

selection list A control element for long lists of options, usually appearing in a list box. JVS 223–227, JVS A27

    creating, JVS A32–A33

    multiple values, JVS 227

selector The element or group of elements within a document to which a style declaration is applied. JVS B30–B36, JVS D2–D13

    applying styles to IDs and classes, JVS B33–B35

    applying styles to pseudo-classes and pseudo-elements, JVS B35–B36

    attributes, JVS B32–B33, JVS D6–D13

    contextual, JVS B31–B32

    pseudo classes, JVS D3

    pseudo-elements and pseudo classes, JVS D2

    @rules, JVS D4

    syntax, JVS D4

    units, JVS D5–D6

    values, JVS D6–D13

self keyword A keyword that refers to the current window and is synonymous with the window keyword, but used to improve clarity when a script refers to many different windows and frames. JVS 611, JVS 612

semicolon (;)

    escape character, JVS 524

    logical operator, JVS F3

sending requests, JVS 739

send() method, JVS 738–740

server A network node that makes information or a service available on the network. JVS A1

    placing AJAX applications onto, JVS 744–745

server-side cookie A cookie stored on a Web server. JVS 521

server-side programming Programming in which a program is placed on the server that hosts a Web site; the program is then used to modify the contents and structure of Web pages. JVS 4–5

    combining with client-side programming, JVS 5–6

server-side validation The browser sends a form to the Web server for checking. If an error is found, the user is notified and asked to resubmit the form. JVS 235

session cookie A cookie that expires when a Web session is completed. JVS 526

Shadow filter, JVS G3, JVS G4

shuffling arrays, JVS 117

single quotation mark (JVS and ')

    escape character, JVS 524

sizing elements, JVS A4, JVS B17–B19

slice() method, JVS 245

slide caption, JVS 467–468

slide gallery

    hiding/viewing, JVS 469–475

    navigating. *See* navigating the slide gallery

slide show, JVS 450–454

    loading slide images, JVS 452–454

    marking slide images, JVS 451–452

Slide transition, JVS G9

sliding menu A menu that is partially hidden either off the Web page or behind another object. JVS 196–197

\<small\> element, JVS C19

snapping to grid, JVS 326–327

sorting an array, JVS 116–117

source document, expanding/collapsing, JVS 409–414

spacing

    tables, JVS A23–A23

    text, JVS B11

spam Unsolicited e-mail sent to large numbers of people, promoting products, services, and in some cases pornographic Web sites. JVS 2

spammer A person who sends unsolicited e-mails, sometimes in bulk e-mailings involving tens of thousands of recipients. JVS 2

\<span\> element, JVS C19

spanning cell A single cell that occupies more than one row or one column in a table. JVS A21–A23

sparse array An array such as the x array with several missing or null items. JVS 114–115

special character, HTML documents, JVS A17–A18

special effects attribute, JVS D13

specific font A font that is installed on a user's computer, such as Times New Roman. JVS B8, JVS B9

Spiral transition, JVS G9

split() method, JVS 538

square brackets ([]), escape character, JVS 524

stacking elements, JVS B27–B28

stateless protocol A protocol that does not record the user's interaction with the Web server. JVS 520–521

statement A single line that indicates an action for the browser to take. JVS 9

statement label, JVS 146–147

static position A style that places an object in its natural position in the flow of the document as determined by the browser. JVS B26

thumbnail, creating with HTML and CSS, JVS 469

time-delayed command A command that is run after a specified amount of time has passed. JVS 88

  anonymous functions, JVS 499

timed-interval command A command that instructs the browser to run the same command repeatedly at specified intervals. JVS 88–90

  anonymous functions, JVS 499

<title> element, JVS C22

toggling, keyboard, JVS 340–342

top alignment, JVS B13

top keyword A keyword that lets you go directly to the top of the hierarchy. JVS 627

<tr> element, JVS C22–C23

tracking A typographic feature that refers to the amount of space between words. JVS B11

tracking cookie A cookie that cannot identify you personally, but that can assign you a random ID number that it can use to track your actions across the Web. JVS 529

tracking mouse movements, JVS 328

traditional binding The application of an event handler as an object property. JVS 303

transient status bar message That message that appears temporarily in the status bar in response to an event occurring within the browser, such as the pointer moving over a link. After the event is over, the transient message disappears, replaced by the permanent message. JVS 591–593

transition A visual effect that is applied to an object over an interval of time. JVS 492, JVS 499–500, JVS G7–G10

  interpage, G12–G13

  running, JVS G10–G12

  scripting, JVS G10

<tt> element, JVS C23

two-sided tag, JVS A5

U

<u> element, JVS C23

<ul> element, JVS C23

unary operator An operator that works on only one operand; can make code more compact and efficient. JVS 67–68

unit of measurement, JVS D5–D6

unordered list A block-level element used for items that do not need to occur in any special order. JVS A10, JVS A11

user-defined object. *See* custom object

V

value

  assigning to variables, JVS 16–18

  Boolean, JVS 18

  null, JVS 18–19

  numeric, JVS 18

<var> element, JVS C23

variable A named item in a program that stores information. JVS 16–21

  assigning values, JVS 16–18

  creating, JVS 17–18

  data types, JVS 18–21

  declaring, JVS 16, JVS 17

  names, JVS 16

  returning data type, JVS 705

VBScript The Internet Explorer scripting language. JVS 7

Vertical Blinds transition, JVS G8

viewing

  CGI script, JVS 769–770

  slide gallery, JVS 469–475

W

watermark A fixed background image used to create the illusion of a translucent graphic impressed into the very fabric of paper and often used in specialized stationery. JVS B16

Wave filter, JVS G3, JVS G4

<wbr> element, JVS C23

W3C. *See* World Wide Web Consortium (W3C)

W3C DOM All of the DOM levels released and supported by the W3C. JVS 170

W3C event model The event model developed by the W3C and supported by Firefox, Netscape, Safari, Opera, and other major browsers. JVS 304

  document events, JVS 304

  this keyword, JVS 316

W3C event object, JVS 312–313

weakly typed language A language in which variables are not strictly tied to specific data types; JavaScript is an example. JVS 19

Web. *See* World Wide Web (Web)

Web browser A program that retrieves a Web page from a server and displays the page on a computer or other device. JVS A2

  automatic navigation, JVS 595–597

  browser cache, JVS 746

  cookies, JVS 521–522

  creating new windows. *See* pop-up window

  non-JavaScript, supporting, JVS 15

  older, supporting, JVS B38

  testing for cookie support, JVS 567–569

Web form. *See* form

Web page A document on the World Wide Web. JVS A2

Web server A computer that stores and makes Web pages available to any device connected to the Internet. JVS A2

  loading Perl scripts, JVS 765, JVS A2

Web table, JVS A19–A27

  border size, JVS A23

  captions, JVS A21

  column groups, JVS A26–A27

  defining structure, JVS A20

  frames, JVS A25, JVS A26

  padding, JVS A24

  row groups, JVS A20–A21

  rules, JVS A25–A26

  sizing, JVS A25

  spacing, JVS A23–A24

  spanning rows and columns, JVS A21–A23

welcome back message, JVS 562–567

Wheel transition, JVS G9

While loop, JVS 125–126

  writing calendar days, JVS 138–140

white space Blank spaces, tabs, and line breaks within an HTML text file. JVS A6

  JavaScript, JVS 14

widow The final few lines of an element's text when they appear at the top of a page, while most of the element's text appears on the previous page. JVS B42